IMPORTANT NOTE: The semester of Microeconomics in this book is independent and entirely self-contained and should be given consideration for first semester coverage, prior to Macroeconomics. An advantage of the "micro first" sequence is that international trade and finance and the economics of the world economy will be studied only after the students have studied both micro and macro principles.

Principles
of
Economics
Theory • Problems • Policies

Fourth Edition

Elbert V. Bowden

Professor of Economics
Chair of Banking
Appalachian State University

Published by

H96 SOUTH-WESTERN PUBLISHING CO.

CINCINNATI   WEST CHICAGO, ILL.   DALLAS   PELHAM MANOR, N.Y.   PALO ALTO, CALIF.

ISBN: 0-538-08960-1

Library of Congress Catalog Card Number: 82-80600

2 3 4 5 6 K 7 6 5 4 3

Printed in the United States of America

Cover Photo: Ulrich Schiller/THE IMAGE BANK

Preface

What's the purpose of a principles text? Should *efficiency* as a teaching-learning tool be one of the essential criteria? Should the principles text try to minimize the effort and frustration required to learn economics? I think so.

STUDENT-IDENTIFIED CHARACTERISTICS OF AN EXCELLENT ECONOMICS BOOK

What do students choose as the essential characteristics of *an excellent text in economics?* My students insist (and this is confirmed by student surveys elsewhere) that an outstanding economics book:

1. must be **Easily Readable! Understandable!**

2. must be **Interesting! Not boring!**

On these two criteria, all three of the previous editions of this book have scored higher than any other principles text. I'm especially happy about that because these were my primary objectives in writing the book.

But what about *the other* desiderata?—the *other characteristics* which students say are essential for an outstanding economics book? On some of those my previous editions have not scored as high. So what's my **paramount objective in this Fourth Edition?** Just this: *To try to make this book truly outstanding on each of the other student-identified characteristics of "excellence"*— while maintaining the previous standards of readability and interest.

What are these additional criteria? And how does this Fourth Edition respond to the need? All of that is explained in the following paragraphs.

Students say that an excellent economics text:

3. must be **Current! Relevant!**

- This Fourth Edition has an entirely new first chapter (Ch. 1, "Economic Principles and the Crisis Issues of the 1980s") which establishes *the reality and critical importance of economics* right at the start.
- New real-world examples have been introduced at several places throughout the text.
- There's an entirely new chapter (Ch. 17, "The Keynesian-Monetarist Debate, Rational Expectations, Supply-Side Economics, and Macro Policies for the 1980s") which explains and illustrates important macro issues and policies and some of the theoretical conflict among economists during the early 1980s.

Students say that an excellent economics text:

4. must have for each chapter a **Clear, Understandable Statement of Objectives!** and a **Comprehensive Summary!**

- In this Fourth Edition each chapter begins with a precise, easily understandable statement of objectives.
- Each chapter in this book ends with a "Summary and Synthesis"—a summary restatement and synthesis of all the key information in the chapter. It is, in fact, *a complete and self-contained abstract* of the chapter itself. I'm sure

iii

that the addition of these "Summary and Synthesis" sections will add significantly to the efficiency of this book as a teaching-learning tool.

- The inclusion of these "Summary and Synthesis" sections has had the important side-effect benefit of permitting *the elimination of intrachapter summary statements and repetition.* The exposition within the chapters now moves along more efficiently than before, and without any loss of readability.

An excellent economics text:

5. must have Clearly Explained Graphs! Easily Understandable!

- In this book, *all graphs* are clearly drawn—large, open, and easy to work with; and
- Each graph is *carefully and thoroughly explained* right on the page on which it's located.

An excellent economics text:

6. must have within each chapter Good Logical Organization! Frequent Headings! Headings which Say Something!

- In this Fourth Edition I have found many opportunities to improve chapter organization, to eliminate some unnecessary repetition, and to insert additional headings.
- Most headings in this Fourth Edition are designed to *say something*—e.g., "The Opportunity Cost Is the Opportunity Lost"; "Bonds Paying Lower Interest Sell for Lower Prices"; "Factor Prices Influence Production Techniques"; "The Key to Macroeconomics Is Total Spending"; etc., etc.

An excellent economics text:

7. must have Clear, Unmistakable Identification of the Key Points!

This Fourth Edition achieves this objective through the use of *six techniques:*
- Emphasis right in the beginning in the *chapter objectives;*
- Use of *frequent sub-headings* which state and/or emphasize key points;
- Use of *color, italics,* and *boldface type* to emphasize key words and phrases;

- Re-emphasis of all key points in the *chapter summary and synthesis;*
- Listing of all important principles, concepts and terms in the *end-of-chapter review exercises;* and finally
- Use of *cartoon characters* to make the very most important points *unforgettable.*

An excellent economics text:

8. must provide ample opportunity for Efficient Review! and Efficient Self-testing!

- In this book the review exercises at the end of each chapter cover all of the important *principles, concepts, terms* and *graphs* in the chapter. Also included are several *essay questions* designed to stimulate thought and discussion.
- The *Study Guide* which I have prepared to accompany this text contains in each chapter more than 60 questions—fill in, true-false, multiple choice, essay, graphs—together with answers to all questions—*including the essay questions.*

Very few textbook authors prepare their own study guide. Truly, *it's a chore.* But I have prepared the *Study Guide* to make sure that it's a "perfect pair" with the textbook—in *style, emphasis, interest,* and *readability.* The widespread use of the *Study Guide* (even sometimes with other texts!) attests to its usefulness and efficiency as a teaching/learning tool.

An excellent economics text:

9. must include an Efficient Glossary! The important terms must be explained for understanding, with no need to go to the dictionary or to look up other terms in order to understand.

- This Fourth Edition contains a glossary—expanded, updated, and revised from the Third Edition—which I believe will thoroughly meet the student's requirements for *completeness, clarity,* and *efficiency.*

An excellent economics text:

10. should have a Complete and Efficient Index!

- This Fourth Edition contains a thoroughly complete and highly efficient index. It now includes every term that any student may seek. And each term is referenced in as many different ways as any student might choose to look it up. (An index may be "a little thing." But as all economic educators know, in learning economics, "little things can mean a lot.")

Should an excellent economics text:

11. include some Mathematical Applications? Some easily understandable illustrations of the Use of Equations in economic analysis? Some introductory examples to generate an awareness of the Power and Usefulness of Math in economics?

People disagree on this. Some fear that the use of equations at the principles level will impede the learning of basic principles by many students. Others insist that some equations should be introduced in the principles course. So, what to do? Include some equations? or not?

- This Fourth Edition includes a brief mathematical appendix at the end of the book. It's there for those who desire it. And it's out of the way where it won't bother anyone who would rather not use it.
- The math appendix is written so that any student (math weaknesses notwithstanding) will be able to understand it and begin to appreciate the usefulness of math—the power of equations—in economic analysis. I believe this easily understandable math appendix can make a significant contribution by giving students an easy, pleasant introduction to this (often frightening) area.

THE EVOLUTION AND CONTENT OF THIS BOOK

This book started out more than a decade ago as a collection of mimeographed pages—handouts for my students—explanations my stu-

dents could understand. Now it's the Fourth Edition of a complete and conceptually rigorous principles text. It includes a sound and thorough treatment of economic principles, applications, problems, and policies.

Explanations Which Students Can Understand

Years have passed, but the original purpose of those mimeographed handouts has not changed. This book still consists of: *explanations which students can understand.* This book is based on a basic theory of economics: that people (including students) will try to be *efficient*—will try to achieve their objectives with minimum cost—in money, time, effort, frustration, whatever.

Recent studies have shown that the student's *concentration span* and *depth of comprehension* diminish rapidly as the readability level approaches the student's maximum comprehension level.* So an economics book from which students can learn *efficiently* must be written at a level at which the exposition itself is not frustrating to the average student.

Contains More Theory and Applications

This book reflects my philosophy that the principles of economics course provides the only

---

*See, for examples:

John Guthrie, "Learnability versus Readability of Texts," *The Journal of Educational Research*, vol. 65 (1972), pp. 273-79.

Walter Kintsch, E. Kozminsky, William Streby, Gail McKoon, and Janet Keenan, "Comprehension and Recall of Text as a Function of Content Variables," *Journal of Verbal Learning and Verbal Behavior*, vol. 14 (1975), pp. 196-214.

Maurice Kurtzmann, "The Reading Ability of College Freshmen Compared to the Readability of Their Textbooks," *Reading Improvement*, vol. 11 (1974), pp. 13-25.

Carol M. Santa, and Joan N. Burstyn, "Complexity as an Impediment to Learning: A Study of Changes in Selected College Textbooks, "*Journal of Higher Education*, Vol. 48 (1977), pp. 508-518.

opportunity most students ever will have to acquire a functional understanding of economic principles and issues. Therefore this book contains more theory and application of theory than the "easy" principles books which recently have been appearing.

I think it's unfortunate that the trend seems to be toward "easy economics by *omission*." The approach of this book is: *easy economics by explanation and by the use of relevant examples and applications*—not by the omission or watering down of essential principles.

Easy Exposition Can Be Deceptive

Because of the intuitive approach of this book, the easy exposition, conversational style, and use of familiar down-to-earth examples, students will find this an easy book to read and understand. Some students may be deceived into thinking that learning economics is relatively easy and effortless.

Some students may read and understand and assume that's the end of the learning process, when in fact it's only the beginning. They may not discover their error until they get the results of their first exam.

The fact is that there's more conceptual depth and rigor in this book than in most of its "apparently more formidable" competitors. But it takes a good economist to see that. Certainly the beginning principles student can't be expected to be aware of it!

For a highly successful course, the instructor who uses this book will need to ensure that the students do more than just read and understand—that they take the time to work with and thoroughly learn the concepts and principles. Instructors may find it necessary to use frequent testing and/or written assignments. Students may find it necessary to use the *Study Guide* to practice with and to test themselves as they go along.

"Easily Understandable Economics Without Omission" Is Not Easy to Write

It is not easy to achieve the expositional objectives set forth in this preface. Explain the complex principles of economics in such a way that no paragraph in the book approaches the frustration level of readability of the average college student? That requires repeated rewriting of the entire book, chapter by chapter, section by section, paragraph by paragraph.

Some economists might believe that the expositional objectives of this book can't be achieved without the loss of some of the rigor and precision which are the essence of sound economic theory. But I don't think that's true. I hope that anyone who is skeptical about this will look up one of the more difficult principles and see how it is treated in this book.

THE SUPPLEMENTS: ALL PREPARED BY THE AUTHOR

I have (personally) prepared all of the supplementary materials for this book: the *Study Guide* (mentioned previously), the *Instructor's Manual*, and the *Test Bank*. Each of these has been significantly improved for this Fourth Edition.

The Instructor's Manual. The instructor's manual has been expanded. It now contains

–many specific suggestions (with alternatives) for planning and conducting a *highly successful principles course*.

–*alternative course outlines* designed to meet the needs of a wide variety of alternative academic schedules, course objectives, and various other special circumstances.

–answers to all of the discussion questions in the text.

–additional essay questions for each chapter to be used in class discussion and/or for testing.

–a complete outline (including *all headings*) for each chapter in the text, to be used in preparing lectures and as a checklist during class discussions.

–transparency masters for the graphs in the text, to be used to prepare transparencies for the overhead projector.

The Test Bank: Expanded. Completely Revised. Computerized! For this Fourth Edition, all of the questions in the Third Edition *Test Bank* have been re-analyzed. I have rewritten many and replaced several. In addition, the total number of questions has been increased by 50%—from an average of 30 to 45 per chapter.

Now you can be *fully confident* that when you use the questions in this *Test Bank* you will have a testing instrument which is *efficient*, *fair*, and *reliable* for almost all students. (Unfortunately there are always a few students who will score unfairly low on M/C exams). Using these questions with my students the computer-scored reliability coefficients are *consistently* in the 80s—that's about as high as you could hope to get on this kind of a test, in moderate-sized classes.

The *computerized testing program* contains all of the questions in the *Test Bank*. It will be made available to all institutions where this textbook is adopted. *Now your computer can make up your multiple-choice exams for you!*

ACKNOWLEDGEMENTS

How does an author "fine tune" a textbook as it goes through its various editions? One thing is sure: It isn't something the author can do alone! It requires a lot of help from students, colleagues and friends.

There's hardly a sub-section in any chapter of this book which doesn't in some way reflect a helpful idea or suggestion from someone. Many have volunteered comments. Many more have helped by their thoughtful responses to questionnaires. And several of my former and present colleagues—at Texas A & M, SUNY-Fredonia, Duke, Appalachian—have read and offered helpful suggestions. Many of the new features in this Fourth Edition reflect the suggestions of students. To all of you I am sincerely grateful—for myself, and for the thousands of students who will have a better book because of your help.

There's one person who must be singled out and mentioned by name: Dr. Caroline Swartz, Department of Economics, Emory University. Dr. Swartz has worked with and assisted me throughout the preparation of this Fourth Edition. Her perceptive touch has had its good influence throughout the book—from the new Chapter 1 on "Crisis Issues" all the way to (and including) the new Math Appendix. For your excellent help Carol, thank you.

Also, my sincere appreciation to Katsuhiro (Ken) Otsuka for his tasteful and sensitive cartoon characters which enliven these pages, and to Marie-Louise van Laarschot Bowden (my wife) for her care and accuracy in drawing many new captions for the cartoons.

During the preparation of this edition and for each of the previous editions, I have been very lucky to have had the help of several outstanding secretaries. My sincere thanks to:

Margie Bailey (College Station, Texas);
Mary Ann Burgess (Fredonia, N.Y.);
Carolyn Champion (Boone, N.C.);
Lois Eggers (Boone, N.C.);
Candy Hall (Boone, N.C.);
Rosemary Jones (Suva, Fiji);
Dinah Lanning (Boone, N.C.).

It has been a privilege and a pleasure to work with each of you.

A FINAL WORD

No student is going to succeed in learning the principles of economics without considerable study and effort. It's a complex and demanding subject. And that's exactly the reason why, for most students, an easily comprehensible text is an essential part of a *successful* principles course.

This book is designed to carry its fair share of the burden of instruction. Students using this book will not find it necessary to rely on their instructor for detailed, repetitive explanations of everything. Less class time is required to generate functional understanding of the principles so more time is avilable for class discussion and for the application of principles to current issues.

This book will maximize the efficiency of the student's study time and efforts (and minimize the student's frustration) in learning economics. Easy exposition can't make all of the principles of economics easy to learn. But it certainly can help.

Experience with the three previous editions has shown that many professors and a great many students appreciate this book's informal style and easily understandable exposition. I hope you'll find that this Fourth Edition succeeds as well on the other student-desired "characteristics of excellence." If you think so (or even if not!) I'd appreciate your comments.

Elbert V. Bowden
Professor of Economics
Chair of Banking
Appalachian State University
Boone, NC

To the Student:
A Few Words of Advice

No professor and no textbook could ever *teach you* economics. All they can do is *help you to learn it*. Much of the learning process *is up to you*.

Understanding Is Only the First Step

If you study the chapters of the textbook and attend all classes, be carefully attentive, take good notes and study your notes, you will learn a lot of economics. *Maybe that's good enough* for you.

But consider this: *This textbook* has been carefully designed to be *easy to understand*. Usually as you read the text you won't have to struggle to get the meaning of a concept or principle. But *understanding is one thing. Learning it well is something else.*

Economics Is a Way of Thinking

Economics isn't a "kit of tools" which you can box up and carry along with you—or leave at home tucked away in the closet. No. *Economics is a way of thinking*. It's something that must be with you all the time. If you're a student of French, you haven't really learned French until you have learned to *think* in French. It's the same way with economics.

In some ways, *learning to think in economics* is easier than learning to think in French. You have been "thinking in economics" to some extent all your life.

But in other ways, learning to think in economics is more difficult than learning to think in French. Sometimes *the concepts and principles of economics can be quite complex*.

This Textbook Is Deceptively Easy

This textbook is written in a style which explains the most difficult parts of economic theory in ways that you can easily understand. But, in a way, *the textbook is deceptively easy*. A careful reading of the text will give you the feeling that you understand a principle even though *you may have missed some of the subtle shades of meaning*. But when you begin to apply the principles and test yourself you'll find that *the precise meanings and distinctions are quite important—in fact, absolutely essential*.

Precise Understanding Requires Practice and Self-Testing

To really understand economic theory, you need to get it *all*. Not just a "general awareness" but *an accurate understanding of all of the precise distinctions*. It isn't likely that you will be able to do that without spending a lot of time *working with the principles* and *testing yourself*.

Only through *exercises and self-testing* will you develop the *precise understanding* which you must have if you're really going to learn economics. No matter how clearly you may understand the explanations in the text you still will need to do a lot of thinking and rethinking and self-testing before the principles become *a permanent part of your way of thinking* about economic issues.

The end-of-chapter review exercises give you a lot of opportunity for self-testing. Be sure that you can draw each graph and explain it to yourself without looking in the book. It's also a good idea to read each heading in the chapter and see if you can explain what that section is about. Also I have written a *Study Guide* (workbook) to go with this textbook.

There's a Wealth of Self-Testing Materials in the Study Guide

The *Study Guide* has a chapter corresponding to each chapter in the textbook. Each chapter in the *Study Guide* gives *a further explanation of the objectives* of the chapter, followed by *further explanations of important concepts and principles*. Then the remainder of each *Study Guide* chapter consists of *a wealth of self-testing materials: fill-in, true/false, multiple choice, and essay questions, and exercises with graphs*—more than 60 questions on each chapter.

The answers to all of the questions and exercises are given at the end of each chapter. The answers to the essay questions and graph explanations provide *concise summary explanations of the most important concepts and principles in the chapter.*

Many students find that the *Study Guide* is *the key to their success* in learning economics. Perhaps you should go to your bookstore and take a look at it.

Study and Practice! Go For An A!

You've probably heard that economics is a tough subject. That's true—but only if you try to get through "the easy way." So do it the hard way!

Follow these suggestions: *Read and study and practice and self-test. Then do more of the same until you can do it all very well. And do all of this regularly. Don't let it slide* until the exam is coming up. By that time, it's too late.

Do It the Hard Way! It's Worth the Effort

I'm urging you to *do it the hard way*. If you take this advice, economics still will not be "easy." But it will not be confusing or frustrating, either. You'll understand it and it will have an important influence on your way of thinking. And on your life. Also, you'll probably make an A in the course. Isn't all that *enough reward to be worth the effort?* Think about it.

Prologue: Why Economics?

Why should anybody want to learn economics? Several reasons. There's a lot you just can't understand until you learn some economics. When you get to the end of this book you'll realize just how true that is.

And another thing. Learning economics is a good exercise in mental development. It leads to new ways of thinking about things. You don't understand what that means, yet, either. But soon you will.

You Can't Escape from Economics

Economics is everywhere. It's at work all the time, in everything. Once you learn to recognize it you can never escape from it.

When you're doing things or making things, cooking breakfast or washing your car, going places, studying math, playing basketball, using up your time and energy and money and things to do one thing or another—all those things involve economics. If economics is involved in everything, then how can you ever get away from economics? That's the point. You can't. You just can't.

Economics is involved in all the things you've been doing all your life. So how have you been able to get along all these years without knowing any economics? You haven't. The fact is, you know quite a lot of basic economics already. Everybody does.

You already know, right now, 40 or 50 or maybe 70 or 80 percent of the economics you will know when you get to the end of this book. But right now you don't call it "economics." You call it "common sense."

Economics Can Sharpen Your Common Sense

So should you study economics because it can expand and sharpen your common sense? Yes! You're going to be surprised how much it can do that. But it can do much more than that. It can let you see much more deeply into so many things that are going on around you.

This book starts with sharpening your own common sense—talking about how you solve your own personal "economic problem." Then it expands the horizon more and more until the first thing you know you'll be working with and understanding the "economic problem" from the point of view of the society, the nation, the entire world.

You're Always Facing an Economic Problem

I suppose you already know that when you're trying to decide if you'll save your money or spend it, you're facing an "economic problem." Or whether to pay your tuition or go to Ft. Lauderdale or someplace, that's an "economic problem" too.

But what about deciding whether to study math or play basketball? or cook breakfast or wash the car? an "economic problem" too? Sure. An economic problem is a problem of having to choose—like whether to have your cake or eat it.

When are you facing an economic problem? All the time! Every moment of every day of your life you're having to decide what to do with yourself—with your time and energy and thoughts—and what to do with your possessions—your money and your things.

Right now you're reading this book. But there are a dozen other things you *might have* been doing right now. Right? Sure.

So many, many choices we all have! We're choosing all the time: to do this or that, to make this or that, to use up this or that, to save this or that. There's just no end to it! And now, already, just from reading this first couple of pages you can see your own personal "economic problem." It's your problem of choosing—of deciding what to do with all the different things available to you. That's *your* economic problem.

Does your family have an economic problem? Like who will wash the dishes or the car and who will get to use the car and who will get to spend how much of the money? Sure. What about your church? Your club? Any organization? Do they have an economic problem? Sure.

What about your city? Your local school board? The corner grocery? The burger drive-in? Your college? Do they have an economic problem too? a problem of deciding what to do with what they have? and of who will get to use how much of what? Of course they do.

Every Society Is Always Making Choices

What about the whole society? Does it face a problem of choosing? of deciding who will do what, who will get to have how much of what, which things to use up and which to save and all that? Of course it does!

It's pretty easy for you to see how you decided to spend your time right now, getting started in this book. It isn't so tough seeing how each person decides.

All of us think about the different things we might do and then we try to make the best choices from our own points of view. But what about the society? How does the society decide what to do and what to make? and what to use up and what to save? and who will get to have how much of what?

Seeing how the society solves its economic problem is not obvious. Not unless you understand economics. That's one of the things you'll learn in the chapters coming up.

Society's Problems Are Economic Problems—and More Than That

Every society has always faced problems. As times change the problems change, but some problems always seem to be there. These days people are concerned about the population problem and about environmental destruction.

Are problems of this sort economic problems? Yes. They're economic problems—but not just economic problems. They're economic problems and more than that.

All real-world problems—all the problems that face the human race—are economic problems. Sure. But they're more than that. You'll never find a real-world problem that isn't both an economic problem and more than an economic problem.

Pick any current problem you're concerned about: the crime rate, inadequate housing, drug abuse, unemployment, poverty—all economic problems? Yes. All economic problems and more than that.

What about the problem of international tensions? wars? rising prices? school integration? urban blight? Are these economic problems? Of course. Not *just* economic problems, but economic problems to be sure. *Economic problems and more than that.*

Without "Scientific Economics," Common Sense Can Mislead You

In many chapters throughout this book you'll be reading about real-world problems. When you do, you'll learn to see each of the problems in a new and different light. Each problem will be more clear to you than ever before. That's one of the important reasons why it's a good idea to study economics.

The study of economics is going to let you really understand many things that will concern you all your life—things which your common sense alone couldn't explain. Sometimes your common sense might even mislead you! There are so many things a person really can't understand without some "scientific-knowledge" of economics.

If the study of economics is so important, then it's worth some effort. Right? But what if it would turn out to be fun too? Impossible you say? Not at all. Just you wait and see.

Contents

Note: For a listing of all Part and Chapter titles, see inside front cover.

PART ONE

You Can't Have Your Cake And Eat It Too!

1

Economic Principles and the Crisis Issues of the 1980s

Chapter Objectives

● This chapter highlights and explains some of the **economic problems**—some of the **crisis issues**—of the **American economy and the world economy** in the 1980s. And it emphasizes the **impossibility** of understanding these issues **without an understanding of the principles of economics.**

● When you finish studying this chapter you will be able **to give a brief explanation of the most important economic crisis issues** of the early 1980s.

● You will be able to give the highlights of the **inflation problem**, the **energy crisis**, the **productivity crisis**, the Reagan **"supply-side economics" program**, the **"guns or butter" problem**, the problem of the **government deficit**, and the crushing impact of the **high interest rates.**

● And you will be able to explain the **most basic law of economics—that there's no such thing as a free lunch—that you can't have your cake and eat it too.**

● **Note: All of the principles and issues** explained in each chapter are listed in the **end-of-chapter Review Exercises.** Some students find it helpful **to review that list** before reading the chapter. Others find it confusing to do this. You should check it out for yourself and **do whatever works best for you.**

THE ECONOMY IN CRISIS?

Do you believe this statement?

THE AMERICAN ECONOMY IS IN A PERILOUS STATE.

In September of 1980 the prestigious Committee for Economic Development (including American economists and business leaders) issued the report: *Fighting Inflation and Rebuilding a Sound Economy*. What you just read was the first sentence of that report.

The cover of the March 24, 1980 *U.S. News and World Report* shows a whirling tornado of dollars. The title of the cover story is ECONOMY OUT OF CONTROL. And the title splashed across the cover of the January 19, 1981 *Newsweek* says THE ECONOMY IN CRISIS.

Do you begin to get the message that in the early 1980s all was not well with the American economy? If that's what you're thinking, then you're right.

And it wasn't just the American economy. The world economy was in some deep trouble and turmoil too.

Economic "Crisis Issues" Touch Everybody

Maybe you're thinking that you, personally, were not a part of all this—that all this economic trouble and turmoil was just "big national and worldwide economic issues"—things for the political and business leaders and social scientists to think about—things that would never touch YOU! Not true.

The "perilous state" of the American and the world economy was touching everybody. Including you.

That was the way it was in mid-1982 when I was getting this book ready to go to press. I'd be surprised if most of these crisis issues weren't still going on. I'll bet many of them are still around—still touching your life as you are reading this.

Something pretty heavy is going on out there in the world of the 1980s. Economic change is blowing in the wind. Wherever it blows it's having a significant impact on all of us—including you.

It's good that you've decided to learn about basic economic principles—about the "laws" of economics. That's going to link up with your own good common sense. And it's going to let you understand a lot better what's going on in your own life and in the world around you.

The "Laws of Economics" Are in Control

Very soon now (in Chapter 2) you'll start the step-by-step process of learning the basic principles—the laws of economics that we all must live by, like it or not.

How do you learn these principles? These laws of economics? By looking at each one, one at a time. You need to work in an "abstract, make-believe world"—a world where everything else can be held constant—where you can watch each principle work out its influence without anything else to interfere.

So what will you be doing most of the time in your econ course? Studying "the whole picture" of what's really happening in the world? No. You'll be learning the principles—the ubiquitous, inexorable (powerful and inescapable!) laws of economics. After you learn the laws, then you'll be able to see them working in real-world situations. And you'll be able to understand a lot better what's going on.

Soon we'll go back and start at the beginning in our abstract "vacuum world." But first, how about a quick look at the real world of the 1980s? What are the major economic problems? The "crisis issues" facing us? The things we're having to deal with as individuals? As businesses? As a society? A nation?

That's what you'll be reading about in the rest of this chapter. After you've been through all that you'll have a lot better idea about what's going on out there. And you'll see why it's so important for you to understand the principles of economics.

When you see how important it is, I hope you'll decide that learning economics is worthy of your best efforts. And I hope you'll resolve to give it all the effort it takes to learn it well.

The "Unusual World" of the 1980s

There has never before been a time and place like the world of the 1980s. What's so special or different or unusual about the world these days? Would you believe, almost everything?

You might call the topsy-turvy world of the 1980s a "back to the drawing boards" world. In many ways it's a new ball game. And nobody has issued the new rule book! We're trying to get it figured out by making our mistakes and getting our penalties. That's the trial and error way we're learning the new rules.

And what does economics have to do with all this? Just this: *It's on center stage!* By the time you finish your study of principles of economics, you'll be able to see that very clearly.

What are the characteristics of this "back to the drawing boards" world of the 1980s? We've been facing inflation, an energy crisis, a productivity crisis, some revolutionary changes in the philosophy and approach of the federal government, huge government deficits, a national debt exceeding one trillion dollars, and our highest interest rates in more than 50 years.

There are revolutionary changes going on in so many aspects of our economy and our lives: in technology, in communications, in labor-management relations, in banking and finance, in international competition, in our international balance of payments, and on and on and on. Those are things you'll be reading about in this chapter.

INFLATION AND THE SHRINKING STANDARD OF LIVING

What's been happening with **consumer prices**? Back in the 1960s, consumer prices during the first half of the decade went up at the annual rate of 1.3%. During the second half of the decade the annual rate of increase was 4.3%.

What about the 1970s? During the first half the rate of increase was 6.8%. During the second half it was 8.9%. From June of 1979 to June of 1980 it was 14.3%!

By the early 1980s, inflation had become the *number one problem* of the American economy. **Controlling inflation** had become the *number one objective* of public policy. Inflation was very much in the news.

The cover story of the March 3, 1980 *Newsweek* was IS INFLATION OUT OF CONTROL?

U.S. News and World Report on October 1, 1979 carried the cover story ROCKETING INFLATION; and on April 7, 1980, HOW TO SURVIVE INFLATION.

The Declining Value of the Dollar

In 1980, what would your dollar buy, as compared with 1970? It would depend on what you bought, of course. Some things (calculators, color TV sets, and a few others) actually were cheaper in 1980 than in 1970. So if you spent all your money for these things the value of your dollar actually increased! But as you very well know, that was the exception to the rule.

Suppose you spent all your money for gasoline. Your 1980 dollar (as compared with your 1970 dollar) was worth 28 cents. What if you bought home heating, and utilities? Your 1980 dollar was worth 38 cents. If you spent your money in exactly the same way as the "average consumer," your 1980 dollar (as compared with the 1970 dollar) was worth 47 cents.

But what about **income**? Some people's incomes increased enough to let them maintain their living standards. A few actually *gained real income* during this period—that is, they could have bought *more goods in 1980* with their 1980 incomes than they could have bought in 1970 with their 1970 incomes. But by the early 1980s most people were losers.

What is being done about all this? And how is "the cure" working? There's been a major effort to control inflation. But you can't really understand it until you know something about the economic principles involved. You'll be learning a lot about that from this book.

The Inflation Rate Slowed

You'll be happy to know that by the end of 1981 the inflation rate had slowed. But the tough **anti-inflation policy** had forced **interest rates** up very high. That was causing some serious problems both at home and abroad. You'll be reading something about that in a minute.

For the whole year of 1981 the inflation rate averaged 8.9%. But it was much slower near the end of the year than it was in the beginning of the year. By the first quarter of 1982 the inflation rate was down to less than 5 percent.

Did the anti-inflation policies help? Sure. But there were some other (what you might call "fortuitious") events that helped a lot too. One of these events was the *decrease in the price of oil*. The next section talks about that.

THE ENERGY CRISIS

You can't go very far in talking about recent economic problems without talking about what has happened to the **price of oil** . That's true for the American economy and it's true for every other place in the world. What happened? How did it happen? And what was the impact? Here are a few of the highlights.

Everything runs on energy. When the **cost of energy** goes up, the cost of everything goes up. When the oil price goes up it pushes up the prices of all other sources of energy. As you learn more about economics you'll understand better why all this is true.

Not only is oil a key source of energy. It is also the basic raw material for the **petrochemical industry** . Look around you right now. Several of the things you are looking at come from oil: synthetic fabrics, dyes, paints, plastics, fertilizers, pesticides, rubber, flavorings, formica, styrofoam, other building materials—even the cover of this book? Probably.

So what happens if the price of oil doubles? Or quadruples? Or goes up by more than 1,000 percent? Worldwide inflation? And other effects

maybe even worse than that? Yes.

Back in the 1960s everybody knew that the "normal price" of crude oil was something less than $2 a barrel. Some kinds of crude are higher quality than others, so prices vary. But in general, the price of a barrel of crude in 1960 was about $1.80. In the early 1970s it was around $2. Then came the crisis.

Impact of the OPEC Cartel

In 1973 the 13 major oil-producing nations got together in their "Organization of Petroleum Exporting Countries" (OPEC) **cartel** and raised the price of oil by more than 400 percent—from $2.40 in early 1973 to about $11 a barrel in 1974.

The shock to the world economy was profound. Both industry and agriculture live on energy—mostly oil. The international financial positions of the non-oil-producing nations were severely hit. The **less developed countries (LDCs)** found their foreign exchange reserves gone—their development programs devastated. But, as it turned out, that was just the beginning.

In 1979 the OPEC cartel doubled oil prices again. Then in 1980 they added on another increase.

In the American economy you can see the effects of all this everywhere you look. **Energy conservation** has become a way of life. And we're substituting other things for oil. That has become "the pattern of life" for businesses, for households and for individuals.

The Powerful Magic of High Prices

By the middle of 1981, the basic laws of economics were catching up with OPEC. **High prices** perform powerful magic! That's one of the most important things you'll learn in economics. OPEC is learning it the hard way.

Since OPEC jacked up the oil price, increased production by both OPEC and non-OPEC producers has been very profitable! Also it has been very profitable for people to find ways

High prices work like magic? That's an economic law?

You bet it is! Just ask OPEC.

to reduce their consumption of oil. So **oil supplies** have been increasing, while **oil demand** has been decreasing.

In 1981, **surplus oil** was flooding world markets. Many OPEC nations couldn't sell all their oil. Some began cutting prices. By early 1982, American consumers found gasoline prices going down.

So is that the end of it? Is the energy crisis over and done with? I doubt it. Throughout the 1980s energy requirements will still be increasing worldwide. Meeting the needs will still be a nationwide and worldwide priority.

During the early 1980s we're having a "breather." It's hard for sellers to raise prices when markets are glutted. But that situation won't last very long. As the world's energy needs expand, the oil markets will tighten again. Prices are likely to resume their upward trend.

What has been the importance of this "energy crisis"? If you dig in very deep on any one of the major "crisis issues" faced by the American economy in the 1970s, what will you find? That the high price of oil has been a contributing factor? Yes. That's what you'll find in every case. The productivity issue (coming up now) is no exception.

THE PRODUCTIVITY CRISIS

What is productivity? And why is it important? Suppose we define your productivity as your "output-value-produced, per hour." Why is that important? Because it puts an upper limit on

your **hourly earnings**. You can't be paid *more than* the value of what you're producing! (that is, not unless some other people are being paid *less than* the value of what they are producing—and nobody likes that very much!)

Income Only Comes from Output

Our productivity as a nation determines the *total value of our output*. And that is what determines the *total value of our income*.

We can't be paying ourselves more than the value of what we're producing! There's just no way! So if we all want to **earn more** per hour, then we're all going to have to **produce more** per hour. Another **basic law** of economics? Absolutely.

Suppose we demand (and get) higher pay per hour, but our productivity doesn't increase. What happens then? The prices of what we produce must go up to cover our higher earnings. When all of us start doing that, all prices go up. Everybody has more *money income*. But all *prices are higher*, so *on the average*, nobody has any more *real income* (goods and services to enjoy) than before. Get it?

Increasing real income depends on increasing productivity. So what's the productivity crisis? Just this: the rate of increase in productivity of American workers has slowed down a lot. In several recent years productivity has actually *declined*.

The Declining Productivity of American Workers

During the 20-year period from 1948 to 1968, productivity grew at an average rate of 3.4 percent per year. So the real income of Americans was growing at this annual rate. So our real income *just about doubled* over this 20-year period. But after then, what?

In the ten years starting with 1968 our productivity grew at only about 1.5 percent per year—less than half the growth rate of the two previous decades. And while we were growing so slowly, what was happening in other countries? Productivity per worker in West Germany was growing at an annual rate of 6.2 percent. In Japan it was growing at 7.9 percent.

If you understand anything about the laws of economics, those productivity figures have got to be telling you something about (a) our "standard of living" trends, and (b) the future of American products in world markets. But in the last of the 1970s it got even worse.

In the three-year period, 1978—1980 productivity in the American economy did not increase at all. In fact it actually declined slightly in each of those three years. Then in 1981 it increased by 0.9 percent. That's hardly enough to mention.

The Impact of the Productivity Crisis

By the early 1980s the declining productivity problem was getting widespread recognition. It was contributing to inflation. Many American producers were having difficulty competing with foreign products—autos, steel, several others.

The news media began to emphasize this problem. The June 30, 1980 issue of *Business Week* is a special issue entitled THE REINDUSTRIALIZATION OF AMERICA. That article suggests basic changes in the economy to meet the special problems of this "productivity crisis."

These two cover stories appear in *Newsweek*:

INNOVATION: HAS AMERICA LOST ITS EDGE? (6/4/79)

THE PRODUCTIVITY CRISIS: CAN AMERICA RENEW ITS ECONOMIC PROMISE? (9/8/80)

U.S. News and World Report carried the following cover stories:

THE U.S. ECONOMY IN THE '80S: CAN WE MEET THE CHALLENGE? (1/21/80)

REBUILDING AMERICA: IT WILL COST TRILLIONS (9/22/80)

The February 23, 1981 issue of *Time* is a special issue with the cover title: AMERICAN RENEWAL.

Why all this focus on productivity? You know the answer. The ultimate survival of the American economy and of the "good life" for all of us depends on it.

But how do we increase productivity? Can the *laws of economics* help us to figure that out? You bet they can!

Increased investment in more and better machinery and equipment is essential. But how do we get that? That's one of the things the "laws of economics" will help you to figure out.

From its beginning in January of 1981, a major thrust of the Reagan administration was to **increase American productivity**. You'll be reading about that in the section coming up.

PRESIDENT REAGAN'S PROGRAM: "SUPPLY-SIDE ECONOMICS" AND THE "NEW FEDERALISM"

What was the Reagan administration's approach to stimulate productivity? One was to get the federal government off the backs of American businesses. Leave them more free to use least-cost production methods. Let them earn profits. And let them keep enough of their profits to make it "good business" to invest in more productive machinery.

Many economists had been saying that our productivity slowdown reflects the discouraging effects of government. If you believe this is the disease, then the prescription is obvious: Free up the productive businesses and people. Allow increased rewards for productivity and innovation and successful ventures. That's what the Reagan administration started trying to do.

Supply-Side Economics

The thrust of the Reagan administration became "supply-side economics." What are the prescriptions for supply-side economics? Things like this: Do what you can to increase productivity. That will increase the supply of goods flowing into the markets. Increased supplies will relieve inflationary pressures. More productive workers can get *real non-inflationary wage increases*.

Increased productivity will let American producers compete effectively with foreign producers—to earn increasing profits—to invest in even more productive equipment to keep the economy going and growing—to result in the ultimate revitalization of the American economy—to let it regain its position of international prominence. But how do you do all that?

The Deregulation Thrust. One major thrust of the Reagan administration was deregulation. Cut out the red tape. It ensnarls businesses, increases their costs, and reduces their productivity.

But cutting regulations is not always as easy as falling off a log! Every regulation is there because somebody (usually lots of people) wanted it there in the first place. In a way it's like cutting government spending. Everything you cut steps on somebody's toes.

The Reagan administration "hit the ground running" on this issue. The title of the cover story of the March 9, 1981 *Business Week* makes the point. DEREGULATION: A FAST START FOR THE REAGAN STRATEGY.

The March 8, 1982 issue of *Fortune* carries the cover story REAGAN'S RELUCTANT DEREGULATORS. This article says that so far the performance of the Reagan administration on deregulation has been "spotty, erratic, and contradictory." Clearly, deregulation won't come easily—or quickly.

The Supply-Side Tax Cuts. Another major thrust of the Reagan administration was to cut taxes. The idea was to reduce the discouraging effect of high taxes on productivity. And taxes were cut. The 1981 *Economic Recovery Tax Act* called for a 5% cut in income tax rates in the first year, and 10% in each of the two following years. But with the tax cut, the problem of the government deficit reared its ugly head.

It was in the fall of 1981 that the federal government debt passed $1 trillion. The deficit in that year was running at the rate of about $100 billion—adding that much more to the debt.

Economists were projecting deficits ranging from $100 billion to as high as $250 or $300 billion a year for the next 2 or 3 years. Congress was nervous about that. A lot of people were nervous about it. The nation's money markets were nervous about it, too. You'll be reading about that in a minute.

Do Tax Cuts Reduce Revenues? Supply-side economics tells us that tax cuts don't always result in revenue decreases! Suppose you cut taxes and businesses become more productive. As they produce more, more income is generated. So the smaller *tax rate* may be more than offset by the *larger income*. So the government may collect more taxes than before!

That's what Reagan's supply-side tax cuts are supposed to do. And maybe that will happen. But it takes awhile. In the meantime how do we reduce the deficits? Cut spending? Right! That's what the Reagan administration was trying to do.

Government Spending Cuts

But how do you cut government spending? Aren't all of the government's expenditures being made to support "necessary and desirable" programs? Sure. And doesn't each kind of spending have its own "voting bloc" supporting it? and fighting to maintain or expand it? Yes. And aren't the costs of all these programs going up, too? Of course.

Cutting government spending is not easy, right? Right! As soon as the Reagan administration took office in January, 1981, it went to work trying to cut spending. The February 16, 1981 issue of *Newsweek* carries a picture of Budget Director David Stockman and the cover story CUT, SLASH, CHOP. The March 2, 1981 issue of *Time* carries the cover story THE AXE FALLS: REAGAN'S PLAN FOR A NEW BEGINNING.

But the "falling axe," and the "cut, slash, chop" didn't apply to military spending. Why not? Because another major thrust of the Reagan administration was aimed toward *building up the military power of the United States*. And that's very, very expensive.

You can't increase military spending by billions of dollars and expect to balance the budget unless you cut out most of the spending for other purposes! And that's why so much cutting, slashing, and chopping was going on.

The Military Build-Up

Even before the end of the Carter administration there were budget clashes in Congress over the question of social programs vs. military build-up. The January 22, 1979 *U.S. News and World Report* carries the cover story: GUNS VS BUTTER: BATTLE OF THE YEAR.

The March 12, 1979 issue of *Business Week* carries a picture of the Statue of Liberty with a tear streaming down her face and the cover story title: THE DECLINE OF U.S. POWER: THE NEW DEBATE OVER GUNS AND BUTTER.

Why "guns vs. butter"? Because back in World War II this phrase was used to symbolize the trade-off: **reduced consumer goods** output to achieve **increased military goods** output—the sacrifice necessary to win the war. Since that time, this phrase **guns vs. butter** has come to mean the **trade-off** between spending for national defense, and spending for social programs and other purposes.

So even before the beginning of the Reagan administration, there was a national debate going on on this issue. But when the Reagan administration's budget projections came forth it was clear that *this administration really means business* on this issue.

In *mid-1981, the administration's plan was to commit $1.5 trillion over the next five years to the biggest peacetime military buildup in U.S. history.*

The cover story of the April 27, 1981 *U.S. News and World Report* is BILLIONS DOWN THE PENTAGON DRAIN. A few weeks later (June 8, 1981) *Newsweek* carries the cover story REAGAN'S DEFENSE BUILDUP: DOES IT MAKE SENSE? CAN WE AFFORD IT? Then the July 27, 1981 issue of *Time* carries a picture of Defense Secretary Caspar Weinberger and the cover story HOW TO SPEND A TRILLION.

The trillion-dollar question was not "Should we spend the money?" The question was "What kind of military hardware should we buy?"

But where was all that money supposed to come from? With all those guns, there's not much left for butter! And that's a fact.

So what can we do? We can't raise taxes. That, says President Reagan, would destroy our new **supply-side economics** thrust. We need to hang tough on that, to increase our **productivity**.

President Reagan's "New Fiscal Federalism"

Another idea is that the federal government could cut out a lot of its non-defense spending. In his State of the Union address in February, 1982, that's what President Reagan suggested.

But if we do that, what about the social programs? President Reagan suggested that we shift the welfare and social service programs back to the state and local governments. The president suggested that ultimately federal taxation (as a share of national income) will be substantially reduced. That will provide the states and localities the opportunity to collect more taxes. So if they wish to continue the welfare and social service programs, they can do so. But that will be up to them.

Throughout this century there has been a continual change in American federalism—in the relations among the local, state, and federal governments. Government programs have been more and more centralized—functions have been shifted from the localities to the states and to the federal government. President Reagan is suggesting that we now take a big step in the opposite direction.

President Reagan's basic argument is that the federal government should only perform those functions which are by nature national—functions which can't be performed by the state and local governments. All other governmental functions should be left to the state and local governments—where they can be performed—or not. The states and localities can decide for themselves what's worth the cost. And what isn't.

What about President Reagan's new fiscal federalism proposal? Will it fly? It would mean basic changes in the American economy, government, and society. That's for sure. But its up to the Congress, of course.

Assuming that Congress is responsive to the people, ultimately it's up to the people. If it happens, it will step on a lot of toes. I don't know what will happen, but it will be one of the interesting things to watch during the 1980s.

THE GREAT DEFICIT DILEMMA

What do we do while we are waiting for "less butter" to make up for the "more guns"? Or while we're waiting for supply-side economics to increase productivity and generate more revenues? Or for Reagan's new fiscal federalism to shift the cost of social services to the state and local governments?

Meanwhile, what about the annual deficits of $100 billion or more? Suppose the Congress goes along with the Reagan administration's budget proposals. Annual deficits of more than $100 billion? How is that possible? Where is all that money going to come from?

That's easy. Just let the government print up $100 billion worth of government securities—bonds (long term) and treasury bills (short term) and sell them. Then they'll have the money. But who will buy all these government securities? Banks. Insurance companies. Some of the OPEC oil millionaires. Private businesses and individuals who are looking for a safe place to invest their money.

Suppose not enough people buy the securities? Then the government can pay more interest. High enough interest rates will induce people to buy the securities. So the government will get the money it needs to finance the deficit. Of course!

The "Crowding-Out" Effect. What happens in the nation's money markets when the treasury is out there selling $100 billion in new government securities? $100 billion a year? That's about $400 million a day, every working day of the year! That's going to pull a lot of money out of the nation's money markets!

What about all the American businesses that depend on these money markets to finance their operations? And their expansions and modernizations? Businesses will be trying to sell their bonds and commercial paper and other "debt securities." That's how they get the money they need for new plants and machinery and equipment—to increase their productivity.

But what do they find? Tight money? High interest rates? Sure. Very discouraging. Businesses are being **crowded out** of the money markets by the government's great demand for money. It's all happening because of the big **government deficits**.

When money is tight and you still want to borrow, what do you do? Pay higher interest rates? Yes. But many private businesses may decide that it just isn't worth it. So they don't modernize. They don't expand. They don't introduce new, more efficient machinery and equipment. So what happens to our program for "supply-side economics?" It doesn't work.

In mid-1982, this "crowding-out" effect was worrying a lot of people. Interest rates were already very high—and with expected deficits of $100 billion? Out of sight!

The Fed Could Create Money. What about this? Maybe the Federal Reserve (Fed) could buy some of the $400 million-a-day government security offerings. Maybe it could buy all of them! No crowding-out effect then! So why not?

If the Fed bought the government securities, that would generate a lot of **new money** and pump it into the economy. You don't yet understand exactly how that works or what it would do to the economy. But before you finish reading this book you'll understand all of that very well.

The effect of the Fed's "new money" would be: **more inflation**. Ultimately that would force **interest rates** up even more. And inflation and higher interest rates, to be sure, are things we don't need any more of right now!

The Basic Dilemma of Reaganomics. So what are we going to do? Go with the Reagan budget? With the $100 billion deficits? Or not?

And if not, what do we give up? Defense spending? Social programs? Or do we forget about those "supply-side economics" tax cuts? And just go ahead and raise taxes to try to balance the budget?

What we are talking about is the **basic dilemma** of the Reagan program. In 1982, this was the "big issue" of "Reaganomics"—very controversial, and very much in the news.

The February 15, 1982 *Time* carries the cover story THE GREAT DEFICIT DILEMMA.

The cover story of the February 22, 1982 *Fortune* is THE BUDGET BIND: HOW TO CUT THOSE DEFICITS—AND WHY.

And in the February 22, 1982 *Newsweek* it's THE DEFICIT REBELLION.

By the time you're reading this I'll bet you already know what happened. I'll bet you could find the answers just by reading newspaper headlines and cover story titles on the news magazines.

THE CRUSHING IMPACT OF HIGH INTEREST RATES

In late 1981 and early 1982, the real rate of interest in the United States was unbelievably high—higher than it had been in more than half a century. The **real rate of interest** is the "stated interest rate" minus "the inflation rate."

Suppose the inflation rate is 10% and the interest you earn on your money is 10%. You aren't earning any *real interest* at all! You're just breaking even. The interest you're receiving is replacing the purchasing power you're losing because of inflation.

But suppose the interest rate you're getting on your money is 16% and the inflation rate is about 4%. The real rate of interest you are receiving is 12%! At that rate you can double your *real purchasing power* every 7 years! And that was approximately the situation in the first quarter of 1982.

The Reason for High Interest Rates

Why were interest rates so high? It obviously has something to do with the *demand for borrowed money*. People and businesses have learned to live on credit. They're out there borrowing all the time.

You already know that the government debt amounts to more than $1 trillion. Would you believe that total private debt in this country amounts to about $6 trillion? That's right. And a lot of this debt (government and private) is always turning over in the money markets. Would you believe billions of dollars every week? That's right!

Inflation's 6%. I am earning 6% on my savings. How much am I really earning? nothin!

Yes, the money markets in this country are very busy markets. It's the high demand for borrowed money (relative to the supply) that keeps interest rates so high. So why doesn't the Federal Reserve go into these markets and buy up some of the bonds and notes? and put in more money? and increase the money supply? That would bring down interest rates! Sure it would.

But you already know what the problem is with that: Inflation! The Fed is holding tight on the money supply to try to hold down inflation. You can't do that and (at the same time) increase the money supply to bring down interest rates! Oh, miserable dilemma.

The Impact on the U.S. Economy

The Reagan administration devised an ambitious "supply-side" program to revitalize the American economy. But in 1981-82 there was one big fly in the Reagan ointment: high interest rates. The high interest rates of the early 1980s had a devastating effect on the housing construction industry, on real estate firms, and on new home ownership. Several savings and loan associations and some banks were forced into near bankruptcy and had to merge with someone else to protect their depositors.

High interest rates forced corporations (and some municipal and state governments) to delay projects needed for modernization, cost-cutting, and growth. High interest rates discouraged investment and played a significant role in forcing the economy into recession, pushing the unemployment rate above 9% in early 1982.

In early 1982 some people were talking about the possibility of a serious depression brought about by the very high interest rates. Several utility companies were cancelling plans to build new power plants because of the high interest cost. Some of the airlines were cancelling orders for new aircraft because of the prohibitively high interest cost.

The International Impact

The high interest rates in this country have had a detrimental impact on our trading partners. Foreigners can trade their money for dollars and then invest the dollars and get high interest!

As more foreigners trade their money for American dollars, that pushes up the international value of the dollar. And that is what happened. So now, Americans can buy foreign goods cheaper. But foreigners can't afford to buy as many American goods. So our export producers have to cut back production and lay off workers.

Another problem was that oil prices in world markets are quoted in American dollars. So when the international value of the dollar goes up, all of the oil-importing countries must pay more for their oil.

When interest rates are high in the United States, that forces up interest rates in other countries. The other nations must push their interest rates up to protect and stabilize the international value of their money. But high interest rates discourage investment, remember? And that fosters recession and increased unemployment. So you can see why the European nations were calling on the Reagan administration to do something to bring down interest rates in this country.

But if we bring down interest rates we may let the inflation cat out of the bag. Nobody wants to do that. A dilemma? Yes. And lots of conflicting opinion on what to do about it.

The Impact on Reagan's "Supply-Side" Program

In early 1982 the news was filled with stories of small businesses and farmers who were facing bankruptcy because of the high cost of borrowing. The Thursday, Feb. 25, 1982 *Wall Street Journal* carries the article MANY FIRMS' DEBT BURDENS ARE INCREASED TO DANGER POINT BY HIGH RATES, RECESSION. The article gives several examples of the destructive impact of the high interest rates on American businesses.

The September 7, 1981 *U.S. News and World Report* carries the article SKY-HIGH INTEREST RATES—THE HAVOC THEY CREATE. This article highlights the impact of the high interest rates on the stock market, on housing, on auto sales, on capital investment by businesses, on government, and on the savings and loan industry. The article shows the losses that are being suffered throughout American industry because of *the high cost of financing.*

Clearly, in early 1982 the Reagan program was threatened by stubbornly high interest rates—aggravated by fear of the "crowding-out" effect of huge government deficits.

PROBLEMS, ISSUES, AND REVOLUTIONARY CHANGES FOR THE 1980s

You can see that the world of the early 1980s was facing some difficult problems. But you haven't seen it all. Not yet. Here's a quick glance at some other things—things you'll understand a lot better when you know more about the principles of economics.

The Changing Population Structure. What's happening to the U.S. *population structure?* It's changing. There are more retired people every year and fewer in the "productive" ages.

This is influencing the directions of the economy: employment, social security programs, education, products produced, housing, recreation—many aspects of the economy. You'll be seeing several important "population-induced" changes throughout the 1980s.

The Technology Revolution. A revolution in technology is going on: new telecommunications and computers, and the widespread use of CAD-CAM (computer assisted design-computer assisted manufacturing) and **robots** This technological revolution will make significant inroads in the areas of production, finance, banking, and in the nature of employment and the labor market.

The October 5, 1981 *Fortune* cover story THE NEXT INDUSTRIAL REVOLUTION tells the story. So does the November 30, 1981 *U.S. News and World Report* cover article THE COMING INDUSTRIAL MIRACLE. The revolution is just getting started. Its impact during the 1980s will be profound.

The Labor Market Revolution. There's a revolution going on in the labor markets, and in labor-management relations. In the early 1980s it's having a significant impact.

Unions are negotiating **give-backs** on fringe benefits—sometimes even wage cuts—in exchange for greater job security. There's a new understanding on the part of labor that, for labor to benefit, the industry must survive! And there is a move toward including **labor representation** on the boards of directors of the corporations.

The "let's all work together and try to survive" attitude promises to revolutionize labor-management relations in this country during the 1980s.

The Revolution in Banking. The revolution in banking and in the money markets is resulting partly from the **high interest rates** you were just reading about. But **deregulation** and **new technology** are having a big impact.

New legislation is bringing banks into greater competition with each other, with the savings and loan industry, and with the non-bank financial businesses such as the brokerage firms, insurance companies, credit card companies, and others. All this will bring **revolutionary changes** in our financial services industry during the decade of the 1980s.

The Invasion of Illegal Aliens. In the late 1970s and early 1980s the influx of illegal aliens appeared to be getting out of control. The January 29, 1979 *U.S. News and World Report* cover story is ILLEGAL ALIENS: INVASION OUT OF CONTROL?

A *Wall Street Journal* article on Wednesday, March 10, 1982 quotes Republican Senator Alan Simpson who says, "Uncontrolled immigration is one of the greatest threats to the future of this country." Simpson is sponsoring a new bill to try to deal with this problem.

Problems of State and Local Governments. The problems of the cities specifically,

and of state and local governments in general were serious in the early 1980s. They were being squeezed by federal budget cuts and the very high interest rates.

In many areas the "taxpayer revolt psychology" was preventing state and local governments from raising additional money through taxes. The October 26, 1981 *Business Week* carries a special report entitled STATE AND LOCAL GOVERNMENT IN TROUBLE. In the early 1980s the solutions to the problems of the state and local governments were not yet in sight.

The Revolution in Antitrust Policy. In the early 1980s there appeared to be a revolutionary change in public policy toward big business. In early 1982 both AT&T and IBM got settlements of their long-pending antitrust cases.

Several big mergers were occurring. The Reagan administration let it be known that our top priority public policy is now concerned with **increasing productivity** and improving the ability of American industry to compete with foreign producers—not with restricting the size of American firms so that they might better compete with each other. It was in the early 1980s that **global competition** (not domestic competition) became the name of the game.

The Underground Economy. The "underground economy" is really the "free economy"—it's the economy which works on its own without the burdens of government regulations or interference or taxes or anything else. In the early 1980s it was becoming a matter of increasing concern.

The October 22, 1979 *U.S. News and World Report* cover story is THE UNDERGROUND ECONOMY: HOW 20 MILLION AMERICANS CHEAT UNCLE SAM OUT OF BILLIONS IN TAXES.

The April 5, 1982 *Business Week* carries the cover article THE UNDERGROUND ECONOMY'S HIDDEN FORCE: MASKING GROWTH, DISTORTING POLICY, UNDERMINING GOVERNMENT. This *Business Week* article says that the total value of activities in the underground economy (legal activities, plus illegal activities) may amount to as much as $420 billion a year (14% of GNP!).

The underground economy is growing rapidly. It distorts the overall growth rate and results in an unrealistic view of what's going on in the economy. It's likely to create some serious problems for us in the 1980s.

The "Balance of Trade" Deficits. The U.S. balance of trade was running large deficits during the late 1970s and early '80s. By 1982 the trade deficit was causing serious concern.

The cost of oil imports had a lot to do with it, of course. But the "strong dollar," supported by our high interest rates, made it expensive for foreigners to buy American goods—and cheap for Americans to buy foreign goods. The deficit worsened.

A Worldwide "Trade War"? In the early 1980s, unemployment increased in the United States, in Europe, and in Japan. Domestic producers in all of these countries were arguing for restrictions on imports. "Keep foreign products out!"

In early 1982 the European Common Market countries called Japan before the Council of the General Agreement on Tariffs and Trade (GATT) on charges of restricting imports in violation of GATT agreements.

At the same time the United States was putting pressure on Japan to try to eliminate some of their barriers to American goods. And the U.S. Congress was considering legislation to restrict imports of Japanese goods if Japan continued to restrict American goods.

Problems of the LDCs. The problems of the less developed countries (LDCs) were serious in the early 1980s. They were hard hit by falling commodity prices, high oil prices, and high interest rates on their borrowed money.

The June 22, 1981 *Newsweek* carries the article HARD TIMES FOR THE THIRD WORLD.

The January-February 1982 issue of *Challenge* carries the gloomy article GLOBAL FOOD PROSPECTS: SHADOW OF MALTHUS.

The January 4, 1982 *Wall Street Journal* carries a headline GHANA'S ECONOMIC SKID ILLUSTRATES BLEAK SPIRAL OF POVERTY IN AFRICA.

All of these articles highlight the serious problems which world conditions of the early 1980s are bringing to most of the LDCs. Their future in the world of the 1980s is not at all secure.

The Twilight of Communism? In the early 1980s the "great economic failure" of Communism as a form of economic system was becoming increasingly clear.

The December 22, 1980 *U.S. News and World Report* cover story TWILIGHT OF COMMUNISM? highlights this issue. So do the October 12, 1981 *Forbes* article THINGS HAVE NOT GOT BETTER, the March 1, 1982 *U.S. News and World Report* cover story COMMUNISM: THE GREAT ECONOMIC FAILURE, and the *Business Week* October 19, 1981 cover story THE STALLED SOVIET ECONOMY: BOGGED DOWN BY PLANNING.

What will happen to the "Communist" form of economic system in the 1980s? Will it "wither away?" Probably not. But it appears that shifts toward using "market system" incentives and rewards and away from "centralized economic planning" will be required. In the early 1980s in China and in several of the Soviet satellite nations, significant moves in the direction of using price and profit incentives were already visible.

Why? What happened? You might say that the basic laws of economics caught up with them. They're learning it the hard way. When you finish studying this book you'll understand what all this means.

Meanwhile, Back at Home . . .

- The U.S. social security system seemed to be in danger of collapsing.
- The automobile producers, airlines, and many other businesses were losing millions.
- The government's program cuts were hurting. The April 5, 1982 *Newsweek* cover story is REAGAN'S AMERICA: AND THE POOR GET POORER.
- The public schools in many places continued to be seriously inadequate.
- Criminal activity worsened and crime prevention was requiring more and more resources.
- The pollution issue wouldn't go away, either. The September 22, 1980 *Time* cover story is THE POISONING OF AMERICA. And the June 29, 1981 *U.S. News and World Report* cover story is WATER: WILL WE HAVE ENOUGH TO GO AROUND?

The "Overwhelming Economic Issues" of the 1980s

You've taken a whirlwind tour through "economic problems and crisis issues" of the 1980s. So how do you feel now? Sort of leaves you breathless, right? Overwhelmed? A little bit bewildered? I guess so.

But that's the way it is in this breathless, bewildering, overwhelming world of the 1980s. And that's one very good reason why you need to understand the basic principles—the **laws of economics**. So you can begin to understand all this—so you can think clearly about these economic issues.

Clear Thinking in Economics Is Not Easy. Clear thinking about economic issues is not something you'll see everywhere you go. It's so much easier to be *emotional* about things than it is to **think clearly** about them. We all know what we like.

We'd a lot rather have what we want than to worry about what economists call "trade-offs" and "opportunity costs." What do we want? Here's a list of some things people argue for:

- Student loans and grants and free college tuition and textbooks.
- A clean environment, no pollution, no "nukes," no pesticides.
- Food and medical care for the hungry children overseas.
- Good job opportunities for everybody, increasing incomes, higher standards of living.
- An excellent teacher or professor in every classroom.
- Excellent books, visuals, study materials, computer services, lab equipment.
- "Decent" living standards for all old people, orphans, fatherless children, handicapped, everyone.
- A powerful America to deter military attack.
- High investment in research and development for increasing American productivity.
- Effective job training and placement programs with equal opportunity for everyone.
- Reasonable prices for housing and utilities and other "necessary" things.
- Good police and fire service.
- No potholes in the streets.

On and on the list could go. I'll bet you could add a few things. Right? I could too. "Other things being equal" I'd be in favor of all those things—and a lot more too.

We Can't Have Everything! But here's the problem—the economic problem: other things are not equal. The most basic law of economics is this: You never get anything without giving up something else. "There's no such thing as a free lunch." "You can't have your cake and eat it too."

We can't have all the guns we want? and all the butter we want, too? No, we can't. We just can't.

In the chapters coming up you're going to be learning the *principles* or *laws* of economics. Sometimes that task won't be as interesting or exciting as reading about the "economic problems" and "crisis issues" of the 1980s. But you need to learn it anyway.

Each "principle" or "law" needs to be learned "in a vacuum." That way you can really understand it. There's nothing else in the picture—no "static" to interfere. After you learn the principles, then you can see how they're working in the real world.

When you look at the real world it's hard to see all the things that are going on out there, all at the same time. So try to learn each principle, each law, one at a time. And learn each one *well*. Then as you get deeper into the book—and into economics—you'll see the principles being put together more and more, and used to analyze the *real world of the 1980s*.

SUMMARY AND SYNTHESIS

In the early 1980s the American economy is facing several serious problems—several crisis issues. The newspapers and news magazines are carrying cover stories emphasizing the inflation problem, the energy crisis, the productivity crisis, the problem of the federal deficit, of government spending cuts, of the crushing impact of high interest rates, and several other "crisis issues."

Economic principles—the basic laws of economics—are playing an important role in all of this. It's impossible to understand these issues without a basic understanding of economics.

Learning economic principles requires dealing in a make-believe vacuum world. Hold everything else constant—then we can see the influence of one variable at a time. That's the way to learn these ubiquitous, inexorable laws of economics.

The inflation rate in this country was very low in the early 1960s. But then it increased almost steadily—to about 15% in 1980. By the early 1980s, controlling inflation had become the number one objective of public policy.

The tough anti-inflation policies of the late 1970s and early '80s, coupled with some "fortuitous" events (e.g., decreasing oil prices), brought the inflation rate down to less than 5% in early 1982.

The energy crisis of the 1970s resulted from the more than ten-fold increase in the price of oil by the OPEC cartel—from less than $3 a barrel in 1973 to more than $30 a barrel in 1980. The shock of this to the U.S. and world economy was profound. Almost nothing in the world was untouched by this "energy crisis."

But by the middle of 1981, the basic laws of economics and the powerful magic of high prices glutted world markets with surplus oil. Prices began going down.

The productivity crisis began to emerge in the late 1960s. During the 1970s worker productivity was growing very slowly, and by the end of the 1970s, was actually declining.

President Reagan attacked the productivity and inflation problems simultaneously with his supply-side economics program. The basic approach was to get the government off the backs of American businesses. Reduce costly regulations. Cut taxes.

The deregulation program was begun immediately after Reagan's inauguration in January 1981. The supply-side tax cuts were made in the Economic Recovery Tax Act of 1981. But by early 1982 the government deficit was running at about $100 billion. Future deficits were projected to be even larger. The crowding-out effect of the large federal deficit was a matter of serious concern.

The administration planned to spend $1.5

trillion over the next five years for **the biggest peacetime military buildup** in U.S. history. But this meant **cutting back on federal spending for social programs**. President Reagan's new fiscal federalism idea was to shift most of the welfare and social service programs back from the federal government to the state and local governments.

In the early 1980s, high interest rates were having a **devastating effect** on several sectors of the economy—discouraging investment, forcing **the economy into recession**.

The basic dilemma of the Reagan program was this **high interest rate dilemma**. If we **ease money** to bring down interest rates: Inflation! But if we don't: Recession!

The decade of the 1980s will see many eco-nomic problems, many crisis issues, many revolutionary changes. Many of these issues are highlighted in the final section of this chapter.

A quick look at all these crisis issues of the early 1980s may leave you a little bit overwhelmed. But it underscores the vital importance of learning the basic principles of economics.

It isn't easy to think clearly in economics, or to accept the constraints. But we can't have all the guns we want and all the butter, too. We just can't. That's economics.

In the chapters coming up you'll be learning the basic laws of economics that we all must live by. When you finish the book you'll understand the world around you a lot better than you did before.

A WORD ABOUT THE END-OF-CHAPTER REVIEW EXERCISES

Each chapter in this book ends with a section of Review Exercises. Each section of Review Exercises contains the following:

1. a list of the *major* concepts, principles, and terms explained in the chapter;
2. a list of *other* concepts and terms mentioned in the chapter;
3. a list of all the graphs and curves explained in the chapter (if any); and
4. a few discussion questions
   (a) highlighting some of the most frequently misunderstood concepts and principles, and
   (b) relating some of the concepts and principles to the "real world."

It is likely that the educational

value of each chapter (to you) will be very much determined by the amount of effort you put into the Review Exercises. The chapters are designed for easy reading and understanding. But beware! There's quite a long jump between *reading and understanding* a concept, and *permanently integrating the concept into your way of thinking.*

You won't get much permanent and lasting value out of just reading—not from *this* book or from *any other* book. The Review Exercises are designed to get you involved—to make this a genuinely educational experience for you. So what should you do? After reading each chapter, without looking back, try to do this:

1. For the major concepts and principles and terms, try to write at least two or three good sentences explaining each.
2. For the other concepts and terms, try to write a brief phrase saying what each one means.
3. For the graphs, try to draw and

label each, then write a few sentences explaining what it means and why it's important.

4. For the discussion questions you might try writing out complete answers. But if you don't have time for that, at least jot down the key points which should be included in a good answer.

After you have tested yourself and practiced explaining everything, look back into the chapter to see how well you did. Then study and practice the ones you didn't do too well on. If you'll do all this you'll learn your economics well and it will serve you well. And now, here are the Review Exercises for Chapter 1. Good luck!*

---

*The *Study Guide* which I have prepared to accompany this text will give you a lot more practice in working with and testing yourself on the concepts and principles in each chapter. It also gives further explanations of the more difficult concepts and principles. Although I don't require it, almost all of my students buy it and use it. For some reason, the bookstore seems to always sell out just before the mid-term exam! So please take a look at it. If it will increase the efficiency of your study time and improve your understanding of the principles of economics, then it would be a good choice, for you.

REVIEW EXERCISES

MAJOR CONCEPTS, PRINCIPLES, TERMS (Explain each carefully.)

the "vacuum world" of economics
the powerful magic of high prices
the economic importance of energy
the relationship between:
—productivity and earnings
—productivity and inflation
—productivity and the trade deficit
—investment and productivity
—deregulation and productivity
—taxation and productivity
supply-side economics

the "crowding-out" effect
supply-side tax cuts
the "guns vs. butter" principle
effect of deficit financing by the Fed
some reasons for high interest rates
domestic impact of high interest rates
international impact of high interest rates

MAJOR ECONOMIC ISSUES OF THE LATE '70S AND EARLY '80S (Give the highlights of each.)

the inflation issue
the declining value of the dollar
the shrinking standard of living
the energy crisis
new international competition

the Reagan deficit issue
the Reagan "guns or butter" issue
Reagan's "new fiscal federalism"
the basic dilemma of Reaganomics

OTHER CONCEPTS AND TERMS (Explain each briefly.)

Committee for Economic Development (CED)
the OPEC cartel
real income
government deficit

federalism
centralized federalism
the real interest rate
The Economic Recovery Tax Act of 1981

OTHER ECONOMIC ISSUES (Explain each briefly.)

the changing population structure
the technological revolution
the labor market revolution
the banking revolution
the flood of illegal aliens
fiscal problems of state and local
  governments

the revolution in antitrust policy
growth of the underground
  economy
balance of trade deficits
fear of worldwide trade war
problems of LDCs
problems of Communism

QUESTIONS (Write down answers or jot down key points.)

1. This chapter says that in learning economic principles (the laws of economics) it's necessary to use an abstract "vacuum world." Can you explain exactly what this means? And why it is true? (You'll know this much better, later. But you should have some ideas about it already.)

2. Following several years in the 1970s of oil shortages and rising prices, in 1981-82 there were worldwide *surpluses* of crude oil and *falling world oil prices*. The book says: "The basic laws of economics were catching up with OPEC." Can you explain what this means? Try.

3. The book says that, in a way, trying to decrease government regulations is difficult for the same reason that trying to cut government spending is difficult. Explain what this means and why it is true. What do you think this basic problem means for the long-run future of the American economy? Discuss.

4. Explain how "supply-side" tax cuts are supposed to result in *increased government revenues*. Is that what happened following the *Economic Recovery Tax Act of 1981*? Why? Or why not? (You'll be able to do a lot better with this question too, after you have learned more principles of economics.)

5. Discuss some of the pros and cons of President Reagan's proposed "new fiscal federalism." Who do you think will go for it? Why? And who do you think will fight tooth and nail to block it? And why? *What do you think* of the idea, strictly from an economic point of view? Do you think it would be good for the U.S. economy over the coming years and decades? Or not? Discuss.

6. In mid-1982 the *basic dilemma of Reaganomics* was this: We must keep interest rates high to prevent a resurgence of inflation. But interest rates must be lowered because high interest rates destroy the effectiveness of the Reagan "supply-side economics" program. But we can't have it both ways!
   a. Explain what all this means.
   b. Check the latest *Economic Report of the President* and/or other sources (including the news media) to find out what happened on this "dilemma."
   c. Whatever happened, try to explain *how* and *why* it happened that way. Do you think that the dilemma will ever be solved, once and for all? and be over and done with? Discuss.

2 What Is Economics? An Introduction to the Basic Ideas

Chapter Objectives

- This chapter gives an **overview of economics**. When you complete this chapter you will be able to **define economics** and to **explain** what the various definitions mean.

- You will understand what economics means from the point of view of an **individual** (yourself), **a business**, and **the entire society**.

- You will be able to explain the important concepts of **scarcity**, **economic value**, and **opportunity cost**.

- You will understand the use of graphs in economics. You will be able to use **expenditure possibility** and **production possibility graphs** to illustrate the economic problem of choice.

- You will have a beginning understanding of the meaning of **microeconomics** and **macroeconomics** and of the **difference** between the two.

ECONOMICS: THE STUDY OF CONSTRAINED MAXIMIZATION

What is economics? Different economists and different textbooks use different words to say it. But the basic meaning is always the same. Economics is the study of **constrained maximization**.

Sounds heavy? It isn't, really. All it means is "You can't have your cake and eat it too"—you must *choose* which to do. So economics is sometimes defined as "the study of **choice**." But what about "constrained maximization"—what does that mean?

The Constraint: Scarcity

Why constrained? Because we don't have *unlimited resources*. The things we have to work with are *limited*. That's the constraint. Economists use the term "scarcity" to express this constraint.

The term scarcity means that there isn't "unlimited abundance." If you think of scarcity in this light, it's obvious that most things are scarce. And it's this "scarcity"—this lack of "unlimited abundance"—that keeps us from doing and having everything we might want to do and have. So *scarcity* is the *constraint*.

The Objective: Maximization

Why maximization? Because we all want to do the best we can at getting what we want: having what we want to have, doing what we want to do, achieving what we want to achieve. And that's what **maximization** means: getting the most we can of what we most want.

What Do Individuals Try to Maximize?

Individuals try to maximize their "satisfaction," or "well-being," or "progress toward their chosen objectives"—whatever those objectives may be. Economists say that individuals try to use their available resources to maximize their **utility** (satisfaction). But "utility" or "satisfaction" is a very personal thing. It's different and unique for each individual.

Economics is about how to use the things you have to get the most of what you want!

Economists have developed some precise ways to analyze the behavior of individuals as they seek to maximize their "utility"—as they face their economic condition of "constrained maximization." You'll be learning a lot about this as you study principles of economics. But for now just remember that individuals try to maximize "utility."

What Do Businesses Try to Maximize?

Business decisions are influenced by a number of objectives. But the overriding objective of a business must be: *to make a profit*. A business must make a profit to survive. So in economics when we analyze business behavior we assume that businesses try to **maximize profits**.

This "profit maximization" assumption is not always precisely true. For example, successful businesses often make charitable and civic contributions. And they do other things which don't necessarily add to profits. But the **profit maximization assumption** lets us build a "first approximation" economic model. It lets us better understand the business decision process—what kinds of decisions businesses make as they face their economic condition of constrained maximization.

What Does the Society Try to Maximize?

The "maximization objective" for the entire society depends on the particular society you are talking about. One society may want to maximize the standards of living of the people. Another may try to achieve maximum military strength, or a maximum rate of economic growth, or economic stability, or perhaps some other objective.

Economics can deal with and analyze different societies which have different "maximization objectives." But much of economics is concerned with this question: "How can a society maximize the **economic welfare** (well-being) of its people?"

"What kind of economic system brings the society the highest level of economic welfare? And how does such a system work? How does it achieve this maximum economic-welfare objective?" These are questions you will be getting into as you study principles of economics.

The Constraint of Scarcity Requires Decisions: Choices

In the real world of limited resources, *the maximization objectives are always constrained by scarcity*. The economic question (the constrained maximization question) is the same for the individual, the business, or the entire society. The question is: "How do we use the limited things we have (constraint) to try to get the most of what we want (maximize)?"

Economics is concerned with *decisions* about what to do with the things we have: which objectives to try to achieve? And which to forego?

Somehow these decisions (choices) must be made by each individual, each business, and each society.

How Are the Decisions (Choices) Made? Given the constraints and the maximization objectives, how are the decisions worked out? By individuals? By businesses? And by society as a whole? That's mostly what the study of economics is all about.

SCARCITY, ECONOMIC VALUE, AND PRICE

The economic value of something is indicated by its price. The price *reflects* the economic value and *protects* the valuable things. People conserve and are very careful to take care of those things which have high prices—things which have great economic value.

But what makes the economic value of something (and its price) high? Or low? One thing: the degree of scarcity. The more it's *wanted* and the more it's *limited*, the more *scarce* it is and the higher will be its *economic value* and its *price*. And then the higher its price, the more carefully it will be protected and conserved. Also, the higher the price, the more likely that more of it will be produced by profit-seeking individuals and businesses.

Scarcity and Economic Value: An Example

Suppose you are out on the desert where water is very scarce. You aren't going to use up the water in your canteen washing your face and hands before lunch! If your canteen runs dry, you will pay all the money you have just for enough water to make it back home. But once you get back home you won't pay nearly so much for water. See how economic value and price depend on the *degree of scarcity*?

Water is not nearly so scarce in the city as it is in the desert. But even in the city, water is a little bit scarce. So people economize water. They don't leave the faucet on all the time, day and night! But if water wasn't a little bit scarce, that's what they would do.

Suppose you're out on the desert wandering around and you stumble into an oasis and find a bubbling spring and a big lake. Suddenly water becomes a free good! It isn't scarce at all. You will drink it, wash your face and hands, water the donkey, splash around in the lake, then splash water on the donkey just for fun. Why not? No reason not to! Water at that time and place is a *free good*. It's economic value is zero.

Marginal Utility Means "Additional Satisfaction"

Suppose, while you are so happy and splashing around in the lake, someone comes along and offers to sell you a drink of water. Will you buy? Obviously not. You would not pay a penny for a hundred gallons. Does this mean that water is of no value to you? Again, obviously not. It only means that *more* water (more than you already have) is of no value to you. Additional water would bring you marginal utility (additional satisfaction) of zero.

This is an important concept in economics. The basic idea is this: The value of something to you (that is, the price you would be willing to pay for it) is never determined by the "total usefulness" of it. The value to you depends on *how useful it would be for you to have more of it than you already have.*

Free Goods Have Zero Marginal Utility

Suppose you have all of something you could possibly ever use. Would you like to have more? Of course not. Any additional amount would have zero value to you. The more of something you already have, the less important it is to you to get even more of it. What we're talking about is called the principle of diminishing marginal utility.

"Marginal utility" is the "extra satisfaction" you get from having a little more of something. Does marginal utility "diminish" as you get more and more? Sure. If *unlimited* amounts are available, then the marginal utility (the extra utility from having more) drops all the way to zero. You saw what happened to the marginal utility of water in the oasis. Right?

Only Scarce Things Have Marginal Utility and Economic Value

Of all the things that people need, air tops the list. Yet, to the individual, air has no econom-

ic value. Why not? Because it is not scarce. The marginal utility you could get from an additional jugful of air would be zero. Therefore the amount you would be willing to pay is zero.

Both of these qualifications must be met if something is going to be called "scarce": (a) people must want it, and (b) the amount of it must be limited. The more it is limited and the more it is wanted, the more scarce it is.

If only a small amount of something is available and many people want very much to have it, then it is very scarce. Its marginal utility will be high and its price will be high. Its use will be carefully conserved, limited, economized.

Economics Is About Conserving and Producing Scarce Things

Most things are scarce. People are willing to work and pay to get scarce things; people econ-

omize the use of scarce things. Also, people work to produce more of the scarce things. Essentially, that's what economics is all about.

Economics is about conserving scarce things, and producing more of the scarce things. It's about choosing—about deciding which scarce things to conserve the most and which to produce the most—which to save, and which to use, and for what.

THE ECONOMIC PROBLEM: WE MUST CHOOSE

The economic problem is the problem of having to decide—of having to choose what to do with our scarce things. The problem faces each individual, each family, each business. It faces each society, each nation. More and more it is coming to face the entire world as a whole.

How are these choices made? By the individual? The business? The society? These are the questions of economics. You'll be finding out the answers throughout this book.

No One Can Escape the Economic Problem

The economic problem—the problem of having to decide what to do with the things we have—faces each of us in each of our roles in life: as parent, executive, worker, student, vacationer, spouse, patron of the arts, homeowner, taxpayer, concerned citizen or whatever. All of us must be constantly deciding what to do with what we have—our money, time, mental and physical energies, everything. If we make the best choices we will make the most progress toward our objectives—toward whatever it is that we want most to achieve.

This same economic problem faces every organization—business, religious, social, educational, political, governmental, etc. It faces every society—totalitarian or democratic, capitalist or socialist, primitive or advanced, civilized or barbaric. No person, no organization, no society can escape it. Those who do the best possible job of solving this problem get the most they can of what they want. Those who don't, don't.

What's Your Most Pressing Economic Problem?

For most students the most pressing economic problem is trying to decide how to use their most valuable resources—their time and "mental energy." How about you? Everyone has lots of conflicting objectives. You want to go out and have fun, get plenty of rest, daydream about your new love, and earn enough money to stay in college. Last (hopefully, not least) you would like to get a certain amount of education. Someday you'd like to graduate. Lots of conflicting objectives, right?

Which Things to Give Up? and Which to Have?

People (and organizations, and societies) want to *do* more and to *have* more than they can do or have. So what happens? We learn to forego some of the things we want. But which to forego? And which to have? That's the economic problem. *It's the problem of having to decide among the alternatives.*

Economizing and Optimizing

Individuals, businesses, and societies must make economic decisions—choices. As they make these decisions they try to **economize** (conserve their scarce resources), and **optimize** (use their scarce resources for maximum progress toward their objectives).

Individuals and businesses do their "economizing and optimizing" consciously. Their *decisions* reflect their *objectives*. For example, a business may decide to expand its output. An individual may decide to spend time and money for a vacation. These are *conscious decisions* aimed

toward their maximization objectives. But what about the total society?

How Does the Society Economize and Optimize? In a "free society"—one in which the important choice-decisions aren't made by government—how are the decisions made? How is the "economic problem" solved? How does the economic system get the answer to the "constrained maximization" question? And does "the answer" bring **maximum economic welfare** for the society? And if so, how does it do that?

When I **economize**, I **optimize**, and I maximize my progress toward my objectives!

Much of the study of economics is concerned with this question: Can the society's maximization objectives be achieved without some kind of "master plan"? Without some overall government plan for the allocation of the society's scarce resources? And if so, how?

The answer is: "Yes." And the "How"? That's one of the most interesting and most important things you will learn from your study of economics.

The Price Mechanism Is the Key. It happens through *automatic price adjustments*— what we call the **price mechanism**. Prices reflect scarcity and indicate people's *values* of things.

Highly valued things have high prices. The high prices protect and conserve these things. At the same time, the high prices stimulate the production of more of these very scarce and highly valued things. Before long you will know a lot more about how all this works.

The Opportunity Cost Is the Opportunity Lost

Choosing is difficult. Each time you choose to use resources for one purpose or objective, that means *you must forego some other objective.* In economics that's what we mean by the term op-portunity cost.

A simple statement of opportunity cost is: "You can't have your cake and eat it too." If you decide to *have* your cake, you give up the opportunity to *eat* it. If you decide to *eat* your cake, you give up the opportunity to *have* it.

Suppose you're deciding whether to buy a new car or to go on a vacation. If you decide on the car, the opportunity cost of the car is the lost vacation. If you decide on the vacation, the opportunity cost of the vacation is the lost car.

Suppose the federal government decides to cut spending for welfare so that it can put more money (resources) into national defense. The opportunity cost of increased defense is the loss in welfare services.

Opportunity cost is always there. Why? Because of scarcity. For most things, "unlimited abundance" just doesn't exist. So we're always choosing—making trade-offs—giving up one thing so we can have another. There's no escape from opportunity cost.

IN ECONOMICS, GRAPHS CAN HELP!

NOTE: Students who already understand graphs may skip this section and go immediately to Figure 2-1. But for the others, here are a few helpful hints about the use of graphs in economics.

Economists use a simple graph to illustrate opportunity cost. You already know the idea: "The more you get of one thing, the less you get of the other." The relationship is easy to show on a graph.

A graph always shows the relationship between two things. One thing is measured along the horizontal (x) axis; the other is measured up the vertical (y) axis. Any point on a graph shows a certain number of units of x and the corresponding number of units of y.

You might say that a curve in a graph is an "if . . . then" line. Each point along the curve tells you "if you have 'this amount' of x, then you will have 'this amount' of y."

Positive Slope? or Negative Slope?

Sometimes the curve slopes downward as it moves to the right (as in Figure 2-1). This is called negative slope. It means that as you get more of x, you have less of y. Or as you get more of y, you have less of x.

Some curves have positive slope. As you get more x, you get more y. For example, if you make a graph showing "miles traveled" on the x axis and "gasoline used" on the y axis, the curve in the graph will have a positive slope. It will show that as "miles traveled" increases, "gasoline used" increases also.

Maybe it would be a good idea for you to draw some graphs showing the relationships between some things you know about. Could you put study time on one axis and your exam grades on the other? Relate how much you eat to how much you weigh? The number of people you smile at to the number who smile at you? Hours of the week spent on study to hours spent on other things? Time in the sun and amount of suntan? (or maybe sunburn?) Sure. Take a few minutes and draw some graphs. You will gain a valuable tool—one which will serve you well.

Learn the Graphs Well!

If you aren't in the habit of reading and drawing graphs (and who is?) it's important that you get started right. Study each graph carefully for about five minutes. (Time yourself.) Then practice drawing the graph until you can draw and explain it without looking in the book.

Figure 2-1 is a graph illustrating opportunity cost. Study the graph and read the explanations. Then practice drawing and explaining it to yourself until you have it down pat. You should do that right now, before you go on to the next section.

Fig. 2-1   The Expenditure (or Consumption) Possibility Curve

This line shows that you have $5 to spend, so if the price is $1, you can buy 5 combos if you want...

...or maybe you want 3 combos and 2 lunches...

If you make this choice you get only one combo and 2 lunches. You don't spend all your money!

...or maybe one combo and 4 lunches...

...or 5 lunches.

The Constraint: Your Consumption Possibility

Giantburger-Shake Combos ($1 each)

Counter-Special Lunches ($1 each)

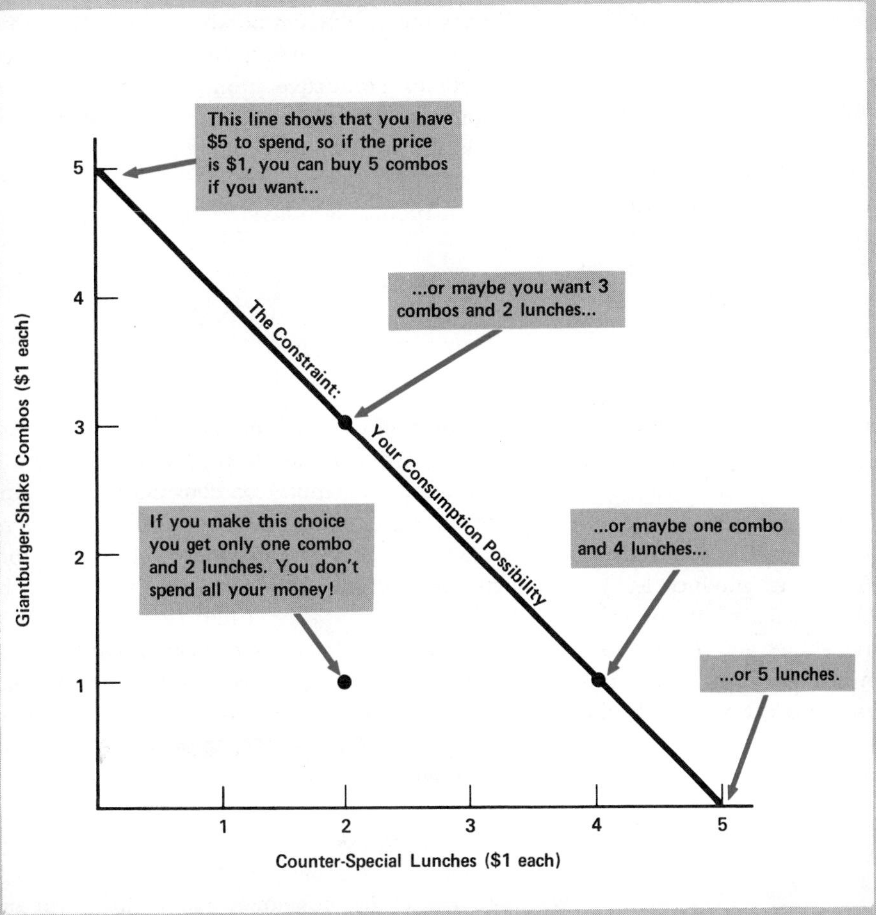

This curve shows the "outer limit" of what you can buy.

You can't buy any more than you can pay for, so you must choose.

This shows the concept of opportunity cost in spending money. You have five dollars weekly to spend for lunch and you must choose between the "counter-special lunch" and the "giantburger-shake combo."

If you only have $5 to spend for lunches this week, you can only spend $1 per day. This graph shows your choices.

The *expenditure possibility curve* is also called the *consumption possibility curve* and the *budget constraint line*. All three terms mean the same thing.

Which combination will you choose? You already know the answer to that—the one that best suits your tastes! You'll choose the combination that brings you the most satisfaction from your five dollars.

If you really go for the combos, maybe you will buy *all* combos. But this you know: each day when you order the lunch, it's costing you the combo; each day when you order the combo, it's costing you the lunch—*opportunity cost*, that is.

PRODUCTION POSSIBILITY CURVES

In Figure 2-1 you saw a picture of opportunity cost from the point of view of the individual. That curve illustrates the "income constraint." The same kind of graph can be used to illustrate the constraint on a business or on the society as it decides which products it wants to produce.

The figure you just studied shows a *consumption possibility curve*—the "outer limit" of what you can buy with your income. The figures coming up show **production possibility curves**. Production possibility curves illustrate the constraint of *limited input resources*. They show the "outer limit" of what you can produce with your resources.

Suppose you're producing corn and tomatoes in your garden. And suppose you'd like to produce more corn. You must produce less tomatoes! How much less? That's what your production possibility curve shows you. It's the *slope* of the curve that shows how much tomato production you must give up to get another bushel of corn.

The Different Shapes of Production Possibility Curves

The **straight-line** production possibility curve shows that your productive resources and energies are all "equally substitutable" between product *x* and product *y*. The "trade-off ratio" between the two is always the same, no matter what combination of *x* and *y* you choose.

On the straight-line curve the ratio might be one *x* for one *y* or two for one or ten for one. But whatever the ratio is, it will always remain the same no matter what combination you choose.

Suppose the production possibility curve is **concave** when viewed from the zero point. That means you have some resources which are better at producing *x* and other resources better at producing *y*. If you want to get maximum output

then you must produce some of *x* and some of *y*.

The *concave* curve is the one which best describes the production possibilities for the society as a whole. Whenever a nation contains a great variety of productive inputs—land and natural resources, factories and machines, skilled and unskilled people, etc.—some of these inputs will be best at producing some things, others will be best at producing others. Here's an example.

The Slope of the Curve Shows the "Transformation Ratio"

Suppose the economy is running along producing at maximum output. It's producing a "normal combination" of consumer goods and industrial products. Now suppose that for some reason the society wants more industrial products. The output of consumer products must be cut back.

How much must the consumer goods output be cut back? Enough to release the inputs needed to produce the extra industrial products. It all depends on the **transformation ratio** between consumer goods and industrial products. When we give up a unit of consumer goods, how much industrial products do we gain?

Figure 2-4 shows what happens. The more we cut back our consumer goods output (*y*) and expand our output of industrial products (*x*), the higher goes the *opportunity cost* of the extra industrial products. As we forfeit consecutive units of consumer goods we get smaller and smaller increases in the output of industrial products. Economists have some big words for this phenomenon! We call it the **diminishing marginal rate of transformation**. The concave production possibility curve illustrates this.

The graphs on the following pages show different kinds of production possibility curves. Each is explained on the page on which it appears. If you did a good job of learning Figure 2-1, the following graphs will be a breeze. But take your time and learn them well.

Fig. 2-2   The Straight-Line Production Possibility Curve

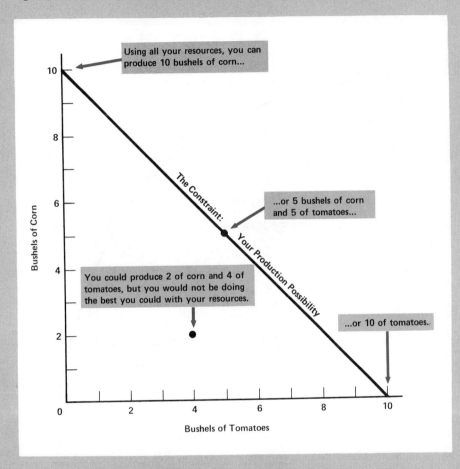

The straight-line (linear) production possibility curve shows that the "transformation ratio" (opportunity cost ratio) between corn and tomatoes is constant.

You have a garden plot, some gardening tools, enough money to buy some seed and fertilizer, and enough free time and energy (labor) to grow a patch of corn and/or tomatoes.

This graph shows your "production possibilites" between corn and tomatoes. It shows that the trade-off ratio (the opportunity cost) is one bushel of corn for one bushel of tomatoes, and that the ratio does not change as you shift output from one to the other. Whenever the "curve" is a straight line, it shows that the ratio does not change. It might be one-for-one, or two-for-one, but whatever it is, if the curve is straight, the ratio will not change as you shift from one product to the other.

The production possibility curve is also called the *"transformation curve"* because it shows how, through shifting your efforts and resources from one to the other, you can (in effect) "transform" corn into tomatoes. In this graph the *transformation ratio* is one for one.

Fig. 2-3 The Concave* Production Possibility Curve

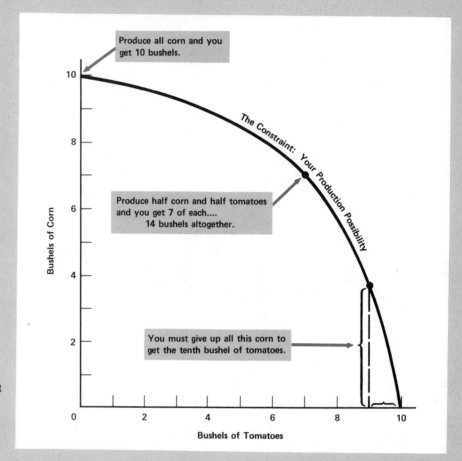

The transformation ratio decreases. As you give up successive units of one, you get decreasing amounts of the other.

You will get the most product by growing corn in the cornfield and tomatoes in the tomato patch.

Inside the figure:

Produce all corn and you get 10 bushels.

Produce half corn and half tomatoes and you get 7 of each.... 14 bushels altogether.

The Constraint: Your Production Possibility

You must give up all this corn to get the tenth bushel of tomatoes.

Bushels of Corn

Bushels of Tomatoes

Sometimes you can produce most by producing a combination of products. Here's a case where half of your land and the other resources are best for growing corn and the other half are best for growing tomatoes. You get the most product by producing corn on the best corn land and producing tomatoes on the best tomato land.

Your maximum output combination is seven bushels of each. Suppose you decide you want nine bushels of corn. You must give up about three bushels of tomatoes to get the two extra bushels of corn. Then suppose you decide you want all corn. To get that tenth bushel of corn, you must give up almost four bushels of tomatoes.

But be careful! The *most* output doesn't necessarily give you the *best output combination.* Suppose corn sells for $10 a bushel and tomatoes sell for 10¢ a bushel. Then you'll produce all corn. Right? Of course.

---

*This curve is called "concave" because it is assumed that you are located at the zero-point of the graph. From that point the curve is concave. If viewed from above, the curve is convex.

Fig. 2-4   Production Possibility Curve for a Nation

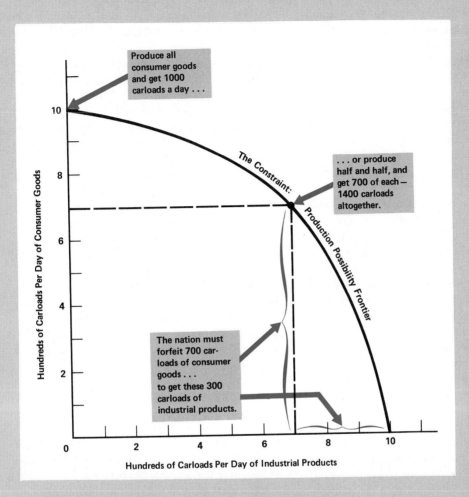

This curve illustrates the economic problem for a nation. It shows the maximum possible output given the limited amounts of available inputs.

If we want more consumer goods, we must produce fewer industrial products. But if we want to build more factories and machines and college libraries and highways and such things, we must cut back on consumer goods.

If the society uses its best consumer-goods inputs to make consumer goods and its best industrial-goods inputs to make industrial goods, it will get its maximum total output. The farther it moves from this combination of output, the smaller the total output will be. Each move from the maximum output position means society is giving up more of one than it's getting back of the other.

What's the *best* combination for the society? You can't say until you know something about the *objectives* of the society. You can see what combination gives the *most* output. But that isn't necessarily the *best* output combination to achieve that society's objectives.

Opportunity Cost Is Everywhere

Perhaps it's a bit sad to realize that all throughout our lives we (as individuals and as a society) are going to have to be constantly de-

ciding to "not get" and "not do" some things, so that we *can* get and do certain other things. But if we always give up the things which are *least* important to us and choose to get (and do, and have) the things which are *most* important to us, then we will have no cause for regrets. The sadness comes when we fool ourselves into thinking that we can have our cake and eat it too.

Individuals can make bad choices. So can businesses and other organizations—and even the society. Some people now are saying we should have been putting less resources into urban thruways and more into mass transit systems. Some people question the wisdom of using our scarce resources in space exploration when the opportunity cost is some other kind of progress—maybe cleaning up the environment. Some criticize the use of so many of our resources for military purposes when the opportunity cost is domestic programs. You can see that the choices aren't easy.

MICROECONOMICS? OR MACROECONOMICS?

Most principles of economics courses (these days) are separated into two major parts: micro-economics and macroeconomics. But that wasn't always true. Back before the depression of the 1930s nobody ever talked about "microeconomics" or "macroeconomics." There was only "economics" or (earlier) "political economy."

During the depression of the 1930s, much of the economics you have been reading about in this chapter didn't seem to make much sense. Scarcity didn't seem to be the problem. There were surpluses everywhere. All kinds of things were going unused.

Businesses had the possibility to produce things, sure. But were they producing things? Many of them weren't. If nobody will buy it, who would be stupid enough to produce it? So the production possibility curve—the "outer limit" of our productive capacity—became irrelevant!

During the period of the 1930s the attention of many economists turned away from the "traditional principles" of economics—of scarcity, constrained maximization, opportunity cost, production possibilities and all that. They began trying to understand why the economy had slowed down so much—why things weren't being produced—why people weren't buying things.

There was widespread unemployment. What was causing all this to happen? It was in this setting that "macroeconomics" came to play a major role.

What Is Macroeconomics?

Macroeconomics is that part of the study of economics which focuses directly on the question of how fast the economy is running. How much output and income are being generated? And why? Macroeconomics tries to understand and explain why the economy speeds up or slows down—why there is unemployment, or inflation—and what (if anything) can be done about it.

Macroeconomics (just as microeconomics) is concerned with understanding why—what would happen if . . . . It's concerned with cause-and-effect relationships: What would cause the inflation rate to increase? Or decrease? What would cause employment and output to increase? Or decrease? What influence can the government have on these things? And how much?

And how? These are basic questions of macro-economics.

What Is Microeconomics?

As you probably already have figured out, **microeconomics** is the study of constrained maximization—of scarcity and opportunity costs—of making choices. Microeconomics tries to understand the cause-and-effect relationships which influence the choices (and the effects of the choices) of individuals, businesses, and the society.

Much of microeconomics is concerned with understanding how the **market process** works. It's concerned with the **price mechanism**, with inputs and outputs, with costs and revenues—and with how all these work in the economy.

You won't really understand in depth what either microeconomics or macroeconomics is until you finish studying the principles of both. For now, it's enough for you to know this:

Microeconomics deals with scarcity and choice and opportunity cost—with the production and consumption and the economic values of individual goods—and with the price mechanism and how it works.

Macroeconomics deals with understanding what determines how fast the economy runs—with total employment, income, output—with inflation and recession—and with what influences all that.

SUMMARY AND SYNTHESIS

Economics is the study of **constrained maximization—of choice.** People, businesses, and societies must choose how to use their **scarce resources** (the constraint) to try to achieve their most **desirable results** (maximization).

Scarcity means everyone can't have all they want for free. How scarce something is depends on two things: how much is available, and how much people want it. If people want something a lot and that thing is very difficult or expensive to produce, then that thing is very scarce—so it's very valuable.

The **economic value** of a thing is indicated by its price. Something very scarce has great economic value and high price. Something not so scarce will have less economic value and lower price.

Prices play a vital role in the operation of the economy. When the price of something is high, people carefully conserve it. Also, when the price is high more of it is likely to be produced by profit-seeking individuals and businesses. Low prices have the opposite effect.

Opportunity cost is forced upon us by **scarcity**. When we choose one thing we forfeit the opportunity to choose something else. The real cost (opportunity cost) of the chosen thing is the loss of the opportunity to have the unchosen thing.

Graphs can be used to illustrate opportunity cost. **Expenditure possibilities** and **production possibilities** can be illustrated with curves showing the maximum attainable combinations of two goods. The **transformation ratio** at any point is shown by the slope of the production possibility curve passing through that point.

Principles of Economics can be separated into microeconomics and macroeconomics. **Microeconomics** deals with scarcity and choice, with individual goods and markets, and with the price mechanism and how it works. **Macroeconomics** deals with total employment and output and income, with inflation and recession, and with what variables influence these conditions.

REVIEW EXERCISES

MAJOR CONCEPTS, PRINCIPLES, TERMS (Explain each carefully.)

economics

constrained maximization

scarcity

the economic problem

the importance of *choice*

the role of *prices*

opportunity cost

diminishing marginal utility

diminishing marginal rate
 of transformation

microeconomics

macroeconomics

OTHER CONCEPTS AND TERMS (Explain each briefly.)

economize

economic value

exchange value

free good

marginal utility

expenditure possibility curve

production possibility curve

transformation curve

budget constraint line

transformation ratio

trade-off ratio

x axis

y axis

negative slope

positive slope

convex curve

concave curve

CURVES AND GRAPHS (Draw, label, and explain each.)

The Expenditure Possibility Curve

The Straight-Line Production Possibility Curve

The Concave Production Possibility Curve

Production Possibility Curve for a Nation

QUESTIONS (Write out answers or jot down key points.)

1. Suppose all the shoe companies made a mistake and produced so many shoes that they had to lower the price to 10¢ a pair to sell them all. Would shoes still be "scarce," according to the "economics" definition of the word "scarce"? Explain.

2. If you inherited ten million dollars, you sure wouldn't have an "economic problem" then. Right? Discuss.

3. What does it mean when we talk about "transforming" consumer goods into industrial goods? That isn't *really* what happens, is it? Explain.

4. When you try to make up an expenditure budget, are you trying to solve your "economic problem"? How about when you work out a time schedule of study hours for each course? How about when the president and Congress try to work out the national budget? Are they working on "the economic problem"? Explain.

5. Can you think of any ways you might shift your own "resource uses" so as to move more rapidly toward *your* objectives? Can you think of any way your *college* might? Your family? Your local city or county government? Your nation? Think about it.

3

The Marginal Concept and Scientific Economic Analysis

Chapter Objectives

- The last chapter gave you an **overview of economics**. This one goes deeper into it.

- What is **economic theory**? What is a **principle of economics**? An **economic law**? And what are all these good for? When you finish this chapter you will know.

- In this chapter you will be learning about the **science of economics**—the **scientific techniques** of modern economics. You will learn more about the **marginal concept** and about its importance in economic analysis. And you will understand the important difference between **positive** and **normative** economics.

- When you finish this chapter you will know what is meant by **economic analysis**. You will know what **economic models** are and how they are used, and you will be able to **build** and **explain** a simple economic model.

- This chapter will alert you to some **hidden fallacies** which sometimes mislead people as they think about economic issues. And finally you'll find out something about the **role of math** in economics.

OPTIMIZING REQUIRES MARGINAL CHOICES

In the last chapter you found out about marginal utility—it means "additional satisfaction." In economics you will be running across the marginal concept in lots of places. Why? Because optimizing—trying to achieve maximum progress toward an objective—requires minor adjustments (fine tuning) to get to the best possible position.

For example, when you're trying to optimize, if a "marginal unit" of something (that is, an additional unit) would be worth more to you than it costs, then you should buy it. If not, then you shouldn't.

Marginal Choices Are "Fine Tuning"

The "marginal choice" question is this: "Is it possible to make small adjustments and come out better?" "If I had a little less of x and a little more of y, would I be better off? Or not?"

If you think about it you'll find that almost all of your "optimizing decisions"—your choices aimed toward your chosen objectives—are marginal decisions. The same would be true for all economic units—all people, all businesses, all societies.

What's so important about making the right "marginal" choices? Suppose each little bit of something used up, is used so that it does as much good as possible. If each choice leads to the best possible move in the best possible direction, then all these little "best moves" must take us to the best possible place! Of course!

Take Care of Your Little Choices

The wisdom of **thinking marginally**—of breaking down the big choices into lots of little choices—is not new. Some 200 years ago Benjamin Franklin told us that we should take care of our pennies—that if we did, our dollars would take care of themselves.

You can see that the whole idea of "marginal thinking" is just good common sense. Still it's a very important concept. Every day small businesses fail and people do foolish things just because they don't know how (or don't bother) to "think marginally."

The Business Manager Must "Think Marginally"

Making "marginal adjustments" is "fine tuning." The idea is that you start from where you are and then consider making little adjustments to see if you might come out better.

Suppose you are running a factory. You ask yourself: "If I expand my output by **one unit** per day, how much will that add to my cost? And how much to my revenue?" If you think the **marginal revenue** will be greater than the mar-

ginal cost, you will expand your output. No matter what your situation was *before*, you are bound to be better off (make more profit) after you expand your output by one unit.

Good Enough Is Best

It's easy to see how *thinking marginally* applies to the business manager. It's just as easy to see how it applies to almost any other "choice situation" you can imagine. Here are some examples.

Suppose you are washing the car or the dishes or the kitchen floor, or you're mowing the lawn or ironing a shirt or a skirt or studying economics. How much time and effort should you put into each task? That's up to you. But you can be quite sure that you will optimize by thinking marginally. That means *doing each job well enough to meet your own personal objectives.* (And it means *not* doing it any *better* than that.)

Perhaps for your brother an absolutely clean, shining, spotless, dust-and-grease-free car, inside and out and under the hood, is just about the most important thing in the world. To him, "good enough" means perfection. Since perfection is impossible, he will never do anything in his whole life except work for and work on his beautiful car. You can't say he's wrong. But you may have a different set of objectives for yourself.

You may be interested in studying economics and making an "A" in the course. You may also be embarrassed about driving a dirty car. So if you have an hour to burn, you will spend fifteen minutes quickly scrubbing down your car. Then you will spend the next forty-five minutes studying economics. Why? Because the marginal utility you got from washing the car during the first fifteen minutes was great. The marginal utility you would have received from spending another forty-five minutes washing the car would be very low—much lower than the **marginal utility** you can get by spending that time studying econ.

How Good Is "Good Enough"? After a person spends a certain amount of time on anything, the extra progress begins to slow down. You could spend all night studying this one page of this economics book. You could memorize it so you could quote it forward and backward. You could count the words and the letters and the commas and periods, and then diagram each sentence.

With your fertile imagination you could think of ways to spend the rest of the semester on this one page! Why don't you? Because your good common sense has already told you that **good enough is best.** You're thinking marginally.

How much time and effort should you put into anything you do? As long as the **marginal progress** you're making is worth more to you than the **marginal effort** you're spending, you're doing just fine.

As long as the additional "value" or "satisfaction" you're getting from your time and effort is *greater* than the additional satisfaction you could get from spending that time and effort in any other way, you are optimizing.

When learning economics, only **very good** is good enough!

Time Is the Coin of Your Life

Are you spending your time and money and things in the best ways for you? Most people seem to be careful with their money, and things. But they waste a lot of their valuable time.

The poet Carl Sandburg once referred to time as "the coin of your life." He said that you ought to be careful how you spend your time—that if you aren't careful, other people will spend it up for you. That idea is worth thinking about. As a student, how you choose to spend your time is likely to be one of the most important economic decisions in your life.

All Intelligent People Think Marginally

Intuitively, all intelligent people think marginally. It's just good common sense. But it's a good idea to stop and remind ourselves that we *really do* have a choice about *how well* to do each task—how to spend each five minutes during each day—how to spend each dollar we have—how to use each thing we have. Success in college (and in life) depends very much on how wisely we make these little choices.

To **think marginally** means to make each little choice so it will do the most good. It means each time you spend each extra bit of effort or time or money or anything, make it do the best it can, for you. It means to optimize the use of everything you have to work with. Only then are you truly optimizing.

There are many reasons for success: in college, in business, and in life. But in most cases the answer rests to a large extent on the way the economic problem is solved.

The most successful people are the ones who do the best job of economizing and optimizing. They are the ones who make the wisest choices about how to "spend up" their scarce time and money and things. It's true that sometimes people are just plain lucky. But I expect the people who do the best job of **thinking marginally** usually come out ahead of the rest.

The Marginal Approach Doesn't Ensure the Best Choices—But It Can Help

Perhaps Benjamin Franklin wouldn't mind if we borrow his idea and say it this way: "Take care of your little choices day by day. Then your

big objectives and goals—like success in economics, or in college, or in life—will take care of themselves."

That's good economics. But recognize that thinking marginally will not always make things come out the way you expected. The marginal approach is essential in making intelligent choices, but it can't insure you (or a business manager, or your college president, or the President of the United States) against making wrong choices.

SCIENTIFIC METHODS IN ECONOMICS

Economics has been the leader among the social sciences in developing scientific techniques of analysis. This has been recognized by the Nobel Prize committee, which ever since 1969 has awarded prizes to distinguished economists for their scientific work in economics.

What are the "scientific techniques of economic analysis"? You already know that economics is the study of "constrained maximization." You know that it is concerned with how people and businesses and societies try to optimize. It's concerned with how everyone decides on the best uses for the limited (scarce) things they have to work with. So what does this have to do with science?

Science Is Concerned with Causes and Effects

Science is concerned with cause-and-effect relationships: What causes what? What would happen if . . . ? So scientific methods in economics are concerned with what influences the

choices—the decisions about what to do with our scarce resources.

How are these decisions made? By individuals? Businesses? The entire society? What would cause these decisions to change? In what ways? And how would these changes alter the economic conditions of individuals? businesses? the entire society?

Suppose we can succeed in understanding what *causes* economic conditions to be as they are—for an individual, a business, or an entire society. Then we can figure out what might be done to *change* those economic conditions. See how important it is to understand the causes and the effects? It lets us know a lot more about what's going to happen. And about what we might be able to do about it.

Techniques of Economic Science: Principles, Theories, Models, Laws

Economic science is concerned with trying to find out what causes what. If you know "what causes what" then you can tell "what will happen if. . . ." If you understand the law of gravity (which could also be called the "principle of gravity" or the "theory of gravity" or the "gravity model") then you could figure out that if you drop a cannon ball and a BB shot off the Leaning Tower of Pisa at the same time, unless something happens to interfere, both will hit the ground at the same time.

In economics, if you understand the law of demand (which could also be called the "principle of demand" or the "theory of demand" or the "demand model") you know that if you're selling tomatoes by the roadside and you put up a sign announcing a big price cut, unless something happens to interfere, you will sell more tomatoes than if you hadn't lowered the price.

Economic science tries to find out things like this. It tries to discover systematic patterns: What causes what? What would happen if . . . ? What depends on what? Economists try to find out these cause and effect (or "functional") relationships concerning production, output, prices, buying, selling—about lots of things.

Economic Models

When economic science discovers a relationship between two or more things, then a model (or principle, theory, or law) can be stated. What is an **economic model**, or theory? It's a simplified picture of reality that tells how some things influence other things. The model leaves out irrelevant variables—that is, it leaves out the "static" of the real world so that we can clearly see what we want to see—so we can see how some things cause other things to happen. All scientists do things like this. For example, the physicists build their law of gravity in a vacuum.

The Ceteris Paribus Assumption. We have our own special "vacuum" in economics. We call it the **ceteris paribus** assumption. Meaning what? Just this: "Everything must freeze!" If everything else remains exactly the same, then we can see how the things we're interested in are influencing each other. Once we understand how one thing (A) influences another (B), then we can predict what will happen to B, if A changes. But that depends on the *ceteris paribus* assumption! Suppose some stronger influences (C, D, and E) all change while A is changing. Then what will happen to B? We don't know.

For example, when you cut the price of your tomatoes we can say *"ceteris paribus,* you'll sell more." Ah, but suppose there's a story on the radio today warning people not to eat local tomatoes because of bugs. So after you cut the price nobody buys any more. People buy less! Does that mean your demand model is wrong? No. It just means "other things weren't frozen." The "other things" had more influence on your customers than the price cut did!

Suppose you dropped a fluffy little feather and a BB shot at the same time out of the little window at the top of the Washington Monument on a windy day. The law of gravity says they'll both hit the ground at the same time. In a vacuum, they would. But will they? Of course not.

Here you can see one of the problems of economic science. The economists may have the best model in the world. But it's always based on assumptions about things staying equal (or about other things changing in a predictable way). But the real world is a very complex place! Things are always changing in unpredictable ways. Some of these changes are bound to cause the results to come out differently than the economists' model would predict.

How Do Economists Build Models? How do economists find out about these cause and effect relationships? We can't easily set up laboratory experiments! One technique is to go back and dig up old data about past happenings.

Suppose you want to find out how buyers respond to changes in the price of chicken. You could go back and find a time when the price of chicken dropped from 60¢ to 30¢ a pound. Then you could find out how much chicken was being bought *before* and *after* the price went down. Then you might build a model saying that when the price of chicken falls from 60¢ to 30¢ a pound, consumers will increase their purchases of chicken by 100 percent.

Of course your model might not work at all next time. Maybe last time the price of beef was going up. Maybe that was mostly why people bought so much more chicken! But economists, especially with the wonders of modern computers, can take a lot of different things into consideration when they build their models.

I'm happy to report that economists using what we call **econometrics** really are building some good models these days. That's one of the reasons economics is the one social science which has been recognized as a science and why the Nobel Prize has been awarded to distinguished economists! In 1980 Lawrence Klein was awarded the Nobel Prize for his economic model building.

A word of warning: Economists often disagree about what causes what, and about how much influence each "cause" has. Which causal factors should be included in the model? And how much weight should be given to each factor? Different economic research groups—all using sophisticated, computerized models—often come out with very different results. The point? Just this: A sophisticated economic model doesn't guarantee accurate predictions about what's going to happen in the real-world economy!

Exactly What Is an Economic Model? An economic model is the same thing as an economic theory or principle or law, depending on what you want to call it. Economists talk about the "**principle** of diminishing marginal utility" and the "**law** of demand" and the "**theory** of the firm." All of these are models: statements of "what causes what" or "what would happen if . . .'' or "**functional relationships** between dependent and independent variables."

An economic model can be stated in an equation which shows the relationships among the variables. For example, in the case of the effect of a price cut for chicken on the sales of chicken, we might use shorthand symbols and say:

Sales of chicken (Sc)	is =	a function of f	the price of chicken (Pc)

This is a model to predict *sales* of chicken, based on *the price* of chicken.

Suppose the price of chicken isn't the only variable you want to take into consideration. Maybe you would also like to include the price of beef (Pb) and the price of fish (Pf) and the rate of employment (E) in your local area. Could the economist build a model which would include all these variables? Sure.

It won't be easy to figure out how much each one of these variables will affect the sales of chicken, of course. So it won't be easy to build an accurate model. Some statistical analysis and some "sophisticated guessing" will be necessary. But it's easy enough to write the model in shorthand symbols:

$$Sc = f\ (Pc,\ Pb,\ Pf,\ E)$$

This says: sales of chicken (Sc) depends on (f) the price of chicken (Pc), the price of beef (Pb), the price of fish (Pf), and the level of employment (E) in your area.

A Macro Model. A model to predict sales of chicken deals with a question in *microeconomics*. Suppose you're interested in a *macroeconomic* model. Perhaps you want to predict the size of the gross national product (GNP). Or maybe the inflation rate. Or the rate of total spending in the economy. Could you do that? Sure. Economists are doing that all the time.

For example, a model to explain the size of GNP might be stated as follows:

$$GNP = f\ (C,\ I,\ G)$$

This says: The size of the gross national product (GNP) depends on (f) consumer spending (C), investment spending (I), and government spending (G). This is a very simple macroeconomic model of the economy. In actual practice macroeconomic models are much more sophisticated and complex than this. You'll learn about some of the complications as you study the macro chapters coming up later.

Economic Models and Economic Policy

In recent years there has been a great increase in the use of economic models, both as a guide to business decisions and as a guide to national economic policy. Several businesses are now in the business of building economic models and making predictions and selling these to other businesses and to government. Businesses use models to try to predict prices and quantities of various inputs and outputs.

In government, economic model builders are predicting everything from next year's income tax receipts to the effects of agricultural policies on grain prices. Government economic policies regarding taxing, spending, and the money supply are constantly being guided by economic models. Models help to predict long-range pollution problems, water needs, expenditure requirements and in fact just about everything you can think of.

Economic models cannot predict with complete accuracy, of course. But usually the predictions are better than we would be likely to get *without* the models. It isn't that economists and their models are always so accurate—because certainly that isn't true. It's just that what the economists are doing is so much better than nothing!

Now aren't you glad you're in economics? And who knows? Maybe you'll get turned on and become an economist. It seems to me that there are lots of *less desirable* ways to go through life!

POSITIVE ECONOMICS AND NORMATIVE ECONOMICS

For more than a century economists have been arguing with each other about whether or not economics and economists ought to get involved in questions of "what should be." Should

economics try to be a "positive science"? to deal only with scientific laws of cause and effect? with questions of "what is?" and "what would happen if?" and stay away from such questions as "what *should* happen?" and "what *would be best* for the society?"

Or should economics be a "normative" field? Should it deal with some of the "less scientific" (more philosophical) questions of *what should be?* Should economics deal with "value judgments"? and try to figure out how *good* or *bad* one choice or another might be, for the society?

Positive Economics Deals with Economic "Laws"— with How Things "Are"

"If you don't pay a person to work for you then that person will not work for you." "If the price of fried chicken doubles and the price of hamburgers goes down, people will buy less fried chicken and more hamburgers." These are statements of positive economics. Positive economics doesn't say it's good or bad—it just tells "what would happen if . . ."

Normative Economics Deals with Questions of How Things "Should Be"

Normative economics deals with "value" issues—the issues of good or bad, right or wrong, better or worse—and of how to make better economic choices for the society.

When economists recommend such things as progressive income taxes and social security programs as "just and equitable," then their recommendations are based on normative economics—on an idea, or philosophy of "social justice." But *the economist's knowledge of positive economics makes possible realistic and feasible normative recommendations.*

Positive Economics is Required for Realistic Normative Recommendations

Anyone who really knows the "laws of positive economics" knows the most basic law: you can't have your cake and eat it too. That's a good thing to keep in mind (and so easy to forget!) when we start making "normative" recommendations.

In the past few years, more and more economists have been getting into the normative "value judgment" issues of economics. Normative economics is much less definite, much less "sure and scientific" than positive economics. For example, it's much easier to say what will happen to a family's food budget if the father loses his job (positive economics), than it is to say what the minimum income of a family of four "should be" (normative economics), or to decide who "should be" required to help to support the family when the father loses his job (normative economics). Yet, even in the face of uncertainties, many economists are willing to get involved in the many pressing normative economic issues of our day.

Realistic and effective involvement in the *normative* economic issues requires a basic understanding of the principles (the "laws") of positive economics. That's why it's good that you are studying economics. When you get to the end of this book you will have a good basic understanding of the principles (the "laws") of positive economics. So you will be able to think more realistically about the normative issues.

ECONOMIC DESCRIPTION, THEORY, ANALYSIS

The ultimate objective of studying principles of economics is to develop the ability to do eco-

nomic analysis. This doesn't mean that you must become a high-powered professional economist! Of course not. What it does mean is this: You will be able to understand what's causing things to happen—to understand how *present decisions and actions* are likely to influence *future conditions.*

Economic Description

Description simply tells you "what is" or "what's happening." It doesn't tell you why. All your life you will be bombarded by descriptions of economic conditions and events. You will hear about what's happening to population, wages, automobile output, employment, prices in the stock market, the balance of trade, beginning wages for college graduates, the inflation rate, changing taxes and government spending and on and on.

As you study principles of economics you need some economic description. Otherwise you wouldn't be aware of what's going on. But description of "what is" at any moment isn't good for very long. The world is changing too fast for that.

As you study principles of economics, don't focus too much attention on remembering "the current facts." The facts are changing rapidly. The important thing is for you to learn the **principles**—the **theory**. The principles and theory will enable you to meet and understand each new situation. How? With your own intelligent use of *economic analysis.*

Economic Theory

You already know about economic theory—about economic principles, laws, models—about statements of cause and effect—of what influences what, and how. *Economic theory provides the basis for economic analysis.*

Economic theory begins with "given certain assumptions," and then it goes on and says "A will cause B to happen." Notice that economic theory, whether stated in a precise model or not, always is based on certain **assumptions**. If these assumptions are realistic (that is, if they fit real-world conditions), then the model or theory can be very helpful as you try to influence and/or predict your own economic future or even the future of the American economy.

Economic Analysis

Economic analysis deals with *new situations*. We see (from economic description) what's going on. We know in general (from economic theory) what kinds of cause-and-effect relationships exist. So now, with **economic analysis**, we try to figure out *why* events are unfolding as they are. Why are we seeing this particular pattern of changing conditions? What's most likely to happen next? What could be done to alter this flow of events? To generate more desirable results?

Economic analysis is the tough part. You can't do it very well unless you have a good understanding of the principles (the theory)—including a healthy respect for the *limitations* required by the *assumptions* underlying each principle or model.

As you study and learn the principles of economics, remember that your immediate purpose is to understand each principle *well*. But your ultimate objective is to sharpen your *analytical ability*—your ability to undertake *economic analysis*—to figure out what really is going on—what's responsible for what—why conditions are unfolding as they are—and what is most likely to happen next.

If you can learn to do this in the stock market you can make a lot of money. If you can learn to do it anywhere, you can certainly come out ahead of most people.

HIDDEN FALLACIES: SOMETIMES COMMON SENSE CAN LET YOU DOWN!

There are some *hidden fallacies* that can slip into economic reasoning and lead you to the wrong conclusions. Some concepts in economics are very tricky. Unless you are very careful your common sense is likely to lead you astray. We need to talk about some of these "tricky pitfalls."

The Fallacy of Composition

In economics there are several things which are true when looked at from the point of view of an individual but which are false when looked at from the point of view of the entire economy, or nation. For example, suppose a farmer clears more land and produces more corn. Does the farmer get more income when the extra corn is sold? Sure. But suppose all the farmers in the country clear more land and produce more corn. What then? The corn price would collapse. All the corn farmers would go broke!

If I can get a lot of money somehow (inherit it or borrow it from a bank or maybe print it up myself in my bedroom) then I can buy more things and live a lot better—bigger house, bigger car, bigger boat, long vacation trips—and I won't have to work anymore. Great! But suppose everybody did this. What would happen then? The economy would collapse. We would all starve to death!

Suppose the government printed up $50,000 in $100 bills and gave it all to you. What a great day for your economic situation that would be! But suppose the government did that for *everybody*. What then? Nobody would be helped. Everybody would be a lot worse off. Probably the monetary system would collapse and the economy would collapse.

This **fallacy of composition** works the other way, too. Free trade can bring great benefits to the people of the society. But does that mean *everyone* in the economy is going to receive great benefit from free trade? Of course not. It may mean that the people who are working at producing sugar beets or hand-tooled leather belts or assembling the movements of watches will lose their jobs. Be careful of the fallacy of composition!

Unconscious Preconceptions

It's almost impossible to begin the study of economics without already having a lot of firm ideas about economic things: maybe about government spending, government debts, business profits, labor unions, taxes, zoning laws, tariffs, immigration policies, minimum wage laws, and lots of other things. Your preconceived ideas will make it difficult for you to understand things in economics which appear to conflict with what you believe. See the problem?

We all have prejudices. We tend to accept everything that reinforces our prejudices. And we reject things which disagree. It's tough not to! But you aren't going to learn economics very well if you go along rejecting things before you even understand them. So try not to do that, okay?

As you study this book, try to understand what's being discussed before you decide to reject it. Ultimately, reject anything you wish. But please: Try to understand it first. Fair enough? Good. You'll learn a lot more economics that way.

Post Hoc Ergo Propter Hoc

This is a Latin phrase that simply means "it happened *after this* (post hoc) *therefore* (ergo) it happend *because of this* (propter hoc)." This is bad reasoning anywhere you find it—in economics and everywhere else. But in economics it's especially common—and especially dangerous.

This is the idea of the rooster who wakes up in the morning and crows and then the sun comes up. He's sure that if he overslept the sun

would never rise! Or if a black cat crosses your path and a few minutes later you stumble into a mud puddle, blame it on the cat. Right? No one with a grain of common sense would fall for that brand of logic! But in economics the fallacy isn't always so easy to see.

The problem in economics is that sometimes it's hard to be sure what causes what. Last year the fishing trawlers caught more fish. This year there are fewer fish. Is it because more were caught last year? Without further investigation, no one knows. In 1975 the federal government gave out some tax rebates. Then the economy improved. Did the tax rebates cause the economy to improve? Without further investigation, no one knows.

It's so easy to say "Look what happened after we did that, last time!" But the trouble is this: *there are so many variables at work all the time.* Unless you know something about the situation other than "one thing followed the other," you really can't conclude anything. So please: Be extremely careful not to fall into the **post hoc ergo propter hoc** trap. And be very careful when someone comes to you with a *post hoc ergo propter hoc* argument about something in economics!

Loaded Terms

Another problem is that often the words we use to express things in economics, aren't "pure." Many words have subtle **"side effect" meanings.** Suppose the government is going to get involved in a new kind of program. The program might be referred to as "government intervention in the free private enterprise system." Or it could be referred to as a "government injection of investment capital for the development of the nation's natural resources." See what a different feeling you get when it's said one way? or the other?

Do we "exploit" resources? Or do we "develop them for useful purposes for the society"? Suppose the govenment levies taxes on high-income people and gives the money to poor people. Is that called "taking money from productive people to support unproductive ones"? Or is it a program of "transfers of money to offset the extremes of income inequality"?

In this book I would like to keep all the words "clean"—no subtle meanings. I don't suppose I'll really succeed in doing it. But I promise to try.

What's True in Prosperity May Be False in Depression

Suppose the economy has full employment. It's operating on its production possibility frontier. So if we want more industrial products we must give up some consumer goods.

But suppose the economy is operating below capacity. There's unemployment everywhere. What then? Then it's possible to have more industrial products and more consumer goods too!

What about the people who are printing up money in their bedrooms? If the economy is seriously depressed, maybe their extra spending will be good for the economy! Do you suppose the economy could be stimulated and prosperity regained if everyone would print up a few dollars and go out and spend them? Think about that for a while!

The "hidden fallacies" in economic reasoning really are good at tripping people up. But after reading about them I'm sure you'll be careful about these tricky pitfalls.

THE ROLE OF MATH IN ECONOMICS

You probably have heard that math is often used in economics. It is. But in this book you have nothing to fear from math. The simple graphs and "economic model" equations you have already studied are examples of the easy way math will be used and explained in this book.

You will see some of these graphs and simple equations again, and you will see a few other mathematical things. But all will be explained in simple, easily understandable terms. So please, don't worry about the math.

The graphs you learned in Chapter 2 illustrate the basic economic problem—the problem of "you can't have your cake and eat it too." By looking at the graphs you can see *exactly* how much of one thing you must give up to get an extra unit of the other. Those graphs helped you to understand opportunity cost. Right?

Equations Can Deal with Many Variables at Once

Sometimes graphs are just great for illustrating economic concepts. But the usefulness of graphs is limited. Why? Because with graphs, it's difficult to work with more than two things at once—one on the x axis, the other on the y axis. But equations aren't limited that way.

The simple "economic model" equations you saw earlier in this chapter show the advantage and usefulness of expressing "cause and effect" in equation form. With equations you can deal with many things—with several products and inputs and other variables all at the same time.

Suppose we want to deal with many things—not just "consumer goods or industrial goods." If we're growing corn and tomatoes we might like to see what happens if we simultaneously use less land and more water and less fertilizer and better seed.

Economists like to try to figure out what's going to happen if the local plant shuts down—what will happen to employment, wages, grocery sales, new car sales, apartment vacancies, tax collections, highway traffic, school enrollments, welfare payments, and other things. With equations we can deal with such things.

You Don't Need Much Math to Learn Basic Economic Principles

Math can be a powerful tool in economics. Advanced algebra, geometry, and calculus permit economists to express and analyze changes in economic variables in very precise ways. These are essential tools in advanced economic analysis. If you are going to become a Ph.D. economist you certainly are going to need to know how to use these mathematical tools.

But what most people need to know about economics can be learned and understood without very much math. In this book you will learn the basic principles and you will get them integrated into your ways of thinking. You will do it by working with words and examples that you can understand and relate to—not by working with highly mathematical techniques. For most beginning economics students, math is neither efficient nor effective as a medium of communication. The principles, by nature, are quite complex. So the medium of communication needs to be the most efficient one available.

A solid, rigorous treatment of economic principles does not have to be highly mathematical. Nor does it have to be dry or heavy or frightening. So fear not.

As you are learning the economic principles, if you have a facility with math you will find yourself translating some of the principles into mathematical terms. If you decide to major in economics, eventually you will need to use some math. What math you will need depends on what specialties in economics you choose and how far you plan to go.

If you major in economics, much of the math you will need will become clear to you and may make good sense for the very first time as you take your advanced economics courses. Some students find it exciting to see how math can be used to help fathom "the economic problem."

But suppose you don't know much math and you don't feel very comfortable with math. Then be heartened by this fact: In this book, English (not math) is used throughout as the language of instruction.

Most "Good Economics" Is "Good Common Sense"

Now that you know something about economics, how does it strike you? Are you beginning to get the feeling that much of "good basic economics" is really "good common sense"? I hope so. Because it really is.

Economics is concerned with the kinds of choice situations you have been dealing with all your life. If you put forth the effort, basic economic concepts and principles will become a permanent part of your way of thinking. Your understanding of economics will help you to make many of your choices throughout your lifetime—for yourself, your family, your society.

Economics, learned well, will provide lifetime support for your own good common sense. I'm happy that you decided to learn it. I hope you'll put forth the time and effort required to learn it *well*. I think you'll be glad you did.

SUMMARY AND SYNTHESIS

Optimizing requires **marginal adjustments** (fine-tuning). You are at your optimum only when it is no longer possible to make any adjustment or trade-off and improve your situation. People who have not yet achieved their optimum position can move toward it by making **marginal adjustments** in the uses of their money, their things, and/or their time.

Scientific economics is concerned with **cause and effect**. It consists of **economic theory, economic principles, economic laws,** and the building of **economic models.** All of these terms refer to "statements of cause-and-effect relationships among variables." Economic theory and economic models now play an important role in guiding the day-to-day decisions (choices) of both businesses and governments.

Positive economics is scientific economics. It studies cause and effect—what will happen if . . . . Normative economics is concerned with achieving desirable economic conditions and goals—of influencing some economic condition in a desirable way.

Economic description tells what is, and what's going on. Economic theory shows the cause-and-effect relationships among economic variables (in general). Economic analysis applies the general theory to new specific situations. Analysis tells us why economic conditions are as they are, what's likely to happen next, and what might be done to change the outcome.

There are several hidden fallacies (tricky pitfalls) in economic reasoning which need to be understood and approached cautiously.

Math can be a valuable tool in advanced economic analysis. But a person who does not know much math can still learn, understand, and profit greatly from a knowledge of economic principles.

REVIEW EXERCISES

MAJOR CONCEPTS, PRINCIPLES, TERMS (Explain each carefully.)

the marginal concept
scientific methods in economics
economic principle, theory,
    law, model
positive economics

normative economics
economic description, theory,
    analysis
hidden fallacies in economics
the role of math in economics

OTHER CONCEPTS AND TERMS (Explain each briefly.)

optimize
economize
welfare economics
ceteris paribus
econometrics
post hoc ergo propter hoc

fallacy of composition
unconscious preconceptions
loaded terms
truth in prosperity may be
    false in depression

QUESTIONS (Write out answers or jot down key points.)

1. Think about "optimizing and economizing" as it applies to your choices
   (a) about using your free time, and
   (b) about using your money.
   Do you agree that "good enough" is best? Explain.
2. One of the things about a "free society" is that each individual has the right to make the wrong choices. Are you making any of the wrong choices for yourself? Is there any way that you might think marginally and shift some of your own time and energy from one direction to another and come out better? Think about it.
3. Explain what economic models are, how they work, and how economic models can be helpful in developing and revising national economic policies.
4. Explain, and give examples that illustrate the difference between economic description, theory, and analysis. Which do you think is easiest? Which most difficult? Why?

4 How Society Chooses: The Market Process and the Price Mechanism

Chapter Objectives

- When you complete this chapter you will know the **three basic questions** which every society somehow must answer: the **output question**, the **input question**, and the **distribution question**.

- You will know the three ways, or **processes** used to make these three basic choices: the **social process**, the **political process**, and the **market process**.

- This chapter explains in some detail how the **market process** works: how it works through the **price mechanism** to **automatically** direct the resources of a "free economy" into the socially desired directions.

- When you complete this chapter you will understand how a society can solve its **economic problem**—how, as it faces its problem of **constrained maximization**, it can work out the choices.

- In this chapter you will begin to understand and appreciate the **importance** of the **market process** and the **power** and **efficiency** of the **price mechanism**.

THE THREE BASIC ECONOMIC CHOICES

Every society which has ever existed has had to solve its economic problem—has had to face its resource-use questions—to make some choices and come up with some answers.

The economic problem of the society can be broken down into three basic questions. First: the output question—what to produce? Second: the input question—which resources to use? And third: the distribution question—who gets to have what share of the output?

You could say the three basic questions are: What? How? and For Whom? That is: What to produce? How to produce it? and Who will get to have it?

The Output Question: What to Produce?

Of all the possible things we might spend our time and resources making, which ones will we choose to make? Will we put more effort into building houses? or into growing food? What kind of food? grain? or beef? Or perhaps we should erect monuments to our ancestors. Or paint beautiful pictures and make beautiful music and write books.

Of all the thousands (or millions) of things

we *might* use our scarce resources to produce, which things and how much of each *will* we produce? Somehow, in every society this question must be answered.

The Input Question: How? Which Resources to Use?

Almost anything can be produced using different combinations of inputs. Roads could be paved with straw, wood chips, boards, gravel, leather, bricks, concrete, asphalt, steel, copper, gold, economics books, or almost anything you could think of. Ridiculous? Well, for some of the examples, yes. Yet it illustrates the fact that almost everything could be produced in several different ways. Somehow it must be decided which resources will be used to produce which things.

Just as we can use different materials, we can use different sources of power and different production methods. For power we can use electricity, steam, draft animals, internal combustion engines, human labor, the wind, water, or sunshine. If we want to make steam we can use wood, coal, oil, gas, nuclear energy, or buffalo chips. As tools we can use steam shovels or hand shovels, conveyor belts or wheelbarrows, paint brushes or paint sprayers, farm tractors or hand plows, adding machines or computers.

No society would have any trouble making the obvious choices. No one is going to pave roads with gold and no one is going to use a steam shovel to plant tulip bulbs. But most choices aren't this easy. Suppose we're trying to decide if we should pave the roads with crushed granite, or natural gravel from the gravel pit, or tailings from the local copper mine—or perhaps some mixture of all three. Now the best choice is not so obvious.

These close choices—where the little marginal "fine tuning" decisions

must be made—are difficult. Should we use a little more land and a little less fertilizer to produce our grain? Should we produce a little more corn and a little less wheat? Should we use migrant labor? or harvesting machines? More account clerks? or a computer?

Not all easy questions to answer. Right? But somehow in every society the answers must be found—the input choices must be made.

The Production Question Involves Opportunity Costs

Sometimes the output question and the input question are lumped together and called the **production question**. In its broadest meaning, the "production question" is concerned with: (a) choosing the specific products to be produced and deciding how much of each will be produced; (b) choosing the specific resources to be used and deciding how much of each will go into making each product; and then (c) stimulating and directing the people and the other inputs to go to the necessary places and to do the necessary things to carry out these choices.

Enough Resources? Never! There are never enough resources to fulfill all our wants and objectives. So somehow we must decide which desired things to have and which to forego.

Isn't there *something* each of us wants more of, for ourselves? or for the society? Maybe not an electric can opener or a bigger car—but maybe a new tire and enough gasoline for a trip to the beach? Perhaps more books? Or maybe more books for the college library. Or more college libraries.

A trip to Singapore? Or France? Maybe better sewage systems in the small towns and villages so we can stop polluting the streams and rivers? Maybe better health and medical care and better food and housing and edu-

What to make? What resources to use? And then who gets to have how much?

I dunno....

cation and transportation for the poor. How about a major effort to develop and install anti-pollution equipment? Or to make automobiles safer? Or to cure muscular dystrophy?

How long is the list? As long as the sheet of paper you have to write it on. Almost everyone sees some desired objectives going unfilled.

Certainly you can disagree with the society's answers to the production question. You can argue that we are producing the wrong things or that we are using up the wrong resources in the process. Probably anyone in any society (anyone who takes time to think about it) will disagree with some of the society's production choices. So long as individuals have different wants, ideas, beliefs, objectives, and different degrees of information and misinformation, how could it be otherwise?

Yes. The production question is difficult. But what about the other basic question—the distribution question? That is difficult, too.

The Distribution Question*: How Much Will Each Person Get?

The **distribution question** asks: "Which individuals will get how much?" Each choice to let one person *have* something means that someone else will *not* have it.

There are lots of ways we could divide up the output. A larger share for educated people and a smaller share for ignorant ones? A larger share for native-born citizens and a smaller share for immigrants? Larger shares for the diligent ones? the tricky ones? the ones whose mothers or fathers got large shares?

How about a larger share for the ones who produce the most? or for the ones who make the most noise and threats? or for everyone who has a monopoly in something? or for everyone who voted for the winner in the last election?

You can see that it won't be easy. But somehow the society must get each person's share figured out.

Everyone Wants a Larger Share. There is no way of working out each person's **distributive share** so that everyone will be completely satisfied. Most people are going to want at least a little more than they get. From the time you first argued about the size of your weekly allowance you probably have been trying in one way or another to increase your "distributive share." Throughout your life you probably will go to all kinds of trouble to try to keep your share rising.

Your Money Income Brings Your "Distributive Share." In all modern nations, people receive their income as *money*. The money you receive gives you a claim to a "distributive share" of the output. You "go into the market and claim your share" of the things produced. The more money income you get, the more output you can buy.

In every modern economy the distribution question is: "How much money income will each person get?" Often the question is stated as the question of **income distribution**. No matter how the question is answered you may be sure that nobody will be completely satisfied with the answer.

Maximum Social Welfare Requires Good Choices

If a society does a good job of choosing—of solving its constrained maximization problem—it will maximize its progress toward its objectives. That's not an easy goal to achieve.

We must produce just the right amounts (proportions) of just the right **output products**. We must use just the right amounts (propor-

---

*The word "distribution" has two different meanings. As used here it is concerned with: "How much of the output each person will receive." A completely different meaning is used in business to refer to the "marketing channel" through which the products are "distributed" to consumers—that is, the movement of products from manufacturer to wholesaler to retailer to final consumer. Be careful not to confuse these two meanings of the word "distribution."

tions) of just the right **input resources**. And we must **distribute** the output among the people of the society in a way that will best satisfy our social objectives.

How can this optimum position be sought? The opportunity costs considered? The trade-offs weighed against each other? And then how can the choices be carried out? It all depends on the **economic system**.

Every society has some kind of an economic system—some systematic way for working out the answers to the output, input, and distribution questions, and for getting these answers implemented. That's what you'll be reading about next.

THE THREE WAYS OF CHOOSING

There are three (and *only three*) different approaches that can be used to answer the three basic questions—to make the three basic choices. First: the **social process**—the choices can be made by the customs and traditions of the society. Second: the **political process**—the choices can be made by the government. And third: the **market process**—the choices can be determined by the free choices of individuals and businesses and worked out through the automatic **price mechanism**.

All three of these processes—the social process, the political process, and the market process—are at work to some extent in every society. In one society, one process may be dominant; in another society, another may be dominant. The one characteristic which distinguishes one kind of real-world economic system from another (e.g., capitalism from communism) is the dominance of one or another of these economic choice-making processes.

The Social Process: Custom and Tradition

Some of the production and distribution questions in every society are answered by the social process. The customs and traditions—the usual ways of doing things—have some influence on all of us. Even in the most modern nations, tradition still tries to force people into customary roles passed down from ancient and medieval times. The movement for "equal economic rights and opportunities for women" is a good example of a modern-world struggle against the ancient bonds of tradition.

The influence of the social process (tradition) on the basic economic choices is much stronger in the more traditional societies—for example in some of the "less developed countries" (LDCs). In a society which operates mostly on custom and tradition, each individual's life—economic, social, and personal—is largely predetermined by tradition.

Three Processes for choosing: social, political, market. That's all.

What determines the activities of the people in the traditional society? Including the work they will do and the share of the output they will receive? Mostly customs and traditions. The same patterns have been repeated by each new generation, century after century.

In most traditional societies the people share the output on the basis of kinship and bloodlines. But usually there also is some special reward for good work. The one who catches the most and biggest fish usually gets a larger share of the catch than the one who brings in no fish at all. But the one who brings in no fish still gets a share.

The Traditional Societies Are Eroding (and Exploding!) Away. Much of the political unrest throughout the world today reflects the erosion and breakdown of the traditional societies. Their customs and traditions have maintained social and political stability, solved the economic problem, and held together and maintained these societies over the centuries. But the breakdown is inevitable. The traditional so-cieties are not designed to encourage—or even to permit—rapid change. But rapid change is re-quired to bring about the higher productivity and increased standards of living which all peo-ple now are demanding.

The day of the traditional society is rapidly passing into history. Sad, perhaps. But not very many of the traditional society's young people (who have glimpsed the "free outside world") seem to want to live in such a society anymore. Most of the people seem to want more personal freedom, and more things—better tools, clean water, modern medicine, outboard motors, cars, transistor radios, and Cokes, beer, and ciga-rettes.

Anthropology and Sociology Explain the Social Process. Economics is not the place to look if you want to understand how the basic economic choices are made through the social process—through custom and tradition. Anyone who is deeply interested in such questions should study anthropology and sociology. It is in understanding the social process—how the so-ciety functions—that you will find the key to understanding how the economic choices are made in the traditional society.

The Political Process: The Government Decides

Billions of dollars' worth of our resources are being used for interstate highways, space ex-ploration, military activities, education programs. How did we decide to do all this? Our govern-ments decided for us. The federal government, state governments, and local governments made these choices.

Governments Make Many of the Choices. All countries rely on the political process for many of their economic choices. In the United States, governmental decisions play a very im-portant role in answering both the production

and distribution questions. You can see the gov-ernment's influence on the production question everywhere you look—streets and highways, post offices and public buildings, parks and rec-reation areas, schools and prisons, and military planes flying overhead.

What about the distribution question? The government requires people to forego some goods and pay taxes instead. When people pay taxes their "distributive shares" are reduced. Govern-ment gives money to unemployed people, poor families with dependent children, disabled veter-ans, old people, students. That increases their "distributive shares."

These examples of government influence (and there are many, many more) show that even in a "free economy" such as that of the United States, the political process (government) makes a lot of the production and distribution choices. Yet the United States is one of the countries in which the government has the least influence on the eco-nomic choices. Political control of the economic choices is the exception—not the rule.

In some countries—for example the Soviet Union and the People's Republic of China—politi-cal control over the production and distribution choices is the usual thing. In those countries the choices which are *not* made by government are the exceptions. Even in the countries of Western Eu-rope, more of the economic questions are decided by government than in the United States.

Governments Direct the Economy by "Command." Whenever a production or distri-bution choice is made by governmental decision (through the political processes of the society), this overrules any other choice which might be made.

When the government levies a tax, the peo-ple pay. There is no choice. When the State Highway Department says a new highway is going to occupy your front yard, sure enough, that's what happens. (You get paid for the land, of course. But you don't have much choice in the matter.)

When the resource-use choices are made by

the political process, this sometimes is called the **command** method for making the choices. You can understand why. Notice that the word "command" does not mean that there is a dictator making the decisions. Your own local city council and county board are making some of these choices every day.

Sometimes the command method involves **direct allocation:** "This piece of land will be used for a naval base; that one for a recreation area. That person will serve in the armed forces."

Sometimes the "command" (political process) method uses the indirect approach. The government simply offers **incentives**—attractive prices for those resources which it wishes to control. Thus the people and resources are persuaded (rather than ordered) to do the government's bidding.

In the United States, most of the government-directed economic choices are carried out by the use of wage, price, and profit incentives. Contractors build government buildings because they are offered payments to do so. Engineers construct dams, aerospace firms make space shuttles, and police officers try to keep the peace all because governments pay them to do these things.

Political Science and History Explain the Political Process. To understand how the choices are made by government, you need to understand the **political process** of the society— how the government functions and makes its decisions.

Why does the government decide to expand the interstate highway system? To cut back the space program? To raise the tuition at the state university? to build a bridge across Oregon Inlet? To increase social security taxes?

In the United States, governmental choices involve decisions by elected representatives and administrative officials and others. In countries with less democratic forms of government the political process is less responsive to the people. But even in the United States, the responsiveness of the political process on economic matters is far from perfect.

The Market Process: Individual Choice and the Price Mechanism

The third choice-making process is called the **market process** or simply, "the market."

Suppose the government isn't getting involved in the production and distribution choices. And suppose there are no traditions directing the economic activities and choices in the society. Without governmental or social control over the economic choices, we're all on our own.

But somehow things must be produced and distributed. Otherwise we will all starve! So what happens? If you want something, produce it for yourself! That seems to be the only way.

But wait! Perhaps you can *induce someone else to produce things for you.* Great idea! But how might you do that? It's easy. Just offer a high enough *price* and someone will produce and sell you whatever you want. Simple? Logical? Yes. And that, in a nutshell, is the *market process.*

How "The Market" Answers the Output Question. Someone produces the things you want because you are buying those things and paying a profitable price. You produce what *others* want, because that's the way you get the money to buy what *you* want.

So, just like that, the society chooses "what to produce." It's automatic! Neither "tradition" nor "command" need to be involved at all. "The market" answers the question automatically.

How "The Market" Answers the Input Question. When I'm making the things other people want, which of society's resources do I use? The cheapest ones I can get to do the job. Of course!

I never use moon rocks to pave people's driveways. Who tells me to conserve the moon rocks? The market. Here's how: Great scarcity puts a high price on moon rocks. The high price convinces me to conserve them—not to use them to pave driveways.

Suppose I did buy and use moon rocks to pave driveways. What would happen then? My "distributive share" would drop to zero. I used up more valuable things than I produced in return!

See what a *high price* can do? It gets people to conserve the society's most valued resources. And, just as with everything else about the market process, it works *automatically*.

How "The Market" Answers the Distribution Question. What about the distribution question. The ones who produce a lot of what I want get a lot of money. That's their income. With that they can buy their **distributive share** of the output.

Where do I get my money? By doing and making things other people are willing to pay a good price for. Of course! The more I produce of the higher priced things others want, the more money I get. So the more I can buy the things I want.

See how distribution is automatically decided by the market process? Your production—the value of what you produce—determines your income. What we're talking about is called the **productivity principle of distribution.** The more productive you are (the more value you produce) the larger will be the distributive share you will receive.

The market process is really only an extension of the way things work in nature. In nature, each living thing must produce to stay alive. Each animal gets to consume whatever it produces. If it produces much, it lives well. If it produces nothing, it starves. That's the way it is in nature with all the animals and birds—and even plants! The productive ones get to consume and live. The unproductive ones die.

The market process modifies this natural "produce and consume cycle" in only one way: It gives each person the opportunity to produce one thing and then consume a different thing. You produce indirectly for yourself by producing directly for others.

The market process lets you specialize in producing something you're good at, and then trade to get the other things you want. When you get into the chapter on specialization and trade you'll see just how important this can be.

To Understand the Market Process, Study Economics. The study of "the market process"—what it is and how it works—will be the most important part of your study of the principles of microeconomics.

Many of the chapters in this book are concerned with explaining the market process. But it can all be summarized in one sentence: The market process works through **demand** and **supply** and the powerful forces of the **price mechanism.** When you finish your study of micro principles you'll understand very well what all this means.

All Three Processes Work in All Economic Systems

Every society has some kind of **economic system**—some procedures for getting the basic production and distribution questions worked out. Every real-world economic system includes some influence from tradition, some from command, and some from the market process.

Each Economic System Is Unique. You've heard about the economic systems of "capitalism," "socialism," and "communism." All of these different systems include all three of the "choice-making processes." So what's the difference between these systems?

The difference is in *how* and *how much* each process is used. For example, suppose the political process of command consists of democratically chosen programs implemented through price-

and-profit incentives. That's very different from a command system with dictator-chosen programs carried out by confiscation and human slavery!

What is "American Capitalism"? In the chapter on "economic systems" near the end of this book you'll find out more about all this. But for now, recognize that the economic system called **American Capitalism** relies fairly heavily on the market process. But the political process also plays a very important role.

An economic system in which the political process plays an important role is usually called **socialism**. So perhaps it would be more appropriate to refer to the American economic system as **mixed socio-capitalism**. And the same name also could apply to the economic systems of "democratic socialism" which exist in the countries of Western Europe.

The Communist Systems Really Are Different. The economic systems of the U.S.S.R. and the People's Republic of China and the other systems called **communism** rely heavily on the political process. Almost all of the production and distribution choices are made and carried out by the government. There's very little "democratic influence" as we know it in this country.

Yes, there are great differences between the "free society" economic systems and the "communist" economic systems. But even the communist systems include some of the influence of tradition. And the market process and the price mechanism, although severely restricted, still play a limited role.

THE MARKET SYSTEM: SOME BASIC CONCEPTS

Now it's time to take a closer look at the market system and at some of the things that make it work.

The Concept of "The Market"

What is **the market**? a place? a thing? Neither, really. It's a concept. If you are growing tomatoes in your backyard "for sale," you are producing "for the market."

If you mow lawns to earn money, you are producing a service "for the market." If your father is a steelworker or a bricklayer or a truck driver or a dentist or a grocer he is "producing" goods or services "for the market," or selling his labor services in the "labor market."

When you spend your income you are buying things from "the market." You may spend money in several stores, supermarkets, gas stations, restaurants. Still you are buying from "the market."

To say that you are "selling in the market" simply means that whoever is able and willing to pay the price can buy what you are selling. If you are "buying in the market" you are buying the things you want from any seller who has them available.

The market may seem to be a fuzzy idea. But for each person (or business) who is making and selling something, it's very real. If the market doesn't want what the seller has to offer, the seller soon gets the message.

Suppose nobody will buy your tomatoes. The market is telling you that you are using energies and resources for something "the market" doesn't want. If you want an income you must do what the market tells you to do—and you must not do what the market tells you not to do!

Market Structure: How Many Buyers and Sellers?

It is useful to think of the market as being "structured" of *buyers* on one side and *sellers* on the other. When economists talk about **market structure** they're talking about the *number* and *relative sizes of buyers and sellers* for that product or service.

Are there many buyers and sellers? or only a

few? Are some buyers and sellers big and powerful? Is it easy for new buyers and sellers to enter this market and start buying or selling? These are the questions you ask if you want to find out about the "market structure."

Market Structure and Market Power. The kind of *competition* existing in a market depends a lot on the kind of "market structure." Suppose you are the only seller of something. Economists call that kind of market structure **monopoly**. You can decide what price you will charge for your product and sell only to those who will pay your price. If that is your situation, you have a lot of **market power** (or **monopoly power**).

"Market power" means the ability to influence or control the price of the product. If there are very few sellers and/or very few buyers, each will be likely to have a good bit of market power. But suppose there are many small buyers and sellers. Then no one will have any "market power" or "monopoly power." Each will simply respond to market conditions. No one will be big enough to have any influence on the total supply or demand or on the market price of the product.

Pure Competition: A Special Kind of Market Structure. One essential condition of the "model market system" is that each market must have a market structure of **pure competition**. If there are many small buyers and many small sellers and no big buyers or sellers, no one has any market power. Everyone must charge or pay the "going price." If you try to charge a higher price, all your customers will go and buy from "your competition." This is the market structure of pure competition.

With **pure competition** no one can do anything but accept the existing market conditions. You can freely enter the market as either a buyer or a seller anytime you wish. You can buy or sell

as much of the product as you want. But you must accept the "going market price."

You will be hearing about pure competition and seeing examples of it several times as you study principles of microeconomics. It's a very special kind of market structure and it's essential in the operation of the "model market system." *

The Market Process Requires Private Property

The market process couldn't work unless people had *private property rights*—to own things—to keep their earnings and the things they buy with their earnings. Your "private property rights" are the rights you have to keep the things you own and use them as you wish.

Anything which interferes very much with a person's private property rights is likely also to interfere with the person's incentive to work. When government collects taxes from people, this reduces the "private property" (income) the people get from working. This may reduce their incentive to work. It is sometimes argued that income taxes in the United States (and in other nations) reduce work incentives so much that the productivity of the economy is impaired.

Property Generates Income. A person with some wealth can invest the wealth and receive income. With investments you can get a *continuing, perpetual income* that you don't have to keep working for! Money invested in bonds or in

*The term "perfect competition" is sometimes used instead of pure competition. Sometimes "perfect competition" is used to mean exactly the same thing as pure competition. Other times perfect competition refers to a theoretical market model where the numbers of buyers and sellers is infinite and where other "perfect model conditions" exist. If you run across the term "perfect competition," usually you can tell which meaning applies.

a savings account *can keep generating income forever!*

If you invest in a house to live in or a car to drive, you are still making an "investment" from which you will receive a continuing "income" for several years—not "money income," but your "real income" will go up because you own the house or the car.

Once you own your house or your car "free and clear," you get the real income of using it without having to make any payments to anyone. You no longer have to pay out your "money income" as rent, or mortgage payments, or car payments. You can use your "money income" to buy more of some other kinds of "real income"—more steaks or lawn furniture or a new stereo system or a trip to Daytona or Lahaina or Acapulco.

The basic "private property right" can be thought of as "the right to receive real income (today) without having to work for it (today)." Many people build up "private property" (money or bonds or real estate or whatever) so that later they can enjoy some real income without having to work for it. Any person who gets wealthy enough—who gets enough private property—will never have to work again!

Most people have a strong incentive to acquire just a little more private property—*just a little more* "real income"—than they already have. Don't you? *This is the driving force that makes the market process work.* The productivity principle of distribution—the idea that how much each person receives depends on how much that person produces—is a vital part of the market process. And it depends on the existence of "private property." If you are going to receive a share according to the value of what you produce, then whatever you receive as your share must become your "private property"—to keep and to use as you wish.

Private Property Rights Are Always Limited. No society gives individuals complete, absolute, unlimited private property rights. As more people get crowded closer together it becomes more necessary to limit the freedoms of individuals to do whatever they please with their property.

The U.S. Constitution says that your property rights cannot be taken away *except* by due process of law. But what this also means is that your property rights *can* be taken away—if it is done by due process of law!

When the State Highway Department decides that a new highway is going to go across the corner of your front lawn, the fact that the land is your private property does not stop the highway! Each time the government collects taxes from you, this takes some of your private property. When a wealthy person dies, the government takes a share of that person's property.

People cannot own certain firearms without governmental consent. No unauthorized person is supposed to own or to transport certain drugs. No one can build anything on his or her property unless the structure is in keeping with the local zoning laws. We are all told what we must and must not do with our automobiles.

How far can the local, state and national governments go in limiting private property rights without upsetting the functioning of the market process? No one knows for sure. The important idea is the obvious one: If the market process is going to work, the people must be permitted to have, to keep, and to use much of what they produce. Otherwise the *incentive to keep producing* is destroyed.

Is "the market" the idea of people buying and selling the things they want to buy and sell?

The Market Process Requires Incentives, Rewards, Inequality

Did you ever stop to think about how reward oriented we all are? Why does a person struggle out of bed in the morning and hurry to get to work on time? What gets the taxi driver to keep fighting the rush-hour traffic? What gets farmers up at dawn to plow, sow, harvest? What gets people to save and invest?

Or .... is "the market" the idea of people trading things they have to get things they would rather have?

Why would a family pull up stakes and move to some distant city where better jobs are available? You know the answer. The promise of rewards. Higher incomes. More and better things.

There aren't very many ways to get the people of the world to do the work that is necessary to keep society fed, clothed, housed, doctored, transported, taught, protected, entertained, etc. One way to get people to do all this work is to reward them. Another way is to order them to do it and punish them if they don't.

If rewards are used, inequality results—some people get more than others. But if rewards aren't used, any other system results in a loss of individual freedom of choice. So which system are we going to use? Either we put up with inequality and use rewards as incentives, or we use something like the military draft to force people to do what the ones in charge tell us to do.

Or .... is "the market" the idea of people producing and selling things so they can get more money and have more things?

Incentives Really Do Work. Incentives, rewards, and the resulting inequality are essential in the operation of the market process. These are the conditions which stimulate and capture and harness and channel the energies of the society and aim them toward the desired objectives. The incentive of reward stimulates and directs the economy and keeps it going and growing.

Would you be just as interested in a college degree if you knew it would have no effect on your lifetime income? Some people would. But many wouldn't.

The market process stimulates and directs most of us. As we try to get ahead, automatically we are working for the entire society. As society evolves, maybe rewards will become much less important, much less necessary as a technique for motivating people. But that hasn't happened yet.

MORE ON THE INPUT QUESTION: THE FACTORS OF PRODUCTION

Whenever something is going to be made, some **inputs** are needed. Obviously. These "inputs" are called **factors of production**.

There are thousands of different factors of production—not just the basic things, but everything from the electricity that runs the machines to the paper that packages the products. With all these different kinds of inputs (factors of production), how do we ever make sense out of what's going on? Easy. We combine and simplify. We group everything under three labels: labor, land, and capital.

Labor, and Wages

People are not factors of production. They are people. But the *effort* they exert to make something is a factor of production. It's **labor**.

Wages are the payments people receive when they sell their labor. The wage rate is "the *price* of a unit of labor."

There are many different kinds of labor. Some kinds sell for low prices, others sell for high prices. Doctors and lawyers sell highly skilled labor and receive high "wages." The efforts of unskilled mill workers and migrant farm workers sell for a much lower price (wage rate). But both are selling labor—their own time, energies, and efforts—in the "labor markets."

Land, and Rent

A second factor of production is land. But like labor, "land" isn't exactly what you would think. To simplify things, economists usually consider "land" to include all the natural resources—all the "free gifts of nature." When we say "land" we include the minerals in the land, the trees in the natural forests, the natural lakes and streams, and even the fish swimming in these lakes and streams, the deer in the forest, and the wild buffalo roaming on the plains. (I don't know why it is that the only thing buffalo ever seem to do is "roam." I suppose it's because "roam" rhymes with "home.") But roaming or not, wild buffalo are "land."

The price paid for the use of land (that is, the income received by the owner of the land) is called rent. If you own a very productive oil well or gold mine or half an acre just off Times Square, the "rent" you receive will put you on easy street. But if you own a barren plot in some secluded spot, better not quit your job and plan to live on your "rent" income!

Capital*, and Interest

The third and final factor of production is capital. Like labor and land, chances are this

---

*The word "capital" has a very different meaning in economics than in accounting. In business finance, "capital" can mean "funds available," or other "liquid assets" such as stocks or bonds. But the economist's definition is quite different.

In economics, "capital" means all of the actual buildings, machines, equipment, materials, and other *produced goods used as productive inputs*. To avoid confusion, economists frequently say "capital goods," or "capital equipment" to make it clear that it is the *real inputs* which are "capital"—not the money or financial assets needed to buy the real inputs. Be careful not to confuse these two *very different* meanings of the word "capital."

---

term doesn't mean exactly what you thought it did. Capital is the only one of the three factors left. So this term must include all the inputs *except* labor and land. And so it does!

"Capital" must include all the inputs except "human effort" (labor) and "natural things" (land). What's left? All the "things" other than the "natural things." That is: The man-made things!

All the "man-made inputs" are called "capital." There are thousands of different kinds of "produced" things which are used as inputs—ranging from buildings and machines and trucks to electricity and note pads and paper clips. All these different things are lumped together and called "capital."

We define "capital" as *produced things which are going to be used as inputs for further production.* Capital is anything which has been produced and which is not available for the immediate satisfaction of someone's desires. Income from capital is called interest. The "interest" is the money you receive because your capital is productive, just as your wage or your rent is the money that you receive because your labor or your land is productive.

Everything produced is aimed either directly or indirectly toward the ultimate objective of "final consumption." If a good is aimed *directly* toward final consumption, it's a consumer good. If it's aimed *indirectly* toward final consumption (if it's going to be used to produce something else) then it's a capital good. All along the "production chain" (for example, from iron ore to an automobile) everything being produced is capital *except* for the good bought by the final consumer (the automobile).

Whether something is a capital good or a consumer good often depends on how it will be used. A small private twin-jet aircraft used by a millionaire movie star to go zooming around the country visiting friends, is a consumer good. An identical aircraft used by a business manager to more efficiently serve distant customers is a capital good.

The tank of oil a person is going to use to heat the house this winter is a consumer good; the tank of oil the power company is going to use to fire its boilers is a capital good.

What About Profit?

Now you know about the three factors of production—labor, land, and capital. And you know about the three kinds of income (distributive shares) the owners of these factors can earn—wages, rent, and interest. You also know that we have defined each factor in such a way that everything is covered. But wait! What about profit?

The market system couldn't work without profit. (If this isn't obvious to you now, you'll see why later.) But is profit a payment to some factor of production? If so, what factor? And what is it a payment for?

One View: The Entrepreneur, and Profits. Economists invented a factor of production to go with profit. What factor? The entrepreneur—the farsighted resource manager who brings together the other three factors, gets them organized and directs them into profitable production.

The entrepreneur is the one who decides what to produce and how much and which inputs to use. The entrepreneur hopes to sell the product and get enough revenue to pay all of the factor owners and have some profit left over.

So we can think of **profit** *as being the payment which goes to the fourth factor of production: the entrepreneur.*

Another View: Risk and Uncertainty and Profits. Another way to explain profit is as an "incentive payment" needed to induce people (factor-owners) to take risks.

Uncertainty is everywhere. Unless people were somehow induced to take some chances the market system couldn't work.

Without the profit incentive, who would quit a steady job at a steady salary and start an auto-repair shop? Who would invest their savings in a McDonald's drive-in? or an organic food store? Who would spend money drilling for oil? or work in the basement every night trying to invent a better antipollution device? Probably nobody.

Profit can be looked at as the reward you get for taking a chance for society, and winning. If you hire some factors of production and make something the people want, and if you do it efficiently, you will be rewarded. Your profit is your reward. But if you guess wrong you get no reward. You lose. Your loss is your "punishment" for using society's resources in ways the society didn't want its resources to be used.

Either way you look at it you can see that profit (and loss) is essential to the functioning of the market process. It can be regulated and taxed and manipulated without destroying the system—but only within limits. Just as private property, wages, rent, and interest are essential, so too profit is essential for the market process to work.

How Many Factors? As Many as You Wish

There are times when it is helpful to break down the factors even further. The labor factor can become several different factors: unskilled, semi-skilled, service, clerical, professional, young, old, male, female, and so on. And capital and land can each be broken into many separate factors.

How many factors are there? As many as you want to define. Use the most useful breakdown—the one that will help you most to observe what you want to observe. For a basic understanding of the market process you can think of either three factors (with profit going to any factor-owner who takes a risk), or four factors (with the risk-taker, resource manager thought of as a separate, profit-seeking factor). You can see the market process working just fine, either way.

HOW THE MARKET SYSTEM WORKS: AN OVERVIEW

By now you're beginning to become familiar with the market process and how it works. This final section of the chapter pulls it together and goes a little deeper. But first, a word of warning.

In this discussion we aren't talking about "the American economy" or about any *real-world economy*. We're talking about the *model market process*—which has never existed in the real world in its "pure" form.

Why do we want to talk about how the "model market process" works if it doesn't really exist? Because it's a useful model. It shows us cause-and-effect relationships. It shows us forces that work in the real world—forces that we must learn to recognize if we want to learn to do any real-world *economic analysis*. So that's why it's worth the effort to learn the model.

The Market Permits Freedom of Choice

With the "model market process" each person would be completely free to choose what and how much to produce and what things to buy with the income earned. Each of us would be free to influence the size of our incomes by deciding how productive we want to be—how hard we want to work. Each of us would be completely free to decide what products we want to buy.

In the model market system, as all the individuals make their choices they automatically determine the choices for the society. The market process just lets nature take its course.

What is the driving force of the market process? Individual self-interest. The desires, hungers, wants of people. All of us are looking out for ourselves. But all of us are working for (producing something for) everyone else. We get rewarded for how much value we produce and how efficiently we produce it.

The Market Answers the Three Basic Questions

All three of the "basic economic questions" are being answered all the time, automatically. As each individual, family, and business works to solve its own economic problem, the society's economic problem is automatically solved.

People buy more of the things they want most. This pushes the price up, and the high price stimulates other people to go into business and make more of those things. So the output question is answered.

The Price Mechanism causes all those things to happen automatically! WOW!

The business is interested in making profit, so it uses the inputs which will do the job at least cost. The business carefully conserves and optimizes the use of society's resources. So the input question is answered.

The owners of the most profitable businesses will get the best incomes. Their most productive employees will get the best wages. The people who supply the best resources and equipment and products to the businesses will receive the highest incomes. The most output goes to the most productive ones. This is the way the distribution question is answered.

The Results: Socially Desirable? Or Not?

Would the pure market process always make "good" choices? Would it always produce the "best" combination of outputs? using the "best" combinations of inputs? Would it always distribute the outputs so that everyone gets the "best," most "socially desirable" share? No. It wouldn't always do this.

Many times throughout this book you will see examples of the inability of the market process to fulfill the wishes of the society. One of the reasons why no "pure market" economic system exists in the world is because (in its pure form) no society would put up with it!

The market process (acting alone) is not capable of making acceptable social choices about everything. About many things, yes. But about some things, no.

In education, antipollution, social security, and in many other areas the market process is "overruled" by the society. The *political process* takes over and tries to do what the society thinks should be done.

But note this well: for *many* things the market process can be very effective in helping society to optimize. It can bring results which are much more socially desirable than would likely be achieved any other way. It's very important to remember that. The more economics you know the better you will understand what this means. Much of your study of principles of microeconomics will be about the market process and about its powerful messenger: the price mechanism.

SUMMARY AND SYNTHESIS

Every society must make choices about three basic economic questions: **output, input,** and **distribution.** These are the questions of "What to produce?" "How?" and "For Whom?"

Societies can make their economic choices by: the **social process of tradition,** the **political process of command,** or the **market process** which responds to the free actions of individuals and businesses and works through the **price mechanism.**

All three of the processes (social, political, and market) are at work to some extent in every society. The kind of economic system which exists in a society depends mostly on the **relative importance** of these three choice-making processes.

"The market" answers the three basic questions as follows:

   a. Those things which are demanded enough to support prices high enough to cover the cost of production will be produced. Those which are not, will not.

   b. The resources which will do the job at least cost (with lowest input prices) will be used as inputs.

   c. The most productive people will be paid the highest prices for their services, will get the most income, and therefore will get the largest shares of the output.

Market structure means the numbers and relative sizes of the buyers and sellers of a product. **Pure competition** is a special kind of market structure in which there are so many small buyers and sellers that no buyer or seller has any **market power** (monopoly power), so the **price mechanism** is in complete control in that market.

The market process requires that **private property** exist, and that **incentives and rewards** be used to direct people's activities. Therefore some **inequality** is necessary to permit the market process to function.

The factors of production are **labor, land,** and **capital,** and (sometimes) the **entrepreneur.** The payments to these factors are **wages, rent, interest,** and **profit.** Profit can be considered to be a return to the entrepreneur or a return for successful risk taking.

It is the **powerful price mechanism** which directs and influences the input-owners and the businesses and consumers in the society and brings the answers to the three basic questions. "Principles of microeconomics" is mostly the study of the market process and the price mechanism and how it works out the choices and arrives at the answers to the three basic questions.

REVIEW EXERCISES

MAJOR CONCEPTS, PRINCIPLES, TERMS (Explain each carefully.)

the three basic questions

the three ways of making the choices

economics of the "tradition-oriented" society

how the political process makes the choices

how "the market" answers each basic question

market structure and competition

the factors of production

the role of demand and prices

the role of profits

the role of competition

the role of inequality

OTHER CONCEPTS AND TERMS (Explain each briefly.)

the output question

the input question

the distribution question

the production question

distributive share

the social process

the political process

the market process

command: the direct approach

command: the indirect approach

productivity principle of distribution

economic system

capitalism

socialism

communism

mixed socio-capitalism

monopoly

market power

monopoly power

pure competition

the concept of private property

private property rights

wealth and income

real income

money income

income redistribution

labor and wages

land and rent

capital and interest

capital good

consumer good

the entrepreneur and profit

QUESTIONS (Write out answers, or jot down key points.)

1. You know that there is no country in the world in which *all* of the economic choices are made by either the social process, or the political process, or the market process, but do you think there ever *could be*? Discuss.

2. What are some examples you have run into *today* (since you got out of bed this morning) of economic choice-making by tradition? by command? by the market?

3. Can you think of any choices that are now being made (in your family, at your college, in your society, in your *world*), where you think the "choice-making process" ought to be changed (from tradition, to command, to market, or vice versa)? Think about it.

4. Suppose there's only one dealer in your city who can repair your small foreign car. What kind of a market structure would you say that is? Suppose you don't like that dealer's repair work or prices. What can you do? Discuss.

5. What's so *efficient* about letting the market process direct the factors of production?

5 Demand, Supply, and Prices: How the Pure Market System Works

Chapter Objectives

- This chapter continues your study of the **market process**—of the **price mechanism** and how it works. When you finish this chapter you will understand and be able to explain the concepts of **demand** and **supply**.

- You will be able to draw and explain a **demand curve** and a **supply curve**. And you will be able to **explain and illustrate with a graph** how the **market price** is determined by supply and demand.

- The ultimate objective of this chapter is to enable you to better understand the workings of the **market process** and the **price mechanism**.

- When you finish studying this chapter you'll be able to explain and illustrate with graphs, exactly how a change in **demand** brings a change in **price** and how the **supply** responds.

- You will be able to use these new analytical tools to explain how the **output choices** of the society respond to the **changing demands of the people.**

Supply and Demand

Much of the study of economics is the study of the market process and how it works. The study of the market process is essentially the study of **supply and demand**.

Demand reflects people's choices; supply reflects scarcity. Demand works through the market process to pull forth the output (the supply). The people who produce (who supply) the demanded output get rewarded with income. See how the "supply and demand" idea ties it all together?

Economists have a great body of economic theory dealing with supply and demand. And curves? Yes. Two basic curves: the *demand curve*

and the *supply curve*. You'll be surprised how much these two curves can help to see how the market process works! So here it is: supply and demand. First, demand.

THE CONCEPT OF DEMAND

Suppose you are ready to give up a lot of money for something. Then your demand for it is high. If you aren't ready to give up any money for something, then you have no demand for it. You may have a *desire* for it. But if you aren't ready to pay a price to get it you do not *demand* it.

64

You aren't going to influence any of society's choices through "the market process" just by wanting something! Unless you are able and willing to spend some money to buy something, your *wants* won't have any effect.

Demand Is "the Propensity to Buy"

Demand is an "if . . . then" concept. The **demand** for something doesn't mean "how much of it people are buying." It only means "how much of it people *would be buying if* . . ." If what? If the price happened to be $5. or $10. or $30. or maybe 50 cents.

For example: If the price is $10 then maybe people will buy 200 units a day. If the price is $5 then maybe people will buy 450 units a day.

So "demand" in economics doesn't mean what it normally means to most people. In economics demand means **propensity to buy**. It means the "ability and willingness," or the "readiness" to buy. It means "how much people would be buying if. . . ."

If you have a "demand" for something, whether or not you *actually will buy* depends on how high the price is. You may be willing to pay to get something, but you may *not* be willing (or able!) to pay a price which you think is too high.

Demand Is a Functional Relationship. Demand is the "functional relationship" between the various prices which might exist and the various quantities people would buy. That is, the **quantity bought** depends on how high (or low) the price happens to be. But when the price changes, the *demand itself* doesn't change. Only the *quantity bought* changes.

I wonder how many eggs you would buy if the price went up to $10 a dozen! (You would still have a demand for eggs—a "propensity to buy"—but would you *actually* buy any? I doubt it.)

The Demand Schedule. One way to illustrate demand is with a table, or schedule, showing various prices and quantities demanded. Here's one:

Weekend Demand for Frying Chickens at Your Local Supermarket

Price (dollars)	Quantity Demanded (lbs.)
1.40	80
1.20	130
1.00	200
.80	300
.60	500
.40	900
20	2,200

See the functional relationship between *price* and **quantity demanded?** Negative relationship, right? The lower the price, the greater the quantity demanded. Economists call this negative relationship the **law of demand.**

The **law of demand** says that people buy more of something at a lower price than they will at a higher price. That is, *the lower the price, the greater the quantity demanded.*

When the price of something goes up, people buy less of it. There are two reasons why: (1) the substitution effect, and (2) the income effect.

Responding to a Price Change: the "Substitution Effect"

When the price of a good goes up, people may spend their money for other things instead—that is, they *shift* their spending to other goods. Maybe they *substitute* breakfast cereal for eggs. Economists call this the **substitution effect** of the higher price.

The "substitution effect" also works when the price goes down. If eggs get cheaper, people will buy fewer breakfast steaks and corn flakes and pancakes and start buying more eggs. They "substitute" eggs for the pancakes and things.

Responding to a Price Change: the "Income Effect"

When the price goes up, you can't afford to buy as much! When prices go up your "money income" can't buy as much "real income" as it could before.

Suppose you are buying eggs and the price goes up. If you keep on buying eggs, the higher price actually reduces your "total purchasing power." Your **real income** (the total amount of things you get to have and enjoy each week) gets smaller.

Suppose you have only two dollars to spend for breakfast foods this month. And suppose that all you really like to eat in the morning is scrambled eggs. If the price of eggs goes up from 50¢ to $2 a dozen, you are in trouble. Before the price increase your $2 bought four dozen eggs. Now it will only buy one dozen.

Your purchasing power has dropped! You still want four dozen. And you might be willing to pay $2 a dozen and buy four dozen if you had the money. But you just don't have the money! So when the price goes up from 50¢ to $2, the quantity you buy drops from four dozen to one dozen—not because you "substitute" other goods for eggs, but because your purchasing power has been reduced. Your real income is lower.

Whenever the price of something goes up, the people who keep buying the good at the higher price actually experience a reduction in "real income." This causes them (really, *forces* them) to buy less. Economists call this the **income effect** of the price increase.

The "income effect" also works when the price goes down. People who are careful to buy what they want only when it's on sale can enjoy more "real income." (Of course this doesn't mean you can save money by buying lots of things you don't *usually* buy, just because they're on sale!)

Demand Change? or Not?

Many students have trouble understanding the very special meaning of the word "demand" in economics. Why? Because everybody already knows the "popular" meaning of demand: it means "how much the people are buying." But in economics it doesn't mean that.

Suppose your local supermarket runs a special sale on hamburger and people buy twice as much. Does that mean there's an increase in the demand for hamburger? No. Or suppose the price of hamburger goes up to $10 a pound and nobody buys any hamburger at all. Does that mean there's no demand for hamburger? No.

Ah, but what if people all suddenly decide that they like hamburger a lot more, so they buy more? Or what if they get more income so they can afford to buy more things, and they decide to buy more hamburger? Increase in demand? Yes!

A person may demand something but not buy any of it at all because the price is too high. I suppose there are lots of people who would like to buy round-trip tickets to the moon. If so, that means there's a demand for trips to the moon. But nobody is buying any. Why not? Because the price is too high!

Here's the idea: Demand is the *basic desire* for something, together with the *ability* and *willingness* to buy it, *at some price*. At a price too high, none will be bought. As the price goes lower and lower, more and more will be bought.

It's the *basic demand* which directs and controls the output choices in the market system. Demand is the basic force which pulls forth the chosen products. The market process works through *the effect of demand on the prices of goods,* and then *the effect of prices on the output decisions of the producers.* When you finish this chapter you'll understand how it all works.

ANSWERING THE THREE BASIC QUESTIONS: THE FUNCTIONS OF PRICE

In the market system, prices perform two basic functions: (1) the **rationing function** and (2) the **production-motivating** function. It is these two functions of price which actually work out the answers to the output question and the input question. And as these two questions are being answered by these two basic functions of price, the distribution question is being automatically answered also.

The Rationing Function of Price: The Demand Curve

If the price of something goes higher, people don't buy as much of it. The substitution effect and the income effect see to that! We can say, then, that one thing which the *price* of something does is to convince the people (the consumer-buyers) to conserve, to limit the use of scarce things. We call this role—the role which price plays to discourage the use of scarce things—the **rationing function of price**.

The more scarce something is, the higher its price will be. The higher the price of something, the more it will be conserved and economized. That's "the rationing function of price."

The demand curve shows the relationship between *prices* and the *quantities* people would buy. The demand curve shows the same thing as the demand schedule. You saw one of those a few minutes ago.

The demand curve is a graphic picture of the rationing function of price. If you think about it you will see that the "rationing function of price" is just another way of looking at "the law of demand." The demand curve shows that the higher the price the smaller will be the quantity demanded.

Figure 5-1 shows a curve indicating the demand for eggs in your metropolitan area. Take a few minutes now to study that graph. While you're there, practice *drawing* and *explaining* a demand curve. Do that right now . . .

Now that you understand the demand curve, you can see that it is a graphic picture of the rationing function of price. The demand curve for eggs in Figure 5-1 shows that at $2 a dozen, only a few eggs would be bought—only about one carload per week. Only those people who really like eggs (or people with lots of money to spend) will continue to eat two eggs for breakfast every morning when the price is $2 a dozen!

People who really like eggs will probably go around scowling and muttering all the time about the high price of eggs. But they should be thankful that the price went up. At a price of $2, every Tom, Dick, and Harry won't be eating up all the very scarce eggs!

High Prices Conserve Things. A price of $2 a dozen saves the eggs for the true egg lovers. If for some reason the price of eggs had not been allowed to go up—if some "consumer protection committee" had convinced the legislature to pass a law holding the price of eggs down to 50¢—soon all the eggs would be used up. Then *nobody* would get any more eggs for awhile. As the price moves up, the people who don't really care very much about eggs stop buying and leave the eggs in the market for those who really go for eggs!

Free goods have no prices. No one tries to conserve or economize or limit or ration the use of free goods. But once a good is scarce it needs to have a price. Then the good will be automatically rationed and conserved. If a high price had been charged for killing them, we would have saved many roaming buffalo!

The **rationing function of price** limits the use of scarce things. Only those people who want something badly enough to pay the price will get any. Things will be used *only* for those purposes which someone considers important enough to be worth the price.

Are you beginning to be impressed by this thing we call "price"? Be impressed. It's truly the key to understanding how the market process works.

Fig. 5-1 The Demand Curve Shows the Quantity Demanded at Each Price

The lower the price of eggs, the more the consumers will try to buy.

Think of this as the weekly demand for eggs in your local metropolitan area.

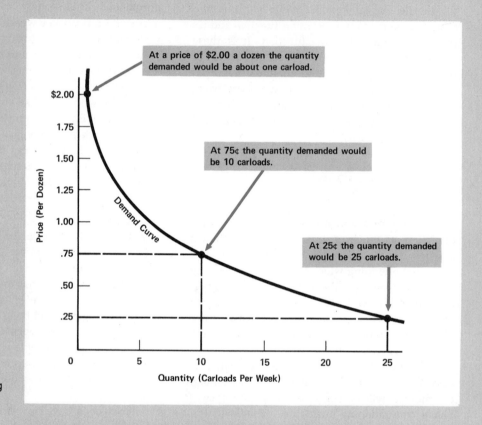

At a price of $2.00 a dozen the quantity demanded would be about one carload.

At 75¢ the quantity demanded would be 10 carloads.

At 25¢ the quantity demanded would be 25 carloads.

Demand Curve

Price (Per Dozen)

Quantity (Carloads Per Week)

The demand curve illustrates the rationing function of price.

The demand curve illustrates the "law of demand." It shows that at lower prices people would buy more. For example, if the price moves down from $1.00 to 75 cents per dozen, the quantity people will buy increases from 6 carloads to 10 carloads per week. This shows that the quantity people buy is very responsive ("stretches" a lot) when the price goes down.

The economist would say that the demand for eggs in this example is *relatively elastic*, or *price elastic*. Elasticity means *sensitivity*, or *responsiveness* to price changes. When the price changes, if the quantity bought does not respond very much we say the demand is *relatively inelastic*, or *price inelastic*. The responsiveness is low.

The concept of elasticity is very helpful in understanding how the market process works. In another chapter, elasticity of demand will be explained thoroughly. For now just remember that it means "responsiveness of buyers to price changes."

The Production-Motivating Function of Price

While the high price is conserving the use of eggs it is also doing something else. The high price is *pulling factors of production*—more labor, land, and capital—into the production of eggs. At a price of $2 a dozen, big profits can be made in the egg business. Of course! So anyone who can get some laying hens and start producing eggs can make a bundle!

The **production-motivating function of price** is what gets the goods produced in the market system. It's what gets the owners of the factors to bring their factors to the right places and to put them into the production of the right products. The factor owners who respond best to the production-motivating function of price are the ones who will get the largest incomes—the largest "distributive shares" of the economy's output.

Suppose that for some reason some product (like eggs in our example) becomes very scarce. Its price goes very high. The high price stimulates increased production. Businesses and factor owners find it more rewarding to shift into the production of the high-priced good.

As all this shifting goes on, the output of the very scarce good expands. Soon the good is not so "very scarce" anymore. So its price comes back down. Isn't that neat?

What we're talking about is the *production-motivating function of price*. And this brings us to the other half of "supply and demand" analysis. This takes us into the concept of *supply*.

THE CONCEPT OF SUPPLY

Every market is made up of buyers and sellers. Goods flow out of the market to the buyers. At the same time, goods are flowing into the market from the sellers.

If the price of the product is going up in the market, then the flow of goods from the sellers tends to increase. That's the production-motivating function of price. But if the price starts moving down, the flow of products from the sellers tends to decrease. What we're talking about now is the concept of "supply."

Supply Is "the Propensity to Sell"

Supply is an "if . . . then" concept just like demand. The supply tells how much the sellers would be trying to sell if the price was $1, or $5, or $10, or $30, or whatever. It is the **propensity to sell**.

Supply Is a Functional Relationship. The word "supply," like the word "demand," has a very precise meaning in economics. You could say that supply is the *"functional relationship"* between the various *prices* which might exist and the various quantities the producers would be trying to sell. Once the "supply" (the "propensity to sell") exists, then the *actual quantity* each producer will offer for sale will depend on the *price*. At higher prices, producers will offer more for sale; at lower prices they will offer less.

The Supply Curve

Now you're ready to look at the supply curve. Do you know what it's going to look like? Of course. Positive slope. At higher prices, greater quantities offered for sale.

Does the supply curve illustrate the "production-motivating function of price"? Yes. Look at Figure 5-2 and that's exactly what you'll see. Take a few minutes and learn to draw and explain the supply curve.

Fig. 5-2   The Supply Curve Shows the Quantity Supplied at Each Price

The higher the price, the more the egg producers will try to sell.

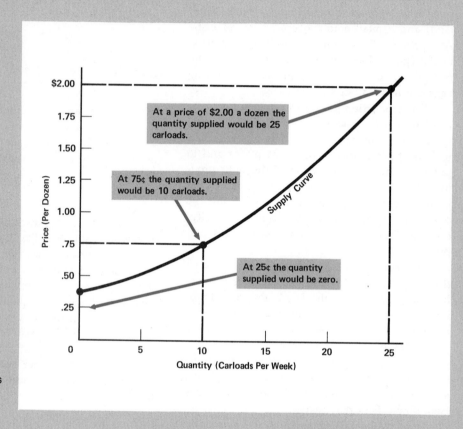

The supply curve illustrates the production-motivating function of price.

Weekly supply of eggs in your local metropolitan area.

The supply curve shows that at lower prices, smaller quantities of eggs will be offered for sale. How much the quantity offered for sale expands as the price rises (or how much it declines when the price falls) depends on the elasticity of supply.

This supply curve only makes sense in the "short run." It could not apply to the industry in the long run because in the long run more producers can enter the industry. Or some of the present producers could leave. If more farmers entered the egg-producing business, or if some left, the curve would shift. More on this later.

As output expands, cost goes up. As price goes higher and higher, businesses will produce more and more. The higher price covers the higher cost and makes the higher output profitable. More on this later, too.

THE EQUILIBRIUM MARKET PRICE

If the price of something goes down, people will try to buy more. The "law of demand" tells us that. Remember? But what about the sellers?

Sellers don't want to sell as much if the price is low. At higher prices sellers like to sell more. But at higher prices buyers won't buy as much!

So how does it all work out? There must be some "just right price"—a price just high enough and just low enough so that the buyers want to buy just exactly as much as the sellers want to sell. Is there such a price? Yes. We call it the equilibrium market price.

Think of supply as "a potential daily flow of the product into the market." Think of demand as "a potential daily flow of the product out of the market."

If the price is just right, the flow being pushed into the market by the sellers will be just equal to the flow being pulled out of the market by the buyers. That means the "equilibrium market price" exists.

Now that you know what the supply of eggs looks like, you know that it doesn't make any difference how many eggs people *would be trying to buy* at a price of 25¢ a dozen. Figure 5-2 shows that at such a low price (25¢ a dozen) the suppliers are not willing to sell *any* eggs at all!

At a price of 25¢ a dozen, the egg producers would put the eggs in cold storage and wait for better times. If better times didn't come, a lot of egg-laying chickens would soon become stewing chickens and a lot of poultry farms would soon become potato farms or something else.

If the society isn't willing to pay the cost of keeping the factors of production working in the egg industry, eventually the egg industry will disappear. The market process and the price mechanism will see to that! Automatically!

What about a price of $2 a dozen? The demand curve shows that people would buy less than one carload a week. But the supply curve tells us that the egg suppliers would ship in 25 carloads! So $2 can't be the right price, either.

The Supply and Demand Graph

The demand curve from Figure 5-1 and the supply curve from Figure 5-2 are shown together in Figure 5-3. This supply and demand graph shows that there is a price (but only *one* price) where the weekly flow of eggs being pushed into the market by the sellers is exactly equal to the weekly flow of eggs being pulled out of the market by the buyers. At what price are the supply flow and the demand flow equal? At the "equilibrium market price," of course.

Figure 5-3 shows that the equilibrium market price *must be* 75¢ a dozen. At any other price there's either too much *supplied* (a surplus) or too much *demanded* (a shortage). Right now you should spend a few minutes learning to draw and explain the "supply and demand" graph.

More About the Equilibrium Market Price

The *equilibrium market price* is the only price that can exist for long in any free market. It is the price where the quantity supplied equals the quantity demanded. Each seller is selling all he or she wants to sell at that price; each buyer is buying all he or she wants to buy at that price.

No one is *completely happy* with the equilibrium price. The buyers would rather get eggs cheaper. The sellers would rather get higher prices. But at this "equilibrium market price" there is no shortage and no surplus. As long as the supply and the demand remain the same, the "equilibrium market price" (75¢ a dozen) and the "equilibrium quantity flow" (10 carloads a week) will continue indefinitely.

The "General Equilibrium" Situation

Suppose the market process is working perfectly. Society is making all its choices through

Fig. 5-3   Supply, Demand, and Equilibrium Market Price

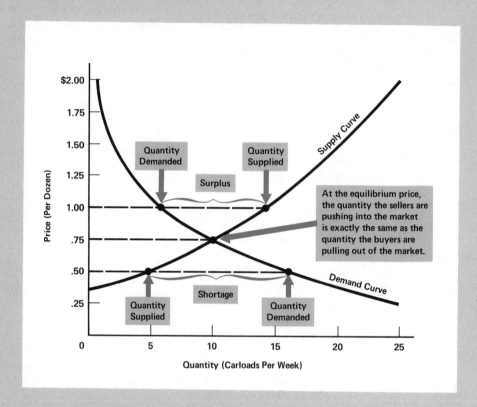

Only when "quantity supplied" equals "quantity demanded," will there be no surplus and no shortage.

It is obvious from the graph that only the price of 75¢ a dozen can be the real price. Any lower price would leave demanders trying to buy more eggs than would be available for sale. Any higher price would have suppliers shipping in more eggs than people would buy.

If the price was too low (say 50¢ a dozen) buyers would be trying to get more eggs than the suppliers would offer. There would be a *shortage*. Some of the buyers would not be able to get any eggs from anywhere! Soon these unhappy buyers trying to get some of the very scarce eggs would start offering more for eggs. They would push the price up.

If the price was too high (say $1 a dozen) sellers would be offering more eggs than people would buy. There would be a *surplus*. Some of the sellers would not be able to sell their eggs. These sellers trying to get rid of their overly plentiful eggs would start offering them at lower prices. This would push the price down.

Everyone who wants to sell at the equilibrium price can find a buyer. Everyone who wants to buy at that price can find a seller. That's what is meant by "equilibrium market price."

the price mechanism. All the prices of everything are "in equilibrium." Just the right amounts of all goods are flowing across all the markets from the sellers to the buyers. There are no surpluses of anything and no shortages of anything. Can you picture that, in a "model situation"?

In this **"general equilibrium"** situation, all the people are carefully conserving the most scarce, most expensive, highest-priced things because of "the rationing function of price." The demand curve for each product shows us that.

Producers are working to produce more of the most scarce, most wanted, highest-priced things because of the "production-motivating function of price." The supply curve for each product shows that.

All of us get rewarded (receive income) according to the market value of what we sell. Our "reward" depends on the price we get for the product we make or for the services of our labor, our land, or our capital.

This view of the market system "in general equilibrium" shows the neat "model system" with all the choices being made automatically. But suppose something happens to disturb the equilibrium. What happens then? Suppose the people decide they want a larger "output flow" of something. Maybe they want more eggs each week. What happens?

HOW DEMAND DIRECTS THE PURE MARKET ECONOMY

First, a word of warning: As you are reading all this, don't be thinking about the present-day American economic system. Think only about the "model market system."

Think about markets of *pure competition*—markets where there are great numbers of buyers and sellers—where no buyer or seller is big enough to have any control over the price—

where buyers and sellers are free to enter or leave the market whenever existing prices attract them, or repel them—and where prices are always free to move up or down whenever the demand increases or decreases. You'll find out later how all this "pure theory" helps to understand the "less pure" markets which often exist in the real world. But now, on to the "model world"—a world where all markets are completely controlled by *demand and supply and prices*.

Suppose the egg market is in equilibrium as shown in Figure 5-3. Then suppose a respected scientist makes a startling announcement: "Eggs, if eaten regularly, will maintain your youthful appearance and your vim and vigor and will add ten years to your life!"

Increasing "Want" Increases the Demand and Upsets the Equilibrium

This idea of "eggs for perpetual youth" causes many people to want to eat more eggs. The "propensity to buy" increases. People who always hated eggs suddenly become egg eaters. With all these people trying to buy more eggs, the weekly supply of 10 carloads gets sold out in a hurry. A shortage of eggs develops.

Everybody's trying to buy eggs but there are no eggs to be found. The disappointed buyers go around offering to pay extra to get some eggs. This pushes up the price.

As the price goes up the rationing function of price will squeeze some of the buyers out of the market. The production-motivating function of price will pull more eggs into the market. These two "functions of price" work together to increase the quantity supplied and decrease the quantity demanded.

How high will the price go? It will continue to go up until the market moves into a new equilibrium. This situation is shown in the supply and demand graph in Figure 5-4. Take a few minutes to study that graph now.

Fig. 5-4 An Increase in Demand: the Demand Curve Shifts

At each price, the quantity demanded is greater.

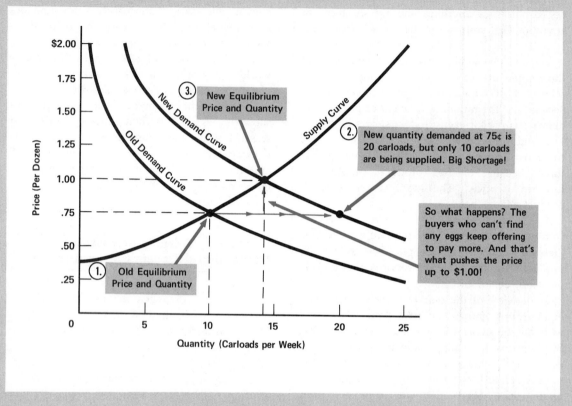

When demand increases it creates a shortage and the buyers push the price up.

The higher price discourages buyers and encourages sellers and the shortage is eliminated!

When people think eggs will bring "perpetual youth," the demand for eggs increases. At any price you choose, the quantity people would buy is greater. The demand curve shifts to the right to show that a larger quantity would be bought at each price. The "propensity to buy" has increased!

Seventy-five cents can no longer be the equilibrium price. At that price people now want to buy 20 carloads a week but the sellers ship in 10 carloads. A serious shortage! The buyers, trying to get eggs, push up the price.

The new "equilibrium market price" is $1 a dozen. This higher price (a) squeezes some of the buyers out of the market (the quantity demanded goes back down from 20 to 14 carloads) and (b) pulls forth more output from the sellers (the quantity supplied increases from 10 to 14 carloads).

Increased Demand Pushes Up the Price.
The graph shows that the price must go up to $1
a dozen. At that price, a lot of buyers are
squeezed out of the market by the rationing
function, a lot more eggs are pulled into the
market by the production-motivating function,
and a new market equilibrium is reached. Four-
teen carloads of eggs will be sold by the sellers
and bought by the buyers each week. But this
new equilibrium price of $1 a dozen can't last for
long. Can you guess why? Competition, of
course!

The High Price Brings Big Profits. Remember I said that everything was in stable equilibrium back when the price of eggs was 75¢ a
dozen? This means that a price of 75¢ was high
enough to cover the production costs and pay
enough profits to the producers to keep them
satisfied to stay in the egg business. So think
what a good deal $1 a dozen must be! Big profits
in the egg business? Right!

Suppose you are producing frying chickens.
You're doing okay, just making "normal profits." Then one day you see your egg-producing
neighbor drive by in her new Cadillac. She's on
her way to the airport to fly to the Virgin Islands
for a three-day holiday.

Big Profits Attract More Producers. You
suddenly realize that you should be producing
eggs instead of fryers! So what do you do? As
soon as you can you'll shift into the egg business
where the big money is. Your neighbor doesn't
mind. She knows that one more little egg producer won't hurt the egg market at all.

What's going to happen? You've already
guessed it. You aren't the only farmer who likes
to make big profits. It isn't long before everyone
who can shift into the egg business starts to do
just that. Everyone wants to get some of the big
profits from those dollar-a-dozen eggs!

This is competition in action. Soon, turkey
producers, cotton farmers, beef ranchers, vegeta-
ble growers and others start producing eggs.

Every day more people become egg producers.
Each time a new producer enters the egg industry and starts shipping eggs to the market, the
total quantity of eggs going into the market increases a little more. Can you see what's going
to happen?

More Producers Bring More Supply. It
isn't long before the quantity offered for sale at a
price of $1 a dozen increases from 14 carloads to
15 carloads a week. But at $1 a dozen, buyers
will only buy 14 carloads. The demand curve already told us that. At a price of $1 a dozen, with
15 carloads a week coming into the market we
have a surplus of one carload of eggs a week.

**More Supply Pushes the Price Back
Down.** Some of the egg sellers can't sell all their
eggs. So what do they do? They start cutting
prices to get people to buy up all the eggs. See
it? The "production-motivating function of price"
is still working! The high price is causing the egg
industry to expand. Each time a new producer
enters the industry, the supply increases. In
terms of the supply and demand graph, the *supply curve* is now shifting to the right—a delayed
response to the *initial* shift to the right, of the
demand curve!

How long will new producers keep on entering the egg business? That's easy. As long as
it is more profitable for them to produce eggs
than it would for them to produce turkeys or
broilers or beef or whatever else they might
produce *instead* of eggs. This means that the egg
industry will continue to expand and the supply
of eggs will continue to increase (the curve will
keep shifting to the right on the graph) until the
price of eggs is pushed *back down* to *"normal."*

The "Normal Price"

You remember that in the beginning the
normal price for eggs was 75¢ a dozen. The
"normal price" is the price that brings the pro-

ducers **normal profits**—that is, enough profits to keep them from leaving the industry, but not enough to entice other firms to stop producing other things and shift into this industry.*

At the "normal price" with "normal profits" being made, an industry will be stable. At prices and profits higher than "normal" the industry will be expanding. At prices and profits lower than "normal" the industry will be contracting. Businesses are always moving into or out of one industry or another, trying to make more profits, or to eliminate their losses.

As the egg industry expands, this may cause production costs to go up. If so the new "normal price" will be higher than before (maybe up to 80¢) because of the higher costs. But let's just suppose that the "normal price" stays at 75¢. How long will the egg industry continue to expand? Until the price is pushed all the way back to 75¢ a dozen.

The New "Long-Run Equilibrium"

There's a graph coming up that shows the new "normal" or "long-run" equilibrium situation in the egg market. The price is back down to 75¢ a dozen. But now, instead of the original quantity of ten carloads, there are *twenty carloads* a week flowing across the market from the sellers to the buyers.

Where did all those extra eggs come from?

*Sometimes economists explain that it might be better not to think of "normal profit" as being "profit" at all. Since the "normal profit" is necessary to keep the firms from leaving the industry, "normal profit" is really a part of the cost of production—a "necessary cost" required to keep the product flowing to the market. It's only when the profit gets higher than "normal" that profit becomes a "surplus" and serves the purpose of attracting new firms into the industry. What's the point? Just this: Be sure to recognize the distinct difference between "normal profit" and "excess" or "surplus" profit. They're different, and they perform different functions in the operation of the market process.

and why? It all happened through the automatic adjustments of the market process. The price mechanism took care of it automatically.

Once the price gets back to normal that's as far as it goes. Until there is some new change in demand or supply, 75¢ a dozen will continue to be the price and 20 carloads a week will continue to be the quantity exchanged.

Figure 5-5 shows each step in the process: (1) the increased demand, (2) the higher price, (3) the increased supply, and (4) the new long-run equilibrium price and quantity.

This graph is very important. It shows the "market process" and the "price mechanism" in action. It shows, in a "model system," how the market process directs society's resources into the production of the desired products. Now, spend enough time with Figure 5-5 to understand and be able to draw and explain each step in the "automatic adjustment process."

The Essential Role of Pure Competition

Think back over the egg example you've just been reading about. Everything worked out just right—very neatly in fact. Why? Because all of the necessary "assumed conditions" existed. The most necessary assumed condition is that **pure competition** exists.*

What's so important about pure competition? Consider this. After the demand for eggs increased, who put the price up from 75 cents to

*There are several other assumed conditions too. But I won't bother you with those until after you understand more about how the "model system" works. When you get into the "real world" chapters of this book you'll find out a lot about how well the assumptions are likely to hold true. For now, just concentrate on learning how the model system works. But be forewarned: It doesn't always work out that way in the real world.

Fig. 5-5 How Consumer Demand Directs the Output Choices in the Pure Market System

Increased demand pushes the price up and in the long run, generates a supply increase.

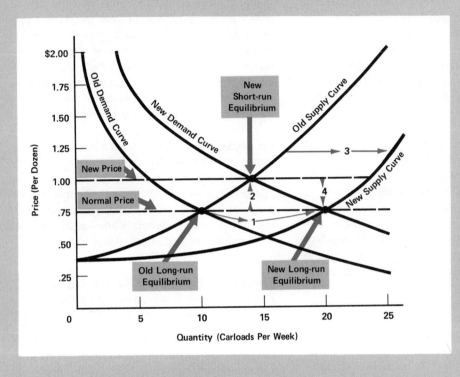

The high price pulls more producers into the industry and the increased supply pushes the price back down to "normal."

If the cost of producing eggs went up as the industry expanded, then the new "normal price" would be higher than 75¢. But in this case, that didn't happen.

Follow the numbers on the graph:

(1) The demand increases. At a price of 75¢ a dozen the quantity the buyers want to buy increases from 10 to 20 carloads a week. This creates a shortage.

(2) The buyers, bidding against each other for the limited eggs, push the price up to $1. At the higher price the new quantity demanded moves back from 20 to 14 carloads per week, and the quantity supplied increases from 10 to 14 carloads. At the price of $1 we have a new short-run "equilibrium market price."

(3) At the price of $1, big profits are made in the egg business. New producers come in and start producing and selling eggs. Each time one more producer adds output to the market this increases the total market supply a little bit. As the supply increases bit-by-bit, the price inches downward.

(4) The supply continues to increase and the price drops until the "normal price" is reached. Then the industry is again in stable long-run equilibrium. The price is again 75¢, but the quantity crossing the market has increased from 10, to 20 carloads per week.

People demanded more eggs—20 carloads a week, at the normal price. And, in the long run, that's just what they got. Automatically! That's how consumer demand directs the output choices in the pure market system.

$1 a dozen? Nobody. The "natural market forces" took care of it. New buyers entered the market. That's what made the shortages develop. And that's what made the price go up.

Then following the price increase, who decided that a lot of the society's resources should be shifted into egg production? Nobody. The natural market forces took care of it. Farmers saw the opportunity for high profits in the egg business so they started producing eggs. They entered the egg market as sellers. That's what made the surpluses develop. And that's what pushed the price back down.

You can see the essential role of pure competition in all of this. Without large numbers of small buyers and small sellers, and without free and easy entry into the market by anyone who wants to buy or sell, it just wouldn't work.

What if there were only one or a few egg sellers? or buyers? or what if there were restrictions on who could produce and sell eggs? or who could buy and eat eggs? The system wouldn't work—at least not the way it did in our example.

How would it work out if the market structure of the egg market was something other than pure competition? Later in this book you'll get into that question. For now just remember this: it would depend a lot on *what kind of market structure did exist*—how much competition and how much monopoly power in the egg market.

CONSUMER SOVEREIGNTY AND THE INVISIBLE HAND

In the model market system who holds the choice-making power? The consumers of course. The consumers are *sovereign*. They have the final control in deciding what will be done with society's scarce resources. That's what **consumer sovereignty** means.

Anyone who has money and spends it, will influence "what is produced." Anyone who produces (or who owns productive factors which produce) will receive money to spend and can influence "what is produced."

You may have heard of **Adam Smith**. In 1776 he wrote an economics book called *The Wealth of Nations*. Adam Smith was the first to give a good explanation of how the market process could work automatically to serve the wants of the society. One of his most famous statements was that if you leave people alone to follow their own personal interests, each will be guided "as though by an invisible hand" to do the things the society wants them to do.

The idea of **the invisible hand** is the idea of the market process at work. It's the idea that society's economic choices will be made automatically, in response to the wishes of the people. The "sovereign consumers," through the market process, will cause the labor, land, and capital to do the things society wants done—as though all were guided by "an invisible hand."

Consumer Spending Really Does Influence the Economic Choices

In the real world, no economy could work just like the model of "consumer sovereignty and the invisible hand." Still, in the economic systems of most countries, the consumer's choice (about what to buy) really does exert a major influence. "Consumer sovereignty" in the real world is far from pure. On the other hand, it's far from dead.

The more a nation allows for and protects open and free competitive markets and private property rights, the more "sovereign" the consumer will be—the more "ultimate power" the consumer will exercise over the society's economic choices.

I'm sure you realize that the "ultimate power of the consumer's choice" is much greater in the economy of a country like the United States or Canada or West Germany or Great Britain or Japan than it is in the Soviet Union or

China. But even in the communist countries, consumers' choices cannot be ignored completely.

The Great Efficiency of "The Market"

When the market is making the economic choices, everything happens automatically. No one needs to run a survey to find out what goods need to be produced, what services need to be produced, etc. (the output question). No one needs to go around contacting workers or the owners of the land or capital to tell them what industries need their services (the input question). All this is taken care of automatically!

When the market is in charge, the distribution question is answered automatically too. Each person's "income share"—wages, rent, interest, or profit—depends upon how well that person is responding to the society's wishes. It depends on how successful that person is in using his or her **factors of production** to do what the society most wants done.

The owner of each factor moves that factor into the activity which pays the most. The price mechanism operates in the *factor market* to accomplish these three objectives:

1. to *move* the factors of production from one activity to another;

2. to *stimulate the development* of new labor skills and new kinds of capital in the areas and activities where society's demands are greatest; and

3. to *discourage* people from using their labor, land, or capital in the kinds of work society doesn't want done.

The Powerful Price Mechanism

The market process works automatically through the **price mechanism**. When the price of a good goes up, that encourages its production and discourages its consumption. When the price of a good goes down, that discourages its production and encourages its consumption. The "signals" of the price mechanism cause businesses, workers, and consumers to shift their production and consumption from one thing to another.

The price mechanism exerts a powerful force. When the price of an item goes up very much, if you will wait awhile you almost always will see more of this item being produced and less of it being consumed. When the price of an item goes down very much, if you wait awhile you almost always will see more of this item being consumed and less of it being produced.

If the price of something goes low enough, eventually none of it will be produced. If the price will not cover the cost, the product will disappear from the market. Or the price of something could go high enough so that none of it would be consumed. People would find an acceptable substitute. The high-priced product would disappear from the market.

The price mechanism is the control mechanism of the market system. Changes in the price of each product automatically stimulate or retard its production. At the same time these price changes stimulate or retard the use of the product. It all happens automatically! Truly, it is the *price mechanism* which regulates and controls the "free market economy."

In the market system the important economic choices— the answers to the three basic questions—are worked out automatically by the price mechanism. In answering the output question, producers will always shift toward the *higher-priced* (most profitable) products. In answering the input question, producers will always shift toward the lower-priced (least cost) inputs. And the distribution question is automatically answered as the productive people earn incomes. Their in-

The key to micro-economics is supply and demand and the Price Mechanism.. Don't forget. Okay?

comes reflect the values (prices) of what they produce—that is, of their contributions to the productive process and to the output of the society.

The price mechanism directs all of us. As buyers we respond positively to low prices and negatively to high prices. As sellers we respond positively to high prices and negatively to low prices. As we do so, our reactions ensure that the market process will work—that the output question, the input question, and the distribution question will be answered automatically.

SUMMARY AND SYNTHESIS

This chapter has explained a lot more about the workings of the **market process** and the **price mechanism**. It works through supply and demand.

Consumer **demand** is the propensity to buy. It's based on the **desire and ability to buy**. Precisely, demand is the **functional relationship** between possible prices which might exist and quantities which would be bought.

The **law of demand** says that the functional relationship is **negative**: the higher the price, the lower the quantity demanded.

The **rationing function** of price is illustrated by the demand curve or schedule. At higher prices, goods are more carefully conserved (rationed). The other important function of price—the **production-motivating function**—is illustrated by the supply curve or schedule. The higher the price, the more production is motivated.

Supply is the propensity to sell. The supply of a product is based on the cost of producing additional units of that product. Precisely, supply is the (positive) functional relationship between possible prices which might exist and quantities which would be offered for sale.

A **supply and demand graph** shows that there is one and only one equilibrium market price for a product. At any higher price there would be **surpluses** which would force the price down. At any lower price there would be **shortages** which would push the price up.

The **price mechanism** responds to **consumer demand** in working out the answer to the **output question. An increase in consumer demand** would cause the price to rise and cause more to be supplied. **In the long run the industry would expand** as firms are attracted to the industry by the **profits** generated by the **high price**. As the industry expanded, the **supply would increase** and push the price back down to **normal. This** illustrates the principle of **consumer sovereignty** and the **invisible hand.**

The price mechanism is the control mechanism of the market system. It operates with great efficiency because everything **adjusts automatically** in response to the **rationing and production-motivating** functions of price.

REVIEW EXERCISES

MAJOR CONCEPTS, PRINCIPLES, TERMS (Explain each thoroughly.)

demand
the two effects of a price change
the two functions of price

supply
demand, supply, and price
the essential role of pure competition
efficiency of "the market"
the powerful price mechanism

OTHER CONCEPTS AND TERMS (Explain each briefly.)

substitution effect
income effect
law of demand
elasticity of demand
rationing function of price
production-motivating function of
  price
equilibrium market price

change in demand
change in supply
normal price
normal profits
price mechanism
consumer sovereignty
the "invisible hand"

CURVES AND GRAPHS (Draw, label, and explain each.)

The Demand Curve Shows the Quantity Demanded at Each Price
The Supply Curve Shows the Quantity Supplied at Each Price
Supply, Demand, and Equilibrium Market Price
An Increase in Demand: the Demand Curve Shifts
How Consumer Demand Directs the Output Choices in the Pure Market
  System

QUESTIONS (Write the answers, or jot down key points.)

1. Explain how supply, demand, and price work together in the "model pure market system." Use supply and demand curves to show how *first price* and then *supply* respond to changes in consumer demand.
2. When you're trying to explain how supply and demand work, it's not easy to always keep it straight whether you're talking about
   a. a change in the *demand*—that is, a change in your overall propensity to buy (a shift of the demand curve) or
   b. a change in the *quantity bought*, which results from a change in the price (that is, a movement along the demand curve, to a higher or lower price and a smaller or greater quantity bought).
   Can you see what would happen to your explanation of how the market mechanism works if you let these two things get mixed up? Think about it and try to explain.
3. The only price that really could exist in a free market would be the equilibrium market price. In the supply and demand graph, all prices above or below

the equilibrium price and all quantities greater or less than the equilibrium quantity are really irrelevant. There's only one price (the equilibrium price) and one quantity (the equilibrium quantity) which would exist in that market at any moment. Can you explain why this is true? What forces guarantee that it must be true?

4. Students sometimes get mixed up between
   a. the two effects of a price change, and
   b. the two functions of price.

Can you clearly explain the difference between the two? Try.

PART TWO

The More We All Spend The More We All Earn

6 Macroeconomics: The Circular Flow of Income and Spending

Chapter Objectives

- This chapter introduces you to the "other side" of your study of the principles of economics. Here you will get **an overview of macroeconomics**.

- When you finish studying this chapter you will appreciate the **interdependence** of a market-directed economic system. You will be able to illustrate this interdependence using the **circular flow diagram**.

- This chapter explains the **basic equality** between **total spending** and **total receipts** and between **real output** and **real income**.

- In this chapter you will learn about the **basic questions of macroeconomics** and how these are **automatically answered by the market process—by the price mechanism**.

THE ECONOMIC SYSTEM IS ALL TIED TOGETHER

What determines whether you will be rich or poor? Is it up to you? Partly, yes. But only partly. In the modern world all our destinies are tied together. Everything you do has an influence on somebody else. And how well-off *you* are depends a lot on what *others* are doing. This is perhaps true in every aspect of life. It is certainly true in economics.

What Happens If the Economy Slows Down?

Suppose you are working in the stockyards and you are told that because of a declining demand for beef you are no longer needed. Many of your friends receive the same notice.

If the stockyards lay you off and shut down, does this mean the economy is slowing down? Maybe yes, maybe no. Maybe people are buying less beef and pork but buying more of other things—maybe poultry. Maybe there is a boom in the egg business and maybe you can get a job there. You start watching the want ads. But you don't see any jobs available. Suppose one day you are talking to your poultry-farming brother. He's thinking about looking for a job at the stockyards. He tells you that the poultry workers are having tough times. Layoffs. No jobs.

You figure that maybe people are buying less food so they can buy more cars and nicer clothes. So you hitchhike to Detroit to get a job in an automobile factory. Then you find that the automobile workers are being laid off too. So you hitchhike down to Burlington, North Carolina and try to get a job in the textile mills. But there you find the same problem. What's going on?

A New Kind of Economic Problem: Recession and Depression

This is a new kind of economic problem—the problem of **recession** or **depression** —a slowdown of the economic system.

The previous chapters were concerned with the question of choosing *which way* to use our resources. What to produce? Which resources to use? How to share the output? These are basic questions of "what to trade-off for what?" Now, suddenly we are looking at a different kind of problem.

Idle factors of production are everywhere. People are trying to sell their labor, but no one wants to buy it. Businesses are trying to sell beef and pork and chickens and eggs but nobody is trying to buy them. The same is true for new clothes and shoes and furniture and automobiles and airline tickets and almost everything else.

As you hitchhike around the country looking for a job you begin to get hungry. You certainly would like to have a steak! The meatcutters would like to have jobs cutting steaks. The cattle ranchers would like to sell their cattle. The stockyards would like to get back into production again and you sure would like to get your job back. Then you could buy a steak!

All the needed inputs—all the factors of production—are available, ready to go to work. So what's wrong? Simply this: The economic system isn't working right. It's suffering from a **partial breakdown** .

When One Thing Slows Down, Other Things Slow Down

If people stop buying things, businesses stop producing things. Then factors of production get laid off. So people's incomes get cut off. So they don't buy as much. So businesses produce even less. They fire more workers. The economy goes into recession.

If people shift their spending from steaks to eggs, there's no problem. The factors of produc-

tion move from where they are less wanted to where they are more wanted. But if people stop spending for steaks and for eggs and for everything else, then the people who make these things—that means all of us, as workers, business managers, clerks, investors, service and repair people and so on—all of us lose our sources of income. Then we are forced to cut spending.

Can you see how different this new kind of economic problem is from the problem of choosing? Now we are looking at the economic system as one big unit—as a big production-consumption circle. Here's a simple example to show how the production-consumption "circular flow" might develop.

The Circular Flow of Production and Consumption

Robinson Crusoe alone on an island would be producing and consuming at the same time. He climbs a palm tree and gets a coconut, then drinks the juice and eats the coconut meat. He catches a fish and tosses it on the coals. As soon as it is cooked he peels off the charred skin and eats the tender, char-broiled meat inside. By the end of the day he has eaten all the food he has produced.

Robinson Crusoe's "circular flow" of production-consumption is a tight little circle! If he wants more output (food or shelter or fishing spears or whatever) he must speed up his "economic system." He can start working longer and harder and produce more. Then he will get more output so he will have more things to have and to consume—that is, more **real income** .

In the Robinson Crusoe world it's very easy to see how **the production-consumption circle** (the output-income circle)

In a modern economic system, everyone is depending on everyone else.

works. It isn't quite as obvious, but the same kind of output-income production-consumption circle also exists in a complex modern economic system.

Suppose you could somehow rise up above and look down on a "transparent economic system." Maybe you could go up in a balloon, then lean out and look down. What would you see? People making things and getting money and buying things and spending money. *Things* going from the sellers to the buyers. *Dollars* going back and forth and around and around.

A person gets some dollars then spends them, then gets them again, then spends them again. It's all sort of like a big circle. For a few minutes, pretend that the "transparent economic system" you're looking down on, *really is* a big circle.

THE CIRCULAR FLOW OF THE ECONOMY

The total amount of money being spent by everybody—all the people and all the businesses—is the **total spending flow**. It's flowing for one reason—to buy things. The buyers push the spending into the market.

As the "total spending flow" pours into the markets, the money goes to people. It pours into the hands of the producers and workers and gets them to keep on producing and working and making the things the spenders are buying.

The people who are working and producing and selling things are the *receivers* of the spending flow. But as they are receiving the money with one hand they are *spending* it with the other. People receive money from the spending flow and just turn around and spend it again. This is the way the spending flow keeps on flowing.

Total Amounts Spent Equal Total Amounts Received

How much do all the people and businesses spend in a week? And how much do they receive? Can you see that the two amounts—the amount spent and the amount received—must be equal?

When a handful of dollars is being spent by somebody, that handful of dollars is also being received by somebody. Obviously! Every spender must have a receiver. So total amounts spent must always be equal to total amounts received.

As long as everyone keeps on spending all the money received, the total spending flow will continue flowing at the same speed and the economy will keep running at the same speed.

Real Output Equals Real Income

What about *real* output (goods produced) and *real* income (goods received)? It's obvious that total spending equals total receipts. Each time someone spends a dollar, someone must receive it. Is the same true for **real output** and **real income**? Yes. The total amount of goods made this week must be equal to the total amount of goods received this week. Why? Because every new thing must have an *owner*!

If nobody makes anything, nobody receives anything. If I produce a thousand dollars' worth of corn and tomatoes, then somebody is going to receive a thousand dollars' worth of corn and tomatoes. If I sell my output of corn and tomatoes to you then you will receive the thousand dollars' worth of corn and tomatoes. If I don't sell my output then I'm the one who receives it as "real income." Maybe I receive it or maybe you receive it. But *somebody* must receive it. It doesn't just pile up in the streets!

If we look at it from the point of view of those who produce it, it's **real output**. If we look at it from the point of view of those who receive it, it's **real income**. But either way, we're looking at the same flow of goods. Real output equals real income? More than that. Real output *is* real income.

Flows of Money Equal Flows of Goods

Now let's tie the *money* flow (total spending equals total receipts) together with the *product* flow (real output equals real income). Your common sense would tell you that the spending flow and the output flow must be closely related. Why do people put money into the *spending* flow? To get some of the things in the *output* flow, of course! Why do people put goods into the *output* flow? To get some of the money in the *spending* flow. Of course!

Do you begin to get the feeling that all these flows must be equal? Everyone is pushing in goods and taking out money and then turning around and pushing the money back in and taking out goods. For every dollar's worth of goods flowing there's a dollar's worth of money flowing. The two amounts must be equal.

Why do people push goods into the flow and take out money and then turn around and put the money back in and take out goods? That seems to be so much wasted energy. But no! They're putting in a lot of one thing—their specialty—and taking out small amounts of many kinds of things—the great variety of things they want.

Specialization and trade is the name of the game! That's what the "market system" is all about. It stimulates people to produce something they're good at and then lets them exchange what they make for the other things they want. And when we're watching the circular flow of the economic system, that's exactly what we see happening.

People are selling goods and factors of production. In exchange for these goods and factors they are on the "receiving side" of the spending flow. These same people, when they are buying goods and services from others, are on the "spending side" of the spending flow. Here's another way of looking at it.

The Circular Flow Between Households and Businesses

Businesses buy factors of production and use them to produce outputs. The factor owners (households) get paid by the businesses. Then the households use the money to buy the outputs of the businesses. This circle keeps on going and the money keeps on flowing from businesses to households and from households to businesses.

Isn't this a neat way to look at any economy? Really, it's a pretty good picture of what actually is going on all the time: People selling factors to businesses and using the money they earn to buy the outputs of the businesses; businesses paying out money to the factor owners, the factors making things, then the businesses selling the things to the factor owners to get the money back.

In this illustration, don't think of "the business" as being "somebody"—some wealthy person—some "business owner." That isn't the idea. The business is sort of "a place where everybody goes to sell factors and receive incomes." Even the person who owns the business—the buildings and machines and all that—is selling those factors to the business in exchange for an income from the business. The business owner doesn't actually "live in the business." Business owners live in households just like everybody else and sell productive factors—capital and managerial skills—to the business.

Actually, when we say **"businesses"** what we really mean is "the *buyer's side* of the *input* markets and the *seller's side* of the *output* markets." Businesses buy inputs and sell outputs. So that's a good way to look at it.

When we say **"households"** what we really mean is "the *seller's side* of the *input* markets and the *buyer's side* of the *output* markets." Households sell inputs and buy outputs. Of course! All the people who are earning incomes are selling in the input markets. And just about everyone is buying in the output markets. We all have to eat!

Figure 6-1 shows a diagram of this circular flow between households and businesses. If you'll study that diagram now, I think all this will become very clear to you.

It's the Total Spending for New Output That Matters

We have been talking about "the spending flow" as though all spending was spent for *new output*, and as though all spending created *new income* for someone. This is not quite true. Here's an example that will explain why not.

If I produce a bushel of corn and sell it to you for $10, then that "sale" is a part of total spending for output. It creates income for me. Then, after you have bought the corn, suppose somebody offers you $11 for it and you sell it to them. The $11 you get does not represent another $11 worth of output, and income. Obviously not. Only one dollar of it would be income for you. That would be your payment for increasing the value of the corn by "buying, keeping, and carrying" the corn to a time and place where it was more valuable—$1 more valuable.

You have increased the value of the output of the economic system by $1, and your income has gone up by $1. But *not* by $11! The value of *your* "output" is the value *you* have added. That's what you get to keep as income. One dollar. Your **value added** is *your* output.

Throughout this book, whenever we're talking about *total spending*, what we'll *really* be talking about is total spending *for new output*. We won't be counting the spending and respending over and over for the same old things. So remember: when I say "total spending," what I really mean is "total spending for new output."

The Interdependence of the Circular Flow

The **circular flow** concept really shows how much we are all dependent on each other. If the flow of money being paid to businesses gets smaller, then the businesses can't pay out as much money to the households. Employment is cut back and output is reduced. As the money flow gets smaller, the real flow gets smaller.

The circle fits together so tightly that if any part of the system speeds up or slows down, all the other parts of the system—both the money flows and the real flows—will be forced to speed up or slow down, too. Once it starts to speed up or slow down, it may go on changing more and more. As you'll see later, that could cause some serious problems.

Each "Economic Unit" Influences the Total Economy

Think about the modern economic system. What a complex thing! Like the inside of a watch. Only instead of dozens of little wheels there are millions of little wheels. Each little wheel is "locked in" and turning with the others. Yet each wheel has its own little engine which it can speed up or slow down if it wants to. But as each tries to speed up or slow down, it influences the speed of all the other little wheels which are "locked in" around it. How fast (or how slowly) the whole machine—the economic system—actually will be going depends on how fast (or how slowly) all the little wheels—the individual economic units—are trying to go.

The more you work and produce and earn and spend, the more you help to speed up the "total mechanism"—the economic system. If you produce a lot, earn a lot, spend a lot, then you push the system to speed up—and it does! When a business buys more materials, hires more people, and steps up production, that pushes the system to speed up. And it does. But when people or businesses produce less and/or spend less, they slow down the system.

Spending Flows Support Employment and Production

How does the market process induce the factors to produce things? By offering them in-

Fig. 6-1   The Circular Flow Between Households and Businesses

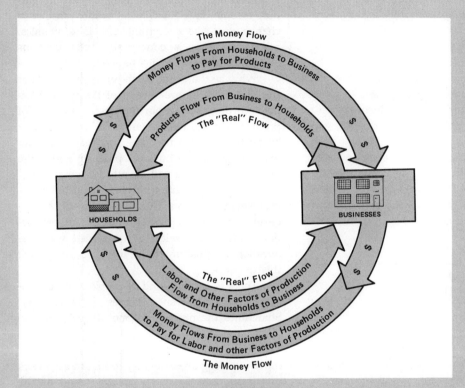

Around and around it goes, with money flowing one way and things flowing the other.

The households own all the factors of production. They sell factors to the businesses. When the businesses pay for the factors, the income goes to the households.

When the households spend the money to buy the products from the businesses, this completes the circle. The households get the goods and the businesses get the money back.

You can see that if anything makes the money flow smaller, the "real flow" will get smaller also. The two flows are completely dependent on each other and are (quite obviously) equal.

This concept of "the circular flow of the economy" is very important. Please be sure to learn it well. A major segment of economics is concerned with analyzing this circular flow—with trying to understand and explain why the economy sometimes speeds up too much and sometimes slows down too much—and with the question of what can be done to stabilize it. All of Parts Two, Three, and Four of this book are directed toward these questions.

come, of course. Where do people get the money to offer other people incomes? From their own incomes. From selling whatever they have to sell. If anything happens to change one person's spending, that affects everybody else's income and everybody else's spending. It's a very *interdependent system!*

If anything happens to reduce the rate of **total spending**, the total output will not be bought, so production will be cut back. We will have unemployed labor, land, capital. People's incomes will fall. People with no income don't spend much. So total spending drops even more.

Are you beginning to get an overview concept of how the total economic system works? Of what keeps it moving? Of what speeds it up and slows it down? If so, you now are beginning to understand *macroeconomics.*

AN OVERVIEW OF MACROECONOMICS

Macroeconomics is concerned with such questions as: Will we operate our economic system at **full capacity**? Will we produce an output which is on the "production possibility curve"? Or will we have **unemployed resources** and produce less than we are capable of producing?

The area of economics we are now talking about is "the economics of full employment and unemployment." Or you could call it "the economics of full production and underproduction," or "the economics of overspending and underspending," or "the economics of inflation and recession," or "the study of the overall level of economic activity." Or you could call it "the study of the causes of speedups and slowdowns of the economic system."

You could call it any or all of these things and all would be right. All these things have essentially the same meanings. But you know the name for this part of the study of economics. It is *macroeconomics.*

What Is Macroeconomics?

When we talk about **macroeconomics** we are thinking about the overall "level" or "rate" of economic activity (employment, production, output, income) and about what might cause it to change. Just like everything else in economics, macroeconomics is concerned with questions about *how* and *why* things happen.

Why is there so much unemployed labor this spring? Why are several of the major business corporations reporting losses instead of profits? Why are department store sales running below the level for this time last year? Why did my boss say unless business picks up within the next two weeks, he will have to let me go?

These are "unemployment" problems— problems of an **economic slowdown**—of the underutilization of the society's factors of production. "Macroeconomics" is concerned with the question of what might be causing things like this to happen.

There is another kind of problem in "macroeconomics." Sometimes it goes the other way. Sometimes the problem is one of "overemployment" and "inflation."

Suppose demand for eggs is up. The price moves up. Egg producers try to hire more factors of production. They try to get some of the stockyard workers to shift to egg production. But people are also demanding more beef. And pork. The stockyards not only are trying to keep their workers—they are also trying to pull in more workers from the poultry business! The automobile companies are looking for extra workers. So are the textile mills and the airlines and the local taxi companies and everybody else.

The lady next door comes by my roadside stand and finds that I have already sold all my corn and tomatoes. She says she will pay an extra 50¢ if I will be sure to save some for her tomorrow. See what's happening? Shortages are developing throughout the economic system. All the resources are fully employed, yet people are still trying to get more output. But the economic system can't possibly produce any more than it is capable of producing! (That's a safe statement.) So what happens?

People keep trying to buy more. Prices rise. What prices? Prices for all the things the people are trying to get more of—almost everything—all products, all factors of production. What do we call this situation? *inflation*. **Unemployment** is one of the major problems of macroeconomics. **Inflation** is another.

The Key to Macroeconomics Is Total Spending

Macroeconomics is concerned with problems of recession, depression, and inflation. It is concerned with the question of how fully we operate our economic system. It is not concerned with the question of whether we use our factors to produce eggs or steaks. It is only concerned with the question of whether or not we use our factors to produce *something*.

What's the key to keeping production levels high? You already know. Keeping *spending* high. It's the level of **total spending** that determines whether or not we will keep our factors fully employed, producing things.

If enough people are spending enough money to buy all the things that all of us want to produce, then all of us will produce. If not, then we will not.

If anybody asks you why so many automobile workers are unemployed, you know the answer. They are unemployed because people are not spending enough money to buy up the "full employment output" of automobiles.

Then someone asks you a very broad question: "Why are so many people and factories and railroad cars and machine tools and processing plants 'unemployed'?" Your answer: "Because the people and businesses throughout the country are not spending enough to buy up the 'full employment output' of the economic system."

Then your question-asking friend asks you the ultimate question—the really tough one: "Tell me *why* the people aren't spending enough

to buy up the 'full employment output' of the economic system. That's *really* what I want to know!" This question stumps you. You admit that you don't know the answer to that one.

Macroeconomics Tries to Explain Why People Don't Buy

You have just discovered another one of those tricky little things that economics has so many of—answers which really aren't answers at all. You've been answering questions by making obvious statements—by stating truisms. When we say that producers don't produce because people don't buy, this doesn't explain very much. But it gives us a start. At least we know the next question to ask: "*Why don't people buy?*" Macroeconomics is concerned with trying to get at the answer to this question—to *find out* and *explain* why people do, or don't buy.

Any number of things might influence the "level," or "rate" of total spending. One important influence is money. How easy is it to borrow money to build a new factory? To buy a new car? How high will the interest cost be? Another important influence is the general outlook of the people— their expectations. If people think times are getting better, they are likely to spend more freely than if they expect hard times ahead.

If we can understand what determines the level of total spending, we can understand why the level of economic activity is high or low. We can understand *why* we have surpluses and unemployment or shortages and inflation. That is what macroeconomics is all about.

Macroeconomics tries to explain what determines the level of total spending (the size of the "total spending flow") in the economic system. Why? Because *in a market-directed economy, total* *spending is the key to understanding total output and total income.* All of Parts Two, Three, and Four of this book deal with macroeconomics.

THE BASIC QUESTIONS OF MACROECONOMICS

The macroeconomic questions are these: "Is the economy running as fast as the people *want* it to run? And no faster? And if so, why? And if not, why not?

Is the **aggregate demand** (total spending) of households great enough to buy all the output the businesses want to produce? And no greater than that? Is the aggregate demand (total spending) of businesses great enough to buy all the factors of production (labor, land, capital) the households want to sell? And no greater than that? If so, the economy will have full employment and there will be no inflationary "excess demand pressures."

Whenever there is unemployment the economic system is running too slowly. The unemployed workers and the owners of the other unemployed factors are not very happy about this situation. If you couldn't get a job, how would you feel? You'd say: "Let's do something to speed up the economy so I can get a job!" Right?

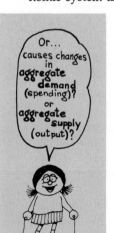

Now look at the opposite situation. Suppose the economic system is trying to run too fast. If aggregate demand (total spending) is too great, **shortages** will appear. Consumers will be trying to buy more goods than are available. Busi-

nesses will be trying to get more factors than are available. Prices will rise. The economic system is trying to run too fast.

You can see that "the basic questions of macroeconomics" can be looked at in several different ways. But all the macroeconomic questions are concerned with the same issue—the issue of *how fast the economic system will run.* For a minute, let's take this basic question apart and look at it from two different points of view.

First, we can look at the **normative** question: "How fast *should* the economy run?" Then we can look at the question economists usually talk about—the **positive** question: "What determines how fast the economy actually *will* run?"

The Normative Macro-Question

The **normative macroeconomic question** is: "How fast do we *want* the system to run?" "What's the best, the most desirable speed of the economic system?" "What speed is 'fast enough but not too fast'?"

Should the economy be running at maximum possible speed? At maximum physical capacity? Of course not. People don't like to put in their absolute maximum effort: Sixteen hours a day? Seven days a week? No holidays? No vacations? That's no fun!

No economic system has ever succeeded in running at its absolute maximum physical capacity over long periods of time. Very few people would want it to. So except perhaps when there is some sort of national emergency, the question is not whether or not the economic machine is running at maximum possible speed. We only want to know if it's running "fast enough"—that is, as fast as we want it to run.

When the society decides to have an eight-hour workday and a five-day workweek and vacation time each year, it's deciding the normative macro-question. When we decide to (or not to) use schools for productive purposes at night and on weekends, we are making a normative macro-decision.

Custom Influences the Normative Macro-Question. In each society, **custom and tradition** are very strong in influencing the answer to this normative question of how hard the economy *should* work—how fast it *should* run. You can see that in the *pure market* economy, the socially desirable rate of output would be reflected in the amounts the people were trying to buy, and in the amounts the producers and workers and farmers and everyone were willing to produce and sell.

In the **model pure market system**, whatever rate of output the society wants, that's the rate of output the society gets. The rate of employment and production automatically reflects the customs, traditions, wishes, and desires of the society. Just automatically!

Even in a completely controlled economy the government planners must build their employment and output goals within the limits of "what the people are likely to be willing to put up with." These limits are mostly determined by the customs and traditions of the society. But even so, if it wants to, an autocratic government can change people's ideas about such things as working on the Sabbath or working long hours or on the night shift.

That's what macro-economics is all about!

The Government Can Force More Output. **Economic plans,** enforced with the power of law, sometimes can result in very large increases in the total rate of employment and output—that is, can push the economy to speed up to a rate much faster than the society "naturally" would want it to go. Very few people seem to want to work a ten-hour day, seven-day week, and forfeit all vacations. But if a government with enough police power decides to enforce this kind of maximum productive effort, it can do so.

The U.S. World War II Experience. During World War II the American economy went on a 24-hour day, seven-day week. Vaca-tions were cancelled. Workers were not allowed to change jobs. Many were urged to work a ten-hour day. Every able-bodied person, male or female, was urged to take a job.

During this period, millions of people were moved out of the labor force and into the armed forces. But even so, the value of the total output of the U.S. economy more than doubled between 1940 and 1945: from less than $100 billion in 1940 to more than $200 billion in 1945. Some of this increase resulted from inflation, but very little. Almost all of it came from the maximum effort speed-up of the economic system.

The Soviet Union. In a *planned economy* (where the political process is in charge of the economic choices) *somebody must decide on the rate at which the system will run.* In the governmentally planned "sectors" of every economy, these planning decisions must be made.

In the Soviet Union the planned production goals and constant push for more outputs have speeded things up. Outputs have been expanded and more capital has been produced. This is the way economic growth has been generated in the U.S.S.R. over the past several decades.

The Positive Macro-Question in the Planned Economy

From what you've been reading about the *normative* macro-question, a good bit about the *positive* macro-question has already come to light. Suppose we're talking about a completely planned economy. You know that **the positive macro-question** (what actually influences or determines the speed of the economy) will be answered by government directives. The administrators give the orders and the people respond. Everyone does what he or she is told to do, so the economy runs at the planned speed.

Of course you know it isn't as simple as

that. People don't always do exactly as they're told. Administrative controls very often are inefficient. Nevertheless the speed of the **planned economy** generally is controlled by the economic planners and resource administrators.

A good course in public administration or administrative management, or one on the Soviet economy, will clue you in to how the "planned economy" carries out its micro and macro decisions. It isn't difficult to see how economic controls and government resource management are supposed to work. But what about the market system?

HOW THE MARKET PROCESS ANSWERS THE MACRO-QUESTIONS

How is the "automatic pure market mechanism" supposed to take care of the positive macro-question? What forces are supposed to determine the overall rate of employment and output and income in the "pure market" system? Then, in the real world where there aren't any *pure* systems (only "mixed economies") how does it work?

In the **model market system** the speed of the economy just takes care of itself. It is automatically determined, just like everything else in the "model market system." The normative question just doesn't arise. In the "pure model," however fast the economy *does* run, that's how fast it *should* run.

If everybody wants to work hard and long, then a lot of output will be produced. A lot of income will be earned by all those industrious people. There will be a lot of spending. If all the manufacturers and farmers and businesses and workers and everyone are really producing as much as they can, pushing hard to make as much income as they can get, then employment and output and income in the society will be high. But if nobody feels stimulated to work very hard or produce very much, the society's output and income will be low. See how the normative

and positive macro-questions are automatically answered in the pure market system?

The more people produce the more they sell and the more they earn and the more they buy. If people decide to produce more they get more income and they buy more. No one needs to decide how fast the economy *should* run. No one needs to plan and direct the people to produce at the right speed. It's all determined automatically by the **natural market forces**—by "the basic laws of positive economics."

Prices Adjust to Prevent Depression

But suppose that for some unexplained reason, suddenly there is too much output for sale in the market. Businesses and farmers are going broke because they can't sell all their products. Many workers lose their jobs. The economy goes into a depression. How does the market process solve this problem of depression?

In the "pure model," it's easy. Prices will adjust themselves until the surpluses are all bought up and until the unemployed workers all have jobs again. Here's how it's supposed to happen.

Product Prices Go Down. The producers who can't sell all their products start offering them for sale at lower and lower prices. As the prices of the surplus products go down, the "buying power" of money increases. All of us now can buy more products with our dollars. Also, people are more willing to spend, to take advantage of all those good bargains! So as the prices fall more and more, people (and businesses) buy more and more. Soon all the surpluses are cleared out of the market and everything's okay again.

Wages Go Down. At the same time that product prices are falling, wages (labor prices) are also falling. The unemployed workers (the "surplus labor") will be willing to work for lower wages. As wages go down, each dollar will buy more labor than before so the cost of producing products goes down. Therefore profit opportunities get better and better. Businesses hire more labor. Soon the unemployment problem is solved.

Interest Rates Go Down. Also there's another "price" working to help get rid of the surpluses and unemployment: the interest rate. Businesses usually borrow much of the money they need to build their factories and to buy their machines and equipment and raw materials and to stock their shelves with inventories. If business is booming and everybody is trying to expand, then everyone will be trying to borrow money. The "money market" will be very "tight." And the interest rate? High, of course!

But suppose the economy is depressed. Not many businesses are trying to borrow. The money market is very "easy." Interest rates are low. As the economy slows down, interest rates go down. With easy money available, businesses can expand at very low interest cost. This induces them to borrow more and expand. This helps to bring prosperity back again.

The Depression Is Self-Correcting. It's easy to see how depression is self-correcting, in the "model pure market system." As soon as surpluses and unemployment begin to appear, automatic price adjustments come into play and begin to solve the problem. The price adjustments keep doing their thing until the problem is solved. It's so neat you just wouldn't believe it! So don't believe it. It doesn't work out quite that way in the real world.

Real-World Prices Don't Move Down Easily

In the real world, all these "market tendencies" really do exist. The tendencies really do try to work in the real world, just as the model says. When there are surpluses and widespread unemployment, it is a fact that prices and wages do *try* to go down.

Some prices and wages actually *do* go down, some. But most prices and wages *can't* go down. People won't let them go down. Most often it's

the *sellers* (not the buyers) who have the most control over prices. So guess which way the prices of most things are likely to move. Up? Yes. Down? No. All modern nations have such things as minimum wage laws, agricultural price controls, and lots of other "price-fixing" laws. But that isn't the really big problem.

Prices don't fall because sellers don't want them to fall, and most sellers have enough **market power** to keep them from falling. Both the sellers of products and the sellers of factors of production fight very hard to prevent price reductions for the things they sell. They would rather see less output and more unemployment than lower prices!

Workers don't want lower wages, land owners don't want lower rents, and the owners of capital and businesses don't want lower interest and profits. How bad does the economy have to get before the steelworkers or the auto workers or the teamsters or the communications workers or the school teachers or anyone else will accept a major wage cut? Pretty bad. Right?

When businesses are faced with declining demands they can cut back output and still survive—sometimes even make profits. But to keep producing and let surpluses pile up to be sold for "whatever the market will bring"—that would be industrial suicide.

In the pure market model, declining demand would have an immediate effect on prices. Prices would fall until the surplus products were bought up and wages would fall until all the workers were hired. (Of course several people might starve while the process was working itself out.) But in the "controlled markets" of the real world, declining demands don't usually push prices down much. In almost all real-world markets, reduced spending results in production cuts and **unemployment**—not declining prices.

If Prices Won't Move, the Market Model Won't Work

Once prices are frozen, the pure market model is of no help in explaining how to get out of a depression. All it can tell us is this: "With inflexible prices, if everything else stays the same the depression will continue indefinitely." That's no help to the hungry workers, the dispossessed farmers, the bankrupt businesses, or the harassed economist who's trying to advise the governments on what to do!

For the market system to maintain **full employment**—that is, to prevent depression—wages and prices must be able to move freely up or down to reflect changes in demand or supply. But are all prices flexible? Of course not.

Generally, prices can move upward without much resistance. But downward? No. Not without a long, hard struggle. Many prices would never move down no matter what!

The "Gut Issues" of Macroeconomics

If we can't depend on price adjustments to bring total spending into line with full employment, then *what* can we depend on? What will keep the economy out of bad depressions? or inflations? Now you have your finger on the really tough questions. These are the real "gut issues" of macroeconomics.

In the real world, price adjustments don't work the way they're supposed to, to keep the economy out of depression. So how can we be sure that the economic system will stay out of depression? That's a good question. You don't yet know enough of the macro concepts and principles for me to give you the answer and explain it thoroughly. That will come in Parts Three and Four. But for now let me give you a tentative answer.

We can pretty well depend on a modern economic system like the U.S. economy to stay out of serious and prolonged depression. To the extent that the economy does it by itself, that's fine. But when the economy doesn't do it by itself, the government will enter the picture and do whatever it must to prevent a serious and prolonged depression. After you have studied Parts Three and Four you will understand how it works.

SUMMARY AND SYNTHESIS

The economy is highly **interdependent** and operates as a **circular flow**. Households sell **input factors** to businesses and receive **income payments** in return. Businesses sell **output products** to households and receive **money revenues** in return.

The size of the **output flow** from businesses depends on the size of the **spending flow** from households to businesses. But that depends on the size of the **income flow** from businesses to households. The system is so interdependent that any speedup or slowdown in any part of the circular flow is felt all the way around the circle.

Macroeconomics is concerned with understanding the factors which influence the circular flow—what might make it speed up or slow down.

The **normative** macro-questions are concerned with how fast we **want** the economy to run. The **positive** macro-questions are concerned with understanding what determines how fast the economy **does** run.

The "model market process" automatically answers both the normative and the positive macro-questions. Flexible price adjustments soon eliminate any surpluses or shortages which might develop. So the economy automatically runs at the speed that the people of the society (as consumers, and as input suppliers) want it to run. But in the real world of inflexible prices it doesn't always work out that way. Much of your study of "principles of macroeconomics" will be concerned with explaining what all this means.

REVIEW EXERCISES

MAJOR CONCEPTS, PRINCIPLES, TERMS (Explain each thoroughly.)

the interdependence of the modern economy
"partial breakdown" of the economic system
total spending equals total receipts
real output equals real income
the basic questions of macroeconomics
the normative macro-questions
the positive macro-questions
how the market process answers the macro-questions

OTHER CONCEPTS AND TERMS (Explain each briefly.)

macroeconomics
microeconomics
the total spending flow
real output
real income
normative
positive
"value added"

DIAGRAM (Draw and explain.)

The Circular Flow Between Households and Businesses

QUESTIONS (Write out answers or jot down key points.)

1. Suppose, next spring, *everyone* decides to really be stingy and save up for a nice long vacation trip, in July. Nobody buys any new cars or appliances or clothes, or goes out to restaurants or shows. Everybody just saves. What do you think will happen? Will all the people succeed in their savings and vacation plans? Discuss.

2. It's interesting to think about how much the normative macro-questions are determined by tradition and custom and habit, even in the highly sophisticated, modern economies of the 1980s. Think about such things as the workday, the workweek, school vacations—how many of these arrangements have been "passed down" to us by the needs of the agriculturally-based, daylight-restricted societies of the past? Do you think it would be a good idea to make some basic changes in some of these "customary" arrangements? Discuss.

3. Explain how depression is supposed to be automatically prevented, and self-correcting in the "pure market economy." Then explain why it doesn't always work that way in the real world of the 1980s.

7 The Magic of Money: What It Is and What It Does, and the American Banking System

Chapter Objectives

- When you complete this chapter you will be able to explain the **nature of money**, the **four functions** it performs, and the **indispensable role** which it plays in the operation of an economic system.

- From this chapter you will understand the **evolution of money** and you will be able to **describe the U.S. money supply**, including the **importance of checkable deposits** as a part of the money supply.

- When you complete your study of this chapter you will be able to **describe the American banking system**, and to **explain how it works**.

- You will understand the **Federal Reserve System** and how it functions. And you will know about the **thrift institutions** and about the important role of **financial intermediation**.

- Finally, this chapter will introduce you to the **revolutionary changes** which are now occurring in the financial services industry in this country. You will find out about the **Depository Institutions Deregulation and Monetary Control Act of 1980** and other important changes now in process, and about the **great impact** these changes are having on the nation's **money and banking** scene.

THE MEDIUM OF EXCHANGE AND THE FUNCTIONS OF MONEY

Everyone has heard that money is a **medium of exchange**. Exactly what does that mean? You know that a newspaper is a medium for spreading the news. We talk about newspapers and radio and TV as being "news media." We talk about trucks, railroads, airlines, pipelines as "transportation media." You have heard of the spiritualist who acts as a medium for contacting spirits. So what is a "medium"?

A **medium** is anything which serves as a go-between. It permits or makes it easier for something to happen. **Money** is a "medium of exchange." Money makes it easier to exchange things—to trade things.

Most of the trade in the modern world could not be accomplished without something to serve as the medium of exchange—that is, without something to serve as money. *Whatever serves as the medium of exchange in a society is money in that society.*

Money is not "the medium of exchange" because it is money. It is money because it is serving as "the medium of exchange." If you

98

want to know what "money" is in any society, look to see what people are using as they exchange things. Anything which is serving as the medium of exchange is (at that time and place) money.

The Need for a Medium of Exchange

I am a fisherman. I just caught a boat load of fish and I want to exchange all these fish for a new suit. Without an "exchange medium" this is very difficult to do. Try to find a suit seller who wants a boat load of fish! But with an **exchange medium** it's easy.

What will I accept as a medium to help me exchange my fish for a new suit? I will accept anything for my fish—I don't care what it is—so long as I am sure the suit seller will accept it in exchange for a suit. If there is any doubt about whether or not the suit seller will accept it for a suit, then I will not accept it for my fish.

Now let's be more realistic. I really don't want to exchange my boat load of fish just for a suit. I want groceries, electricity and water, housing (rent), and maybe a few glasses of beer and some jukebox music at the local tavern. So whatever I accept in exchange for my fish cannot be something acceptable *only* to the suit seller. It must be acceptable to all those other people, too.

Why might all those other people accept it? Only because they are confident that everyone they do business with will accept it too. See how it all ties together? When everyone is confident that everyone else will accept something as money, then that something becomes **generally acceptable**. Then—and only then—it is money.

The Functions of Money

As soon as something becomes generally acceptable in exchange for things, it becomes money. Then it begins to perform all the functions of money. There are four functions of money. The first is to serve as medium of ex-

change, of course. But there are three more functions.

Money serves as the standard for valuing things. People automatically compare the values of things in terms of how much "money" each thing is worth. Is my boat worth more than your car? How can we tell? Just translate both into money. A $3,000 car is worth more than a $1,500 boat. Right? Of course. So money serves as the **standard of value**, or **unit of value** for the society.

The "value unit" function and the "medium-of-exchange" function are sometimes called the two *primary functions of money*. The **primary functions** are the functions which money performs at the present time. You might call them the "current functions" of money—the functions of valuing things and exchanging things *now*.

The two other functions of money serve the purpose of "transferring value" from one time to another. These are called the **secondary functions** *of money*. You might call them the "future functions" of money.

Whenever a person or a business takes on an obligation and agrees to make some future payment, the obligation (debt) is usually stated in money. The money unit (for example, dollars) is usually the most convenient way to express the amount of the debt. When money is used this way, we say that it is functioning as the **standard of deferred payments**.

In its other secondary function, money serves as a convenient form in which to hold savings. It is a thing which can be used to "store up value" for the future. When you save money, your money is serving as a **store of value**. That's the fourth and final function of money.

If you want to save you must have some way to store up the value you are saving. You could buy and hold land or buy and store steel ingots or mahogany lumber or antique furniture or stocks and bonds or anything else you think will hold its value. Money is a very convenient form of stored up value. If you save money (instead of land or steel or whatever) you can always exchange it for other things in a hurry. You know that you can use the money anytime for whatever you might want to buy. No other kind of asset is as **liquid** (as easily and rapidly exchangeable into other things) as money.

The four functions which money performs for the society—medium of exchange, unit of value, standard of deferred payments, and store of value—are *vital* in the operation of the market process. Even in tradition or command-oriented societies these functions must be performed. It would be difficult for even a primitive society to operate without something to serve as money. A modern economic system just couldn't exist without it.

HOW MONEY MIGHT EVOLVE

Sometimes a simple model of an economic system can be helpful in understanding basic principles. Here's an example. When you finish reading this little story you will have a much better understanding of what money is and how it works in the modern world.

Suppose there's an island somewhere in the Pacific Ocean inhabited by four large families (clans, maybe). Each family lives in its own village—one on the north side of the island, one on the south; one on the east side and one on the west. It's called "Tubaland Island." There's a map of it on the next page.

Does this little island economy need money? Something to serve as the medium of exchange? Yes.

It just so happens that the northsiders are the only ones who know how to make "tuba." Tuba is the coconut palm wine which is served at all important ceremonies. The southside, eastside, and westside islanders all must get their tuba from the northsiders.

In the beginning the northsiders were accepting all sorts of things in exchange for tuba— yams, fresh fish, turtle meat, dried fishsticks, breadfruit, taro—anything the other islanders wanted to trade. But now the northside islanders no longer accept "any old thing" in exchange for their tuba. Here's what happened.

Fishsticks Become Money

One day the westside islanders took several baskets of breadfruit and taro to the northside islanders to trade for tuba. But it happened that on that day the northside islanders already had all the breadfruit and taro they could use. So they refused to accept the breadfruit and taro in exchange for tuba. They explained that the breadfruit and taro would all be spoiled before they could eat it. Then the northside chief, King Ratukabua, made a suggestion.

"Why don't you trade your breadfruit and taro to someone for dried fishsticks? We will sell you all the tuba you want, for dried fishsticks. Dried fishsticks last forever. If we get too many we can always ship them and sell them in Japan. The Japanese call them "katsuobushi" and value them highly."

So the westside islanders go around trying to find somebody who will give them dried fishsticks in exchange for their breadfruit and taro. Sure enough, the eastside islanders are willing to trade fishsticks for the breadfruit and taro. So the westsiders make the trade, then go and exchange the fishsticks for jugs of tuba. In this trade, what function did the fishsticks perform? Medium of exchange? Of course.

Soon the word gets around that the northside islanders will always accept fishsticks in exchange for tuba. Because of this, other people around the island begin to accept fishsticks in exchange for the things they want to sell. Soon everyone realizes that everyone else will accept fishsticks in exchange for things. So no one hesitates to accept fishsticks. Fishsticks have become money? Just automatically? Yes.

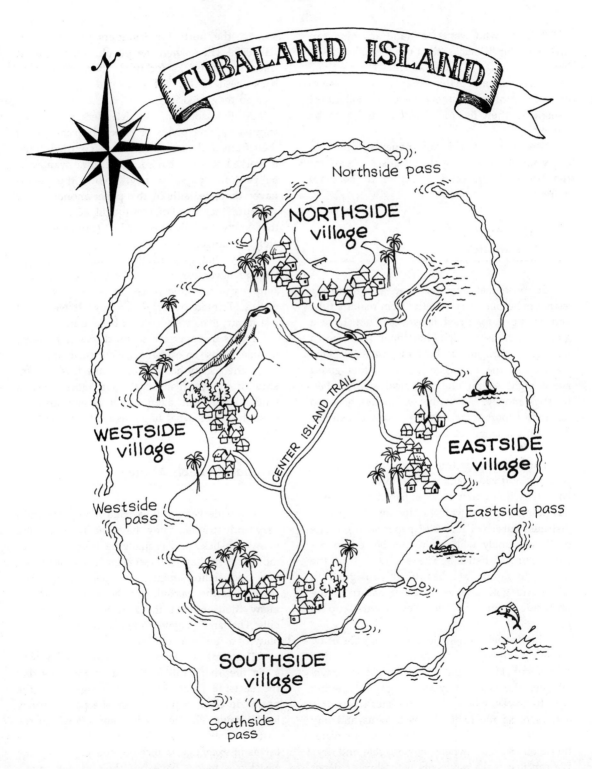

Anyone who wants to trade anything can first sell it for fishsticks, then use the fishsticks to buy other things. As long as fishsticks continue to be generally acceptable—that is, as long as everyone is confident that everyone else will accept fishsticks—then fishsticks will continue to be money.

See how easy it is for money to arise? In every society something always arises to perform the functions of (and therefore to become) money.

Specially Printed Paper Becomes Money

Suppose that over the years the northside islanders become very wealthy from making tuba and selling it for dried fishsticks. They have a great warehouse which they built from hewn mahogany logs, just to hold the fishsticks. One member of the northside family stands guard every night so no one will steal any of their fishstick money. When the warehouse gets too full they export some fishsticks (katsuobushi) to Japan in exchange for better tuba-making equipment and for all kinds of luxury items to enjoy.

These days, when the members of the wealthy northside family travel around the island, they don't carry sacks of fishsticks to use to buy things. If they want to buy something they just give out small pieces of paper saying: "The northside family will pay to the bearer on demand, one fishstick." These "IOU's" of the northside family are beautifully designed in green and gold and carry the signature of the northside chief who had them printed up in Japan.

The "paper money" idea was thought of by the northside chief as a way to make trade more convenient. He thought: "Why should we travel all over the island buying things and paying with fishsticks, when a few days later the people always bring the fishsticks back to us and buy tuba? Why not keep the fishsticks in our warehouse all the time, where they are safe and dry? We can just make payments with slips of paper saying 'the northside islanders owe you one fishstick.' Then when the people come to us to trade the fishsticks for tuba, they can give us back these IOU's." This seemed to be a good idea so they tried it.

At first some of the islanders were wary about accepting pieces of paper in exchange for their fruits and vegetables. But a few tried it and it worked so well that soon everyone wanted to be paid in "paper money." Now, the people have complete faith in the paper money. They are sure that everyone else will accept it and they know it's fully "backed by" (can be immediately exchanged for) fishsticks.

Now that modern times are here, the islanders never carry fishsticks with them. They simply use the little pieces of printed paper as money. Printed paper? as money? If we didn't use it ourselves we wouldn't believe it!

Pieces of paper are so much easier to keep, to hide, to use in exchange. How easily and naturally the society has moved from a less efficient kind of money (fishsticks) to a more efficient kind—paper. But even paper is not efficient enough. Watch what happens next.

The Eastside Islanders "Deposit" Their Money

Over the years the eastside family has been very industrious. They have been producing many fishsticks and exchanging them for paper money. Also they have been making other products and selling them for paper money. The savings of the eastside family now amount to many thousands of the fishstick-backed paper bills. The family begins to worry about the possibility of a fire or a robbery.

The northside family has a stone house with a big fireproof vault in the basement. One day the eastside chief, King Tuituranga, asks the northside chief to please store the paper money in the vault. The northside chief agrees. So the eastside chief delivers the paper money and receives in exchange, a receipt. You might say the eastside islanders have put their money into a "bank account" for safe keeping.

A week or two later the eastside family wants to buy some breadfruit tree logs from the westside family so they can make outrigger canoes. First they go to the northside chief and get (withdraw) some of their paper money from the vault. Then they buy the logs and pay the westsiders. The westsiders don't want to keep all this cash lying around either. So they take it to the northside chief and ask him to keep it in the vault. They "deposit" their money and get a receipt.

A week or two later the eastsiders withdraw more money and buy taro from the westsiders. As soon as the westsiders get the money they take it right back to the northside chief and ask him to put it back in the vault. They "deposit" it again. This sort of thing continues to happen every week or two.

Bank Accounts Become Money

One day the northside chief has an idea. He says to the eastside chief: "Every week or two you come and get some of your money from your vault box and you go and spend it to buy things from the westsiders. Then the westsiders bring the money right back. So I have to open the vault and let them put the money into *their* vault box. That seems to me like a lot of trouble for nothing. Let me make a suggestion.

"When you want to buy something, why don't you just write a note to the westsiders authorizing me to take the money out of your vault box and put it into their vault box? That will save you both a lot of trouble, and I will only have to open the big heavy door to the vault one time for each transaction. Here. Write your authorization on these special pieces of paper I had printed up in Japan. These are called 'checks.' All you do is write who gets the money (whose vault box I should put it in) and how much and then sign your name. I'll take care of transferring the money, and I'll keep a record. I'll send you a statement once a month showing how much you have deposited, how much has

been paid out, and how much is left in your vault box. Want to try it?"

The eastside chief thinks this is a little bit unusual, but he decides to give it a try. When he tries to buy something the westsiders are wary about this flimsy way of doing business. But soon they decide to take a chance and accept the eastside chief's "check." Lo and behold, the system works fine! So now whenever the eastsiders want to buy from the westsiders, they write checks. It works so well that soon all the people on the island start keeping their paper money in the northside vault and writing checks when they want to buy things.

An Efficient Money System Has Evolved

Notice how far the island's monetary system has evolved. And how efficient it is! Seldom does anyone exchange checks for paper money. Almost all of the paper money just stays in the vault. The most efficient way of doing business is by writing checks to each other. Paper money is only used for small, day-to-day transactions. No one ever uses the actual fishsticks to make payments. Not anymore. How medieval that would be! The islanders now have a modern monetary system. But it isn't through evolving yet. Just watch.

As the years go buy, trade picks up on the island. In a few years it gets so busy that the northside chief, King Ratukabua, has to spend much of his time going into the vault and moving paper money from one owner's box to another. One day he says to himself: "This is ridiculous. All these fishstick bills are exactly the same. Why should I keep moving them from one box to another? Why not count the number of bills in each box and make a record. Then I will know how much belongs to each 'depositor.' After that, I can dump all the bills in the same pile and not worry about which ones belong to which people. Then I won't have to be going into the vault all the time and moving cash from box to box.

"I will keep the account books upstairs in my office. When the westside chief (Queen Isaleilani) comes in with a check from the eastside chief, I will just add the amount to her account and subtract it from the eastsiders' account. How easy that will be! I will also keep some fishstick bills up there in the office safe so that if anyone wants any cash I'll have it right there. I may *never* have to open this big, heavy door to the vault, ever again. (How stupid I was not to have thought of this sooner!)"

Account Figures Begin to Be Used as Money

The northside chief puts his plan into action. It works beautifully. Sometimes someone comes in and wants cash (fishstick bills). But before the wall safe gets empty, someone else comes in and deposits cash and replenishes the supply. Last year just before Christmas, many people came in to get cash because they were making lots of small gift purchases. The wall safe was emptied and the northside chief had to open the vault and bring more cash upstairs. But right after Christmas all the cash came back. The wall safe got overstuffed with cash and the chief had to take some of the currency to the basement and put it back in the vault.

The monetary system is working just great. The dried fishsticks never leave the warehouse. Most of the cash never leaves the vault. People do business mostly by writing checks. Whatever you "spend" is subtracted from your account and added to someone else's account. Whatever checks you receive are added to your account and subtracted from someone else's account.

The account figures are being transferred back and forth. So what's serving as money? Would you believe, the account figures? That's the truth.

How neatly it all works—just like a modern monetary system. And it all came about so naturally! Why? Because the benefits of an efficient monetary system are so great and so obvious! The islanders couldn't enjoy the full advantages

of specialization and trade without an efficient medium of exchange. So one evolved. But look out! A disaster is about to happen.

The "Backing" for the Money Is Destroyed

Let's suppose that one spring the tuna from which the fishsticks are made all migrate away so that no more fishsticks can be produced. Also, that same spring, a midnight fire breaks out in the warehouse. The flames leaping skyward can be seen all over the island. Everyone awakens and hurries anxiously, apprehensively, to see what is burning. When they arrive the entire warehouse is ablaze. They stand dumbfounded, watching the flickering reflection of the flames lighting the circle of sad, tearful faces of their friends from all over the island. The fire is beyond control. Everyone knows that their money—the island's store of treasure—is gone. And they know it can never be replaced.

Almost overcome by grief, the eastside chief speaks: "Woe be unto all of us. Our money is gone. Our savings of paper money now are only paper. Our checking accounts mean nothing. We are all poor again. We must all go back to the hard, primitive life we had to lead before our fishstick money freed us from all that. Truly, this is the saddest day in our lives, and the saddest day in the entire history of this island."

Then the wise old northside chief who earlier had withdrawn from the crowd to think, came forth and began to speak. Everyone's attention was captured by his deep, reassuring voice: "Do not despair, my friends. Truly, nothing is lost. The kindly gods have relieved us of a burden. No longer will we need to waste our energies guarding and repairing the warehouse or producing fishsticks which no one will ever eat.

"You have my word that your paper money and your checking accounts are as good as they ever were. You can't exchange them for fishsticks. But you never wanted to do that anyway. You *can* exchange them for tuba anytime you want to, and you can still spend your fishstick money for anything else you want to buy from us. We will all miss the delicious flavor of dried fishsticks. But except for that, nothing is lost. Your money is still just as good as it was before."

At first the others can't see how "fishstick money" can be any good if there are no fishsticks to back it up. What good is paper money if the *backing* is gone? But then the westside chief announces: "As long as the northside chief will continue to accept this money in exchange for tuba, we will accept it in exchange for breadfruit and taro."

The eastside chief announces: "As long as we are sure we can use this money to buy tuba and breadfruit and taro, we will accept it for smoked lagoon fish, turtle meat, and anything else we have to sell."

The Monetary System Doesn't Need Any "Backing"

The monetary system has been saved by the wisdom and quick, reassuring action of the northside chief. He was wise enough to know that it is not what "backs up" the money that gives it its value—it is what you can *buy* with it. It is "faith in its **general acceptability**" which makes money, money. The northside chief knew that if he could assure everyone that the currency and checking accounts were still acceptable then the monetary system would continue to work just as before. But if the people lost confidence in the money, the monetary system would collapse.

It is always true in every society that the monetary system operates on confidence. If the American people, for any reason, lost confidence in the future general acceptability of the U.S. dollar, the U.S. monetary system would collapse. The dollar would cease to be money. Unless something was done quickly to reestablish some kind of money, production would stop. Drastic action would be required to prevent most of the

people from starving.

The wise old northside chief saved the monetary system and the island's economy. Before he spoke, the monetary system had been destroyed because the people *thought* it had. After he spoke the money was good again. Why? Because everyone was confident that it was.

The only thing the island's fishstick money can now be used for is to buy things. But that is what money is always wanted for anyway! Do people want money so they can turn it in for whatever backs it up? Of course not. They want it so they can buy things.

The value of money is determined, not by the number of fishsticks or grains of gold you could get for it, but by what you can buy with it. This is true in every society. You accept dollars, not because they are backed by gold (which they are not), but because you can use them to buy things. The more you can buy, the more valuable is your dollar.

Most of the Paper Money Is Destroyed

Even though the backing behind the fishstick money is gone, the monetary system functions as well as it did before. Everyone has complete confidence in the money. As time goes on, the northside chief occasionally looks into the big vault and sees the great pile of paper money lying there. One day he picks up one of the aging pieces of paper money and reads what it says: "King Ratukabua will pay to the bearer on demand, one fishstick." Suddenly it hits him.

"These are nothing but my old IOU's! Each one says that I owe the bearer one fishstick. Why should I have to keep and store and guard all these old IOU's? If I could get rid of them we could use the vault space as a wine cellar for aging our tuba. Why shouldn't I just burn up all this old money? If I ever need more of these bills (because people want to carry more cash, like at Christmas time) I can always get a new batch printed up in Japan. So why keep this pile of old paper money?"

The chief ponders over this question for quite awhile. But try as he will, he can think of no good reason to keep the paper money. So one day he clears out the vault and burns the money. He is very careful not to be seen. He doesn't think they would understand.

Now the island has no fishsticks backing up the paper money, and almost no paper money backing up the checking accounts. Then one day before long the eastside chief comes and wants to see his money, just to be sure everything is all right. The northside chief opens the account book and shows the eastside chief his balance. But the eastside chief says: "I want to see the *money*, not a *number* in your account book!"

"The number in the account book *is* your money, my friend," says the northside chief. "It's perfectly good money. You can spend it by writing checks. But you can't change it into fishsticks. And you can't change it into paper money either, unless you wait for two weeks until I have the paper money printed up."

The Eastside Chief Demands Cash

The eastside chief is really upset. He has heard of many strange things, but this takes the cake! The idea that the *number* showing his *checking account balance* is his money—the idea that *the number in the account book is the only form in which his money exists*—that is just too much for him to comprehend. He says "I'll be back in two weeks to get my cash and you'd better have it ready for me when I get here. Otherwise, be ready for war!"

The northside chief orders the bills printed. Two weeks later the eastside chief returns, gets his cash, closes out his checking account, and goes home with a big basketful of new paper money. He really doesn't have any more money than he had before. He has just changed the form of his money—from an accounting figure to printed pieces of paper.

As the weeks go by the eastside family finds that using cash is not nearly as convenient as using checks. Also they get worried about theft or fire. One day the eastside chief finally realizes he did the wrong thing. He takes his basketful of cash back to the northside chief, apologizes, re-opens his checking account and deposits the cash. Now he has changed the form of his money from paper bills back into an accounting figure.

The paper bills really aren't money any longer. They aren't serving as a medium of exchange anymore. They are old IOU's of the northside chief and as long as they are in his vault they are not serving as money. That night the northside chief discreetly takes the cash out and burns it. The eastside chief has regained his confidence in **checking account money**. Once again everyone is happy and all goes well.

The Island Now Has a Modern Monetary System

Now a modern monetary system has evolved on the island. Most of the money exists only in the account books of the northside chief. The accounts are not fully backed by paper money (currency), and the currency is not backed by anything. People make most payments by writing checks. Each check results in a subtraction from one account and an addition to another. That's all. No currency changes hands. Currency representing these accounts doesn't even exist.

What do you think of the island's monetary system? Would you believe that's the way it works in every modern society? This example really does fairly well describe the money system of the United States and of every other modern nation in the world.

MONEY IN THE UNITED STATES

To see just how similar the monetary systems of the modern world are to our island example, let's take a quick look at money in the United States. In this country most of the money is made up of checking account balances in the banks. Each depositor has an account balance. Each depositor's account balance is that person's money. Paper money ("currency" or "cash") doesn't exist to back up these checking accounts. If the currency did exist, all the vaults of all the banks in the country would be stuffed full and there still wouldn't be enough space to store all the currency.

People don't like to use paper money except for small transactions. They would rather have most of their money in the form of an account figure at the bank than in the form of paper bills. If enough paper money existed to pay off all the checking accounts in the country, no one would want to hold all that cash.

Nobody wants several thousand dollars in cash lying around the house. The banks certainly don't want several billions in cash lying idle in their vaults! If all this cash existed someone would have to arrange for it to be taken out and burned. That's just what would happen. Just like on the island.

The Federal Reserve Banks Issue Paper Money

In the United States the twelve Federal Reserve Banks are the ones that issue the currency (paper money). As people go to their local banks and cash checks, the banks pay out the cash they have on hand. If they run short they get more paper money from the Federal Reserve Banks which get it from the Bureau of Engraving and Printing of the U.S. Department of the Treasury in Washington, D.C.

The paper money in the United States consists of *Federal Reserve Notes*—simply the IOU's of the Federal Reserve Banks. Just as the northside chief could have a little piece of paper printed up to say: "This piece of paper represents one fishstick," so the Federal Reserve Bank of New York (or St. Louis or Chicago or Minneapolis or Kansas City or Dallas or any other) can have a piece of paper printed up to say: "This is one dollar."

Reach in your wallet and pull out a Federal Reserve Note. The black numbers on the face of the bill and the letter and the printing on the black seal tell you which Federal Reserve Bank issued the note. The number "1" and the letter "A" indicate Boston; 2 and B-New York; 3 and C-Philadelphia; 4 and D-Cleveland; 5 and E-Richmond; 6 and F-Atlanta; and so on to 12 and L for San Francisco.

Currency is Printed Up As Needed

The number and sizes (denominations) of the notes issued by each Federal Reserve Bank are determined by the currency needs in their district. That depends on the desires of the people and businesses to hold and use "cash money" instead of "checking account money." If people want to hold more cash (perhaps at Christmas time), they cash checks. Then their banks ask for (buy) more currency from the Federal Reserve Banks.

The Federal Reserve Banks get more currency printed up, as needed. If the people decide to change their form of money from "currency" back to "checking account money" they simply deposit the Federal Reserve Notes (currency) in their bank accounts. The banks send the surplus dollar bills back to the Federal Reserve Banks where some (the newest) are kept for future use and the others are destroyed.

Be careful to say "money" when you mean

money, and "currency" when you mean only "the paper kind" of money, and coins. You know that money is anything people will generally accept in exchange for things. And you know that "the paper kind" is only about one-fourth of the total.

The Present U.S. Money Supply

In the United States in the early 1980s the total amount of money in existence (the money supply, often referred to as M_1) was approaching $500 billion. About three-fourths of it consisted of **checkable deposits**—that is, the "transferable-by-check" account balances of people and businesses.

About three-fourths of the U.S. money supply is really nothing but little numbers in the account books and computer memories of banks, savings and loans, and credit unions! Total currency (paper money and coins) adds up to about one-fourth of the total money supply.

None of the money being used in the United States is backed by gold or silver or anything but the promises (and the assets) of the Fed and the banks and other financial institutions. It has been about fifty years since a person could go to the bank and exchange paper money for gold coins. It has been several years since a person could turn in paper money and get silver coins. But no matter. Money is money because people accept it as money—because you can use it to buy things.

THE EVOLUTION OF MONEY IN THE REAL WORLD

Money is so useful and it evolves so naturally that in every society something has evolved into money. Seashells, stones, various kinds of metals, diamonds, cigarettes, fish hooks, grain, bullets—almost every imaginable thing has been

money at one place or another at one time or another throughout history.

At First, Money Must Be Full-Bodied

How does something get to become money? Usually it starts out as something useful—some commodity or tool, something used and wanted by most people. At first, people will not be sure whether other people will accept it as money. Still they are willing to accept it because it is **full-bodied**. It has as much value as a "thing" as it has as "money." Otherwise people would not trust it and would not accept it.

Over the centuries, precious metals have been valued for their own sake. It was almost inevitable that gold and silver would evolve into money—so convenient, so attractive, so permanent, so easily made into bigger or smaller sizes, and such a little bit can be worth so much! So gold winds up performing the functions of money.

Full-Bodied Coins Emerge. If the little pieces of gold were melted down into carefully measured sizes, trade would be much easier. No longer would everyone need a scale for weighing gold. Gold would become a better medium of exchange—better money.

This idea lead to the development of uniform little pieces of metal, each stamped to indicate its weight. But who can you trust to stamp the right weight on the pieces of gold? Not everybody! So before long, coins are being made and certified by the government.

Once the government gets involved, the next step is to reduce the amount of precious metal in each coin. So long as people continue to accept the smaller or less pure coin at face value, the "un-full-bodied" coin (**token coin**) works just as well as a full-bodied one. Smaller coins are more convenient, anyway.

The next step in the evolution of money comes with the introduction of paper money, backed by (convertible into) the gold or silver coins. Then as time goes on, people stop carrying so many metal coins and begin to use paper money almost entirely.

The Valuable Substance Is Removed from Money. The two final steps in the evolution of a modern monetary system are taken (1) when the precious metals are entirely withdrawn from the monetary system, and (2) when the people begin carrying out most of their exchanges by writing checks.

Most of the money supply becomes the checkable account balances of the people and businesses. Why? Because the people choose to hold their money this way. It is the most convenient, most efficient form of money for most transactions.

It would be impossible to overstate the importance of money in the operation of any modern economy. Money is the medium which permits the market process to function. Truly, *money is the lifeblood of the market process.*

The Banking System Is the Heart of the Money System

Another thing you have learned in this chapter is the critical role of the banking function in an economic system. How important is the banking function? It's this important: *the money function* can't be separated *from the banking function.*

Think back to the island example. What would life on the island have been like without the northside chief, King Ratukabua, to serve as the island's banker? And suppose he wasn't honest? and prudent? The economic welfare of the people on the island really depends on their banker!

Don't you think the islanders should do something to ensure the safety of their "money and banking system"? Of course they should. It works that way in the real world, too.

In every modern society the banking function is recognized as vital in the functioning of the economy. For this reason every nation exercises some controls over the banks.

THE AMERICAN BANKING SYSTEM AND THE FEDERAL RESERVE SYSTEM

There are about 14,000 different banks in the United States. In addition, there are more than 4,000 savings and loan companies (S&Ls) and more than 20,000 credit unions. And in addition to that, many of the banks, S&Ls and credit unions have many branches.

All of these financial institutions play an important role in the money and financial operations of the country. During the 1980s the distinctions between these different kinds of financial institutions are eroding rapidly.

Most of the banks and other financial institutions are small, with total assets of less than $50 million. They are located in cities and towns all over the country. But some are huge, with assets in the billions and branches all over the world.

Two banks—Citibank in New York and Bankamerica in California—have assets of more than $100 billion. It would take *several thousand* of the smallest banks to equal the assets of these two biggest ones.

Traditionally there has been a strong sentiment in the United States in favor of decentralized banking. Most modern nations have only a few banks with many branches scattered throughout the country. But not so in the U.S.A.!

For more than 50 years the banks in this country have generally been prohibited from interstate branching. Many states don't let banks branch at all! But all this seems to be changing. By the time you are reading this, it may not be true anymore.

Even the "central bank" in this country—the *Federal Reserve System*—is decentralized. It's made up of twelve different banks. Here's a quick look at the history.

A Brief History

In the past the United States has had recurrent problems with its money and banking system. Most of the time, almost anyone with a few assets (like King Ratukabua) could set up a bank and then do just about anything—hold demand deposits, make loans, and all that. There has always been some, but usually not very much government regulation or control.

The states have always been chartering banks. Since the **national banking system** was set up during the Civil War, the federal government (the Comptroller of the Currency in the U.S. Treasury Department) has been chartering "national banks." Both the state banking authorities and the Comptroller of the Currency have always examined banks to see if they are being honest with their depositors and prudent in their investment policies—that is, not putting their depositors' money in unproven oil wells or gold mines. Often, the safeguards haven't been good enough. But that hasn't been the big problem.

The big problem has been "financial panics." Every few years there would be a business slowdown or something would happen to shake people's confidence. People would be afraid the banks might fail. So they would hurry to the banks to get their money. This is called a "run on the banks" or a "panic."

When a **panic** occurs the banks can't possibly pay off all the depositors. They would have to sell all their investments, and billions of dollars of new currency would have to be printed up first! So the banks are forced to fail. All of the depositors (except the few who got there first) lost their money. When all this money just ceases to exist that's no good for the depositors or for the economy, either!

In 1907 there was a really bad one. Many banks failed and the depositors lost their money. With no money, the people couldn't buy much.

The economy went into a depression. A lot of people were fed up with the instability of the American banking system. They demanded that the government do something about it. A commission was set up to study the situation. Ultimately, over the protests of the bankers, legislation was passed (in 1913) establishing the Federal Reserve System.

The Creation of the Federal Reserve System

To satisfy the demands for decentralized banking, Congress divided the country into twelve Federal Reserve districts. A separate **Federal Reserve Bank** was established in each district. All commercial banks which became members of the Federal Reserve System were required to buy a specified amount of stock in the Federal Reserve Bank in their district. So do these stockholders exercise *policy control* over the Federal Reserve Banks? No. Control rests with the Board of Governors of the Federal Reserve System (usually called the **Federal Reserve Board**) in Washington.

All national banks (banks chartered by the federal government) were required to join the Federal Reserve System. State-chartered banks could join if they wanted to—that is, they could join if they had enough assets and if they could meet all the other requirements for membership.

What was the Federal Reserve System (usually called the **Fed**) set up to do? Several things:

—to issue currency,
—to act as banker for the federal government:
  • to hold deposits for the Treasury,
  • to buy and sell government bonds,
  • to aid in the collection of taxes,
—to act as banker for and to provide banking services to the commercial banks,
—but most important: the "Fed" was set up *to hold the reserves and regulate the lending activities of the commercial banks.*

Banking Problems of the 1920s and 1930s

One of the things that the new Fed was supposed to accomplish was *safety*. The depositors shouldn't have to worry about the banks collapsing. Another thing was to provide for a *flexible money supply*. The money supply needs to expand when business is expanding to support the prosperity and growth of the economy.

Both of these problems—lack of **safety** and lack of **flexibility**—had been serious before 1913. Did the creation of the Fed solve these problems? You know the answer. It certainly did not.

Even during the prosperous years of the 1920s, hundreds of banks failed. Millions of dollars' worth of depositors' money were lost. And you know what happened in the 1930s.

Between 1930 and 1933 *more than 8,000 banks failed*. Many billions of dollars of "demand deposit money" were destroyed. By 1933 the American economic system hung on the verge of total collapse.

The depression of the 1930s wasn't entirely a "monetary phenomenon." The interrelated causes were very complex and are difficult to sort out. But here's one thing you can be sure of and it's worth remembering: in an economic system, *when the banking system goes, money goes. And when money goes, everything goes.*

Banking Changes of the 1930s: Deposit Insurance and Tighter Controls

Since 1933 the role of the government in money and banking in the United States has been quite different than before. The government now takes the position that it should do whatever necessary to protect bank depositors from the loss of their money. If the bank fails, the government pays back the money to the depositors.

The federal government, through the Federal Deposit Insurance Corporation (FDIC) now insures bank deposits and through the Federal Savings and Loan Insurance Corporation (FSLIC) it insures non-bank savings accounts. Credit union accounts are also insured. So depositors don't have to "run on the banks."

State bank examiners (for state-chartered banks) and the examiners for the Comptroller of the Currency (for national banks) now keep a careful eye on the banks. In addition there are now two more examining agencies: the FDIC and the Fed. All of these different examining agencies coordinate their activities so that no one bank is hounded to death by examiners. But there's a lot more examining going on!

Present Membership in the Federal Reserve System

Which banks are members of the Fed? All the banks chartered by the federal government (about 4,000) plus about 1,000 state-chartered banks. But that still leaves some 9,000 which are not. Most of the non-member state banks are small. But a few are large.

There are now about 5,000 member banks in the Federal Reserve System—much less than half of the banks in the country. But don't forget this: (1) most of the big banks are members of the Fed, so more than two thirds of the bank deposits in the nation are in "Federal Reserve member" banks. And more important: (2) the Fed's policies and actions don't just influence the member banks. The Fed influences the entire money and banking situation in the nation.

Structure of the Federal Reserve System

The Federal Reserve System consists of the twelve Federal Reserve Banks, the Board of Governors in Washington, and two committees: the Federal Open Market Committee, and the Federal Advisory Council. The Board of Governors establishes the policies for the entire system.

The **Federal Open Market Committee** (FOMC) decides when and how much the Fed will buy or sell government securities (bonds, etc.) in the "open market." Later you'll find out all about this. But for now just remember this: The FOMC plays a very important role because its decisions have an important influence on interest rates and on the money supply of the nation.

The **Board of Governors** is made up of seven members. Each is appointed to a 14-year term by the President with the advice and consent of the Senate. One member's term expires every two years.

The FOMC consists of the seven members of the Board of Governors plus the presidents of five of the Federal Reserve Banks. The **Federal Advisory Council** consists of twelve prominent commercial bankers, one chosen by the Federal Reserve Bank in each district.

Figure 7-1 shows a map of the Federal Reserve System. Although the System is geographically decentralized, its policies are not. The money and banking policies of the Fed really are *national policies*—not twelve different "regional" policies. Take a few minutes now and study that map.

The Functions of the Federal Reserve System

What does the Fed do? It performs the central banking function in the United States. Here's a quick rundown of the Fed's functions:

1. Serves as a banker for the commercial banks: holds their deposits, and lends money to them.
2. Supplies currency (dollar bills and coins) to the banks, who then supply them to the public.
3. Helps in the "clearing and collection" of checks—checks deposited in one bank and drawn on another bank.
4. Serves as fiscal agent for the federal government: holds deposits for the U.S. Treasury. Aids in the buying and selling of government bonds and other securities. Aids in the collection of taxes.

5. Supervises, examines, and regulates the activities of the member commercial banks.
6. Plays an important role in foreign exchange transactions.
7. Most important: the Federal Reserve System exercises control over the money supply of the nation.

The policies and actions of the Fed determine whether or not the money supply will be expanding or contracting. The Fed's decisions play a critical role in influencing the levels of employment, the stability of prices and the growth of the economy. Clearly, the Fed is at the center of the financial structure of the nation.

Commercial Banks and Other Financial Institutions

What are the important financial functions which banks and other financial institutions perform? One is to hold *checkable deposits* which make up most of our money supply.

The "Checking Account" Function. Traditionally, only commercial banks could hold checking accounts. But now the S&Ls with their "NOW" (negotiable order of withdrawal) accounts and credit unions with their "share draft" accounts can also offer check-writing privileges.

What's so important about checking accounts? Just this: money in a "checkable account" is *immediately spendable in its present form.* So it's *money.*

Suppose you put your money into a non-checkable savings account. Or into a certificate of deposit or treasury bill or a savings bond or some such. After that, can you spend it? No. So you aren't holding immediately spendable *money* anymore. You must change it back into "money" before you can spend it.

But what if you put your money into a *checkable account?* You can still spend it by writing checks. So it's money! That's the important thing about checkable deposits. Checkable deposits are

Fig. 7-1 The Federal Reserve System

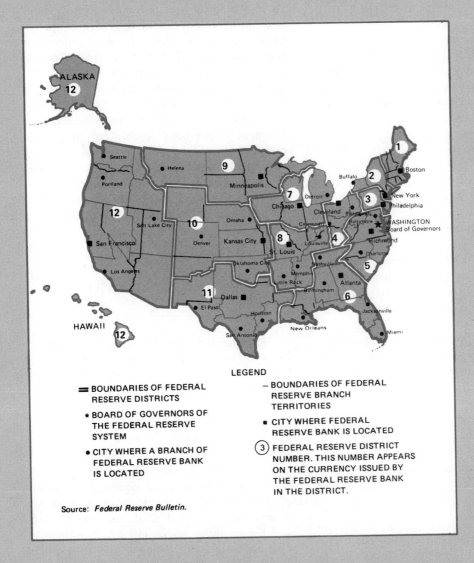

LEGEND

= BOUNDARIES OF FEDERAL RESERVE DISTRICTS

★ BOARD OF GOVERNORS OF THE FEDERAL RESERVE SYSTEM

● CITY WHERE A BRANCH OF FEDERAL RESERVE BANK IS LOCATED

— BOUNDARIES OF FEDERAL RESERVE BRANCH TERRITORIES

■ CITY WHERE FEDERAL RESERVE BANK IS LOCATED

③ FEDERAL RESERVE DISTRICT NUMBER. THIS NUMBER APPEARS ON THE CURRENCY ISSUED BY THE FEDERAL RESERVE BANK IN THE DISTRICT.

Source: *Federal Reserve Bulletin.*

A map of the Federal Reserve districts showing the locations of the 12 Federal Reserve Banks and their 24 branches.

This map shows the "decentralized" central banking system of the United States. Each Federal Reserve Bank performs banking functions for and holds deposits of the member banks in its district. But policy for the entire system is established by the Federal Reserve Board in Washington, D.C.

The Federal Reserve Banks aren't all equal in size and importance, of course. The biggest and most important one (by far) is the one located in the financial center of the nation, right in the middle of the money market. Which one? The Federal Reserve Bank of New York, in New York City, of course!

the most important part of the nation's money supply. When the dollar value of checkable deposits increases, the nation's money supply increases.*

Every financial institution which offers checkable deposits can influence the size of the nation's money supply. That's important. Until recent years only commercial banks could do that. But now a lot of other financial institutions can do that too. In the next chapter you'll find out exactly how these checkable deposits affect the nation's money supply.

The "Financial Intermediary" Function. What's the financial intermediary function? Essentially this: to channel money from *savers* to *investors*. A very important function. Think about it.

When you save money and put it in a savings account where it will earn interest, you're making a personal investment. But from the point of view of the economy you aren't investing at all. You're only saving.

Now it's up to the financial intermediary— the bank or savings and loan association or whoever—to channel your *savings* into *investment*. To become **investment** (from the point of view of the economy) your **savings** must be spent to buy capital or to build something or to produce something productive. See the important role of **financial intermediation**?

In addition to the banks and savings institu-

tions there are some other important financial intermediaries. The "consumer finance" companies gather up savings and use them to make small loans to individuals. Insurance companies gather up money from millions of individuals and businesses and then invest this money in productive ways in the economy.

In the big city finance markets there are the so-called "factors" who provide working capital for corporations. There are "small business investment corporations" (SBICs) which provide capital for (invest in) small businesses. The "investment bankers" help to finance corporations by selling their stocks and bonds for them.

How important is financial intermediation? This important: it wouldn't be possible for a modern economy to function without it.

THE BANKING REVOLUTION OF THE 1980s

Banking and the entire financial services industry in this country entered the decade of the 1980s in a state of rapid change. Sometimes near-crisis conditions existed in the money markets and in the industry.

Interest rates reached the highest levels of the century. Many banks were dropping their Fed membership to avoid holding non-interest-bearing "reserve deposits" in the Fed.

Many people who had money in savings accounts were taking their money out and putting it into money market funds and other assets which paid much higher interest. The financial intermediaries were prohibited from paying high interest rates on these savings deposits. This "disintermediation" soon began to create a serious problem for the financial intermediaries— especially for some S&Ls.

The S&Ls usually hold most of their assets in home mortgages. Mortgage loans made in the 1970s and earlier pay interest rates much lower than the interest rates of the early 1980s. So, many of the S&Ls found themselves with assets (mortgages) bringing in less than 10 percent

*Are non-checkable savings deposits money? Or not? That all depends on how you choose to define money. Economists use different definitions of the money supply.

We define M_1 as "immediately spendable money"—that is, all checkable deposits, currency, and travelers checks in the hands of the public. A broader definition of the money supply (M_2) includes M_1 plus non-checkable savings deposits and money market mutual fund shares. An even broader definition (M_3) includes M_2 plus certificates of deposits and some other highly liquid assets. The Fed also defines an even broader measure of liquid assets (L) which includes M_3 plus some additional kinds of liquid assets. But it's usually most appropriate to think of money as M_1: checkable deposits plus currency and travelers checks.

while their liabilities (sources of funds, such as certificates of deposits, etc.) were costing them 14 or 15 percent, or more. When you're paying out more than you're bringing in, it's just a matter of time before you go broke! And that's what was happening to some of the S&Ls.

The Depository Institutions Deregulation and Monetary Control Act of 1980 (DIDMCA)

It was in the near-crisis conditions of the early 1980s that a new and revolutionary banking act was passed. The Act requires that all banks and other financial institutions which have checkable deposits must hold reserves for those deposits at the Federal Reserve Bank in their district. This stopped the exodus of banks from Fed membership.

The Act calls for the elimination of "Regulation Q" which limits the amount of interest which financial institutions can pay on their depositors' accounts. The Act also permits S&Ls and credit unions (the so-called "thrift institutions," or "thrifts") to offer *checkable deposits* and to make new kinds of *commercial and consumer loans*. So the Act permits the thrifts to engage in activities which previously had been the exclusive domain of the commercial banks. The provisions of the Act are to be phased in over the next few years.

How important will be the effects of this new Act? To answer that question, here's a quote from a book I wrote following the passage of the DIDMCA.*

> As the provisions of the Act are phased in, fundamental changes will be occurring among the financial institutions throughout the country. . . . The competitive impact of these changes among the nation's financial

institutions, and the ways in which the various financial institutions will respond to this new competitive environment will significantly change the nature of the financial services industry in this country.

It is clear that this piece of legislation is the most significant, the most far-reaching, the most revolutionary change which has occurred in the banking and financial industry in this country since the depression of the 1930s. The new legislation signals great change in the structure and operation of the banking and other financial services institutions. The impact of these changes will be felt throughout the economy.

It is clear that small savers will receive more return on their savings as the banks and S&Ls and other depository institutions compete for the small saver's deposits. And borrowers in all segments of the market are likely to find themselves paying interest rates which more accurately reflect the "time value" of the funds which they are borrowing. . . . As the effects of this new Act work their way out in the economy during the decade of the 1980s, the changes will be profound.

The New Competitive Environment

The 1980 Act brought much new competition into the financial services industry. It permits new kinds of competition among the banks, S&Ls, credit unions, and mutual savings banks. But this kind of "new competition" only goes a short distance in explaining the "new financial services competition" of the 1980s. Two other kinds of competition are generating revolutionary changes in the financial services industry. One is *geographic* (spatial) competition. The other is competition from *outside the banking and thrift industry.*

---

*Elbert V. Bowden, *Revolution in Banking: Regulatory Changes, The New Competitive Environment, and the "New World" for the Financial Services Industry in the 1980s* (Richmond: Robert F. Dame, Inc., 1980), p. 128.

Geographic "Spatial" Competition: Interstate Banking? For more than 50 years it has been illegal for banks to own branches in other states. But in the early 1980s the barriers to interstate banking began to crumble. What happened? Several things.

For one thing, some foreign banks had been permitted to establish branches in more than one state in this country. Another, some banking corporations had been able to establish branches in other states through legal loopholes. But even more important, many banks, while not actually "establishing branches" in other states, are actively competing across state lines: in attracting deposits, in making loans, and in providing other kinds of financial services. So we do in fact have intense *interstate competition* among the larger banks and thrifts.

Non-Bank Competition: What Is a Bank? In the 1970s and early 1980s, several very large non-bank corporations began to offer banking-type financial services. Such firms as Merrill Lynch and other brokerage companies, American Express and other credit card companies, some insurance companies, and even Sears Roebuck began to offer a wide range of financial services in direct competition with the banks and thrifts. And these financial services are offered interstate— that is, *nationwide*. The large banks are asking: "Is that fair?" And they are calling for new laws to give them equal opportunities to compete with the non-bank companies.

Some financial institutions are facing a **tough transition!**

"Failing-Bank" Mergers. The difficult financial circumstances of the 1980s are threatening the survival of some banks and thrifts. Suppose a bank (or a thrift institution) is in danger of failing. The Federal Deposit Insurance Corporation (FDIC) (or FSLIC for the S&Ls) tries to arrange for a merger with a stronger partner. But suppose an appropriate "stronger partner" can only be found in another state. Should an interstate merger be permitted? Or suppose the most appropriate "stronger partner" for a failing S&L turns out to be a bank? Or vice versa? Should the merger be permitted?

During 1981 and 1982 several *interstate mergers* were arranged between S&Ls to prevent failures. Several banks were arguing for permission to merge with (acquire) S&Ls. Many bankers were also calling for legislation which would permit open interstate banking. But there was strong opposition from some small banks who didn't want competition from out-of-state banks.

Many bankers were also calling for legal permission to compete across-the-board with their non-bank competitors. "If stock brokers and insurance companies and others can compete in the banking business, then banks should be able to compete in the stock brokerage, insurance and other businesses."

As this book goes to press, these important issues are very much alive but still unresolved. In Congress, both the Senate and House banking committees are considering various bills dealing with these controversial issues. It's impossible to know what legislation will be forthcoming. But the general directions of change seem fairly clear.

By the end of the decade of the 1980s, the financial institutions in this country will look much more alike than they did at the beginning of the decade. The distinctions between commercial banks, S&Ls, and non-bank financial institutions will be reduced—possibly eliminated.

Competition will be keen in the financial services industry. The most dynamic and aggressive institutions will reach for broader and deeper markets for their services. Small banks and S&Ls (and some large ones) will choose not to fight this competitive battle and will be merged into the larger, more aggressive firms.

Of this you can be quite sure: The next few years will be a period of interest, excitement and dynamic change in the financial services industry in this country. In a few years this industry will look very different from the way it looks today.

SUMMARY AND SYNTHESIS

A modern economy could not operate without something to perform the function of **medium of exchange**. Whatever performs this function is **money**. The three other functions of money are: **standard of value, standard of deferred payments**, and **store of value**.

Because of the need for something to serve as "medium of exchange," money naturally evolves. At first money is **full-bodied** (worth as much as a commodity as it is as money). But as time goes on money tends to evolve into paper, and bank accounts, both of which perform the medium-of-exchange function more efficiently than full-bodied money.

The essential characteristic of money is that it be **generally acceptable**. If people are confident of the general acceptability of something, then that something will serve as money and therefore will be money. But if there is any question about its general acceptability, it will not be accepted and it will not be money.

Money in the United States consists of **checkable deposits** at the banks and other financial institutions, and **currency**: paper money issued by the Federal Reserve banks and coins issued by the Treasury. The total size of this money supply (M_1) in the early 1980s was approaching $500 billion—about three-fourths of it checkable deposits and the other one-fourth currency and coins.

In a modern economy, **checkable bank deposits** make up most of the money supply, and most of the **paper currency** is issued by the banking system—so the "banking function" and the "money function" are inseparable.

The other indispensable role of the banking system (broadly defined to include all financial services institutions) is to perform the function of **financial intermediation**—the "go-between function" which channels savings into investment.

In the early 1980s there were some 14,000 banks, some 4,000 S&Ls, and more than 20,000 credit unions providing financial intermediation services and facilitating the performance of the "money function" in the economy. But the few largest of these firms held most of the assets, and provided most of the financial services.

The **Federal Reserve System** is the **central bank** in the United States. It provides **financial services for the banking system** and for the **government**. But its most important function is to control the size of the money supply. Its **money-control function** is carried out through the **Federal Open Market Committee (FOMC)**.

The early 1980s brought **revolutionary change** in the nation's banking and financial services industry. The **Depository Institutions Deregulation and Monetary Control Act of 1980 (DIDMCA)** is the most important banking legislation in many decades. It reduces the distinction between the commercial banks and thrifts, extends control of the Fed over non-member financial institutions, and includes other significant changes.

During the early 1980s the **competitive environment** in the financial services industry changed dramatically. There was **new competition** between the banks and the thrifts, some erosion of the barriers to **interstate banking**, and competition from **non-bank** and **non-thrift** institutions entering the financial services industry.

The outlook for the 1980s seems to be for more interstate competition, more competition between the banks and thrifts, and more competition with non-bank financial services institutions. In the coming years the number of banks and thrifts will decline as the weaker and/or smaller firms merge with the stronger and/or larger ones.

REVIEW EXERCISES

MAJOR CONCEPTS, PRINCIPLES, TERMS (Explain each carefully.)

the meaning and importance of money
how "full-bodied" money might evolve
how paper money might evolve
how "checking account" money might evolve
two "current functions" of money
two "future functions" of money
the functions of the Federal Reserve System
the importance of "checkable deposits"
the functions of financial intermediaries
the "banking revolution"
impact of the DIDMCA

OTHER CONCEPTS AND TERMS (Explain each briefly.)

medium of exchange
standard (or unit) of value
primary functions of money
secondary functions of money
standard of deferred payments
store of value
liquid
monetary "backing"
currency
token coin

FDIC, FSLIC
Federal Reserve System
Federal Reserve Bank
Federal Reserve Notes
demand deposits
full-bodied money
investment bankers
"checkable" deposits
spatial competition
thrift institutions

QUESTIONS (Write out answers or jot down key points.)

1. Do you think *tuba* (instead of fishsticks) might have evolved into money on the island? Explain in detail.

2. During the great U.S. and worldwide depression of the 1930s, not very many people had very much money. A lot of banks had collapsed—gone bankrupt. Where do you suppose most of the money had gone? Did the rich people have it squirreled away somewhere? Or what? Discuss.

3. If you lend your friend $5 to buy a few glasses of beer, that doesn't create any money. But suppose you were so rich and well known that everybody knew your signature and would accept your IOU. If you write your friend an IOU for $5 and your friend goes and "spends" the IOU at the local bar and the barkeeper uses it to pay the waitress and the waitress uses it to pay the taxi driver and the taxi driver uses it to buy gas . . . Does that mean that your loan has *created money*? Discuss.

4. Describe the American banking system.

8 How the Banking System Creates Money: The Deposit Multiplier

Chapter Objectives

- After you study this chapter you will be able to explain **how money is created and destroyed through the banking system.**

- In this chapter you will find out about the importance of **required reserves** and **excess reserves,** and how **monetary expansion** occurs as banks **lend their excess reserves.** And you will find that excess reserves are a **necessary** (but sometimes not a **sufficient**) condition for **monetary expansion** in the economy.

- When you finish studying this chapter you will be able to explain why: "**Lending money creates money and repaying loans destroys money.**"

- You will find out about the **deposit multiplier,** and how its size depends on the **reserve requirement.** And you will learn the **formula** for the **deposit multiplier,** and how to use the formula.

- In this chapter you will see how the **Fed** operates as a **bankers' bank,** holding **deposits** and **reserves** of member banks. And you will see how commercial banks settle their individual accounts with each other through **transfers** of their **Federal Reserve deposits.**

The Money Supply Expands and Contracts Automatically

If the economy is going to speed up very much, the money supply—the actual number of "spendable dollars" in existence—must somehow increase to permit the increased spending to occur. So where does the extra money come from?

It's newly created. Nobody "creates" it. It just expands by itself through the normal workings of the banking system. First, a look at how it might happen on Tubaland Island. Then you'll see how it actually does happen in the U.S. economy.

LENDING MONEY SOMETIMES CREATES MONEY

Suppose the eastsiders want to buy a plot of land from the westsiders but they don't have enough money in their account. The eastside chief goes to see the northside chief who, as you know, is operating as the island's banker. The eastside chief asks if he can borrow 10,000 fishsticks (FS 10,000) to buy some land from the westsiders.

Lending can **create money!** Crazy!

The northside chief realizes that the eastside chief doesn't want cash—he only wants the amount added to his checking account so he can write a check to buy the land. Then the westsiders will deposit the check to their account and the "loaned money" (FS 10,000) will be subtracted from the eastsiders' account and added to the westsiders' account.

The northside chief, knowing the eastside chief's credit is good, says "Certainly. We will lend you as much as you would like." The northside chief adds FS 10,000 to the account of the eastside chief.

What has happened to the supply of money on the island? It's FS 10,000 bigger than before! The eastside family now has FS 10,000 which it did not have before. Nobody had it before. It didn't exist! The northside chief, acting as the banker, simply created that FS 10,000 when he added that amount to the eastsider's account.

Look at it this way. Suppose *before* the FS 10,000 loan, you went around the island and found out how much money each person had (in cash and in checking accounts). If you added up all the figures you would come out with the total size of the island's money supply. Then *after* the FS 10,000 loan, suppose you did it again. You would come up with a larger total than before. How much larger? FS 10,000 larger. Where did the extra FS 10,000 come from? It was *created* by the northside chief? That's right.

The eastside family will now buy the land from the westside family and pay them by check. Then the new FS 10,000 will be subtracted from the eastsiders' account and added to the westsiders' account. The new FS 10,000 will become the westsiders' money. Before the eastside chief borrowed it, whose money was it? Nobody's. Where was it? Nowhere. It didn't exist.

All the Money on the Island Is Really "Debt"

All the money on the island consists of debt. It's the debt of the northside chief. The "bal-ance" in each account is the amount the north-side chief owes to the owner of the account. And it's those "account balances" which make up most of the island's money supply.

Since the debt of the northside chief serves as money, any increase in that debt is an increase in the money supply. What happens when the eastside chief borrows? He gives the northside chief a promissory note saying, "I owe you FS 10,000." What does the eastside chief get in return? He gets a FS 10,000 addition to his checking account. He gets a "deposit slip" from the northside chief which says (in effect), "I owe *you* FS 10,000."

See what has happened? Each has given the other a debt in exchange for a debt! Each owes the other an additional FS 10,000! But the important thing is that the northside chief's debt is **monetized debt**—that is, *his debt serves as money.* This transaction creates money because the debt of the northside chief *is* money. When the northside chief is issuing more *debt,* he is issuing more *money!* Get it?

Increasing the Checking Account Balances Creates Money

Whenever the northside chief is lending money to people by adding to their checking accounts, he is adding to the island's total money supply. The people are getting more money to spend. But whenever a person pays back the northside chief by writing a check, that reduces the person's checking account balance and destroys money. It reduces the size of the total money supply of the island.

The total money supply is made up of the checking account balances of the people, plus the paper money they carry around. Anything which increases the size of the checking account balances increases the money supply; anything which reduces the size of the checking account balances reduces the money supply.

If anything happened to cause the northside chief's bank to collapse, all of the checking account balances would be gone so all of the "checking account money" would be gone. That's about the way it is in the real world, too. If the bank where you keep your money suddenly collapsed, your "checking account money" would be gone. But the Federal Deposit Insurance Corporation (FDIC)—the government agency which guarantees the safety of your bank account—probably would reimburse you.

This simple island example of "creating money by making loans" is more true to life than you might think. Most of the money in the United States and in other modern nations is actually created by bank loans. It doesn't happen exactly as in the island example, but almost!

So now you know *what* happens. Here's a little story that will show you exactly *how* it happens.

HOW ONE BANK CAN CREATE MONEY

Mr. Zimmer, the local banker, is sitting at his desk one morning musing about the ups and downs in the banking business. "The **money market** is a strange 'market'," he says to himself. "Six months ago we had more money to lend than we knew what to do with. I was buying government bonds just so we could earn some interest on all the money we had on deposit. But today? It's hard to believe. We're all loaned up and the demand for loans seems to just keep on increasing.

"Interest rates are going up too, but people keep on borrowing. I guess those 'monetary policy' people in Washington are doing something to make money hard to get. Anyway, it's sort of good to be all loaned up. No need to worry about having to keep our money busy by buying government bonds! On the other hand, it's tough to tell old customers, old friends, that you can't lend them any money because you're all loaned up. Ah well, such is life . . . ."

Banks Can't Lend Unless They Have Some Money to Lend

While Mr. Zimmer is thinking all these thoughts, Mr. Baker walks into the bank. He interrupts Mr. Zimmer's thoughts with a shocking request. Mr. Baker had an economics course in college some years ago. He flunked it, but he remembers the part that said the banking system really does create money. So, full of desire to show his sophisticated knowledge about banking, he says: "How about creating $4,000 and lending it to me? I'd like to buy a camping trailer that's on sale."

Zimmer calms himself enough so that he says nothing worse than: "Don't be ridiculous! You think I can create money for you, right out of thin air? Preposterous! I can only lend you the money I have available to lend. And I don't have any money available to lend. Money is very tight these days."

Baker is confused. He's *sure* he remembers the part about banks creating money. That's the only question he go right on the final! He's thinking, "No money to lend? Is this guy pulling my leg?"

A New Deposit Creates Excess Reserves. About that time one of Mr. Zimmer's good customers, Mr. Alber, comes striding into the bank, waving a government check, saying: "I knew the government would finally understand my case and refund all those unjustified taxes I have been paying over the past five years!" The man is carrying a treasury check for $5,000. The check is drawn against the U.S. Treasury's account in the Federal Reserve Bank of New York.

(The Treasury has accounts in the Federal Reserve Banks. Remember? So when the government spends money it can write checks against those accounts. When it collects taxes or sells bonds it can deposit the money in those accounts.)

Mr. Zimmer's bank is not a very big bank. In fact there's only Mr. Zimmer, one teller, and a secretary. Right now the teller is out to lunch so

Mr. Zimmer has to interrupt his conversation with Mr. Baker to take Mr. Alber's deposit. Baker doesn't mind the interruption. In fact he isn't too happy about the way things are going so he's getting ready to leave anyway. He heads for the door.

Zimmer calls him back: "Mr. Baker, wait. Now I will be able to lend you the money!"

A Bank Can Lend Its Excess Reserves. Baker looks puzzled. He turns and slowly walks over to the other two men and says, "I'm afraid I don't understand. You just said . . . ."

Zimmer interrupts: "I know what I just said. But that was before we received Mr. Alber's $5,000 deposit. Now we have money to lend! Now we have some excess reserves! Let me introduce you to Mr. Alber. Why don't both of you have a seat here at my desk and let me explain to you something about banking procedures.

"We keep checking accounts for people. We call them **demand deposits** because they are payable 'on demand' to anyone the owner tells us to pay them to. Whenever Mr. Alber writes a check to somebody he's just telling us to pay that somebody some of the money out of his (Mr. Alber's) account. Right, Mr. Alber?"

Alber nods.

"Mr. Alber has had demand deposits in this bank for several years. He's one of our best customers. But we have lots of good customers. In fact would you believe that in our little bank we have a total of one million dollars in demand deposits? Don't ask to see the money in our vault. We only keep about $50,000 in the vault. There's no profit made on money in the vault! But on the books we really do have total deposits of $1,000,000. I'll bet that surprises you!"

Baker doesn't look too surprised or too impressed either. In fact he's a little bit bored listening to Zimmer brag about how "big" his little bank really is. "Okay," he says. "So what's the point?"

"The point I was coming to is this: The way we make money in this business is to lend out the money our customers deposit in their ac-

counts. Mr. Alber just made a deposit. So now we can make you a loan."

"There, he said it again," Baker thinks. "He keeps trying to tell me that banks don't create money when I know they do! And I'm getting kind of tired of all this. . . ."

Zimmer continues. "Mr. Alber just deposited $5,000 but we can't lend you all of that. The banking regulations of the Federal Reserve System require that we keep some money 'on reserve.' The more money we have in our demand deposit accounts, the more we must keep 'on reserve.' So how much must we keep?

"Right now the **reserve requirement** is something less than 20 percent, but let's say it's 20 percent just so the numbers will come out even. Twenty percent of what? Twenty percent of the total amount of money our customers have in their demand deposits, that's what! So you can see that whenever our customers deposit more money in their demand deposit accounts, we also must keep more in our reserve. Understand?"

Baker nods, "I think I see it, but I'm not sure."

Federal Reserve Banks Hold Reserve Deposits

Baker is beginning to get interested. "You said you're holding a million dollars in demand deposits, and suppose the reserve requirement is 20 percent. That means you must be holding $200,000 on reserve. (20% of $1,000,000 is $200,000.) Right? And you just said you only keep about $50,000 in your vault. Where's the other $150,000? Or are you just pulling my leg?"

"No, no leg pulling. It's all very true. And you're right. There is another $150,000. It's in our bank account at the Federal Reserve Bank in this district."

"You mean your *bank* has a bank account? Like a demand deposit account? At the Federal Reserve Bank?"

"Right!" says Zimmer.

Banks Pay Each Other Out Of Their Federal Reserve Accounts. Zimmer goes on. "My bank has an account in our Federal Reserve Bank, but we can't write checks to people or businesses on our *Federal Reserve bank account.* The account is only used for making payments to other banks. Whenever another bank has a 'money claim' against this bank—that is, whenever we owe money to another bank—the other bank gets paid out of our account at the Federal Reserve Bank. It's a neat system!"

"But wait!" Baker thinks something's a little bit fishy here. "If you are going to be using that account to pay off other banks, you aren't going to have enough left. You're supposed to keep that $150,000 there on deposit all the time to meet the 'reserve requirement' you told me about. If you pay some of the $150,000 to another bank, you won't have enough left to meet the 20 percent requirement."

Zimmer's eyes sparkle. "Aha! Now you see it! That's why I couldn't lend you the $4,000 you wanted to borrow awhile ago. You would sign a promissory note and I would open a checking account for you. Then what would happen? You would go right over to Mr. Culver, the sporting goods dealer in Tonawanda and spend the money. You would write him a check for $4,000. Then what do you think would happen after that?"

Baker says, "The sporting goods dealer would come right over here and cash the check and get the money out of my account."

No One Ever Cashes a Large Check. "Come now, Mr. Baker," Mr. Zimmer says. "Who would ever cash a $4,000 check? No, Mr. Culver will deposit the check in his own demand deposit account at the bank where he does business in Tonawanda. The bank will have the check. So what do you suppose the Tonawanda bank will do with the check?"

"Come over here and cash it and get their money out of my account?"

"There. You said it again. No. Nobody *ever*

cashes a $4,000 check! The Tonawanda bank will send the check (along with a bunch of other checks) for deposit to its account at the Federal Reserve Bank of New York (or maybe to the Buffalo branch). The Federal Reserve Bank will then deposit the check—that is, add the $4,000—to the account of the Tonawanda bank. But the Federal Reserve Bank is not just going to add $4,000 to the Tonawanda bank's account without getting the money back from somewhere. Where does the $4,000 come from? Can you guess?"

"I'll bet they take that $4,000 out of your $150,000 deposit at the Federal Reserve Bank. Right?"

"Right!"

Insufficient Reserves Must Be Made Up Somehow

Zimmer goes on. "If they take $4,000 out of my reserve account, I'm suddenly in an illegal position. I won't have enough left to meet the 20 percent reserve requirement, to back up my demand deposits. I will have to do something quick to make up the difference. I might *borrow some money from the Federal Reserve Bank* to make up the difference. Or maybe I would *sell some of my government bonds to them, or to somebody.* Or I might *borrow some of the excess reserves of other banks.* Or when someone comes in to renew a loan I might *refuse to renew it.*

"Anyway," Zimmer continued, "I'd rather not have to do any of those things. The Federal Reserve Bank is charging a high **discount rate**— that is, high interest on the loans it makes to banks—these days. And the bond market is depressed. Bond prices are so low that if I sell my bonds now, I'll have to take a loss. As for refusing to renew loans, I certainly don't want to do that to my good business customers. They would have to sell off their inventories to pay off their loans. They would never do business with me again!"

NEW EXCESS RESERVES PERMIT NEW LOANS

Mr. Zimmer continues. "Now you see why, before Mr. Alber's deposit, I couldn't lend you any money. I had only enough to cover my required reserve. No excess at all. But now, with Mr. Alber's $5,000 deposit I do have some excess reserves. I can lend you any amount you want, up to the amount of my excess reserves. Can you figure out how much excess reserves I have now? Can you tell me how much I can lend you!"

"Let's see. Mr. Alber deposited a government check for $5,000. You're going to send that check to the Federal Reserve Bank and they will deposit it to your account. Right?"

"Right!"

"Then you will have $155,000 in your account. You only need $150,000. So you can lend me $5,000. Right?"

"Almost right, but wrong. You forgot something."

Part of a New Deposit Becomes Required Reserves

"When Mr. Alber deposited his check he added $5,000 to my bank's total demand deposits. So now I must . . ."

Baker interrupts. "Wait! I see it! Now you must have more reserves, because now you have more deposits! You must have enough new reserves to cover Mr. Alber's new deposit. If the required amount is 20 percent (one-fifth) then for $5,000 more of deposits you must have $1,000 more in reserves (20 percent of $5,000 equals $1,000). So you only have $4,000 in 'excess reserves.' You can lend me any amount up to $4,000! Right?"

"Right. Now you understand. So how much do you want to borrow?"

"I'll take the whole thing! That's exactly how much I want to borrow anyway. Let's draw up the loan papers. I have about $6,000 worth of

GM and Exxon stocks here to leave with you as collateral. You can open a checking account for me. Then you can just deposit the $4,000 in my new checking account. Okay?"

"Fine. It will only take about 10 minutes to get the papers ready for your signature."

While the loan papers are being prepared, Mr. Baker is re-thinking this whole banking process. "They only need a 20 percent reserve to back up their checking accounts. I'm borrowing $4,000 and it's going to be put into my checking account. Well then! All they *really* need to have on reserve to back up my account is 20 percent of $4,000—only $800!"

He thinks about this a few more minutes and then decides to confront Mr. Zimmer with this new bit of logic. "You really only need $800 behind this $4,000 deposit of mine! Why do you insist on having $4,000 in your Federal Reserve account to 'back up' my checking account balance of $4,000? You said you only needed 20 percent. If you're only holding $1,000 behind Mr. Alber's $5,000 deposit, how come you insist on holding $4,000 behind my $4,000 deposit?

"You're holding a 100 percent reserve behind my new checking account, but only 20 percent behind Mr. Alber's. How come? I don't want to borrow but $4,000 anyway. But I sure would like to know what's going on!"

Loaned Money Soon Leaves. Mr. Zimmer seems pleased that Mr. Baker has gotten so interested. "That's an intelligent question! But I'm sure that if you thought about it awhile, you'd figure out the answer. Really, *your* account is very different from Mr. Alber's account. Both accounts look exactly the same on the bank's books, but still they're very different. Mr. Alber's account consists of *deposited* money. Yours consists of *borrowed* money. Let me explain the difference to you.

"You are going to go out and spend that $4,000 right away. When you spend it to buy the camping trailer, the check is going to be deposited in the sporting-goods dealer's account in the Tonawanda bank. Then the Tonawanda bank is going to send the check to the Federal Reserve

Bank. Remember?

"The Federal Reserve Bank will deposit the check to the Tonawanda bank's account. Then what? The Federal Reserve Bank will take the money away from my account. How much money? $4,000 of course! Then they will send the check back to me and I will take it off your checking account. Then, poof! Your money (account balance) will be gone!

"See what would have happened if I only had $800 in my reserve account to back up your $4,000 demand deposit? When your check clears, I am going to lose $4,000 from my reserve account at the Federal Reserve Bank. So I *must* have a "100 percent reserve," or $4,000 behind your account. Your account was created not by a *deposit* but by a *loan*. That's what makes it different. Do you understand?"

Deposited Money "Never Leaves." Baker is still puzzled. "But then, why do you feel so confident about keeping only $1,000 behind Mr. Alber's $5,000 deposit? Suppose he goes out and writes a check tomorrow for $5,000? When the check clears, aren't you going to be in trouble? What about that?"

"You're right," Zimmer admits. "If that happened tomorrow, and if that's the *only thing* that happened tomorrow, we would be in trouble. But that's not going to happen. Or if it does, it's not going to be the only thing that will happen. I guess you would say that we are 'protected by the law of averages.' Let me explain it this way.

"We have many customers who come in and make deposits every day. These regular customers are also writing checks, spending their deposit balances every day. We know that on the average day in the average month, the number of people coming in and *depositing* money, will be almost exactly equal to the number of people who are going out and writing checks and *spending* their money. So the two balance each other. There's no 'net change' in our Federal Reserve account."

In a Growing Bank, Deposits Keep Expanding. Zimmer continues. "Look at it this way. On November 1 of *last year* we had total demand deposits of about $990,000. On November 1 of *this year* we expect to have total demand deposits of slightly more than $1,000,000. *Next year* on the same day, we expect to have even more demand deposits on our books. Do we need to worry about the fact that any one individual is spending some of his or her demand deposit money, and that some of our reserves are going to other banks?

"So long as the money coming back and being deposited in our Federal Reserve account is more than enough to make up for the money leaving our Federal Reserve account, we have nothing to worry about. As long as we are a growing bank, our deposits will always be more than enough to offset the 'spending withdrawals.' Doesn't that make sense?"

Mr. Baker sort of understands. But he asks, "What about me? Why don't I fall into the same category?"

"Because you are borrowing money. Borrowers go out and spend money *immediately*. The amount you borrow will be leaving our reserve account right away. We can be certain of that. There won't be any 'average return flow of deposits' to offset your expenditure. So you don't fit into the normal pattern. Therefore we can't lend you any more money than we actually have free to lend—that is we can't lend you any more than we have in **excess reserves**.

"We can only lend you as much as we can afford to lose from our reserve account. Why? Because we know that when we lend it to you, you are going to spend it and we are going to lose it. Right away."

Mr. Baker seems to understand. Anyway, now the secretary has prepared all the loan papers, ready for signature. Mr. Baker signs the promissory note. Mr. Zimmer signs a receipt for the stock certificates Mr. Baker is leaving as collateral to guarantee that he will repay the loan.

The teller who has returned in the meantime gets Mr. Baker to sign a signature card, then gives Mr. Baker a new checkbook and a deposit receipt for $4,000. Mr. Baker writes down the balance in his checkbook ($4,000), waves goodbye to Mr. Zimmer, and starts walking toward the door. Mr. Alber, who has been quietly listening, walks out at the same time.

Mr. Baker smiles and comments to Mr. Alber that this has been a very educational day. "I always thought banks created money. They taught me that in college. But today I found out how wrong that is. Banks don't create money at all. Banks don't lend money unless they already have that money to lend, dollar for dollar! How about that?"

Lending the Excess Reserves Creates Money

Mr. Alber, who happens to be taking college courses at night working on his MBA, looks back and smiles, "I think you missed something," he says. "Banks really do create money. You just watched this bank create $4,000."

By this time they are in the parking lot. Baker stops for a second before entering his car and says, "No, I think you must have misunderstood."

"No, my friend," says Alber. "It is you who has misunderstood. Open your checkbook and look at your account balance. What do you see there?"

Baker says, "There's no need for me to look. I already know. But let me show you. Here's the balance: $4,000! That's just the amount of money the bank had free to lend. That's not bank-created money. It's real solid money that has existed all the time."

Then Alber says: "Yesterday I had to pay my fall semester tuition and buy books. This morning I was flat broke. My deposit balance was zero. Then I got the tax refund check in the mail. You saw me deposit it. Right?"

Baker nods. He has no idea what Alber is getting at.

Alber continues: "Here. Look in my checkbook and read the balance. See? $5,000. That's my money. Now look in your checkbook there. See? $4,000. That's your money. Between the two of us we have a total of $9,000. Right?" Baker nods again.

Alber goes on. "When I walked in the bank I had $5,000. A government check. Now the two of us are leaving the bank and we have a total of $9,000 between us. An extra $4,000 came from someplace. Where do you suppose the extra money came from? Where could it have come from? Only one place. Our banker friend, Mr. Zimmer, created it."

Baker's jaw drops. He just stands there, looking at the balance in both checkbooks. There's $9,000 all right, and he knows it's true. But he only half believes his eyes. Sort of half-consciously he mutters, "Well, I'll be!"

HOW THE BANKING SYSTEM CREATES MONEY

Yes, the banking system really does create money. Do you see how it happened in the Alber-Baker-Zimmer case? Alber brought in some "new money" and deposited it in his checking account. This was a **primary deposit**—a deposit of new money, new reserves flowing into the banking system. The "new money" went into the bank's reserve account.

Only 20 percent of the newly deposited money had to stay in the reserve account to "back up" the new deposit. So 80 percent of the amount deposited is now in "free reserves" or "excess reserves." It can be lent to someone else. It is through this process of *lending the free reserves*, that money is created. Once the process gets started—once the new "primary deposit" enters the banking system—the money expansion can go on and on from bank to bank to bank. The potential expansion of the money supply is limited by the size of the reserve requirement.

The Lower the Required Reserve, the More the Money Supply Can Expand

Suppose the reserve requirement was 100 percent. Then how much money could be created by Mr. Zimmer's bank? None. All the money deposited would be held in reserves. Suppose the reserve requirement is 50 percent. How much can be re-lent? Half of it.

So the lower the reserve requirement the more the bank can lend. The more money it can create, so the more the money supply can expand. *The whole purpose of having a reserve requirement is to limit the extent to which the money supply can expand.*

We just watched Mr. Alber's $5,000 turn into $9,000. Alber still has $5,000 and Baker has $4,000. The money supply of the nation has been expanded by $4,000. There's no question about that. But all you have seen so far is the first step in the expansion process.

In terms of the nation's money supply, Mr. Alber's $5,000 government check has already grown into $9,000. Before it's all over with, *that check can grow into $25,000!*

How do we know $5,000 can grow into $25,000? Because if the required reserve ratio is 20 percent (that is, 1/5), then $5,000 in new bank reserves can "back up" $25,000 in new demand deposit money. Of course! The supply of money can expand by *five times* the amount of the new $5,000 in reserves.

Suppose the reserve requirement is only 10 percent (that is, 1/10). Then $5,000 in new reserves can "back up" $50,000 in new demand deposit money because $5,000 is 10 percent of $50,000. The money supply can expand by *ten times* the amount of the new reserves. If the reserve requirement is 25 percent (¼) the money supply can expand by *four times* the amount of the new deposit.

The Deposit Multiplier

This idea of a new deposit in the banking system permitting a multiple expansion of the money supply is what economists call the **deposit multiplier.** The idea is that any new reserves introduced into the banking system permits a multiple expansion of demand deposits—and therefore, of the money supply. As you might guess, we have a way of assigning a number to this "deposit multiplier." What determines the size of the number? You already know—the reserve requirement.

If the reserve requirement was 100 percent, the deposit multiplier would be 1. That is, the new deposit wouldn't multiply at all! In our case, it would mean that Alber's $5,000 deposit would be the only increase in deposits permitted by Alber's new addition of $5,000 of reserves. But suppose there was no reserve requirement. Then the deposit multiplier would be infinite! The money expansion could go on forever.

You know there's going to be a formula to explain this in simple, shorthand form, right? Sure. You could figure it out by yourself. But here it is anyway:

$$\text{Deposit Multiplier} = \frac{1}{\text{Reserve requirement}}$$

This formula simply tells you that the deposit multiplier is the reciprocal of the reserve requirement. In terms most students use: "turn the fraction upside down."

So to find out how much deposits *in total* can be supported by any given addition to reserves just "turn the reserve requirement fraction upside down" (that gives you the deposit multiplier), then multiply the increase in reserves by the multiplier. If the reserve requirement is 20 percent, change it to a fraction (1/5) and you know the multiplier is 5. You know an increase in new reserves of $1,000 will permit an increase in demand deposits of $5,000. It isn't very complicated, but it's very important in the functioning of the economic system.

As soon as the initial deposit (Mr. Alber's

deposit) brings new reserves into the banking system, the money supply can start to expand. You saw the first part of that expansion when Mr. Baker borrowed $4,000. From there, the money supply can keep on expanding until all the new reserves are being used to "back up" new demand deposits. If the required ratio of reserves to deposits is 20 percent (*one* to *five*) then every one dollar of new reserves can "back up" five dollars of new demand deposit money. If the required ratio is 10 percent (*one* to *ten*) then every dollar of new reserves can "back up" ten dollars of new demand deposit money. That's all simple enough to see. But how does all this expansion come about?

The Money Expansion Process Goes from Bank to Bank

You know all about the first step in the expansion process. Mr. Alber, Mr. Baker and Mr. Zimmer have shown you that. But what happens next? Let's watch.

Mr. Baker drives over to the Tonawanda dealer to buy the camping trailer. He writes a check for $4,000 to the dealer, Mr. Culver. As soon as Baker has hooked up the trailer and pulled it away, Mr. Culver jumps in his car and speeds off to his bank in Tonawanda. He parks in the lot and dashes into the bank waving the $4,000 check in the air saying, "I finally got my money out of that old-model trailer!"

He fills out a deposit slip and walks up to the teller's window to deposit the check. As he is making the deposit he notices a sad-faced young man walking slowly toward the door leading to the parking lot. Then he hears Ms. Yeager, the loan officer, call out:

"Mr. Dover! Come back!" As Mr. Dover comes back and approaches Ms. Yeager's desk, Mr. Culver hears Ms. Yeager say: "Mr. Dover, I think we are going to be able to handle your request for a loan, after all. We have just received a new deposit for $4,000. With a required reserve of 20 percent we only need to keep as reserves, one-fifth of the amount ($800). We will be happy

to lend you the other four-fifths. That's $3,200. Isn't that the amount you need to pay the contractor for the new plumbing in your house?"

So Mr. Dover gets his $3,200 loan. That's new money. Mr. Culver still has his $4,000 in his checking account and Mr. Dover has $3,200 in his. And remember, Mr. Alber still has his $5,000 in his checking account. The original $5,000 has now grown to a total of $12,200 ($5,000 + $4,000 + $3,200 = $12,200).

Notice that Mr. Baker doesn't have his money any more. He spent it. The one who borrows it *always* spends it. His money went to Mr. Culver, so Mr. Zimmer's bank's "excess reserves" went to the Tonawanda Bank. That's why that bank can now make the loan to Mr. Dover.

So what's Dover going to do? Spend his borrowed money right away to pay the plumbing contractor, Mr. Elder. And Mr. Elder will go into his bank waving the check in the air, then deposit it in his account. His bank must hold one-fifth of the amount in its reserves ($640) but it can lend the other four-fifths ($2,560) to Ms. Fuller who wants to build an addition and more shelf space so her shoe store can carry more inventory.

Ms. Fuller will write a check to pay Mr. Garner, the carpentry contractor. Mr. Garner will deposit the check in his bank. The bank will keep one-fifth ($512) as reserves and lend the other four-fifths ($2,048). The borrower will spend the money. And on and on it goes. Until when? Until there aren't any excess reserves left to lend!

The money supply can continue to expand until *all* of Mr. Alber's initial $5,000 of new reserves is being used as reserves to "back up" new demand deposits. That is, the expansion can continue until the total of new demand deposits amounts to $25,000. The $25,000 will include Mr. Alber's original demand deposit of $5,000, plus another $20,000 of demand deposit money created through bank lending. Figure 8-1 shows a summary of this money expansion process. It would be a good idea for you to take a few minutes to study that figure, now.

Fig. 8-1 How Money Expands as Banks Make Loans

A Summary of the Steps in the Depositing-Lending-Spending-Redepositing-Relending-Respending Process

Deposited by		Amount of Deposit		Required Reserve (20%)		Excess Reserve (80%)		Lent to		Paid to
Alber	→	$ 5,000	→	$1,000	→	$4,000	→	Baker	→	Culver
Culver	→	4,000	→	800	→	3,200	→	Dover	→	Elder
Elder	→	3,200	→	640	→	2,560	→	Fuller	→	Garner
Garner	→	2,560	→	512	→	2,048	→	Horner	→	Ilter
Ilter	→	2,048	→	410	→	1,638	→	Joker	→	Keller
Keller	→	1,638	→	328	→	1,310	→	Lester	→	Miller
Miller	→	1,310	→	262	→	1,048	→	Nader	→	Olter
Olter	→	1,048	→	210	→	838	→	Palmer	→	Quaver
Quaver	→	838	→	168	→	670	→	Richter	→	Salter
Salter	→	670	→	Etc., etc., etc...................................						
		―		―						
Ultimate Totals		**$25,000**		**$5,000**		**-0-**		No more loans are possible		
(assuming		(total		(total		(total		until new reserves come from		
maximum		demand		required		excess		somewhere.		
possible		deposit		reserves)		reserves)				
expansion)		money)								

This table shows Mr. Alber's original deposit of $5,000 growing into a total of $25,000—that's twenty-five thousand real, spendable dollars of demand deposit money. Mr. Alber has $5,000 of it, Mr. Culver has $4,000 of it, Mr. Elder has $3,200 of it, Mr. Garner has $2,560 of it, and so on.

Only $5,000 existed in the beginning. Where did the extra $20,000 come from? It was created by the banks. The banks created it just by lending their excess reserves.

But don't forget: If times are bad, this expansion in the money supply may not occur. If Mr. Baker and Mr. Dover and Ms. Fuller and those other people ever get pessimistic and decide not to borrow, then the expansion will stop, right there!

You can always figure out what the maximum possible expansion is by using the deposit multiplier. Here, with a reserve requirement of 20 percent (1/5) the deposit multiplier is 5. So the maximum possible expansion is $5,000 (amount of new reserves entering the banking system) times 5 (the deposit multiplier)—which equals $25,000, of course!

Note: This table assumes (1) that *all* excess reserves are borrowed and (2) that no one withdraws any cash. In reality, as the money supply expands, some cash always is withdrawn. This "cash drain" significantly limits the size of the deposit multiplier and therefore reduces the extent of money expansion.

THE RESERVE REQUIREMENT LIMITS THE MONEY EXPANSION

Alber's new deposit sets off a process of lending, spending, and relending which continues from bank to bank. As the excess reserves move from bank to bank they leave a trail of newly created money in their wake. Every bank they pass through has an increase in its demand deposit money.

But in each succeeding bank the addition gets smaller and smaller. Why? Because each bank keeps a part of the "moving excess" as it goes by. Each bank must hold some of the moving excess as new reserves, to back up the new demand deposit—that is, the demand deposit (like Alber's) which brought the excess reserves to the bank in the first place.

If there was *no reserve requirement*, the "moving excess" could go on and on from bank to bank, leaving a new $5,000 demand deposit in *each* bank. The money supply could just keep right on expanding. A new $5,000 "primary deposit" could go zooming around, touching banks, creating $5,000 more at each stop. It could create millions and millions!

Unlimited Expansion Would Destroy the Value of Money

Can you see why a reserve requirement is necessary? If we didn't have the reserve requirement the money supply could continue to expand indefinitely! There would be no way to limit the size of the money supply. Each time a bank received a new deposit it could re-lend it all. Each time this happened the money supply would get larger. It would just be a matter of time before the money supply would increase so much that runaway inflation would occur and the monetary unit would be destroyed.

In the "olden days" of gold-backed and silver-backed money, the limited availability of these metals limited the expansion of the money supply. But in modern times, when the account numbers on the books of banks serve as our money, the only effective limit on money expansion is the reserve requirement. The reserve requirement is vital!

For money to have value, its supply must be limited. In the United States and Canada and other modern nations, the supply limitation rests on the legal reserve requirement. If you want you can go around telling people that *the money supply of the United States is backed by the "legal reserve requirement" of the Federal Reserve System!* That might not be precisely true. But it's a lot more true than telling them it's backed by gold!

In the last chapter you learned that more than three fourths of the total money supply in the United States is bank deposit (checking account) money. Where do you suppose all this bank deposit money came from? From bank lending? Most of it, yes. Just like in the illustration you just read about.

New Reserves Come from the Federal Reserve System

Where did all the new reserves come from, to permit the money supply to expand? Most of the new reserves came from the Federal Reserve System. You just saw Alber's $5,000 come from the Treasury's deposit at the Fed and become new reserves, to permit a monetary expansion to begin.

Whenever the government runs a deficit—spends more money than it collects in taxes—it makes up the difference by selling bonds. If people and businesses and insurance companies and other private corporations buy the bonds then no new reserves go into the banking system. But suppose the Federal Reserve banks buy the bonds. That's different!

What Happens When the Treasury Borrows from the Federal Reserve Banks?

When the Treasury borrows money from an insurance company or a savings and loan association or from individuals and gives them bonds in exchange, that doesn't create any money. All the Treasury is doing is gathering up existing money. When it borrows existing money and spends it, there's no expansion in the money supply.

But when the Federal Reserve banks buy the government bonds from the Treasury, that *does* create new money. In fact it's exactly like what happens when Baker borrows $4,000 from Zimmer. Remember? And it's exactly like what happened when the eastside chief, King Tuituranga borrowed FS 10,000 from the northside chief, King Ratukabua. It creates money!

But the money which gets created when Baker borrows from Zimmer is a lot different than the money that gets created when the Treasury borrows from the Federal Reserve banks. What's the difference? Just this: The money the Federal Reserve banks create is **high-powered money.** This is money that will become *new reserves* for the banking system!

What will the Treasury do with its newly created money? Pay it out in government checks to pay the bridge builders and the civil service workers and the welfare recipients and all the others. When all those people receive their checks, what will they do with them? Take them and deposit them in their banks. Of course.

Then what happens? The banks will send the checks to the Federal Reserve banks. That is, they will deposit the checks in their Federal Reserve accounts. So the Federal Reserve banks will take the Treasury's newly created "high-powered money" deposits out of the Treasury's account and add them to the member banks' reserve accounts. See what happens? The banking system gets a lot of new excess reserves! So now a lot of new money can be created!

Not just Mr. Zimmer's bank. *All* the banks get new excess reserves. So now they can *all start making more loans.* The money supply can begin to expand, and it can keep on until a five-fold expansion has occurred. High-powered money? You bet! A dollar will get you *five!* And is this where most of the U.S. money supply really came from? That's exactly right.

Did you ever wonder where the government would get the extra money if it wanted to run a deficit?—that is, to spend more than it collects in taxes? Now you see how the government can get all the money it wants. It can print up bonds and sell the bonds to the Federal Reserve banks in exchange for new Treasury deposits! Then it can write checks and spend these new deposits.

The federal government can spend as much as it wants to. It never needs to worry about not being able to get the money! But you can see how such a program pumps new reserves into the banking system and lets the money supply expand. It could create some serious problems. You'll be reading a lot more about this, later.

Excess Reserves Do Not Guarantee an Expansion

Putting new reserves into the banking system is not certain to result in a multiple expansion of the money supply. For example, suppose Mr. Baker is out of a job and has already had to sell his stocks to pay the rent and buy groceries. And suppose no one else comes in to borrow the $4,000 of excess reserves created by Mr. Alber's deposit. What will happen? Nothing. New reserves *permit,* but don't *guarantee* an expansion of the money supply.

The money supply will not expand unless people want to borrow. People will not borrow unless they want to go into debt for the purpose of *spending.* If people don't want to spend these days, no amount of free reserves in the banks' reserve accounts will force an expansion. (Someone once said that trying to force a monetary expansion by pushing excess reserves into the banking system is like trying to push with a string!) Excess reserves *permit* people to borrow. That's all.

When excess reserves are high, banks want to lend. There is no profit in keeping money in excess reserves! If the banks have excess reserves and borrowers aren't borrowing, interest rates will go down. Money will be easy to borrow. This may stimulate borrowing. But it may not. It all depends on how bad things are. How much unemployment? How much overstocked inventories? How many shut-down plants? How gloomy and pessimistic is the outlook? But let's not get ahead of our story. We'll get into all of these issues later.

Loan Repayments Destroy Money

Now that you know about how the money supply expands through the banking system, it's easy to see how it contracts.

Remember when Mr. Baker borrowed $4,000 from Mr. Zimmer? Well, that was a year ago. Meanwhile Baker has been putting money into his checking account at Zimmer's bank, trying to get enough money in the account to be able to pay off the loan.

He has already paid the interest so he doesn't have to worry about that. But now the $4,000 note is due. Luckily he has been able to build up a balance of exactly $4,000 in his account. So today he goes into the bank and writes a check for $4,000 and gives it to Mr. Zimmer to pay off the loan. Zimmer gives him back his note, stamped "paid." Baker's account balance is now zero. So he closes his account, says goodbye, and leaves.

What did this transaction do to the money supply of the nation? It destroyed $4,000 in checkable deposits. It reduced the money supply by $4,000. That's *always* what happens when people pay off their loans.

Throughout the banking system people and businesses are paying off loans (destroying money) every day. And other people and businesses are borrowing (creating money) every day. So what's the net effect of all this on the size of the nation's money supply? It's obvious. Right?

When the volume of new loans exceeds the volume of repayments, the money supply ex-

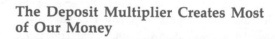

pands. When new loans equal debt repayments the money supply stays the same size. When repayments exceed new loans the money supply contracts.

When everyone is in debt and business is bad, people try to pay off their loans and get out of debt. Businesses try to sell off their inventories and pay off their loans. The money supply gets smaller.

Unless someone wants to borrow, a bank can't lend. Obviously. And who wants to borrow and build inventories when times are bad?

The businesses sell hard to get the consumers' dollars. Then they use the dollars to pay off loans. Poof! The dollars are gone! The businesses are gathering back up and destroying the dollars they were creating and paying out, before. The money supply is contracting. Total spending is getting smaller. No wonder we're having hard times!

Excess reserves are piling up in the banks' Federal Reserve accounts. The banks can always use their excess reserves to buy government bonds. Then they will earn some interest income. But this doesn't expand the money supply. It doesn't help to generate any business spending or consumer spending. It doesn't help to speed up the economy.

The Deposit Multiplier Creates Most of Our Money

How important is this "deposit multiplier"?—this "money creation through the banking system"? Consider this: In the early 1970s the total money supply of the United States was less than $200 billion. By the early 1980s, it was about $500 billion. Where did all that new money come from?

The new money was created through the "deposit multiplier" process. The Fed created new reserves and the lending-spending-redepositing-relending process did the rest. It happened just as you saw in this chapter except that in reality a money expansion usually doesn't begin with just one bank. When the Fed permits new reserves to flow into the banking system, the new reserves flow into many banks simultaneously. So the deposit expansion (money expansion) process begins to take place in many banks all at the same time.

In this chapter you have seen how the money expansion process works. This process has been responsible for the creation of by far the largest part of the nation's money supply.

Over the next several years our money supply will expand further. How? Through the banking system—through this "deposit multiplier" process.

The way money is created and destroyed through the banking system is a fascinating subject. The problems of inflation and unemployment which seem to be continuously—sometimes simultaneously—attacking the economies of today's world can't be understood without an understanding of all this. So take your time and learn it well.

SUMMARY AND SYNTHESIS

The money supply of the nation **expands automatically** as the banks make loans and it **contracts** as those loans are repaid.

To make loans, banks must have **excess reserves.** As banks lend their excess reserves they create new **checkable deposits,** which are money.

As new **primary deposits** flow into the banking system (from the Fed) this creates excess reserves and permits a **multiple expansion** in the nation's money supply. For the money supply to expand, people and businesses **must want to borrow** the excess reserves.

The amount by which the money supply can expand is limited by the size of the **reserve requirement.** The greater the reserve requirement the smaller the size of excess reserves and the smaller the possible expansion of the money supply.

The **deposit multiplier number is the reciprocal of the reserve requirement.** So the smaller the reserve requirement the larger the multiplier.

Bank loan repayments destroy money in the same way that bank borrowing creates money. If repayments are offset by new borrowing, the money supply does not contract. But if not, it does.

Most of the expansion in our money supply occurs through this **deposit multiplier process —** this process of **money creation through the banking system.**

REVIEW EXERCISES

MAJOR CONCEPTS, PRINCIPLES, TERMS (Explain each carefully.)

how banks create money
why borrowed money always leaves
why deposited money "never leaves"
role of the reserve requirement
how the government creates money
how new reserves are generated
how loan repayments destroy money

OTHER CONCEPTS AND TERMS (Explain each briefly.)

the money supply
demand deposits
reserve requirement
deposit multiplier (concept, and formula)
Federal Reserve account
discount rate
excess reserves
primary deposit
"high-powered" money

QUESTIONS (Write out answers, or jot down key points.)

1. Try to describe in detail the step-by-step process through which money is created by the banking system. Start with a new "primary deposit" coming in from somewhere, and take it from there.
2. Suppose Zimmer's bank finds that its Federal Reserve account is too small to meet its reserve requirement. How might it get more money to deposit in its Federal Reserve account?
3. If the federal government can create all the money it wants just by printing up bonds and selling them to the Federal Reserve Banks, then why don't they do that? Why does the federal government keep making people miserable by collecting taxes all the time? Why don't they just print up the bonds and get the Federal Reserve Banks to create new government deposits as needed? What would happen to the money supply (and to the value of our money and to the economy) if they did that? Discuss.
4. There seems to be a sort of "natural tendency" for the money supply to adjust to the wishes of the consumers and businesses. When buying and spending are picking up, people and businesses are going into debt and the money supply is expanding. When things are slowing down, loans are being repaid and the money supply is contracting. Can you explain just how this all happens? Try.

9

How to Measure National Output and Income: GNP and Price Indexes

Chapter Objectives

- In this chapter you will learn how to **measure** the **rate of flow** of the economic system.

- **How big is the circular flow?** How can you tell? And what if **inflation** distorts the figures? What can be done about that? When you finish this chapter you will be able to answer these questions.

- You will be able to describe and explain the **national product and national income account.**

- You will be able to define **gross national product (GNP), net national product (NNP), national income (NI), personal income (PI),** and **personal disposable income (PDI).** And you will be able to explain the **important differences** among these **rate-of-flow measures.**

- In this chapter you will learn **to make and to use a price index.** You will find out about different kinds of **price indexes,** and you will find out how important it is to **deflate macroeconomic statistics** when comparing one year with another.

HOW TO ESTIMATE THE SPEED OF THE ECONOMY

There are lots of ways to see if the economy is booming or depressed. If you see lots of trucks on the highway, trains going by, factories running night shifts, crowds of people spending lots of money in the supermarkets and department stores and bars and everywhere, then you know the economy must be booming. If you see a lot of idle factories and glum people pinching pennies and looking for work then you know the economy must be depressed.

But isn't there some more exact way to observe and measure the speed of the economy?

Can't we use some *numbers* to show the overall level of economic activity? You bet we can!

Remember the circular flow diagram? Money flowing one way, inputs and outputs flowing the other way? Couldn't we just measure the size of those flows? Sure. In fact that's just what we do!

We look at **total employment**—which could mean "the total use of all the productive factors," or it could mean just "the total employment of labor." Or we look at "the total amount being produced"—**total output.** Or we look at "the total amount being received as income by the owners of all the factors of production"—**total income.** Any one of these figures gives us a measure of "total economic activity"—the speed at which the economy is running.

Suppose you look at the figures for "total employment" and "total output" and "total income" and see that all three figures are getting larger from month to month. You know that economic activity is increasing. Right? But do you really need to look at all three figures? Of course not. All three figures will be moving along together. Total output is equal to total income. And more employment brings more output and income.

Now you know what to look at. But where do you look? How can a person find out what these "employment" and "output" and "income" figures really are—for the American economy, or for any other economy?

THE NATIONAL INCOME AND PRODUCT ACCOUNT

Most nations of the world actually try to add up their "national output" and "national income" to see how much is being produced in the country. Everyone wants to know "how's business?" Probably you have heard about **gross national product** (usually called GNP) and about **national income**. These, together with the employment and unemployment figures, are the most often used measures of "the overall level of economic activity"—that is, the rate at which the economy is running.

How the Government Gathers the Statistics

How does the government get the "national product" and "national income" numbers? To get the "product" statistics the government statistics gatherers ask each business to fill out forms telling how much they are producing.

As Willie Wonka is operating his candy factory, one day he will get a questionnaire asking about the size of his output. They will ask him to send in a report several times a year indicating his "rate of production." They won't ask for his daily or weekly or monthly rate. They want his *annual rate* of output. So instead of telling them he is producing 10 truckloads a week, he tells them he is producing "at the annual rate of 520 truckloads per year" (10 truckloads times 52 weeks = 520 truckloads). But he needs to tell them more than that.

They need the *dollar value* of his "annual rate of output." Why? Because they are going to add up his output of candy together with everyone else's output of everything else. How can they possibly do that? Only by translating each output into its dollar value. Then they add up the dollar values. This gives them one number, a dollar figure, to indicate the "rate of flow of output" for the entire economic system. That dollar figure is called the *gross national product*—GNP.

So Willie Wonka tells them that during the first quarter of this year he was producing at the rate of 10 truckloads of candy a week @ $10,000 worth of candy per truckload for a total of $100,000 worth per week. So he's producing at the rate of $5,200,000 worth of product per year ($100,000 worth per week times 52 weeks = $5,200,000 worth per year).

When they get Willie Wonka's and everyone else's figures for the first quarter, they add them all up. Suppose they come up with a total figure of $3,000,000,000,000 (three trillion dollars). Then the U.S. Department of Commerce publishes a report saying that during the first quarter (January-March) gross national product (GNP) in the United States was being produced *at the annual rate* of three trillion dollars' worth of goods and services.

The GNP Rate of Flow Changes During the Year

Suppose this rate of output continues for all twelve months of the year. Then the total GNP for the year will amount to three trillion dollars' worth of output. But that isn't the way it's really going to happen. The "annual rate of output flow" isn't going to stay the same for all twelve months of the year. During some months people may buy more candy and Willie Wonka may put on an extra shift of workers to produce enough to meet the extra demand. During other months, demand may slack off and he may cut back production.

During July he may shut down the plant for two weeks while everybody goes on vacation. This will cut his July output almost in half. Even if nothing else happens, he won't produce as much candy in the month of February. Why? Because there aren't as many days in February!

If this turns out to be a good year for business, then the annual rate of flow of the GNP will probably get larger from month to month. But if this turns out to be a bad year for business, the flow will get smaller. As the year progresses we can watch these GNP figures and see how fast the economy is running and whether or not it is speeding up or slowing down.

The National Income Figures

So much for the "product" figures. Now how does the government get the "national income" figures? The same way they get the product figures. They ask the businesses how much they are paying out to the owners of the factors of production—for labor, land, and capital.

The government's national income statisticians try to find out the total amount of income being received as wages, rents, interest, and profits. Then they add up all the figures and come up with the "national income." You can see that these figures would not be too difficult to find. All the businesses and several govern-ment agencies keep records of all these payments anyway—for income tax purposes and for several other reasons. It's a simple matter for the national income statisticians in the Department of Commerce to get the figures.

Why the GNP and National Income Figures Are Not Equal

Suppose all the figures of "income payments to the factors of production for the first quarter" have been reported. Then all the figures are adjusted to annual rates and added up. And suppose the total comes to $2,400,000,000,000 (two trillion, 400 billion dollars). The government issues a report saying national income during the first quarter was running at the annual rate of $2,400 billion." But you know that's got to be wrong. A minute ago you found out that the GNP was running at the annual rate of three trillion.

You know that if *output* in the first quarter is being produced at the annual rate of three trillion, then the rate of *income* being received must also be three trillion. Output is *always* equal to income. Right?

Every dollar paid for output must go to somebody as income. There's no other way! Still, the government *does* come out with a three trillion dollar GNP figure, and a figure of only 2,400 billion for national income. How can this be? The answer is easy. The GNP figure isn't really the *true value* of the output. The GNP figure is partly fictitious. It includes some make-believe values, and it overstates the "value added" by the output flow. But for the national income figure the government statisticians stick to the true values. So the national income figure is always smaller. Here's an example.

Suppose you are talking to me about my backyard corn-producing business. I tell you that, using only my own labor, I produced and sold $2,000 worth of corn last year. I produced 200 bushels of corn and sold it all for $10 a bush-el and collected $2,000. You congratulate me for making $2,000 of income from my garden. (You know that if I produced and sold $2,000 worth of product I must have received $2,000 of income). But I say, "No. I really didn't earn two thousand dollars. I only made about $1,700. Let me explain why."

Deduct Depreciation from GNP to get NNP

"First of all, I really didn't produce an additional two hundred bushels of corn. I had ten bushels of corn to begin with, which I planted as seed corn. So really, I didn't add two hundred bushels of corn (or $2,000 worth) to the society's output. All I added was 190 bushels, or $1,900 worth. See? My net product was only 190 bushels. That's all the 'value' I really added through my production process."

It's easy to see why the seed corn must be deducted to find the "net product." It's just as easy to see why *all* the capital used up in the productive process must be "replaced in its original condition" before we can start bragging about how much we have produced—about how much product value we have added.

If you wear out a thousand dollars' worth of tractor parts producing a thousand dollars' worth of corn, or tear up a thousand dollar fish net catching a thousand dollars' worth of fish, or wear out a thousand dollars' worth of canning machinery producing a thousand dollars' worth of canned peas, you haven't added any product value at all! So really, you haven't "produced" *anything!*

So the first reason the GNP figure is inflated is that it's too "gross." We must take out enough of this "gross product" figure to make up for the *capital* we used up and wore out in producing the product. We call this deduction the **depreciation deduction.**

When we subtract the "depreciation deduction" (also called the "capital consumption allowance") from the GNP figure, we get a *net product* figure. We call it **net national product** (NNP). That's closer to a true measure of the product

value added during the year than is the *gross* GNP figure.

But even the NNP figure includes some fictitious value. So we must subtract something else. Let's go on with the corn example and you'll find out why.

Deduct Indirect Business Taxes from NNP to Get NP = NI

The "seed corn replacement deduction" (depreciation) takes off $100 from the $2,000 I received when I sold my corn. My "net product" is $1,900. But my income from my corn garden was only about $1,700. Remember? So what happened to the other $200? Why did my $1,900 worth of net product only bring me about $1,700 in income? Here's why: The *true* value of the corn I sold really wasn't $10 a bushel. The corn was only worth $9 a bushel. The price was pushed up to $10 a bushel by "embodied taxes" (indirect taxes) of one dollar a bushel. I collected $2,000 from my customers, but the corn I sold them was really only worth $1,800. I only got to keep $1,800, not the whole $2,000. Let me explain.

Last year the local county board levied their "dollar-a-bushel and pass-it-on-to-the-tourist" corn tax. All roadside-stand corn sellers must pay this tax. If it wasn't for the tax, corn would be selling for $9 a bushel. So the corn is really only worth $9 a bushel. The tax pushes the price up to $10 a bushel.

Since I really only added a net product of 190 bushels, the true value of my total output was really only $1,710 (190 bushels @ $9 = $1,710). And that's exactly the amount of income I received from my corn-producing operation! (I had to pay the county $200 for the indirect taxes I collected, of course. And the true value of the seed corn I used up was really only $90: 10 bushels @ $9 = $90.)

I collected $200 in "indirect taxes" for the county by raising the price of my corn from $9 to $10 a bushel. Indirect taxes are meant to be collected that way. **Indirect taxes** become embodied in the prices of the products people buy.

The buyer pays the "indirect tax" without even knowing it. But because of the tax, the price of the product is higher than the "true value" of the product. That's the reason why all indirect taxes must be deducted from the prices of things—that is, from the total value of the net national product—in order to get the "true value" of the output of the economy.

After we deduct all of the fictitious value added by indirect taxes, then we arrive at the *true value* of the national product—the value of national product which is equal to **national income**.

From GNP to NI: Summary

The gross national product (GNP) is a "partly fictitious" figure. It includes two kinds of "fictional value" which must be taken away before we get down to the true "output value added" of the economy.

First we must deduct an allowance for all the capital used up in the production process. We call this the *depreciation* deduction. *"Depreciation" simply means "the rate at which we are using up capital in the production process."* It doesn't make much sense to talk about the "additional value of the output we're producing" unless we first replace the things we're using up in the process.

Second, we must get rid of the inflated prices which result from indirect taxes. The prices of almost everything bought—in the United States or Canada or Great Britian or Germany or anywhere else in the world—reflect some embodied indirect taxes.

The prices of automobiles, tires, TV sets, furniture and almost everything else are pushed up quite a bit by indirect taxes. For some products—for instance cigarettes and whiskey—the embodied indirect taxes account for more than half of the price! We must get rid of these "embodied taxes" if we want to get to the true value of the national product.

After we subtract depreciation and indirect taxes from the GNP figure, what do we have? We have the "real, honest value added by the newly-produced national product." Is this "true value added by the national product" exactly equal to the "national income" received by the owners of the factors of production as wages, rents, interest, and profits? You bet it is!

National Income Equals National Product

The **national product** figure is exactly equal to the national income. The two *must be equal.* Each dollar paid for new output is a dollar received by someone as new income. The income is shared among the owners of the factors— labor, land, and capital—which helped to produce the product. After all the factor owners are paid their shares, any money left over is profit.

All the money received from the sale of the product is distributed: as wages, rents, interest, and profits. All of it goes as income to somebody. The money received for the sale of the national product *is* the national income. Of course!

The national product and income statisticians actually go through this very process we have been talking about. (1) They add up all the payments to the factors of production to get the "national income." (2) They also take the gross national product and subtract depreciation and indirect business taxes.

When they do both of these things—figure "national income" one way, and figure "the real net value of the national product" the other way—do they come up with exactly the same figures for "product" and for "income"? No. Not exactly. But they would if all their figures were precisely accurate.

We know that national product and national income are equal. Any differences in the figures are obviously statistical errors. When the government statisticians do it both ways, the two figures usually come out very close.

Sources of Income and Product Statistics

Now you know what we look at to measure the speed of the economic system. You know that the government statisticians collect the figures and publish the "national income and product account" showing the figures for GNP, NNP, NI, and all.

This work is done by the Bureau of Economic Analysis in the U.S. Department of Commerce. Their monthly magazine, *Survey of Current Business,* is a good source of information on national income and output. I'm sure you can find it in your library.

The Bureau of Labor Statistics in the U.S. Department of Labor publishes statistics on employment and unemployment. Their *Monthly Labor Review* is an excellent source of labor market information and statistics.

Several other agencies of the federal and state governments and several local governments and regional planning commissions and chambers of commerce and industry groups and labor groups and others are busy gathering statistics to see and measure the speed of economic activity in the various parts of the economy. You'll find many of these statistics in your own local newspaper.

Finding Personal and Disposable Income

The *income and product account* does more than show national product and national income. The account also shows how much of the national income the people actually get to keep, and how much they actually spend for consumer goods.

So I really made $1,170 last year on my corn operation. That was the real value I added to the national product and that was my part of the national income. Did I get to spend it all? Did all of it flow to my "household"? You know it didn't. The government made me pay $340 in income taxes. All I actually got to spend out of my corn crop was $1,370 ($1,710 − $340).

You know that all the "national income" doesn't stay in the hands of the people who earned it—that is, it doesn't all become "disposable personal income." You just saw me pay $340 in taxes. That's one example of why all the national income doesn't become disposable personal income. People must pay taxes.

Anything which prevents you from spending a part of your income *reduces* your disposable personal income. Anything which gives you *more* money to spend, *increases* your disposable personal income. Let's talk about some of these adjustments.

Social Security Taxes. First of all, some of your income never actually gets to you. Social security taxes for the federal "retirement, survivors and disability insurance and medicare" programs are taken right out of your paycheck. You never see it. All the social security taxes collected must be deducted from national income before we get to "personal income." But that isn't all.

Corporate Taxes and Retained Earnings. The government takes about half of a corporation's income in taxes. Also, most corporations hold about half of their "after-tax" income and use the money for growth. "High growth" companies sometimes retain *all* their after-tax earnings and use the money for growth.

So how much of the total national income gets distributed to the people as **personal income?** Only what's left after the social security taxes and the corporate profits taxes and the "retained earnings" (undistributed profits of corporations) are deducted. All these dollars are pulled out before the people ever get their hands on them.

Transfer Payments to Individuals. But what about the people who are on the receiving end of all those social security taxes? What about the retired people and the dependent children and all the other people who are receiving the government's retirement and welfare and disabled veteran benefits and all the other money-sharing payments? All those people get money from the government as *personal income*, don't they? Sure they do.

After the statisticians finish *subtracting* the social security taxes and the corporate profits taxes and the retained earnings of corporations, then they *add* the amount of money the governments are giving to people. These "government gifts of money" are called "transfer payments." Income is taken from the people who originally earned it and then "transferred" (given free) to other people.

Personal Income. If we take the national income figure, then *subtract* social security taxes and corporate profits taxes and corporate retained earnings, then *add* government transfer payments to individuals—what figure do we wind up with? Personal income, of course! Then what do we do to get the disposable income figure? Just subtract all the *other taxes* (the direct taxes) the people have to pay out of their incomes. Then you have **disposable income**. That's what the households *really* get to spend.

Direct Taxes. What taxes are deducted to get to disposable income? All of them. All the taxes you pay directly out of your income. The income taxes are the biggest for most people. But sales taxes and property taxes and all the others take away personal income and leave less disposable income.

You may wonder why the social security taxes are treated differently than the income taxes. Income taxes are deducted from most people's paychecks. The wage earner never gets to see that money. It doesn't ever become a part of *personal income*. So why the difference? It's just that the national income statisticians decided to

do it this way many years ago, back when income taxes weren't being deducted from everybody's paychecks. It isn't precisely logical anymore, but as long as we all understand, it's okay. No harm done.

The Purpose and the Logic of the Income and Product Account

Now you understand the U.S. system of national income and product accounting. Other nations have very similar systems. But often other nations call their GNP by a different name: gross domestic product (GDP). But it means the same thing.

The important thing is that you understand the purpose and the logic of the national income and product accounting system. The national income and product account measures the economic flows—the size of the spending stream—the output and income flows in the economy.

This account represents the real-world application of the output and income concepts of macroeconomics. It lets us keep an eye on the changing macro-condition of the economy. If something goes wrong it helps us to see what the problem is and maybe figure out what to do about it. This account can be very helpful. But there's a lot this account does not show. You should know something about that, too. That's the subject of the next section.

SOME LIMITATIONS OF THE "GNP APPROACH" TO NATIONAL ACCOUNTING

The national income and product account doesn't do all we might want it to. There are two problems: (1) the account really can't accurately measure the value of the nation's output, and (2) the account doesn't reflect the "economic welfare" (conditions of life) of the people. We need to spend a few minutes on each of these problems.

Why the GNP Account Isn't an Accurate Measure of Output

It's a pretty tough task to add up the value of everything produced in a complex economy like the United States! Some things are almost impossible to measure.

Household Production. For example, take the economic value of all the services performed by family members who work in the home—cooking, cleaning, washing, entertaining—and teaching, directing and supervising children. What would be the value of all these productive activities if they had to be bought and paid for in the market? High, of course. But the value of all this production doesn't even show up in the GNP account.

Suppose all the do-it-yourself householders work in each others' houses and pay each other for all that work. Then their services would be sold and paid for and would be included in the GNP figures. So GNP would go up quite a bit! But did national product really go up? Of course not. See the problem?

The Underground Economy. Some transactions don't show up in the GNP because of tax evasion. If you eat at a restaurant and pay in cash, the restaurant owner may decide not to report it. Waitresses, cab drivers, hairdressers and others don't always report all of their tips. Teenagers who babysit or mow lawns or do odd jobs don't usually report the value of their production.

What about illegal production? Do bookies, drug dealers, moonshiners, and prostitutes report their outputs and incomes? All perform desired and valuable products and/or services. But they never tell! So their outputs and incomes are not counted in the national product and income accounts.

How much "underground" production is omitted from the GNP accounts? No one knows. But it's big enough to be a matter of concern. It probably amounts to several billion dollars each year.

Government Services. There are some kinds of goods to which it's difficult to assign values because they aren't "sold" in the market. Government services are the best example. How do you value the services of schools? police and fire departments? other government services?

Usually the approach is to assume that the output value of the services is equal to whatever the services cost, and just let it go at that. We know this kind of measure isn't accurate. An inefficient and costly school or fire department gets assigned a higher output value than an efficient one! But that's what we do because we don't have a better way to do it.

Year to Year Changes. Other problems arise when we try to compare "the state of the economy" from one year to another. In the real world, things don't always change in an orderly way as the years go by. Prices sometimes do and sometimes do not reflect product changes. And new products are always being introduced. That even further confuses the issue.

One big problem is that prices are always changing (going up). We can use price indexes to eliminate the worst effects of price changes (as you will learn in a few minutes). But these techniques don't give us precisely accurate comparisons from year to year.

Yes, there are problems with trying to get an accurate measurement of the national product. But that isn't usually the big complaint about the GNP account these days. The major complaint is that GNP is not a very good indicator of economic welfare in the nation. If the GNP was increasing would that mean the people were getting better off? that their welfare was improving? Not necessarily.

GNP Doesn't Measure Economic Welfare

There are several reasons why the GNP figures might be going up while economic welfare in the nation was going down. Usually it probably wouldn't work out that way. But sometimes it might. The point is this: we just don't know. Why not? Because we don't have any way to measure the level of or changes in economic welfare in the nation! That's exactly the problem.

All Products Count the Same. For one thing, when the GNP figure is being added up there is no distinction between one kind of product and another. The production of cigarettes and fighter planes and porno flicks counts the same as the production of housing and education and hospitals and pollution control. Surely all these things don't bring "equal national welfare per dollar's worth"! But in the GNP account they're all equal.

Negative Utility of Increased Production. Sometimes, producing more of what we want means also producing more of things we *don't* want—like garbage or pollution or health hazards. GNP includes the value of the "goods" we produce—the steel and chemicals and electric power, etc. But we don't adjust GNP for the costs of the "bads"—the things we *don't* want that get produced along with the things we *do* want.

Air and water pollution, noises, messing up beautiful landscapes, crowding people into towns and cities, destroying the harmony of peaceful neighborhoods and communities, requiring people to commute long distances to work—all these things have very important effects on our quality of life. How many more cigarettes or fighter planes or porno flicks—or for that matter, houses and schools and hospitals and pollution control devices and cars and boats and steaks and stereos and everything else—must we produce to make up for all these social costs?

Over the past 10 or 20 years, GNP has risen quite a lot. But on balance, are we really any better off? Most economists would say: "Yes, on balance we probably are (at least most of us are) better off. But we probably aren't as much better

off as the increase in the GNP figure might lead you to believe."

Less Work and More Leisure. On the other side of the picture consider this: the average work week has decreased by almost one half over the last 100 years. Even if people didn't have any more products they would have a lot more free time. And surely that's worth something in human welfare! These days instead of working more than 70 hours a week most people work 40 hours or less. But the GNP figure doesn't in any way reflect this.

Population and Income Distribution. There are a couple of other things you need to think about when you're on the welfare implications of GNP. First, population size must always be considered. If GNP doubles and population doubles, that's no increase in the output available per person! Secondly, income distribution is important. If a large share of the GNP of a nation goes to a few people, then even if *GNP per capita* is high, most of the people still may be living in poverty.

What About an "Economic Welfare" National Accounting Figure?

Most economists agree about the shortcomings of the GNP approach to national accounting. Some economists are now trying to work out a new system—one which can do a better job of measuring economic welfare. Some experimental accounts have been put together which try to take into consideration the factors which the GNP account leaves out.

NEW and MEW. Economist Paul Samuelson has worked with a new measure he calls "Net Economic Welfare" (NEW). William Nordhaus and James Tobin at Yale University have worked out a system they call MEW—"Measure of Economic Welfare." But so far we still don't have a generally accepted national accounting system that measures economic welfare. Maybe someday we will. But until then, please don't forget: the GNP account certainly doesn't do it.

Are the best things in life really free? If they are, measuring economic welfare is going to be a tough task! When you stop to think about it, clean air and refreshing surroundings and lots of good weather and sunshine may be more important to our welfare than most of the goods we buy!

What is GNP Good For? If GNP isn't a measure of welfare, then what's it good for? Just this: *GNP is a measure of the speed at which the economy is running.* That's all. It isn't a precisely accurate measure but it's pretty good. It's good enough to tell us when the economy is clicking along well and when it's slowing down and by about how much. That isn't everything. But it's a lot.

National Income and Product in the United States: 1929-1981

Table 9-1 shows the national income and product figures for the United States over the past several decades. Can you see the Great Depression of the 1930s? Sure. And the big boom of World War II? And then the economic expansion of the 1950s and the 1960s? Sure. But one word of warning: much of the increase you see in the table represents rising *prices*—not just rising *outputs*.

So how do we get rid of this "rising prices" illusion? How can we find out how much the output *really* increased over these years? We have to **deflate** the figures to get rid of the effect of rising prices. That's easy enough to do. You'll learn how to do it in the next section.

But first you need to study Table 9-1. The table gives a good summary of all the GNP account "subtractions and additions" explained earlier in this chapter. It also gives an indication of the growth, and of the ups and downs of the

American economy over the past half-century. Study the table now. Then, on to the next section.

Comparing GNP from Year to Year

Now when a friend asks you "how's business?" you will know how to find the answer. You will be able to say: "During the first quarter of this year, GNP was flowing at an annual rate of more than three trillion dollars. This is an increase of more than ten percent over the rate of flow of GNP during the first quarter of last year. It looks like business this year is doing just fine."

But that isn't quite all. You must also remember to say: "Of course some of this increase in the GNP figure doesn't really represent an increase in real output in the economy. Yes, prices have increased. And yes, we are valuing each unit of output at a higher price.

For example, I hear that Willie Wonka's candy output is up from an annual rate of $5,200,000 last year, to $5,720,000 this year. But guess what? He is still producing at exactly the same rate: 10 truckloads a week. What's the difference? It's just that this year the price is up from $10,000 to $11,000 a truckload. Costs and prices went up. If Willie's candy business is any indication, the economy really isn't producing any more this year than last."

So your friend wants to know whether or not Willie Wonka's case is typical. "Has there really been any increase in the rate of output of the economy between the first quarter of last year and the first quarter of this year? How can I find out?" You explain that the way to find out is to "deflate" the GNP figures, using a **price index.**

Anyone who is going to compare "levels of economic activity" from one year to another needs to know something about price indexes. A price index is one of the world's simplest things. But lots of people don't understand it. In a few minutes, you will.

Table 9-1 National Income and Product Figures for the United States, Selected Years* 1929-1981 (in Billions of Dollars)

	1929	1933	1939	1944	1950	1960	1970	1978	1981
GNP	103	56	90	210	285	504	976	2,108	2,922
− depreciation	8	7	7	11	18	44	84	217	321
NNP	95	49	83	199	267	460	892	1,891	2,601
− indirect taxes (and other minor adjustments)	8	9	10	16	26	45	92	187	257
NI (= NP)	87	40	73	183	241	415	800	1,704	2,344
− social security taxes	a	a	2	5	7	21	57	164	240
− corporate taxes	1	a	2	13	18	23	37	84	76
− retained earnings	3	−3	1	7	11	13	14	69	50
+ payments (transfer, etc.)	4	3	5	7	23	43	109	325	426
PERSONAL INCOME	86	47	73	165	228	401	801	1,708	2,404
− direct taxes	3	2	3	19	21	51	116	256	388
DISPOSABLE INCOME	83	45	70	146	207	350	685	1,452	2,016

Source: *Economic Report of the President*, and *Survey of Current Business*. (a = less than one billion)

---

*Some of the figures presented in this table are not precisely accurate because of adjustments made by the author to take care of statistical discrepancies and to make the table internally consistent without introducing unnecessary detail.

This table shows annual rates of flow of output, income, tax payments, etc. You can see a lot of interesting things by looking at these figures.

You can see that the rate of flow of GNP, NNP, and NI have all increased by about 30 times since 1929. But taxes and government transfer payments have increased much faster. The rate at which direct taxes are flowing to the government has increased by about 100 times,

and transfer payments flowing from the government to the people have increased by about 100 times.

Just look how much change there has been since 1970! Most of the flows have doubled or tripled.

You might guess that one of the reasons for the big increases in all these numbers is *inflation*. That's right. You are getting ready, right now, to find out what to do about that.

HOW TO MAKE AND USE A PRICE INDEX

Let's suppose that just for fun you wanted to make your own price index for the cost of mailing first-class letters. Back in 1970 the cost was 6¢. But by 1982 the cost was up to 20¢. Suppose you decided to use 1970 as your base year—that is, your reference point—the year to start from. Then you want to find out what the "first-class postage price index number" was after the cost went up to 20¢. How do you do it? Easy.

Divide the Base-Year Cost Into the Present Cost to Get the Index Number

You know how much it cost to mail a letter in 1970 (the base year)—6¢. And you know it costs 20¢ in 1982. Simply divide the base-year cost (6¢) into the present cost (20¢) and you will have your index number for the current month. (20 divided by the base-year cost of 6, comes out to 3.33 or 333 percent, or an "index number" of 333.) What could be easier than that?

The price index for the base year is always 100. Why? Because you are dividing a number into itself! You must come out with one, or 100 percent, or an "index number" of 100! In our postage case, you would be dividing 6¢ (cost in the base year) into 6¢ (cost in the base year). (6/6 = 1, or 100 percent, or an index number of 100.) In order to show that 1970 is your base year, you might say: "1970 = 100." That means that 1970 is the base year.

Divide the Index Number Into Present Cost to Find "Base-Year Cost"

Now that you know how to get an index number, the next question is: "how do you use it?" For one thing, you can use your "first-class

postage price index number" to find out how much it *would have cost* to mail your letters, back in the base year. The index number is 333. This tells you that it's now costing you $3.33 to get as much "first-class postal service" as you got for $1.00 in 1970.

Last month suppose you spent $12 for first-class postage. How much would this have cost you in 1970? Just divide $12 by the index number of 333 and you'll see! ($12 divided by an index number of 333 equals $3.60). The value of your "first-class postage dollar" has gone down, all right. In 1970, $3.60 would have bought as much first-class postal service as $12 can buy, now!

Divide the Index Number into a Dollar to Compare "Present Value" of the Dollar

Suppose you say to yourself: "As compared to 1970, what is the present value of my 'first-class postage dollar'?" To find out, just divide the index number into a dollar. You come out with 30¢. ($1.00 divided by an index number of 333 equals 30¢.) So for first-class postage services, the dollar this year is worth only as much as 30¢ was worth in 1970. Sad, isn't it?

Suppose this little exercise intrigues you and you decide to build a first-class postage price index on a 1960 base. In 1960 it only cost 3¢ to mail a first-class letter. So with 1960 as your base year (1960 = 100), what is the first-class postage "price index" for 1982? It is 20¢ divided by 3¢, or 6.66 or an index number of 666.

So to get as much postal service as you are now getting for $12, how much would you have had to pay in 1960? You find this out by dividing your index number into $12. In 1960 it would have cost you only about $1.80 to mail as many letters as you are mailing these days for $12. ($12 divided by an index number of 666 equals $1.80.)

There's been a big decline in the value of your postage dollar! In order to buy as much postal service in 1982 as you could have bought for $1 in 1960, you had to pay (in 1982) $6.66!

So what was the value of your first-class postage dollar in 1982 as compared with 1960? Only 15¢! ($1.00 divided by 666 equals 15¢). Now that you know what a price index is and how to use it, let's take another look at the problem of trying to compare GNP figures when our "measuring rod" (the value of the dollar) keeps shrinking from year to year.

Divide the Index Number into the GNP Figure to See How Much the Output Really Changed

When the gross national product is added up, it includes a figure for first-class postal services. The figure will be considerably larger now than it was in 1970. Why? A big flurry in first-class correspondence? No. The higher figure comes partly from the higher price charged for postage services, and only partly from the higher volume of mail.

How do you get rid of the "fictitious product value" which results from the inflated postage prices? Simply divide the present "value of first-class postal services performed" figure, by the index number (index number 333, 1970 = 100). This will give you a figure which accurately reflects the *real* increase in "the output of first-class mail services" between 1970 and 1982.

You know that postal services make up only a very small part of the GNP. But suppose you could go around and do, for *each* product and service, exactly what you just did for postal services. Then when you got the dollar value of *each* product and service "deflated" you could add up the deflated figures and get a new GNP figure. The new figure would show the present output, not measured by the *inflated* "current" dollar units, but measured by the *same size* "constant" dollar units that were used to measure the gross output back in 1970. The new (deflated) "constant dollar" GNP figure would show how much the output of the economy really has changed

since 1970.

Can you see it? If prices go up and output value gets bigger, you don't know if more is *actually* being produced or not. But if prices stay the same and output value still gets bigger, you know for sure that more is being produced. Right? Of course.

So, do the government statisticians make up a price index for postal services and one for tonsillectomies and one for hamburgers and gasoline and tires and heating oil and subway fares and beer and dorm rent and phone calls and textbooks and everything else, and then "deflate" the "present output value" of each, and then add up all the "deflated output values" to get a new (deflated) GNP figure? That's sort of the way they do it.

The Bureau of Economic Analysis of the U.S. Department of Commerce works out the **GNP price deflator**. This is an index number which reflects the "average change in all output prices." With this index number you can deflate the whole GNP figure at one time! How? Divide the current GNP figure by the index number! That brings the GNP figure down in size so that it's comparable to the base year GNP figure.

Remember in Table 9-1 how GNP in the United States has changed so greatly since 1929? How much of the change was caused by increased output? And how much of it was just caused by higher prices?

You know how to find out! Just go back and revalue the output produced during each year. Only instead of using the "current prices" which existed in each year, use the *same* prices for each year. Use "constant prices"—the prices which existed in the year you choose as your "base year."

How do you do this? How do you convert the "current dollar" GNP figures into "constant dollar" GNP figures? Simple. Just divide the "current dollar" GNP figure for each year by the "price index" (the "GNP price deflator") for that year. That's all there is to it!

Table 9-2 shows that when you deflate the

GNP figures it can make quite a lot of difference! Take a few minutes now and study Table 9-2. After that we'll get into some other kinds of and uses for price indexes.

The Consumer Price Index (CPI)

There are many kinds of price indexes. One of the most often used is the "consumer price index," also called the "cost of living index." This index is put together by the Bureau of Labor Statistics, U.S. Department of Labor. What they do is make up a list of all the things that the "average consumer" would buy and in what quantities in the average year. This list will include postal services, medical services, tires and gasoline, meat and potatoes, clothing and everything else bought by "the average family."

It isn't always easy to decide exactly how much of which things to put into this list. But the government statisticians make the best estimates they can and go ahead. Once they get the list made up they then assign a "base year" cost figure (say, 1967 = 100) to each item on the list. Then they add up all the costs of all the things. This gives them the "cost of living" of the "average family" in the base year. That's the first step.

The next step is to take the same list of things and assign the *present* cost of each item on the list, then add up the total. This shows the "cost of living" of the "average family" at the present time (present month, or week). Then the *base year cost* is divided into the *present cost* to get the consumer price (cost of living) index.

Suppose the list of things would cost $8,000 in 1967, and $9,300 in September of 1971. Then the index number for September, 1971 (on a 1967

Table 9-2 A Comparison of Current Dollar Values and Constant Dollar Values of U.S. GNP, Selected Years, 1929-1981 (in Billions of Dollars) 1972 = 100

	1929	1933	1939	1944	1950	1960	1970	1972	1978	1981
GNP (current dollars)	103	56	90	210	285	504	982	1,171	2,108	2,922
GNP (constant dollars 1972 = 100)	315	222	320	567	534	737	1,075	1,171	1,399	1,510
PRICE INDEX (GNP Deflator)	32.7	25.2	28.1	37.0	53.4	68.4	91.3	100	150.7	193.6

Source: Economic Report of the President, and Survey of Current Business.

What a difference price changes can make!

The "current dollar" figures show a 30-fold increase in GNP since 1929. The deflated (constant dollar) figures show that the real rate of flow of output has increased by only about five times. That's still a lot of increase, but it's a lot less than 30 times!

The rapid price increases which have occurred since 1972 are easily visible in this table. The "current dollar" figure has increased by about 150 percent since 1972. But the "constant dollar" figure shows that the rate of flow of real output has increased by only about 30 percent.

base) would be 116. ($9,300 divided by $8,000 equals about 116.) This means that it would have cost the average family $1.16 to buy in September, 1971 what they could have bought for $1.00 in 1967. It means that the "average family's consumer dollar," in September, 1971 was only worth as much as 86 cents would have been worth to the "average family" in 1967. ($1.00 divided by the index number of 116 equals $.86.)

By May of 1974 suppose the cost of the things on the list had gone up to $10,400. Then the consumer price index (CPI) would be 130. ($10,400 divided by $8,000 equals 130.) The May, 1974 dollar would buy only about as much as 77 cents would have bought in 1967. ($1.00 ÷ 130 = about 77¢.)

By September of 1977 suppose the cost of the list of goods and services—that is, of the average consumer's market basket full of things—has gone up to $13,000. What's the price index? On a 1967 base its 163 ($13,000 ÷ $8,000 = 163.) On the average, the September 1977 dollar would buy only about as much as 66¢ would have bought ten years earlier. ($1.00 ÷ 163 = 66¢.)

Other Price Indexes

Price indexes are interesting, simple, and helpful numbers. The best known and most widely used index is the one you just heard about—the consumer price index. Then there is the producer price index (formerly called the wholesale price index) which compares prices of things that businesses are buying. There are lots of indexes for individual products, such as the construction cost index, the housing cost index, the medical cost index, the food cost index, the transportation cost index, and so on.

Each of these indexes gives a quick and easy way of finding out how much the prices of these things have changed, on the average, since the "base year." You can look at the index and tell immediately how much it would cost you *now*

(on the average) to buy what was "a dollar's worth" in the base year. If the index is 130, it now costs you $1.30 to buy what you could have bought for $1.00 in the base year.

If you want to find out how the "real purchasing power" of your present income compares with the real purchasing power of your income in the base year, simply divide your present income by the cost of living index (CPI). Just as the GNP figure can be "deflated" by dividing by an index, so can your own income.

If the price index is 200, it means that your income now must be twice as large as it was in the base year, for you to have as much "real income" now as you had then. Your income must have doubled just to keep you in the same place. Also it means that the pension funds or insurance policies that you contracted for in the base year are now going to bring you only *half* as much real goods and services as you thought you would get when you made the contract. That, of course, is one of the major problems and one of the great social injustices of inflation.

A Dollar's Value Depends on What It Buys

One small word of warning about price indexes. An index number always refers to one thing, or to an "average list" of things. If you are spending your dollars exactly the same way as represented by this "average list" then your dollars will change in value exactly as indicated by the index number. But no one spends money exactly like the "average list." Let's take a wild example.

Suppose medical services, automobiles, gasoline and related products and meats and bakery products are all items which have increased considerably in price since 1967. But suppose you use very few of these things. You have decided to sell the car and ride a bike. No one in your family has been sick. You and your family are vegetarians and you do all your baking at home. Further, you always go camping on your vacations and you buy winter clothes for the children at the local rummage sales. You make your own wine and beer in your basement. So what does the consumer price index have to do with the value of *your* dollar? Not very much!

The actual value of each individual's dollar is de-termined, not by the consumer price index, but by how much that individual gets when spending each dollar. One family may live better on $9,000 a year than another family would on $12,000. Why? Because the people in the first family spend their money carefully and maximize the value of their dollars!

All this does not mean that the cost of living index is not a valuable tool. It really is. But recognize that it doesn't apply in a precise way to anyone. You can have considerable control over the value of *your* dollars—if you want to. A good course in consumer economics can help you learn how!

SUMMARY AND SYNTHESIS

The **National Income and Product Account** shows the **speed** at which the economy is operating. This account shows the **size** of the **circular flow** of the economy—of inputs and outputs flowing one way and dollars flowing the other way. In short, this account shows us the **macroeconomic condition** of the economy.

The **gross national product (GNP)** figure in the account shows the total dollar value of the annual output of goods and services. GNP is a **rate of flow** figure, always stated on an **annual basis**—e.g., "The economy last month was operating at the rate of $3 trillion (gross output) **per year.**"

In producing the GNP, the economy uses up and wears out some of its capital. If we want to know the **net output value (net national product,** or NNP) we must first replace all of the used up capital. This deduction from GNP is called **depreciation.** GNP minus depreciation equals NNP.

Many of the output items included in NNP have artificially inflated prices. Indirect taxes (levied on the manufacturer, for example) are added into the prices of goods and passed along to consumers. If we want to know the true economic value of the nation's output, we must deduct in-direct taxes to get rid of these artificially inflated prices. NNP minus **indirect taxes** equals the **true value of the national product**—which is equal to **national income (NI).**

National income doesn't all go to individuals and become **personal income (PI).** Corporations don't pay out all of their earnings, and the government collects social security taxes out of your paycheck. That subtracts from PI. But government payments for social security and other benefits add to PI.

Personal disposable income (PDI), or just **disposable income (DI)** is what's left of your personal income after you pay all of your **direct taxes.**

Inflation distorts the output and income values shown in the national product and income account. **Price indexes** are used to eliminate the **inflationary distortion** of the output and income figures.

To construct a price index, (1) choose a **base year** to serve as the "constant-price year," (2) find out the prices of the various goods and services in the base year, (3) find out their **current prices,** and (4) divide the **base year cost** of these things into the **present cost.** If current prices are higher than base year prices, the index number will be greater than 100 (> 100 percent).

To eliminate the effect of changing prices on GNP, divide the index number for each year into the **current value GNP figure** for that year. To find out how much one dollar is worth today as compared with the value of one dollar in the base year, divide $1.00 by the price index. But remember: the value of **your** dollar depends on how wisely you choose to spend it!

The price indexes most frequently used in this country are: the **consumer price index (CPI)**, the **producer price index (PPI)**, and the **GNP price deflator**. Also there are specific price indexes for many kinds of products and services.

In the American economy, the **current dollar** GNP figure increased thirty-fold between 1929 and the early 1980s. But **constant dollar** (real value) GNP increased only five-fold, over this five-decade period. Since 1972, **current dollar GNP** increased more than 150 percent, but the **constant dollar** (real) increase was only about 30 percent. For the latest national product and income statistics, consult the *Survey of Current Business* which is published monthly by the Bureau of Economic Analysis, U.S. Department of Commerce.

REVIEW EXERCISES

MAJOR CONCEPTS, PRINCIPLES, TERMS (Explain each thoroughly.)

the purpose of the national product and income account
why depreciation is deducted
why a price index is needed
what determines the value of *your* dollar
limitations of the GNP figure

OTHER CONCEPTS AND TERMS (Explain each briefly.)

gross national product
national income
depreciation deduction
net national product
indirect taxes
personal income
transfer payments

price index
base year
GNP price deflator
consumer price index (CPI)
cost of living index
NEW and MEW
Survey of Current Business

QUESTIONS (Write out answers or jot down key points.)

1. Suppose you produced macrame belts and sold them to people at the concession stand at Seashore State Park last summer, and you took in $1,000. Do you think all of that thousand dollars would be included as part of the "national income"? Or what deductions do you think would need to be made? Make up a list, and then explain why each deduction would be necessary.

2. I'm sure you don't spend your money exactly like the "average family." Think about the specific things *you* usually buy, and about how their prices have been

changing in the past year or two. Do you think you could make up a sort of "roughly estimated" personal price index? and then figure out what has been happening to the value of *your* dollar? (Maybe you've found out how to buy things cheaper—wholesale, maybe—and the value of your dollar is going up!) Want to take a few minutes and try to make up your own personal price index? It might be interesting to see what you come up with!

3. Can you list each of the income and product measures in the NP-NI account (from GNP all the way to Disposable Income) and explain what adjustments are required to get from each one to the next? and why? Try.

PART THREE

The More We Earn, The More We Spend—
And The More We All Save, Too!

10 National Income Analysis I: The Components of the Income-Spending Stream

---

Chapter Objectives

- Understanding **total spending** is the key to understanding **macroeconomics.** What influences total spending? That's what you will be learning in this chapter.

- In this chapter you will learn to break down the **total income-spending stream** into its sources: **consumer spending (C), investment spending (I), government spending (G),** and spending by foreigners for our **exports (Ex).** And you will learn about some of the things which influence these spending sources—these components of the spending stream.

- Also in this chapter you will learn about the **withdrawals** from the spending stream which occur because of: **savings (S), taxes (T),** and spending for **imports (Im),** and you will find out how these withdrawals affect the size of the spending stream.

- When you finish your study of this chapter you will be able to write and explain the **expenditure and income equation** and the importance of this equation in understanding the macroeconomic condition of the economy.

- You will be able to explain the **foreign trade balance (F)** and its importance, and you will know about **John Maynard Keynes (KAYns)** whose writings in the 1920s and 1930s marked the beginning of modern macroeconomics.

- In this chapter you will also find out about the **monetary approach** to analyzing total spending, focusing on the **quantity (Q)** and **velocity (V)** of money.

An Overview of Macroeconomics

It is total spending which supports the total level of employment and production—the total level of economic activity. Total spending pulls forth total output. If spending goes down, total output goes down: Recession .

As spending increases, output increases—that is, output increases until the economy reaches full capacity. If spending continues to increase after full capacity is reached, there will be shortages. Prices wll rise: Inflation .

The total level of spending must be just right if we are going to have "full employment and stable prices." But what determines the total level of spending? What makes it just right? Or too low? Or too high?

Who spends? People, businesses, governments, and foreigners all spend to buy things.

Aside from government and foreign spending (discussed later) there are *two basic motives* for spending. One is to consume for personal satisfaction. The other is to buy capital and become more productive. People spend for **consumption** purposes and businesses spend for **investment** purposes. First, a look at things that influence consumer spending—then later, business spending.

WHAT DETERMINES TOTAL CONSUMER SPENDING?

What might make people spend more? Or less? Various things. People with more income usually spend more. No mystery about that!

Suppose the economy is depressed and many people are unemployed. Then for some reason business picks up. Unemployed people are hired. The "unemployed" buildings are rented. Idle factories start producing things. So what happens next? You could guess.

Size of Income: The Consumption Function

When the unemployed workers and the factory owners and other people start earning incomes again, what do you suppose will happen to the total level of consumer spending? Do you think people will buy more TV sets? Movie tickets? Frozen lobster tails? All sorts of things? Of course. Consumer spending reflects people's incomes. You know it does.

Economists have a name for this idea—the idea that the more income people are getting the more they will be spending for consumer goods. We call it the **consumption function**.

Why "consumption function"? Because people's consumption (meaning, in this case: "spending for consumer goods") is a function of (meaning: "depends on" or "is determined by") the size of their incomes. The higher their incomes, the higher will be their spending for consumer goods.

You can see how the idea of the "consumption function" makes sense for each individual.

It makes sense for the total economy, too. As *national income* gets larger, what happens to consumer spending? It gets larger too. Of course.

The Role of Expectations

Consumer spending also reflects people's expectations. If people are concerned about their economic future they will usually spend less (save more). People will save more if they think they are going to lose their jobs. Or if they think the union is going to call a long strike. Or if they expect that all their teenagers will need some money to help them go to college. Or if they expect they will have to retire early or quit work because of poor health. Or if for *any* reason they expect their incomes to fall or their expenditures to rise. And the opposite is also true.

If people expect to be earning more (or if they expect their spending obligations to go down) they will be willing to spend up their present incomes right away. They may even buy lots of things "on time." Why should they try to save if they think they are going to be earning more and more all the time?

Anything which makes people more optimistic or more pessimistic is likely to influence their rate of consumer spending.

Consumers Can Spend Past Income or Future Income

People don't just spend their current incomes. What about the big items people buy? When you buy a new car you are spending either your past income (your savings) or your future income. So consumer spending is influenced by how much savings people have and their willingness to spend these savings. Also it is influenced by how much the consumers are already in debt and their willingness to go further into debt.

Consumer spending is influenced by how easy it is to buy things on credit. You probably could go out and buy a $500 TV set today by spending less than $50 (the down payment). Maybe you could buy one with *no* money down. With easy credit you don't have to have much current income to be able to buy things. But then your future income is already spent before you get it. That will force you to cut down on your future spending.

You can see how consumer spending is influenced by how much savings and how much debt the "average consumer" already has, and by the availability of easy credit. You can also see why a really big boom in the sales of autos, appliances, and furniture *last* year is likely to be followed by a slump in the sales of these consumer durables *this* year. If everybody bought new things last year, this year they'll all be paying off their debts!

See how the amount of a person's current income doesn't really determine the amount of that person's consumer spending? Sometimes individuals spend more than their incomes. Sometimes they spend less. For this reason it's very easy for shortages to develop (like in consumer durables last year, when everyone was trying to buy new things) or for surpluses to develop (like in consumer durables this year, when everyone is trying to pay off debts).

Taxes Reduce Consumer Spending

When you pay taxes you don't have as much money left to buy things. Income taxes take hundreds (or thousands) of dollars from most people. Social security taxes take a good bit, too. Then in addition you must pay property taxes and automobile taxes and gasoline taxes and utility taxes and alcohol and tobacco excise taxes and state and local sales taxes and lots of

other taxes. Taxes put a real crimp in the amount you have to spend. Taxes reduce your *disposable income*. So you spend less for consumer goods.

An important reason for taxing by the federal government is to hold down spending—to get all of us not to spend so much, so some things will be left in the market. Then the government can buy what it needs without pushing up total spending and causing inflation.

The Consumer Spending Decision: A Summary

In capsule form, we can summarize the highlights of the "consumer spending decision" this way:

The amount the consumers are going to spend will be determined by how much current income they have, as modified by how much taxes they have to pay, how much money they already have saved up, or how far they are in debt, how easy it is to borrow or to buy things on time, and what they expect to happen to their *future* incomes and expenditure needs. Anything which causes any of these factors to change is likely to cause consumer spending to change.

WHAT DETERMINES BUSINESS INVESTMENT SPENDING?

There are many reasons why businesses spend. But in general, businesses spend whenever they expect the expenditure to be a "good deal." Suppose a business is considering an additional investment of some sort. If the business expects a high enough return (a big enough addition to revenue or a big enough reduction in cost) then it will make the additional investment. If not, then it won't.

How high does the **expected return** need to be to induce the business to invest in a machine—that is, in a piece of "capital equipment"? High enough to pay off all the expected costs of the machine (including the interest cost) and leave a *reasonable profit* for the business.

Anything which causes the "expected return" to increase (or anything which causes the "expected cost" to decrease) is likely to cause businesses to increase their investment spending. Anything which lowers the expected return or raises the cost is likely to slow down investment spending. Of course.

Investment Spending Is Influenced by Expected Returns and Interest Rates

Why would anyone spend money for **capital goods**? Why would anyone want to buy a tractor to use to produce corn and tomatoes? Why might you buy a machine to expand the output of your macrame belt shop? How do you decide? You consider the "expected returns" you will get from the investment. And you consider the "interest cost" you will have to pay on the borrowed money you will use to buy the machine.

(If you plan to use your own money to buy the machine, the interest cost is still just as real. You must consider the *interest income* you will have to give up—the opportunity cost—when you withdraw your savings or sell your bonds to get the money to buy the machine.)

You already know that capital equipment is *productive*. An extra piece of machinery has a marginal "value product" just as does an extra worker. Whether or not you will buy a piece of capital depends on whether or not you expect the **marginal value product** of that piece of capital to be greater than the cost of the piece of capital to you.

If you think the additional output will be worth more than the cost of the capital, then you will invest in it. But if you don't think the piece of capital will add enough value to your output to justify its cost, then you will not buy it. Nobody pays more for something than it's expected to be worth!

John Maynard Keynes and the Marginal Efficiency of Capital

Everyone who is producing something has some "demand for capital." Your demand for capital will be high or low depending on whether or not you think the capital will add a lot or a little to the value of your output (or perhaps subtract a lot or a little from your cost of production). Is your demand for the capital *high*? Then that means you expect a *high return* from the capital. Of course!

The idea of **expected return** as the thing which determines the demand for capital was developed by John Maynard Keynes (pronounced KAYns) in his famous and somewhat revolutionary economics book, *The General Theory of Employment, Interest, and Money* (1936). Keynes emphasized the importance of expectations in determining whether or not a business will invest in a piece of capital.

Keynes referred to the additional return the business expects to get from an additional piece of capital as the **marginal efficiency** of the capital. He said that if the capital is expected to be productive enough to more than cover its cost (including the interest cost) then the business will invest in the capital. If it is not, then the investment will not be made.

If a new factory or a new gear grinder or a new truck or a new pile of coal is expected to bring a marginal profit—that is, if its marginal "value product" is expected to be greater than its marginal "input cost"—then the business will buy it. If not, then the business won't buy it.*

Keynes developed quite elaborate theories of macroeconomics—theories explaining the different things which influence the total spending flow—things that might cause it to change. As you might guess, he worked out theories ex-

---

*For those who would like to go deeper into the Keynesian theory of business investment spending, this chapter has an appendix dealing with that subject. You'll find it just after the review exercises.

plaining both consumer spending and investment (business) spending. The theory of the consumption function is one of his ideas for explaining consumer spending.

Many of the concepts and theories of macroeconomics in this book are based on Keynesian ideas, as those ideas have been refined and modified over the past 40 years. If you can think of something like macroeconomics as having a father, then surely Keynes is the father of modern macroeconomics. The ideas in the next section on the components of the total spending stream are straight from Keynes.

equal to the total value of the consumer goods and capital goods being bought. The total amount of money received by the people producing all this output is equal to the total amount being spent by all those buyers.

Expenditures for consumer goods (C) plus expenditures for investment goods (I) equals total spending for consumer goods and capital goods (C + I). It must be so. And it also equals the total value of the output of these goods and it equals total income received by those who produced these goods. But that doesn't tell the whole story. So let's take another step to complete the picture.

THE COMPONENTS OF THE TOTAL SPENDING STREAM

The whole purpose of breaking down total spending is to identify and understand each "spending source." If we can understand how each "spending source" decides how much it will spend, then we will better understand how *total spending* is determined. Then we will know much more about macroeconomics. Perhaps sometimes we can even predict what is going to happen. And perhaps then we can establish government policies to bring better macro-conditions in the economy.

Consumer Spending (C) and Investment Spending (I)

You know that total spending by people for consumer goods (consumption) plus total spending by businesses for capital goods (investment) add up to total spending for the economy's output of consumer and capital goods. The total rate of spending in any day, week, month, or year for these goods must be

Government Spending (G)

Since all things produced are either produced to be consumed or to be saved and reused later, you could say that all goods produced must be either consumer goods or capital goods. That's all there is! But what about "government goods"?

The governments—*all* levels of government—spend money. They buy goods which would have been consumer goods if individuals had bought them and they buy goods which would have been capital goods if businesses had bought them. But since the government buys them we call them "government goods." So now we add a third "spending source." We simply refer to this as **government spending** (G).

Government goods include everything from school buildings and highways and teacher's services to Polaris submarines and the canned peas to be used to feed the crew of the aircraft carrier *Enterprise*.

So now you know that total spending in the economic system (the total spending stream) generates from at least three sources: spending by individuals for consumer goods (C), spending by businesses for investment goods (I), and spending by government for "government goods" (G). We might say that "C + I + G equals total spending, which is equal to the total value of the output, which equals total income in the economy." We could say that. But as you will see in a moment it wouldn't be precisely correct.

Why do we put *government spending* into a separate category? Couldn't we just include government under "investment spending" and only have two categories? Yes, we could do that. Why don't we? Because it's useful to look at government spending separately. The spending choices (how much to spend, in which ways, at what times) are based on different *motives* and therefore are made *differently* by the government than by businesses or by individuals.

Foreign Spending for Our Goods (Ex)

The fourth and final spending source we break out and identify separately is "spending by foreigners for our goods." Just as with the government, this "spending source" could be included in the "C + I" two-way breakdown. But you can see that it might be helpful to separate "spending by foreigners for our goods" into a category all its own. The term usually used to mean "spending by foreigners for our goods" is exports. We can use "Ex" as the symbol for this.

Suppose Monsieur Champenois in Paris decides he would like to have a case of Del Monte canned peas. He goes to the Bank of France and exchanges some of his deposit account francs for some of the dollars which the Bank of France has on deposit in an American bank. Now he can use those U.S. dollars to buy the Del Monte canned peas. So he does. This adds to total spending in the American economy.

Suppose Signor Costanza in Rome decides to buy an Oldsmobile Cutlass. He goes to the Bank of Italy and exchanges some of his lira deposits for some dollar deposits and he sends the American dealer a check to pay for the Cutlass.

Suppose Mr. Smythe in London decides to buy an oyster-breading machine from a Baltimore manufacturer. He goes to the Bank of England and trades some pounds for dollars and then sends the manufacturer a check for the machine.

Suppose a Japanese business decides to buy a shipload of American chemicals to be used in making plastic toys. The business manager goes to the bank and exchanges yen for dollars and sends a check to pay for the chemicals. (These "foreign exchange" checks may be called "bills" or "drafts" or "orders." But they're really checks.)

All purchases by foreigners add spending into the spending flow. The effect on spending, output, and incomes is the same as if the canned peas had been bought by someone in Willimantic, Connecticut and the oyster-breading machine by someone in Pascagoula, Mississippi and the chemicals by someone in Rahway, New Jersey and the Cutlass by someone in Snook, Texas! Can you see that from the point of view of the seller of the goods, or of the effect on the total spending stream, it really doesn't make any difference whether the buyer lives in Paris or Poughkeepsie? In Tokyo or Kokomo? Bangkok or Little Rock?

Some of the foreign buyers are buying consumer goods. Others are buying capital goods. But still we lump both together and treat them the same. Why do we do it this way? Only because it's convenient and useful. This gives us our fourth and last spending source: "spending by foreigners for our goods." Exports (Ex).

The Four Spending Sources

Now we have the entire four-way breakdown of the spending stream. Each spending source is identified in the most useful way. Now our "spending flow breakdown" becomes C + I + G + Ex.

Now can we say that C + I + G + Ex = GNP? Can we say that? Or not? Think about it.

When you buy French perfume, your spending leaks overseas. Right?

Sure. But when they use the money to buy Kodak film, the spending "leaks" back!

You know that anything which would cause any one of these "spending sources" to get smaller would pull down the size of total spending.

Reduced spending means reduced output and reduced income. GNP would fall.

You also know that anything which might happen to cause spending by any one of the "spending sources" (C, I, G, or Ex) to increase, would push total spending upward. GNP would rise. Yes, C, I, G, and Ex are the only sources from which spending can flow into the total spending stream to support total income and total output (GNP). So can we say that C + I + G + Ex must be equal to total spending and total output? to GNP? No. Almost, but not quite.

There's another adjustment we must make because C + I + G + Ex doesn't *exactly* equal GNP. Why not? Because we must account for the part of the spending flow which is "leaking out" to foreign countries.

THE FOREIGN TRADE BALANCE

Some of C, I, and G is leaking overseas! Some of the spending for consumer goods (C) is *not* for consumer goods *produced in this country,* but for consumer goods produced in foreign countries and imported to this country. Some of the capital goods bought by the investment spending (I) are capital goods *produced in other countries* and imported to this country. Some of the things that the government is spending for

(G) are things that are being *produced in other countries.* Do you begin to get the point?

Some of the Spending Flow Is "Leaking to Other Countries" (Im)

You know that this country's GNP is pulled forth by the flow of spending in *this* country, spent for *this* country's output. Right? So we must be careful not to include the part of our spending flow which is "leaking overseas"—that is, the part which is going to foreign sellers to pay for foreign-produced goods.

The part of the "C + I + G flow" which flows to other countries *does not* support output and income in this country. So how do we handle this part of the spending flow which is "leaking overseas"?

We must subtract from "C," that part which is being spent for imported goods and subtract from "I" that part which is being spent for imported goods, and so on. Then we add up all these dollars "leaking overseas" (to pay for imports) and subtract it. We call the subtraction items **imports** (Im). What it means is "total spending by buyers in *this* country for goods produced in foreign countries."

You know that the spending flow in this country is always being *increased* by foreign spending for our goods (Ex.) Now you also know that the spending flow in this country is always being *decreased* by the amount that buyers in this country are spending for foreign goods (Im). So wouldn't it be a simple thing just to subtract the "spending outflow" (Im) from the "spending inflow" (Ex)? Sure. That's exactly what we do. It looks like this:

$$C + I + G + (Ex - Im) = GNP$$

We May Have a Positive or Negative Foreign Trade Balance (F)

You can see that if the *spending outflow* for foreign goods (Im) is *greater* than the *spending inflow* for our goods (Ex), then "Ex − Im" will be a *negative* number. More spending is flowing out than is flowing back in. This holds down the size of output and incomes in this country. In this case we would say that the foreign trade balance (F) is negative.

If the *spending inflow* from foreigners for our goods (Ex) is greater than our *spending outflow* to buy foreign goods (Im) then "Ex − Im" (F) will be a *positive* number. There will be a net addition to the spending flow in this country. The positive "foreign trade balance" (F) will help to support our total employment, output, and income.

If you want to, you can say it this way:

$$C + I + G + (Ex - Im) = GNP$$

or you can say it this way:

$$C + I + G + F = GNP$$

Either way, our equation is now exactly and precisely correct. You know that F can be either plus or minus, depending on whether foreigners are spending more for our goods or we are spending more for theirs. If imports and exports should happen to be exactly the same, the foreign trade balance (F) will be zero.

OTHER WAYS TO BREAK DOWN THE TOTAL SPENDING STREAM

We can look at the total spending stream any way we want to. We can look at it as one big flow going on all the time. Or we can look at it as thousands of little flows going on all the time.

Remember the circular flow diagram? It shows the spending flow as one big flow. When we look at GNP we are looking at it as one big flow. The same is true if we look at "national income." These are ways of looking at the spending flow (and the output flow) as "one big flow."

Then there's the "four-sector" flow you've

just been reading about. Each sector is defined by the source of the flow: consumer spending, investment spending, government spending, and the foreign trade balance. That's a useful way to look at the spending flow, too.

Each one of these four sectors could be broken down into much smaller parts. The consumer spending flow (C) might be broken into expenditures for: consumer durable goods (automobiles, appliances, furniture, etc.), nondurables (gasoline, canned peas, paper towels, toothpaste, etc.), and services (auto repair, attorney's fees, doctor bills, airline tickets, motel bills, etc.). The investment spending flow (I) can be broken down into fixed capital (buildings, machines and equipment, etc.), and circulating capital (raw materials, gasoline for the tractor, seed corn, etc.).

Government spending and foreign spending can be broken down in many ways, too. And each of the smaller spending categories can be broken down even more. For example, expenditures for nondurables can be broken down into food and other things. Expenditures for food can be broken down into meats, canned goods, etc., etc.

Why Should We Break Down the Spending Flow?

Why would anyone ever want to break down the total spending flow into all these little component parts? Because we want to try to understand what is going on. Sometimes it's helpful to know *what kinds* of consumer spending are increasing or decreasing, or *what kinds* of investment spending are increasing or decreasing.

How far do economists go in breaking down the total spending flow? As far as necessary to do what they want to do—to find out what they want to find out. Sometimes the basic "C + I + G + F" breakdown is sufficient. At least that's usually a good way to start. But often it's necessary to go farther. If something is "going wrong" with consumer spending, a more detailed breakdown of the consumer spending flow (C) may help us to see what's going wrong and why.

Sources of "Spending Flow" Statistics

Do government statisticians actually break down the spending flows into these smaller parts? You bet they do! Where do you think you could find the figures? In the *Survey of Current Business* (monthly) from the Bureau of Economic Analysis, U.S. Department of Commerce? Right! Or in the *Economic Report of the President* (annual), or the *Federal Reserve Bulletin* (monthly), or on page two of *Business Week* magazine (weekly), or from time to time in the *Wall Street Journal* (daily), in the *New York Times,* or in almost any news magazine or big city newspaper or in any publication or article entitled: "Indicators of Economic Activity." It might be fun for you to look up some of these figures sometime, just to see what's going on in the economy. (Why don't you go to the library and do it right now?)

Another View: The Money Supply and the Velocity of Circulation

Here's an entirely different way of looking at the total spending flow: the **quantity of money** (number of dollars) in existence, and the **velocity** (speed) at which the money (each dollar) is circulating.

For example, suppose the total money supply consisted of $500 billion. If each dollar was spent for new output six times each year, then the total size of the spending flow in the country would be $3 trillion a year. ($500 billion in existence, each dollar spent six times a year equals $3 trillion.) The total amount of output bought in the country would amount to $3 trillion dollars' worth. Total spending for output equals total output. Right?

Can you see that this is another way to look at the spending flow? The quantity of money in existence times the velocity at which each dollar is flowing equals total spending. If we wanted to understand what was going on using this approach, we would try to find out (a) what might cause the total money supply to get larger or smaller, and (b) what might cause the velocity,

or speed at which each dollar is turning over, to get faster or slower. This "quantity of money" approach to understanding total spending has been used by economists for more than 100 years. You will be reading a lot more about it later.

Other Breakdowns Can Be Useful

There are many other ways the total spending-income flow might be broken down for the purpose of analysis. We might look to see which parts of the country are doing the most of which kinds of spending (geographic breakdown). Or we might look to see how much and which kinds of spending are being done by young people or older people. Or we might find out how much spending is done by cash or on credit.

Several different ways of breaking down the spending stream actually are used. When? Whenever someone thinks such a breakdown will help to find out something, of course! The basic "four-sector" breakdown by spending source (C + I + G + F) and the basic breakdown whch focuses on the *quantity* and *velocity* of money, are generally the most useful. Those are the two we will use.

Right now we need to go farther with the four-sector breakdown (C + I + G + F). After that, we'll go deeper into the "monetary" approach and you will learn more about "the quantity of money (M) times the velocity at which it is circulating (V)." But that must wait until another chapter.

INJECTIONS INTO AND WITHDRAWALS FROM THE SPENDING STREAM

People stand on the receiving end of the total spending stream. They get checks in payment for the use of their labor, land, and capital. Each of us receives a little share of this total spending stream as our income. When we receive it, what do we do with it? What are our choices?

Income Must Be Used In One of Four Ways

We have four choices about what to do with our income: spend it for consumer goods (C), save it (S), pay taxes (T), or buy imports (Im). That completes the list. Those are our only choices. Of course we could spend it for capital goods, for business purposes (I). But that's sav-ing—*and then* investing.

The spending-receiving-spending cycle is going on all the time, every moment of every day. The consumers, investors, government and foreign buyers (C + I + G + Ex) are pushing money into the spending stream. The people who are receiving the money are pushing some of it back into the stream to buy consumer goods (C). They are pulling the rest of it out as savings, to pay taxes, and to buy imports (S + T + Im).

Withdrawals and Offsetting Injections

Notice that when the income receivers spend their money for domestically produced consumer goods (C), the money goes right back into the income stream. But the parts of their income they use for savings (S), taxes (T), and imports (Im), do *not* go right back into the stream. So does the stream get smaller? Not nec-essarily.

If the system is running along smoothly and you look at it at any moment, what you will see is this: consumer spending is flowing at a con-tinuous level, around and around. Taxes (T) are being pulled out of the stream and flowing away to the governments. Savings (S) are being pulled out of the stream and going into idle pools where they may be available for investment. Payments for imports (Im) are being pulled out of the stream and flowing into the bank accounts of foreigners.

At the same moment you will see govern-ment spending (G) flowing into the stream. You will see business investors pulling money out of the idle pools of savings and from the banks (creating money) and adding spending (I) back into the stream. Foreigners will get some dollars and push them into our spending stream to pay us for our exports (Ex).

All these withdrawals and injections are going on simultaneously, every moment, all the time. If you were to look at the overall macroeco-nomic picture at any moment, that's exactly what you would see.

It's obvious what would happen if the *injec-tion* flows (I, G, Ex) should either fall below or rise above the withdrawal flows. The size of the spending stream would change—would get smaller or larger wouldn't it? Sure.

The Expenditure and Income Equation

We have an equation which summarizes the spending-income flow. It shows the four ways money can get pushed into the spending stream: people spending for domestic consumer goods (C), businesses spending for domestic invest-ment goods (I), government spending for do-mestic goods and services (G), and foreigners spending to buy our goods (Ex). And it shows the four ways people can dispose of their in-comes: spend for domestic consumer goods (C), save (S), pay taxes (T), or spend to buy foreign goods (Im). *The amounts the spenders are spending* (putting into the income stream) *must be equal to the amounts the receivers are receiving* (taking out of the stream). You recognized this right off as an equality, didn't you? The equation looks like this:

$$C + I + G + Ex = C + S + T + Im$$

Figure 10-1 on the following page explains this equation in detail. You should study Figure 10-1 now.

Fig. 10-1 The Expenditure and Income Equation

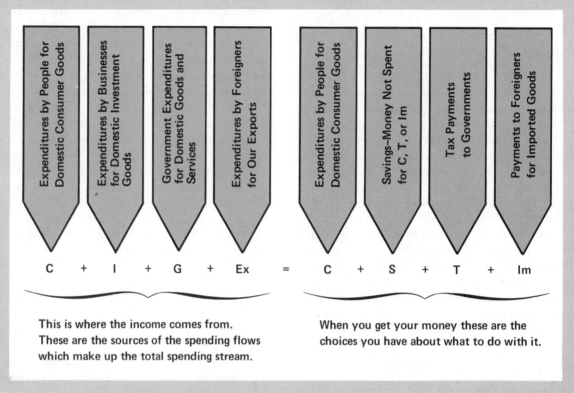

This is where the income comes from. These are the sources of the spending flows which make up the total spending stream.

When you get your money these are the choices you have about what to do with it.

The expenditure and income equation shows where the income comes from, and then how it is used by those who receive it.

You receive income because consumers, businesses, governments, and foreigners are spending to buy your output. You dispose of your income by spending for domestic consumer goods, or by saving, paying taxes, or buying imports.

An Overview of the Injections and Withdrawals

Income (spending) is flowing in a circle all the time. Consumer spending for domestic goods stays in the circle and goes around and around. At each instant, some of the money in the income stream is being pulled out, but simultaneously new spending is being added in. The stream has a stable level only when the amounts being drained off are equal to the amounts being added in.

The spending stream will be the same size only if the sum of the withdrawals is exactly "neutralized" or offset by the sum of the injections. The important thing is that S + T + Im (total withdrawals) must be exactly offset by I + G + Ex (total injections). Otherwise the economy will be speeding up or slowing down. No doubt about it. Now here's another way to look at it.

A "Fire Hydrants and Drainpipes" View of the Economy

Try to visualize this **total spending stream** as a stream of water flowing around in a big circle. There are three big "drainpipes" (savings, taxing, and imports) draining off the water as it flows around. There are three big "fire hydrants" (investment spending, government spending, and exports) gushing water into the stream as it flows around. It's easy to see that if the hydrants keep gushing exactly as much water into the stream as the drainpipes are draining out, then the total size of the stream will stay the same.

The **basic flow** in the stream is consumer spending for domestic goods and services. That just keeps going around and around. The savings drainpipe drains off some of this basic flow. So do the taxes drainpipe and the import drainpipe. But if the outflow through these drainpipes is just offset by the inflow from the investment, government spending, and export hydrants, then the size of the stream will not change. A lot of water will be gushing in from the hydrants at the top and a lot will be gurgling out through the drains at the bottom. But the size of the stream will stay the same. Can you picture it?

There Are Millions of Little Faucets and Drainpipes

Now that you have the basic picture, let's complicate it a little. You know that in the real world all the savings and taxes and import spending don't really drain off in one big pipe. All the investment spending and government spending and export payments don't gush in at one place, either. Actually, it's more like millions of little faucets and millions of little drainpipes. Each of us is in charge of regulating the withdrawal flow through our own tiny little "savings drainpipe." Each business is in charge of regulating the reinjection flow through its own little "investment faucet."

With all these people involved in the savings and investment decisions it seems that only a miracle would make the savings withdrawals and the investment injections come out even! The same is true for foreign buyers of our goods and domestic buyers of foreign goods. Each of us decides on our own whether to buy a Saab or a Pinto or a Datsun. What we decide determines whether or not we will be draining income out of the U.S. spending stream.

The government's decisions on taxing and spending are not quite as scattered as this. But when you think about all the state and local governments, you'll see that there's a lot of scatter! Governments usually try to adjust the "tax drain" to be about the same size as the "expenditure injection"—but not always. And even when they *try* to "balance the budget," they aren't always successful.

The Federal Government Has a Big Hydrant and a Big Drainpipe

There is only one spending unit which has control of a really big "spending hydrant" and "drainpipe." Which spending unit? The federal government, of course!

Even the largest business corporations are not big enough to have a major influence on the total spending flow. But the federal government has control of a big enough injection hydrant (government spending) and a big enough drainpipe (taxes) to have a really big effect on the size of the spending flow if it wants to.

We will talk more about these issues later. For now, just be sure you understand how it all fits together. And remember that all these withdrawals and injections must offset each other to keep the economy in "macroequilibrium."

Figure 10-2 shows a diagram illustrating the injections into and the withdrawals from the total spending stream. It shows the *sources* and the *uses* of the national income. It would be a good idea for you to study that diagram now.

Fig. 10-2 A Diagram of the Total Spending-Income Stream, Showing Injections and Withdrawals

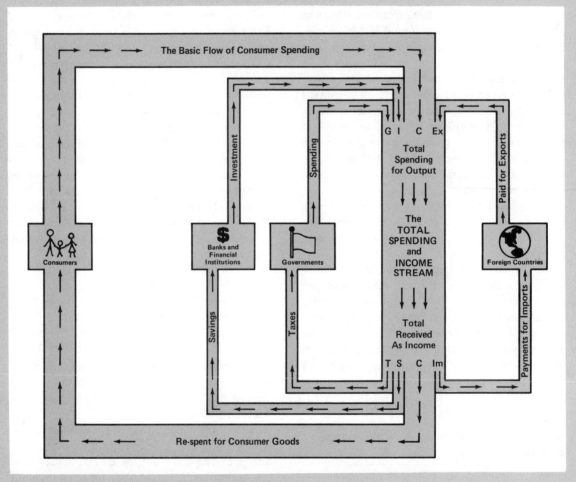

The spending-income diagram is just a picture of
the expenditure and income equation.

The total spending stream is generated by the basic flow of consumer spending, plus spending injections from the investors, the government, and the foreign buyers. All these "spending sources" are spending to buy outputs of goods and services.

The total spending stream flows as incomes (as wages, rents, interest, and profits) to the owners of the factors (labor, land, and capital) and then is "disposed of" either as consumer spending or for savings, taxes, or imports.

From this diagram you can see what would happen if any of the spending injections got larger or smaller. The spending flow would get larger or smaller. Right? Of course!

You can see from Figure 10-2 that if the total amounts people are trying to withdraw (drain off) are not exactly equal to the total amounts the people are trying to reinject, then total spending will be changing. Inflation? Recession? Yes.

SUMMARY AND SYNTHESIS

Total spending is the key to understanding **macroeconomics**. This total spending flow can be thought of as consisting of: consumer spending (C), investment spending (I), government spending (G), and foreign spending for our goods (Ex).

Consumer spending (C) is influenced by the **consumption function**. As people's incomes rise, they tend to spend more for consumer goods. Also **expectations** influence consumer spending, especially since consumers can spend not only present income, but also past or future income. Consumer spending is reduced by **taxes**.

Business **investment spending** (I) is greatly influenced by the **expected return** from potential investments. If the **marginal value product** is expected to be **greater than the cost**, then businesses will spend for **capital goods**. But if not they will not.

John Maynard Keynes (KAYns) introduced much of modern macroeconomics in 1936 in his book *The General Theory of Employment, Interest, and Money*. Keynes emphasized the importance of the **marginal efficiency** (expected return) of capital in influencing the size of the investment spending flow in the economy.

The **government spending** (G) part of the total spending flow responds to the political process choices at the federal, state, and local levels. The **foreign spending** (exports—Ex) component of the total spending stream depends on foreign demand for and relative prices of our goods. The foreign trade balance (F) is "exports (Ex) minus imports (Im)." If positive, it makes our spending flow larger; if negative, it makes our spending flow smaller.

We can think of the spending flow as one big "circular flow." Or we can focus on these four components: C + I + G + Ex. Or each of the spending sources can be further broken down. Detailed output and spending flow statistics are published monthly in the *Survey of Current Business* and are frequently reported in the news media.

The expenditure and income equation indicates the **sources** of the spending flow, and the **uses** of the income generated by the spending flow. The equation is: C + I + G + Ex = C + S + T + Im. Consumer spending is the basic flow. The injections are I + G + Ex, and the withdrawals are S + T + Im. Whenever total injections exceed total withdrawals, the spending stream will be getting larger. Whenever withdrawals exceed injections the stream will be getting smaller.

Another way to analyze the total spending flow is as a "mass of moving dollars"—the **quantity of money** (M) times the **velocity of circulation** (V). The quantity of money in existence multiplied by the rate at which the average dollar turns over each year gives the size of the total spending flow. Anything which increases or decreases either M or V causes the size of the spending flow to change in the same direction.

REVIEW EXERCISES

MAJOR CONCEPTS, PRINCIPLES, TERMS (Explain each thoroughly.)

the expenditure and income equation
what influences consumer spending

what influences investment spending
how investment spending offsets consumer saving
the components of the spending stream
the foreign trade balance
the "quantity and velocity of money" idea

OTHER CONCEPTS AND TERMS (Explain each briefly.)

consumer durables
consumer expectations
investor expectations
expected return
John Maynard Keynes (KAYns)
C, I, G, Ex, Im, F
the "four-sector" breakdown

QUESTIONS (Write out answers, or jot down key points.)

1. There are several ways in which *optimism* can be very stimulating to the economy. Can you explain several of the ways? Try.
2. What would be likely to happen to investment spending in the economy if the interest rate suddenly went up from 8% to 16%? Can you explain why?
3. If there's too much spending, and lots of inflationary buying in the U.S. economy, then it would be good for the economy if some people would stop buying Omnis and Pintos and Gremlins and Dusters, and start buying Volkswagens and Toyotas and Volvos instead. But if the economy is in a recession, it would help for more people to "buy American." Discuss.
4. Explain how a change in the size of the money supply might influence the size of the total spending flow.

APPENDIX

Business Investment Spending: Expected Returns, Interest Rates, and Capitalized Value

In this chapter you have read a small section about business investment spending. If that section didn't tell you as much about it as you would like to know, here's more.

If we want to understand investment spending in the economy we need to understand expected returns to capital and the interest rate. And we need to know how to use both of these to find out if the business will (or will not) invest. That's what this appendix is about.

What Determines the Expected Return?

What causes a business to think some piece of capital—some machine—will bring a high return? First, what kinds of "returns" can a capital investment offer? Two kinds. It can add to the output value, or it can reduce the production cost. Often the business expects a new piece of capital equipment to do some of both.

If the local union gets a big wage increase, labor cost goes up. This increases the expected return to capital. The business will be more likely to invest in labor-saving machinery. If the demand and price for the product are expected to go up, this also increases the expected return—the "marginal efficiency of capital."

Some Examples of the Investment Decision

Harry Walker owns the local sawmill and joinery shop. Suppose he thinks bad times are coming. He sees the marginal efficiency of capital as being low. His investment spending is likely to be low. Of course!

When Mr. Walker sees the expected return of a certain piece of capital as "high," he will have a "high demand" for that piece of capital. But will he buy it? Or not? How does he decide? It depends on the price. Actually, it depends on two prices. It depends on the *cash* price Mr. Walker must pay for the piece of capital. It also depends on the price he must pay for the *money* he will have to sink in the investment. That is, it depends on the *interest rate*. Let's look at some hypothetical cases to see how it all works out.

The Seafood Packing House Case. Suppose a small seafood packing house down on the eastern shore of Virginia is considering investing in an oyster-breading machine. This is a "latest technology" piece of equipment. It has a stainless steel breading mixer, then a small conveyor belt to carry the oysters from the mixer through a roller to flatten them and on into the final package for freezing. The minimum wage law has just pushed up the cost of labor and the seafood packing houses have raised their prices for frozen breaded oysters. Several restaurants and hotel chains have complained about the high prices of frozen breaded oysters. Some customers have shifted from Chesapeake Bay oysters to Gulf Shrimp and Cape Cod flounder fillets. The oyster-dependent economy of the Chesapeake Bay area is hurting.

The oyster-breading machine sells for $20,000. It is designed for a small operation. Remember your uncle who runs the Seaside Seafood Packing House in Chincoteague, Virginia? He remembers you! And he knows you

are taking a course in economics so he writes to you and asks you whether or not he should pay $20,000 for this new stainless steel oyster-breading machine. You are going to have to answer the letter and say something. What are you going to say?

The Iron Ore Pelletizing Case. Before you get too upset about having to make such a tough decision, think of the plight of your roommate's father. He is a high-powered management consultant receiving $500 a day to help a major steel company decide whether or not to install a new iron ore pelletizing plant at Ishpeming, Michigan. The steel company is already operating a pelletizing plant which is less than 10 years old. The present operation crushes the iron ore and tumbles it around and gets the good part—the iron part—to stick together in little pebble-type pellets. Each pellet comes out about 40 percent iron and 60 percent other stuff—"inert ingredients" you might say.

But suppose that a new process has been developed. It would cost $2.8 million to install the new equipment, but it can turn out pellets of 75 percent iron and only 25 percent other stuff. And it operates with only half as much labor. Also, it can handle twice as much iron ore per hour as the present equipment. A shipload of the 75 percent pellets will actually have in it about twice as much usable iron (and only half as much "inert ingredients") as a shipload of the 40 percent pellets. So in addition to all the other benefits, the cost of transportation will be cut almost in half. But remember? The present plant is less than 10 years old!

Should the steel company buy the new equipment and scrap its existing plant which is still working as good as new? Or should they keep using the old plant until it wears out? And then put in the new equipment? Your roommate's father is going to advise them. Tough task, huh? But these are the kinds of questions on which real world investment spending decisions are based. And you'll see that it's really not so difficult to figure out.

In both the oyster-breading case and the iron ore pelletizing case there is no question that there is a *demand* for the capital. That is to say, there is *some* price at which it would be "good business" to buy the capital. But is the price right? Would it be good business to pay $20,000 for the oyster-breading machine? Or $2.8 million for the new iron ore pelletizing plant?

How Much Will Output Value Increase and Cost Decrease?

How does a business decide in cases like these? The first step is to estimate each way in which the piece of equipment is expected to reduce the cost. Next, estimate each way it is expected to increase the revenue. Then you put the two together.

When you make these estimates you would like to be as precise as you can. But don't try to overdo it. Make-believe accuracy in the face of real-life uncertainty is a luxury you can't afford! Remember that over the life of this piece of equipment, *all* the cost and revenue conditions are going to change in several unforeseeable ways. Some of the changes may be completely unexpected. The situation in three or four years may not even resemble today's situation. So there is no need to knock yourself out trying to achieve precise accuracy. That's a waste of energy.

How much cost and effort should Mr. Walker spend in trying to estimate the "expected returns" of a piece of capital? He should follow the marginal principle. Each time he puts any more effort or money into trying to increase the accuracy of his estimates, he should expect the increased accuracy to be worth at least as much as the cost of the extra effort. It would be a waste to try to get more accuracy than that! Good enough is best. Right?

EXPECTED RETURNS AND "CAPITALIZED VALUE"

You know that the new oyster-breading machine will bring your uncle some savings in labor costs and perhaps in other input costs—maybe in transportation costs, power costs, or other

costs. And you know that the value of the output probably will increase as a result of the new machine. But how much decreased cost and increased revenue will there be? Enough to justify the investment? How can you figure this out?

Just take it step by step. It isn't difficult to work out an "expected return" for the first year. Then you project to the second year, third year, and so on for the estimated life of the capital. Suppose you figure that during the first year the oyster-breading machine would save about $2,000 in labor costs and other production costs and would probably increase your uncle's output ("value added") by about $1,000 worth. So you estimate that the "expected return" of the machine is about $3,000 in the first year.

Next you might try to guess what is going to happen to wages and to other costs of production and to the prices of breaded oysters in the following years. Then you could make a different calculation for each year, depending on your cost and revenue projections. Or you might take the more practical approach—the easy way—and assume that the return for each year will be approximately the same: $3,000 each year.

Suppose you figure this machine will last about 10 years and its expected return will be about $3,000 each year. Then its total "expected return" over its life will add up to $30,000. Does this mean the machine is worth $30,000 to your uncle? To get at the answer to this question, and to emphasize the importance of the interest rate, let's look at it another way.

The Effect of the Interest Rate

Would you give me $30,000 today if I agreed to give you back $3,000 each year for the next 10 years? You certainly wouldn't! Why not? Because you could put your money in a savings account or in government bonds or in AT&T bonds or in GM stocks or in any kind of investment you could think of and get back *more than* $3,000 each year for the next 10 years! If you could invest your $30,000 at an interest rate of 10 percent, you would get back $3,000 a year *forever*! And always own the $30,000 to boot! See what a bad deal it would be to invest $30,000 when you only expect to receive a return of $3,000 a year for 10 years?

So how much would you advise your uncle to pay for the oyster-breading machine? Certainly not $30,000. But how much? $25,000? $20,000? $15,000? $10,000? How do you figure it out?

Suppose your uncle bought the machine. By the end of the first year it would have brought him an "expected return" of $3,000. Just to make it easy, let's assume that he receives all his "return" on the last day of the year. So looking at it from the point of view of the *first* day of the year, how much is that $3,000 return (to be received on the *last* day of the year) worth? If he had the $3,000 on the *first* day of the year, he could invest it or lend it out, or just put it in a savings account, and by the *last* day of the year he would have the $3,000 *plus* one year's interest. At a 5 percent interest rate, he would have $3,000 plus $150. So: $3,000 to be received a year from now is worth about $150 less to you than the $3,000 would be worth if you had it right now. That is, if the interest rate is 5 percent, "the right to receive $3,000 a year from today" is worth only about $2,850, today ($3,000 minus the $150 you lose by *not* having the money now).

Sometimes people have trouble with this concept because it seems strange at first. But it's really quite simple. For example, suppose your wealthy sister offers you a choice. She will give you $3,000 now, or she will give you $3,000 one year from now. Which would you prefer? You would rather have it now, of course. How strong would be your preference to have the money now? That depends on "the going interest rate" for the kind of investment you are thinking about. If you are thinking about investing the money at an interest rate of 5 percent, then it "costs" you $150 to wait a year. If you are thinking about an 8 percent rate, then it "costs" you $240 to wait a year. (8 percent of $3,000 is $240.)

Future Receipts Must Be "Discounted"

Suppose someone comes to you and says: "Here's a piece of paper which says I will pay you $3,000 one year from today. How much will you pay me for this piece of paper (promissory note) right now?" If you're thinking of a 5 percent interest rate you will pay about $2,850.

($3,000 minus $150.) If you are thinking of an 8 percent rate, you will pay about $2,760. ($3,000 minus $240.)

What you are doing is buying a $3,000, one-year promissory note, at a discount. If the interest rate is 5 percent, you will "discount" it about $150; if the interest rate is 8 percent, you will "discount" it about $240. Suppose it is a *two*-year promissory note. At 5 percent per year the discount would be about $150 each year, or about $300, total. The present value would be about $2,700. At 8 percent per year the discount would be about $240 per year, or $480 total. The present value would be about $2,520. (You will notice that these figures are not exactly correct, because of the "compounding effect." But don't worry about that now).

See how the present value of an expected future return goes down more and more as we look farther and farther into the future? Also, notice how much difference it makes whether the interest rate is 5 percent or 8 percent! Maybe you have always thought of the interest rate as something small and insignificant. But as the years go by, the interest rate can become a very big thing. (Find out how much of the average car payment or house payment goes for interest. You may be surprised!)

Discounting the "Expected Return"

Your uncle expects a return of $3,000 at the end of the first year. If the interest rate is 8 percent, the present value of that expected return is only about $2,760. At the end of the second year he expects to receive another $3,000. But the present value of that is only about $2,520. Actually it's a little less than $2,520, because of the "compounding effect"—he's losing the chance to earn interest on the interest!

It's just the opposite of having your money in a savings account. The longer you *have it* in your account, the more you *gain*; the longer you *don't have it* in there, the more you lose. Get the idea? So the *present* value of the $3,000 your uncle is going to receive in the third year, the fourth year, the fifth year and so on, gets smaller and smaller and smaller.

So what do you advise your uncle to do?

		First year	Second year	Third year	nth year
Present Capitalized Value	$(V) =$	$\dfrac{\text{Expected return (X)}}{1 + \text{interest rate (i)}}$	$+\ \dfrac{X}{(1 + i)^2}$	$+\ \dfrac{X}{(1 + i)^3}$	$+\ \ldots +\ \dfrac{X}{(1 + i)^n}$

Should he pay $20,000 and buy the machine? How do you decide? Simply find the discounted value of the "expected return" for each of the years over the expected life of the machine. Then add them all up. How simple! This little exercise will give you the capitalized value of the machine. It will tell your uncle how much the machine is worth to him, on the basis of your estimates. *The "capitalized value" of any asset is the present value of the asset, as figured on the basis of how much money that asset is expected to bring to its owner over its lifetime.*

Suppose you spent a thousand dollars (or a million dollars for that matter) building a machine, and then found out that it would cost more to run the machine than the output would be worth. What would be the capitalized value of the machine? Zero, of course. The machine might have some scrap value or some "aesthetic value" or something, but capitalized value? No. Anything which won't make you any money doesn't have any capitalized value. The more money it will make for you, the more its capitalized value will be.

You can see that the higher the interest rate happens to be, the greater the discount which must be subtracted from the expected returns. So *as interest rates rise higher and higher, capitalized value gets lower and lower.* At higher interest rates, fewer capital investments appear profitable. High interest rates can have a very discouraging effect on the flow of investment spending. Now you can understand why.

How do you figure out the capitalized value of a machine or of any other asset? First you figure out what you think the expected return is going to be in each year over the expected life of the asset. Then you "discount" the dollar figure for each year. This gives you the present value of each future year's expected income. Then you add up all the *present values* of all the future-year

incomes. And what do you have? You have the present capitalized value of the asset. Of course!

Computing the Capitalized Value

By now you could probably figure out what the "capitalized value," or "capitalization" formula looks like. It shows how to discount the expected return for the first year, for the second year, the third year, etc. And once you have done all that you just add up all the figures and you have it!

First, study the formula in the box at the top of this page. Then you'll be able to work through the following examples.

Example (using 8% interest rate)
Present value of $3,000 to be received:

in 1 year: $V = \dfrac{\$3,000}{1 + .08} = \dfrac{\$3,000}{1.08} = \$2,777.78$

in 2 years: $V = \dfrac{\$3,000}{(1.08)^2} = \dfrac{\$3,000}{1.1664} = \$2,572.02$

in 3 years: $V = \dfrac{\$3,000}{(1.08)^3} = \dfrac{\$3,000}{1.2597} = \$2,381.52$

(You can work it out the rest of the way if you want to.)

Sidelight: What about a perpetual income?
Suppose you're thinking about investing in a piece of land which you think will pay you (and your heirs) a rental of "X" dollars a year *forever.* How much would you pay for the land? Here's the formula:

Present Capitalized Value	$\Big\}$ $V = \dfrac{X \text{ (expected annual return)}}{i \text{ (assumed interest rate)}}$

Examples:

Suppose the annual return is $3,000 and the interest rate is 8%:

$$V = \frac{\$3,000}{.08} = \$37,500$$

Suppose the interest rate is 5%:

$$V = \frac{\$3,000}{.05} = \$60,000$$

Suppose the interest rate is 10%:

$$V = \frac{\$3,000}{.10} = \$30,000$$

(See how much difference it makes which interest rate you choose?)

The easiest way to do the discounting is to look up the figures in a "present value" or "interest and discount" table. (Ask your friendly banker to show you one.) I looked up the present value figures for your uncle's investment problem and found out that at an interest rate of 5%, the present capitalized value of the oyster-breading machine comes out to about $23,000. This assumes, of course, that the machine really will last exactly ten years, and that it really will bring your uncle a return of $3,000 a year. And of course it assumes that the opportunity cost (or the interest cost) of the money he invests in the machine really will be 5 percent. These are big "ifs"!

Should the Business Manager Allow Some "Margin for Error"?

So what do you advise your uncle to do? Should he buy a machine that costs $20,000,

when it looks like the machine is going to be worth $23,000 to him? Probably so.

But suppose the interest rate is considered to be 8%. What then? Then the capitalized value of the machine comes out at about $20,000. Should your uncle buy it? Probably not. Not much margin for error! It's chancy at best. Maybe you should just send your uncle all the facts and figures and let him decide. Do you see how uncertain the investment spending decision can be?

Your roommate's father goes through the same process. The only difference is that he deals with bigger figures and he may use a computer to make it easier. Besides, the computer makes everything look so scientific and precise! If he comes up with a "capitalized value" for the iron ore pelletizing machinery *greater* than the $2.8 million it will cost (plus some satisfactory margin for error and risk) then he will advise his client to buy and install the equipment. If not, he won't.

You can see that both of these decisions will be highly sensitive to *changes in expectations* about future returns. Also, the decisions are sensitive to *changes in the rates of interest* in the "money market." So what determines the level of investment spending in the economy? **Expected returns** and **interest rates** have a lot to do with it. Higher expected returns are likely to stimulate investment spending; higher interest rates are likely to retard investment spending. Common sense? Sure.

Appendix: New Concepts, Principles, Theories

capitalized value
capitalization
discounted value
two formulas for finding capitalized value

11

National Income Analysis II: Savings, Investment, and Macroequilibrium

Chapter Objectives

- The size of the **total spending flow** determines the **macroeconomic condition** of the economy. **Injections and withdrawals** cause the spending flow to **increase or decrease.**

- **Macroequilibrium** in an economic system occurs where the **injections and withdrawals are in balance.** What determines the balance (or imbalance) between these injections and withdrawals? That's what you will find out in this chapter.

- When you complete your study of this chapter you will be able to explain **forced savings** and **forced investment,** compare these with **planned savings** and **planned investment,** and explain the important role these play in influencing the macroeconomic condition of the economy.

- You will be able to explain the concept of **macroequilibrium** and how it is influenced by **planned and unplanned savings and investment.**

- You will understand the **paradox of thrift** and you will be able to state and explain **Say's Law** and to explain how the **secondary functions of money** can keep Say's Law from working.

SAVINGS CAN SLOW THE CIRCULAR FLOW

Remember Tubaland Island? With its modern monetary system? Well, bad news. The existence of this efficient monetary system is going to bring them a new problem. Just watch.

Last October when some of the Eastside islanders were out fishing they were talking about Christmas and bragging about the presents they were going to buy for their friends and loved ones. Then they realized that if they really were going to buy all those things they had better start saving some money!

That day, after they sailed to shore they sold their fish to the waiting buyers on the beach just as always. But instead of going around the island and spending all their money for breadfruit, bananas, tuba, and other things, they all decided to spend only *half* of their money. They all decided to save the other half—to just deposit it and leave it in their bank accounts.

These thoughtful, thrifty eastside islanders are doing a fine thing, saving for Christmas. Right? But look what happened next.

Savings May Leave Surplus Products in the Market

At sundown that day the westside, northside, and southside islanders couldn't understand why they had so much left over—breadfruit, bananas, coconuts, tuba, everything. Why all the surpluses? You know why. The thrifty eastside islanders didn't spend all their money, so the other producers can't sell all their products. So what's going to happen next?

Maybe the surpluses of breadfruit, bananas, tuba, and all will force the prices to go down. At the lower prices, maybe all the surpluses will be bought up and everything will be all right again. Do you think it really will happen that way? Maybe. But probably not.

Over the years the breadfruit gatherers and banana growers and tuba makers have established trade associations and unions. They now insist on "fair and just wages and prices." Each family has made it quite clear that the "going price" is the rock-bottom price they will accept. If the demand for their product happens to drop, they will not permit the price to go down. They will cut back production instead.

You can see that all the sellers on the island have enough **monopoly power** or **market power** to keep their prices from falling. If demand drops they will hold their prices up and just cut back production. They would rather *dump the surpluses in the ocean* than to let their prices go down!

So here we are with the eastside islanders not spending all the money they are getting from the other islanders. They are saving for Christmas. But as a result of their saving, surpluses develop. Then the westside, northside, and southside islanders cut back their production rather than let their prices go down. While all this is going on, what do you think is happening to the demand for fish?

Increased Savings Sets Off a Chain Reaction

Yesterday when the eastsiders decided to save half of the income from their catch, the demand for fish was as great as it always had been. But today, what about it? When the outrigger

canoes come sailing in to the beach this afternoon there aren't as many buyers as before. Can you guess why?

Where do the westside, northside, and southside islanders get the money to buy fish? By selling their own products, of course. When they can't sell all their products, they don't get as much money. So they can't buy as much fish.

Today the eastside islanders find that they can't sell all their fish. Several baskets of fish are left over. The eastsiders can't understand what happened. Today the eastsiders face the same problem the others faced yesterday. And today the eastside chief decrees that tomorrow, fewer people will go out fishing. No sense producing more fish than can be sold for the going price!

What's going on, on our happy little island? We have unemployment! The incomes of all the island people are now lower than before. Both their money incomes and their real incomes are lower. What about the eastsiders' Christmas savings plan? That's out the window, too! Their incomes are now so low that *they can't save*.

The economy is depressed. Total economic activity—total production, output, and income in the economy—has declined. The GIP (gross island product) is smaller. The eastside islanders didn't want to cause trouble. They only wanted to save for Christmas. But look at the trouble they caused! Why?

Money Makes It Easy to Defer Spending—to Save

What is "saving"? In *real* terms it means producing something and then not using it up. It means keeping something so you'll have it later when you may need it more. It means to "not-consume" some of the goods you've produced or earned.

In *money* terms "saving" seems to mean about the same thing. It means to "not-spend for consumer goods" some of the income you've earned. So what's the difference? Just this:

Real saving is economizing by "not-using-up" some of the things you've produced—some of the things you own.

Money saving is "not-spending" some of your income. It's "not-buying" things.

Can you see what kinds of problems *money saving* could cause? When you decide to "not-

spend," this means you are selling more products and services to others than you are buying back from them. When the eastside islanders started saving, they stopped giving the others the money they needed to buy all the fish.

You know that the economy operates as a big circle. What you have just seen is what happens when somebody doesn't keep the money moving around the circle. Whenever someone receives some of the money from the spending circle and doesn't put it back, soon everyone winds up getting less. Any such withdrawal from the spending circle is felt all the way around the circle.

Back when the eastsiders and westsiders were meeting at 4 o'clock and trading fish for breadfruit, there was no problem. When the fish sellers "sold" (traded) their fish, they automatically "bought" (received in trade) an equal value of breadfruit and took it home with them. There was no way a person could "sell" fish and then "not-buy" an equivalent amount of breadfruit. It always came out even. Obviously!

But once *money* is introduced, this permits a lot of *slack* in the system. When money is used, the people can take their fish to the market, get their money and go home. They don't have to take home the breadfruit! They can leave all the baskets of breadfruit just sitting there in the market! That's the problem.

Money Is a "Claim Check"

Money is really a sort of "claim check," or "credit slip." It's your "right to claim the goods which society owes you." When you place goods in the market or perform services for the market, you get "claim checks." You can use these claim checks to claim whatever other goods or services you want from the market. When you claim the things you want, you pass along your "claim checks" to other people who can then claim the things they want. But when someone gets "claim checks" (money) and doesn't use them, some of the goods in the market will be unclaimed, "surplus" goods.

The owners of the surplus (unsold) goods will not get as many "claim checks." So they can't claim the goods they want from other sellers. So the other sellers soon will have surpluses too. The chain reaction just keeps going on and on and the economy slows down more and more. See the problem *money* can cause?

With barter, the total value of products a person takes into the market must be equal to the total value of products that person takes back out of the market. So long as *things* are being traded for *things*, it must work this way. But with a medium of exchange (money) people can put more products *in the market* than they take back *out of the market*. Some people may decide to hold their "claim checks" so they can claim goods later. That's when the trouble starts.

Say's Law: the Amount Supplied Determines the Amount Demanded

The more a person sells in the market the more that person can buy. When people produce goods and take them to the market, they receive money. With this money they can buy an equal value of goods from the market and take them home.

A Frenchman, Jean Baptiste Say (in the early 1800's), explained this concept, saying that the more a person produces and puts into the market the more the person will take from the market. The more a person supplies, the more that person demands. This principle is sometimes called "Say's Law of Markets," or just **Say's Law.**

Say's Law says "supply creates its own demand." If a person supplies more, that person will demand more. Obviously Say's Law is not precisely true. Otherwise there would never be surpluses in the market. The market would always be "cleared"—that is, everything placed in the market always would be bought up and taken away.

If everybody who sells something in the market turns right around and buys something of equal value, the total amount taken to the market will equal the total amount taken home. There will be no surpluses and no shortages. Everything will work out even. But when people take things and leave them in the market and take their money and go home, this breaks the production-consumption circle. Some producers will not be able to sell all their output. This is what you saw happen when the thrifty eastside islanders started saving for Christmas.

The "Secondary Functions of Money" Allow Some Slack

What happened to the economy of our happy island? I suppose you could say that the island's economy was "wrecked by one of the *secondary functions of money*." The eastside islanders were using some of their money, *not* as a medium of exchange, but as a *store of value*, instead. That's what created the problem.

It's those *secondary functions*, those "future functions" of money that bring the slack in the system and keep Say's Law from working all the time. The *store of value* function lets people save—to spend *less* than they earn. The *standard of deferred payments* function lets people go into debt—to spend *more* than they earn.

The two "secondary functions" have offsetting effects on the economy, of course. When people spend *less* than they receive, that *slows things down*. When people spend *more* than they receive, that *speeds things up*. If everyone would just use each dollar immediately as a medium of exchange, then Say's Law would always hold true. But people don't. So we have speedups and slowdowns in the economy.

Savings, Economic Growth, and the "Paradox of Thrift"

The island people are facing hard times. Why? Because the eastside islanders wanted to be thrifty and save for Christmas. They were putting more goods into the market than they were buying and taking home from the market. They were *saving* money. Saving money must be a very bad thing. Look at the trouble it brought to our happy little island!

Say's Law was "repealed" by the secondary functions of money! Howbout that ?!

How can *saving* money be *bad*? People who save can be more secure and do more things they like to do. And saving is absolutely essential for economic growth. Economic growth provides opportunities for everybody to get more things and not have to work so hard. So how can saving be bad?

Just like most of the other answers in economics, the solution to this dilemma is really very simple. Your common sense probably could figure it out for you. But here's the answer: The savings must be *invested* to bring **economic growth.** If the savings are *invested*, then there's no problem of surpluses or unemployment! But if the savings are not invested—well, you saw what happened.

INVESTMENT CAN TRANSLATE SAVINGS INTO GROWTH

When people save money they leave some of the current output unbought in the market. "Economic growth" occurs when this "leftover output" is then bought up by businesses and used to increase future production.

For growth to occur, the surplus must be bought up and used as capital. The surplus can't be left lying around in the market! That's what causes depressions!

To have growth, there must be saving. But just saving is not enough. In order to link savings to growth, there must be investment. Savings cannot be translated into growth, without "investment." *People can save as much money as they want to, just as long as investors buy up everything the savers decide to "not-buy."* *

Suppose the economy is clicking along at just the right speed—no unemployment problems and no overspending. As long as investors spend as much money as the savers save, no slowdown will occur. There will be no problem of surpluses or unemployment. And everything will be fine. The economy can be growing all the time.

Think of "saving" as "leaving some output in the market." "Investing" means "buying up this leftover output." If the amount of investing is equal to the amount of saving, then there's no problem. All the markets are "cleared"—no left-over surpluses.

---

*From one person's point of view, saving money and putting it in a savings account may be thought of as "saving and investing." But from the point of view of the economy: not so! For your deposited savings to become investments in the economy, someone must take those deposited dollars and *spend them for capital goods*. Otherwise your savings withdrawal from the income stream will not be offset by a corresponding *investment injection*. The income-spending stream will get smaller. The economy will slow down and there will be unemployment.

Also, notice this: In order for the investors to be able to buy things, somebody *must* be saving. If there isn't anything left over, then there won't be any goods for the investors to buy.

Let's see what would have happened on our island if investment spending had increased enough to offset the savings of the eastsiders. Suppose, on the day the eastsiders decided to save their money, the son of the northside chief, Prince Hafakaloa, decided he would like to go into the business of producing pearl necklaces. He thinks he could sell a lot of necklaces at Christmas time.

He needs to buy some canoes, underwater goggles, other diving equipment, oyster knives and some other things. But he doesn't have the money to buy all these things. So (just to make it all work out neatly) let's suppose he goes to the eastside islanders to borrow some money. He promises to pay them back (with interest) one week before Christmas. They agree to lend him their savings. They arrange it so that each day they will turn over to him all the money they save that day.

Investment Demand Stimulates Capital Goods Production

When Prince Hafakaloa (our business entrepreneur) takes his borrowed money and goes into the market to buy things, he doesn't buy up the surplus breadfruit and bananas and all. He wants pearl-diving equipment and canoes and such. So he starts spending money for canoes and other capital goods.

His spending for capital goods is just great enough to exactly offset the eastsiders' reduced spending for consumer goods. The shift in spending convinces some of the people who previously were producing consumer goods—breadfruit, bananas, tuba—to start producing capital goods—canoes, diving masks, oyster knives and other pearl-necklace-making equipment.

See how the factors of production will shift from the production of *consumer goods* to the production of *capital goods*? This is a temporary problem which the "market process" can take care of. There is no problem of unemployment, no drop in outputs or incomes—no hard times at all! Why?

Because the increase in investment spending (for capital goods) is exactly the right size to off-set the decrease in consumer spending (for consumer goods). That is, the new rate of investment spending is exactly equal to (and exactly offsets) the new rate of savings. The new injections offset the new withdrawals. See how neatly it works out?

If Investment Spending Offsets Savings: No Surpluses, No Shortages*

If the total value of the things people *don't buy* as consumer goods is exactly equal to the total value of things that investors *do buy* as capital goods, then the total size, or "speed" of the circular flow, just stays the same. Total outputs and total incomes do not change. Total economic activity continues at the same level.

But the minute total investment spending for capital goods gets *smaller* than the total amount the people are leaving in the market (saving) then there will be surplus goods in the market. Whenever this happens, output will be cut back. Unemployment will develop. Total economic activity will slow down. Outputs and incomes will decline.

The only way the surplus goods left by the savers can be bought up and cleared out of the

market is for someone to get the money the savers took home (or get an equal amount of money from somewhere—like borrowing from banks) and go into the market and buy up those surplus goods. Whenever this happens there isn't a problem. Whenever it doesn't, there is.

As long as the investors are spending as much as the savers are saving, the markets will be cleared and the economy will keep on operating at the same level. No surpluses will pile up in the market because total spending or aggregate demand is great enough to "clear the market." The investors are deciding to spend exactly enough to offset the amount the savers are deciding to "not-spend." All goes well.

Too Much Investment Spending Brings Inflation

Now suppose the investors want to start spending *more* than the savers are saving. What happens? The investors will still be in the market looking for goods after the goods are all gone! What would happen then? Shortages. Of course.

Maybe producers would try to produce more, to meet the demands of the investors. But suppose we already have a "full employment" economy. The producers are producing all they can produce. Then, no matter how you slice it, that's all they can produce!

Given enough time, producers can build more and better capital. Then they can produce more. But isn't that just what they're trying to do now? They're trying to spend more money to invest in more capital. But the consumers are buying too much! Businesses can't invest any more in growth than the people are saving—that is: "producing but not consuming." So what happens meanwhile? The shortages continue.

The investors who are trying to buy more capital goods than the economy is producing start bidding against each other, trying to get the capital goods they want. They entice some of the factors of production away from making consumer goods and into making capital goods. When

---

*You will notice throughout this discussion that all of the withdrawals and injections except savings and investment are being ignored. I think you will get a better picture of the critical savings-investment relationship if for the time being we ignore taxes and government spending and imports and exports. Near the end of this chapter all of the withdrawals and injections will be brought back into the picture.

that happens *the consumers* start facing shortages.

All the people are employed in good jobs these days, and they want what they want—new cars, new refrigerators, new houses, you name it. And they're spending their money to try to get the things they want. But shortages are everywhere. Prices begin moving up. You know what we call this: **Inflation**. The investors and the consumers are all bidding against each other, trying to get the available goods and factors of production. Prices go up faster and faster. Times are tough.

Too Little Investment Spending Brings Recession

Now let's take another look at the opposite case. Suppose savings are high. There is a large amount of output that the consumers are not buying. Lots of goods and factors of production are available for the investors. Now, if they want to, the investors can build new factories, buy new machines, order fleets of new trucks—they can get plenty of everything they need. But suppose they decide they don't want to invest very much right now. Then what? I'll bet you know what.

If the businesses don't think this is a very good time to expand, then we have a problem. The amount the consumers are leaving in the market by *saving* (not-spending) is greater than the amount the businesses want to take out of the market by *investing*. So there lie all those goods, waiting unbought in the market. The consumers don't buy them. The investors don't buy them. What happens?

The producers who produced the unbought goods will just hold on to them. Not because they want to, but because they don't have much choice. They are caught with unwanted surpluses. They will cut back production and lay off workers. Some producers will shut down their plants. We will have an economic slowdown. Unemployment. **Recession**. If it continues and

unemployment gets really bad, then we will call it a **depression**. Times are *really* tough then!

Does Total Output Still Equal Total Income?

A while ago you saw the eastside islanders catching and selling fish and getting income. The more "dollars' worth" of fish they produced, the more "dollars' worth" of income they got, of course. The total value of their product was equal to the total income they received when they sold it. Output always equals income. Remember?

Suppose one day the eastside islanders couldn't sell all their fish. Then their *money incomes* would be smaller. They would have to take a *part* of their income in the same way Robinson Crusoe always took all of his income—that is, in goods instead of in money. Their *money income* is equal to the value of the output they produce and *sell*. The rest of their income is made up of *real income*—their unsold fish.

So their total output is still equal to their total income, even though part of their income is money and the other part is fish! It's as though they had invested a part of their money income in fish.

Whatever the value of the unsold fish happens to be, that's the value of that part of the output. So that's the value of that part of their income, and that's how much money they have tied up ("invested") in fish! See how, if the eastsiders can't sell all their fish, they are forced to "invest" in fish? Here's another example of this "forced investment" or **unplanned investment**.

Realized Investment Is Always Equal to Savings

When Mr. Hebert the boatbuilder hires labor, buys materials, and builds boats, he is investing in those boats. He hopes to sell them. He doesn't want to keep his money invested in boats. But suppose the boatbuyers decide to save—to "not-buy" the boats? Then Mr. Hebert is forced to take his "income," not in money, but in boats. He is forced to invest in boats.

As the boat-buyers save more, Hebert is forced to invest more in boats. If this sort of thing goes on for very long, what happens? Hebert will stop producing boats. He'll fire his workers, stop buying lumber and screws and paint and things. He'll stop investing in boats and just shut down his boatyard.

If the same thing is happening to lots of other businesses, soon the whole economy will slow down. Outputs and incomes will go down. Unemployment will be everywhere. Soon those boat-buyers who decided to save (to "not-buy" boats) will lose their jobs too. No work. No income. No money to spend. No money to save, either.

Now think about what you just saw happening. Savers saved more and forced investors to invest more. Then pretty soon the investors cut back, invested less, and forced savers to save less. This is a very important principle in macroeconomics. Suggestions: Read this section again and watch how it happens. You'll be needing a good understanding of this principle, later.

MACROEQUILIBRIUM: A SUMMARY OVERVIEW

The total income is just exactly big enough to buy the total output. So unless all the income is spent for output, some of the output will be left unbought in the market. The producers of the unbought output soon will cut back production. They will fire workers and buy less raw materials. The rate of production will slow down. Incomes will drop. The macro-level of the economy will go down.

If all the *output* is going to be bought, that means all the *income* must be spent to buy it. But we know that some of the people who receive income are *not* going to spend it all for output. Some of the income will be saved.

So will we have unemployment? Will a depression come? That depends on whether or not somebody else—the businesses—the investors—will buy up the goods left in the market by the savers.

Investment Spending Must "Clear the Market"

To keep the economy in macroequilibrium, investment spending must be just great enough to "clear the market." The investors must buy up all the goods left by the savers.

If the businesses try to buy *more* output than the savers are leaving, then there will be shortages in the market. These shortages will stimulate producers to produce more, up to the point where all of them are producing all they can. Output will expand until the economy reaches full capacity. We could say that the economy will "move up to a higher macroequilibrium."

But suppose the rate of savings is not offset by the rate of investment spending. Some output will be left in the market unbought. The unbought surpluses will result in reduced production and unemployment. The economy will "move down toward a lower macroequilibrium." Perhaps the lower macroequilibrium will be one of widespread unemployment and depression.

You can see that sometimes the issues of macroeconomics could give us some things to worry about. Surpluses, unemployment, and depression; or shortages and inflation—not very pleasant to contemplate! Sometimes these problems can get really serious.

Also consider this: whenever macroeconomic conditions start getting bad, there's a tendency for them to get even worse. Unfortunately, macroequilibrium in the economy is not a stable and dependable condition.

Macroequilibrium Is Unstable—Like a "Perched Boulder"

Macroequilibrium is always sort of shaky. The injections and withdrawals from the spending stream determine the macro-level of the economy. All these injections and withdrawals are sort of unstable.

Macroequilibrium is like a round boulder resting at the very top of a gently sloping mound, or hill. Anything which pushes the boulder off balance is likely to cause it to roll quite a distance before it once again comes to rest—that is, before it finds a new equilibrium. That's the way it is with total spending. So that's the way it is with macroequilibrium.

Do you know what has the most to do with macroequilibrium? It's what you've been reading about so far in this chapter. Macroequilibrium depends mostly on what's going on with *savings* and *investment*. The next section goes deeper into that.

DO INJECTIONS EQUAL WITHDRAWALS? OR NOT?

Something may seem illogical to you about this "spending, receiving, spending" discussion. There's a dilemma here that must be resolved. The next section explains it.

Does "Total Spending" Equal "Total Receipts"? Or Not?

You know that every time a dollar is spent, somebody is receiving it. So total spending must equal total receipts. Right? No doubt about it. If people are receiving dollars, somebody must be spending them. So the amounts being received must be exactly equal to the amounts being spent. That's obvious. But now, the dilemma.

You also know that if all the income received is respent—that is, if spending is as great as receipts (and no greater)—then the total spending flow will stay the same size—no larger, no smaller. The macroequilibrium of the economy will be maintained.

The only time the macroequilibrium (the rate of spending, employment, output, and income) can possibly change is when the rate of spending changes. And the only way the rate of spending can possibly change is for total injections (I + G + Ex) to be smaller or greater than total withdrawals (S + T + Im).

Do you see what all this means? It means that for us to have an increase in spending (and output and income), total *spending* must be *greater* than total *receipts*! And you know that spending and receipts are (must be!) equal. What a dilemma!

You can easily see that there's something wrong with the logic of this statement:

> Since every dollar *spent* must also be *received*, total spending (C + I + G + Ex) must always equal total receipts (which must always equal C + S + T + Im). But whenever the national income flow is *increasing*, spending must be *greater* than receipts (injections greater than withdrawals); whenever the national income flow is decreasing, spending must be *less* than receipts (injections less than withdrawals).

This is a dilemma all right! What's the answer? The key to the dilemma is this: the words "spending" and "receipts" don't always mean the same thing. It's a question of *which* spending equals *which* receipts. Let me explain.

Which "Spending" Equals Which "Receipts"?

As I am standing here receiving income, *somebody* must be spending it. No question about that! People only receive what other people spend. So spending equals receipts.

The amount of income I am receiving is equal to the amount of spending by somebody else for my output, or services. Of course. But then, as I am receiving the money, am I going to be *spending* the same amount I am *receiving*? Not necessarily! (And that's the point.)

The total income everybody is receiving right now obviously is equal to the total amount being spent (to generate income) right now. But the amount the people are receiving right now as income is not necessarily the amount that they are going to turn right around and spend!

We can't say that the total amount of money the people are *receiving* today is necessarily equal to the total amount of money they are going to be *spending tomorrow*! That's the key to the dilemma.

Since the amount being spent today is equal to the amount being received today, savings (and other withdrawals) today must be equal to investment (and other injections) today. Every injector-spender must have a withdrawer-receiver. Of course.

It's obvious that C = C, today. (It's the same thing!) It's obvious, too, that the total of the spending injections (I + G + Ex) must be exactly offset by total withdrawals (S + T + Im). At any moment, spending equals receipts, of course. Therefore, since C = C, total withdrawals must be equal to total injections. It *must* be so!

How is it ever possible for withdrawals and injections to become unequal? Only when we compare today's injections with tomorrow's withdrawals, or today's withdrawals with tomorrow's injections. That's the way injections and withdrawals can be (and often *are*) unequal. And that's the kind of inequality which explains increases and decreases in the size of the national income-spending stream.

Each Economic Unit Is Locked into the Macro-System

Let's go back to something we were talking about before, back in the very first chapter that

introduced you to macroeconomics. Remember how the economic system is a "total mechanism," and that all the "little wheels" are locked in and turning together? Yet each little wheel has its own engine. Each "little wheel," by itself, can try to speed up or slow down. But just the same, all the little wheels are locked in together so they *must* all be turning together!

Suppose most of them are *trying* to speed up. What then? The total mechanism will be speeding up. Right? Or if most of them are *trying* to slow down, then the whole mechanism will be slowing down. Do you begin to see what I'm getting at?

Let's forget about the government sector (G and T) and the foreign trade balance (Ex and Im) for a few minutes. Pretend that the only withdrawals are for savings (S) and the only injections are for investments (I).

Whenever investors are "trying to" spend less than the savers are trying to save, the economy will be slowing down. Whenever investors are "trying to" spend more than the savers are trying to save, the economy will be speeding up. Nevertheless, at any moment the *actual amount* of the investment injection is going to turn out to be exactly the same size as the *actual amount* of the savings withdrawal. This will be true whether the investors and the savers like it or not!

Increased Investment Can Force an Increase in Savings

If the investors are trying to invest *more* than the savers are trying to save, the increased investment buying will *force* people to cut back on their consumer buying—that is, to save more. At any moment, suppose the investors are buying more of the output. How is that possible unless the consumers are buying *less* of the output? And to say that people are *buying less consumer goods* is just another way of saying that people are *saving more*.

As it actually turns out, S = I. But look. *Be-*

cause the investors are *trying* to spend more for investment than the savers want to save, there are shortages. Producers expand output. The total spending flow begins to increase. There is more employment, more output, more income.

As long as the investors are trying to spend more than the savers want to save (want to "leave in the market for the investors") there will be some forced saving. The people can't spend as much for consumer goods as they want to, so they are *forced* to save. Shortages exist, and output, employment, and incomes expand. The pace of the economy quickens.

What If "Planned I" Exceeds "Planned S" at Full Capacity?

As long as the economy has "excess capacity" (unemployed workers and machines and things) output can continue to expand. But when all the people and factories and machines are busy producing all they can, then if the *desired rate* of spending by the investors ("planned I") continues to be greater than the desired rate of saving by the consumers ("planned S")—that is, if the investors are still trying to buy more than the savers want to leave in the markets for them to buy—then the shortages can't be overcome. Output cannot be increased because the economy is already producing all it can produce. So what happens?

The consumer-goods buyers really want what they want. They offer to pay more for consumer goods. They try to "bid things back" from the investor-buyers. But the investor-buyers want what they want, too. They offer to pay more for the investment goods they want, to "bid things back" from the consumer-buyers. If there aren't enough goods for everybody, then somebody is going to come up short. The ones who will pay the most will get the goods. What's happening? Inflation, of course.

Why are we having all these shortages? and inflation? Because the economy is producing as much as it can and still planned I is greater than planned S. The investors are trying to buy more goods than the savers want to leave in the markets. The investors are trying to buy more of the output than the consumers want to release. Total "spending pressure" is too great. Prices go up.

Increased Savings Can Force an Increase in Investment

Now you know what happens when "planned I" is greater than "planned S." You already knew about what happens when "planned S" is greater than "planned I." You saw it happen back on Tubaland Island when the eastsiders tried to save (planned S) for Christmas.

And you saw it when Mr. Hebert found himself with an unplanned investment in boats, and then shut down his boatyard. But here's a review of the principle, and then some real-world examples.

Suppose the consumers start leaving more things in the market than the investors want to buy. This means that some of the businesses can't sell all the output they have produced. So what happens to the unsold output? The businesses are forced to keep it. That's called "forced investment," or "unplanned investment."

An Example of Unplanned Investment

Suppose Chrysler Corporation discovers one day that its cars are piling up in the dealers' lots. The dealers are saying: "Don't send any more cars! We have already invested to the limit in our new car inventory! People just aren't spending enough for cars these days."

It seems that people are *saving* too much. So Chrysler Corporation finds itself with a lot of cars it can't sell. It has unwillingly *invested* a lot more than it had planned to in its "stock of new car inventories."

See how, if the consumers decide to save

more—that is, to leave more in the markets than businesses want to buy up—that *forces* businesses to increase their investments? Sure. And you know exactly what is going to happen next. The economy is going to slow down.

Chrysler Corporation isn't going to keep on producing more cars and pushing them into its new-car inventory. Of course not! It has invested more in its new-car inventory than it had planned to already. So it cuts back production.

See what's happening? Output and employment and incomes are getting smaller. Total spending is going down. Why? Because people are trying to save more than businesses want to invest; "planned S" is greater than "planned I."

All this time, while Chrysler Corporation is having its problems, what's going on at GM? and Ford? and American Motors? The same thing: unplanned investment in new car inventories. What's happening at RCA and Magnavox and GE and Westinghouse and Whirlpool and Maytag? The same thing. Unplanned investments in inventories of new TVs and refrigerators and stoves and washing machines and things.

It's obvious what's going to happen. All these producers are going to cut back production. The economy (total spending and production and output and employment and income) will slow down.

The Economy Begins to Adjust Immediately

The moment the consumers begin to save more, that's the moment the unplanned inventory investments begin. It doesn't take long after that for the companies to start cutting back their production. The economy slows down.

The response is just as fast when the opposite occurs—when the investors are trying to spend more than the savers want to save—when "planned I" is greater than "planned S." As soon as shortages begin to show up in the mar-

kets (that is, as soon as the businesses see their new-product inventories being completely sold out) they quickly order more. The producers begin to produce more.

The economy can start speeding up very quickly whenever "planned I" is greater than "planned S." It can start slowing down very quickly whenever "planned S" is greater than "planned I."

Planned Savings and Planned Investment: An Overview

At any moment, the amount the savers are *trying* to (want to) pull out of the spending stream may be *greater* or *less* than the amount the investors are trying to (want to) pour back in. So "planned S" may be *greater* or *less* than "planned I."

If "planned S" (withdrawal) is greater than "planned I" (injections), surplus products will be left in the market. Businesses will cut back. Total spending will get smaller. The economy will slow down.

But if "planned I" (injections) is greater than "planned S" (withdrawals), total spending will get larger. There will be shortages of things. The economy will speed up. If the economy is already working at "full capacity," there will be inflation.

Does "S" always equal "I"? Sure. It always comes out that way. But if by "S" you mean "the amount people are *trying* to (want to) save" and if by "I" you mean "the amount businesses are *trying* to (want to) invest," then S doesn't equal I unless the economy is in macroequilibrium.

Whenever "planned I" is *greater* than

"planned S," the spending flow will be increasing and the economy will be speeding up. Whenever "planned I" is *less* than "planned S," the spending flow will be decreasing and the economy will be slowing down. If anybody ever asks you if savings are equal to investment, tell them: "Yes. Or maybe no. It all depends on what you mean by 'savings,' and 'investment'."

Planned Withdrawals and Planned Injections: An Overview

Now, just to be sure it's all tied together, let's bring all three kinds of "withdrawals" and "injections" back into the picture. You can be sure that at any moment the total flow of injections (I + G + Ex) into the income stream is exactly equal to the total flow of withdrawals (S + T + Im) out of the income stream. You can be *perfectly sure* of that. Could someone be spending money and no one receiving it? Or someone receiving money and no one spending it? Ridiculous!

However, as people, businesses, governments, and foreigners are *receiving* their money, they are *planning* the amounts they are going to save and to spend. In this *planning process* there's no assurance that the planned injections (I + G + Ex) will be equal to the planned withdrawals (S + T + Im).

If the planned injections are greater than the planned withdrawals, the size of the total spending flow will be increasing. The economy will be speeding up. But if the planned injections are less than the planned withdrawals, the size of the total spending flow will be decreasing. The economy will be slowing down.

Macroequilibrium Depends on What the Spenders Are Trying to Do

It is the *equality* or *inequality* between what the "injectors" (I, G, and Ex) and the "withdrawers" (S, T, and Im) are *trying* to do, that

determines whether the economy will be speeding up or slowing down. *Macroequilibrium requires that injection plans be exactly large enough to offset the withdrawal plans.* Really, that's all there is to it. Now, how would you like to see it on a graph?

THE KEYNESIAN NATIONAL SPENDING AND INCOME GRAPH

As you might have guessed, economists have a graph to show the relationship between spending and income. We call this a "Keynesian" (KAYn-zian) graph after John Maynard Keynes.

The Keynesian national spending and income graph shows total spending on the vertical axis (the y axis) and the total income on the horizontal axis (the x axis). Think about that: spending on one axis; income on the other. What kind of a curve will that make on the graph? As spending goes up, what happens to income? As income goes up, what happens to spending? Both go up together? Sure!

The curve is going to be positive (sloping upward) and linear (a straight line). And more than that. If the vertical (y) axis and the horizontal (x) axis are marked off on the same scale, the straight line will be rising at a 45-degree angle, exactly. You can see why, can't you? (When you increase by one unit on the spending (y) axis you must increase one unit on the income (x) axis.)

For example, suppose businesses start spending more. That's an increase in investment spending. Increased investment spending (*ceteris paribus*, of course!) means increased *total spending*. Increased *total spending* means increased *total income*. Here's the point: *Anything which causes total spending to increase also causes total income to increase.* That's exactly what the graph shows.

Now, spend awhile studying and drawing the graph on the next page. Then go on and read the chapter summary.

Fig. 11-1   The Keynesian National Spending and Income Graph

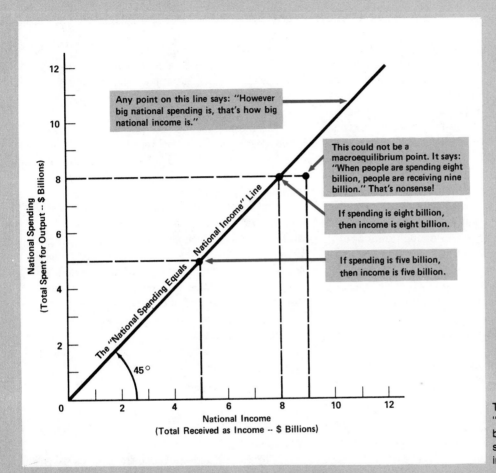

Any point on this line says: "However big national spending is, that's how big national income is."

This could not be a macroequilibrium point. It says: "When people are spending eight billion, people are receiving nine billion." That's nonsense!

If spending is eight billion, then income is eight billion.

If spending is five billion, then income is five billion.

The "National Spending Equals National Income" Line

45°

National Spending
(Total Spent for Output -- $ Billions)

National Income
(Total Received as Income -- $ Billions)

This graph shows the "if. . .then" relationship between national spending and national income.

This graph shows that the total amount being spent for output always equals the total amount being received as income. Of course! It's the same flow. But how large will the national spending (and national income) be? From this graph you can't tell.

If spenders (C, I, G, and Ex) are *trying* to spend more, then spending and income will be moving up along the line. If people are *trying* to withdraw more, then spending and income will be moving down along the line.

Soon we will draw in more curves so that you can see where the macroequilibrium is. But you may be sure that it will always be shown by a point somewhere along the "national spending equals national income" line. Obviously!

SUMMARY AND SYNTHESIS

The **circular flow of the economy** will speed up or slow down in response to changes in total spending. For macroequilibrium to be maintained and the circular flow to continue at the same speed, **withdrawals** from the spending stream **must be offset by injections** into the spending stream.

An increase in the **savings withdrawal** can result in surplus products being left unsold in the market. When this happens, prices of the surplus products will tend to fall. But if the producers of the unsold products have enough **monopoly power,** they will be likely to cut back their production and hold up their prices. This was the case in the Tubaland Island example used in this chapter. Also, it's usually the case with manufactured products in the real world.

Say's Law says that supply creates its own demand—that as people supply more goods to the market they demand more from the market. Therefore there can never be a "general glut" of surplus products in the market. But the **secondary** (future) **functions** of money permit suppliers to place their goods in the market and take their money and go home. Sellers can supply things without demanding things.

The **paradox of thrift** refers to a situation where increased savings result in surplus products in the market and cause a slowdown in economic activity and lower incomes and more unemployment. Incomes go down so people are forced to stop saving—maybe even spend up their past savings!

Investment spending can offset **savings** and translate savings into **growth,** thus bypassing the "paradox of thrift." When there is an increase in saving and investment, fewer consumer goods and more capital goods are produced. This in-creases the society's rate of **economic growth.** For any level of savings in the economy, too much investment spending would be inflationary; too lit-tle would lead to recession.

Macroequilibrium is not very stable because it depends so much on the equality between what the savers would like to withdraw and what the investors would like to inject into the income stream.

The most **critical "equality"** for maintaining the size of the circular flow is this equality **be-tween planned investment** and **planned savings.** If busiesses are planning (trying) to spend more than the savers are planning (trying) to save, then the economy will be speeding up. But if busi-nesses are planning to spend less than the savers are planning to save, then the economy will be moving into recession.

Whenever planned investment drops below savings, the immediate effect is likely to be **un-planned investment**—that is, producers have their money tied up in output which they cannot sell. The immediate response is to cut back pro-duction. Unemployment increases. The circular flow slows down.

It is the equality or inequality between what all of the "injectors" (I, G, Ex) and the "with-drawers" (S, T, Im) are trying to do that deter-mines whether the economy will be speeding up or slowing down. Macroequilibrium requires that the sum of all of the injection plans and the with-drawal plans be exactly equal.

The **Keynesian national spending and in-come graph** illustrates the equality between spending and income in the economy. It shows that as national spending increases, national in-come increases—and by exactly the same amount.

REVIEW EXERCISES

MAJOR CONCEPTS, PRINCIPLES, TERMS (Explain each carefully.)

the concept of macroequilibrium
how investment spending offsets saving
how increased investment can force increased saving
how increased saving can force increased investment

OTHER CONCEPTS AND TERMS (Explain each briefly.)

John Maynard Keynes	unplanned investment
full capacity	unplanned saving
planned investment	Keynesian (KAYnsian)
planned savings	Say's Law
planned injections	paradox of thrift
planned withdrawals	money as a claim check

CURVES AND GRAPHS (Draw, label, and explain each.)

The Keynesian National Spending and Income Graph

QUESTIONS (Write out answers, or jot down key points.)

1. What does it mean to say that macroequilibrium is sort of unstable, like a "perched boulder"?
2. If people could really understand and predict the *planned injections into* and the *planned withdrawals from* the spending-income stream, then they would be able to tell with certainty whether the economy was going to speed up or slow down. Explain.
3. Total spending must equal total receipts because every dollar spent must have a receiver. But total receipts are not necessarily equal to total spending. The only time national spending and income can change is when the two are *not* equal. Can you explain this apparently illogical statement?
4. Suppose "consumer spending" at your macrame belt concession stand at Seashore State Park dropped off, and you got caught with a lot of money tied up in belt-making materials and in finished belts you couldn't sell. Is that "unplanned investment"? Do you think you would slow down your future investment spending? maybe all the way to zero? If this sort of thing was happening all over the economy, what do you suppose the result would be? Explain.

12 National Income Analysis III: Keynesian and Monetary Theories

Chapter Objectives

- The last chapter introduced you to the **Keynesian national spending and income graph.** When you finish this chapter you will be able to use that graph to find the **macroequilibrium of the economy.**

- You will know much more about **what determines the size of the total spending flow.**

- You will be able to explain the **average propensity to consume (APC)** and the **marginal propensity to consume (MPC)** and you will be able to illustrate these important concepts using the **consumption function curve,** and to explain how the MPC generates an **income multiplying effect.**

- You will learn more about the **monetary approach** to macroeconomics—about the importance of the **quantity of money** and the **velocity at which it circulates** in influencing **total spending** and the **price level.**

- When you finish studying this chapter you will be able to write the **equation of exchange (MV = PQ)** and to explain how it is used in macroeconomic analysis. Also, you will know something about the controversy between the **"monetarists"** and the **"Keynesians."**

THE PROPENSITY TO CONSUME

In Keynesian national income analysis, what determines the total size of the national income? Total spending, of course! And what's the basic flow? You already know. It's "spending for consumer goods" (C).

What determines the rate of total consumer spending (C) in the nation? It's influenced by several things. One of the things is: "How big is the national income?"

You know that if people are receiving high incomes they are likely to be spending more for consumer goods—more than if their incomes were low. That's just common sense. But also there are statistics to prove it.

We know that as a person's income gets higher, that person is likely to save a larger share—a larger percentage of it. People with very low incomes usually don't save anything.

How about you? If you are like most college students you're spending more than you're receiving in income. Maybe you worked awhile and saved some money and now you are living off your savings. Or maybe your parents are helping you out. Or maybe you borrowed. But one way or another, almost all college students are consuming more than they are receiving as earned income.

If the income of the whole nation was very low, most people probably would be trying to spend more for consumer goods than they were receiving as income. Suppose your income (disposable personal income) was only $5 a week. Would you spend it all for consumer goods? and save nothing? I'll bet so. I'll bet you'd be trying to borrow, too, so you could spend more. Most people would.

People With High Incomes Usually Save More

Suppose your income was $1,000 a week. Most people would save some of it. But pretend that somehow you managed to spend it all for consumption. No savings.

Then suppose your income suddenly *doubled*, to $2,000 a week. What then? Would you double your rate of consumer spending? I doubt it. But suppose you did. Then suppose your income doubled again. Do you suppose your spending for consumer goods would double *again*? And suppose it happened again? and again?

Do you get the point? The idea is that the higher a person's income, the more likely that he or she will save some. Usually, the larger a person's income the larger proportion (percentage) that person will save.

The Propensity to Consume Is an "If . . . Then" Concept

Economists call this idea the **propensity to consume**. "Propensity to consume" answers the question "what would you do if. . .?" "If your income was such and such, then what fraction of it would you be spending for consumer goods?"

Keynes suggested that if the national income was low, then the "propensity to consume" (the proportion or fraction of it that people would spend for consumer goods) would be high. If the

national income was high, then the propensity to consume would not be so high.

The propensity to consume tells us what fraction *would be* spent for consumer goods at all the *various levels* of national income that *might* (sometime) exist. For each level of national income you might choose, there would be an **average propensity to consume**—that is, some fraction (percentage) of the total income which would be spent for consumer goods.

For example, if national income was $10 billion and total consumer spending was $8 billion, that would mean that out of every ten dollars being received as income, eight dollars were being spent for consumer goods. Then the average propensity to consume (APC) would be 8/10ths (or 4/5ths). The **average propensity to save** (APS) would be 2/10ths (or 1/5th). Out of every five dollars of income being received, one dollar would be saved—that is, not spent for consumer goods.

Or suppose the national income was $8 billion and consumer spending was $7 billion. Then the APC would be 7/8ths. The APS would be 1/8th.

THE APC AND THE SPENDING FLOW

What does all this have to do with total spending and total output and macroequilibrium and all that? Quite a lot! Just think. Consumer spending is the basic flow in the income stream. The average propensity to consume (APC) tells us, for any level of national income, just how big that *basic flow* would be!

Suppose, at a national income (NI) of $10 billion, consumer spending would be $8 billion (APC would be 8/10ths). Then the only way the NI could *ever* get up to $10 billion would be for $2 billion of spending to come from someplace to *add* to the "basic consumer spending flow" of $8 billion. See how important the APC is?

Suppose I told you that if NI was $5 billion, then APC would be 5/5ths, or "100 percent."

APC tells what share of your **total income** you'll spend for Consumption.

mPC tells what Share of some **extra income** you'll spend for **C!**

That means that if NI was $5 billion, consumer spending would be $5 billion. Consumer spending would support the entire national output and national income, by itself!

With APC of 100%, the average propensity to save (APS) would be zero. There would be no "savings withdrawals." So if the APC is 100 percent when the national income is $5 billion, then NI can *never* drop below $5 billion! How about that? (That is, it can't unless taxes or a negative foreign trade balance are draining off some of the basic consumer spending flow.)

At any level of national income the APC tells how much of the income received will be *automatically* returned to the total spending flow (as consumer spending). So it tells you (implicitly) how much "spending injection" (investment spending or government spending or positive foreign trade balance) would be required to bring national spending (and income) up to any level *above* the size of the basic consumer spending flow!

These relationships can be shown very clearly on the Keynesian national spending and income graph—the one you learned in the last chapter. We'll get into that in just a minute. But first we need to talk briefly about one other concept: the **marginal propensity to consume**.

THE MARGINAL PROPENSITY TO CONSUME

What happens when you get an *increase* in income? What proportion (fraction) of the in-

crease will you spend to buy consumer goods? Suppose you're almost starving. You may spend it all! Suppose you're very wealthy. You may save it all.

The "marginal propensity to consume" (MPC) is concerned with the question of how much consumer spending (C) would go up if national income (NI) went up. *The MPC tells you what fraction of an increase in income, would be spent for consumer goods.*

Suppose NI increases by $4 billion and C increases by $3 billion. Then MPC would be 3/4ths. So you know implicitly that the **marginal propensity to save** (MPS) would be 1/4th. Right? If 3/4ths of the increase is spent for consumer goods then the other 1/4th *must* be saved.

Now, to get some practice with this new idea, look at the marginal propensity to consume (MPC) from the point of view of an individual. You. Suppose you were receiving an income of $1,000 a week. Not bad!

And suppose your average propensity to consume (APC) was 8/10ths. That means you would be spending $800 out of your $1,000 income for consumer goods, and saving $200. Then suppose your income increases by $100, to $1,100 a week. How much of the *extra* $100 will you spend for consumer goods? Maybe none of it. Maybe $800 a week is all you want to spend for consumer goods. See how MPC is likely to be low if your income is high?

But let's guess that you would spend an extra $50 a week for consumer goods. That means you're spending half of the extra $100 and saving the other half. So your marginal propensity to consume (MPC) is 1/2 and your marginal propensity to save (MPS) is 1/2.

Suppose income increases. Will consumer spending increase? Sure. How much? It depends on the MPC—on *the slope of the consumption function.*

The consumption function can be shown on the Keynesian national spending and income graph. There are four of these graphs coming up. The graphs show exactly the same things you've been reading about. Take time to learn each one well.

Fig. 12-1   The Consumption Function: How Large We Expect the Basic Flow of Consumer Spending to Be at Different (Assumed) Levels of National Income

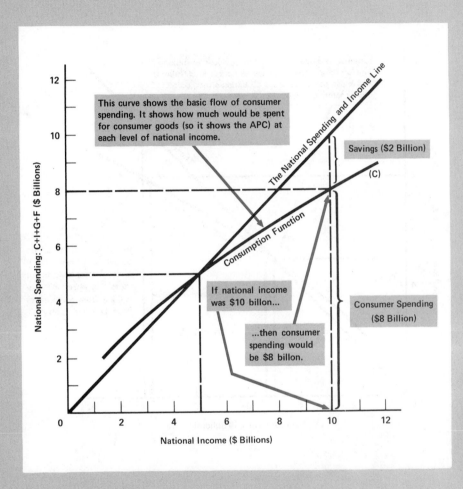

The "consumption function" line shows what fraction of the income will be spent for consumer goods.

The basic flow of consumer spending would be larger at the higher levels of national income. But also, notice how much more the people would *save* if the national income was high!

The higher the national income, the smaller the proportion (fraction) that would be spent for consumer goods.

Just look how high the savings withdrawals would be if the national income was $12 billion! A lot of spending injections would be required to keep national income up as high as $12 billion!

Fig. 12-2   The Consumption Function: The Average Propensity to Consume (APC) Would Be Smaller at Higher Levels of National Income

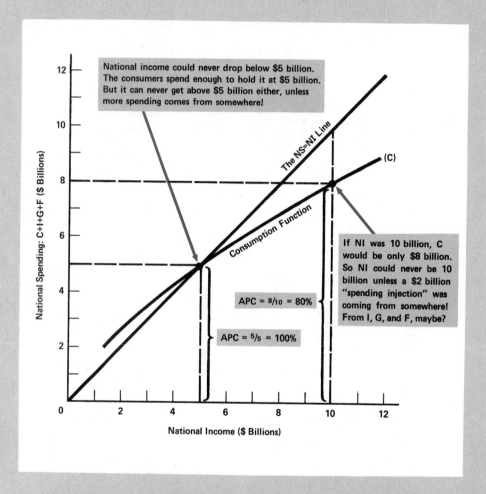

National income could never drop below $5 billion. The consumers spend enough to hold it at $5 billion. But it can never get above $5 billion either, unless more spending comes from somewhere!

The NS=NI Line

(C)

Consumption Function

APC = $^8/_{10}$ = 80%

APC = $^5/_5$ = 100%

If NI was 10 billion, C would be only $8 billion. So NI could never be 10 billion unless a $2 billion "spending injection" was coming from somewhere! From I, G, and F, maybe?

National Spending: C+I+G+F ($ Billions)

National Income ($ Billions)

The higher the national income, the greater the *amount*, but the smaller the *fraction* spent on consumer goods.

You can see that as long as the "consumption function" line stays where it is, the only way national income can ever get above $5 billion is for some *other* source of spending to be added to the income stream.

If the consumers are spending only $5 billion and if they are the only ones spending, then total spending will be $5 billion. And that's all. So national income will be $5 billion. And that's all!

But suppose investment spending and government spending and a positive foreign trade balance are all injecting spending into the income stream. Then national income will be a lot bigger than $5 billion! Of course.

Fig. 12-3   The Consumption Function and the Savings Function: Two Different Ways of Looking at the Same Thing

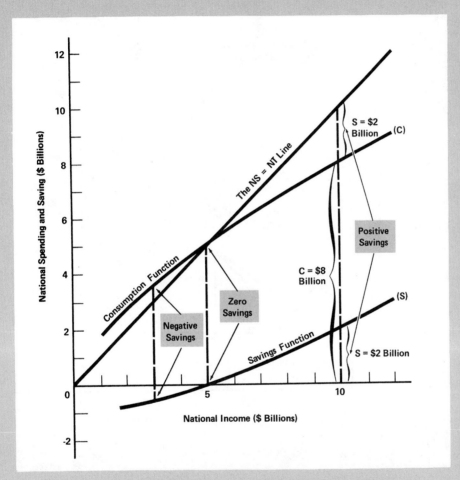

As income gets higher, the "savings gap" gets larger.

The relationship between the "savings function" (S) and the "consumption function" (C) is obvious. The two together must always add up to "100 percent" of national income. For example, if C = 80% (8/10ths), then S = 20% (2/10ths). If C = 100% (10/10ths), then S = 0.

What about "negative savings"? If S = −10% (people are borrowing, and spending more than they are earning) then C must equal 110% of national income—which means: "Total *consumer* spending is 10% bigger than total spending"—which you know has got to be nonsense!

Some people can spend more than their total incomes, but *all* people can't. If they tried, NI would be forced up by the amount of the increased spending. Of course!

**Fig. 12-4   The Marginal Propensity to Consume and the
Average Propensity to Consume**

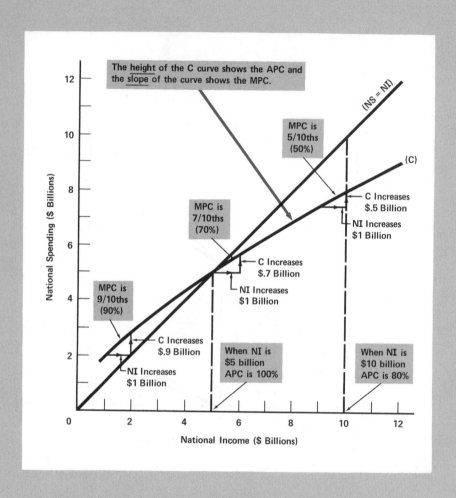

A prosperous nation
requires a big
spending injection to
maintain its high level
of national income.

For any level of national income, the *marginal* propensity to consume is not as high as the *average* propensity to consume. So no matter what the existing consumption rate (APC) might be, an *increase* in NI is going to bring a lower consumption rate (a higher savings rate) than before.

Therefore: the higher the national income, the higher the *savings* rate; and therefore, the higher will be the *investment* rate required to sustain the high level of national income.

So therefore a very prosperous nation must depend on investment spending (reinjections to offset the savings withdrawals) to sustain its prosperity.

The graphs you've just been studying are all hypothetical, of course. They show the macroeconomic picture of a small hypothetical country—one with a national income of only around $10 billion. But these graphs could be drawn (not precisely, but with some degree of accuracy) for a nation like the United States.

You can look at "national income and product" figures for several years and you can get some idea of what the consumption function and the savings function have looked like in the past. But the real purpose of these graphs is not to plot curves and show an accurate dependable macroeconomic picture of the economy. Things change too fast for that anyway.

The purpose of the graphs is to illustrate some principles which *are* dependable: as incomes increase, consumer spending increases, but savings increase faster, and it requires higher rates of investment to support higher levels of national spending.

The MPC Causes a Spending Increase to Multiply

The graphs also show that an increase in spending (in income) has a "multiplier effect" on national income. If your marginal propensity to consume is high, then when you receive an increase in income you will spend a lot of the increase to buy consumer goods. That way you will pour most of your new income right back into the basic spending flow. So the basic spending-income flow expands.

If everyone has a high MPC, any increase in people's incomes will have a high **multiplying effect**. Any initial increase will pour a lot of spending into the basic consumer spending flow and will push up total spending more and more.

Suppose that when you receive an increase in income, you decide to save most of it. That means your marginal propensity to consume is low. You don't put much of it back into the basic spending flow. Can you see the difference it could make if everyone had a high MPC? or a low MPC? *The higher your income the higher your marginal propensity to save (MPS) and the lower your marginal propensity to consume (MPC) is likely to be.*

You probably didn't see the multiplier effect as you were studying the previous graphs. So let me first give you a numerical example of how it works; then I'll show it to you on a graph. In the numerical example I'll use exactly the same figures as shown on the four graphs you just studied. It might be helpful for you to keep looking back at the graphs, or to draw one for yourself to keep looking at as you read.

The "Full Employment" Level of National Income

Suppose this little make-believe nation we're talking about would like to have a national income of $10 billion. Let's say that a $10 billion NI would bring full employment, an acceptable rate of economic growth and no problems of shortages or inflation. But if NI was $10 billion, the average propensity to consume (APC) would be only 8/10ths ($8 billion). Remember?

If NI was $10 billion, the people who received the $10 billion would only be spending $8 billion of it for consumer goods. If the consumers are the only ones doing any spending, the national income can't be $10 billion. That's obvious. Unless $2 billion of spending is coming from somewhere else—from investment spending or government spending or from a positive foreign trade balance—NI can *never* get up to $10 billion.

Now, for the next step, there are two questions which need to be answered:

Question one: In this little make-believe nation if the only people doing any spending were the consumers then the national income would be just $5 billion. Right? That would continue to be the macroequilibrium level of NI until some new spending injections were introduced from somewhere—or until something happened to cause the consumption function (the APC) to change. Nothing to worry about yet. So, on to the next question.

Question two: Suppose our little nation was dragging along with a national income of only $5 billion, and then the businesses decided to start spending at the rate of $2 billion a year. That would push national spending and national income up to $7 billion. Right? No. Wrong. It would push national spending and income up to *more than* $7 billion because of the multiplier effect. Let me explain.

THE INCOME MULTIPLIER AND MACROEQUILIBRIUM

Remember how much investment spending it would take to reach the desired level of NI ($10 billion)? Look at Figure 12-3. Only $2 billion, right? But $5 billion (the NI with zero investment injection) plus $2 billion (the investment injection) only adds up to a total spending flow of $7 billion. Where does the other $3 billion of spending come from?

[$5 billion (C) + $2 billion (I) + $3 billion (?)
= $10 billion (NI)]

I think you know the answer already. The extra $3 billion comes from *more consumer spending*. It comes from the *marginal propensity to consume* (MPC). Remember? There is one level on NI (and only one level) at which consumers would spend exactly $5 billion. What level of NI? NI = $5 billion. Look at the graphs again and you'll see.

At any level of NI *higher* than $5 billion, consumer spending will be *higher* than $5 billion. As incomes rise, people spend more for consumer goods. Of course! So it's nonsense to talk of NI = $7 billion and consumer spending of only

$5 billion. That just couldn't be.

If the NI was $7 billion, the people would *not* be spending *all* of their incomes on consumer goods (as they would be if the NI was $5 billion). But they certainly would be spending more than $5 billion! Let's say they would be spending $6.5 billion and saving $.5 billion. (That's what it looks like on the graphs.) So can we say that the new level of national spending and income will be:

[$6.5 billion (C) + $2 billion (I)
= $8.5 billion (NI)]?

No, we can't say that, either. Why not? Because if NI was up to $8.5 billion, spending for consumer goods would be up to *more* than $6.5 billion. See how NI and C seem to be working back and forth on each other, pushing each other up higher and higher? If NI was $8.5 billion, C would be up to about $7.4 billion. The graphs show that. So can we say that the new equilibrium level of national spending and income will be:

[$7.4 billion (C) + $2 billion (I)
= $9.4 billion (NI)]?

By now you already know the answer. No, we can't say this either. It just can't be true! If NI was $9.4 billion then C would not be $7.4 billion any more. Therefore $9.4 billion can't be the new level of national spending and national income!

When the rate of investment spending is $2 billion a year, what will be—what *must* be—the macroequilibrium level of national spending and national income? It *must* be that level which will induce the people to want to *save* $2 billion.

With *investment spending* of $2 billion, the national income automatically will move up to the level where the *savings withdrawals* become $2 billion. The national income must expand to that rate of flow at which the savings withdrawals are equal to the investment injections. Remember? Of course! So here it is:

[$8 billion (C) + $2 billion (I)
= $10 billion (NI)]

How do we know that this is the equilibrium level? Because we know (that is, we assumed in the beginning) that APC would be 8/10ths ($8 billion) when NI was $10 billion.

The Macroequilibrium Level of National Income

It's all as simple as 1, 2, 3.

1. If we know what the average propensity to consume would be at each "might exist" level of national income, and

2. if we know how much "injection spending" (investment) there is going to be, then

3. we can see right off what the macroequilibrium level of national income must be—where withdrawals (planned savings) are equal to injections (planned investments).

Isn't that neat? You can see it on the Keynesian national spending and income graph, too.

In the Keynesian graphs you have already studied, the only equilibrium level of national spending and income you can see is NI = $5 billion. If consumer spending is the *only* kind of spending in this nation, then $5 billion is just where NI is going to be. That's where it *must* be! If the consumers are the only ones spending and if $5 billion is all they're spending, then $5 billion is all there is.

We know that the consumers really aren't the only ones spending. So we know that the macroequilibrium for our little nation will come out higher than $5 billion. But how much higher? That depends on the size of the *injections*. Let's introduce some investment spending and see what happens to national income.

First there's a table and then two graphs all

showing exactly the same picture you've been reading about. When you finish studying these I think you will really understand about the multiplier effect—that is, about the income multiplier. Now would be a good time for you to study Figures 12-5, -6, and -7.

Fig. 12-5   The Income Multiplier (or Investment Multiplier)

The NI will keep increasing until S = I (planned S = planned I, that is!)

If NI level is		Then basic consumer spending will be		If investors inject		Then NI will be
$5	→	$5	→	0	→	$5
5	→	5	→	$2	→	7
7	→	6.5	→	2	→	8.5
8.5	→	7.4	→	2	→	9.4
9.4	→	7.7	→	2	→	9.7
9.7	→	7.9	→	2	→	9.9
9.9	→	7.95	→	2	→	9.95
9.95	→	etc., etc., etc. . . .				

until the new level of macroequilibrium is reached, where:

$10	→	$8	→	$2	→	$10

Once we assume a "consumption function," then the size of the **basic consumer spending flow** is determined by the size of the national income. An investment injection into the income stream increases NI, so it causes C to increase. But the increased C pushes NI up even more.

As C increases, NI increases. And each NI increase causes a further increase in C. For how long? Until a new macroequilibrium is reached. Until NI increases to where the consumers are withdrawing as much in savings as the investors are injecting as investment spending.

Fig. 12-6   The Effect of an Injection of Investment Spending (the Multiplier Effect)

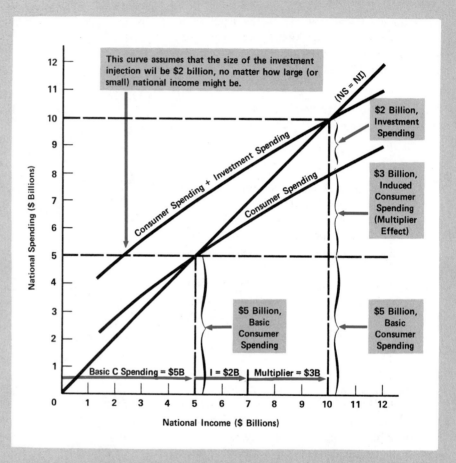

Investment spending has a "multiplier effect" on national income.

Investment spending of $2 billion brings an increase in national spending and income of $5 billion. Why? Because of the income multiplier!

National spending and income are increased by 2½ times the amount of the investment spending. How? By causing (inducing) consumer spending to increase by $3 billion.

This multiple effect of an increase in investment spending (caused by the induced consumer spending) is called "the multiplier." In this case the multiplier is 2.5. [$2 billion (I), times 2.5 (the multiplier) equals $5 billion. This $5 billion is the *total* increase in spending, resulting from the initial increase of only $2 billion. The initial increase, times the multiplier, always gives the total increase in spending and income.]

Can you see that the size of the multiplier depends on the size of the marginal propensity to consume (MPC)? The MPC is "the respending effect" of an increase in income. The more respent, the steeper would be the "consumption function" line in the graph, and the higher would be the multiplier.

Fig. 12-7   More Investment Spending Induces More Savings; Macroequilibrium Is Where S = I

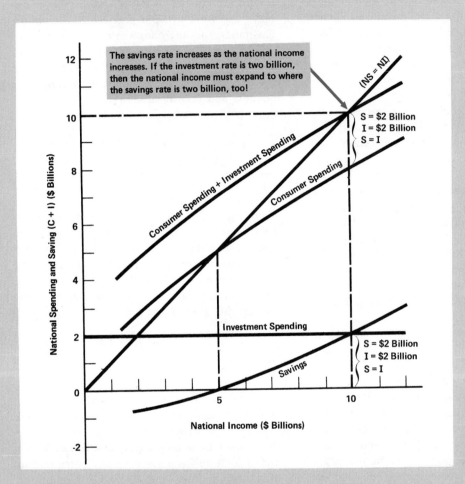

The savings rate increases as the national income increases. If the investment rate is two billion, then the national income must expand to where the savings rate is two billion, too!

(NS = NI)

Consumer Spending + Investment Spending

Consumer Spending

S = $2 Billion
I = $2 Billion
S = I

Investment Spending

Savings

S = $2 Billion
I = $2 Billion
S = I

National Spending and Saving (C + I) ($ Billions)

National Income ($ Billions)

More investment spending causes national income to increase, which causes savings to increase.

National income must continue to increase until the size of the flow of savings withdrawals is great enough to equal and exactly offset the flow of investment injections.

When investment spending is zero then the savings rate also must be zero. That means APC must be 100%. All income received is spent for consumer goods. The economy is in macroequilibrium at a very low level of employment, output, and income (NI = $5 billion).

With the injection of $2 billion of investment spending, NI must rise—not just by $2 billion, but by enough to induce the income receivers to withdraw from the consumer spending flow (that is, to save) $2 billion, to offset the investment injection. National income must rise to that level at which the income receivers will be saving $2 billion—that is, to where NI = $10 billion.

Other Injections and Withdrawals

We've been talking about investment injections as though the investors were the only ones who ever inject anything into the income stream. What about the other kinds of injections? How would they influence the macroequilibrium? And how would it look on the graph? Just exactly like the investment injection looks, in Figures 12-6 and 12-7.

Government spending (G), or a positive foreign trade balance (F) would shift the curve upward, just as the "investment injection" did. Then NI would expand to a new level of macroequilibrium.

What about withdrawals? The savings withdrawal is already shown in the graph. But how would taxes or a negative foreign trade balance influence the picture? Just as you would guess.

These withdrawals would pull down the basic consumer spending flow. The "consumption function" curve would shift downward. The withdrawals would cause the macroequilibrium level of NI to be smaller.

What about the "consumption function" curve itself? Is that a stable, dependable thing that just stays where it is until some injections or withdrawals push it up, or pull it down? Not really. But it doesn't usually jump around much.

During times of high expectations and optimism we would expect the consumption function curve to shift upward. There would be more consumer spending at any level of NI you might choose. But during gloomy times, or when everyone is deep in debt and trying to get things paid off, we would expect the average propensity to consume (APC) to be smaller. The curve would shift downward.

The Keynesian Graph Provides a Useful Approach

It would be good, just for practice, if you would stop for a few minutes now and draw a few of the Keynesian graphs and move the consumption function curve around. If you do, you will notice that anytime you move it there will be a multiplier effect.

By now you're getting a real feel for this Keynesian national spending and income graph, right? See what a helpful framework it gives for illustrating and analyzing the effects of all these different kinds of withdrawals and injections? As soon as you're sure you have it down pat, move on into the next section and learn about the quantity and velocity of money.

A MONETARY APPROACH TO MACROECONOMICS

All this time we have been looking at total spending as the sum of its parts. We have defined four basic parts, or sectors, or spending sources: consumers (C), businesses (I), government (G), and foreigners (F). Now we are going to do something entirely different. We are going to look at total spending as "a big mass of dollars flowing around and around."

The Spending Flow Is a Mass of Moving Dollars

Total spending can be looked at as "the total amount of money in existence in the nation" and "the speed at which it is flowing." You can see that if the total money supply is a billion dollars and if each dollar is spent to buy some output once each month, then the total size of the spending flow will be one billion dollars each month. Right? Or $12 billion a year. Nothing very mysterious about that.

Economists use the symbol "M" to mean "the supply of money in existence" (the money stock), and the symbol "V" to mean "the velocity of circulation of money" (the number of times each dollar is being spent). It is obvious that the quantity of money in existence (M) times the velocity at which "the average dollar" is being spent (V) equals total spending. So we can say that M times V (or just "MV") equals total spending.

If each dollar is turning over one time each year, then total spending during the year is equal to the size of the money supply. The **velocity of circulation** is one. If each dollar is spent three times during the year, then the velocity is three and the total spending flow is three times as large as the total money supply. Simple. Right?

In this discussion we are not going to count all "spending velocity." We are only going to count the velocity of spending for *new* output— that is, only the "output velocity" or "income velocity" will be counted. Economists frequently use the "MV" approach and consider *all* transactions in figuring "velocity of circulation." But for our purposes it's best to count only the **"output and income"** velocity because we're looking at national output and income.

Why should anyone ever look at the total spending flow as a big mass of dollars flowing around? What's the purpose? It's just that when we look at it this way we can see things that otherwise we couldn't see. The "MV" breakdown lets us concentrate on the *size* of the money supply (the money stock). It lets us see how the **quantity of money** (and changes in the quantity of money) might influence the rate of spending.

What Determines the Income Velocity of Money?

What determines V? What influences the number of times each dollar will be spent during a week, month, or year? Several things. Some of the things are built into the system. If people get paid once a week, then each dollar will turn over faster than if people get paid once a month. If everyone in the economy was on a weekly pay period, the money stock would support a higher rate of total spending than if everyone was on a monthly pay period. Each dollar would be changing hands more often, "doing more work"—buying more things.

If your uncle earns $100 a week but only gets paid every four weeks, then it takes four-

hundred dollars of "money stock" to pay him for his four weeks' work. But if he earns the same wage and is paid at the end of *each* week, then only $100 of money stock is needed to pay him. When he gets paid $100 at the end of the first week, he spends it. Then he could get paid the same $100 at the end of the second week, then spend it, then get it back again, spend it again, and so on.

Of course he wouldn't get back the *same* dollars, week after week. But I think you get the idea. It's simply that the more frequently people get paid, the more work each dollar will do.

Velocity Is Fairly Stable

At any moment the velocity of circulation is fairly stable. Like the consumption function, it has a tendency to stay where it is. But it can move up or down in response to people's changing conditions, moods, or expectations. Still, it isn't unrealistic to think of V as being fairly constant and stable.

The Money Stock Is Closely Related to Total Spending

Since the velocity of circulation of money is fairly stable, it's obvious that *an increase in the size of the total spending-income flow requires an increase in the size of the money supply! Also, if spending and income are slowing down, the money supply must be contracting.* That's just what happens, too! How? Automatically. Through the banking system. Remember?

In order for the economy to speed up, bank loans (and therefore, the money supply) must expand. But as the economy slows down, bank loans are repaid and the money supply contracts. See how important the money supply can be? And see how it can be useful to look at the total spending flow as "a mass of moving money"?

Since velocity is fairly constant, if the money supply also stays fairly constant then the total spending flow will stay fairly constant. But if "M" increases, spending increases; if M decreases, spending decreases. So, if we want to, we can say that *all* increases or decreases in spending can be "explained" by increases or decreases in the money supply!

As "M" Increases, Total Spending Increases—and Vice Versa

We can say that *no matter what the consumers and investors and the government spenders and the foreign buyers are doing, as long as "M" is gradually increasing, total spending and output and income will be gradually increasing and everything will be just fine!* So why don't we just forget about C + I + G + F and just concentrate our attention on the money supply? Wouldn't that be easier and neater? Sure. But it may not be wise. Perhaps we should talk a little bit about the question of "cause and effect."

The whole purpose of our macroeconomic analysis—taking the spending flow apart—is to try to find out what *causes* changes in the size of the spending-income flow. We know that the size of the money supply and the size of the spending flow move very closely together. That's important. But here's the real question: Is it changes in the size of the money stock (M) which *cause* the spending flow to expand or contract?

Do you see the problem? Spending doesn't increase unless "M" increases. But M doesn't increase unless spend-

ing increases! What causes what? Do you suppose that each could have some causal influence on the other? Sure. That's why it's a good idea not to ignore either "MV," or "C + I + G + F" as ways of looking at the total spending-income flow.

Economists Disagree About the Causal Role of M

Many economists these days disagree about the best way to look at and analyze the macroeconomic forces at work in the economy. The "monetarist school of thought," which includes Professors Milton Friedman (Nobel prize winner in economics), Paul McCracken (former Chairman of the Council of Economic Advisers under President Nixon) and many others, emphasizes the necessity of controlling the size of the money supply. The monetarists emphasize the importance of the "money stock" as the key to understanding economic conditions and prices in the economy. *"Keep a watchful eye on the money supply!"*

On the other side of this argument stand the followers of Keynesian economics. These economists focus their attention directly on the spending sources which contribute to the total spending flow. This group includes Professors Paul Samuelson (Nobel prize winner in economics), Walter Heller (Chairman of the Council of Economic Advisers under President Johnson), and many others. They believe that the supply of money is very important. But they also believe that in order to understand and/or influence macroeconomic conditions it is necessary to focus on the "Keynesian components" of the total income-spending flow: C + I + G + F.

Who is right? The monetarists? The Keynesians? Until a few years ago the Keynesian approach was clearly dominant in macroeconomics. But the monetarist philosophy has gained in acceptance in recent years.

You'll be finding out a lot more about these policy issues later on. But first, on with the basic theory.

Another Way to Look at "Output": Price Times Quantity

Now you know two ways to look at the total spending flow: by "spending source" (C + I + G + F) and by "money supply times velocity of spending" (MV). So now it's time to look at *output* a new way: as "the number of units produced" times "the average price per unit."

Here's an example. Suppose we are producing a thousand units of output per day. Suppose the average price (per unit) is one dollar. Then the total value of the output flow will be one thousand dollars per day. Right? Then suppose the total output flow increases to *two* thousand units and the average price is still one dollar. Then the total value of the output flow will be two thousand dollars per day. Obviously.

Let's say it this way: total output value is equal to the total quantity (number of units) produced (Q) times the average price per unit (P). You can see that "Q" times "P" is really "the value of the national product." It's gross national product (GNP) stated in a different way. Now that we have the output flow defined in this way (Q times P) we can put together what economists call the "equation of exchange."

The Equation of Exchange

The **equation of exchange** is another way of showing that the total spending flow is equal to the total output flow. We say it this way:

$$MV = PQ$$

This only tells us that the total spending flow (looked at as the total money supply times the average velocity at which each dollar is being spent for output) is equal to the total value of the output (looked at as the total quantity of units produced times the average price per unit). The statement is obviously true. But what can we do with it? Just watch.

The velocity of circulation (V) is fairly constant and stable. Remember? But what about the quantity of output (Q)? Sometimes that can decrease and increase a lot when the economy is speeding up or slowing down. But usually the economy runs along on a fairly stable course most of the time. So the quantity of output (Q) usually doesn't change greatly. Now do you see where this leaves us?

If V is fairly constant and Q is fairly constant, this gives us a direct tie between M (the money supply) and P (the average level of prices). It tells us that if the money stock (M) does not increase, then "prices in general" absolutely cannot rise. Inflation is impossible! Now do you understand the monetarists' position on fighting inflation? "Don't let M increase any more than Q increases; then there can be no inflation!"

The following chapters will go further into these interesting issues of how to fight inflation and unemployment. But now it's time to stop and summarize.

THE COMPONENTS OF THE SPENDING FLOW ARE ALL LOCKED TOGETHER

You can think of the spending flow as made up of the four spending components (C + I + G + F), or you can think of it as a total quantity of money circulating at a certain rate (MV). Either way you look at it you are looking at the same thing.

If any one of the "spending components" slows down (unless something else speeds up) spending and income will get smaller. If this is happening it means that either M or V (or both) are getting smaller.

You can look at the output flow as the quantity of units of output (Q) times the average price per unit (P). Or you can look at it as "GNP." GNP, really, is figured up by adding the outputs of things times the price of each. Remember? So in both cases you are looking at the same thing: output times prices. The two *must* be equal. Obviously.

If anything happens to cause the total spending flow to increase, then the value of what the spending flow is buying (the output flow) must also increase. Either the size of the output must increase or prices must rise. One or the other (or some combination of both) must happen!

See how all this is "locked-in" together? Everything moves together. So it's impossible simply to look at what is happening and decide *what is causing it* to happen. Let's take an example.

What's Causing What?

Perhaps I look and see an increase in investment spending. The investors borrow money from the bank (which expands the money supply) and spend the money to buy more goods. But if the economy is already fully employed, output cannot increase. So prices are forced up. What I see is: "increased investment spending bringing inflation."

Someone else looks at the same situation and says: "the expansion in the money supply resulted in inflation." Was it the increase in investment spending? Or was it in the increase in the money supply which brought the inflation? The answer is obvious. It was both!

The increased investment spending could not have occurred without the increase in the money supply; the increase in the money supply could not have occurred without the increased

borrowing and spending by the investors!

If it happens that next spring consumers start going into debt and are spending more for appliances and automobiles and things, the money supply will increase. The economy will boom and prices may rise. What's responsible? The increase in the money supply? Or the "upward shift in the consumption function"? See the problem?

Changes Are Likely to Be Cumulative

Another problem is that these macroeconomic variables are so closely interrelated that any change is likely to set off a chain reaction. If total spending begins to increase for any reason, this may bring a wave of increased spending.

If consumers spend more, businesses may think this is a good time to make profits. So they spend more. So incomes rise and consumers spend even more. The money supply expands. Employment increases. Output increases. Probably prices rise, too.

It works the other way too. If businesses start cutting back spending and paying off loans, the money supply gets smaller. Workers receive less income. Some lose their jobs. Consumer spending drops. So businesses cut back even more. The money supply shrinks farther. More jobs are lost. Things get worse and worse.

See how macroequilibrium is sort of like a "perched boulder"? You'll find out even more about that in the chapters coming up in Part Four. But it's time to stop now and give you time to review. It's essential that you learn the basic concepts and principles *well* before you go on into Part Four.

SUMMARY AND SYNTHESIS

In Keynesian national income analysis, **total spending** holds the key to macroeconomics. The **basic spending flow** in the economy is "spending

for consumer goods" (C). The size of this basic flow may be thought of as "a function of the size of the **national income (NI)**." So we can define the consumption function [C = f(NI)] as the size of the consumer spending flow which would exist at each possible level of national income.

The **average propensity to consume (APC)** is that fraction of income received which would be spent for consumer goods (not saved). The **marginal propensity to consume (MPC)** is that fraction of an increase in income which would be spent for consumer goods (not saved).

It is the marginal propensity to consume which causes the **respending effect** which is the **income multiplier.** The higher the MPC (the lower the MPS), the higher the income multiplier. The income multiplier may be thought of as the "consumer respending effect."

The Keynesian national spending and income graph shows the consumption function curve. The curve illustrates APC. Each point along the curve shows how high C would be at that level of NI, so it shows the APC (C/NI). The MPC is shown by the **slope** of the curve at each point.

The consumption function curve shows that as national income gets larger, the "savings gap" gets larger. So progressively larger investment (or other) injections are required to support a continually increasing national income. The more steep the consumption function curve, the higher the MPC (the lower the MPS), the higher the income multiplier, and the smaller the amount of investment (and other) injections required to enable the economy to achieve any desired level of national income.

The **monetary approach** to macroeconomics focuses on the **size of the money supply** and the income velocity, or speed at which the average dollar is being used to buy output. Velocity tends to be fairly stable, so changes in the size of the money supply are closely related to changes in total spending.

But economists disagree about whether a money supply change is the **cause** or the **result** of a change in total spending.

The "monetarist school of thought," including Professor Milton Friedman and others, emphasizes the importance of the size of the money supply as a **causal** influence. The economists who emphasize Keynesian economics (Professor Paul Samuelson, and others) focus more attention on the **spending-decision process** by each of the **spending sources** as causal factors. To the Keynesians, changes in the size of the money supply are thought to be more **permissive** than **causal.**

The monetarist approach uses the **equation of exchange** to illustrate the equality between the **spending flow** and the output flow. The **equation of exchange** is: MV = PQ. This says: "Money times velocity equals prices times the quantity of output." The left side of the equation gives "total spending for output." The right side gives "total value of output bought." Equal? Of course.

The monetarist approach and the Keynesian approach both look at the same situation but they analyze it differently. Each approach provides insights which cannot be gained from the other, so almost all economists agree that both are useful ways of looking at, analyzing, and trying to understand macroeconomics.

REVIEW EXERCISES

MAJOR CONCEPTS, PRINCIPLES, TERMS (Explain each carefully.)

the propensity to consume
the multiplier effect
why money times velocity (MV) equals total spending
why output times prices (PQ) equals GNP
why MV = PQ
the problem of "what causes what"

OTHER CONCEPTS AND TERMS (Explain each briefly.)

average propensity to consume (APC)

average propensity to save (APS)

marginal propensity to consume (MPC)

consumption function

full employment

the money supply (M)

the velocity of money (V)

"income (or output) velocity"

Milton Friedman

$C+I+G+F=MV$

Paul McCracken

the "monetarists"

the "Keynesians"

Paul Samuelson

Walter Heller

CURVES AND GRAPHS (Draw, label, and explain each.)

The Consumption Function

The Consumption Function and the Savings Function

The Effect of an Injection of Investment Spending

Macroequilibrium, Where S = I

QUESTIONS (Write out answers, or jot down key points.)

1. Can you think of anything that might cause *your* "consumption function" to shift up or down (either temporarily or permanently)—that is, things that might cause you to spend more or less for consumer goods, even though your income didn't change? Can you think of things that might cause the consumption function to increase or decrease for the entire nation? Explain.

2. What do you think of the "relative usefulness" of the Keynesian and monetary approaches to understanding macroeconomics? For which purposes would you prefer to use the Keynesian approach? the monetary approach? Discuss.

3. Using the "MV = PQ" approach (and thinking back to things you learned in the previous chapters) it becomes pretty obvious why it's necessary to prevent unlimited expansion of the money supply, and why the government must be very careful about how much it finances its spending programs by creating new money (high-powered money) by selling bonds to the Federal Reserve banks. Right? Explain.

PART FOUR

It's Feast Or Famine, Drought Or Flood; Whenever It Rains, It Pours!

13 Business Cycles: The Income Multiplier and the Acceleration Principle

Chapter Objectives

- What makes total spending sometimes increase so much? Or decrease so much? That's what you'll be reading about in this chapter. You might call this chapter "Macroeconomics in Action."

- When you complete this chapter you will better understand the **real-world operation** of the income multiplier—the **consumer respending effect**. You will be able to **explain it** and to **give examples** showing how it works.

- This chapter will introduce you to **another cause of instability**: the **acceleration principle**—the **induced investment effect**. In this chapter you will learn to explain how a change in **consumer demand** can cause a much greater change in **derived demand**.

- You will find out how the **accelerator** and the **multiplier** work together **to generate business cycles**, and that **monetary expansion and contraction** play an essential role in this process of **economic expansion and contraction**.

- You will see why a **rapid expansion** usually leads to a **serious contraction**, and you will read about the great **social costs** of **depression** and **inflation**.

THE INCOME MULTIPLIER: THE CONSUMER RESPENDING EFFECT

You already understand the concept of the multiplier. When businesses (or governments or foreigners—or consumers, for that matter) increase their spending, what happens? People's incomes increase by the amount of the increase in spending. But ultimately, people's incomes will increase by *more* than the amount of the initial increase in spending.

The multiplier concept is simply a way of looking at the **consumer respending effect**. If the people spend almost all of the increases in their incomes, then the multiplier will be high because the marginal propensity to consume is high. (The marginal propensity to save is low.) But if people don't spend much of the increase—that is, if they save most of it—the multiplier will be low.

The "income-increasing effect" of an initial increase in spending will continue for how long? Until the daily rate of savings withdrawals is high enough to offset the higher daily rate of spending injections. Once the "savings withdrawal rate" increases enough to exactly offset the new "spending injection rate" the spending flow will be stable again—at a higher level than before.

An Example of the Multiplier

Suppose the economy has a lot of unemployed student labor—people who really would like part-time jobs. The economy is in "macro-equilibrium"—that is, it isn't expanding or contracting. But we have productive capacity that is not being used. So what happens?

Suppose Christmas is coming so the toy manufacturers decide to expand and hire the unemployed students. This increases total output and total income. But that's not the end of it. As the students' incomes increase, their spending also increases. They add more dollars to the spending stream.

Suppose that one afternoon you go by the toy shop and work a few hours to earn some income. Then you go on down to the shopping center to buy a new pair of shoes. The store manager, Mr. McCoy, seems to be in a very good mood. He tells you that his business is much better this month. Guess why? You know very well why. It's the multiplier effect of the new income from the toy factory!

Students now have more money to spend, so they're spending more for shoes. That shouldn't be a surprise. You're spending money at the shoe store today. That's what the multiplier says you will be doing. When you spend your money for shoes that's going to increase the incomes of a lot of people, each a little bit. Mr. McCoy will get to keep some of it for his own income, but not much of it.

Some of the increased spending goes to the shoe store employees. Some goes to the wholesaler who supplies the shoes. The wholesaler gets to keep a little of it and some goes to the wholesaler's employees. Then some goes to the shoe manufacturer.

The manufacturer keeps a little bit of the income and some goes to the workers. Then some goes to the leather company. The leather company gets to keep a little bit and some goes to the workers. Some goes to the bank as interest on loans. The banks keep a little and pay the employees a little. Some goes to the electric company and to their suppliers and employees. On and on it goes.

Ultimately, all of the increased spending for output must go as new income to somebody. Each person who receives some of it, responds some. All this new income is being generated by the multiplier. *The multiplier is the re-spending effect*, don't forget.

The toy factories keep on paying the students, so the students keep on buying more things. Those who sell to the students are receiving more income. So they're spending more too. The income stream is increased by (a) the amount of the initial spending injection (new student incomes) plus (b) the amount of all this "multiplier-induced" spending.

The multiplier carries total income to a higher level, where ultimately it stabilizes. The new stable level must be the level at which the new (induced) rate of planned withdrawals (savings) is equal to the new rate of planned injections (investments).

If you understand all this, then you really understand the income multiplier. That's good, because it really does work in the real world. It isn't always neat and predictable. But it really does work.*

---

*If you would like to know the formula for the income multiplier, it's: "the reciprocal of the marginal propensity to save:"

$$\left(\frac{1}{\text{marginal propensity to save}} \right),$$

or $\left(\dfrac{1}{1 - \text{marginal propensity to consume}} \right).$

The MPC plus the MPS equals one, of course. So 1 − MPC = MPS!
(Think about how similar this is to the formula you learned for the deposit multiplier!)

This multiplier can be very powerful. But the multiplier effect is only half of the "induced spending" picture. Here's the other half. We call it "the acceleration principle."

THE ACCELERATION PRINCIPLE: THE "INDUCED INVESTMENT" EFFECT

While you are in the shoe store trying on shoes you hear hammering in the back. You ask Mr. McCoy what's going on. He says he is expanding his shelf space. He is going to expand his inventory. He explains that when sales are faster, he likes to have a larger inventory. That way he can be sure he won't run out of particular styles or sizes just when sales are going best.

As Sales Increase, Inventories Increase More

The "accelerator" is induced investment. It's the "inventory stocking-up" effect.

"Each time you run out of someone's style, or size, you lose a customer," he says. "In the past, we have been selling at the rate of about $1,000 worth of shoes per week and we have been keeping about a $10,000 inventory of shoes on hand. But now our sales are up to almost $2,000 per week, and we think we should keep a much larger inventory, maybe even as much as $20,000 worth." That seems reasonable to you. You commend Mr. McCoy for his quick response to the increased demand for shoes. Then you pay for your shoes and go on your way.

As you are leaving you happen to think about the shoe *manufacturers*. How happy they must be to get Mr. McCoy's order! He has been ordering about $1,000 worth of shoes a week through the wholesalers, from the factory. Now, suddenly Mr. McCoy is going to place an order for $12,000 worth of shoes all at one time! What an order! He needs $2,000 worth to cover his (larger) weekly sales volume, and he needs another $10,000 worth to build up his inventory.

You say to yourself, "Just think. His sales of shoes increased from $1,000 to $2,000 a week. That's an increase of 100 percent. But his order for more shoes from the manufacturer is going to *more* than double, or triple, or quadruple, or even quintuple. His order is going to increase by *1200 percent!* He is going to order *12 times as many shoes* as he did before. Wow! I'll bet the economists have a word to describe a situation like this!"

And so we have. We call it the **acceleration principle**. If you think about it you can guess exactly what's going to happen next. Shortages? Right!

Acceleration Principle: Tidal Wave of Derived Demand

Throughout the economy, students are working at toy factories earning extra money. Then they are buying twice as many shoes as before. So shoe stores all over the country are sending in big orders to the shoe manufacturers—orders suddenly *12 times as great* as their previous orders. Now I ask you, how in the world are those shoe companies going to fill all those orders?

They aren't. They can't! There's just *no way* they can produce all those shoes. They hire all the extra workers they can find. They start working three shifts a day. They try to lease more buildings and buy new shoe-making machines.

The shoe machinery people are next to get hit by this tidal wave of derived demand. When a Wilmington manufacturer calls in a rush order for more machines, the shoe machinery people respond by saying: "You have been ordering only two machines a year from us, just to replace your old machines as they wear out. Now, suddenly you want to buy twenty new machines so you can set up a new factory. Would you believe that every shoe manufacturer in the country has called us and tried to buy 20 new machines? There's just *no way* we can produce all those machines.

"We will go on overtime, hire all the extra labor we can get, and expand our plant as quickly as we can. But we should warn you that we can't ship you more than one new machine every three months until we get tooled up to expand our output. That may take more than a year. Please understand that *we can't get the machines we need* to expand our plant, either!"

See how the "acceleration principle" blows up an increase in consumer demand, all out of proportion? Of course this example is a little bit exaggerated. Used with discretion, exaggeration sometimes can serve a useful purpose as "the microscope of the social scientist." (But *always* with discretion!)

Shortages Appear in Almost All Industries

Now look back to the day you bought your new shoes. Suppose you had gone into the local appliance store or hardware store or sporting goods store or music store or automotive accessories store or almost anywhere else. You would have seen the same thing going on. Fast sales. Expanding orders for inventories. Then, shortages. It's happening everywhere!

Here's the pattern: Consumer demand increases some. Why? Usually because of some increase in incomes—from increased I or G or F, or from a tax cut, maybe. Then the initial increase sets off the multiplier.

It's all this increased consumer demand that triggers the acceleration principle. Retailers will increase their orders *much more* than consumer demand increases. Then wholesalers and manufacturers "accelerate" the demand even more. *Total demand* goes right out of sight!

If only shoes were involved, resources could be shifted out of other things and into shoe production. But when *everything* is in short supply there's nowhere to get the needed resources. There's just no way all this inventory buildup can happen in a week or a month or even in a year! So there will be tight markets, waiting lists, and people offering extra money to get on the top of the lists. And inflationary pressures? You bet.

What started all this? The increased spending by the toy companies. That is what set off the multiplier. Remember? Then the increased consumer spending (multiplier effect) set off the accelerator. Consumer demand has gone up. **Derived demand** has gone out of sight! But that's not all. There's more.

THE ACCELERATOR, THE MULTIPLIER, AND THE BUSINESS CYCLE

What kind of "spending" do we call it when the shoe store spends for inventory? "Investment spending," of course! People buy shoes as *consumer goods*, but retail shoe stores buy shoes as *investment goods*, for investment purposes. So when the shoe store increases its spending for shoes, this is an increase in investment spending. Also when the shoe manufacturing company leases and renovates the building next door and buys new machines, what kind of "spending" is all this? "Investment spending," of course!

Remember what happens to people's incomes and to consumer spending when investment spending increases? If the initial increase in spending by the toy companies caused all this havoc, what do you suppose will happen when all these retailers and wholesalers and manufacturers and everybody else start increasing their spending by leaps and bounds?

What's going to happen? How long can these high demand, shortage, inflationary conditions last? You could guess. *Until total production has caught up with and satisfied the pent-up demand* for factories and machines and inventories. But this could take quite a long time.

Each increase in consumer demand works up through the retailer and wholesaler and manufacturer and further accelerates the demand for inventories and factories and machines.

At the same time, each increase in investment spending for inventories and factories and machines works down through the multiplier to further increase consumer demand. Things are really tight. They're going to stay tight for a long time.

When Shortages End the Boom Ends

The boom doesn't keep on going this way forever. One day Mr. McCoy heaves a big sigh of relief and says: "Finally I have my inventory built up to the right size. I have been trying to do that for almost two years. Finally, I've made it. My sales of shoes are now up to $5,000 per week and my inventory is up to $35,000 worth of shoes. All my shelves are full. My sales seem to be stable at $5,000 and I think I will just let my inventory stabilize at the $35,000 level."

Mr. McCoy notifies the wholesaler and the manufacturer that in the future he will be satisfied with $5,000 worth of shoes per week. No longer will he write nasty letters saying that he must have another $15,000 worth. So the pressure is off, at least from Mr. McCoy's store.

What's the situation throughout the rest of the economy? The same. The level of sales is much higher than before and inventories are much larger than before. Everywhere you look, outputs and incomes are much higher than before. Spending is high. People are buying shoes and everything else like crazy. Prices of everything are higher, too.

But one thing is different now. There is no longer a need for the shoe store to build its inventory. So it cuts back its demand for shoes.

What's going to happen when every shoe store and clothing store and appliance store and music store and automobile dealer and furniture store and paint store and all the others stop building inventory? The manufacturers are going to be in for a real jolt!

Manufacturers Are the First to Feel the Slump

It took the manufacturers a long time to build up enough productive capacity to meet the "accelerated" demand. But now things are different. The wholesalers and retailers are all stocked up. Their orders drop to a trickle.

The shoe manufacturers start closing down some of their plants. Other manufacturers do too. Soon it happens to several manufacturing firms. See what kind of a problem is sneaking up on us?

What do the manufacturing workers do when they get laid off? They buy fewer shoes and things. Is this the multiplier going the other way? It sure is. The manufacturers are reducing their spending for labor and other inputs. Down go incomes. So down goes consumer demand.

How about the acceleration principle? Does it work in reverse, too? I'm afraid so. It looks like the boom is all over. The economy is on the brink of a recession.

The Process of Recession

Here's how it happens. First a few manufacturing workers are laid off. They reduce their spending for consumer goods. With reduced sales, retailers don't need as much inventory. So they stop ordering from the manufacturers for awhile. They just sell out of inventory. When this happens the manufacturers' sales drop to *zero*!

What do the manufacturers do? They close down their plants and lay off their workers for a few weeks. The laid-off workers don't have any income so they don't spend much. That means retail sales drop even more. So the retailers decide to reduce inventories even more. No sense in carrying the expense of high inventories if it isn't necessary! More manufacturers close down.

How Bad Is the Slump?

How far does total spending (aggregate demand) go down? Is this a really bad recession? a depression? Who knows? We could exaggerate it enough to show a time when *all* retailers would be trying to sell out of inventory and *nobody* would be ordering anything from the manufacturers. Then nobody would be making any money working in the factories, so nobody would be buying very much from the retail stores.

If nobody is buying much of anything, how long is it going to take the retailers and wholesalers and manufacturers and everybody to get rid of all their overstocked inventories? A very long time. Such a depression would last a very long time.

This is the kind of situation that existed in the United States in the 1930s. The inventory problem wasn't the only thing that caused the Great Depression of the 1930s to be so bad and to last so long. But it was one of the important things. I'm sure you can understand that now.

Economic Instability: the "Business Cycle"

It's easy to see how the multiplier and the accelerator reinforce each other. Any increase in spending by businesses (or by anybody) triggers the multiplier. Consumer spending increases. The increase in consumer spending triggers the accelerator and pushes investment spending up. The two work together, first to speed things up too much, then to pull the rug out from under us.

The boom keeps going until the plant and inventory expansions have been completed. Then everything turns around. The investment spending cutback brings consumer spending cutbacks which bring more investment spending cutbacks—down, down, down we go.

This "boom and bust" we are talking about is sometimes called the business cycle. The multiplier and accelerator reinforce each other and create a natural tendency for the economy to overexpand and then overcontract—to go from boom to recession. Sometimes this tendency is referred to as "the problem of the instability of capitalism."

This business cycle of "boom and bust" isn't desirable from anybody's point of view. The times of declining demand, recession, unemployment and low incomes are usually thought of as the worst times. But the times of shortages and upward pressures on prices really aren't satisfactory either.

I don't need to tell you that depressions and inflations are undesirable. Everybody knows that. But maybe it won't hurt, just for a few minutes, to talk about some of the undesirable effects of depression and inflation.

THE GREAT SOCIAL COST OF DEPRESSION AND INFLATION

Think for a minute. What's the purpose of "the economy"? What is the "economic system" supposed to do, anyway? Why should all these people be working and burning up energy and using up resources and making things and all that? The purpose is to feed and clothe us and to try to improve our lives—to let us live better.

We produce for the good of ourselves. We do and make what "we the members of the society" think will benefit us—will bring us better lives, or a better world. Anyway, that's what we're *trying* to do, I suppose.

The Tragedy of Unemployment and Depression

When we say "there is widespread unemployment," exactly what does that mean? It means that there are people who want to be productive, to produce something of value for the society. But because of some hangup, some snag, some flaw in the way the economic system is working, these people don't have the opportunity to produce things for the society.

When there's a lot of unemployment, there's a lot of waste. Labor is being wasted. And not just labor. Factories are sitting idle, depreciating. Trucks, railroad cars, machines, all sitting around, doing nothing. Becoming obsolete. While there's so much that needs to be done!

When unemployment exists it means that the economic system somehow is failing in its job. The things society could be doing for its own benefit are going undone, while the society's productive resources are wasting away. Really tragic.

If we *decided* to produce less—maybe to conserve natural resources or to go on a 32-hour work week or to slow down the economy for some other reason, that's okay. But that's different! When we are talking about unemployment and **depression** we are talking about people *wanting* to be productive and society *wanting* the output, but nothing happens. The pieces just aren't fitting together.

People are walking the streets looking for jobs, suffering the shame of having to admit failure. People having to accept handouts, losing their self respect. Sometimes just giving up. Sometimes turning against the society which has done this to them.

How would you measure the "social cost" of depression? We can't, really. But everyone knows that the cost is great. Not just *economic* costs, but *many kinds* of social cost. The breakdown in family harmony. The rise in the crime rate. Delinquent taxes. State and local governments facing fiscal crises. The quality of services—education, health, hospital, social welfare—going down. The list goes on and on. The social costs of widespread unemployment are appalling. Intolerable.

Persistent Depression Is No Longer Tolerable

You can understand why people refuse to put up with depression. If any modern nation began to experience serious depression, the government would be forced to do something about it. If it was necessary to change the economic system to solve the problem, then you may be sure that the economic system would be changed. An economic system which would permit persistent depression and widespread unemployment is no longer acceptable in today's world.

The American economic system has been greatly changed during the past five decades. Much of the change has resulted from the people's feelings of economic insecurity. People really fear the threat of unemployment. They demand that the economic system be set up to do something positive to prevent it whenever necessary.

The following chapters explain what the government can do. But first, what about inflation? What's so bad about inflation?

Inflation Tears the Society Apart

What's **inflation**? Prices are going up. That's all. Is that so bad? Yes. It's very bad. Much worse than you think. It hurts the society. It brings really serious injustices to people. It actually *robs* people of the economic assets the society owes them. It forces people who, by all rights, deserve a comfortable retirement, to live their retirement years in poverty. But that isn't all. Not by a long shot.

Inflation really does tear the society apart. It forces every one of us to fight to see that the value of *our incomes* and the value of *our assets* keep going up at least as fast as prices are going up.

Inflation forces workers to fight for "exorbitant" wage increases. It forces businesses to announce "exorbitant" price increases. It forces the state and local governments to pass "exorbitant" tax increases, while costs of government services surge forward even faster. "Austerity budgets" are forced on the public schools, colleges, health and welfare services, highway departments. College students are forced to pay higher tuition and fees. People feel more and more cheated, and get more and more angry.

What does inflation do? You can see how it tears the society apart! Everyone must fight as hard as possible just to stay in the same place—to keep from being left behind. Inflation breeds unreasonableness, dissension, mistrust, unhappiness, and even hate among otherwise reasonable people.

If inflation continues, people lose interest in saving money. Nobody wants to hold money. Spend it! Hurry, before prices go up any more! Buy a new car. Buy land. Or stocks. Anything. But don't hold on to any money.

Once the people get afraid to hold money, they spend fast. Then prices really skyrocket! The next step is the complete collapse of the markets of the economy.

Never in this country, but a few times in other countries inflation has gone this far. People just *refuse* to accept money. Suddenly, there is no medium of exchange. The markets collapse. When the markets collapse, production stops. The economy collapses. Depression!

Gouge Thy Neighbor

Inflation instills in all the people—children and adults, workers, investors, business managers, police officers, teachers, college professors, everyone—the philosophy: "Gouge thy neighbor because thy neighbor is certainly out to gouge thee!" We are all forced to get involved in bargaining and pushing and trying to get our own incomes up enough so that (if we are lucky) we at least stay in the same place.

We might all be surprised if we knew just how many of today's economic and social problems are born of the distortions and injustices of inflation. Inflation distorts the economic relationships among all the people of the society. Businesses which sell in markets where they can raise their prices can come out all right. Workers who work where they can keep their wages rising fast can make out all right too. But many people have incomes which are not easy to adjust upward. They are seriously hurt. Usually the burden falls most heavily on the ones least able to carry it.

It isn't "just a few people" who are hurt by inflation. Most of the "ordinary people"—those of us who make up most of the society—are depending on some savings, some insurance policies, perhaps some government bonds, and a retirement program of some kind to bring us goods and services in our later years. For many years, most people produce and contribute more to the society than they consume. They save. The extra value they produce for the society (but don't consume) is supposed to flow back to them (as goods and services) so they can help their children through college, and so that in later years they can have the things they gave up earlier. But what happens?

Inflation Robs the Thrifty

Inflation robs savers of what the society owes them. If the inflation rate is high, the people simply aren't going to be getting the things they've saved up for. The things they gave up earlier will be going to the businesses and workers and governments and others who have the power to "increase their take" and come out on top. Everyone else gets left behind.

Do you begin to understand what inflation does to a society? If so, then you can understand why it is essential that inflation be held in check. The farther it goes, the more the people push to get their prices and wages up. Ultimately it can destroy the economy, the government, the entire society.

Economic Stabilization

As the economy expands and contracts, what happens to the money supply?

It expands and contracts, too. Of course!

In the following chapters we will be talking about "monetary and fiscal policy"—techniques used by the government to stabilize the economy. While we're talking about what these policies are and how they work, try not to lose sight of the *vital purpose* of economic stabilization. Modern society cannot tolerate and somehow must prevent the social costs of serious depression or inflation.

Now, before we go on into the issues of preventing and overcoming depression and inflation, there's one more thing we need to talk about. We need to ask this question: When the multiplier and the accelerator get going and everything is speeding up, where does all the *money* come from to finance such a boom?

THE MONEY SUPPLY EXPANDS TO FINANCE A BOOM

What role does money play in this whole "boom and bust" cycle of economic instability? The money supply must expand, or else the boom couldn't occur!

Remember the toy manufacturers? Where do you suppose they got the money to pay the students for all that part-time work? Where do you suppose Mr. McCoy got the money to build up the value of his shoe inventory from $10,000 to $35,000? What about the money to lease and renovate buildings and to buy all those shoe machines and to pay for all the labor and other

things? The multiplier couldn't get going very well without some new (bank-created) money to finance all those payments. Right?

Now think of the consumer goods boom. Where do you suppose all those people got the money to buy all those TV sets and the new automobiles and furniture and all those things? All this buying, building, and stocking up of things just couldn't be going on unless a lot more money was coming from somewhere. Where did it come from? It was being created through the banking system.

Could the money have come from savings that consumers are making out of their current incomes? Obviously not. The consumers are spending up their incomes and going into debt! Maybe the consumers are spending up the money they have been saving for a rainy day? Not a chance. Who is paying cash? Nobody. Well, almost nobody. Everyone's buying on time.

How about the money the businesses have saved up? Or the money they're taking in from current business profits? No chance. The businesses are all going into debt, too. And selling things on credit. So *where could* the money be coming from? It's newly created. Of course.

The money to finance the boom is newly created, just for the purpose of financing the boom. It's created by the banking system, to meet the loan demands of businesses and consumers.

But what about the new excess reserves needed to let the money supply expand? Where did they come from? Do you suppose the government or the Federal Reserve System permitted bank reserves to expand? Of course. What if they hadn't? Suppose they didn't want this boom to go so far, so fast. Could they have held down the money expansion and slowed down the boom and relieved some of the shortages? You bet they could! And they would, too.

The "monetary control tools" can be used to work against both inflation and depression. In the next chapter you will find out what these tools are, and how they work. The next chapter is all about **monetary policy**. As soon as you're sure you understand all about the multiplier and the acceleration principle and the other concepts in this chapter, you'll be ready to go on into "monetary policy."

SUMMARY AND SYNTHESIS

This chapter has carried you farther in your understanding of macroeconomics. Now you better understand some of the factors at work in the actual **process** of economic expansion and contraction—how the **income multiplier** and the **acceleration principle** work together to generate **economic fluctuations**, or **business cycles.**

The **income multiplier is the consumer respending effect.** Whenever people's incomes are increased by **new spending injections** (from increased investment spending or from any other source), this **initial** increase in income is not the end of it. As people receive more income, they **spend more for consumer goods.** The greater their **marginal propensity to consume,** the more they spend, so the greater the income multiplier will be.

The **acceleration principle is the induced investment effect.** The acceleration principle refers to the speed-up in **derived demand** caused by an increase in **final demand.** For example, if final demand increases by only 10%, derived demand may increase by as much as 100% or more.

The **acceleration principle** might be called the **stocking-up effect.** When final demand is increasing, businesses find it profitable to carry **larger inventories.** But when businesses throughout the economy are trying to increase the size of their inventories, this creates **shortages and inflationary pressures** throughout the economy.

The acceleration principle is set off by an increase in final demand. The increase in final demand usually results from **new injections into the income-spending flow.** Once the increased spending begins, the process tends to reinforce itself and speed up. This happens as the **multiplier** and the **accelerator** interact and reinforce each other.

The **accelerator stimulates investment spending** that pours more income into the economy. As people get more income, their **consumer spending** increases. This induces more income multiplier effects. It also stimulates more **derived demand** and speeds up the accelerator. The income multiplier and the acceleration principle can work together to push the economy into a period of **rapid expansion, shortages, and inflation.**

The **economic downturn (recession)** occurs when businesses decide that their inventories are adequately stocked up. As they cut back their orders, manufacturers see a drop in sales. So they cut back production. This reduces **employment and income** in the economy.

People who have less income, spend less. Businesses of all kinds soon feel the slowdown. So they cut back. Unemployment increases.

Incomes drop even more as the accelerator and the multiplier work in reverse. Businesses stop placing new orders and just sell off their inventories. The more the businesses are overstocked with **excess inventories,** the more **serious and prolonged** the recession is likely to be.

There is great social cost of a "boom and bust" business cycle. During depression there is **economic waste of labor and capital,** there is **social cost to individuals and families,** and **fiscal crises reduce the effectiveness of local and state government services.**

Inflation forces people and businesses to fight just to stay in the same place in the **wage-price-increasing game.** Inflation generates **"gouge thy neighbor"** attitudes. It robs the thrifty people of the goods and services that they have saved for.

Inflation discourages thrift and encourages spending. "Spend now, before prices go up!" "Go into debt and pay off later—with inflated (less valuable) dollars!" In some countries **runaway inflation** has occurred, destroying the medium of exchange and resulting in complete collapse of the economy.

Economic stabilization policies are undertaken by all modern "free market" nations to try to **reduce economic fluctuations.**

The **money supply must expand and contract** to permit the business cycle to occur. One obvious approach to **economic stabilization** would be to try to **adjust or stabilize the size of the money supply**—i.e., to use **monetary policy.** Another approach would be to try to influence the **spending flow by adjusting government spending and taxes**—i.e., to use **fiscal policy.**

The following chapters deal with the issue of **economic stabilization.** There you'll find out how **monetary policy** and **fiscal policy** can be used to deal with this problem.

REVIEW EXERCISES

MAJOR CONCEPTS, PRINCIPLES, TERMS (Explain each carefully.)

the multiplier
the acceleration principle
the business cycle
the tragedy of depression

the injustice of inflation
a boom requires a monetary
   expansion

OTHER CONCEPTS AND TERMS (Explain each briefly.)

macroeconomic change
inflation
depression
derived demand

the "consumer responding effect"
the "induced investment effect"
economic stabilization

QUESTIONS (Write out answers, or jot down key points.)

1. Can you explain the relationship between the marginal propensity to save and the multiplier? Try.
2. Why is it that when the *shortages* end, the boom ends? Explain.
3. The multiplier and the accelerator always tend to work together and to reinforce each other, yet each one is a *distinctly different thing* than the other. Can you explain the distinct difference between the two principles?
4. When prices continue to rise year after year (as they have been in recent years in the United States and in the other countries of the world) the continuing inflation affects the lives of everyone in the society. What are some of the ways inflation has touched *you personally*? Explain.
5. If the business cycle really does try to work the way it's explained in this chapter, and if recurrent depression and inflation really are as bad as this chapter says, then it's pretty obvious that we can't let the economy just go its own way, and "let nature take its course." It's pretty obvious that the government must play an active macroeconomic role—that it must carry out some policies of "economic stabilization." The next two chapters will be talking about that. But already, right now, you should be able to think of some of the things the government might do. Can you?

14 Monetary Policy, the Bond Market, and the Stabilizing Role of the Fed

Chapter Objectives

- **Economic expansion and contraction** require **monetary expansion and contraction.** Is it possible to smooth the business cycle by **limiting monetary expansion and contraction?** Yes. How? That's what you'll find out in this chapter.

- You will find out about the **monetary control tools** and how they are used to try to **prevent undesirable** (and/or **induce desirable**) changes in the **size of the money supply**—to try to **stabilize the economy.**

- When you finish studying this chapter you will know about **monetary policy** and about the monetary control tools: (1) **changing the discount rate,** (2) **open market operations,** and (3) **changing the reserve requirements.**

- You will be able to discuss the question of the **effectiveness of monetary policy,** and of each of the **monetary control tools.**

- You will be able to explain why **interest rates rise as bond prices fall** (and vice versa). And you will be able to explain why the **most frequently used and most useful tool of monetary policy** is **open market operations.**

The President Wants a Healthy Economy

How would you like to be President of the United States? Maybe just for a while? I wouldn't either. But would you be willing to make believe? Do you have enough imagination to think of yourself as the President?

This chapter is concerned with "economic stabilization." We'll be talking about the government's efforts to influence total spending, income, output, and employment in the economy. If you could visualize yourself as the President—as "the one who's really in the hot seat," you might be able to get into it. You might get a feel for the techniques and tools, and for the difficulties and frustrations involved in **economic stabilization.** So will you try? Then okay, Mr. or Ms. President, let's have a go at it!

Now that you're the President you realize what a tough job it is trying to run the government. But you've become sort of attached to the White House and you really would like to be elected to another four-year term. You know that if everyone is happy about everything that's going on in the nation, you probably will be voted in again next November. But if the people are unhappy they will blame you and out you will go! So is there any problem? Yes. The economy is sort of depressed.

The average unemployment level throughout the country is about 7 percent. That means that 7 out of every 100 people in the labor force are out of work and looking for jobs. In some sections of the country the unemployment percentage is more than 10 percent. For some segments of the labor force—young, unskilled, minorities—the percentage is over 20 percent in some areas.

You know that these unemployed people aren't going to be very happy with your administration. Neither are their families or their friends or the grocers who sell them groceries or any of the others who are hurt by all this unemployment. Unless something can be done to improve conditions in the economy before election time, you may find yourself out of a job!

WHAT ABOUT MONETARY POLICY?

The first thing you think about is: "Maybe we could stimulate the economy by using monetary policy." You think: "If we had 'easy money'

One way to stabilize the economy is to stabilize the growth of the money supply!

Monetary Policy

(all the banks with excess reserves, and low interest rates for borrowers, and low down payments and easy credit terms for autos and appliances and all) then maybe people and businesses would borrow and spend. Then the economy would speed up. Unemployed people would be able to get jobs and the spending-output-income flow would be all right again." (And if all that happens, you will be reelected in November!)

You call together your top economic advisers: Chairman of the Council of Economic Advisers, Chairman of the Board of Governors of the Federal Reserve System, the Secretary of the Treasury, and the Director of the Office of Management and Bud-

get. You ask them, "What can we do with monetary policy to stimulate the economy, *quickly?*"

Depressed Conditions Call for Easy Money

Everyone agrees that with monetary policy you can make it easier and cheaper for people to borrow money and to buy things on credit. Your advisers agree that there will be some danger of inflation if you follow this policy. But they also agree that a policy of "easy money" at this time would probably stimulate both business spending and consumer spending. Then this initial spending increase would increase employment, output, and incomes, and perhaps would set the economy on the path to prosperity.

That sounds good to you, Mr. or Ms. President, so you urge your four top economic advisers to do whatever they can to bring about "easy money." You try to impress on them the need for haste. The political future of a great national leader is at stake!

When the meeting breaks up, your four economic advisers go their separate ways. The Chairman of the Council of Economic Advisers goes back to his office in the building next door to the White House and starts preparing some reports which he thinks will make bankers more willing to lend. But he recognizes that there really isn't very much he can do to help. There isn't very much the Director of the Office of Management and Budget can do either. He can say the right things and hope to help to get the people in the right mood. But he really doesn't have any "monetary policy tools" to work with.

The Secretary of the Treasury has some direct dealings in the money market. The Treasury "markets" the government debt, so it is constantly dealing in the "money market." But it is the Chairman of the Board of Governors of the Federal Reserve System who really is in the driver's seat when it comes to monetary policy. First, let's talk a little bit about what the Treasury does, then we will be ready to really dig in on the Federal Reserve and its role in "monetary policy."

The Treasury Deals in the Bond and Money Markets

The Treasury is dealing in the bond and money markets every day. It must do this to "manage the government debt." In the early years of the Reagan Administration (1981-82) the federal debt amounted to more than $1.0 trillion.

The federal debt increases each year by the size of the federal deficit—that is, by the amount that the government's *expenditures* exceed its *revenues*. When the government runs a deficit the Treasury makes up the difference by borrowing—that is, by selling government securities (mostly bonds and Treasury bills).

In 1982 the size of the deficit was approaching $100 billion a year. One of the administration's stated objectives was to **balance the budget**. But as this book goes to press the achievement of that objective is not yet in sight. If you want an up-to-date figure of the size of the debt you might check the *Economic Report of the President* or the *Federal Reserve Bulletin* or maybe the *Statistical Abstract of the United States*. You'll find them all in your library.

Suppose the government succeeds in balancing the budget. What then? Will the Treasury stop selling government securities in the bond and money markets? It certainly will not!

There's more than a trillion dollars' worth of government securities out there now. Every week *several billion dollars' worth* of these securities come due and must be "rolled over"—that is, paid off with money obtained by selling *new* securities. So the Treasury will always be very much involved in the bond and money markets.

The government debt is made up of government securities: bonds (long-term) and Treasury "notes" and "bills" (short-term). The people, banks, insurance companies, business corporations, local governments, Federal Reserve Banks, and others hold these government securities. The securities are sold by the Treasury in the "open market"—that is, to anyone who wants to buy them.

Where are these bond and money markets? Scattered around the country in cities and towns, wherever there are banks and securities brokers. Securities brokerage companies and banks deal in government securities. The "money market headquarters" (if there is such a thing) is in New York City.

So what can the U.S. Treasury do to bring easy money? It might try to pay off more of its bonds. It could create some new money by selling bonds, not to individuals and businesses, but to Federal Reserve Banks. Then it could use this "Fed money" to buy up bonds held by individuals and businesses. That would increase the money supply.

For example, suppose Mr. Alber cashes a bond. He receives a government check and goes into his bank, waving it in the air shouting: "Look! Some new excess reserves for the banking system! High-powered, multiple expansion money! Happy days are here again!" Well, maybe he doesn't do all this. But you get the point.

Notice that the Treasury must depend on the Federal Reserve if it wants to do anything to bring easier money. Suppose the Fed doesn't want to buy all these new securities? What could the Treasury do then? Not much. So you see, it's really the Fed which holds the key to monetary policy in the United States. So before we go on, here's a little review of what you already learned about the Fed.

OUR INDEPENDENT FED

The Federal Reserve System is the "central banking system" of the United States. It is controlled by a seven-member Board of Governors appointed by the President of the United States. The major function of this board is to decide on and carry out monetary policy for the nation.

The Federal Reserve System isn't a part of any of the "three branches of government." The system was set up by Congress as "an independent agency" to keep an eye on the nation's money. The Board isn't under anyone's direction or control. If it wants to, it can be as free and independent as the Supreme Court! Except that the Congress could pass a law to restrict, change, or even abolish it at any time.

Maybe the Federal Reserve won't go along with the Treasury. It doesn't have to buy all those bonds if it doesn't want to. Maybe the Federal Reserve Board won't even go along with your policy, Mr. or Ms. President! They may decide that the advantages of easy money look too small and that the dangers of inflation look too great. If that's what they decide, then unless you can persuade them or pressure them into changing their minds, there isn't much you can do to bring easy money.

Maybe you can persuade Congress to pass a law to change the Federal Reserve System and give you more control. Some people have suggested that. Others strongly disagree. But no matter. It would take forever to get such controversial legislation through Congress, anyway. If it ever did pass, by then it would be too late to do *your* program any good.

So, Mr. or Ms. President, the success of your proposed "easy money" policy—and of your economic recovery plan, and perhaps of your bid for reelection—seems to hinge on the decision of the Federal Reserve Board. If you want things to go your way, now would be a very good time for some of your very best aides to start to do some gentle but persuasive arm-twisting!

The Fed Usually Goes Along With the President

As it turns out, Mr. or Ms. President, you didn't have to be concerned about the Fed's de-

cision after all. Following your meeting, the Chairman of the Board of Governors called a meeting with the other six members of the Board. After some arguments they agreed to go along with your suggested "easy money" policy. They decided that they will take the necessary action to make money readily available to borrowers, and at low interest rates.

Can the Fed really do it? Can they bring easy money if they want to? Yes, they really can. They have several techniques—several "tools of monetary policy"—which they can use. The major tools are: (1) changing the discount rate, (2) open market operations in government securities, and (3) changing the reserve requirements. Most of the rest of this chapter will be talking about these tools and about how (and how well) they work.

Lowering the Discount Rate Can Bring Easier Money

Perhaps the first thing the Fed would do is to announce that they are going to lower the **discount rate**. What does that mean? Think back. Remember when Baker was first trying to talk Zimmer into lending him $4,000? Zimmer's bank didn't have any excess reserves.

One way to get excess reserves is to borrow the extra money from your Federal Reserve Bank. The "discount rate" is the "interest rate" the Federal Reserve Bank would charge Zimmer's bank for "borrowed reserves." That's all.

You can see how a lower "discount rate" could make it easier and cheaper for people and businesses to borrow money. This "easy money" can stimulate more spending, output, and employment.

The lower rate at the Fed's "discount window" pushes down the interest rates in every nook and cranny of the economic system. Even the corporations which are borrowing money by selling their own bonds don't have to pay such high interest to get people to buy their bonds. This makes expansion cheaper. So they may sell more bonds and expand more as the lower rates are reflected throughout the money market.

When the Fed offers to make loans to banks at a lower discount rate, money becomes easier to borrow, and at lower cost. In some cases this "monetary policy tool" (adjusting the discount rate) may be very effective. But it isn't used on a daily basis. And it isn't used by itself. Really, it operates as a backup for open market operations.

OPEN MARKET OPERATIONS

A second and even more important technique the Federal Reserve uses to bring "easy money" is called "open market operations in government securities," or just **open market operations**. This is a neat and simple little trick for pushing more money into (or pulling money out of) the economy, and into (or out of) the reserve accounts of the banks.

You can see that if this tool lets the Fed put money into or take money out of a bank's reserve account (whether the bank likes it or not!) then it's a very powerful tool of monetary policy. Right? Yes. And that's what it does. So it is. In addition, it's the most *sensitive* and *flexible* tool of monetary policy. So it's *the most useful tool* the Fed has for controlling the money supply.

You'll see exactly how it works in just a minute. But first, a few words about "bonds" and "the bond market". . .

What Are Bonds? And What's the Bond Market?

A bond is a piece of paper which brings interest income to its owner. There are many trillions of dollars' worth of these pieces of paper in existence in this country. They are owned by individuals and banks and insurance companies and savings and loan companies and businesses and just about everybody. The Fed holds billions.

Where did all these bonds come from? Mostly from businesses (mostly large corpora-

tions) and governments (federal, state, and local). There are a lot more corporation bonds than government bonds, but government bonds are the ones the Fed uses in its "open market operations." But don't forget this: Whatever the Fed does with government bonds will influence what's going on with all the other bonds.

How does it work? The governments and the businesses have bonds printed up, then they sell them. That's how governments and businesses borrow money. Each bond has printed on it a face value (usually $1,000), an interest rate, and a maturity date. Each bond is a "promise to pay" two things to the owner of the bond: (1) interest, and (2) the face value at the maturity date.

Why do people and banks and insurance companies buy bonds? Because bonds pay income. How much income? That depends on the interest rate on the bond. The higher the rate, the more it pays and the more it's worth to its owner. Obviously? Sure.

What's going to happen someday when all these billions and trillions of dollars' worth of bonds reach maturity and have to be paid off? All these people and banks and insurance companies will get all that money back? And the governments and the businesses will all go broke trying to pay off their debts? No. That isn't the way it works at all.

Billions of dollars' worth of bonds are maturing and have to be paid off every week! Ah, but guess what? Billions of dollars' worth of new bonds are being printed up and sold every week, too. So it all works out about even.

New Bonds? Or Old Bonds? When people buy bonds do they have to hold them to maturity to get their money back? No. And when they buy bonds, do they have to buy new bonds, just being issued? No.

When people or banks or businesses buy bonds they usually aren't buying newly issued bonds and they usually aren't thinking of holding the bonds to maturity. They usually buy old bonds "in the bond market." They just call a stocks-and-bonds broker and place a "buy" order. Where do the bonds come from? From the previous owners who decided to sell—who called in "sell" orders to the brokers.

It works just like buying and selling stocks. You can buy as many as you want of any kind you want any day you wish—just so long as you're willing (and able) to pay the price. And you can sell your bonds any time you please if you're willing to accept the existing price in the bond market. That's the way old bonds are being bought and sold all the time.

Banks, businesses and individuals buy and sell millions of dollars' worth of bonds every day. Some buy, and plan to hold them for a while. Others (speculators) buy because they think the prices of the bonds they're buying will go up. If so, they can sell and make a profit.

From the point of view of the buyer in the bond market, a bond is an investment like any other investment. You might consider putting your money into rental housing or building lots or a small business or bonds or stocks or antique furniture or whatever. How do you decide? You choose the one you think will bring you the most suitable combination of risk and income—and profit when you decide to sell it.

If people don't think much of bond investments these days, then a lot of them will be selling bonds. Prices in the bond markets will go down. Or maybe just now people would like to shift more of their investments into bonds. Demand for bonds will go up. Bond prices will rise.

See how the bond markets work? Just like other markets. And now that this little "familiarization tour" is complete you are ready to understand the Fed's "open market operations."

What Is Meant by "Open Market Operations"?

"Open market operations" means planned, purposeful, manipulation of the bond and money markets, by the Fed, through the buying and selling of government securities. That is, the Fed changes the supply of or the demand for (and therefore, the prices of) government securi-

ties. Then the effect spreads all throughout the money market and makes money easy or tight, and interest rates high or low. It's really neat how it works.

You already know that the Federal Reserve Banks hold billions of dollars' worth of government bonds. The Federal Reserve Banks can make interest rates move up or down and can make money "easier" or "tighter" just by buying or selling these bonds "in the open market."

The bonds are bought and sold through "normal investment channels" including banks and stock and bond brokers. If the Federal Reserve is selling government securities (bonds), then *anybody* can buy them. If the Fed's buying, it buys from anyone who wants to sell. That's why it's called "open market operations." The Fed is buying or selling bonds in the "open market"—on Wall Street—in the regular, normal bond and money markets of the economy. But how does all this make money easy or tight? and interest rates low or high? Watch.

The Fed Buys Bonds, Pushes Bond Prices Up, and Increases the Money Supply

Suppose Mr. Alber, a businessman who's going to night school working for his MBA degree, owns five $1,000 marketable government bonds. Each is a 6 percent, $1,000 bond. So it pays its owner $60 a year in income.

Mr. Alber thinks these bonds are a pretty good investment. That's why he bought them in the first place. But now the Fed is buying bonds in the open market. Will Mr. Alber sell his bonds? That depends on how much the Fed is offering to *pay*, of course!

Suppose the Fed offers to pay $1,200 for each of Mr. Alber's 6 percent, $1,000 bonds. Do you think he will sell? Perhaps. Let's suppose he does.

Mr. Alber turns his five bonds over to his banker or a local "stocks and bonds" broker. Then the banker or broker sends the bonds to the Federal Reserve Bank and the Federal Reserve Bank sends Mr. Alber a check for $6,000 (for 5 bonds @ $1,200 each). (The broker gets to keep a little bit of the money as a commission, but we won't worry about that.)

The Fed's Payments for Bonds Become New Money and New Bank Reserves

What does Mr. Alber do with the $6,000 check he just received? What *can* a person do with a $6,000 check? Deposit it in his bank account, of course.

When Mr. Alber does that, what does the banker, Mr. Zimmer, do with the $6,000 check? What *can* a banker do with a $6,000 check drawn on the Federal Reserve Bank? He sends it to the Federal Reserve Bank for deposit to his reserve account, of course.

See what has happened? Just automatically the amount of money in that bank has gone up by $6,000 (Mr. Alber's account, which he can now spend). The money supply is now $6,000 bigger than before!

But that's not all. The bank now finds itself with excess reserves! The bank has $6,000 more in its reserve account. If the reserve requirement is 20%, then $1200 is required reserves for Alber's deposit and $4800 is excess reserves, free to be loaned out.

Now Mr. Zimmer has to worry about what to do with all that excess money—how to use it to bring in some income. He would like to lend it to someone. See how the Fed's "open market operations" are bringing easy money?

Mr. Zimmer is going to try to expand his loans so he can start earning interest on the $4,800 he has in excess reserves. He hopes Mr. Baker will come in and borrow the $4,800. Then Mr. Baker will go out and spend it and the increased spending will help to stimulate the economy. Then Mr. Culver, who receives the $4,800 check from Baker, will deposit it in his bank. Then Culver's bank will have excess reserves. You know how this process can continue until the money supply expands to five times the amount of Mr. Alber's $6,000 deposit.

Yes, the money supply can expand by as much as $30,000, or maybe more, depending on the exact size of the reserve requirement. But will it? Maybe not. If conditions in the economy are really bad, maybe nobody will want to borrow and spend.

It's easy to see how the Fed, by buying bonds, places new money in the hands of the people who are selling the bonds. Also it's easy to see that this new money is "high-powered money." It flows directly into the reserve accounts of the banks. It permits a multiple expansion of the money supply to begin.

If the Fed is buying bonds it is pushing new excess reserves into the accounts of banks all over the country. Does this bring easy money? You bet it does! But wait. You don't know the whole story yet.

To see the full effect of open market operations on the bond and money markets (on interest rates and bond prices and easy credit and all that), you first must know about the interesting relationship between *interest rates and bond prices*.

BOND PRICES AND INTEREST RATES

Open market operations push interest rates up or down, two ways. First, a banker with excess reserves would be likely to offer loans at lower interest rates. So excess reserves push interest rates down. But there is another, more direct way that buying bonds in the open market pushes interest rates down.

To understand this, you need to understand this fact: When the market price you pay for a bond increases, the "interest yield" you will get from that bond decreases. Therefore, as the market prices of bonds go up, the interest yields earned by the buyers of those bonds, go down.

A bond pays interest (say 6%) on its face value (say $1,000). The owner of that bond earns $60 a year—no more, and no less. If you pay $1,200 for the bond, you *still only get $60 a year!* That's only 5% on your $1,200 investment (5% of $1,200 is $60). This idea is really simple, but sometimes it seems confusing. Let's go through it step by step.

Market Prices of All Kinds of Bonds Rise and Fall

First of all, we aren't talking about the "savings bonds" (E and H bonds) that most individuals are familiar with. The E bonds and H bonds are special, *non-marketable* bonds. They don't fit into this discussion.

When the Fed is trying to ease money it buys "marketable" government bonds and pushes up the prices of these bonds. This entices people, banks, insurance companies and others to sell their bonds. As the Fed pushes up the open market prices of government bonds, the prices of *all* bonds react the same way.

The Fed buys bonds, pushes up bond prices, and pushes down interest rates. Easy money!

All the money and bond markets are very closely tied together. When the prices of government bonds are being forced up, this pushes up the prices of AT&T bonds, U.S. Steel bonds, General Motors bonds, Amoco bonds, and all other marketable bonds in the country. As the bond prices in the market go up, what happens to the actual interest you receive on your money when you buy one of the higher priced bonds? It goes down.

Bonds Paying the Highest Interest Sell for the Highest Prices

The face value of a bond may not be very close to its market price. For example, a 20-year,

$1,000, 3% bond would not bring as much in the open market as a 20-year, $1,000, 9% bond. That's obvious, isn't it? When the 3% bond was issued, interest rates were low. But as interest rates (interest rates on new bonds) got higher and higher, the market value of the 3% bond got lower and lower.

That's the way it always is. *If interest rates are rising, prices of existing bonds are falling.* Or we can say it the other way and it's just as true: *if prices of existing bonds are rising, interest rates are falling.*

Suppose you paid $1,200 when you bought a $1,000 bond which pays 6% per year. How much income would it pay you per year? Only $60, of course. That's what the bond says. It says it will pay 6 percent on $1,000.

Even if you paid $1,200 when you bought the bond, you still aren't going to receive but $60 annual return. That happens to be a return of only 5 percent on your $1,200 investment. The bond is still paying 6 percent on its face value ($1,000). But *you* paid $1,200 so you're only getting a 5 percent return on your investment.

Why would anyone ever pay $1,200 for a $1,000 bond? Because they think it's the best investment for them available in the bond market, that's why! Suppose the new bonds being issued these days carry an interest rate of only 4 percent. Would you be willing to pay $1,200 for a long-term $1,000 bond that pays 6 percent? I would!

Very-Long-Term Bond Prices Reflect Only the Interest Return

Just to make the point, let's suppose we are talking about 500-year bonds. You can get 3 percent ones for $500 each or 6 percent ones for $1,000 each or 9 percent ones for $1,500 each. They're *all* $1,000 bonds, but they are selling at such different prices! Which ones would you buy? It really wouldn't make any difference, would it?

You are going to earn 6 percent on your money, no matter which bonds you buy. Guess what the going rate of interest is on new bonds, these days? It's 6 percent, of course! The 3 percent bonds were issued sometime back when money market interest rates were low. So what happened to the value of the 3 percent bonds when the money market rate went up from 3 percent to 6 percent? The bond values dropped from $1,000 to about $500.

The 9 percent bonds were issued sometime back when money market interest rates were high. So what happened when the money market rate went down from 9 to 6 percent? The bond values went up from $1,000 to $1,500. If you hold marketable bonds while the money market rates of interest are *rising*, the open market value of your bond will be *falling*. But if the money market rates of interest are *falling*, the market value of your bonds will be *rising*.*

Now you can see that whenever the open market values of existing bonds are being forced up, interest rates are automatically being forced down. Whenever interest rates are moving down, open market values of existing bonds are moving up.

As market rates of interest change, market values of existing bonds also change—but always in the opposite direction. It must be true, and now you understand why.

Open Market Operations Directly Influence Bond Prices and Interest Rates

Now you can see what happens when the Fed goes into the market and pushes up the

---

*In real world markets at any moment this relationship may not be *precisely* true. Why? Because not only *current* conditions but also *expected future* conditions affect open market bond values and interest rates. But don't worry about this—not unless you're planning to speculate in the bond markets—in which case, please get some professional advice!

prices of government securities—like when it paid $1,200 each for Mr. Alber's $1,000, 6% bonds.

Now suppose Mr. Turner decides to buy a 6%, $1,000 government bond. How much must he pay? $1,200? Right! The Fed has pushed the price up!

But Mr. Turner still only gets $60 a year. So how much interest is he making on his $1,200 investment? Only 5 percent.

So when the Fed goes into the open market and pushes the price of $1,000, 6% bonds up to $1,200, it automatically pushes "the effective rate of interest (the interest *yield*) on government bonds" down to 5 percent. But that isn't all. When the effective rate of interest on government bonds is pushed down, the rate of interest on everything else goes down. All interest rates move together (more or less).

Buying Bonds Eases Money Two Ways

As the Fed buys bonds and forces up bond prices, interest rates throughout the economy automatically are forced down. That's one effect. At the same time, new excess reserves pour into the banking system as the Fed pays for all those bonds it's buying. That's the other effect.

So interest rates are low and banks have lots of excess reserves. What a great time for people and businesses to borrow and spend! You, Mr. or Ms. President, are hoping that more businesses and consumers will borrow and spend. This could set off the multiplier and the accelerator. Then soon the economy would be booming again.

Will the open market operation of "buying securities" really work? Nobody knows for sure. If conditions are really bad, then no. It won't work. It might help a little but it will not be likely to bring a quick recovery. But if conditions aren't really *too* bad the open market operations may work very well.

One of the best things about the open market operations approach to monetary control is that the policy can be adjusted gently and quickly as circumstances change. The Fed has an "open market committee" which meets frequently to consider what the Fed's open market policy should be. This flexibility adds to the effectiveness of this *most important monetary control tool*—open market operations.

OTHER MONETARY POLICY ACTIONS

Now you understand the two most frequently used tools of monetary policy—"discount rate changes" and "open market operations in government securities." A third "tool" consists of changing the **reserve requirement**.

Suppose the amount required in reserves to back up the banks' demand deposits is 20 percent. Remember Mr. Zimmer and his bank? He had $1,000,000 in checking accounts and $200,000 in reserves. If the reserve requirement was 20 percent then Zimmer's bank had just enough reserves to be "legal." What would happen if the reserve requirement was changed?

Changing the Reserve Requirement

Suppose the Fed wants to ease money, so it decides to lower the reserve requirement to 19 percent. Suddenly Mr. Zimmer's bank has $10,000 in excess reserves. So do other banks all over the country. Every one dollar of these excess reserves can support an expansion of about five dollars in the nation's money supply.

Billions of dollars of lending power have been created! Talk about a meat cleaver effect! Reserve requirements can't be changed or adjusted as easily and sensitively as the other monetary policy "tools." For this reason, this "tool of monetary policy" is used only infrequently and with caution.

For Tight Money, Use the Same Tools the Other Way

We have been talking about using monetary policy to bring **easy money** to overcome unemployment, recession and depression. Now let's look at the opposite kind of problem. What kind of monetary policy should we use to slow down a runaway boom? Suppose the people and businesses are trying to buy more than the economy can produce. Shortages and waiting lists are everywhere. Inflationary pressures are serious. Prices threaten to break loose and skyrocket.

What would be the proper monetary policy to slow down total spending? That's easy to figure out. **Tight money!** Make money difficult to borrow, and push interest rates up. How? Raise the discount rate. Sell bonds in the open market. We might even consider raising the reserve requirement.

Raising the discount rate will discourage banks from lending and it will cause them to charge higher interest rates on their loans. Selling bonds will push down open market bond prices. That will push up interest rates. And the checks people write to the Fed to buy the bonds will be taken right out of the banks' reserve accounts. Bank reserves will be reduced, so banks will have to restrict their lending.

When people and businesses pay off their loans the banks will have to deposit this money (this repayment money) in their reserve accounts. They can't use the money to make more loans. So the money supply will get smaller. People will have less money to spend and it will be more difficult to borrow or to buy things on time. Will total spending slow down? You bet it will!

Open Market Operations Can Force Down Lending and Spending

Let's look at the process of tightening money using open market operations. Suppose our friend Mr. Alber recently received a tax refund so he has some excess cash in his bank account. He has been thinking about buying some government securities but he just hasn't gotten around to it yet. Today he hears that $1,000, 6% government bonds are available for a price of $800 each. This seems like a good deal so he decides to buy some.

He buys five of the bonds—total par value of $5,000—for $4,000. He writes a $4,000 check. The check goes from the bond broker to the Federal Reserve Bank. There, $4,000 is deducted from the reserve account of Mr. Zimmer's bank. Then the check is sent to Mr. Zimmer's bank where $4,000 is deducted from Mr. Alber's account. The bank has lost $4,000 in deposits and also $4,000 in reserves. Is it in an illegal position? Yes!

The bank needs less reserves because it has less deposits. But *how much* less reserves does it need? Only $800 less. It has $4,000 less!

The bank must get another $3,200 from somewhere to make up the "illegal deficit" in its Federal Reserve account. Where can it get the money? It could borrow the money from the Fed. But remember? As a part of its tight money policy the Fed has just raised the discount rate. So borrowing from the Fed is expensive!

Zimmer's bank might sell some of their securities to get more money to deposit in their reserve account. But that's expensive, too. Bond prices are depressed now. Remember?

What the bank is likely to do is to reduce its lending. As old loans are repaid the bank just won't relend the money. They'll put the money in their reserve account instead. That will get their reserve account built up again. Meanwhile they will temporarily borrow from the Fed to avoid being in an illegal reserve position.

As the bank cuts back on new loans and refuses to renew old loans, businesses will not be able to expand so much. Some may have to sell inventories and reduce their expansion plans.

The higher interest rates will reduce the demand for machines and equipment and materials, and for inventories. At the higher interest rates it becomes more expensive to carry inventories and it's more costly to buy new machinery and equipment.

It seems that this tight money policy is going to succeed. Will it? Maybe. That's what we'll be talking about next.

HOW EFFECTIVE IS MONETARY POLICY?

Considering all the approaches, all the tools, how effective can monetary policy be? The Fed has several decades of experience. How well have they done? Sometimes, apparently all right. Sometimes not so well. We can't really be sure. Everything the Fed has done with monetary policy has been criticized by someone.

The Fed has been accused of moving too slowly and doing too little. It has been accused of doing too much, of doing the wrong things, and of doing things at the wrong times. Even looking back with all the wisdom of hindsight it's hard to be sure which times the Fed did the right things, and which times it didn't. It's difficult to be sure just how effective the tools of monetary policy have been.

Our Picture of the Economy Is Always Late

One of the frustrations in trying to use monetary policy (or any kind of stabilization policy, for that matter) is that we really don't know what's going on in the economy at any moment. We can't see what's going on today. We only see what was going on some weeks ago. Trying to prescribe stabilization policies in the real world is sort of like a doctor trying to prescribe treatment for a patient who hasn't been examined for several weeks.

Try to picture this situation: You don't feel

very well so you go to "a council of doctors" for tests in mid-June. Then you wait. In late July the doctors figure out what was wrong with you back in June. But the opinion is not unanimous. Several eminent doctors disagree with the diagnosis. But anyway, medicine is ordered. By the time the medicine starts you may be well again. Or you may be dead! But once the medicine starts coming, you must take it.

It may be several months before anyone can tell for sure if you're getting better or worse. Can you see why monetary policy—and all economic stabilization policy—is sort of chancy? Only when conditions in the economy *really get serious* do the economists begin (more or less) to agree on what needs to be done and how.

People Will Spend Only If They're Ready

In general, we can say this: If businesses and consumers are about ready and have been waiting for some little nudge to shake them loose, then "easy money" is likely to have a quick effect. But if businesses are very pessimistic about the future and if the people are out of jobs and deep in debt, then no amount of "easy money" is likely to induce very much increase in spending.

No business is going to borrow and buy a new machine unless the owner expects to be able to sell the output! And if things are really bad, consumers won't start borrowing and buying things. Who would lend money or sell on credit to an unemployed person who's already facing overdue debts, anyway? You can see how unresponsive the economy might be when

things get really bad.

What about the opposite kind of macroeconomic problem—the problem of overexpansion, shortages, and inflation? How effective can monetary policy be in tightening down on an "overheated economy"?

We know for sure that if money gets tight enough, people and businesses will spend less. Very tight money can definitely slow down spending in the economy. There is absolutely no question about that.

What we don't know is *when* to tighten and *how much*. And still more serious, we don't know whether the induced *slow down in spending* will have most of its effect in *reducing inflation* or in *reducing production and employment*. That's an important issue you'll be getting into later.

Tight Money Could Result in "Overkill" and Recession

How much "tight money" do we need to "just do the job and no more"? A little bit of "overkill" when we are trying to curb the boom could result in a serious downturn in the economy. Then the multiplier and accelerator, working downward, could bring widespread unemployment and depression. We just don't know how sensitive the economy will be, when we start to tighten money.

If a slight increase in the discount rate happens to shatter business optimism, the economy could move into an immediate recession. On the other hand, the business community may completely ignore a small change in the discount rate. If the business community overreacts it may be impossible for the monetary policy to be changed back in time to avoid a recession. With your knowledge of the accelerator and the multiplier, you know how hard it is to stop a cumulative expansion or contraction once it gets going!

The tools of monetary policy are being used

all the time. That's right. Every day, even! You will be hearing about and feeling the effects of these things all your life.

Monetary policy is very important in every modern economy. But it isn't the only approach to economic stabilization. Fiscal policy is another approach. You'll learn about that in the next chapter.

SUMMARY AND SYNTHESIS

Monetary policy means government policy to influence or control the size of the money supply and/or interest rates, for the purpose of influencing macroeconomic conditions. Monetary policy focuses on the availability and cost of credit (money). It usually aims toward the **economic stabilization** objectives of **full employment, stable prices, and steady economic growth.**

In the United States, monetary policy is exercised by the **Federal Reserve System (Fed)**—by the **Board of Governors,** and by the **Federal Open Market Committee (FOMC).** The Chairman of the Board plays a very important role. The Fed was created by Congress as an **independent agency.** It is not responsible to the administration. No one has the power to tell the Fed what to do—except that the Congress could pass laws restricting or changing its structure or functions.

The important tools of monetary policy are (1) **changing the discount rate,** (2) **open market operations in government securities,** and (3) **changing the reserve requirements.** All three of these tools are used in cooperation with each other.

Open market operations are most frequently used (actually, on a daily basis). **The discount rate** is changed occasionally to reflect and/or influence money market conditions as required to support and strengthen the effects of the Fed's open market operations. **Reserve requirement** changes occur less frequently because the desired results usually can be more flexibly achieved using the other two tools.

The prices of **marketable bonds** move in opposite directions to money market interest rates. **When the market price of a bond goes up, the interest yield received by the buyer of that bond** goes down. Is it the higher prices of the bonds which push down interest rates? Or lower interest rates which push up the prices of the bonds? It's both.

Each **open market transaction** by the Fed eases or tightens money in **two different ways,** simultaneously. If the Fed buys bonds, this (1) forces bond prices up, so it pushes interest rates down. That's one effect. At the same time (2) new excess reserves are being pushed into the banking system as the Fed pays for the bonds it's buying. That's the other effect.

Suppose the Fed sells bonds. Both effects operate in the opposite direction. (1) The increased supply of bonds in the market pushes bond prices down and interest rates up. (2) The bond buyers pay with checks which the Fed uses to pull down the reserves of banks. The result? Tight money.

The **effectiveness** of a given amount of "easing or tightening in the money market" is impossible to predict. It depends a lot on what conditions exist in the economy at the moment. What "stage of the business cycle" is the economy in? How ready is the economy to respond to a change in the availability and/or cost of credit (money)? It's difficult to know when to ease or tighten, and how much.

How much will the monetary policy influence **production and employment?** And how much will it influence the **inflation rate?** Those, too, are tough questions! Economists and political leaders spend a lot of time trying to figure out (and arguing about) the answers. You'll be reading a lot about all this in the chapters coming up.

REVIEW EXERCISES

MAJOR CONCEPTS, PRINCIPLES, TERMS (Explain each thoroughly.)

monetary policy
changing the discount rate
open market operations
changing the reserve requirement
bond prices and interest rates
how open market operations affect bank reserves
how open market operations affect interest rates

OTHER CONCEPTS AND TERMS (Explain each briefly.)

easy money
tight money
government securities
the "money market"
the bond market
"old bonds"
the discount rate
the "overkill" problem

QUESTIONS (Write out answers, or jot down key points.)

1. For many years there has been a continuing controversy among some economists over the question of the "independence" of the Fed. Some say independence of the Fed is essential to insulate the nation's monetary policies
   from the whims of politicians. Others say the president is supposed to be
   responsible for the health of the economy, but because the Fed is independent the president is denied control over the monetary policy tools needed to
   do the job. What position do you take on this issue, Mr. or Ms. President?
   Why?

2. Under what kinds of economic conditions in the nation would you expect
   monetary policy to be most effective? or ineffective? Explain.

3. Can you explain how open market operations work, *both* (1) through the direct effect on the money supply and bank reserves *and* (2) through the direct
   effect on bond values and interest rates? It's important that you be able to do
   that.

4. After all is said and done, how effective do you think monetary policy really
   is in stabilizing the economy? Do you think it's more effective in overcoming
   depression? or inflation? Explain.

15

Fiscal Policy, the Automatic Stabilizers, and the National Debt

Chapter Objectives

- In the last chapter you learned how **monetary policy** can be used to try to smooth out the **business cycle** and **stabilize the economy.** In this chapter you will learn how **fiscal policy** can be used for the same purpose.

- When you finish studying this chapter you will know about the **tools of fiscal policy: what** they are, **how** they work, and **how effective** they can be.

- You will learn how **expenditure adjustments** and **tax adjustments** work to stabilize the economy through "**discretionary compensatory fiscal policy.**" And you will know about the **non-discretionary "automatic stabilizers."**

- You will be able to explain the idea of **fiscal drag,** the **"burden" of the federal debt,** and factors which influence the **effectiveness** of "compensatory fiscal policy."

- You will be able to explain the **cheer up approach,** the use of **public works programs,** about **government deficit financing,** and the creation of **monetized debt.** And you will be able to discuss **the effects** of each of these.

If Easy Money Doesn't Work, What Then?

How do you like pretending you are the President of the United States? A little credibility gap? Well, I guess so. But now that you are experienced at it, please stick with it awhile longer. Okay?

Let's go back to where we were at the beginning of the last chapter. The economy is depressed. You, Mr. or Ms. President, are looking at the high unemployment figures and thinking, "Something must be done quickly! At least before election day!"

You are quite sure that the Fed is going to do something to bring "easy money." But sup-

pose nobody wants to borrow and buy? Suppose people put their money in savings accounts and it just sits there? Then what good will all this monetary policy do? No good! So that's why you're worried.

USING FISCAL POLICY TO INDUCE PROSPERITY

You are impatient, Mr. or Ms. President. You say, "Isn't there some way we can take *more direct* action to solve this problem? Can't we just take the bull by the horns and do something that doesn't depend on what a lot of consumers and businesses decide to do?"

Increase Government Spending or Cut Taxes

Yes, there is something. If you could *increase government spending* that would be *sure* to put more spending into the total spending flow.

How obvious! Instead of trying to do something to induce the consumers and businesses (C + I) to increase their spending, why not just come in and increase government spending (G) directly? The surest way to increase total spending is to increase it yourself! So you decide to go to Congress and persuade them to pass some new "appropriations legislation."

You might try to persuade Congress to appropriate enough money so the government could *hire all the unemployed people.* That certainly would be the most direct way to solve the unemployment problem! Or you might get the Congress to appropriate money to build new school buildings and post offices and highways and recreation areas and military bases. That would create more jobs, more incomes, more spending. Maybe the multiplier and the accelerator would catch on and take it from there. Do you try it? Maybe not.

Maybe you decide that this is not a good time to try to get Congress to increase government spending. Maybe you decide to try to get them to cut taxes instead.

If the government takes less taxes out of people's paychecks, the people get to keep more money. Very likely they will spend more. If enough people spend enough more, that will solve the problem.

Or maybe the government will cut taxes on business profits. Then businesses will be likely to spend more for investment and hire more people and produce more. That might do the trick.

So which will you do, Mr. or Ms. President? Why not try some of both? Increase spending some and cut taxes some. Use both "tools" of **compensatory fiscal policy.**

When you adjust taxes or spending to "compensate" for too little (or too much) spending by consumers and businesses, this is called "compensatory fiscal policy." Suppose you decide to try it. First you plan to cut personal income taxes and leave more money in everybody's paycheck. This should push total consumer spending up and help to get things going again. So you get some of your friends in Congress and some lawyers to start drafting a tax-cut bill.

The Program Must Meet Political Realities

While the tax-cut bill is being prepared, you begin working with a group of Congressional leaders drafting a program of expenditures for federal **public works projects**—new highways and streets, water and sewer systems, public buildings, things like that. Each senator wants several projects "for the old home state." All the members of Congress want one or more projects in their home districts. All the "party faithful" governors and mayors throughout the country expect to be rewarded for their party loyalties.

This could get out of hand! They can't all have everything they want. Too much government spending would create much more factor demand than there are factors available. *Surplus* would suddenly become *shortage.* Total spending or "aggregate demand" would be too great for the productive capacity of the economy. Prices would break loose and go up. You don't want that to happen. You want to do enough, but *not too much!*

Finally, after many precious weeks have

been lost in haggling, your legislative program for "compensatory fiscal policy" is ready to be offered to Congress. You go to Congress and give an impressive speech in support of the tax cut and the "public works" spending program. You urge Congress to take speedy action on these high priority measures. But then what?

The weeks drag by and nothing much seems to happen. Several leaders of Congress express concern about your program. "Spend more, and tax less? Blatant fiscal irresponsibility!" Some of your own party, but mostly the opposition, keep making noises about your proposed government deficit.

Some members of Congress (and their economic advisers) say the program is one of overkill. They say: "The economy is about ready to start booming anyway. This big push by government will bring shortages and inflation for sure!"

Others say the opposite: "We are really on the verge of a serious depression. Inventories are high and general confidence is low. Just look at the recent stock market slide, for example! The President's proposed program is too little and too late. It's only a drop in the bucket. Let's build a public works program big enough to do the job!"

How Much Fiscal Action Is Needed?

Who is right? Is your program the right size? With the right emphasis? Or not? What about your economic advisers and the economist-statisticians (econometricians) with their highly refined computerized models of the economic system. Can't they tell you the answer?

No. Unfortunately, they can't. They can make scientific estimates but there's no way they can tell what the people and businesses are going to do, once your program gets started. They can *estimate*, but they can't tell for sure.

Suppose inventories are down to low levels and businesses are looking for some little excuse to begin restocking their shelves. Suppose consumers only need some little indication that things are going to get better. They are just waiting for some excuse to run out and start buying new vacuum cleaners and refrigerators and stoves and furniture and TV sets and automobiles and new designer jeans and all. The multiplier and the accelerator are lying just under the surface, poised for action. In these conditions not much government spending or government hiring or tax cutting will be needed to speed up the economy. But under different circumstances, things could be quite different.

The More the Economy Is Overstocked, the Slower the Recovery

Suppose most businesses—manufacturers, wholesalers, retailers—are overstocked with (and deep in debt for) excess inventories. And suppose most consumers have just recently been on a buying binge. Every family has a new car, new refrigerator, new furniture, new everything and is up to their ears in debt. Now how much must the government cut taxes and increase spending to get the economy to speed up? Quite a lot!

The multiplier and accelerator are buried deep under all this mass of inventory and excess plant capacity and debt. Until some of the inventories and debts are cleared away the "multiple expansion process" will work only very sluggishly, if at all. That's what happens in a big-big boom. We build big inventories and big debts. Now you can see why a very big boom is likely to lead to a very bad depression.

Is there any way that you, Mr. or Ms. President, can find out whether or not the economy is about ready to surge forward? Or if it is buried in excess inventories and debt? Luckily, there is. During the past few decades great progress has been made in keeping tabs on what's going on in the economy.

Reports from the Departments of Commerce, Labor, Agriculture and others, from the Fed, and from many other sources tell how much the consumers are in debt, how old the average automobile is, how much inventory is being carried in each industry, what the businesses and consumers are buying these days, and all sorts of things. These statistics help a lot. But they can't tell you everything.

Reactions of Consumers and Businesses Are Hard to Predict

It's much easier to tell how old a person's car is than to tell whether or not that person will buy another car this year if taxes are cut by 8 percent. It's much easier to tell the level of debt in an industry than to tell how much sales must increase to set off an inventory expansion.

Individuals make their economic choices on the basis of their outlook—their expectations. They seem to all move at the same time. Now you know how a cowboy feels when he's trying to figure out how much noise it will take to move the cattle without stampeding the herd! It's the same kind of question. Sometimes the cattle are spooky and poised for a quick move. How much noise? Just a little! At other times the cattle are feeling overfed and lazy. It takes quite a lot to make them move.

We take all kinds of surveys and opinion polls to find out what people and businesses *think* they are going to do. This information helps. But sometimes people don't really know what they're going to do until the time comes. People and businesses have a tendency to do whatever the people and businesses just down the street are doing. This makes **economic forecasting** very hazardous.

The very best program you and your advisers could design might hit far from the mark. But no matter. The program you design isn't going to get through Congress anyway.

Congress Doesn't Always Cooperate

Tax cuts and spending projects are of *great* interest to Congress. So no matter what you do, Congress is going to have the last word on this taxing-spending program. Some members of Congress will be fighting for what they see as

"the good of the nation." Others will be fighting for reelection or to pay back a political favor or for some other reason. Some of them may even be fighting for your job!

Which taxes will be cut? and by how much? and what projects will be undertaken? and where? and when?—all of these matters will ultimately be decided by Congress. Not by you. Political considerations are likely to outweigh the economic considerations in *every one* of these taxing and spending decisions. Even though you and your advisers had known with absolute certainty what *should* be done, it is almost an absolute certainty that your "perfect program" couldn't have gotten through Congress anyway!

You, Mr. or Ms. President, are facing a tough problem. I suppose the best thing you can do is, first: be sure you have good economic advisers. Then work with them to design a program which you think will be effective and which you think Congress will pass. Then cross your fingers and go ahead. If you do everything carefully (and if you're lucky) maybe you will get to have a second term in the White House after all.

What we are talking about is "compensatory fiscal policy," or just **fiscal policy**. It's a powerful tool if you get it to work right. You can adjust taxes and spending to overcome depression. You can also use fiscal policy to hold down a boom and fight inflation.

USING FISCAL POLICY TO CURB INFLATION

Suppose almost everyone is trying to buy a new TV set and a new car and a new washing machine and new furniture and new designer jeans and other things. And suppose every manufacturer of automobiles and home appliances and furniture is trying to double plant capacity and every wholesaler and retailer is trying to expand inventory. Can all these demands be met? Obviously not. There's just no way!

Do you see the picture? It's a booming economy, all right. The acceleration principle is working full force. An economy booming at this pace is headed almost certainly for two disastrous results: first, inflation. Then depression.

The Threat of Inflation

Rapid price inflation will eat up a lot of the purchasing power which is now making Mr. and Ms. Average Consumer feel so wealthy. They're going to find out that they won't really be able to buy the cars and the appliances and all the other things that they thought they were going to buy with all of their money. They're going to pay higher prices than they thought and run out of money sooner (and/or be in debt deeper) than they expected.

What's the situation with the business firms? All businesses are trying to expand as fast as they can. They're ordering more inventories, machines, factories, everything. But deliveries are very slow. These are "good times" from the point of view of employment. Everybody who wants a job gets a job. Income is good. Producers are begging workers to work overtime. That's great. But shortages are everywhere. Prices and wages are under serious pressure to break loose and start leap-frogging each other until they go out of sight over the horizon!

The Threat of Overbuilding then Collapse

Yes, serious inflation is the first threat. But another disaster also is threatening. This rate of expansion can't possibly be sustained for very long. Then what will happen? Recession? Of course.

Eventually the inventory buildup will cease. "Normal" levels of demand will return. The factories which have been producing to meet the boom-time demand for the build-up will no longer be able to stay busy. They will cut back production. Overtime work will cease. Some un-employment will develop. You know what happens next.

The unemployed people stop buying as much. So retail stores stop ordering as much. Soon the wholesalers and retailers stop ordering altogether and just sell out of their overstocked inventories. Spending slows down even more. Unemployment spreads. Businesses and consumers stop spending and start trying to pay off their debts. Here comes our depression again! Scary, isn't it?

How do we cool down this excessive boom before it's too late? You already know about the monetary policy tools of raising the discount rate and the reserve requirements, and selling bonds in the open market to pull money out of the economy. But what about the *fiscal policy* tools?

Cut Government Spending or Raise Taxes to Hold Down the Boom

One way to curb the boom with fiscal policy is to increase taxes on businesses and consumers. This will force them to cut back their spending. The other way is to cut back on government spending. Delay all new government projects and slow down or stop ongoing projects. This reduces the demand for labor and the other factors of production. Reduced government spending will release factors of production so they can shift to (and relieve shortages in) the "private sector" of the economy.

Would this "counter-inflationary fiscal policy" (increasing taxes and cutting back government spending) really work? Yes, it really would. Except that you will have all the problems you had before. Here are some questions to be considered:

How much to raise taxes? Which taxes? How much to cut back spending? Which projects to stop? Slow down? Delay? Which government employees to lay off? Which private business contracts to cancel? And then: how do I get the Congress to go along?

Cutting Spending and Raising Taxes May Mean Political Suicide

Suppose you could get the "exactly right" answers to all these questions (which you can't). Would you then prepare a message and go to Congress urging the tax increases and the spending cuts? Do you want to go down in history (or into the next election) known as the tax-raising, project-cancelling boom-killer? Suppose you're willing to take that chance. How many members of Congress do you think will go along with you?

Later, when you're out stumping the country campaigning for the next election, you will explain to the people why it was necessary to raise taxes and cut back their favorite projects.

• You will explain that the tax increase didn't take nearly as much of their purchasing power away as the *inflation* would have taken, so they're really better off paying more taxes!

• You will explain that the reason you cancelled all their government projects—the new hospital and the pollution-free sewer system and the manpower training program and the promised bridge across the river—is that "they, the people" were spending so much for new cars and appliances and things that there weren't enough factors of production left over to keep the government projects going.

• You will tell them all about opportunity costs—that "You can't have your cake and eat it too. The economy can't produce any more than it can produce."

You will teach them all sorts of good lessons in sound economics. Guess what they'll tell you! (I'm sure you can guess.) Even if they know you're telling the truth, this isn't the kind of truth people like to hear.

They might ask why you didn't cancel the foreign aid programs instead of the domestic programs, and why you didn't cancel any of the programs in *your own* home state. Can you begin to see the difficulty of raising taxes and cutting government spending to fight inflation? It can be made to work, yes. But it isn't easy.

Even if you didn't have to worry about the political repercussions and even if you could get Congress to go along with your program, counter-inflationary fiscal policy is tricky business. How much should you increase taxes or reduce spending? That's hard to say. You always face the problem of choosing the right "dose"—between ineffectiveness and overkill.

THE AUTOMATIC STABILIZERS

By now you know for sure that fiscal policy is not an easy, quick way to stabilize the economy. But wait. Here's some good news for a change. To some extent compensatory fiscal policy works automatically!

Some Taxes Adjust Automatically

The federal income tax is progressive. That means the *tax rate* gets higher as your *income* gets higher. So as the economy booms and people get more income they *automatically* pay higher tax rates. As the income stream gets larger and larger the government keeps pulling out a larger percentage of it. Just automatically! Here's an example.

Suppose Mr. Snyder is a construction worker, but construction has been slow. He only managed to earn $6,500 last year. Considering that he has a wife and three children, he had to pay only about $200 in federal income taxes. That's only about 3% of his income.

This year things are much better. Mr. Snyder's income is up to $13,000. That's twice as much income. And his federal income taxes? Up to $1,400. That's seven times as much! This year his taxes are up to about 11% of his income. But that's not all. For every additional dollar he earns (over $13,000) he's going to have to pay 22% of it in taxes!

Suppose the economy really goes into a boom next year and Mr. Snyder gets higher wages and works a lot of overtime. His income doubles again—up to $26,000. He will have to pay about $5,000 (about 3½ times as much as this year) in federal income taxes. Now his tax rate is up to almost 20% of his income. For each additional dollar he earns now (over $26,000) he's going to have to pay 32% in federal income taxes.

See how the federal government automatically pulls a lot more money out of the spending-income stream when the economy starts to boom? It works the other way too, of course. When the construction boom slows down and Mr. Snyder's income goes down, his "effective federal income tax rate" will automatically go down, too. If his income ever drops down to $5,000, his "effective tax rate" will drop to zero!

Is this **automatic tax adjustment** big enough to really have any effect on the economy? It sure is! It results in billions of dollars of extra tax withdrawals when the economy is expanding.

Sometimes the effect of the automatic tax increase is so strong that it chokes off the economic expansion too soon. When this happens it's called **fiscal drag**. Sometimes a tax cut may be needed to cut down the "fiscal drag" and let the economy continue to expand toward full employment!

Some Spending Adjusts Automatically

Government payments for unemployment compensation and for welfare programs work against the business cycle. When times are bad more people draw unemployment compensation and more people go on the public welfare rolls. When business picks up, most of these people become self-supporting again.

When the economy slows down, billions of government dollars flow to individuals and families. Their marginal propensity to consume (MPC) is likely to be high so the "induced consumer spending" (and therefore the income multiplier) is likely to be high.

Over the years, as the welfare and unemployment programs have been increased, the "automatic stabilizing effect" of government spending has increased. Later in this book you'll be reading about ideas for a **negative income tax**—that is, automatic payments to people whenever their incomes fall below some minimum size. If the negative income tax is ever established in this country it will provide even more automatic stabilization.

Stability of Consumer Spending

You've already learned a lot about the consumption function. You know that people's spending for consumer goods is determined by the size of their incomes. Right? Well, the purpose of this little section is to tell you "It ain't necessarily so." Not exactly, anyway. Not for any short period of time.

It usually takes people a while to adjust to a new "income situation"—especially if the new income is a *lower* income. People who are hit by hard times usually try to hang on to their old standard of living as long as they can, hoping things will soon get better. For a while they can spend their savings or sell some things or go into debt to keep up their old standard.

If hard times continue long enough, sooner or later they must learn to get by on less expensive housing, food, clothing, transportation, recreation, medical and dental care, etc. But the important thing is this: during times when people's incomes are falling, consumer spending tends to stay high—at least for a while. This "consumer spending buoyancy" helps to support the economy, to use up excess inventories, and to get the economy on the upswing again. If the recession is short, people may get their jobs back soon enough so that their consumer spending doesn't have to be cut back at all!

What about boom times? You know how savings increase as incomes increase. Suppose people's incomes are going up fast. Some people will spend it as fast as they get it. Sure. But many people won't.

Many people will let some savings pile up before they move into a better place, buy another car, start wearing more expensive clothes and eating steak and lobster twice a day. See how these savings withdrawals could hold down the boom? They really do, too. It's hard to say just how much this **consumer spending stability** helps. But it does help.

"Stabilized Dividend" Policies

There's another automatic stabilizing influence that needs to be mentioned: corporate dividend payments to stockholders. In the early 1980s corporations were paying out between $60 and $70 billion a year in dividends. That isn't a "massive amount" when compared with a national income of more than two trillion dollars. But it's at least big enough so that its "marginal stabilizing effect" can be important. How does it work? Like this.

Suppose there's a big boom and big profits. Do corporations pay out more in dividends? Usually, yes. A little more. But not *much* more. They just hold most of the extra profits as "undistributed profits," to reinvest.

Suppose the economy slows down and the corporations don't make much profits. Maybe many of them have losses. Do they pay out less in dividends? Usually, yes. A little less, but not much less. Usually they pay out some of the "undistributed profits" from previous years.

What's the effect of all this? It pulls some "consumer spending money" out of the spending stream during boom times and pushes some extra "consumer spending money" into the stream when things are slack. The net effect is to help to stabilize the economy.

How Effective Are the Automatic Stabilizers?

The "automatic fiscal stabilizers" (automatic spending and taxing adjustments) can help a lot. When aided by the stabilizing effects of consumer spending stability and corporate dividends policies, they can certainly help to stabilize the economy.

The economy has been more stable since World War II. Has it been because of the automatic stabilizers? No one can say. They deserve some of the credit, that's for sure.

But the automatic stabilizers are not enough. Sometimes **discretionary stabilization policy**—compensatory monetary policy and fiscal policy—is required. That is, when things get bad enough, Mr. or Ms. President, you have to make up your mind that it's time to do something and you have to decide what to do and then you have to find a way to do it. That's "discretionary stabilization policy." Will it work? Maybe.

HOW EFFECTIVE IS "DISCRETIONARY COMPENSATORY FISCAL POLICY"?

So what can we say about "discretionary compensatory fiscal policy?" Is it effective? Sometimes. If we are willing to take enough fiscal policy action during depression—cutting taxes, increasing expenditures, hiring people on government payrolls, buying up surplus outputs and so on—we can definitely overcome the depression.

We can also be sure that if we are willing to take enough fiscal policy action during times of shortages and inflationary pressures, we can cut back the inflationary pressures. But in both these cases we run the risk of "overkill." Each time we move to overcome depressed conditions we run the risk of driving the economy into inflation. Each time we move to hold down inflationary spending we run the risk of generating unemployment and recession.

Fiscal policy is not a "fine-tuning knob" for economic stabilization. We can't hope to use it to maintain "just the right level" of spending, employment, output, and income. When we try to solve our macroeconomic problems with fiscal policy, we go after them not with a surgeon's scalpel but with a meat cleaver. Any time "meat cleaver action" is justified, fiscal policy will work. It may work too much or it may work too little, but it will work.

Whenever serious depression threatens, you may be sure that Congress will take some fiscal policy action. And you may be sure that *it will work*. For this reason you may be sure there will never be another disastrous depression in the American economy. The government will not let it happen.

We might overdo it and run into inflation. But no doubt we will take that chance. We might have to establish wage and price controls—maybe government rationing, even. But it seems clear that the people would prefer widespread economic controls to widespread unemployment. The point is this: there are, today, *known alternatives* to serious depression. It seems to be a safe bet that fiscal policy will be used to whatever extent necessary to prevent serious and prolonged depression.

Yes, the government will use fiscal policy sometimes—and it will work. If it doesn't work well enough at first, then more and different things will be done *until it does work*, at least "well enough."

The government will unbalance the budget and run deficits and add to the debt as much as necessary to get things going again. But what will all these deficits and debts do to the economy? Let's talk about that.

FISCAL POLICY AND THE UNBALANCED BUDGET

Maybe you haven't thought about it, but "discretionary compensatory fiscal policy" really is a policy of *unbalancing the federal budget on purpose!*

If total spending is too small, let's increase government spending! That will *directly* increase the size of the spending flow in the economy. And let's reduce taxes! That will *indirectly* increase the size of the spending flow.

Increasing spending? while cutting taxes? That means "unbalancing the budget"! It means "deficit financing." It means "increasing the national debt." What about that? Isn't that bad?

A Budget Deficit Increases the Debt

When the budget is unbalanced, tax revenues don't provide enough money to support the government's spending. How does the government make up the difference? It sells bonds and Treasury bills, of course.

If it sells the bonds to individuals and businesses and banks and insurance companies and all, this pulls money out of the economic system. Then when the government spends the money it puts the money back into the economic system. When the government does this the federal debt gets larger. The government owes the debt to the people who are holding the bonds.

Suppose the government did not sell the bonds to individuals and businesses and banks and insurance companies and all, but sold them to the Federal Reserve Banks instead. What difference would that make? Quite a lot!

A "Federal Reserve financed government deficit" would be much more stimulating to the economy. Why? Because that would be *creating new money* and putting it into the economy. New *high-powered* money!

When the Fed buys new Treasury bills, notes, or bonds, the Fed simply creates the money. It creates a new demand deposit (Treasury deposit) for the government (just like Zimmer's bank created a new demand deposit for Baker). With the new deposit the Treasury can write checks to hire people or can buy things or start new programs or whatever.

Borrowing from the Fed Creates High-Powered Money

When the Treasury borrows from the Fed, it works like this: the Federal Reserve Banks receive newly printed government bonds. Then the Federal Reserve Banks add the amount to the

Treasury's deposit.

The Treasury now has more money—a larger deposit balance—in the Federal Reserve Banks. The national debt is larger, and the Treasury has that much more money to spend.

Soon the Treasury will start spending the new money. Checks will be paid to people and businesses throughout the country. What do you suppose all those people and businesses are going to do with their government checks? Deposit them, of course!

When each check clears, see what happens? The new money is pulled out of the Treasury's deposit at the Fed and goes into each bank's reserve account. The new money soon becomes *new reserves for banks* all over the country! A multiple expansion of the money supply can result.

When the government uses deficit financing and "covers the deficit" by selling bonds to the Fed, that can have a very stimulating effect on the economy. The increase in government spending pays money to people and businesses. That's the initial increase in the total spending flow. Then if the people have an MPC greater than zero (that is, if they spend *any* of their new income) there will be a multiplier effect. Spending will increase even more.

This kind of fiscal policy has a strong "easy money" policy locked into it—but only when the Federal Reserve Banks buy the government bonds. When the government sells the bonds to individuals and businesses and banks and insurance companies, that just gathers up existing money—money they wanted to invest in government bonds. Then when the government spends the money, that just pushes the money back into the economy again. No new money is created. See how much difference it makes whether or not the deficit is financed by the Fed buying the bonds?

WHAT ABOUT THE NATIONAL DEBT?

From what you know about the government debt, what do you think of it? Do you think it

would be good if we could just "wish it away"? Would we be better off?

To get at this question, first think about debt, in general. Surely I'd like to "wish away" the mortgage on my house! If you owe anybody money I'll bet you'd like to "wish away" that debt too!

But suppose somebody owes you money. Do you want that debt "wished away"? Do you have a savings account? Or a checking account? Then the bank or savings and loan *owes you* your money. Right? How would you like it if their debt to you was suddenly "wished away"? Not so good, huh?

If the mortgage debt on my house was "wished away," then your savings account in the savings and loan that lent me the money would have to be "wished away" too. So when we look at it from both sides, maybe debt is not such a bad thing.

Is the debt on my house a good thing? I must think so or else I wouldn't have agreed to create it. I would not have borrowed. The savings and loan company must think it's a good thing too, or else they wouldn't have agreed to create it. They wouldn't have lent me the money.

The people who sold the house to me thought the debt was a good thing, because it enabled me to buy the house. I wouldn't have been able to buy the house unless I could borrow the money and create the debt. That's for sure! So, all things considered, I guess the mortgage debt on my house must be a good thing.

All of Our Money Is Debt*

What do we use as money in this country? Debt? That's exactly right. Nothing but debt. *Absolutely* nothing but debt! The money supply is made up of checkable deposits and currency. The deposits are the debts of the banks, savings

*Economists sometimes define money as different from other kinds of debt—but no need to get into that issue here.

and loans, etc. If you have an account in a bank, that bank *owes* you your money. It's their debt to you.

What about the currency in your pocket? Currency is issued by the Federal Reserve Banks. Each one-dollar bill or ten-dollar bill or fifty-dollar bill is a debt (a "liability") of one of the twelve Federal Reserve Banks.

What do the banks use to "back up" their deposit money? You remember: their Federal Reserve accounts. More debt? Sure. Where did all those Federal Reserve deposits come from, anyway? Where did we get all that "high-powered money" to back up all these billions of dollars of demand deposit money? Can you guess? From the federal debt, maybe? Of course.

The government printed up bonds and "sold" them to the Federal Reserve Banks. That gave the Treasury new deposits, which they spent. The money went to the businesses and people and then was deposited in the banks. Next the new money became new reserve deposits at the Federal Reserve Banks. That's exactly what happened.

Government Debt Can Create Money

The growth of the money supply in the United States (and in all other modern countries) has come about through the creation of new government debt. The government debt becomes **monetized**. It becomes money! The newly created money moves into the banking system and creates new reserves. Then the new reserves support the multiple expansion of the money supply.

So is government debt good? Or bad? Would you like to "wish away" that part of the government debt which is supporting our money supply? You wouldn't want that any more than I would. Furthermore, as the economy grows, national income and national product grow. More people and more businesses are doing and making and buying and selling more things. So do we need a larger money supply? Of course. How do we get it? From the expansion of loan-created

demand deposit money? Sure. And where do the new reserves come from to permit all these new demand deposits? The new reserves are created by the expansion of **monetized government debt.**

So some of the government debt helps to support (and through the Fed's open market operations, helps to regulate) the money supply. That's okay. But what about the part of the federal debt which wasn't sold to the Fed?

What about the "non-monetized" part of the debt—that is, the bonds and notes which were sold to the people and banks and insurance companies and all? What effect does that have? Would it be good if all this part of the debt suddenly could be "wished away"?

Non-Monetized Government Debt Serves a Purpose, Too

One thing is sure. The two government bonds I own are not going to be "wished away"! (Not if I can help it.) And my bank holds millions of dollars' worth of government bonds. If that part of the debt is "wished away" my bank is going to go broke and all my money (deposits) will be wiped out. I'm not in favor of that!

The insurance company that I am depending on to help me in my retirement years or to pay my survivors if something happens to me—that company holds millions of dollars' worth of government securities, too. If that part of the debt is "wished away" the company is going to go broke and my retirement years will be lean and hungry!

I suppose the government could collect more money in taxes and then use the money to pay off (buy back) all those privately-held bonds. But that would take a lot of taxes. A lot of money would have to be pulled out of the spending-income stream. I don't think we want to do that. You can guess what the economic (and political!) consequences of that would be!

The people and companies holding the bonds don't want to get rid of the bonds. They own government securities because they've decided that's the best thing for them to do with their money. That's the best kind of "asset" for them to invest in. If they wanted to they could get cash for their bonds any day. Since they don't, it's pretty obvious that they don't want to.

So what do you think about the government debt? Is it good? Or bad? By now I think you can see that it is more good than bad. It's certainly a lot better to have it than it would be to get rid of it!

As time goes on the federal debt is going to get bigger. I think you can be sure of that. But there's no reason to get excited about *the size* of it. When people get excited about the size of the government debt it's usually because they don't understand it.

Federal Debt, GNP, and Private Debt: A Comparison

If the size of the federal debt is alarming to you, perhaps it will be comforting for you to look at these comparisons:

1. At the end of World War II (1945) the federal debt was about the same size as the gross national product. It totaled about $200 billion. At that time, total private debt in this country was about $150 billion.
2. By 1960, the federal debt had increased by 25 percent (to about $250 billion). The gross national product had increased by 150 percent (to $500 billion), and total private debt had almost quadrupled (to almost $600 billion).

See what's happening? The federal government debt is getting larger, but not nearly as fast as either GNP or total private debt.

3. From 1960 to the early 1970s, the federal debt increased by more than 60 percent (to more than $400 billion), gross national product increased by more than 100 percent (to more than $1,100 billion), and private debt *almost tripled* again (to about $1,500 billion).

4. During the early 1980s the federal debt passed $1 trillion, GNP passed $3 trillion, and private debt was more than $5 trillion.

Just look at the growth in that private debt! Should we be worried about that? My home mortgage is a part of that. Should we be worried about that part? Suppose the total size of the private debt started coming down? Would that be good? What would that mean?

It would mean that people were paying off their home mortgages and that fewer people were buying houses. Or it would mean that businesses were paying off their loans and were not re-borrowing to expand and produce more. It would mean that the economy was slowing down. Unemployment would be high. Hard times would be here.

Private debt and government debt are very different in many ways. But both are functioning parts of our economic and monetary systems. It just doesn't make sense to look at the size of either and be alarmed.

The "Burdens" of Debt

Aren't there any burdens of debt? Of course there are. Debt sometimes can be very oppressive to people. When people try to consume at a higher rate than they are producing, they go deeper and deeper into debt. If they keep it up, someday their past will catch up with them. They may have a miserable time trying to pay off all those debts!

But government debt and the great mass of private debt in this country and in all the other modern countries aren't that kind of thing at all. Debt is an essential part of the market system. It is a part of the exchange mechanism. As the economic system grows, debts will grow.

If anyone ever asks if debt is bad, ask them these questions: Is money bad? Are government bonds bad? Are savings accounts bad? Are mortgages bad? Debt isn't bad. Back in the early chapters of this book you saw how efficiently debt can provide for the monetary needs of the society. You saw the wise old northside chief create all that money. Those checking accounts. Those "bank debts." Remember?

To be sure, debt can create problems. The "borrowing privilege" can be (sometimes is) abused. This is as true for the federal government as it is for an individual. But consequences of "debt abuse" by the federal government are different—are in fact *completely unrelated*—to the consequences of debt abuse by an individual or a family or business. That's one reason why there's always so much misunderstanding about the federal debt.

The Consequences of "Debt Abuse" by the Federal Government

There are several kinds of problems associated with the federal debt. But the greatest danger results from the *opportunity to be irresponsible*—to go to extremes. A rapid increase in the debt can create too much money. This can generate inflation and do serious harm to the economy.

Some members of Congress may try to use government debt to "make political hay." Congress can run a large deficit, create money, and undertake many projects to "woo votes" from the people back home. When a member of Congress comes up for reelection (every two years) if he or she can show the people back home lots of government projects and increased jobs and incomes—with no increase in taxes—you can guess who is likely to get the votes! See how great the temptation might be?

It isn't the *existing size* of the federal debt that creates the problem. It's the rapid expansion in the money supply and in total spending which can result from the *rapid expansion* in the size of the debt.

What About "Crowding Out"?

Sometimes there's good reason to be concerned about too much increase in the government debt. Rapid increases must be financed in the money markets. The Treasury must sell new government securities to get the money it needs.

Suppose the Fed buys the new government securities. That puts new high-powered money into the banks' reserves. A multiple expansion of the money supply can begin. Inflation! Nobody wants that!

But suppose the Fed *doesn't* buy the government securities. What then? The new government securities increase the supply of securities for sale in the money markets. As people buy these securities it pulls a lot of money out of the nation's money markets. The increased supply forces down the prices of all bonds. And all of this forces up interest rates, of course.

The government is selling bonds and gathering up billions of dollars to finance its programs. At the same time, businesses throughout the economy are depending on these money markets to finance their continuing operations and planned expansions. So what's happening? The government's deficit financing (selling bonds) is **crowding out** the private investors!

The government is absorbing so much of the available funds that money is very tight. Interest rates are pushed so high that many businesses can't afford to borrow. So they cut back. The economy slows down.

How serious is this "crowding out" problem? Economists disagree. But during the early 1980s many economists blamed "crowding out" for seriously impeding the growth and productivity of the American economy. The fear of "crowding out" was one of the reasons why so many national leaders in the early 1980s were demanding that the federal government deficit be reduced or eliminated.

What About Stimulating the Economy?

If the economy is depressed and needs to be stimulated (and if there's no threat of inflation), then deficit financing is a different story. An increase in government spending may stimulate the economy, and the creation of monetized debt may ease money and stimulate private investment. All this may help the economy to get going again.

"Deficit financing" (spending more than is collected in taxes) can support public works projects and reemploy people. This can increase incomes and spending. If it does, it will generate more tax revenues for the government.

If the "deficit financing fiscal policy" is completely successful, the economy will regain its prosperity. People will have good incomes and will pay a lot more taxes. All those extra tax revenues may bring the government budget back into balance.

In 1981, President Reagan called on Congress for a tax cut. He argued that people and businesses should be permitted to retain more of their earnings. This would stimulate more productivity and growth—and more income in the economy.

The higher income would produce more tax revenues—enough more, in fact, to balance the budget—automatically. You can see that as national income increases, tax revenues increase. But will the government budget move into balance?

Congress passed the tax cut bill in 1981. As this book goes to press, it's much too early to draw any conclusions about the ultimate results. By the time you're reading this, you may already know the answer.

THE "CHEER UP" APPROACH TO OVERCOMING DEPRESSION

You know about the importance of expectations in influencing the economy. Expectations influence the amount businesses will spend for factories, equipment, inventories, everything. Expectations play a big role in influencing consumer spending for new cars, TV sets and other consumer durables.

If everyone expects high employment and good times, the spending rate is likely to be high. But people who expect unemployment (and surpluses and special sales and price-cuts)

tomorrow, will not go out and spend today. They will wait until the surpluses and price cutting begin. They may also be waiting to see if they still have jobs!

Expectations and the "Self-Fulfilling Prophecy"

See how important expectations are? If everyone thinks there is going to be high employment and a great demand for things and rising prices, then that is exactly what will happen. Everyone goes out and buys before the shortages occur and before the prices rise.

So what happens? All this spending *creates* the shortages and rising prices the people are *expecting!* Maybe if they hadn't expected it, it wouldn't have happened.

Here's a specific example: In February, 1976, the Chinese Lunar Year of the Dragon began. Well-informed Chinese know that the dragon will bring financial success and prosperity. The prophets prophesied profits. So what happened? As the Year of the Dragon began, Asian investors began buying heavily. Stock prices soared in Hong Kong, Singapore, Taipei and Manila!

We can say it this way: If people expect rising prices and shortages and high levels of employment, that is exactly what they will get. But if people expect unemployment, surpluses, and widespread price cutting, then everyone waits.

Because of the waiting and the drop in spending, the people get exactly what they expected! Many lose their jobs. The economy goes into recession. It's sort of a **self-fulfilling prophecy**. Whatever the people *expect* to happen, that's what *will* happen.

If you're still playing the role of President and trying to overcome a depression, maybe this discussion of the importance of "expectations" will give you some ideas.

Maybe you should go on radio and TV and try to convince all the people that a big boom is about to begin. Tell them there will be shortages, lots of jobs, and overtime for everybody. Tell them if they want to buy anything they should go out and do it *tomorrow.*

Maybe everyone will believe you and go out and borrow and spend. If they do, sure enough, it will turn out that you were right. But if they *don't* believe you it will turn out that you were wrong.

All Presidents Use "Cheer Up" Speeches

In the early part of the depression of the 1930s President Herbert Hoover announced to the nation: "Prosperity is just around the corner." If all the people had really believed him he would have been right. But they didn't. So he wasn't.

In 1933, President Franklin D. Roosevelt in his "fireside chat" radio broadcasts told the people: "All we have to fear is fear itself." But we had plenty of fear to fear. Until we got rid of some of the fear we weren't going to have much prosperity.

Every president since Roosevelt has tried to influence the public mood—and usually with some success. So why shouldn't you? Really, a powerful force for economic downturn and depression or for economic upturn and prosperity is the psychology of the people. If the people are convinced that the economy really is getting ready to go soft, then it will. If they are convinced that it is getting ready to improve, then it will.

The People Need Confidence in the Government's Policies

Suppose the people are confident that the government has the necessary tools and can guarantee prosperity. Then this confidence is likely to make it unnecessary for the government to use the tools.

If you, Mr. or Ms. President, have been able to inspire confidence to such an extent that all the people are *sure* that you can and will handle any serious economic problem which may arise, then the people will not be spooky or gun-shy. They will all just keep going along, doing things in the normal way. No big "rush for the hills" for security and no big "dash for the valley" to make a killing.

If people expect stability and long-term growth in the economy, then they will act as though stability and long-term growth are going to occur. As long as they *act* that way, stability and long-term growth are *exactly what will occur.* But suppose there's serious doubt in the minds of the people. Then the stabilizing tools are not going to work very well.

It's almost like this: If the people believe you can handle the situation, then you can—maybe without even trying. If they think you can't, then you can't—no matter how hard you try!

SUMMARY AND SYNTHESIS

Compensatory fiscal policy (usually called just "fiscal policy") means **adjusting taxes and government spending** for the purpose of **stabilizing the economy.** Fiscal and monetary policy are the two kinds of economic stabilization policies. Governments try to use these to smooth out the business cycle—to reduce the seriousness of economic fluctuations.

To increase total spending (and employment, incomes, etc.) the fiscal policy approach would be to cut taxes and increase government spending. A tax cut leaves consumers and businesses with more of their income to spend. An increase in government spending adds a direct injection into the spending stream. These actions should **speed up the economy and overcome depression.**

Government spending and taxing decisions are made by Congress—not by the Administration. The Administration can propose more spending for public works projects or for other purposes. But the final decision is up to Congress.

There is always a problem trying to estimate how much fiscal action is needed. If the economy is depressed, the more overstocked the economy is, the slower the recovery is likely to be and the more fiscal policy action may be required.

What about appropriate fiscal policy to slow down inflation? Increase the "tax withdrawal" from the spending stream and reduce the government spending injection, of course! But it's difficult to know how much to raise taxes. And which taxes? And how much do we cut government spending? And which programs or projects? And (don't forget) it isn't easy for politicians to raise people's taxes while cutting out their favorite projects!

There are some automatic stabilizers in the modern economy. Progressive taxes tend to increase automatically as incomes rise, and some kinds of government spending automatically increase as incomes fall. The stability of consumer spending, and the stability of dividend payments by corporations both have a stabilizing effect on the economy. These automatic stabilizing effects are important enough to be significant.

The idea of fiscal drag is that sometimes the automatic tax increase may be so strong that it chokes off the economic expansion and prevents the economy from achieving the desired full employment. Discretionary compensatory fiscal policy is not a "fine-tuning knob." But when things get far enough out of balance, it can be used effectively and it can be made to work. Its effectiveness depends on (1) the existing conditions in the economy at the moment, and (2) the appropriateness of the taxing and spending adjustments.

Compensatory fiscal policy requires unbalancing the government budget. When tax revenues are reduced and expenditures are increased, there's a deficit. This adds to the federal debt.

If a government deficit is financed by selling bonds to the Fed, new high-powered money is created. So the money supply can expand. This could lead to inflation.

If a deficit is financed by selling bonds in the open market (to individuals and businesses) this could squeeze out private investors. This crowding out effect could force interest rates up to investment-discouraging levels and hold down employment, productivity, and economic growth.

Debt performs an essential function in the economic system. All of our money is debt. Most of it was created by expansions in monetized government debt. That's what provided the bank reserves to permit our money supply to expand to its present level.

For several decades the federal debt has been increasing—but not nearly so fast as private debt, or as GNP. In 1981 the federal debt passed $1 trillion. But "relatively speaking" it has declined.

Their borrowing power lets governments be irresponsible—to provide goods and services without levying taxes to pay for them. But sometimes deficit financing can stimulate productivity, increase income and generate more tax revenues—maybe even bring the government budget into balance. This was what the Reagan administration was hoping would result from its 1981 tax cut.

Expectations play an important role in macroeconomics. The self-fulfilling prophecy idea says: "Whatever people expect to happen, will happen because their expectations will cause it to happen." Presidents give speeches to try to influence the mood of the nation because they know that a healthy economy requires optimistic expectations. The government's stabilization policies can't work without the people's confidence.

We can't use fiscal and monetary policy to smooth out all the little ups and downs in the total spending stream. Anyone who thinks we can "fine tune" the economy on a perfectly stable course—either with fiscal or monetary policy or with any other approach—simply doesn't understand. When you get into the next chapter you'll see more about how difficult this stabilization problem can be.

REVIEW EXERCISES

MAJOR CONCEPTS, PRINCIPLES, TERMS (Explain each carefully.)

fiscal policy
how expenditure adjustments work
how tax adjustments work
the automatic stabilizers
the "burden" of the federal debt
the "cheer up" approach

OTHER CONCEPTS AND TERMS (Explain each briefly.)

the "excess inventories" problem
the "excess debt" problem
the "excess manufacturing
  capacity" problem
public works programs
government deficit financing

fiscal drag
crowding out
progressive tax
unbalancing the budget
monetized debt
self-fulfilling prophecy

QUESTIONS (Write the answers, or jot down key points.)

1. Supppose you were a member of Congress and the president was trying to get you to vote to cut off the money for a planned (and badly needed) interstate highway in your home district. Also, the president wants you to vote to increase taxes. (You're up for reelection, of course.) Do you think you will vote for the president's program? In view of such problems, do you think it's politically feasible to use fiscal policy to fight an "over-boom" or inflation? Discuss.

2. The government can get all the money it wants just by printing up bonds and "selling them" to the Federal Reserve Banks, but this is a dangerous procedure because a multiple expansion of the money supply is likely to result. Explain what this means and how it happens.

3. Write an essay on "the government debt"—what's good about it and what ought to be done about it, if anything.

4. What do you suppose President Franklin D. Roosevelt meant (in 1933) when he told the people "The only thing we have to fear is fear itself"? Was it true? Do you think the same thing could be said of *all* periods of economic recession and depression? Or are there some *basic economic causes* to blame (totally, or partially) for recession and depression? Discuss.

5. After all is said and done, how effective do you think fiscal policy really is in stabilizing the economy? Do you think it's more effective in overcoming depression? or inflation? Explain.

16 The Economic Stabilization Dilemma: Unemployment with Inflation

Chapter Objectives

- In the last two chapters you've been reading about the **monetary and fiscal tools** of stabilization policy. In this chapter (and the next) you'll find out about the **serious problems and disagreements concerning stabilization policy.**

- When you finish studying this chapter you will understand and be able to explain and draw graphs illustrating **the basic dilemma of economic stabilization.**

- In this chapter you will see examples of **runaway inflation** and of **creeping inflation.** And you will find out about the **inflationary bias** and the **unemployment bias** in a modern economy.

- You will learn to draw and explain the **Phillips Curve** and to explain how it has **shifted** in recent years. Also you'll find out why some economists say the Phillips Curve **doesn't exist in the long run,** and what the **natural rate of unemployment** has to do with all this.

- This chapter also explains **incomes policies**—that is, **wage-price controls: when, why, and how they have been used** in this country, the **problems involved,** and the **future outlook** for direct controls on wages and prices.

What's So Bad About Unemployment? or Inflation?

You've already read about the great social cost of unemployment and inflation. Remember? Unemployment wastes resources—valuable human resources and other resources too. It frustrates and degrades people. It leads to poverty, lack of self-respect, family breakdown, crime, social and political stress.

If unemployment gets bad enough it spells collapse for the economic system. Sooner or later the hungry people will likely revolt. That's what has happened in several places in the world just during this century. It almost happened (to some

extent it did happen) in the United States during the 1930s. Read Steinbeck's *Grapes of Wrath* if you want to feel what it was like.

What about inflation? It robs most people of the things they have worked for and saved for. Then it gives those things to other people (or sometimes to the government). It forces everyone to get the "gimmies." Anyone who can't do something to keep up gets robbed the most.

Inflation breeds clash between unions and management, between businesses and their customers, between government officials and their constituents. It forces teachers and police officers to unionize and go on strike. It creates financial crisis in all the programs of the state and local

252

governments. It turns college administration into a financial nightmare. It creates problems and generates stresses and disharmony in every nook and cranny of the society.

If inflation is moderate—say, if prices rise only two or three percent or maybe even four or five percent per year—we can work out ways to live with it. But if it runs away, inflation destroys the "general acceptability" of money. What happens then?

Without money, trade stops. Production stops. Employment stops. Income stops. Complete collapse of the economic system? Right! That's what happened in Germany in the 1922-23 inflation. And it happened in the 1940s and 50s in Hungary and China and to a lesser extent in several other countries. Here's an example of what it was like.

AN EXAMPLE OF RUNAWAY INFLATION

Suppose you go camping up in the mountains for a few weeks. Then when you get back to your car and back on the highway heading home, you stop at a drive-in for a double-decker burger and a chocolate shake. The counter girl says: "That'll be fifty dollars."

"FIFTY DOLLARS! Don't be ridiculous!" You leave the bag on the counter and go stomping out to your car, get in, slam the door and drive away. Soon you stop at a gas station and say: "Fill'er up."

"You got the cash? We don't take checks from out–of–staters and we don't take credit cards anymore. We have to have cash so we can spend the money *today*. Prices are going up too fast to wait until tomorrow."

You are confused. "Sure, I have the cash. It won't be all that much anyway. I only need about ten gallons." "Let's see. Ten gallons, at twenty dollars a gallon, that'll be two hundred dollars. You got two hundred dollars on you?"

This nonsense is really beginning to get to

you! "What do you mean, twenty dollars a gallon? What is going on around here?"

Prices Go Up Several Times a Day

Then he explains it to you, step by step — about how prices have broken loose. How every hour the oil company calls in a new price list. Prices are getting higher and higher, faster and faster.

While he's talking the phone rings. He answers it, then comes back shouting. "Ten gallons will cost $220 now. The price just went up again!"

You don't have $220. You ask him how much he'll give you for your spare tire. He offers you a thousand dollars. You think, "It's good that inflation works both ways." So you sell the tire and get your tank filled.

Then you think. "By tomorrow, gas is going to cost a lot more. I'd better buy some gas cans and spend up the rest of my money right now. That way I'll be sure to have enough gas to make it home." So that's what you do. It was a wise thing to do, too. Why? Here's why.

This time next week gas is going to cost $140 a gallon! And next month it will cost $2,400 a gallon. A couple of months later it will cost *seven million dollars* a gallon. A few weeks after that it will go to a billion, then to a hundred billion, then to a trillion—but long before then the economy will be in a state of total disruption—total collapse.

The German Inflation of 1922-23

The kind of runaway inflation you've been reading about is an example of exactly what happened in Germany in 1922-23. In the fall of 1923 a new administration took over in Germany. They called in all of the old, inflated marks and issued a new kind of marks in exchange. Would you like to try to guess what the exchange rate was? Would you believe a *trillion to one?* That's right.

Suppose you had lived in Germany then and had a million dollars' worth of marks in your savings account before the inflation. What would all that money be worth in the fall of 1923? Think of it this way: Suppose there were one million people and each one of them was a millionaire—each one had a million dollars' worth of marks before the inflation. Then in the fall of 1923 if the *entire million* of those millionaires turned in their money on the same day, what would they get back? At the exchange rate of a trillion to one? They would get back *one penny's worth of marks* to split between them!

Suppose something like that happened in the United States today. If you had enough money to buy the whole GNP of the United States before the inflation, then you'd have just enough to buy a double-decker burger and a chocolate shake afterwards. Such is the nature of runaway inflation. Is it any wonder it disrupts the market process and brings total collapse of the economic system?

The Problem: Moderate but Chronic Inflation and Unemployment

It doesn't seem likely that either runaway inflation or serious, prolonged depression will occur in the United States or in any of the other advanced economies. Not that it's impossible. It's just that I think we will do enough of the right things to prevent any such catastrophe.

No, what we have to worry about is not total collapse of the economic system. It's the continuing, eroding effect of moderate but chronic inflation and moderate but chronic unemployment, both going along together.

THERE'S NO "FULL EMPLOYMENT AND STABLE PRICES" RATE OF SPENDING

What supports (holds up, or pushes up) total employment and output and income in the economy? Total spending? Of course. And what supports (holds up, or pushes up) prices in the economy? Total spending? Of course.

See the problem? *That which pushes up employment also pushes up prices.* There you have it. That's the reason for this basic dilemma of economic stabilization.

The Inflation-Unemployment Overlap: the Basic Dilemma

In the real world there is a wide "overlapping area," where "inflationary-level spending" and "full-employment-level spending" overlap. As total spending speeds up, inflation gets going before full employment is reached.

As total spending slows down, unemployment starts increasing even before all the inflationary pressures are cooled down. Whatever you do with monetary or fiscal policy to try to make one better (say, reduce unemployment) is likely to make the other worse (increase inflation). That's the basic macroeconomic problem—that's *the basic dilemma of economic stabilization.*

So what can we do with monetary and fiscal policies? Try to speed up spending to reduce unemployment? We get more inflation. Try to slow down spending to reduce inflation? We get more unemployment. Oh, miserable dilemma!

There are some graphs coming up that will help you see the problem more clearly. The first (pure model) figure shows a level of spending which brings "full employment and stable prices." The second (real world) figure shows some unemployment and some inflation *at any level of spending* you can choose.

Why doesn't the real world look like the model? Essentially, for this reason: There are things *other than total spending* which are always pushing upward on unemployment, and on prices. More on that in a minute. First, stop and study Figures 16-1 and 16-2.

The Inflation Bias: "Upward Price-Inching"

In the real world, almost all sellers can do things to push up the prices of what they sell. This is true of consumer goods sellers and it's true of the sellers of the factors of production—labor, land, capital. Each seller wants to be sure not to get left behind in the game of **upward price-inching.**

All of us are "price-inchers"! We give all sorts of reasons for pushing our prices up—some of our "reasons" are excuses. Some are valid.

Labor talks about the increased cost of living and increasing output per worker and such things. Businesses cite increased costs of labor, materials, transportation, utilities, interest and other inputs. Both labor and businesses have some power to push up their prices—so that's just what they do.

The lower income people are getting organized and are pushing hard for higher wages. There's great pressure for wage and price increases. And there's great resistance to wage and price decreases. So the economy is biased toward inflation. But during the early 1980s, competition from foreign products was seriously limiting the "upward price-inching" of American businesses and workers.

The Unemployment Bias: Unsuitable Workers

What about the unemployment problem? When spending increases, why don't employment and production and output increase until full employment is reached? That's easy to figure out too, if you think about it.

Just as the "inflationary bias" in the real world can be explained in terms of one thing: "upward price-inching"—also the "unemployment bias" in the real world can be explained in terms of one thing: *all labor is not alike.*

As total spending increases, more people get jobs. True. But the ones most suited to work in the expanding industries are hired first. As spending increases more, only as prices go higher will people be hired at jobs they aren't well suited for. Total spending would have to go very high for unemployed teachers to be hired as bricklayers! or bricklayers as teachers!

Another real-world consideration is that some businesses are always cutting back while others are expanding. Some people are always changing jobs for one reason or another. While they're moving between jobs they're unemployed. But this kind of temporary unemployment is not a real problem. It's only when the "between jobs" period stretches on and on that some action may be taken to try to get things going again—hopefully, without throwing gasoline on the fires of inflation.

If total spending is already high, an increase in spending is likely to bring a little more employment and a lot more inflation. You already saw this on a graph. There's another graph we use to show the "inflation-unemployment trade-off." It's called the "Phillips Curve."

The Phillips Curve: the Inflation-Unemployment Trade-Off

The Phillips Curve is named for the economist, A. W. Phillips, who developed the "curve" in the 1950s. What Professor Phillips did was to look back over the years and see, for different times, what the rate of inflation had been and what the rate of unemployment had been. He found out that when unemployment was high, the inflation rate was low and when unemployment was low the inflation rate was higher. You can understand why.

More spending brings more employment, sure. But it also supports higher wages and prices. So the rate of inflation picks up. When total spending slows down that brings more unemployment. But when things are slow, there is less demand to support wage and price increases. So when unemployment gets higher, inflation slows down.

The Phillips Curve illustrates this idea: *We can have a smaller unemployment rate, only if we are willing to accept a larger inflation rate.* It's a "trade-off" situation, where we would like to have *minimum amounts* of both—minimum unemployment and minimum inflation. But to get

less of one, we must put up with more of the other. The Phillips Curve illustrates the "real-world dilemma of economic stabilization."

A Production Possibility Curve for Unwanted Products?

Now that you understand what the Phillips Curve illustrates, what do you suppose it will look like? Negative slope? Of course. As you give up some of one thing (inflation) you get back more of the other (unemployment). This curve is going to look like a "production possibil-

Fig. 16-1   Total Spending, Employment, and Prices: the "Model" Case

Increased spending brings first full employment and then inflation

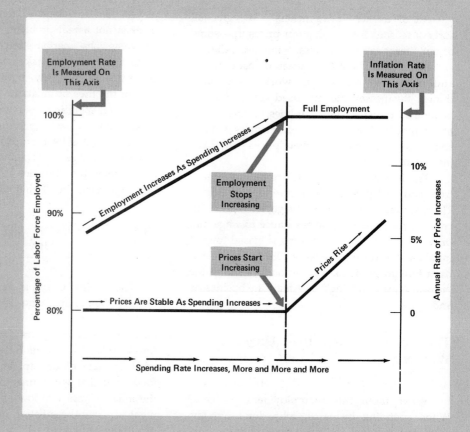

In the model market system there is no "inflation-unemployment overlap." As spending increases, prices wll remain stable until full employment is reached.

ity" or "opportunity cost" curve. Right? Sure. But in a way, it's very different from the production possibility curve.

The production possibility curve shows you *how much you can get of the good things you want*, and how much of one you must give up to get more of the other. You would be happy if the production possibility curve would shift upward and outward. You could then have more of either product or a larger combination of both.

What about the Phillips Curve? It shows you *how much we must take of the bad things we don't want*—unemployment and inflation. Would we be happy if the Phillips Curve shifted upward and outward? Certainly not! More unemployment, or more inflation, or a larger combination

of both? Not if we can help it!

We would like for the Phillips Curve to shift downward and inward. We would be most happy if it would shift all the way down to zero and disappear! Then we could have full employment and stable prices and the whole dilemma would be solved. But has that been happening? Unfortunately, no. In fact the opposite has been happening.

Figure 16-3 shows the Phillips Curve. It's just another way of looking at the same picture you saw in the employment-inflation graphs earlier. In fact this Phillips Curve was derived from the two curves in the figure below (16-2). Now, take a few minutes and study Figures 16-3 and 16-4.

Fig. 16-2 Total Spending, Employment, and Prices: the "Real World" Case

Increased spending brings inflation before full employment is reached

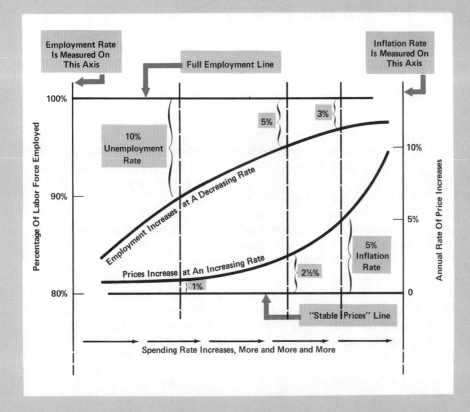

In the real world, as spending increases more and more, each extra increase in spending is likely to add less to employment and more to inflation.

Fig. 16-3   The Unemployment-Inflation Trade-Off: The Phillips Curve

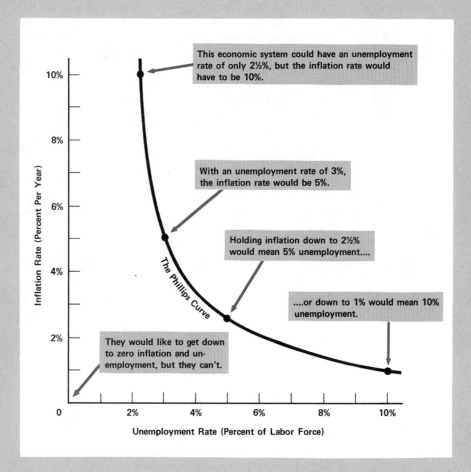

As total spending increases, unemployment drops. But inflation gets worse.
As total spending decreases, inflation slows down. But unemployment gets worse.

The Phillips Curve says that when the inflation rate is low the unemployment rate is high; when the unemployment rate is low, the inflation rate is high. If we use monetary or fiscal policy to get less of one, we get more of the other.

The Phillips Curve you see here was derived from the "employment function" and "inflation function" curves shown in Figure 16-2. Nobody knows just exactly where this Phillips Curve will be for any economic system at any particular time. All sorts of things might cause it to shift.

The Phillips Curve illustrates the fact that something *other than* total spending must be influencing (holding up or pushing up) wages and prices. Whenever these "other than" influences get stronger, the curve shifts upward and outward; whenever they get weaker the curve shifts downward and inward.

Whenever the "other than" influences are changing, it may be more helpful to try to understand why the curve shifts than to try to understand why it is shaped as it is. The next graph shows you an example of "the shifting Phillips Curve."

Fig. 16-4   The Shifting Phillips Curve—1960s–Early 1980s

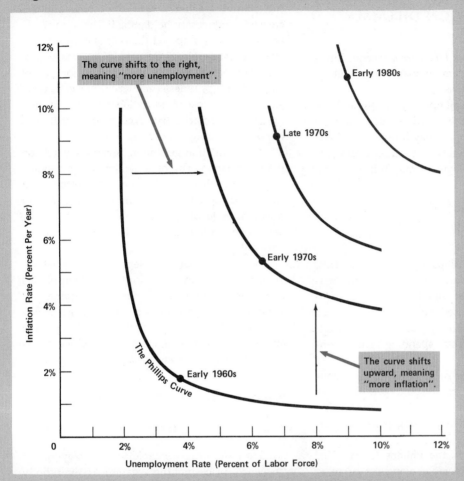

No matter where the economy happens to be at the moment, attempts to *reduce unemployment* are likely to *increase inflation*. Attempts to *reduce inflation* are likely to *increase unemployment*.

In the early 1960s the unemployment rate in the United States was less than 4 percent and the inflation rate was less than 2 percent. Then in the early 1970s the unemployment rate was about 6 percent and the inflation rate was more than 5 percent. A big shift in the Phillips Curve, upward and outward!

In the inflation-recession years of the early 1980s the unemployment rate went up to more than 9 percent and the inflation rate went up to more than 12 percent!

If the Phillips Curve is going to be shifting around all over, what good is it? Just this: It illustrates a concept—the concept of the basic dilemma of economic stabilization—of the unemployment-inflation trade-off. We really don't know where the curve is going to be or exactly how it will be shaped. Still, it's a useful way to illustrate an important concept—the concept of the basic dilemma of economic stabilization.

THE PHILLIPS CURVE AND THE U.S. STABILIZATION DILEMMA

The Phillips Curve *illustrates a concept.* But it can't *predict* what unemployment rates will go with what inflation rates.

When both the unemployment rate and the inflation rate are high, cutting back on total spending to curb inflation may bring a disastrous depression. But increasing total spending to overcome the unemployment may bring a disastrous inflation!

Some Causes of the Recent Inflation

Why has the Phillips Curve for the U.S. economy shifted upward so much? Several reasons. During the mid and late 1960s, government spending increased rapidly. Tax increases were delayed. More money was created through the banking system. Total spending in the economy kept increasing.

The economy was running along just about as "fully employed" as it could get. So what happened as spending kept increasing? Inflationary pressures began pushing prices up. Of course.

Was this a shift in the Phillips Curve? No. Not at all. It was just a move along the curve — a move which brought a little more employment and a lot more inflation. Once the inflation was triggered off, it began to get worse and worse.

Each time wages in one industry would move up, the workers in other industries would push for higher wages, each trying to outdo the others. Each time one business would raise prices, others would do the same. As wages increased, prices increased; as prices increased, wages increased. Everybody kept fighting to stay ahead.

In some industries, productivity was increasing, so wages could increase. But then everybody (whether they happened to be in high productivity industries or not) started pushing to get just as much increase as the other guy.

When the auto workers get a wage increase, the school teachers want one, too—and increased productivity be damned! The auto worker's wage can go up, yet the cost of each car may stay the same. How? Because of increased productivity per worker. But if wages for school teachers go up, unless each teacher teaches more students, the cost of education per student goes up. That's inflationary. And that's what was happening throughout the economy.

Once inflation gets going, everybody gets on the bandwagon. The high-demand, high-productivity industries may be the pace-setters. But soon, throughout the economy, wages and prices start leapfrogging each other across the landscape until both go out of sight over the horizon!

Increased spending sets off the inflation. Total demand is too great for the total supply, so shortages develop and prices start going up. Then soon everybody starts trying to get ahead of everybody else. The inflation speeds up more and more. Inflation begets inflation. Once it gets going it tries to run away.

What Causes the Phillips Curve to Shift?

How do we get people to stop playing the "upward price-inching" game? If everybody would stop trying to play "wage-price leapfrog," that would help a lot. Then we might be able to have low unemployment and low inflation at the same time. But how do we get people to quit pushing all the time for higher wages and prices?

It could do a lot of good if we could make it easier for people to be employed, too. Can anything be done to help the unemployed people become more productive? or more mobile? or more aware of available jobs? or more responsive to the changing demands for labor in the economy? Anything like that would help.

Even lowering the wage rate for inexperienced, untrained, unskilled workers would help. Anything which would reduce the resistance to full employment would reduce unemployment without pushing up prices. That would shift the Phillips Curve to the left.

It isn't difficult to figure out that manpower training and job placement programs are needed to reduce the resistance to full employment. That will shift the Phillips Curve to the left. But what about the inflation problem? Can anything be done to get the people and businesses to stop playing the "wage-price leapfrogging game"? How do we get rid of these "built in" inflationary pressures which push the Phillips Curve up?

You know that if it were not for the economic power held by businesses and labor unions and governments and professional people and just about everybody, then wages and prices would respond a lot more to the "natural forces" of supply and demand. But nearly everybody has some power to push up the prices of what they sell. So what are we going to do about it?

Anything that can be done to reduce monopoly power and increase competition, will help. But are we going to eliminate big businesses? and labor unions? and everyone else who has any power to influence wages or prices? I don't think so.

Kinds of Inflation: Demand-Pull, Cost-Push, Structural

Once inflation gets going, there are three kinds of inflation that start working together, reinforcing each other. Demand-pull inflation results from too much total spending. Cost-push inflation occurs when businesses raise their prices because their *costs* are going up—usually because the wage rate goes up. Structural inflation can occur when the "structure" (the industrial makeup) of the economy is changing (as it always is, of course).

"Structural inflation" can result from shifts in the buying patterns of the consumers. As demand increases in one segment of the economy (say, the tire industry) this pushes up prices and wages in that industry. But in the industries where demand is declining (say, the wagon

wheel industry), wages and prices don't go down to offset the increases in the expanding industry. Of course not! What really happens is that the people in the declining industry fight to get their wages and prices to go up, too!

President Nixon and the Monetarists

When President Nixon took office in January, 1969, he brought in a new group of economic advisers—economists with a different idea about what ought to be done and how. Several were "monetarists," members of "The Chicago school" of economic theory, anti-Keynesian, allies of Milton Friedman. They believe in carefully limiting the size of the money supply. But except for that, they were for a *hands-off policy toward the economy on issues of both micro- and macroeconomics.* "Let the money supply increase a little each year—enough to support the real growth of the economy—and leave everything else alone. Never fear. If you'll do that, the natural economic forces will make everything work out all right—or, at worst, things will be better than any discretionary government policy could achieve."

President Nixon's economic advisers, alarmed by the rapid rate of increase in the money supply and the high rate of inflation, called for tight money. "Stop the money supply from expanding. That will hold down total spending. Soon prices will stop rising."

The Fed tightened money. The tight money succeeded in holding down total spending, sure. But instead of the inflation rate slowing down, employment slowed down. Prices just kept going up.

Unresponsive Inflation

Cost-push inflation and structural inflation don't respond quickly to tight money—or to increased unemployment either, for that matter. And inflation begets inflation, remember? The longer the inflation continued, the harder it was to stop.

What could be done? One approach would be to stick steadfastly to the monetarist prescription. Hold the size of the money supply in close check. Also, hold down government spending and keep taxes up. That will eliminate any inflationary effect of the government budget.

With a tight budget and tight money, *total spending absolutely cannot expand very much.* But does that mean that prices will suddenly be stopped dead in their tracks? Unfortunately, no. It doesn't mean that.

What it does mean is this: If prices continue to rise, total spending will not be big enough to buy up all of the output. Suppose output prices double. Then total spending must double to buy up all of that output. Right? Sure.

If output prices go up 10%, then total spending for that output must go up 10% to buy it all. But what if tight money prevents total spending from increasing by 10%? Suppose total spending is not permitted to increase at all? Then 10% of the output will not be bought! So as businesses see their "unsold output inventories" piling up, either they will cut back their prices (thus solving the inflation problem) or they will cut back their production (thus creating an unemployment problem). Which will they do? Cut prices? Or cut back production?

Monopoly Power and Administered Prices

When manufacturers see their sales dropping off they have a choice: to cut output, or to cut prices. Which choice do they make? Usually they try to make the most profitable (or least-loss) choice.

In the economist's pure competition model, there's no question what will happen. Prices will go down until the output is all being sold. There will be no problem of unemployment, and the inflation problem will be solved. But in the real world of monopoly power and administered prices, will it happen that way? No. Too bad, but in the real world it never works exactly that way.

How can a business survive if it cuts prices while costs are rising? It can't. Of course not. So what do businesses do? They cut output. The unemployment problem gets worse. So surpluses develop in the labor and other input markets.

Won't the surpluses cause input prices to go down? In the "model pure market system" that's what would happen. But usually it doesn't happen that way in the real world. Most input prices are "administered"—are controlled to some extent by someone—and no one likes to go home with a smaller paycheck—not if they can help it!

So will the monetarist prescription work? Will it stop inflation? There's no question that sooner or later, steadfastly pursued, *it will work.* But meanwhile the economy must slow down. Recession? Probably. How bad? How much unemployment must we have, and for how long, before prices are stabilized? Nobody knows. Many distinguished economists disagree a lot on this issue.

WHAT ABOUT WAGE-PRICE CONTROLS?

The classic argument against wage-price controls has been this: "If we want to keep the pot from boiling over we must turn down the fire under the pot (tighten money), instead of trying to clamp the lid on (control prices)!" That's a good analogy. It makes very good sense whenever we're dealing with demand-pull inflation. But when we're dealing with the upward price-inching, leapfrogging game, the analogy doesn't fit very well.

Sometimes it might make more sense to think about a pot of live fiddler crabs, each one trying to crawl over the backs of all the others and get out of the pot. It might help to put the pot in the refrigerator to cool them down. But to be sure it would be more *effective* to clamp the lid on! But that doesn't mean we can ignore the need to limit the money supply. Of course not!

Remember what happened in Germany in 1923? What could wage-price controls have done then? Nothing! Government **incomes policies** or **wage-price guidelines** designed to hold down the wage-price leapfrogging game couldn't possibly work if the money supply was permitted to expand unchecked.

If the total spending is permitted to expand more and more, the pressure for "demand-pull" inflation gets greater and greater. The longer the "price control lid" is held on, the harder it is to keep the prices from breaking loose. People start to offer more money "under the table" for the things they want. When this "black marketing" gets widespread it becomes impossible to stop. It becomes the name of the game. Everybody does it. All the goods disappear from the controlled markets. The natural market forces take over. When this happens, the sooner the government abolishes the controls, the better.

No, controls can't replace the need for responsible monetary and fiscal policies. But many businesses and labor unions and professional associations have enough economic power to keep inching up their own wages and prices. So tight money, acting alone, sometimes may be an insufficient tool for inflation control.

Sometimes, some prices may keep going up even as total spending declines and unemployment increases. This was happening in the U.S. economy in the early 1980s. In February of 1982, Federal Reserve Board Chairman Paul Volcker mentioned this problem in his address at The Conference Board's Financial Outlook Conference in New York. Volcker said that it may be necessary to identify those prices which do not respond well to monetary and fiscal restraints and to establish some kind of *direct controls* over these prices.

Controls Prevent the Market Process from Working

It's good to hold down inflation. So unless there is something bad about direct controls, why not have direct controls on all wages and prices, all the time? You already know the answer. Wage-price controls block the operation of

the market economy!

Suppose the government would set up rigid incomes policies—saying that each business should get a certain amount of profit and no more. Each worker should get a certain wage and no more. Every product price should be no higher than it was last June. What would happen?

If everything in the economy is in "general equilibrium" when the controls are established, then the "set" prices and wages and profits will all be in line at that moment. There won't be any immediate problem. But the longer the controls stay on, the more things are likely to get out of line.

Demands change. Production costs change. Technology changes. As these changes occur, prices will need to adjust to the new conditions. If the adjustment can't be made, then shortages will begin to show up in some markets and surpluses will pile up in others. The longer the prices stay frozen, the worse the distortions will get. Shortages of some products will get worse and worse while surpluses of other products grow bigger and bigger.

Black Markets Develop. Suppose prices were frozen when there was an oversupply and very low price of corn. So the corn price is fixed at 10¢ a dozen. Everybody quits producing corn. Soon the shortage of corn is very great. But some people like corn very much—enough to be willing to pay $2.50 a dozen! Suppose I'm growing some corn for myself in my backyard plot and someone sees it growing there, ready to harvest. One night I hear a knock on the door and a voice says "If I leave a $5 bill under the doormat will you look the other way while I steal two dozen ears of corn?" What temptation! I just might look the other way.

As time goes on, the word gets around that you can "steal" corn from my field without anybody catching you if you leave $5 under the doormat for every two dozen ears you "steal." Soon I'm making lots of money and people who really like corn are getting some. But what about the price controls? They aren't working anymore.

Not for corn, anyway. And not for lots of other things, too.

When the "black markets" (free markets) begin to develop, they catch on like wildfire. If the controlled prices are very far out of line with the "real-world supply and demand conditions," then black markets are almost certain to arise. So if controlled prices are going to work for very long, the prices will have to be adjusted to reflect changing market conditions. But isn't that hard to do? Yes. It sure is.

Political Influence Comes In. All sellers want their prices to go up a little bit. All workers want their wages to go up a little bit. Every business wants its profits to go up a little bit. Everybody is putting pressures on their members of Congress and on their local political party representatives and writing letters to the President to try to get some "special consideration." Everybody can think of some very special reasons for a favorable price adjustment.

How does a system which responds to political pressures withstand this sort of thing? It doesn't, of course. As time goes by, *politics* is likely to decide more price adjustments than *economics!*

Wage and price controls are a bad thing—a real no-no for the "free enterprise system." They're hard to design, hard to administer, hard to police. So what is the government going to do about wage-price leapfrogging? And about those prices which don't respond well to monetary and fiscal restraints? Impose direct restraints? Probably.

A New Approach: TIP

In recent years a new approach has been suggested by three well-known economists: Henry Wallich, Sidney Weintraub, and Arthur Okun. The idea is to use **tax credits and penalties** to induce businesses and workers to limit wage (and indirectly, price) increases. This suggested approach is called **TIP** (Tax-based Incomes Policy).

As you might guess, economists disagree about whether this suggested TIP approach should be tried. In two interviews reported in *Newsweek* (May 29, 1978) Professor Paul Samuelson comments that "some experimentation (with TIP) might be in order to improve our inflation-unemployment trade-off." Professor Milton Friedman says such plans are "another form of price and wage control (which) would prove no less monstrosities than earlier price and wage controls."

Several of the world's most outstanding economists disagree about the need for and effectiveness of wage-price guidelines or controls. But usually when push comes to shove, controls are imposed. Half-heartedly, yes. Because almost nobody likes wage-price controls. But the government uses them just the same.

When Have We Used Direct Controls?

Over the past four decades, most countries most of the time have tried to use *direct restraints* to hold down wages and prices. The United States has been no exception.

In the United States, wage-price controls were imposed in August, 1971. That was the first time wage-price controls had been imposed since the early 1950s during the Korean War. It had happened during World War II also, and during other wars. But what about the period from the mid 50s to August of 1971? Were wages and prices completely free to seek their own levels? Sometimes, yes. But most of the time, no.

In the early 1960s, President Kennedy set up wage-price guideposts spelling out the "appropriate conditions" for wages or prices to be increased, and by how much. The guideposts were not "legal requirements." They were only "urged upon" the industries and the labor organizations. But both President Kennedy and President Johnson used the power of the presidency to "twist some arms," to convince some businesses and labor leaders to go along with the guideposts. This "arm-twisting"—this unofficial but sometimes quite powerful technique for holding down wage-price increases in some of the major industries—is known as **jawboning.**

The "jawboning" polices of the Kennedy-Johnson era were continued until the beginning of the Nixon Administration in 1969. Then President Nixon instituted a "tight money" policy and denounced all other approaches to the inflation-control problem.

So what happened? Interest rates rose rapidly and the economy headed into a recession. But the rate of inflation didn't slow down. Instead, it kept getting worse. In August, 1971, President Nixon established a wage-price freeze. That was followed by continuing (off and on) direct controls.

In 1975, President Ford called for voluntary restraints to slow inflation—his "WIN" (Whip Inflation Now) program. In 1977 when he took over, President Carter did not use any direct controls. But in 1978 as the inflation rate picked up, he established "voluntary" wage-price guidelines with "jawboning" penalties for non-compliance.

When the Reagan Administration began in 1981, all direct wage-price restraints were eliminated. The anti-inflation battle was left to the tight money policies of the Fed. And how well did that succeed? I can't tell you because I don't know. As this book gets ready for press (in 1982) there are two big questions in the air.

First: How much recession must we endure, and for how long, to bring down the inflation rate? And will the administration stick by its policy of tight money and spending cuts if serious recession threatens?

Second: If the tight money policy doesn't work well enough, will direct controls be imposed? On what? And if so, what then?

If you've been keeping up with the news, I'm sure that you already know the answers to these questions. If you haven't been keeping up with all this, next time you're in the library why not spend half an hour looking in the back issues of the *Wall Street Journal* or *Business Week* or any news magazine and find out what happened? I think you'll find it interesting. Educational, too!

THE PROBLEM OF UNRESPONSIVE UNEMPLOYMENT

Just as some kinds of *inflation* don't respond very well to *reductions* in total spending, some kinds of *unemployment* don't respond very well to *increases* in total spending. One kind of unemployment which total spending could never bring down to zero is **frictional unemployment.** People who are changing jobs for one reason or another don't "flow smoothly and instantaneously" from the old jobs to the new ones. The person may be unemployed a day or two, or maybe a week or two, or maybe longer.

Sometimes the "frictional unemployment" results from structural changes in the economy. Remember about structural inflation? With **structural unemployment,** what do the old line, highly skilled wagon-wheel workers do when the demand shifts to automobile tires? They get unemployed. If total spending in the economy picks up, will they get new jobs? Most of the younger ones will learn new skills. Some of the older ones may. Others, no. Their "day in the sun" has passed. That's the way it is with structural unemployment.

There's another kind of unemployment you hear a lot about these days: **technological unemployment.** That's what happens when people are replaced by machines—"automated out of a job," so to speak. That's what's happening to the migrant farm workers. Everywhere you go you see more "mechanical pickers" instead of "hand pickers" harvesting crops. In every modern economy, jobs are constantly being eliminated by improved technology. As wages get higher, more capital is introduced. "Technological displacement" speeds up.

The more the economy is dynamic, growing, introducing new technology, the more serious structural and technological unemployment will be. What can be done about it? Manpower training and development programs? Job training subsidies? Helping people to find new jobs? Yes. All these and some other things too. But one thing's sure. An increase in total spending can't solve the problem by itself.

New People in the Labor Force

Another kind of unemployment which can't be eliminated is the unemployment of the **young and inexperienced people** who are constantly joining the labor force. In the early 1980s when the average unemployment rate for the nation was about 8 percent, the unemployment rate for teenagers was more than 20 percent. In several places in the country it was much higher than that.

If all the members of the labor force were identical, how simple it would be to solve the unemployment problem. Just get total spending to increase, that's all! Soon everyone would have a job. But the labor force is very diverse—young and old, male and female, skilled and unskilled, black and white, educated and uneducated, brilliant and stupid, industrious and lazy, and on and on and on. So it's obvious that just increasing total spending would create a lot of inflation before it would ever bring unemployment down near zero!

Unresponsive Unemployment Keeps the Phillips Curve Out

What happens to the Phillips Curve as more young, unskilled people join the labor force? And as more people get trapped by structural and technological and other "unresponsive" kinds of unemployment? The curve shifts to the right. At any "inflation rate" you choose, the "unemployment rate" is larger than before. This is the other side of the stabilization dilemma.

The "Natural Rate" of Unemployment

Do you suppose it would ever be possible to get unemployment all the way down to zero? No people between jobs? No new people in the labor force looking for jobs? No structural or technological unemployment? Nobody having to read the "Help Wanted" ads? Not possible, right?

Some unemployment is a necessary, "natural" condition in a modern economic system. Economists generally agree that there is some "natural rate" of unemployment. But they disagree about how big it is. The more dynamic, growing and changing the economy is, the larger the natural rate of unemployment is likely to be. The better the education, training and job placement facilities are, the smaller the natural rate is likely to be.

What's so important about the natural rate of unemployment? Just this: if we try to stimulate total spending to overcome some of this "natural unemployment," we're going to (a) fail in our objective, and (b) push up the inflation rate. Bad scene!

Before the policymakers set out on a monetary/fiscal policy to reduce unemployment, they had better know about this "natural rate" idea. And they had better not increase total spending to try to overcome it. Because they can't.

Some economists these days are saying that much of our inflation problem comes from ill-conceived macroeconomic policies—policies which do not adequately consider the "natural rate of unemployment" idea. Here's the argument:

1. Politicians (guided by some misguided economists) want to reduce the rate of unemployment. So they initiate monetary and/or fiscal policies to increase total spending. The increased spending will increase demand for goods and services

so production will be stepped up and the unemployed people will be hired. Hooray! But . . .

2. The increased spending causes output demand to increase, true. But no new output is produced! The unemployed people either weren't suited for or weren't available for the new jobs. So producers began bidding against each other for workers, offering more wages, and charging higher prices for their products. Inflation!

3. In the short run, the government's policies can succeed in reducing unemployment a little below the "natural rate," because poorly qualified people will be hired as output prices rise. But this pushes up costs and adds to inflationary pressures.

4. In the long run, unemployment in the economy will again increase to the "natural rate." The only difference will be that the rate of inflation is higher than before. If the government keeps on trying to reduce unemployment, inflation will keep getting worse.

The Long-Run (Vertical) Phillips Curve

If there is a "natural rate" of unemployment, then is there really an inflation-unemployment trade-off? Yes.

Anytime spending slows down, (1) unemployment will increase and (2) the inflation rate will decrease. Anytime spending speeds up, (1) unemployment will decrease and (2) the inflation rate will increase. That's what the Phillips Curve shows. And it's true.

But what about the long run? Isn't there a "natural tendency in the long run" for the "natural rate of unemployment" to exist? And regardless of how big the dollar volume of total

spending happens to be? A lot of economists think so. So what does this mean?

Suppose total spending doubles. In the long run, unemployment will be just as big as if spending had stayed the same—it will be the "natural rate." So what doubles? Prices. Of course. Figure 16-5 shows how it looks on a graph. Take a minute and study that graph now.

Fig. 16-5   The Long Run: A Vertical Phillips Curve?

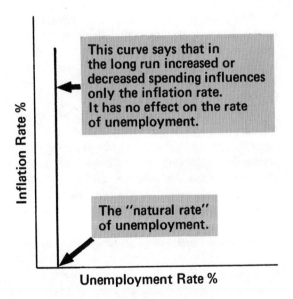

This curve says that in the long run increased or decreased spending influences only the inflation rate. It has no effect on the rate of unemployment.

The "natural rate" of unemployment.

As you look at Figure 16-5 you may say: "This is no Phillips Curve! It doesn't show any inflation-unemployment trade-off!" Well, you're right.

What Figure 16-5 says is: "There's no Phillips Curve in the long run." Not all economists would agree with that. And not all economists would agree that "the long run" is a very useful concept when dealing with macroeconomic analysis and policy. In the next chapter you will find out a lot more about this and other macroeconomic disagreements among economists.

SUMMARY AND SYNTHESIS

The basic dilemma of economic stabilization stems from this basic truth: it is **total spending** which supports both (a) **total employment** and (b) **the level of prices.** Any action to increase total spending for the purpose of **supporting employment** also (like it or not) **pushes upward on prices.** The inflation rate increases. The opposite action—holding down total spending to stabilize prices—also (like it ot not) reduces the support for employment. The unemployment rate increases.

The **Phillips Curve** illustrates the basic stabilization dilemma. It shows that there is no "full employment and stable prices" level of spending. It shows that any **total spending adjustment** involves a **trade-off** between the **unemployment rate** and the **inflation rate.**

The **Phillips Curve** says: no matter where the economy is at any moment, the policymakers certainly can use monetary and fiscal policy to increase total spending and bring us **less unemployment**—if we are ready to suffer the **inflationary consequences.** Or they certainly can bring us less inflation—if we are ready to suffer the **unemployment consequences.**

Runaway inflation is possible, and has actually occurred in Germany, Hungary, and several other countries during this century. It results in the collapse of the money supply, and of the economy.

The **inflation bias** results from the **monopoly power** of sellers of both outputs and inputs. They are all in the game of **upward price-inching.** The **unemployment bias** results from the **poor fit** between the available workers and the available jobs. Many people, especially new entrants into the labor force, are not qualified for the available jobs, so they remain unemployed.

Inflation, once started, **tends to speed up.** As workers and businesses see their purchasing power eroding, they push hard for **wage and price increases** just to try to stay in the same place. As costs throughout the economy go up, prices must go up to cover these costs. So the **inflation generates more**

inflation. The Phillips Curve shifts upward. **Demand-pull, cost-push,** and **structural** inflationary pressures all play a role in this.

Wage-price controls, also called **incomes policies,** have been used off and on over the past 40 years. Usually these incomes policies have taken the form of **wage-price guidelines** and **jawboning penalties** for non-compliance. But during the early 1970s there was a **wage-price freeze** followed by **legally enforced controls.**

The **Reagan Administration** as of mid-1982 had not imposed any direct controls or limits on wage-price increases. But **Fed Chairman Volcker** had suggested that some prices which don't respond well to other anti-inflation measures might require some kind of **direct controls.**

Wage-price controls **distort** the operation of the market system. **Shortages** develop in those areas where prices are kept artificially low. Eventually **black markets** (free, but illegal markets) develop and **undermine** the controlled prices. Some price adjustments are necessary to make the system work. But the adjustments are likely to be more **political** than economic.

The proposed **tax-based incomes policy** (TIP) approach would use **tax credits and penalties** to induce business and workers to hold down wage (and indirectly, price) increases. Economists disagree about the desirability of this plan. As of mid-1982 it had never been tried.

Unemployment could never be zero because of **frictional unemployment** (when people change jobs it isn't instantaneous), **structural unemployment** (some industries are contracting while others are expanding), **technological unemployment** (some workers are being replaced by machines), and **new entrants** (young and/or inexperienced people joining the labor force). All of these factors contribute to the "natural rate" of unemployment.

Economists disagree about the size of the "natural rate" of unemployment. Policies which support increased spending to try to reduce unemployment below this rate would only produce inflation. This leads to the idea of a **vertical long-run Phillips Curve**—which says: "There's no inflation-unemployment trade-off in the long run." Economists disagree about the **truth** and **relevance** of this state-ment. In the next chapter you'll be reading more about this and other (related) disagreements among the leading economists of the 1980s.

REVIEW EXERCISES

MAJOR CONCEPTS, PRINCIPLES, TERMS (Explain each carefully.)

the basic macroeconomic dilemma
runaway inflation
the inflation-unemployment overlap

the inflation-unemployment trade-off
the Phillips Curve
the "natural rate" of unemployment

OTHER CONCEPTS AND TERMS (Explain each briefly.)

demand-pull inflation
cost-push inflation
structural inflation
the monetarists
the "Chicago School"
Milton Friedman
incomes policies

wage-price guideposts
jawboning
TIP
frictional unemployment
structural unemployment
technological unemployment

CURVES AND GRAPHS (Draw, label, and explain each.)

Total Spending, Employment, and Prices: The "Model" Case
Total Spending, Employment, and Prices: The "Real World" Case
The Unemployment-Inflation Trade-Off: The Phillips Curve
The Shifting Phillips Curve—1960s–Early 1980s
The Long Run: A Vertical Phillips Curve?

QUESTIONS (Write out answers or jot down key points.)

1. Can you think of any specific examples (examples you are personally familiar with) of wages and/or price increases which are *not* likely to be stopped by a slowdown in spending? Discuss.
2. Can you think of any specific examples of unemployment which aren't likely to be overcome, even if total spending increases? Discuss.
3. Explain how the Phillips Curve is similar to, and how it is different from, a production possibility curve.
4. Mention and explain as many things as you can think of that would be likely to make the Phillips Curve shift up or down, or to the right or left.
5. What is the basic position of Milton Friedman and the monetarists regarding stabilization policy?
6. There are many reasons why wage-price controls are undesirable in general, and why it's very hard to make them work. But under some circumstances they *can* be made to work. Try to explain all this, in as much detail as you can.

17

The Keynesian-Monetarist Debate, Rational Expectations, Supply-Side Economics, and Macro Policies for the 1980s

Chapter Objectives

- In the last chapter you found out that **economists disagree** about **macroeconomic theory and policy.** In this chapter you'll find out a lot more about these disagreements.

- When you finish studying this chapter you will understand **Keynesian "demand-side" economics.** And you will know about the **synthesis of Keynesian ideas** into the pre-Keynesian **neoclassical economic theory.**

- You will find out about the **monetarist challenge** to Keynesian economics, and about the **key issues** in the **great debate** between the **Keynesians** and the **monetarists.**

- This chapter explains the theory of **rational expectations,** and how this theory relates to the theories of both monetarist and Keynesian economics.

- In this chapter you will learn about **supply-side economics,** about the **Reagan administration's** supply-side program, and about the **"Laffer Curve"** illustration of a **supply-side tax cut.**

- Finally, from this chapter you will get an **overview** of the **macroeconomic conditions, policies and outlook** for the 1980s.

KEYNESIAN "DEMAND-SIDE" ECONOMICS

Much of the macroeconomics you've been reading about in this book has been Keynesian "demand-side" macroeconomics. In Keynesian economics the focus is on **aggregate demand.**

What determines the *speed* of the economy? What determines *how much* (in total) will be produced? What determines whether or not all the labor, capital, land (the factors of production) will be employed as fully as their owners (and

the society) want them to be employed? Aggregate demand, right?

Keynesian economics focuses on *the rate of spending* in the economy. Spending is what pulls forth the *output*, and thus supports *employment* and *incomes*. Keynesian economics tells us that if we can understand what determines the level of spending (aggregate demand), we will know what determines the level of employment and production—of output and income in the economy.

Keynesian economics tells us that public policies which *change the level of spending* in the

270

economy will *change the level of employment and production, and output and income* in the economy. Keynesian economics offers the government a *positive* approach to overcoming depression:

Make total spending increase and the economy will speed up. Increase government spending. Cut taxes so people and businesses will have more money to spend. Permit the money supply to expand. As the government and the businesses and the people all spend more, people will receive more income. As people's incomes increase, their spending will increase. The result: prosperity!

If the Keynesian prescription works, the economy will boom. Soon the government will need to cut down on its spending and raise taxes to keep the boom from running away into inflation.

Keynes Focused on the "Spending Sectors"*

Keynes analyzed total spending. He took it apart and looked at *who* was doing the spending, and why. Essentially, he split the "spending stream" into two sectors—spending for consumer goods, and spending for capital goods. Then he tried to get at the *motives* underlying each kind of spending—to try to see what underlies, what determines how much *each sector* of the spending stream will spend. If we can understand the *causes* of spending increases or decreases by each sector, then maybe we can induce total spending to adjust to the desired level. See what a neat approach Keynes thought of? (Like so many things, it seems quite obvious once someone else works it out and explains it to us!)

*Much of this section and of the remainder of this chapter consists of excerpts from my recent book, *Economic Evolution: Principles, Issues, Ideas—Through the Looking Glass of Time* (Cincinnati: South-Western Publishing Co., 1981), Book Two: "The Troubled World and Disagreeing Economists of Modern Times," pp. 105-165.

So Keynesian economics is the economics of understanding why each sector of the spending stream (essentially consumers and businesses) spend as much as they do, and what makes their spending change. Also, Keynesian economics tries to explain how adjustments in government spending and taxes can influence the total spending flow and thereby influence the speed at which the economy will run.

The Keynesian Prescription: Unbalance the Budget

The basic idea of the Keynesian prescription for overcoming unemployment and depression was to unbalance the government budget. The government would reduce its "tax withdrawals" from the income stream at the same time that it would increase its "spending injections" into the income stream. The idea was for the government to unbalance the budget, run a deficit, create more money to finance its expenditures, and thereby push more money into the spending and income flow of the economy.

It was not until the early 1960s—actually, not until 1963, the year of President Kennedy's death—that Keynesian economics was explicitly stated as public policy. It was stated by President Kennedy in his speech at the Harvard graduation in June 1963. This is the basic idea of what he said:

Even though we are already running a government deficit, we are going to cut taxes and even further unbalance the budget. The economy will be so stimulated by the tax cut that soon people and businesses will be making so much more income that they will be paying much *more* to the government in taxes. The extra *tax revenues* will be big enough to bring the budget into balance.

A radical idea! Cut taxes in order to collect more taxes? (The idea was that *raising taxes* to try to balance the budget—which was what the Eisenhower administration had done—would only slow down the economy even more, and make the deficit *larger!*)

What had happened during the years following World War II to prepare the nation to accept such a radical idea?—the idea of *further* unbalancing the budget *on purpose?*—the idea that *cutting* taxes will produce more revenue than *raising* taxes? What had happened to ready the policymakers for such an unorthodox economic policy? Such a policy would have been considered nonsense only a few years earlier. What brought about the change in thinking?

The Synthesis of Keynesian and Neoclassical Economics

Perhaps the most important influence was the synthesis, or integration, of Keynesian economics into neoclassical economics—that is, into the general body of accepted pre-Keynesian economic principles. As time went on, most economists (and apparently most people) came to accept Keynesian economics—not as a substitute for, but as a necessary complement to neoclassical economics.

But *note this well:* Not *all* economists accepted Keynesian economics into their "theoretical models" of how the economy functions. Milton Friedman was the leader of the "anti-Keynesian school" of economic thought. He and his followers held out and ultimately emerged with the powerful "monetarist challenge" to Keynesian economics. You will be reading more about that soon.

Exactly what was this synthesis?—this integration of Keynesian and neoclassical ideas? Quite simple, really. The neoclassical model was still accepted as a valid statement of the *market forces* which are constantly at work in the society. But the Keynesians emphasized that there were many other forces, too—forces *outside* the neoclassical model—some outside of *economics*

even—which sometimes would be strong enough to overpower the neoclassical market tendencies to maintain full employment—maybe even carry the world in the *opposite* direction. And when that happened, the neoclassical model would not be the best place to look for an explanation of what was going on.

The Focus of Neoclassical Economics. Neoclassical economics is based on a different set of assumptions about the world and how it works, than is Keynesian economics. Neoclassical economics focuses on the forces which, if left free to operate without impediment, will always bring the economy fairly quickly and smoothly into a "long-run equilibrium" of full employment and stable prices.

In this long-run equilibrium, all resource uses will be optimized—that is, all labor, land, and capital will be directed in the most efficient ways toward the true objectives of the society. A beautiful system! But not everyone believes that it works out that way in the real world.

The Focus of Keynesian Economics. The Keynesians also believe in the neoclassical model as an essential tool for explaining what the market forces are and how they work. But they don't believe those forces always work out in the same predictable ways. They don't believe in the "inevitable mechanistic determination" of real-world economic events, as described in the neoclassical model. They don't believe that the real-world economic condition looks like the long-run equilibrium of the neoclassical model. Therefore, when they see high unemployment and other signs that the economy isn't running as it should, they look to the ideas of Keynesian economics to help them to understand what's going on.

As an economy grows and prospers, people's incomes go up. People with high incomes save a lot. They may pull so much savings out of the income stream that a depression will result. Prices may not easily adjust to end the depression as the neoclassical model says. That's when the Keynesians say *the government should take action:* follow the Keynesian prescription! Spend enough to offset the savings withdrawals. Or cut taxes so people and businesses will be able to spend more. Or promote "easy money" (low interest rates) so businesses and people may borrow and spend more. Most economists these days agree with some Keynesian ideas.

Without Keynesian economics we would be right back where we were before the depression of the 1930s, with no way to prescribe effective action to revitalize the system. So who, pray tell, would throw out Keynesian economics? Milton Friedman and the other monetarists, that's who. Why? Because they don't think it's needed. And they don't think it works. They think the Keynesian prescription, although perhaps *seeming* to help to stabilize the economy, actually has the effect of *worsening* the problem of economic instability.

CHALLENGE TO KEYNESIAN ECONOMICS: THE KEYNESIAN-MONETARIST DEBATE

In the way the monetarists perceive the world, Keynesian economics is unnecessary, wrong, harmful. If the monetarists' perception of the world is correct, then Keynesian economics is wrong and harmful. But if the monetarists' perception of the world is *not* correct, then the monetarists are doing serious harm by discrediting these prescriptive tools which the Keynesians offer for dealing with economic instability, economic stagnation, and depression. So in the real world of the 1980s, this issue is very serious business.

The Anti-Keynesians: Milton Friedman and the Monetarists

Throughout the period of the 1940s, '50s, and '60s, while Keynesian economics was being integrated into the mainstream of economic understanding, a few economists were speaking out loud and clear against Keynesian economics.

They were arguing and building their case against the whole idea of government fiscal policy—of adjusting taxes and spending to influence the economy. The leading challengers have been (and are) Milton Friedman and his colleagues who make up the **"monetarist" school** of economic thought.

To the monetarists, macroeconomic conditions are to a very large extent determined by the natural forces of the market mechanism (the forces of demand and supply and price). Any attempt by government to alter the results would interfere with the natural market forces and therefore would be harmful—and doomed to failure.

The Monetarist Creed: Keep Your Eye on the Money Supply

According to Milton Friedman and his followers, the government should never take any kind of direct discretionary action to influence employment or spending or wages or prices. A 4 or 5 percent limit on the expansion of the money supply will take care of the problem of inflation; automatic price adjustments and the automatic forces of the market system will take care of unemployment and depression. The government shouldn't do anything to try to make the economy run better than it runs naturally.

"Keep your eye on the money supply. Let everything else alone. If times are bad, there's nothing the government can do. If the government tries to do something it will only slow down the natural adjustments and delay the coming of good times. The government has no business fooling around

Keynesians say: Use compensatory fiscal and monetary policies! Monetarists say: Don't! Who's right?

I dunno.. ......

with the economy." So say Milton Friedman and his colleagues, the monetarists.

To the monetarists, there's just no need to get involved with the Keynesian prescription. To do so would do more harm than good. The government's *only* economic policy should be to control the size of the money supply and its rate of increase. As total output and trade increase, the money supply should be permitted to increase enough to finance the increased trade. But that's all.

The Monetarist "Long-Run" View

The very basis, or "root cause" of the disagreement between the monetarists and the Keynesians stems from a basic difference of opinion about how to view the economy, and how the macroeconomic forces in the economy actually operate.

The monetarists take a long-run view, and assume that the short-run ups and downs of the economy—inflation, unemployment, etc.—are just that—short-run conditions which the natural market forces will work out in due time.

The monetarists assume that the economic forces of price and competition will work more effectively than would any government attempt to stabilize or offset undesirable changes in prices or production and employment.

Because of the great power and effectiveness of the "natural market forces," these forces should be allowed to control the economy. We should not try to offset or overthrow them in order to achieve short-run price-level or production and employment objectives.

The Keynesian "Short-Run" View

The Keynesian view of the economy is different. The Keynesians accept the proposition that the natural market forces are powerful. But the Keynesians do not believe that these forces are sufficiently powerful to guarantee a healthy economy. The Keynesians focus on the fact that the world only operates in the short run.

Keynes said it this way: "In the long run, we are all dead!" So according to Keynesian economics, whether or not *in the long run* the equilibrium conditions of full employment and stable prices *might arrive*, is irrelevant—and certainly should not be used as the *only guide* to government policy in macroeconomics.

Keynesians Emphasize "Unresponsive Prices"

The Keynesian position is that actual conditions in the modern economy are quite different from the *assumed conditions* in the "model economy"—that the model therefore cannot be relied on as the complete guide to appropriate public policy. Keynesians emphasize the condition of *inflexible prices*, and the constant upward pressure on prices from business and labor organizations all trying to push their prices up.

The Keynesians would agree with the monetarists that if spending in the economy slows down *enough*—so that surpluses in markets are widespread and unemployment is very high—it isn't likely that prices will be going up under such depressed circumstances. Keynesians also would agree that when the economy is in a depression, some workers would be willing to take jobs for less than their previous wages. Some businesses would be willing to sell their products for lower prices.

But the Keynesians hold that in order for these conditions to arrive, the economy must be in a *serious* depression. The Keynesians don't believe that such suffering and misery are necessary. And they don't believe that such misery should be forced on the people—not when appropriate Keynesian-type government policies and programs are available to prevent and/or overcome such depressed conditions.

Keynesians Emphasize Fiscal Policy

Those who accept the Keynesian view of the economy see an important role for government in **economic stabilization**. The government is supposed to maintain a stable, growing economy primarily through **fiscal policy**—taxing more and spending less to hold down excess demand; taxing less and spending more to speed up spending when the consumer and business sectors are not spending enough to maintain full employment. The government is supposed to support its fiscal policies with appropriate **monetary policies**—tightening money and raising interest rates to help to hold down excess demand; easing money and lowering interest rates to speed up spending when the economy is depressed.

The Monetarist Fear of "Overkill"

The monetarists hold that if the government tries to follow these Keynesian policies, not only will it be unsuccessful, it will *worsen* the short-run fluctuations in employment and prices. The monetarists say that whenever the economy has a problem of either unemployment or inflation, the problem soon will be corrected through **natural market forces**.

The monetarists say that if the government tries to come in and offset a "too fast" or "too slow" rate of total spending, it will be adding its "corrective" influence into the economy *at the same time* that the natural market forces are exerting *their* corrective influence. The total effect will be to *over-correct* and force the economy to respond too fast. So the economy will overshoot the "desired equilibrium" rate of spending and wind up with *the opposite* problem.

If the government tries to correct for *too little spending* (recession and unemployment), soon the economy will find itself with *too much spending*. Serious inflation is likely to result. If the government tries to correct for *too much spending* (inflation), soon it is likely to wind up with *too little spending* (recession and unemployment).

The Monetarist Problem of "Response-Lags"

The monetarist position is that there is a **natural pattern** of almost "mechanical relationships of causes and effects" in the economy. ("When you pull this lever, then this result is certain to occur.") But the important problem is this: No one can tell you *how soon* these results will occur.

The monetarists say that when we have inflation, if you bring down the rate of growth of the money supply, you will bring down the rate of inflation. They agree that the reduced money supply will result in reduced spending and some increased unemployment—a recession—but they are absolutely certain that the inflation rate will come down. But there are "lags"—some time delay—between the slowing of the money supply growth rate and the slowing of the inflation rate. The monetarists believe that in general these lags are not very long—no more than a few months—so we should hold tight on the money supply and wait.

The monetarists are **sure what's going to happen. They just aren't sure When.**

The Experience of 1979-80

In the late 1970s and early 1980s, **money supply growth** was held down to a very slow rate. There were periods of several months when the rate of money growth was approximately zero. During that time several Keynesian economists (and some business leaders—and Senator Edward Kennedy) were saying that the reduced growth of the money supply *alone* was *not sufficient* to handle the serious inflation problem. They were suggesting that other government policies (such as **direct controls** on wages and prices) were also required.

But the monetarists were saying that maintaining the slow growth rate of the money supply *was* a sufficient policy—was in fact the *only* effective policy available—and that other government action to try to stop inflation (such as any kind of direct controls on wages and prices) ultimately would do much harm, and no good.

The monetarists blamed the apparent lack of responsiveness of the inflation to the tight money policies and slow money growth on "lags." They said that the lags between the slowing of the money supply growth and the slowing of the inflation rate turned out to be longer than they had expected—probably because of the "built-in inflationary psychology" which was causing people and businesses to behave as though they *expected* inflation to continue.

The importance of expectations in influencing economic behavior (and therefore economic conditions) is well recognized. Expectations play an important role in Keynesian economics. But here's a new theory of expectations—one that strikes at the heart of Keynesian economics.

A NEW THEORY: "RATIONAL EXPECTATIONS"

During the 1970s a new attack was mounting against the Keynesians—the theory of "rational expectations." This new theory leads to the conclusion that any government stabilization policy which the government might decide to undertake (and which the spending units in the economy—businesses, consumers, financial institutions, etc.—might have "rationally expected" the government to take) would be doomed to failure.

The basic idea of the "rational expectations" theory is this: When economic decision-makers (consumers, businesses, etc.) expect the government to initiate a certain economic stabilization policy, then these decision-makers will take action to protect themselves—to "maximize their own positions" in the light of the "rationally expected" effects of the government policy. As they do this, they will make it impossible for the government's stabilization policy to work.

The Logical Steps of the Theory

The theory of "rational expectations" is quite complex. But the basic outline of the theory can be summarized in the following steps:

1. First, we must assume that the old saying, "Everybody makes mistakes but only a fool makes the same mistakes over and over," is true. Not very many people would disagree with that.
2. After the first basic premise, the theory goes on with a series of steps with which not everyone would agree. The second step is that when government takes Keynesian-type actions to try to stabilize the economy, that tricks people into doing things which *ultimately* will hurt them—that is, ultimately will worsen their economic condition.
3. After the government has done its "Keynesian-type stabilizing tricks" once or twice, people catch on. They realize that if they do what the government policymakers expect them to do, they will wind up being hurt again, just as before.
4. Since people (and businesses, financial institutions, etc.) "rationally expect" to be harmed if they respond to the government policies in the way that the government policymakers *expect* them to, they look at the situation differently now. They *do not* do what the government stabilization policymakers *wanted* and *expected* them to do.
5. Because people's "rational expectations" tell them not to respond to government stabilization policies in the "expected way," the government stabilization policies are doomed to failure. For example, anti-recession policies would cause inflation—not increase production and employment. So any attempt to use Keynesian policies to overcome recession would only make matters worse.
6. Following these logical steps the conclusion is obvious: Government should *never*

introduce any Keynesian-type stabilization policies. Instead, government should make it clear that it is *never going to use* any Keynesian-type stabilization policies.

The government should emphasize that its only "stabilization policy" will be to permit the money supply to expand by a slow and constant rate (four or five percent per year). Then the economic decision-makers (consumers, businesses, etc.) will make their decisions based on this assurance that the government will not "meddle" in the economy to try to overcome or lessen the effects of any recession which might appear.

The "rational expectations" theorists (now led by Robert Lucas of the University of Chicago) put forth the hypothesis that when everyone in the economy knows that the government will maintain slow and constant money growth, then they will know that they have no cause to "rationally expect" continued inflation. In this stable environment they will be able to make proper decisions and thereby ensure that the economy will be as stable as it ever could be—that recessions which may occur will be short-term and self-correcting.

Recessions are thought to be a natural part of the functioning of the market system. People should learn to accept them as that. They should not call on government policy to try to do anything about them because active government stabilization policies can't help and will make matters worse.

Rational Expectations, and the Traditional Monetarist Position

You can see that the rational expectations theory leads to exactly the same government policy recommendations as Friedman and the monetarists have been advocating all along. But rational expectations theory arrives at the same conclusion in a different way.

The logic of the more **traditional monetarist position** is this: The natural market forces for overcoming recession and inflation are *powerful*,

and *effective*, but they operate with *time lags*. The economy *ultimately* will correct itself—but not *immediately*. If the government undertakes any stabilization policies to try to achieve a *more immediate* correction of either recession or inflation the *ultimate* result will be overkill. The government's corrective actions will be added to the already powerful corrective forces of the market. So the economy will overshoot the objective of long-term stability and growth. Government anti-inflation efforts will cause recession; anti-recession efforts will cause inflation.

The **rational expectations theory** doesn't focus on the effect of these "time lags." It focuses on the way in which people's *expectations* of the effects of government stabilization policies cause them to behave differently—and how this "change of behavior" renders the government's stabilization policies not only ineffective but also destabilizing. The following section gives some examples so you can see how the rational expectations theory explains this.

Examples of "Rational Expectations" at Work

Exactly how do the "rational expectations" of people and businesses prevent government stabilization policies from working? This section gives two examples of ways in which Keynesian-type stabilization policies are *supposed* to work. Then for each it explains the way in which the new theory says that people's "rational expectatons" will prevent these policies from working.

Example 1. One way government tries to overcome unemployment and recession is to *create new money and increase its own spending*. It spends on such things as public works projects and it buys products from businesses. This stimulates businesses to hire more labor and buy more material inputs and increase their outputs.

The Keynesian theory says that as the government does this, the spending flow in the economy will increase. The newly-employed workers will spend more money, and demand throughout the economy will increase. Soon the recession will be overcome as business activity (production and employment) speed up. The "rational expectations" theory says this won't happen. Here's how the theory explains why not:

1. Suppose government increases its spending to try to induce production and employment to increase. Businesses will respond by producing and selling more to government. They will do this because their "rational expectations" tell them that government spending will cause their output prices to go up *faster than* their costs will go up. Workers will be working for wages which don't go up as fast as prices go up. So businesses will make more profits. This is what stimulates businesses to expand their operations, employ more workers, and speed up the economy.

   Note: Keynesian and other non-monetarist economists would argue that this is not a picture of the real world—that in the real world, businesses will sell more as government stimulates demand even if prices do not rise—or even if wages rise as rapidly as do prices.

2. The "rational expectations" theory says that after the government has used its "increased government spending" approach two or three times, labor catches on. They see what happens to their *real wages* when government spending increases.

   Workers soon come to realize that when the government starts creating new money and spending more, that will cause prices to rise. So they realize that unless they get wage increases right away (at least as much wage increase as the "rationally expected" price increase) soon they will wind up as losers.

   So workers demand (and get) higher wages. This chokes off the possibility for increased profits by businesses and prevents businesses from expanding their outputs and employing more workers as the Keynesian theory predicts. In this case it's the "rational expectations" of labor which doom the government's anti-recession policy to failure.

   Note: Keynesian and other non-monetarist economists would argue that this also is a distorted view of the real world because:

   a. Wage rates are not under such complete control of labor—that it isn't realistic to assume that labor would get higher wages just because they decided that's what they wanted and what they deserved; and

   b. Depressed businesses would be happy to produce and sell more output even if their labor cost increased as rapidly as their output prices might be increasing.

3. The conclusion of the "rational expectations" theory, again, is that the government's attempt to overcome recession won't work. It will only succeed in forcing prices up—causing inflation.

The theory says that only if the government could count on "catching people by surprise" (so they wouldn't have any "rational expectations" about the policy) would it be possible for the policy to work. But "catching people by surprise" usually isn't possible. People are too sharp and have too much information about what's going on. So the obvious conclusion, again, is that *the government should not try to overcome recession or depression by creating money and increasing government spending*—so say the rational expectations theorists.

Example 2. Another "Keynesian stabilization policy" designed to speed up the economy and overcome recession or depression is the *"easy money"* approach. It's supposed to work like this:

The Federal Reserve buys bonds from banks, businesses, and individuals, and pays for the bonds with newly created money. This increases the money supply, pushes down interest rates in the money markets, and provides banks with more money to lend.

Banks with more money to lend offer loans at lower interest rates. At the lower rates, businesses are more willing to borrow and invest. With lower interest cost, more investment opportunities become profitable. Also, consumers are more willing to buy durable goods (such as automobiles, and appliances) because the interest cost is lower. As businesses spend more, the economy begins to speed up. Businesses hire more people and generate more income, so people spend even more. This is the way the "easy money" policy is supposed to overcome the depression. This process continues until the economy reaches full employment.

The "rational expectations" theory demolishes this Keynesian scenario in one sentence: "Banks will not make loans at low interest rates because their 'rational expectations' tell them that the 'easy money' policy will cause *inflation*, which will push interest rates up and make low-interest loans unprofitable." Certainly banks don't want to make loans on which they expect to wind up losing money! So *the "rational expectations" theory concludes that the government should not try to use "easy money" policy to try to stimulate a depressed economy. The policy would fail and would only cause inflation.*

Note: It is generally recognized by economists and other informed people that widespread *inflationary expectations* do in fact influence people's economic decisions and therefore also influence the functioning of the economy. For example, in the high inflation period of the 1970s and early 1980s, banks were making loans with "floating interest rates" so that if interest rates went up after a loan was made, the interest rate

on the loan would also go up. Some savings institutions were lending to home buyers on "variable-rate" mortgages. But this does not lead all economists to conclude that "rational expectations" prevent businesses and consumers from borrowing more when there is "easy money" and lower interest rates, or less when there is "tight money" and higher rates.

Summary Analysis

One positive thing that economists can agree on about the "rational expectations" theory is this: It reemphasizes the importance of *expectations* in economic decision-making, and it offers us a new idea about the way in which some expectations are formed. Most economists agree that *expectations play an important role in influencing the functioning of the economy.*

The Keynesians focus on the *short-run changeability* of expectations as an important factor influencing economic decisions, contributing to the *short-run instability* of the economy (recession and inflation).

The rational expectations theorists focus on the *long-run rationality* of expectations—based on the expected long-run effects of government policies—as an important factor influencing economic decisions and (assuming government policies are appropriately stable) contributing to the *long-run stability* of the economy.

So again, the basic difference in the "mental set" between the Keynesians and the neoclassical economists carries on into the basic difference between Keynesian economics and the rational expectations theory. That is, **Keynesian economics** is concerned with understanding and explaining the *dynamic short-run changes* which occur in the economy—the process by which it gets itself into recession or inflation and the process by which it gets itself out. The rational expectations theory concentrates on *long-run equilibrium* conditions and doesn't focus on the dynamic process of causes and effects which move the economy to (or away from) this long-run equilibrium position.

A NEW EMPHASIS: SUPPLY-SIDE ECONOMICS

Another important development in economic thinking which occurred during the 1970s and early 1980s was the shift in emphasis toward "supply-side" economics. This also was to some extent an attack on Keynesian economics. But it was a different kind of attack than the monetarist attack.

The monetarist attack says that Keynesian economics has always been basically wrong about the economy and about what the government can (and should) do to stabilize the economy. Keynesian economics prescribes stabilization policies, and monetarist economics prescribes "hands-off" policies. "Supply-side" economics doesn't focus primarily on this controversy.

What is "Supply-Side" Economics?

The basic idea of "supply-side" economics is this: If we want to slow inflation, we need to generate *more output*—more supply of products in the market. If we can succeed in doing that (assuming nothing else changes to upset the results), then the increased *supply* will help to hold down prices.

How do we increase the total (aggregate) supply of output in the economy? Primarily by increasing the *productivity* of the average worker in the economy. So "supply-side" economics focuses its attention on *increasing worker productivity* and on ways to achieve that.

Recent "Supply-Side" Conditions in the U.S. Economy

The idea of supply-side economics is very relevant to the situation in the American economy in the early 1980s, because the economy was not increasing its productivity very rapidly during this period. During 1979 there was an *absolute decline* in productivity (in average output per worker).

When productivity growth is slow, that means that output per person is not increasing much. So the "amount per person" being supplied into the nation's markets is not expanding much. That's what was happening in the American economy. Productivity just wasn't increasing as it had been in previous decades. Yet employees were receiving increasing incomes for their work—even though their outputs were not increasing commensurately with their incomes. The result: People were *receiving more money* at a faster rate than they were *producing more goods*. So people had more money to spend, but there weren't that many more goods in the market to buy! You know what happens in a situation like that—prices go up. Inflation.

In the late 1970s and early 1980s, economists and business, labor, and government leaders were seriously concerned about this productivity problem. Various explanations were offered as to *why* average productivity was so low. Various prescriptions were suggested as to *how* the problem might be solved.

"Supply-Side" Economics and the Keynesian-Monetarist Debate

Where does "supply-side economics" fit in the Keynesian-monetarist controversy? It doesn't, really. But it makes the Keynesian prescription somewhat irrelevant.

Keynesian economics focuses on "demand-side" economics. Keynesian economics is concerned with the forces which determine total spending (total, or "aggregate" demand) in the economy. It's concerned with the ways in which government actions can adjust this total spending or **aggregate demand** flow to achieve full employment and stable prices. "Supply-side" economics looks at the *other side* of the question.

Supply-side economics recognizes that the economic circumstances which exist in the American economy in the early 1980s are greatly different than were the circumstances during the depression of the 1930s—back when Keynes was offering his stabilization policy recommendations. During the depression years, the economy was glutted with supply. The demand to buy the output just wasn't there. It made sense, both pragmatically and in Keynesian theory, to concentrate on the demand-side problem. The question then was: "How do we increase the spending flow enough to get all these surplus products bought up and get the economy back into production again?"

In the American economy of the early 1980s the situation was very different. A slow rate of productivity growth throughout most of the 1970s, together with constantly increasing incomes of the people, had clearly led to a "supply-side" problem.

Does the World Need a "New Keynes"?

In the early 1980s some people were suggesting that what we need now is a "new Keynes"—someone who will focus on the new, different situation and provide a new theory— and a new policy prescription.

But the monetarists are not calling for a new Keynes. The monetarists are sure that we already have the theoretical understanding we need. We already know what to do: Cut back the influence of government in the economy. Maintain a slow, steady rate of increase in the money supply. Then let everything be controlled by the **natural market forces**—the forces of supply and demand, and prices and competition.

Conflicting Ideas on How to Increase Productivity

In the late 1970s there was developing a general awareness of the seriousness of the "low productivity" problem. Then in early 1980 when the 1979 productivity figures showed an *absolute decline* in output-per-worker it became clear that this problem was becoming critical. In the early 1980s, not only the economists and business and political leaders, but also most of the informed members of the general public were aware of the problem and of the need to do something about it. But everyone *did not* agree on how this might best be achieved.

Almost everyone can agree that increasing productivity requires *increased efficiency* in the production process—that more efficient technology, machinery and equipment, resource management, and use of the labor force, are required. But how do we achieve that? Here are some suggested approaches which were being put forward by various individuals and groups in the late '70s and early '80s:

- A reduction of cost-increasing government regulations;
- Reduced taxes on businesses to provide more incentive and more cash flow for investment in more and better capital;
- More emphasis by corporations on long-run productivity improvement and less emphasis on "maximizing profits in the present quarter";
- Improved education and training programs and personnel policies for employees;
- Changing the "reward structure" to reward *productivity* more than seniority;
- Stimulating and rewarding truly innovative activities of any kind by anybody, either labor or management;
- Eliminating government prohibitions to competition and letting the inefficient businesses fall by the wayside to make room for more efficient ones;
- Reduced concern about "equal opportuni-

ty" and "consumer protection" and more concern with increasing productivity and competition and "let the devil take the hindmost";

• Eliminating productivity-reducing "job rules" required by some labor-management contracts which slow the introduction of high-technology production techniques;

• Reducing welfare, unemployment, and other kinds of payments which "reward people for not working";

• Developing lower-cost energy sources and reducing the dependence on high-cost imported oil;

• Eliminating government restrictions on (potentially environmentally harmful) energy developments and uses, such as nuclear power, high sulphur coal, strip mining, etc.;

• Increasing the rewards for invention and innovation;

• Convincing the labor force and the general public of the "basic truth" of the "work ethic" and that "the good life" for an individual and for the society comes from increasing productivity;

• Working out "social contract" arrangements between management and labor in each industry and firm (with government's assistance and support) so that management and labor will become partners (not adversaries) in working for increased productivity;

• Establishing government "targets" for productivity increases in each industry and providing rewards and imposing penalties on those businesses which fail to meet their established targets;

• Establishing government "labor force plans" and inducing people to take training and to move into high productivity occupations;

• Nationalizing the big corporations and establishing government management teams to plan and manage the activities of these businesses for maximum increases in productivity;

• And the list could go on and on.

The Choices Will Not Be Easy

As you look at this list of possible approaches you can see why there would be much disagreement about what should be done. Nobody would suggest that *all* of the possible approaches should be tried. Obviously not. Several of the approaches conflict with each other. And as you can see, some of them would involve basic changes in the nature of the American economic system.

One thing is clear. If we are going to have very much success in solving the problems of inflation, reduced productivity, and the declining competitive position of the United States in the world economy, we're going to have to do some things differently in the future than we have in the past. During the decade of the 1980s you are likely to see an increasing number of these "possible approaches"—and some other ones too—actually being put into practice.

Supply-Side Fiscal Policy

Suppose the government cuts taxes to try to stimulate productivity. If businesses then decide to invest in high technology equipment, great! Worker productivity will increase. There will be more output (supply) in the market. Inflationary pressures will be eased.

But what about the effect on government revenues? When taxes are cut, the government runs a big deficit, right? And financing the deficit with *monetized debt* would be inflationary, right? Or financing it in the money markets would cause *crowding out* and choke off business investment, right? Well, maybe all these things might happen. And then again, maybe not.

What if the tax cut stimulated productivity so much that tax revenues actually increased? Suppose tax rates were cut 10% and that caused incomes to increase by 20%. Then the government's tax revenues would be higher than before! There wouldn't be any deficit. Is this possible? Some supply-side fiscal policy theorists think so. They even have developed a curve to illustrate this possibility. It's called the Laffer Curve after Arthur Laffer, its creator.

The Laffer Curve. The Laffer Curve illustrates the basic idea that as tax rates go up, productivity is discouraged. So (beyond some point) a *tax rate increase* will reduce productivity so much that it will result in a *tax revenue decrease*. When tax rates are already discouragingly high, how can we get more revenue? And increase the productivity of the economy at the same time? Cut taxes.

Figure 17-1 shows the **Laffer Curve.** You'll notice that as tax rates increase from zero (moving up along the *y* axis), government revenues increase from zero (measured along the *x* axis). But as tax rates keep going up more, revenues go up less and less (point b), reach a maximum (point c), and then decline (point d).

You will notice that there aren't any numbers on the axes of Figure 17-1. That's because nobody knows where the numbers should be. Which point on the curve illustrates where we are at this moment? We don't know.

Suppose you think we're at point "a" and I think we're at point "e." You and I aren't going to support the same tax policies. That's for sure!

MACROECONOMIC OUTLOOK AND POLICIES FOR THE 1980s

In the early 1980s the macroeconomic problems of the American economy were clear and serious: *inflation, unemployment,* and *low productivity.*

Inflation. During the 1960s the average annual inflation rate was less than 3%. In the 1970s it was about 7%. In 1980 it was more than 13%. But in mid-1982 it was down to less than 6%.

Unemployment. During the 1960s, unemployment ranged from about 3% to 7%. In the 1970s it ranged from about 5% to 8%. In 1980 it was about 7%. But in mid-1982 it was about 9%.

Productivity. During the 1960-65 period, productivity (output per worker/hour) increased at an average annual rate of 2.6%. In the 1974-79 period the rate of increase was only 0.7%. During 1979-81 it actually declined.

Figure 17-1   The Laffer Curve

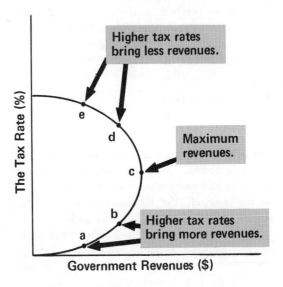

The Reagan Administration's Recovery Program

Presidential candidate Ronald Reagan campaigned on a platform which promised reductions in: taxes, federal deficits, federal spending increases, and government regulations. After his election his administration moved to follow through on all of these promises. **Supply-side economics** became the guideline.

The *Economic Recovery Tax Act of 1981* cut taxes, hopefully to stimulate productivity. (Remember the Laffer Curve?) New tax legislation was designed to stimulate savings and to make investment more profitable.

The following quotes from the 1982 *Economic Report of the President* (p. 23) highlight the key elements of the administration's economic recovery program:

—cutting the rate of growth in federal spending;

—reducing personal income tax rates and creating jobs by accelerating depreciation for business investment in plant and equipment;

—instituting a far-reaching program of regulatory relief; and

—in cooperation with the Federal Reserve, making a new commitment to a monetary policy that will restore a stable currency and healthy financial markets.

The Fed's Program

In October of 1979 the Federal Reserve Board had announced a new decision about how it was going to control the money supply. Until that time, the Fed had looked more at *interest rates* as an indicator of "the tightness of money." But since October, 1979 the Fed has looked at and tried to control the "monetary base"—that is, the reserves available to banks. If the monetary base is not permitted to expand, this cuts off the ability of the banking system to make new loans.

The significance of this shift in Fed policy is this: By controlling the monetary base, the Fed can *absolutely prevent* the money supply from expanding. When it does this, if the demand for money goes very high, then interest rates are pushed up very high—and not only do they go high. They also become very volatile. Since the supply of money is more or less fixed, demand changes cause interest rates to fluctuate widely. And that's what has happened.

High and volatile interest rates deter investment. And that interferes with "supply-side" objectives. But easing money would be inflationary. The Fed's position (in mid-1982) is that as soon as tight money breaks the inflation, interest rates will come down and (non-inflationary) productivity growth can proceed. But meanwhile, there are supply-side problems.

In agriculture the very high interest rates have pushed up production costs and caused cutbacks in inputs. So we are almost certain to see reduced outputs of some farm products—which will mean higher agricultural prices.

In the housing construction industry, the high interest rates have forced nationwide cutbacks approaching 50%. That means that only a little more than *one-half* of the usual number of new houses are being constructed. This reduced supply of housing will show up in coming years and housing prices are likely to go up to reflect that.

Adjustments of the Humphrey-Hawkins Timetable

In 1978 the Congress passed the *Full Employment and Balanced Growth Act* (known as the Humphrey-Hawkins Act). This Act provided specific target rates for *unemployment* and *inflation*. The Administration is legally bound to take the necessary steps to try to achieve these targeted rates.

The targeted unemployment rate was set at 4%; the targeted inflation rate was set at 3%. The Act says that these rates are supposed to be achieved by the end of 1983—but it says that the president can amend this timetable if necessary.

In his January, 1980 *Economic Report*, President Carter amended the timetable. He set 1985 as the target year for achieving 4% unemployment, and three years later (1988) as the target year for lowering the inflation rate to 3%.

In his February, 1982 *Economic Report*, President Reagan not only amended the timetable. The *Report* also amended the target figures, saying (p. 215): "The Federal Government cannot fully anticipate the course of the economy; neither can it direct economic outcomes precisely." Then it goes on to give the projections.

President Reagan's projections show **unemployment** in 1985 of 6.4% and 1987 of 5.3%. The **inflation** rate is projected to be, in 1985, 4.6% and in 1987, 4.4%. Is that what will happen? Only time will tell.

The Reagan administration promised its steadfast pursuit of its supply-side policies—no more "stop and go" economic policies. And

Chairman Volcker and other Fed Board members promised the same—no surrender in their commitment to hold down the size of the money supply. They vowed that *inflation would be brought under control.*

This book goes to press in a Congressional election year (1982). Election years have a way of bringing economic policy surprises. So after you finish this chapter, try to spend some time with the news magazines in your library. There you can find out what really did happen!

SUMMARY AND SYNTHESIS

Keynesian economics is "demand-side" economics. It emphasizes **aggregate demand** (total spending) in the economy and focuses on the individual **spending sectors.** It tries to understand what causes these sectors to speed up or slow down.

The **Keynesian** prescription for macroeconomic policy is to **influence total spending.** One way is by adjusting **government spending** and/or **taxes** (i.e., fiscal policy). The other is by adjusting the **availability and cost of credit** (i.e., monetary policy). Both of these policies can be used to **compensate** for adverse changes in the size of the total spending flow. So say the Keynesians.

Monetarist economists—Milton Friedman and many others—challenge Keynesian economics as **unworkable** and **destabilizing.** The **monetarist** prescription is "hands off!" Let the forces of **demand, supply, and price adjustments** control the economy. Then, macroeconomic problems will be **self-correcting.** Only one rule: Let the money supply expand just fast enough to permit the desired rate of economic growth.

The monetarists point to the long-run **"tendency toward equilibrium"** in the economy. Policies to try to reduce short-run difficulties (e.g., unemployment) will be destabilizing because they will cause the economy to overshoot equilibrium (e.g., cause inflation). When real-world conditions don't seem to be going as the monetarists predicted, the explanation usually is that there are

response lags—sometimes quite a bit of **lead-time** is required before the forthcoming response can be seen.

The Keynesians focus on the fact that **the short run is all that ever exists in the real world.** They emphasize the existence of real-world **monopoly power** and **inflexible prices** which differ from the neoclassical "long-run equilibrium" model. The Keynesians say that sometimes **compensatory fiscal and monetary policies** can result in a more healthy and growing economy than the "natural market forces" would bring.

The **rational expectations** theory says that individuals, businesses, financial institutions, etc., **get hurt by Keynesian-type fiscal and monetary policies. But after awhile they catch on and stop responding** as the government expects them to. When this happens, **any Keynesian-type compensatory policy is doomed to failure.** The conclusion of the rational expectations theorists and the monetarists is the same: **"Hands off! Leave the market forces in control."**

Supply-side economics emphasizes the importance of increasing productivity. The greater the output per person, the higher each person's income can be without creating inflationary pressures. And also, the more the average person can consume! **Supply-side economics bypasses the Keynesian-monetarist debate** and focuses on the other side of the **"aggregate demand-aggregate supply"** equation.

Supply-side economics emphasizes increasing productivity. The Reagan administration's tax cuts were designed to stimulate savings and investment and productivity. The Economic Recovery Tax Act of 1981 is aimed toward this objective.

The Laffer Curve shows the hypothetical relationship between various tax rates and the size of government revenues. It indicates that sometimes tax cuts will generate increased revenue by stimulating greater productivity and more income.

The U.S. economy entered the 1980s with high rates of inflation and unemployment and declining productivity. The Reagan administration outlined a program of supply-side tax cuts, stimulating savings and investments, cutting the rate of growth of federal spending, reducing regulations, and a commitment to the Fed's policy of holding down the size of the money supply. And both President Reagan and Fed Board Chairman Volcker promised no more "stop and go" policies. By the time you're reading this you probably already know what happened after that.

REVIEW EXERCISES

MAJOR CONCEPTS, PRINCIPLES, TERMS (Explain each carefully.)

Keynesian economics
demand-side economics
supply-side economics
the Keynesian prescription

the monetarist position
the Keynesian-monetarist debate
short run vs. long run view
rational expectations theory

OTHER CONCEPTS AND TERMS (Explain each briefly.)

aggregate demand
Milton Friedman
response lags
The Economic Recovery Tax Act of 1981

CURVES AND GRAPHS (Draw, label, and explain each.)

The Laffer Curve

QUESTIONS (Write out answers or jot down key points.)

1. Explain the highlights of the Keynesian-monetarist debate. Do you think there are times when the Keynesians might be more right? And other times when the monetarists might be more right? Explain and discuss.
2. What policy change did the Fed announce in October of 1979? Why? And what happened after that?
3. Do high and volatile interest rates interfere with supply-side economic policies? Explain and discuss.
4. Describe some of the macroeconomic problems facing the U.S. economy in the early 1980s. Then give the highlights of the Reagan administration's program for dealing with these problems. In view of recent events, how do you think it's working out? Discuss.

PART FIVE

I Wonder If It Knows We're Going Back Into Microeconomics?

18 Exchange and the Market Process: Comparative Advantage, Specialization, and Trade

Chapter Objectives

- This chapter re-introduces you to **microeconomics** and explains the critical role of **specialization and trade** in the functioning of the market system.

- When you finish studying this chapter you will be able to explain **comparative advantage** and **the gains from trade.** And you will be able to use straight-line **production possibility curves** to illustrate these principles.

- You will be able to explain how specialization and trade are **generated automatically** by the operation of the **price mechanism.**

- In this chapter you will learn about the importance of **opportunity cost ratios** in generating trade. And you will learn about **economic integration,** about the **law of comparative advantage,** about **division of labor,** and about the **economic interdependence** which always results from specialization and trade.

- When you finish this chapter you will understand that **specialization and trade** are responsible for the **high standards of living** which so many people now enjoy, and that the **most basic function of markets** is to **permit and facilitate** this all-important **specialization and trade.**

Microeconomics, Again!

Welcome back to *microeconomics*—back to the study of *opportunity costs,* of *scarcity* and *choosing,* of trying to *optimize,* of *substituting* this for that—to the study of how the *market process* automatically carries out the choices of the society.

How does it happen? First, *demand and supply* work against each other to set the *price* of each good. Then the *rationing and production motivating functions of price* go to work to carry out the society's choices.

You remember how it all works, right? How demand changes and causes a shortage or a sur-plus? And how that pushes the price up or down? And how the two functions of price work? And how eventually they bring the production and consumption patterns of the society into line with the new demand situation? Sure.

The chapters back in Part One were explaining the basic concepts and principles of microeconomics. If your memory is a little fuzzy on any of that, better go back and review Part One before you go on into this Part. Especially, be sure you remember about *the factors of production* and about *demand and supply and the functions of price.* And then: On to the study of more microeconomics!

THE GAINS FROM TRADE

Suppose a society's economic system is operating *entirely* on the "pure market process." (None ever did, but just suppose.) Why do people produce? Because they would get pretty hungry if they didn't. They produce because they want to consume.

Some people may be producing their own food and clothes and shelter and all. But most people will be producing just one thing (or maybe a few things). Why? Because it's more efficient to **specialize** in producing something you're good at and then **trade** to get the other things you want. It's "the market" that lets you do that. After you read this chapter you'll see how all this "specializing and trading" helps the people to live much better.

An Island Example

Suppose there are four large families (clans, maybe) living on a tropical island. Each family is located some distance from the others. If you'll look back in the chapter about "the magic of money" (Chapter 7) you'll see a map of this island.

One family lives on the east side of the island and one on the west side; one on the north side and one on the south side. Each family is entirely self-sufficient and produces only for itself. There is no trading between one family and another. If you'll look on the next page you'll see a close-up of this island.

Different "Opportunity Cost Ratios" Generate Trade

Now suppose that the family living on the east side of the island finds fishing to be very good. But the family on the west side has very poor fishing. Ah, but the westside family has very fertile soil. Coconuts, breadfruit, and other tropical vegetables and fruits are plentiful.

You can see that the eastside family is more productive in producing fish. The westside family is more productive in producing vegetables and fruits. And you know what's going to happen. Right?

The eastside islanders will catch fish and trade for breadfruit; the westside islanders will grow breadfruit and trade for fish. Everyone will benefit. But exactly how does all this **specialization and trade** get started?

To the Eastside Islanders Breadfruit Is Very Scarce and Valuable. Suppose the eastside islanders can work all day and catch five baskets of fish. Or if they wanted breadfruit and worked all day at that, they could gather one basket of breadfruit. So what is the **opportunity cost** of a basket of breadfruit? Five baskets of fish! So the value of breadfruit is high: one basket of breadfruit is worth five baskets of fish.

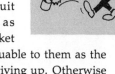

Back to the world of scarcity and opportunity cost. Oh, well...

How do we know that breadfruit is five times as valuable as fish to the eastside islanders? Because the only time they will go after breadfruit (and give up five times as much fish) is when one basket of breadfruit is at least as valuable to them as the five baskets of fish they are giving up. Otherwise they would be fishing instead.

The eastside islanders will conserve breadfruit and eat mostly fish. At suppertime, an eastside child who reaches for a second slice of breadfruit gets a slap on the hand!

To the Westside Islanders Fish Is Very Scarce and Valuable. Now let's look at the westside islanders where the situation is exactly reversed. In one day's work they can produce five baskets of breadfruit or one basket of fish.

When the westsiders spend a day fishing, the one basket of fish they catch "costs" them five baskets of breadfruit. So fish are *five times* as

valuable to them as breadfruit. They eat mostly breadfruit. Woe be unto the westside child who reaches for another piece of charbroiled fish!

Eastside Fish Will Be Traded for Westside Breadfruit

Let's suppose that both families spend half their productive time catching fish and the other half gathering breadfruit. In their normal twenty-workday month the eastside family will produce 50 baskets of fish (10 days of fishing, five baskets a day = 50) and 10 baskets of breadfruit (10 days gathering breadfruit, 1 basket a day = 10).

Over on the west side the situation is exactly reversed. They wind up with 50 baskets of breadfruit and only 10 baskets of fish. They also get a total of 60 baskets of food per month. Figure 18-1 uses transformation (production possibility) curves to show this situation. You should study that Figure for a few minutes now.

Trade Permits Specialization and Increased Output for All

There is really a great opportunity for the eastside islanders and the westside islanders to gain from trading fish and breadfruit. If the eastsiders could trade *less than five baskets* of fish and get *one basket* of breadfruit in exchange, they would be better off.

Suppose they could trade four baskets of fish for one basket of breadfruit. They would be ahead by one basket of fish. If they could trade *one basket* of fish for *one basket* of breadfruit they would wind up with *five times* as much breadfruit as they are now getting. With a one-to-one trade ratio, breadfruit would become as easy to get and as cheap as fish!

Even if the eastside islanders had to pay four and a half baskets of fish for one basket of breadfruit, they still would be one-half basket of

fish better off than if they didn't trade. They could spend a day producing five baskets of fish (instead of producing one basket of breadfruit). Then they could trade four and a half baskets of fish for one basket of breadfruit, and wind up with one basket of breadfruit and one-half basket of fish. That's better than one basket of breadfruit and no fish at all! (which is what they would get if they produced the breadfruit themselves).

The Production Ratio Is Different from the Trade Ratio

For the eastside islanders, the "trade-off ratio" in production (between fish and breadfruit) is 5 for 1. If the trade-off ratio *in trade* is anything *less than* 5 for 1, then they should get their breadfruit by trading—not by producing it.

Isn't it obvious? When they *produce* to get a basket of breadfruit the trade-off cost is 5 baskets of fish. If they can *trade* and get a basket of breadfruit for *less than* 5 baskets of fish, then they will come out with more by trading.

Any individual, family, business, or society will get more of what they want if they will follow this general principle: If the opportunity cost is higher *in production* than it is *in trade*, then you should trade to get what you want. You should get what you want at the **lowest opportunity cost** (the lowest "trade-off" cost) you can arrange. That way you'll get the most of what you want with what you have to work with.

Now take a look at the westside islanders. They are facing the same kind of situation the eastside islanders are facing. But the "trade-off ratio in production" (the transformation ratio) between the two products is exactly reversed.

To the westside islanders the opportunity cost of *one basket* of fish is *five baskets* of breadfruit. If they could trade *less than five baskets* of breadfruit and get back *one basket* of fish, they would be better off. So we have a beautiful setup, just waiting for trade to begin.

Fig. 18-1   Economic Independence—Production Possibilities Without Trade

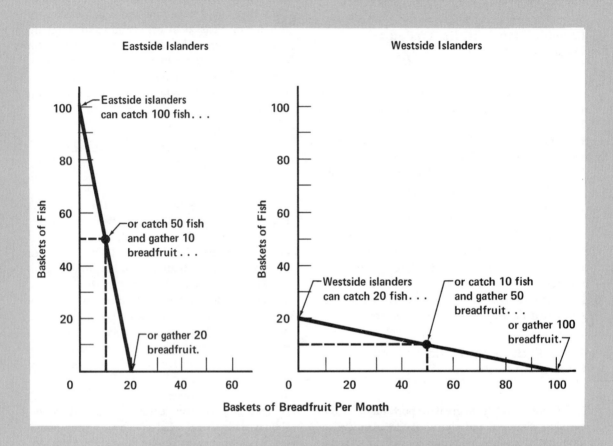

These curves show the production possibilities of the eastside islanders and the westside islanders in producing fish and breadfruit. By looking at these curves you can see the relative value of each product, in each place. How? By looking at the opportunity cost of each, in terms of the other.

The "opportunity cost ratio" or "transformation ratio" for the eastsiders is one basket of breadfruit for five baskets of fish, or a 1 to 5 ratio of breadfruit to fish. Breadfruit is 5 times as valuable as fish.

The transformation ratio for westsiders is five baskets of breadfruit for one basket of fish, or a 1 to 1/5 ratio of breadfruit to fish. Fish is five times as valuable as breadfruit.

To the eastsiders, fish is not very valuable. It is worth 1/5 basket of breadfruit. But to the westsiders, fish is very valuable. It is worth five baskets of breadfruit. What a great opportunity to gain from trade!

The Island Chiefs Discover the Gains from Trade

Suppose that one day the chief of the eastside islanders, King Tuituranga, is walking down Center Island Trail and meets the chief of the westside islanders, Queen Isaleilani. They stop to talk. Soon King Tuituranga begins to brag about the good fishing. Queen Isaleilani responds with stories about the fabulous breadfruit harvest. Each challenges the other: "Prove it!"

Soon they have worked out an agreement to meet regularly, and to trade. They agree that they will trade one for one—one basket of fish for one basket of breadfruit.

Once the bargain is made, the eastside chief hurries home as fast as he can, hardly able to contain his glee. What a great trick he has pulled off! He knows breadfruit is *five times* as valuable as fish. Yet he has arranged for one-for-one trade! Such a bargain! And at the expense of the westside islanders! He rushes on home to tell his people.

At the same time, guess what the westside chief is doing and thinking? The same things, of course! She knows that fish are *five times* as valuable as breadfruit. But she has talked the eastside chief into trading each basket of fish for only *one* basket of breadfruit! Each chief keeps thinking, "What a steal! What a steal!"

The Gains from Trade: More Output for Everybody

The beauty of this situation is that both chiefs are right. It is "a steal." But they're both wrong about where all the extra fish and breadfruit are coming from. The gains of one obviously aren't coming from the other. Both are gaining equally. Nobody is losing. The "steal" that each chief has made, is coming from the increase in total output!

The "steal" is coming from the **gains from trade**. A great increase in output of both fish and breadfruit is going to result when each family specializes in the production of the thing they

can produce best. "The gains from trade" come from **increased productivity**. The increased productivity comes from **specialization**. And **trade** is what makes it possible.

Once the trade arrangement is set up, the eastside islanders produce only fish. They produce a total of 100 baskets of fish per month and trade 50 baskets of fish to the westsiders for 50 baskets of breadfruit. The westsiders produce 100 baskets of breadfruit and trade 50 baskets of breadfruit for 50 baskets of fish. Now both families have much more food than before.

Now all the eastside kids and the westside kids can reach for all the second helpings they want. Even the chickens and pigs are finding that life is easier these days. See the great gains from trade? The entire society benefits. Chickens and pigs too.

THE PRICE SYSTEM AUTOMATICALLY STIMULATES TRADE

In a society where the market process is functioning, the *price system* automatically gets people to specialize and trade. In our example, if the market process with its **automatic price system** had been working on the island, the trade would have developed automatically. Here's how it would happen.

To the eastside islanders who catch so much fish, breadfruit is highly valued. It is very scarce, so its *price* (on their side of the island) is very high. But to the westside islanders (the good breadfruit growers) breadfruit is *low-priced*. Fish is the highly valued, very scarce, *high-priced* item.

For example, suppose breadfruit is worth $10 a basket to the westside islanders. How much is a basket of fish worth? Fifty dollars!

And suppose fish is worth $10 a basket to the eastsiders. How much is a basket of breadfruit worth? Fifty dollars! So what's going to happen? It's obvious.

One day the eastside islanders will hear about the high westside price of fish. They will start catching more fish and selling them to the westsiders. Big profits! But as fish become more available to the westsiders, what happens? The more available the fish become, the less scarce they become. So the less valuable they become. The price goes down.

What about breadfruit? It works the same way. The westside breadfruit growers will hear about the eastside price of breadfruit. They will start producing more baskets of breadfruit and selling them to the eastsiders. As more breadfruit is supplied to the eastsiders some of the scarcity is relieved. So the price goes down.

Trade Brings the Prices into Balance

Without trade, eastside fish would stay low-priced and breadfruit would stay high-priced. Westside fish would stay high-priced and breadfruit, low-priced. But *the market process will generate trade and bring the prices into balance.*

If the market process is working, the ultimate result will be the same as what happened when the sly island chiefs outfoxed each other. The *price mechanism* will induce the eastside islanders to specialize in fish and the westsiders to specialize in breadfruit. Then each will sell to the other. See how efficiently the **price mechanism** can get the right production choices made? Automatically!

THE BENEFITS OF ECONOMIC INTEGRATION

Economic integration permits the free movement of goods and resources (of inputs and outputs) among economic units. The benefits can be really great. In our island example no one is working any harder than before. Yet the total product of the society is almost doubled.

Perhaps they will decide to go on a four-day work week, or a six-hour day. Or perhaps they will spend more time building better houses or developing a better water supply. Or maybe they

will build a harbor so they can export dried fish and copra (dried coconut meat). Then they will be able to gain even more by trading with other islands and other countries.

Figure 18-2 adds together the production possibility curves of the two families. The "combined" production possibility curve shows the great gains in output which result from the **economic integration** of the two formerly separate economies.

In the production of fish and breadfruit, these two units—the eastside economy and the westside economy—are now integrated into *one economic unit*. The transformation curve in Figure 18-2 shows the production possibilities for this "newly integrated" economic unit. First review Figure 18-1. Then study Figure 18-2 on the next page.

COMPARATIVE ADVANTAGE

In our example, both the eastside islanders and the westside islanders have a clear and obvious advantage in something. The eastsiders are definitely more productive in producing fish. The westsiders have an obvious advantage (sometimes called "absolute advantage") in producing breadfruit.

But suppose one family doesn't have an obvious absolute advantage in *anything*. What then? To find the answer to that we need to go on with our example.

It's the Comparative Advantage That Counts

Suppose the family living on the south side of the island doesn't have very good fishing or very good growing conditions either. Suppose it takes them a *whole week* (five days) to produce a basket of fish. In one day they can only produce 1/5 of a basket of fish. With breadfruit, things are not quite as bad. They can produce three baskets of breadfruit a week (3/5ths of a basket a day).

Fig. 18-2 Economic Integration—Production Possibilities with Trade

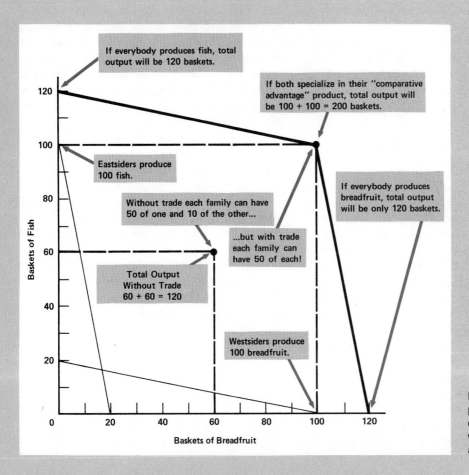

If everybody produces fish, total output will be 120 baskets.

If both specialize in their "comparative advantage" product, total output will be 100 + 100 = 200 baskets.

Eastsiders produce 100 fish.

Without trade each family can have 50 of one and 10 of the other...

If everybody produces breadfruit, total output will be only 120 baskets.

...but with trade each family can have 50 of each!

Total Output Without Trade 60 + 60 = 120

Westsiders produce 100 breadfruit.

Baskets of Fish

Baskets of Breadfruit

Much more can be produced when the eastsiders and westsiders specialize and trade.

This concave production possibility curve puts together the two curves (eastsiders and westsiders) as shown in Figure 18-1. The great bulge in the curve shows how much more product it is possible to get by letting each specialize and then trade.

This "integrated east-west economic unit" can produce 100 baskets of fish *and* 100 baskets of breadfruit per month—a total product of 200 baskets a month. Without trade, each could produce only 50 of their specialty and 10 of the other, for a total of 60 for each family—120 for the two families combined. Specialization and trade almost doubles their food output!

If the southsiders fish all week they wind up with one basket of fish (1/5th basket a day for five days). That's all they get to eat that week. If they spend the week gathering breadfruit they get three basketfuls (3/5ths basket a day for five days).

The southside islanders aren't nearly as productive as either the eastsiders or the westsiders. Can they possibly gain anything from entering the on-going trade between east and west? Yes! They certainly can!

Opportunity Cost Ratios Determine Comparative Advantage

For the southside islanders, the **opportunity cost ratio** between breadfruit and fish is three for one. Each time the southsiders decide to *not* produce breadfruit for a week so they can produce fish, how much breadfruit do they lose? Three baskets. How much fish do they get? One basket. So whenever they produce their own fish, each *one basket* of fish is costing them *three baskets* of breadfruit.

Suppose that the "going exchange rate" between fish and breadfruit is one-for-one. Then if the southsiders produce breadfruit and trade to get fish, how much breadfruit will they have to give up to get a basket of fish? Only one! So can they gain from trading? Of course!

The southsiders can give up one basket of fish (by not producing it) and get three baskets of breadfruit (by producing it for themselves). Then if they want fish they can trade the three baskets of breadfruit for three baskets of fish. So they wind up with three times as much fish!

When they trade, the cost of fish is only one-third as much as when they produce the fish themselves! Now study Figure 18-3 and you'll see what it looks like on a graph.

What Is Comparative Advantage?

The southside islanders don't seem to have an advantage in anything. They are very unpro-

ductive as compared with the eastside and westside islanders. Still the southside islanders have a **comparative advantage** in the production of breadfruit. So, what is comparative advantage?

"Comparative advantage" means "the opportunity cost in production" is less than "the opportunity cost in trade." When you have a comparative advantage in something (like breadfruit) you don't trade to get it. You produce it yourself. Then you trade to get other things (like fish). You trade to get the things in which you have a **comparative disadvantage**.

Comparative disadvantage, quite obviously, means the opposite of comparative advantage. It means *"the opportunity cost in trade"* is less than *"the opportunity cost in production."* You don't produce the things in which you have comparative disadvantage (like southside-island fish). You produce something else (like breadfruit) and then trade.

Let's say it another way. Can you get more of product x by producing product y and then trading to get x? If so, you have a comparative advantage in y. You have a comparative disadvantage in x. You can get more x by producing y and trading for x than you could by producing x yourself.

You can see that the low total output makes no difference in determining whether or not the southsiders can gain from trade. Perhaps they will always be poor. But they will be *less poor* if they will specialize and trade.

Both Trading Partners Have Comparative Advantage. Whenever one trading partner (individual, business, or nation) has a comparative advantage in one thing, the other party automatically has a comparative advantage in the other thing. Anytime it's possible for one "trader" to come out better, that means the other "trader" has the opposite opportunity to come out better also.

If the "trade-off ratio" (opportunity cost ratio, or transformation ratio) between two products is different for any two economic units—individuals, businesses, or nations—then one of the units will have a comparative advantage in

Fig. 18-3 Production Possibilities and Trade Possibilities Compared: The Case of the Southside Islanders

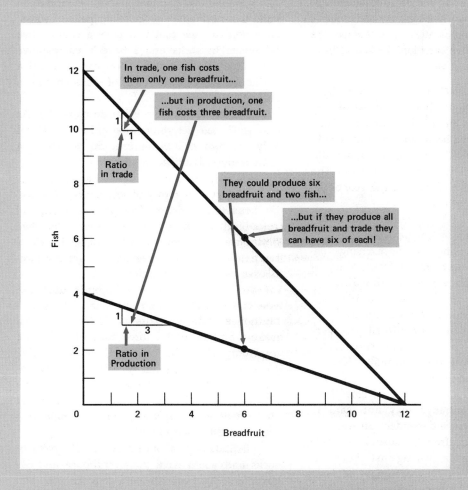

In trade, one fish costs them only one breadfruit...

...but in production, one fish costs three breadfruit.

Ratio in trade

They could produce six breadfruit and two fish...

...but if they produce all breadfruit and trade they can have six of each!

Ratio in Production

The southside islanders have a disadvantage in everything, but still they have comparative advantage in breadfruit.

In production, the opportunity cost (transformation) ratio between fish and breadfruit for the southside islanders is 4 to 12 (or 1 to 3). If the southsiders produce their own, the opportunity cost of one basket of fish is three baskets of breadfruit.

Since the "going exchange rate" on the island is one-for-one, the southsiders could trade one basket of breadfruit and get back one basket of fish. So the opportunity cost of one basket of fish *in trade* is only one basket of breadfruit. So by specializing in the production of breadfruit and trading, the southsiders can get three times as much fish as if they had produced their own.

The effect on the southsiders' food supply is the same as if they had discovered some new technique to make them three times as productive in catching fish. All hail the gains from trade!—(even when—or *especially* when—you have an absolute disadvantage in everything).

one of the products and the other will have *exactly the same amount* of comparative advantage in the other product. Your comparative advantage is my comparative disadvantage; my comparative advantage is your comparative disadvantage. It's the same "comparative situation" looked at from two different points of view.

What About International Trade? Suppose there are national boundaries separating these island families into different nations. Then all this trade we have been talking about would be international trade. Would that make any difference? No. Not from the point of view of the economics involved.

With international trade, there might be some difficulty working out the exchange because of the different kinds of money used in the different countries. Also, the Westside Fishing Association and the Eastside Breadfruit Growers Association may scream for protection against "foreign competition."

Or the eastside chief King Tuituranga may not want to become dependent on westside breadfruit because he's planning a war against the westsiders. Or there might be some other complications. *But from the point of view of the opportunity for both to benefit, it makes no difference whether the trading partners are in the same city, in different states, or on opposite sides of the world.*

Another Example of Comparative Advantage

Here's another example, closer to home. Suppose that in one weekend you can build two birdhouses or knit six pairs of socks. Do you have a comparative advantage in socks? or birdhouses? You can't say. Why not? Because you don't yet have anything to *compare it* with.

Suppose I tell you that in one weekend I can build two birdhouses or knit four pairs of socks. Now you can see that you have a comparative advantage in socks and I have a comparative advantage in birdhouses. You can give up a birdhouse and get three pairs of socks—but I can only get two pairs.

Let's say it this way. What do pairs of socks cost you? You get three-for-a-birdhouse. Me? I only get two-for-a-birdhouse. So you have a comparative advantage in socks.

Ah, but turn it around. What about the cost of birdhouses (in terms of lost socks)? My two birdhouses only cost me four pairs of socks. So I get a birdhouse for two pairs of socks. Your two birdhouses cost you six pairs of socks. So a birdhouse costs you three pairs. I get my birdhouses *cheaper* than you do!

So let's specialize—me in birdhouses and you in socks. If we *don't* specialize, I'll make a birdhouse and two pairs of socks and you'll make a birdhouse and three pairs of socks and total output will be two birdhouses and five pairs of socks. But when we specialize, I'll produce two birdhouses and you'll produce six pairs of socks. So total output is two birdhouses and *six pairs* of socks. Specialization and trade generated an extra pair of socks? Right!

I'll trade you a birdhouse for 2½ pairs of socks and you'll have your birdhouse and 3½ pairs of socks. See? An extra sock for you, and for me! Now look at Figure 18-4 and you'll see how all this looks on a graph.

The "Law of Comparative Advantage"

In the real world, every economic unit, every country (no matter how rich or poor) has comparative advantage in some things and comparative disadvantage in others. *Each unit will get more output if it concentrates on producing the things in which it has comparative advantage and then trades for the other things it wants. Economists call this idea the* law of comparative advantage.

Fig. 18-4   Production Possibility Curves Illustrate Comparative Advantage

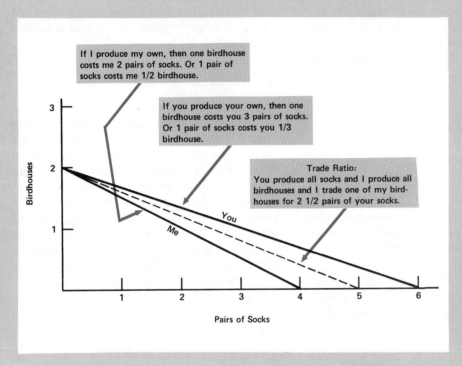

If I produce my own, then one birdhouse costs me 2 pairs of socks. Or 1 pair of socks costs me 1/2 birdhouse.

If you produce your own, then one birdhouse costs you 3 pairs of socks. Or 1 pair of socks costs you 1/3 birdhouse.

Trade Ratio:
You produce all socks and I produce all birdhouses and I trade one of my birdhouses for 2 1/2 pairs of your socks.

Birdhouses

You

Me

Pairs of Socks

Comparative advantage results from a different opportunity cost ratio for one producer than for the other.

In this case, you have a comparative advantage in producing socks. You can produce socks at a lower opportunity cost than I can. Each pair of socks you produce only costs you ⅓ of a birdhouse. Each pair of socks I produce costs me ½ of a birdhouse. So I have a comparative disadvantage in producing socks. Socks cost me more "lost birdhouse production" than they cost you.

My comparative advantage is in producing birdhouses. Each birdhouse I produce costs me only two pairs of socks. But each birdhouse you produce costs you three pairs of socks. You have a comparative disadvantage in producing birdhouses. Birdhouses cost you more "lost sock production" than they cost me.

To illustrate the idea of comparative advantage you need at least two different producers and two different products. Then, if the two producers have different opportunity cost (transformation) ratios between the two products, comparative advantage (and comparative disadvantage) exist.

The "comparative advantage" product of one producer is the "comparative disadvantage" product of the other producer. The greater the *difference* in opportunity cost ratios between the two producers, the greater will be the total gains from specializing and trading.

The "law of comparative advantage" emphasizes the potential benefits of trade. It says that the plumber should work as a plumber, then buy shoes from the shoemaker. The shoemaker should concentrate on making shoes and hire the plumber to do the plumbing. Through this arrangement the society will have more and better shoes and more and better plumbing. Everyone will benefit.

ADVANTAGES OF SPECIALIZATION

You know that almost any "economic unit" could produce almost anything if it was willing to work at it hard enough. Any individual, family, business, farm, or nation could use its resources to make a hundred different kinds of things. You could go to Iowa and become a farmer and produce all sort of things: corn or tomatoes, chickens or eggs, coconuts or bananas or polar bear skins. How could you decide which to produce?

Specialize in the Most Profitable Product

If the market process is working, it's easy. First you figure how much it would cost to make each product and how much revenue you would get from it. Then you produce the most profitable product, or the most profitable combination of products.

You don't go to Iowa and produce bananas or coconuts or polar bear skins! The cost would be ten times as high as the value of the product! You might be able to break even on chickens and eggs, or tomatoes. But for *your* farm, *corn* is the thing. You own some of the best corn land in the state. So what will you grow? Polar bears? Ridiculous.

If the market process is working as it's supposed to, if you're a producer you will automatically make the most efficient, most productive (the optimum) use of your (the society's) resources. You will produce the **highest-priced outputs** (the ones your society values most) and use up the **lowest-priced inputs** (the ones your society values least).

Specialization Requires Trade

People who concentrate on doing the things they can do best usually produce more, receive higher incomes, and enjoy higher standards of living than those who don't have any "specialty." But **specialization requires trade.**

For people to specialize, other people must want to buy what they're producing. If you're going to specialize in medicine, then you must depend on many people to buy your services. Unless the **market demand** is great enough to buy up what you are producing, you cannot specialize.

Specialization and Division of Labor

The word "specialization" is frequently used together with *division of labor*. Actually, "division of labor" is a special kind of specialization. It doesn't mean "I'll concentrate on producing my 'comparative advantage' product and you'll concentrate on yours." It means: "Let's break the production process into a series of simple steps and let one person (or machine) become highly specialized in performing each step." The total production operation is divided up so that each task can become specialized.

Different people have different skills and abilities. By specializing, most people can become even more productive at their specialties. With division of labor comes the opportunity to use *more advanced technology*—that is, more efficient ways of doing things.

As new **technology** is discovered, new kinds

of machines are built. Workers are trained to use the new machines. Output gets larger. The productive capacity of the economy increases. This is an important part of the process of **economic growth**.

The society gets more output as technology develops and the different parts of the production process become more specialized. It tends to come about all by itself. If you just let people alone in a society where the market process is working, they will figure out ways of specializing and trading to get more of the things they want.

The Remarkable Results of Specialization

The only way it's possible for people to have more than just the bare necessities of life is through specialization and trade. One of the important differences between the poverty-stricken economies of the underdeveloped world and the affluent societies of the modern world, is the degree of specialization.

Think about it for a minute. What would you be eating today if all you had to eat was what you produced yourself? What would you be wearing? What kind of house would you be living in? What kind of medical care would you get? What sort of transportation would you use? Things would be sort of primitive, right?

The effects of specialization and trade are truly remarkable—so remarkable, in fact, that it's almost impossible for us to visualize a world without specialization and trade. It's a basic, essential part of modern society.

Specialization influences every moment of the lives of each of us. And the results—in terms of fewer hours, easier work, and more and better things of all kinds—are truly phenomenal. Yet we are so accustomed to it that we just take it for granted.

Specialization is great. Still, there is a cost. We all become dependent on each other.

The Cost of Specialization—Interdependence

When there are many people all producing and trading with each other, no one stands alone anymore. All of us are dependent on and influenced by what all the other people decide to do. Whatever happens anywhere has an effect everywhere.

The more specialized and interdependent the economy becomes, the more productive it can be. And the more speedily the society can achieve whatever objectives it seeks. But what about the **costs of interdependence**?

If I produce eggs and you egg-buyers decide you don't like eggs, it hurts me. If I am depending on you to produce the gasoline I use in my car and suddenly you go on strike, it hurts me. If the workers in my steel mill demand a wage increase and I can't raise my price to cover it, it hurts me.

If I do raise my price and then my customers start buying their steel from foreign producers, I go out of business and fire my workers. It hurts me. It hurts my workers. Before it's all over it's going to hurt the grocers and the bakers and a lot of other people in my town.

With specialization and exchange we live much better. We're happy about the easier work and the free time, the warm houses and fast cars, the eyeglasses and dentures and allergy shots. Specialization and division of labor "cost us" our economic independence. But it's a cost that most of us are willing to pay.

SUMMARY AND SYNTHESIS

Gains from trade are the extra outputs which result from specializing and trading. These gains are possible whenever the **opportunity cost ratios** between two products are different for one producer than for another. If an apple costs you two oranges and costs me four oranges, then your **comparative advantage** is in apples and mine is in oranges. **The greater the difference in opportunity cost ratios, the greater the comparative advantage and the greater can be the gains from trade.**

The law of comparative advantage says that an economic unit (person, family, business, nation) will maximize its economic welfare by specializing in its "comparative advantage" products and trading to get its other desired (comparative disadvantage) products. If the **price mechanism** is permitted to operate freely, prices will automatically induce economic units to specialize in their comparative advantage products, and to trade. Profit-seeking businesses are forced to specialize in their comparative advantage products in order to survive.

Every producer, every person, every nation **has comparative advantage in something, and comparative disadvantage in many things.** Even if you have an **absolute disadvantage** in everything, you still have **comparative advantage in something.**

Economic integration is what occurs when **trade barriers are eliminated between economic units.** Producers in the "integrated economic unit" are free to follow the law of comparative advantage and can profit by doing so. The lack of trade barriers between the states in the United States, and the reduction of barriers between the European "Common Market" countries provide examples of "economic integration"—and of the economic advantages which can result.

Division of labor means breaking down the production process into a series of small operations (like an assembly line) to increase efficiency by letting each worker (and machine) become highly specialized. This permits **improved technology** and contributes to **economic growth.**

The results of **specialization and trade** are remarkable. The **high standards of living** which so many people now enjoy, couldn't exist without specialization and trade. The **basic function of markets** is to permit and facilitate this all-important specialization and trade.

Specialization and trade require **adequate markets and a sufficient demand** for the specialized outputs. Without this we can't specialize. Also, with specialization there's a cost: we become **interdependent.** Our economic well-being becomes **vulnerable to the decisions and actions of others.**

REVIEW EXERCISES

MAJOR CONCEPTS, PRINCIPLES, TERMS (Explain each carefully.)

the gains from trade
the advantages of specialization
trade requires different "opportunity cost ratios"
how the "price mechanism" generates trade

OTHER CONCEPTS AND TERMS (Explain each briefly.)

economic integration
comparative advantage
comparative disadvantage
the law of comparative advantage
international trade
economic growth
division of labor
specialization and technology
specialization and interdependence

CURVES AND GRAPHS (Draw, label, and explain each graph.)

Economic Independence—Production Possibilities without Trade
Economic Integration—Production Possibilities with Trade
Production Possibilities and Trade Possibilities Compared: the Southside
    Islanders
Production Possibility Curves Illustrate Comparative Advantage

QUESTIONS (Write out answers, or jot down key points.)

1. The westside islanders *really* shouldn't be buying their fish from the east-siders. They should "buy locally" from the Westside Fishing Association. That would be good for the local economy. Support your local businesses! Keep the money at home! Right? Discuss.
2. One impediment to the economic development of the poor nations of the world is that the poor nations can't benefit from the gains from trade. As compared with the advanced nations, a poor, underdeveloped nation couldn't possibly have a comparative advantage in *anything*. Discuss.
3. Most of the European countries have joined the European Community (the Common Market) to eliminate trade (and other) restrictions on things (and people) moving among the member countries. If it's such a good idea for Europe, why not the whole world? Discuss.
4. Suppose stringent restrictions were imposed on trade between all the states in the United States. What difference do you suppose that would make? Do you think it would have any effect on you *personally*, in your daily life? Think about it.

19 Income Distribution, and the Input Question: How Prices Are Determined in the Factor Markets

Chapter Objectives

- You already know how to use **supply and demand analysis** in **output markets** to explain **how the market process directs the output choices** for the society. In this chapter you will learn to use **supply and demand analysis** in the **input markets**, to explain **how the price mechanism works out both the input choices and the distribution choices** in the "model market system."

- You know that **input choices are based on least cost**, and that **distribution is based on productivity.** In this chapter you will learn more precisely what all that means and how it is worked out in the **input factor markets** through **demand and supply, and the price mechanism.**

- When you finish studying this chapter you will be able to draw a **factor demand curve** and to explain why it is **shaped** as it is, what might influence its **elasticity**, and what might cause it to **shift.** Also you will be able to explain the **law of diminishing returns** and what it has to do with **factor demand.**

- You will learn to draw an **input factor supply curve**, to explain why it is **shaped** as it is, and what would cause it to **shift.** And you will learn about the important difference between **factor supply for one business** and **factor supply for the entire economy.**

- Finally, in this chapter you will find out how the **distributive results** of this **positive automatic process** are being modified in pursuit of **normative objectives.**

Income Distribution: Factor Ownership and Factor Pricing

What determines your income? In the model market system it depends entirely on what inputs you have to sell and how much they sell for. If you own a lot of high-priced inputs you'll get a big income. If you don't, you won't. So the question of income distribution in the pure market system is one of factor ownership and factor pricing.

In micro-theory we don't deal much with the question of factor ownership. We can sort of take it as "given." We can assume that everyone owns some labor and that the hard-working and thrifty people (and maybe some lucky ones) will own some land and capital, too.

So now, with the "factor ownership" question assumed away, the question of income distribution becomes: What determines the *prices* of labor, land, and capital in the factor markets? We'll be talking about that throughout this chap-

304

ter. Mostly we'll be concerned with: What might cause the price of an input to be high or low? or to go up or down?

Suppose you can find out *why* the labor of a cherry picker is priced lower than the labor of a bulldozer operator—or why the labor of a school teacher is priced lower than the labor of a bricklayer or an accountant or a pediatrician. Then you will know why cherry pickers and school teachers don't get as much income as bulldozer operators or bricklayers or accountants or pediatricians.

Factor Prices Have Special Names: Wages, Rent, Interest

As you know, the price of each factor of production has a special name. But it's only a price just the same. If labor is being sold we call the price "the wage rate." For land we call it "rent." For capital it's "the interest rate." The fourth distributive share—the one the business gets to keep after everyone else has been paid their wages, rent, and interest—is called "profit."

Profit is the only one of the distributive shares which is not really a "price." Profit is what's left over after the prices of all the "hired factors" have been paid. Profit is determined by (1) the value of the output, as compared with (2) the cost of the inputs (wages, rent, interest).

The size of the wages, rent, interest, and profits will determine which people will get large incomes and which ones will get small incomes—which ones will be rich and which ones will be poor.

Most people work for wages. If the average wages received by the people in a country are low, then most of the people in that country will be poor. If the average wages received by the people are high, most of the people will enjoy a high standard of living. But what might cause the average wage rates in a country to be high? Or low? *That* is the question.

Supply and Demand Determine Factor Prices

What determines the price of the factors you have to sell? In the model world, it's supply and demand, of course. So you need to understand what determines the supply and what determines the demand.

Just about all you need to do to understand the question of income distribution in the pure market system is to understand factor demand and factor supply. First, factor demand.

FACTOR DEMAND REFLECTS PRODUCTIVITY

What determines the demand for (the propensity to buy) a productive factor? The value of what it produces, of course! It depends on *the value the factor adds to the output.*

A factor of production is demanded only because it is productive. The more productive it is, the greater the demand for it. Obviously! So all we need to understand the *demand* for *any* productive factor—labor, land, or capital—is to understand what determines its *productivity.*

The firm's **cost** is the factor owner's income!

If the marginal "value product" of the factor is high, the demand for the factor will be high. The price paid for the factor will be high. Whoever owns it and sells it will get a high income.

MVP Is MPP Times Price

The marginal "value product" (MVP) of (and therefore the demand for) a factor of production depends on (1) the amount of physical product the factor produces, and (2) the price per unit the business gets when it sells the MPP.

For a business selling in a market of pure competition, we can say it this way: the marginal value product (MVP) is equal to the marginal physical product (MPP) times the price (P), that is: MVP = MPP × P.

How much you are worth to a business (MVP) depends not only on how much you produce, but also on how much your output sells for.

Factor Demand Is Always Derived Demand

There are only two reasons for demanding something: (1) for *consumption* (to bring "final satisfaction"), or (2) for *production* (to produce something that is wanted). The production demand (demand for input factors) always reflects the fact that somewhere there is a consumption demand. If there was no consumption demand for a product then there would be no *production demand* for factors to be used to make it.

When we talk about the *productivity* (marginal "value product") of an input factor we are talking about the *value which one additional unit of that factor would add to the output. All of that added (marginal) value is derived from (results from) the demand for the final product.*

If there's no final product demand, there's no derived demand. Nobody will hire a worker to produce something that no one will buy! Obviously not.

Marginal Productivity (MVP)—Some Examples

Suppose you are running a factory producing jeans. How many workers will you hire?—

that is, how many "units of labor per day" will you buy?

If you think an additional unit of labor will bring you more "value product" than it costs (if it adds more to your revenue than it adds to your cost) you will buy it. So your "propensity to buy" a unit of labor is determined by your estimate of its marginal "value product."

Suppose the kind of labor you use in your plant costs $20 a day. You are currently employing 25 people (using 25 "units of labor" per day). Should you increase your daily rate of labor input by one unit? That depends on how much more revenue you expect to get. Right?

Suppose with one more worker (without increasing any of your other costs) you could produce enough more to increase your total revenue by $25 a day. Would you hire one more person? At a wage rate of $20 a day? Sure you would!

Marginal Value Product (MVP) and Marginal Input Cost (MIC). When you increased your labor input that added more to your revenue than it added to your cost. That increased your profit. That's good business!

You will continue to hire more labor and expand your output as long as the marginal value product (MVP) is greater than the wage rate—that is, as long as the marginal "value product" is greater than the marginal "input cost" (MIC). But as you hire more labor, the MVP of labor goes down. When the two become equal (when MVP = MIC) that's the "rate of production" where your profit is at a maximum. You won't hire any more.

Suppose you have adjusted your output to the most profitable daily rate. That means you are using the most profitable amounts of labor and other inputs. *If, for each factor of production, the marginal "input cost" is equal to the marginal "value product" then you are operating at your maximum profit output.*

Higher Output Prices Increase Factor Demand. Now suppose the market price of jeans goes up—say from $100 a carton to $150 a carton. What happens to the productivity of the labor you're hiring? It goes up!

When the price goes up for the product, suddenly the output of each factor becomes more valuable. Suddenly your demand for input factors goes up! See how an increase in the demand (and price) for your output can bring an increase in your demand for inputs?

Marginal Productivity Reflects the Law of Diminishing Returns

What determines how much more output you will get if you hire one more unit of labor? The most important thing is this: "How much *other factors* is the new worker going to have to work with?" If the worker is going to have lots of efficient machinery and plenty of materials to work with, then that worker will add a lot of extra product.

But suppose all the machines and everything else are already being overused. All there is for the new worker to do is to go around and clean up and straighten up a bit. Then the extra worker isn't going to add much product.

We're talking about what economists call the law of diminishing returns. The law of diminishing returns says that if a factory or a farm (or any kind of productive activity) expands its output more and more without adding any more land or buildings, sooner or later some overcrowding and inefficiencies will occur. The variable inputs won't have enough fixed inputs to work with. Costs will go up.

You can increase your output some by adding more "variable inputs" (say labor) even though the amounts of some other inputs are fixed (say the size of your jeans factory). But there's a limit to how far you can go. Sooner or later the extra output you get when you hire each successive "unit of the variable input"— labor, materials, etc.—will get smaller and smaller. The returns (extra product) received from the extra variable input, will diminish.

You can see why the law of diminishing returns is also called the law of variable proportions. It is talking about varying the proportions of the inputs. The reason the returns (extra outputs) diminish is because there is too much of the variable input (labor and materials and all) in proportion to the amount of the fixed input (the factory and machines). Each worker has too little of the fixed input (machines) to work with. So the extra output you get when you hire an extra worker isn't very big.

A Flowerpot Wheat Farm?

The law of diminishing returns is obviously true. If it was not it would be possible for you to grow enough food for the world in your backyard garden (or in a flowerpot!) just by adding enough labor, seed, and fertilizer. Being ridiculous, let's suppose one worker is growing wheat in a flowerpot and another worker decides to come along and help. How much added output do you suppose will result from the added efforts of the second worker? Zero? I guess so.

Why is the marginal product (the additional product obtained from the efforts of the second worker) zero? Because of laziness? Incompetence? No. It's because of the law of diminishing returns. It's because not enough fixed inputs are available to work with. That's what makes it impossible for the second worker to produce anything.

What About Adding More Fixed Inputs?

Suppose the second worker could manage to find another flowerpot someplace. Then the second worker could produce just as much as the first! The law of diminishing returns wouldn't be working anymore. Why not? Because nothing is fixed anymore. All of the input factors have become variable!

A silly example, sure. But it illustrates something. It tells us that the more and better land, machines, and other things a worker has to work with, the more productive that worker can be.

Suppose you are already running your jeans plant at its maximum efficiency and then you decide to hire more workers and produce more. The law of diminishing returns tells you that the more extra workers you hire the less extra output per worker you're going to get—and therefore the more each extra unit of output is going to cost you.

If you expand your output of jeans beyond the maximum efficiency rate (say, 10 cartons a day) the marginal physical product (MPP) of the added variable factors will go down. Why?

The MPP diminishes because you are trying to produce faster than your plant is designed to produce. The extra workers don't have enough fixed inputs to work with. So they aren't very productive. You probably wouldn't hire extra workers and push your output beyond 10 units anyway. But then again, you might.

Would You Add Factors When MPP Is Low? What might cause you to hire additional workers even when you know they aren't going to add very much output?—that is, even when you know they won't add very much marginal physical product? Either one (or both) of two things: (1) a very high price (per unit) for the output (MPP), or (2) a very low price (per unit) for the input (labor). We could say it this way:

(1) The demand for your product in the market might go up and push the price

up so high that the little bit of extra product added by an extra worker would bring in enough extra revenue to more than cover the extra cost of hiring the worker; or

(2) The price of labor might go down so low that even though the additional worker doesn't add much output, the output value is still great enough to more than cover the very low wage cost.

How Many "Variable Factor Units" to Employ? As the product price goes higher or as the price of the variable factor goes lower, you will employ more of the factor. How much more? Enough to push down the marginal productivity (MVP) of the factor to where it is no longer profitable to hire any more—that is, to where the cost to hire an extra unit of the factor (MIC) is as great as the extra output is worth to you (MVP). Once you get to this input (and output) rate (where MIC = MVP) you don't hire any more.

The law of demand applies in the factor markets just as it applies in the consumer goods markets. The lower the price of the factor the more the businesses will buy. Why does the law of demand hold true in the factor markets? Partly because of the *law of diminishing returns*. As more variable factors are hired, marginal value product goes down. So the price of the factor must go down to get more to be hired!

HOW ELASTIC IS THE FACTOR DEMAND?*

Suppose the price of your jeans goes up a lot. You will hire more "units of the variable factor." How many more units of the variable

---

*If you don't remember much about "elasticity of demand," be sure to review that concept before you read this section.

factor will you hire? *How many more you will hire depends on how fast the returns diminish as you expand your output.*

How Fast Does Marginal Productivity (MVP) Diminish?

Can you see that the elasticity of the demand for "units of the variable factor" depends a lot on the law of diminishing returns? As new units of the variable factor are hired, if the MPP goes down quickly, then not very many more units will be hired. But if the MPP diminishes slowly, then a lot more units will be hired.

Suppose the productivity of the variable factor diminishes rapidly. Then the demand for that factor will be very inelastic. That means, if the price of the factor goes down, not much more of it will be hired.

But suppose the MPP diminishes very slowly. If the price of the variable factor goes down, will you hire a little more? or a lot? A lot more, of course. So the demand is very elastic.

How Elastic Is the Final Product Demand?

Suppose the demand for the output product is *highly elastic*. If its price drops a little, people will buy a lot more. So a lot more input factors will be demanded.

Suppose input prices go down. Cost of production goes down. So producers find it profitable to produce more. The supply increases.

Increased supply pushes the selling price down. If the product demand is highly elastic, at the lower price a lot more will be bought. So a lot more output will be produced. A lot more inputs will be hired.

See how *the lower input cost causes a lot more output to be bought? And that causes a lot more inputs to be bought?* Sure. That's how *a highly elastic product demand causes the input demand to be highly elastic too.*

How Variable Is the "Input Mix"?

The elasticity of a firm's demand for a variable factor depends a lot on how easy (or how difficult) it is to substitute one factor for another. Elasticity of demand always depends a lot on the availability of acceptable substitutes.

How critical are the ratios (proportions) among the input factors? Is there much variability in the "input factor mix"? or not? Is each factor an absolutely essential ingredient? Maybe like flour when you're baking a cake? Or is there more variability? like whether to use butter or margarine? or whether to use more or less eggs?

You can see that in some kinds of production and for some inputs there is a lot of variability. For others there is less. But there is almost always some (and usually quite a lot) of variability (substitutability) in the "input mix."

Fixed Proportions? or Variable Proportions? Suppose that in order to produce anything at all, each worker's position in the plant *must* be filled. Then the factor proportions of labor and capital are absolutely fixed. The plant's short-run demand for workers will be absolutely inelastic, right up to the "shut-down factor price" (where the factor price gets so high it would be cheaper for the firm to shut down than to operate).

On the other hand, suppose we're talking about a trucking company that can lease more trucks and hire more drivers at a moment's notice. There really isn't much "fixed factor" in this case, so the returns don't diminish much. The trucking company can hire a lot more "variable inputs" with very little "diminishing" of the marginal value product. So the firm's demand for the variable inputs (trucks and drivers) probably would be very elastic.

Most plants are designed to use a certain amount of labor and other variable inputs. If the price of any one of these inputs goes up or down the quantity can be adjusted some. But it isn't likely that the "input mix" will be changed very much in the short run. But what about the long run? That's a different matter!

Factor Demand Is More Elastic in the Long Run. Firms will respond to factor prices *much more* in the *long run* than in the short run. Suppose the wage rate goes up. What are you going to do about it?

All you can do in the short run is try to minimize your losses. But as soon as you can, you'll get out of this business. Or else you'll install labor-saving machinery and fire a lot of workers.

See how the demand for labor is more elastic in the long run? The quantity of labor bought will respond a lot more to the wage increase if you'll just wait awhile—until the firms in the industry have time to work things out!

When a business is designing a new plant it insists on using minimum quantities of the highest-priced factors and substituting more of the lower-priced factors. This is where the demand for each factor becomes really elastic. So this is where the rationing function of price really works to conserve the scarcest, most valuable of society's inputs.

Employment Effects of Factor Demand Elasticity. Suppose there's a lot of unemployed labor throughout the economy. And suppose the demand for labor is highly elastic. A small drop in the wage rate will induce businesses to hire a lot more people and unemployment may be eliminated!

But what about the inelastic demand case? If the demand for labor is highly inelastic, then what happens when the wage rate goes down? Not much. Unemployment continues.

Suppose the demand for labor is highly elastic throughout the economy. What does that mean? It means that a small increase in the price of labor would cause many businesses to hire less labor and use more capital.

What do you suppose would happen if the government passed a minimum wage law? Do you suppose there would be a lot of unemployment among young, inexperienced people?—high-school dropouts and high school graduates and college students looking for summer jobs? You bet there would.

This is the argument that McDonald's has been using to try to get an exemption from minimum wage laws. The management of McDonald's has been saying that if they must pay the minimum wage, then they must use less labor and more automatic equipment. They argue that the minimum wage is going to force them to stop hiring many of the young people who come to them looking for jobs.

Can you see that the whole idea of minimum wages doesn't make sense if the demand for labor is highly elastic? If capital is going to be used instead of labor, what good is the minimum wage? It sure won't help all those unemployed people!

The Factor Demand Curve

Would it be possible to draw a curve to show the demand for a productive factor? No question about it. We could call it a "diminishing returns curve" or a "marginal value product curve," or a "factor demand curve." Either way, it's the same curve. After you finish studying Figure 19-1 you will understand it better. Right now would be a good time for you to do that.

RELATIVE SCARCITY, FACTOR PRICES, AND MVP

The greater the marginal value product of a factor, the greater will be the demand for it. But consid-

Fig. 19-1   Demand for a Factor of Production: the Marginal Value Product Curve

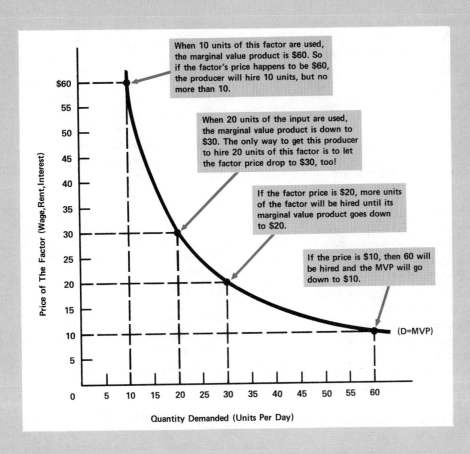

When 10 units of this factor are used, the marginal value product is $60. So if the factor's price happens to be $60, the producer will hire 10 units, but no more than 10.

When 20 units of the input are used, the marginal value product is down to $30. The only way to get this producer to hire 20 units of this factor is to let the factor price drop to $30, too!

If the factor price is $20, more units of the factor will be hired until its marginal value product goes down to $20.

If the price is $10, then 60 will be hired and the MVP will go down to $10.

(D=MVP)

Price of The Factor (Wage, Rent, Interest)

Quantity Demanded (Units Per Day)

The law of demand works in the factor markets too! Why? Mostly because of the law of diminishing returns.

If the price of the factor goes down, the business will use more. So, as the law of diminishing returns tell us, the MPP will go down. So therefore the marginal value product will go down too. *How much more* of the variable factor the business will use depends on *how fast* the marginal value product goes down. And that's what the curve shows you.

If the price is high you will use only a few units of the factor so the marginal value product of the factor will be high (high enough to be worth the high price). As the price goes lower you will use more units of the factor. Its marginal value product will diminish. The lower the price of the factor the more you will use and the lower its marginal value product will be.

This curve will shift only if there is a change in "the marginal value product situation" for this factor. The curve will increase (shift to the right) if (1) the selling price of the product goes up, or if (2) more of the *other* factors become available for this one to work with, thus increasing the marginal physical product of this factor.

er this: *Is the high marginal value product of a factor the cause of (or simply a reflection of) the high price of the factor?*

The rationing function of price will cause a high priced factor to be carefully economized—to be used very sparingly. If a factor is used very sparingy its marginal value product will be high! So a factor's price can be the cause of (not just the *result* of) its high marginal value product. Causality goes both ways!

The Scarcest Factor Has the Highest Marginal Productivity

The productivity of an additional unit of any factor of production depends on the availability of "other factors."

If a lot of capital and land are available then an added unit of labor will be highly productive. If a lot of labor and land are available then an added unit of capital will be highly productive. As the quantity of any one factor is increased, it becomes increasingly important to get more of the other factors to work with it.

Suppose a farmer is running a big farm and has lots of land and labor but only one tractor. That farmer will be much more interested in getting another tractor (more capital) than in getting more land or more labor. Why?

Because an additional tractor would be much more productive—would add much more value to the output than would more land, or labor. Why? Because the tractor is the relatively scarce factor, that's why!

Which factor are you willing to pay the most to get more of? The relatively scarce one, of course. Your demand for the relatively scarce factor is higher because of its higher productivity. That's why you will pay more to hire it. And that's why its owner will receive a high income.

These concepts apply just as much to *specific* factors as they do to "labor, land, and capital *in general.*" Suppose the *kind* of capital or land you own is relatively scarce. Or suppose the kind of labor you have for sale is relatively scarce. Then the marginal value product of your kind of capi-

tal or land or labor will be high. The demand for your inputs will be high and your income will be high. Lucky you!

An Example Of "the Relatively Scarce Factor"

Suppose you live in the "Grape-belt" area of Chautauqua County in western New York State and you're the only person in the county who has a grape-picking machine. When harvest time comes you will have plenty of opportunity to keep your machine running day and night!

Your relatively scarce piece of capital will have high productivity. It will be in very high demand. You will be able to make a lot of money with it. One more grape-picking machine would have a high marginal value product in Chautauqua County! Chances are somebody else (maybe everybody else?) will buy one soon. Maybe *very soon.*

Now, suppose every grape farm in Chautauqua County finally has its own grape-picking machine. But suppose you are the only person in the county who knows how to repair one. You may be sure that the marginal productivity of your labor services will be very high! Your efforts will be in great demand. You will make a lot of money.

The marginal value product of an additional grape-picker mechanic in your county would be very high. Chances are that pretty soon someone else will learn to fix those monsters. Or else some skilled mechanic will move in from Canandaigua or Bass Island, or maybe even from St. Joseph or Roseburg or Fresno or Yakima! Why? You know why. Because the "production motivation function" of the high price for this specialized kind of labor will pull this new mechanic to Chautauqua County. That's why!

As a Factor's Supply Increases, Its Productivity Decreases

What about the marginal productivity of grape-picking machines in Chautauqua County now that everybody has one? It's much lower. Still, if the cost of buying and owning capital is low enough (as compared with the high price of labor), more machines will be bought.

The reason all the farmers in the United States and Canada and in the other advanced nations are using so many mechanical harvesters—grape-pickers and corn-pickers and tomato-pickers and cotton-pickers and pickle-pepper-pickers—is because of the relative scarcity (and the high price) of labor. Each time farm workers get higher wages, more "mechanical pickers" take over. Elasticity of the demand for labor? Right!

The high-priced factor is conserved. It's used very sparingly. An extra unit would have high marginal productivity (like skilled grape-picker mechanics in Chautauqua County). The low priced factor is used more freely and abundantly. It is used so freely and abundantly that the marginal productivity of another unit of it would be low (like grape-picking machines in Chautauqua County).

High Prices Make Factors More Productive

The "rationing function of price" will restrict the purchase of everything (every resource, every good, every input) so that *nothing will be bought for any purpose (consumption or production) unless the buyer thinks the use is going to be worth at least as much as the cost.*

In the factor markets it says this: No business will pay a dollar for a unit of input unless the unit of input is expected to add at least a dollar's worth to the output. If a factor is selling for $10 then you can be quite certain that the marginal value product of the factor is at least $10. If not, the factor wouldn't be hired. The $50 factor has a marginal value product of at least $50. It will be used sparingly enough to *ensure* that its marginal productivity is at least $50.

High-priced factors will be used only in highly productive uses. They will be used together with an abundance of other factors. *So a*

high price for a factor will guarantee high productivity for that factor. It is true in the model market system and it is true in the real world. (Exception: Short-sighted administrators sometimes forget this principle and let a $40,000 a year professor or executive do the work that a secretary or student assistant could do.)

When wage rates are high, labor will be conserved. Lots of labor-saving machinery will be used. The productivity of labor will be high. Suppose the wage was high and the productivity of labor was not high enough to cover it. Then the labor would not be hired. If it was hired the businesses would go broke.

Factor Prices Influence the Input Choices

The organization and techniques of production in a society (that is, the input choices) always reflect the relative scarcities and the relative prices of the productive factors. In the United States and other advanced nations we use steam shovels and conveyor belts. In countries where labor is very cheap, they use hand shovels and wheelbarrows.

If lumber is plentiful and low-priced while steel and other building materials are very scarce and high-priced, the society will cut down the forests and build things out of wood. But if lumber is very scarce and high-priced and other building materials are plentiful and low-priced, lumber will be used sparingly and other building materials will be used instead.

You can think of all kinds of ways that production would be organized differently if we had different prices on our labor, natural resources, and capital. If you look at a highly developed country and compare it with a less developed country, you will see many differences in the way production is organized. In each case the production organization reflects the relative scarcities, the relative prices, and therefore, the *relative productivities* of the factors of production in the economy.

Demand for One Factor Reflects the Supply of Other Factors

The demand for an input reflects its marginal productivity (MVP). But what is the most important thing that determines the productivity (and the demand) for the factor? Its relative scarcity!

If a factor is relatively plentiful, then it will be used in abundance. Its productivity will be pushed down low. Its price will be low. But if a factor is relatively scarce it will be used sparingly and its productivity and price will be high.

Suppose the price of a factor is high. If the supply of the factor is free to expand, then as time passes the supply will increase and the price will fall. The marginal productivity of this factor will get lower and lower. That's what has happened in the case of capital in the United States and in the other highly developed nations. Capital has become more plentiful, so labor and natural resources have become more scarce. Labor and resources are now higher priced (and are economized more) than in the past.

If you want to analyze the demand for any factor of production, then you must look closely at the supply of the other factors. That's what the next section talks about.

THE SUPPLY OF INPUT FACTORS: LABOR, LAND, CAPITAL

How much of each factor (labor, land, capital) will be offered for sale at each price (wage, rent, interest)? That's the "factor supply" question. The answer is different for one factor or another and it depends on several things. Partly it depends on which way we choose to look at the question.

Factor Supply to the Individual Business. Suppose a small business wanted more labor or land or capital. If it offered to pay more, could it get more? Sure. So the supply of any factor to any individual business is likely to be highly elastic. The quantity offered for sale to an individual business will be quite responsive to a change in the price.

If a firm or an industry is expanding, it pulls in input factors. Factors shift from one industry to another. When higher prices are offered, more inputs are supplied.

But we can't understand *the income distribution question for the society as a whole* by looking at the individual firm, or industry. For example, if we want to find out what market forces are setting "wages in general," we can't figure it out by looking at the egg industry. To get at the issue of "factor price determination" for the economy as a whole, *we must look at the nation's total supply and total demand for each factor.*

Factor Supply for the Entire Nation. For the nation as a whole the supply of each input factor is *highly inelastic.* At higher prices how much more *total* labor or *total* natural resources or *total* capital would become available? Not very much. The quantity supplied isn't very responsive to price. In a short period of time the *total* quantity supplied may not be responsive to price at all!

The Supply of Labor

The nation's total labor supply might respond a little bit to increases or decreases in the wage rate, but we aren't sure about that. Higher wages may induce more married women to join the labor force. On the other hand, higher wages might induce more women to quit their jobs and live on their husbands' incomes.

Higher wages may convince more students to quit college and take jobs; but higher wages may make it possible for students to make it through college by working only part time, or on their parents' high income. Low wages might even force students to quit college and take full-time jobs. (The "production motivating function of price" may work in reverse!)

In High Wage Countries, People Work Less. It's hard to say anything definite about how "the total quantity of labor offered for sale" responds to *price*. As the wage rate gets higher some people will offer more of their labor for sale. But others will offer less.

In the low-wage countries, people work longer and harder than in the high-wage countries. In the United States where wages are high, many adults are not even in the labor force (wives, students, retirees, etc). Those who are in the labor force work fewer "hours per year" than in low-wage countries.

We can't say that our high wages are inducing people to offer more labor for sale. It seems to be working the other way!

A Backward-Bending Supply Curve for Labor? We really don't know very much about how the "quantity of labor supplied in the nation" would change if all wage rates went up, or down. Some studies suggest that if wages start out very low and then increase a little bit, more labor will be offered. But then if the wage continues to increase, after awhile people start dropping out of the labor force, or demanding a shorter workday or workweek and more time off. This leads to the idea of the "backward-bending supply curve for labor."

Figure 19-2 shows a backward-bending supply curve. It shows how the wage rate in this "hypothetical nation" would be determined. But don't put too much stock in this backward-bending supply curve. The truth is that we really don't know much about the relationship between "the wage rate in general" and "the quantity of labor that would be supplied." So, remembering this word of warning, it's time now for you to study the graph.

The Supply of Land

It's easy to see that the nation's supply of labor is not likely to be very responsive to wage rate changes. It's more or less fixed by the size, age, skills, habits, economic conditions (etc.) of the population.

What about the nation's supply of land and natural resources? That's even more fixed and unresponsive than labor. The production motivating function of price will not have much influence on the *total quantity offered*—either of labor, or of land and natural resources. On labor or land for a *specific purpose*? Yes. But on the *total quantity offered*? No.

What about the nation's supply of capital? Does that respond to price? Capital is made up of *produced* goods. So surely it would seem that a higher price for "capital in general" would soon bring forth more capital. Right? Well, don't be so sure. Better think about that for a minute.

The Supply of Capital

How does a nation increase its supply of capital? By saving (not consuming) and investing (building capital). Capital formation requires less consumption. What would make people consume a smaller proportion and businesses invest a larger proportion of the nation's output? That's the key to capital formation.

If capital is bringing a high return to its owners, that means the interest rate is high. Will that induce more people to "not consume"? To save? Maybe so. Then again, maybe not.

A high return to capital, just like a high wage rate, might work either way. Some people might save more (to build more capital to get the high return); others might save less (the capital they already have now brings them enough income, so they're all set).

For capital in any particular industry, or for any one *kind* of capital—grape-pickers or IBM computers or shoe repair machines—the supply will be very responsive to the production motivating function of price. But for the nation's *total*

Fig. 19-2 The Supply and Demand for Labor, Showing the Hypothetical Backward-Bending Supply Curve

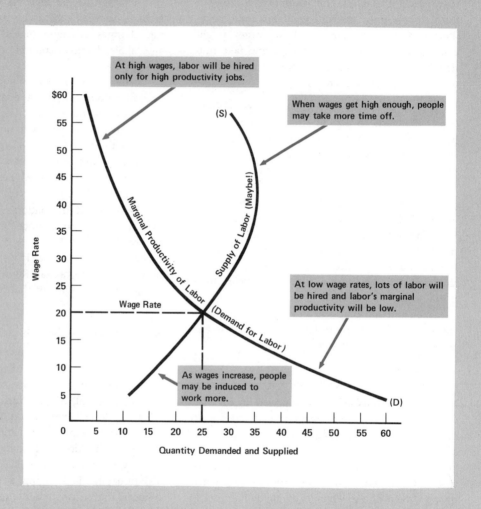

After the wage rate gets just so high, a higher wage rate may cause a *decrease* in the amount of labor people will offer for sale!

If "the wage in general" goes up for "labor in general" this may get more people to take jobs and workers may be willing to work overtime and to forego vacations. But if the general wage rate in the nation keeps on going up, after awhile people may start cutting down on their work time so they can take time to enjoy all those things they can buy with their high wages.

High wages may *induce* people to work more. True. But it's also true that high wages *permit* people to get by without working so much. For some, the inducement may win out. For others, the opportunity to take more leisure time may win out.

So is the labor supply curve backward bending? I don't know. What do you think?

supply of capital? Maybe not.

Why do people save more (or less) this year, than last? Many reasons. Some of the other reasons may be much more important than the "price" (interest rate) they get paid for saving.

How to Handle the Problem of Factor Supply

Here we are, faced with a dilemma. To understand income distribution we must understand factor pricing. So we must understand factor demand and factor supply for each factor. But we don't know much about factor supply. About all we really know is that *for the economy as a whole, factor supply is not very responsive to price changes.*

Neither the supply of labor nor land nor capital responds much to factor price changes. But wait! Maybe that's all we need to know! Maybe there's no dilemma after all.

Absolutely Inelastic Factor Supply?
Suppose we assume that the elasticity of the nation's supply of each of the "factors in general" is *zero*. That would mean "zero responsiveness of the total quantity to a price change." *Absolutely inelastic supply.* The quantity available would be the same whether the price was high or low.

We know this assumption isn't exactly true. Still, it isn't so far from the truth, either. If it will help us to understand factor pricing—that is, income distribution in the market system—then it's a good assumption. And it does, so it is. Just watch how neatly all the pieces now fall together.

Each Factor's Demand and Price Depend on the Supply of the Other Factors. If the supply of a factor is fixed, then what will determine the price? *Demand*, of course!

The demand for each factor is determined by its productivity; its productivity is determined by the availability of other factors.

• The productivity of *labor* is determined by the amounts and kinds of land and capital available.
• The productivity of *land* is determined by the amounts and kinds of labor and capital available.
• The productivity of *capital* is determined by the amounts and kinds of labor and land available.

See where all this is leading us? It's taking us directly to the answer about factor pricing—and to the answer to the distribution question for the model market system!

If one factor is relatively scarce, that means that the other factors are relatively plentiful. The productivity of the relatively scarce factor (and the demand for it) will be high. And the price? High, of course!

The strong demand and the limited supply will keep the price high. Whoever owns and "sells" some of this relatively scarce factor will receive a large income—that is, a large distributive share of the output of the society.

It's the Relatively scarce factor that's most productive! It gets the highest income!

Demand and Supply Curves for Factors of Production

Figure 19-3 shows the factor demand and the "absolutely inelastic" supply. This graph could apply to any one of the factors.

To show the relatively plentiful factor, shift the supply curve to the right. The factor price (and its owner's income) is low.

To show the relatively scarce factor, shift the supply curve to the left. The factor price (and its owner's income) is high.

Now spend a few minutes studying Figure 19-3. Practice drawing and explaining it. Practice shifting the curves to illustrate the prices of (and incomes of the owners of) different factors of production.

Fig. 19-3   The Supply and Demand for a Factor of Production

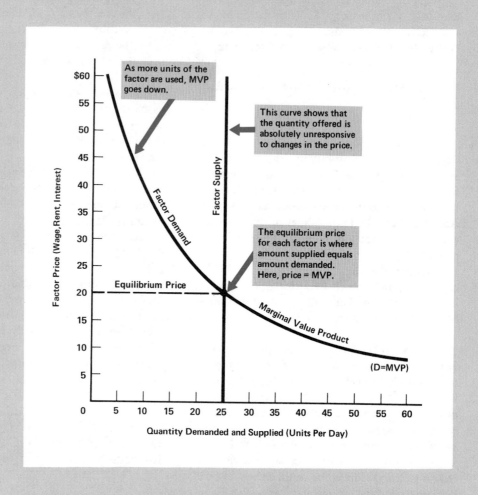

The total supply of a factor of production usually isn't very responsive to price. That is, it's highly inelastic.

The factor supply wouldn't really be a straight vertical line. But this is a useful approximation, at least for prices not too far from "the equilibrium price." (At very low prices the factor owners might not offer any of their factor for sale!)

Any increase in the amounts of other factors available would cause this factor's demand curve (MVP) to shift to the right. The price of the factor would increase.

Anything that would cause the supply of this factor to increase (shift to the right) would lower the price of this factor and would automatically increase the productivity of (and demand for) the other factors.

Anything which would cause the supply of this factor to decrease (shift to the left) would raise the price of this factor and would decrease the productivity of the other factors. For the economy as a whole, *the productivity of each factor depends on the supply of other factors.*

THE MARKET MODEL
AND THE REAL WORLD

Figure 19-3 can help you to understand why the general level of wages, rent, or interest in an economy would be high or low. But this doesn't answer all of the "real world" questions. Not by a long shot. It just gives us a place to start.

Real-world input markets (like real-world output markets) never work exactly like model markets. Most of the variables which always exist in real-world markets are "frozen" in our model markets. Our *ceteris paribus* assumption takes care of a lot of that problem. Also, the model assumes that all labor is identical. It assumes all land is and all capital is, too. Is that true? Of course not.

There Are Many Kinds of
Labor, Land, and Capital

Each particular kind of labor, land, or capital has its own relative scarcity, it's own marginal value product, and its own "supply and demand situation." One kind of labor or land or capital may be highly productive. Another may be of no value at all in the production process.

While the total quantity supplied of labor or land or capital may not respond at all to a change in demand and price, *each kind* of labor, land, or capital may be quite responsive to price changes. If the price of one kind of labor is unusually high (like grape-picker mechanics) this will "motivate the production" of more of this kind of labor. But in the meanwhile, the owner of the high-priced kind of labor will enjoy an especially high income.

In this "constant shifting about" *within* the various factor categories, the production motivating function of price really does its work. It entices the factors to do the kinds of things most valued by the society. It stimulates the development of new and better labor skills and new and better capital. It even stimulates the discovery of more of the most productive kinds of natural resources.

The person who is most successful in developing the kind of labor which is highly valued in the market (or the person who gains ownership of the kinds of land or capital which are highly valued) will receive a high income—that is, a large distributive share of the society's output.

The Normative Questions
of Income Distribution

In this chapter, most of the time we have been talking about income distribution in the pure market system. The theory of the model system really does relate to what goes on in the real world. But it doesn't answer all the questions. It doesn't get into the issues of extreme affluence or poverty. It doesn't talk at all about how the society's income and output *should* be distributed.

Most people in every society seem to agree that the distribution of income in their society is something less than perfect. How bad is it? What should be done about it? Why isn't a better distribution arrangement being worked out?

Most societies are working on this problem constantly. Each price change or wage change makes a difference. Each tax or social security or unemployment compensation or medical program change is a change in the distribution system. Each manpower training program, minimum-wage law, and anti-poverty program exerts some influence. Yes, people are always trying to work through the political process to change the distribution system. And sure enough, it's being changed all the time.

The issues we're talking about now could take us far beyond the theory of income distribution. This book will not be able to go very deeply into these normative questions. But later on there's a chapter that deals with real-world income distribution problems. For now, be sure you understand what the "distributive forces" are and how they work in the "model market system." Then when you get to the real-world problems, you'll be ready.

SUMMARY AND SYNTHESIS

In the model market system, income distribution depends on factor ownership and factor prices. Assuming factor ownership to be "given," the price you get for the factors you own (and sell) determines your income and your share of the output of the economy. Wages, rent, and interest are special names for factor prices.

Supply and demand determine factor prices. The demand for a factor reflects its productivity (MVP). The MVP is MPP times the price of the output product. A change in either MPP or price will cause MVP to change in the same direction.

Factor demand is always derived demand—the demand for inputs is derived from the demand for outputs. A producer will hire additional inputs only as long as the value of the additional output (MVP) is expected to be great enough to cover the additional input cost (MIC). So the factor demand curve is really the MVP curve for that factor.

The law of diminishing returns (variable proportions) says that MVP goes down as more variable factors are employed in combination with a given amount of fixed factors. This causes the factor demand curve to have negative slope. The faster the MVP diminishes, the less elastic the factor demand.

Factor demand elasticity also tends to reflect the elasticity of the demand for the output product, and the variability (factor substitutability) within the "input mix." Factor demand analysis tells us that the more elastic the demand for labor inputs, the more unemployment will be generated if wages are pushed up above their "market equilibrium" levels.

The relatively more scarce, higher priced factors will be carefully conserved—used only in highly productive ways. So their marginal productivity (MVP) will be high and their owners will receive high incomes.

Both the input choices and the distribution choices of the society automatically adjust to reflect the relative scarcities of the input factors.

The organization and techniques of production (the input factor combinations) are worked out in ways that guarantee that factor productivities will be in line with the relative scarcities and relative prices of the factors.

A high factor price tends to generate increased supply of that factor in the long run. As its supply increases its productivity (and price) will decrease. How fast? That depends a lot on (1) the law of diminishing returns, and (b) the elasticity of the demand for the output product.

To one business, the supply of any input factor is likely to be very elastic. For example, if you offer a little higher wage you can hire a lot more labor. But for the entire nation the supply of each factor is very inelastic. The labor supply curve may even bend backward to indicate that less labor would be supplied as wages increase!

To get at the question of factor price determination for the economy as a whole, it is useful to think of the supply of each factor as a fixed quantity, absolutely unresponsive to price changes—i.e., absolutely inelastic supply. Given this fixed supply, the demand for each factor will determine its price.

A factor's demand reflects its productivity. Its productivity reflects the availability of other factors for it to work with. So it all comes down to a question of relative scarcity. If you think about it, the law of diminishing returns tells you that. Right?

Anything which increases a factor's relative scarcity will increase its productivity and its price and its owner's income, and will cause it to be more carefully conserved—will reduce its "quantity used" in the input mix. Anything which reduces a factor's relative scarcity will have the opposite effects.

In the real world, each kind of labor, land, and capital has its own relative scarcity and productivity and price. So there are really hundreds of different "factors of production" to which these principles of factor pricing apply.

In the real world, **normative considerations about income distribution** result in political process choices which significantly alter the results which would be generated by **factor demand and supply** and the **price mechanism.**

REVIEW EXERCISES

MAJOR CONCEPTS, PRINCIPLES, TERMS (Explain each carefully.)

law of diminishing returns
how MVP influences factor demand
how the law of diminishing returns influences factor demand
how time influences factor demand
how "output demand elasticity" influences factor demand
how factor prices influence economic growth and change
how relative scarcity influences factor prices
how factor prices influence factor productivity
how factor demand is determined by other factor supplies

OTHER CONCEPTS AND TERMS (Explain each briefly.)

law of variable proportions
marginal value product (MVP)
marginal input cost (MIC)
derived demand

variable inputs
fixed inputs
the normative question of income
   distribution

CURVES AND GRAPHS (Draw, label, and explain each.)

Demand for a Factor of Production: the Marginal Value Product Curve
The Hypothetical Backward-Bending Supply Curve
The Supply and Demand for a Factor of Production

QUESTIONS (Write the answers, or jot down key points.)

1. In the real world, each "factor of production" (labor, land, capital) is really made up of a great number of different factors of production. Each *kind* of labor is really a different "factor of production." What are you doing these days to try to develop a more productive, more highly valued kind of labor, so the "price" you can get for your labor will be higher in the future? Discuss.

2. Explain as much as you can about what influences (1) the demand for a factor of production and (2) the supply of a factor of production.

3. In a completely planned economy, should the planners try to use each kind of labor, land, and capital in the same proportions as the market process would direct? or not? Also, do you think the planners should try to distribute the income in the same way the market process would direct? Explain.

4. Think back over the past 100 years or so. What do you think was the effect of the U.S. "open immigration" policy on wage rates? and on the returns to the owners of capital? and on the rate of economic growth? And today, what do you think are the effects of the *more restrictive* immigration policies? Discuss.

20 Consumer Demand Analysis: Indifference Curves, Marginal Utility, Elasticity

Chapter Objectives

- You already know about **the importance of consumer demand** in directing the market economy. In this chapter you will learn about the **theories of consumer behavior** which underlie consumer demand, and about the two basic approaches to analyzing consumer behavior: **indifference curve analysis** and **marginal utility analysis.**

- You will learn to use **indifference curves** to show **consumer satisfaction trade-offs,** and **budget lines with indifference curves** to show the **consumer's equilibrium position.** And you will learn to use these curves to **derive a consumer demand curve.**

- You will also learn to find the **consumer's maximum utility equilibrium position** using (a) **fictitious utility measurement units** (called **utils**) and (b) **equations** which illustrate the **principle of equal utilities.**

- Finally, you will find out about **elastic, inelastic,** and **unitary demand;** about **price elasticity, income elasticity,** and **cross elasticity** of demand, and about the **importance** of these concepts.

INDIFFERENCE CURVE ANALYSIS

When you lose a certain amount of good x, how much of good y must you get to make up for it?—that is, to leave you at exactly the same "level of satisfaction" as before? That's what an indifference curve tells you.

You can see already that an indifference curve must be a very personal thing. "Chacun a son gout." "Each to his or her own taste." Remember? But before we get into the indifference analysis there are a few assumptions you need to know about.

The Assumptions

Let's assume that you are the "typical consumer." If this indifference analysis is going to work in your case, then the following three things must be true about you:

1. **You Can Decide What You Prefer.** When you are faced with a choice between two bags of goods, a and b, you can decide:
   —If you prefer a over b;
   —if you prefer b over a; and
   —if you are indifferent between the two—that is, if a and b are of such close "utility value" to you that you

would be just as happy to have one as the other.

2. **Your Preferences Are "Transitive."** Suppose you are faced with a series of choices:

—if you prefer a over b; and

—if you also prefer b over c;

—then you also prefer a over c. If you prefer horseback rides to boat rides and boat rides to bike rides, then you'd rather go horseback riding than bike riding. Right?

3. **You Would Always Prefer to Have More (Rather Than Less) of Something You Like.** Suppose you like pumpernickel bread and pepperoni sausage. If you had a choice between a bag containing a loaf of pumpernickel and *half a pound* of pepperoni and a different bag containing a loaf of pumpernickel and a *whole pound* of pepperoni, which would you choose? You'd better choose the one with the whole pound of pepperoni. Otherwise this analysis won't work.

The Model Situation: Your Choices Between Food and Fun

If you are ready to accept the three assumptions (and surely they are true for most people most of the time) then we can use indifference curves to illustrate your pattern of preferences. And we can do some interesting things.

Now assume that you are a college student living on campus and that almost everything you need is provided to you. You get free housing, tuition, clothing, medical attention—just about everything you can think of except *food*. You also get an allowance of $100 a month which is supposed to take care of your needs for *food* and for all kinds of *recreation*; music, travel, entertainment, etc. So your spending choice is between two goods: food and recreation. Let's call it "food and fun."

The "Two Consumer Goods" Model. As you can see, we're building a little model. We

are assuming there are only two goods for you to spend your money on: food, and fun. You could spend your entire $100 a month on food and nothing on fun. Or you could spend it all on fun and starve to death!

What will you do? How much food will you buy? and how much fun? That depends on your personal preferences, of course. Some people would spend more for food. Their "indifference curves" will be shaped to show that. Maybe you'll spend most of your money for fun. If so, your indifference curves will be shaped to show that.

Finding the Points on Your Indifference Curve. Suppose I asked you if you would rather have 10 units of fun and 10 units of food, or less fun (6 units) and more food (15 units). And suppose you said "I'm indifferent between those two combinations. To me, 10 fun and 10 food would be just as good as (but no better than) 6 fun and 15 food." So already we've identified two of your "equal satisfaction combinations" of food and fun. We have located two points on a "food-fun indifference curve" for you.

THE INDIFFERENCE CURVES

Now it's time for you to see what all this looks like on graphs. So here they come, five in a row. All of the principles are explained right on the graph pages. Each graph builds on the previous one so take your time and learn each one well.

Fig. 20-1 The Indifference Curve: Combinations of Equal Satisfaction

Your trade-off preferences between food and fun

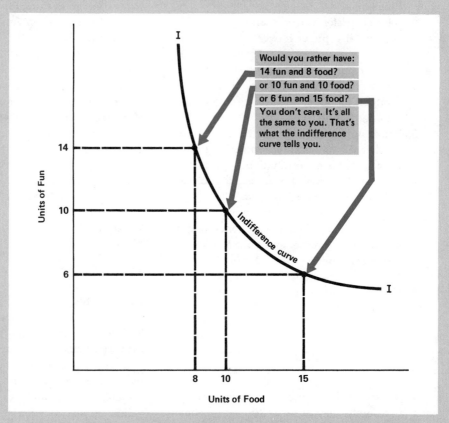

Would you rather have:
14 fun and 8 food?
or 10 fun and 10 food?
or 6 fun and 15 food?
You don't care. It's all the same to you. That's what the indifference curve tells you.

The slope at each point on the curve shows your "satisfaction trade-off ratio" between good x (food) and good y (fun).

Indifference curves join "points of equal satisfaction." Since each point on the curve is a "point of equal satisfaction" that means the satisfaction lost by giving up one unit of food is *exactly equal* to the satisfaction gained by getting the extra amount of fun indicated by the curve.

The "satisfaction trade-off ratio" between food and fun is different for different points along the curve. Why? Because of the *principle of diminishing marginal utility*. As you get more units of fun, the marginal utility of getting additional units of fun goes down. Remember from Chapter 2 about the marginal utility of water on the desert? Sure. And as you're getting more units of fun you're getting less food. So the marginal utility of food is increasing. (You'll be reading more about marginal utility soon).

Do indifference curves always have negative slope? Yes. A positive slope wouldn't show a trade-off between food and fun. It would say "you are receiving more fun and more food too but your level of satisfaction is staying the same." Nonsense.

Fig. 20-2   An Indifference Curve Map

Higher Indifference curves show higher levels of satisfaction

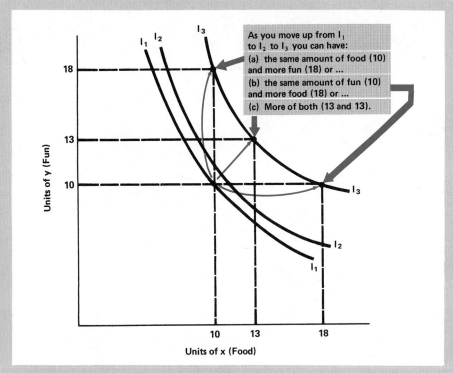

As you move up from I_1 to I_2 to I_3 you can have:

(a) the same amount of food (10) and more fun (18) or ...

(b) the same amount of fun (10) and more food (18) or ...

(c) More of both (13 and 13).

Each consumer's "individual preference map" shows the relative satisfaction values and trade-off ratios of these two commodities for that person.

You can draw in as many indifference curves as you wish to illustrate a consumer's "preference pattern." Each higher indifference curve indicates a higher level of satisfaction. Each consumer would like to get to as high a level of satisfaction (to as high an indifference curve) as possible. Of course. And you can draw in as many curves as you'd like. But the only ones that matter much are the ones your income will let you reach!

Why don't consumers move all the way up to the highest conceivable indifference curve? Because they can't afford to. But if your income goes up you can move up to a higher curve. Or what if there's a drop in the price of food? or fun? Then you can move up to a higher curve because your money will buy more.

Can indifference curves touch? or cross? Never. Two touching indifference curves would say "This consumer has a higher level of satisfaction and a lower level of satisfaction at the same time." A person would really have to have a split personality to achieve that!

If we knew how much money you had to spend and the price per unit of food and of fun, then we could draw an "expenditure possibility curve" or "budget line" just like the one you learned in the very first figure back in Chapter 2. Remember? Then we could see exactly how much you could buy: of food, of fun, and of various combinations of the two. The next graph shows you some of these "budget lines."

Fig. 20-3   Expenditure Possibility Curves I: Income Changes

Your consumption possibility curve shifts when your income changes

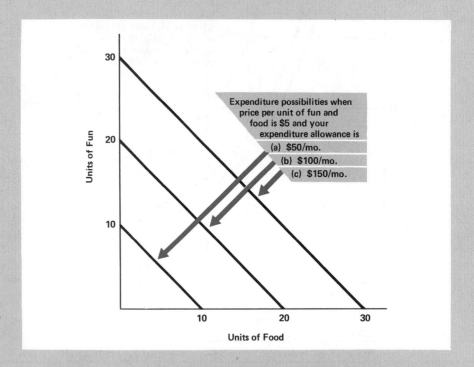

Expenditure possibilities when price per unit of fun and food is $5 and your expenditure allowance is
(a) $50/mo.
(b) $100/mo.
(c) $150/mo.

Units of Fun

Units of Food

As your income increases you can buy more of either good, or more of both.

Here you are again faced with the problem of trade-offs. You can't have everything you would like, so you must choose. What are your constraints? The amount of money you have to spend and the prices of the things you want to buy. The more money you have and the lower the prices of the things you want to buy, the higher the level of satisfaction you can achieve.

When your monthly expenditure allowance is $100 you could spend all of your allowance on food and buy 20 units. Or you could buy 20 units of fun, and starve! Or you could buy any combination in between: 19 and 1, 18 and 2, 17 and 3, etc.

If your expenditure allowance goes up to $150 you can buy more. You can buy either 30 units of food or 30 units of fun or any combination in between.

Chances are you will not buy all food or all fun but will buy some combination of the two. Why? Because that's how you will reach your highest level of satisfaction. But we can't tell for sure about that until your preferences are revealed—that is, until your *indifference curves* are drawn in to show your "equal satisfaction combinations" of food and fun. When your indifference curves reveal the relative importance to you of food and fun (at all of the possible different consumption ratios between the two) then we can see your "maximum satisfaction combination."

Fig. 20-4 Expenditure Possibility Curves II: Price Changes

Your consumption possibility changes when the prices change

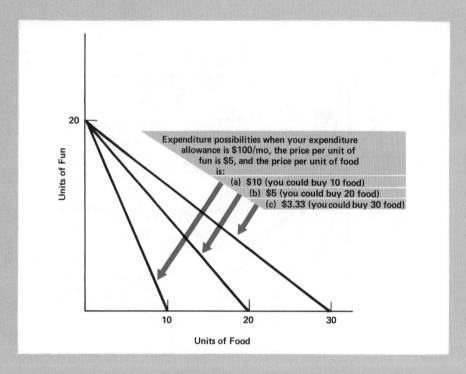

Expenditure possibilities when your expenditure allowance is $100/mo, the price per unit of fun is $5, and the price per unit of food is:

(a) $10 (you could buy 10 food)
(b) $5 (you could buy 20 food)
(c) $3.33 (you could buy 30 food)

Units of Fun

Units of Food

As the price of food decreases you can buy more food, or more of both.

When the price of food goes down from $10 to $5 a unit, your consumption possibility for food increases from 10 units per month to 20 units per month (if you spend all of your money on food). If the price goes down to $3.33 per unit for food you can buy 30 units of food.

As the price of food goes down you almost certainly would buy more food. But you might also spend more for fun. That depends on your own personal "satisfaction trade-off ratios" between food and fun at different consumption combinations of food and fun. That is, it depends on your food-fun indifference curves.

If the price of food is $10, all you can afford is 10 units of food per month. Maybe you'll spend almost all of your money for food. But if the food price is down to $3.33 where you can buy 30 units of food per month, chances are you won't want all that food. So probably you'll spend more of your money for fun. But how do we know?

It's easy to find the answers to these questions in our model. All we need to do is put your indifference curves into the picture. Then your "highest satisfaction combination" for each of the expenditure possibility curves will become obvious. On the next page, you'll see how to do it for one expenditure possibility curve. Then later you'll see how to do it for all three.

Fig. 20-5   The Consumer's Equilibrium Combination

How to choose your "highest satisfaction" combination of food and fun

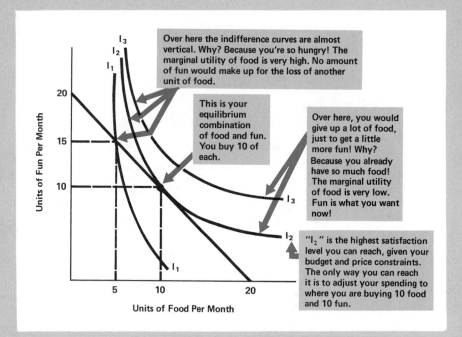

When you have (a) the indifference curves and (b) the budget line, then you can find the consumer's equilibrium combination—the combination of highest satisfaction.

This figure shows your consumer equilibrium position, given your current preferences, your income, and the prices of the two goods. If your income changes or if the price of either good changes or if your personal preferences change, you will need to shift to a new equilibrium. But until then, you're doing the best you can.

Indifference curve I_2 shows the highest level of satisfaction you can reach. The only way you can get to the I_2 level of satisfaction is by spending half your money for food and the other half for fun. That way you'll get 10 units of each. Any other combination you choose will give a "total satisfaction level" lower than I_2.

You will choose that combination of food and fun which gets you up to the highest possible level of satisfaction, given the constraints of:

(a) your limited income—that is, your "expenditure allowance," and

(b) the price per unit of food, and fun.

Is this what consumers really do? Do consumers really adjust their spending between goods to achieve their highest levels of satisfaction? In general, yes. At least this is what most people are *trying* to do. Aren't you?

What's the Use of Indifference Curve Analysis?

Now that you've had a chance to learn the graphs, what's the value of this model of consumer behavior? It highlights and further clarifies the economic problem. It focuses attention on the trade-offs consumers make as they are adjusting their spending between alternative goods.

Indifference curve analysis is a way of getting at the question of "diminishing marginal utility" without having to actually measure utility. As you'll see in a moment, that's important.

DIMINISHING MARGINAL UTILITY, AND CONSUMER EQUILIBRIUM

Throughout this chapter you've probably suspected that the **principle of diminishing marginal utility** influences the shape of the indifference curves. Of course it does! What does a person's "indifference curve map" show? It shows that person's **marginal utility** pattern!

In Figure 20-5, why do the indifference curves get so steep when the number of units of food is low? Because when you are consuming so little food your marginal utility of additional units of food is very high. No amount of extra fun could make up for the loss of another unit of food. If you lost another unit of food per month you might starve to death!

But look what happens as you get more and more units of food. If you're getting about 20 units of food per month, you could give up several units of food and get back only one unit of fun and still be as well satisfied as before. Why? Because of the diminishing marginal utility of food as you get more and more food and the increasing marginal utility of fun as you get less and less fun. Make sense? Sure.

What is utility? It's the "want satisfying quality" of a good. Utility is a very subjective thing, of course—you get the most utility from the things you prefer and I get the most utility from the things I prefer. There's no way to know if you're getting more utility from your preferred things than I'm getting from mine.

Is Utility Measurable?

If we could measure utility we could compare different levels of satisfaction, for you. We could tell exactly how much more satisfaction you would get from the bag with a whole pound of pepperoni than you would get from the bag with only half a pound of pepperoni. Also we could compare your level of satisfaction from "bag x" and "bag y," with mine. Too bad, but we just can't do that.

But we can measure utility "ordinally"—that is, we can rank things in your *order of preference.* When given the choice between the bag with half a pound of pepperoni and the bag with the whole pound of pepperoni, you know in *which order* to rank these two alternatives. Right? But we can't say *how much more* utility you will get from the bag with more pepperoni in it.

Suppose you gave me half of your pumpernickel and pepperoni? Would my total utility go up more than yours went down? It would be nice to be able to answer questions like this. But we can't.

Do you suppose we could get at this by seeing how much more you would pay for the bag with the full pound of pepperoni than for the other bag? Suppose you would pay one-third more. Then aren't you expecting to get one-third more utility from it? Maybe so. But not necessarily.

Maybe it's just that you have a low preference for the other things you might buy with your money. Or perhaps it's just that you have a low preference to hold dollars! So what can we do on this issue? We can give up. And that's just what we have to do.

After we give up on the idea of measuring utility, then we come back and say: "Okay. So we can't measure it. Not *cardinally* (that is, in specific units) anyway. But we can measure it *ordinally*. We know which combinations rank higher or lower than others. So from that *we can pretend we can measure it cardinally*. We can assign a make-believe number of "utility measurement units" to each combination in your preference pattern.

Utils: Utility Measurement Units (Fictitious of Course!)

Suppose we had a unit of measurement called the **util**. And suppose we could assign numbers of "utils" to the marginal utility a person gets from additional units of some good. Now suppose a person's monthly consumption of something keeps getting larger and larger. We know that sooner or later the extra utility that person receives from the additional units will go down. That's all we need to know! Watch.

Let's assume that the tenth unit per month of something adds 20 "utils" to your satisfaction. Then we know that the eleventh unit of it per month is likely to add *less than 20 utils* to your satisfaction. See how we could assign numbers? The numbers won't be the right size. But they will be in the right order. And that's good enough for what we're going to do.

Consumers Spend to "Buy Utils." Now, with our trusty "utils" on our side, we can analyze your expenditures this way: we can say you really aren't buying units of food or fun. You are buying utils! You are buying "units of utility" or "satisfaction."

What you'd like to get, of course, *is the most utils you can for your* money!

Buy all your utils at the lowest price and get the most utils for your money!

Suppose you're getting ready to buy another unit of something: either fun or food. Which do you buy? The one that gives you the most utils per dollar, of course!

Suppose food and fun cost the same amount: $5 per unit. Then you'll buy more units of the one that brings you the most utils (say, food). But soon the utils you get from a unit of extra food will get smaller than the utils you could get from a unit of fun. Why? Because of diminishing marginal utility, of course! So then you'll spend for fun until the marginal utility of fun goes down. Then you'll spend for food again. And on and on it goes.

Where Is Your Consumer Equilibrium? Your consumer equilibrium is where the last $5 you spend for a unit of food brings you just as many utils as the last $5 you spend for a unit of fun. It's where you're getting as many utils as you can for the last dollar you spend.

Suppose the price of food was twice as high as the price of fun—$10 per unit. What then? Then for you to be in consumer equilibrium, the last unit of food you buy must bring you *twice as much utility* (twice as many utils) as the last unit of fun you buy. Why? Because the unit of food costs you twice as much as a unit of fun.

You're paying *twice as many dollars* for the unit of food. So for it to be a good deal, it must bring you *twice as many utils*! Of course. Your equilibrium is where you're getting the same number of marginal utils for each dollar you're spending.

Consumer Equilibrium: Equal Utils per Dollar. Suppose you're spending most of your money on food and haven't thought much about it. Then when you stop to think about it: How good it would be to have some fun! You figure a unit of fun would bring you more than a hundred utils! And you figure you could give up a unit of food and lose only about 20 utils. So what do you do? You buy less food and spend some money for fun. Of course!

But then what happens? Your marginal utility of fun goes down and your marginal utility of food goes up. After awhile you get to where the next unit of fun you're thinking about would bring you less utils than you will lose by giving up another util of food. Do you shift any more, from food to fun? No. You're in equilibrium.

Figure 20-6 shows two tables to illustrate the consumer equilibrium situation. You should stop now and study that figure before you go on to the next section.

The Principle of "Equal Marginal Utility per Dollar"

Figure 20-6 shows consumer equilibrium when there are only two goods. What about when there are lots of different goods? How would consumer equilibrium be defined then? You could guess.

The total number of utils you're receiving must be as great as possible, given your constraints of income, and prices. So the number of utils you get for each dollar you spend must be as great as possible. If any one good costs you twice as much as another then it must bring you twice as many utils as the other. If one good costs you five times as much as another then a unit of it must bring you five times as many utils as a unit of the other.

You Shift from the More Expensive to the Less Expensive Utils. If any one good brings more utils per dollar than any other good, then you can't be in equilibrium. Why? Because you could reach a higher level of satisfaction—could get more utils—by shifting your spending from the "less utils per dollar" goods to the "more utils per dollar" good.

How long would you keep shifting your spending? As long as this kind of opportunity exists. As long as any one good brings more utils per dollar than any other good, you will contin-ue to shift. And each time you shift you'll get back more utils than you give up.

So where is your "maximum satisfaction consumer spending equilibrium"? It's where you're getting the same amount of "utils per dollar" on each good in your monthly market basket. If you weren't, you would put back some of the goods in the basket (the "*less* utils per dollar" goods) and take some different ones (the "*more* utils per dollar" goods). Of course.

The "Equal Utilities per Dollar" Equation. This principle of equal marginal utility per dollar as a way of stating the consumer spending equilibrium can be shown by an equation. The equation doesn't tell you anything more than what you just read. But maybe you'd like to see it anyway. So here it is.

Consumer spending equilibrium is where:

(1) Utils received for each dollar spent on the last unit of good A = utils received for each dollar spent on the last unit of good B = utils received for each dollar spent on the last unit of good C = . . . = utils received for each dollar spent on the last unit of good n.

How do we get the "utils received per dollar spent" for a good? We just divide the marginal utility (number of utils) received from the last unit bought, by the price of that unit. Like this:

$$(2) \quad \frac{\text{Marginal Utility (Utils) from the unit of A}}{\text{Price per unit of A.}}$$

= Marginal utility (utils received) per dollar on the last unit bought of A.

or to abbreviate:

$$(3) \quad \frac{\text{MU of A}}{\text{P of A}} = \text{utils per dollar from the unit of good A}$$

$$\frac{\text{MU of B}}{\text{P of B}} = \text{utils per dollar from the unit of good B; etc.}$$

Therefore equation (1) of consumer spending equilibrium—where the consumer's total utility (total utils received) is maximized—can be stated as being where:

$$(4) \quad \frac{\text{MU of A}}{\text{P of A}} = \frac{\text{MU of B}}{\text{P of B}} = \frac{\text{MU of C}}{\text{P of C}} = \ldots = \frac{\text{MU of n}}{\text{P of n}}$$

Fig. 20-6   Finding Consumer Equilibrium

Using fictitious "util measurements" to illustrate diminishing marginal utility and to show the consumer's "highest satisfaction combination" of food and fun

NOTE: Price per util is $\dfrac{\text{price per unit}}{\text{utils added per unit}}$; in this case $\dfrac{\$5.00}{\text{utils added}}$.

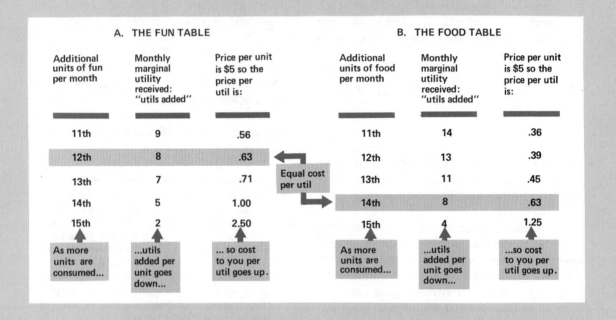

A. THE FUN TABLE				B. THE FOOD TABLE		
Additional units of fun per month	Monthly marginal utility received: "utils added"	Price per unit is $5 so the price per util is:		Additional units of food per month	Monthly marginal utility received: "utils added"	Price per unit is $5 so the price per util is:
11th	9	.56		11th	14	.36
12th	8	.63	Equal cost per util	12th	13	.39
13th	7	.71		13th	11	.45
14th	5	1.00		14th	8	.63
15th	2	2.50		15th	4	1.25
As more units are consumed...	...utils added per unit goes down...	... so cost to you per util goes up.		As more units are consumed...	...utils added per unit goes down...	...so cost to you per util goes up.

Suppose you have $130 per month to spend. You could buy 13 of fun and 13 of food. But will you? No. You can get more satisfaction—more utils—from buying 12 fun and 14 food.

The 13th unit of fun would cost you $5 and brings you only 7 marginal utils. That's 71 cents a util. Should you buy it? No. Instead, you could buy the 14th unit of food and get 8 marginal utils. That's only 63 cents a util. A better deal, right?

So what's your consumer equilibrium in this case? You'll buy 12 units of fun and 14 units of food per month and you'll be maximizing your utility. You'll be getting the greatest possible number of utils per month, given your constraints of (1) $130/mo income, and (2) a price of $5 per unit for both food and fun.

This equation is just another way of saying what you already knew: that for your spending pattern to be in equilibrium, the cost to you "per util" must be the same among all the things you're buying. How does a consumer get to this equilibrium? By adjusting spending among different goods and letting the principle of diminishing marginal utility bring the "utilities per dollar" into balance.

After you've taken advantage of every possible opportunity to shift your spending pattern and get more utils per dollar, then you've pushed yourself into equilibrium. You're getting all the satisfaction you can get, given your constraints of income and prices.

The Principle Applies to All Spending Decisions

The principle of "equal marginal utility per dollar" applies to any situation where spending decisions are made. It applies to every person, household, government agency, business, or any other organization.

Maximum progress toward desired goals comes only when each dollar is spent in the way it will do the most good. When that's happening, that's the best you (or anyone) can do.

Is a precise "consumer spending equilibrium" always achieved? Of course not. The equilibrium in this case—as in so many cases (as you will see later)—is the ultimate position toward which things tend to move. But certainly the principle of equal marginal utility per dollar does show the direction in which most people are trying to move most of the time. So it's a valuable tool for analyzing consumer demand.

Suppose you're trying to find the consumer's "maximum satisfaction" equilibrium position. What's the relationship between this "equal marginal utilities" approach and the indifference-curve-budget-line approach? You could guess. Both are saying the same thing in a different way.

The principle of *equal marginal utility per dollar* is satisfied by the indifference-curve-budget-line point of tangency. The *price ratio* between the products is shown by the *slope of the budget line*. The *marginal utility ratio* between the products is shown by *the slope of the indifference curve*.

At the point of tangency the slopes are equal. So the price ratios and utility ratios are also equal.

So $\frac{MUx}{Px} = \frac{MUy}{Py}$. Or, if you prefer: $\frac{Px}{Py} = \frac{MUx}{MUy}$. Consumer equilibrium? Of course.

HOW TO DERIVE AN INDIVIDUAL CONSUMER DEMAND CURVE

Now that you understand the indifference analysis and the principle of diminishing marginal utility you are ready for a much better understanding of consumer demand.

How can we figure out the demand curve of one individual? Using your "indifference curve map" we can construct one for you! How? Suppose we want to derive your demand for *food*. Here's how:

—First we set up your indifference map showing your "preference trade-off ratios" between food and fun.
—Next we assume (a) that you have a certain amount of income to spend, and (b) that the price for a unit of fun is fixed.
—Finally, we change the price of food and shift the budget line. Then we see what quantity of food you would buy at each price. And that's all we need to know to construct your demand curve for food!

Figures 20-7 and 20-8 show and explain the entire process. You should take a few minutes to study those figures now.

Fig. 20-7   Deriving the Individual's Demand Curve

Using indifference curves to derive your demand curve for food

Assume: You have $100/mo to spend and the price of fun is $5/unit. The Question: How much food would you buy at various possible prices for food?

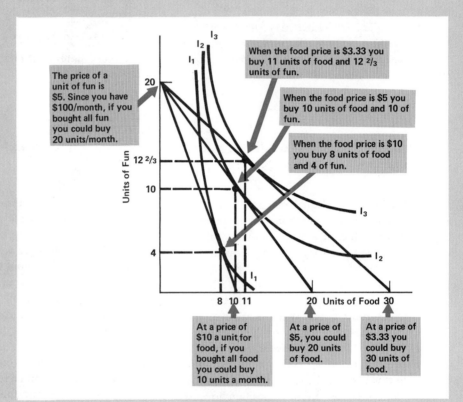

The price of a unit of fun is $5. Since you have $100/month, if you bought all fun you could buy 20 units/month.

When the food price is $3.33 you buy 11 units of food and 12 2/3 units of fun.

When the food price is $5 you buy 10 units of food and 10 of fun.

When the food price is $10 you buy 8 units of food and 4 of fun.

At a price of $10 a unit for food, if you bought all food you could buy 10 units a month.

At a price of $5, you could buy 20 units of food.

At a price of $3.33 you could buy 30 units of food.

Notice that each time the price of food goes down, you move up to a higher level of satisfaction. The income effect? Right!

The three points derived on this graph can be used to build your demand curve for food. You will see that in the graph on the next page.

The three indifference curves shown here are the same ones you saw in Figure 20-5. The three budget lines are the ones you saw in Figure 20-4. The curves are brought together here to show how the quantity bought responds to price changes.

As you look at this graph, think about how much difference it could make if the indifference curves were situated or sloped differently. If the consumer had a very different pattern of preferences the *quantity response* to each price change could be very different.

What do you suppose would happen to your food purchases if your *income* went up? or down? or if *the price of fun* went up? or down? These questions are concerned with various kinds of *elasticity of demand*. Later in this chapter you'll be reading about elasticity of demand. When you do you may want to refer back to this graph.

Fig. 20-8 Your Demand Curve for Food

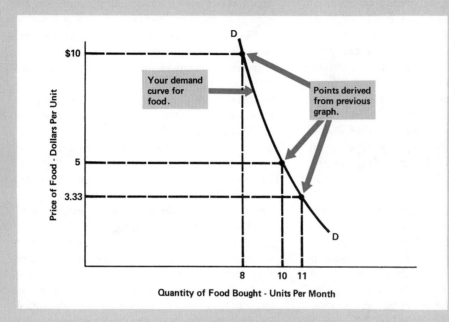

This curve shows your individual demand for food, as derived from (a) your preferences, as shown by the indifference curves on the previous graph, and (b) the various prices of food which might exist, assuming a fixed price of $5 a unit of food.

Could your demand for fun be derived in the same way? Sure. Why don't you do it? It will give you some food for thought. And who knows? It might even be fun!

DERIVING THE MARKET DEMAND CURVE

Figure 20-8 shows your *individual demand curve* for food. Suppose you wanted to get the *market demand curve* for food for everyone on your campus. Or for everyone in the United States, for that matter. How would you do it?

Add Individual Demands to Get Market Demand

Conceptually, it's easy. In practice it's not so easy. Conceptually, all we need to do to get the market demand curve is to add up the individual demand curves of all of the people who make up the buyers' side of the food market! If your "quantity demanded at each price" is added to my "quantity demanded at each price" and then everybody else's "quantity demanded at each price" is added on then we'll have the total

quantity demanded in the market, at each price. That is, we'll have the total market demand curve for food.

Suppose you wanted to look at Figure 20-8 and change that demand curve into a market demand curve. The easiest way to do it would be to increase the quantity scale. For example, suppose you assume that there are 100 people in this market and that each has a demand curve for food exactly like yours. To get the market demand, just add two zeros to each number on the x (quantity) axis of Figure 20-8. Your new market demand curve will show at a price of $5 a quantity demanded not of 10, but of 1,000. At $10 the quantity demanded will not be 8, but 800, and at $3.33 the quantity demanded will not be 11, but 1,100.

What If Individual Demands Differ?

Suppose different people have different demand curves for food. Then you can't assume everybody is just like you. You will have to add up the demand curves of all the individuals, one by one. At a price of $10 you must add your quantity demanded (8) and mine (say 6) and your brother's (say 10) and my wealthy cousin's (say 13) and on and on until every person's quantity demanded at a price of $10 is added up.

When you finish all that, what you get is one point on the market demand curve. Then you must do the same for all the other prices. When you finish you will have several points on the market demand curve. Then draw in the curve and you have it. Pretty obvious, right? So what's the point?

The point of all this is simply that the market demand for any product in any market is made up of the demands of all the individuals who are on the buyer's side of that market. These individual demands, of course, reflect the preferences and incomes and "satisfaction trade-off ratios" of all these consumer-buyers. As individuals, through their demands, are influencing and responding to market conditions, they are determining the buyers' side of the market. That is, they are determining the market demand.

What About Market Demand for Real Products?

Do businesses try to figure what the market demand for their product is like? Does the U.S. Department of Agriculture try to figure out how price changes would influence the amount of wheat being bought? and bread being eaten? Does the Federal Power Commission care about what would happen to the quantities demanded of natural gas at various prices that might be

charged? And is anybody in Washington concerned about the effect of high oil prices on the amount of gasoline, fuel oils, etc. being bought?

The answers to all of these questions are: yes! yes! yes! But how can any of these businesses or government organizations or anybody figure out the market demand for a product? Well, they have a head start in the beginning. At any moment they know approximately what the price is and what quantity is being bought. Usually they also have information about some time in the past when the price was different. They know how much was being bought then, too. So by looking at historical prices and quantities it's possible to make some estimates of market demand for some things.

Also, sometimes businesses "test market" products in special areas, with special prices, just to see what the effect will be on the amount people will buy. It's very important to know how the buyers will respond when the price changes. That is, it's important to know about "elasticity of demand."

ELASTICITY OF DEMAND

You already know that when the price goes down, people will buy more. That's the "law of demand." The elasticity of demand answers the question: "How much more?" You already know that if it is a *lot* more, that means the demand has a *lot* of elasticity. If it is "only a *little* more" then the demand has only a little elasticity.

If the price goes down a little and a great deal more is bought, then we say that the demand is "highly elastic." If the price goes down

The **slope** of the **indifference** curve at any point shows the **marginal utility ratio** between the two goods?

Naturally! And the **slope** of the **budget line** shows the **price ratio**. Where they're tangent the ratios are **equal**, of course. That's **consumer equilibrium**! Now get back to work.

a lot and only a very little bit more is bought, we say the demand is "highly inelastic" (meaning "very little elasticity"). What we are talking about is the **price elasticity** of demand—the sensitivity, or responsiveness of buyers to *price* changes.

Elasticity Depends on Percentage Changes

We say it this way: If a 1 percent change in price would cause a *larger* percentage change (say, a 2 percent change) in the quantity people would buy, the demand is **relatively elastic**. "Relatively elastic" demand means the *percentage change in the quantity bought* would be greater than the *percentage change in the price*. It means the quantity bought is highly responsive to price changes—that the quantity people would buy "stretches a lot" when the price goes down and "shrinks a lot" when the price goes up. That's all it means. We also use the term **price elastic** to mean the same thing.

If the 1 percent change in price would cause a *smaller* percentage change (say, a .5 percent change) in the quantity bought, we say that the demand is **relatively inelastic**. "Relatively inelastic" demand means the *quantity* changes by a *smaller percentage* than the *price* changes. The quantity people would buy isn't very responsive to price changes—that is, it doesn't "stretch" (or "shrink") very much if the price goes down (or up). We also use the term **price inelastic** to mean the same thing.

Elastic, Inelastic, Unitary. Suppose it happens that the one percent change in price causes an exactly equal percentage change in the quantity bought. Then we say: "the elasticity of demand is unitary." Why unitary? Because if you *divide the percentage change in price (1 percent) into the percentage change in quantity (1 percent) what do you get?* You get *one*, which is *unity*, of course!

If you got a number *larger* than one you would know the demand was *relatively elastic*.

The "quantity response" was *greater* than the price change. If you got a number smaller than one you would know the demand was *relatively inelastic. The "quantity response" was less* than the price change. Why *relatively* inelastic? Relative to what? Relative to *unitary elasticity*! Of course. Here's an example.

A "Percentage Change" Example. Suppose American Airlines decides to offer a 25 percent reduction in air fares for students. Following the announcement of the reduced fare, suppose twice as many students start buying tickets and flying American. The demand turned out to be relatively elastic—highly elastic, in fact. A 25 percent price cut brought a 100 percent increase in "quantity bought." The elasticity of demand would be 4. The 100 percent quantity increase, divided by the 25 percent price decrease, equals 4 (100% ÷ 25% = 4).

What if there had been only a 15 percent increase in ticket sales to students? Then we would say the demand was relatively inelastic (elasticity of less than one). The elasticity of demand would be .6 (15% ÷ 25% = .6). What if the student ticket sales increased exactly 25 percent? Well, unitary elasticity, of course! (25% ÷ 25% = 1.)

Elasticity Affects the Amount Spent

When the price of something goes down, people will buy more. But will they spend more money? Or not? The lower price *saves* them more money. But the greater quantity *costs* them some money. Which one will win out? The price change? Or the quantity change? It all depends on *how much the quantity changes* in response to the price change. Right?

Here's the general principle:

1. If the quantity does not change enough to offset the "expenditure effect" of the price change, then the total amount spent for the good will move the same direction as the price moves. If price goes up, total amount spent goes up. If price goes down, total amount spent goes down. Demand is *inelastic*. (Quantity doesn't "stretch" enough to offset the "expenditure effect" of the price change.)

2. If the quantity changes by enough to *more than offset* the "expenditure effect" of the price change, then the total amount spent for the good will move the *opposite* way from the price. If the price goes up, total amount spent goes down. If price goes down, total amount spent goes up. Demand is *elastic*. (Quantity "stretches" enough to *more than* offset the expenditure effect of the price change.)

3. If the quantity changes just enough to exactly offset the expenditure effect of the price change, the total amount spent for the good will stay the same. The elasticity of demand is *unitary*.

Now that you know all this about elasticity of demand, what's the purpose? Its just that this is one of the most significant concepts in economics, that's what! It's *responsiveness to price* that makes the market process work!

The following sections will tell you about two other kinds of demand elasticity: *income elasticity*, and *cross elasticity*. Then, following the review exercises at the end of this chapter there's a brief appendix explaining two easy ways to compute *price elasticity of demand*— in case you (and/or your professor) are interested in that sort of thing.

Income Elasticity of Demand

Think about your demand curve for food, as derived back in Figure 20-7. Your income was fixed at $100 per month. Remember? Suppose your income had increased—say to $200 a month. Would that cause your demand for food to increase? Of course! Your demand for food responds to a change in your income. *How much* does it respond? That depends on your *income elasticity of demand* for food!

The income elasticity of demand for a good can be defined as: the percentage change in quantity bought caused by a 1% change in income. If your income goes up 1% and you buy 2% more food then your demand for food is income elastic. But if you buy only 0.5% more food then your demand for food is income inelastic.

What do you think about the income elasticity of your demand for food? If your income goes up are you likely to spend much more for food? Or only a little more? Most people seem to have an *income inelastic demand for food but an income elastic demand for fun.*

Income Elasticity and Inferior Goods.
What are the things you would buy more of if your income went up? Everything? Probably not. I have an idea that if you get wealthy enough you may never buy another recapped tire in your life! Can you see how some goods would have negative income elasticity?

As people's incomes rise they buy less instead of more of some goods. What goods? Economists call them inferior goods. "Inferior goods" are goods people buy when their incomes are low (such as recapped tires and hot dogs instead of steak) but which they will buy less of if their incomes go up high enough.

Cross Elasticity of Demand

Here's another kind of demand elasticity. Again, think back to Figure 20-7 where your demand for food was derived. What would have happened to your demand for food if the price of fun had gone up? or down? These are questions of cross elasticity of demand.

Complementary Goods. Suppose you still like pepperoni sausage and pumpernickel bread. But you don't like one without the other. Then suppose your local supermarket runs a half-price sale on pepperoni. Will that increase your demand for pumpernickel? Of course!

In this example we're talking about **complementary goods**. When the price of one goes down, the demand for the other goes up. Why? Because when the price of one goes down you buy more of that one. So you are induced to demand more of the other to go with it!

What about the prices of lumber and nails? Or gasoline and big cars? Or milk and corn flakes? When the price of one goes down, the demand for the other goes up? Sure. All complementary goods? Yes.

Suppose the price of pepperoni doubled. Would your demand for pumpernickel go down? Sure. At the higher price you buy less pepperoni. So you also buy less pumpernickel—even though the price of pumpernickel didn't change.

Substitute Goods. What about cross elasticity and **substitute goods**? Suppose you like eggs on toast for breakfast. But you also like grilled cheese on toast just about as well. Suppose the price of eggs doubles. Will you demand more cheese? Sure. Suppose the price of eggs goes down. Will you eat more eggs and demand less cheese? Of course.

Eggs and cheese are substitutes for each other. When the price of one goes down the demand for the other goes down.

How much does the quantity bought of pumpernickel *increase* when the price of pepperoni *goes down* by 1%? *How much* does the quantity bought of cheese *decrease* when the price of eggs *goes down* by 1%? These are questions of the *cross elasticity of demand*.

Independent and Interdependent Goods. The demands for many goods are independent of each other—like soap powder and toothpaste or fishhooks and pantyhose. A price change for one doesn't cause you to buy either more or less of the other. There isn't any cross elasticity of demand between them.

But the demands for many goods are interdependent. Some are complements. Some are substitutes. Sometimes the interdependence is close and the cross elasticity is high—a price change in one will bring a big quantity change in the other. Other times the interdependence is not so close. So the cross elasticity is low.

When we talk about elasticity of demand, unless we specify otherwise, we are talking about *price* elasticity of demand. We are talking about the responsiveness of the *quantity bought* to a change in the *price of the product*.

SUMMARY AND SYNTHESIS

The analysis of **consumer demand** requires an understanding of the **theories of consumer behavior**. The most basic of these are indifference curve analysis and marginal utility analysis.

An **indifference curve** indicates different consumption combinations of two goods. All points on the curve indicate **combinations of equal satisfaction** to this particular consumer. Indifference analysis is based on the assumptions that: (1) **you know** what you like, (2) your preferences are **transitive**, and (3) you'd prefer to have **more of** the things you like.

You can draw as many indifference curves in a graph as you wish. The **higher the curves the greater the satisfaction** indicated. You would like to get to the highest possible curve. But you're limited by (a) your budget constraint which reflects **how much money you have** to spend and (b) by the **prices of the goods**.

Your expenditure possibility (budget constraint) line can be drawn in the graph and it will show (by point of tangency) the **highest indifference curve** (level of satisfaction) you can reach. The point of tangency indicates your **equilibrium** combination between the two goods.

Another way of defining the consumer's maximum satisfaction equilibrium is with **equations which show equality in the marginal utility-to-price ratios among goods.** Equilibrium exists when the MU of A divided by the price of A is equal to the MU of B divided by the price of B and this same equality holds for all goods. Whenever this equality **is not satisfied,** the consumer then has the opportunity to gain satisfaction by spending **more** on the **higher MU-per-dollar products** and **less** on the **lower MU-per-dollar products.** Economists sometimes use a fictitious utility measurement unit—the util—to illustrate this principle.

This principle of **equal marginal utility per dollar** is satisfied by the indifference curve-budget line point of tangency. The price ratio between the products is shown by the slope of the budget line. The marginal utility ratio between the products is shown by the slope of the indifference curve. At the point of tangency the slopes are equal, so the price ratio between the goods is equal to their **marginal utility ratio.**

You can **derive an individual consumer's demand curve** using indifference curves and budget lines. On the indifference curve graph, vary the price of one good and locate the various consumer equilibrium points. Then, on a supply and demand graph, **plot the various prices and quantities** of that good and you'll have a demand curve for that good.

To build a **market demand curve** it is necessary to add up the individual demand curves for all of the buyers (and potential buyers) in that market.

Price elasticity of demand is concerned with this question: "How much does the **quantity demanded** change in response to a **price change?"** Suppose the price changes by 1%. If quantity changes more than 1% we say the demand is **relatively elastic;** if less than 1%, **relatively inelastic;** and if exactly 1%, **unitary.**

Income elasticity of demand indicates how **changes in income influence the quantity purchased of a good. Cross elasticity** indicates how **changes in the price of one good influence the quantity purchased of some other good.**

With income elasticity we can identify **inferior goods.** With cross elasticity we can identify **complementary, substitute, and independent goods.**

Unless some other kind of elasticity is specified, the term "elasticity of demand" always means **price elasticity of demand**—i.e., the responsiveness of buyers to a change in the price of the good.

REVIEW EXERCISES

MAJOR CONCEPTS, PRINCIPLES, TERMS (Explain each carefully.)

indifference curve
diminishing marginal utility

equal utilities per dollar
price elasticity of demand

OTHER CONCEPTS AND TERMS (Explain each briefly.)

transitive (preference)
marginal utility
individual preference map
satisfaction trade-off ratios
consumer equilibrium
budget line
expenditure possibility curve
the consumption constraints
cardinal measure

ordinal measure
utils
individual demand curve
market demand curve
income elasticity
cross elasticity
relatively elastic
relatively inelastic
unitary elasticity

CURVES AND GRAPHS (Draw, label, and explain each.)

The Indifference Curve: Combinations of Equal Satisfaction
An Indifference Curve Map
Expenditure Possibility Curves I: Income Changes
Expenditure Possibility Curves II: Price Changes
The Consumer's Equilibrium Combination
Deriving the Individual's Demand Curve
Your Demand Curve for Food

QUESTIONS (Write out answers, or jot down key points.)

1. Explain the assumptions on which the indifference curve analysis depends.
2. Suppose you know of someone who really has a taste for expensive food. As that person's income goes up, the food expenditure keeps going up, up, up. There isn't much spending to buy more fun. Could you draw an indifference curve to illustrate this unusual preference pattern? Try.
3. What functions does "elasticity" perform? What would happen without it?
4. Explain what the relationship is between indifference curves and these two principles: (1) *diminishing marginal utility*? and (2) *equal utilities per dollar*? Try.

APPENDIX

Some Ways of Figuring Price Elasticity of Demand

This brief appendix shows two different ways of calculating price elasticity of demand. If you really understand elasticity of demand then it's almost obvious how you would calculate the "elasticity of demand."

Price elasticity of demand can be defined as: the percentage change in *quantity* resulting from a 1% change in *price*. If the quantity percentage change is greater than 1%, demand is "price elastic." If it's less than 1%, demand is "price inelastic." To find the elasticity of any point of the demand curve you could use this formula.

The Point Elasticity Formula

$$\frac{\text{Change in Quantity}}{\text{Initial Quantity}} \div \frac{\text{Change in Price}}{\text{Initial Price}}$$

Which means: Percentage change in quantity divided by percentage change in price.

Example: Suppose the price of something went up by $1: from $100 to $101; and the quantity bought decreased by 4 units: from 200 units to 196 units a day. (See bottom of page.)

The demand for this product (at prices around $100) is "relatively elastic" or "price elastic." How do we know? Because the elasticity is greater than 1. The quantity change (expressed as a percent) is greater than the price change (expressed as a percent). The quantity responsiveness is relatively high.

The point elasticity formula works just fine for figuring elasticity if you're dealing with a point on (or a very small move along) the demand curve. But suppose the price changes quite a lot. That means there's a movement of some distance along the demand curve.

If you want to figure the elasticity of demand based on a big change in price, no longer are you dealing with a *point* on the curve. You're dealing with an *arc* of the curve. And since elasticity can be very different at different prices and quantities, when you're dealing with arc elasticity there's a different formula.

$$\frac{\text{Change in Quantity } (\Delta Q) = 4}{\text{Initial Quantity } (Q_1) = 200} \div \frac{\text{Change in Price } (\Delta P) = 1}{\text{Initial Price } (P_1) = 100} = .02 \ (2\%) \div .01 \ (1\%) = 2$$

Arc Elasticity of Demand

When price and quantity changes are fairly large and we're dealing with an arc (a segment) of the demand curve, we need a formula with a "center of the arc" basis—that is, a formula that is not based on the initial price and quantity position *at one end of the arc.*

How do we do it? It's simple. Instead of dividing by the initial quantity and the initial price (as in the "point elasticity" formula) we divide by the "mid point of the arc" quantity and the "mid point of the arc" price.*

The Arc Elasticity Formula

$$\underline{\text{Change in quantity } (\Delta Q)} \div \underline{\text{Change in Price } (\Delta P)}$$

$$\left(\begin{array}{l}\text{midpoint between}\\ \text{initial quantity } (Q_1)\\ \text{and final quantity } (Q_2)\end{array}\right) \qquad \left(\begin{array}{l}\text{midpoint between}\\ \text{initial price } (P_1)\\ \text{and final price } (P_2)\end{array}\right)$$

$$\text{that is: } \left(\frac{Q_1 + Q_2}{2}\right) \qquad \text{that is: } \left(\frac{P_1 + P_2}{2}\right)$$

Example: Suppose the price of something goes up by \$20; from \$100 to \$120, and the quantity bought drops by 60 units: from 200 units to 140 units per day. This works out as follows:

$$\frac{(\Delta Q) = 60}{\left(\dfrac{Q_1 + Q_2}{2}\right) = \left(\dfrac{200 + 140}{2}\right)} \div \frac{(\Delta P) = 20}{\left(\dfrac{P_1 + P_2}{2}\right) = \left(\dfrac{100 + 120}{2}\right)} = \frac{60}{170} \div \frac{20}{110} = .35 \div .18 = 1.94$$

If you had used the *point elasticity formula* to figure this out you would have:

$$\frac{60}{200} \div \frac{20}{100} = .30 \div .20 = 1.5$$

But 1.5 is not a very good approximation of the elasticity of this arc of this demand curve. That's why the arc elasticity formula is needed.

Figure 20-9 shows a graphic example of arc elasticity of demand. I think a look at that Figure will make all this very clear to you.

New Concepts and Principles from the Appendix

Point elasticity: the concept and the formula
Arc elasticity: the concept and the formula
Graphs: arc elasticity of demand

Fig. 20-9   An Example of Arc Elasticity of Demand

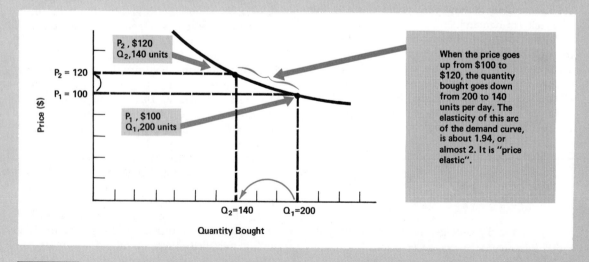

When the price goes up from \$100 to \$120, the quantity bought goes down from 200 to 140 units per day. The elasticity of this arc of the demand curve, is about 1.94, or almost 2. It is "price elastic".

*Actually, the formula gives us a "midpoint of the arc" price and quantity only if the arc between the two points is a straight line.

PART SIX

Better Keep A Close Eye On Your Inputs and Outputs!

21

Short-Run Cost Analysis: How Efficiency Changes as Output Changes

Chapter Objectives

- The **price mechanism** works through supply and demand. In the last chapter you learned a lot about **demand**. In this and the following chapters you'll learn a lot about **supply**.

- In this chapter you'll be learning about **cost of production**, because **cost determines supply.**

- When you finish studying this chapter you will be able to explain how both **total and average (per unit) costs of production change as a business firm's output changes.**

- You will be able to **draw curves** illustrating these "cost/output" relationships and to **explain**, for each curve, **what it means and why it is shaped as it is.**

- You will be able to draw a **marginal cost curve**, explain how it is a **graphic illustration of the law of diminishing returns**, how it **influences the other cost curves**, and how it influences the **maximum efficiency rate of output** of the firm.

Supply: An Overview

Supply (the propensity to sell) is determined by the cost of production. Producers are likely to be willing to sell a lot more of something if they can produce it at low cost than if the cost is high. If the *production cost is higher* than the *selling price* they won't want to produce and sell *any!* What if the selling price is much higher than the production cost? Then the producers will want to produce and sell a lot.

It's easy to see how cost determines "the propensity to sell." But the next step is to really understand a business firm's cost situation and

see exactly *how* supply is determined by the cost of production.

TOTAL COST IS MADE UP OF FIXED COST PLUS VARIABLE COST

Now, for a while, try to think of yourself as a business manager who owns and runs a small manufacturing plant. Your plant is located up in the Appalachian mountains at Cullowhee, North Carolina. You produce jeans. Let's talk about your cost of production and about how the cost increases as your daily output increases.

Fixed Cost Doesn't Change as Output Changes

Suppose your daily output last week was zero. You didn't produce anything. What do you suppose your total cost was last week. Zero? No. More than zero.

Even if you produce nothing you still have to pay your fixed cost. You must pay the rent, and the interest on the money you owe. And you must pay insurance and the night guard and the maintenance worker who cuts the grass around the plant and lubricates the machines to keep them from getting rusty. And taxes. Seems that you can't ever escape from paying some taxes.

What Is Fixed Cost? "Fixed cost" is all of the costs you must pay even if you don't produce anything. If you produce nothing or if you produce a thousand units a day it makes no difference to your fixed cost.

Does the fixed cost tell you anything about how much output you should produce? No. But you know that the greater your rate of output the lower your "per unit fixed cost" will be.

For example, suppose your fixed cost is $150 a day. If you produce only one unit of output per day, what will be your "per unit fixed cost"? The whole thing: $150. But if you produce 10 units a day your "average" or "per unit" fixed cost will be only $15. If you produce 150 units a day the fixed cost per unit will be only $1!

Spreading the Overhead. The concept we're talking about is what business managers call "spreading the overhead."

Every business manager knows that if the volume of output is high, the overhead (fixed cost) will not be anything to worry about. But when output slows down, high overhead can bring heavy losses.

Cost of production determines supply?

Yes. You'll supply what's profitable and that depends on cost.

Variable Cost Increases as the Rate of Output Increases

If you're going to produce any output you're going to incur some *additional* costs. Why? To buy some *variable input factors*, of course!

The Cost of the Variable Factors. To make jeans, you are going to have to buy some denim and some thread and some zippers (and maybe some brass buttons and rivets to jazz 'em up a bit) and some other things.

You're going to have to buy some cardboard cartons and gasoline for the delivery trucks and electricity to run the machines too.

What about labor? You are going to have to hire some people to run the sewing machines and some cutters and some supervisors and inspectors and all. And some sales people to sell your jeans to the department stores and clothing stores over in Asheville and Knoxville and Rock Hill and Texarkana.

All these *additional* costs—costs which increase as your rate of output increases—are called **variable costs.** When output is zero the variable cost is zero. But as soon as you produce something you must pay some variable cost. The greater your daily output the higher your variable cost will be. That's obvious. But here's something else.

Variable Cost Per Unit Is High When Output Is Low

The *rate* at which the variable cost increases (as your daily output increases) isn't always the same. Suppose you are trying to produce at a very low rate of output—maybe just a few pairs of jeans a day. Then your variable cost per unit of output may be very high. Maybe you must keep a full shift of workers, even if you only produce a few pairs. So if you produce at a very low rate, your *cost per unit* will be very high.

What's Your Most Efficient Output Rate?

Suppose your plant is designed to operate most efficiently when you are producing 10 cartons of jeans per day (two dozen pairs of jeans per carton). So ten cartons per day is your output rate where your *per-unit cost is lowest.*

If you operate your plant at less than 10 cartons a day the operation will not be as efficient; if you operate at more than ten cartons a day the operation will not be as efficient. "Efficient" means "low cost per unit."

Now, an example. Suppose you aren't producing anything. Then you decide to start producing two cartons a day. The per unit cost of those two cartons will be very high. So maybe you decide to increase your output to five cartons a day. Your variable cost will go up, sure. But not as fast as your output goes up.

Next, suppose you decide to expand your output to ten cartons a day. Your variable cost will go still higher. But your output will go up more than your cost goes up. Why? Because you are getting closer to your "maximum efficiency rate of output."

What happens if you decide to increase your output to *more than* ten cartons a day? Suppose you decide to produce eleven or twelve or thirteen? or maybe more? Your variable cost will increase much more than your output will increase. Why? Because you're producing more than your plant was designed to produce!

Fixed Cost Plus Variable Cost Equals Total Cost.

What makes up your total cost for any rate of output you might choose? The "fixed cost" plus the "variable cost"? Sure. If you produce nothing, the fixed cost is your "total cost." If you produce something your total cost is the fixed cost plus the variable cost.

The higher the rate of output the higher will be the variable cost. So the higher will be the total cost. But the per unit cost will be lowest if you operate at your most efficient rate of output: ten cartons per day.

Minimum Cost Is Not the Objective

Which rate of output should you choose? Don't worry about that yet; we'll get to it later. But one thing you know already. The output you choose will not be the one of *minimum total cost.* The "least total cost" rate of output is where you produce nothing! You pay only your fixed cost. But it wouldn't make much sense to run that kind of operation! Right?

Exception: If nobody wanted to buy your output, or if the price was so low that you couldn't even make enough to pay for your denim, brass buttons, labor, and other variable factors, then it would be best not to hire any variable factors.

Produce nothing! That will minimize your losses. Pay your daily fixed cost as long as you have to. But make plans to get out of this business as fast as you can!

THE COST CURVES: VARIABLE AND FIXED, TOTAL AND AVERAGE

Now you know a little bit about how your costs change as your *rate of output* changes. Wouldn't it be helpful to see how this looks on a graph? We could show the *rate of output* along the horizontal axis and the *cost* on the vertical axis.

The variable and the total cost curves will have positive (upward) slope—more output, more cost. But these cost curves won't be straight lines. Why not? Because variable and total costs don't increase *at a constant rate* as output increases. Remember?

What about fixed cost? That will show up on the graph as a straight, horizontal line. Why? Because fixed cost is just as high when you produce nothing as it is when you produce as much as you can!

Now you're ready to start learning the cost curves. Here they are, five graphs in a row. Each one is illustrating exactly the situation we have been talking about.

Take time to really understand each one of these curves. You'll need to practice drawing them and talk to yourself about them as you go along. So your roommate thinks you've flipped out? Oh well . . .

Fig. 21-1 Fixed Cost and Average Fixed Cost

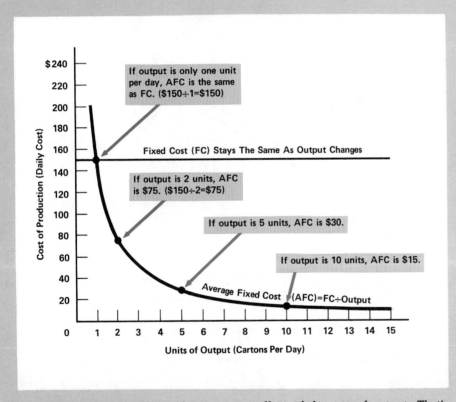

Even if you don't produce anything you still must pay the rent and taxes and interest. And the night guard, of course!

The fixed cost is always the same regardless of the rate of output. That's why the total fixed cost curve is horizontal. The average fixed cost is the total divided by the number of units of output. That's why the average fixed cost curve gets lower and lower as output gets larger and larger.

At low rates of output, the fixed cost is an important part of the cost of each unit. At high rates of output the fixed cost is only a small part of the cost of each unit. If output is expanded enough, fixed cost (overhead cost) per unit gets so small that it's hardly worth considering.

You can see that a business which has a very high fixed cost must produce and sell a large volume of output. Otherwise it wouldn't be able to cover its "overhead"—that is, its fixed cost.

Fig. 21-2   Variable Cost and Average Variable Cost

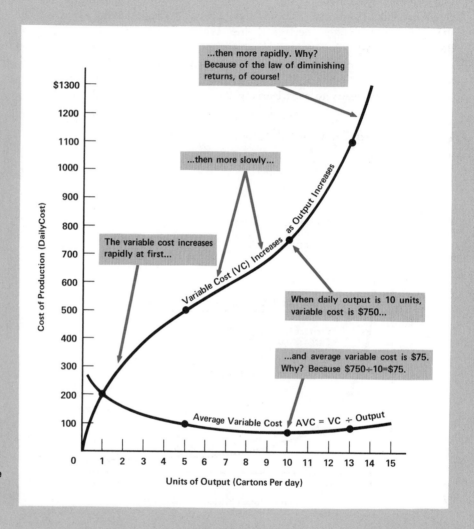

The more you produce the more variable cost you must pay.

The variable cost is the cost of all of the inputs except the fixed inputs. It includes such things as labor and materials and power—everything that causes your total cost to go up as your output increases.

As the rate of output increases, variable cost increases rapidly at first, then more slowly, then more rapidly again.

Notice that as output increases, the *total* variable cost increases all the time. But the average variable cost goes down for awhile. Then if you expand beyond the most efficient output rate, the total variable cost increases rapidly and pulls the average upward again.

(You will notice that this graph has a smaller vertical scale than the previous figure. We had to squeeze down the vertical axis to keep this "variable cost curve" from running off the top of the page.)

Fig. 21-3   Fixed Cost Plus Variable Cost Equals Total Cost

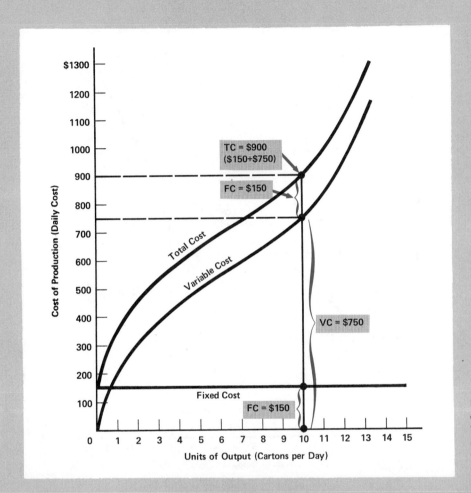

Fixed cost is the cost
of being in business.
Variable cost is the
cost of producing
things. Add them up
and you get total cost.

When output is ten cartons per day, fixed cost is $150 (as always) and variable cost is $750. So total cost is $900 ($150 + $750 = $900).

When output is zero, the total cost equals fixed cost. Then as output expands, total cost is pushed up by the variable cost.

The total cost curve is exactly the same shape as the variable cost curve. The only difference is that the variable curve starts at zero and the total curve starts at $150 (the fixed cost).

The *vertical distance* (the dollar difference) between the two curves is always $150 (the fixed cost). (Note that the only distances that mean anything on this graph are the *vertical distances*, which show what the costs are at different rates of output.)

Fig. 21-4 Total Cost and Average Total Cost

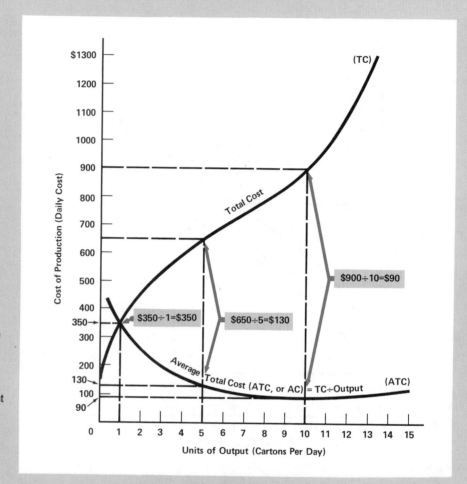

The total cost curve shows the sum of the fixed cost plus the variable cost at each daily output rate.

The average total cost curve shows the sum of the average fixed cost plus the average variable cost at each daily output rate.

You know that as output expands, total cost goes up. But the average cost (the per unit cost) goes down. Average cost keeps going down until your plant reaches its "maximum efficiency" rate of daily output (10 cartons per day). If output expands beyond that the average (per unit) cost will go up.

When output is low the average cost is high. You aren't producing many units to "spread" the high fixed cost. But if output is increased to more than 10 cartons per day, the average cost goes up again. Why? Because of the law of diminishing returns (the law of variable proportions). Of course!

This plant was designed to operate most efficiently at an output rate of 10 cartons per day. You can see that by looking at the average total cost curve.

Fig. 21-5 The Average Cost Curves: Total, Variable, and Fixed

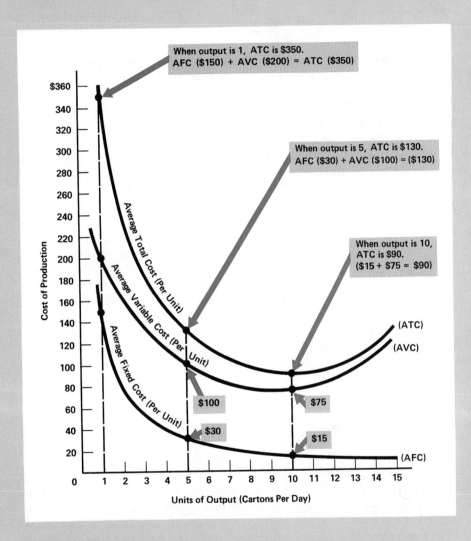

When output is 1, ATC is $350.
AFC ($150) + AVC ($200) = ATC ($350)

When output is 5, ATC is $130.
AFC ($30) + AVC ($100) = ($130)

When output is 10, ATC is $90.
($15 + $75 = $90)

Average Total Cost (Per Unit)

Average Variable Cost (Per Unit)

Average Fixed Cost (Per Unit)

Cost of Production

(ATC)

(AVC)

$100

$30

$75

$15

(AFC)

Units of Output (Cartons Per Day)

Average total cost is "total cost per unit." As output expands, ATC goes down as production gets more efficient. But too much production is inefficient so ATC goes up again.

Average total cost is the average fixed cost plus the average variable cost. Your per unit cost is lowest ($90 per carton) if you produce ten cartons per day. But you don't know whether or not you will produce at that rate because you don't know what the price is. You'll find out about that, later.

These curves are the same ones you saw on the preceding graphs. They look different here because the vertical axis has been stretched out again. When there aren't any *total* curves (when there are only *average* curves) in the graph, you can use a much larger scale on the vertical axis. That lets you see the "ups and downs" of the curves much better.

The Cost Curves Are Hypothetical

The cost curves show what the costs of a business "would be if . . ." If what? If the business was operating at each of the various output rates. But the business is not ever going to operate at all those different daily rates of output. Not ever!

You would never operate your jeans factory at the daily rate of only one unit of output. If you did your total cost would be $350. And you would have only one unit of output to sell! The only way you could break even would be to sell that unit of output for $350. Think for a minute. Suppose you *really could* sell that one unit for $350! Think how much profit you could make by producing and selling a lot more!

At a Very Low Selling Price You Would Shut Down

No, if the market for your jeans was so bad that all you could sell was one carton a day, you would just shut down your plant. You would lose the $150 of fixed cost. But the variable cost you would have to pay to produce that first unit is $200. The fixed cost plus the variable cost would be $350. Better for you to lose your fixed cost ($150) than to produce one unit and lose even more!

If someone happened to be willing to pay *more* than $200 for that one unit per day, and if that was all anyone would buy, what would you do then? You would produce 10 units a day for a few days and build up some inventory in your warehouse. Then you would shut down and sell one carton per day out of the inventory.

The very low output range of these cost curves is purely hypothetical. It's interesting to know what would happen to costs if daily output was only one unit. But really, most businesses only operate somewhere fairly close to their most efficient operating rate. If the market demand isn't great enough to let you operate your factory near your most efficient daily rate of output, then you will shut down until the mar-

ket gets better. Or you will produce some other product instead of jeans.

What about the very high outputs shown on the graphs? Are the curves only make-believe there, too? Usually, yes. You really can't expand your output very much beyond your most efficient operating range. The curves tell you that. If the demand was very strong and prices very high you would increase your output some. But not very much. You can't!

Look back at the last figure and see how steeply your total cost goes up when output goes beyond eleven units a day. The price would have to be very high to induce you to expand your daily output to as much as twelve or thirteen cartons.

Why is your "efficient range" of output so restricted? Why can't you just produce 2 or 3 units a day and still make a reasonable profit? And if the demand is great and the price goes up high, why can't you just go ahead and produce 15 or 20 or 30 cartons a day and make lots of profit? You can't do it because it's against the law. What law? The law of diminishing returns. Remember?

The Law of Diminishing Returns, Again

The way the variable (and total) costs change at different rates of output illustrates the **law of diminishing returns**. This "law" says that if a factory or a farm (or any kind of productive activity) expands its output more and more without adding any more land or buildings, sooner or later inefficiencies will occur. The **variable inputs** won't have enough **fixed inputs** to work with. Average (per unit) costs will go up.

You can increase your output some by adding more "variable inputs" (say labor) even though the amounts of some other inputs are fixed (say the size of your jeans factory). But there's a limit to how far you can go.

Sooner or later the extra output you get when you hire each successive "unit of the variable input"—labor, materials, etc.—will get smaller and smaller. The returns (extra product) received from the extra variable input, will diminish. So the more extra workers you hire the less extra output per worker you're going to get—and the more each extra unit of output is going to cost you.

The law of diminishing returns is one of the most important concepts in economics. In our "theory of the firm" it explains the shape of the variable and total cost curves. In the real world it influences decisions and costs and profits of all businesses. Think about it and be sure you understand it well.

MARGINAL COST

You know very well the importance of approaching economic choice situations (decision situations) by looking at marginal differences. So why has nothing been said in this chapter about marginal cost? I have waited until now to bring it up because the marginal cost curve confuses a lot of students. I believe you'll find it much easier to understand now that you have all the other cost curves clearly in place in your mind.

If you don't quite understand all the other cost curves (Figures 21-1, 2, 3, 4, 5) please go back now and study them. If you have a good command of all those graphs I don't think you'll have any difficulty understanding the marginal cost concept or the marginal cost curve. First, an overview of the marginal cost concept.

The "Per Unit Rate of Increase" in Total Cost

"Marginal cost" means "the addition to the total cost when you expand your daily output by one unit." Or you can say it this way: The marginal cost is the "per unit rate of increase" in the total cost as daily output expands one unit at a time. Or you can say it this way: If you increase

your daily output by one unit, your daily total cost will go up. By how much? By the amount of the marginal cost.

Suppose the marginal cost is high. Then as the output rate increases the total cost will go up fast. But if the marginal cost is low, total cost will rise slowly. What causes the total cost to increase as the rate of output expands? The marginal cost! Of course.

Suppose you are producing 10 cartons a day and I tell you that your marginal cost (at that rate of output) is $90. What does that mean? It means that your total cost is $90 higher when you're producing 10 cartons a day than it would be when you're producing only 9 cartons a day.

As you go through the graphs coming up, remember this: the marginal cost is what you have to pay for the additional variable factors needed to increase your rate of production by *one additional unit* of output. At any rate of output (output x) the marginal cost can be found by subtracting total cost at the one-unit smaller output rate (output x-1) from total cost at the present rate of output (output x).

Now you're ready for the marginal cost curve. The first figure (21-6) shows that "marginal cost" is "the rate of increase in the total cost." It shows that the *steeper* the total cost curve, the *higher* the marginal cost.

Then the next figures (21-7 and -8) show the marginal cost curve. There you'll see the important relationship between the marginal cost curve and all of the other cost curves.

So finally, here it is: the marginal cost curve. Study it carefully. Take your time and learn it well.

Fig. 21-6 Total Cost and Marginal Cost

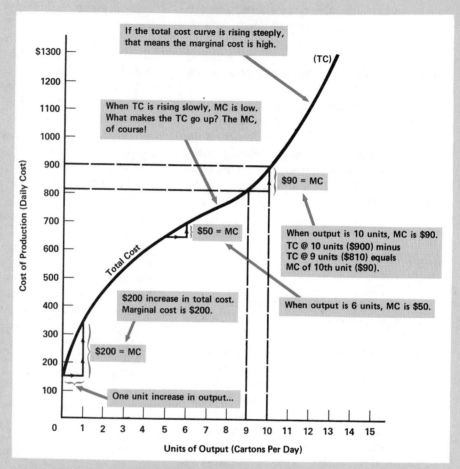

The marginal cost is the cost you have to pay for the extra variable inputs when you expand your output by one unit a day.

If you draw a "one-unit increase triangle," the altitude of the triangle (i.e., the height of the vertical line) is the marginal cost.

The marginal cost is the rate of increase in the total cost. It's how much the total cost goes up when output is increased by one unit. To figure the marginal cost for your 10-unit output, subtract the total cost of your 9-unit output from the total cost of your 10-unit output.

The marginal cost curve is a different kind of curve than anything you've run across yet. The marginal curve doesn't refer either to *the total* of anything or to *the average* of anything. All it tells you is this (and you should memorize this statement): *the marginal cost tells you how much greater the total cost would be at that daily rate of output than it would have been at a one-unit smaller daily rate of output.* That's all it tells you. But that's important. Why? Because it lets you know how much *extra cost* you must pay to get each additional output unit.

Would you expand your output if the marginal cost was high? Or not? That depends on how much you expect to get when you sell that "marginal output unit." If you expect to get enough for the "marginal output unit" to more than cover the "marginal cost" then you will produce it. It's ok to pay high *marginal cost* if the *marginal revenue* you're going to get is even higher!

Fig. 21-7 Deriving the Marginal Cost Curve

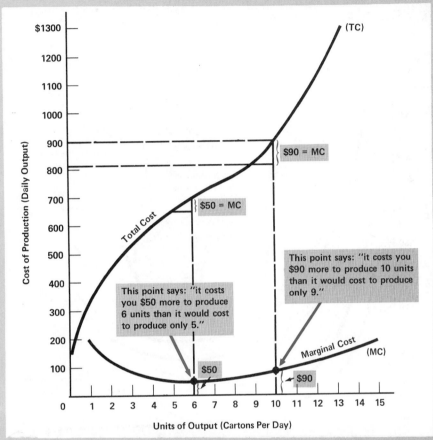

The marginal cost tells you how much extra cost you must pay to get each additional output unit.

When output is very small or very large, the marginal cost is high, because of the law of diminishing returns.

If you don't have to buy very many variable inputs (that is, if the inputs are highly productive) or if the price of the inputs is low, then the marginal cost will be low. But if you have to buy a lot of inputs (they aren't very productive) or if the price of the inputs is high, then the marginal cost will be high.

When you plot the altitude of each "marginal cost triangle" what you get is the marginal cost curve. On this graph the marginal cost curve looks very flat because the vertical scale is squeezed down so that the total cost curve won't run off the top of the page. In the next graph (21-8) you will get a much better picture of the marginal cost curve.

Be careful. Think very carefully about the marginal cost curve. Practice deriving it from the total cost curve, and practice drawing it and explaining it to yourself. It looks really simple. But it's quite tricky, and it's very important. So take time to learn it well.

The marginal cost for any rate of output is found by taking the total cost for that rate of output (output "x") and subtracting the total cost for the one-unit-smaller rate of output (output "x − 1"). The marginal cost for any rate of output is the *extra cost of expanding your output up to that rate (x) from the "one unit smaller" rate (x − 1).*

Fig. 21-8   Average and Marginal Cost Curves

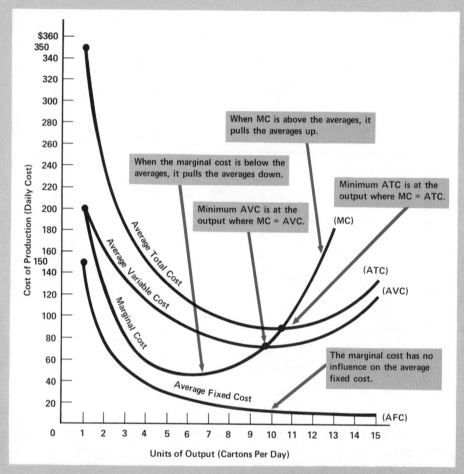

The marginal cost is the extra cost of the additional unit. If the cost of the unit is above the average it pulls the average cost up. If it's below the average it pulls the average cost down. Of course!

The marginal cost curve must go through the average total and the average variable cost curves at the place where the average curves are lowest. Why? Because as the rate of output is increased, if the extra cost of each extra unit is below the average, then the average will come down. If the extra cost of each extra unit is above the average, the average will go up. Of course!

If you are familiar with calculus you will see immediately that the marginal cost curve is the *first derivative* of the total cost curve. That is, marginal cost is the *rate of change* (increase) in total cost as output increases.

Therefore, when total cost is increasing fast (the TC curve is steep) marginal cost is high. When TC is increasing slowly, marginal cost is low. But if you aren't familiar with calculus you still won't have any trouble understanding marginal cost. You'll see.

Marginal Cost Pulls
the Averages Up or Down

When the marginal cost is below the averages it is pulling the averages down. When the marginal cost is above the averages it is pulling the averages up. Why? Because *the marginal is the addition!* If the "addition" is above the average, the average goes up. Here's an example.

Suppose your average in Econ is 80, then you take an additional (marginal) quiz and make 90. The average goes up because the marginal is above the average. But if you make 70 on the marginal quiz what happens to your average? It goes down. It works the same way with marginal cost.

If you expand your daily rate of output by one unit, the cost goes up. How much? That's the marginal cost. If your cost goes up $50, then your marginal cost is $50. If that $50 is higher than the average cost per unit, it's going to cause your average cost to increase. If the $50 is below your average (per unit) cost, then your average (per unit) cost will decrease. Higher "additional cost per unit" pulls *up* the "average cost per unit." Lower "additional cost per unit" pulls *down* the "average cost per unit." Of course!

When you look at the marginal cost at any rate of output it really doesn't tell you very much. It only tells you *how much more* it costs to produce at that rate of output than it would have cost if you had produced at a rate one unit less. That isn't very much information. It doesn't tell you anything about the overall per-unit cost of your product. It doesn't give you any idea whether your business is making a profit or not.

There is much that the marginal cost doesn't tell you. But the one thing it does tell you—how much extra cost you must pay to get each additional unit of output—is very important to know. Why? Because that's something you need to know before you can figure out *your most profitable rate of production!*

All this will be explained in the next chapter where you will find out about *revenues and profits.* But first we need to get this discussion of *cost curves* all tied up. At this point, Note: be sure you can draw and explain the cost curves!

HOW ALL THE COST CURVES ARE INTERRELATED

All these cost curves are different ways of looking at the same thing. Suppose you knew what your *total cost* would be, at each rate of output. Could you draw your *total cost* curve? Sure. But what about the other curves? Could you figure out your *total fixed cost?* and your *average fixed cost?* and your *total variable cost* and *average variable cost?* your *marginal cost?* Sure. No problem. Think about it for a minute and you will see that:

1. Your total cost curve tells you what your fixed cost is. When output is zero, then the total cost *is* the fixed cost.

2. The total cost curve tells you what your variable cost is. If you subtract your fixed cost from your total cost at each output what you have left is the variable cost.

3. Your total cost tells you the marginal cost, too. For any daily rate of output (output "x"), the marginal cost is the total cost at "output x" minus the total cost at "output x minus 1."

It's easy to get the fixed cost, the variable cost and the marginal cost when you know the total cost. But what about the average cost curves? That's just as easy. To convert totals to averages, just divide by the number of units of output. If output is 10 units and total cost is $900, the *average* total cost is $90. If fixed cost is $150, the *average* fixed cost is $15.

Suppose you know what the fixed cost is, and you know what the marginal cost would be for expanding output from zero to one unit, from one unit to two units, from two to three, and so on. Could you then figure the total cost? and the variable cost? and the average costs? Of course! The variable cost, for any output rate, would be the sum of all the marginal costs up to that rate of output. Add fixed cost to that and you have the total cost for that rate of output.

How neatly all these cost curves tie together! Surprising? Not really. They have to tie together. After all, we're looking at the same picture all the time—just in different ways.

Which Cost Curves Are Most Helpful?

What are all these curves good for? When should you want to look at the total cost curve? And when should you look at the average curves? That depends on what you are trying to find out. The total curves tell you immediately what your total costs would be at each output rate.

If you are interested in finding out the "per unit cost," the average cost curves will show you that immediately. Also they will show you immediately what rate of output gives you your lowest per unit cost, how much fixed cost is embodied in each unit at each rate of output, and how much variable cost is embodied in each unit. If these are the kinds of things you want to know, then you should look at the average curves.

Now You Need to Know the Selling Price

Now you know all about your costs at your Cullowhee jeans plant. So at what daily rate are you going to produce? And will you make a profit? or a loss? and how much? You can't yet say, can you? Of course not. You can't answer any of these questions until you know what *price* you're going to get for those cartons of jeans.

It's pretty obvious that if the price per carton was only a dollar, you wouldn't produce any at all. The best thing you could do would be to shut down your plant and pay the $150 daily fixed cost. As soon as you could you would either get rid of the plant and equipment, or shift into producing something else that pays enough to cover the cost of production.

If the price per carton was $1,000 you would produce all you possibly could. If the price is high enough, you can add to your profit by expanding your output and producing inefficiently!

Before you can go any farther in understanding "the theory of the firm" you're going to have to find out something about *revenues*—something about the *market demand and price* for your product. That's what you'll be reading about in the next chapter.

SUMMARY AND SYNTHESIS

Microeconomics is mostly concerned with understanding **how the market process works.** That means: **understanding supply and demand and the price mechanism.**

Understanding supply means understanding cost of production. Why? Because the **supply of a product** (i.e., the quantities which would be offered for sale at the various prices which might be offered for that product in the market) is determined by that product's **cost of production.** The **higher the cost the smaller the supply tends to be.**

A business firm's costs consist of **fixed cost** (overhead) which **must be paid even if nothing is** produced, and **variable cost** which **increases as the rate of output increases.**

The **total cost is lowest when nothing is produced.** It increases (fast at first, then more slowly, then faster again) as the **output rate increases.**

The **average (per unit) cost is lowest when** the business firm is operating at its **maximum efficiency rate of output.** The more the firm's actual output rate departs from this **maximum effi-**

ciency rate (either above or below) the higher the average cost will be.

As the firm's output rate increases, it is the law of diminishing returns which explains how the firm's costs will change. The marginal cost curve illustrates this "law."

At each output rate the marginal cost tells how much it would cost to expand from the "one-unit-smaller" output rate, to this output rate. So the marginal cost at each output rate is the additional cost (extra total cost) of producing this last additional unit.

If the marginal cost is high, total cost will be going up fast. If marginal cost is above the average (per unit) cost, then the average will be pulled up by the (higher) marginal cost.

All these cost/output relationships can be shown on graphs, with output on the horizontal (x) axis and cost ($) on the vertical (y) axis. Fixed cost (FC) will show up as a horizontal line. Variable cost (VC) will be a positive, non-linear curve, rising more steeply at very low or very high output rates and less steeply nearer the maximum efficiency output rate. The total cost (TC) curve is the variable cost curve shifted upward to reflect the size of the fixed cost.

In the "average" or "per unit" cost graph the average fixed cost (AFC) curve will be downward sloping to indicate that fixed cost per unit gets smaller as output increases. The average variable cost (AVC) and average total cost (ATC) curves will be high at very low or very high output rates. This illustrates the inefficiency (high cost) of inappropriate input proportions.

The lowest point on the average total cost curve indicates the maximum efficiency output rate. This indicates the most efficient proportions of variable input factors to fixed input factors.

The marginal cost (MC) curve is high at a very low output rate. This indicates that total cost would be pushed up sharply if output was increased from zero to one or a few units. Then the MC curve goes down low indicating a slow rate of increase in total cost as the firm expands output toward its "maximum efficiency" rate. The low MC is what pulls down AVC and ATC as output expands.

As the output rate increases more, the MC curve moves higher. Finally it cuts through the AVC and ATC curves, goes above them, and pulls them up. Average costs rise.

Considering these cost curves, which do you think would be the "best" output for the firm? Least total cost? (Zero output?) Of course not! Least average cost? (Maximum efficiency?) Maybe. But not necessarily. The best output is always the maximum profit output.

You can't choose the "best" (maximum profit) output for a firm on the basis of costs alone. You must know about the demand for this product and about prices and revenues. That's what you'll be reading about in the next chapter.

REVIEW EXERCISES

MAJOR CONCEPTS, PRINCIPLES, TERMS (Explain each carefully.)

the law of diminishing returns
the nature and influence of "marginal cost"
the relationships among the cost curves

OTHER CONCEPTS AND TERMS (Explain each briefly.)

total cost
fixed cost
overhead
variable cost

variable factors
average total cost
average fixed cost
average variable cost

CURVES AND GRAPHS (Draw, label, and explain each.)

Fixed Cost and Average Fixed Cost
Variable Cost and Average Variable Cost
Fixed Cost Plus Variable Cost Equals Total Cost
Total Cost and Average Total Cost
The Average Cost Curves: Total, Variable, and Fixed
Total Cost and Marginal Cost
Deriving the Marginal Cost Curve
Average and Marginal Cost Curves

QUESTIONS (Write out answers, or jot down key points.)

1. Draw a total cost curve and mark off and number both axes. Then derive from the total cost curve (a) the total fixed cost and (b) the total variable cost. Then derive: (c) the average total cost, (d) the average variable cost, (e) the average fixed cost, and finally (f) the marginal cost. If you can do all that you understand the relationships between the curves. If you can't, you don't. (Use graph paper if you have any around. Graph paper makes it easier.)

2. Suppose the wage rate goes up. What does that do to the total cost curve? Or suppose local property taxes are doubled. Or suppose electric power gets more expensive. Or suppose you tear down your old jeans plant and build a new one twice as big. Can you see how each of these changes would change your total cost picture? Can you draw a new total cost curve to reflect each of these changes? Try.

3. A producer would not produce jeans or any other product at a *very low* rate of output. Explain why.

4. Can you see how important the law of diminishing returns (variable proportions) can be in helping to understand "the economic problem" as seen by the business manager? Discuss.

22

Revenue Analysis: Market Demand, Prices, and the Firm's Revenues

Chapter Objectives

- In this part of the book we're concerned with **supply.** In the last chapter you learned a lot about **the business firm's costs,** which influence supply.

- But you can't tell **how much** a firm will produce and **supply to the market** until you know about the **demand and price of the product**—i.e., about **the firm's revenue opportunities.** That's what you'll learn in this chapter.

- When you finish studying this chapter you will know **how the business firm's revenue changes** in response to **changes in the rate of output and sales.**

- You will be able to **draw and explain the total revenue curve, the average revenue (demand) curve,** and the **marginal revenue curve** both (a) for businesses in **pure competition** and (b) for businesses with **monopoly power.**

- You will be able to draw and explain graphs which illustrate: (a) the **changing elasticity** of the **straight-line demand curve,** (b) **consumer's surplus,** and (c) **price discrimination.**

Businesses Produce to Earn Revenue

Why do businesses produce? To sell things, of course. To bring in money. Hopefully to make profits.

When a business sells its daily (or weekly or monthly) output, what it receives in return is its daily (or weekly or monthly) revenue. If the revenue coming in is greater than the cost going out, then the business is making a profit.

You know what determines the cost. It's the fixed cost plus the variable cost. The total cost curve shows how high the cost would be for any rate of output you might choose. You learned all about that in the last chapter.

HOW REVENUE CHANGES AS OUTPUT CHANGES

What determines the daily (or weekly or monthly) revenue? The *number of units* sold and the *price per unit.* Obviously. If the quantity sold increases or if the price per unit increases, total revenue goes up. If either the quantity sold or the price goes down, the revenue goes down.

If you want more revenue, all you have to do is produce and sell more output for the same price (if you can). Or sell the same amount at a higher price (if you can). But that may not always be easy to do! It *depends on the market demand for your product.* Right?

Also here's something else to consider: When you produce more, your cost goes up. Remember? We'll talk more about that later. Right now you need to know about how *the revenue goes up as output and sales go up.*

Total Revenue: The "Constant Price" Case

If you sell more, or if you sell the same and charge more, you get more revenue!

Suppose you're still operating your Cullowhee, N.C. jeans plant. But you got tired of the uncertainty of wholesaling your jeans to all those department stores in Asheville and Rock Hill and Texarkana and all over. So you made a special deal to sell all your output to a big retailing company (maybe Sears). They will buy all the output you can produce and they will pay you a flat rate of $100 a carton. Now you know *exactly* what your total revenue is going to be for each rate of output you might choose.

If you produce one unit a day your total revenue will be $100 a day. If you produce two units your total revenue will be $200. If you produce 10 your revenue will be $1,000. Obviously.

Marginal Revenue: The "Constant Price" Case

What about the **marginal revenue**? How much "extra revenue" do you get when you expand your daily rate of output and sales by one unit? When you expand from zero to one, how much does that add to your total revenue? Or when you expand from one to two, how much does that add? Or from nine to ten? The marginal revenue is always the same: $100. *If the price is always the same, the marginal revenue must*

be always the same.

What about the **average revenue** per unit (per carton)? You can see right off that it must be $100. If you get $100 for each carton, then the average revenue per carton has to be $100. Anytime you sell your entire output all for the same price then that price obviously will always be the "average revenue received per unit sold." Of course! So in this case the marginal revenue and the average revenue are always the same—always $100, no matter what rate of output you choose.

Can you guess what the *total revenue* and the *marginal revenue* and the *average revenue* are going to look like on a graph? Sure. The **total revenue** is going to be a straight line with a positive slope. The higher the rate of output and sales, the higher the total revenue. If you want to impress somebody, you can say "the total revenue is a positive and linear function of output and sales."

What about the marginal revenue curve? It's a straight line too. But it will be perfectly horizontal and located at the $100 level. The marginal revenue curve will show that the marginal revenue never gets any higher or lower than $100 no matter what rate of output and sales you choose.

What about the average revenue curve? It will be the same as the marginal revenue curve. Of course! And you already know why. Figure 22-1 shows the picture. Take a few minutes now and be sure you understand that graph.

DEMAND FOR ONE SELLER'S OUTPUT: THE "PURE COMPETITION"CASE

When you can sell all you want to for a fixed price of $100, what does the demand for your output look like? Think about it. You can sell as little or as much as you wish, all for the same price. So *from your point of view,* how elastic is the demand for your jeans? It's infinitely elastic!

Infinitely Elastic Demand

You could increase your output to four or five times as much and the price wouldn't go down at all. *The quantity bought will respond greatly, with no price change! That's what is meant by "infinitely elastic" demand.*

This situation—where you have a contract to sell as many cartons as you wish for a fixed price—usually wouldn't happen. Usually a contract between a buyer and seller would specify both the price and the quantity to be delivered. But what about sellers in a market structure of pure competition?

Can't firms in **pure competition** sell all they wish at the going price? True. So from each seller's point of view the demand would be infinitely elastic? Right!

Suppose the price of eggs goes up and your brother over in Gatlinburg, Tennessee decides to stop producing broilers and start producing eggs for the Nashville market. If the going price of eggs in Nashville is a dollar a dozen, how much does your brother expect to get for his eggs? A dollar a dozen, of course. And how many dozen does he expect to be able to sell? As many as he wants!

Fig. 22-1 Total Revenue and Marginal Revenue When Price Is Constant

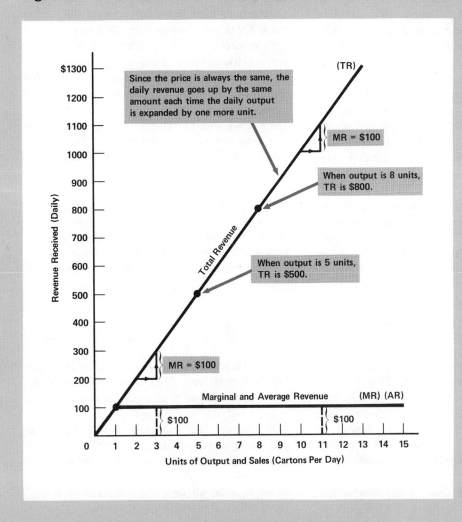

Since the price is always the same, the daily revenue goes up by the same amount each time the daily output is expanded by one more unit.

MR = $100

When output is 8 units, TR is $800.

When output is 5 units, TR is $500.

MR = $100

Marginal and Average Revenue (MR) (AR)

$100 $100

If the price doesn't change, the total revenue curve will be a straight line. The higher the price, the steeper the line.

The more you sell the more revenue you take in.

When output expands one unit, revenue goes up $100. MR is always $100.

If the price dropped to $50, the marginal revenue curve would shift downward and the total revenue curve would rise by only $50 a unit.

The Demand for the Seller in Pure Competition

Your brother is a seller in pure competition. He can produce and sell one dozen or 10 dozen or 50 dozen and he expects to get the going market price. So your brother sees the demand for the output of his "individual firm" as infinitely elastic. Zero change in price while quantity increases or decreases without limit? Sure. Infinite demand elasticity!

Of course you and I know that if a lot of farmers start doing what your brother is doing, pretty soon the price of eggs will go down. But no one farmer feels any responsibility for the drop in price. All the egg farmers just accept the market price as "given." They don't expect it to change because of anything they might do. And for each farmer individually, that's true. But for all of them together, as you very well know, it is not true.

If many new sellers enter the market, the increased supply will force the price down. But at any moment, no matter how high or low the market price happens to be, the individual seller will still see the demand as being infinitely elastic at the price which exists.

Now here are two graphs that show all this. Figures 22-2 and 22-3 first show how supply and demand set the market price. Then they show how the market price sets the "level of the demand curve" as seen by the individual seller in pure competition. Take a few minutes to study those figures now.

Pure Competition in the Real World

There are many producers in the real world who are selling in markets where there is something like pure competition on the sellers' side. Most agricultural producers sell for whatever the market price happens to be at harvest time.

Farmers don't like to have their fortunes hanging on the uncertainty of the market price. Not if they can help it. Sometimes they try to organize and limit the flow of supplies to the market to try to keep prices up. And governments are often called on to stabilize prices of farm products. You'll be reading more about this later. But now it's time to get into the other kind of market structures—where the seller *isn't* selling in pure competition.

DEMAND FOR ONE SELLER'S OUTPUT: THE "MONOPOLY POWER" CASE

For the rest of this chapter we're going to be talking about market structures where the number of sellers is small enough so that each seller's output does have some influence on the market price. Or to say it differently: We'll be concerned with market structures in which the sellers have some **market power** or **monopoly power.**

When a seller is big enough to have some influence on the market price then that seller has some monopoly power. That seller can't look at the market price as "given." Monopolistic sellers can never forget about the effect of their output rate on the market price. Otherwise they would go broke!

Monopoly power results in some very different output decisions by businesses. So to give you a personal view of how businesses behave in this kind of market structure, here you are back again in your jeans business. But the situation is different. Now you have some "monopoly power."

The "Decreasing Price" Case

If you're selling all your jeans to Sears for $100 a carton, you don't have to worry about whether or not you're going to be able to sell all of your output. You can sell all you want to for $100 a carton. That's the easy way. But suppose you thought you could do better by going it alone. You could just send your sales force out to sell your "Cullowhee True-Forms" to the stores in Asheville and Texarkana and all over.

Fig. 22-2   Market Demand and the Demand for One Seller's Output in Pure Competition

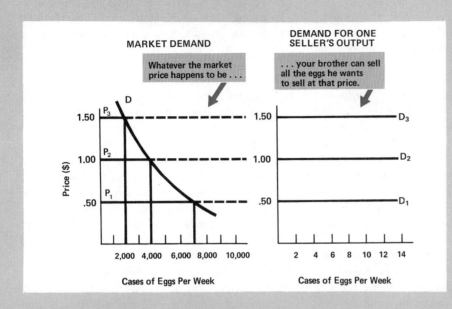

MARKET DEMAND

Whatever the market price happens to be . . .

DEMAND FOR ONE SELLER'S OUTPUT

. . . your brother can sell all the eggs he wants to sell at that price.

The demand for the output of one seller doesn't slope downward, because each seller in pure competition produces such a small part of the total supply. Suppose your brother produced 6 or 8 or 12 or 14 cases. What difference would that make in a market where 4,000 cases are being exchanged? No difference.

Fig. 22-3   Market Demand Increases so the Price Goes Up

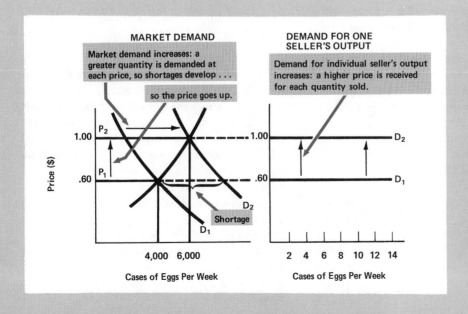

MARKET DEMAND

Market demand increases: a greater quantity is demanded at each price, so shortages develop . . .

so the price goes up.

DEMAND FOR ONE SELLER'S OUTPUT

Demand for individual seller's output increases: a higher price is received for each quantity sold.

Shortage

When the market demand increases, shortages develop. Some buyers offer more. The price goes up.

The individual seller in pure competition sees the demand as being "the market price." That's all.

Now things are going to be very different! The lower the price you charge the more you can sell. If you sell the jeans for $100 a carton you can sell more than if you charge $150 a carton. Maybe you could sell a few cartons for as much as $200. (Probably not many.)

The lower the price you charge, the more profit the stores can make when they sell your jeans to their customers. So the lower the price, the more they will buy. That's what the law of demand says: at lower prices, buyers will buy more. The law of demand works in the wholesale markets too? Sure.

What a different situation this is! Now you have two things to worry about: (1) how many cartons to produce, and (2) how much to charge per carton. If you decide on a high price then you will be able to sell only a small quantity; if you decide to produce and sell a large quantity, you won't be able to sell all of them unless you lower the price.

Now what does the demand for your product look like? It's no longer a straight horizontal line! Now, at high prices you can sell a few. At lower prices you can sell more. The demand for your output has negative slope!

How much more can you sell at lower prices? That depends on the **elasticity of the demand** for your jeans, of course!

How Elastic Is the Demand? Can you see why you are now very interested in knowing the elasticity of the demand for your jeans? Suppose you set the price up high: $200. And suppose you could sell only one carton a day at that price. Then what would happen if you lowered your price to $190?

If the demand happens to be highly elastic then maybe you could sell 3 or 4 or maybe even 5 a day at the lower price. But what if the demand is highly inelastic? You might have to lower the price all the way down to maybe $100 to get the stores to buy more than one carton a day.

How Demand Elasticity Affects Total Revenue. If the demand is relatively elastic, the quantity changes more than the price changes. So with relatively elastic demand, when the price is cut, the "upward effect" of the increased quantity brings in enough revenue to more than offset the "downward effect" of the lower price.

If the demand is relatively inelastic, the quantity changes less than the price changes. The "upward effect" of the increased quantity would not bring in enough revenue to offset the "downward effect" of the lower price.

See what happens? *With relatively inelastic demand a price cut will reduce total revenue.* Marginal revenue will be negative! See how important the elasticity of demand can be when a producer is thinking about lowering the price to try to sell more?

Demand and Total Revenue for the Monopolistic Seller

Here's an example. Let's suppose: if you set the price at $200 you could sell only one carton a day. If you lower the price to $190 you could sell two cartons a day. If you lower the price to $180 you could sell three cartons. To make it easy, let's just assume that each time you want to increase your daily sales by one more carton you must cut your price by another $10.

Suppose we build a demand curve showing this. What would it look like? Straight line? Negative slope? Sure. And what about the total revenue at different price-and-quantity combinations? The table and graphs on the next three pages show and explain all this. So now, on to Figures 22-4, 5, and 6.

Fig. 22-4   The Demand and Marginal Revenue Schedules and Curves for the Monopolistic Seller

If there are only a few sellers of jeans in your territory, then each of you has some monopoly power. Here's a picture of your price-and-quantity alternatives.

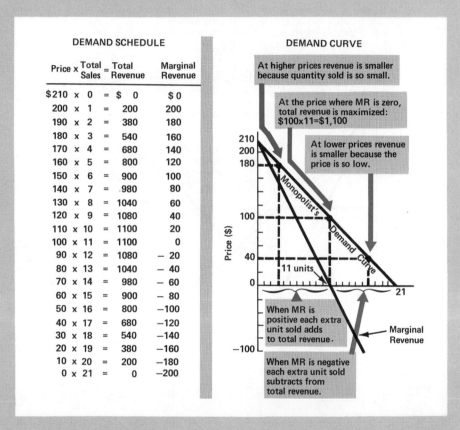

The demand and marginal revenue curves show exactly the same things as the demand and marginal revenue schedules.

Can you see that the rectangles drawn under the demand curve are really *total revenue* rectangles? The bigger the rectangle the higher total revenue? Sure. Each rectangle shows quantity times price. That's total revenue, of course.

The quantity times price is also "base" times "height" for that rectangle. And what's "base times height"? It's the area of the rectangle! So the size of the rectangle represents the size of total revenue.

Looking at the total revenue rectangles, do you get any ideas about the *price elasticity* of this demand curve? Think about it. Then go on to the next graph and see if you figured it out right.

Fig. 22-5   Elasticity of the Straight-Line Demand Curve

When you lower the price, if the demand is "price elastic" you'll get more revenue. If it isn't, then you won't.

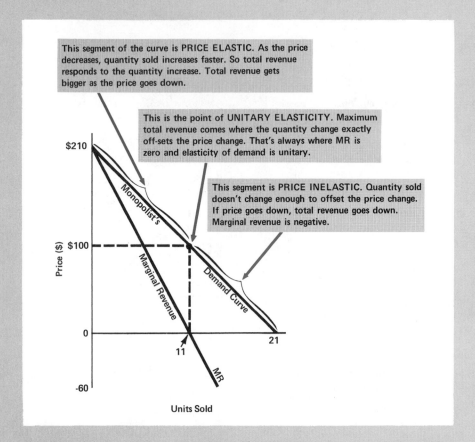

This segment of the curve is PRICE ELASTIC. As the price decreases, quantity sold increases faster. So total revenue responds to the quantity increase. Total revenue gets bigger as the price goes down.

This is the point of UNITARY ELASTICITY. Maximum total revenue comes where the quantity change exactly off-sets the price change. That's always where MR is zero and elasticity of demand is unitary.

This segment is PRICE INELASTIC. Quantity sold doesn't change enough to offset the price change. If price goes down, total revenue goes down. Marginal revenue is negative.

Monopolist's

Marginal Revenue

Demand Curve

MR

Units Sold

Each point on a straight line demand curve has a different elasticity—the lower the price, the lower the elasticity.

Why is the marginal revenue curve so far below the demand curve? For example, when you sell the eleventh carton of jeans, you receive $100 from the sale of that carton. But the marginal revenue curve says that the eleventh item doesn't add anything to your total revenue? Why not?

What did you have to do to sell the eleventh carton? You had to cut your price from $110 to $100. So how much did you lose when you cut the price? You lost $10 on each of the units you could have sold for $110. How many units was that? Ten units. So you lost $100!

Your "price cut" cost you $100. Your "quantity increase" (the sale of the eleventh unit) brought in $100. So what's the net addition to your total revenue? Zero. That's exactly what the marginal revenue curve shows you.

The next graph shows a picture of the total revenue. It also shows the same demand and marginal revenue as shown in this graph. But as you will see, on the next graph the scale is much smaller.

Fig. 22-6 Total, Average, and Marginal Revenue for the Monopolistic Seller

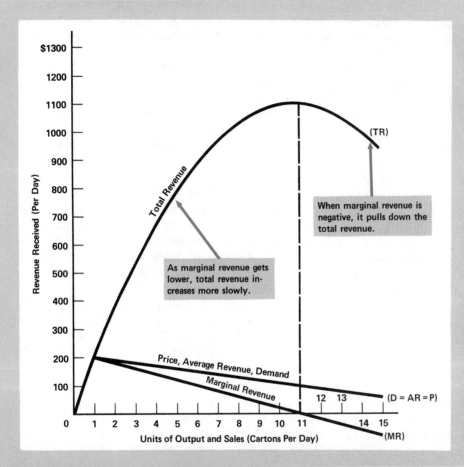

As marginal revenue gets lower, total revenue increases more slowly.

When marginal revenue is negative, it pulls down the total revenue.

As you lower the price to sell more, total revenue increases more slowly all the time. If you keep cutting the price, after awhile your total revenue will go down!

This graph shows the same picture as the two previous graphs. But here the vertical scale is much smaller and the total revenue is shown as a *curve* instead of as *rectangles beneath the demand curve.*

This graph and the two previous ones show you that your "maximum revenue" price-and-quantity combination is $100 and 11 units. So is that the best price and quantity for you to choose? No. That is, not unless your cost of production is zero! We'll get into the question of *cost of production* very soon. Until then, just remember this: You can't make any decisions on the basis of revenue alone. You must also know what your costs are.

(*Note:* You may have noticed that on this figure and the two previous ones, total revenue is just as high at a price of $110, where 10 units are sold. Actually, if the units were divisible, your maximum profit would occur at 10.5 units at a price of $105. That would give you a total revenue of $1,102.50. That's $2.50 higher than the total revenue you could get at an output of either 10 units or 11 units.)

Monopolistic Pricing, Output, and Total Revenue: A Summary

The three figures you just studied brought you a long way in understanding demand as seen by the monopolistic seller. Also, they tell you quite a lot about elasticity of demand. Here's a brief summary of the situation.

When you have monopoly power in the market it means you can raise the price if you want to. But if you do, you can't sell as much. Or if you want to, you can lower the price and sell more. You're caught between these two opposing movements: price and quantity. *It makes a lot of difference to you whether it's the price or the quantity that changes most. And that's determined by the elasticity of the demand.*

Demand Elasticity and Total Revenue. When you're producing at a low rate and the price is high, chances are the demand is price elastic. So you can lower your price and sell more and get more revenue. Why?

(1) because the price is so high it adds a lot to your revenue, and

(2) because you don't lose much revenue when you lower your price. You don't have much "previous revenue" to lose!

What happens as you lower the price more and more? Your total revenue increases less and less with each additional "$10 price cut and one more unit sold." The curve bends and gets more nearly horizontal.

Marginal Revenue. What about the *marginal revenue*? When total revenue isn't going up as fast that means the marginal revenue is get-

ting smaller. It *must be* getting smaller.

What's the marginal? It's the increase in the total when you increase your sales by one unit. "Smaller increase in the total" means the same thing as "smaller marginal." Of course.

Average Revenue. As the price gets lower the average revenue gets lower too. Why? Because if you're selling all of your output at the same price per unit, then the price per unit is the "average revenue per unit." "Average (per unit) revenue" means "price (per unit)." Of course.

Elasticity Usually Decreases as Sales Increase. When prices are high and quantities are low the straight line demand curve shows relatively elastic (price elastic) demand. When prices are low and the quantities are high the curve shows relatively inelastic (price inelastic) demand. You can see that in Figure 22-5. But why is this true?

Suppose a producer is selling *ten units a day* and then lowers the price a dollar to try to sell more. The price cut "costs" $10 of "previous revenues" ($1 per unit lost on 10 units). Will sales increase enough to more than make up for the ten dollar revenue loss? If so, demand is **price elastic.**

Now suppose the producer is selling a *thousand units a day* and then lowers the price a dollar. How much "previous revenues" will that "cost"? A thousand dollars! Are sales likely to increase enough to make up for the thousand dollars of the lost revenue? Probably not. So when the price goes down it pulls the total revenue down. Demand is **price inelastic.**

Price Line, Average Revenue Curve, Demand Curve. The price line, the average revenue curve, and the demand curve are all the same thing. You know that the price is always the average revenue. It has to be.

If you are selling things for $100, then the average revenue per unit is $100. If you are selling things for $20 each then the average revenue per unit is $20. Price and average revenue are always the same thing. (Unless you are using price discrimination—that is, charging different prices to different buyers. We'll talk about that in a minute.)

What about the demand curve? How is it that the demand curve is the same thing as the price line? Think about it. What's a demand curve? It's a "price line." It shows price-and-quantity combinations. That's all. Any *price* you choose shows the *quantity* the buyers will buy. So sure enough: Your average revenue curve, price line, and demand curve are all the same curve.

PRICE DISCRIMINATION AND CONSUMER'S SURPLUS

As you have been thinking about what price you might charge for your Cullowhee jeans, you may have thought about the idea of using **price discrimination**. It's a profitable thing to do—if you can make it work. Why so profitable? Because when you lower the price to sell more, *you don't lower the price to everybody!*

Here's the idea: Some buyers will pay $200 a carton for your jeans. Others will pay only $190. Others will pay only $150. Also, buyers who would pay $200 for one, might buy a second if they could get it for $100.

What if you could somehow *get all buyers to pay the maximum amount they would be willing to pay* for each unit bought. Then you could really make a killing! To understand this idea you need to know something about the concept economists call **consumer's surplus**.

Consumer's Surplus: Satisfaction You Don't Have to Pay For

Suppose it's a hot day and you just finished a fast game or you just ran across campus or you just rode your bike up a long hill—anyway,

whatever you did, now you're all hot and thirsty. How good it's going to be to get a big drink of cold water!

How much would you pay for a big drink of water if you had to? Suppose someone had monopolized the supply of water and was charging a dollar a pint. Would you pay it? Yes. If you had to, you would. Maybe you'd get mad and hold out until tomorrow. But sooner or later you'd pay it. Why? Because when you're really thirsty, water is worth more than a dollar a pint to you.

See how lucky we all are? We get several dollars' worth of "utility value" from the water we drink every day. If we had to pay several dollars, we would. But we don't have to pay several dollars! Water sells for such a low price that it's almost free!

Now do you get the idea of what consumer's surplus is? Sure. *Consumer's surplus is the utility or satisfaction you get that you don't have to pay for.* Whenever you can get something for less than you would have been willing to pay for it, then you're getting "consumer's surplus." Now look at Figure 22-7 and you'll see what it looks like on a graph.

Price Discrimination: Charging What the Traffic Will Bear

What does consumer's surplus have to do with **monopolistic pricing**? And price discrimination? Just this: suppose the monopolist can somehow split up the market—that is, separate the *different buyers* of the product or separate the *different uses* of the product—and charge higher prices in the higher demand markets and lower prices in the lower demand markets.

Fig. 22-7   Consumer Demand and Consumer's Surplus

The demand for water in your local metropolitan area.

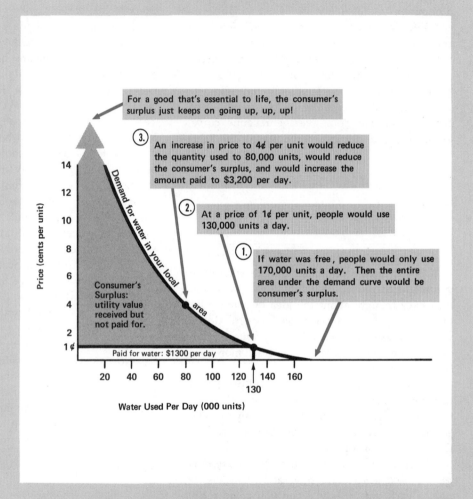

For an essential good like water you receive a lot of satisfaction that you don't have to pay for. The consumer's surplus is very high!

This graph illustrates the idea of consumer's surplus. For almost every good, some people who are buying it are receiving some consumer's surplus.

If the price of something went up, would some people still buy it? If the answer is yes, then that means those people are now receiving consumer's surplus.

The idea of consumer's surplus gives a vivid illustration of the fact that "value received" from a good—in terms of personal satisfaction—does not necessarily depend on how many dollars a person must pay to buy it!

Nobody charges you anything for the pleasure you get from watching a beautiful sunset or from hearing the voice of someone you love. And think how great it is to be able to take a big breath of air without having to pay for it! Talk about consumer's surplus! Wow!

Suppose someone really did monopolize the water supply and charged a dollar a pint for water. They wouldn't sell much water, true. But they would sure make a big profit on what they did sell! If they lowered the price would they make more profit? Probably not. But if they could use price discrimination, *yes, they would!*

Suppose they decided to keep selling "A-grade" water for drinking at a dollar a pint, but to sell "B-grade" water for washing clothes at 10¢ a gallon and "C-grade" water for flushing toilets at 2¢ a gallon. Of course, they would have to do something to make B-grade water unfit for drinking and C-grade water unfit for washing clothes. But if they did that they could make millions!

The purpose of price discrimination is to "gather up" the consumer's surplus and turn it into monopoly profits.

Is there any way you might use price discrimination in selling your jeans? If some people are standing there ready willing and able to pay more, you wouldn't mind giving them an opportunity to do so, would you? So how might you do it?

One way would be to "differentiate" your product—to put out "different quality" packages. Perhaps the quality of all of the jeans might be about the same, but you could label the $200 carton as "very exceptional quality." And you might offer buyers of the $200 carton a 10% discount on the second carton and maybe half price on the third.

You might even put out a dozen or so different grades of jeans. You could label some "standard quality," some "low-priced, economy" and you could have all sorts of variations in between. Also, you could use various ways of discounting each kind. See the possibilities?

Another method I'm sure you're familiar with is this: Set your price high enough to bring you a comfortable profit, and keep it there most of the time. Then once every spring or fall or maybe right after Christmas, run a big sale. Then the people who wouldn't buy at the regular price will come rushing in to buy!

Businesses use all kinds of price discrimination techniques to try to increase their profits. Sometimes the product is differentiated. Other times the high-priced buyers may be given special attention—maybe treated to free cocktails in the VIP lounge. But the idea is always the same: charge the higher price to the buyer who will pay the higher price.

"But," you say, "price discrimination is not fair! Why should some buyers have to pay more than others for the same product?"

You may have a point. And maybe that's why there are laws—both federal laws and some state and local laws—prohibiting *some kinds* of price discrimination. But many kinds of price discrimination are perfectly legal.

Some kinds of price discrimination are economically and socially desirable. To some people it's very important to buy the most prestigious brand names, and the higher the price the greater the prestige—so the more they like it. And some people want what they want when they want it. They don't want to wait until things go on sale.

Total Revenue of the Monopolistic Seller Using Price Discrimination

In the real world, price discrimination of one kind or another can be found almost everywhere. Why? Because it's such good business! Look at Figure 22-8 and you will see! That graph shows nearly perfect price discrimination—the monopolist gets nearly all of the consumer's surplus. No seller is likely to succeed in getting it all. But some sellers probably succeed in getting quite a lot of it! Now, take a minute and study the graph.

Now that you understand something about price discrimination, we're going to put it aside for a while. In the chapters coming up we will be assuming that the monopolistic seller can't use price discrimination—that is, if you cut your price to anyone you must cut it to everyone. Later (in Part Seven) you'll run into price discrimination again.

Fig. 22-8   Total Revenue of the Monopolist Using Price Discrimination

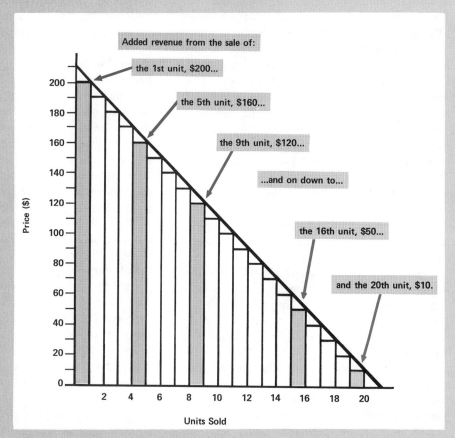

Added revenue from the sale of:

the 1st unit, $200...

the 5th unit, $160...

the 9th unit, $120...

...and on down to...

the 16th unit, $50...

and the 20th unit, $10.

With price discrimination you sell at a high price to the buyers who will pay a high price and you find some way to cut the price to other buyers. That way you can sell to them too, without cutting the price to the high-price buyers!

If you could sell one carton for $200 and take in $200, while also selling one for $190 and one for $180 and one for $170 and one for $160, etc., your total revenue would then be equal to all these little rectangles. With "perfect price discrimination" you could turn the entire area under the demand curve into your total revenue area!

The greatest total revenue you could collect would be $2,310. It's the sum of all of the revenues received—of all the prices shown on the vertical axis (or in the table, back in Figure 21-4): $200 + $190 + $180 + . . . + $10 = $2,310. That's a lot more than the $1,100 you can get without price discrimination!

If you could use "perfect price discrimination" your marginal revenue curve would not be below your demand curve. Why? Because you aren't lowering the price to the "high-demand" buyers! There's no "subtraction from revenue" from price-lowering—only the "addition to revenue" from selling each additional unit. So all the money you take in when you sell an additional unit is additional revenue. Your demand curve is your MR curve!

SUMMARY AND SYNTHESIS

A firm produces output and sells it to get revenue. How much revenue it gets depends on (a) how much it produces and sells and (b) the selling price.

Suppose you produce and sell more. Does that make the price go down? In pure competition, no. But if you have monopoly power, yes.

So if you're selling in pure competition the demand curve for your output is horizontal—infinitely elastic. The price stays the same—i.e., the "average revenue" is constant.

If you have some monopoly power, the demand curve for your output slopes downward. Your price and average revenue (AR) get lower as you increase your output and sell more.

In pure competition, each additional unit you produce and sell brings you the same revenue—i.e., the marginal revenue (MR) is constant. So the marginal revenue curve also shows the average revenue, the price, and the demand for this seller's output. It's a horizontal line.

The total revenue (TR) curve is positive and linear. How fast it goes up (how steep it is) depends on how high the price is. When the price goes up, the horizontal MR curve shifts upward and the positive and linear TR curve becomes steeper.

If you're running a business firm which has some monopoly power (some control over the price of what you're selling—and most firms do), that's different. You must cut the price to increase your sales.

The demand curve (price line, or AR curve) for your output slopes downward. So as you sell more and more, your total revenue (TR) goes up less and less. Your TR curve goes up steeply at first, then less steeply. If you keep cutting your price and selling more and more, eventually the TR curve will turn down (become negative).

Your MR curve goes down even more steeply than your demand curve because it reflects both (a) the lower price of the marginal unit sold (as indicated by the "price line"—i.e., the demand curve) and (b) the revenue which you forfeit on all of those other units which you could have sold at a higher price if you hadn't lowered your price to enable you to sell that "marginal unit."

The elasticity of a downward-sloping straight-line demand curve is different at each point along the curve. The higher the price (the smaller the quantity demanded) the higher the elasticity. The higher the elasticity, the higher the marginal revenue the monopolistic seller could get by lowering the price and selling more.

When demand elasticity is high, a small price cut can induce a great increase in sales (and in total revenue). But when demand elasticity is low, you'll lose revenue if you cut the price. That means marginal revenue is negative. Any monopolistic producer in this situation would certainly raise the price!

Consumer's surplus means satisfaction you get but don't have to pay for. Suppose it's raining hard and you'd be willing to pay $20 for an umbrella to keep from getting soaked. But you can get an umbrella for $4.98. So you get $15.02 of consumer's surplus. Great!

Price discrimination means charging different prices to different buyers. It means trying to charge each buyer as much as that buyer is willing to pay, so that the consumer's surplus is turned into monopoly profits. On rainy days, the price-discriminating seller puts $20 price tags on umbrellas!

Many (most?) businesses use some forms of price discrimination. When you have monopoly power it's very profitable to use price discrimination whenever you can.

REVIEW EXERCISES

MAJOR CONCEPTS, PRINCIPLES, TERMS (Explain each carefully.)

effect of elasticity of demand on total revenue
elasticity of demand for one seller's output
elasticity of a straight-line demand curve
consumer's surplus
why marginal revenue is lower than price for a monopolistic seller
why elasticity decreases as sales increase
why "Price line" = "AR curve" = "Demand curve"

OTHER CONCEPTS AND TERMS (Explain each briefly.)

total revenue	monopoly power
marginal revenue	market power
average revenue	monopolistic seller
price elastic demand	price discrimination
price inelastic demand	perfect price discrimination
infinitely elastic demand	total revenue rectangle

CURVES AND GRAPHS (Draw, label and explain each.)

Total Revenue and Marginal Revenue When Price Is Constant
Market Demand and the Demand for One Seller's Output in Pure Competition
Market Demand Increases so the Price Goes Up
The Demand and Marginal Revenue Schedules and Curves for the Monopolistic Seller
Elasticity of the Straight-Line Demand Curve
Total, Average, and Marginal Revenue for the Monopolistic Seller
Consumer Demand and Consumer's Surplus
Total Revenue of the Monopolist Using Price Discrimination

QUESTIONS (Write out answers or jot down key points.)

1. Suppose you owned a mineral spring and you were charging people for coming and getting jugs of water. Your cost of production is zero, so you want to maximize your total revenue. That will bring you your maximum profit. You would set the price where the elasticity of the demand is unitary. Explain why.

2. Now suppose you use price discrimination in selling your jugs of water. Explain it and draw a graph illustrating it.

3. It is necessary for the monopolistic seller to lower the price to sell more. But all the pure competitive seller needs to worry about is how much to produce. There's no limit on the amount that can be sold! So really, the seller in pure competition has the advantage. Right? Discuss.

4. Once you start thinking about consumer's surplus you begin to realize just how much of the total satisfaction or utility most people receive in life really *doesn't* have to be paid for. Think of some examples, and then discuss this question: "Is it true that the best things in life are free?" What do you think?

23

Short-Run Costs and Revenues: The "Optimum Output" Decision, and the Market Supply Curve

Chapter Objectives

- In the two previous chapters you learned about the **costs and revenues of the individual firm.** In this chapter you will find out how to use these curves (a) to find the **most profitable output,** and (b) to find out **how much profit or loss** the business is making.

- When you finish studying this chapter you will be able to explain **marginal cost, marginal revenue,** and **marginal profit** and to draw graphs illustrating these principles.

- You will be able to draw and explain the **total cost, total revenue, average cost and average revenue (demand) curves,** both for sellers in **pure competition** and for sellers with **monopoly power.**

- You will be able to show and explain: **maximum profit output, the amount of profit or loss,** the **break-even point** and the **shut-down point.** And you will be able to draw and explain the **break-even chart.**

- You will also be able to look at these curves and tell (in pure competition) **how much the individual firm will supply to the market.** From this you will be able to build the **short-run market supply curve** for this product, and to explain why this curve is a **diminishing returns curve.**

How Much to Produce?

How does a business decide how much product to make? It wants to produce the most profitable quantity, of course. But how does it do that?

If a business produces "too little" its revenue will be too low. So its profits will be less than "maximum." But if it produces too much, its costs will be too high. So its profits won't be "maximum" then, either!

Each time a business expands its output by one more unit per day, that adds something to its cost that also adds something to its revenue. So what determines how far the business should go in expanding its daily output? It all depends on how much the *revenue* is going to go up and how much the *cost* is going to go up.

Suppose you are running a business and you're thinking about expanding your daily output by one unit. And suppose you think your cost will go up by $10.

Suppose you expect to sell the extra unit for $20. Will you produce it? Sure. But suppose you think you could only sell it for $5. Will you produce it? Certainly not!

MARGINAL COST, MARGINAL REVENUE, AND MARGINAL PROFIT

As you know, the cost of expanding the rate of output by one unit is called the marginal cost. The extra revenue gained from the sale of the extra unit of output is called the marginal revenue. If the marginal revenue (say, $15) is greater than the marginal cost (say, $10), the business makes a marginal profit on the extra unit of output ($15 marginal revenue minus $10 marginal cost = $5 marginal profit).

How long should a business keep expanding and adding "marginal output units" to its daily output? As long as each expansion brings a marginal profit. Of course!

If the extra revenue received from the sale of the one unit larger output is *greater than* the extra cost of producing the one unit larger output then there's a marginal profit. Total profit goes up.

If Marginal Profit Is Available, Produce More!

Whenever marginal profits can be made by expanding the rate of output, then the profit-maximizing business will be expanding output. Obviously. But as the output of a factory or mill or a processing plant (or even a hamburger stand, for that matter) gets larger and larger, pretty soon inefficiencies begin to develop. The law of diminishing returns at work? Sure.

The inefficiencies cause the marginal cost to go up. As the marginal cost goes up, what happens to the marginal profit? It goes down.

If the marginal revenue is $15 and the marginal cost is $10, then the marginal profit is $5. Great. Expand the output. But as the daily rate of output expands more and more, the marginal cost creeps up more and more.

Sooner or later (probably pretty soon) the marginal cost is going to inch its way up to where it's as high as the marginal revenue. That means the marginal profit is going to inch its

way down to zero. ($15 marginal revenue minus $15 marginal cost equals $0 marginal profit!)

Maximum Profit Is Where MC = MR, and MP = O.

When the marginal profit is zero that's as far as the profit-maximizing business will expand. At that rate of output the business has "gathered up" all of the marginal profits it can get. It has expanded its output rate to the point where its marginal cost is equal to its marginal revenue. So marginal profit has inched down to zero.

The most profitable output rate for a business is always where its marginal cost equals its marginal revenue (MC = MR). At any smaller output rate (MC < MR) the business would be passing up the chance to make marginal profits. It could expand output and make more profit. At any larger output rate (MC > MR) marginal cost would be too high and the business would be making marginal losses. The business could cut back and make more profits.

As you see all this illustrated on graphs you will understand it better. But for now there's only one important thing to remember:

The most profitable rate of output for a business is always that output at which marginal cost and marginal revenue are equal. That's where marginal profit is zero and total profit is maximized.

THE COST AND REVENUE CURVES

Several graphs are coming up now. These graphs will put the revenue curves and the cost curves together. There are no new curves on any of these graphs. You have seen them all before. But please, don't go on to these graphs unless you understand all the cost and revenue curves. If you haven't already learned them, go back and learn them now. Otherwise, when you see them all together you may get confused. And now, whenever you're ready . . .

Fig. 23-1 Total Cost, Total Revenue, and Total Profit for the Seller in Pure Competition

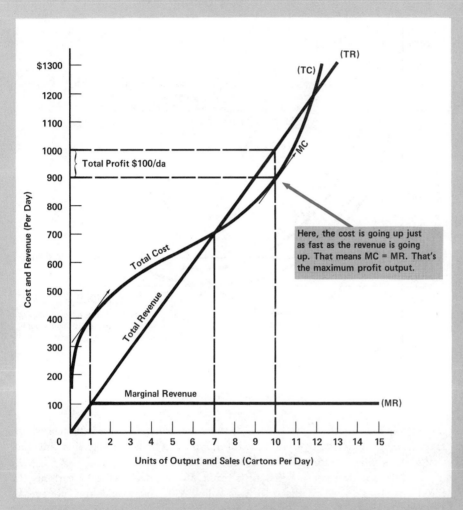

Total revenue just keeps on going up, but after ten units a day, total cost goes up even faster!

This graph shows that you can sell all you want to, and you can get $100 for each carton you sell. So why don't you produce and sell 50? or maybe 100? Because your cost would be so high you'd lose a lot of money, that's why!

If you increase your output from zero to one unit, that will add a lot to your cost ($200) but not as much (only $100) to your revenue. But then as you expand your daily output rate from one unit to two to three and on up to ten units, each time you expand your rate of output your total revenue goes up *more* than your total cost goes up. That means your MR is greater than your MC.

Total revenue is rising faster than total cost all the way between the output of one unit and the output of ten units. But beyond ten units, your total cost rises more rapidly than your total revenue. That means your MC is greater than your MR. If you produce more than ten units your profits will shrink.

Fig. 23-2   Average Cost, Marginal Cost, and Marginal Revenue for the Seller in Pure Competition

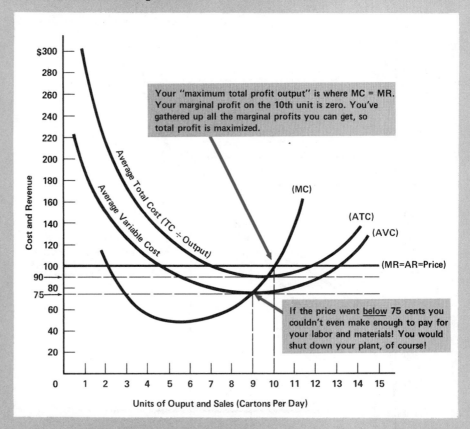

If you divide the total cost and revenue curves by the number of units of output, you get the average cost and revenue curves.

This is just another way to look at the same things shown in the previous graph, except that here everything is on a "per unit" basis. (Note that this vertical scale is much larger.)

At $100 a carton you are making a profit. If the price was $90 a carton, you could only break even. If the price was below $90, you would lose money. At any price above $75, you earn enough to pay for all your variable inputs, plus something left over to help pay for your fixed inputs. At a price less than $75 you couldn't even pay for your variable inputs. So you wouldn't produce anything.

Note: 1. Average revenue ($100) times quantity sold (10 units) equals total revenue ($1,000).

2. Average cost ($90) times quantity sold (10 units) equals total cost ($900).

3. Average revenue ($100) minus average cost ($90) equals average profit ($10).

4. Average profit ($10) times quantity sold (10 units) equals total profit ($100).

Fig. 23-3   Total Cost, Total Revenue, and Total Profit for the Monopolistic Seller

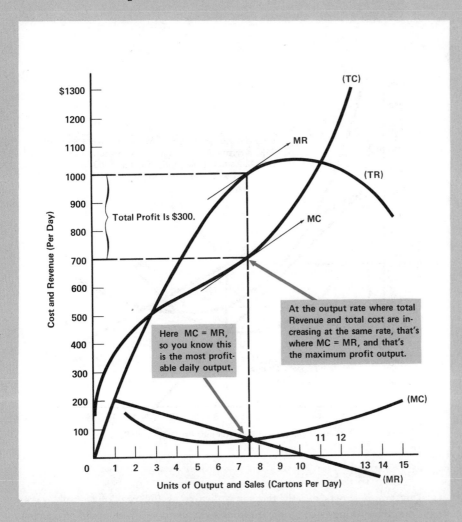

Here MC = MR, so you know this is the most profitable daily output.

At the output rate where total Revenue and total cost are increasing at the same rate, that's where MC = MR, and that's the maximum profit output.

Total Profit Is $300.

If you must cut your price to sell more, you will not produce and sell as much. Of course not!

To increase your sales by one unit you must lower your price by $10. The increased output tries to push your total revenue up. But the decreased price tries to pull it down. When output is small and the price high, the increased quantity more than offsets the reduced price. But when the output is large and the price low, the quantity doesn't increase enough. The price cut pulls the total revenue down.

The shapes of these revenue curves depend on the elasticity of demand. Remember? When demand is relatively *elastic*, marginal revenue is positive and total revenue is rising. When the elasticity is *unitary*, marginal revenue is zero and total revenue doesn't change. When demand is relatively *inelastic*, marginal revenue is negative and total revenue is falling.

I'll bet you wish you could use price discrimination! But here, we're assuming you can't.

Fig. 23-4   Average Cost, Average Revenue, and Average Profit for the Monopolistic Seller

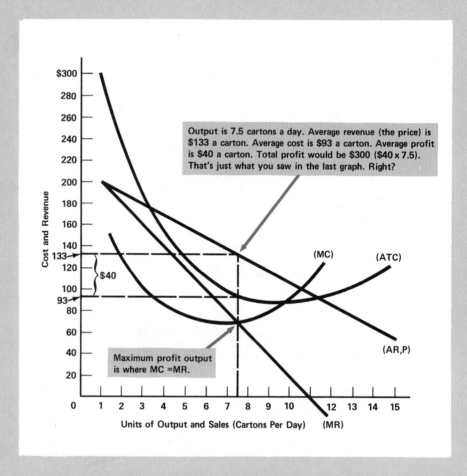

Output is 7.5 cartons a day. Average revenue (the price) is $133 a carton. Average cost is $93 a carton. Average profit is $40 a carton. Total profit would be $300 ($40 x 7.5). That's just what you saw in the last graph. Right?

Maximum profit output is where MC =MR.

The producer with a declining demand curve has some monopoly power. Output will be restricted to keep the price from falling too far.

This graph shows exactly the same picture as the previous graph, except that here, everything is on a per unit basis (totals, divided by units of output).

As you lower the price to sell more, the marginal revenue drops rapidly. Soon you reach a point where you lose as much money by lowering the price as you get back when you sell the extra unit of output. That's where marginal revenue is zero and total revenue is maximum. But that isn't the maximum profit output. Your maximum profit is where your marginal cost equals your marginal revenue (7.5 units). If you expand beyond 7.5 units a day you will be adding more to your cost than to your revenue. So if you lower the price and sell more, your profits will shrink.

(The AR and MR curves are the same ones on the previous graphs. Here they look much steeper because of the larger vertical scale. The average variable and the average fixed cost curves are excluded here to keep from cluttering up the graph.)

Now you know how the costs and the revenues fit together and relate to each other. You know how to find your most profitable rate of output—where MC = MR. Then at that output you can look at your ATC curve and see exactly what your average cost is per unit.

And you can look at your average revenue (price, demand) curve and see your per-unit revenue. So you can see how much profit you will be making per unit (if any). Yes, now you know quite a lot about "the theory of the firm." But of what use is all this?

HOW BUSINESSES USE THE COST AND REVENUE CURVES

In this chapter and the two previous ones you have learned a lot of curves which illustrate the costs and revenues of a "typical business firm." Do businesses actually use these curves? Generally, no. But they *certainly do go by the concepts and principles* which these curves illustrate!

The purpose of the curves is to illustrate the concepts and principles which guide business decisions. You may be quite sure that *any good business manager* when thinking about increasing the rate of production, *considers the extra cost and compares it with the extra revenue expected.*

The economist uses the cost and revenue curves to make explicit these ideas and concepts and principles—many of which are "just common sense" to a good business manager. The concepts and principles which these curves illustrate are very important. If you are thinking about going into business (or if you're just thinking about "the ordinary business of life") there are many times when these concepts and principles can help you.

Sometimes businesses actually use these curves. A modification of the economist's total cost and total revenue graph is frequently used. Business analysts call it the "break-even chart."

The Break-Even Chart

The break-even chart is a simplification of the "total cost and total revenue" graph. It shows a straight-line total cost curve (starting part way up the vertical axis to reflect the fixed cost) and a straight-line total revenue curve beginning at zero.

The total revenue line is going up faster than the total cost line. By increasing its output and sales to where the total revenue is high enough to equal the total cost, the firm "breaks even." At higher outputs than this, the firm makes a profit. At lower outputs it loses money.

Who uses break-even charts? The automobile producers, for one. They use a break-even chart to relate to a "model-year." By the time the company is all set up to produce a new car they have already incurred big costs. So they must sell a lot of them to break even. But beyond the break-even point, additional sales add to profits.

Figure 23-5 shows a typical break-even chart. This graph shows that if the demand for the product is great enough to buy an output of 500 units, the business will break even. If not, they will lose money. If they can sell more than 500 units they will make a profit. You'll see all this in Figure 23-5, on the next page.

It's the Concepts that Count

The graphs economists and business analysts use to illustrate costs and revenues provide

If price is below **AVC** what can you do?

Shut down and lose all your FC. Or don't, and lose all your FC plus some VC, too!

Fig. 23-5   A Modified Version of the Total Cost and Total Revenue Graph: The Break-Even Chart

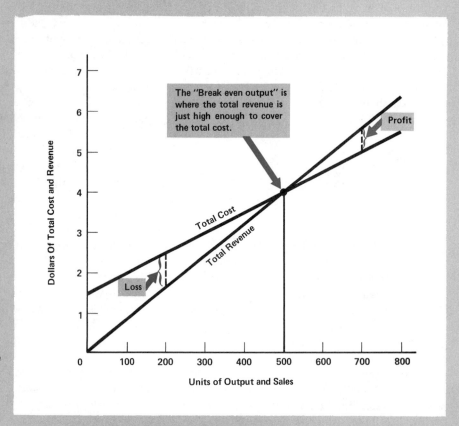

If a business is going to make a profit, its total revenue must rise fast enough to get above the total cost before the business runs out of customers.

This chart shows that when output is zero, total cost is already high. But revenue is zero. Then the larger the output the higher the revenue.

If the demand for the product is great enough so that 500 units can be sold, then the business will break even. If more than 500 can be sold they will make a profit.

What would happen if the price was increased? The total revenue line would get steeper and the break-even point would be at a smaller output. A lower price would have the opposite effect.

What about a cost change? If the cost drops, the break-even point will move to the left, indicating a smaller break-even output. But if the cost was higher the cost curve would be steeper. More output would have to be sold before the business could break even.

a way of seeing more clearly the process by which the business makes its "economic choice" decisions. The curves serve well to illustrate the important concepts.

The "marginal cost equals marginal revenue" concept is an excellent way of conceptualizing the business decision process.

The business manager who thinks marginally when making decisions is likely to be right more often than one who does not, just as the individual who "thinks marginally" in deciding how to use his or her scarce money, time, and other resources is more likely to achieve the desired objectives than one who does not. But there's no guarantee.

Anyone who guesses wrong about the marginal cost or the marginal revenue will make the wrong decision—in spite of the good use of a sound principle. Also, this analysis leaves out many of the important practical questions which the business decision-maker must face:

"How can I reduce my costs?" "What will happen to my revenues if I improve my product?" "What will happen to the cost of my inputs in the future?" "Will the demand for jeans continue to expand?"

These and many other unanswerable questions face all businesses in the real world. So it takes more than an understanding of economic concepts to be successful in business. But the economic concepts sure can help!

Why do you need to understand the firm's cost and revenue picture? So you can understand supply! So you can figure out how much the firm would produce and sell at various market prices. Of course.

You haven't yet seen *the supply curve for the output of the individual firm.* That's the next step, coming up right now.

THE INDIVIDUAL FIRM'S SUPPLY CURVE

Suppose you are producing 10 cartons of jeans a day and selling them to Sears for $100 a carton. Then suppose this particular style of jeans really begins to catch on. There's a big increase in demand. Maybe Sears offers you $140 a carton and urges you to supply more. Will you increase your daily output and supply more? Yes, you will!

If Price Is Fixed, the Marginal Cost Curve (above AVC) Is the Firm's Supply Curve

When your marginal revenue (price) goes up to $140 you will expand your output until your marginal cost goes up to $140. That way you will maximize your profit. If you'll look back at Figure 23-2 you'll see that you will increase your output to 11 cartons a day. And look how much profit you will be making! More than $50 per unit. About $600 a day! With all that profit, this is a pretty good business to be in.

You may decide to expand your plant as soon as you can and produce more and make even more profit. Other firms are likely to start producing jeans too. Looks like the jeans industry is about to expand. Why? Because people are demanding more. The price is high. This is a very profitable industry to be in!

It's going to take awhile for the industry to expand. Meanwhile, in the short run, how much will you supply to the market? You will supply as much as your marginal cost tells you to supply. If the price rises higher you will produce more.

You will expand your output to where the marginal cost goes up as high as the new price (marginal revenue).

Suppose the price goes down. You will produce less. You will reduce your daily output to where your marginal cost equals the new (lower) price (marginal revenue). So in the short run, see what determines your supply (propensity to sell)? Sure. Your supply—that is, the amount you will produce and offer for sale at each possible price—is determined by your marginal cost.

Why Is Maximum Profit Where MC = MR?

When you adjust your output to exactly where your marginal cost becomes equal to the market price, that's exactly the output which brings your maximum profit. Why?

1. Because at that output every unit which will bring a marginal profit—that is, every unit which can be produced for a *marginal cost less than the price*—is being produced. You're getting all the marginal profits you can possibly get, and

2. Because you aren't producing any units that would have a *marginal cost greater than the price*. Those units would bring marginal losses and reduce your profits!

So at the output rate where MC = Price you're getting all the marginal profits you can get. And no marginal losses. So your total profit is as big as it possibly can be.

What if the price drops so low that the business can't even pay for its variable inputs (labor and materials and all)? Then it won't produce anything. It will **shut down** and wait (1) for the price to go up or costs to go down; or (2) for a chance to get out of this industry (whichever comes first). For a seller in pure competition, here's the rule:

For each price higher than the average variable cost, it's the marginal cost curve that tells how much the producer will produce and supply to the market.

Since the marginal cost curve shows "how much the producer will offer for sale at each possible market price," that means the marginal

cost curve (at prices above AVC) really is the supply curve for the output of the individual firm.

(*Note:* This rule is true only if the firm is selling in the kind of "fixed price" situation we're talking about—that is, in a pure-competition-type situation. For the monopolistic seller who must lower the price to sell more, MR < P. So the maximum profit output (where MC = MR) is where MC< P also. You can see this back in figure 23-4, where the price is $133 and the MC and MR are down around $70. So the maximum profit output for the monopolistic seller will always be an output smaller than the output where P = MC).

The Marginal Cost and Marginal Revenue Curves

It might be a good idea to see a graph showing only the marginal cost, marginal revenue, and average variable cost for the seller in a pure-competition-type-situation. Then you can see this supply concept without any other curves in the graph to confuse you.

You will see that the marginal cost really does show how much you will supply at various selling prices. So the marginal cost curve really is your supply curve.

The next two graphs (Figures 23-6 and 23-7) show the marginal cost-marginal revenue relationships. Study the graphs carefully and I believe all this will become perfectly clear to you.

FROM THE FIRM'S SUPPLY TO THE MARKET SUPPLY

Figures 23-6 and 23-7 show your marginal cost curve as your firm's supply curve. But that's only true (a) if the price is higher than your average variable cost, and (b) if you are selling in a market where you can sell all you wish at the going market price—that is, you see the demand for your product as infinitely elastic. You have

Fig. 23-6 Marginal Cost and Marginal Revenue and Marginal Profit and Marginal Loss for the Seller in Pure Competition

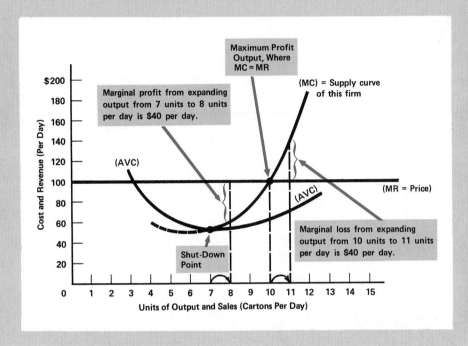

The producer who thinks marginally will keep adding output as long as the addition to revenue is greater than the addition to cost.

At a price of $100 you will produce and sell 10 cartons a day. If the price goes up to $140 you will sell 11 cartons a day. If the price drops below $100, you will sell less than 10 cartons. Your MC curve is your supply curve.

If the price ever gets down to where it's so low it will just barely cover your average variable cost, then you're operating at your "shut-down point." When you are operating at this price you are losing an amount equal to your fixed cost. You are just getting back enough to cover your variable cost. You would be just as well off to shut down since you are already losing as much as your fixed cost. But at any price higher than the shut-down price you get enough revenue to cover all of your variable cost and some left over to pay for some (or all) of your fixed cost.

This graph doesn't tell if you are making any profit. It only shows you your "maximum profit" (or "minimum loss") rate of output.

The marginal cost and marginal revenue curves only tell you what daily rate of output will be "most profitable" for your plant. That's all. After you find the most profitable rate of output (where MC = MR) then you must look at the average total cost curve to see what the cost per unit is at that rate of output. Then you can see how much profit (or loss) you will be making on each unit. The next graph will show you that.

Fig. 23-7   Costs, Revenues, and Profits for the Seller in Pure Competition: The Case of a Price Increase

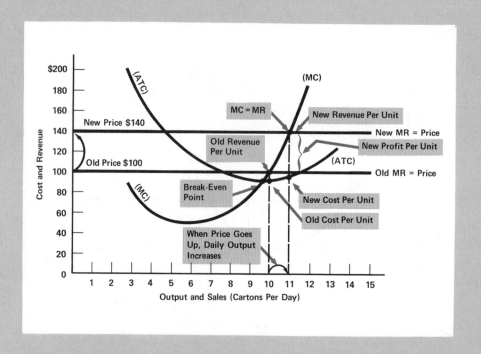

When the price goes up, the firm produces more.

An increase in price brings increased profit. If you know your Average Cost (ATC) you can see how much profit you're making per unit. So you can figure out your total profit. (Average profit times quantity sold equals total profit.)

When the price goes up from $100 to $140 per carton, output expands from 10 units per day to 11 units per day and average cost per unit goes up from $90 per carton to $95 per carton. Marginal cost increases to $140 where it is equal to the new marginal revenue. Profit increases from $10 per carton to $45 per carton!

This is going to be a *very rapidly expanding* industry. The high demand for jeans has forced up the price. More competitors will keep entering the industry and pushing more product into the market until the price is pushed back down to the "normal" level.

The normal price is the break-even price. It's just high enough to cover all costs, including a reasonable return (normal profit) for the business owner.

At prices above the break-even point, firms will be making surplus profits and new firms will be entering the industry. The industry will be expanding and the price will be moving down. At prices lower than the break-even price, firms will be making less than normal profits. Firms will be leaving the industry. The supply will be getting smaller and the price will be moving up.

no monopoly power at all.

What we really are talking about is: *market supply in a market which has pure competition on the seller's side.*

Suppose we are thinkng of your local egg market and suppose your brother is still running his poultry farm. He can sell two cases or ten cases or fifteen cases of eggs each week at the going market price. He doesn't see his output as having any effect on the price at all.

So what do you know about the seller's side of this egg market? It's pure competition. There must be hundreds or maybe thousands of other sellers like your brother, supplying that market.

What will determine how many cases your brother will supply to the market next week? The price as compared with his marginal cost? Of course! If the price goes up he will produce and deliver more eggs to the market. If it goes down he will produce and deliver less. His marginal cost will tell him *how much more or how much less.*

What about all of the other hundreds or thousands of egg sellers? Do they all produce more when the price is higher? And less when the price is lower? Do they adjust their output to where MC = price? Sure.

Market Supply Is the Sum of the Individual Firm Supplies

It's obvious that the market supply of eggs consists of all of the individual firm supplies of eggs, all added together.

Remember how to get from the *individual demand curve* to the *market demand curve*? Sure. Just add up the individual demand curves. Now can you see how we are going to get from the *individual supply curve to the market supply* curve? Exactly the same way. Hypothetically it's easy.

The market supply is the sum of the quantities that would be supplied by all of the individual firms, at each possible market price. So pick a price—say 75¢ a dozen. How many cases of eggs will your brother supply per week? And how many will the next farmer down the road

supply? and the next? and the next?

You just keep going along and adding the amount each individual producer would supply at that price. When you get them all added up that gives you *one point on the market supply curve.*

You have found out what total quantity would be supplied if the market price was 75¢ a dozen. So pick another price—say $1 a dozen. Then do the same thing and you'll get another point on the market supply curve. Then do it again and again until you get as many points as you want. Then just draw in the market supply curve connecting all of the market supply points. Simple!

A Graph Deriving the Market Supply Curve

How might you do it on a graph? The easiest way is to just change the scale on the quantity axis!

The individual firm in pure competition doesn't supply very much. So the quantity scale for the individual firm's supply curve shows only a few units. For the market supply curve you can just increase this number of units to reflect the number of firms in the industry. For example, you might let 12 units become either 1,200 units (assuming 100 identical firms are supplying this market) or 12,000 units (assuming there are 1,000 identical firms). Now if you'll look at Figure 23-8 you'll see an example of this.

Short-Run Market Supply—a Diminishing Returns Curve

The market supply curve you just looked at is a short-run supply curve. You have known about short-run market supply curves since you were first introduced to supply and demand

Fig. 23-8   Deriving the Market Supply Curve

The market supply of eggs is the sum of the eggs supplied by all of the individual firms at each price.

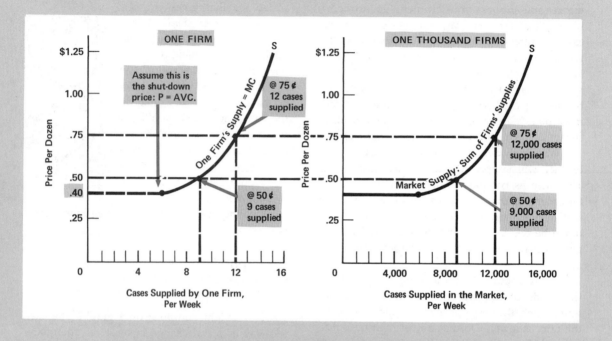

Going from the individual firm's supply curve to the market supply curve is just like going from the individual's demand curve to the market demand curve. If you assume all firms are identical then it's easy. All you need to do is change the numbers on the quantity scale.

What if some of the firms are large and others are small? And what if some have marginal costs rising more rapidly than others? Then to get each market supply point you would need to add up the amount supplied by each firm. In this example we are assuming there are 1,000 identical firms. Surely this assumption isn't likely to be true in the real world! But it illustrates the point.

What's the point? Just this: In a market of pure competition the market supply is determined by the marginal cost curves of the individual firms which supply that market. To get the market supply curve it is only necessary to add up the outputs of the individual firms at each price—as indicated by their marginal cost curves.

This illustration shows what happens as more firms come into the industry, or as firms leave. Suppose there weren't 1,000 firms, but only 500? Then the quantities of the market supply curve would only be half as great. Suppose there were 2,000 firms? Then the quantities on the horizontal scale would be double. The market supply would be twice as large.

back in Part One.

Why is this market supply curve "short-run"? Because it will only stay as it is as long as (1) the costs of the individual firms do not change, and (2) the number of firms in the industry doesn't change.

The short-run market supply curve depends on the existing *number* and *sizes* of the firms in the industry. You could say it this way:

The short-run market supply curve *depends on the amount of* fixed inputs *now existing in the industry*. That is, it depends on all of the buildings, machines, equipment, and all of the other "fixed factors of production" already installed in this industry.

In the short run, how do firms adjust their output when the price goes up or down? They buy more variable factors: labor, materials, power, etc. Why does the marginal cost (and therefore the supply curve for the individual firm) go up so steeply as output increases? Because of the law of diminishing returns. The added variable factors have less fixed factors to work with. So they aren't as productive.

The short-run market supply curve for a product is really a "diminishing returns curve" for the industry that supplies that product.

What about the long run? In the long run, firms have a chance to build more buildings or install more equipment. Or they can shift out of this industry and produce something else altogether. What about that?

In the long run, the short-run market supply curve can shift. How? By fixed factors (plants, machines, new firms) shifting into or out of this industry. You'll be finding out all about that in the next chapter.

SUMMARY AND SYNTHESIS

Each business tries to adjust its output so as to produce the **most profitable** quantity. If **marginal profit** is available, then if **the output rate is increased, profits will be increased.**

It all depends on the **relative sizes** of **marginal cost** and **marginal revenue.** If marginal revenue is greater than marginal cost, then the business has the opportunity to make a **marginal profit.** It will expand its output and increase its profits.

As a business speeds up its operation and increases its output, its **per-unit cost** of production goes up. The **law of diminishing returns** says so. So how far does the business go on expanding its output? Until **marginal cost equals marginal revenue**—that is, until **marginal profit is zero.** When no more **marginal profits** (only **marginal losses**) are available, there's no reason to expand any more!

A **total cost-total revenue graph** shows the **profitable output range**—where total revenue is above total cost. The **most profitable output rate** is where the total revenue is as high above total cost as possible. This is where the **total cost and total revenue** curves are parallel—where **marginal cost** (rate of increase in total cost) equals **marginal revenue** (rate of increase in total revenue).

Using average cost, marginal cost, and marginal revenue curves, the **most profitable output** is where the **marginal cost and marginal revenue curves intersect.** Then the question is: at this output is the business making a profit? That depends on the average cost and the average revenue (price). **If price is above ATC you're making excess profits!** If it's equal to ATC you're making **normal profits**——enough to keep you in this industry but not enough to attract new firms into the industry.

If the price is **below ATC,** you're making **losses.** If the price happens to be **below AVC** you're losing all of your **fixed cost** and part of your **variable cost too.** So you would **shut down your** plant and lose only your fixed cost. You'd plan to get out of this industry as soon as possible.

The cost and revenue curves are quite different for the **monopolistic seller** than for the **seller in pure competition**. But the basic principles are the same: the "maximum profit" rate of output is where MC = MR, and the amount of profit or loss is indicated by the cost and revenue curves at that rate of output. This is true whether the curves are straight or curved, and whether price equals marginal revenue or not.

The break-even chart (a modified version of the total cost-total revenue graph) is used by some businesses in marketing planning for new products. The chart shows linear total cost and total revenue curves. It shows, for each possible price of the product, how many units would have to be sold to break even.

For the seller with some monopoly power, the break-even analysis can be helpful in deciding (a) whether or not to produce the new product, and (b) what price to charge. The chosen price would depend a lot on the firm's estimates of the elasticity of the demand.

The supply curve of the individual firm in pure competition is its marginal cost curve at prices above its average variable cost. Why? Because the firm will produce and sell where MC = MR.

In pure competition, MR is the horizontal "price line." Where it intersects MC, that's the maximum profit output, so that's how much the firm will produce and offer for sale. The quantity supplied at each price is indicated by the MC curve, so the MC curve is the firm's supply curve.

For the seller with monopoly power, where price is not equal to marginal cost (P $\gtrless$ MC) the amount supplied to the market will always be smaller than the amount which would be supplied by a producer in pure competition. Why? Because the marginal revenue is always less than the price (MR < P), so the intersection where MC = MR is always at an output rate which is smaller than where MR = P.

Sellers in pure competition have no power over the price. They are "price takers," not "price makers." So in an industry of pure competition (where MC = MR = P) an increase in demand will increase the market price, and the increase in market price will have its full impact on output. But in a market where monopoly power exists (where MC = MR < P) an increase in demand will bring forth more output—but not as much more as in pure competition.

The market supply curve can be derived from the supply curves of the individual sellers. How? In the same way that the market demand curve is derived from the demand curves of the individual consumers. Just add them up. When you're dealing with theoretical numbers, the easiest way to turn the supply curve of one firm into the market supply curve is to change the numbers on the horizontal (x) axis to hundreds or thousands, instead of individual units.

In pure competition the short-run market supply curve for a product is a diminishing returns curve for the industry. But in the long run there are no fixed input factors so the law of diminishing returns doesn't apply. You'll be finding out about that in the next chapter.

REVIEW EXERCISES

MAJOR CONCEPTS, PRINCIPLES, TERMS (Explain each carefully.)

marginal profit
marginal cost
pure competition
where MC = MR is maximum profit output

for the monopolistic seller, MR < P
the shut-down price is the lowest point on AVC
the break-even price is the lowest point on ATC
the MC curve is the firm's supply curve

CURVES AND GRAPHS (Draw, label, and explain each.)

Total Cost, Total Revenue, and Total Profit for the Seller in Pure Competition

Average Cost, Marginal Cost, and Marginal Revenue for the Seller in Pure Competition

Total Cost, Total Revenue, and Total Profit for the Monopolistic Seller

Average Cost, Average Revenue, and Average Profit for the Monopolistic Seller

A Modified Version of the Total Cost—Total Revenue Graph: the Break-Even Chart

Marginal Cost and Marginal Revenue, and Marginal Profit and Marginal Loss for the Seller in Pure Competition

Costs, Revenues, and Profits for the Seller in Pure Competition: the Case of a Price Increase

Deriving the Market Supply Curve

QUESTIONS (Write out the answers, or jot down key points.)

1. Your marginal cost curve (at prices higher than the average variable cost) is the supply curve for your jeans plant. But the MC curve at prices lower than AVC is not a part of your plant's "supply curve." Explain why all this is true, and draw a graph to illustrate.

2. For the seller in pure competition, the MC curve is the supply curve for the firm. But for a seller with monopoly power, this isn't true. Can you explain this, and illustrate with graphs? Try. (Hint: Only in pure competition does MR = P.)

3. The cost and revenue curves are a way of explaining and making explicit the implicit "common sense" concepts and principles which guide the intelligent decisions of managers. Try to state, in your own words, as many as you can of the "common sense" concepts and principles which the cost and revenue curves illustrate. How much do you think the curves help you to see and understand the concepts and principles? Discuss.

24

Supply and Cost in the Long Run: Market Structure, and the "Optimum Input Mix"

Chapter Objectives

- In the last three chapters you have been learning about **supply and costs in the short run**. In this chapter you will learn about **long-run supply**.

- In this chapter you will learn about the **three different supply periods**, and about the importance of **normal price** and **pure competition** in influencing the long-run supply.

- When you finish studying this chapter you will be able to draw and explain **long-run supply (LRS) curves** for an industry in pure competition, for the **constant cost case**, the **increasing cost case**, and the **decreasing cost case**.

- You will be able to explain **returns to scale** and to explain the effect of this on **plant size** and on **market structure**. And you will be able to draw and explain **long-run average total cost (LRATC) curves** illustrating these concepts.

- Finally, you will be able to define the **least-cost input combination** using **marginal physical product per dollar** equations and also using **isocost and isoquant curves**.

Short-Run Supply

Suppose you're still in the jeans business. Your marginal cost curve is the supply curve for your *existing* plant. Suppose you build a new plant. What then?

Your new plant might be built to operate most efficiently at a daily output of only five cartons. Or it might be made to operate most efficiently at an output of 30 cartons. What a big difference that would make!

The marginal cost curve is the *short-run supply curve* for your firm. The law of diminishing returns is working. In the short run you're stuck with your existing situation whether you like it or not.

LONG-RUN SUPPLY

When we talk about the long-run supply for a product we're thinking about how much would be produced if we wait long enough for new plants to be built. More businesses could come into the industry.

If you wait long enough, all factors can be increased or decreased. In the long run, all factors are variable. Therefore all costs are variable. There are no fixed costs in the long run.

How Long Is the Long Run? The long run is as long as it takes for an industry to fully respond to a change in the prices of inputs or

394

outputs—that is, to expand or contract in response to a change in demand or cost conditions. The long run is however long it takes to increase or decrease *all* the factors of production—not just the "variable factors."

What would determine whether or not an industry would be expanding "in the long run"? Suppose someone comes up to your Cullowhee plant and says: "Are you going to stay in this business? Perhaps even expand your plant? Or are you going to try to get out of this business?"

Your answer would depend on your present and expected profits. Right? If your business is very profitable, probably you will stay in it and maybe expand. Chances are that other people are going to start producing jeans, too. So in the long run the industry will be expanding.

But suppose you're losing money. That's different! As soon as you can you'll get out of the jeans business. Other producers will too. This is going to be a declining industry.

Maybe you will start producing pleated blouses or sleeping bags or something else. Or maybe you will get out of the textile industry altogether. Maybe you will sell out and go to the West Coast and set up an almond processing plant in Chico—or an abalone plant in Arcata— or a toy plant in Eugene—or a ski shop in Bellingham. But one thing is sure: If you're losing money in the jeans industry, you're going to get out and get into something else in the long run.

See the beauty of the long run? You can do anything you want to. *All factors are variable.* But you must plan it ahead of time and work it out as times goes by.

The amount of time required for the long run is very different from one industry to another. In some industries it's only a few days. In other industries it would take years for a major expansion or contraction to occur.

Supply Is Much More Elastic in the Long Run. The production-motivating function of price works *to some extent in the short run.* But *it works a lot more in the long run.*

In the short run the **production-motivating function of price** is limited because the fixed factors can't be increased. Outputs are limited by the law of diminishing returns. But in the long run the supply response is much greater. Supply is much more "elastic."

In the short run, costs go up fast as output expands. But not so in the long run. Why not? Because in the long run all factors are variable. So if the price goes up and you wait long enough, the supply response can be great. For most things, supply is somewhat responsive to price in the short run and *highly responsive* in the long run.

The Very-Short-Run, or "Momentary" Supply

Economists sometimes talk about the **very-short-run supply period**—a time period so short (maybe one day) that you don't even have time to adjust your daily rate of output. All you can decide is what to do with the products you have already produced. You can only decide whether to hold your inventories or to sell them. That's all.

In the "very short run," the only function "price" can perform is to ration the existing goods. There isn't time for the production-motivating function of price to work *at all*. But when does the production-motivating function of price really work well? In the long run, when all input factors are variable of course!

NORMAL PRICE AND THE LONG-RUN SUPPLY CURVE

The "normal price" is that price which is just high enough to bring a "normal profit" to the "average firm" in the industry.

A price higher than "normal" will bring abnormally high profits and *will attract new firms* into the industry. The industry will expand and the market supply will increase. The increased supply will push the price down to "normal." Then the industry will be in long-run equilibrium.

A price below "normal" is one which is too low to cover all the costs (including "normal profits") of the "average firm" in the industry. If the price is below "normal," firms will be leaving the industry. The industry will be getting smaller.

As the supply flowing into the market decreases, the price will go up. This will continue until the price gets up to the "normal" level. Then the industry will be in "long-run equilibrium."

Higher Cost Increases the Normal Price

The only thing that could change the normal price would be a change in the cost of production. Why? Because the cost of production is the only thing that determines the normal price!

If anything happens to make the "average firm's" cost go up, the normal price goes up. If the cost of production goes down, the normal price goes down. So what happens when the "normal price" moves up or down? The industry expands or contracts until the *market price* is pushed up or down to the "normal price" level. Of course!

Suppose you're going along producing ten cartons of jeans per day and selling them in a market of pure competition. Then for some reason the cost of denim goes down and maybe some of your other costs go down. Suddenly you're making big profits. Can you guess what's going to happen?

Before long the market price is going to go down too. Why? Because before long, more firms, seeking profits, will come into the jeans industry and increase the supply. That will push the price down. How far down? Down to where

the "excess profits" are gone. Down to the new (lower) "normal price"—the price which reflects the new (lower) cost of production.

Suppose production costs went up. It would work the other way. The firms would be losing money so they would cut back production and start getting out of the industry. Supply would decrease. Prices would be forced up. How far up? Up to the new (higher) "normal price"—the price which reflects the new (higher) cost of production.

Do the Buyers Have to Pay the Normal Price?

In the long run, how much are the people of the society going to have to pay for jeans? If we assume that jeans are produced and sold in pure competition (which they aren't, of course) then in the long run the buyers are going to have to pay the normal price.

In the pure market model, in the long run, cost increases always get passed along to the buyers. Lower cost always gets passed along to the buyers, too. Each person must pay the true, full cost of whatever he or she buys.

Of course you know it doesn't work out exactly this way in the real world. Still, even in the real world these market forces are strong. But how the market forces work depends a lot on the kind of competition existing in the market.

The Role of Pure Competition

The "normal price" is also called the normal competitive price. Can you see why? It is the force of competition (new firms coming in when the price is too high) that pushes the price down to "normal."

Without pure competition this "normal price" idea wouldn't work. An increase in demand might not generate much new supply. It might only generate a lot of profits for the monopolistic producers!

Of course the price of each product must be high enough to cover the cost of producing it. If the price is too low to cover the costs, firms will get out of the industry. The supply flowing into the market will decrease. So the price will increase.

If the costs were higher than the price and the price *didn't* increase, ultimately all the producers would go out of business. The product would disappear from the market. You can see that pure competition isn't essential to keep the price up *high* enough—that is, "up" to normal. That would happen anyway. But pure competition *is* essential to keep the price down *low* enough—that is, "down" to normal.

A producer with complete monopoly could keep the price up above "normal" indefinitely! If a producer (monopolist) can keep other firms from entering the industry, then *that producer can keep the supply permanently restricted.* So the price can be kept high, with big profits going to the monopolist. See how monopoly can interfere with the operation of the market process?

You'll be reading a lot more about the monopoly issue later. But now it's time to take a close look at long-run cost and long-run supply.

LONG-RUN COST AND LONG-RUN SUPPLY

The concept of "long-run supply" involves two different kinds of questions: First, "how many firms will be in the industry?" and then, "how big will each firm be?"

1. **How many firms?** *The long run in a market for some product is a time period long enough for firms to enter into or to exit from the industry.* As price and cost conditions change, firms move in or out and keep pushing the price "back to normal." As long as the industry is expanding or con-

tracting, the "long run" hasn't yet arrived. How long does it take for an industry to complete its adjustment to a change in price and cost conditions? That's how long the long run is. Now, the other aspect of the long run.

2. **How big will each firm be?** *The long run is a time period long enough to permit the individual firm to change all of its fixed factors.* A company can expand or contract as much as it wishes. It can build a new factory (or 5 or 6 new factories). It can get new machinery and equipment, establish new sites, automate and computerize— it can undertake and complete any change it wishes to make. That's the long run from the point of view of the individual firm.

From the point of view of the individual firm it's sometimes useful to think of "the long run" as the "planning horizon" for the firm. The long run never exists, of course—except in people's minds. But it does exist in the mind of the entrepreneur who is planning future plant expansions or alterations. Every business needs to have somebody looking ahead "at the long run" and deciding what changes need to be initiated now in order to move the business in the right direction "in the long run."

Long-Run Supply in Pure Competition

Is it possible to develop a long-run supply curve? Can we use a curve to show what quantity would be offered for sale at various possible prices, in the long run?—that is, if you wait long enough for the industry to complete its long-run adjustment to each price? Yes, we can!

Back in Chapter 5 in the egg market example you saw the price of eggs go up from 75¢ to $1. At the higher price, new firms were attracted into the egg industry. As the new firms came in they added more supply in the egg market. The increased supply pushed the price down. Remember?

Firms kept coming in and the price kept going down until the price was pushed all the way back down to 75¢. So what could we say about the long-run supply of eggs in that market? Is it a horizontal line at a price of 75¢? That's right! At least, that's the long-run supply curve for quantities between 10 carloads and 20 carloads per week. The very last figure in Chapter 5 shows you this.

Whenever the industry expands and the normal price stays the same, that means the long-run supply curve is horizontal. It means that the cost of producing eggs doesn't increase as new firms enter the industry. It means that the people can have all the eggs they might ever want, for that price—in the long run.

But suppose the cost per dozen *does increase* as the industry expands. That means the normal price will go up. It means the long-run supply curve has positive slope (slopes upward).

Figure 24-1 shows a graph of the *constant cost* (horizontal long-run supply) situation. Then Figure 24-2 shows and explains the *increasing cost* case. You should study those two figures now.

LONG-RUN COST, RETURNS TO SCALE, AND MARKET STRUCTURE

In Figures 24-1 and 24-2 you've been looking at "the long run" as the period during which *the industry* can adjust to changes in market conditions. Now it's time to look at "the long run" as the time during which *the individual firm* can adjust by increasing or decreasing in size.

Now we're back at the question of whether or not you should expand your Cullowhee jeans operation or not. And we're up to this question: "What would happen to your average cost (cost per unit) if you did expand your plant?"

In Pure Competition You Must Try for Maximum Efficiency

Is your operation already big enough to be efficient? If you doubled the size of the plant could you use some better kinds of machinery?

Or maybe your plant is already too big to be efficient. Maybe you don't have any good supervisors—and you can't *personally* keep an eye on everything! So maybe some of your workers are wasting materials. And time. Maybe with a smaller operation you could keep things really shipshape and get more output per unit of input.

How big should your plant be? If you are producing and selling in a market of pure competition, then in the long run your plant must be exactly big enough to operate at maximum efficiency—that is, *the plant must be just the right size to bring the lowest possible cost per carton of jeans.* Why? Because other *efficient sellers* are going to keep entering the industry and pushing the price down. If you aren't as efficient as they are you will go broke!

The Monopolistic Seller Must Consider Both Efficiency and Demand

What if you aren't selling in pure competition? Suppose you have some "monopoly power"—that is, you must lower your price if you want to sell more. What about that? Should you build the *most efficient* plant size? Or should you build just the right plant size to serve your market?

Fig. 24-1 Long-Run Supply in Pure Competition: The Constant Cost Case

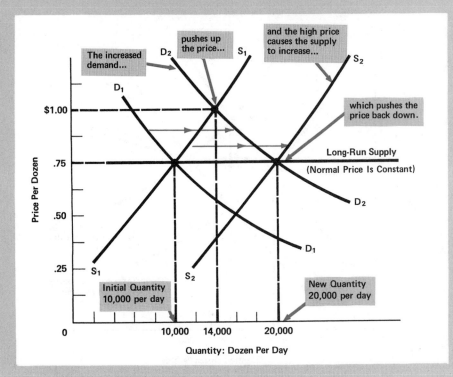

When the industry expands, if the cost of production does not go up then the normal price will stay the same so the industry will continue to expand until the price comes back down to where it was before.

The long-run supply shows what quantities would be offered for sale at various prices, assuming you wait long enough for the industry to adjust to each price. This graph shows that if you are willing to wait long enough for the industry to adjust completely, you can get all the eggs you want for 75¢ a dozen.

While the industry is not in long-run equilibrium—that is, while it is expanding or contracting—you will find the price of eggs sometimes higher and sometimes lower than 75¢. But you will always know that the price is tending toward 75¢. If you wait long enough and if nothing happens to change the cost situation, then sooner or later the price will once again come to rest at 75¢.

This graph works both for an increase and for a decrease in demand. If the demand *increases*, there are shortages. The price is forced up, excess profits are made in the industry, and new firms enter. The supply keeps increasing until the price is pushed back down to 75¢. If the demand *decreases*, there are surpluses. The price is forced down, and firms lose money and begin leaving the industry. The supply keeps decreasing until the price works its way back up to 75¢.

This graph assumes that costs don't change as the industry expands or contracts. But suppose that as the industry expands (or contracts) the cost of production goes up? (or down?) What then? That's what the next graph will show you.

Fig. 24-2   Long-Run Supply in Pure Competition: The Increasing Cost Case

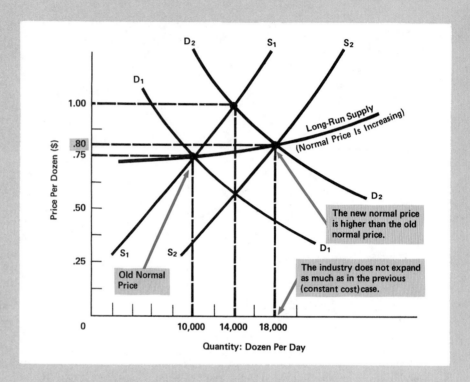

As the industry expands, if that causes the cost to go up then the normal price will go up. The long-run supply curve will slope upward.

The upward-sloping long-run supply curve says: "as the industry expands, the normal price goes up." In this graph it is *higher cost* which causes the long-run supply curve to slope upward.

Why might the cost increase as the industry expands? Maybe there aren't enough of the needed kinds of labor and land and resources. Maybe some less efficient factors must be used. Or maybe the prices of some of the specialized inputs will go up.

The long-run supply will slope upward for industries with some "physically limited" input factor—such as mining, crop production requiring special soils, businesses requiring special locations, etc. If such an industry expands much, costs will go up. So after the increase in demand, the price will never go all the way down to the previous "normal price" level.

There may be problems of overcrowding, or of pollution. When there's only one egg producer using the local road, no problem. But when more producers use it, maybe transport costs will go up. When there's only one egg producer on the river, nobody complains. But as the industry expands, new laws may require the use of costly anti-pollution equipment.

When you have monopoly power you *must* consider this: If you produce too much you're going to force the price down to where you'll reduce your profits! The producer in pure competition only needs to be concerned about adjusting plant size to increase efficiency.

The producer who has monopoly power must consider *efficiency*, sure. But the monopolistic producer must also consider the *size* and the *elasticity* of the demand for the product.

The Question of "Returns to Scale"

When we talk about different "efficiency" for different "sizes of firms" what we're talking about is the question of **returns to scale**—also called **economies of scale**.

If you increase the size of your plant (that is, the scale of your operation) and that increases your efficiency (lowers your per-unit cost) then we say you are receiving **increasing returns to scale**. That means you're getting back more product per dollar (and getting more revenue, per dollar of cost) as your business increases in size. The "more product" (and more revenue) you're getting per dollar of input-cost, is the "increasing returns" you are getting.

Suppose you increased the size (scale) of your business and found that your per-unit cost went up instead of down? Then that's a case of **decreasing returns to scale**. You are getting back less output (and therefore less revenue) per dollar of input cost as you increase the size (scale) of your plant. And suppose you increased your plant size and the per-unit cost didn't change. Then that's a case of **constant returns to scale**.

Economies of Scale Influence Plant Size

Think for a minute about the idea of "returns to scale." Suppose you are producing something in an industry where the only *efficient*

plant is a *very small* plant. Does that give you any ideas about the kind of market structure that will exist in that industry? Sure. Lots of small sellers. Maybe pure competition. Right?

But what if the only *efficient* kind of plant is a *very large* one? What kind of competition do you suppose will exist in that industry? Pure competition? Of course not! Most likely pure monopoly!

Whether or not there are any "returns to scale" depends on engineering considerations—that is, it depends on the technology of production in each industry. Industries differ

The LRATC curve tells **how big** the most efficient firm is. That's all.

quite a lot in this respect. In some industries, returns to scale are great. In others there's little or nothing to be gained from "bigness." That's true in theory; it's just as true in the real world.

THE LONG-RUN AVERAGE TOTAL COST CURVES

Suppose you're traveling around the country. You'll see lots of small businesses everywhere you go. But how many "mom and pop" steel mills do you see? Or electric power companies? Or automobile manufacturing companies? Not many, right? In fact, you'll see *exactly none*. Why? Could it be that the idea of *returns to scale* might be involved? You bet it could!

Economists have developed some curves to illustrate these concepts. That's what you'll be studying on the pages coming up. When you finish studying these graphs you'll be able to understand all of this much better.

Here they are: Figures 24-3, -4, -5, -6—four in a row. And Figure 24-6 contains five small graphs. So there are eight of them altogether. Take your time and learn them well.

Fig. 24-3   Long-Run Cost: Constant Returns to Scale

Size has no effect on cost. The average total cost (cost per unit) is the same for the large plant (or firm) as for the small one.

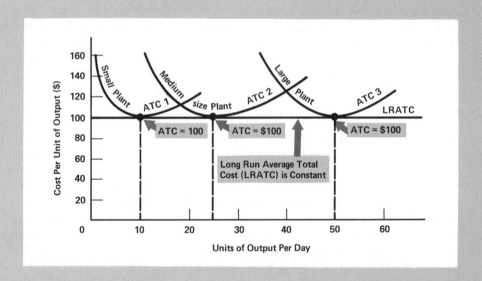

This figure shows the average total cost curve for a small (10-unit) plant, a somewhat larger (25-unit) plant, and a much larger (50-unit) plant. You can see from the graph that if each plant is operated at its most efficient rate of output the ATC (cost per unit) will be the same for each plant.

If you were a producer in this industry, would you rather have a large plant? or a small plant? It really wouldn't make any difference. The small one is just as efficient as the big one. There are no increasing returns or decreasing returns to scale—no economies of scale at all.

Both large firms and small firms could exist in this industry. Large firms would have no cost advantage over small ones. (Of course the large firms might try to use underhanded methods to cut out their smaller competitors. But that's something else, and it's illegal. We'll be talking about that sort of thing later.)

(Note: The ATC curves in this figure can be used to represent either *plant size* or *firm size*. A firm may have one plant or several plants. Also *plant size* can refer to one factory operation or to a group of several different factories and operations. Either way you think of it, the principles still hold true.)

Fig. 24-4   Long-Run Cost: Increasing Returns, then Decreasing Returns to Scale

In this industry there is one certain plant size (or firm size) which is just right for maximum efficiency. Plants (or firms) of any other size will be less efficient.

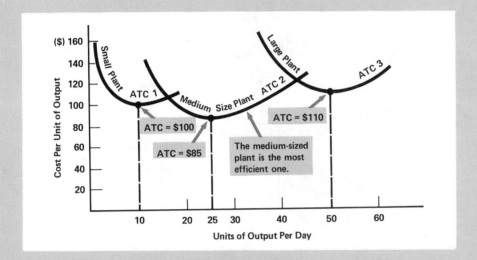

This graph shows the small (10-unit) plant is not as efficient as (has higher cost per unit than) the larger (25-unit) plant. But the graph also shows the largest (50-unit) plant is even less efficient than the small one.

If there is pure competition in this industry, then the only size firm that can survive is the medium size one (ATC_2). Why? Because if the price is high enough to let the ATC_1 and ATC_3 firms break even, the ATC_2 firms will be making excess profits! New producers will enter the industry and build ATC_2 size plants to get some of the excess profits. The supply will keep increasing and the price will keep going down until only ATC_2 firms can survive.

Suppose you were a producer with monopoly power. And suppose you didn't think your market was big enough to take 25 units—that is, not without a big price cut which would wipe out your profits. What would you do? You have a choice:

(1) You could build the most efficient size plant and operate it at a small (inefficient) output rate, or

(2) You could build a smaller plant and operate it closer to its maximum efficiency output.

Which choice would the monopolistic seller make? The one expected to result in maximum profit, considering both (1) the cost alternatives of different plant sizes, and (2) the revenue alternatives of different volumes of sales. Of course.

Fig. 24-5   Long-Run Average Total Cost: the Envelope Curve

If plant size is completely divisible and variable, then the long-run average total cost (LRATC) curve is tangent to all of the possible short-run average total cost (ATC) curves.

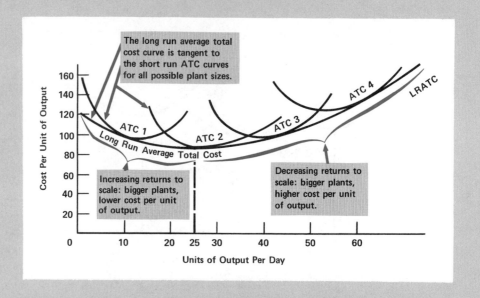

The long-run average total cost (LRATC) curve shows the most efficient plant size (or firm size) in this industry. This curve shows that smaller firms can expand and get increasing returns to scale. But if a firm expands beyond the most efficient (25-unit) size, then decreasing returns will result. Cost per unit will go up.

Can the shape of the LRATC curve influence the number of producers in an industry?—that is, the number of sellers in a market? Definitely! If the most efficient firm size is very small, then there will be lots of producer-sellers. Most likely pure competition will exist.

But suppose it takes a very large plant (and therefore a very large firm) to be most efficient. Then there won't be many producers in the industry. The market certainly won't have pure competition on the seller's side! The graphs on the next page (Figure 24-6) illustrate this idea.

Fig. 24-6 How Long-Run Average Total Cost (LRATC) Influences Market Structure

These different LRATC curves illustrate the influence of long-run average cost (returns to scale) on market structure. If the most efficient size is very small, then *pure competition* can exist; if the most efficient size is very large, then the market will have *monopoly* on the seller's side.

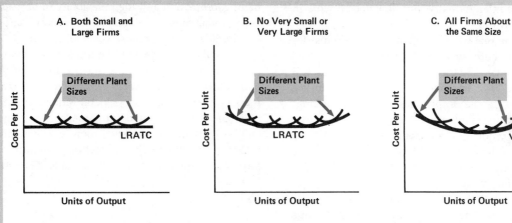

A. Both Small and Large Firms

If the LRATC is constant (showing constant returns to scale) there can be all sizes of firms in the industry -- big ones and small ones, all existing together.

B. No Very Small or Very Large Firms

With this shape of curve there won't be any very small firms or any very large ones. But there will be a broad range of sizes, ranging between "not very small" and "not very large."

C. All Firms About the Same Size

With this curve, all of the firms in the the industry will be the same size. Smaller firms must expand to the most efficient size; larger firms must reduce their size.

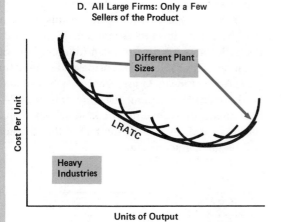

D. All Large Firms: Only a Few Sellers of the Product

With this shape of curve, there are increasing returns to scale until the plant gets quite large. After that, there are decreasing returns to scale. In this industry all the firms will be large. This curve describes "heavy industries" such as automobile, steel, aluminum, and other such industries.

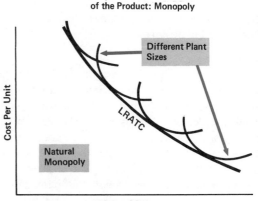

E. Only One Producer-Seller of the Product: Monopoly

With this LRATC curve there can be only one firm. The only firm which can exist is one which serves the entire market. This illustrates LRATC in the public utilities. This industry is a "natural monopoly."

What About Returns to Scale in Real-World Industries?

From all the graphs you just studied you know that the long-run average total cost (LRATC) curve can be very different from one industry to another. And you know that the shape of LRATC has a lot to do with the market structure in an industry. But how does it work in the real world?

In the real world there are several industries in which both small and large firms can exist side-by-side—like the situation shown in graph B in Figure 24-6. You see this in such industries as: furniture, some appliances, food processing, meat packing, brewing, retail groceries, trucking, clothing production and some others.

Then there are some industries in which the firms seem to tend toward the same size (although not really very close) as shown by graph C in Figure 24-6. Firms in retail trade and some kinds of light manufacturing seem to fit this pattern.

Returns to Scale Can Destroy Pure Competition. In some industries economies of scale *absolutely require* that only big businesses can survive. In such an industry, pure competition couldn't exist! (But note this: increasing returns to scale *isn't the only explanation* for the existence of big businesses!)

Why Are Big Firms Sometimes More Efficient? What is more efficient about big firms than small ones? Big firms can use some techniques which small firms can't. The very latest technology sometimes requires the use of very large machines. With a large firm there can be more specialization, more division of labor. Assembly lines, mass production, computerization of the production process all require big plants.

The opportunity for specialization by supervisors and management people can sometimes add to efficiency. A big firm may be able to make use of by-products, or produce a variety of related "joint products" at lower cost than each product could be produced separately. There are likely to be more possibilities for resource exploration, research into new technology, etc. with a large firm than with a small one.

But big firms sometimes can be less efficient than smaller ones. The difficulties of management coordination and the inflexibility of bureaucracy sometimes cause problems for very large firms and sometimes cause costs to go up.

Usually there seems to be quite a lot of variability in how large or how small a firm can be and still be efficient. Most economists agree that massive corporations like General Motors or U.S. Steel could be separated into smaller firms and still be efficient—maybe even more efficient. But a firm in the automobile or steel or aluminum or any of the other heavy industries could never be "small."

The Heavy Industries Have High Fixed Cost. Very high fixed costs are required to "tool up" a firm in the heavy industries. With high fixed costs the volume of output must be large to make the operation profitable. But this doesn't mean that several giant plants must be tied together and owned by the same giant corporation!

You'll be seeing a lot more on this issue of "big business" in Parts Seven and Eight of this book. But now it's time to ask a different kind of question: How does the business decide *what combination of inputs to use?* That is, what should be the *proportions* among the different inputs?—how much of each different kind of labor and resources and capital? All the rest of this chapter will be talking about that.

THE PRODUCTION FUNCTION

For several chapters you've been reading about how a business adjusts its *output* in order to influence its costs. And you've been reading about the effect of output adjustments on revenues and profits. But what about the question of adjusting the *inputs*?

Adjusting the "Input Mix"

What about maybe using more machines and less labor? or different kinds of materials? or maybe different kinds of labor? with different skills? What about that? Isn't it possible to adjust inputs and reduce costs? and increase profits? Of course it is.

All along we have been assuming that the business somehow finds the right combination of inputs. Now it's time to look into this question. So it's time to talk about the **production function**.

The output of a firm is a "function of" the inputs. That means the output "depends on" or "results from" the inputs. Nobody could disagree with that. Right?

What are the inputs? Labor and land and capital. And we could break down the inputs into different kinds of labor, land, and capital. If we wanted to we could define 50 or 100 or maybe 1,000 different "inputs." Businesses have to deal with lots of different kinds of inputs. But that kind of detailed breakdown isn't necessary to let you see the principles at work.

Output Is a Function of the Inputs

You can guess right away that *for each output* a business might want to produce, there would be *a variety of input choices*—that is, there would be a variety of possible "production functions." Each production function would contain a certain amount of: various kinds of labor, various kinds of land and resources, and various kinds of capital.

The "production function" shows the "input mix" and the "maximum achievable output" using *that combination of inputs.*

Each production function is a set of "input-use rates" showing how much of each input factor will be used and showing the rate of output flow to be generated. We could say it this way: Output (O) is a function (*f*) of the following inputs: Labor (l), land and resources (r), and capital (c). Or, in symbolic shorthand:

$$O = f\,(l, r, c)$$

That's a production function. But it doesn't tell you any more than you already knew. All it tells you is that the output is a function of the inputs.

For any given output rate you choose, some production functions (input combinations) will cost more than others. Some might cost a *lot more*. (Using moon rocks to pave driveways? Ridiculous.) So which production function do you choose? The one that produces the desired output for the lowest cost? Sure.

THE "LEAST COST COMBINATION" OF INPUTS

Each business must choose among a variety of different production functions (input combinations) for any chosen output rate. And it isn't easy to choose. There's a lot of "substitutability" among the input factors.

Capital can be substituted for labor. One kind of labor or capital can be substituted for another. Different kinds of material inputs can be used. Some materials will require more labor and/or more capital than others. The range of input combination choices is almost unlimited.

Producer Choices are Like Consumer Choices

The task of a business choosing among inputs is about like your task of deciding which consumer goods to buy. How does the business decide? In about the same way the consumer decides. The business tries to adjust its spending so that each dollar spent will do as much good as possible—that is, *so that each dollar spent will add as much marginal product as possible.*

The consumer tries to get each "marginal dollar" to bring in as much "marginal utility" as possible. The consumer's equilibrium combination (the "maximum utility consumption mix") is where the marginal-utility-per-dollar-spent is the same for each good being consumed. That means there's no opportunity to shift spending from one good to another and gain any more utility. You learned all about that back in Chapter 20.

When the business seeks its "least cost combination input mix," exactly the same principle applies. The business tries to get the maximum "marginal physical product (MPP) per dollar" for each marginal dollar spent for a unit of input. Of course!

Here's an example: Suppose you could hire another worker (unit of labor) for $1,000 per month. And suppose this worker would add a marginal physical product (MPP) of 10 cartons of jeans per month. Suppose you could also rent a computerized cutting machine for $1,000 per month which would add 20 cartons per month to your output. Which would you hire? It's obvious, isn't it? You will spend your $1,000 where it will bring you a marginal physical product (MPP) of 20 cartons—not 10 cartons. Of course.

Now suppose you have rented a few of those machines for $1,000 per month and you've laid off some workers. Now the situation is dif-

ferent. Suppose the MPP of your latest additional machine is only 12 cartons per month, but the MPP you lost on the latest worker you fired was 16 cartons per month. Looks like you've gone too far! Now you need to adjust your production function back the other way—to use more labor and less capital.

The Least-Cost Input Combination: Equal MPP Per Dollar

Can you see where the least cost combination is going to be? Of course! It's where the extra product (MPP) per dollar spent is as large as it can be. And where is that? Where the "MPP per dollar spent" is the same for each input factor you are using. It works out exactly the same way as the principle of "equal utilities per dollar." Exactly!

Remember the "equal utilities per dollar" equation? Well, here's the "equal productivity per dollar" equation. You'll see that it looks exactly the same.

The Least-Cost Combination Equation. This equation shows "equal marginal physical product per dollar." It's just another way of saying exactly what you have been reading. It doesn't tell you anything more. But it does give you a convenient shorthand method of expressing it. So here it is. The producer's least-cost input combination is where:

(1) Marginal physical product (MPP) received *per dollar spent* on input A = MPP received *per dollar spent* on input B = MPP received *per dollar spent* on input C = . . . = MPP received per dollar spent on input n.

How do we get the "MPP received per dollar spent," for each factor? Like this:

(2) $\dfrac{\text{MPP received from a marginal unit of input A}}{\text{Price per unit of input A}}$

= MPP received per dollar spent on input A

or to abbreviate:

(3) $\dfrac{\text{MPP of A}}{\text{P of A}}$ = MPP *per dollar* on input A;

$\dfrac{\text{MPP of B}}{\text{P of B}}$ = MPP *per dollar* on input B; etc.

Therefore the equation showing the producer's least-cost combination (equation 1) now becomes:

(4) $\dfrac{\text{MPP of A}}{\text{P of A}} = \dfrac{\text{MPP of B}}{\text{P of B}} = \dfrac{\text{MPP of C}}{\text{P of C}} =$

$\cdots = \dfrac{\text{MPP of n}}{\text{P of n}}$

This is the equation which shows the producer's least cost input combination. If you will adjust your *combination of inputs* to where the conditions shown in this equation are met and simultaneously adjust your output to where your marginal cost equals your marginal revenue (MC = MR) then that's absolutely the best you can do. You're making as much profit as you possibly can within the constraints of your given situation.

Least-Cost Input Combination: The Isocost and Isoquant Technique

Now here's another way of getting the least-cost combination. It's just exactly like the "indifference curves and budget lines" technique that you learned in Chapter 20. Only now, instead of "consumption combinations which bring equal utility" we are dealing with "input combinations which produce equal output."

Here's how it works: Suppose you want to produce a certain quantity of output—say 10 cartons of jeans per day. You could produce that output using a few workers and a lot of specialized machines. Or you could use more workers and less capital. Which combination will you choose? The least-cost one of course! It's easy to

see this on a graph.

In Figure 24-7 you'll see an isoquant (equal quantity of output) curve. That curve shows you the various combinations of labor and machines you could use to produce an output quantity of 10 cartons per day. You'll also see some isocost curves (equal-cost input combinations) which show you what the various labor-and-capital combinations will cost you.

If you are familiar with weather maps, the names of these curves will seem familiar to you. On the weather map an "isotherm" is a line joining points of equal temperature. An "isobar" is a line connecting points of equal barometric pressure. In Figure 24-7 you see "isocost" curves joining points of equal cost and an "isoquant" curve joining points of equal quantity of output. What does "iso" mean? Equal. Of course.

What labor-and-capital combination do you choose? The combination which lets you produce your 10 cartons per day at lowest cost! Of course.

This graph shows quite clearly what your "least-cost input combination" is, between machines and labor. Now study Figure 24-7 and you'll see it's exactly like the "indifference curves and budget lines technique" which you already know from Chapter 20.

Now that you have studied Figure 24-7, you know the two basic ways of analyzing the "optimum input decision" of a business. You know the optimal position is where the marginal physical product per dollar is the same for each input factor. And you know how to indicate this combination (a) using the MPP/P equation, and (b) using the isocost and isoquant technique. If you understand all this, then you understand the basic principles of least-cost combination. And if so, that's enough for now.

Fig. 24-7   **Finding the Least-Cost Input Combination: The Isocost-Isoquant Technique**

Where the isoquant is tangent to the isocost line that's your least-cost combination between labor and capital. The only way you can get as much output as the isoquant indicates, with a cost that low, is to use the input combination indicated by the point of tangency.

At the point of tangency the isoquant and isocost curves have the same slope. So at that point the marginal productivity ratios and the price ratios of the two inputs are equal:

$$\frac{MPPx}{MPPy} = \frac{Px}{Py}$$

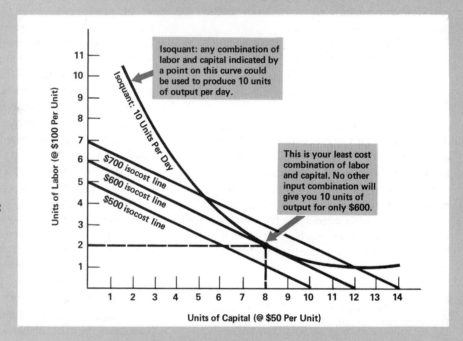

Isoquant: any combination of labor and capital indicated by a point on this curve could be used to produce 10 units of output per day.

This is your least cost combination of labor and capital. No other input combination will give you 10 units of output for only $600.

The lowest cost of producing 10 units a day is $600. You buy 8 units of capital at $50 per unit: total, $400. You buy 2 units of labor at $100 per unit: total, $200. Your total capital and labor input cost is $600.

If you used some other combination of labor and capital, you would have to pay more for inputs—or else you would get less than 10 units of output.

The slope of the isoquant indicates the "marginal rate of substitution" of capital for labor (or vice versa). That is, it shows how much capital is needed to offset the loss of a unit of labor (or vice versa) and still produce the same quantity of output.

You can see the marginal rate of substitution keeps changing as you move along the curve from one labor-and-capital combination to another. Why? Because of the law of diminishing returns. Because as the proportions between capital and labor change, the marginal rate of substitution of one for the other changes also.

SUMMARY AND SYNTHESIS

The elasticity of the supply—i.e., the **responsiveness of the quantity supplied when the price changes**—depends a lot on how long you wait. The supply curves you saw in the previous chapter were for the **short run**—that's a time period long enough for businesses to change their **variable factors** and produce more, or less. But it's not long enough for them to change their **fixed factors.**

Economists define the **long run as a period long enough for all input factors to be adjusted.** It's long enough to build a new plant, or even to get out of this business and go into something else.

In the **very-short-run** time period there isn't enough time to change the output at all. So the only function which price can perform is to **ration the existing goods among the buyers.** The production-motivating function of price doesn't work at all in the very short run. It operates **some in the short run, but it operates much more in the long run.**

The **normal price** is a price high enough to bring the typical producer a **normal profit,** but **no excess profit.** When the normal price exists in an industry, the industry is in **equilibrium**—neither expanding nor contracting. At a price **above normal,** the industry will be **expanding; below normal,** contracting. But **sufficient competition** is necessary to guarantee that these supply adjustments will occur.

The concept of **long-run supply** involves two questions: (1) **how many firms will there be in the** industry? and (2) **how big will each firm be?** In pure competition, when an industry is expanding that usually means **more firms are coming in.** But in an industry where **monopoly power exists,** increasing output in the long run may mean **the firms in the industry are getting larger.**

In pure competition, the **long-run supply (LRS) curve** consists of **points of normal price** as the industry expands. The shape and slope of the curve shows if (and how much) the **normal price**

would change as the industry expands or contracts.

A seller in **pure competition** is forced (in the long run) to build **the most efficient-sized plant** and to operate it at the **most efficient rate.** Firms which do not do this will not survive because the **normal price** will cover only **maximum-efficiency costs**—and no more than that.

A seller with monopoly power must consider the **size and elasticity of the demand** for the product. Sometimes a monopolistic seller may find it most profitable not to build the **most efficient-sized plant** or to operate it at the most efficient rate. Maximum efficiency might require producing **too much, pushing the price down, and reducing profits.**

When economies of scale are possible, that means **larger plants are more efficient than** smaller ones. So pure competition can't exist in this industry. But where there are **constant returns to scale** (constant costs) or **decreasing returns to scale** (increasing costs) pure competition is **technically feasible.** So the question of "returns to scale" has a lot to do with the **market structure** in an industry.

The **long-run average total cost (LRATC)** curve indicates **returns to scale:** increasing, constant, or decreasing. The curve shows how high the short-run ATC curve would be for different sized plants, or firms.

A **production function** says that the **output is a function of** (depends on, or results from) the **input mix.** For example, a production function might say:

$$O = f (l, r, c)$$

which says: "output (O) is a function (f) of the labor (l), land and resources (r), and capital (c) inputs."

Different production functions are simply different combinations of inputs. The most profitable production function would be the **"least-cost combination"** of inputs capable of producing the desired output.

The least-cost combination occurs where the $\frac{MPP}{P}$ ratio is equal for all input factors—where $\frac{MPP \text{ of } A}{P \text{ of } A}$ equals $\frac{MPP \text{ of } B}{P \text{ of } B}$ etc., for all inputs. This says that if a unit of one input costs twice as much as another, then that input must be producing twice as much as the other.

The least-cost input combination can also be found using isocost and isoquant curves. These curves are exactly the same as indifference curves and budget lines except that we are now comparing **marginal-productivity-to-price** ratios instead of marginal-utility-to-price ratios.

A final word: long-run supply (LRS) reflects **cost changes (if any) as more firms enter the industry. Long-run average total cost (LRATC) reflects cost changes as the size of the individual firm or plant gets larger.** Try not to confuse these two related but nevertheless distinctly different things.

REVIEW EXERCISES

MAJOR CONCEPTS, PRINCIPLES, TERMS (Explain each carefully.)

why all factors are variable in the long run
long-run supply
the difference between long-run supply and LRATC
the effect of returns to scale on market structure
the production function
the "equal MPP per dollar" equation
the isocost-isoquant technique

OTHER CONCEPTS AND TERMS (Explain each briefly.)

long-run supply
long-run average total cost
normal price
normal profit
long-run equilibrium
the short run

the long run
very short run
momentary supply
economies of scale
increasing returns to scale
decreasing returns to scale

CURVES AND GRAPHS (Draw, label, and explain each.)

LRS in Pure Competition: (a) Constant Cost. (b) Increasing Cost.
Long-run Cost: (a) Constant Returns. (b) Increasing, then Decreasing.
Long-run Average Total Cost: (a) Envelope Curve. (b) Market Structure.
Least-Cost Input Combination: Using Isocost-Isoquant Curves

QUESTIONS (Write out the answers, or jot down key points.)

1. Explain how normal price comes about automatically.
2. The long-run supply curve and the long-run average total cost curve are quite different. Explain exactly what determines the shape of each.
3. In pure competition, only the most efficient firms could survive. Why?
4. Explain the relationships between the (1) equal MPP per dollar approach and (2) Isocost-Isoquant technique. Why must both always come out the same?

25

Input Markets and Output Markets: Cost, Supply, and Normal Price

Chapter Objectives

- This chapter **applies the principles** you have learned in previous chapters. It gives an **integrated view** of how the model market system works: through **demand** and **supply** and the **price mechanism.**

- When you finish studying this chapter you will have a good understanding of the **interrelationships between the input markets and the output markets**—of consumer demand and **derived demand** and how the **functions of price** operate in both the **input and output markets.**

- When you finish studying this chapter you will be able to **explain** and **draw graphs to illustrate** the effects of **changing input prices** (changing costs of production) on **output quantities** and prices—short run and long run.

- You will be able to explain the important role of **price elasticity** in influencing (specifically) the **input and output responses,** and (in general) the **functioning of the market process** and the **effectiveness of the price mechanism.**

- From this chapter you will gain an **integrated understanding** of the **functional interrelationships** among the input and output markets.

Input Markets Are Like Output Markets

In the "model market system" what happens when the demand for a product increases? It creates a shortage and the price goes up. Then producers produce more. In the long run, the industry expands.

When the producers expand their output, where do you suppose all the extra labor and capital and materials and other inputs come from? They're bought in the **input factor markets,** of course!

There is a demand for each input factor, just as there is a demand for each output product. When the *demand* for an input factor increases, its *price* increases (just like in the output markets). Remember?

FACTOR DEMAND IS DERIVED DEMAND

Increased *factor demand* results from increased *consumer demand.* That's why economists refer to "consumer demand" as **final demand** and to "factor demand" as **derived demand.**

When people demand things to "consume," this means they want to use things for their own personal desires, needs, pleasures, objectives. It is from this *final consumer demand* that all factor demands are derived.

It's easy to see that if there's no *final demand* for something there will be no "derived demand" for the factors to produce that "undemanded something." *The greater the final demand for a product the greater will be the derived demand for the factors needed to produce that product.*

Suppose I demand a tractor to help me to raise my backyard corn crop. My demand for the tractor results from the fact that there is a demand for my corn.

If there was no demand for corn then there would be no demand for tractors to be used in growing corn. There would be no demand for tractor tires to go on the corn-producing tractors. There would be no demand for labor to produce the tires or for steel to build the tractor or for iron ore to make the steel or for steam shovels to scoop up the iron ore.

All demands for all things ultimately result from the final demand to consume things. When you think about it, how obvious that is!

All kinds of basic and intermediate products are being produced all the time. But if there wasn't any consumer demand for the final products, all this productive activity would stop! Anything which increases the final demand for a product *automatically* increases the demand for the input factors used to produce it.

Factor Markets Respond to Changing Demand

In the model market system, whenever consumer demand for a product increases, the price goes up. Then the demand for the factors needed to make the product will go up. Shortages will show up in these factor markets and will push up the prices of these factors. The higher factor prices will pull in additional factors.

Increased *consumer demand* pushes up the price and signals the need to expand the industry. Then it is through the increased *derived demand* for the factors of production that society's wish is carried out. It's "consumer sovereignty" and "the invisible hand" in action!

When the consumer demand for eggs increases and the price of eggs goes up, businesses start to pull together the needed factors and go into the egg business—factors attracted by the highly profitable price that eggs are bringing these days.

Some profit-seeking business will offer a good price to buy or lease your land. Businesses will run ads in the *Chicago Tribune* offering good wages for workers who would like to shift into egg production. Also they will contact the farm equipment people and place orders for egg-producing machinery and equipment.

As the businesses get the needed input factors they will start producing more eggs. Society's wish for more eggs is being fulfilled. See how neatly it all fits together? Consumer sovereignty and the invisible hand. Great!

As One Industry Demands More Inputs, Another Demands Less

As the egg industry is expanding, where are all the extra input factors coming from? From somewhere else, of course. But where? In the model market system it works like this:

As the demand for eggs increases, the consumers who are eating more eggs are eating *less* of something else. They are buying less cheese or meat or pork sausage or pancake mix or corn flakes or something. The increased demand for eggs brings an increased price for eggs and increased derived demand for the factors of production needed to produce eggs.

But at the same time the *decreased demand for the other products* is bringing decreased prices and decreased derived demands for the factors needed to produce the other products. Of course!

The egg producers are expanding their operations, demanding more factors of production and paying higher prices for the factors (land, labor and capital). Sure. But the businesses in the declining industries are reducing their operations, demanding fewer factors of production and paying lower prices for the factors. They're trying to get out of the "declining demand" industries and into something better as soon as they can.

The whole scene is one of resources moving out of the areas of declining demand and lower prices and into the areas of increasing demand and higher prices. It is the shift in consumer demand (from other things to eggs) which initiates this process. It is the shift in the demand for the factors of production which carries out and completes the process.

Consumer Demand and Derived Demand: A Summary

What you have read in this section describes a major segment of "the market process in action." In capsule form it's essentially this:

When the consumers demand more eggs the price of eggs goes up. Businesses seeking more profits demand more egg-producing factors. The higher demand brings higher prices for the egg-producing factors. The higher prices attract more factors into this "shortage" industry and get them to do what the society wants them to do—produce more eggs.

You already know this, but another word of warning just now won't hurt. Don't forget: this very neat way in which the "model market system" operates is not exactly the way the market process works in the real world.

All of Part Seven (coming up soon) will deal with "real-world imperfections" in the operation of the market process. There you'll find out something about how well (or how poorly) the "imperfect real-world market process" really does work—how well it serves the interests of society. But before you get into that, here's more that you need to know about the model system.

HOW THE SUPPLY RESPONDS TO COST CHANGES

Let's go back to the initial egg market (back in Chapter 5) before the increase in demand. The price of eggs was 75¢ a dozen and the equilibrium quantity flowing across the market was 10 carloads per week. Then the demand increased. The price went up to $1.00 and the higher price brought forth more eggs. Remember?

Now let's look at it another way. Suppose the demand for eggs didn't change. But suppose something happened to *change the supply* instead. What might happen to cause the supply to change? Then what would happen next?

You already know that for sellers in pure competition, the marginal cost curve (at prices above the average variable cost) is always the supply curve. And you know that the supply curve for the entire market is nothing more than a composite curve made up by adding together all the marginal cost curves of all the little firms in the industry.

So implicitly you already know the two things that would cause the market supply curve to change: (1) more little firms or less little firms in the industry, or (2) higher or lower marginal costs for each little firm. Let's talk about both of these kinds of changes in market supply.

Supply Changes as Firms Enter or Leave the Industry

If the number of firms in the industry increases, this will increase the supply. It adds more "little marginal cost curves" to the total "composite market supply curve." If more firms are producing and adding their outputs to the market, then the total amount arriving in the market is greater. Obviously.

You have already seen how the supply increases as more firms enter the industry. Remember (in Chapter 5) how the industry expanded following the increase in the price of eggs to $1.00 a dozen? As the industry expanded, the supply increased—shifted to the right on the graph—to show that more eggs would be shipped into the market at each price. The extra carloads of eggs came from the new egg producers—the new little firms in the industry.

It works the other way too, of course. If firms leave the industry the amount coming into the market at each price gets smaller. The supply curve shifts to the left.

Supply Changes as Factor Costs Change

The other way for the supply to change is for the cost of production to change. Any change in the firm's marginal cost will change the amount the firm will produce and sell at each price.

1. If the variable input factors get more expensive (or less productive) the marginal cost will increase. As the marginal cost increases, the *supply will decrease.* Less will be produced and offered for sale at each price.

2. If the input factors get cheaper (or more productive), the marginal cost will go down and the *supply will increase.* More will be offered for sale at each price.

It is obvious that changes in the prices you have to pay for variable factors will change your marginal cost. But when factor prices change, this changes *more* than just the *marginal cost.* It changes the *entire cost and profit picture* for each firm in the industry. The *long-run* effects of such changes can be really big!

How a Cost Increase Affects a Business

Suppose that for some reason there is a big wage increase in the garment industry. Your jeans plant feels the effect right away.

The higher wages push your marginal cost way up. This changes the amount you will supply in short run. But that isn't all. Now you have higher average costs per unit and higher total costs for each daily rate of output. The higher costs wipe out your profits. You are losing money!

What happens to your cost per unit (as shown by your average cost curve)? The per unit cost goes up. *The average cost curve shifts upward.* The per unit profit you were making (shown by how high your price was above your average cost curve) is all gone. Now, even at your "most profitable output" your price is *below* your average cost.

When your *per-unit cost is higher than the price,* you're losing money on each unit you're selling! Figure 25-1 shows the picture and tells the story. Spend a few minutes studying that graph now.

How to Choose Your "Minimum Loss" Output

Now you know what happens when the cost goes up. Your average cost is higher than the price. You lose money no matter what output you choose. But *the output where your marginal cost equals your marginal revenue is your "minimum loss" output.* You produce at that rate and plan to get out of the jeans business as soon as you can.

Let's suppose that the retailer you sell to won't pay you any more than $100 a carton even after the cost increase. Then maybe you will just go out of business. Or maybe you will produce something else or find another market where you can sell your jeans. Let's talk about how it would work out in a market of pure competition in the model market system.

In the Long Run, Firms Will Leave the Industry

The higher cost means that all the little firms in the industry are losing money. They will be trying to find something more rewarding to do so they can get out of this industry. The most

Fig. 25-1   When Cost Increases, the Cost Curves Shift Upward

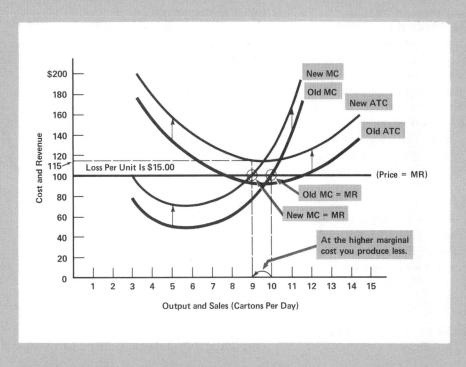

When the wage rate goes up, output is cut back. The "most profitable" output is 9 cartons, and you're losing money!

When the cost goes up, you cut back your output to where MC = MR: 9 cartons a day. You are losing $15 a carton, for a total daily loss of $135 (9 units @ $15 = $135).

If you shut down your plant you lose $150 per day (your fixed cost). It's better for you to produce and lose $135 than to shut down and lose $150. But you must find some way to reduce your cost or increase your revenue or else you must get out of this business. Otherwise you will go broke.

The cost increase is shown on the graph as an upward shift of both the ATC and MC curves. It's the ATC curve that tells you whether or not you are making a profit or loss. It's the MC curve that tells you how much to produce and supply to the market.

Notice that the cost increase shifts the MC curve upward. But when you think of the MC curve as the supply curve this amounts to a *leftward* shift in the curve—indicating a smaller quantity offered for sale at each price you might choose. You will see this idea more clearly in Figure 25-2, coming up soon.

This graph does not show your average variable cost. (The graph looks cluttered enough as it is!) But don't forget: the marginal cost curve is the supply curve for your firm *only* at prices equal to or above the average variable cost. At prices below the average variable cost you will not produce and supply anything because if you did your losses would be greater than if you shut down and lost your entire fixed cost of $150 per day.

flexible firms can get out first. As they leave the industry one by one this will reduce the supply (shift the market supply curve to the left).

The increased cost already reduced the market supply (shifted the curve) once. It caused each "typical firm" to cut back from 10 units to 9 units (as shown in Figure 25-1). Now, as the money-losing firms start leaving the industry the market supply will be reduced even more. The curve will shift to the left even more.

As time goes on, more and more firms get out of the industry. The market supply is reduced more and more, step by step. Each reduction in supply causes a little *shortage* in the market and *pushes the price up a little bit*. Each time the price inches up it cuts down a little bit on the losses of the firms remaining in the industry. You can look at Figure 25-1 and see what will happen as the price line inches up from $100 to $101 to $102 and on upward as more firms leave the industry.

The Price Goes Up Enough to Cover the Cost

As long as there are losses in the industry, firms will keep on leaving, seeking "normal profits" (or better) elsewhere. How long will the decrease in the market supply (the leftward shifting of the supply curve) continue?

Firms will continue to leave until the market price goes up enough to cover the increased costs and to provide "normal profits" to the firms remaining in the industry—that is, until the new normal price is reached. At the new normal price, all of the buyers who are still buying the product will be paying the full cost of production, including (a) enough to cover the higher wages, and also including (b) a normal profit for "the average firm" remaining in the industry.

The Effects of a Cost Increase: A Summary

The wage increase at first shifted the cost curves upward. That's what *reduced the short-run*

supply. That caused some shortages so the price increased some. But the firms in the industry still were losing money.

The money-losing firms began to leave the industry. They kept on leaving the industry, reducing the supply little by little until the price was pushed up to "normal" again.

The "long-run condition" arrives. The industry is stable again. Now this product is more expensive. Society is more carefully conserving its higher-priced, scarcer, more valuable factor of production—labor.

What we've just seen is how this adjustment process looks from the point of view of "the typical firm." Now let's take an "egg market" example and watch how this process works itself out in the total market.

A COST INCREASE AFFECTS THE ENTIRE MARKET

Let's begin by supposing that cost of production has increased in the egg business and has forced up the "normal price" from 75¢ to $1 a dozen. Eggs will now have to sell for a dollar a dozen in order for the egg producers to make enough profit to keep them from leaving the egg business. What might cause such a cost increase to occur? Let's look at some of the possibilities.

Why Does Cost Increase?

Any one of the factors of production might have become more scarce or more expensive. A wheat blight or corn rust disease might have made grain very scarce and forced up the price of chicken feed. Something might have happened to cause more of the egg-laying hens to die. Transportation costs might have gone up. Or electricity or water rates might have gone up.

Strong demands for labor in the economy might have pushed up wage rates. Or maybe the poultry workers decided to unionize and strike for higher wages. Or maybe the government passed a minimum wage law or some new health and safety regulations which require expensive equipment or more skilled personnel or more expensive procedures.

Or maybe a new anti-pollution regulation requires more expensive equipment and procedures to eliminate the smell of chickens (or other chicken-related smells). Or perhaps the state and local governments decided to impose higher taxes.

Many things could happen to cause an increase in the cost of producing eggs. No matter what makes the cost go up, the effect on the supply in the long run will be the same. But in the short run it can make a difference.

A Fixed-Cost Increase. Suppose the cost increase is a *fixed cost increase* (like higher property taxes on your buildings). Would that increase your marginal cost? No. Not at all.

Fixed cost has no influence on marginal cost. Remember? So the market supply would not shift immediately. The price would not start moving up until firms began to leave the industry.

A Variable-Cost Increase. The marginal cost only reflects the *variable costs,* of course. So if the marginal cost curve shifts upward (causing an immediate shift in the short-run supply curve) then that means the cost increase is an increase in variable cost (like higher wages, or feed prices). The supply curves in Figures 25-2 and 25-3 show that the cost increases in both these cases are increases in *variable costs.*

Whenever the variable cost increases because of higher-priced variable inputs, the marginal cost will shift upward, the supply curve will shift to the left, and shortages will develop in the egg markets. All the egg buyers will start bidding against each other, offering more money to try to get their "normal amounts" of eggs. The price will go up.

At the higher price the shortage will be eliminated. Once again we will have a *short-run equilibrium*. The quantities shipped into the market by the sellers will be equal to the quantities taken out of the market by the buyers. But the quantity flowing across the market will be smaller than before.

High Prices Conserve Scarce Products and Factors

Eggs are now more scarce and more valuable than before. Eggs will be more carefully conserved. The factors of production used to produce eggs will also be more carefully conserved.

If the higher cost results from corn rust destroying much of the corn crop, the higher price of eggs will reduce the amount of corn needed for chicken feed. So more of the very scarce corn will be available for other purposes. If the higher cost is a result of a higher demand for labor in the economy, the higher price for eggs will conserve the use of labor in egg production and will let more of the labor be used to do some of the other things the society wants done.

Figure 25-2 shows how this situation looks in the egg market and explains what happens. Study that graph now and I think it will all fit together for you.

Supply Keeps Changing to Bring a New "Normal Price"

Figure 25-2 shows that the new short-run equilibrium market price moves up to 90¢ a dozen. At this price the producers will ship in more eggs than they would at 75¢. But at 90¢ the producers will supply less than the 10 carloads they were selling before the cost increase. The graph shows that the new (temporary) equilibrium quantity flowing across the market will be 7½ carloads a week.

The higher price (90¢) partly offsets the higher cost of production, but not completely. The egg producers are still losing money. As soon as they can make the shift, some egg producers will stop producing eggs and start producing turkeys or broilers or maybe pork or beef or something else. Or maybe some of them will

Fig. 25-2 Increased Cost of the Variable Inputs Decreases the Supply in the Short Run

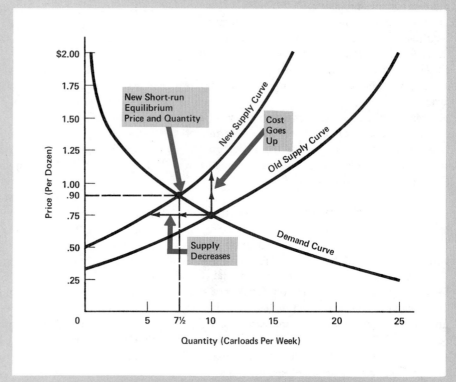

When the marginal cost curve shifts upward that means the supply curve shifts to the left.

(*Note:* This graph would not apply to an increase in fixed cost, such as a property tax increase.)

At each level of *output* the marginal cost is higher. (The marginal cost curves of all the little firms shift *upward*.) Therefore at each *price* the quantity offered for sale is smaller. The *supply curve* represents both these shifts—upward for cost and leftward for the supply.

The shift of the supply curve to the left shows that after the cost goes up, the quantity of eggs offered for sale at a price of 75¢ drops back from 10 carloads to 5 carloads a week. So no longer can 75¢ be the equilibrium price.

People are trying to buy 10 carloads of eggs and only 5 are available. There is a shortage. Eggs are more scarce—harder to get. Up goes the price. Hungry buyers keep offering higher prices until the price of eggs moves up to where the quantity offered by the sellers is equal to the quantity demanded by the buyers.

The new price of 90¢ provides a new equilibrium flow of eggs across the market, with a total of 7½ carloads per week being exchanged. But remembering Figure 25-1, you should expect that even at this higher price the egg-producing firms are losing money. In the long run some firms will leave the industry. So in the long run the supply will shift even more to the left and the price will rise even more.

just go broke, move to the big city and go on welfare. It wouldn't be the first time something like that has ever happened!

As each producer shifts out of the egg industry, the supply of eggs will decrease a little more and the price will move up a little more. Producers will continue to leave the industry and the supply will continue to get smaller (shift to the left). For how long? Until the price gets high enough to provide normal profits to all those who are still producing eggs.

If we assume the new "normal price" is $1 a dozen, then we know that the supply will continue to get smaller until the market price moves up to $1 a dozen. When the market price reaches $1 a dozen the egg producers will find that once again they are making normal profits. There is no longer any reason for them to want to get out of the egg business.

When eggs start to sell for $1 a dozen, the "normal price" (the "long-run equilibrium price" or the "normal competitive price") again exists in the market. The normal price has been brought about by the long-run adjustment (decrease) in supply. The egg market and the egg industry are once again in **long-run equilibrium.**

Figure 25-3 shows all this on the supply and demand graph. The graph shows how (1) *increased marginal cost* shifts the supply in the short run. Then (2) the exodus of the firms leaving the industry shifts it even more in the long run. The shifting continues until the market gets back to a new "normal price." Then the egg market and egg industry are once again in long-run equilibrium. Take a minute now and study Figure 25-3 before you go on.

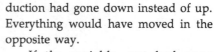

duction had gone down instead of up. Everything would have moved in the opposite way.

If the variable cost had gone down, the supply would have increased and the price would have gone down. But even at the new lower price this probably would be a very profitable industry. If so, other producers soon would shift out of the turkey, broiler, pork, beef, grain, and other businesses and start producing eggs. Each time a new egg business added its output to the market this would increase the supply a little more and inch the price down a little.

How long would new producers continue to come into the egg business? You know the answer: until all the excess profits are eliminated. The supply would continue to increase and the price would continue to inch down until a new "normal competitive price" is reached. The new normal price would reflect the new, lower cost of production in the egg industry.

When the new normal price (perhaps 60¢ a dozen) is reached, the egg market and the egg industry will again be in stable, long-run equilibrium. The price and the flow of eggs across the market from sellers to buyers will continue at a stable level until some new change occurs to upset the equilibrium—that is, until something happens to change either the supply (cost) or the demand.

Reduced Cost Brings a Lower Price

You can look at Figure 25-3 and figure out what would have happened if the cost of pro-

In the Pure Market System, in the Long Run You Must Pay for What You Get

The *cost of production* of each product is reflected in the *supply*. Through supply, cost is re-

Fig. 25-3 In the Long-Run the Supply Decreases More

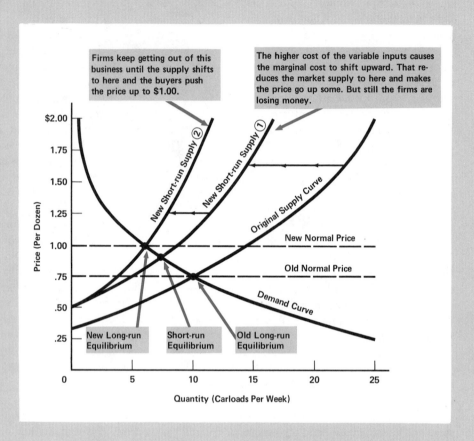

Firms keep getting out of this business until the supply shifts to here and the buyers push the price up to $1.00.

The higher cost of the variable inputs causes the marginal cost to shift upward. That reduces the market supply to here and makes the price go up some. But still the firms are losing money.

New Short-run Supply ②

New Short-run Supply ①

Original Supply Curve

New Normal Price

Old Normal Price

Demand Curve

New Long-run Equilibrium

Short-run Equilibrium

Old Long-run Equilibrium

Price (Per Dozen)

$2.00
1.75
1.50
1.25
1.00
.75
.50
.25

0   5   10   15   20   25

Quantity (Carloads Per Week)

Eventually all the increase in cost is passed on to the ones who eat the high-cost eggs.

The initial cost increase reduces the supply by increasing the marginal cost of the producers in the industry. This decrease in supply creates a shortage. The quantity being shipped into the market drops back from 10 carloads a week to 5 carloads a week. Many buyers can't find any eggs so they begin offering more—bidding against each other. That forces the price up.

In the short run the price moves up to 90¢. The producers then increase their shipments from 5 to 7½ carloads a week. But at 90¢ a dozen the egg producers are still losing money.

Producers start getting out of the egg business. As the producers leave, the supply decreases and the price inches up. The price finally reaches the new normal price of $1 a dozen. At this price, 6 carloads per week are crossing the market.

Notice that throughout all of this the demand has not changed. First the people were buying 10, then 7½, and finally 6 carloads per week. They are buying less as a reaction to the higher prices—because of the income effect and the substitution effect. But the demand (the "propensity to buy") has not changed. They buy less, true. But that's a reaction to the market conditions—to the shortages and higher prices. It isn't a change in the "propensity to buy"!

flected in the *price* of the product. This is the way the market process in the long run requires each consumer to pay the full cost (and no more than the full cost) of whatever he or she buys.

Lower cost of production increases the supply and lowers the price. The consumer doesn't have to pay as much as before. Higher cost reduces the supply and increases the price. The consumer who still wants to use the higher cost, scarcer, more valuable product, must pay more for the privilege.

It is through this process—cost changing the supply and supply changing the price—that the market process requires the people who buy each product to pay the full cost of producing that product—including as a part of the cost, a normal profit for the producers.

Normal Profit Is the Entrepreneur's Income. Whenever the price of a good isn't high enough to provide a "normal profit," then firms will leave the industry and go elsewhere. As the businesses leave, the supply flowing into the market will get smaller. The price will rise. The price will keep on rising until the businesses stop leaving the industry—that is, until the normal price is reached.

The "normal profit" is really a part of the cost of getting the good produced. If "normal profits" aren't being paid, the entrepreneur who puts it all together and takes all the risk isn't receiving any income!

"Normal profit" is the entrepreneur's "just reward" in the same way that the wage is the "just reward" for labor, or rent for land. If the consumers are not willing to pay a price high enough to provide "normal profits" then in the long run the product will disappear from the market.

Ultimately It's the Consumer Who Pays the Cost. In the model market system all the costs (including normal profits) ultimately are paid by the people who buy the products. Even in the real world this result comes close to being true most of the time.

This simple truth needs to be understood by people who suggest that businesses should pay more taxes or spend more to overcome poverty or to clean up pollution or to make automobiles safer or to give their workers better wages or retirement benefits or whatever. I'm not saying you *shouldn't* argue for all these things. I'm only saying that you should understand the full effects of what you are suggesting.

Ultimately it is not the owners of the business but the buyers of the product who must pay the costs. When the buyer reacts to the higher price by buying less or by ordering from some other (perhaps foreign) producer instead, the business may wind up "out of business."

Any cost increase or decrease—for labor, land, capital, taxes, pollution control or anything else—sets into motion a chain reaction. The effects ripple throughout the economic system, going many places, doing many things. The one thing you can be sure of is that the people who ultimately pay most of the increased cost are the people who buy the product. As long as the market system is working there's just no way around it.

ELASTICITY OF DEMAND AND RESPONSIVENESS OF SUPPLY

When the cost of production changes, the supply changes. When the supply changes, the price changes. The price *must* change. But *how much* does the price change? A little? Or a lot?

If you think about this question for a minute you will see that the answer depends on this: How responsive are the buyers to price changes? Or say it differently: How elastic is the demand?

If the demand is **highly inelastic,** that means the buyers are *not very responsive* to price changes. They buy almost the same quantity no matter whether the price goes up or down. So a *small change* in the supply would cause a *big change* in the price.

So what happens if cost increases and demand is highly inelastic? A small decrease in supply can push the price right up to the new "normal price." Of course!

What if the demand is **highly elastic**? As the supply decreases the price goes up. What do the buyers do? They buy a lot less when the price goes up just a little. A lot of firms will have to leave this industry before the price will move up to the new "normal equilibrium" level!

Suppose the cost goes up and the supply gets smaller, as you saw in the last graph. How many firms must get out of the industry before the price moves to the normal level? Will the price go up very quickly to bring a new long-run equilibrium? Or will the price increase come about very slowly and only after many firms have left the industry?

The answers to all these questions depend entirely on this question: "How elastic is the demand?"

The "Highly Inelastic Demand" Case

If the demand for something is highly inelastic it means that people really would like to keep on buying about as much of it as they are buying now. If the price goes down they will buy a little more, but not very much more. If the price goes up they will buy less, but not very much less.

How far up would the price of salt have to go before you would use less salt on your eggs in the morning? Or how much more salt would you use on your eggs if salt was a penny a pound? Your demand for salt is highly inelastic, wouldn't you say?

When the demand is highly inelastic, if the cost goes up and decreases the supply, the price will move upward quickly to cover the increased cost. The new normal price will come about very soon. Not many firms will have to leave the industry. Maybe none will.

If salt starts to get more expensive, no mat-

ter. You will pay twice as much to get the amount you want. Won't you? Let's look at this on a graph. It's much easier to see that way.

Figure 25-4 shows exactly the same picture as Figure 25-2 except that a new, highly inelastic demand curve has been added. With highly inelastic demand, the price really goes up when the cost goes up! Look at the graph now, and you'll see.

If Demand Is Highly Inelastic, Firms Should Fear a Cost Decrease. When demand is highly inelastic, producers don't have to be worried about a cost increase. The price can go up and the buyers will buy almost as much as before.

But what if the cost goes *down*? The supply will increase. The curve will shift to the right. What then? Disaster!

When the demand is highly inelastic, a supply increase will create a surplus and the price will move down to try to "clear the market." But as the price moves down, people don't buy much more. The surplus persists. So the price just keeps on falling and falling.

How low would the price of salt have to go to get people to use more salt on their eggs in the morning? Very low, right?

Those who produce and sell a product like table salt, for which the demand is very inelastic, do not need to worry about their costs going up. Increased costs will be easily and quickly passed forward to the consumer. But such producers are really vulnerable to a *decrease* in costs which would increase the supply!

The Case of Agriculture. The demand for most agricultural products is relatively inelastic. Whenever there is a bumper crop of some farm product, this creates a surplus and causes the price to drop very low.

This is a part of the reason why the government has set up various programs to "stabilize" the prices of many farm products. The govern-

Fig. 25-4 When Demand Is Highly Inelastic, an Increase in Cost Is Passed Along Very Quickly to the Buyers

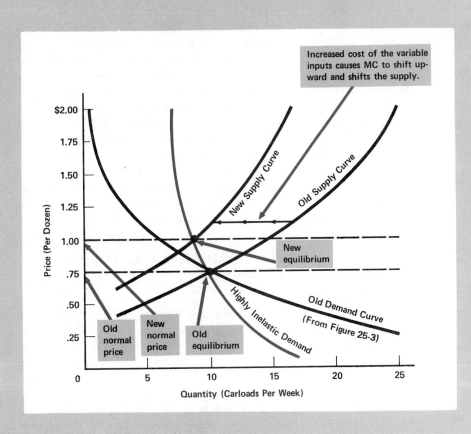

When the demand is highly inelastic the rationing function of price doesn't work very well. Right?

In this case the demand is so inelastic that the price immediately jumps up from 75¢ to the new "normal price" of $1 a dozen!

The "inelastic demanders" insist on getting their eggs, even if they have to pay a dollar a dozen! At the initial normal price of 75¢ a dozen, 10 carloads per week were bought. But at a price of $1.00 a dozen, 9 carloads are bought.

The price increased from 75¢ to $1.00 (an increase of ⅓ or 33%) and resulted in a decrease in quantity bought from 10 carloads to 9 carloads (a decrease of only 1/10th or 10%). The price change is much greater than the quantity response. The demand is highly inelastic.

What might cause the demand for a good to be so inelastic? There are several possible causes, but no matter what the basic cause of this you can be sure: people want their desired quantities of this thing and to most people's way of thinking, there's no good substitute available to take its place.

ment sometimes sets minimum prices, buys up surpluses, and limits the acreages for certain crops to try to keep prices from falling too low.

It's paradoxical, but the farmers might get more income if half of everybody's crops got eaten by grasshoppers! Inelastic demand is great for the producer who has enough market power (monopoly power) to be able to keep the supply low and the price high. But for the producers in an industry where the supply is likely to increase (or maybe where the supply is likely to fluctuate up and down from year to year) highly inelastic demand can be disastrous.

The "Highly Elastic Demand" Case

The producer faced with *highly elastic demand* has a problem, too. But the problem is exactly opposite from that of the farmer. With highly *elastic* demand, if the supply increases and pushes surpluses into the market, what happens?

When the price moves down a little, everybody buys a lot more. Soon all the surpluses are bought up. So when cost goes down and the supply increases, the price moves down only very slowly, a little bit at a time.

When the cost of production goes *down*, the firms in the industry make excess profits. The effect is about the same as if the *price* had gone *up*.

Each firm produces more in the short run. Then in the long run the excess profits attract more firms into the industry. But if the demand is highly elastic, as the industry expands and the supply increases, the price doesn't go down very fast.

How long will it take for the price to be pushed down to where the firms are making only "normal profits" again? How long will it be before all of the cost decrease is passed along (by lower prices) to the buyers? A long time!

When the demand for a product is highly elastic, when cost decreases, a big expansion in the industry will be required to increase the supply enough to push the price down to the new normal level. But what about the opposite case? Suppose the cost has *increased* instead. That's a sad story. Study Figure 25-5 and you will see what a sad story it is!

The Market Mechanism Depends on Elasticity

Now you can see how important elasticity is in the "equilibrium adjustment process." Elasticity means responsiveness. We have been talking about the responsiveness of buyers and sellers to price changes. *Price elasticity of demand and supply is what makes the market system work.*

The system flexes in one way or another in response to price changes. The price changes are responses to the changing demands (propensities to buy) of the people, working against the built-in (cost) constraints of supply. As prices move around, it's the elasticities (of demand and supply) that determine how well the price mechanism does its job.

The supply curve is a graphic picture of the production-motivating function of price. The demand curve is a graphic picture of the rationing function of price.

The elasticity of supply (short-run or long-run) determines how well the "production motivating function of price" will work. The elasticity of demand determines how well the "rationing function of price" will work.

Fig. 25-5   When Demand Is Highly Elastic, an Increase in Cost May Destroy the Industry

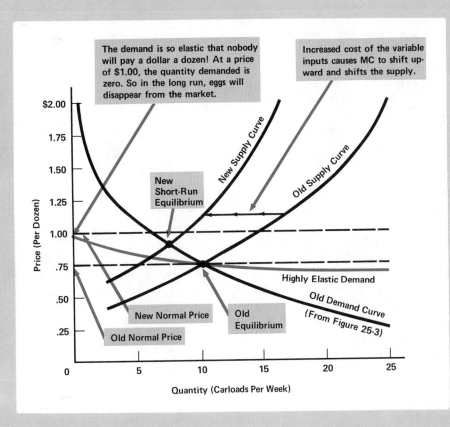

The demand is so elastic that nobody will pay a dollar a dozen! At a price of $1.00, the quantity demanded is zero. So in the long run, eggs will disappear from the market.

Increased cost of the variable inputs causes MC to shift upward and shifts the supply.

New Supply Curve

Old Supply Curve

New Short-Run Equilibrium

New Normal Price

Old Normal Price

Old Equilibrium

Highly Elastic Demand

Old Demand Curve (From Figure 25-3)

Price (Per Dozen)

Quantity (Carloads Per Week)

When demand is highly elastic, the rationing function of price works so well it may destroy the industry!

At the new normal price of a dollar a dozen the quantity of eggs demanded would be zero. Unless the demand increases or the cost decreases, all the firms will leave the industry and eggs will disappear from the market. The society doesn't want eggs enough to continue to pay the cost of producing them. Society wants those egg-producing resources shifted into some other industry. The market process will see to it that that's exactly what will happen!

Of course the demand for eggs really isn't this elastic. But think of some product with close substitutes—say saturated-fat margarine. If the cost of producing such margarine went up to where the price would have to be higher than the price of butter, then the cost increase might destroy the industry. Why? Because the elasticity of the demand is so great. Why is the elasticity so great? Because an acceptable substitute (butter) is available at a lower price!

The price of $1 in this graph and in the previous one has been "assumed" as the new "normal price" resulting from an increase in the cost of production. If the cost went up more, the new normal price would be higher than $1, of course. If the cost went up less, then the new normal price would be less than $1.

SUMMARY AND SYNTHESIS

The market process automatically integrates and synchronizes the input and output markets throughout the economy. How? With supply and demand and the price mechanism. Of course.

In the model market system, when the demand increases for a product, its price goes up. At the higher price, firms in the industry make excess profits and expand their outputs. New firms enter the industry. One effect of all this is: increased demand for the required inputs.

If this industry is very large, then as more inputs are demanded, the prices of the inputs will go up. That's what attracts more inputs to the expanding industry. But at the same time, up goes the cost of production for this product! (The long-run supply curve slopes upward.)

As the cost of production in an industry changes, the supply changes. Of course! Changing costs shift the cost curves for the firms in the industry. And the cost curves are supply curves. Remember? The marginal cost curve for a firm selling in pure competition is that firm's short-run supply curve.

There are two ways that the supply can change in a market of pure competition:

1. The number of firms in the industry can change. If more firms come into the industry, that increases the supply.
2. The cost of production of the "typical firm" can change. If the costs change, the cost curves shift, changing the "maximum profit output rate."

Increased input prices will shift the cost curves upward and decrease the supply. Decreased input prices will shift the cost curves downward and increase the supply.

The supply change induced by a cost change will be greater in the long run than in the short run. In the short-run supply period the supply response is limited by the inevitable law of diminishing returns. The supply response is limited to output adjustments by firms already in the industry. But in the long run, firms will enter (or leave) the industry in response to the excess profits (or losses) which result from the lower (or higher) costs.

The supply adjustment in the industry will continue until the market price is pushed down (or up) to where it is equal to the new normal price—i.e., where excess profits (or losses) have been eliminated and normal profits are being made.

How much will the industry need to expand (or contract) to bring the new "normal price"? That depends on the elasticity of the demand for the product.

Suppose the demand for the output of an industry is highly elastic. If the production cost goes up, many firms must leave the industry. Why? Because the supply will have to be cut back greatly to push the price up high enough to cover the higher costs. Or if the cost goes down, the industry will expand a lot because the price will go down very slowly.

But suppose the demand is highly inelastic. If the cost goes up, only a few firms will leave the industry. The price moves quickly up to the new "normal price." Or if the cost goes down, the price will drop quickly! You can see an example of this in the agricultural product markets where demand is not very elastic. In those markets, anything which causes an increase in supply will be likely to cause a serious drop in the price.

Is it true that everyone must "get what they pay for"? and "pay for what they get"? In the model market system? with pure competition? in the long run? Yes. It is true. Everyone who buys a good must pay exactly as much as it costs to produce that good—including a "normal profit" for the producer. So everyone is getting exactly as much economic value as they're paying for—no more, and no less.

Now you know how supply and demand and the price mechanism integrate and synchronize the input and output markets throughout the economy. And you know that elasticity of demand has a lot to do with how the results work out. At least you know how all this works in the model market system. In the next several chapters (Part Seven) you'll find out a lot about how all this works in the real world.

REVIEW EXERCISES

MAJOR CONCEPTS, PRINCIPLES, TERMS (Explain each carefully.)

how to choose your minimum loss output
how high prices conserve the scarcest input factors
the role of "price elasticity" in the market process
how factor markets influence product outputs and prices

OTHER CONCEPTS AND TERMS (Explain each briefly.)

final demand
derived demand
highly inelastic demand
highly elastic demand
"full cost" of production

CURVES AND GRAPHS (Draw, label, and explain each.)

When Cost Increases, the Curves (ATC and MC) Shift Upward
Increased Cost of the Variable Inputs Decreases the Supply in the Short Run
In the Long Run the Supply Decreases (Shifts Leftward) More
When Demand is Highly Inelastic, An Increase In Cost is Passed Along Very Quickly to the Buyers
When Demand is Highly Elastic, An Increase in Cost May Destroy the Industry

QUESTIONS (Write the answers, or jot down the key points.)

1. How does the market process get the factors of production to respond to the society's desires—to move into the industries where demand is increasing and out of the industries where demand is decreasing? Explain the process, step by step.

2. Suppose the consumer demand for eggs really did increase by 30% this year. Would you expect the price of eggs to increase in the short run? What about in the long run? Would you expect the "normal price" of eggs to go up? Explain.

3. If the "model pure market system" was working perfectly, then it would always be true of everything and for everybody, that: "You get what you pay for." Also it would always be true that: "You must pay for what you get." Explain exactly what

all this means and exactly why it must be true.

4. If a business is producing a product which has a highly elastic demand, the business is likely to go broke if its costs go up very much. But businesses producing products for which the demand is highly *inelastic* have more to fear from a *cost decrease* than a *cost increase*. Explain.

5. The "market process" is really nothing more (or less) than the rationing function and the production motivating function of price at work in the output and input markets. How well each "function of price" works depends on the elasticity of supply and demand—that is, the responsiveness to price—in the input and output markets of the economy. Can you explain all this? Try.

PART SEVEN

If It's Supply And Demand That Sets Prices, How Come So Many Prices Turn Out To Be $4.98?

26 The Market System in the Real World I: Microinstability, Inequality, Externalities

Chapter Objectives

- This chapter begins your careful look at **how the market process—supply and demand and the price mechanism and all that—works in the real world.**

- In this chapter you'll find out that **long-run equilibrium is a direction** toward which markets tend to move. And you'll find out why in some markets **instability tends to perpetuate itself.**

- You will learn about the problem of **delayed supply-response** and how this is responsible for **corn-hog cycles** and **the cobweb theorem.**

- You will be able to **draw supply and demand graphs** illustrating the cobweb theorem, showing both the **converging** and the **diverging** cobwebs and to explain the importance of **supply elasticity** in influencing cobweb-type markets.

- You will find out more about **inequality,** about the **self-perpetuating nature** of wealth, and about **income redistribution.**

- You will learn about the problem of externalities—of "spill-over" or "third party" costs and benefits—and how these externalities can be **internalized.** And you will find out that the achievement of **long-range social goals** sometimes requires involvement by the political process.

Did you ever go down on the beach and watch the waves come rolling in to the shore? The booming surf keeps frothing and pounding, the water surges far up on the beach, then rushes back. You say to yourself, "What a restless thing this ocean is!"

As you stand there watching the ocean frothing and foaming, the waves peaking, curling, breaking, you might say to youself, "If that ocean was in equilibrium it would be completely flat and smooth. The children could build sand castles here at the edge of the water and they would last all day. As it is, their sand castles only last until the next big wave comes up." Can you see where this story is leading?

LONG-RUN EQUILIBRIUM: AN ELUSIVE MOVING TARGET

Equilibrium is the condition we would have if everything "came to rest." Have you ever seen the ocean in "long-run equilibrium"? I don't think so. The ocean always "tends toward" equilibrium. But it never gets there. The same is true of markets.

Equilibrium Is a Concept, Not a Condition

The "normal equilibrium price" is like the normal equilibrium of the ocean. It's important to know which way things are tending. You know that a high wave is going to go down; a deep trough in the ocean is going to get filled up. It's important to know that. But don't get confused about **the equilibrium concept** and think of it as a description of a real-world *condition*. Certainly it isn't. It couldn't be.

Demands and costs are changing constantly. Prices and quantities are moving in response to these demand and cost changes. The movement of demand, supply, and price goes on forever.

The concept of equilibrium shows which direction things will be changing and it sets some limits within which fluctuations will occur. Because you know about the equilibrium ocean level you know how high to build the fishing pier to be sure no wave will ever break over it; you know how deep to dig the channel crossing the bar to be sure that the trough between two waves will never be so low that boats will hit the bottom. But you don't ever expect to see a perfectly placid ocean. This is the way it is in the real world with the free operation of competitive markets.

In markets, the constant change in demands and supplies of outputs and inputs keep equilibrium conditions "chased after but never caught." So the market process (like the ocean) never reaches a smooth, stable equilibrium.

But sometimes the problem may be worse than you think. Why? Because *market fluctuations can be much more violent and unpredictable than ocean waves!*

The Delayed "Supply Response"

Suppose the demand or the supply shifts and forces the price to a level above or below the "normal equilibrium" level. It may be a long time before any visible "corrective response" will start to move the price back to normal!

A Corn-on-the-Cob Example. The agricultural markets offer good examples of the slow and uneven supply response.

Suppose you are producing corn in your backyard plot. It just happens that at about harvest time there's an article in *Newsweek* saying that a medical research team has just discovered that fresh corn-on-the-cob steamed in the husk has heretofore unrecognized nutritional value!

The Demand For Corn Increases But the Supply Does Not. What happens to the demand for corn? It increases. But what happens to the supply of corn? Nothing.

Nothing *can* happen to the supply of corn on such short notice! The corn crop was planted months ago. It has been growing all this time. Now it will be harvested and sold for whatever prices the market may offer.

The pure market process doesn't work just right in the real world. Too bad!

But why are you so happy as you watch your corn tassels waving in the breeze? Because you understand enough about basic economics to know that there's going to be an increased demand for corn; that the increased demand is going to bring a higher price—and that *lucky you* are going to be one of the beneficiaries of this fortuitous turn of events!

Yes, lucky you. The demand is going to increase for sure. The price is going to go up from 75¢ a dozen for those fresh, succulent ears of corn, to $1.50. Then to $2 or $2.50 or maybe even $3. You are *really lucky!*

But what about all those corn-loving people who live in the cities and dream all winter long of the pleasure of having fresh corn-on-the-cob in the summertime? They aren't so lucky.

"But," you say, "the high price will bring forth more corn. Then the price will go down to normal and everyone will be happy again." Will this happen? Maybe sometime. But not this summer.

The Rationing Function of Price Works Just Fine. The market process is supposed to work by bringing forth more output in response to an increase in price. But what is happening in the corn market?

As the price goes up, this rations the available supply of corn. Those who are willing to pay a high price are the only ones who will get to eat any of it. A person who doesn't like corn very much will stop eating corn and leave it for somebody else.

The high price guarantees that people who are having corn-on-the-cob will not cook a dozen ears when all they really need is seven. At the higher price they probably will buy only four ears and cut each one in half. The rationing function of price is working fine. But the price keeps going up and no new supply comes forth.

Everything is going great for you. Each day someone comes by and wants to buy your entire corn crop. (Everybody is trying to make a buck!) One of your neighbors has a big truck and wants to harvest your crop and take it to New York City where the price is really going wild. You're tempted to sell. But you decide to sit tight, to harvest each ear just when it's ready and take your chances at your little roadside stand.

As it turns out, the longer you wait the higher the price goes. What a lucrative summer! You can hardly believe it. You finally sell your last dozen ears for $3.75. That's *five times as much* as the "normal price" you expected to get when you were planting the corn last spring. What a summer! What a profitable business corn farming can be!

Getting Ready for the Supply Response. After your corn is all sold you feel very wealthy. You sit thinking for a while, then you call the owner of the seven acres of land which adjoins your backyard plot. You ask him if he would like to sell. After some haggling you make a deal.

Then you start contacting agricultural equipment dealers to see if you can get a tractor, a cultivator, a planter, a harvester, a sprayer and all of the other things you need. It's obvious to you that if you are going to grow seven more acres of corn in your spare time, you need to use a lot of capital to increase your productivity.

You call the county agricultural agent to ask about how to increase the corn output per acre. Why? Because you're planning to cash in on the gold mine you discovered this summer!

But wait. What do you suppose the wheat farmers out in Kansas are doing? And the egg producers in New Jersey? And the cattle ranchers in Texas? And the potato growers in Idaho? And all the others who have land which could be used to grow corn? They are doing the same thing you're doing.

When Everyone Responds at Once the Price Collapses. Everyone is planning to cash in on the gold mine—the high price and high profits from producing corn. You know what's going to happen.

In this market for corn there will be no "step-by-step increases" of the supply and "inching downward" of the price. Next summer when the corn begins to be harvested, the supply is going to be *so much greater* than it was this year that the market is going to be glutted. The price is going to collapse.

The demand for corn is not very elastic. As the price plummets downward people still aren't going to eat but just so much corn. Even at a price of 10¢ a dozen not many people are going to eat five ears of corn a day! The quantity people eat does increase as the price goes down, yes. But it doesn't increase very much. Before the summer is over, lots of hogs and cows and chickens are going to get to enjoy some high-quality corn!

Well, after it was all over, you lost money

on your seven acres and all that equipment and fertilizer, didn't you? But you are no fool. You won't get caught making the same mistake again! So you curse the day you planted all that corn and resolve that from now on you will grow tomatoes instead. So next summer, guess what? Fickle fate has done it again! Corn is very scarce. The price is very high.

This is no way for an economic system to serve the society! Things are out of balance! When does all this "disequilibrium"—this "microinstability"—work itself out? Never, right? (Sorry about that).

This example is a little over-dramatized. But it isn't *completely* unrealistic. Recurring fluctuations in prices and quantities do happen, especially in farm products. The problem can be very serious if the weather happens to be especially good, or bad, to accentuate the fluctuations.

CORN-HOG CYCLES AND THE COBWEB THEOREM

The over-dramatized example you have just been reading about has shown you a part of what is sometimes called the corn-hog cycle. The idea is that during years when corn prices are high, producers can't afford to feed so many pigs. So they sell them off.

The supply of pork is high so the price of pork is low. But the high price of corn causes lots of farmers to produce more corn. So next season what happens? The corn market is glutted. The price of corn is very low. But what about the price of hogs? It's high, of course.

The pork producers sold off their hogs back when the price of corn was high. Now that the corn price is low they're trying to build up their breeding stock of hogs. So they aren't sending many hogs to the market. See the picture?

The Corn-Hog Cycle in the Real World

Is there a corn-hog cycle in the real world? There sure is! And it works with feed grains other than corn and it works with livestock other than hogs.

Back in 1972 the U.S. government sold about 20 percent of the entire American wheat crop to the Soviet government. What happened to the price of wheat? It went up from $1.70 a bushel to a peak of about $5 a bushel a year later. What happened to the price of other feed grains? They all doubled and tripled and some quadrupled, too. Soybeans went up from about $3.50 to a high of $12.00 a bushel!

Suppose you were a farmer raising beef and feeding your cattle on these high-priced grains. What would you do? You would try to reduce the size of your herd, of course.

Any way you look at it, unless the price of beef goes sky high, you're losing money every day your cattle keep eating that high-priced grain! So you start selling off your beef. But what are the other beef farmers doing? The same thing of course.

The Feed Grains-Beef Cycle. While the price of feed grains goes up high the price of beef is pushed down low. Corn-hog cycle? Sure. But what's going to happen to the price of beef later on? It's going to go up? Sure. Because less beef is going to be produced.

Steers were selling for about 37 cents a pound in 1972. As the price of feed grains rose the price of steers dropped to about 33 cents. Then later, the price of steers rose to more than 50 cents a pound!

This "corn-hog" or "feed grains-beef" cycle goes on to some extent all the time. Why? Because farmers are always adjusting their outputs—always responding to the changing prices in their input and output markets.

If they didn't respond they would go broke! But when everybody responds the same way, you can see what happens. Over-response of supply? And big price fluctuations? Right.*

---

*Later on there's a chapter dealing with problems in American agriculture. When you read that chapter you'll see that much of the problem stems from the "corn-hog" cycle, and the "delayed supply response" in agricultural markets.

Finding "Commodities" Prices—The Wall Street Journal. Go to your library and pick up a copy of the *Wall Street Journal*. On the front page at the very bottom of the second column you'll find "today's index." Look to find out what page "commodities" are listed on. Then turn to that page.

Look under the "cash prices" section and you'll find the prices of flour, coffee, cocoa, potatoes, sugar, orange juice, butter, eggs, broilers, beef, ham, hogs, steers, all kinds of grains and feeds, fats and oils, textiles and fibers, metals, and just about any other kind of commodity you might want to know about. It even includes gold and silver—and old newspapers, by the ton.

You could go back through several past issues of the *Wall Street Journal* and find out what has been happening to the price of steers and the price of feed grains over the past few years. I'll bet you could find some traces of a "corn-hog cycle" between feed grains and steers. Why don't you try it?

The Cobweb Theorem: Microeconomic Instability

Corn-hog cycles have been going on for more than a hundred years and economists have tried to work out ways to explain it. The **cobweb theorem** does just that. In fact, everything you have been reading in this chapter fits within what we call the "cobweb theorem."

The essential idea of the cobweb theorem is this: Suppose the quantity of something offered for sale is determined by the price that existed some time ago—that is, *the quantity supplied today is not responsive to the price which exists today*. The quantity supplied reflects *past prices*—not *existing prices*.

If the past price was high, then the quantity supplied will be great. So the present price will be low. The future quantity supplied will respond to the low present price. So the future quantity will be small. And the future price? It will be high. Of course.

On the following pages you will see graphs

showing how the "cobwebs" work. You'll see how in competitive real-world markets the supply sometimes doesn't adjust smoothly to a change in demand—how sometimes the price may go very high. Then when the response comes it may glut the market.

The Cobweb Reflects Supply and Demand Elasticity

As you study the graphs you'll find out that some "cobwebs" are diverging, destabilizing—getting worse year after year. Why? Because the supply is too elastic. The supply responds too much to the high or low price of the previous year. *Whenever the supply from one season to the next is more elastic than the demand, a diverging, destabilizing cobweb will result.*

It's obvious if you think about it. What makes the violent fluctuation in price? The *supply response!* Of course. The more elastic the supply from one year to the next, the greater the supply response will be. So the more the price will be pushed up or down.

On the other hand, *the more elastic the demand, the less serious the "cobweb fluctuations" will be.* With highly elastic demand, when the price begins to drop because of a big surplus, people will run out and buy up the surpluses fast. So the price won't go down very far.

In a cobweb-type situation, anything which would cause the supply to be more elastic (or the demand to be less elastic) will cause the fluctuations to be more destabilizing. But if the supply is less elastic (or the demand is more elastic) the cobweb will move toward equilibrium—that is, the fluctuation will get smaller from year to year. Finally, *ceteris paribus*, equilibrium will be established.*

Take time now to study Figure 26-1 and the ones that follow it. Those graphs explain the cobweb theorem, step-by-step.

——————

*Ceteris paribus: if nothing else changes in the meanwhile. Remember? (But something will, of course.)

Fig. 26-1   The Supply and Demand for Corn This Season

When the demand increases, the price goes up. But no more is supplied.

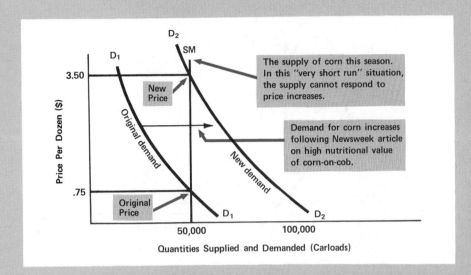

The supply of corn this season. In this "very short run" situation, the supply cannot respond to price increases.

Demand for corn increases following Newsweek article on high nutritional value of corn-on-cob.

The price goes up from 75¢ to $3.50, but the quantity supplied does not change.

During this "very short-run" supply period (which in the case of corn is the entire season) no more can be supplied, no matter how high the price may go. So the production motivating function of price can't work. But the rationing function of price works! Look at this graph and see how much corn would be demanded if the price stayed at 75¢ a dozen! Almost 100,000 carloads!

Even this season the supply of corn wouldn't be *absolutely* fixed. There is always a possibility for *some* variability. Farmers might hire extra workers to go into the field and be sure the mechanical harvesters pick every ear of corn. Also there might be possibilities for better (more expensive) methods to prevent any corn from being damaged in harvest or damaged by insects.

Also the farmers might stop feeding the smaller ears to the pigs and chickens. And they might stop giving each of the workers a dozen ears of corn at the end of each workday. And they might decide to let their own families eat less corn and more potatoes and bread and dumplings instead.

But even with all the things farmers do, the quantity supplied at $3.50 per dozen is not going to be but slightly larger than the quantity supplied at a price of 75¢.

But what's going to happen next season? You already know. Look on the next page and you'll see it on a graph.

Fig. 26-2   The Demand and Supply of Corn Next Season

Next season the supply of corn is much larger and the price is much lower.

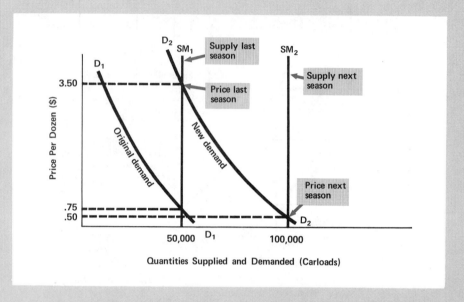

Quantities Supplied and Demanded (Carloads)

Look what happened to the supply of corn! There's twice as much as last season. And what about the price? It's down from $3.50 to 50¢!

Last season, the price was $3.50 and only 50,000 carloads were available. Now the price is down to 50¢ and 100,000 carloads are marketed. Sounds backwards, doesn't it? When the price is high, more is supposed to be supplied. Not less! And when the price is low, less is supposed to be supplied. Not more! What's the problem?

The problem is this: The supply in the market next season is determined by the high price in the market *last season*. That's what the "cobweb theorem" explains. The next graph tells more about it.

A Note about the "Reservation Price"

The supply curves show that the price of corn could go all the way to zero and the quantity the sellers would offer would still be the same. Of course that isn't true. Before the price got that low, the corn would be withdrawn from the "human consumption" market and used for animal feed. Or it would be left to rot in the fields instead of being harvested and shipped to the market at a price of zero! There is always some "reservation price" below which no corn would be supplied. But for convenience we draw the "very short-run" or "momentary" or "market" supply curve as vertical, all the way to zero.

Fig. 26-3 The Diverging (Explosive) Cobweb

The "unstable equilibrium" model: disequilibrium gets worse.

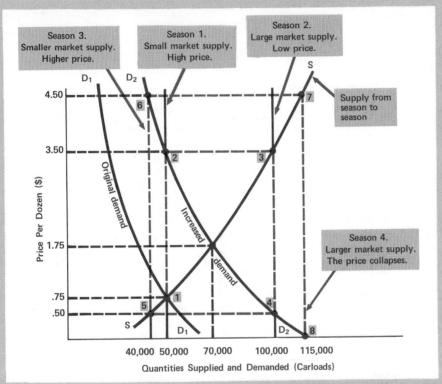

This is a picture of the corn market you've been looking at all along. Only here, things don't get better. They get worse. Unless something happens to stabilize this industry, the consumer's desire for corn will never be properly taken care of. One year there will be a great oversupply and farmers will go broke. The next year there will be a great shortage of corn.

Follow these numbers on the graph:

1. This is where it all started out, with a price of 75¢ a dozen for corn and 50,000 carloads available for the season.
2. Then demand increased and forced the price up to $3.50. But the quantity available that season did not increase.
3. The high price brings forth a much greater supply (100,000 carloads), next season.
4. The 100,000 carloads forces the price down to 50¢ a dozen. But at a price of 50¢ the supply that season is still 100,000 carloads!

5. The following season the corn producers respond to the low price of 50¢ a dozen. Only 40,000 carloads are produced.
6. The market supply of only 40,000 carloads pushes the price up to $4.50.
7. The high price ($4.50) brings forth 115,000 carloads of corn in the following year.
8. The price collapses. There's so much corn around you can have all you want just by going and picking it up. Next year there's really going to be a shortage of corn!

If the price could ever get to $1.75 a dozen, then 70,000 carloads of corn would be supplied and demanded. That would be a satisfactory equilibrium. But with a diverging cobweb, equilibrium never comes.

Fig. 26-4 The Converging Cobweb

The supply is less elastic so the market moves toward equilibrium.

Each vertical dashed line shows the "market supply" for one season.

Each horizontal dashed line shows the market price for one season.

One look at this and you can see why they call it the cobweb theorem. Right?

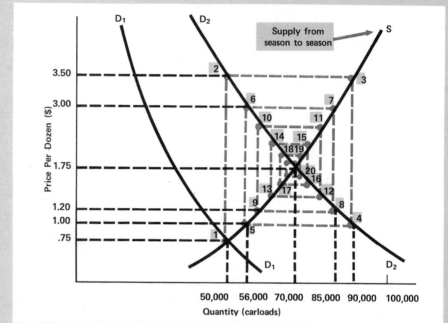

This graph is just like the previous one, except that here the supply from one season to the next is less elastic—it doesn't over-respond as much.

Follow these numbers on the graph:

1. The price is 75¢ and quantity is 50,000 carloads.
2. The demand increases and the price goes up to $3.50, but the quantity available does not increase.
3. Next season the market supply is much larger. But instead of expanding to 100,000 carloads as in the previous graph, here the output only expands to 90,000 carloads. And that's what makes the difference between this graph and the previous one. That's what's going to make this cobweb converge toward equilibrium!
4. The 90,000 carloads pushes the price down, of course. But it doesn't push it all the way down to 50¢ as in the previous graph. It only pushes it down to $1.00.
5. The following season, suppliers produce a lot less

than 90,000 carloads, of course! But they supply more than 50,000. They supply 56,000 carloads. The market is converging toward equilibrium!
6. With only 56,000 carloads in the market, the price is pushed up to $3. But that isn't as high as the $3.50 of the last high-price year! Sure enough, the market is converging toward equilibrium.
7. The price of $3 brings forth 85,000 carloads.
8. The 85,000 carloads push the price down to about $1.20. But that's not as bad as in the last low-price year. In the following year the quantity will be cut back again, but not as much as previously. . . .etc. (You can follow the steps on the graph and see the cobweb converge to a stable equilibrium where the price is $1.75 and the quantity is 70,000 carloads).

No demand and supply situation is going to stay the same year after year and wait for the cobweb to converge to stable equilibrium! So in "cobweb-type" markets, fluctuations are likely to be so great as to be intolerable. You'll be reading more about that in a minute.

The Government Sometimes Stabilizes Outputs and Prices of Farm Products

After all you've been reading about cobwebs, you can see why governments might sometimes be called on to do something to stabilize agricultural markets. Right? Sure. And that's what has happened. Not just in this country. In most countries.

Not that the government always does it right! But there are times when whatever the government does is better than the violent fluctuations which happen in a divergent-cobweb-type market!

Ag Markets Are Like the Model

The markets for agricultural products are the markets in which the requirements of the "model market system"—with pure competition, lots of small producers and all that—comes closest to reality. These are the markets in which the market process is supposed to work best.

What a shame that these are the very markets in which we can't let the process work! But when the natural market forces result in recurrent fluctuations, both the consumers and the producers are hurt. So the political process (government) comes in and exercises control.

What can the government do? It can set minimum prices, establish output (acreage) restrictions, buy up surpluses, pay subsidies to farmers. Often it does all these things. Why? Because the people of the society are not satisfied with the way the market process works things out. The automatic adjustment process described in the pure market model doesn't always work out right for agriculture in the real world. You'll be reading more about this when you get to Part Eight.

Recurring violent fluctuations of prices and outputs are socially intolerable. But that isn't the *only* problem with the market process as it works in the real world. Here's another problem, coming up.

THE PROBLEM OF INEQUALITY OF WEALTH AND INCOME

Over the past 200 years or so the market process has been a major force influencing and directing the economies of most of the modern nations. But all this time, some people have been criticizing and attacking it. Why? On what grounds? Usually *because of the way the* distribution question *is answered.*

No society has ever permitted the market process to have *complete* control over the distribution question. Of course not! It would never work. All the little children would starve to death! Some of society's output must be distributed to the unproductive children. It must be done by some "process" other than the market process—either the political process or the social process must do it.

The Family Is a "Social-Process-Income-Redistribution Unit"

Throughout history *the family unit* has played an essential role in answering the distribution question. In modern times, even in the advanced nations the family continues to play an important role in modifying the harshness of the pure market process.

For many centuries, most people gained most of their economic security from their family unit. But in modern society, traditions are breaking down. The family unit is no longer so strong.

Today, many individuals feel that they belong—not to a family, with responsibilities to the family—but to themselves. No longer can the family perform the "income redistribution and economic security" function for everyone. The babies still get fed, but a lot of kinfolk get left out. Private and religious charities help some, but they have never been big enough to do more than supplement the family's redistributive role. So they can't take over the job.

Governments Redistribute Wealth and Income

As people have become more dissatisfied with the way the market process distributes the output and income they have looked to the government to do something about it.

The only way the unacceptable inequality of the market process can be overcome is by some kind of government action. The unproductive members of the society—young, old, infirm, others—are not left to starve just because there is no family to take care of them! To meet the problem, governments undertake income redistribution and economic security programs such as the U.S. unemployment compensation and social security programs.

The Rich Make the Choices and the Poor Go Hungry

Just as the pure market system is intolerable because some people don't get enough, it is also intolerable because some people get too much. Suppose you inherited a million dollars. How much influence could you have on your society's choices? on the production and distribution questions? Quite a lot!

Now compare that with Danny O'Shaughnessy who just lost his job on the delivery truck. Danny didn't inherit any money at all. He's hungry and broke. How much influence do you suppose he's going to have on whether or not you will plant corn or tomatoes? You know the answer. In the market system, people with no money don't influence *any* choices.

You might say: "If he's broke, then *he should be broke*. He isn't producing anything for the rest of us so there's no reason why we should be producing anything for him! If he will do something productive he will have some income. Then he can go out and buy what he wants and influence some of society's choices just like the rest of us can."

Of course you can say that. That's the basic justification for the inequality which (at least to

some extent) is an essential condition in the market system. After you've said it you may feel better, but that's no help to Danny.

The Question Is: How Much Inequality?

No economic system has ever operated on the principle of "equality." It isn't likely that one ever will. So that isn't the real issue. The real issue is the question of *how much* inequality there will be. How many will be how poor? And what opportunities will they have to improve their circumstances? Will people have something approaching *equal opportunities* to be productive? to earn good incomes? Or not?

In the real world, equal opportunities don't exist, either. "Unequal opportunity from birth" is a fact of life. One person is born to an uneducated, poverty-stricken, unwed mother. Another is born into a family of millionaire economic and political leaders. Equal chance? Of course not. But what can the market process do about it? Nothing. That's the problem.

People Don't Have Equal Opportunities

If you have some wealth you can have the income you get from that wealth and you can also have the income you receive from your own efforts—your "labor." Furthermore, if you have wealth to begin with you can get a high-priced education and increase the value of your "labor" greatly—like from janitor to corporate lawyer!

If your family is wealthy enough to let you finish high school without having to stop and go to work, you are lucky. Not all people are that lucky. In almost all countries for most people, such extravagance is out of the question.

Suppose your family is wealthy enough to lend you the money you need to buy some land and capital so you can go into business. Wouldn't you say you had more than an equal chance? In a wealthy nation quite a few people have such good breaks. But not *all* people have this kind of head start toward economic success in life.

If you start out with such a big head start and then work reasonably hard you may be a very wealthy person when you die. Then your children may have so much wealth that they will not need to sell their labor at all. They just need to keep their wealth (land and capital) invested and working for them and they will get richer and richer.

If your father leaves you a million dollars and if that million dollars is invested in productive capital earning a return of only five percent, the income on your inheritance will be $50,000 a year—about $1,000 a week. Unless you work at it, you will not be able to fritter away all that money every week. A thousand dollars a week? That's a lot of fritterin'! So what happens? You'll automatically get richer and richer.

Wealth Generates Income and More Wealth

Suppose your father leaves you a *five million dollar* investment, paying a five percent return. That will bring you an income of $250,000 (a quarter of a million dollars!) every year. That's about $5,000 a week. Almost a thousand dollars a day! You'll have to spend it all up (for nothing of value) in order to keep from getting even richer!

If you spend it for capital or any other valuable property you will just keep piling up more wealth. To keep from getting richer you must spend it *for fun*. I don't think you could do it. So unless you just give the money away you can't help getting richer and richer.

The Process of "Snowballing Enrichment"

As you get richer, your income keeps going up more too. So you get even richer. And richer and richer and richer! Through no fault of your own you are going to gain more and more con-

trol over society's choices. You can't help it. Then your children (or other heirs) are going to be wealthy. And they won't be able to keep from getting more and more wealth. That's the way the market process makes it turn out.

Your heirs really will be able to make a lot of the society's economic choices! Should they be? Is this just? If so, on what grounds? If not, should the political process intervene?

Maybe the government should take away some of your big income. ($5,000 a week? WOW!) Then when you die maybe the government would take away a lot of your wealth. People disagree about whether it should or shouldn't. But you may be quite sure of one thing: It does—on both counts.

The Marxian Prediction

The process of "snowballing enrichment," where the rich keep getting richer and richer, is something like the process Karl Marx was talking about when he said that capitalism had within itself "the seeds of its own destruction." He said that the richest people (the bourgeoisie) would get constantly richer and more powerful, and that more and more people would be pushed into the ranks of the poverty-stricken.

Marx predicted that economic (and political) power would become concentrated in the hands of a very few people and that someday the poverty-stricken masses (the proletariat) would rise up and take over.

In the century which has passed since Marx was observing and writing, the political process has proved its ability to soften the harshness of the market process. The "total concentration" of wealth and power in the hands of a few people has not occurred. Most people are enjoying *more* wealth these days—not less.

Income Redistribution, Private and Government

Many of the wealthiest people have decided to give away much of their great fortunes. For example, look at the Ford, Rockefeller, Carnegie, and many other foundations, and at Duke, Vanderbilt, Carnegie-Mellon, and many other universities which have been financed by gifts of private wealth.

The government has become increasingly demanding of the wealthy and increasingly helpful to the poor. The society through its democratic processes has demanded these changes in the government's attitudes toward the rich and toward the poor.

Governments have been increasing taxes on incomes, property, inheritance, and other things while increasing the payments for welfare, social security, medical care, job training and other aids to the "less wealthy" people. These reforms have worked together to redistribute some of the wealth and income among the people of the society.

A "New Deal"?

When too few people are holding all the "high cards," maybe it's time to call in the cards and have a "new deal." This is the sort of thing President Franklin D. Roosevelt was talking about during the depression of the 1930s when he announced his "New Deal" programs. Of course we didn't really "pull in all the cards and start over." But several "income redistribution programs" were started at that time.

Each time the government takes some of my "property" (income, or wealth) and uses it to feed a fatherless child or to subsidize college education for a worthy student or to put picnic tables in a national park, isn't that sort of a "new deal"?—a move away from the productivity principle of distribution? Yes. It really is.

What about the problem of poverty and inequality of wealth and income in the United States, today? Specifically, how serious is it? And what is being done about it? And what are the ultimate answers?

These are important questions—unsolved problems, really. We'll be talking about them soon in another chapter—one dealing with the problem of poverty and with other current problems.

For now, just be sure you understand that the market process has never been left in *complete charge* of the distribution choices for any society. The results would be intolerable. In all market-oriented societies, both the social process and the political process are called on to modify the results which the market process would bring. In the last few decades the political process has become increasingly involved.

EXTERNALITIES: SOCIAL COSTS AND BENEFITS OUTSIDE THE MARKET

Sometimes important *social values* are not reflected in the market. *If the true value of the social benefit of something is not reflected in the market demand, or if the true value of the social cost of something is not reflected in the market supply, then the market price will not reflect society's true values.*

Whenever the market price doesn't reflect society's true values, then the "production motivation" and the "rationing" which such a price accomplishes will be misdirected.

Suppose the price is "too high." Uses will be more severely limited and production more strongly motivated than would be required for the "social optimum." Suppose the price is "too low." Resources will not be conserved enough, and new production will not be motivated enough to achieve the "social optimum."

The resources which move in response to a "socially erroneous" price will not move to where society, all things considered, would most *want* them to go. Why not?

Because some of the true social benefits or true social costs of the product *are not being re-*

flected in the market price of the product. These extra social benefits or extra social costs, outside of (external to) the market process, *are called externalities.*

Cost Externalities and Benefit Externalities

Many people are talking about "externalities" these days. Industrial pollution is a cost externality—a social cost which does not show up in the market price of the product. But when you plant trees on your land, there are benefit externalities. The whole neighborhood gains some benefits from your "reforestation project." But those external (neighborhood) benefits are not reflected in the demand for your land or in the price you will get if you sell it. There are many kinds of "cost" and "benefit" externalities. Let's look at a make-believe example.

An Example of Cost Externalities: Cutting Timber

Suppose you lived in a village in a beautiful green valley. The hills surrounding the valley are covered by a virgin forest of fir, spruce, and hemlock. These forest lands around the village are owned by the heirs of old Sam Johnson, the man who founded this village many years ago. There's a monument to his memory in the village square. But all his heirs have long since moved to Seattle.

One day the logging crews arrive with their heavy equipment and begin clear-cutting the forest on the hillsides around the village. Everyone in the village is terribly upset. It is the only presence of those timberlands which make this valley a pleasant place to live. But more important: Those timberlands prevent the heavy spring rains and melting snows from turning the surrounding hills into a mudslide that would bury the village!

To the village, those stands of timber may mean life or death. But to the present owners—the heirs of Sam Johnson—the timber is simply an economic resource, ready to be used in response to market demand and price. The timber owners mean no harm to the village. They are just responding to the market demand for timber in the way everyone is supposed to in a market-directed economy.

From the social point of view, this stand of timber is a very valuable asset. At stake is the property (and maybe the lives!) of the people of an entire village. So how can the market process which is supposed to restrict the use of things which are very scarce and valuable—how can it permit the clear-cutting of timber on these hills?

The price of the lumber isn't nearly high enough to cover the great social cost of destroying the village! How can the market permit such a thing to happen? I think you already know the answer.

External Social Values Do Not Influence the Price

The *values* we are talking about are "external" to the market. The "external social cost" of cutting the timber is not reflected in the price of the lumber. *The "external social cost" doesn't affect the supply of the lumber; therefore it doesn't push up the price and conserve the lumber.*

If the owners of the timberlands valued their timber at its *true social value* then they wouldn't cut it unless the market price of lumber went very, very high. But since the high "external value" of the timber is not reflected in the "economic value" of the timber, the present owners see no reason why they shouldn't cut it and sell it.

The timber owners have the "property rights" to do whatever they please with their trees. They have chosen to do what the market has *directed* them to do—cut the timber and sell it. What a perfect case of cost externalities!

What can the villagers do? What would you do? The villagers meet in the town hall and decide to talk to the foreman of the lumbering crews. Then if that does no good they will try to sabotage the equipment. At the same time one member of the village will be rushing to the county seat to try to get a court order prohibiting the cutting of the timber. Perhaps the property rights of the owners to cut the timber can be taken away "by due process of law."

The lumbering foreman has a job to do and he doesn't want to get fired. He appears sympathetic to the pleas of the villagers. He says: "I would like to help you. But you know I can't. My hands are tied." Then the people of the village decide to take the law into their own hands. They pour sugar in the fuel tanks of the bulldozers, shoot holes in the tires of the logging trucks and chop up the ignition wires on the draglines. These (usually) law-abiding citizens decide to take the law into their own hands to protect their village. They are forcibly denying the "private property rights" of the timber owners. They are breaking the law.

If the system and the law are right, then what the villagers are doing is very wrong. If what they are doing is right, then the system and the law in this case are very wrong. Luckily we live in a society in which it is possible to change the system. That's why they sent someone to the county seat.

But change takes time. If the timber is cut, no amount of "system changing"—of restricting the owner's property rights—will bring the timber back! And maybe the court will not agree to protect the timber anyway. The law doesn't always do what every group of dissatisfied people wants done! What a mess. How could such a thing happen in an economic system directed by the market process?

Externalities Require Government Intervention

This is just one of those cases in which the *true values* of the society are not reflected in the market. Most of the social cost is external to the market. The villagers bear the cost. The timber market (made up of the sellers and buyers of timber) is not influenced by this "villagers' cost."

In a society in which the market process plays a major role, these external social costs must be protected either by the government or by social traditions and customs. Otherwise wasteful, non-optimal choices will be made through the market process.

Whenever there are large "externalities"—either external social *costs* or external social *benefits*—the society usually demands that the government modify the results which the market process would bring.

Everyone knows that it isn't going to do your friend any good or society any good if your friend gets hooked on heroin. But if your friend offers to pay *enough*, someone will supply the heroin and make the profit.

The people who produce and sell illegal drugs are responding to the market process. The fact that the *social cost* doesn't show up in the market is not a matter of their concern. So what happens? The political process—the government—comes in and *overthrows the market* and changes the results.

In the case of Sam Johnson's valley where the wooded slopes are in danger, legal action probably will be taken to prevent the owners from cutting the timber. Then the owners will be given some court-determined "fair compensation" to make up for the loss of their "property rights" to cut and sell the timber. In the case of illegal drugs, the government tries to *abolish* the market—to make it impossible for the drugs to be bought and sold.

In both cases the society is using its political process to overthrow the market. Why? Because in these instances the market does not reflect the true values of the society. The most important considerations (social values) lie outside (are external to) the market.

An Example of Benefit Externalities: Urban Housing

Externalities (social benefits and social costs which are not reflected in the market) show up in many places in every market-oriented society.

Here's another example: urban housing.

It is said that people who live in decent houses in decent neighborhoods are more likely to be stable, law abiding citizens. They will be more serious about educating their children. They will be better contributors to society and less likely to be on welfare. It is said that slum housing contributes to crime and violence and social disruption. If this is true, then there are externalities—external social benefits—in urban housing.

Investors Respond to Market Costs and Prices—Not to Externalities. Suppose Alice Larken, a local real estate investor, is thinking about building a new real estate development to serve poor people in the urban area.

She can't afford to make the investment unless she expects to get her money back, plus a reasonable interest and profit. The return she can get in this investment must look at least as good as what she could expect to get in any other investment opportunity she might be looking at—maybe suburban houses or wholesaling warehouses or factories or maybe stocks and bonds. Obviously!

It doesn't matter that the new urban real estate investment would result in reduced crime, better education for young people, growth of new businesses, new employment opportunities, better social harmony for the people in the area, and all that. All these benefits are *externalities*. *These are benefits which the investment will bring to the society but for which the investor will not get paid.*

Ms. Larken is a prudent businessperson. So unless she has some money she wants to give away she cannot consider external social benefits as she is deciding where to invest. So chances are the urban housing development will never get off the ground.

From the point of view of the *society* the benefits might justify the costs. But from the point of view of the market—that is, the return the investor can expect—the investment is not justified. It will not pay itself off and provide the investor a "normal profit." So she will invest in something else—something which will pay its

way. That's what she *must* do. Otherwise she will go broke.

Should Urban Housing Developments Be Subsidized? What should the society do about urban housing? Should we call on the government to modify the market process? Should we get the government to pay subsidies or give special tax breaks or otherwise support the construction of housing to serve the urban poor? Perhaps so. If there are external social benefits, then there's no way the "housing investment market," operating by itself, can produce enough housing to achieve the social optimum.

If you look around you, you will see many examples of "externalities." Suppose the local coal mine spreads dust over the countryside for an area of twenty miles. If the coal producers don't have to pay for all this pollution, then this is an "externality." It's a social cost. But it isn't a cost that shows up in the cost (and price) of coal.

If I decide to plant Christmas trees on the barren hillside so that I can make profits from selling the trees, my tree farm provides externalities. The trees stabilize the soil so the spring rains will not wash topsoil into the stream and muddy the water and kill all the fish. But do I get paid for this external benefit? No.

The only way the market can take externalities into account is for a way to be found to **internalize the externalities.** *That means: to get market costs and prices to reflect the full social costs and full social benefits.*

How to Internalize the Externalities

The obvious way to "internalize" a cost externality (say pollution) would be for the government to require that the business pay an additional cost as a penalty for polluting—or else have the business pay the full cost of eliminating the pollution.

If the business must pay for the *full social cost* then the cost externality becomes internalized. As the cost goes up, the price the consumer pays will go up. Only those consumers who are willing to pay the higher price covering the *full social cost* (including the pollution cost) will get the product.

In the case of the timberlands surrounding the village, after internalizing all of the great social costs of cutting the trees, the price of the lumber would be so high that nobody would ever buy it. If nobody is going to buy it then nobody is ever going to cut it and sell it. Of course not. So the village will be saved.

In general, the government can "internalize" externalities by taxes and subsidies.

External social *costs* can be internalized by levying taxes or by imposing other government charges to *push up the cost* (and the price). This will discourage the production and limit the use of the product.

External social *benefits* can be internalized by paying government subsidies—some kind of "bonus payments"—to the producers of the beneficial products. This will *push down the cost* and the price and will encourage the production and the use of these beneficial products.

The "village destruction tax" the government levied on the cutting of Johnson's Valley timber is very high! The loggers all go home. Can't you just hear the village mayor's speech when he says: "The timberlands have been saved by the timely internalization of the externalities!" Oh, well . . .

There Are Many Kinds of Externalities

The term "externalities" has broad meaning in economics. It is used to refer to any kind of "outside the market" influence. If a new type-writer repair shop opens up in my town, this may let my local business get its typewriters repaired faster and cheaper. This is a beneficial externality for my business. Ultimately my customers will benefit.

Or if a new processing plant opens up in my area and causes more overcrowding of the already overcrowded highways and railroads and telephone services, my costs will go up. I would see this as an undesirable externality. Ultimately my customers will have to pay more.

In both these examples the ultimate result is for the society to have extra benefits or extra costs which do not show up in the "profit and loss statements" of the new typewriter shop or the new processing plant.

The Political Process Must Influence The Choices

Whenever externalities exist, the entrance of the government into the market process is understandable. Sometimes it's essential. When externalities exist, the only way society can arrive at the best choices is to change the results the market would bring.

One approach is to subsidize the external benefits and place extra charges on the external costs. Another approach is to *prohibit the production or use of some things*.

As population expands and more people get crowded together, externalities multiply. Everything you do has "spillover effects" on somebody else! So the problem of externalities is likely to become even more serious in the future.*

THE MARKET CAN'T ACCOMPLISH ALL OF OUR LONG-RANGE GOALS

There's another kind of "social consideration" which is external to the market. How does

---

*Chapter 30 goes much deeper into externalities—specifically, into the economics of the pollution problem in a modern, industrialized society. The basic conceptual knowledge you have gained in this section will serve you well when you get to Chapter 30.

the market handle the question of society's long-range objectives and goals? For many, it doesn't. It can't.

If the society is going to establish long-range "non-market objectives" and work out long-range plans for achieving the objectives, it must do these things through the political process.

We know that over the next 40 years the market process, with some modifications, can generally provide for the efficient use of our resources. In that way it can help us to reach our objectives. But some long-range objectives and goals and general plans for their achievement must be worked out through the political process.

Might it be possible to work out some plans and achieve something better than would happen if we just "let nature take its course?" Should the society through its political process decide on some objectives and develop some programs to move us toward these long-range objectives? Most people agree that there are some long-range objectives which require government planning.

An Example: the Interstate Highway System. During the early 1950s some people in the Bureau of Public Roads and some members of Congress and some others worked up plans and legislation for the construction of a 41,000 mile "interstate highway network." The planned network was to link all the major cities of the United States and to be completed over a 20-year period. Soon the plans were worked out and the engineering and construction of the interstate highway system was begun.

Today most of the system is complete. Why? How did it happen? Because the objectives and the plans were made by the government more than a quarter of a century ago.

The U.S. Space Program. Another example is the U.S. space program. Decisions were made to put a man on the moon in the decade of the 1960s—and to have a "space shuttle" operating in the early 1980s. All this was possible only because the objective was established

and the plans were made by the government. This kind of long-range planning and programming is not a function which the market process can be expected to perform.

The Market Process Can Implement the Plans

The market process isn't designed to choose for the society all of its "long-range objectives," or to decide how much "opportunity cost" we will accept as we seek these chosen objectives. But once the goals are decided and the plans made, most of the day-to-day implementation of the plans can be carried out very efficiently by the market process—by letting prices pull the resources into the "chosen" places to do the "chosen" things.

But some of the objectives and the plans—to reach the moon, to revitalize the cities, to build a new and exciting education system, to eliminate poverty, to protect the environment—must be the brainchildren of the political and social processes. We can't make all of these choices through the market process.

So some of the objectives and programs needed to meet the long-range needs of our society (and our world) will have to be approached, not through the market, but through the political and social processes.

Where does this leave us? We've spent several chapters talking about the market process and how it works. Do we scrap it now and take off with political process to try to solve some of the big problems of our na-

tion and our world?

When we come out of the "model market system of pure competition" and move into the real world, what do we have left? Anything of value? Yes. Nothing pure or perfect. But certainly something valuable. The chapters coming up will go much deeper into all this.

SUMMARY AND SYNTHESIS

Real-world market systems don't work out exactly like the model market system. In the model system, the "normal condition" is long-run equilibrium. There's long-run balance in all input and output markets—no surpluses or shortages, and normal prices and normal profits everywhere you look. But not so in the real world.

Real-world markets are dynamic. They are always changing in response to changing demand, supply, and price conditions—both in the input and the output markets. They always tend toward long-run equilibrium, but mostly never get there.

In the markets for most products this disequilibrium—this microeconomic instability—is not a serious problem. Supply adjustments come fairly smoothly in response to demand, price, and cost changes. But in some markets (e.g., for agricultural products) the supply response is delayed.

When demand increases and the supply doesn't respond much (is very inelastic) then the price can go very high. Ultimately the high price will motivate a huge supply response and flood the market. The price will collapse.

The corn-hog cycle is a real-world example of this "microinstability" which occurs in some markets. The cobweb theorem describes this and uses supply and demand graphs to illustrate how it works.

In one year (agricultural season) the supply will be low and the price, very high. In the next season the supply will be high and the price very low.

In the corn-hog cycle, when the corn price is high the hog price is low (and vice versa). Why? Because farmers shift their outputs back and forth between corn and hogs, responding to present (not future) prices and costs.

The supply and demand cobweb may tend toward "ultimate equilibrium," or not. If the season-to-season supply curve is not very elastic (less elastic than the demand) then the "supply over-responses" will get smaller and smaller and the cobweb will be converging toward equilibrium. But if the supply curve is highly elastic (more elastic than the demand) then the over-responses will get larger and the cobweb will be diverging away from equilibrium.

This microinstability in the agricultural product markets is partly responsible for some of the past and present governmental controls over agricultural outputs and prices, both in this country and in other nations.

Inequality of wealth and income is a necessary condition for the operation of the market process. Everybody knows that the use of incentives requires inequality. But there's serious disagreement about how much inequality is needed, or should be permitted in a real-world economic system.

There's a tendency for the rich to get richer because wealth generates income and produces more wealth. Both private and government income redistribution activities are aimed toward reducing the inequality, hopefully without seriously reducing people's incentives to produce.

Externalities exist whenever market values (prices) of things don't accurately reflect the social values involved in the production or consumption of those things. Externalities are sometimes called "spillover" or "third-party" effects. People who are outside that market are experiencing costs or benefits which are generated in that market and are "spilling over" on them.

Whenever the **cost to society** of a product is greater than the **cost to the producer,** then there's an **external social cost.** The supply (and the price) of this product will not reflect the full social cost. The supply will be too great, and the price, **too low.** The social cost of **unregulated pollution** would be an example.

Whenever the **benefit to society** of a product is greater than the **payment received by the producer** then there's an **external social benefit.** The supply of the product will be **too small** and its price too high to achieve the "social optimum." The social benefits from **building a new plant** during a recession, or in an area where there's widespread unemployment, would be an example.

Externalities can be internalized by forcing the supply-demand-cost-price conditions in the market to reflect the **external (social) costs and benefits** as well as the **internal (economic) costs and benefits.** We can impose taxes or other government charges to reduce the supply and push up prices of the "cost externality" products. And we can give grants, subsidies, tax exemptions, etc. to increase the supply and push down prices for the "benefit externality" products.

Some kinds of **long-range objectives and goals** can't be identified and pursued entirely by the "free forces of the market process." So the political and social processes sometimes must get involved. But once the goals are decided and the plans are made, most of the implementation **can be carried out most efficiently by the market process.**

REVIEW EXERCISES

MAJOR CONCEPTS, PRINCIPLES, TERMS (Explain each carefully.)

disequilibrium is the "normal" thing
the role of supply elasticity
the role of "income redistribution"
the role of inequality
the process of "snowballing enrichment"
the idea of a "new deal"
the basic problem of externalities
the problem of long-range goals

OTHER CONCEPTS AND TERMS (Explain each briefly.)

the corn-hog cycle
the cobweb theorem
the delayed "supply response"
income redistribution
social cost

social benefit
externalities
cost externalities
benefit externalities
internalizing the externalities

CURVES AND GRAPHS (Draw, label, and explain each.)

The Supply and Demand for Corn This Season
The Demand and Supply of Corn Next Season
The Diverging (Explosive) Cobweb
The Converging Cobweb

QUESTIONS (Write the answers or jot down key points.)

1. If "long-run equilibrium" doesn't ever exist in the real world, then exactly what good, if any, does it do to learn how it looks in the model and to describe how the "model market system" would move into "long-run equilibrium" following a change of demand, or cost? Do you think your understanding of the "long-run equilibrium" concept helps you to understand anything about what goes on in the real world? Discuss.

2. The markets for agricultural products are "triply treacherous," since:
   a. the market supply can't increase for many months, then suddenly the market may be flooded;
   b. the weather may bring a bumper crop and low prices or it may create shortages and high prices; and
   c. the demand for most agricultural products is inelastic so the price must move drastically for people to buy much more (or less) of the product.
   Can you explain what all this means? Then what do you think ought to be done about "the farm problem"?

3. Can you give a good explanation of the corn-hog cycle? Try.

4. I don't suppose anybody likes inequality for its own sake but some inequality seems to be essential to permit rewards to be given to those who produce the things wanted by the society. No economic system has ever been able to function satisfactorily without rewards, and the resulting inequality. So *inequality* is not the question. The questions are: "How much inequality do we want to permit?" and "In the real world of economic uncertainty and practical politics, how do we achieve the 'desired amount' of inequality—no less and no more?" Discuss some of the difficulties you see in trying to get this complex socio-economic problem worked out.

5. In our complex, densely populated modern societies, almost all activities have some "spillover effects" which have either favorable or unfavorable influences on other people. If the "spillover effects" occur in some kind of market-directed activity, then that's what we mean by "externalities." List some "social benefit externalities" and some "social cost externalities" that you are personally familiar with and explain how each one might be internalized.

27

The Market System in the Real World II: Monopoly Power and Administered Prices

Chapter Objectives

- You already know a good bit about the importance of **market structure** and **competition** in the functioning of the market system. In this chapter you'll learn a lot more about that.

- When you finish studying this chapter you will be able to **describe different kinds** of **market structures** and to **explain** the **kinds of competition** which would be found in each.

- You will be able to **draw and explain** the **kinked oligopoly demand curve** and to use this to show why **price leadership** is likely to arise in **oligopoly markets.**

- You will be able to explain the great appeal of **product differentiation,** and **the essential role of advertising** in a market structure of **monopolistic competition.**

- Finally, from this chapter you will get a brief overview of the evolution of and the **unresolved dilemma** concerning U.S. **public policy** toward **big business** and **monopoly power.**

PURE COMPETITION AND MONOPOLY POWER

You know a lot about how the model market system works. You know how changes in the demand and the supply change the market price. You know how prices move freely, responding to shifts of demand or supply. But things won't happen quite that way unless there is **pure competition** in all the markets. *Without "pure competition" the adjustment process can't work out the way the pure market model says it will.*

Competition Protects the Buyer

Back in our "island economy" there was a big demand for tuba (coconut-palm wine). Remember? The northside chief, King Ratukabua, was the only seller of tuba. In response to the great demand for tuba, he might have simply raised the price (instead of increasing the output). But suppose he had lots of competitors all selling tuba. Then he couldn't just raise the price and make lots of profits. Right? Of course not.

Competition is the thing which prevents businesses from limiting their output and raising the price sky high. Suppose there's competition and one factory limits its output and holds up the price. What happens? Nobody buys! Everybody buys from the lower-priced sellers. If there are *many* buyers and sellers of a product we say the **market structure** is one of pure competition. Remember? Here's a brief review.

Pure Competition Again

In a market of pure competition *no producer thinks of cutting back output to hold up the price.*

Competition forces all sellers to do a good job of serving the buyers!

Would you cut back your "backyard plot corn production" to keep the price of corn from falling? Obviously not. Then you are producing and selling under conditions of pure competition. Would any one of your roadside stand customers stop buying corn to force the price to go down? No. So the buyers are buying under conditions of pure competition.

Buyers and sellers simply "react" to the market price. They don't try to change the price. So it's a market of pure competition. But *as they all react, "the market" changes the price.*

In a market of pure competition, the price moves upward only if many buyers are trying to buy more (or if there are a lot more buyers) or if many sellers are selling less (or if there are a lot fewer sellers).

With pure competition, the price is a true reflection of society's demand (reflecting the society's marginal utility of the product) and of society's supply (reflecting the cost of production of the product). But what if one buyer or seller gets big enough to create a shortage or surplus? Then pure competition no longer exists.

Without pure competition, no longer can we say that the price is a true reflection of society's demand for and cost of the product.

A Producer with Monopoly Power Can Set the Price

Suppose one seller gets large enough to influence the total supply for a product. Then that seller can restrict output and keep the price up high and make big profits. This power to restrict output and hold up the price is called **market power** or **monopoly power.** Remember?

Is pure competition the usual thing? You know it isn't. In all the modern economies in which "free markets" play an important role—the United States, Canada, Western Europe, Japan, and most of the other nations of the modern world—pure competition usually exists only in the markets for farm and fishery products. Most manufactured products are made by only a few producers.

Sometimes there is strong competition among these manufacturers. But the competition is very different and brings different results than pure competition would bring.

Outputs still adjust to changes in demand. But *the adjustment process is very different.* Also the equilibrium price and the quantity flowing across the market may be quite different from the results described in the "model market structure of pure competition."

Producers Can Respond Directly to Demand Changes

Manufacturing firms usually set the selling prices of their products. They try to set and hold the prices at levels they believe will cover their costs and bring some profits. Once the price is set it will not change in response to every little change in demand, or cost. The price stays constant.

In a market of pure competition a demand change causes a price change. Then production responds to the price change (as was the case in our egg market and corn market examples). But in the markets for manufactured products (toothpaste, TV sets, automobiles, ball-point pens, economics books and almost anything else you can think of) output usually responds directly to the strength of the demand. The manufacturer sets the price and doesn't change it very often.

Administered Prices? Or "Competitive" Prices?

How different the markets are in the real world from the market model of pure competition! In markets of pure competition the price moves freely in response to changes in demand and supply. It's the *price* as it moves up or down, which carries the message from the consumers to the producers. It's the *price increase* which pulls the factors into the industries which society wants expanded and it is the *price decrease* which moves the factors out of those industries which society wants contracted. But in the real world very few prices are free to move around like that.

The prices for almost everything you can think of are set by someone. The economist calls these "set prices": administered prices. Manufacturers, wholesalers, retailers, barber shops, doctors, lawyers, taxicab companies and airlines all sell their products and services at "administered prices." The wages received by most people are "administered prices." Interest rates are "administered prices." Even many of the farm products are now sold at prices which are "administered" either by government or by farmers' organizations.

All administered prices reflect demand and cost conditions, at least to some extent. The administered prices for manufactured products generally are set on the basis of cost and demand estimates. Then the prices are held firm and the output is expanded or contracted, depending on how much is being sold.

Figure 27-1 illustrates the situation in which the individual producer is producing a brand-name product—perhaps Ford Pintos or Bobbie Brooks knitwear, or whatever. The producer fixes the price and then adjusts the output in response to the quantity people are buying. Take a few minutes now to study Figure 27-1.

The Effects of Administered Prices

Economists have spent a lot of effort and have written many volumes on the issue of "administered prices." Yet we still don't know for sure exactly how to assess the effects of administered prices in the real world. We know that administered prices reduce the responsiveness of market prices to shifts of demand. But that isn't always bad.

Violent price fluctuations resulting from sharp changes in demand don't do anybody any good. Administered prices do introduce a degree of stability. That's desirable. But on the other hand, *administered prices permit sellers to bend the economic choices of the society toward their own interests.* This would not be possible in the pure competitive model.

Another problem is that *administered prices tend to inch upward year after year.* Workers want bigger paychecks. Businesses want increasing profits. Everyone who is selling anything would like to get more money year after year. When prices are administered, sellers usually have the opportunity to inch up their prices—so they do. So what happens? There's a tendency for a *continual upward movement* of prices.

Now you have an overview of the issues of pure competition, market power, and administered pricing. But there's a lot more to it than that—as you'll be finding out in the next section.

"COMPETITION" IS DETERMINED BY MARKET STRUCTURE

You already know that each market is "made up of"—that is, built of, or structured out

Fig. 27-1   The Administered Price (Horizontal) Supply Curve

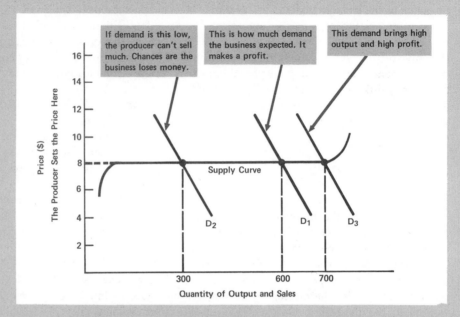

The price is set by the producer and the amount produced and offered for sale responds directly to changes in demand.

This illustrates the supply of a manufactured product marketed under normal circumstances in an economy like the United States. For a broad range of output, the *price* will stay the same.

If the quantity people are buying is large, production will be stepped up; if the quantity people are buying is small, production will be cut back. The producer would go on a four-day work week, or perhaps close down for one week each month rather than lower the price.

If the demand is low the output is low; if the demand is high, the output is high. The price stays the same. But notice that if the demand goes very high (shifts far to the right) the price *will* go up. Or if the demand gets very low (shifts far to the left) the price will go down. Sales and discounts will be used to get rid of the surpluses. If the demand does not soon pick up, the business will stop producing this unprofitable product.

This graph shows about the same picture you saw back in Figure 23-5—the break-even chart. Remember? The price stays the same and the producer sells more (or less) depending on the strength of the demand. You can see that if the demand is at D_1, 600 units will be sold at a price of $8; total revenue will be $4,800. Figure 23-5 shows that, too. And Figure 23-5 shows that the total cost would be about $4,400 and profit would be about $400.

of—buyers on one side and sellers on the other. All the buyers and all the sellers are not standing there glaring at each other, of course! But they are there just the same.

No more than two people—one buyer and one seller—may meet face to face at any one time. But if each buyer and each seller knows that there are a thousand other buyers and a thousand other sellers just waiting to appear, then we have a "market structure" of **pure competition.**

When we talk about "pure competition" we are talking about one form of "market structure"—a structure of *many buyers and sellers—so many that no one of them acting alone could have any noticeable effect on the market—either on the price or on the quantity flow.* You've heard quite a bit about pure competition already. But now here are some other kinds of market structures that you don't yet know much about.

Bilateral Monopoly: One Seller and One Buyer

What kind of market structure would be the complete opposite of pure competition? **Complete monopoly,** of course! It would be a market where there is only one buyer and one seller. This market structure is sometimes called **bilateral monopoly.** Other times it is called **monopsony-monopoly** (one buyer-one seller).

When the steel workers' union bargains with the steel industry that's a labor market of "bilateral monopoly" or "monopsony-monopoly." The union has complete control of the supply. It's the only seller. The steel industry has complete control of the demand. It's the only buyer.

Whenever a market structure of bilateral monopoly exists, both the buyer and the seller must consider their market power. Anything either one does will change conditions in the market. Both must take this important fact into consideration. So the monopolist's decision-making process is more complicated than that of the "pure competitor." The monopolist must consider costs and revenues, just as a "pure competitor"

would. But *the monopolist must also figure out what effect each decision will have on the price!*

Now you have seen the two most extreme forms of market structure. All other market structures are variations of these extremes. There's one seller and many buyers (monopoly), one buyer and many sellers (monopsony), a few on each side of the market, and so on. All kinds of variations in the sizes and numbers of buyers and sellers are possible.

Most Product Markets Have Few Sellers and Many Buyers

Most consumer product markets in the real world consist of a few sellers and many buyers. All the *buyers* know that no matter how much they buy, it won't force the price up. But all the *sellers* know that if they increase their output very much they will have to cut the price to sell it all. They can all set their own prices. As long as each seller's prices are not higher than the prices of their competitors then each seller can continue to sell some.

How many products and services can you think of which are produced and sold by "a few sellers"? How about metals—steel, aluminum, copper, etc.? Or coal, oil, and natural gas? And what about the railroads, trucking companies, bus companies, airlines? Producers of automobiles, washing machines, refrigerators, TV sets, tires, paints, chemicals? Local building contractors, shipbuilding firms, computer companies? Toothpaste, deodorants, hair spray, after-shave lotion, headache pills? Just about everything you can think of, right?

Market **Structure** means how <u>many</u> and how <u>strong</u> are the buyers and the sellers.

All Producers Must Keep Their Prices "In Line"

Most of the products you buy are produced and sold by a few large sellers. Each company sets the price for its product. But each company knows that the price it charges must not be very far out of line with the prices other companies are charging for similar products. If one company's price is so high that it's out of line, no one will buy that company's product.

If one company is selling only half as much as it would like to, one way it could sell more would be to lower the price. But any company that lowers its price will take customers away from its competitors. The competitors would not be very happy about that! So what would they do?

They would lower their prices too, just like in a gasoline "price war." In the end where will they all wind up? In about the same place except that everybody's prices will be lower and probably everybody will be losing money.

Suppose you were a producer in this industry. What good would it do to lower your price? No good. You would wind up hurting your competitors and yourself, too. Every producer already knows that. So usually, nobody lowers the price.

All Producers Limit Their Outputs

In the kind of market structure we are talking about (where there are a few sellers and many buyers) does each firm produce as many as it can? Not on your life! The rate at which each plant operates is determined by the rate at which people are buying the output. Each business keeps its production regulated so that no unwanted surpluses will be produced and no price cutting will occur.

Each firm is responsive to demand. But their responsiveness does not result from *price movements* in the market. Each firm responds *directly* to the strength of the demand. If their customers start buying more, the firm produces more. Isn't that the way you would operate if you were selling jeans to the department stores in Asheville and Knoxville and Nashville and all over?

In most real-world markets, the response of production to demand is *direct*, rather than

through the movement of price. If Bethlehem Steel finds that people aren't buying as many hot rolled sheets as before, Bethlehem doesn't wait around and let a glut on the market push the price down! Production is cut back immediately.

OLIGOPOLY: A MARKET WITH FEW SELLERS

The kind of market structure we have been talking about is one with lots of buyers but only a few sellers. Each seller must be very careful not to push the price down. Economists call this kind of market structure oligopoly.

"Oligopoly" is an important kind of market structure in the world today. You need a good understanding of what it is and how it works. So let's resurrect our island example and talk some more about "palm-tree wine." What do we call it? Tuba! Of course.

The Island Example Again

Remember when King Ratukabua (the northside chief) had the monopoly on tuba? That was a market structure of complete monopoly on one side and several buyers on the other. The northside chief (monopolist) had the power to restrict the output, raise the price and make profits. Why should he produce a lot of tuba and force the price way down? His maximum profit will come if he limits output and sells his tuba at a high price.

That's a very important thing about a market structure of monopoly. Once King Ratukabua has it he *cannot ignore the fact that he has it*. He cannot ignore the effect of his rate of output on the market price.

If he does ignore his monopoly position he loses the opportunity for more profits. What kind of businessman would he be if he didn't take advantage of his profit opportunities? That's a problem with monopoly. *Once monopoly exists, the seller must restrict output to keep from pushing the price down.*

In order to introduce *oligopoly* to our island we need more people. So let's assume there are several more islands just like our island, all scattered within easy trading distance. Soon trade develops among all these islands. Also, let's suppose that the only island on which the people know how to make tuba is *our* little island—Tubaland Island. (You knew I named it that for some good reason. Right?)

Suppose that as the years have passed, all of the families on our island have learned to make tuba. Now there are four big tuba-making operations on the island—north, south, east, and west. All the operations are approximately the same size, and all four families are selling tuba to the people on the nearby islands.

Oligopoly Discourages Price Competition

The northside chief always sells his tuba at the "going price." He is wise enough to know that if he tries to charge more than that, no one will buy from him.

He realizes also that if he tries to sell more by cutting his price, his "oligopolistic competitors" will cut their prices too. Otherwise they would lose all of their customers! In the end all of the producers would be selling for lower prices and all of them would be worse off. So he doesn't cut his price either.

Is there "competition" in the tuba market? Yes. **Oligopolistic competition.** But notice how different this "oligopolistic competition" is from pure competition! Remember the case of the egg market? One egg producer doesn't care if the next farmer down the road goes into the egg business or not. Each producer knows that one more or less producer isn't going to have any effect on the market.

But what about "oligopolistic competition?" That's very different. Each seller is acutely aware of the interdependence in the market. You know that everything your competitors do will affect you. Everything you do will affect your competitors. Each seller is very careful to restrict output to that amount which can be sold at the going price. No one wants to rock the boat!

What Happens If Someone Cuts the Price?

Suppose the westside islanders are not careful enough about limiting their production of tuba. One day the westside chief (Queen Isaleilani) realizes that they have produced so much tuba that the only way they can sell it is to cut the price. So she decides to pull a quick price cut and sell off the surpluses before the other tuba sellers know what's up.

She decides to cut the price from eight fishsticks (FS 8.00) to six fishsticks (FS 6.00) per jugful. She sends out a boatload of tuba. As the boat approaches a neighboring island the crew unfurls a huge banner saying: "SPECIAL PRICE! TUBA FS 6.00 A JUGFUL!" The minute the boat gets to the beach the people begin to clamor for the tuba. In less than an hour all the tuba is sold. The boat heads back home for a new supply.

It just so happens that about two hours after the westside boat leaves, an eastside boat arrives and tries to sell tuba for FS 8.00. No one will buy. They explain that they can now get tuba at FS 6.00 from the westside islanders and that they are not going to buy any more tuba from anyone else unless they can get it for FS 6.00 a jugful.

The eastside islanders realize immediately that they can't sell any tuba on that island unless they lower their price to six fishsticks. Those westside islanders! Trying to get away with a trick like that! They should know this basic principle: *With a market structure of oligopoly, "price competition" lowers the profits for everybody!*

Everyone Must Cut the Price

The eastside islanders reluctantly agree to sell their boatload of tuba for FS 6.00 a jug. They would rather do this than to take back a boatload of tuba, or try to make the long run to the next island before nightfall. By the time they arrive home the eastsiders are in the mood to convince the westsiders of the error of their ways—by fair means or foul!

By the time the eastside chief, King Tuituranga, arrives at the westside village, Queen Isaleilani has already been thinking about this thing. She begins to realize that it probably would be more profitable for her (and for everybody) if she would just dump the surplus tuba in the lagoon and keep the price at FS 8.00. She is already planning to send a messenger around saying that she made a mistake and announcing that from now on all westside tuba will be sold for no less than FS 8.00 a jugful.

Since the demand for tuba is not very elastic, the total amount people would buy at a price of FS 6.00 probably isn't very much greater than the total amount they would buy at a price of FS 8.00. As the price moved down to six fishsticks, the producers would be able to sell a little more—but not much more. They wouldn't sell enough to make up for the loss (FS 2.00 a jug) caused by lowering the price. Everybody would get less revenue. So believe me, no one is ever going to be so foolish as to cut the price of tuba again!

Oligopoly Generates Price Leadership

Will anyone ever *raise* the price of tuba? Maybe. If one seller raises the price, all the others must also raise their prices or else the initial price increase will be withdrawn in a hurry! Suppose the northside chief raises the price to nine fishsticks a jugful. Unless everyone else

immediately does the same, the northside chief will not be able to sell any tuba.

Here's a new idea. Perhaps the northside chief can become recognized as the "price leader" in the tuba market. If so, he can raise the price to FS 9.00 and be confident that all the other tuba makers will immediately follow. Then all will get more profits at the higher price. Can you see why price leadership sometimes develops in oligopolistic industries? Sort of obvious, isn't it?

In the United States, if Bethlehem Steel announces a ten percent increase for hot rolled plates, unless the other steel companies soon announce similar price increases Bethlehem will probably announce that it isn't going to raise the prices after all. Bethlehem doesn't want to lose all of its customers! They know that no one is going to buy steel from Bethlehem when they could get the same product from USS, Republic, Inland, J & L (or maybe from Germany or Japan) for ten percent less!

Characteristics of Oligopoly Markets

All oligopoly markets have three special characteristics:

1. All producers must quote prices which are identical (or nearly identical).
2. No producer can profit by using price competition—by cutting the price to less than the "going price."
3. The only way any producer can raise the price and then stick to the higher price is for all the other producers to move their prices up, too.

If you understand why these three things are true, then you have a good basic understanding of oligopoly. You can see how each seller must be very careful in a market of "pure oligopoly" (where the product of all sellers is identical). Each seller must always be mindful of what those other sellers are doing. It's a watchful, nervous kind of situation!

Oligopolists Would Like to Form a Cartel

Producers don't like the limitations and restrictions imposed on them by this "pure kind" of oligopoly. No producer can change the price without considering what the other producers are going to do. Producers would like to escape from such restrictions.

One way to escape is to have a little conference with all the other oligopolists and agree on what prices to charge. You might even agree which market territories each one will sell in. A cartel agreement like this sure would make life easier! (Like OPEC maybe? Sure!)

An agreement among the oligopoly sellers would let all of them know just how everything is going to go. Everybody can have high prices and carefully restrict outputs and make high profits. How? By eliminating the nervous, watchful kind of "oligopolistic competition" and replacing it with an agreement which, in effect, creates a "pure monopoly." When all the big sellers get together and form a "cartel" and plan market strategy, they become "one seller."

An "oligopolistic conspiracy" is great for the producers! But it can be expensive for all the rest of us. This is the kind of agreement "in restraint of trade" (limiting the amount sold and holding up the price) which the U.S. antitrust laws are designed to prohibit.

A GRAPHIC EXPLANATION OF OLIGOPOLY

As you have been reading all this about oligopoly you may have been wondering about the strange nature of the demand for tuba as seen by each seller:

—If you lower the price, everybody else is going to lower the price. So you aren't going to sell very much more. Inelastic demand. Right? Sure.

—But what if you raise the price? Other sellers probably won't raise their prices. So who will buy from you, with your price so high? Maybe nobody! Everybody may buy from other sellers whose prices are lower.

So your little increase in price causes your quantity sold to drop maybe all the way to zero. Highly elastic demand? Right?

Can you see what this is saying? Inelastic demand if you lower the price (you don't sell much more). Elastic demand if you raise the price (you sell a lot less)! How can that be?

Look at Figure 27-2 and you'll find out about it. After that, go on to Figure 27-3 and you'll find out even more about oligopoly markets.

PRODUCT DIFFERENTIATION GENERATES MONOPOLISTIC COMPETITION

There is another way—a legal way—which producers may be able to escape from the nervous, watchful conditions of "oligopolistic competition." It's called product differentiation.

One day the northside chief decides to order from Japan some beautifully designed, multicolored tuba bottles with interesting figurines on the bottle caps. Then when the new bottles arrive he fills them with tuba and labels them with the slogan THE ONLY MONEY-VAULT-AGED AND DECORATIVELY-BOTTLED TUBA IN THE WORLD. Then he makes a ceremonial trip to the other islands and donates one bottle to the chief of each village.

Now Advertising Becomes Important

On each island the northside chief makes a speech. He says: "Of all the very, very finest things in the entire world, by far the most outstanding and regal is this. This is the only Money-Vault-Aged and Decoratively-Bottled

Fig. 27-2   Oligopoly I: Demand as Seen by the Individual Seller

The demand is very elastic if you raise the price (you lose your customers) and not very elastic if you lower the price (you don't sell much more).

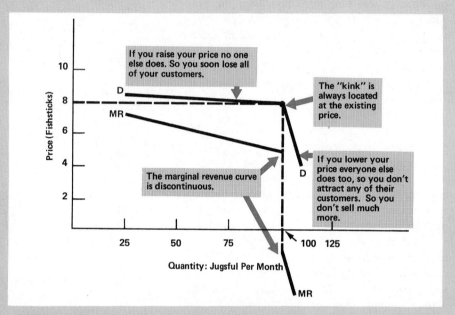

Why is there a kink in the demand curve? With the upper segment "price elastic" and the lower segment "price inelastic"? It's simple. There are really two demand curves put together.

The upper segment is "the demand curve for your product assuming all other sellers keep their price the same." The lower segment of the curve is "the demand for your product assuming that any price you choose will also be the price chosen by all the other sellers."

Why do we build the demand curve for the oligopolist using the lower segment of one of the curves and the upper segment of the other? Because that's realistic. That's the way it works in oligopoly markets.

If you raise your price it's profitable for the other producers *not* to raise their prices. They get your customers and make more profits. But if you lower your price the other sellers must lower theirs or else you will get all their customers!

So when you lower the price, everyone follows so that's the demand curve that applies. When you raise the price, no one follows, so the other demand curve applies. Get the idea?

Now you can understand why the marginal revenue curve is discontinuous. The upper segment of the marginal revenue curve really goes with the "nobody follows" demand curve. The lower segment of the marginal revenue curve goes with the "everybody follows" demand curve.

So when should an oligopolist either raise or lower the price? According to this, never! The next graph tells more about that.

Fig. 27-3 Oligopoly II: Total Market Demand, and Sales by Each Seller

If all the sellers get together and raise their prices, everyone can make more profits. They can escape from the "frozen situation" of the kinked demand curve.

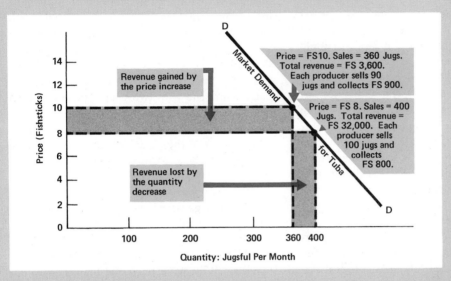

At the higher price, everyone gets more revenue! And since they are all selling less, their total costs also must be less. It's obviously very profitable to raise the price *if everyone raises the price at the same time!*

Here it is assumed that each seller will have one fourth of the entire market. As long as all of the sellers increase their price at the same time there is no reason why the price increase should disturb the "market shares" of any of the sellers. But if any one seller raises the price and the others don't? Then we have a kinked demand curve again!

You can see that the market demand for tuba between the prices of FS8 and FS10 is price inelastic. Each increase in price brings an increase in total revenue. All the producers will make more money (but all the buyers will be worse off) when the price goes up to FS10. The buyers will get less tuba and pay more money. The sellers will produce less tuba and will get more money.

What about a price of FS12? It looks like at a price of FS12 about 320 jugsful would be bought. So would it be good business to raise the price to FS12? It sure would! The total revenue received would go up to FS 3,840. The revenue each producer would receive would increase to FS 960. And what about the producer's costs? They would go down even more! When you produce less, your total cost goes down.

How far up should the price go? You can't tell for sure from this graph because there are no cost curves. But it would be easy to put in some cost curves and see where profits of the firms in the industry will be maximized. That might be at a price of FS18 or FS20 or more! See why competition (and the prevention of monopolistic collusion) is so important to protect consumers? Of course.

Tuba in the world. This tuba should be used only by those who have that highly developed sense of taste which will enable them to appreciate the very finest. You should never give this tuba to anyone unless you care enough to give the very best!"

The northside chief then announces that the price of this special money-vault-aged tuba will be 22 fishsticks a jugful and that he can supply only 12 jugful per month.

You wouldn't believe the reaction! Everyone wants some vault-aged tuba. The high price appears to be no deterrent at all. There is a long waiting list of people who want some of this special tuba.

In actual fact the tuba is no different than the other tuba. But in *economics* it is different. If the people think something is different, it will carry a higher price. So *from the point of view of economics, it is different!*

The northside chief is making beautiful profits. How did he swing it? He escaped from the "oligopolistic competition" by using product differentiation—by making his product different from those of his oligopolistic competitors. Now, he has escaped from that nervous, cautious oligopolistic competition!

The northside chief is still selling ordinary tuba in the "oligopoly" market. But in his special "vault-aged tuba," he has himself a **little monopoly,** all his own. He has hit upon a truly profitable scheme—a scheme recognized by business people all over the world—"differentiate your product, and advertise!"

But how long do you suppose he is going to be able to enjoy this great special advantage? Can he keep this "separate little monopoly" all his own? Forever?

Other Producers Differentiate Their Products

The other tuba producers are not stupid. They too are going to think up some special brand names, get some special bottles, differentiate their products, advertise, and create some "little monopolies" of their own. Soon they will start cutting in on the northside chief's little monopoly. Just watch.

Soon Queen Isaleilani gets a bright idea and orders some pink food coloring from Japan, mixes it with some of her tuba, bottles the tuba in smaller containers of clear glass so the pink can be clearly seen, puts on a label showing a strong man with big muscles, and the words: WESTSIDE TUBA FOR HEALTH, STRENGTH, VITALITY. She runs her own advertising campaign, complete with two giant-type strong men borrowed from a traveling carnival. She prices the bottles at 27 fishsticks each and announces that because of the great difficulty of producing this special tuba she can only supply 14 bottles a month. Soon she too has a long waiting list of customers for her special "health-type" tuba.

You can guess what happens from now on. Soon the eastsiders develop their own brand; then the southsiders develop their own brand. As all this is going on the northside chief asks himself, "Why have only one brand? Why not one brand to sell for FS100.00, in a goldplated jug, and only sell two each month? And maybe another brand to sell for FS 15.00? And several others?"

Soon There Are Many Brands of Tuba. Before long each family has five or six or eight or ten different brands of tuba, all sort of competing with each other, but no two brands exactly alike in the minds of the buyers. The northside chief still has his monopoly in "money-vault-aged" tuba and the westside chief still has her monopoly in "health, strength, and vitality" tuba. Each family has, in effect, a "little monopoly" in each of their brand name products. What the producers are doing now is *competing by advertising.*

Each family is trying to convince the people that their kinds of tuba are the best. But by now the island people are beginning to get a little immune to all the advertising and "medicine shows." Several people are beginning to suspect that the different kinds of tuba really aren't all that different. Some strong-willed people are beginning to buy the brands that are priced lowest—and without even being apologetic about it.

Price-Consciousness Must Be Carefully Undermined! The producers do all kinds of things to try to stop this intelligent "price consciousness" on the part of their customers. They pay people to put on fancy clothes and go around drinking expensive tuba. They spread the word that only "low-class" people drink low-priced tuba. They put on "educational programs"—movies and guest speakers and free wall posters and all that—for the school children, to convince them early in life about such "truths" as:

> "You get what you pay for"—"expensive things are good things and show good breeding and good taste"—"low-priced things are shoddy and only the very poor or the 'country clods' would buy such things"—"a truly refined person never asks about the price"—"anyone who is really intelligent will be glad if the price is high because high prices signify *good* goods."

So goes the propaganda campaign. You would be absolutely astonished how many otherwise intelligent people fall for it! The sales of the higher priced brands of tuba increase quite a bit, then stabilize.

Each family is now competing with all the other families in selling tuba at each "price level." Each family continues to have its own little monopoly in each of its brands, but each brand is in close competition with other brands. This kind of market structure should not seem strange to you. You've been living with it all your life! You have been bombarded with it by radio and TV ever since you were old enough to hear and see!

The kind of market structure we are talking about now is called **monopolistic competition.** "Monopolistic competition" is simply competition among "little monopolies." Each "little monopoly" is a "brand name" or "differentiated product" monopoly, just as in our island example. With monopolistic competition, most of the competing is done through advertising and trying to improve (or differentiate) the product.

Monopolistic Competition Is Everywhere

In the United States and throughout the world, monopolistic competition exists almost everywhere you look. We find it in toothpaste and cigarettes and soaps and detergents and candy bars and beer and cola drinks and gasoline and swimming pools and TV dinners and almost everything else. It exists with big, nationally known products, and also on the main street of every town and village.

Each store is trying to advertise a little better, trying to compete for customers, trying to display its products better, to run attractive sales and do all kinds of things to get more customers to come in and buy. Each of these businesses, just like each of the brand name products, is really a "little monopoly." The amount of "monopoly power" or "market power" each holds is really very small. Why? Because there are so many "little monopolies," all with similar products and services and all trying to take customers away from each other.

Is "monopolistic competition" a kind of market structure? Sure. But it isn't quite as neat and easy to describe as the market structures of pure competition or pure monopoly or pure oligopoly. Why? Because with monopolstic competition, instead of having one product we have many *slightly different* products. The competing products are very much alike. Still, the products aren't *exactly* alike.

With Monopolistic Competition, Each Producer Has Some Freedom

A "monopolistic competitor" has a little bit of freedom to change the price. Once you differentiate your product, you will have customers who will stay with your product even though you raise the price some. All producers would prefer to have "brand name loyalty" among their customers because this gives them more freedom from competition. It lets them raise prices without losing so many customers.

Just think how profitable it can be to advertise effectively. How long will people continue to pay more for a dozen brand name aspirin than it would cost to buy 100 non-brand name aspirin? For a long time, I suppose.

The difference which advertising can create in the minds of your customers is as real to them as if the difference *really was real!* So it pays to advertise. That's the way it is with monopolistic competition.

MONOPOLY POWER IN THE REAL WORLD

How does the market process really work, when we get away from pure competition? Does the market still get the choices made *in response to the wishes of society?* Or does the market process *serve the producers, at the expense of the rest of the society?*

This is a difficult question. Many aspects of the "real world" answer aren't even known—not by anyone.

No producer, not even one with pure monopoly, can escape the influence of consumer demand. At prices which are too high, the monopolist will lose customers.

Also, *if the monopolist is making high profits, the magnetism of these profits to potential competitors is very strong.* So we might say that no producer, no seller ever has complete, *absolute* "monopoly power." Some kind of actual or potential competition—either in the same prod-

There's Competition out there! domestic, foreign... actual, potential.....

uct or in some substitute product—seems to always be lurking there, somewhere.

"Bigness" Is Not All "Badness"

Another fact to consider is that "bigness" is not all "badness." Specialization is limited by the size of the market. You can't specialize in something unless the market is large enough to use up all of your specialized output.

It takes large markets to support large firms. Large firms can introduce new technology. They can spend money for research and development and for new, more efficient machines and techniques and processes.

A big firm can look more to the long run than to the short run. It can smooth out some of the ups and downs in its production operations by stockpiling things during times of slack demand and then selling out of inventory when demand picks up.

There are several very real economic advantages of bigness, both in production and in marketing. But the problem of "market power" always exists when a few big firms make up the seller's side of the market.

The modern societies of "mixed socio-capitalism" are faced with this dilemma:

Each society wants all the advantages which bigness can bring: good management, effective planning, production efficiency, stability, sound financing, industrial growth and all that. Yet each society wants each business to have many competitors, so that no one will have much monopoly power.

See the dilemma? What should the public policy be? How far should the government go in trying to pass and enforce laws and regulations to prevent businesses from getting big, from joining together, from doing things which the businesses themselves claim are necessary for increased efficiency? Where and how should the lines be drawn? This is the dilemma.

We Want to Have Our Cake and Eat It Too

The "market model" tells us that the best interests of the society will be served by markets in which there are many competitors. With pure competition, each producer will be forced to respond to market prices which reflect (a) the wishes of the buyers in the market, and (b) the true cost conditions in the society. Any producer who doesn't respond to market prices soon goes out of business.

If we absolutely prevent bigness we will force inefficiency on our economic system. The standards of living of all the people will suffer. There isn't much logic in that!

On the other hand we can hardly afford to let the markets become monopolized. The market model tells us that sellers with a lot of monopoly power can (and will) guarantee themselves large profits at the expense of society. So what do we do?

The "Monopoly Power" Question Is Unresolved

Are we certain that the market model really is close enough to the real world to be trusted as our guide on this vital matter? A good understanding of basic economic concepts can be of great help in approaching the problem. But the truth of the matter is that we don't yet have a body of "real-world theory" which is capable of taking us all the way to clear and indisputable answers on these vital public policy issues.

So what do we do? Do we pass laws to limit "bigness"? and monopoly power? Yes we do. No nation permits the unlimited creation and exercise of monopoly power. Of course not! You can understand why.

Even before the first antimonopoly or antitrust laws, if sellers got together and agreed to limit their output and keep their prices up, this was held to be illegal by the courts. It was considered to be a "conspiracy" against the public—a conspiracy to restrain trade.

This area of evolving antitrust law and public policy toward big business is one of the interesting and important parts of the subject of economics. The following section presents a few of the highlights.

U. S. Antitrust Policy

In the late 1800s in the United States, there was rising sentiment against the economic power of big business. In 1887, the *Interstate Commerce Act* was passed to limit the monopoly powers of the railroads. Then three years later (1890) the *Sherman Antitrust Act* was passed to prohibit all businesses from trying to monopolize any market, either by joining together in some sort of "trust" arrangement, or by merger, or by any other means.

The Sherman Act was not very strictly enforced. In fact, it was hardly enforced at all. Only a few of the most obvious and flagrant violations were prosecuted. By the early 1900s Standard Oil had managed to get control of most of the oil companies in the country, and American Tobacco had managed to monopolize the tobacco industry.

Then, in 1911, the U.S. Supreme Court forced both these companies to split up— but not until after the Rockefeller family (Standard Oil) and the Duke family (American Tobacco) had made many millions of dollars in profits!

In 1914, two new laws, the Clayton Antitrust Act and the Federal Trade Commission Act, were passed to strengthen the government's position against monopoly. After that, enforcement was somewhat better. Since 1914 there have been several additional laws and a great many court cases. Some have strengthened the government's antimonopoly position. Some have weakened it.

Why has U.S. antitrust policy been somewhat inconsistent? Partly because of strong political pressures. But perhaps the major cause of the inconsistency is the uncomfortable fact that we really don't know what we want. We want all the advantages of bigness and all the advantages of smallness. Which to give up? and which

to have? That's the question. Sound familiar? The economic problem—the problem of choosing. Right?

Today multi-billion dollar corporations make up a major segment of the U.S. economy and of all the other modern economic systems. In Part Eight you will be reading a lot more about it. But that's enough on the "monopoly power" issue, for now.

It's time now to move on into direct confrontation with the questions: "How does the market process work in the real world, anyway? After all is said and done, do we wind up where the 'model' says we will? or not?" That's what you'll be reading about in the next two chapters.

SUMMARY AND SYNTHESIS

Market structure means the **number and relative sizes of buyers and sellers** of a product—including the question of **ease of market entry and exit**. The kind of market structure which exists is the most important thing in influencing the **kind of competition** you'll find in that market.

Suppose there are **so many buyers and sellers** that no one (acting alone) can have any noticeable influence on the price. That's **pure competition**. But in real-world markets, most sellers can set an **administered price** and then adjust output in response to **quantities demanded**. So they have some **monopoly power**. The horizontal **administered price supply curve** illustrates this situation.

Bilateral monopoly means one seller and one buyer of a product. This market structure means a real bargaining situation!

Another market structure is oligopoly. **Pure oligopoly** means a **few sellers** of an **identical product**. If any seller cuts the price, all the other sellers will cut their prices too—or else they'll lose all their customers! Suppose a seller in oligopoly **raises the price**. That's a sure way to lose all your

customers!

The oligopoly seller sees a **kinked demand curve**, with the "kink" at the existing price. Raise the price and lose all your customers! Or lower it and lose revenues.

In oligopoly a **price leader** is likely to emerge—one who can announce price increases with reasonable confidence that other sellers will follow.

Monopolistic competition is a market structure with several sellers of **non-identical** products. **Product differentiation** is the important characteristic. Sellers compete by **brand names** and **advertising** to make their products **more different** (in a desirable way, of course) in the minds of their potential customers.

Most sellers in most real-world markets have some **monopoly power**. But no producer, not even one with **pure monopoly** can escape the influence of **consumer demand**. Raise your price and you **lose some sales**. The longer you wait the more **elastic** the demand becomes and the more sales you'll lose. The OPEC nations found out about that. Right?

The higher you raise your price the sooner you'll see other sellers coming in with **substitute products**. Your sales will drop. So don't forget: **monopoly power is never complete, or absolute, and the more it's used to exploit the buyers the** more its likely to turn out to be **only temporary.**

The creation or exercise of monopoly power is limited by law in all modern nations. In the United States the first **antitrust (antimonopoly) law** was the **Sherman Antitrust Act (1890)**. That Act is still the basic anti-monopoly law of the land. Since 1890, public policy toward monopoly has

been continually evolving. There have been several more acts and hundreds of court decisions. Generally the trend in recent decades has been toward **more restrictive public policy toward mo-**nopoly.

But there has been a continuing and **unre-solved dilemma: we want all of the advantages** (efficiency, stability, etc.) which **big businesses can bring,** and we also want all of the consumer protection and other **advantages of competitive markets.** We want to have our cake and eat it too. Right?

REVIEW EXERCISES

MAJOR CONCEPTS, PRINCIPLES, TERMS (Explain each carefully.)

pure competition
pure monopoly
oligopolistic competition
monopolistic competition

OTHER CONCEPTS AND TERMS (Explain each briefly.)

market power
monopoly power
antitrust laws
administered prices
bilateral monopoly
monopsony-monopoly
oligopoly

cartel
price leadership
product differentiation
Sherman Antitrust Act (1890)
Clayton Act (1914)
FTC Act (1914)

CURVES AND GRAPHS (Draw, label, and explain.)

The "Administered Price" (Horizontal) Supply Curve
Oligopoly I: Demand as Seen by the Individual Seller
Oligopoly II: Total Market Demand and Sales by Each Seller

QUESTIONS (Write out answers or jot down key points.)

1. Explain why pure competition is essential to the functioning of the "model market system."

2. Discuss some of the advantages and disadvantages of administered prices.
3. Can you think of any specific ways you have seen businesses "raise the price, without *announcing* that they were raising the price?" Discuss.
4. Explain why oligopoly tends to eliminate price competition and to generate price leadership.
5. Explain why, when oligopoly exists, there is a strong incentive for product differentiation to arise and for the market structure to move toward monopolistic competition.
6. Discuss some of the advantages and disadvantages of business "bigness."
7. Mention some of the highlights in the "evolution of public policy toward big business" in the United States.

28 Real-World Markets: How Prices Are Set and How Buyers and Sellers Respond

Chapter Objectives

- You already know some reasons why **real-world markets** don't always work out so well. But how do they actually work? And what results do they bring? That's what you'll be reading about in this chapter and the next.

- When you finish this chapter you will be able to explain (in general) **how the price mechanism works in the real world.**

- You'll be able to explain **how prices are set** both for **output products** and for **input factors.** And you'll know about the **real-world market constraints** on this price-setting process.

- You will be able to explain **how buyers and sellers** in both **output and input markets respond** to the **administered prices** which are set. And you'll know about the great importance of **waiting for the long run.**

- You will be able to use supply and demand graphs to illustrate some real-world conditions in the agricultural, money, and labor markets. And you will know how all this affects **income distribution** in the real world.

The Price Mechanism Is the Key

The model market process *lets you see some of the forces which are at work in all markets.* Once you understand these market forces you can look at the real world to try to see how they're working there. Do they? Or don't they? And how well?

It's difficult to generalize about *real-world markets.* Whatever you say can't be very precise. Precise statements probably would be *wrong* more often than right! Every rule is bound to have many exceptions. See the problem?

Each market at each moment is in some ways unique. How impossible it would be for anyone to see all the little details! Still, there are some "general conditions" at work in most real-world markets.

You have been seeing and living in real-world markets all your life. You will recognize the characteristics of the real-world markets the moment I begin to flash them at you. How different they look from the pure market model! And yet looked at more closely, how surprisingly similar! But first, a quick review of the key role of the price mechanism. Then we'll get into "real-world markets."

What About the Functions of Price?

You know that the model market process works its magic through the price mechanism.

The demand of the people acting against the restraint of supply, sets the price of each good at the level which reflects society's wishes. Then both the producer-sellers and the buyer-consumers respond to the price.

What induces them to respond? to follow society's wishes? The two functions of price—the *rationing function* and the *production motivating function,* of course!

Each **real-world** market, and each transaction is a unique, **special case!**

Suppose we want to look at real-world markets and see how they're working. What do we look at? At the price mechanism? Sure. Are demand and supply setting prices? If not, what (or who) is? And how?

Once the prices are set, what then? Do the prices in real-world markets induce the proper responses? That is, do the **rationing function** and the **production motivating function** of price really work? How well?

Suppose "real-world prices" are set the way "model prices" are set. And suppose "real-world responses to price" are the same as "model responses to price." What then? Real-world markets would work out exactly the same way the market model works out!

But everybody knows that *in the real world both the setting of prices and the responses to prices are different than in the model.* So the real world results are different. Why? and How? That's what we're getting into now. First a look at product prices in the real world.

HOW OUTPUT (PRODUCT) PRICES ARE SET IN THE REAL WORLD

You've bought lots of things in your life. How do you suppose the prices were determined on all those things you've bought? Do you suppose somebody *set* most of the prices? Probably so.

You've seen enough "output pricing in the real world" to know a good bit about how it actually happens. You know that businesses set their prices. Sometimes they advertise and run sales and all that.

Most Output Prices Are "Administered Prices"

Almost anywhere you look, almost any price you see has been "set" by somebody. That is, almost all prices are **administered prices**.

Remember from the last chapter how the seller sets the price and produces more (or less) in response to the quantity demanded? Usually that's how it works in the real world. A few output prices may be set by pure market forces. But not many.

Sometimes agricultural prices are set by pure market forces. But there's usually some kind of price *administering* going on.

For some products there are government price supports. And producer co-ops sometimes try to restrict supplies to keep prices up. I'll bet that in your state, milk is marketed by dairy co-ops and that the prices are set by the "State Milk Commission" (or whatever the "milk price control board" is called in your state).

So even in the "pure competition-type" farm product markets, prices are pushed around (administered) by monopoly influences and by the government.

Figures 28-1 and -2 use supply and demand graphs to show two different methods governments use to keep agricultural prices up above the "equilibrium price." Spend a few minutes studying those graphs now.

The "Administered Price" Must Reflect Reality

When you get right down to it, almost every price you can find is either set or manipulated or influenced by somebody or something *other than* "the pure market forces of supply and demand."

Fig. 28-1   One Way of Keeping Agricultural Prices Up: Price Supports

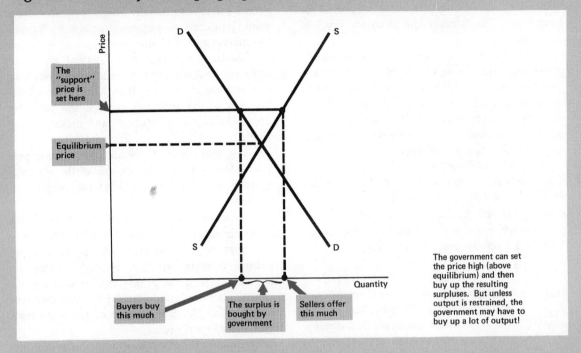

The government can set the price high (above equilibrium) and then buy up the resulting surpluses. But unless output is restrained, the government may have to buy up a lot of output!

Fig. 28-2   Another Way of Keeping Agricultural Prices Up: Output Restraints

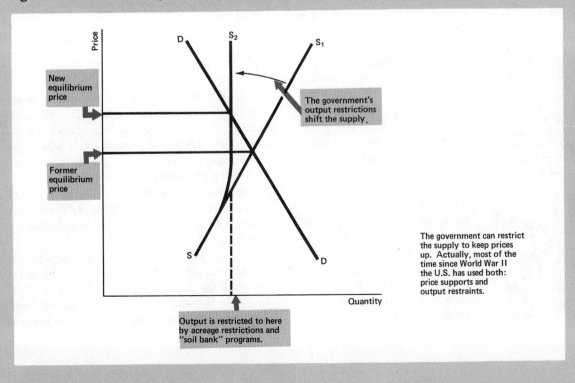

The government can restrict the supply to keep prices up. Actually, most of the time since World War II the U.S. has used both: price supports and output restraints.

Does this mean that supply and demand are irrelevant in the setting of real world prices? Of course not. That's really the issue we need to think about.

How far are the "set" or "administered" prices from the prices which "the pure market forces of supply and demand" would set? That's the important question. What's the answer? It's different from one industry to another, from one product to another, from one market to another, and from one time to another.

Generally speaking, in the market-oriented economic systems, for most things and at most times, most prices probably aren't very far from what the model would call "the normal price"—that is, the price which will cover the cost of production, including a normal profit for the producer.

Most Prices Really Do Reflect Production Costs.

In the real world you'll seldom see anything like pure competition in most markets. Still there's usually *enough* competition to keep most prices in line with the cost of production. What competition? *Competition from substitute goods from both domestic and foreign producers.*

If any producer's price gets very far above the cost of production, new competition will arise. This threat really does influence the pricing decisions of most sellers. It convinces them not to set their prices "too high."

Real-world markets have administered prices and production schedules and all that. Prices are less volatile and outputs are more controlled and stabilized than real-world markets of pure competition have ever been. So maybe the "limited monopoly power and administered prices" of real-world markets bring us the best that we can hope for!

Some Prices May Be Exorbitantly High.

What about exorbitantly high prices? Surely some producers sometimes manage to "corner the market and soak the public."

Maybe a company has a patent on something (or maybe a secret process) so nobody else can produce it. Then if there's no good substitute for it, the producer can set the price far above the cost of production and make a lot of profit!

Yes, that's true. There are always some sellers making a killing. That's one of those exceptions to the rule. Some of those are going on all the time.

What about the producers whose prices are many times as high as the cost of production—the ones with advertising and promotion expenses burning up the society's scarce resources—fooling the people into making unwise choices. Is this a good way for an economic system to run? No. But it's one of the ways real-world markets do run.

The government comes in and tries to force producers to tell the truth about their products. But this effort is not always successful.

Deceptive Advertising May Distort the Market

A problem of deceptive advertising really does exist in real-world markets. Deceptive advertising—with exorbitantly high prices for the deceptively advertised products and with most of the buyer's dollar going to pay the advertising cost and with society's valuable resources flowing into this socially harmful use—this is one of the most often criticized failings of "the market system" as it works in the real world. Yet it's hard to get at.

It's hard to separate good advertising from bad advertising. Informational advertising is essential in the functioning of real-world markets. Deceptive advertising is the scourge of real-world markets. The system would work better if we had some way to handle this problem.

Public Utility Services and Prices Are Regulated

In some markets the "tendency toward monopoly" is so strong that it can't be resisted; competition just can't work to ensure the consumer a quality product at a reasonable price. When that happens there's no way the market process can work. The government must come in and perform the "consumer protection function." That's what happens in the public utility industries.

When you buy electricity or gas or telephone service or bus or subway tokens, the price you pay is regulated by the government. Why does the government set the prices for these "public utility type" products and services? Because it's not easy for competition to work to protect the consumer in these industries.

The public utilities are just naturally "monopoly-type" industries. That's why the public utilities are called natural monopolies. You saw some "natural monopoly" cost curves back in Chapter 24. Remember?

Free, open competition among the public utilities would be highly inefficient. Can't you see several electric companies setting up poles and stringing wires or several gas companies digging trenches and burying pipes down your street? No way!

So the government (sometimes the city, sometimes the state and sometimes the federal government) has regulatory commissions to decide which company will provide what kinds of services and where. And how much they will be permitted to charge.

Regulatory Commissions Try to Do Competition's Job

What do the regulatory commissions do? They establish "required standards of services," then they set the prices for these services.

First they try to figure out the average cost. Then they try to set the price just high enough to cover the "per-unit cost plus normal profit."

The regulatory commission tries to do what competition would do, that's all.

Whenever a natural monopoly exists, it has to be regulated. Otherwise the buying public would have no protection from low quality and high prices. In competitive markets, if a producer doesn't produce a good product and sell it for a reasonable price, all the customers leave. They buy from competitors! But in natural monopoly markets there aren't any competitors! That's why the government must come in and regulate.

Do the regulatory commissions do a good job of figuring out "average costs" and "normal profits"? Then do they really set the prices and standards of services where they "should be"? Sometimes they do and sometimes they don't. It isn't as easy as you might think.

It's a constant struggle between the government regulators and the utility companies. The firms are busy trying to convince the commissions to let them reduce their services (to cut their costs) and to push up their rates. The government regulators are busy trying to ensure "adequate services" and to hold the rates down. Constant struggle? Litigation too? Right.

The history of public utility regulation in the United States provides plenty of proof that government price-setting doesn't always work out so well in the real world.

Consider this: A small increase in the average electric bill could add thousands of dollars of profits to the electric company. The electric company can afford to put a lot of effort into convincing the regulatory commissioners that the price needs to go up a little. What a great opportunity for bribes and graft!

There have been several scandals about crooked deals by regulatory commissioners. Probably some crooked deals have been pulled and never discovered. But in view of the great opportunity to make millions and not get caught, I suppose it's surprising that the regulatory commissions have been so honest!

How close do public utility prices come to where they ought to be? They're probably not too far out of line in most cases. But it would be so much simpler if we could just let competition take care of these things. Too bad that with the natural monopolies we can't do that. So the regulatory commissions keep on struggling with the problem.

Real-World Price-Setting Is a Constant Struggle

Mostly, real-world output prices are administered. They're set by somebody. And mostly they're pretty close to "the cost of production plus normal profit."

What about the *cost of production?* Costs may be higher in the real world than in the model. True. "Inefficient plant size" may be responsible—or there may be other reasons. Still it seems to be *generally* true that real-world markets usually do generate a high degree of efficiency.

Real-world markets are scenes of constant struggle—opposing and balancing forces offsetting each other. Businesses trying to push down costs, to expand their markets, to raise their prices—but being hemmed in: by various kinds of competition, by government restrictions, by labor and consumer organizations—all pushing and pulling—all trying to get things to be a little better from their own point of view.

Somehow real-world markets seem to work out pretty well—not at the optimal condition described by long-run competitive equilibrium. Of course not. But for the most part, probably not *too far* from it. So it appears that price-setting in the output markets usually doesn't work out badly, all things considered. But what about price *responses?*

REAL-WORLD RESPONSES TO OUTPUT PRICES

In real-world markets, do prices really ration (cause people to conserve and limit the use of) things? Sure. That's obvious.

What about the production motivating func-

tion? Do prices really motivate people to produce? Of course.

The Rationing Function of Output Prices

Generally speaking, the **rationing function of price** really does work. As prices go up, people really do shift to other products. And you know what people do when things go on sale! Right?

Higher prices really do squeeze out some buyers. And lower prices get people to buy more. Yes, in almost all of the markets in the real world the rationing function of price works all right.

The Production Motivating Function of Output Prices

The **production motivating function of price** really does work in the real world, too. But it doesn't always work quite the way it's explained in the model.

If one product is selling at a very high price (much above its average cost) then pretty soon some competitors will come in and start selling acceptable substitutes. This is the production motivating function of price at work.

Usually though, in the real world the "motivating process" works in a different way than in the model. You might say that real-world markets get into balance "backwards" from the way the model explains it. Here's an example.

Suppose Polaroid has developed a new kind of camera. The price is set at $19.95 and Polaroid is going to produce and sell as many as people will buy. They think they will be able to sell enough to go beyond the "break-even point" and make profits. They put on a nationwide advertising campaign and introduce the new camera. So what happens?

The new camera sells just great! The price stays at $19.95 and Polaroid keeps producing and selling more and more. Is Polaroid responding to the production motivating function of price?

Really they're responding *directly* to the quantity demanded! They're responding to the **production motivating function of sales.** As more cameras are sold, more are produced. The price doesn't change. That's what you saw back in Figure 27-1.

Polaroid sells more and more cameras and makes high profits. What's going to happen next? You can guess. Kodak wants in. Leica and Nikon want in too. These other companies come out with competing models as soon as they can.

Are Kodak and Leica and Nikon entering this market in response to the "production motivating function of price"? Sort of. What they're after is some of the high profits, that's for sure.

But is wasn't an upward movement in *price* that attracted Kodak and Leica and Nikon into this market. It was the high volume of *sales.* It's the high volume of sales that makes this little camera so profitable.

In the real world, the "production motivating function of price" usually works out to be the "production motivating function of sales."

Businesses Offer New Products: Buyers Get a Multiple Choice

In the market model, when the demand increases, the price increases. So the producers make excess profits. The profits attract more firms into the industry, so the supply increases.

In the real world it usually works differently. In the real world the business firm chooses a product it thinks will sell, sets a price it believes will be profitable, then produces the product and pushes it out to let it stand the test of the market place.

Of course the firm doesn't introduce the product and leave it out there lying all alone in the market! It advertises and does everything it can to convince the buyers to buy it. So really, the buyers are offered a "multiple choice."

All the competing products are out there in the market vying for the buyer's favor. The buyers will choose some and ignore others. The chosen ones will continue to be produced. They will be imitated by other producers. The ignored ones will disappear from the market.

Those products which nobody thinks about producing or which nobody thinks would be profitable, will not be offered. A product can't be chosen if it isn't offered. The consumer usually doesn't "generate" new products. Businesses do that.

Each business is always trying to develop profitable products. Some producers guess right. They succeed, make profits, and get more chances to develop new products and to offer more "multiple choices" to the buyers. Some producers guess wrong. They don't make it.

The "Chosen Ones" Survive and Prosper

This process goes on all the time. You see it working in all kinds of products and services. The well-managed businesses with good products and services and good customer appeal will survive and grow. The ones that can't stand "the test of the market place" will fail and disappear.

The process works with all products and with all services. It works with drug stores, department stores, clothing stores, variety stores, candy stores, grocery stores, appliance stores and record stores; with beauty parlors, barbershops, gas stations, laundries and cleaners, taverns and bars, restaurants, hotels and motels, dance halls, movies, campgrounds, recreation areas; with auto repair services, building contractors, plumbing shops, hamburger drive-ins, and just about everything else you can think of.

Consumers keep making their "multiple choices." The "unchosen ones" fail the test of the market place. They just fade away. The "chosen ones" survive and prosper. They expand their outputs. Soon other producers imitate them.

So now you know how "the production motivating function of price" works in the real world. It isn't exactly what you see in the model, but most of the time it seems to come out pretty close to the same place.

Most of the time, in most real-world markets, the things people are demanding are being produced in about the right quantities. Most prices are pretty close to the cost of production. Anyone who is ready to pay the price can get the product.

There are always some businesses making good profits while others are going broke. And there's always a movement of input resources toward the profits and away from the losses. That's what you would expect from the model, and that's the way it works in real-world output markets.

HOW INPUT PRICES ARE SET IN THE REAL WORLD

Now we need to get into these questions: "How are input prices really set?" and then, "How do the 'rationing' and 'production motivating' functions of price really work in the real-world input markets?"

Are real-world wages, rents, and interest rates set by pure market forces? You know the answer. *Nothing in the real world is determined entirely by the pure market forces described in the model.*

There Are Many, Many Input Factors

In the model we talk about three factors of production. We talk about labor, land, and capital as though all "labor" was identical and all "land" and all "capital" were identical. But really there are all *kinds* of labor, land, and capital. One kind of labor may be very scarce, very productive, and very highly paid. Another kind may be very plentiful, unproductive, low-paid, and maybe unemployed.

Each decision to hire or not to hire and which to hire and how much to hire reflects the principles illustrated in the model. The productive kinds of factors will be hired; the more pro-

ductive a factor is the more the business will be willing to pay for it. It really does work that way in the real world—except that there's a lot of guessing going on—and usually there are lots of pressures influencing the decisions.

Most Factor Prices Are "Administered Prices"

You probably won't be too surprised to find out that most *input* prices (like most *output* prices) are administered. Can you think of any real world wage rates that are actually set by "pure market forces"? Probably not. In a minute you'll find out that you can say the same thing about interest rates.

In the case of land and natural resources, the market forces of supply and demand really do sometimes set some prices. But almost always there's some kind of monopoly power or government regulation or something and the prices wind up "administered" after all. So we need to talk about each of these factor prices—about how wages, interest, and rents are set in the real world.

How Wage Rates Are Determined

I suppose everyone knows that wage rates aren't set by the "free market forces of supply and demand." Everybody knows about minimum wage laws. The "minimum wage" started out several years ago at less than $1.00 an hour and has been increased several times. Now it's over $3.00 and Congress is always talking about increasing it even more.

You can be pretty sure that the minimum wage will keep going up. Woe be unto the member of Congress who votes against an increase in the minimum wage!

Most big companies bargain with labor unions to set wages. The sellers of professional labor (doctors and lawyers and public accountants and such) usually set their charges (wages) by following the pattern recommended by their "professional association." Government employees usually have some sort of salary scale approved by the legislature or the civil service commission or somebody. It's hard to find any "unadministered wages."

Are the **administered wages** somewhere close to where the free market forces of supply and demand would set them? Maybe yes, maybe no. But if the administered wage is pushed up very much higher than the free market wage would be, then there's likely to be some inflation and/or some unemployment. Why?

Because businesses will not hire people who can't produce enough to pay their way. The *marginal physical product* must increase and/or the *price of the product* must increase. That's almost as true in the real world as it is in the model.

How MVP Adjusts to Equal the Wage Rate

Suppose the "administered" wage rate is set very high. What will the company do? What *must* it do? Either it must respond (a) by hiring less labor, or (b) by bringing in more or better capital to make labor more productive, or (c) by raising the price enough to cover the higher wage. Prices will be increased and/or more capital will be added and/or employment will be decreased to where those workers who are still employed will have enough "value product" to be "worth" the high wage.

See what happens? *The value product adjusts itself to the wage rate*—either (a) more physical product is produced or (b) the price is raised. Either way, the "value product" goes up!

When the wage goes up, those businesses which *don't* do something to increase labor's value product soon will be out of business! Now study Figures 28-3 and -4 and you'll see what all this looks like in the "labor market."

How Interest Rates Are Determined

Most people can't understand interest rates because they don't understand money. But you can, because you *do!*

Banks lend money to consumers and businesses. If the banks have lots of excess reserves and want to make more loans, interest rates go down. It really does work that way.

If the banks are all loaned up and consumers and businesses are clamoring for more loans, interest rates really do go up. So is the market model working perfectly? with supply and demand setting interest rates in the real world? In a way, yes. But not exactly. Why not? Because in the real world the market is "rigged."

The Fed "Rigs" the Money Market. What determines if the banks are all "loaned up," or if they have lots of excess reserves? Many things. But the very biggest of these "many things" is what the Federal Reserve decides to do.

The Fed is always trying to follow a monetary policy "easy" enough to let the economy be prosperous and growing but not "easy" enough to let the economy slip into rapid inflation. Remember? Sure!

The Fed is always manipulating bank reserves by using open market operations and adjusting its discount rates. That means the Fed is "rigging" the supply side of the money market. That's how it makes interest rates high or low.

Also, the Fed's open market operations influence interest rates directly, through the effect on bond prices. When the Fed sells bonds that pulls money out of the banks' reserves. Sure. But it also pushes down the prices of bonds and that automatically pushes up interest rates. Remember?

Interest rates really are determined by supply and demand, more or less—but not "free" supply and demand! The Fed always has its hand on the "supply control knob" and can make the money market as "tight" or "easy" as it wants to. Then the big banks set (administer) their interest rates to reflect the "tightness" of the money markets, and all the little banks follow along.

If lots of businesses suddenly decided to borrow lots of money and do a lot of expanding

**Fig. 28-3   Minimum Wages Set by Government or High Wages
Bargained by Unions Can Result in Unemployment**

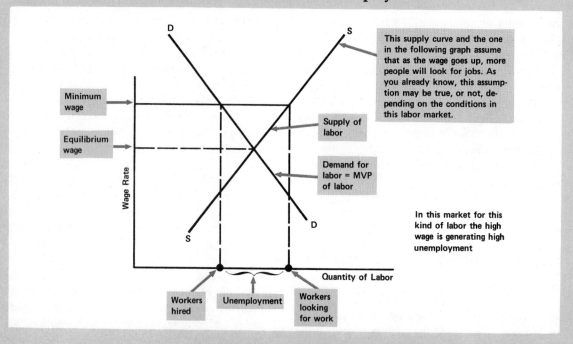

Minimum wage

Equilibrium wage

This supply curve and the one in the following graph assume that as the wage goes up, more people will look for jobs. As you already know, this assumption may be true, or not, depending on the conditions in this labor market.

Supply of labor

Demand for labor = MVP of labor

In this market for this kind of labor the high wage is generating high unemployment

Wage Rate

Quantity of Labor

Workers hired

Unemployment

Workers looking for work

**Fig. 28-4   When the Wage is Pushed Up, the MVP of Labor
Must Go Up: the Curve Can Shift, or Less Can be Hired**

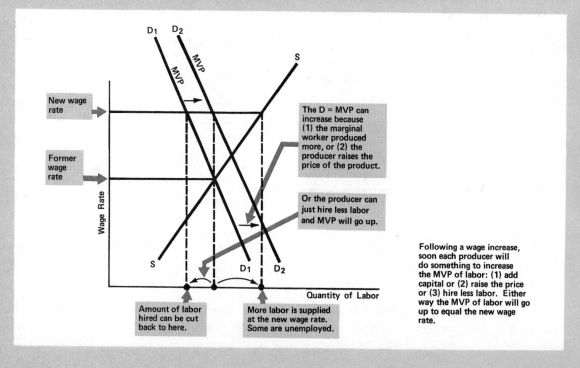

New wage rate

Former wage rate

The D = MVP can increase because (1) the marginal worker produced more, or (2) the producer raises the price of the product.

Or the producer can just hire less labor and MVP will go up.

Following a wage increase, soon each producer will do something to increase the MVP of labor: (1) add capital or (2) raise the price or (3) hire less labor. Either way the MVP of labor will go up to equal the new wage rate.

Wage Rate

Quantity of Labor

Amount of labor hired can be cut back to here.

More labor is supplied at the new wage rate. Some are unemployed.

would this push interest rates up? Sure it would. How far up it would push interest rates would depend on how much the Fed would permit the money supply to expand—that is, how much new bank reserves the Fed would be willing to generate. If the Fed would permit the money supply to expand a lot, interest rates would rise only a little.

Suppose the Fed didn't want the money supply to expand very much. The money market would get very tight and interest rates would go very high. The high interest rates would discourage businesses from investing. That's what was happening in the early 1980s.

It wouldn't be wrong to say that in general, interest rates are set by "supply and demand." But since the Fed controls the supply, it can and does control the general level of interest rates in the country all the time.

The States Have "Usury Laws" Setting Maximum Interest Rates. In addition to the controls by the Fed, the states have various kinds of "usury laws" limiting the maximum interest rates banks and other lenders can charge for various kinds of loans.

For example, many states limit interest charges on "revolving charge accounts" and "overdue credit card charges." Several have limited the interest rate on home mortgages. But in the high interest rate environment of the early 1980s, many states raised or abolished their usury ceilings.

What About the Productivity of Capital? Doesn't the demand for (the productivity of) capital have anything to do with the setting of interest rates? The productivity (marginal value product) of capital makes up the *demand side* of the "money market" (where interest rates are determined), doesn't it? Sure.

If businesses expect capital to be productive enough to be profitable, they will be trying to borrow more money to buy more capital. The borrowing will push upward on the interest rate. But will the interest rate actually go up? That depends on what the Fed decides to do.

Suppose the Fed "holds the line" on money expansion. Interest rates will go up more and more. Does that mean the businesses think the productivity of capital (the marginal value product of the new machines and things) will be high? Of course. Only when businesses expect a high productivity of capital will they borrow and buy the capital and pay the high interest. Obviously!

If the Fed is trying to curb inflation (using a "tight money" policy) interest rates will be high. Only those businesses which have *highly productive* uses for capital will borrow and invest. Only that capital which is expected to be productive enough to pay the high interest cost will be bought.

Seems like everywhere you look in output and input markets, prices are administered.

See how *a high interest rate can force an increase in the productivty of new capital investments*? Just as *a high wage rate* can force an increase in *the productivity of employed labor*? Labor that isn't productive enough to be worth the high wage won't be employed. Capital that doesn't look productive enough to be worth the high interest won't be "employed" either! Now study Figure 28-5 and you'll see how this looks on a graph.

How Rents Are Determined

See what's happening in the case of wages, and interest? In the model, factor productivity determines factor prices. But here in the real world it looks like *factor prices are determining factor productivity!* More on this interesting issue in a few minutes. But first, what about *rents* in the real world?

Suppose you own a piece of land or some natural resource—maybe a puddle of oil about half a mile down in the ground. How much money can you get from your land? or from your oil? That depends on how high the demand happens to be.

You can set the land rent or the oil price as high as you want to. But if the price is too high, no one will buy. There are many "substitute pieces of land" and "substitute puddles of oil" which people can buy instead of yours. If for some reason people want very much to have *your* land or *your* oil, then they will pay an especially high price to get it. But if they don't, they won't.

Perhaps the prices of land and natural resources ("rents") are somewhat more responsive to pure market forces than wages or interest rates. But not necessarily. Some monopoly power usually exists on both sides of most real-world land and natural resource markets. Still it's fairly safe to say that the price which is paid for each bit of land or natural resource usually reflects the strength of the *demand* for it.

If you happen to own forty acres in central Florida near Disney World, you're going to make a lot more money on your land than if you owned forty acres someplace in the Everglades. Why? Because there's more *demand* for Disney World land! If you own a pool of oil down in your land and I own a pool of salty water down in mine, you will get rich and I will stay poor. Why? Because there's more demand for oil than for salty water.

There are many reasons why the price in the real world doesn't work out exactly as it does in the model. You may sell your oil too cheap to the first person who comes along. Or you may sell your forty acres near Disney World for half a million dollars when someone else would have been willing to pay you five million. But if the demand for some kind of land goes up, pretty soon the word gets around and the price re-

Fig. 28-5   When Interest Rates Are High, Businesses Will Only Invest in Highly Productive Capital

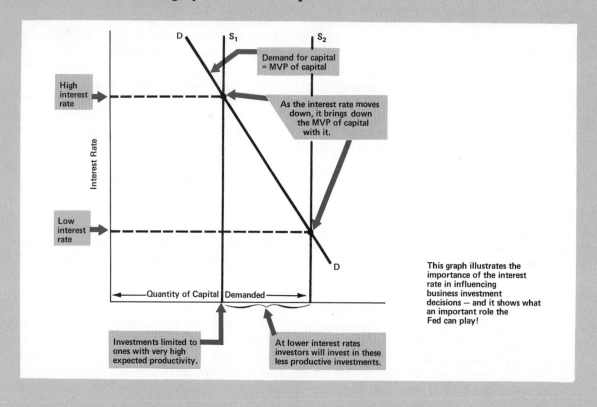

sponds. When something happens to push up land prices in an area it's just amazing how fast the word gets around!

Most land and natural resource prices are "administered" to some extent, either by the buyers or the sellers. Governments sometimes regulate these prices, too. But in general, prices of land and natural resources really do come fairly close to reflecting the strength of the demand. And the demand for land really does generally reflect its marginal productivity (its marginal "value product").

Summary: Productivity Adjusts to Equal the Input Price

In real-world markets, input prices (like output prices) are usually administered prices. But the price of each input factor really is pretty close to its productivity. Why?

Because the business can't afford to pay a factor much more than its value product. If it did, the revenues wouldn't be high enough to cover the costs. The business would go broke!

If the factor's price is much *less* than its value product, then as time goes by, more of the factor usually will be hired. As more of the factor is hired its value product really will go down.

So in the real world the *ultimate results* look very much like what you would expect from looking at the model. But just as in the case of the output markets, the input markets seem to get there via a different route—sort of "backwards" from the way the model works.

In the real world, the usual thing is for the price to be set first—that is, "administered" by the seller or the buyer or the government or somebody. Then *the productivity of the factor adjusts itself to equal the price.* That's what you saw back in Figures 28-3, -4, and -5. After you read the next section about how real-world input markets *respond* to factor prices, you will understand this even better.

HOW INPUT MARKETS RESPOND TO FACTOR PRICES

Do input markets respond to price changes? Of course. The rationing function of price *conserves* the higher-priced factors; the production motivating function of price *pulls in more* of the higher-priced factors.

In this section you'll be reading about input-price-fixing. There's a lot of it going on. And the results? Usually not so good.

The Rationing Function of Factor Prices

What happens when the wage for some kind of labor goes up? Everyone using that kind of labor tries to use less of it. When less of the higher-priced labor is used, its productivity goes up—that is, the *units which are still employed* are more productive. The rationing function of price causes it to work out that way.

The rationing function of price works for all factors of production—for every kind of labor, capital, land, and natural resource. The rationing response is much smaller in the short run than in the long run, of course. It takes awhile to automate the plant to cut down on the high-priced labor. But the longer you wait after the price goes up, the greater the response you're likely to see.

"Featherbedding" Practices Impede the Rationing Function. There are many real-world restrictions which keep this rationing function from working out the way the model says it will. Restrictions can be severe in the labor market.

Suppose you were working in a plant and your union had just gotten a big wage increase. Then suddenly you found out that you were going to be "automated out of a job." You wouldn't like that much. Right? Nobody else does, either. So labor unions fight hard to keep high-paid workers from being replaced by machines.

Ever hear of **featherbedding?** Labor unions sometimes get employers to agree not to lay off people, even though their jobs no longer need to be performed. The classic example is the fireman (the man who is supposed to stoke the steam boilers) who always rides along on the diesel locomotive (which has no steam boilers, of course). The idea of "featherbedding" is that the surplus workers might as well take along featherbeds and sleep—since there's no work for them to do! Now take a look at Figure 28-6 and you'll see what the labor union tries to accomplish by its "featherbedding" practices.

There's no way of knowing just how much the efficiency of the economy is reduced by featherbedding practices. Certainly it's significant. It's more serious in the old, established in-

dustries (railroads, steel, coal, etc.) than in the new and growing industries (petrochemicals, computers, etc.). Also it's more serious in the older industrialized centers than in the newer industrializing areas.

In the United States it's more serious in New England, the Northeast and Midwest than in the South, Southwest, and far West. The newer industries and the newer areas can develop without the restrictions of obsolete techniques and practices to impede them. Is that why these newer areas have had so much prosperity and economic growth in recent years? Maybe. But don't just jump to that conclusion. Beware of *post hoc ergo propter hoc!* Remember?

We Must Wait for the Long Run. The owners of the other inputs (land and capital) are less likely to be able to interfere with the rationing function of price. If the cost of investing in

Fig. 28-6 "Featherbedding" Tries to Force the Firm to Hire More Labor than the Demand Curve Shows

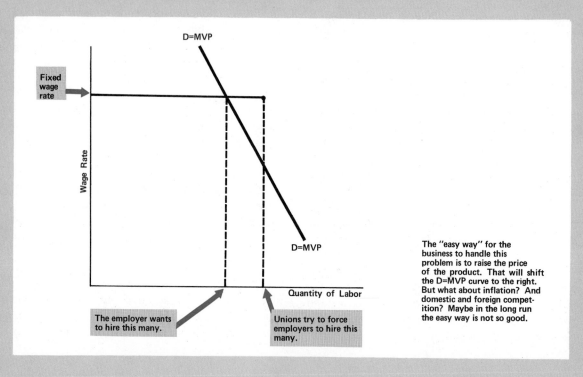

The "easy way" for the business to handle this problem is to raise the price of the product. That will shift the D=MVP curve to the right. But what about inflation? And domestic and foreign competition? Maybe in the long run the easy way is not so good.

capital goes up, some businesses will invest less. That's true in the real world just as in the model. The only serious restriction to the response is that of "waiting for the long run."

After the investment is made—the note is signed at the bank, the money is spent, the concrete is poured, the machines are all in place and all that—it's going to be awhile before all this process can be "undone." So that's a natural limitation on the responsiveness to a factor-price change. You learned about "waiting for the long run" from the model. But if you'll just wait long enough *everything can change.*

What about featherbedding and other such restrictive arrangements? Will the long run work these things out, too? Sure. Either one way or another: either *employment* will be adjusted (reduced) so labor's productivity can increase, or *competitors* from other parts of the country or from other parts of the world will come in and take over the markets and force the "old-line producers" out of business. Some of that has been happening lately. Right?

Many kinds of things can be done to slow or stop the adjustment process. For example import restrictions can be imposed to prevent foreign competition—and choke off the gains from trade. But the pressure to adjust will be there, constantly "pushing against the dike" until something gives and lets the adjustment occur. When all the opportunity costs are considered, usually *the harm done by trying to prevent the adjustment is greater than any good effects that might result.*

The Rationing Function Really Works. So even with all the restrictions and limitations, *the rationing function of price* seems to work fairly well in most real-world input markets.

As factor prices for different kinds of labor or land or capital go up, these higher priced factors really are more carefully conserved. There's some effect in the short run. Then the response gets much greater as time goes by. In the model, the demand for a factor of production is *much more elastic* in the long run. Remember? That's how it is in the real world, too.

The Production Motivating Function of Factor Prices

What about the production motivating function? Does a high price for a certain kind of labor bring in more of that kind of labor? What about land? or capital? Sure it does. Here's an example.

Suppose you heard that people who can read English are being recruited and paid $250 a day to go overseas to read to people in some of the mid-east oil producing countries. Do you think anybody will sign up? Sure. See how labor really does respond to a high price?

What about land? Suppose wealthy Mr. Gotrocks just moved into your neighborhood. He doesn't want to park his car on the street overnight. But he has no driveway. He's looking for some little place—some land—where he can park his car. He's willing to pay $20 a night. Do you think somebody will supply him some "land"? I might. How about you? Yes, land also responds to high prices.

What about the interest rate? Suppose you have a few thousand dollars in savings, drawing about 6% at the local savings and loan. Then you hear about a money market fund that's paying more than 15%. Do you suppose people will shift their savings? Will you? Me too!

During the early 1980s more than $100 billion were shifted from low interest savings accounts to high interest money market funds. Does money flow to where the interest rate (price) is highest? Sure.

The Production Motivating Function Really Works. Now you know the answer to the general question: "Does the production motivating function of price work in the factor markets?" Of course it does.

Whenever the price offered for a factor is *high enough* you may be sure that factors will shift from other uses into the high-priced use. It really does work that way in the real world—sometimes. But that isn't *usually* the way it happens. Just as in the case of the output markets, the production motivating function of price seems to work itself out "backwards" in the input markets, too.

Inputs, Like Outputs, Respond Directly to Demand

Suppose a new business opens up and wants to hire workers. Does it offer a high wage rate (price) to attract the people it wants? Not usually. It just advertises to let people know it has jobs available at the "going wage." Then do workers who are already getting the "going wage" quit their jobs and come to work for the new business? No.

It works like this: In a dynamic real-world economic system some people are always changing jobs. Some businesses are going broke; others are expanding. New people are always entering the labor force. There is always some unemployment—some "slack" in the labor markets. Jobs are constantly being eliminated; new jobs are being created.

The "structure" (make-up) of the economy is always changing. New products and new technology eliminate old jobs and create new ones. These **structural changes** in the economy are constantly displacing workers who (if they are young and flexible enough) can shift into new kinds of jobs that are always opening up.

So it usually isn't necessary for an expanding firm to offer more than the "going prices" for the inputs it needs. Inputs flow in direct response to the increased quantity demanded. Usually it isn't necessary for the price to go up to attract the needed inputs.

Summary: Factor Movement Balances the Market

Constant turnover is always going on, not just in labor markets but in all factor markets. Factor prices always are being set by various "administering forces." Then at those set prices, labor and other inputs flow across the markets

from sellers to buyers.

If the set price of a factor is "too high" then businesses will start using less of that factor and more of the other (less expensive) factors. That's how it works its way out.

At a higher price, less of a factor will be used so its *marginal productivity* will be higher (high enough to cover the high price). It really does work that way in real-world markets.

Anyone who wants to hire people at the "going wage" usually can find workers. The same is true in the land and capital markets.

There is a constant flow of all kinds of inputs moving across the real-world factor markets at the going prices. Usually anyone who wants more of an input can get it at the going price.

So does the production motivating function of price actually work in the input markets? Yes. But just as in the output markets, *the inputs usually respond directly to demand*. If people are demanding more Polaroid cameras, more of them will be produced. The price doesn't have to move. The same is true in the input markets.

If a producer is demanding more of a certain kind of labor, or land for a certain purpose, or a special kind of capital, usually the response will be direct and almost automatic. No change in price is required. That's the way it really does work in the real world. Figure 28-7 shows a graph which illustrates this "real-world factor market supply" situation.

WHAT ABOUT FACTOR PRICES AND INCOME DISTRIBUTION?

How is the income distribution question really answered in real world markets? Is each person's share determined by the value of what his or her labor and land and capital produce?

Do owners of the scarcest, most productive factors really get the highest incomes? And if so, how does it happen? That's what you'll find out in this section.

Income Really Does Go to the Productive Ones

You may be surprised how closely income distribution in the real world really does reflect what the pure model predicts. (We're not counting "income redistribution programs," of course.) Think about it. People who own and sell the high-priced factors really do receive the high incomes.

People who "sell" highly skilled or professional or managerial labor receive high incomes. People who own a lot of highly productive capital or land or natural resources receive high incomes. People who work overtime and those who go out of their way to seek high paid jobs really do receive more income than those who don't.

If the demand for your kind of labor is going up, then your income will be rising. You will be able to get more of the society's output. If you own a very scarce and productive kind of land or capital, you will receive a high income. It really does work that way.

You know (in the model) what creates a high demand and a high price for an input. High productivity? Of course! And you know what makes a factor's productivity high, too: lots of other good factors to work with. Is that the way it is in the real world? Sure.

Suppose a society has an abundance of good capital and land and natural resources, and a relatively small population and labor force. Will the wage rate be high? Will the working people enjoy good incomes and high standards of living? Yes! It really does work out that way.

The Scarcest Factor Gets the Highest Return

When labor is the **relatively scarce factor** then labor is highly productive. Workers receive high wages and most people enjoy high stan-

Fig. 28-7   Most Small Businesses See the Supply of an Input Factor as Infinitely Elastic

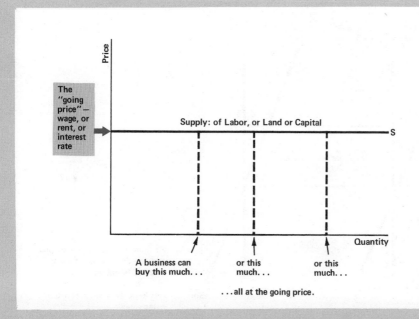

Price

The "going price" — wage, or rent, or interest rate →

Supply: of Labor, or Land or Capital   S

Quantity

A business can buy this much. . .   or this much. . .   or this much. . .

. . .all at the going price.

There are many factor markets in which this infinitely elastic supply would not apply, of course. If the market is small and the factor buyer is big then an increase in factor demand will push up the factor price.

dards of living. But what if there's a great abundance of labor?

Suppose there are great hordes of people but not much capital or land or natural resources. What then? The productivity of labor will be low. Wages will be low. Most people will be poor. That's the way it works in the model and that's the way it works in the real world too.

Compare different countries in the world. Or look at different areas within this country. Or any country. What do you see? In places where there is an abundance of highly developed land and natural resources and highly productive capital (so that each worker has a lot to work with) wage rates are high. Most of the people enjoy a good living. But in places where there is lots of labor and not much capital or land or resources, wages are low. Most of the people are poor.

An Example from History

In the late 1800s and early 1900s millions of people moved to the United States. Why? Jobs were available. Lots of land, natural resources and capital were available so labor was more productive.

As more land and resources were opened up and as more capital was built, more labor was needed. More and more labor came in to meet the demand. All the labor coming in kept wages from rising much. Look at Figure 28-8 and you'll see a graphic picture of this.

The immigrants kept arriving and increasing the supply of labor and holding down wage rates. This kept the productivity of capital high, kept the profits of the capitalists high, and kept the economy growing by leaps and bounds!

Suppose the massive flow of immigrants had been stopped. What then? Labor would have been more scarce. Wages would have gone up. Living standards would have gone up and profits would have gone down.

There would have been less savings and investment. More consumer goods and fewer capital goods would have been produced. The growth of the economy would have slowed

Fig. 28-8   Supply and Demand in the U.S. Labor Market: The Effect of Past Immigration Policies on Wage Rates

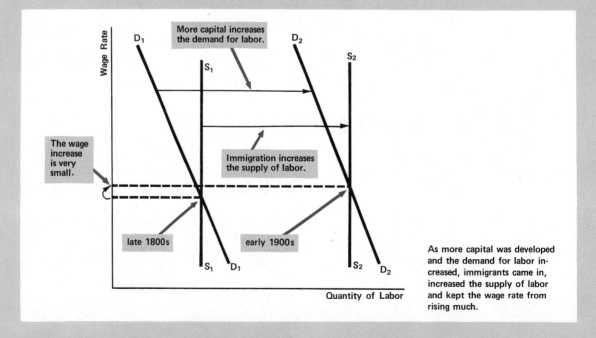

As more capital was developed and the demand for labor increased, immigrants came in, increased the supply of labor and kept the wage rate from rising much.

down.

Today the rapid inflow of labor has been stopped. Capital is relatively plentiful and labor is relatively scarce. Wages are high; the returns to the owners of capital are low. Most of the people are enjoying high incomes. Why? Because of the high productivity of their labor, which results from all of the highly efficient capital they have to work with.

The owners of land and natural resources have been receiving higher and higher incomes too. Why? Because with more people and more capital, land has become relatively more scarce.

The more labor and capital there is, the more productive and higher priced the land becomes. Of course! So the landowners get a bigger **distributive share**. That's the way it works in the model and that's generally the way it works in the real world too.

Some Kinds of Labor Are Very Scarce; Others Are Not

In general, incomes in real-world markets seem to be fairly close to the results described in the model. But for any *particular* worker or piece of land or machine, the "in general" condition may not be very relevant.

In any economic system or in any area, some kinds of labor or land or capital are relatively scarce and some kinds are not. So be careful about generalizations.

If "labor on the average" is scarce, that isn't going to be much help to a person who is uneducated, unskilled, inexperienced, unproductive, or unwilling. The same thing goes for the other input factors too.

If "capital in general" is relatively plentiful in a country, that doesn't mean that some new kind of highly efficient machine isn't going to bring its owner a very high return. There's always some "relatively scarce" kind of labor, land and capital. You can always beat the average if you're smart enough or lucky enough—or both!

A Normative Question: "Distributive Justice?"

Do real-world markets bring a "socially just" distribution of the society's income and output? Since it appears that income distribution in real-world markets really does reflect factor productivity, does that mean the distribution is equitable? Does each person actually get the amount of income he or she really *should* get? the amount he or she really *deserves*?

This **normative question** of the social justice of income distribution can't be answered by the concepts (the principles, theories, models, or laws) of positive economics. Each of us can have our own opinion about what is and what is not "socially just."

And suppose we don't like what's happening? We're all free to work through the market process, the social process, and the political process to try to change things. Maybe we can cause the society to move toward the conditions we consider to be more "just" or more "desirable."

Everyone Is Trying to Influence Income Distribution

Some people acquire great fortunes and then give them away. Why? Some people dedicate their lives to trying to improve the conditions of the poor. Why?

Almost everybody seems to be doing something to try to redistribute some of the income—from contributions to the Red Cross and to the church to trying to get the government to increase payments for unemployment and social security. *Why? To change the society's distribution of output and income!*

Most people seem to agree that the income

distribution which results from "the ownership and sale of productive factors" is not entirely socially acceptable. It seems to be generally accepted that some **redistribution** is essential.

One problem is that the ownership of wealth (capital and land and natural resources) is so unevenly distributed. Another problem is that some people are incapable of producing enough to live on.

The government does many things to redistribute income from the people whose "factors" produce it, to those who need it. Taxes are collected from the income earners and some of the money is paid to the poor. The governments offer various kinds of public facilities and services—parks and playgrounds and schools and many other things. All these "income redistributions" change the results generated by the real-world market forces.

But there's another approach that can be used. The government can "rig the markets" so that larger incomes will go to the disadvantaged people. How does the government rig markets? By doing things to push prices up or down—by **price-rigging** and **price-fixing**.

How do they do that? And what happens when they do? Doesn't price-rigging and price-fixing generate some unplanned **reflex effects**? Yes! And that's what the next chapter is all about.

SUMMARY AND SYNTHESIS

Markets work through the operation of the **price mechanism**. The most important reason for studying the **model market system** is to understand how the price mechanism works—that is, to understand **supply and demand**, and the rationing and production motivating functions of price.

Real-world markets don't work exactly like the model of pure competition. If we want to know how real-world markets work, we need to look at the **price mechanism** and find out how it works in the real world. But each real-world market is a **special case**. So it's difficult to generalize.

In most real-world output markets, prices are **administered** by the sellers. But most of the time these administered prices seem to come out fairly close to the **normal price** as defined in the model. Why? Because of **actual and/or potential competition**, both domestic and foreign.

In the **public utility** (natural monopoly) industries competition would result in inefficiencies. So competition's function is taken over by **regulatory commissions** which decide what standards of services will be required and then try to figure out what the **normal prices should be**. And that's where they set the prices. But there's a **constant** struggle, with the buyers of the services trying to hold down the prices and the companies trying to push them up.

The **rationing function of output prices** works all right in the real world. The more carefully the consumers spend their money—the more "price conscious" they are—the better it works. **Price competition advertising**, including special sales, rebates, etc., helps to make the rationing function work.

The **production motivating function of output prices** works all right, too. But it's different than in the model. In the model, **price changes are necessary to induce output changes**. But in the real world of administered prices, outputs are adjusted in **direct response to changes in quantities demanded**. A business will introduce a product to the market, set the price, advertise, and then **adjust the output in response to the volume of sales**.

Like output prices, most **input prices** also are administered. In the labor markets there are minimum wage laws, labor-management bargaining contracts and several other "administered wage" arrangements. If the "set wage" is higher than the productivity, then either **worker productivity** or the product price must go up.

Usually, higher wages will result in less employment—and higher productivity for those who still have jobs. This is the way the MVP adjusts itself to the wage rate.

The Fed rigs the money markets and influences interest rates. But **loan demand** plays an important role, too. So do government "usury laws" and other regulations.

If interest rates are high, businesses will borrow and invest only in capital which is **productive enough to pay the high interest rates.** So, as in the case of labor, the **MVP will be brought into line with the price** (interest rate) by adjusting the **quantity used.**

These same principles hold true for land and natural resources. There's a good bit of **price administering** going on in most input markets. But the administered factor prices usually closely reflect factor productivity. Why? Because anytime they don't, the input mix (production function) is likely to be adjusted until they do. That's the **rationing function of price,** conserving (and increasing the productivity of) the most scarce, highest priced factors!

Inputs (like outputs) **respond directly to quantity demanded.** A business which wants to employ more labor or land or capital can usually get it at the "going rates." But if an industry is expanding, **the prices of any special kinds of labor, land, or capital needed in that industry will likely go up.**

Income distribution in real-world markets (excluding redistribution) works out quite closely to the results described in the model. The **relatively scarce factors are more productive** so have higher prices, and their owners do receive the highest incomes. But in the real world **income redistribution programs** are used to reduce the degree of inequality generated by the market process as it works in the real world.

REVIEW EXERCISES

MAJOR CONCEPTS, PRINCIPLES, TERMS (Explain each carefully.)

how output prices are really set
how buyers and sellers respond to output prices
how input prices are really set
how factor buyers and sellers respond to input prices
how the Fed rigs the money market

OTHER CONCEPTS AND TERMS (Explain each briefly.)

public utilities
natural monopoly
minimum wage laws
usury laws
"featherbedding" practices
structural changes
distributive justice

input price-fixing
administered prices
market structure
freedom of entry
elasticity of demand
Federal Trade Commission (FTC)
regulatory commissions

CURVES AND GRAPHS (Draw, label, and explain each.)

One Way of Keeping Agricultural Prices Up: Price Supports
Another Way of Keeping Agricultural Prices Up: Output Restraints

Minimum Wages Can Result in Unemployment
When the Wage Is Pushed Up, the MVP of Labor Must Go Up
With High Interest Rates Only Highly Productive Capital is Bought
"Featherbedding" Tries to Force the Firm to Hire More Labor
Small Businesses See the Supply of Inputs as Infinitely Elastic
The Effect of Past Immigration Policies on Wage Rates

QUESTIONS (Write out answers, or jot down key points.)

1. To understand real-world markets you need to find out (a) how real-world *prices* are set, and then (b) how the functions of price work in the real world. Explain why this is true.

2. Explain several conditions which would require the "administered price-setter" to keep the "set prices" fairly reasonable.

3. Price-setting in the real world is almost always a constant struggle among conflicting forces. Try to explain this and then give some examples of this from your own personal experience.

4. Input price-fixing has a much greater impact in the long run. Explain this, then give some examples.

29

The "Basic Law" of Real-World Markets: Administered Pricing and the "Reflex Effect"

Chapter Objectives

- In the last chapter you found out a lot about **how markets actually work** in the real-world—about **how prices are set** and **how buyers and sellers respond.**

- When you finish studying this chapter you will know a lot more about **real-world price-setting** and **price responses.** You'll know about and be able to explain what I call the **"Basic Law of Real-World Markets",** and the **"reflex effect"** which makes this "basic law" work.

- You will be able to **explain** and to **draw graphs illustrating** the **supply and demand conditions** which **limit the range** in which **administered prices** can be set.

- You will be able to give several **real-world examples** of **price-rigging** in various kinds of markets. And you will be able to explain **alternative ways** in which the **reflex effect** can work to **bring these rigged markets into balance.** You will find out that **ultimately** (given enough time) **it always does.** That's what the basic law says.

- Finally, in this chapter you will get an **overall evaluation** (a) of the **"imperfect market process"** as it works in the real world, and (b) of the **relevance** or **helpfulness** of the **pure market model** in understanding the functioning of **real-world markets.**

The Beautiful Market Model

The model of the "pure market system" is really beautiful. But much of its beauty results from its many make-believe conditions: freely-moving prices and freely-moving factors of production, plenty of competition among great numbers of small buyers and sellers in all the markets, everybody getting a fair and equal chance to produce and to consume, everybody free to follow his or her own interests, demand directing the resources of the society to do and make the right amounts of all the chosen things, and all the adjustments coming about smoothly and easily. With all the "assumptions in place" it's really neat!

With all the make-believe conditions, the "model pure market system" looks like a most attractive, most appealing kind of economic system. The demand reflects the wishes of the people. The supply responds to the demand. Any person can choose to have or to eat any of the things produced, just as long as that person will pay the honest cost of what it takes to make it, including a fair profit for the producer.

Society's most scarce, most valuable things are most carefully conserved, automatically. The most wanted things are the things that are produced. All the "economic choice" questions are answered and with freedom and justice for all. Beautiful! But what about the real world?

Market Forces Are Powerful in the Real World

Even in real-world markets of monopoly power and administered prices and market-rigging and all sorts of un-model-like conditions, *the market forces still exercise great power in directing the economic activities and choices of the society.*

Prices and wages can be administered. Markets can be tampered with or "rigged" in various ways. But the tampering or "rigging" will set off a chain reaction which will immediately begin to try to bring everything back into balance. This indirect "balancing effect" is what I call the reflex effect of real-world markets.

This "automatic balancing force" or "reflex effect" really does exist. It really is there at work in all real-world markets. *Always.*

In the model the "direct effect" is in control. Prices move to bring things into balance. In the real world, more often than not it's the indirect "reflex effect" that brings things into balance. This "reflex effect" really explains how real-world markets work.

You can't understand real-world markets without understanding this "indirect balancing force." To emphasize its importance I call this reflex effect the **"Basic Law of Real-World Markets."**

THE REFLEX EFFECT: BASIC LAW OF REAL-WORLD MARKETS

What is this "reflex effect"? *It's the irresistible power of prices as they work in the real world to bring everything into balance—to move every market toward "long-run equilibrium."*

Be sure you understand it. Most of the rest of this chapter will be explaining it in detail. There will be many real-world examples so you can see how it works.

A Specific Statement of the Reflex Effect

What exactly, is this "reflex effect"? It goes like this:

1. Almost all real-world markets are controlled or influenced or "rigged" to some extent—by the buyers or the sellers or the government or maybe all three.
2. Whenever these "market riggers" force *any change* in a market (in supply, demand, or price) that puts the market in an unbalanced condition. Immediately the "reflex effect" goes to work to try to put the market back into balance.
3. The "reflex effect" will exert its influence either (a) to overthrow the "rigged" condition or (b) to bring all the other conditions into line with the "rigged" condition or (c) maybe both.
4. Unless the "reflex effect" of the market-rigging action is foreseen and planned for, the "market riggers" probably won't achieve their objectives. Things might even wind up *worse* than before!

Nobody likes to try to achieve some objective by fixing a price or rigging a market and then find out that things wind up worse than before! Of course not. But people who don't understand this "reflex effect" are always doing things like that. After you've read the next several pages of explanations and examples you'll be able to see these "reflex effects" almost everywhere you look!

The Reflex Effect Brings "Rigged" Markets into Balance

It's the reflex effect which causes real-world markets to look so much like the markets described in the market model. In the real world the cause and effect roles often get reversed—what the model describes as the "cause," in the real world becomes the "effect."

In the model, supply and demand set the prices. In the real world, businesses or labor unions or producer co-ops or professional associations or governments or other organizations usually set the prices. It's the reflex effect which then brings each market into balance.

Administered Prices Cannot Ignore Market Conditions

In real-world markets the administered price can't be set too far out of line with basic supply and demand conditions. The price can be set "a little too high" or "a little too low." But the price can't be set "much too high" or "much too low."

Suppose the price is set "much too high" or "much too low." What happens? The automatic balancing forces of the market (that is, the reflex effect) either will force the price to change or will destroy the market.

If the price stays "much too high" or "much too low" for very long, the market will cease to exist. At a price much too high, nobody will buy. A market can't exist without buyers! At a price much too low, nobody will sell. A market can't

exist without sellers! Of course not.

If the price is set "a little too high" the market will adjust to the high price; if it's set "a little too low" the market will adjust in the opposite direction. But for any price to be "administered"—that is, "set" by business or government or labor or anyone else—certain conditions must be met:

1. Setting the price "too high" requires *the power to restrict supply* and/or *the power to increase demand*. Otherwise what will happen? The high price will pull forth a large supply but buyers won't buy very much. The market will be flooded! The price will break loose and go down.
2. Setting the price down "too low" requires *the power to restrict demand* and/or *the power to increase supply*. Otherwise what will happen? At a low price, buyers will be trying to buy a lot but the sellers won't supply very much. There will be severe shortages! The price will break loose and go up. Now study Figure 29-1 and you'll see how all this looks on a supply and demand graph.

How the Reflex Effect Works

Suppose the administered price is set just "a little" too high or too low. You might say the price is set "within the permissible range" as determined by basic supply and demand conditions in the market. Then if the price-setters have enough power (monopoly, monopsony, or governmental) to control the demand or supply (or both) they can make the price stay where they set it.

What happens then? The "automatic reflex forces" will go to work and start to bring everything into balance again.

As time passes, both supply and demand will become more and more elastic—that is, buyers and sellers will respond more and more to the "administered price." The reflex forces will keep pushing to try to rebalance the market.

The reflex forces will become stronger and stronger and push more and more, either (a) until all the other conditions in the market are brought into line with the administered price (so that the administered price becomes the "right price") or (b) until the set price is overthrown. That's *what* happens. Now here are some examples to show *how* it happens.

The "Monopolistic Competition" Product Markets.

In the output markets, setting the price "too high" on your product will attract more competitors. Everyone will be trying to cut in on your profits! Do the competitors flood the market and force the price to go down? Not usually. It works the other way.

As more competitors enter the market, prices don't come down. Costs go up instead. Up how high? Up to where the "administered price" becomes the "right price" and the market is in balance again.

In the last chapter you saw what happened when Polaroid introduced a very successful new camera for $19.95. Many other producers entered the market. Soon there were so many different models competing against each other that no one was making very much profit anymore. But the price didn't go down; the per-unit cost went up.

The reflex effect eliminates the excess profits in the markets of monopolistic competition, not by pushing the price down, but *by pushing the cost up.* It pushes up per-unit costs and pushes down the profits. When the excess profits are all gone the market will be in balance. The industry will stop expanding. Figure 29-2 shows this on a graph.

The Agricultural Product Markets.

In the agricultural product markets (for corn or wheat or cotton or tobacco or whatever) a "too high" price pulls in more supply than the buyers want to buy. As time goes on, more and more

Fig. 29-1   Supply and Demand Curves Show How the Reflex Principle Works

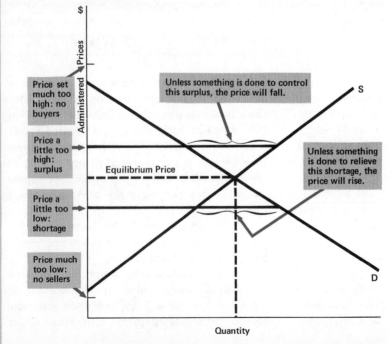

The longer you wait, the more elastic both the supply and demand will become. As time passes, the surplus or shortage will become greater and greater.

The only way administered prices can be kept above or below the equilibrium price for very long is to work out some way to take care of the problem of surpluses or shortages. Otherwise the reflex principle will take over!

people will stop growing other things and start growing the high-priced product.

If the cotton price, for example, is held up high enough, long enough (and unless the government makes it illegal to produce so much cotton) one day the pile of surplus bales of cotton will reach to the moon! But before that happens, the reflex effect will either force the price to break or force the government to change its policy. You can be sure of that!

The Public Utilities. Suppose the regulatory commissions set public utility rates "too low." People will use lots of electricity and all, but the low-paid companies won't invest much in new equipment. The quality of the service will decline.

If the regulatory commissions set the rates "too high" the utility companies are likely to expand their services too much—to make wasteful expenditures. Their costs will rise. There will be excess capacity (a) because of too much invest-

ment, and (b) because the people will be careful to conserve (not use so much of) the high-priced services.

See how the costs tend to go up and down to make the "set" price become the "right" price? And see what happens if the society tries to get its utilities without paying the full cost of production? The society winds up with inadequate utility services. The reflex effect strikes again!

THE REFLEX EFFECT DEPENDS ON ELASTICITY OF SUPPLY AND DEMAND

Whenever supply is *highly elastic* that means sellers are *highly responsive* to price changes. So if supply is highly elastic it's difficult (maybe impossible) for the price-setters to set the price either "too high" or "too low" and make it stick.

Fig. 29-2 The Reflex Effect Eliminates Excess Profits in Monopolistic Competition: the Cost Goes Up!

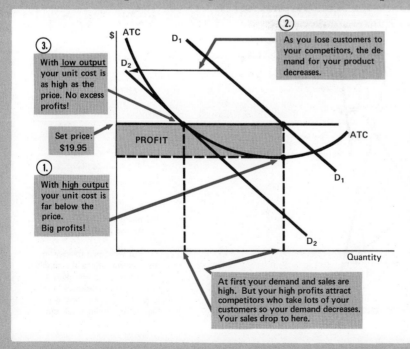

(3.) With **low output** your unit cost is as high as the price. No excess profits!

(2.) As you lose customers to your competitors, the demand for your product decreases.

Set price: $19.95

PROFIT

(1.) With **high output** your unit cost is far below the price. Big profits!

At first your demand and sales are high. But your high profits attract competitors who take lots of your customers so your demand decreases. Your sales drop to here.

You introduce a new product-- a real winner! At first, there's a high volume of sales--and big profits! Then other sellers begin to compete. You lose some customers. So you produce less and unit cost goes up. Excess profits are gone! Reflex effect? Right.

The suppliers respond too much!

Suppose the price is set "too high." Great surpluses will be generated and the high price will be forced to collapse. If the price is set "too low" very little will be produced. There will be *severe shortages*. The price will break loose and go up.

It's very difficult to administer a price if the supply is *highly elastic*. If the demand *also* is highly elastic that will make it *twice as difficult* to administer the price.

Suppose the supply is highly inelastic. Then the price can be set "too high." The sellers won't offer much more for sale. If the demand is inelastic too, there won't be much of a surplus.

Or if the supply and demand are inelastic and the price is set "too low" the sellers still will offer almost as much and the buyers won't buy much more. There won't be much of a shortage. What then? Can the price-setters set the price "too high" and make it stick? Yes. They can. Figure 29-3 shows this on a graph.

So what about the reflex effect when supply and demand are highly inelastic? Do the automatic balancing forces still work? You bet they do. It may take longer, and sometimes the reflex effect has to work itself out a different way. If so, then that's just what it does.

Migrant Farm Workers Are Being Replaced by Machines

Right now there's a strong push to unionize and increase the wages of farm labor—especially the migrant workers who move from place to place harvesting crops. So what else is happening in the agricultural input markets? More and more capital being demanded? and less and less labor? Of course.

There's a rapid increase in the development and use of agricultural harvesting equipment.

If you don't look out the **reflex effect** *will come around and* **zap you** *from behind!*

Fig. 29-3   Administered Prices: The Case of Highly Inelastic Supply and Demand

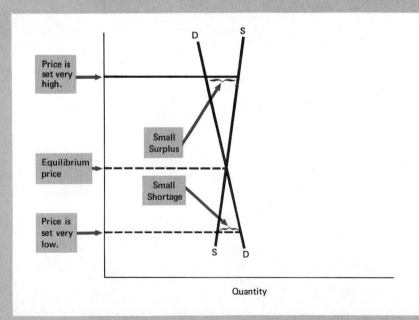

It's much easier to set prices and make them stick when supply and demand are inelastic.

But what will happen in the long run? Both the supply and the demand are likely to become more elastic. So the surplus or shortage will get bigger. And then: Look out for the reflex effect!

The reflex effect again? Of course. The higher wages stimulate more investment in labor-saving capital. More capital is used and that brings the market back into balance again. But there's likely to be a lot of unemployed (surplus) farm workers, until they can develop new skills and move into other occupations.

What do you think will happen in U.S. farm labor markets? Will farm workers get higher and higher wages? Sure. Then will more and more farm workers be replaced by machines? Of course.

If the migrant worker works for a low wage, farmers can afford to have their crops picked by hand. But if migrant workers insist on a "living wage" (comparable to what more highly-productive, semi-skilled workers receive in a factory) then farmers can't afford to hire them!

As Wages Rise, Mechanize!

So what happens as the farm workers' wage goes up? Mechanical equipment must be developed to take over the harvesting task. If not, the farmer will have to go into something else

(maybe poultry or dairying, or growing wheat or corn) where mechanical equipment *can* be used.

Is this another example of how the reflex effect works itself out? Sure. As wages rise, mechanize! If you can't mechanize, then either prices must rise to cover the higher wage or you must get out of that industry. It's one or the other. You have no choice. Figure 29-4 shows this on a graph.

During the next few years, hand labor may be virtually eliminated from crop-harvesting in the United States. The crops which can't be harvested mechanically simply won't be produced in this country. Perhaps they will be produced in Mexico or Central or South America (or somewhere else where wages are not so high), then shipped to U.S. markets. Either that, or the prices of the hand-picked crops will have to go up very high!

Whenever *wage rates* go up very much, then either (1) the *output per worker* must go up or (2) the *price of the product* must go up. If neither of these can happen quickly enough, then (3) the firms in that industry must go out of business or shift into the production of something else. You can be absolutely sure that one of these three

**Fig. 29-4 Farmer's Demand for Migrant Labor:
If the Wages Rise the Farms Will Mechanize!**

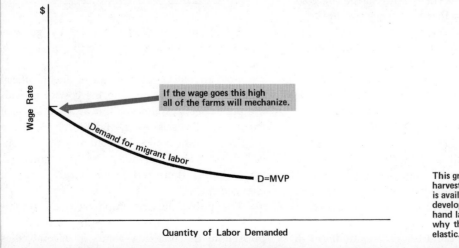

things will happen.

As wages rise, if capital cannot be introduced to reduce the use (and increase the productivity) of labor, then output prices must go up. If the market won't stand the higher prices, or if *foreign producers* ship their products in and undersell the domestic producers, then the domestic industry will decline. Unless the trend is reversed, ultimately that industry will die out completely. *Under no circumstances can businesses pay workers more in wages than the value of what the workers produce.* There's just no way.

THE SERVICE INDUSTRIES AND THE REFLEX EFFECT OF INFLATION

In an economy which has a rising wage rate, industries which can't mechanize and automate have a special problem. People who buy the products of the nonmechanized industries have a special problem, too. They pay high prices! Look at the repair and service industries, for example.

The Private Services

As wages rise, some of the service industries can't mechanize very much. The productivity of the workers can't be increased by adding labor-saving capital. But workers (and maybe the government) will insist that their wages go up.

Then how can the "value product" of the worker go up enough to justify the higher wage? There's only one way. The price of the service must go up.

If the worker's "physical output" can't be increased, then how can the "value product" be increased? *By raising the price of the physical output?* Of course. That's exactly what has been going on in the U.S. economy.

Can you begin to understand why it's so expensive to get your car worked on or to get your shoes shined or your plumbing repaired or a broken windowpane replaced or anything else done that requires hand labor? We can afford to buy new cars but we can't afford to have much work done on our old ones!

It really pays, these days, to "do-it-yourself." If you can fix your car or your roof or your TV or your plumbing you can save yourself some money. It's going to get even more that way in the future. Can you see why?

The Reflex Effect of Inflation. As the wages of the service workers have gone up, the prices of the services have gone up. That has helped to push up the cost of living for everybody. As the cost of living has increased, everybody has pushed for more wage increases.

Is this an example of **the reflex effect of inflation** working to wipe out the "artificial productivity increases" (the wage increases) in the service industries? Right! When "prices in general" go up as much as the service workers' wages went up, where are they? All back in balance again? Yes. Right back to square one.

How much of the present inflation problem in the United States results from this kind of see-saw action? from each group trying to get ahead while the reflex effect of inflation constantly erodes their gains? We don't know. But a lot. Maybe most of it. But even if we knew, that wouldn't help much. This kind of problem is not easy to handle!

The Public Services

The public services (financed by government) face the same problem as the private services.

Ask any local or state government official what has been happening to the cost of providing public services and you'll hear a sad story of frustration. The salaries of school teachers, police officers, administrators, sanitation workers, social workers and everybody else have gone up, up, up. But their *real productivity?* It hasn't changed much.

The public service employees feel underpaid. Yet the taxpayers who support them feel pressed to the breaking point. In several cities and states the financial problem has reached crisis proportions. Why? Partly because wages have been going up faster than productivity and partly because of the rapid increase in the demand for more and better public services.

This financial problem is not going to go away until better ways are found to increase the efficiency (productivity) of labor in the public services. When we're talking about teachers and social workers and such, that isn't going to be easy to do!

Wages Rise but Productivity Doesn't: Inflation

How does the reflex effect work in the service industries? Primarily by inflation. The service workers get their wage increases, but prices go up. So they don't get much of a "real increase" after all. *Unless "the people in general" really do produce more output, they can't have more income.*

We can't give ourselves more than we're producing! Unless we're producing more we can't have more. There's just no way. Whenever we try to pay ourselves more than the value of what we're producing, the reflex effect of inflation brings things back into balance.

Manufacturing workers (and others with increasing productivity—and perhaps with bargaining power) lead the way in gaining wage increases. Then everyone else demands similar increases. Ultimately they get them, so prices must rise. Then just about everybody winds up no better off than they would have been if the whole thing hadn't started.

Those whose wages run ahead of the price increases get some increase in their standards of living. For the others, the wage increase is only an illusion. The reflex effect (in this case, inflation) reduces people's real incomes enough to wipe out the effects of inflationary wage increases—increases which go beyond the real increases in output.

You might say that inflation is the "last in line" of the automatic balancing forces in real-world markets. If something else doesn't get the markets pushed back into balance, inflation probably will.

PUBLIC POLICIES CANNOT IGNORE THE "REFLEX EFFECT"

Society's ideas of social justice demand that we sometimes rig some markets. But whenever anybody sets out to rig a market, all the reflex effects should be considered. Otherwise the planned objectives are not likely to be achieved.

The "market riggers" must try to foresee the direct and indirect effects of each action they're planning to take. They need to know about all the automatic balancing forces which will come into play following any price-fixing or supply-rigging or demand-rigging action they may take.

Suppose the market-riggers succeed in foreseeing all the reflex effects of their actions. That's only half the battle! Foreseeing is one thing; forestalling is something else.

Minimum Wage Laws and Other "Government Price-Fixing"

Governments sometimes set input prices to try to improve the conditions of low-income people. Minimum wage laws try to guarantee that everybody who works will earn a decent living. Maximum interest laws try to prevent lenders from "gouging" the poor. Rent ceilings are sometimes used to prevent landlords from overcharging.

What are the effects of all this input-price-fixing? You already know enough about "the functions of price" to be able to guess. Let's look at some examples.

Interest Rate Controls. Suppose the legal limit is 9 percent on home mortgages and the market rate on government bonds goes up to 12 percent. Who will lend you money at 9 percent so you can buy a house? Nobody.

So what does the law accomplish? It keeps

the lender from "gouging you" all right! It also keeps you from buying the house you want to buy. Too many people are trying to borrow the low cost loans; too few banks are willing to lend. *Holding a price down always creates shortages.*

Rent Ceilings. Maximum rents work the same way. Suppose the rent ceiling on a certain type of apartment is $100 a month. Then suppose maintenance and repair costs and interest and taxes and other costs go up so that landlords can't break even. What happens?

Landlords start to cut corners and let the apartments run down. More people want to rent the low-cost apartments but fewer and fewer are available. Ultimately these apartments will vanish from the market. So what does the rent ceiling do? It creates a shortage of apartments. *Holding a price down always creates shortages!*

Minimum Wage Laws. Minimum wage laws create problems too. Suppose the minimum wage goes up to $4.50 or maybe $5.00 an hour. Will businesses use less labor and more capital? Of course. Which workers will be hired? The highly skilled, most productive ones.

Who will hire the thousands of inexperienced young people who are constantly joining the labor force? At $5.00 an hour? Nobody. So how do all these "surplus workers" get jobs and get a start? They can't. The price of their unskilled, inexperienced labor is too high. *Holding a price up always creates surpluses.*

What Can Be Done About the Reflex Effects?

You can see that the reflex effects can cause serious problems. Does this mean that the government shouldn't set minimum wages? or rent ceilings? or maximum interest rates? Maybe so. But maybe not.

What it does mean exactly, is this: Whenever the government decides to regulate any input price, *unless preventive action is taken, the price-fixing will do some harm.* Why so?

Because both the buyers and the sellers respond to the "manipulated" price. How great the response will be depends on the *elasticities* of both the supply and demand.

In the short run the elasticities are likely to be low. So the response is likely to be small. But as time passes, the response will become greater and greater.

If rent ceilings are imposed this month there isn't much the landlord can do but go along. But the apartments can be allowed to run down. Then ultimately they can just be abandoned! In some big cities, apartment buildings actually have been abandoned because they wouldn't pay their way.

Price Ceilings Require Action to Prevent Shortages. What can be done to prevent the undesired effects of **price-fixing?** It's very simple: *If the government is going to try to hold a price down then it must do something to prevent shortages. It must guarantee that there will be an adequate quantity supplied—either by supporting the supply or by restricting the demand, or both.*

If rent ceilings are imposed, the government must ensure a supply of rental units. It can build them itself or subsidize private landlords or it can take other approaches.

If the government is going to hold the interest rate down to 9 percent for home mortgage loans, some arrangement must be made to guarantee the supply of loanable funds to those who want to borrow to buy homes.

"Minimum Price Laws" Require Action to Prevent Surpluses. *If the government is going to try to hold a price up then it must do something to prevent surpluses. It must do something to guarantee that there will be an adequate quantity demanded—either by supporting the demand or by restricting the supply, or both.*

If a minimum wage law is passed, the government might subsidize businesses to induce them to hire inexperienced workers. Or it might establish job training and placement programs to increase the workers' productivity and help them to find jobs. Or it might take some other approach.

If the government is going to support the price of peanuts, then it had better do something to restrict peanut production and to get the people to eat a lot of peanut butter! It's much easier to pass minimum wage laws and rent ceilings and maximum interest rates and farm price supports than it is to design effective programs to take care of the total problem!

Forestalling the Reflex Effect of Price Supports. Suppose the legislature wants to help the cotton farmers. So it sets a high price for cotton. What happens next?

The textile producers start using more nylon and other synthetic fibers. And they start buying more Egyptian and Mexican and Brazilian and other foreign cotton. At the same time the corn and wheat and tobacco and chicken and beef and lettuce producers decide to produce cotton. Soon there are big surpluses of cotton. Finally, the high price collapses.

Couldn't a system of controls be built to make the high cotton prices stick? Sure. Cotton production could be carefully limited. Government agents could go around checking to be sure that nobody was growing any more cotton than had been alloted. Imports of foreign cotton could be prohibited. The government could police all the borders to keep people from smuggling cotton into the country.

Special taxes could be levied on nylon and other synthetic fibers to make them more expensive so the textile producers wouldn't substitute synthetic fibers for cotton. The government could buy up all the surplus cotton and burn it. That would keep the price from collapsing. Or the government might build a lot of warehouses and store up the cotton just in case we should ever want to stack up cotton bales all the way to the moon!

Figure 29-5 shows how the government might try to "rig the cotton market" to keep the price up. Take a minute and study that figure now.

Can We Block the Reflex Effect?

Can the reflex effect be prevented from working? Sure, if we're willing to exert enough effort and energy and resources and money. But it isn't easy. And the social costs—the harm done to the people—may be high.

The longer we "hold the line" the more difficult it gets to keep on holding the line. As time passes, enterprising citizens always seem to figure out some way to get around all the controls and restrictions, and to profit from the artificially high (or low) price.

As people do this more and more, the artificial price breaks loose. The reflex action of the market overthrows the controls and brings things back into balance. The more the "rigged condition" departs from the natural condition in the market, the more difficult it is to block the reflex effects.

Who rigs the market? Everyone who has (or who can get and exercise) some monopoly power. Many buyers and sellers have market-rigging power. But the really big "market rigger" is the government. Many of the government's economic policies are specifically designed to rig markets.

All people seem to think they are good economists so they argue for whatever they think looks good—more progressive income taxes, tariffs on foreign cars, more aid for dependent children, minimum wage laws, tuition-free universities, tax incentives to stimulate investment, higher unemployment benefits, etc.,

etc.—without any regard at all for the reflex effects.

So what kinds of economic policies does the nation wind up with? Not perfect. Not by a long shot. But it's surprising how good the economic policies work out to be, much of the time. Why? Because outstanding economists who really understand the reflex effects are in charge of things? No.

Then how does it happen to work out reasonably well, much of the time? Through trial-and-error? pragmatism? Right!

The Reflex Effects Usually Are Handled After They Appear

First, people decide that every worker should earn a "living wage." So they get the government to pass a minimum wage law. Then pretty soon we see high unemployment of young, and unskilled workers. So then the government sets up job training and economic development programs.

One thing leads to another. Each time some "reflex effect" shows its ugly head, the government takes a swat at it. Not very scientific, right? Still we will keep doing it this way, more or less. Why? Because it isn't easy to find any other workable approach.

We might hope that all of our policymakers will be learning more about the reflex effect—about this **basic law of real-world markets**. That kind of understanding might improve the government's economic policies. More of the indirect effects might be foreseen and contained or circumvented or offset right from the beginning.

Reflex Effects and Golden-Egg-Laying Geese

I'm sure that when Aesop told his fable about the man who killed the goose that laid the

Fig. 29-5   Adjust Demand and Supply to Keep the Price of Cotton High

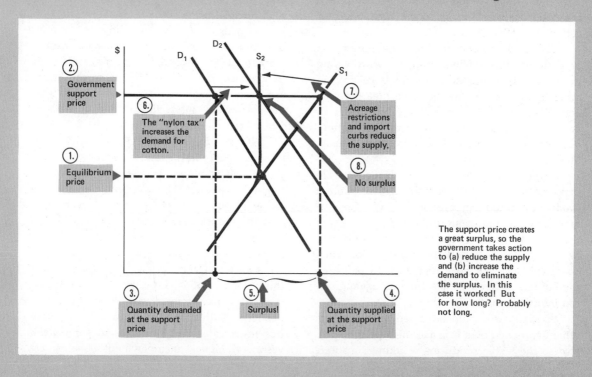

2. Government support price
6. The "nylon tax" increases the demand for cotton.
7. Acreage restrictions and import curbs reduce the supply.
1. Equilibrium price
8. No surplus
3. Quantity demanded at the support price
5. Surplus!
4. Quantity supplied at the support price

The support price creates a great surplus, so the government takes action to (a) reduce the supply and (b) increase the demand to eliminate the surplus. In this case it worked! But for how long? Probably not long.

golden egg, he must have had in mind the idea of the reflex effect. If you kill the goose to try to get all of the golden eggs today, you lose all of the eggs. That's a pretty powerful reflex effect all right!

To rig a market without considering the reflex effect is as ridiculous as to kill a golden-egg-laying goose. It would be a good idea to keep that in mind as "appealing shortcuts" seem to appear.

Usually, in reality, there's no "easy way." The opportunity costs, the trade-offs, are always lurking there beneath the surface, ready to zap you! That's the "reflex effect."

Each time we manipulate the market it's a good idea to try to figure out what the reflex effects will be and to make plans for handling them. Otherwise we may wind up killing the goose that lays the golden egg—or maybe jumping out of the frying pan into the fire.

Policymakers Need to Understand the Reflex Effect

No one will ever be able to foresee all the reflex effects of any government economic policy or program. Still, the better the policymakers understand the reflex effect, the more realistic their programs are likely to be. The less likely the policymakers will be to fall into the trap of offering quick and simple answers to chronic and complex problems.

The market process in the real world is headstrong and powerful. It tries to insist on working things out its own way. Government policymakers need to be very careful about how they choose to manipulate markets. Otherwise you know what can happen. Out of the frying pan, into the fire!

In view of all the things we have been talking about, perhaps we should junk the market process. Then what would we do? Governmental planning and administration would be the only answer, of course. All the market-oriented economies are using a good bit of governmental planning already. Why not just get rid of the market and use governmental planning and administration all the way? No, we'd better not try. You just can't kill these market forces!

If you think the market creates problems, you're right. But compared with the task of trying to administer and direct all the resources and production activities and everything in the economic system? Forget it.

The people in the world simply aren't going to be able to make it without the market process working for them. The inefficiencies of trying to get along without it would be intolerable.

THE MARKET PROCESS: MANKIND'S MOST VALUABLE TOOL

It's good for you to be aware of the many real-world imperfections in the workings of the market process. But please, don't throw out the baby with the bath water!

The market process—intelligently and realistically modified and, when social objectives and goals require, manipulated—has been and is the world's single most valuable tool for serving the material needs of mankind.

The personal feelings of freedom which it permits, the careful conservation of most of society's resources which it accomplishes, the stimulation of production which it generates—all these are going to be essential in building the kind of world the people of tomorrow will want and demand.

Some Advantages of the Market Process

The needs of the world simply cannot be served through the inefficient process of "resource administration." The idea of each input and output being controlled by many "experts" who spend all their time working on such things? Ridiculous. It's just too inefficient, too wasteful, as compared with the neat way the market process can handle it. The needs of the people of the world will never be met if we waste our resources and talents trying to "administer" everything.

The market process doesn't always work right. It presents many problems and has many flaws. But the people of the world would always be poor except for the market. Even the communist countries are finding that out.

The Market Process Works Automatically

The "market model" certainly isn't a true picture of how things happen in the real world. But the forces which operate in the model really do operate in the real world.

People work hard to get more money and things—more private property. They work, study and struggle to get more income. Usually the ones who work at it *really do* get more income. And most people really do work at it!

By now you know many good things about the market process. You know that it is very efficient in stimulating production. For most things, most of the time, it really does a great job of conserving and optimizing the society's things, too.

The efficiency of the market process as a "resource-directing mechanism" is truly impressive. Somehow the market finds the needed factors and moves them to the right places and gets the right things produced.

How could you get all the factors to do the right things, without prices and wages and profits as incentives? Sure, resources can be "directed" by government administrators. But this usually is an inefficient (and often dis-

What's a good way to conserve our scarce things?

Let the rationing function of Price do it!

tasteful) way to do it. The price mechanism is **far** more efficient.

"Private Property" Gets Us to Conserve Society's Things

The market system appeals to the natural self-interest of each person. By a sort of "neat trick" it gets all of us to become full-time custodians of society's resources. A big part of this "trick" depends on the concept of private property.

Look how neatly it works! A patch of forest can be "mine," a house can be "mine," a truck can be "mine," and I will work like a slave (harder, really!) to take care of these things. I will put forth great effort to care for pieces of the society's land and capital. Which pieces? The pieces which happen to be "mine."

Why will I fight the forest fires and stay awake all night to keep the wolves from the cattle? Fear of punishment? No. Offer of high wages? No. Then why? Because these things are *mine*. I will fight and struggle and exert every effort I can to protect those things which are *mine*. Do you see the great custodial, economizing role of private property? How efficiently it works!

The truck will be lubricated when it needs to be because it's mine and I want to take care of it. It will be used to haul the bricks to build the new factory because that's where it's demanded. It's my truck, sure. But it's society's truck too. I take good care of it and I use it to serve the wishes of the society. See how neatly the market gets things taken care of and used for the desired purposes?

Suppose the truck was owned by the government and I was just the driver. Would I take such good care of it? Maybe so. But probably not. Would you be lubricating, fixing, washing, or otherwise taking care of a government truck during your time off on Saturday afternoon? Not likely.

My forest will be protected from insects, from fire, and from disease so the timber can grow. My forest is one of the natural resources of the nation. Really, it's *society's* forest. But I'm taking care of it because it is also "mine." No "government supervisor" must waste energy watching over me to get me to take care of the forest. I do it automatically because it's mine. The "private property" thing tricks me into taking care of it.

If I work hard and I'm lucky, all my efforts will be rewarded. I'll earn more income. Then I'll be able to buy more things and become society's custodian for *even more* of its resources!

Efficiency and Freedom Are the Big Advantages

The great **efficiency**—this custodial role of all the people, and the automatic response of everyone to the price mechanism—is one of the two great advantages of a market-directed economic system. The other great advantage is that each individual really does have a lot of **freedom** to choose his or her own way of life.

In the real world the harshness of the pure market forces can be modified to give each person a reasonable chance. Then each is free to decide where to live and what kind of work to do and how hard to work. Each person can work hard and produce more and get more things or work less and own fewer things and have more free time.

The relatively high degree of freedom of each of us to choose our own work pattern and life style is often considered to be the greatest advantage of a "free enterprise" or "market-oriented" economic system. The same feelings which support democracy as a form of government also support "free enterprise" as a form of

economic system. Both strongly emphasize the importance of the individual—our "rights to choose."

Of course you recognize that neither political democracy nor economic "free enterprise" operate quite as neatly in the real world as they do in theory. But, praised be, both do work!

A Summary Overview of the Market Process in the Real World

You know that there are several ways in which the model market process doesn't fit the real world. Administered pricing and monopoly power result in major changes.

There are many socially desirable conditions which the market cannot bring about. The market permits over-use of some natural resources and pollution of the environment while letting desirable projects (reforestation, urban housing, etc.) go wanting. The unequal distribution of wealth and income lets a few people have a lot of control over society's resource choices while many people have very little influence.

No society would permit the market process to have full control over its resource-use choices. Every society departs from the market process. The political process forces the people to turn some of their private property into public programs: police and fire protection, highways and streets, hospitals, urban renewal, education, manpower training, nuclear submarines, lunar excursions.

All societies practice some forms of income redistribution. Suppose a person's "welfare level" drops below the level which the society's conscience will permit. Then the society does something about it. Either by the social process or the political process, more of the society's outputs are transferred to the poor.

It isn't likely that anyone would ever suggest that the market process be given complete charge over all of the society's economic choices. On the other hand, history has shown the great power and efficiency of the market process. As we continue to modify it, perhaps we should take care not to destroy it completely—at least not until we are sure we have found something good enough to take its place.

HOW RELEVANT OR HELPFUL IS THE "PURE MARKET MODEL"?

The model of the "pure market system" certainly doesn't describe the real world. That's for sure! Nothing in the real world works exactly like the model. So why have you had to go to all the effort to understand the model?

Why don't we forget about the concepts of pure competition and easily moving prices and about supply and demand determining prices and about "productivity theories" of wages and rents and interest? Why don't we just study the things we can see going on in the real world? What good is the model anyway?

The Model Is Not Supposed to Describe the Real World

Everybody knows that the model of the pure market system really doesn't describe the real world. *It's not supposed to do that!* What it's supposed to do is to illustrate the forces at work in the real world.

The law of gravity can explain how things would drop in a vacuum. But that sure doesn't describe what's going to happen if you drop a fluffy little feather out of the little window at the top of the Washington Monument!

It's a good idea to know about the force of gravity. But that doesn't describe what will happen when you drop the feather. Not by a long shot! That's sort of the way it is with our model of the "pure market system."

The "pure market model" can't describe the real world. Of course not. But can't you look at the world, now, and see things you couldn't see before? Could you understand the reflex effect— the **basic law of real-world markets**—if you

didn't know anything about the workings of supply and demand? or about the rationing and production motivating functions of price? or about the effects of surpluses and shortages? Could you? Probably not, right?

The Model Shows the Market Forces "in a Vacuum"

In the real world, the results of the pure market forces are always modified by special circumstances. Still, it's very helpful to know what these forces are and how they work.

The model gives us a "solid rock foundation" to start from as we try to understand real-world markets. It lets us see the forces at work. Also it gives us a way to "pre-test" proposed policies to see how each might work out in a model setting—"in a vacuum" so to speak.

An overemphasis on the model sometimes hides the real world from people. Try to be careful about that. The neatness and beauty of the model is so great that it's easy to get carried away. Try not to. But on the other hand, do try to be aware that in real world markets the supply and demand forces and the two functions of price *really are* in there. They're working all the time.

Sometimes the market forces are in *direct* control; more often, prices are "administered" and the "reflex effect" keeps things moving into balance. But either way, market forces are always influencing things. You can't learn the economics of the real world just from studying the model. But studying the model sure can help.

The Model Is True, Just as Aesop's Fables Are True

The economist's model of pure competition is like Aesop's fables. Surely Aesop didn't want us to believe that there really was a fox looking up and saying the grapes must be sour because he couldn't reach them! But Aesop did manage to put his finger on a very human tendency, right? If all you knew about humans and their tendencies was what you could learn from reading Aesop's fables, you would have a very distorted view of the world and its people!

If all you knew about real-world economics was what you learned from the economist's pure market model, you would have a very distorted view of real-world markets too. But everybody has some awareness of what's going on in the real world. By studying the economist's model you can learn to understand it so much better. (But don't forget what you *already* knew. That's an essential input, too!)

Is the model necessary? Helpful? You decide, for you. For me, I have already decided. I need it. Without it I wouldn't be able to understand how a modern economy "gets it all together." Could you? And I probably couldn't do nearly as well at distinguishing between "sound economic policy" and "shortsighted political demagoguery." Could you?

In the next two chapters you will be reading about some current real-world problems. With your understanding of how the market forces work I think you'll be able to look at each of these problems with greater insight than ever before.

SUMMARY AND SYNTHESIS

Most real-world markets don't work quite like the model of the "pure market system." Yet the results in most real-world markets seem to come out fairly close to the results described in the model. How does that happen? Through what I call the reflex effect—the Basic Law of Real-World Markets.

This "law" says that there are powerful, automatic balancing forces (reflex effects) which will come into play whenever a market is rigged or pushed out of balance in any way—and that it's just a matter of time before (one way or another) the market is pushed back into balance.

The "reflex effect" works out balance in the market backwards from the way markets are balanced in the model. In the model, changes in demand or supply conditions will change the price. The price mechanism will take it from there. But in most real-world markets, prices are administered and don't change easily. So it's up to the reflex effect to bring things into balance.

In monopolistic competition markets the reflex effect eliminates excess profits—not by pushing down the high administered prices but by creating excess capacity and pushing up per unit cost to where it equals the price. Reflex effect? Yes.

In labor markets, high administered wage rates result in more unemployment and mechanization. This increases the productivity of the employed workers enough to equal the high administered wage rate—until MVP = P. Reflex effect? Sure.

If workers get higher wages and there's no increase in their physical productivity (as is the case in many service industries) then there must be an increase in the prices of the services they are producing. That's inflationary. By the time prices in general go up as much as their wages went up, the service workers are "right back to square one." Reflex effect? Of course.

Whenever prices are fixed or controlled or set too high, surpluses will be generated. Whenever too low, shortages. Unless something can be done about the surpluses or shortages the "fixed prices" can't stay fixed for very long. They'll break loose and move toward equilibrium. Do price controls generate black markets? Yes. Do high income taxes stimulate the development of an underground economy? Sure. Reflex effects again!

How are reflex effects usually dealt with by government policy-makers? Usually pragmatically—only after they appear and start making trouble for somebody.

The market process—the price mechanism—imperfect though it is as it works in the real world, is still mankind's most valuable tool for allocating resources and providing for the material welfare of the society. It's automatic. It tricks people into conserving society's resources. It works with a high degree of efficiency. And it leaves individuals a lot of freedom to choose their own way of life.

The model of the "pure market system" shows the market forces (of demand, supply and the price mechanism) "in a vacuum." It doesn't exactly describe real-world markets. But it certainly does describe and illustrate clearly the forces which are at work in all real-world markets.

These market forces described in the model are what create (in the real world) the reflex effect—the powerful automatic forces which work inexorably to balance real-world markets—to achieve the kind of results stated in the Basic Law of Real-World Markets.

REVIEW EXERCISES

MAJOR CONCEPTS, PRINCIPLES, TERMS (Explain each carefully.)

the reflex effect and how it works
how labor productivity adjusts to wage rates
the reflex effect of inflation
some reflex effects of high wages
some ways to try to block the reflex effect
how private property "tricks people"
the efficiency of the market process
the purpose and helpfulness of the "pure market model"

CURVES AND GRAPHS (Draw, label, and explain each.)

Supply and Demand Curves Show How the Reflex Effect Works
The Reflex Effect Eliminates Excess Profits in Monopolistic Competition
Administered Prices: the Case of Highly Inelastic Supply and Demand
The Farmers' Demand for Migrant Labor
Adjust Demand and Supply to Keep the Price of Cotton High

QUESTIONS (Write out answers or jot down key points.)

1. Can you explain in detail what is meant by the Reflex Effect—the "Basic Law of Real-World Markets"? Try.
2. What would happen if the government came in and set the price of *anything* (gasoline, or shoes, or houses, or economics books, or you name it) *much too high?* Or what if it set the price *much too low?* Explain exactly what would happen, and why, in each case. Draw some supply and demand graphs to illustrate your answer.
3. Why do the reflex effects get stronger and stronger as more and more time goes by? (What happens to the elasticity of supply and demand as time goes by, and

does that matter?) Explain. Draw some supply and demand graphs to illustrate your answer.

4. The "reflex effect" helps to explain why producers who sell in markets of monopolistic competition often have high average cost of production, and a lot of excess capacity. Can you explain why? and, illustrate with a graph? Try.

5. If you were a farm worker, knowing what you know about the reflex effect and how it works, would you be pushing hard to get your wages up higher? or not? Try to look at this from all sides and explain the various possible points of view.

6. Do you really believe that the market process is humanity's most valuable tool for meeting the economic needs of the people? Explain, in as much detail as you can.

30 Micro Problems of Modern Society I: Progress, Pollution, Population

Chapter Objectives

- In the previous chapters you have been reading about **how markets work** in the real world. This and the following chapter focus on some **real-world problems.** What are they? and what can be (and/or is being) done about them?

- When you finish studying this chapter you will be able to discuss **different meanings of progress.** And you will know how **progress** toward chosen objectives has sometimes **uncovered** and/or **created new problems,** requiring **new objectives** and **new directions** for the allocation of society's resources.

- You will be able to explain the **economics of the pollution problem.** You will be able to describe **environmental externalities** and to use graphs to **illustrate the trade-offs** which society must make as it decides: "**How much pollution?**" and "**How much cleaning up?**"

- You will be able to explain **various ways** of approaching the **pollution problem,** including the selling of "rights to pollute."

- Finally, you will be introduced to the problem of the **population explosion,** and to some of the impacts it's having on our society and our world.

In an economy like the United States the microeconomic forces do a lot to direct things and to protect things for the society. But these microeconomic forces don't take care of everything.

Some of the serious problems these microeconomic forces don't take care of for us are: pollution, population growth, urban blight, poverty, and discrimination. All these problems are already serious. Some are getting more serious. This chapter and the following one will give you some insight into the economics of these issues.

PROGRESS AND PROBLEMS: WHICH OBJECTIVES SHOULD SOCIETY PURSUE?

Many of the **problems** which have become so serious in the advanced modern nations seem to be related to all the **progress** which has occurred in these nations. Does progress create more problems than it solves? Some people are saying "maybe so."

But it's really a question of what we mean by progress—that is, of which objectives we want to pursue. Modern society's objectives must reflect its changing ideas about what's important and what isn't. More on that in a minute. But first, a little more introduction to this chapter and the next.

The Economic Considerations: Alternatives and Opportunity Costs

In this chapter and the next you'll be reading about the *economics* of some real-world problems. A few statistics describing the problems will be presented, but not many. What I want you to get from all this is a good understanding of the *nature of each problem and of the economic influences at work.*

If you can learn to be realistic about the choices available to society as we tackle these problems—if you can recognize the opportunity costs which the choices will require—then you'll be far ahead of most people. And you'll be able to better recognize the basic economic forces working in the real world, too.

For now, please don't worry about memorizing a lot of detailed statistics on pollution or population or urban problems or poverty or discrimination or any such things. Textbook statistics are always out of date anyway. And up-to-date statistics are easy to find.

From time to time as you go along I'll tell you where you can find current figures. But in general, remember this: The *Statistical Abstract of the United States* is an excellent place to go to find statistics when you don't know where else to look. (I'm sure your friendly librarian would be glad to help.)

All of Us Are to Blame for the Major Problems of Our Society

When something is going wrong we usually try to find someone to "blame it on." It's frustrating to discover there's *nobody* to blame it on! But in this case you're going to find out that's the way it is.

If the problem is poverty or population or

pollution or unemployment or inflation or a balance of payments deficit or whatever, you're going to find that you can't "blame it on" the rich people or the labor unions or the landowners or the government or big business or the foreigners or the southerners or the northerners or the younger generation or "the system" or any other easily available scapegoat. Why not? Because mostly, for all of these problems *all of us are to blame.*

Progress to me, is going after whatever **matters most** to me!

What I'm trying to say is this: There aren't any easy answers. The answers are *tough* answers. The opportunity costs are high. You can't have your cake and eat it too, remember?

Even if we all decided that we were willing to pay the opportunity costs—to make the sacrifices needed to overcome all of these problems—most of the problems still couldn't be solved very fast. The problems are *too big. Quick solutions are physically impossible!* (As this chapter and the next unfold, you will see just how true this is.)

Progress Uncovers or Creates New Problems

People and societies have always faced problems. Now that the age-old problems of hunger and disease have been pushed back, new problems are coming to the surface. So now society's objectives—the directions of progress—are having to change.

As one set of problems is solved, new problems are uncovered or created. We solve the problems of hunger and disease. So what happens? People stay alive longer, live better, consume more. Population explosion? Yes. Environmental problem? Sure! Who's to blame? High technology and high productivity have done it. So let's get rid of high technology and high productivity? We'd better not!

Without our high technology and high productivity we wouldn't have a chance of handling the environmental effects of the world's exploding population! Not nearly enough progress has yet been made in bringing the population explosion under control or in dealing with the environmental crisis. Everybody knows we've barely scratched the surface. But we've made more progress than we ever could have without our high technology and high productivity to help us.

Sometimes people suggest that because of the environmental problem, we should try to stop economic progress—have **zero economic growth (ZEG).** But surely zero growth isn't the answer. Even if it was a good idea it wouldn't work. People always try to change the things they don't like—that is, to improve things. That's what progress is all about—making things better—moving toward the objectives we desire.

Progress Means Moving Toward the Desired Objectives

What "progress" means to each person depends on what that person wants most. Think about William Wellsford, an unemployed worker whose family has been subsisting on nothing but dandelion greens and corn meal mush. Mr. Wellsford is a lot more interested in seeing a new factory open up where he can get a job than he is in protecting the clean air in the valley or the pure water in the stream. To him, a new factory would bring progress.

But what about the retired stockbroker who lives in the valley or the local school teacher who heads the environmental protection committee or the wealthy family that owns most of the land and raises horses? A new factory that might mess up the water and air? And bring a lot of low-class outsiders who might have Saturday night brawls in our peaceful little city? That's progress? Forget it!

Suppose there's a public hearing on the issue of re-zoning some land to permit the new factory to be built in the area. Will all the local people agree? Of course not! What a tough situation this creates!

Each of us will work for the things that are most important to us. We will try to change those conditions which we see as problems. But is a problem to *me* a problem to *you?* That all depends on *your* point of view!

Many choices have to be made by "society as a whole"—by the government. Whenever this happens, disagreements are inevitable. In every society, no matter what the economic or political system, people disagree about issues such as these. Only when a problem becomes very obvious and very serious will everyone agree that something must be done. Even then they still will disagree about exactly *what* should be done, and *how much*, and *how.*

There are many kinds of economic issues and "public policy" problems which fit into this discussion. This chapter talks about only two: pollution, and population. First, the pollution problem.

THE ENVIRONMENTAL CRISIS: THE ECONOMICS OF THE POLLUTION PROBLEM

I suppose everybody knows that the pollution problem is bad. And it has been getting worse. All of us are in on it.

All of us are dumping cans and bottles and garbage and trash and all kinds of junk ("solid wastes") into the environment. And that's only the beginning. We're dumping liquid wastes (effluents) from all the industrial plants and processing plants and from all the sewage systems of all the cities all over the country and all over the world. All these effluents wind up in our streams and lakes and rivers and oceans and everywhere.

We're spreading all kinds of chemicals all over the landscape to control insects and weeds and all. We're puffing out smoke and all kinds of "gaseous emissions" into the air from the smokestacks of all the factories and from the exhaust pipes of all the automobiles and trucks and from city incinerators and home furnaces—even from burning steak fat from the backyard barbecue grills.

We're pulling fresh water out of the rivers and streams: to drink, to bathe in, to use for industrial purposes. So now less fresh water is flowing into the salt water estuaries—Chesapeake Bay and Galveston Bay and Puget Sound and Pamlico Sound and all the others. So the water in the estuaries is getting more salty. Maybe it's getting too salty to continue to serve as a breeding ground for many kinds of marine life. That's bad. At the same time the power plants and other plants are dumping warm water into the streams and increasing the temperatures. That may be upsetting the natural balance of life there.

The Seriousness of the Pollution Problem

I know figures like this are hard to comprehend. But to get some idea of the extent of the problem, consider this:

—The United States has about a quarter of a million miles of rivers and streams in its major watersheds. More than one fourth of that mileage is polluted.

—More than 100 million tons of carbon monoxide are being released into the air every year. Other air pollutants: hydrocarbon, sulphur oxides, nitrogen oxides, and others amount to millions of tons each, per year.

—There's more than 150 million tons of garbage and trash being thrown away every year. And billions of tin cans, billions of bottles, and even *several million junk cars every year.*

It isn't a question of whether or not these pollutants and junk will be thrown away. They must be thrown away. It's a question of *where* they will be thrown, and how—that is, of what we will do to make them clean and safe before we throw them

away.

Another way of getting at the seriousness of the pollution problem is to figure what it is costing American industry to try to control it. More than $5 billion a year is being spent. But many people say that isn't enough. Certainly it hasn't stopped pollution!

It would take a lot of polluting to pollute all the land and water and air of the earth and kill off all the wild life and marine life—and human life. But some scientists say we are moving in that direction at a rapid clip! Everyone knows that the trend can't be allowed to continue. Something must be done. But what? And how? These are tough questions.

We All Contribute to the Pollution Problem

Who pollutes? Everybody. Every living person. Every organization, every business, every school, every factory, every store. Everybody! We are all responsible for this pollution problem.

All pollution results from either final consumption activities or from production. If it results from final consumption activities, the final consumers are the ones who are *directly* responsible. If it results from productive activities then the final consumers are the ones who are *indirectly* responsible. You might say that all pollution is either **final pollution** or **derived pollution**.

"Ask not for whom the industrial plant pollutes. It pollutes for thee!" And who is going to make the sacrifices required to pay the cost of overcoming the problem? Make no mistake about it. "Thou art."

All industrial activity and all of the normal processes of life require some "environmental destruction" and some "waste disposal." Until recently everyone has been thinking of the "environmental destruction effects" and the "waste disposal task" as sort of trivial aggravations—to be ignored—to be dealt with only when absolutely necessary.

Throughout history the task of environmental protection and waste disposal has been treated as "an afterthought in the total economic process of life." But now that isn't good enough. Not anymore. With so many people on the earth, consuming so many things, environmental protection has become critical. It's becoming more critical every day.

We Are "Living High" by Not Fully Paying Our Way

In the past, most of the environmental costs—the costs of waste disposal and resource destruction and all that—have been **external** to the market. In adding up their costs, businesses haven't had to pay much attention to the resource destruction and waste disposal effects of their activities. Consumers have been able to buy all kinds of products without having to pay for the "full social cost" of producing them.

Also, people have been getting by without having to pay the full cost of disposing of their trash and garbage and sewage. All of us have been enjoying the temporary pleasure of "living high" at the expense of our environment. But it won't be long before we aren't going to be able to do that any more.

What does all this mean? It means that some things which have always been thought of as "cheap" are suddenly going to become expensive. Why? Because the cost of environmental protection from now on is going to be included in the prices of things. It's already beginning. But it still has a long way to go.

In recent years paper manufacturers have been putting many millions of dollars into equipment and processes to protect the environment. You helped to pay for some of that when you paid the high price of this book! Get the point? Already we're beginning to feel the pinch. But it's only just begun. We will all grumble. But we will pay. We just don't have any choice.

Cleaning Up Is Part of the Job

The environmental protection task must become an important part of every productive ac-

tivity—really, of *every aspect of life*. A larger and larger percentage of the national output will be directed toward environmental protection. A lot more labor and equipment and power and other resources will have to be directed toward this task. Maybe before it's all over, we will have to learn to get along with less—fewer cars, less electricity, less gasoline, less plush college buildings, less of lots of things. Maybe. We can't have our cake and eat it too. Remember?

How much more of the GNP will have to go for environmental protection? How much are we going to have to transform "consumer goods" and "industrial goods" into "environmental protection goods"? Nobody knows. But we do know that the cost will be high. And we know that all of us are going to have to give up some things (things we otherwise could have had) to help to pay for it. There's no doubt about it. There's just no other way.

How Much Pollution Should Be Allowed?

How much "gaseous emissions" or "liquid effluents" or "solid wastes" should be permitted? And by whom? And under what circumstances? Absolutely none? Zero? That's really going to be tough!

Be careful. Don't exhale and pollute the atmosphere with your used breath! Don't drive your car because if you do you'll pollute the air with exhaust fumes and you'll support the "derived pollution" of all those gasoline and tire companies! Don't eat or drink anything out of cans or bottles or paper bags. And please! No trips to the bathroom!

Zero pollution? No. That can't be the answer. So how much then? That's a tough question. Nobody really knows the answer. The biologists and chemists and other scientists are working on it.

Luckily the environment has much ability to rejuvenate itself. It can give up a lot of resources and absorb a lot of wastes. But there's a limit. Everybody knows that in the big cities and in the industrialized areas we have gone too far. We've got to cut back. But to zero? No. That would be an impossible, unnecessary, ridiculous objective. But we must cut back from where we are now. Some scientists are saying that if we do the very best our technology will permit, that will be barely good enough.

The Political Process Must Solve This Problem

The environmental protection problem is a problem of externalities. It's "external" to the market. That's why the problem must be solved through the political process. There's just no other way it could be done. But that doesn't mean that the market mechanism can't be used to help. Of course it can. And it will be.

Essentially there are three different ways the government can approach this problem:

1. By a system of regulations, with constant policing to see that everyone follows the law;
2. By charging "prices" for the use of the society's environment (that is, selling nature's "waste disposal services") and letting *the rationing function of price* take care of the problem; or
3. By subsidizing the businesses by giving them tax concessions or direct payments to pay for the installation and operation of pollution control equipment.

The first two of those approaches will internalize the externalities and pass along the "environmental protection costs" to all of us who buy the products. The third approach will charge the general public. Economists generally favor approach number 2. Why?

Approach number 3 is usually rejected because it doesn't internalize the externalities. Consumers buy the good for less than its true social cost. That's socially wasteful.

Approach number 1 usually is not preferred because the policing problem is not easy to handle, and because it's difficult to design anti-pollution regulations which reflect the unique input-output requirements of the individual firms.

For example, suppose regulations are established. The firm which can clean up its pollution at relatively low cost is placed in the same situation as the firm which can clean up its wastes only at very high cost. Perhaps the high cost firm will have to go out of business. Perhaps its production processes make it impossible for it to reduce its pollution to the required minimum. And perhaps this firm produces a very "socially desirable" product.

But suppose the firm which could clean up its pollution completely would do so. Then it might not be necessary for the other firm to go out of business. It could simply reduce its pollution and that would be sufficient. Get the idea?

There's no reason why all firms should have to meet the same "standard of cleanliness" if what we're aiming for is optimum social efficiency in our economic system. You'll be reading more about this later in this chapter. But now, here's an example to illustrate the differences between approach number 1 and approach number 2.

As you drive along the highway you see signs saying: DO NOT LITTER. $50 FINE. That's the first approach. It's against the law to throw beer cans out of your car window.

Another approach might be for the government to require a nickel deposit on each beer can. Then when you turn in the used can for proper disposal or recycling you get your nickel back. If you throw the beer can beside the highway or in the lake it costs you a nickel. If people still throw away too many beer cans, raise the price to a dime, or a quarter—or to a dollar, or two, or five! Can you see how effective this approach might be? (But be careful of the reflex effect! Someone may set up a factory to produce used beer cans and make millions!)

Internalizing the Environmental Externalities

Which approach should the government use? regulations and policing? or the price mechanism? Probably both. Whenever the price mechanism can be used, it's likely to cut down on the "policing cost." But no matter which approach is used, the results are going to be far from perfect.

There will be all kinds of special interest groups pushing for more protection or less protection, for tighter or easier regulations, for stricter or more lenient enforcement, for higher or lower "environmental protection prices." That's the way the political process always operates.

Remember Mr. Wellsford? The unemployed father of five who feeds his family on dandelion greens and corn meal mush? The one who wants a local factory so he can get a job? He detests the environmental protection program and writes nasty letters to the mayor and to the governor and to congress.

The local gas station operator and the local real estate agent do the same. They want to see business pick up. What about investors who want to build the factory? They write letters, too. All these people want to kill (or soften) the environmental protection program.

But what about the retired stockbroker and the civic-minded school teacher and the wealthy landowner who raises horses? They get together and visit city hall and the state capital and Washington. They're urging that the environmental protection programs be tightened!

Who will win out? Who knows. If we're lucky the final decision will be made with an eye to *what ought to be done*. But the final decision is almost certain to depend partly on who is a member of which political party, who contributed how much to the last political campaign and such things as that. That's too bad, I suppose. But that's the way it is. Such is the nature of the political process.

How Fast Should the Government Move on Environmental Protection?

What ought to be done? And how quickly? Nobody knows, really. The "doomsday proph-

ets" say it's already too late. We've blown it. Human life on earth is on the way out. Others say that we must move as fast as we can because there's no time to lose.

At the other end of the range are those who say that this whole problem has been blown completely out of proportion—that we are working on it too fast already. They say we're distorting the progress of our economy by turning too much effort toward environmental protection.

Many people seem to agree that we should work on the environmental protection issue as fast as we reasonably can. But how fast is that? We could impose enough controls to absolutely "shut down" the economic system! We might say: "Okay. Let's do it." But after we've been going without food or water for a few days we might all decide to change our minds.

This is a tough question, with opportunity costs staring us in the face every step of the way. As long as we recognize that, and go after the problem realistically, I think we'll find the ways to handle it. We'd better all hope so!

The Problem Provides the Means for Its Own Solution

One thing is sure. The great human population is going to have to become compatible with its limited environment—with its city, its nation, its "spaceship earth." Solutions will not be easy to find. The cost is going to be higher than most people would like to admit. But *the cost must be paid*. Soon everyone will realize that we don't have any choice about that.

Can we do it? Sure. High technology and economic growth have let the problem arise. That same high technology and economic growth will now provide us the means to solve it.

So is the solution to the environmental problem at hand? No. Far from it. But we have the means to develop the solutions. Now it's time for the economic system, through the political process, to redirect more energy and effort toward environmental objectives. "Progress" in the decades ahead is going to have to be redefined, and *aimed much more toward achieving environmental objectives and less toward other objectives*.

It's good that we have the means. Now let's hope we will be wise enough to pay the opportunity costs and take care of the problem. Try not to grumble too much as more and more of the costs come to rest on you. Sorry, but there's just no other way. Let's all pay the cost and be glad we got around to it in time! (I hope.)

AN ECONOMIC ANALYSIS OF "ENVIRONMENTAL EXTERNALITIES"

Can the tools of economic analysis help in deciding what to do about pollution? Or in understanding who bears the burden of pollution control? Or deciding how much pollution we should put up with? How clean the air and water and landscape should be? Sure.

If the environmental problem was not external to the market, then the market forces would take care of it. If *production costs* really did reflect *social costs* then the rationing function of price would limit the amounts of pollution to the "socially optimum" levels.

If it cost something to pollute the rivers, then there would be an incentive to develop techniques to *prevent* polluting the rivers. But since the "waste-disposal services of the ecosystem" have been offered as a free good, there has been no incentive to limit the use of those "waste-disposal services."

When the waste-disposal services of the ecosystem are available free, then they will be used right to the point where the last little bit used has zero marginal value. Why not? Nobody restricts or conserves or limits the use of free goods!

So we must prevent people and businesses and communities and cities from using the "waste disposal services of the ecosystem" as a

free good! We can pass laws prohibiting them from doing it. Or we can charge prices for "nature's waste disposal services."

The Increasing Cost of Cleaning Up Wastes

Suppose we decided to levy a charge for using nature's waste disposal services. Even a low charge might result in a lot of cleaning up. Why? Because a lot of cleaning up can be done at low cost.

Think of it this way. Suppose a factory is putting out a lot of very dirty smoke and very dirty effluent. It wouldn't be difficult or expensive to remove a lot of pollutants from the very dirty smoke and effluent. But as the smoke and effluent get cleaner it becomes more difficult to clean it up even more.

So if the government puts a "pollution measurement meter" on the smoke stack and one on the effluent discharge pipe and places even a low charge per unit of pollution, suddenly it becomes profitable for the firm to clean up more. So the "demand for nature's waste-disposal services" probably would be fairly elastic when the prices (charges for nature's waste-disposal services) are low. At higher prices where firms have already cleaned up a lot and it's difficult to clean up more, demand probably would be much less elastic. In Figure 30-1 you'll see all this on a graph.

A Graphic Picture of "Optimum Pollution Levels"

When you look at the four figures coming up you'll see that zero pollution wouldn't make much sense. The social cost of "total clean-up" would be much greater than the social cost of allowing tolerable amounts of pollutants to enter the atmosphere and the water. Now take time to study Figures 30-1, -2, -3, and -4, and you'll find out a lot more about the economics of pollution controls.

Fig. 30-1   The Increasing Cost of Cleaning Up Wastes

The cleaner the wastes become, the more expensive it gets
to clean them up even more.

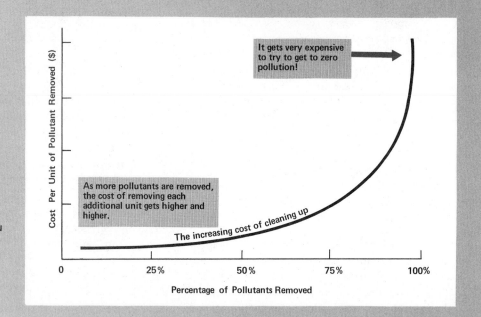

It gets very expensive
to try to get to zero
pollution!

As more pollutants are removed,
the cost of removing each
additional unit gets higher and
higher.

The increasing cost of cleaning up

Cost Per Unit of Pollutant Removed ($)

0   25%   50%   75%   100%

Percentage of Pollutants Removed

On this graph, as you
move to the right you
get less pollution, but
a lot more clean-up
cost per unit of
pollution removed.

For liquid effluents there are stages in the clean-up process. "Primary treatment" takes the large particles out. Primary treatment is not very expensive and
gets rid of a lot of pollutants. But then secondary treatment costs a lot more. It
takes out a lot less pollutants per dollar spent.

The same principles apply to smoke stacks. The cleaner you get the "air"
coming out of the stack, the more expensive it may get to clean it up even more.

Would this same principle hold for the society as a whole? Could society go
a long way toward cleaning up pollution at a fairly low cost? Then would it
become terribly expensive to get all the way to zero pollution? Right!

The U.S. Environmental Protection Agency has estimated that about $60
billion would be sufficient to remove more than 85 percent of the water pollutants of industries and municipalities by 1982. But to reduce the pollutants to
zero? That would cost $320 billion! That's *more than five times the cost, to clean up
about one-seventh as much!*

Fig. 30-2   The Producer's Demand for Nature's Waste-Disposal Services

At a price of zero the producer will dump everything. So even a low pollution charge will make it profitable to clean up quite a lot.

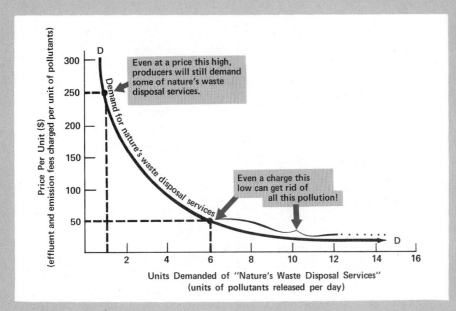

Units Demanded of "Nature's Waste Disposal Services"
(units of pollutants released per day)

On this graph as you go to the right you get more pollution—that is, more demand for the use of nature's waste-disposal services.

This graph derives from the previous one. If the cost of polluting is zero, then a great amount of nature's waste-disposal services will be used. It's a free good. Why not use it?

A low charge on pollution will provide an incentive for firms to eliminate all those kinds of pollution which can be eliminated for low cost. But after that, what happens?

As the pollution charges get higher and higher and the businesses get their effluents and emissions cleaner and cleaner, it becomes more and more expensive for them to clean up even more. That's why it would be so very expensive to try to get to zero pollution—either for a firm or for a society.

You can see that this demand curve, just as the increasing-cost curve on the previous graph, applies to the society as well as it applies to the individual firm. Society can clean up quite a lot of pollution without very much cost. But as it gets closer to zero pollution the marginal cost gets higher and higher for each additional unit of "pollution removal."

Fig. 30-3   The Supply and Demand for Nature's Waste-Disposal Services

The government could decide how much liquid and gaseous "dumping" to permit, and then auction off that number of "dumping rights."

Each "dumping right" would permit the holder to release one unit of pollutant into the ecosystem.

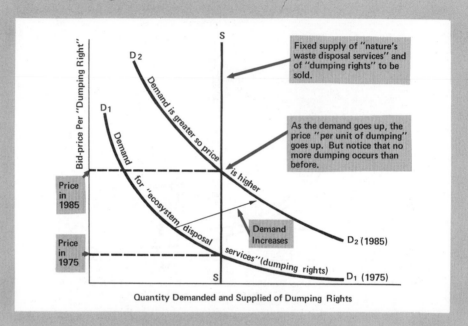

Quantity Demanded and Supplied of Dumping Rights

Would it be possible for governments to find out how much "dumping" into the air and water could be permitted without seriously undesirable results? And then allow that much dumping? and no more? And could they sell the "rights to dump" to the highest bidder? Probably. It would be hard to get people to agree on how much is acceptable and how much is too much. But it would be a very efficient way to internalize the externalities and protect the environment.

You can see from the graph that as industrial activity in some area expands and the demand for the disposal services of the ecosystem go up, the price of the fixed supply of "dumping rights" would go up. The cost of production in that area would go up, too. It would be necessary to spend more on pollution control equipment in that area. Perhaps firms would move to other areas where "dumping rights" could be obtained at lower cost because the pressure on the environment there was not so great.

With this approach, producers who could use cheaper equipment to clean up their wastes instead of buying the high priced dumping rights, would do so.

It won't be easy to work out the details. It won't be easy to get people to agree on the quantity and kinds of dumping to be permitted in each area. Some will say "none." Others will say "much more." But the approach (if it can be made to work) is a good one.

Fig. 30-4   Finding the Optimum Social Level of Dumping into the Ecosystem

Society should try to minimize social cost. If the social cost of cleaning up pollution gets greater than the social cost of the pollution itself, then we've gone too far.

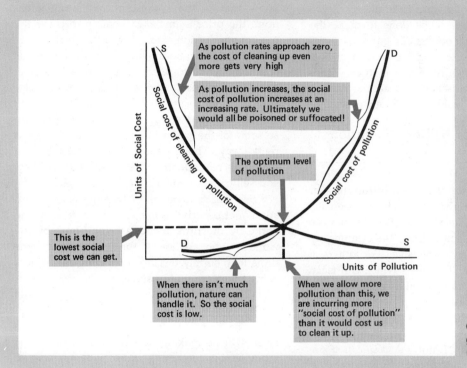

As pollution rates approach zero, the cost of cleaning up even more gets very high

As pollution increases, the social cost of pollution increases at an increasing rate. Ultimately we would all be poisoned or suffocated!

The optimum level of pollution

Units of Social Cost

Social cost of cleaning up pollution

Social cost of pollution

This is the lowest social cost we can get.

Units of Pollution

When there isn't much pollution, nature can handle it. So the social cost is low.

When we allow more pollution than this, we are incurring more "social cost of pollution" than it would cost us to clean it up.

On this graph, as you go to the right you get more pollution.

As pollution gets worse and worse, the social cost goes up very fast. But going the other way, as pollution gets lower and lower, the social cost of cleaning up even more gets higher and higher. So what is the "optimum pollution level"? Where the social cost is at a minimum. Of course.

If the amount of pollution in an area gets greater than the "optimum" level, then society can improve its welfare by cleaning up. The "social cleanup cost" is less than the "social pollution cost."

But suppose pollution is held to less than the optimal level. That means the society is incurring greater cleanup costs than the pollution costs they're preventing! That's not a very good deal.

This looks all very clear and straightforward on a graph. But wait until you try to get people like the environmentalists of the Sierra Club and the business leaders in the public utilities and heavy industries to agree on where to put this "social cost of pollution" curve! It isn't going to be easy to get people to agree on the social cost of different levels of pollution!

When you see a smoke stack, something's coming out of it. Usually you can't see the smoke anymore. It isn't really smoke. But something's coming out other than pure clean air. Or when you see an effluent pipe flowing into the river, it may look like it's dumping clear water. But I don't think you'd want to drink it.

What would have to be done to make the smoke stack release nothing but pure clean air? Or the pipe release nothing but pure drinkable water?—and at normal river temperature? That's what would be necessary to go all the way to "zero pollution." It would be very expensive.

An Advantage of Selling "Pollution Rights"

An advantage of using **pollution fees** or selling **"dumping rights"** is that this approach allows each firm to decide how far it should go in cleaning up. For some firms, the cleaning up process may be very expensive. For others it may be inexpensive. The firms which can clean up at low cost certainly should—and with this approach they certainly will.

The firms which can clean up only at very high cost should be permitted to dump wastes within tolerable limits. If not, *the social cost of prohibiting the dumping will be greater than the social cost of the dumping.*

What happens when a producer's costs go up, either because of pollution regulations or dumping charges? The next section explains that. Then there are some graphs that explain it more.

Who Pays the Cost of Pollution Control?

Earlier in this chapter you already heard that "thou art" going to pay the cost of protecting the environment. Ultimately it's the people who must pay. But what about the steps in the process? How does it come about?

Suppose the government requires a local manufacturing plant to put "scrubbers" or "elec-

tronic precipitators" into their smokestacks to reduce air pollution. Who is going to pay the cost?

The Model Market System. First look back at the model pure market system. You know that in the "long-run equilibrium situation" the price is just high enough to cover the cost of production, including a "normal profit" for the producer. So the increased waste disposal cost is going to force the firms into a loss position. The increased cost is going to reduce supply.

The reduced supply will push the price up so some of the cost will be shifted to the buyers right away. Then some firms will start leaving this high-cost industry. They will lay off workers and sell off equipment.

See what's happening? During the short-run adjustment period some of the cost is being borne by the firm. Some is being borne by the workers who are losing their jobs and by the firms who supply the industry. Only part of it is being borne by the consumers.

What about the long run? In the model market system you know exactly what will happen. The firms remaining in the industry once again will be making normal profits. All of the input factors remaining in the industry will be receiving their normal returns. So who will be paying the cost of the pollution controls? The consumers of the product? Of course.

What About the Real World? In real-world markets it usually works the same way, only quicker. When producers see the cost go up that gives them an immediate excuse to increase the price. So they do.

But then don't they lose their customers to other sellers? Not usually. The other sellers are faced with the same problem. So they raise their "administered prices" too. Otherwise all of them would lose money. But sometimes producers in other parts of the country may not have to clean up so much and that may give them an advantage.

As all the prices go up to reflect the higher cost, don't the buyers buy less? And doesn't that result in reduced profit for the producers? Maybe so. In the short run the cost probably is shared by both the consumer-buyers and the producer-sellers.

What about the workers and other input suppliers for this industry? As this industry produces less, some of the workers will lose their jobs. Some of the suppliers will sell less and maybe lose money, too. You can see that some of the workers and suppliers may bear a part of the burden too.

What about the long run? That's going to be different? Of course. The demand is going to be much more elastic. People who were buying the output of the "high polluting" industry are going to find other acceptable substitutes to use instead.

The supply will adjust, too. The industry is going to decline. How much the industry declines will depend a lot on the *relative seriousness* of the pollution problem in the industry. An industry which is by nature very "dirty" and difficult and expensive to clean up is going to be hit much harder than one which is naturally cleaner.

Some of the dirty industries may be put out of business entirely! Then who is hurt? Who bears the ultimate cost? All three: the consumers (who can't get the product), the producers (who are forced out of business) and the workers and other input suppliers (who lose their sources of income).

Of course, in the very long run there will be time for the workers to be relocated elsewhere, for all the suppliers to shift over and start supplying other industries, and for the producers who were losing money in this industry to get out and go into something else.

In the Long Run It's the People Who Pay

Here's the point: For a while the producers and the workers and the suppliers are likely to share the increased waste disposal cost with the consumers of the product. But if you wait long enough, things will all shift around so that the buyers are the ones who will be paying the cost.

You'll probably get a truer picture of the situation if you'll think of it as "the society" paying the cost. People in general are going to have a somewhat lower standard of living than otherwise would have been attainable. The increased costs of waste disposal are going to be shared by all of us.

In the years to come, waste disposal and environmental protection costs are going to become a part of the cost of just about everything being produced. Some pollution control cost is going to be included in the price of just about everything.

Textbook publishing companies certainly don't pollute the environment. But the paper companies which supply them paper? and the gasoline companies which supply them fuel? and the petrochemical companies which supply them ink? and the utility companies which provide them electricity? The list could go on and on. Get the point? The cost of protecting the environment is going to get embodied in everything. We are all going to pay for it.

The political process might work fine if everyone could **agree** on everything.... But they can't!

When production cost for everything goes up, that means we can't produce as many things as before. So we can't have as many things as before. More of our output is going to be shifted from consumer goods and industrial goods into environmental protection and waste disposal goods. And you can't eat those things!

Figure 30-5 shows the market for a product which is suddenly hit with an increase in waste-disposal cost. Then Figure 30-6 shows a picture of the cost curves of one firm in this industry. I think these two figures will round out your understanding of the economics of the pollution problem.

Fig. 30-5   How Output Markets React to the Cost Increase When Pollution Controls Are Imposed

This shows the short-run and long-run effects of the increased cost from pollution controls, or from effluent fees.

This graph assumes that as firms leave the industry and the supply is shifting from S_2 to S_3, the pollution control cost gets lower—either because of new, more efficient technology, or because as the industry gets smaller the pollution problem becomes easier to handle. That's why the new long-run price is lower than the short-run price.

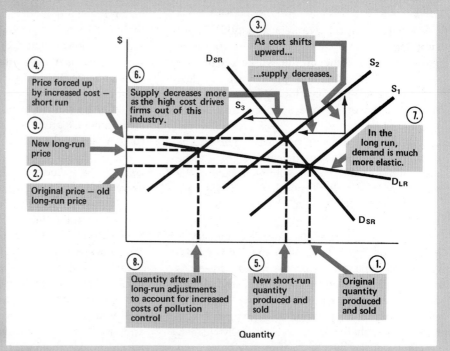

How much smaller the output of this industry is, if you wait long enough for the buyers to find acceptable substitutes! Less than half as much of this product is produced! But isn't that the way it should be?

This is a product which generates a lot of pollution. The cost of the pollution has been included in the price of the product and in the long run the rationing function of price is taking care of the pollution problem for us.

As you look at this graph you can see the adjustment problem for the people in this industry. It will be tough. More than half the workers will lose their jobs. The towns and cities where this industry is located are going to lose jobs and tax revenues. Investors in these businesses are going to lose money. All these people will be unhappy about this and they will fight hard to prevent it from happening to them. Wouldn't you?

It's one thing to be "highly in favor of" a clean environment. It's quite another thing to know that a specific regulation is going to wipe out your life's savings or throw you out of a job or make you lose your house or lose your ability to help your kids through college.

Some of the social costs of cleaning up pollution are going to be very high. We must get on with the task of course. But we shouldn't make believe that it's going to be easy.

Fig. 30-6   How the Firm in Monopolistic Competition Reacts to the Increased Costs of Pollution Control

It works out just like any other cost increase. You learned about that for markets of pure competition back in Chapter 25. Here you can see what happens when a firm has some monopoly power—as in the real world most firms do.

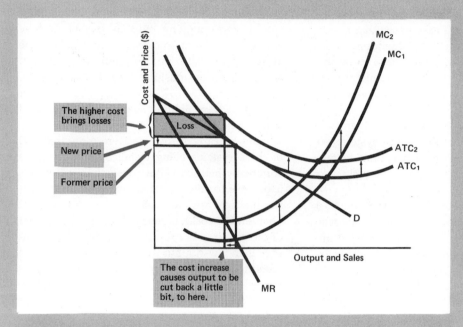

You can look at this graph and see that this firm is selling its product in a market structure of monopolistic competition.

A shift in the cost curves will shift the maximum profit position. Why? Because MC = MR at a different rate of output than before.

This graph shows that this producer was making no excess profits before the pollution control costs were imposed. After the cost increase the firm is losing money.

If the producer had been making profits before, the demand and marginal revenue curves in this graph would simply be shifted up higher. The pollution control cost would wipe out some of the profit. Maybe all of it.

In the long-run what will happen? This firm is going to get out of this business—that is, unless something happens to increase the demand and the price, or to reduce the cost.

As some firms leave this industry, the demand for the output of the remaining firms will increase. So they can raise their prices and sell more at the same time! When the demand for the output of the remaining firms increases enough, their losses will be eliminated. No longer will it be necessary for them to get out of the industry. The industry can stabilize at that level.

How much less will the industry be producing, when it's stabilized? The previous Figure (30-5) showed it would be quite a bit smaller. It all depends on the elasticity of the long-run demand for the product, of course.

How Much Pollution? It's a Matter of Choice

It's not easy to keep the questions of pollution controls and environmental protection in proper perspective. It is easy to argue for zero pollution. But you know the idea of zero pollution just doesn't make sense.

It's easy to blame environmental problems on economic growth. It's easy to see that as economic growth has occurred, the environment has gotten messed up. But it didn't have to be that way. The defect wasn't in the economic growth. The defect was in our own socio-economic institutions.

The problem was that the environment was outside the protection of the market-system. We were depending on the market system to take care of things which it couldn't possibly take care of!

There is no reason to conclude from the past that we must now stop all economic growth in order to stop pollution. No. That isn't the answer. It's just a matter of *choice among alternative directions of progress.*

The economic, social and political processes which have permitted the pollution and environmental destruction to occur now must be turned toward solving the problem and preventing it in the future. That's all.

It's only recently that the United States and most other countries began to take a serious interest in the problem. For many years environmental protection groups—the Sierra Club and others—have been pushing to get something done. But it's only in the last decade or so that some definite action has been taken.

In 1969 the Council on Environmental Quality was set up. In 1970 the Federal Environmental Protection Agency was established. If you want to find out something about the seriousness of the pollution problem and about what's being done, go to your library and find the annual reports of these two agencies. Or write either of these agencies in Washington—or to your congressional representative or senator. You'll get a wealth of interesting things. Why not try it?

New Technology Can Help: the Example of the Coal Scrubber

Environmental protection in an economy like the United States is a very complex thing. There aren't any easy answers. But definite progress is being made. New pollution control-waste disposal technologies are being developed.

Take the example of the coal scrubber. It's a system for removing sulphur oxides so they won't escape from smokestacks and pollute the atmosphere. The Environmental Protection Agency has been pushing for the coal scrubber, but as recently as 1975 the major electric power companies were fighting against it as "unproved and unreliable."

But by early 1976 there were more than 100 of these systems being installed. The system is admittedly high cost. But consider this: It makes it possible for the power companies to use high-sulphur coal without polluting the atmosphere. That kind of coal happens to make up 90 percent of the coal in this country. It produces more energy than low-sulphur coal and it's located in the eastern part of the country where most of it is needed.

Furthermore, the high-sulphur coal can be taken from deep mines. This doesn't destroy the landscape as does the surface-cut "strip mine" operation which is used in the West to produce most of the low-sulphur coal.

The externalities of waste disposal and environmental destruction are being internalized. So incentives and efforts to develop new technologies are being greatly increased. You may be quite sure that a lot of progress is going to be made.

All is not yet perfect with the coal scrubber, of course. But this example is good enough to illustrate the idea that technology can go a long way in helping us to solve the problem.

Increased Population Brings Increased Pollution

Some people blame the pollution problem on the fact that population has been expanding too fast. We know that population has been ex-panding fast. No question about that. But it isn't just a question of population size.

Population can continue to expand and the environmental problem can still be solved. It's a question of choice among alternatives. But the population issue is a serious one. If it could be solved that would help on the environmental problem. So what about the population issue? The next section talks about that.

THE POPULATION EXPLOSION: THE ECONOMIC PROBLEM OF WALL-TO-WALL PEOPLE

Human beings have been on earth for thou-sands of centuries. But it was "only yesterday" that suddenly there were *lots of people* on the earth. At the time of the first Crusade (about 1100 A.D.) the population of the world only amounted to about 300 million people. Then in the 4 centuries between the first crusade and the time Columbus discovered America, the world's population expanded by about 50 percent—to abut 450 million.

Then in the next 3 centuries (by the time the United States was created as a nation) the world's population *doubled*—to about 900 million. Then in the next *one* century (the 1800s) it almost doubled again! Now it appears that the number of people in the world may double again (may increase by *three billion*) in only 40 years (1960-2000). You can see what is happening!

The World's Population Is Exploding

Just think. In 1900 when the world entered this century there were about 1.5 billion people on earth. By 1960 there were about 3 billion. By the end of this century (by the year 2000) the number could reach 6 billion. Three fourths of the total (4.5 billion) is being added just during this century. Explosion? You bet. Is there any wonder we have a pollution problem? And lots

of other serious problems?

It has been said that "of all the people who have ever been alive on earth since the begin-ning of time, half of them are alive today." That's a sobering thought. Here's another. The number of children who will be born during *your* lifetime will be greater than the total number of children who have been born before you, *since the beginning of time!*

It's just hard to conceive of the dimensions and seriousness of the population problem. Un-less mankind can work out the means for drasti-cally curtailing the number of births, then nature will take care of the problem for us—probably by arranging for most of us to die off!

People Are Pouring into the Cities

Where are all these people? These three billion, going on six billion, most of whom are in their teens and younger? They're all over the world. They're in the high-in-come advanced countries, they're in the low-income ad-vancing countries, and they're in the poverty-stricken under-developed countries. They're everywhere. They're in India and China, Mexico and Brazil, Japan, western Europe, the United States, Canada, Russia, Australia, Africa, South Ameri-ca, Indonesia—everywhere.

Wherever they are, masses of them are moving to the cities—thousands every day—a constant, steady, increasing stream. Why do they pour into the cities? Because there's nowhere else for them to go. The greatest migration the world has ever known is the one that's going on right now—the millions of people pouring into the cities. It's happening everywhere the world over. Every day it gets larger.

Suppose a peasant farmer has enough land to get by on. Then there are six or eight or a

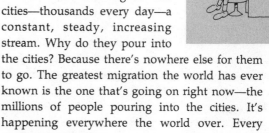

dozen children. Maybe all of them can eke out a semi-starvation existence from the little bit of land. But then by the time the children are in their mid-teens the girls start having babies and raising families of their own—perhaps each of them having six or eight or a dozen children.

Where can all these people go? What can they do? They go to the cities to try to find something to do—some means of existence. But wherever they go, whatever they do, they keep having children. Babies, babies, babies, everywhere babies.

Yes, it's true that more than half of the people alive on the earth right now are in their teens or younger. In China the number of children under ten is greater than the total population of the United States! In most countries most of those in their teens are already having more babies. And the flood of surplus population keeps pouring faster and faster into the already overburdened cities. How long can it continue? Not very long, now. Not very long at all.

Population Growth Is Very Difficult to Control

The flood of babies pouring into the world is going to have to be stopped. But how? Every individual has feelings about this. Every society has its taboos, its restrictions, its religious beliefs about the "right" or the "obligation" to bear children. Getting around all of that is going to be a tough task.

Here's another tough one. Some people, some organizations, some groups, some nations see *strength in numbers*. Having lots of children can provide a kind of "social security"—the children can care for their aging parents. Or if a "good Democrat" or a "good Episcopalian" raises a dozen children, chances are most of them will turn out to be good Democrats or good Episcopalians. If the French-Canadians or the Irish Catholics or the Southern Blacks want to gain political control of some area, if they just keep having enough babies, sooner or later they "tip the balance"—especially if all the other peo-

ple are all trying to have small families and slow down the population boom. Even the leaders of some nations still see "strength in numbers" and hesitate to curb the baby boom.

"Everybody just like me, who agrees with me, who wants what I want, should have lots of babies. Everyone else should stop!" See the problem?

Cooperative and Decisive Action Is Essential

Several of the nations of the world are aware of what must be done. Many of them are trying. The U.N. is working on it. In India where the problem is very serious, the government has been trying to slow the birthrate but without much success. In 1976 Mrs. Gandhi's government announced that several of a person's rights, privileges, and government benefits would be removed if they had a third child. Also, government employment would be denied.

Drastic measures such as this may help some. But they don't reach the remote rural areas where most of the problem stems from.

The technology of birth control is just now getting good enough so that a solution is becoming *technically* possible. But technology is not enough. The socio-cultural problems are going to be really tough to overcome. Multibillion dollar programs—a massive thrust of energy and effort to bring down the birth rate—are going to be required. Nobody knows where these billions of dollars' worth of energy and effort are going to come from.

What's the ultimate answer? First a lot of people are going to have to become aware of the imperative need for population control. The international community, all nations, must work together to convince the people of what must be done. Then the governments must provide the assistance and the incentives required to do the job. The *political process* must direct resources toward this objective.

The tidal wave of new babies will be brought under control, because it must. The only questions are: how soon? and in what ways?

In the meantime, what happens to the ones who already have been born? and to the ones who will be born? What about today's little babies, young children, teenagers?

They will continue to grow up. Many of them will pour into the already overcrowded cities. The population crush in the metropolitan areas—just from those who are already born—will continue to get worse. It's in the cities where the full force of the population explosion does its damage. It's going to get a lot worse before it gets better.

The next chapter is going to begin by talking about the problems of the urban areas. Then it will go into the problems of poverty and discrimination.

But before you go on, be sure you understand the nature of the environmental problem. That's really a critical issue for modern society. It's an issue on which popular discussion often generates more heat than light. Spend enough time to really understand it. That will put you far ahead of most people.

SUMMARY AND SYNTHESIS

The **meaning of progress in any society, is relative. Progress means movement toward the desired objectives. And objectives are different** from one society to another and from one time to another.

Progress frequently **uncovers or creates new problems.** Several of the problems of modern society have been created by the economic progress which has been made in the past. So now **directions of progress are being changed to aim toward some of these new problems.**

Everyone in a modern society **contributes to the pollution problem, either through direct (final) pollution or derived pollution.** Most of us have not been required to **pay the cost of preventing or cleaning up this pollution. But that's changing as costs of production and prices are going up** to reflect the cost of protecting and cleaning up the environment.

Since the pollution problem is a problem of **externalities, the political process** must get involved. The government can approach this problem by (1) **regulations and enforcement,** (2) **selling waste disposal rights,** or (3) **providing incentives to businesses** to induce them to install anti-pollution equipment. Economists generally favor the second approach because this relies on **the rationing function of price.** This approach would be most likely to achieve the desired results

with **minimum detrimental effect** to the efficiency of the economy.

Modern technology has helped to create the pollution problem, and modern technology **must now be relied upon to deal with it.**

As wastes are cleaned up, **the cost of cleaning up even more, increases. But the greatest social benefit of the cleanup occurs when the pollution problem is worst.** This means that the **social benefit goes down while the social cost goes up** as addtional cleanup occurs. So where is the **optimum social level of pollution?** Where the **total social cost** (the sum of the cleanup cost plus the pollution cost) **is lowest.**

An **advantage of the sale of "pollution rights"** as an approach to cleaning up pollution is that these pollution rights can be marketable. So those firms which can **clean up cheaply will sell their pollution rights** to those firms which would have **very high costs** of cleaning up. In this way, the limited amount of pollution permitted would be permitted to those firms where the **cost of cleaning up would be greatest.** This would be the **most efficient way** to approach the pollution problem.

In the long run **the people who buy the product must pay the cost** of preventing pollution. The higher cost **discourages production and reduces the supply.** Ultimately the price of the product **must include the cost of cleaning up.** This is true in monopolistic markets as well as competitive markets. In monopolistic markets the adjustment may come more quickly as the administered prices are adjusted upward.

The world population explosion is very real and very serious. In 1900 there were only about **1.5 billion people** on the earth. By 1960 there were 3 billion, and by the end of this century the number **could reach 6 billion.** Three-fourths of the total is being added just during this century. The world cannot support that rate of growth for very long.

Many governments throughout the world are acutely aware of the **serious problems** which this population explosion is generating in their countries. But the problem is **difficult to control.** The most serious focus of this "population crush" is in the **exploding urban areas.** You'll be reading about that in the next chapter.

REVIEW EXERCISES

MAJOR CONCEPTS, PRINCIPLES, TERMS (Explain each carefully.)

the meaning of "progress"
progress and problems
the "socially optimal" level of pollution
who will pay for pollution controls, and why
the population explosion

OTHER CONCEPTS AND TERMS (Explain each briefly.)

externalities
final pollution
derived pollution
dumping rights
Environmental Protection Agency
Council on Environmental Quality

CURVES AND GRAPHS (Draw, label, and explain each.)

The Increasing Cost of Cleaning Up Wastes
The Producer's Demand for Nature's Waste-Disposal Services
The Supply and Demand for Nature's Waste-Disposal Services
Finding the Optimum Social Level of Dumping into the Ecosystem
How Output Markets React to the Cost Increase When Pollution Controls Are
  Imposed
How the Firm in Monopolistic Competition Reacts to the Increased Costs of
  Pollution Control

QUESTIONS (Write out answers or jot down key points.)

1. The "desired directions of progress" in a society are always changing some. In recent years the desired directions have been changing very rapidly. Can you

think of several shifts in the directions of progress, just during the last few years? Discuss.

2. "We have all been 'living high' by not paying the full costs of the things we've been using up." Explain.

3. Can you think of several ways in which you personally are helping to pay some of the cost of environmental protection? Can you think of ways in which you are likely to have to pay more of those costs as time goes on? Discuss.

4. "The reason the environmental problem has grown so rapidly and become so serious is that in the 'market-directed' economies, most of the things which create and contribute to the environmental problem are free from the major control mechanism of the society—that is, are external to the market process." Discuss.

5. "Two ways the environmental problems can be handled are these: (a) force the social costs of each bit of 'environmental destruction' to be reflected in the market process, or (b) establish regulations and prohibitions to protect the environment. Both these approaches require decisive (and sometimes unpopular) actions by the political process." Discuss.

6. Explain some of the reasons why the population problem is so difficult to control.

31

Micro Problems of Modern Society II: Urbanization, Poverty, Discrimination

Chapter Objectives

● This chapter continues where the last chapter left off, discussing some of the **problems** of modern, **real-world market systems**. In this chapter you will find out about the problems of the **urban areas**, and about **poverty, discrimination**, and **anti-poverty programs**.

● When you finish studying this chapter you will be able to **identify** and **explain** several of the problems of the urban areas, including **population spillover, neighborhood deterioration**, and the **urban transportation** problem.

● You will know about some of the **approaches to overcoming these urban problems**, including developing **new towns**, and **federal aid programs**.

● You will know more about the **poverty problem**: about **how serious** it is in the United States, about **how it has changed**, and about **what can be (and is being) done** about it.

● You will know about the difference between programs for "**curing the disease**" **of poverty**, as compared with those designed to "**lessen the discomfort**" **of poverty**. And you will know that there is **no easy solution** to the poverty problem.

FOCUS OF THE POPULATION CRUSH: THE URBAN AREAS

We don't have to wait for a serious problem to appear in the urban areas. That problem is already here.

In the urban areas the population crush and all of the other problems of modern society come into sharp focus. We need to spend a while talking about these urban places—these places where the *acute* symptoms of the *chronic* "population disease" weigh so heavily on so many people.

The Explosive Growth of Urban Areas

About three fourths of the people in the United States are living in urban areas now. More are pouring in all the time. Some forecasters estimate that in the United States, by the end of the present century another 100 million people will be living in urban areas.

That's enough people to make up ten metropolitan areas as large as New York City! Can you picture that? Or it would make up fifteen metropolitan areas the size of Chicago, or Los Angeles-Long Beach. It would make twenty more

Philadelphias or Detroits. It would make up between fifty and a hundred Buffalos or Cincinnatis or Dallases or Denvers or Indianapolises or Kansas Citys or Miamis or Milwaukees or New Orleanses or San Diegos or Seattles.

If you live in a city of only 100,000 population it would take a *thousand more* cities like yours to accommodate all these people! Get the picture? All this is likely to be happening just during the next three or four decades of your lifetime!

All over the world the same thing is going to be happening. In many countries it will happen much faster and it will create many more serious problems than in the United States. Much human suffering is likely to result and there doesn't seem to be much that anybody can do about it.

The Problems of the Urban Areas

The problems of the urban areas are the problems of modern society. Not that all the people with problems are located in the urban areas. Of course not.

Many people live in rural areas and some of them face serious problems, to be sure. In the United States there are several government programs aimed toward overcoming the poverty of people who live in Appalachia, the Ozarks, and in other rural areas. The rural area problems can be very stubborn and difficult to solve. But the really tough challenge to the wisdom, the ingenuity, and the technology of modern society is the challenge of the exploding urban areas.

It is in the urban areas where the serious problems of modern society are concentrated and magnified—expanded into crisis proportions. It is in the urban areas that the environmental crisis is most acute. It's there that the problems of unemployment, inadequate education, inadequate medical

and health facilities, inadequate housing, high crime rates—all the things which are heralded as the "major problems of our society"—come into focus. And it is in the urban areas that the problems are so resistant—so difficult to overcome.

One problem of the urban area is that it is made up of such different parts. Urban areas contain healthy places and sick places. There are the wealthy suburbs and there are the poverty-ridden ghettos. It is in the ghettos—these "isolated cities within the cities" where the problems come most sharply into focus. It is in the ghettos where the solutions to the urban problem will be most difficult. But it's in the ghettos where the solutions are most needed.

The Problem of "Population Spillover"

Yesterday, there was a city. It had its boundary and its people lived within the boundary. Then suddenly, almost overnight the population of the city exploded—spread itself out beyond its own boundaries. When that happened, the city lost control of itself. It lost the means for governing itself, for working out its problems.

Why Did People Move to the Suburbs? As low income people began moving into the city seeking jobs, residential property values began to go down. Then more people began moving out to the suburbs.

Everybody had a car. There were highways connecting the suburbs with the central city so commuting was no serious problem. Once this trend began, the "natural forces of the market" guaranteed that it would continue. The "laws of positive economics" can explain it.

Suppose you live in a neighborhood where the people next door have sold their house and the house has now been subdivided into four apartments. Now there are four families living next door.

As more people move into your neighborhood there's overcrowding in the schools. There are more social welfare costs. There's more congestion. More noise on your street. Life there isn't so pleasant anymore. Then to provide the additional services needed, city tax rates go up.

This is the last straw! You move to the suburbs. You sell your house. Soon it is subdivided into apartments. The process continues.

Neighborhood Deterioration.

Do the buyers of your house and the other houses keep up all this real estate in tip-top condition to "protect their investment"? Of course not.

The market value of each one of these places depends more on what happens to the neighborhood than it depends on what the owner does to the property. So each owner lets the property "go with the neighborhood." So what happens? The neighborhood goes down. It's absolutely guaranteed!

Once it starts, what can reverse this trend? Local governments try to use zoning laws to prevent the single family residences from becoming apartment houses and to require that property be maintained. This may slow the process. But once the process gets going, it isn't likely that much private money is going to be risked on the future of such a neighborhood!

The people moving out will go to the suburbs and establish zoning laws requiring each house to be expensive and built on a large lot. If all your neighbors' properties are as expensive as yours then your neighbors will carry as much of the local property tax burden as you do. Also, in the suburbs it isn't likely that there will be costly programs for welfare or crime control or fire prevention.

The Fragmentation of the Metropolitan Area.

All over the country and all over the world we see metropolitan areas sliced up into many local government jurisdictions— people living in the county, working in the "central city," visiting their friends in another "little city" nearby—when really it's all one metropolitan area. Usually there's not much coordination among all these local government units. Each "local government unit" has its own leadership, its own tax system, its own local programs, its own little problems to take care of. But the metropolitan area as a whole really doesn't have a "government." Nobody is in charge of the whole thing!

For example, the New York City metropolitan area is made up of some 1,400 different local governments. The San Francisco area includes about 1,000 and the St. Louis metropolitan area includes almost 500 with half of them in Illinois and half of them in Missouri. The pattern is the same in the big metropolitan areas all over the country.

Most of the problems of a metro-area can't be solved in little pieces. The problems are area-wide. It's obvious that the transportation problem, or the problems of education, law enforcement, fire protection, welfare, housing, air and water pollution, employment and such things just can't be solved piece-meal. So what can be done? In the United States, the federal government tries to force some coordination and area-wide program planning in the metropolitan areas.

The federal government now requires that "councils of government" (COG's) or "regional planning councils" be set up to coordinate the programs and plans for the entire metropolitan area—either that, or else the federal government will cut off the grants for the sewer systems and the urban transit systems and such things. The "COG movement" has helped quite a bit—more in some places than in others—but the problem still is far from being solved.

The "Metro Government" Approach.

The city of Toronto, Canada, and a few other cities in the world have established "super governments" that encompass the entire metro-area. The results appear to be very good—but apparently not good enough to convince the "small town" residents of any U.S. metro-area to give up their own independence and toss in with a "metro-area government."

While the urban areas have been growing and their problems multiplying, a financial crisis has been emerging. The "financial base" of the city has been eroding from two sides: (1) the more wealthy taxpayers have moved outside the city where they no longer pay city taxes, while (2) the cost of providing city services have been going higher and higher. So now many of the cities just can't make it on their own.

The Urban Transportation Problem

You'll be surprised how much the urban area problem is tied in with urban area transportation. Without the development of the freeways and everyone (except the very poor) owning a car, the "flight to the suburbs" wouldn't have occurred.

If, instead of the development of freeways, urban mass transit systems had been developed linking the downtown areas with the outlying areas, then the pattern of urban development would have been very different.

Congestion in the downtown areas has gotten worse. Tax rates and property costs and costs of utilities and other services have gone up. Many downtown businesses have moved to the outlying areas to escape all this.

But what of the low-paid workers living in the ghettos and other areas of the central city? When the firms move, how do these people get to work? Many don't own cars. If they did they would have no place to park them and they

couldn't afford to operate them.

Why don't they move out near the jobs? They can't do that either. They can't afford to. And there are various kinds of regulations to prevent them from coming out and "breaking down" the new suburban neighborhoods. Many are locked into the central city with no way to get out.

Urban Mass Transit?

As urban areas grow in the future, it will make a lot of difference what kind of urban transportation system exists in each area. But what will that pattern be? That's hard to say.

Everyone seems to agree that there should be some kind of mass transit system. But most people don't want to ride buses or subways and give up the convenience of driving their own cars.

If no one is going to ride the mass transit except the poor, then mass transit is going to be a losing proposition. Are the taxpayers going to want to pay for it? And maintain adequate standards? Just so the poor can ride? These are important issues. They won't be solved easily.

Federal Government Programs

In the 1950s conditions in many urban areas kept getting worse. So the federal government was called on for help and it began to get involved. The Department of Housing and Urban Development (HUD) was set up. Various "urban renewal" programs began to be undertaken.

Under the urban renewal programs, hundreds of thousands of ghetto housing units have been demolished in various cities throughout the country. Low-cost housing has been built. Urban throughways have been built to speed automobile traffic.

More recently (1964, 1966, and later) urban mass transit acts were passed providing federal funds to help provide mass transit systems. In 1975 the federal government for the first time subsidized operating expenses on some urban mass transit systems.

Federal grants have been given to the cities for many different purposes. The programs have been expanded over the past 25 years. Several approaches have been tried—urban renewal, community renewal, model cities, various housing programs and others.

There is no question that some impressive things have been done. A look at Atlanta or Norfolk or Buffalo or Philadelphia or Dallas or Houston or St. Louis or many other cities throughout the nation shows the physical success of several urban renewal programs. Still, most of what has been done so far has been more "panic relief" than carefully planned, long-range problem-solving.

Some progress has been made, but we haven't yet aimed enough resources, enough effort at this "urban problem" to get very many things really "solved." In the future, more permanent solutions are going to be required. Many people are worrying about it and working on it.

The U.S. Advisory Committee on Intergovernmental Relations has recommended (1) that some kind of effective coordination among the local governmental units—between the cities and villages and counties and townships and all the others which make up each "metro-area"—be worked out; (2) that the cost of public education be taken over entirely by the state governments; (3) that the cost of the welfare program be taken over entirely by the federal government; and (4) that the federal government give "no strings attached" grants to help out the local governments in the urban areas.

Developing "New Towns"

Another recommendation of the Advisory Committee (and of others) is that we develop many more "new towns." That would take some of the population pressures off the existing cities. This means that we go out into the rural areas and find suitable undeveloped sites and develop entirely new cities.

In recent years several "new towns" have been developed in the United States and in other countries. It's likely that many more "new towns" will be developed. These new towns will absorb some of the (perhaps 100 million) people who will pour into U.S. urban areas (and some of the thousands of millions who will pour into urban areas throughout the world) during the next few decades.

New towns will help. But they won't solve the problem. For one thing, "new towns" won't necessarily be "better towns." But more serious than that, it's the already overburdened *existing* cities which are going to feel most of the pressure. They are going to have to be greatly strengthened, both politically and economically, if they are going to be able to handle the task without worsening "the mess" which we have already allowed most of them to get into.

The Impediments Are Many and Serious

The problems of the urban areas will not be solved by economics alone. Some of the major impediments are political, social, traditional, psychological, cultural. The key individuals in each little borough or suburb or county government don't want to give up their positions of status or power. Racial, nationality, religious, and cultural groups within the metropolitan area don't want to give up whatever "local government control" they may have and toss in with some distant, impersonal "metrogovernment."

Urban Renewal May Harm the Poor. Many people fear change. The people who feel at home in the ghetto may be very wary about those "social planners" who are out to tear down their neighborhoods and disrupt their familiar pattern of life—the only pattern of life they have ever known.

And what about this? After the urban renewal demolishers come through, where will these people live? The government may provide "low cost housing" at maybe $200 a month. But in their slum dwellings some of these families have been paying less than half that much!

So maybe they did have to walk down a dark hallway to get to the cold-water bathroom. And maybe they would step on a cockroach on the way. Not very pleasant, true. But at least they could pay the rent and have money left for enough food to get by on. After they move into the government "low cost housing" how are they going to make it? They were already living on a malnutrition budget!

Don't forget why all these people drifted into the ghetto in the first place. It isn't necessarily because they prefer the surroundings. It's because *they can afford to live there.*

A person who only has $200 a month to live on would rather give up housing than food. If urban renewal means forcing more housing (and less food) on the poverty stricken people, then it isn't a very humanitarian program. It may make the city look prettier for visiting dignitaries. But it doesn't solve the problem of people who inhabit the central city. Sometimes urban renewal programs have not given enough attention to this problem.

Urban Renewal Will Be Expensive. Fixing up the cities will not be easy. Just think of the many billions of dollars' worth of resources it's going to take just to get the "physical plant" in shape: all the tearing down and rebuilding; the development of transit systems; greatly improved waste disposal and anti-pollution services; better housing, schools, hospitals.

And what about the "people oriented" programs? Better education, training, manpower development, health, recreation, job development and all that? And with the constant flood of new people pouring into the area, while costs keep going higher and higher? This is a tough one, right?

The Population Problem Doesn't Help. Ultimately it could help a lot if the *population problem* could be solved. Think of a problem of modern society. Just pick a problem—any problem. Does the population explosion have anything to do with it? Chances are it does.

The population problem is a major cause of the urban problem and the pollution problem and of many of the other problems of our society. When the flood of births is brought into check, many of our problems will become more manageable.

While we are waiting to get the flow of births slowed down we must keep working on the problems in the urban areas, and on the environmental crisis. Another is the *poverty problem.* It's time to talk about that now.

POVERTY: WHAT IS IT? AND HOW BAD IS IT IN THE UNITED STATES?

What is poverty? Poverty is not being able to have what most people have—not being able to live like most people live. It's like hearing the jingle of the ice cream truck and peeking out from behind the curtain, watching the other kids buying ice cream and knowing that you can't have any.

It's like hearing your mother in the bedroom crying because she has no money to give you for lunch. It's like having to be always pleading with people not to disconnect the electricity or the telephone or to repossess the car or the TV set—like being forced to move from one shabby apartment to another because you can't pay the rent—like trying to hide from your "well-off" friends so they won't see how poor you are and feel sorry for you.

The kind of poverty I'm talking about is the poverty of an affluent society like the United States. In less developed countries poverty means something quite different. It may mean having no home, sleeping in the streets, getting wet when it rains—going for days with no food—having no access to medical care—someday dying of sickness and malnutrition.

Poverty Is Always Relative

Poverty is always "relative to the people around you." It means "being deprived of the things the people around you have." It may be defined as: "not having enough to meet basic needs." It's easy for everyone to agree on that.

But what do we mean by "basic needs"? And how much money does that take? That's where people disagree. In the United States in the early 1970s the government defined the "basic needs" income as being about $4500 for a family of four. By the early 1980s, this figure had been adjusted upward to about $8,500.

You can see that these minimum basic income figures couldn't be very exact. Picture a family of four healthy people living on a farm, growing much of their own food and living in their own house and receiving a cash income of a little less than $6000 a year. By the government's definition they might be living in poverty. But they might think of themselves as quite well-to-do. Probably they're living as well as (or better than) most of their neighbors and friends!

Now put that same family in a tenement house in the heart of a big city where they must pay for everything, with no relatives or friends to share vegetables and hand-me-downs. Suddenly they're poor. Where you live and how you live and who your neighbors are can make all the difference! Also it makes a lot of difference whether the family includes young children or teenagers or grandparents and whether or not any of them have chronic illnesses.

Any income definition of "the poverty line" is bound to be too high for some families and too low for others. Still, if we're going to set up any practical programs to cure poverty we must have some way of deciding who qualifies and who doesn't! We must have some measurable definitions. Since there is no "right" definition let's hope our programs can be flexible enough to take care of the injustices which will result from the definitions we choose.

In the United States the Social Security Administration has developed measurements of "basic needs" and estimates of how much income is required for a family to be above the "poverty level." In their measurement, the Social Security Administration makes an adjustment to

account for the rural or urban location of the family.

If you would like to see what some of the current estimates are of the income required for "basic needs" and of the numbers of people who fall below this "poverty line," go to your library and look in the *Current Population Reports*, published by the U.S. Department of Commerce.

How Many Americans Are Living in Poverty?

Using these (admittedly inexact) "minimum income" definitions of poverty, how many people in the United States are "living in poverty"? More than one family in ten. More than five million families. A lot of people, to be sure. If you look just at the black and other minority families, you see about one family in four with incomes below the poverty line. Also, if you look at families headed by very young men or very old men or by women, you will see a high incidence of poverty.

About a third of all the Americans living in poverty are living in fatherless households. Most of them, of course, are children. There are about ten million children and teenagers under 18 living in households with incomes below the government's poverty line.

None of these measures or indicators of poverty is very precise or accurate. Still, there's enough evidence to be convincing. Yes, we can be quite sure that a very real poverty problem does exist in our affluent American society.

Changing Patterns of Income Distribution in the United States

If you look at the trend in income distribution over the past several decades, there are two clear conclusions:

(1) The percentage of the population living in poverty has gone down greatly since World War II. In 1947 about 30 percent of Americans were living below the pov-

erty line. By 1960 the percentage was down to about 20 percent. By the early 1980s the number had dropped to less than 12 percent.

That kind of reduction in the percentage of people in poverty is gratifying, of course. But it still leaves more than 25 million Americans living with less than a "basic needs" income. Many of these are victims of some kind of disability, or are living in a household where there is no husband to help to support the family.

(2) Since World War II, the extent of inequality of income distribution in the United States hasn't changed very much. Rising incomes, supplemented by the social security program and other programs have done a lot to overcome the poverty at the low end of the income scale.

But in terms of "percentage of income received" the 20 percent of the people who receive the lowest incomes are still receiving about the same percentage of the total as they were receiving 30 years ago (between 5 and 6 percent of the total income). The 20 percent of the people who receive the highest incomes are still receiving about the same percentage of the total as they were receiving 30 years ago (about 40 percent of the total income.)

We use a Lorenz curve to show the percentage breakdown of income distribution. A "Lorenz curve" showing the income distribution pattern for the United States in the early 1980s is explained in Figure 31-1. If you will study that Figure now I think you'll get a clear picture of income distribution in the United States.

Profiles in Poverty

It's difficult for most people to visualize a poverty situation. If you're from a middle or upper income family, how can you picture a family in poverty? If you begin by picturing a family like *your* family, you'll never make it. A family like your family wouldn't be in poverty.

Try to picture what your family would have been like if your father had died before you were old enough to remember. Or suppose he had contracted some kind of disabling disease that required a lot of medical expenses. And suppose there were no well-to-do relatives to help out. And suppose there were already three young children ahead of you, and another due in a few months. What would life have been like for you, then? Very different. Right?

The most frequent, most serious profile of a poverty family is the profile of a fatherless household where there are small children. Other "profiles in poverty" would include families with disabled or otherwise unproductive fathers, and families of high school drop-outs who get married in their teens, start producing children and try to make it on their own.

For another profile, you might picture a household headed by a middle-aged or older man, perhaps not too bright, not too flexible, whose skills have been made obsolete by changing times. If the man happens to be a member of a minority race or has a poor employment record or a prison record or some other "undesirable characteristics" (or even if he doesn't) he may not be able to get another job. After months or maybe years of looking, he may just give up. Many do.

Other profiles in poverty would show you families living on seasonal employment, working at part-time jobs, temporary jobs, low-paying jobs. Often the poverty is worsened by a large number of people depending on one low-wage earner. If the family includes aging relatives, plus several children, the paycheck just won't meet the needs.

The Poor: Who Are They? Where Are They? A lot of poor people are old people—people who can no longer be self-supporting who are living on what they can get from relatives, savings, and government assistance pro-

Fig. 31-1   Income Distribution in the United States by Population and Income Groups: the Lorenz Curve

This income distribution pattern has been approximately the same for the past 30 years.

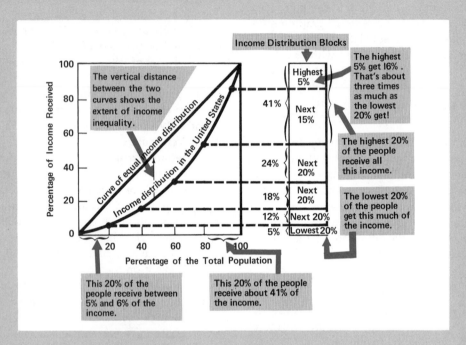

THE LORENZ CURVE

The Lorenz curve keeps adding more people as you go to the right along the horizontal axis, and adding more income as you go up along the vertical axis. You add the low income people first. So as you start at the zero point and go to the right along the horizontal axis the curve doesn't go up very much. Then as you go farther to the right along the horizontal axis you begin to add people with higher incomes. So the curve gets steeper.

For the last few people added, the curve goes almost straight up. Those people are making millions! But look over near the zero corner at how little income is earned by the first few people. The lowest five percent of the people have almost no income at all!

Generally speaking, there isn't much mobility of individuals or families along the horizontal scale of this graph. The poor usually stay poor and the rich usually stay rich. But there are many exceptions to this general rule. Poor people sometimes work their way into better income situations. And some affluent families are struck by disaster and forced down into poverty.

Before the 1930s, income distribution in the United States was more unequal than it is now. In 1929 the top 5 percent of the population received 30 percent of all the income. These days the top 5 percent receive about 16 percent.

This curve shows income before taxes. What about after taxes? Do taxes reduce income inequality in the United States? Not much. Economists disagree about how much. There are some progressive (soak the rich) taxes like the income tax. But there are lots of regressive (soak the poor) taxes like sales taxes, too. You'll see more about this when you get to the chapter on taxation.

grams. About one in every twelve people over 65 in the United States is living in poverty.

There is a lot of poverty in agriculture, especially in the South. About one-fourth of all the rural people in the country are poor.

You will find poverty in homes where health problems (physical or mental) are interfering with the ability of the adults to earn money. Sometimes unemployment is responsible. Some jobs—in hotels and motels and retail stores and some others—pay such low wages that even a full-time worker couldn't earn enough to lift the family income above the poverty level.

Poverty occurs four times as often among non-whites as among whites. About one third of all Southern blacks and about one fifth of all Northern blacks are living in poverty.

About one third of all the poor people in the United States live in households which have no man—no husband, no father—to help to support the family. In our society when the mother attempts to take care of the children and earn enough money to provide for the family she is faced with a herculean task. Throw into the picture the sex discrimination which exists in the American labor market and the task for most husbandless mothers becomes impossible.

Poverty Is Self-Perpetuating

An important *cause* of poverty is the *existence* of poverty. Poverty begets poverty. Many people are born and raised in poverty, in neighborhoods where poverty is a way of life. All the influences point toward the poverty pattern of life rather than toward ways to get out of poverty. Avenues of escape are difficult to find. Many people feel beaten before they start—so why try?

A person who is bright, strong, healthy, and capable will find a way to get out of poverty. But only a certain percentage of the people born in any generation are going to be bright, strong, healthy, and capable. The others, if they had been lucky enough to be born into affluent mid-

dle class families, would have been able to do okay. They would have been educated and trained and given all the necessary advantages and "conditioned to succeed." They would have succeeded. But when born in the ghetto and conditioned to the poverty way of life their chances for success are very slim. They will just stay in the ghetto and be the "perpetuating group" left behind when the strongest and most capable ones break out and leave. The ones left behind are trapped by and are the ones who perpetuate the "vicious circle of inherited poverty."

What Can Be Done About Poverty?

When you look at the poverty profiles it's easy to see that simple solutions are not going to solve the problem. No longer is it possible to quip: "If people are poor, let them go to work. If they are unskilled, offer them training and then let them go to work. If they won't take the training and won't go to work then let them go hungry."

How simple this solution seems to be! But how do you apply it to the widowed or unwed or deserted pregnant mother of four small children? How do you apply it to the aged person? or couple? Or to the worker who is not too old to work but is too old to be able to get a job? Or to the men and women who are physically or mentally incapable?

Much, probably *most* of the poverty in the United States can't be "cured" by getting people to go to work. In so many poverty families there

just *isn't anybody* to go to work! Often, even if there is someone who possibly *could* work, there's no *feasible* way to train them and fit them into an available job.

What About Manpower Development?

We need to emphasize manpower training and job development. Obviously. We need such programs as worker education and skill development and on-the-job training, supplemented by job placement services, and subsidies to stimulate new employment opportunities. Of course!

Many such programs are already operating, and progress is being made in overcoming some of the "curable" kinds of poverty. But no matter how far we go in job development, this approach cannot *completely eliminate* the poverty problem. Obviously not. So what can be done?

The Fatherless Household.

What's the most serious "profile in poverty" we see in this country? The fatherless home with small children. Do you suppose the population problem is lurking under the surface here, somewhere? You know it is. If the number of children born into these homes could be reduced, that would help a lot. Improved birth control technology and liberalized abortion laws may lessen the seriousness of this "profile in poverty." But still the problem isn't going to be completely solved that way.

The only way we can really hope to handle the incurable kinds of poverty is to have some programs which will provide money to the families who have no way to generate their own incomes. There's just no other way. What kinds of programs? And how much money? To whom? Under what circumstances? Those are the tough questions. The choices usually reflect more political and social considerations than economic ones. Near the end of this chapter there's a section that talks about programs for overcoming poverty. But first we need to get into the issue of discrimination.

THE PROBLEM OF DISCRIMINATION BY RACE AND SEX

Discrimination is one important cause of poverty. But discrimination is a deep issue. It goes far beyond the problem of poverty. How serious is discrimination as a cause of poverty? It's hard to say. One problem is: it isn't easy to separate present discrimination from the results of past discrimination.

Discrimination Against Blacks

We know that less than 10 percent of the whites and about 30 percent of the blacks live in poverty. Does that mean the blacks are poor because of discrimination? We can't conclude that unless we know more about the situation. Beware of *post hoc ergo propter hoc!* Remember? (But we do know more about the situation.)

We know that blacks generally have not had past opportunities for education, development of skills, job experience, etc., as have whites. And we are seeing some of the results of that, now. Also we know that in almost every field of work blacks have usually received less for doing the same jobs. But progress has been made.

Less than 20 years ago the "average" (median income) black family only earned a little more than half as much as the "average" (median income) white family. By the early 1970s the average black family was earning three fourths as much as the average white family. That shows a lot of progress. And progress is still being made. But we're still a long way from equality.

Blacks have been discriminated against by being hired last and fired first, denied education and training and access to other programs which would permit them to advance. And discrimination in housing helps to lock them into the ghettos where their economic opportunities are seriously limited. Their incomes reflect this discrimination.

The New Economic Role of Women

More than 45 percent of all working-age women are now in the labor force. That's almost one out of every two. In the mid-1970s there were more than 36,000,000 women in the labor force.

Since World War II the role of women in the American economy has really changed! Before World War II—back in the 20s and before—women never made up more than about 20 percent of the labor force.

Now the percentage of women in the labor force is up from about 20 percent to about 40 percent. These days, *two out of every five employed people in the United States are women.*

These figures show the very important role that women are playing in the American economic system. No longer can "working women" be thought of as being "at the fringe" of the economic system, to be taken not too seriously and to be discriminated against.

Discrimination Against Women

Women often are employed in "appropriate female tasks" such as retail sales, clerical work, elementary teaching, nursing, etc., while men are the doctors and lawyers and dentists and engineers and craftsmen and the important business decision makers.

This kind of job separation makes it easy to maintain wage differentials between men and women because "it has traditionally been that way." But even in occupations where men and women compete openly, the men often earn more than the women.

In the early 1970s while men sales workers were averaging more than $10,000 a year, women sales workers were averaging less than $5,000. Men school teachers were averaging more than $10,000 while women were averaging only $8,000. The same patterns existed among clerical workers and among service workers.

As in the case of discrimination against blacks, discrimination against women is under serious attack. The Equal Pay Act of 1963 and the Civil Rights Act of 1964 bar discrimination in hiring and firing and in other job practices and require equal pay for equal work. The actions of the women's liberation movement in court cases have made some significant progress in getting equal pay and job rights for women.

Progress is being made to be sure. But the barriers and traditions are strong. The road is much more open for women and for blacks and other minorities today than in the past. But there are several stretches of that road which are still very rocky for one of unfamiliar sex or color who tries to travel it.

Now it's time to talk about what government has been doing to overcome poverty—about programs we have now and other programs we might have. That's the subject of the next section.

PROGRAMS FOR OVERCOMING POVERTY

Essentially, there are two ways to approach the poverty problem. One way is to try to "cure the disease"—that is, to help the poor people become more productive so they can lift themselves out of poverty and be self-sufficient. The other is to redistribute some of the income from those who earn it to those who need it. Government agencies, private charities and various religious and other organizations are working on this problem, both ways. I'm sure you know that. This section will be talking about government programs, but don't forget that the efforts of the private charities and religious organizations also are important.

Curing "the Disease of Poverty": Manpower Development

The United States has a long tradition of manpower training and development through public education, vocational education, extension services and many other programs. Since the "New Deal" days of the 1930s, the U.S. government has become more involved in these programs. During World War II the government undertook a massive manpower training effort, not to cure poverty, but to increase the output of the economy. But the wartime manpower program cured a lot of poverty. You can be quite sure of that!

In the late 1940s and throughout the 1950s, traditional kinds of manpower training were continued. Then in the early 1960s the Manpower Development and Training Act increased the size and scope of this effort. But it wasn't until the mid-1960s that the *Economic Opportunity Act* was passed, setting up the "anti-poverty program"—that is, the "war on poverty."

The "Economic Opportunity" Program—The "War on Poverty"—1965. The thrust of this new program was to get local people, including poor people, involved in working out innovative ways to overcome poverty. Many things were tried—neighborhood information and help centers, legal aid for the poor, "black capitalism" programs to help small businesses, job development activities, volunteer counseling and help for the poor, and of course, education and training and manpower development.

Several of the efforts supported by OEO (the U.S. Office of Economic Opportunity) failed miserably. Others, including some of the legal aid and counseling and education programs, were generally thought to be very successful. The OEO-sponsored "headstart" program—preschooling to help "culturally deprived" children to get ready for school—was a most popular and apparently very successful program.

The OEO also sponsored educational programs—Sesame Street, the Electric Company, and several programs offering special help (in primary and secondary schools and in college) for students from poor minority families. In 1973 the Democrat-born Office of Economic Opportunity was "phased out" by the Republican administration and its surviving programs were distributed among the other agencies. The Community Services Administration now performs several of the OEO-created functions.

Lessening the Discomfort of Poverty: Income Redistribution

Most of the people drawing welfare are too old, too young, or too unhealthy to work. For these people who can't stand alone, their only chance for a share of the society's output is for the society to donate something to them—a gift from the productive people to the unproductive people.

No matter how effective the "poverty curing" programs may become there always will be a need for some income redistribution to take care of those who are either temporarily or permanently incapable of self-support.

In the United States we have three big "income redistribution" programs: (1) the "social security" program, (2) the "unemployment compensation" program, and (3) the "welfare" program.

Social Security. The social security program is the largest income redistribution program in the country. It was set up during the depression of the 1930s and has been growing ever since. This is the so-called "Old Age, Survivors, Disability and Health Insurance" (OASD-HI) program. This is the same as the "Retirement, Survivors, and Disability Insurance and Medicare" program.

Under the social security program, taxes are automatically deducted from people's paychecks and payments are automatically made to people who qualify—by retirement, disability, or poor health. If the wage earner dies, payments automatically go to the dependents. You can see that this program would help a lot to soothe the hurt of lost income.

This is a federal program and the taxes and benefits are the same nationwide. The program is financed by social security taxes which are paid both by workers and employers. This is the "payroll tax" you will be reading about later.

Medicare. The social security program was initially set up back in the 1930s. But it has been expanded frequently since then. In 1965 there was a major new addition to the program: Medicare.

This is a program of hospital insurance which covers people over 65 and pays almost all of their hospital costs for up to 90 days. The program also provides a low-cost (optional) insurance program to help on doctors' fees.

Unemployment Insurance. The unemployment insurance or "unemployment compensation" program gives payments (for a limited number of weeks) to anyone who gets laid off. This is a federal-sponsored, state-administered program. The amount of money you get per week and the number of weeks you can get it depends on rules adopted by your state. The program is financed by a tax on employers. It usually pays around $50 a week but there are wide variations among the states.

People "sign up" for their unemployment payments at the state employment office in their area. Usually the only requirement is that they be ready to take any appropriate job that might become available. If you're interested in how the program is working in your state, go down to the local employment office and ask. I'm sure someone there would be glad to explain it to you.

There are many things to complain about, about the social security and unemployment compensation programs. The payments aren't high enough to provide for basic needs, and what does a person do after the unemployment payments run out? There are other questions, but generally these two programs seem to be functioning reasonably well. It's in the welfare program where most of the serious problems seem to arise.

The Welfare, or Public Assistance Program

The welfare program includes several kinds of aid. "Aid to Families with Dependent Children" (AFDC) (to families without a father's support) and Medicaid take most of the "welfare" money. But some is also paid to others.

This "welfare program" is supported with federal and state money and some local money. Generally, the federal government sets up the guidelines and each state sets up the rules for its own program. The procedures and the benefits are a lot different from one state to another. (I suppose everyone has heard stories about poor families moving from one state to another so they can get more welfare benefits.)

The cost of the "welfare" or "public assistance" program has been growing very rapidly in recent years. In New York and California this program supports about *twelve percent* of the children in the state. In other states the percentages are smaller.

In addition to AFDC, welfare payments go to "needy" people who are elderly, blind, disabled, or otherwise unable to work and who for some reason don't qualify for payments under the social security program. A person must be able to really prove a need for the money. How hard it is to do that may depend a lot on which state you happen to be in and which person at the public assistance office you happen to be talking to.

In 1974 a new federally financed and administered program called the Supplemental Security Income (SSI) program was initiated. It provides payments to the aged, the blind, and the disabled. More than 3 million people are covered under this SSI program.

Another recent addition to the welfare program supported by the federal government (with some matching funds paid by the states) is *Medicaid*. This is a medical care program for the poor who would not be eligible for Medicare. Before Medicaid, AFDC was the biggest user of welfare money. But it didn't take Medicaid long to take the lead.

In 1977, of the total expected federal welfare expenditure of about $28 billion, Medicaid was expected to use up about $14 billion. AFDC was expected to cost about $9.5 billion, with day care centers and emergency support amounting to another $4.5 billion.

> The political process might work fine if everyone could **agree** on everything.... But they can't !

In addition, there are the food stamp programs costing about $5 to $6 billion a year, school lunch programs and various other programs operated by several different departments of the federal government and by the state and local governments, all aimed toward relieving some part of the poverty problem.

There is a lot of confusion about who does what on the anti-poverty front. The federal programs are administered by the departments of Education; Health and Human Services; Agriculture; Housing and Urban Development; and various others. Each has different criteria for eligibillity. In some cases eligibility is left up to the states. Requirements differ greatly from one place to another.

In 1976 President Ford was trying to do something to coordinate all these programs. In 1978 and '79 President Carter was trying to get his own welfare reform plan through Congress, but without much success. In the Reagan administration's 1981-82 budget cutting to try to reduce the deficit, welfare spending was an area

of big disagreement. Some cuts were made, but no major reforms.

The idea of some "new and different" approach to the welfare program is still very much alive. President Reagan wants to transfer more functions to the states. But this book will be going to press before any "bold new action" is likely to be taken.

Everyone seems to agree that we need to reform our "public welfare" program. One suggested approach is the "guaranteed annual income"; one suggested way to achieve it is the "negative income tax."

The Guaranteed Annual Income and the Negative Income Tax

Maybe the government should stop providing welfare payments and simply guarantee each family a minimum income. People whose paychecks were large could still have taxes deducted, but people with paychecks too small could have "taxes" *added!* People with no job (no paycheck) could receive checks from the government. If your income is high, you pay. If it's low, you receive. See how this approach can be called the "negative income tax"?

Another approach might be to give *everyone in the country* a certain sum of money (say $1,000 a year) and call the money "taxable income." People who had no other income wouldn't have to pay any taxes on the grant but those with high incomes would have to repay most of it in taxes.

As part of a guaranteed annual income program, any able-bodied recipient could be required to work, and/or to participate in a job training program. Day care centers could be set up to permit mothers of dependent children to take jobs and/or training. The continuation of the family's "guaranteed annual income" could require that a person take any suitable job that became available.

What about this "guaranteed annual income" approach to getting rid of the "welfare mess"? Is it a good approach? Can it be made to work?

The answer is "probably, yes" to both questions. But it isn't going to be easy to work out, not only because of the economics involved, but even more, because of the political and administrative problems. Unless it's done right it could turn into an administrative nightmare of red tape, high costs, and injustices. That would be no improvement! That's what we're trying to get rid of now.

There Is No Easy Solution to the Poverty Problem

The poverty problem isn't going to be easy to solve. Much progress has been made, sure. The number of people classified as "living in poverty" has decreased considerably—by about *half*—over the past twenty years.

But the more we reduce the number in poverty the more difficult it becomes to do more. The more we succeed, the closer we get to the "hard core" of families who have no way of becoming self-supporting—families which have no choice but to depend on the "social process" or the "political process" to provide them a distributive share of society's output.

Proposals for overcoming the poverty problem are among the most controversial public policy proposals of our time. It's obvious that the U.S. economy is productive enough to provide for everybody. There's enough so that the rich can still be rich and the middle income people can keep on living well, while the poor can be brought up above the poverty level. The physical means to solve the problem certainly exist. But to try to design a realistic program or plan to put it all together—that's really tough. It involves hard choices—difficult trade-offs.

How do we serve the needs of the "honestly poor" without indulging the "fast-buck artists"? and without destroying the incentives, and the feelings of personal worth of the recipients? How do we get the needed flexibility into our programs? And withstand selfish political pressures and bypass entangling bureaucracy? How do we balance off the insensitive snobbism of the "hard-nosed" against the unworkable idealism of the "willing bleeders"?

Can we go far enough to really take care of the problem without perpetuating it? Or without creating other problems more serious than the one we're trying to solve? Are there reflex effects to think about? Are we endangering any golden-egg-laying geese by trying to reach the best of all possible worlds?

Anyone who knows for sure what the ultimate answer is, either has great wisdom—or else doesn't understand the complexity of the problem! So far, all we have been able to do is go along experimenting—taking various steps as they have become politically feasible. Probably that's what we will continue to do.

There will be tough choices every step of the way. And it isn't likely that anybody will be completely satisfied with the results. But that seems to be the way it is with the income distribution problem. Remember?

SUMMARY AND SYNTHESIS

The **growth of urban areas** in this country and throughout the world has been **explosive** during recent decades. It has been estimated that by the end of the present century **an additional 100 million people** will be living in urban areas in this country. That would make up 15 metropolitan areas the size of Chicago, or 100 the size of New Orleans or Seattle.

Urban areas consist of some **healthy places** and other places where **economic deterioration is** serious. When neighborhoods start going downhill, the people who can leave, do so. The neighborhood deteriorates.

People move out of the central city into the suburbs. They escape from city taxes, and belong to a different local government unit. So **metropolitan government becomes fragmented,** with no one unit capable of dealing with the problems of the urban area.

The "councils of government" (COG) movement and the "metro-government" approach are two ways of trying to **coordinate metropolitan planning** to provide services and overcome this "fragmentation" problem.

Urban transportation, with the development of **freeways,** has contributed to metropolitan area fragmentation, and has left "islands of poverty" in the ghetto areas. Most urban planners now look to **mass transit systems** as more effective than urban highways in helping to overcome these problems.

The federal government has supported **urban renewal programs** through the Department of Housing and Urban Development (HUD). Ghetto housing has been demolished, **low-cost housing, urban thruways,** and **mass transit systems** have been subsidized. But the problem is far from solved.

One recommended approach is to develop "new towns" to take some of the growth pressure off the existing urban areas. Several "new town" developments have been undertaken, with mixed results.

Urban renewal programs need to be sensitive to the realities and **needs of the urban poor.** Otherwise the result may be structural beautification, but a worsening of the conditions of the urban poor.

Poverty in the United States (according to our not very precise measurements of it) has been **declining** as a percentage of the population. It is now only about one-half as large as it was about twenty years ago. Rising incomes and **various**

government programs have helped to overcome the poverty at the low end of the income scale. But the **overall inequality of income distribution** in the United States hasn't changed very much over the past thirty years.

The **Lorenz curve** shows the **percentage breakdown** and **degree of inequality** of income distribution. For the United States it shows that the lowest 20% of the people receive about 5 or 6% of the income, and that the highest 20% of the people receive about 41% of the income.

Income distribution was **more unequal before the 1930s.** In 1929 the highest-income 5% of the population received about 30% of all the income. These days the top 5% receive about 16% of the income.

There is a tendency for **poverty to be self-perpetuating,** and this tendency is not easy to overcome. **Manpower development** programs and **job placement** can help. But the most serious "profile in poverty" is the **fatherless household.** There's no way to get at this problem through manpower development programs.

The problem of **discrimination by race and sex** contributes both to poverty and to **income inequality.** The government has programs to make job discrimination against blacks or women illegal, and progress is being made. But indications are that **economic discrimination continues,** and that the incomes of blacks and women continue to reflect this.

Programs designed to **"cure the disease of poverty"** have been emphasized over the past four decades, with considerable success. In the mid-1960s the **"war on poverty"** program mounted several thrusts designed to break the self-perpetuating links of poverty. *Sesame Street* and *The Electric Company* were two programs sponsored by this "war on poverty."

For many people in poverty, there is no cure because the people are too young, too old, or too unhealthy to be productive. So for them, **income redistribution** is required. The most important income redistribution programs include the **social security program, Medicare and Medicaid,** unemployment insurance, and the "welfare" or "public assistance" program which includes aid to families with dependent children (fatherless households).

In recent years there has been much discussion about the need to cut the cost and improve the effectiveness of our income redistribution (welfare) programs. One suggested approach is the "guaranteed annual income," perhaps using the "negative income tax." These approaches have been recommended, but so far, not tried.

The poverty problem is very difficult to approach, because of the impossibility of separating the payments to the truly needy from those sought by the "fast-buck artists." The basic dilemma inherent in all anti-poverty programs is that payments to people reduce their incentives to produce.

REVIEW EXERCISES

MAJOR CONCEPTS, PRINCIPLES, TERMS (Explain each carefully.)

the neighborhood deterioration problem
the urban transportation issue
the metro-government approach
poverty
U.S. social security program
the U.S. welfare program
negative income tax

OTHER CONCEPTS AND TERMS (Explain each briefly.)

population spillover
urban renewal
HUD
Lorenz curve
Civil Rights Act of 1964

unemployment insurance
Medicare
AFDC
Medicaid
SSI

CURVES AND GRAPHS (Draw, label, and explain each.)

Income Distribution in the United States by Population and Income
Groups: the Lorenz Curve

QUESTIONS (Write out answers or jot down key points.)

1. Discuss some of the characteristics—the "nature"—of the urban problem. Explain some of the reasons why the problem is not going to be easy to handle. Can you see examples of any of these characteristics and impediments in *your own* local area? Discuss.
2. Do you think New York City's financial crisis will have much effect on the speed with which the urban problems are worked out in the United States? Discuss.
3. Explain some of the important causes of, and impediments to overcoming poverty

in the "affluent societies."

4. What are some indications of discrimination in the U.S. labor markets? Do you think these indications are conclusive? Discuss.

5. Do you think the negative income tax would be a good idea? Why or why not? Discuss.

6. The poverty problem is *especially* difficult to handle, because just about everything you can think of to *overcome* poverty, seems to interfere with something else—seems to generate reflex effects: "Adequate" payments to support fatherless children may result in more fatherless children; "adequate" payments to the unemployed may result in more unemployment. When a person receives "adequate" payments to eliminate the discomfort of poverty that automatically takes the pressure off. It relieves the urgency to work out a permanent solution to the uncomfortable situation. It tends to perpetuate the problem. This basic dilemma is inherent in all "anti-poverty" programs. It's because of this dilemma that the "degree of success" in overcoming poverty is likely to always fall short of the "desired social objective." Discuss.

PART EIGHT

The American Economy: Agriculture, Labor, Business, Government

Things Sure Have Changed Around Here Since Our Last Visit! Wow!

32 The Evolution of the American Economy and the Changing Role of Agriculture

Chapter Objectives

- In this chapter and the ones that follow, you will be looking at **the American economy—what it is,** various **parts** of it and **how they work,** how it has **evolved,** and some of the **current problems and issues.**

- When you finish studying this chapter you will be able to give some of the **highlights** in the history of **the growth of the American economy.** You will be able to distinguish between **the American Economy (1) before the Great Depression and the "New Deal,"** and **(2) afterwards.**

- You will be able to **name** and **describe** several **sources of current statistics** on conditions and trends in the American economy.

- You will be able to describe the **changing role of agriculture** in the American economy, and to explain some of the **indications that** and **reasons why** American agriculture has become so **highly productive.**

- Finally, you will know about the **special problems** of the **inelastic demand agricultural product markets,** about government **price support programs** designed to stabilize agricultural markets, and about **recent changes** in agricultural **conditions** and in **government policies** toward agriculture.

Introduction to Part Eight

Here in Part Eight you will be reading about the details of the American economic system— about what it is and how it works. You'll be reading about how it developed, about its component parts, and about how the parts all fit together.

When you get to the end of Part Eight you will know a lot about the American economic system. Especially you will know about the importance of big labor, big businesses, and big government. But you will also know about agriculture and small businesses and households and consumers, and about how all these big units and small units mesh together to make up the American economic system.

The American Economic System: an Overview

You know that the American economic system is a mixed economy—that is, it responds to the market process and also to government planning and influences. You know that in general people get their shares of income from the work they do, then they buy the things they want. The producers try to be as efficient as possible and to produce the things people are buying. And the government influences a lot of income distribution choices and a lot of production choices, too.

That, in broad general terms, really is the way it works. But Part Eight is going to tell you a lot more than that.

First, some historical perspective—a quick look at the way the American economy has evolved since colonial times.

THE AMERICAN ECONOMY IN HISTORICAL PERSPECTIVE

Back in colonial times the American economy was based almost entirely on agriculture. People produced mostly for their own consumption and for local trade, but some products (tobacco, lumber, others) were produced for export. In the developing cities some artisans were producing implements and clothing and other goods for local sale—but the real base of the economy was agriculture.

Growing Industrialization and Increasing Output

As the years went by the textile industry began to develop. The textile industry was the leader in the Industrial Revolution in England. It wasn't long before the secrets of improved textile manufacturing were brought to the United States. Businesses saw the opportunity to make money producing textiles and they outdid each other in building more and better textile mills, seeking more profit. The industry grew rapidly. The economy became more industrialized.

By the time of the Civil War the American economy had changed greatly. Already it had become an industrial-based economy. Agriculture continued to be a very important sector of the economy, of course. But no longer was it the predominant occupation of the country.

Rapid Industrialization. In the period following the Civil War the industrialization continued. The population grew, business grew, the economy grew. The railroad system was developed almost overnight. The coal, iron, and steel industries grew rapidly. Machinery and equipment manufacturing expanded. The oil industry got started, then grew by leaps and bounds. Big banks and financial interests were involved in financing all this rapid growth—and they gained great economic power and influence.

Growth of Monopoly. In the late 1800s the people began to criticize the growing power of big businesses and banks. Farmers' organizations and labor organizations tried to get the government to limit the powers of the big businesses and banks.

It was during this period that the Sherman Antitrust Act (1890) was passed. But the Sherman Act was not very effective in stopping the growth of giant businesses. It wasn't until the 1930s that the government enforced much effective restraint on the growth of the monopoly powers of business. You'll be reading all about this later.

U.S. Per Capita Output Leads the World. Over its history the American economy has shown remarkable growth, both in total output and in output per capita. The number of people in the United States doubled and redoubled. But output increased much more rapidly.

By the time of the Civil War, output and income per capita in the United States was already greater than that of Britain. The baby had outgrown the parent! Ever since that time output and income per capita in the United States has continued to lead the world—and (most of the time) by an increasingly wide margin.

Laissez-Faire and Government Intervention

Throughout most of its history the United States government has followed a "hands off" policy toward the economy. The United States was born with a deep philosophical commitment to individualism: each person should go it alone—should be permitted to go as far and as fast as possible, or to fall by the wayside if that's the way it turns out.

The Philosophy of Laissez-Faire. This was Adam Smith's philosophy of laissez-faire, strongly expressed in Smith's *Wealth of Nations* in 1776. The government followed this philosophy and was reluctant to restrict or regulate individuals or businesses. It was also reluctant to assist organized groups—workers or farmers—in getting together to improve their own circumstances by group action.

Yes, the spirit of laissez-faire and individualism was very strong in 19th century and early 20th century America. It stood as a strong deterrent to any kind of government action in the economy. The idea was that the rewards people receive are the "just rewards" of their hard work.

"Those who make great gains deserve to keep what they make. Those who don't gain very much haven't produced very much and therefore shouldn't have much." This was the basic idea underlying American capitalism, so the government was slow to intervene in the workings of the economy. But there were many ways the government did intervene.

Government "Public Lands" Policies. In the 1800s the government's public lands policies influenced the economy significantly. Great strips of land were given to the railroad companies to induce them to extend their railroads.

The government also influenced the economy through its homesteading policies and by establishing land grant colleges and by its policies on releasing mineral rights to individuals and companies.

The Interstate Commerce Act and the Sherman Antitrust Act. In the late 1800s when the clamor against monopoly began to get serious, the government took some action. The Interstate Commerce Act was passed to regulate the railroads; the Sherman Antitrust Act was passed to discourage the growth of monopoly. Notice that one act was aimed in one direction (regulating) and the other act was aimed in the other direction (maintaining competition). But neither of these acts was greatly successful.

The Interstate Commerce Act (1887) was based on the idea of "government regulation of monopolies"—the idea that there are some industries (such as railroads) in which competition can't work to protect the interests of the society. So government regulation is necessary: (1) to stabilize the industry, (2) to keep the rates at reasonable levels and (3) to assure adequate standards of service for the economy. The Interstate Commerce Act thus recognized railroads as a kind of "natural monopoly."

But the Sherman Antitrust Act aimed in the opposite direction. The idea was to prevent monopoly power from growing. With enough competition the interests of the public would be protected automatically. With competition maintained, there's no need for regulation. Laissez-faire can reign! You'll be reading a lot more about all this in the chapter on American business, coming up soon.

The 1920s Boom. The American economy rolled into the 20th century growing rapidly. Industrialization was increasing. Outputs of industry and agriculture were increasing. The trade and service industries were expanding rapidly.

By the late 1920s, productivity and outputs and incomes had gone beyond anyone's expectations. Business was booming. Prosperity and perpetual economic advancement seemed to be the permanent condition of the American economy. But as it turned out the economy was riding in a bubble. In October of 1929, the bubble burst.

The Great Depression

During the 1930s the economy went into the longest depression in history. There had been depressions before. As you already know, depressions had occurred at such frequent intervals in the past that economists for many years had referred to these recurrent periods of bad times as "business cycles."

Ever since the Civil War, periods of prosperity had been limited. Things would be prosperous awhile. Then would come the depression. But each depression would only last a while—maybe a year to so—then business would start to pick up again. Soon the unemployed workers would get jobs and the economy would be prosperous again. But in the 1930s it was different.

In October of 1929 the stock market tumbled. It wiped out the assets of many people and organizations. Banks, insurance companies, and savings institutions saw the values of many of their assets wiped out. Many went bankrupt. The whole financial structure of the economic system was just about knocked out. After the stock market crash, conditions just kept getting worse and worse—1930, 1931, 1932. In March of 1933 when President Franklin D. Roosevelt took office, the economy was close to a standstill.

Each day more businesses and banks were going broke. Millions of people had lost their jobs—had no source of income. As the banks collapsed, the savings and checking accounts of many people were wiped out. Not many people had any money. Not many were spending. The economic system was near total collapse.

What happened to the American economic system during 1933 and the years that followed? It changed. It wasn't a matter of just minor adjustments, either. The changes were basic and permanent.

The American economic system before the 1930s and the American economic system afterwards are two distinctly different economic systems.

The section coming up is something I wrote just a few years ago. I think it will give you a feeling of what happened in the American economy in the 1930s.

THE NEW DEAL: BASIC CHANGES IN THE ECONOMIC SYSTEM*

With things so bad and getting worse following the stock market crash in October 1929, people were urging the government to do something. Many voices clamored for government action. The clamor came from businesses large and small, from state and local governments, from welfare agencies and private charities, from religious organizations, from groups of irate citizens, from just about everybody. . .

When Franklin D. Roosevelt was inaugurated on March 3, 1933, he promised to do something. He promised a "New Deal." He promised action. A real flurry of action is what he delivered. When he was all through the American economic system was a different economic system than it had been before. A better system? Perhaps. Some people disagree on this. But everyone agrees that it was different.

What Was Roosevelt's "New Deal"?

What was meant by the "New Deal"? You can answer that question in many different ways. One way would be to list the fifteen or so major pieces of legislation which were pushed through Congress during the first 100 days after Roosevelt took office, and to describe the impact of these important federal acts on how the American economic system functions.

Another way to answer the question "What was the New Deal?" is to say that it was an idea, a con-

---

*This section is reproduced from Elbert V. Bowden, *Economic Evolution: Principles, Issues, Ideas—Through the Looking Glass of Time* (Cincinnati: South-Western Publishing Co., 1981), Part IV, "The Great Depression and Keynesian Economics," pp. 86-89.

cept, a vision of major change in the American economic system—a change away from the philosophies and policies of laissez-faire. The idea was that we were going to "reshuffle the cards and deal them out again"—to give the people with "bad hands" a chance to do better—that is, a "new deal."

This New Deal means that we will give the farmers some help and some economic power to protect themselves from economic adversity. We will let workers join unions and bargain with (and if they wish, strike against) their employers. We will establish a social security program so that the welfare of each individual will be a responsibility shared by all members of the society.

The New Deal tried to do something specific, something direct to help those who were in difficulty—and that included farmers, workers, businesses, young people, old people, city people, country people: just about everyone. The government started programs to employ people and buy up surplus food and give it to people.

Increasing the Economic Role of Government

Ideas about the proper role of government were changing fast. The New Deal idea was that wages and farm prices need to be kept high enough to support people adequately; that people have a right to live in decent housing—and that the government has a responsibility to do something to bring about these results.

The New Deal also included the ideas that the banks and stock markets and other financial businesses should be watched over and regulated by the government to be sure that the interests of the people are protected; that the government should watch over and regulate employment practices: should prohibit child labor, should set limits on the length of the work week and should require that higher wages be paid for overtime work. And there were many other changes to the economic system—all away from laissez-faire and toward more influence and control by government in the economy.

A New Philosophy: Challenge to Laissez-Faire

Perhaps we could summarize the philosophy of the New Deal this way: "It is the responsibility of the government to be concerned about the operation of the economic system, and about the material welfare of the people. The government has a responsibility to keep the system running properly, to oversee all of the activities within the economic system which might adversely affect the lives and conditions of the people of the society, and to see to it that everyone has an opportunity to share in the high level of well-being which this 'modern economic system' can produce. Even those people who are unproductive—because of health or age or unemployment or some other misfortune—should still get a share of the output. The government should take some income from the productive people and give it to the unproductive ones."

What a basic change this New Deal was! The American economic system before the New Deal was quite a different system from the American economic system after the New Deal. Quite a different system! It's no wonder that many people—especially those who had been enjoying most of the benefits of the pre-New Deal system—were violently opposed to President Franklin D. Roosevelt's New Deal.

But in 1933 and the years following, almost everyone was feeling the squeeze of the depression. Most of the people were disillusioned, confused, bewildered. The depression had been dragging on, getting worse and worse each year. People who in 1929 would have considered the New Deal subversive and un-American (or maybe even a Communistic takeover!), in 1933 were ready to try anything. By then it was obvious to most people that sitting around waiting for the natural forces of the laissez-faire market system to solve the problem just wasn't the answer. . . .

It has been said that when Roosevelt took office he mounted his horse and galloped off in several directions at once. And really, that's sort of what he did. So many programs, each aimed at overcoming some visible problem, and some of the programs inconsistent and conflicting with each other—but there was no question that something was being done. Action was *being taken.*

The depression years of the Roosevelt administration are a truly unique period in American history. The things which happened during these years brought major changes both in economics and in politics. The greatest changes were in the rapidly increasing functions of government in the economic system. . . . Many of the programs were temporary. But many initiated permanent changes in the nature of the American economic system and in the role of government in the economy.

It would hardly be correct to say that following the years of the depression, laissez-faire in the American economy was dead. But certainly laissez-faire had been significantly reduced. The role of the political process in the economic system had been greatly expanded.

The New Deal philosophy is embodied in the social security program. It's also embodied in the *Employment Act of 1946* and in the *Full Employment and Balanced Growth Act of 1978* (the Humphrey-Hawkins Act). Both these acts require the administration to take action as necessary to keep the economy near "full employment with stable prices."

As you go through the following chapters you will see many more indications of the expanded functions of government: in agriculture, in labor-management relations, in business, and in the taxing and spending policies of government itself. But before you go on into that, take a minute to think about the American economy today. That's what the next section talks about.

THE AMERICAN ECONOMY IN THE 1980s: AN OVERVIEW

What is the American economy? It's an economy made up of and serving a population approaching a quarter of a billion people. Most of the people are living in households in urban areas. Most of the households own some property. But they get their incomes from the work that some of the members of the household do.

Most of the people have more material goods (more real income) than the average in any other nation of the world. Most of them have more freedom in using their time and money and "doing their own thing" than people elsewhere—more than "average people" anywhere in the world previously have ever known.

One Way to Look at It: Big Business, Big Labor, Big Government

The American economy is made up mostly of big businesses. Most of the value produced in manufacturing, transportation, utilities, banking, insurance, finance, wholesale and retail trade, and services is produced by big businesses. But there are also a great many small (and many tiny) businesses. There are millions of tiny "business firms" in agriculture and in retail trade and services.

The households are earning and spending and earning and spending and influencing the direction of the economy. The governments—federal, state and local—are taxing and spending and borrowing and influencing the production and distribution choices in the economy. So you could say that mostly the economy is made up of big business, big labor, and big government, and the millions of households. That's one way to look at it.

Another Way to Look at It: Attitudes, Institutions, Factors of Production

The American economy is made up of an exceptionally favorable endowment of natural resources, capital, and labor.

The world's greatest industrial plant stands at the heart of the American economic system. The system has a highly efficient network of transportation and communications, and a "free trade common market" throughout the fifty states. There's highly developed technology, efficient business organization, highly skilled management, an educated and experienced labor force and a population with attitudes and habits that support high productivity and responsiveness to incentives.

The American economy is blessed with governmental stability, a dependable legal system, highly developed financial institutions, and effective techniques for the introduction of innovations. All these characteristics—some tangible, some intangible—are important parts of the American economic system. All of them help to support the high productivity of the system.

Another Way to Look at It: What It Produces—the "Final Output Mix"

What's in the pile of goods and services called "the U.S. GNP"? There are manufactured products and agricultural products and all of the services. Here's a look at the breakdown.

Trade and Services. Would you believe that more than half (in fact about 60 percent) of the value of the U.S. GNP is made up of trade and services? That's right. Here's a rough breakdown:

1. Wholesale and retail trade (18% of GNP)
2. Finance, insurance, and real estate (13% of GNP)
3. Transportation, communications, and utilities (11% of GNP)
4. Government goods and services (9% of GNP)
5. All other kinds of services (9% of GNP) TOTAL TRADE AND SERVICES: 60% of GNP

You can see why some people refer to the American economy as a "trade and service" economy. One of the things that seems to happen when an economy gets more advanced and incomes go up is that there is an increased demand for services. That's what you would expect. If everyone is already well-fed and owns a house and a car and appliances and things, their demand for services is likely to go up. Right? As the American economy has developed, the percentage of GNP made up by trade and services has increased quite a lot. It's still increasing.

Manufactured Goods. About one third of the U.S. GNP is made up of manufactured goods. And about 60 percent of the manufactured goods are *durable goods*—machinery, equipment, automobiles, household appliances, etc. The other 40 percent are *nondurable goods*—clothing, soap, toothpaste, processed foods, gasoline, pencils, cigarettes, shoe polish and all the thousands of other nondurable goods people use every day.

Agricultural Products. What about agriculture? Agriculture was the big thing, back in the beginning. But if trade and services make up 60 percent of the GNP and more than 30 percent is in manufactured goods, that comes up to more than 90 percent! So what about agricultural products?

As a percentage of total GNP, agricultural output is very small. Would you believe it only makes up about 4 percent? That's right. And that 4 percent includes all the products of agriculture, forestry, and fisheries. But be careful. That 4 percent figure doesn't really give you a true picture of the importance of agriculture in the American economy. Here's why.

Most of the output of agriculture goes into manufacturing, so it shows up in GNP as "manufactured goods." So agriculture continues to be important. It provides these basic inputs into manufacturing. More than that: it feeds the people! You'll be reading more about the role of agriculture later in this chapter.

Other Products. The remainder of the GNP is made up of contract construction (3 or 4 percent) and mining and all other outputs (about 2 or 3 percent).

The "Final Output Mix" Doesn't Tell You Everything. This broad breakdown of what the American economy is producing (the "final output mix") tells you something. But there's a lot it doesn't tell you. It doesn't tell you about the importance of the industries which are producing the basic and intermediate products—like agriculture and lumbering and mining and such.

Here's something else. This breakdown doesn't tell you that in recent decades the historically great industries—coal, railroads, iron and steel, cotton textiles, and some others—have lagged behind as the economy has surged forward. And that other industries have forged ahead. Rapid expansions have been made in aircraft, chemicals, trucking, utilities, electrical machinery, computers, instruments, plastics, natural gas, and some others.

The shifts in emphasis have come about as a result of changing technology, changing demands for various products, the introduction of new products and processes, and last but not least, by government spending for military goods.

The Important Role of Big Corporations

Most of the expanding products were produced by big corporations. Of course! Just as most of the declining products were produced by big corporations. How could it be otherwise? *Big corporations make up almost all of the productive capacity of the American economy!*

In manufacturing and mining and even in the services, giant corporations are the pacesetters in almost all fields. It's true in transportation, communications and utilities; in wholesale and retail trade; in finance and insurance. In retail trade the big chain stores prevail. In most services (for example, the auto service stations all over the country) big businesses are setting the pace.

Many of the services in the American economy are provided by government. Education, police and fire protection and medical and social welfare programs are mostly government pro-

vided. And the national defense services are too, of course.

Integrating the Component Parts of the Economy

If you could understand each of the various parts, would that give you some insight into the American economy? Sure. Then if you could get all those parts pulled together you might see how the economy works—how it functions as an integrated system. That's exactly what Part Eight is going to try to help you to do.

We'll be getting into that in a minute. But first, if you're going to see what the economy looks like, you'll need some facts and figures. So here are some suggestions about where to look for statistics on the American economy.

Sources of Statistics on the American Economy

As you read about the American economy in this textbook (or in any textbook) you will see statistics on GNP, employment, output, population, labor force, government taxing and spending, per capita income, business earnings, and lots of other things. But it takes a long time to publish a textbook. So by the time the book comes off the press the statistics are always out of date.

As you're going through this chapter and the following ones, why not spend some time in the library looking up some current figures? Where should you look? Here are a few suggestions:

1. *The Statistical Abstract Of The United States.* U.S. Department of Commerce. Annual.

Whenever you don't know where else to look always go to the *Statistical Abstract*. The full title of it is: *The Statistical Abstract of the United States and National Guide to Data Sources*. It really is what the title says. It gives statistics on almost everything. In addition it will direct you to the original sources of the statistics so you can find even more recent and more detailed figures if you wish.

Everyone should be familiar with the *Statistical Abstract*. If you aren't, go ask your reference librarian to show it to you right now. You'll be surprised what a valuable source it is.

2. *Economic Report of the President*. Council of Economic Advisers. Annual.

This report comes out about February or March of each year. It gives a detailed analysis of the American economy for the previous year, and carries a statistical appendix with figures on GNP, employment, money, taxes, profits, and many other kinds of data on the American economy.

3. *Survey of Current Business*. U.S. Department of Commerce. Monthly.

The *Survey of Current Business* carries articles and statistics on GNP and national income and employment and prices and most of the other kinds of statistics you'll want on the American economy.

4. *Federal Reserve Bulletin*. Board of Governors of the Federal Reserve System. Monthly.

The *Federal Reserve Bulletin* carries excellent and timely articles on the economy, on such things as employment, production, spending, inflation, monetary conditions, international trade, etc., and has a statistical appendix on the American economy.

5. *Monthly Labor Review*. U.S. Department of Labor. Monthly.

The *Monthly Labor Review* carries timely articles and data on the economy with emphasis on conditions and changes in the labor markets and on changes in prices and in the cost of living.

There are dozens of other excellent sources of statistics on the American economy put out by various government departments and agencies and by business, labor, consumer, and other organizations. But the five sources listed here will get you well on your way. The *Statistical Abstract* will lead you to other sources if you need them.

For the most current statistics as they appear, you need to depend on the news media. Weekly news magazines: *Time, Newsweek, U.S. News and World Report, Business Week,* and the business and finance section of the *Sunday New York Times* all are excellent sources. So are the major daily newspapers, especially *The New York Times* and *The Wall Street Journal*.

I wouldn't recommend that you spend all your study time trying to "stay current" on what's going on in the economy. You can waste a lot of time that way. But it sure is good to know where to go to find out what's going on whenever you need to know. As you're studying these chapters, an occasional trip to the library to find out "what's going on right now" may help to bring it all to life for you.

And now it's time to get into the substance of Part Eight. First, a discussion of agriculture in the American economy.

THE ROLE OF AGRICULTURE IN THE AMERICAN ECONOMY

There aren't very many farmers in the United States. But they sure do produce a lot! Most of the people in the world are working in agriculture. They're all trying to produce enough food to feed themselves and their families.

But in this country farm employment only involves about 3.4 million people. Farmers make up less than one out of every thirty workers in the country. Farmers make up *less than one out of sixty* of the total population. That means on the average *each farmer is producing enough to feed more than sixty people!*

Even so, the "farm problem" in the U.S. economy for the past 40 years or so (until very recently) has been a problem of *too many farmers,* and of *surplus agricultural outputs.* The great productivity of American agriculture is an almost unbelievable example of what can be done with modern technology.

Rapid Increase in Output per Farm Worker

The history of agricultural production in the United States is a history of doubling and redoubling of output per farm worker. Just since the 1930s the farm output per hour input has increased by more than six times. It has more than doubled just since 1960!

When you think of 3.4 million people working in agriculture, that may seem to be a lot of people. But in terms of the total U.S. population of over 230 million or the total labor force of well over 100 million people, 3.4 million is a very small number.

Present Outputs of Farm Products

What about outputs? In the early 1980s the value of farm products in the GNP was running at about $90 billion per year. When compared with the total GNP of about $3,000 billion, $90 billion isn't very big. But don't forget that agriculture plays a key role in providing inputs to other industries—and in feeding the people.

About half of the farm output goes into processing industries and doesn't show up as "agricultural output" in the GNP. The GNP counts only *final* goods. Remember? Actual output value from American farms amounted to more than $150 billion in the early 1980s. But that's still not very much, by comparison.

Even though by comparison it isn't very big, still you can't have an accurate picture of the American economy without an understanding of the role of agriculture. No need for you to go into it in great detail, but an accurate overview is essential.

How did American agriculture get to be so productive? And how did it get to be so small as a part of the total economy? A look at the historical highlights helps to answer these questions.

THE EVOLUTION OF AMERICAN AGRICULTURE

In the colonial years, America was a land of agriculture, fisheries and forestry. The fur trade, forest products (timber, tar, rosin, turpentine), tobacco, corn, wheat, livestock, rice, indigo, fish and whale oil provided most of the exports and much of what was needed at home. Americans in the early days were "living off the land."

During colonial times some of the colonies encouraged manufacturing. People were offered land and sometimes monopoly rights to induce them to start industries. Some industries did develop. Domestic production was started in iron, flour, lumber, shoes, hats, furniture, textiles, candles, and some shipbuilding. But at the time of the American revolution nearly all of the people still were engaged in agriculture.

The Early 1800s: New Crops and Livestock

Agriculture expanded during the early 1800s. New and improved crops and livestock were introduced, including cotton, grains, sugar, and better breeds of cattle and sheep.

There was a lot of effort in "spreading the word" about the new and better agricultural products and how to produce them. County fairs were held and prizes were given for outstanding agricultural specimens. Agricultural magazines and pamphlets described the new and better crop and livestock varieties and explained the new techniques of production.

The Homestead Act, the Morrell Act, and the USDA

In the period following the Civil War there was even greater emphasis on expanding and improving agriculture. In 1862 the Homestead Act offered free land to those who would establish farms. In the same year the Morrell Act established the land grant colleges by donating to each state a segment of public land, to be sold to raise money to establish agricultural-vocational colleges.

It was from the Morrell Act that the nationwide system of "State" [Agricultural and Mechanical (A & M) and Agricultural and Industrial (A & I)] Colleges evolved. Also, in that same year (1862) the U.S. Department of Agriculture (USDA) was set up to help in the agricultural development in the nation.

Rapid Improvement in Technology

In the late 1800s the development of agricultural technology moved fast. Plows were improved. New reapers, threshers, mowing machines, hay rakes and other kinds of agricultural machinery were developed. Total output, and output per farmer increased rapidly. Why? Because of mechanization and better knowledge of where and how to grow various things, and the introduction and improvement of fertilizers.

Cattle breeds were improved. Cattle-raising spread westward into Texas and then northward throughout the Midwest and the plains. Wheat spread throughout Illinois and into Kansas. Corn stretched through the corn belt from Illinois throughout Iowa and into Kansas. Cotton spread from the eastern seaboard to the South and Southwest. Dairying became a major industry in Wisconsin while it continued to grow in New York and in several other states.

Declining Agricultural Employment

By the mid-1800s the nation was industrializing rapidly. But even so, in the 1860s about 60 percent of the work force still was employed in agriculture. *It was during the 1870s that the employment balance between agriculture and other occupations was tipped with more employees in other occupations than in agriculture.*

By 1910, agricultural employment made up only about one third of total employment in the American economy. By the 1920s agricultural employment had dropped to *one fourth.* By 1980 it's down to *less than one thirtieth!*

The use of fertilizers and agricultural implements increased greatly between 1870 and 1900. As a result, output per worker during this period increased rapidly. Would you believe a 15 to 20 percent increase in output per worker per decade? That's right. There's no question that American agriculture was on the move.

Farmers' Complaints in the Late 1800s

In the late 1800s farmers began to get together and complain about some things. Some said that railroads were setting their rates too high and that the commodity exchanges such as the Chicago Board of Trade and the New York Cotton Exchange were controlling prices and hurting the farmers. Also there was a problem with rural credit. Farmers had trouble getting the money they needed to buy seeds and fertilizers and equipment.

In this country the political ear usually has been able to hear the voice of the farmers. The establishment of the Interstate Commerce Commission to regulate the railroads (in 1887) was a response to the farmers' voice expressed through the National Grange movement founded in the 1880s. Then in the early 1900s the Federal government did several things to aid agriculture.

Government Aid to Agriculture in the Early 1900s

In 1912 and 1913 the government began regulating the agricultural exchanges. Two farmers' organizations, the Farmers' Union and the American Society of Equity, had been pushing for this. A special office in the department of Agriculture was set up to carry out this "market regulation" function.

In 1914 the Smith-Lever Act was passed, providing for federally sponsored "county extention agents" to assist the farmers. In 1916 the Rural Credits Act was passed to help to provide farm financing. In 1917 the Smith-Hughes Act provided Federal support for agricultural and vocational education. So even in the laissez-faire days of the early 1900s the government was willing to intervene in several ways to help agriculture.

There is no question that sometimes agriculture needed help. Throughout the history of the nation (and the world) agricultural prices have been unstable. Sometimes prices of agricultural products drop destructively low. That's the natural way agricultural markets sometimes work— with corn-hog cycles, cobwebs and all that. Remember? Here's more about it.

PRICE INSTABILITY AND PRICE SUPPORTS FOR FARM PRODUCTS

What determines how much wheat will be produced this year? Weather conditions have a lot do with it. But one thing is sure. *The price of wheat this year* isn't going to have much influence on *the amount of wheat produced this year*. It's too late for that. There isn't time for this year's output to respond to this year's price. You already know all about that.

The price of wheat this year will influence the amount of wheat the farmers *will try to produce* next year. But even so, what they try to produce and what they actually produce may be quite different. For example, in the United States and throughout the world in 1973, grain was in short supply. Prices moved up. The U.S. government abolished all acreage restrictions and urged maximum production. So in 1974 a big increase in American grain output was expected.

But what happened? The weather didn't cooperate. In 1974, instead of bumper crops, grain production suffered the largest setback in nearly 40 years. So what happened to food prices in 1974? Up they went. Of course.

What's the point? Simply this: The output of agricultural products is likely to be much smaller or much greater than planned. It depends a lot on the weather and other circumstances. But here's the problem: If the output is much greater, prices will go very low. Why? Because of the inelastic demand for most farm products.

The Inelastic Demand for Farm Products

When prices for food products go up or down, do the buyers respond? Do people buy less bread at 95 cents a loaf than they would at 60 cents a loaf? Do people buy fewer tomatoes at 80 cents a pound than they would at 50 cents a pound? Sure they buy less at the higher prices. But *they don't buy very much less.* And that's the point.

When agricultural products are in short supply, prices rise. But the higher prices don't discourage the buyers very much. So prices go up even more. The rationing function of price doesn't work very well to limit the consumption of the very scarce food products. So the price must go very high to eliminate the shortages. Take a look at Figure 32-1 and you'll see this on a graph.

Now look at it the other way. Suppose there's a bumper crop of some food items. Prices will fall. Will people buy more at the lower prices? Yes. But *they won't buy very much more.* As the price goes down some, people

don't buy enough to buy up the surpluses. So the price falls even more. How low must the price of food go to get people to eat six meals a day? Very low, right?

Here's the problem: The amount supplied hardly responds at all to current prices. If the price is very low, producers can hold their output instead of selling it. They can feed more of their grain to livestock. But even so, the amount offered for sale is not going to be very responsive to the current price.

What does all this have to do with the incomes of farmers? Just this: When farm product supplies increase, prices tumble. Farmers lose money. In a bountiful year it might be impossible for a farm even to cover its costs! Just look at Figure 32-1 and see what will happen to the price if the supply curve shifts very far to the right!

But what about a year of drought when output supplies are low? Prices shoot up. The farmers whose crops aren't destroyed will make big profits.

Unstable prices in the farm product markets have always been a problem. Since the depression of the 1930s one of the major farm policies of the government has been to support the prices of farm products.

The Idea of Parity Prices

During the depression of the 1930s the price of farm products collapsed. Farmers were left

Fig. 32-1 Supply and Demand for an Agricultural Product

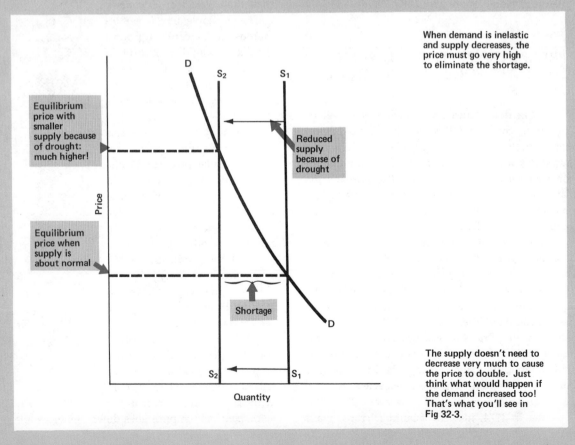

When demand is inelastic and supply decreases, the price must go very high to eliminate the shortage.

Equilibrium price with smaller supply because of drought: much higher!

Reduced supply because of drought

Equilibrium price when supply is about normal

Shortage

The supply doesn't need to decrease very much to cause the price to double. Just think what would happen if the demand increased too! That's what you'll see in Fig 32-3.

with little or no income. Many farm families who were producing cash crops for sale didn't even have enough food to eat! The prices of some farm products fell so low that it would cost more to ship the product to the market than the product was worth when it got there. Potatoes rotted in the fields while people in the cities went hungry. It was a sad situation.

Remember about the New Deal? About all the legislation passed, with something for everybody? For the farmers the Agricultural Adjustment Act (AAA, 1933) set the policy. The AAA established the principle of "parity prices."

This is the idea: *When prices (on the average) go up for the things farmers buy* (consumer goods and building materials and water pumps and tractors and tires and gasoline and all), *then the prices should also go up just as much for the things farmers sell* (potatoes and beef and cotton and tobacco and wheat and corn and peanuts and all).

Back when farm product prices were high (1910-1914), when the farmers sold their products they received enough money to buy an "adequate" quantity of goods. But as time went on, the prices of the things farmers bought (manufactured goods and services) went up quite a bit. The prices of the things farmers sold (farm products) didn't go up as much. So what happened? Farmers who kept producing the same amount as before kept selling their products and getting back less and less manufactured products in return.

The idea of "parity prices" is that farmers should get enough money for what they sell to be able to buy as much as they were buying before. If prices of things bought by farmers double and at the same time prices for farm products double, that's parity. But if prices of other things double while prices of farm products don't go up as much, the farmer gets less. Farm incomes are "below parity."

If a bushel of potatoes could be sold for enough to buy a pair of shoes at some time in the past, then a bushel of potatoes should sell for enough to buy a pair of shoes *now*. That's the idea of "parity."

During the depression of the 1930s when the prices of farm products tumbled, prices of manufactured goods went down, too. But not as much as the prices of farm products went down. You can guess why.

Producers of manufactured goods don't keep producing more and more and shoving the goods into the market and pushing the price down. Of course not! They cut back production and keep the prices up.

If the farmers had been able to cut back their outputs to restrict the supply, prices would not have fallen so much. But farmers are selling in pure competition. So they just keep on producing. So in the 1930s farm products prices fell disastrously.

You can see why in 1933 the farmers organizations would be very interested in the idea of "parity prices." And you can see why they would like to define "parity" as what existed at a time when agricultural prices were high (1910-1914). Of course! In 1933 that's just what was done. And the same idea of "parity" has been continued for more than 50 years—right into the 1980s.

Government Price Supports Create Surpluses

Since 1933, the federal government has been supporting farm product prices. Suppose the free market price falls below the government support price. Then the higher government price prevails. So what happens? What always happens when a price is set too high for the supply and demand conditions in the market? More is supplied than demanded? Sure. Surpluses? Of course. Look at Figure 32-2 and you'll see it on a graph.

The U.S. government has bought up a lot of surpluses. It never bought so many bales of cotton that you could stack them up and climb to the moon, but it bought so much wheat that the storage cost in some years was more than a billion dollars!

The big surpluses were a subject of much discussion and embarrassment during the 1950s.

The government tried to hold down agricultural output to cut down on the mounting surpluses. Acreage restrictions (limits on the number of acres a farmer could plant) were carefully defined and enforced. The "soil bank" program was set up to pay farmers for taking land out of production.

The supply-limiting measures all helped. But they didn't solve the problem. The American farmer turned out to be very ingenious. Produce more output on fewer acres? Sure. So the surpluses continued to mount. But then the kindly course of world history intervened to solve the problem.

The 1970s: World Shortages of Grain

In 1973, just about everywhere in the world the grain harvests were disappointingly low. World supplies of grain dropped dangerously. Demand for American grain suddenly was very strong. More than 70 million tons of grain were exported from the United States that year. That's about three fourths of the total amount of the world grain trade! It sure took care of the problem of surpluses.

By the mid-1970s it was a brand new ball game in the American agricultural markets. Totally different! You'll be reading about that in a minute. But first, here's more about "parity prices."

The idea of parity prices is simple. It seems like "true justice for the farmer." Be careful or you'll get pulled right into the trap.

Parity Prices Aren't Necessarily "Fair and Just" Prices

First, consider this: Which farmers are helped by "parity price supports?" The big, highly efficient commercial farms producing hundreds of carloads of output? Right! And what about the small farmers who only produce two or three truckloads? They get a little help. But not much.

The small, inefficient farm gets little dribbles

Fig. 32-2 Price Supports Always Create Surpluses

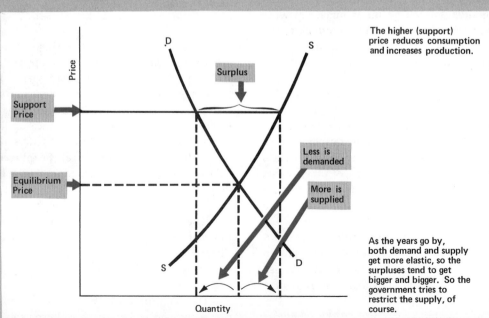

The higher (support) price reduces consumption and increases production.

Surplus

Less is demanded

More is supplied

As the years go by, both demand and supply get more elastic, so the surpluses tend to get bigger and bigger. So the government tries to restrict the supply, of course.

of extra income from the parity price program—often just enough to let the people keep living there, in poverty. But the big money goes to the big producers. Here's why.

Back in the 1910-1914 "base period," farming was very different than today. Very different! Horses and mules and human beings were doing most of the work. The labor input was high and the productivity of labor was low. But since then just look what has happened!

Now we have large mechanized commercial farms. The human effort required to produce a bushel of potatoes in 1910 might produce three *truckloads* of potatoes on a modern farm in the 1980s! Get the point?

If parity prices (the 1910 ratio between bushels of potatoes and pairs of shoes, for example) is maintained, it makes the efficient farmers very wealthy! And potatoes for everybody unnecessarily expensive! While the small, inefficient farmers still don't produce many potatoes. They live in poverty. What kind of program is that? It's the kind we've had most of the time in this country since before you were born. Sad, but true.

If productivity in farming increases more rapidly than productivity in industry, and if "parity prices" are maintained, then some farmers are going to get very rich. And under the parity pricing program, some really did!

Parity Prices Are Arbitrary

One more point: The whole thing is entirely arbitrary. When your wheat-growing friend suggests to you that parity pricing is a good idea, all you need to say is: "Good. Let's take 1933 as our parity year and let the government maintain the 1933 price ratios between agricultural and industrial products!" Chances are the discussion will end right there.

About all that can be said about the idea of parity pricing is this: It illustrates the effectiveness of using a fair-seeming and scientific-sounding statistical technique to influence public policy. When you can use a statistical technique

(hopefully using a computer in the process) to come to a conclusion which you've already decided to come to anyway, it's amazing how you can get most people to go along with you!

No, the "parity prices" approach hasn't really been aimed at the problem of the *rural poverty* which exists in the households of the very small, low-productivity farmers. There are about 5 million rural Americans living in poverty. Parity prices haven't helped them much.

What to Do with the Surpluses?

During the 1950s and 1960s the federal government tried various ways to get rid of the embarrassingly large surpluses of grain. In 1954, public law 480 permitted foreigners to buy American wheat with their local money. That is, they didn't have to pay for it with U.S. dollars.

The U.S. government was accepting a lot of foreign money in exchange for surplus wheat. Unless we wanted to buy something from those countries, we certainly didn't need the foreign money. But we didn't need the surplus wheat, either. And money is easier to store than wheat! With foreign money there's no storage cost—and no need to worry about the rats eating it!

What about school lunch programs? And programs for distributing food to the needy? Both are programs to help people to have better nutrition. Have these programs helped to get rid of agricultural surpluses? Sure. If we didn't have surplus farm products maybe these programs wouldn't have been developed.

From Surplus to Shortage

When surpluses are stacked up in silos and barns and warehouses and everywhere else, that influences government policy. It sure is different than when the nation and the world are facing food shortages and rising food costs!

That's the kind of change the world went through during the remarkable decade of the 1970s. You might even ask: "Doesn't anything ever stay in one place anymore?" In the 1970s and early 1980s things sure didn't.

RECENT FARM POLICY CHANGES: MOVING TOWARD FREER MARKETS

In the early 1970s, agricultural markets in the United States and the world did a complete flip-flop. Prices of grain shot upward. Doubled. Tripled. Some more than tripled. It seems that everywhere in the world something went wrong with production.

What happens when the supply curve shifts to the left and the demand curve is inelastic? The price goes up a lot. That's what happened.

Remember those embarrassing surpluses of wheat? They were loaded on ships and sent overseas, mostly to the Soviet Union. After the wheat had gone, prices kept going higher. People were wondering why we hadn't held on to our surpluses until the price went way up! (All your life you will notice how much better economic forecasting is by hindsight!)

The Agricultural and Consumer Protection Act (1973)

This is the Act which set forth the new U.S. agricultural policy. What did it do?

1. Most of the land in the "soil bank" was released for production.
2. Export subsidies on agricultural commodities were reduced or eliminated.
3. Import restrictions on agricultural commodities were reduced.
4. Most important: Price supports based on the idea of parity were eliminated for almost all products. Only peanuts, tobacco, rice and long-staple cotton were continued under the price support program (mostly for political reasons).

This 1973 act was the biggest shift in U.S. government agricultural policy—the first major change of direction, really—since the 1930s. It was the shortages and high prices that made the move toward freer markets economically and politically acceptable.

Nobody cares about "parity prices" when farm product prices are shooting up faster than other prices! In 1972 corn was selling for about $1 a bushel. In 1975 it was about $3 a bushel. Prices of other feed grains were doing likewise. So who cares about parity prices?

The Russian Wheat Deal and Other Price Influences

It was in the summer of 1972 that "the biggest agricultural transaction in history" was announced by the Nixon administration. Twenty percent of the American wheat crop had been sold to the U.S.S.R. That's what touched off the soaring grain prices. But that was just the beginning.

As the months (and then the years) passed, it became more and more obvious that world demands for grain were increasing while supplies seemed to fall short, season after season.

In 1973, year-end stocks of feed grains amounted to more than 30 million tons. In 1975 the year-end stocks were only about half that large. "Normal" U.S. output of feed grains amounted to about 200 million tons. In 1974 the output was only 165 million tons. Prices continued to rise. Of course.

There were sharply higher costs of agricultural production, too. Why? Because of the 4 fold (400 percent!) increase in the price of oil brought about by the OPEC cartel (Organization of Petroleum Exporting Countries). Energy shortages and high fuel prices interfered with agricultural production, worldwide.

Recent Demands, Supplies, and Prices for Grain

In 1975 the U.S. grain harvests recovered from the low outputs of 1974. But the U.S.S.R.

suffered the worst crop disaster in a decade. We worked out a 5-year grain agreement in which the U.S.S.R. agreed to purchase at least 6 million tons of grain from the United States each year for five years: 1976-1980. What do you suppose was happening to the prices of beef cattle? and hogs? You could guess.

The very high grain prices of 1973 and 1974 caused the cattle and hog raisers to cut back—to raise fewer animals. So by 1975 the marketing of grain-fed cattle dropped to the lowest level since the mid-1960s. The number of hogs marketed in 1975 fell to a 35-year low! And what about prices of hogs and steers in 1975? They shot up to the highest levels ever! Of course.

Meanwhile the U.S. government was increasing its own demands for farm products through expansion of its food assistance programs. Figure 32-3 shows a picture of what was going on.

In January of 1980 President Carter announced an embargo on wheat shipments to the Soviet Union, in response to the Soviet invasion of Afghanistan. This obviously reduced the foreign demand for American wheat and the price dropped from about $4 a bushel to about $3.60 immediately. A look at Figure 32-3 shows what a decrease in demand does to the price of grain!

Recent Developments, and the Outlook for American Agriculture

In the early 1970s most American farmers were doing very well. Farm income in 1973 reached a peak of $33 billion. At that time people were interested in reducing government controls over agricultural production and prices. But by 1976, farm income was back down to less than $20 billion. So what happened after that?

During the late 1970s many farmers began to push hard for more and higher government price supports and for more restrictions on agricultural imports. Early in 1978 a new organization called

Fig. 32-3   American Grain Markets in the Mid-1970s: Increased Demand and Decreased Supply

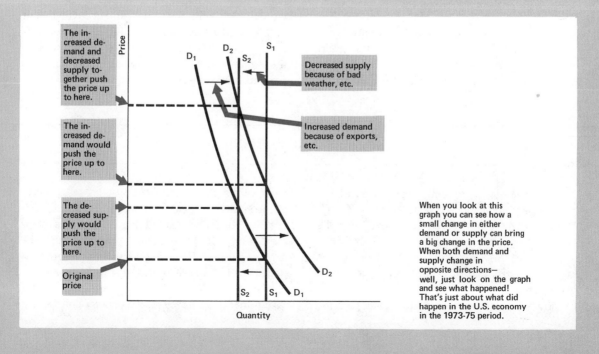

the American Agriculture Movement (AAM) organized tractor parades around the country and in Washington, calling for more price supports. The government responded with a fourfold increase in payments to wheat growers.

In 1979 the AAM led a bigger tractor parade to Washington. The farmers took over the Mall and stayed awhile, but without much success in influencing government policy. Farm incomes in 1978 were up by 30% over 1977 (up about $26 million). Also in early 1979 the Carter administration was much too determined to fight inflation to easily give in to the farmers and push up farm prices (and the inflation rate)! So the "tractorcade" of 1979 didn't achieve much.

Another thing that was happening in the late 1970s was increased political activity by local chapters of all of the farmers' organizations. As farmers have become a smaller percentage of the population, their political power has declined. So now they are trying to build more influence in Congress by lobbying and by making campaign donations and trying to get their chosen candidates elected.

President Reagan's Position

When he was campaigning for the presidency, Ronald Reagan promised to lift the grain embargo, and he did that in April, 1981. But the Reagan administration during its first two years maintained a strong position against the idea of agricultural price supports, in general—while continuing to go along with price supports for a few selected products.

One big problem of agriculture in 1982 was the high interest cost generated by the "tight money" stance of the Fed. Interest costs were pushing up agricultural production costs, leading some economists to predict reduced supplies and increased prices of agricultural products later in the year.

Farm income in 1978 and 1979 was around $30 billion, but in 1980 and 1981 it was hovering around $20 billion. If you look at "constant dollars" to eliminate the effect of inflation, farm income in the early 1980s was only about half that of the mid-1970s. Pressures were mounting for the government to do something about that.

It wasn't that the value of farm output wasn't increasing throughout this period, it was just that production expenses were going up much more rapidly than output values. If you check the agriculture tables in the latest *Economic Report of the President,* you will see what has been happening more recently, on all this.

What will be the effects of all these recent happenings in agriculture? It seems likely that we will have continued government involvement in the markets for farm products. Whatever is done I expect we'll still see ups and downs in these markets. After you look at Figure 32-3, it's hard to think otherwise.

SUMMARY AND SYNTHESIS

The American economic system has undergone great change since colonial times. Originally it was an **agriculture-based economy.** Then the textile industry lead the **industrial revolution** in this country. Following the Civil War there was a **rapid industrialization** and a rapid growth of **giant businesses.**

Throughout its history, **until the depression** years of the 1930s, the United States was mostly a nation of **laissez-faire,** although **"public lands"** policies supported railroad and industrial development, and there were several **programs supporting agriculture.** Also the antitrust movement was beginning to **impose limits on big business behavior.** But it wasn't until the **New Deal** of the 1930s that basic policy in this country changed.

The **Great Depression** of the 1930s and the **New Deal** brought basic changes in the philosophy, policies, and conditions in the American economy. The net effect was a significant move **away from laissez-faire.** The New Deal philosophy is that **the government has a responsibility** to look out for the **material welfare of the people,** and to **keep the economic system operating smoothly.**

The New Deal philosophy is embodied in the social security program, in the **Employment Act of 1946** and in the **Full Employment and Balanced Growth Act of 1978** (the Humphrey-Hawkins Act). Both these acts require the administration to take action as necessary to keep the economy near "full employment with stable prices."

There are **several ways** you might **look at or describe the American economy.** You might look at the **individual sectors,** big business, big labor, and big government. Or you might look at it on the basis of the **attitudes, the institutions,** or the **factors of production.** Or you might look at what it produces—the **"final output mix."** If you really want **to understand the American economy of the 1980s,** you need to spend some time looking at **each of these.**

In the 1980s some 60% of our total GNP is made up of, not physical products, but our production of valuable **trade and services** activities. About one third of the GNP is made up of manufactured goods—about 60% **durable goods** and the others **nondurable. Agricultural output** only makes up about **4%** of the final output of the economic system! (But understand that **most agricultural output enters the economy as manufactured goods,** including everything from cotton sheets and wooden furniture to cigarettes and peanut butter.)

All of Part Eight of this book (which you're just getting into now) will be **explaining and describing various aspects and sectors of the American economy.** The final chapter in Part Eight will try to integrate these component parts so that you will gain **an integrated understanding of the American economic system**—what it is and how it works. As you study Part Eight it would be very helpful if you would

spend some time with the statistical sources mentioned in this chapter to find out what is happening currently in various sectors of the economy.

Productivity in American agriculture is much higher than anywhere else in the world. In this country, farmers make up less than one out of every 30 workers. One farm worker (on the average) produces enough to feed more than 60 people. Just since the 1930s, the **output per hour** on the farms in this country has increased by **more than six times.**

The great productivity in American agriculture has come about from the **"free private enterprise"** efforts of profit-seeking farmers, with considerable help in **educational and extension work** by the federal and state governments. The **Homestead Act (1862)** offered free land to people who would establish farms, and the **Morrell Act** (in the same year) established the land grant (A & I and A & M) colleges to support agricultural education.

In the 1860s about **sixty percent** of the work force was **employed in agriculture.** By the 1920s that was down to about **one fourth.** By the 1980s it's down to **less than one thirtieth!**

Between 1910 and World War I the Federal Government expanded its assistance programs for agriculture. The **Smith-Lever Act (1914)** provided for the federally sponsored **"county extension agents."** The **Rural Credits Act (1916)** provided **farm financing,** and the **Smith-Hughes Act (1917)** provided federal support for **agricultural and vocational education.**

The **inelastic demand** for farm products has resulted in **price instability** in agriculture and has supported the development of the **"parity prices"** idea—that when the prices go up for things farmers buy, the prices of the things farmers sell should also go up by the same amount—and that **the government should support farm prices** to guarantee this result. The idea of parity prices and government price supports **has played an important role in the** agricultural markets since the 1930s.

During the 1970s and early 1980s the **government's influence** in agricultural markets has been **significantly reduced.** There are still a few agricultural commodities with "support" prices. And **farmers' organizations** continue to have sufficient **political strength to influence public policy**

Part Eight • The American Economy: Agriculture, Labor, Business, Government

whenever the feeling among farmers is strong enough to go "all out" to get government support. But the trend in recent years definitely has been toward a reduction of government involvement in the agricultural markets even though there have been some notable exceptions to this trend.

REVIEW EXERCISES

MAJOR CONCEPTS, PRINCIPLES, TERMS (Explain each carefully.)

The New Deal
parity prices

IMPORTANT ACTS (Explain each briefly.)

Sherman Antitrust Act (1890)
Interstate Commerce Act (1887)
Homestead Act (1862)
Morrell Act (1862)
Smith-Lever Act (1914)
Smith-Hughes Act (1917)

Agricultural Adjustment Act (1933)
Employment Act of 1946
Agricultural and Consumer
    Protection Act (1973)
Humphrey-Hawkins Act (1978)

CURVES AND GRAPHS (Draw, label, and explain each.)

Supply and Demand for an Agricultural Product
Price Supports Always Create Surpluses
American Grain Markets in the Mid-1970s: Increased Demand and Decreased
    Supply

QUESTIONS (Write out answers or jot down key points.)

1. Give some of the highlights in the development of the American economy from colonial times to the present.
2. Describe some of the changes in the American economic system which occurred in the depression of the 1930s.
3. Explain and give some examples of what is meant by this statement: There are several different ways to "look at" or describe the American economy.
4. Why do you suppose trade and services make up such a large part of the U.S. GNP? Discuss.
5. Mention some sources of statistics on the American economy, and describe each briefly.
6. Give some of the highlights in the evolution of American agriculture.
7. Explain what it means, and some of the effects of the *inelastic demand for farm products*.
8. Explain the "hidden fallacy" of the idea of parity prices—why it sounds so "just and fair," and why it isn't necessarily just and fair at all.
9. Describe some of the recent developments in the U.S. agricultural product markets.

33 Population, Labor Force, Wages, and Labor-Management Relations

Chapter Objectives

- This chapter continues the look at specific aspects of **the American economy,** focusing specifically on **population, labor force, and labor-management relations.**

- In this chapter you will find out about **recent changes in the structure** of the U.S. **population and labor force,** and about some of the **effects** of these changes.

- When you finish studying this chapter you will be able to give some of the **highlights** in the **history of American labor.** You will be able to **trace the development** of the **labor movement** and explain some of the **important events** and **major legislation** relating to labor.

- You will find out about the **"language of labor-management relations,"** and you will learn a good bit about the labor movement as you learn this **unique** (sometimes colorful) **terminology.**

- Finally, from this chapter you will gain some economic insight into some of the **current labor issues** and into some **unresolved questions** concerning labor in the American economy.

It makes a lot of difference whether the population of a nation is growing rapidly or not. A nation with a rapidly growing population will have a lot of children to support, to take care of, to educate. A lot of people will be tied up in the homes, the schools, the hospitals and other places, taking care of all of the babies and young people.

A nation with a stable population will have more people in the productive ages and more in the retirement ages, but fewer children to take care of. A nation with a declining population will have a larger percentage of retired people. There will be even fewer children.

U.S. POPULATION AND LABOR FORCE: CHANGES SINCE THE 1940s

What does it look like in the United States? The rate of increase in the U.S. population has been slowing down over the past 20 years. So has the age distribution of the population been changing? You bet it has!

Ten or fifteen years ago, school systems all over the country were overcrowded. Teachers were in short supply. But now? Teachers are having trouble finding jobs! Let's take a look at what's been happening to the number of people in some of the age groups.

Children Under Five: Increase, Then Decline. From 1940 to 1960 the number of children under five just about doubled: from about 10 million to about 20 million. But after the early 1960s the number turned around and started going the other way. By the mid-1970s the number of children under five had decreased by about 4 million—down to about 16 million. It declined to 15.2 million in 1977, then began to increase. In 1980 it was up to about 16 million again.

School-Age Children: Increase, Then Decline. At the end of World War II (1945) the United States had about 24 million children and teenagers in the 5-to-15 age bracket. By the mid-1950s the number had increased to more than 30 million and by the early 1960s, to more than 40 million.

In the early 1970s the number reached about 45 million. Then it turned around and went the other way. By the mid-1970s there were less than 42 million in the 5-to-15 age bracket. By 1980 the number was down to 39 million.

Retirement-Age People: Increase, Then More Increase. In 1940 there were only about nine million Americans ages 65 and over. By 1950 the number had increased to about 12 million, and by 1960 to about 17 million. The number almost doubled in twenty years!

By 1970 there were more than twenty million people over 65. As the years of the 1970s kept going by, the number in this over-65 age group kept getting larger. By the mid-1970s the number had passed 22 million. In 1980 it was 25.5 million and was increasing at the rate of about half a million a year.

Recent Rates of Population Increase

Why has the age pattern of the American population changed so much over the past 30 years? Because lower birthrates have caused population growth to slow down. When the growth rate changes, the age groups change. Of course.

The population of the United States is not increasing very fast these days—only at about 1.7 million people per year. In the early 1980s the total U.S. population passed 230 million. (That was about the time the world population passed 4 billion!) An increase of only about 1.7 million per year, with the population already at 230 million gives an annual growth rate of only about 0.7 percent per year. That's almost no growth at all! It's only recently that the growth rate of the U.S. population has been so low.

A Spectacular Slowdown in Growth Since the Early 1960s. As recently as the late 1950s and early 1960s (back about when you were born?) the U.S. population was increasing by about 3 million per year. With a total population of about 180 million at that time, an increase of three million amounted to a 1.7 percent increase per year. That's still quite low as compared with the less developed countries of the world where population growth rates range up to more than 3 percent per year. But 1.7 percent is very high as compared with 0.7 percent.

After the early 1960s, the rate of population growth moved into a continuous decline. By the mid-1970s it stabilized at about 0.7 percent where it remained for the last half of the decade.

The population increased almost 20 percent during the decade of the '50s. It increased only a little more than 10 percent during the decade of the '70s.

Some Economic Effects of the Slowdown. I don't suppose population statistics like these are very exciting to you. But they're important. Just think of all the things that must change when population growth slows down. The economic system has a lot of adjusting to do.

The makers of baby oil and baby powder and baby powder and baby shampoo begin telling you how good their products are for grown-ups, too! College counselors begin advising students not to prepare for careers in teaching. People begin worrying about how much of the national income and output will be needed to support so many retired people. The building of "retirement cities" becomes big business. When you see all these things start happening you can be sure the effects of the new population age-structure are beginning to be felt.

The Labor Force

What about the labor force in the American economy? How big is it? Is it increasing fast? Or slowing down? With a population of more than 230 million, how big would you expect the labor force to be? About half that size? Less than half? Yes. Less than half.

Not Everyone Is in the Labor Force. Some of the people in the population are less than one year old. To be sure they are not in labor force! And some are over 100. I would hope they wouldn't have to work, either.

School students, retired people, a parent who decides to stay home and raise children—these people wouldn't be in the labor force. Also there are always a lot of "institutionalized" people: in hospitals, prisons, other institutions. They aren't in the labor force either.

The Changing Size of the Labor Force. In the early 1980s there were about 110 million people in the U.S. labor force. That's about 43 percent of the population.

The labor force has been increasing fairly steadily over the past 30 years. Since the early 1970s it's been increasing by more than two million people a year. Faster than the population! Why?

Because all the people born back when birth-rates were higher (back when you were born) are now entering the labor force. Also because more women are shifting out of "the homemaking role" and entering the labor force. Immigrants (most of them illegal) are playing a role, too.

But before very long the rate of growth in the labor force will slow down (if illegal immigration doesn't interfere). Why? Because there are now fewer people in the younger age brackets—fewer to become adults and start looking for jobs. So in a few years it probably will be easier for new people entering the labor force to find jobs.

But also, there will be fewer people working to support each retired person. Some people think this will create a serious problem for the economy. Others think increasing productivity will take care of it so it won't be a problem at all. Maybe as new technology and more mechanization are introduced, more retirement and fewer workers is just what the economy will need.

But we don't know for sure about that, of course. Some jobs—like the trade and service jobs—are not easy to mechanize. Only time will tell how it will all work out. Now it's time for a quick glance backward at the way the population and labor force developed in the United States.

POPULATION AND LABOR FORCE: SOME HISTORICAL HIGHLIGHTS

One of the striking things about the economic development of the United States is the speed at which the population grew. In the early days the doors were wide open to immigration. People poured in. Why? For jobs. For income.

Working people in the United States have had it really tough sometimes. But even so, on the average they have had it better than workers in any other nation in the world. As early as 1840, income per capita in the United States was as high as in France. By 1860 it was as high as in Britain. From then on it has continued to lead the world.

The streets weren't paved with gold as some foreigners thought. But they came and found out. And they stayed anyway. And they became Americans and they built America.

"Open Immigration" Slowed the "Labor Movement"

During the late 1800s and early 1900s immigrant labor poured in. Without the immigrants the rapid industrialization of the American economy couldn't have happened. The United States gathered itself a "melting pot" labor force—and gathered it in a hurry.

Different nationalities were flowing into the United States and taking jobs. The U.S. labor force became a motley bunch to be sure! No other nation in the world had ever had anything like it. There were differences in nationality, language, religion—and a strong tendency for each group to stick with their own kind.

So the working people in the United States really didn't form into a close-knit "laboring class." They didn't develop a feeling of togetherness—a consciousness of brotherhood. They didn't all identify with each other. You can see why "labor solidarity" was not an easy objective for the union organizers to achieve!

Open immigration policies provided a constantly increasing labor supply. So shortages and upward wage pressures didn't develop. Also, it was risky for workers with jobs to talk about going on strike or to argue with their employers.

Workers who would join unions or go on strikes could be kicked out. Usually they were. There were always lots of new workers waiting to be hired. Troublemakers could be fired and blacklisted so they couldn't get jobs anywhere. It's no wonder "the labor movement" didn't move very fast in the United States!

Shift of Workers from the Farms

Not all of the new workers pouring into the expanding industries were from overseas. Lots of kids were being raised on the farms. Some of them were growing up and moving off the farms and taking jobs in the factories and mills. It's a good thing that so many people moved off the farms and took jobs in industry. The birth rate on the farms was high. As new technology was developed and more farms were mechanized, the farms just didn't need all those workers.

In 1860, six out of every ten workers in the U.S. economy were working on farms. By 1920 there were a lot more workers in the American economy, of course. But only three out of every ten of them were working on farms. The other seven out of ten were in manufacturing, mining, trade, and other nonagricultural jobs.

You remember from the last chapter what happened after that. By the early 1980s, out of every one hundred workers in the American economy, less than four were working in agriculture.

More Women Are Joining the Labor Force

As the labor force has expanded, the number of women in the labor force has expanded too. Women have had a long, slow struggle for acceptance in many occupations. Traditional discriminatory attitudes still persist. Even in the 1980s in an "advanced and enlightened nation" like the United States, the entrance of women into many occupations is inhibited.

But much progress is being made. Throughout the past two decades, employment of women has been increasing at a much higher rate than employment of men. In recent years, much of the annual increase in the labor force has been made up of women joining the labor force, getting jobs.

In the years following the Civil War there were only about one million employed women in the American economy. By 1920, women had come to be accepted as employees in several industries: food processing, cigarette manufacturing, textiles, and some light metals industries. There was general acceptance of women as telephone operators, nurses, retail clerks, and secretaries. But in the 1920s, men employees still outnumbered women by more than 3 to 1.

In 1950 there were about 15 million employed women. By 1960 there were 20 million. By the mid-1970s there were more than 30 million. The number more than doubled in 25 years. Then by 1981 (in only 6 years) the number was up to almost 40 million—another 33 percent increase! In 1981, 43 percent of the employed people in the country were women.

Is it possible that as the size of the labor force declines (because of the changing age structure of population), some of the decline can be offset by more women joining the labor force? Yes. Not only is it possible. It's already happening.

Also, consider this: the lower birthrate means that many women have fewer homemaking responsibilities. So they have more opportunity to join the labor force and work for wages. And that's just what they're doing. If present trends continue it won't be long before women make up 50 percent of the labor force.

Fewer Hours and Higher Wages

In the early 1800s the usual workday was about 14 hours. Even that long ago there were some labor organizations trying to improve conditions for workers. One objective was to reduce the length of the workday to ten hours. That hardly seems unreasonable by present standards!

But would you believe it wasn't until about 1900 that the workday for most workers got down to ten hours! Even as recently as the 1920s the workday in some industries was still twelve hours! And in some industries a seven-day work-week was not unusual. (And we sometimes think we have it tough!)

What about wages? Throughout the 1800s they were low. The constantly increasing labor supply helped to keep them that way. By the late 1800s wages in several occupations began to move upward. Wages continued upward in the early 1900s, but still only slowly.

When did the great increases in wages and standards of living occur for "the average American"? Only yesterday! Just since the end of the Great Depression and World War II—that is, in the past 30 years or so. If you'll think about that for a few minutes it may help you to better understand some of the attitudes of your parents—or your grandparents.

Increasing Productivity Supports Higher Wages. You know that if the average worker's wage is going up, then the value of output per worker must be going up, too. To get higher wages, workers must produce higher product value. The wage might go up first and then technological advance and mechanization and increased productivity might come afterwards. Or it might happen the other way around. But one way or the other, it has to happen. Remember the reflex effect of real-world markets? Sure.

Wage increases in recent decades have been unprecedented. *Just since 1950 the average wage earner in the United States has achieved a doubling of real income per hour of work. In agriculture, the increases have been even greater.*

The recent increases have been most spectacular. But the productivity of American labor has been increasing at a fairly rapid pace for more than 100 years. Why? New technology and highly efficient machinery and equipment have played a key role. It couldn't have happened without that. But there were other things that helped too.

Labor Mobility. Many American workers are very mobile. They go to the places where the jobs are available—where they can make more money. That is, they go to where their productivity is higher.

Would you believe that six or seven million Americans change their state of residence each year? And that doesn't even count the ones who move to some other place in the same state! How much does all this labor mobility add to productivity? Nobody knows for sure. But it's important.

Emphasis on Education. Education has always been a big thing in America. For more than 100 years the federal government has been assisting the states in vocational and agricultural education. During the present century the emphasis on vocational education has increased even more.

In the 1960s the federal government initiated new manpower development and training programs. It supported programs of on-the-job training, retraining for workers with obsolete skills, and improved job placement services to help people to find jobs.

How much has this emphasis on education and training increased the productivity of the average American worker? Nobody knows for sure about that either, of course. But everybody knows it's important. (You'll be reading more about government support of education in the chapter on government expenditures.)

Labor Problems in the Early Days

In the days following the Civil War the American economy was industrializing rapidly. Immigrants were pouring in. Wages were low and hours were long. Workers often faced tough times.

Most American workers were making out better than the average worker overseas. But that isn't saying much. Conditions were bad. Looking back from the 1980s it's hard to understand how people could put up with such conditions. I guess the answer is that they had no choice. And they didn't think any other way of life was possible. They were right, of course. For them, given the conditions of the times, it wasn't.

Sometimes the workers tried to get together and force the employers to give them a better deal. It's interesting to look back at what the workers did and how they did it—how they tried to organize and work together to improve their lot.

When you finish reading the next sections you'll understand how labor-management relations have evolved in this country. And you'll know about the important role organized labor will be playing in the American economic system of the 1980s.

THE LABOR MOVEMENT IN THE AMERICAN ECONOMY

Labor unions in this country have had a long (and sometimes stormy) history. Skilled workers in the various trades—carpenters, plumbers, shoemakers, etc.—have been getting together in their own organizations for hundreds of years. As the various trades developed in this country, organizations of tradesmen also developed. But when these trade organizations began to argue with their employers about wages and hours, that's when the trouble began: (a) trouble with the employers, and (b) trouble with the law.

The Early Trade Unions and Criminal Conspiracy

In the early 1800s if the trade union members threatened to take any joint action against their employers (such as to strike) they were charged with criminal conspiracy. In those days there wasn't much pro-labor sentiment either in the government or in the courts. The economy was agriculture-based. Industrial workers were a small minority. Remember?

What about **reform unions**? Unions that work to change the harsh system of capitalism? Unions that argue for political action to change the system to one of mutual sharing and brotherly love? During the mid-1880s there were a few "utopian reform unions" in the United States, speaking out for the reorganization of society along more humanitarian lines. But their long-run influence on the American labor movement was negligible. Their approach just didn't catch on in this country.

The Knights of Labor

In 1869 the Knights of Labor (K of L) was formed. This new nationwide union invited just about everybody to join. Lots of people did. Many existing unions and union members joined up. By the mid-1880s the K of L had about 700,000 members.

The K of L had a platform dedicated to improving conditions for working people. They were for the 8-hour workday, equal pay for women, abolition of child labor, arbitration of labor disputes, and other changes. They stood strongly for **labor solidarity**—the idea that working people of all occupations and trades should stick together and work together for their mutual benefit.

The Haymarket Square Incident

The Knights of Labor lacked strong leadership at the top. So its member organizations throughout the country went off in several different directions. In May of 1886 there was a general strike for the 8-hour day. But the different K of L groups were all doing their own thing.

In Chicago, violence broke out. Some strikers were killed. In Haymarket Square (Chicago) a bomb was thrown and policemen were killed. Some union members were tried and executed. There was a wave of public sentiment against unions and the K of L got much of the blame. After that its membership dwindled. In the 1890s the K of L just died out.

The American Federation of Labor

As the Knights of Labor was withering away, membership in a new labor organization, the American Federation of Labor (AFL) was growing rapidly. The AFL was formally established in 1886 under the leadership of Samuel Gompers, the man who was destined to provide leadership for the American labor movement until his death in 1924. In less than 10 years, membership in the AFL had expanded to about 1.7 million. By 1920 the membership was more than 4 million.

What was the AFL? A federation. It brought together already existing national **trade unions** into one big union. Each national "member union" continued to have complete control of its own affairs. But the AFL insisted on certain policy objectives.

The general policy of the AFL was to work for day-by-day improvement of the conditions of working people. That is, their objectives were to try to achieve higher wages, shorter hours, better working conditions. They were not out to reform the world.

The Industrial Workers of the World (IWW)

In 1905 a radical-socialist-pacifist reform union, the Industrial Workers of the World (IWW) was formed. The IWW members (called "Wobblies") were in favor of changing the system and were willing to go about it militantly.

Membership in the IWW was never very large and it didn't have a great impact on the American labor movement. The union was harrassed almost out of existence as "unpatriotic" during World War I.

The Changing Legal Status of Unions

During the 1890s and early 1900s, union activities were dealt with severely under the law. The court held union activities to be illegal under the "conspiracy in restraint of trade" provision of the Sherman Antitrust Act. The Clayton Act in 1914 had a statement exempting labor from the antitrust laws. But the statement was not very effective. It really didn't give any legal status to organized labor.

During the industrial boom of World War I, harmony existed between labor and management. Union membership grew. But following the War, strong anti-union policies were followed by businesses, often led by the National Association of Manufacturers (NAM). Many firms refused to recognize and deal with unions, and insisted on hiring non-union workers.

The anti-union efforts during the 1920s were successful in reducing union membership. Then, after 1930, the economy went deeper and deeper into the depression. More and more people lost their jobs. Many dropped out of the unions. By 1933 union membership had dropped by about 50 percent from the 1920s. But then, in the mid-1930s, legislation was passed giving unions a clear legal right to exist.

The Norris-La Guardia Act and the Wagner Act

In 1932 Congress passed the Norris-La Guardia Act. This Act removed some of the weapons businesses had been using to attack unions. No longer could yellow-dog contracts be enforced in federal courts. (A **yellow-dog contract** is a worker's signed statement swearing not to join a union.) The Act also made it more difficult for businesses to get injunctions (court orders) to prevent unions from going on strike.

The Norris-La Guardia Act was a small step forward for organized labor. The really big step came in 1935 with the passage of the National Labor Relations Act—the so-called "Wagner Act."

The Wagner Act. The Wagner Act made it legal for unions to organize, and illegal for employers to interfere. The Act required employers to bargain collectively with the "recognized" union—that is, with the union which represented the majority of the company's workers.

Under the Wagner Act, organized labor finally obtained its long-sought legal basis on which to exist—its right to function as a recognized part of the American economic system. The Wagner Act set up the National Labor Relations Board (NLRB) to keep an eye on employers and prevent unfair labor practices.

The NLRB. Over the years the NLRB has been performing an increasingly important function in looking out for labor in the American economy. It gives the worker a place to call and complain about unfair labor practices. In recent years the Board has been handling between 40,000 and 50,000 cases per year of workers' complaints against their employers.

Most of the complaints aren't found to be valid. But many are. In 1975 more than 7,000 employees were awarded total payments of more than $11 million in back pay because of unfair labor practices by their employers.

During 1975 the NLRB conducted elections at about 9,000 businesses to determine which union (if any) would represent the workers. In about half of the elections, unions were voted in. In the other half, the workers voted to stay non-union.

The Congress of Industrial Organizations (CIO)

In 1935 a new labor organization was created: the Congress of Industrial Organizations (CIO). The CIO was a federation of unions, just as was the AFL. But the CIO dealt with a different kind of union.

The AFL was a federation of national *trade* unions. Each national union was made up of local trade unions. So each union was made up entirely of members of one particular trade, or craft. Each of the building trades—carpentry, bricklaying, glazing, roofing, plumbing, painting, etc.—had its own trade union. Machinists had their own union, printers their own, teamsters their own, etc. But the CIO was different.

The national unions which joined together to make up the CIO were not trade unions. They were unions of all workers in an industry. In a

CIO union, the skilled, semi-skilled and un-skilled, the painters, plumbers, welders and clean-up people all joined the same union.

At the beginning the CIO had one big mem-ber-union: the United Mine Workers (UMW) which had started in 1890. By 1920 about 50 percent of the miners in the country were UMW members. When the new CIO was started in 1935 it was headed by the fighting UMW Presi-dent, John L. Lewis.

Rapid Unionization of the American Economy

The miners had been organized for some time. But at the time the Wagner Act was passed in the mid-1930s there were several major in-dustries without unions. The biggest two were the steel industry and the automobile industry. John L. Lewis went right to work to unionize the steel workers and the automobile workers. He also soon went to work on the rubber industry, petroleum refining, textiles, electrical machinery, and others. Unionization in the American econ-omy spurted forward.

In the late 1930s, union membership in the American economy grew explosively. By the end of the 1930s there were about 10 million union members in the United States. By 1945 the num-ber had increased to 15 million.

Not all industries and not all workers were unionized, of course. Only about two out of every five non-farm workers were union mem-bers. But it was already easy to see that the wages and working conditions of American workers from then on were going to be in-fluenced quite a lot by what went on at the bar-gaining table.

Labor Unrest and the Taft-Hartley Act

Right after World War II, workers began in-creasing their demands. In May, 1946, the rail-road workers threatened to go on strike. Presi-dent Truman tried to work out a compromise but

couldn't. So to prevent the national paralysis of a railroad strike, Truman took over the railroads. He even went so far as to ask Congress to pass emergency legislation to permit him to draft the strikers. (But Congress didn't do it.)

Several other instances of strong and disrup-tive labor action led to a growing popular re-sentment of unions. Some people began to say that the unions had gotten too much power under the Wagner Act—that something ought to be done to cut down on the power (and some-times, irresponsibility) of the unions. In 1947 Congress responded to this mood and passed the Labor Management Relations Act of 1947—the so-called "Taft-Hartley Act."

The Taft-Hartley Act spe-cifically prohibits certain "un-fair labor practices." It makes it illegal for unions to require the hiring of unneeded employees. And it outlaws the "closed shop" (where only union mem-bers can be hired). But most important, it provides for the federal government to prevent strikes for up to 80 days. It au-thorizes this "cooling off peri-od" of almost three months during which the government can work with labor and man-agement to try to work out a settlement.

Our Labor unions weren't very strong 'til the 1930s!

The unions weren't happy about the passage of the Taft-Hartley Act. Perhaps that's one of the reasons the two big national labor federations—the AFL and the CIO—decided to join forces. That's what they did in 1955.

The Combination of the AFL and the CIO

In 1955, following several years of disagree-ment and negotiation, the two big labor federa-tions came together and merged. So now there's one federation of labor for the entire country: The AFL-CIO. So is there now one voice which speaks for American labor? No. That isn't really the way it works.

In the first place, some of America's biggest national unions are not now AFL-CIO members. But more important, the real power of the American labor movement is exercised by the national unions and by some of the local unions—not by the national AFL-CIO federation.

The unions in the various trades, and the massive industrial unions: steel workers, automobile workers, mine workers and others—are the ones that really exercise the power. They are the ones who sit across the bargaining table and work out the "terms of sale" of American labor.

The Landrum-Griffin Act (1959)

During the 1950s there was a growing feeling that the "bosses" might be running the big unions and that there wasn't enough democratic control by the "rank and file" members. In 1959 the Labor-Management Reporting and Disclosure Act (the Landrum-Griffin Act) was passed to deal with this.

The Landrum-Griffin Act requires democratic procedures in the election of union officers; it holds union officials responsible for union property and money; it guarantees the right of the individual worker to participate in the union's proceedings; and it gives the U.S. Secretary of Labor broad power to look into union governance to see what's going on.

But it is clear that the problem of union corruption has not been totally solved. The September 8, 1980 issue of *U.S. News and World Report* carries the article "Union Corruption: Worse Than Ever." This articles says:

> Twenty years after Congress enacted legislation to rid organized labor of corruption, government records show that racketeers still rule some of America's major unions.

This article names several union officials who have been charged and found guilty of criminal activity, ranging from the embezzlement of large sums of union funds, to close ties with organized crime. The sums of money involved amount to millions. Apparently the issue of union corruption is adding to the effect of crippling strikes to cause a decline in the public sentiment toward labor unions in the early 1980s.

Recent Trends in Union Membership

The most rapid growth in union membership came between 1935 and 1945. But unions continued to grow until the mid-1950s. Since that time union membership hasn't grown very much. There are still many segments of the U.S. workforce which are primarily non-union. Most of the white collar workers, who make up a large and increasing proportion of the labor force, are non-union.

One area in which unions are growing rapidly is in government employment—federal, state and local. The rapid inflation of the late 1960s and the 1970s has put serious pressure on government employee incomes. So how do the people in these jobs get their incomes up? Many of them have joined unions and turned to collective bargaining.

Today, less than one out of every four non-agricultural workers is in a union. Still, the influences of unions (and of their collective bargaining agreements) are felt throughout the labor market and in every segment of the economy.

The Weakening of the Unions?

The election of Ronald Reagan and many of his Republican supporters in November of 1980 was a definite setback for organized labor. Unions had campaigned against the Republicans. The AFL-CIO strongly opposed the Reagan tax-cut plan, but the plan was enacted anyway. Before the end of 1981, several members of Congress were working on legislation which would reduce the power of organized labor.

In the air-traffic controllers' strike in 1981, President Reagan fired the strikers, and won. But the entire nation felt the impact. In April of

1980, the transit workers in New York City went on strike and paralyzed the city. In 1979 a United Airlines strike brought serious harm to the airline industry, and to business and tourism in Hawaii. There seemed to be mounting public disillusionment with organized labor.

Also, the unions themselves were having some trouble with their own internal disputes. In the late '70s and early '80s, one of the big efforts of organized labor was to "get together." Large unions were merging into even larger unions, and the AFL-CIO, which had lost two big unions—the Teamsters and the United Auto Workers with a combined membership approaching 4 million—was trying to bring these unions and others back into the fold.

The financial problems of the American automobile industry led to historic "roll-back" agreements between the automobile companies and the United Auto Workers. In these agreements (essentially) the unions gave up some of their previously gained (costly) benefits in exchange for promises of greater job security. In some cases, union representatives were given a role in management.

The events of the early 1980s promise that this decade will be an eventful one for organized labor.

THE LANGUAGE OF
LABOR-MANAGEMENT RELATIONS

Over the years the labor movement has developed a terminology all its own. This section explains the important terms. In so doing, it explains a lot about the labor movement and about the development of labor-management relations in the American economy.

1. Labor-management relations means the same thing as *industrial relations* which means the same thing as *labor relations*. All three terms are talking about the relationships and dealings between management and organized labor—including collective bargaining procedures, ways of settling disputes, etc.

2. Organized labor simply means "unionized labor." It means "workers who are union members." An *organized firm or plant* is a company or a factory which recognizes one union to speak for all of its workers. All discussions about wages, working conditions, etc., are carried on between representatives of the *recognized union* and representatives of the firm or plant.

3. The labor movement refers to the development of "organized labor." It means how labor gets organized and what organized labor does. The history of the labor movement is the history of organized labor.

4. Collective bargaining is what happens when management and labor representatives get together and work out a *contract,* or *collective bargaining agreement.* The collective bargaining agreement (contract) specifies wages, hours, working conditions, fringe benefits, seniority rights, grievance procedures, hiring and firing procedures, etc. The agreement usually is for three years, but usually there are built-in provisions for annual wage increases and often "cost of living" adjustments to protect the workers from inflation.

5. Fringe benefits, seniority, grievance procedures are important collective bargaining issues. *Fringe benefits* are employer payments for such things as medical insurance and retirement. *Seniority* concerns the question of how much importance will be placed on *length of employment* in determining promotions and salary increases, and in deciding who will be laid off first when business slows down. The *grievance procedure* explains how an employee can go about voicing a complaint about unfair treatment and how that complaint will be given fair consideration, and by whom.

6. The local union is the basic unit in the organized labor structure. There are three levels of unions: local unions, national unions, and federations of national unions. In the case of a *trade union* the "local" would be made up of all of the members of a specific trade, in that locality. The local might cover a small city and its suburbs. A big city might have several locals in the same trade. In the case of an *industrial union* a "local" would include all the union members employed in one factory or plant, or by one local firm.

There are many thousands of local unions in the United States. Some have only a dozen or so members; others have several thousand members. The local union is the one that bargains with employers. But usually the national union helps them to prepare and present a good case and to get the best possible terms in their "collective bargaining agreement."

7. The national union is made up of local unions all over the country. (Often Canadian local unions are included in American national unions.) Union members pay dues to the local and a percentage is passed on to the national. The national unions make broad policies which the locals must follow. The national helps the local and give it much more clout than it would have on its own—especially in collective bargaining.

There are about 200 of these national unions. The largest is the Teamsters with some 2.3 million members. The United Auto Workers' Union has about 1.5 million members and the United Steel Workers, about 1.3 million. The Electrical Workers, the Machinists, and the Carpenters all have memberships approaching one million.

Most of the national unions have fewer than 200,000 members. One fourth of them have fewer than 5,000 members. The role of the national union is very important in influencing labor-management relations, in establishing broad policies, and in influencing the collective bargaining process at the local level.

8. The federation of national unions is the AFL-CIO. The national unions are members of the federation. The federation tries to bring organized labor together, to harmonize their interests, to speak for them and to work for improved conditions of organized labor in the economy. The federation really doesn't have very much power. Each of the national unions keeps on running its own affairs and maintains its right to go its own way.

9. The company union is an "independent" union made up of people who work for a specific company. It is not connected with a national union. "Company unions" have often been promoted by the companies themselves. If a company can get its own plants "organized" before any outside union does it, then it will have a "company union" to "collective bargain" with. It won't have to deal with the tough bargainers of the national unions.

Many companies have found the most effective way to prevent their plants from being unionized by national unions is to form a "company union" and be generous in granting good wages, hours, working conditions, fringe benefits, etc. As long as the "company union" is the recognized bargaining agent for the employees, the national union (or its local) must stand on the sidelines.

But if the national union thinks it can get enough support among the workers in the plant, it can petition the National Labor Relations Board (NLRB) for an election. If the outside union wins, the "company union" is pushed aside and the national union (or its local) becomes the bargaining agent.

10. The exclusive bargaining agent for a plant is the union which has been chosen by the workers, by secret ballot. Once the "exclusive bargaining agent" has been chosen, that "agent" does all of the collective bargaining for the workers—that is, until some other union challenges them and wins an election and takes over.

11. Business unionism, also *bread and butter unionism,* means union polices aimed at dealing with the "bread and butter" issues: wages and hours, working conditions, vacations, fringe benefits, effective grievance procedures, etc. "Business unionism" concentrates on improving the immediate economic conditions of the workers. It isn't concerned with broad areas of social reform or with political or revolutionary actions to change the economic system.

American labor unionism in modern times has been almost exclusively "business unionism." Although communists have sometimes managed to get some control in a few of the national unions, American workers generally have been strongly opposed to radical, revolutionary, and reform movements. Usually the communists who work their way in, soon get pushed out.

12. Closed shop, union shop, and open shop are the three "degrees of unionization" which may exist in a plant. Suppose a plant has recognized a union as the exclusive bargaining agent. If it is a *closed shop* , no one except a member of the chosen union can be hired to work in that plant. If it is a *union shop,* non-union workers can be hired. But after they are hired they soon must join the union. If it is an *open shop* the employer may hire anyone, union member or not, and the person hired may join the recognized union or not, as he or she wishes.

You can see how much control a union would have if it could get a closed shop! Before the Taft-Hartley Act there were some closed shops. But not anymore. The closed shop is now illegal. But there are a lot of union shops.

The "union shop" is outlawed by about 20 of the states under what are called *right-to-work laws.* The arguments pro and con are: (a) that a person should have the right to work without being forced to join a union, vs. (b) that all the employees who enjoy the benefits gained by the union at the bargaining table should be required to join up and help to pay the cost—that is, there shouldn't be any "free-riders."

13. Conciliation, mediation, and arbitration are techniques for breaking a deadlock between management and labor. In all three, some "disinterested and unbiased" person or group of persons is brought in to help to work things out when the collective bargaining process breaks down—that is, when the labor and management representatives can't reach an agreement and a strike is threatening.

Conciliation means trying to soothe the ruffled feathers and get the labor and management representatives to be more reasonable to each other and sit down together and work things out themselves.

Mediation means more involvement by the outside party. The mediator usually works out a proposed settlement and tries to get everyone to agree.

Arbitration is stronger still. It involves a final decision by an outside person: the arbitrator. The decision of the arbitrator is binding on both parties.

14. Strikes and lockouts. You already know what a strike is. The workers don't work. This is the "ultimate tool" of organized labor. Without the right to strike, organized labor doesn't really have much power. But when workers can strike they can force businesses to listen to their demands.

A *wildcat strike* is an "illegal" strike—one which has not been ordered by the union. It means some of the local workers get angry for some reason and walk off the job in violation of the union contract.

In a *sit-down* strike the workers go to work, then occupy the plant. They refuse to work and refuse to leave. This is the kind of strike which was used in 1936 by the United Automobile Workers (CIO) to get General Motors to recognize their union as the sole bargaining agent for GM. This strike lasted for several months. In the end it was a big victory for the union.

A *lock-out* is the opposite of a strike. It means the employers close the plant and lock the workers out. Sit-down strikes and lock-outs were techniques used in the earlier, "rough and tumble" days when "big labor" was getting organized. Neither the sit-down strike nor lock-out has been used much in recent years.

Picketing is usually used along with a strike. Picketing means walking back and forth outside the entrance to the plant, usually carrying signs identifying the local which is on strike and saying the plant is UNFAIR TO LABOR. When workers are picketing a plant, other union workers usually refuse to "cross the picket line." So when one local strikes and pickets the plant, that can shut down all of the operations at that plant site.

15. Scabs and free riders are the bad guys in union lingo. A *scab* is someone who would cross a picket line and take a union worker's job while the union worker is on strike. A *free rider* is not quite as bad. A free rider is someone who enjoys all the benefits that the union gets for the workers at the plant but doesn't join the union.

Free riders are not appreciated by the union, of course. I remember a union newspaper cartoon showing a rat crawling up a mooring line to get on a ship. The caption read: "The Original Free Rider." Not as bad as a "scab." But not so good, either!

16. Injunctions, blacklisting, strike breakers, Pinkerton men—all are terms which belong to the earlier "rough and tumble" era in labor management relations. All refer to ways used to block the labor movement.

An *injunction* is a court order saying that someone must not do some specified something. It's a restraining order. After the order is issued, if it's broken that's contempt of court. For several decades employers used injunctions to prevent union members from striking and picketing.

Blacklisting was a technique used back in the early years of the labor movement. A union member or organizer or "troublemaker" could be identified and "blacklisted." The "blacklist" was circulated and nobody would hire a person whose name was on the blacklist.

Strikebreakers are people brought in to take over the jobs of the workers who go on strike. In the late 1800s and early 1900s this technique was often used by employers. The arrival of strikebreakers at the plant site often led to violence.

Pinkerton men were men employed by the famous Pinkerton Detective Agency which specialized in anti-labor activities. Pinkerton men were used as spies to find out who the union organizers were so they could be kicked out and blacklisted. Sometimes strikebreakers were Pinkerton men. The Pinkerton men were "private cops." They came in very handy for those who wanted to break the labor movement.

So now, enough of what went on in the past. The next section talks about some of the current labor-management issues.

SOME CURRENT LABOR ISSUES

There are now about *twenty million union members* in the American labor force. Most (but not all) of the locals to which these members belong are affiliated with national unions. Most (but not all) of the national unions are members of the AFL-CIO.

Some Unresolved Questions

There is no question that unions are an important part of the American economy. Unions have considerable power and influence over conditions in the labor market and on the relationships between employers and workers. They hold considerable power in the American economic system. Is that good? Or bad? And good or bad from whose point of view? Let's take a look at some of the issues.

The Issue of Crippling Strikes. What about the strikes which sometimes cause serious problems to the American economy? Every U.S. president from Truman (1940s) to Reagan (1980s) has stepped in and interfered in key industries to deal with the issue of crippling strikes. The Taft-Hartley Act says the government may require an 80-day "cooling off period" before a strike begins. But after the cooling off period, what then?

Usually the 80-day period has been long enough to get things worked out. But not always. Should there be a further limitation on the right to strike? Should there be an arrangement for compulsory arbitration (instead of strikes) in key industries? That's what some people have suggested.

The Issue of Cost-Push Inflation. What about cost-push inflation? You know about the bad effects of inflation—distorting things, tearing the society apart, over-pricing American goods in world markets. Unions can (and do) push for higher wages without being too concerned about the inflationary effect.

Each union is "only catching up with the others." But when everybody starts pushing hard to catch up, the race is on! What should be done about this? Should there be limits on the amount of wage increase a union can ask for? And if wages are going to be controlled, shouldn't prices also be controlled? And where does that leave us?

What About Free Riders? The union works to get better wages and working conditions for everyone at the plant. So shouldn't everyone be required to join the union and help to pay the cost?

With the union shop there aren't any free riders. That's why the unions advocate the union shop, of course. But with the union shop the worker is forced to join the union. Some people don't think that's such a good arrangement, either. That's why more than one third of the states have passed "right to work" laws outlawing the union shop.

What About the Question of Monopoly Power? What's the major purpose of a union? To get some monopoly power? Sure. And then to use that power to "rig the labor market" to improve wages and other conditions for their members? Of course.

But the labor market certainly wasn't a market of pure competition, in the first place! Some monopoly power always existed *on the buyer's side* of the labor market. So what do unions do? They provide some monopoly power *on the seller's side* of the labor market. Wages never have been determined by "the free action of the market forces of pure competition and supply and demand." Of course not.

There's no question that unions have gone a long way in "evening up" the monopoly power. Now it exists *on both sides* of the labor market. Some people say the monopoly powers of

unions have gone too far. Others say they haven't gone far enough.

Have Unions Really Raised Wages?

Have the unions really been successful in getting higher wages? Isn't it true that wages and productivity are locked in together? That with the great productivity increases in the American economy, wages would have gone up about as much, anyway? Even if there hadn't been any unions?

Of course wages would have been rising even if there hadn't been any unions. As industrialization has proceeded and as immigration has been limited, the "natural market forces of supply and demand" would have pushed wages up. But in imperfect markets (such as the labor market) where there's so much monopoly power on the buyer's side, these "natural adjustments" can take a long time in coming!

It's not much consolation to a worker to know that "in the long run" the monopoly powers of the labor-buyers probably will be overcome by market forces, and then wages will rise. Working people want wages to rise *now*. And there's no question that for millions of workers, labor unions have helped to cause that to happen.

Also, consider this: Without the pressure of unions pushing up the cost of labor, would businesses have been so quick to develop and introduce the highly productive labor-saving machines and techniques? Of course not. So was it the high productivity that pushed up the wages? Or was it the unions that pushed up the wages? and then the higher wages stimulated more mechanization and that's what pushed up productivity?

Which was it? You know the answer. It was both, working together? Right.

Some Straws in the Winds of Change

In the late 1960s and on into the mid-1970s there were some indications that some of the local unions were losing some of their iron grip. This section gives some examples.

The Building Trades. The trade and craft unions in many localities throughout the country have long been very powerful. In some areas the building trades have "make work" requirements written into local building codes. Building costs are sometimes much higher because of trade union practices.

High building costs interfere with government programs to provide better urban housing. In the late 1960s the federal government initiated its "operation breakthrough" program to try to reduce housing costs. The idea was to try to develop mass production methods for building houses—with preassembly of sections of houses, and other efficient techniques. Pressure from the federal government succeeded in breaking some of the tight control of some local building trade unions. (But there's still a lot of control, to be sure.)

The Printers' Unions. The newspaper printers are another group with powerful local unions. During the 1960s the International Typographical Union (ITU) killed off several newspapers by striking to prevent the newspapers from introducing more efficient printing equipment.

Another powerful printers' union is the International Printing and Graphic Communica-

tions Union. In October of 1975 this union went on strike against the *Washington Post*. The union refused to agree to changes in the "work rules" to permit new processes to be introduced.

Some of the striking union members damaged the presses before leaving. But even so the *Washington Post* was able to keep on publishing. As the months passed, new people were hired to fill the jobs of the strikers. The union members were left without jobs.

This same kind of thing had already happened to the locals of this union at newspapers in Miami, Portland (Oregon), Dallas, Kansas City, and New Haven. Why? Because the unions refused to accept work-rule changes to go along with technological developments in the printing industry.

Some Locals Are Accepting Changes. But some of the local printers' unions (those in St. Louis and in Charlotte, North Carolina) have shown flexibility. They have negotiated contracts accepting work-rule changes, in exchange for assurances of job security.

The ITU locals in New York and Washington and some other cities have also seen the light. The ITU locals have made long-term agreements which protect the jobs and earnings of the people now employed, but which permit work-rule changes so that new electronic typesetting equipment can be installed.

For many years these unions have exercised life-or-death power over the newspapers. But by the mid-1970s the economic forces had become so strong—technological changes had gone so far—that the power of these unions no longer could stop it. Some of the unions have had good leadership and good counsel and have been able to bend with the winds of change—to make the best of a declining situation. Others have stood inflexible and have been broken.

It seems clear from the case of the *Washington Post* that public opinion (even including members of other unions) will not support a craft union which is inflexible and violent in trying to block technological advance.

The Union's "Range of Control" Is Limited. The range within which a craft union can exercise control is limited by the basic economics of the situation. Those unions which can recognize and work within these boundaries can survive in these rapidly changing modern times. They can serve their members well. But those which cannot bend with the changing times are not likely to survive.

Population and labor force are important elements in the American economy. The changing structure of the population, the changing labor force, and the evolving relationships between labor and management are all things which must be understood by anyone who wants to understand the American economy. But there's a lot more to the American economy than that, of course!

Another major sector of the economic system is *business*. That's what the next chapter will be talking about. As soon as you've finished reviewing all the things in this chapter, go on into the next chapter and find out about the important and changing role of business in the American economy.

SUMMARY AND SYNTHESIS

The **age structure** of the population in an economy is of considerable significance. In the United States in the years following World War II (late '40s and '50s) the age structure of the population was "bottom heavy" with **large numbers in the lower-ages.** Since that time **the birth rate has slowed** and the rate of population growth has slowed. So now the numbers in the **upper ages are increasing** while the numbers in the **lower ages are decreasing.**

The **changing age structure** of our population is shifting emphasis toward **retirement-age people, has eliminated the overcrowding in the** schools, and is now **slowing down** the rate at which **new people are entering the labor force.** Several of the **production and distribution choices** of the society during the decade of the 1980s will feel the effects of the changing age structure of our population.

During the 1800s and early 1900s the **open immigration policies** of the United States resulted in **rapid growth in the working-age population and in the labor force.** This rapid increase in the number of workers supported the **rapid development of capital** and the **rapid growth of the American economy.** The labor force also was growing in this period due to the rapid **shift of workers from the farms** to the factories and urban areas. More recently, the growth of the labor force has been significantly augmented by **women entering the labor force.**

During the last century and the early part of this one the usual **workday was 12 or 14 hours.** It was not uncommon for the **work week to be seven days.** It was not until **the depression years** of the 1930s that the **"eight-hour day, forty-hour week"** became the "norm" for American working people.

The **productivity of American workers has** increased greatly over the last century. It has approximately doubled just since World War II. But during the **decade of the 1970s this productivity growth slowed almost to a standstill.**

In the early days of the labor movement, **union** efforts to bargain with employers, or to strike were considered to be **"criminal conspiracy"** punishable by law. To be legal, organizations of working people could not get involved in such things as bargaining for higher wages or better working conditions.

The **Knights of Labor** was a nationwide organization which grew in the 1870s and '80s to about 700,000 members. But this union was **discredited by the Haymarket Square incident,** and after that time it lost membership and finally just "withered away."

While the Knights of Labor was withering away, the **American Federation of Labor (AFL)** was growing, led by **Samuel Gompers** who was to be the leader of the American labor movement from the late 1800s until his death in 1924.

After the passage of the **Sherman Antitrust Act** in 1890, unions were held to be **illegal conspiracies in constraint of trade.** It was not until the 1930s that unions received their legal right to exist, to bargain collectively, and to strike, in the **National Labor Relations Act (Wagner Act)** in 1935. This Act is still the basic labor law of the land, and the **National Labor Relations Board,** established by the Wagner Act, still **conducts elections** among workers in plants to determine which (if any) union will represent them.

The Wagner Act created a lot of **union power.** In response to this the **Congress of Industrial Organizations (CIO)** arose. This new union organized an **entire industry,** not just the workers in a specific trade or craft. The CIO started with the **United Mine Workers,** organized the **United Auto Workers,** then workers in the rubber industry, petroleum refining, textiles, and others.

Fear of (and some instances of) **crippling strikes** resulted in the passage of the **Labor Management Relations Act of 1947** (the **Taft-Hartley Act**). This act limits somewhat the rights of unions to strike, and was considered to be a "backward step" by organized labor.

The AFL and CIO struggled against each other many times during the 1930s and '40s, but during the 1950s they decided to combine and since that time it has been the "AFL-CIO."

The **real power** of unions is exercised by the national unions which work out the contracts with the employers—that is, the **United Steel Workers, United Automobile Workers, Teamsters,** etc.

The special "language" of a subject often gives insight into the nature of the subject itself. In this chapter the **language of labor-management relations** serves as an aid in tracing **the history of the labor movement.**

There are several **current unresolved labor issues.** One is the issue of **crippling strikes.** Although strike activity slowed down significantly during the recession period of 1981-82, the issue is still alive and has not been resolved. The issue of **union corruption,** although perhaps aided by the **Landrum-Griffin Act** (1959) is still a continuing problem. According to the September 8, 1980 *U.S. News and World Report* article "Union Corruption: Worse Than Ever," racketeers are still said to rule some of America's major unions.

The questions of **cost-push inflation,** and of **union monopoly power** are still very much alive. Have unions raised wages? In imperfect markets, **prices can be raised by** "price administering" techniques. Labor unions have helped to do that. Productivity has been forced to respond, with the more rapid introduction of more **efficient labor-saving capital.**

It seems clear that **change is in the wind** for American labor and labor unions. Workers and management are getting a better understanding of the fact that they are both in the same boat together—and that there is no "natural law" that assures that the boat will not sink—if you aren't careful.

REVIEW EXERCISES

MAJOR CONCEPTS, PRINCIPLES, TERMS (Explain each carefully.)

criminal conspiracy
collective bargaining
company union

OTHER CONCEPTS AND TERMS (Explain each briefly.)

reform unions
business unionism
Knights of Labor
Haymarket Square
American Federation of Labor
Samuel Gompers
Industrial Workers of the World
National Labor Relations Board
Congress of Industrial
    Organizations
John L. Lewis
the AFL-CIO

fringe benefits
local, national, and federation of
    unions
closed, union, and open shop
right-to-work laws
conciliation, mediation,
    arbitration
strikes, lockouts
scabs, free-riders
injunctions, blacklisting,
    strikebreakers, and Pinkerton
    men

IMPORTANT ACTS (Explain each briefly.)

Norris-La Guardia Act (1932)
Wagner Act (1935)
Taft-Hartley Act (1947)
Landrum-Griffin Act (1959)

QUESTIONS (Write out answers or jot down key points.)

1. Describe some of the changes now going on in the U.S. population. What are some of the differences you think these changes are going to make? Explain.
2. The changing age structure of the U.S. population is important to people who are now of college age. Can you think of ways it's going to affect you? Discuss.
3. Describe some of the changes now going on in the U.S. labor force. What are some of the differences you think these changes are going to make? Explain.
4. Explain some of the effects of the open immigration policies followed by the United States during the late 1800s and early 1900s.
5. What do you think are the *causes* and the *effects* of the rapid increase in the number of women in the U.S. labor force? Discuss.
6. Describe and explain the improving conditions of American labor over the past 100 years or so.
7. Give the highlights in the history of the labor movement in the United States.
8. Have unions really raised wages in the American economy? Discuss.
9. Unions have a lot of power and influence in the American economy. But so does big business. Do you think the power of unions is too great? and should be more limited? Or do you think union powers should be increased? Discuss.

34 Big Business, Antitrust, Foreign Competition, and Social Control

Chapter Objectives

- This chapter explains the **evolution** and rapid growth of **American businesses** and the development of **giant corporations.** Then it gets into the important **public policy issues** concerning the role of **"big business"** in the American economy.

- When you finish studying this chapter you will be able to describe the **role of business in the American economy** and give some indications of the **extent of concentration**—of "business bigness" in the economy.

- You will be able to give the **historical highlights** in the development of "big business" and in the development of **antitrust legislation and policy.** And you will be able to discuss the issue of **big business and social control** and to explain different positions and **conflicting opinions** on this issue.

- You will be able to explain how **intense competition in the world economy** and **the "new economic philosophy"** of the Reagan administration are affecting American businesses and **public policy toward business** in the early 1980s. And you will be able to explain the **important recent changes** in public policy toward business.

- Finally, for those who have not been introduced to it in other courses, **this chapter has an appendix** which presents the highlights of **business organization, finance,** and **accounting.**

How important are businesses in the American economy? So important that you wouldn't be very far wrong to say: "The American economy is made up of businesses." If you use the word in its broadest sense, "business" can include every kind of productive activity. After all, the original meaning of business was "busy-ness"—that is, being busy. Doing something.

BUSINESSES IN THE AMERICAN ECONOMY: AN OVERVIEW

In the American economy it's mostly businesses which are responsible for getting the work done—for getting the products produced and delivered. So when you're thinking about the American economic system, think about business (busy-ness). That's mostly what it's all about.

The Role of Business in the Economy

In the American economy, *businesses* organize most of the production activities. They make the resource-use choices. They decide what machines to use, which raw materials, how much and what kinds of labor, which products to produce, how to transport the products to markets, which markets, and usually, what prices to charge.

Of course the businesses must respond to buyer demands. And they must respond to changing technology and costs in the input markets too. Each firm is constantly reassessing its situation—looking at the output markets and input markets—considering the alternatives: Which products to produce? In what quantities? Using which inputs? Which technology?

All the millions of American business firms are deciding about these issues all the time. In very small businesses it's usually done by common sense. In the giant corporations it's done using the latest techniques of scientific management. But either way, when the decisions are made and the actions taken, that's what detemines the directions the American economy will go.

About nine tenths of all the productive activity in the United States is done by business firms (including agricultural as well as industrial businesses). The remaining one tenth is done by federal, state and local governments and by nonprofit organizations (hospitals, universities, etc.)

What is the role of businesses in the American economy? Truly, business firms make up the American economic system. They control the flows of productive wealth of the economic system.

The American economy? **Business** is mostly what it's about!

How they do it makes up a large part of the story of how the economic system works.

What Kinds of Businesses?

Businesses range from very small to very large—all the way from the one-worker farm producing a few acres of corn and tomatoes or the high school student who has a pick-up truck and hauls away junk for people on weekends—all the way up to General Motors, IBM, Exxon, and other giant corporations, with sales in the billions.

Businesses are involved in every kind of activity: agriculture, forestry, fisheries, manufacturing, mining, construction, transportation, communications, storage, wholesale and retail trade and all kinds of services.

How Many Businesses?

There are millions of businesses in the American economy. Would you believe about *ten million*? The next time you are out driving around, look at the businesses: groceries, restaurants, taverns and bars, laundries, bus and trucking companies, lumber yards, building supply firms, clothing stores, drug stores, jewelry stores, law offices, real estate companies, service stations, and on and on.

Of the total of about 10 million business firms, about half of them (5 million) are in wholesale and retail trade and services. The next largest group—about 3 million or so—are in agriculture, forestry, and fisheries. Then there are about one million or so firms in the financial field.

That only leaves about 2 million firms in manufacturing, construction, mining, transportation and communications. But

596   Part Eight ● The American Economy: Agriculture, Labor, Business, Government

as you might guess, a large part of the economy's output comes from the 2 million firms in this last group—especially the manufacturing firms.

How Big Are the Businesses?

How big are these 10 million firms? Most of them are small. But a few of them are massive. Most of the businesses—in fact about 80 percent of them—are one-owner businesses. They are "proprietorships."

Only about 13 percent of the businesses are corporations. But the big corporations are the ones that own and control the great majority of the productive assets of the economy.

But not all corportions are "big business." In fact, most of them are small. Some are tiny.

Although there are more than one million corporations, more than half of the corporate assets are controlled by the largest two hundred. That means .02 percent of the corporations control more than 50 percent of the assets! What does this tell us? Simply that *big business is a dominant characteristic of the American economy.*

There are about half a million manufacturing corporations in the United States. But of all of the assets of those 500,000 corporations, half of those assets are owned by the 100 largest corporations. That is, 50 percent of the manufacturing assets are owned by .02 percent of the businesses.

Market-Concentration Ratios—a Measure of Bigness

Another way of looking at the bigness of business is to look and see how much concentration there is in the **market structure.** Market structure means "how many and how big are the buyers and sellers." Remember?

Economists use the term **concentration ratio** to indicate the number of sellers of a product. *The "concentraton ratio" is usually defined as the percentage of the total output of the product which is produced by the four biggest producers.*

Here's an example. Suppose there were only four firms in the industry. Then 100 percent of the output would be produced and sold by the four largest firms. So what would be the concentration ratio? One hundred (100 percent) of course. If there were 100 firms, each producing 1 percent of the output, then the largest 4 would be producing only 4 percent. So the concentration ratio would be 4. Not much concentration, right?

Concentration Ratios in American Industries

How about concentration ratios in the American economy? In some industries it's low. But in other industries it's very high. Take the automobile industry. What would you guess? A high concentration ratio? Of course. Would you believe 99?

In aluminum the concentration ratio is about 96. In cigarettes, soaps, and automobile tires the ratio is around 75. The aircraft industry and the steel industry have concentration ratios in the neighborhood of 50.

In petroleum and cement the concentration ratios are about 35. In the market for shoes the ratio is about 25. In some manufacturing industries (for example soft drinks and wood furniture) concentration ratios get down to less than 10. In the non-manufacturing industries (agriculture, for example) concentration ratios are much lower—often less than one.

What is responsible for high concentration ratios in some industries? There's no easy answer to this of course. But it seems to be related to *fixed capital requirements* (high fixed cost) in the industry. In an industry where a large capital investment is required, the concentration ratio is likely to be higher than in an industry which does not require much initial investment.

You wouldn't expect a very high concentration ratio in roadside stands selling fresh corn and tomatoes. But in the production of automobiles, aircraft, steel, and petroleum it's different.

High concentration in the heavy manufacturing industries is a fact of life in the American economy.

What About the Small Businesses?

It's easy to see that a few big businesses hold the central position and play the key productive role in the American economy. But all those millions of small businesses are there too. And you should know something about them.

Most Small Businesses Soon Go "Out of Business." Most of the really small businesses don't survive for very long. Many don't make it even for one year. The average life expectancy of a new small business is only about 5 or 6 years. But as yesterday's little businesses are folding up, new optimistic and venturesome people are striking out anew or taking over the failures of others—fulfilling the American dream of going into business for themselves.

Millions of the small businesses are the tiny "mom and pop" businesses. Most of them are grocery stores, drug stores, service stations and other retail stores and services. Usually the owners work long hours and get less than the minimum wage for their efforts. Before long, most of them are looking for a chance to sell out and get a job working somewhere else for steady wages.

There seems to be something magic about the idea of "going into business for yourself." Many people dream of doing it—of being their own boss. When you go into business on your own, one thing is sure: You are your own boss. But when the customers don't seem to be making their payments and your banker is after you and your suppliers are after you, "being your own boss" may not be so pleasant after all.

Some Small Businesses Survive and Prosper. Luckily, the story doesn't always turn out bad. Many small businesses make it. They prosper and grow. Sometimes they get incorporated and sell stock to get money to buy more

capital to keep on growing.

The venturesome people who make good (the minority, unfortunately) gain financial freedom. It's these few successes, I suppose, which keep so many people going into businesses for themselves. "If they can make it, so can I." And even those who fail gain something: a valuable educational experience in applied economics!

Big Business Is the Heart of the American Economic System

The millions of small businesses in the American economy are important, to be sure. But the heart of the productive system is big business.

The state of the economy depends a lot on the decisions and actions of big businesses. Big businesses play a key role in influencing productivity, employment, wages, prices, outputs, incomes, technology, growth—everything. As you already know, even the questions of prosperity or depression depend a lot on the decisions of the big businesses.

The decisions and actions of the big corporations have a lot to do with the daily lives of all of us. But is wasn't always that way. In the beginning the U.S. economy was based on agriculture. So how did these big corporations come about? What brought such big changes in the American economic system?

THE GROWTH OF AMERICAN INDUSTRY

How long did it take this agriculture-based new nation to become an industrial nation? Only a few decades. Historically speaking it happened overnight.

The Early Years

In the beginning, Alexander Hamilton was impressed with the potential of industry and he worked for policies to support the growth of industries. In the late 1700s and early 1800s efforts were made to induce foreigners with experience in textiles to come to this country and set up enterprises. People with know-how in metals were also attracted, and the latest kinds of machinery sometimes were smuggled out of Britain and brought to the United States.

The Beginnings of Mass Production. In the metal industries, much new technology was developed in this country. I suppose you've heard about Eli Whitney. He is best known for developing the cotton gin. But he did more than that. He was a pioneer in the development of mass production.

In the late 1700s he worked out a way of producing muskets by first producing a lot of identical parts and then having the parts assembled. That seems like a simple enough thing to do? But when no one has done it before, it's quite a breakthrough.

During the early to mid-1800s there were new high-speed machines for metalworking: lathes, milling machines, others. The new machines could make high quality identical parts. So mass production became easier and more efficient.

Increasing Capital Investment. The population of the United States was growing rapidly. With no barriers to interstate trade, markets for products also grew rapidly. Industrial growth spurted forward. Between 1820 and 1860 the total capital value in U.S. industry increased from about $50 million to $1,800 million. That's a thirty-six fold increase in only 40 years!

The pre-Civil War years were years of rapid growth, to be sure. But it was the decade following the Civil War that the industrialization of the American economy became breathtaking. Manufacturing outputs in the United States increased by twelve times between 1860 and 1914. By the early 1900s the United States already had become the world leader in industrial production. How did it happen?

Rapid Growth After the Civil War

Throughout the late 1800s the new construction was like something the world had never seen. Whole cities were built. Hundreds of factories. Thousands of miles of railroads. Ships. Everything. Unbelievable! But just the same, it happened.

Population, industries, cities, all exploding at the same time. The government climate was favorable. New machinery was being developed and introduced rapidly. Mechanization came fast in coal, oil, steel. With mechanization there came giant plants, massive investments, super-big businesses. Heavy capital investments were required in railroads, pipelines, mines, oil wells, refineries, iron and steel plants.

The Age of the Robber Barons

During this time there developed a special breed of American business leaders. Industrial giants? Or robber barons? Call them what you will. But they played a big role in the development of the economy.

They were ready and able to take the risks of experimentation and change. They were riding the crest of the wave of economic expansion—with a rapidly expanding labor force, easily available high-quality raw materials, and massive profits to help to provide the capital. With good (often tough) business management, they kept the profits high and the investments high and kept the ball rolling faster and faster.

Mass production spread from plant to plant and from industry to industry. An industrial plant became a whole system of interrelated automatic machinery. As you might guess, the investment cost was very high. With all that investment, the business investors really wanted to keep their plants operating at full speed. They all wanted high outputs, big markets and profitable prices.

Sometimes businesses would cut prices to

try to sell more. But what would happen? Other businesses would cut prices too. Why? To keep from losing their customers. Maybe to try to get some new customers themselves. What ideal circumstances for price wars and cut-throat competition!

Think back. Remember about **oligopoly**? About the nervous watchfulness of oligopolistic competition? You learned about that from the tuba-producing island chiefs. Right? It's just that way in the real world, too.

In the decades following the Civil War, waves of cut-throat competition broke out among the firms in the railroad, steel, oil, and coal industries. The business giants (robber barons) began looking for ways to "stabilize" their industries—ways to get together and eliminate all this nervous, watchful, disruptive "oligopolistic competition."

The Trust Movement

In the 1880s John D. Rockefeller solved the problem of oligopolistic competition in the oil industry. He created the Standard Oil Trust. A **trust** worked like this: All of the stockholders in the competing firms would turn over their stocks to a board of trustees. In exchange they got trust certificates. So the board of trusteees held the stock. That gave them control over all of the competing businesses. A neat way to eliminate competition, right?

With a trust setup it's as though only one firm exists! Complete monopoly? Maybe. But usually, not quite. Usually there were owners of a few firms who refused to join up. But for practical purposes, yes. Complete monopoly.

The "trust" approach was not the only approach used. There were several other ways the oligopolistic businesses got together to eliminate competition. Sometimes the separate businesses would merge and form one new big business. Sometimes one business would buy up the other businesses. Sometimes the businesses just got together and quietly agreed not to cut prices, not to sell in each other's territories, etc.

What was the effect of all these moves to eliminate competition? They eliminated a lot of competition. They created a lot of monopoly.

The Antitrust Movement

The trust and **merger** movements of the late 1800s soon got the public eye. The people didn't like some of the things big businesses were doing. As you know, in 1887 the Interstate Commerce Act was passed, setting up the Interstate Commerce Commission (ICC) to regulate railroad rates and services. Then in 1890 the Sherman Antitrust Act was passed.

The Sherman Act wasn't very specific. In fact it really didn't say very much. Essentially what it did was to put into statute form the prohibitions which already existed in common law. The prohibitions were against sellers' conspiracies to benefit themselves by restraining trade—that is, be getting together with other sellers and agreeing to restrict the supply of something to keep the prices up high.

The Sherman Act says:

Section 1. Every contract, combination in the form of trust or otherwise, or conspiracy, in restraint of trade or commerce among the several states or with foreign nations, is hereby declared to be illegal. . . .

Section 2. Every person who shall monopolize, or attempt to monopolize, or combine or conspire with any other person or persons, to monopolize any part of the trade or commerce among the several states, or with foreign nations, shall be deemed guilty of a misdemeanor. . . .

In the years following the passage of the Sherman Act, public policy against trusts and mergers really wasn't very strong. The Attorney General wasn't very interested in prosecuting cases under the Sherman Act, and the courts weren't very much interested in handing out guilty verdicts. In fact, after the act was passed there were a lot more "combinations in restraint of trade" and "attempts to monopolize" than there ever had been before!

In the period between 1897 and 1903 there was a wave of mergers which far surpassed anything that had ever happened before. Several multi-billion-dollar industrial combinations were created. The granddaddy of them all was the giant U.S. Steel Corporation. It joined together under one ownership about 800 different plants previously owned by more than 200 separate firms. And what action did the government take under the Sherman Antitrust Act? None.

Financing the Corporations

As businesses grew, more and more of them decided to get incorporated—that is, to become corporations. Between 1860 and 1914 the number of corporations multiplied by nearly 60 times. There are some advantages that go with being a corporation. Corporations can have many stockholders, all providing money to support the growth of the business and all sharing in the ownership.

Also, consider this: It's quite easy for corporations to merge with each other. The stock of all of the competing firms can be turned in. Then stock in the new "combined firm" can be issued in exchange. The new combined firm will then own all the assets of the previously competing firms. What a neat way to eliminate competition and get monopoly power!

With the rapid growth of corporations and all the trusts and mergers going on, how did it all fit together? How were the financial deals worked out? Who was buying and selling and exchanging all these stocks? all of these "ownership shares" in all of these businesses? And how?

You could guess that there were stock markets and stock brokers (dealers in stocks). And that bankers would be involved. Of course. Bankers played a very important role.

The Investment Bankers and Industrial Control

In 1869 the New York Stock Exchange was set up. The purpose was to enable people to buy and sell stock in the railroads and some other corporations. But when companies would issue new stock and sell it to get money to finance a business expansion, the stock usually wouldn't be sold on the exchange. It would be sold through an investment banker.

An investment banker is a person (or firm) who sells newly issued securities for the issuing corporation. It works like this: Suppose a company needs a million dollars to buy buildings and machinery and equipment. And suppose it decides not to borrow the money or to save it out of profits, but to sell new stocks instead.

They have a million dollars' worth of new stock certificates printed up. Then they turn over the new stocks to an investment banker who proceeds to sell them to banks, insurance companies, private investors—anyone who will buy them.

In the late 1800s investment bankers played an important role in financing the rapidly growing corporations. Some of the investment bankers got very wealthy. They had enough money to buy and hold great blocks of stock themselves. And they did.

You know what a person who holds a block of stock in a company can do. Control the company? Right! Did you ever hear of John Pierpont (J.P.) Morgan? He was an investment banker (and also a regular banker and also a lot of other things). He managed to get enough financial control in several firms to make things go his way.

Can you see how the investment banker might contribute to the growth of monopoly power? First, get a controlling interest in the stocks of several competing corporations. Then get all of them to raise their prices at the same time! and to stop competing in the same market areas! Sure.

Then all of them make lots more profits than they made before. And without the worry that some competitor might undersell them. And who gets to enjoy a big chunk of the profits? J. P. Morgan and Co.? You bet.

The Investment Bankers and Monopoly Power

It's easy to see how the investment bankers could get influence in lots of competing corporations and eliminate the competition between them. J. P. Morgan wasn't the only one. But he was the biggest. Here's an example of what it was like.

J. P. Morgan and Company held a major stockholding in the National City Bank and was also tied in with the First National Bank of New York. By 1912, J. P. Morgan and Company, First National Bank, and National City Bank held directorships in more than one hundred corporations, involving a total value of more than $22 billion in assets. These corporations included several of the major ones in the American economy—in the railroad, industrial, public utility, and banking business.

How competitive was the American economy? At the heart—at the financial-industrial-public utility-railroad core—there wasn't much competition. In fact it was quite the opposite. There was a great concentration of economic power in the hands of very few people.

What about today? In the 1980s? As you already know, even today there are great concentrations of economic power. But probably not as much as then.

Today we don't have anything that quite compares with the J. P. Morgan and Company example. And government, through Congress and the Department of Justice and the courts, has decided to take a much stronger position against monopoly. The next section gives a quick run-down on the changing attitudes and public policies toward monopoly power—that is, to-ward these "combinations and conspiracies in restraint of trade."

HIGHLIGHTS IN THE HISTORY OF U.S. ANTITRUST POLICY

Antitrust policy in this country has followed an interesting but not always logical evolution. At some times in the past, big businesses have been able to get away with just about anything. More recently they haven't been able to get away with as much. Here's a chronological listing and explanation of the highlights.

1. The Common Law. Before the Sherman Act was passed, common law prohibited conspiracies among businesses to "restrain trade"—that is, to enrich themselves at the expense of their customers.

2. The Interstate Commerce Act (1887) set up the Interstate Commerce Commission (ICC) to regulate railroad services and rates.

3. The Sherman Antitrust Act (1890) makes it illegal to attempt to monopolize, or to enter into combinations or conspiracies in retraint of trade.

4. The E. C. Knight Case (1895). The American Sugar Refining Company had worked out an arrangement to control 95 percent of the sugar refined in the country. But the Supreme Court declared that this was not illegal. Why? Because the monopoly was in *manufacturing*, not in *commerce*. This was exactly the kind of combination the Sherman Act was supposed to prevent. But the Supreme Court at that time was not in the mood to enforce the Sherman Act. So it didn't.

5. The Northern Securities Company Case (1904). In this case the Supreme Court decided that the Northern Securities Company—a combination of several railroads put together by J. P. Morgan and others—was illegal. The Theodore Roosevelt administration was happy with the decision. Immediately the Department of Justice went to work against the American Tobacco Company and the Standard Oil Company—both gigantic combinations, monopolizing entire industries.

6. The American Tobacco and Standard Oil Cases (1911). In these cases the Supreme Court ordered the breakup of both of these giant combinations. So several separate oil companies and tobacco companies were established.

7. The Rule of Reason (1911). This "rule" was created by the language of the Supreme Court in the Standard Oil an American Tobacco Company decisions. The idea was that "every contract or combination" which might tend toward monopoly was not necessarily illegal. Only *unreasonable* ones were illegal. The rule of reason further weakened antitrust enforcement—which as you know by now had never been very strong anyway.

8. The Clayton Act (1914). This was the second antitrust act passed by the U.S. Congress. It spelled out some of the things which were illegal. It replaced some of the vagueness of the Sherman Act. The Clayton Act outlawed price discrimination by manufacturers in selling to wholesalers and retailers. (You can't sell cheaper to one retailer than to another.) It outlawed tying contracts and exclusive dealing arrangements. (If you're a manufacturer you *can't force a retailer to carry all of your products and deal exclusively with you.*)

The Clayton Act also outlawed interlocking directorates (where the same people are on the boards of directors of two or more competing corporations), and acquisitions of stocks or assets by one corporation in a competing corporation. (You can't buy out your competitors.) With all these prohibitions you would think that the Clayton Act was a powerful tool of antitrust enforcement. But it didn't turn out that way. Here's the problem: All these things that were outlawed *really weren't entirely outlawed!*

In each case, the illegal acts were not illegal unless the effect was "substantially to lessen" competition. So how much could a company do before it was illegal? How much (of price discrimination and tying contracts and exclusive dealing arrangements and interlocking directorates and intercorporate acquisition of stocks and assets) could you get away with before someone would blow the whistle? As the courts interpreted it, you could get away with quite a lot.

The Clayton Act may have caused some businesses to be cautious—perhaps not to do some things they might otherwise have done. But there wasn't much actual enforcement. The Clayton Act didn't get much use during the first twenty years or so of its lfe. (You remember from the previous chapter that the Clayton Act had a clause exempting labor from the antitrust laws—and that clause was so weakly worded that it also was ineffective.)

9. The Federal Trade Commission Act (1914). This Act specifically prohibited "unfair methods of competition" and "unfair or deceptive acts of practices" in commerce. This Act also set up the Federal Trade Commission (FTC).

The FTC was given broad powers to investigate and issue orders to prevent unfair methods of competition. But it too had most of its powers eroded by the courts. It was not until 1938 when the Wheeler-Lea Act gave it the task of policing false and deceptive advertising that the FTC began to do very much.

10. The U.S. Steel Case (1920). In this case the Supreme Court ruled that U.S. Steel was not an illegal monopoly and that *size alone* did not make a giant combination illegal. *It was only when unreasonable things were done that the monopoly was illegal.*

11. The Robinson-Patman Act (1936). This Act was aimed at reducing price discrimination by spelling out some things left unsaid in the Clayton Act. But the actual effect was that of protecting small and inefficient businesses from the competition of larger more efficient firms. This act probably did more to reduce competition than to strengthen it.

12. The Miller-Tydings Act (1937). This Act was passed to reduce competition among retail firms. It supported state laws permitting manufacturers to fix the retail prices of their products. The retail firms were legally required to charge the manufacturer's quoted price.

This is called resale price maintenance or fair trade. The effect of this Act and the state "fair trade" laws was to reduce competition between retailers. In effect, it permitted the monopolized manufacturers to extend the long arm of monopoly all the way to the retail level.

13. The Wheeler-Lea Act (1938). This act outlawed deceptive or misleading advertising and gave the FTC the task of policing advertising to see to it that the businesses "keep it straight and honest."

If you ever watch television I'm sure you know that lots of advertising is not designed to tell "the truth, the whole truth and nothing but the truth." Some of the things done by the headache-pill pushers, for example, are carefully designed to be deceptive and misleading.

The FTC has had some success. Also, perhaps businesses prepare their advertising programs more carefully because they know the FTC is there watching. Maybe it helps more than we realize.

14. Thurmond Arnold's Trust-Busting (late 1930s). Thurmond Arnold, the trust-busting Assistant Attorney General who was head of the Antitrust Division of the U.S. Department of Justice, pushed hard for antitrust enforcements in several industries. These were the depression years and the climate was right to attack big businesses. Thurmond Arnold went after them in a way they had never been gone after before.

The industries he brought cases against included glass, cigarettes, cement, and several others—including the giant Aluminum Company of America (Alcoa) which supplied about 90 percent of the aluminum market. Both the general political sentiment and the attitude of the Supreme Court were ready to make Thurmond Arnold's prosecutions stick. He achieved considerable success. In fact he played the important role of bringing in the new era of antitrust enforcement in the United States.

15. The Aluminum Company of America (Alcoa) Case (1945). In this case the Supreme Court reversed the position taken in the U.S. Steel Case (1920) and said that *mere size alone is all that is necessary for a giant firm to be illegal under*

the antitrust laws. (Other court cases since 1945 have reaffirmed this position.)

The Court said that even though Alcoa had not used any illegal means in trying to gain its monopoly position, and even though it might not be possible to show that Alcoa had used its monopoly position in any "unreasonable" way, the mere fact of its size gave it a monopoly position. And that, by itself, was illegal. The Court ordered Alcoa to split. Reynolds Metals was created as a result.

16. The Cement Institute Case (1948). This case abolished the basing point pricing system—a system of "geographic price discrimination." With basing point pricing, each buyer is quoted a "delivered price" which will be higher or lower depending on how far the buyer is located from the nearest "basing point." Buyers located at a basing point get the lowest prices, of course!

Basing point pricing had been under attack ever since the Pittsburgh plus system (pricing all steel in the country with Pittsburgh as the basing point) was the first set up in the early 1900s. But it wasn't until 1948 that basing point pricing was held to be illegal.

17. The Cellar-Kefauver Anti-Merger Act (1950). This Act prevents competing businesses from merging with each other. Under this act the Supreme Court has been very strict in preventing firms from merging. Several mergers which would never have been questioned during the first 30 years of this century, in recent years have been held to be illegal.

18. The DuPont-General Motors Case (1957). In this case the Supreme Court held that DuPont's holdings of General Motors' stock lessened competition. The Court required DuPont to sell its GM stock. The issue was that GM buys a lot of paint for its cars and buys the paint from DuPont. Since DuPont held enough GM stock to influence GM decisions about where to buy its paint, the stock-holding was held illegal.

19. The Electrical Equipment Price-fixing Case (1961). In this case General Electric, Westinghouse, and other sellers of electrical equipment were found guilty of price-fixing. Some of the executives were sent to jail.

Fines of more than one million dollars were levied on the companies by the government, and the companies were required to pay *triple damages* (three times the amount of the loss) to all of the buyers who had been over-charged. The triple damage payments by the companies amounted to about half a billion dollars! This case let businesses know that the government was deadly serious about prosecuting for collusive price-fixing.

20. The Conglomerate Merger Movement (1960s). Throughout the history of business growth in this country, mergers generally have been among firms involved in similar or closely related activities. There were **horizontal mergers** (one company with steel rolling mills might merge with another company with steel rolling mills) and there were **vertical mergers** (a company with steel rolling mills might merge with a company making basic steel and with a company producing iron ore). Sometimes there were giant mergers like the case of U.S. Steel Corporation which involved a lot of both horizontal and vertical merging.

But in the 1960s there developed a new kind of merger movement: **conglomerate mergers**. There was a lot of this in the 1960s. As a result, several giant "conglomerate corporations" were created in the American economy.

A conglomerate corporation is one which joins several different and unrelated kinds of businesses together under one top management. For example, LTV Corporation started out primarily as an aircraft manufacturer. Then it started taking over other corporations: meat packing, sporting goods, pharmaceuticals—on Wall Street it was called "meat balls, golf balls, and goof balls." Then it took over J & L Steel, and others.

Many well-known corporations began "diversifying." Several of them changed their names to better reflect the "conglomerate" nature of their expanded operations. U.S. Rubber Company became Uniroyal; Warner Brothers pictures became Warner Communications, United Fruit became AMK Corporation and later, United Brands.

These were the days when International Telephone and Telegraph (ITT) took over several things, including the Sheraton hotel chain; Reynolds Tobacco went into the food and beverage and other businesses; Litton Industries got involved in just about everything; Tenneco (formerly Tennessee Pipeline Company) went into shipbuilding, agricultural equipment and lots of other things.

What was the effect of all this conglomerate merging? As long as firms were diversifying and not merging with their competitors, what's the harm? But then look at it this way: What's the good of letting one corporation gain control over so many billions of dollars' worth of corporate assets? Over such big pieces of the American economic system?

During the late 1970s there was considerable disagreement in Congress about what to do about conglomerate mergers. Senator Phillip Hart, one of the long-time champions of maintaining competition and of protecting the consumer, was working on a bill that would tighten antitrust enforcement. Senator Edward Kennedy, chairman of the Senate Judiciary Committee, was pushing a bill which would stop a large firm from acquiring or merging with another firm, just because the firm was already "large enough." But no congressional action was taken. Instead, conditions changed, and the direction shifted.

The 1980s: New Policy Direction

By the early 1980s, it was becoming increasingly clear that the ability of American firms to compete with foreign firms was in jeopardy. An American firm might have a complete monopoly and still go broke because of inability to compete with foreign firms! So the emphasis during the early part of the Reagan Administration changed: from *antitrust and government regulation* of industry, to *trying to create conditions which would stimulate increased productivity* by American industry.

In the late 1970s and early 1980s, antitrust actions were pending against several firms, and anti-conglomerate legislation was pending in Congress. But with the Reagan election, both the idea of passing new legislation and of proceeding on several of the antitrust cases was deferred, or abandoned.

The AT&T and IBM Cases (1982)

In January of 1982 two historic antitrust decisions were made. The American Telephone and Telegraph Company (AT&T), the world's largest corporation, agreed to its own breakup.

The Antitrust Division of the U.S. Department of Justice had been trying for 7 years to break up the AT&T system. Under the agreement, AT&T agreed to divest itself of two-thirds of its assets. All of the local operating telephone companies which had been part of the "Bell System" will be split off from AT&T.

On the same day that the AT&T divestiture was announced, the Justice Department announced that it was dropping its other massive antitrust case—i.e., the case against International Business Machines Corporation (IBM).

Without its operating companies, AT&T may be a strong competitor for IBM. AT&T still has its research, product development, and long-distance telephone connections. So it is in an excellent position to move into modern telecommunications and data transmission markets. And that's where it will meet IBM as a major competitor.

Deregulation

A major thrust of the Reagan administration policy aims toward increasing the efficiency and productivity of the American economy. Backing off on antitrust enforcement seems to be one of the directions. Another direction is clear: *deregulation.*

The cost to American businesses of complying with governmental regulations in 1980 was estimated at about $125 billion. The Reagan administration promised to reduce that figure significantly. The regulation cut-back affected many departments and agencies, ranging from Energy, Interior, and Agriculture, to the Environmental Protection Agency, Occupational Safety and Health Administration, and Consumer Product Safety Commission, and many more.

The objective stated was that only those regulations found to be "cost effective" would be continued. If the *costs* were to exceed the value of the *benefits*, then the regulation would not be permitted.

As this book goes to press in mid-1982 it is clear that much is changing in the area of public policy toward business. Not everyone is happy with the changes. But the present direction of the Reagan administration seems clear. But the future? Who knows. There are Congressional elections coming up in November, 1982. The results of those elections may cause some changes in some of the policies. By the time you are reading this it might be a good idea to check some of the current news magazines and see what's happening.

EXEMPTIONS TO THE ANTITRUST LAWS

Government policy hasn't always been against monopoly. Many things have been done *to aid the growth of monopoly power.* Here are three important examples:

1. The patent system gives the inventor a monopoly. Sometimes patents have been used to monopolize entire industries.
2. Governments sometimes have fixed prices and sometimes have made price competition illegal. You know about the "fair trade" laws. But that isn't all. In 1933 the National Industrial Recovery Act (NIRA)

permitted entire industries to enter into cartel agreements. The firms in the industry could get together and fix prices and divide up market shares and act as a complete monopoly.

3. Special exemptions from the antitrust laws have been made for farmers' organizations and labor unions, and for manufacturers selling in competition with foreign monopolists.

The Public Utilities

The public utilities are a special group of big businesses. They are regulated by governments—federal, state and local—and in some cases they are owned and operated by governments. Why? You already know, right?

The public utilities are **natural monopolies**—that is, there's something about the nature of the industry that doesn't let competition work to safeguard the public interest. So what happens? The governments come in and regulate and control to "protect the public interest." And sometimes the governments just decide to own and operate the businesses. For example, many cities operate water systems, power systems, gas systems, and transport systems.

Everywhere in the country, in the utilities industries, prices are set and minimum service standards are prescribed by government. The states have various kinds of **public utilities commissions** regulating rates and services. ·

At the federal level, regulations are imposed by such agencies as the Interstate Commerce Commission and the Federal Power Commission. The provision of utility services in the American economy often depends more on government direction than on the "free workings of the market system."

An Evaluation of U.S. Antitrust Policy

Has American antitrust policy done any good? Yes. It has. Most foreign countries seem to have more monopoly than the American economy. American antitrust policy hasn't been all that strong, but it has been stronger than in most other countries.

Even during the times when the courts and enforcement agencies have been lenient, perhaps the corporate directors and officers have still been aware of the laws—perhaps have been less bold in their moves to "monopolize and conspire to restrain trade." I'll bet right now, in the 1980s, corporate executives looking back on the jailing of G.E. and Westinghouse executives for price-fixing, are a little more careful about what they do.

BIG BUSINESS AND THE QUESTION OF SOCIAL CONTROL

Giant corporations play the key productive role in the American economy. They exercise most of the economic power of the nation. So how the big corporations go, so goes the economy of the nation.

So what determines how the corporations go? Who makes the decisions? How are these multi-billion dollar organizations controlled? That's what this section talks about.

Divorce of Ownership from Control

How is the big corporation controlled? One thing is sure. Most of the stockholders don't control it. Usually there are many thousands of stockholders. Often the number of stockholders runs into millions. Do they all participate in running the corporation? Of course not.

In four out of every five of the major corporations, no identifiable group of people holds more than about 10 percent of the total stock. Usually the managers and officers and directors don't own much of the stock, either. What does all this mean? Just this: The people who own the corporation don't really run it; the ones who run the corporation certainly don't own it. That's a far cry from the era of the robber barons!

Each corporation holds an annual stockholders' meeting. At the meeting, members of the board of directors are elected and some other issues are usually decided. But most of the stockholders don't come.

Most stockholders simply sign and mail in their "proxy cards" authorizing management to vote their shares. As long as you think the managers are doing a good job running the corporation, why not let them decide the issues? So you sign your proxy card and send it in, expressing your confidence in the management of the corporation to make the right decisions.

Day-by-Day Control of the Corporations

Who runs the corporations on a day-to-day basis? Professional management people. Usually there's a president in charge. Then there are several vice-presidents, each taking care of a department. The board of directors is legally in charge, but it doesn't meet very often. Usually a small executive (steering) committee meets more often. The committee is usually headed by the chairman of the board of directors, and includes perhaps two or three of the other members of the board.

It's the chairman and the steering committee (and ultimately the board of directors) who have the power to call the shots. But usually they don't. As long as they have confidence in the president and vice-presidents they usually leave them free to run the corporation. Of course, if the board loses confidence in the management people, things will be different! Soon the corporation will have some new management people.

Galbraith and the Technostructure

When it's the professional managers making the decisions in the major corporations, and the major corporations setting the tenor and the pace

of the entire economic system, how can we be sure the decisions are being made in the best interest of the country? Is it possible that these managers might be more interested in looking out for themselves personally? And let the corporation, and good business practices, and all that be damned? John Kenneth Galbraith has had a lot to say on this question.

Galbraith uses the term **technostructure** to refer to the professional managers and technicians and others who are in a position to decide the day-to-day activities and directions of the corporation. He says it's the technostructure that really runs the corporation—decides what it does, which directions it goes and how fast.

Galbraith says the goals of the technostructure are different than the goals of an owner-manager of a business would be. The technostructure is interested in stability, avoiding risk, making sure of the survival of the corporation. Growth is desirable—but not if it's risky. The management people may like to have good salaries, plush offices, efficient and attractive secretaries, chauffeur-driven limousines, private jet planes, and business conferences at Waikiki.

Galbraith's Government-Industrial-Labor Complex

Galbraith sees the people in the technostructure as having a lot in common with the political leaders and the labor leaders in the country. All would like to see harmony and stability and growth—but without too much risk. He sees the business, government, and labor leaders all interested in working together and planning for long-range stability and "reasonable rates" of growth.

What about competition in this kind of a "planned" economic system? Galbraith says there isn't much between the firms in any one industry. But *between industries, competition is still important.* The steel industry must be careful not to lose its markets to aluminum, plastics, other metals and metal substitutes, for example.

In his book, *Economics and the Public Purpose,* Galbraith recommends that since the big corporations are planning anyway, the government should be involved, just to make sure that the planning aims in the right direction. That is, the government should direct the long-range planning and overall policies of the big corporations. For the smaller businesses Galbraith suggests that they should be given a stronger position—not having to live so much in the shadow of the big corporations.

Most economists and political leaders wouldn't go as far as Galbraith suggests. But he gives us some interesting ideas to think about. And ideas help, because nobody knows the answers. We know that the giant corporations need to be under the control of the society. And we suspect that to some extent they aren't. People disagree widely about what (if anything) to do about it.

President Eisenhower's Military-Industrial Complex

About twenty years ago President Eisenhower warned the American people about a dangerous power-block that seemed to be growing in the American economic system. He called it the **military-industrial complex.** In his farewell address in January 1961 Eisenhower said:

In the councils of government, we must guard against the acquisition of unwanted influence, whether sought or unsought, by the military-industrial complex. The potential for the disastrous results of misplaced power exists and will persist. . .

Only an alert and knowledgeable citizenry

can compel the proper meshing of the huge industrial and military machinery of defense with our peaceful methods and goals, so that security and liberty may prosper together.

Since the time Eisenhower issued the warning, the danger may have increased. The Pentagon now directs the flow of many billions of dollars. The money goes into important job-creating activities in many states. It goes into the production of many kinds of products and into the research programs of private firms, and universities.

Lots of people and lots of places are enjoying the flow of this money. They all would like for it to keep on flowing. Can you see the problem? Can you see how this could get so big that it would be political suicide for a member of Congress to vote for big cuts in military spending? The people back home don't want their local plant to shut down!

The military leaders want all the money they can get to carry out their programs; the people in the bureaucracy of the Pentagon don't want to lose their jobs; labor isn't in favor of getting fired from defense plants; the universities don't want to lose their research contracts; and the big corporations certainly don't want to lose their billions of dollars in military contracts! All of these people let their wishes be known to their representatives in Congress. Of course!

A major cutback in military spending would create a lot of discomfort for a lot of people. Can you see how this interlocking "you scratch my back and I'll scratch yours" situation could get out of hand? Truly, it could become uncontrollable. Some people think that maybe it already has.

It isn't that the people in the military-industrial complex are evil and sinister people. Of course not! It's just that they are all pursuing their own objectives. But maybe that's all it takes! We don't want to lose congressional control over defense spending. That would be a serious blow to our political democracy.

(In the next chapter you'll find that defense

spending as a percentage of GNP and as a percentage of total government spending has been going down in recent years. Figures like that should be heartening to those who think the military-industrial complex has already taken over the country!)

Who's in Charge?

The day-to-day control of things is in the hands of the few. There's no question about that. The corporation certainly isn't under the day-to-day control of the stockholders—or even of the board of directors.

The military establishment certainly isn't under the day-to-day control of Congress, either. Nor is Congress under the day-to-day control of the American people, for that matter.

When there's a big "policy question" to be decided, more people get involved, to be sure. But even so, most important things are (and no doubt will continue to be) decided by the very few.

Corporate Directors Are Being Held More Responsible

During the late 1970s, in the light of the "investigative attitude" in the aftermath of the Watergate scandal, several corporations were found involved in illegal and unethical activities. Mostly the activites involved illegal bribes and political campaign contributions.

Are the members of the board of directors responsible when the management of the corporation does something illegal? Several things that happened in 1975 and 1976 seem to answer the question: "Yes!" In January of 1976 the Securities and Exchange Commission (SEC) announced that it was investigating some 30 companies suspected of illegal contributions and bribes.

A few months earlier the SEC had successfully sued two directors of the Stirling Homex Corporation on the grounds that their "performance as directors was not adequate." The SEC charged that as directors, they had the legal responsibility to find out what was going on in the corporation, and to take action if necessary to prevent illegal activities. The illegal activity in this case was the fraudulent concealment of the company's financial situation.

Surely the time will never come when the members of the board will be in complete touch with everything that goes on in the giant corporations. But straws in the wind in the late 1970s indicate that people who accept the responsibility of being on the board of directors are going to be held legally liable for what the officers of the corporation do.

In this chapter you've been reading about big businesses. But when you get into the next chapter you're going to read about a *really big business*. What business? The United States government! That's bigger than any other business in the United States—by far!

But first, this chapter has an appendix. It's about business organization, finance, and accounting. If you haven't already studied these things, it would be a very good idea for you to study the appendix.

SUMMARY AND SYNTHESIS

It is mostly businesses which make up the American economy. Businesses are in charge of assessing the situation and choosing which products to produce, in what quantities, using what inputs and what technology. So they are the ones actually directing the flows of resources on

610 Part Eight • The American Economy: Agriculture, Labor, Business, Government

a day-to-day basis in the economic system.

There are about 10 million businesses in the country. Most of them are small one-owner proprietorships. There are more than 1 million corporations. But the largest 200 of them control more than one-half of the corporate assets. Obviously big business is a dominant characteristic of the American economy.

Concentration ratios indicate something about the market structure. The "concentration ratio" figure tells what percentage of the output of the industry is produced by the four largest firms in the industry. The higher the ratio, the greater the concentration in that industry.

Small businesses are important in the American economy, of course. There are so many of them! But the productive heart of the economic system is big business.

In the beginning the United States followed mostly policies of laissez-faire, but tried to stimulate business growth. Population flowed to the United States, capital was developed very rapidly, and by the early 1900s the United States had become the world leader in industrial production.

In the period between the Civil War and the end of the century the economy grew rapidly. This was the age of the "robber barons." Monopoly power developed rapidly during this period and in 1890 the Sherman Antitrust Act was passed to limit the growth of monopoly power.

More businesses became incorporated. Inter-corporate stockholding and inter-corporate directorships developed. The investment bankers got involved and monopoly power was difficult to limit.

In 1911 the American Tobacco Company and the Standard Oil Company were both split up under the Sherman Act. In this Supreme Court decision the rule of reason was stated: that only unreasonable restraints of trade were illegal under the antitrust laws.

In 1914 the Clayton Act and the Federal Trade Commission Act were passed to try to tighten antitrust enforcement. But neither of these acts was very effective.

It was not until the 1930s under Thurmond Arnold's trust-busting thrust that a serious anti-

trust effort was mounted in this country. Since that time there have been several important cases and additional legislation. Antitrust law enforcement has been significantly tightened.

In the early 1980s the new international competition began to be recognized as a much more important matter of concern than antitrust enforcement. The thrust of the Reagan administration was toward reducing government regulation and increasing industrial productivity to permit the economy to grow, to overcome unemployment, and to compete favorably in the international markets. Pending antitrust legislation and enforcement activites were slowed down or stopped. Pending regulations were held up while a start was made at cutting back on some of the existing regulations.

There are several exemptions to the antitrust laws, including patents and copyrights and special exemptions for farmers' organizations and labor unions. In the past there have been "fair trade" laws reducing competition at the retail level. Also, during the 1930s, cartel agreements among oligopoly firms were legalized for a short time. The public utilities are natural monopoly industries and regulated monopoly is the legal form of market structure there.

How can we evaluate antitrust policy in this country? It's difficult. How can we know how much "deterrent effect" the laws and enforcement activities have had? We can't. But most people seem to believe that the growth of monopoly in this country has been significantly retarded by our antitrust policies.

Real-world markets don't function like the model market system, where the price mechanism is in control of everything. So how are the giant corporations controlled? The managers of the corporations are responsible to the board of directors. The members of the board are responsible to the stockholders—who can vote out the board members if they wish. But not much effective control is actually exercised by most stockholders.

Galbraith says that the technostructure (professional managers and technicians in corporations) exercises control and aims for stability and risk-free growth. Galbraith warns of the "government-industrial-labor complex" controlling the economy and consumers losing their "sovereignty." President Eisenhower warned of the "military-industrial complex" which could lead to ever-increasing military spending. Everybody is in favor of increasing defense production and employment in their area, while the military people would like to get the best weapons systems possible.

Direction and management on a day-to-day basis moves along, with the managers in control. But when a big policy issue comes up, a lot more people get involved. Then there is an indication that social control of some form is being exercised. But is this adequate? This ultimate veto power by a larger number of people who may become dissatisfied by the way things are going? I don't know.

So is there adequate social control over big businesses in the American economy? People disagree about that. Those who favor more regulation and government involvement seem to think "No." Those who are in favor of the Reagan deregulation thrust seem to think "Yes." What do you think?

REVIEW EXERCISES

MAJOR CONCEPTS, PRINCIPLES, TERMS (Explain each carefully.)

market concentration ratios	conglomerate merger movement
the robber barons	government-industrial-labor complex
investment bankers	military-industrial complex

OTHER CONCEPTS AND TERMS (Explain each briefly.)

cut-throat competition	stock broker
trust	common law
New York Stock Exchange	John Kenneth Galbraith
J. P. Morgan	technostructure

IMPORTANT ACTS AND CASES (Explain each briefly.)

Interstate Commerce Act (1887)	Robinson-Patman Act (1936)
Sherman Antitrust Act (1890)	Miller-Tydings Act (1937)
E. C. Knight Case (1895)	Wheeler-Lea Act (1938)
Northern Securities Co. Case (1904)	Alcoa Case (1945)
American Tobacco and Standard Oil Cases (1911)	Cement Institute Case (1948)
Rule of Reason (1911)	Cellar-Kefauver Act (1950)
Clayton Act (1914)	Du Pont-General Motors Case (1957)
FTC Act (1914)	Electrical Equipment Price-fixing Case (1961)
U.S. Steel Case (1920)	

QUESTIONS (Write out answers or jot down key points.)

1. Give some facts and figures about businesses in the American economy—how many, how big, and all that.

2. Some industries (automobile, aluminum, several others) have high concentration ratios. Why do you think that's so? Do you think anything should be done about it? Discuss.
3. Discuss the situation of small businesses in the American economy.
4. Give some of the highlights in the industrial development of the U.S. economy since colonial times.
5. Explain the role of the investment bankers in the development of the American economy.
6. Trace the highlights in the history of U.S. antitrust policy.
7. Describe the U.S. antitrust policy of the 1970s. In general, what is illegal? and what isn't? And what are the exemptions to the antitrust laws?
8. Do you think there should be some changes in U.S. antitrust policy? Discuss.
9. Discuss the issue of big businesses and social control.

APPENDIX

The Language of Business, Finance, and Accounting

This appendix takes a closer look at business—a look inside business itself: at the forms of business organization, at business financing, and at accounting.

This appendix is organized around the "language of business"—that is, around the terms which you need to know. But as the terms are explained, so are the concepts.

First there are terms about business organization, then about business finance, and finally about accounting.

Business Organization: Proprietorship, Partnership, Corporation

This section talks about the three forms of business organization: proprietorship, partnership, and corporation. But before we start, here are three terms people sometimes get confused about: plant, firm, and industry.

A plant is a physical structure. It's a factory. It's a building (or group of buildings) with machines, etc.

A firm is a company. It's a business. A firm may operate one plant or several plants. A small corner grocery is a business firm. So is General Motors with plants all over the world.

An industry includes all of the firms which produce the same product. All of the automobile-producing firms make up the automobile industry, the garment-producing firms make up the garment industry, the steel firms make up the steel industry, etc. And now, the three forms of *business organizations*.

The Proprietorship. This is the simplest form of business organization. Any person can start one. Suppose you decide to start making macrame belts in your room at night and selling them to the people standing in line at the college cafeteria at lunchtime. Then you are running a business. You are running a proprietorship.

Some day you may decide to hire some people so you can produce more belts. And you may set up a roadside stand to sell them to the tourists. Or you might even rent a store downtown, or sell them wholesale to the Whatnot Shop. You're still running a proprietorship.

Anyone who wants to (and who has the money to buy whatever is needed) can go into business—that is, can start a proprietorship. The real problem with setting up and running a proprietorship is that you must have the money to start with. It's hard to find someone who will lend you money to start your own business! So sometimes people take in partners.

The Partnership. A partnership is like a proprietorship except that there are two or more partners who share in the business. Partnerships are frequently used in law farms and other firms of professional people. The partners can share the work and each one can specialize in some aspect of the profession. In other businesses a partnership might be used as a way of getting together enough money to start the business.

One problem with a partnership is that each partner is legally *totally liable* for anything any other partner does. You have to trust people quite a lot to go into a partnership with them!

Another problem is that if the business goes broke, *if you're a partner you can be sued for everything you own* to pay off the debts of the business. You have **unlimited liability** for all of the obligations and debts of the business. The same is true if you are the individual proprietor, of course. But *if the business is incorporated, nobody can sue you for your personal property.* They can only take what you have put into the business—no more.

The Corporation. As you know, corporations make up the productive heart of the American economic system. A **corporation** is a fictitious person. It has a legal right to buy and sell things, to own things, to enter contracts with other people and corporations, to direct the movements of resources, to hire labor, to set prices—it can even break the law, be sued, fined, or even split apart.

The corporation is a *perpetual* "fictitious person." It lives forever. It is owned by those who own the shares of it—that is, the stock certificates.

If you own stock in a corporation and the corporation goes broke, you'll lose all the money you put into it. But that's all you'll lose. The bill collectors can't come and take your house and car as they could if the business was a proprietorship or a partnership.

The corporation is a great way to get money together to finance a business. Many people can participate. Each can put up a little bit of the money and each can share a little bit of the risk.

Although about 80 percent of all the business firms in the United States are proprietorships (only 13 percent are corporations), almost all of the business assets are owned by corporations. Most of the proprietorships are tiny; many

of the corporations are multi-billion dollar businesses.

Business Finance (Corporation Finance): Stocks and Bonds

What is the subject of "business finance" all about? It's about how the corporations get the money they need to do business. They sell **stocks and bonds,** of course.

Corporations get money from profits, too (sometimes). Usually when a corporation makes profits it pays out some to the stockholders as dividends and it keeps the rest to be used for more investment—for new plants, new equipment, research, etc.

Stocks and bonds are traded on the **stock exchanges,** located in important financial cities all around the world. There are several stock exchanges in the United States. The most important are the New York Stock Exchange and the American Stock Exchange, both located within a few blocks of each other in downtown Manhattan. But wherever you may happen to be you can easily buy and sell stocks and bonds.

Stock and bond **brokers** are scattered all over the United States. In almost every little town you can find a broker who will be glad to buy or sell almost any stock for you.

If you want to find out more about it, do this: Look in the Yellow Pages of your phone book under Stocks and Bonds. Find out where the nearest brokerage office is located and go talk to them about it. You'll probably come away with a handful of free pamphlets and knowing a lot more than you did.

Common stocks are ownership shares in the corporation. A person who owns **common stock** can vote for the board of directors and on other issues at the annual stockholders meeting.

The more stock you have the more votes you have. You can vote either in person or by proxy. Just mark your proxy card, mail it in, and let the management cast your votes for you.

The common stockholder has a right to share in the profits of the corporation. If the corporation doesn't make any profits then the common stockholder doesn't get a share.

Most corporations lose money during some years. It's only when losses come year after year that the corporation is in danger of going broke. If it does, of course, the holder of common stock loses everything invested in the stock.

Bonds issued by a corporation are debts of the corporation. When the government borrows money from you, you get a bond in exchange. When a corporation borrows money from people it gives them bonds too. If a corporation is selling bonds and you are buying them, what you are doing is lending money to the corporation.

A **corporation bond** is just like a government bond or any other bond. It has a certain face value (usually $1,000) and a stated interest rate—maybe 6 percent or 8 percent or 10 percent.

If you buy a bond you are supposed to receive a payment of interest each year—no matter whether the corporation makes a profit that year or not. If it's a $1,000 bond and the interest stated on it is 8 percent, then you are supposed to receive $80 a year. At *maturity* (the date when the bond comes due) the corporation is obligated to pay off the full face value ($1,000) to the owner of the bond.

Bonds are bought and sold on the exchanges through stock and bond brokers, just like common stocks. If you own a corporation bond you don't have to wait until the maturity date to get your money out of it. You can sell it any day you want to.

If the corporation is in financial trouble, or if the interest rate on your bond is low as compared with interest rates on the new bonds being issued these days, then you'll have to sell your bond at less than its face value. But if you're willing to accept the market price, you can always sell it!

If you own a bond, you can't vote at the stockholders meeting, of course. You aren't an owner. You're just a lender. Bonds are safer investments than common stocks. But during profitable times common stockholders make out better.

One problem with bonds is the problem of inflation. As prices rise and the value of the dollar goes down, the annual interest becomes smaller and smaller in "real value" terms. Also, by the time maturity arrives, the $1,000 may not buy anywhere near as much as it would have back when you bought the bond! So with inflation you might lose two ways: on interest income and on the face value (the principal) too!

Convertible bonds help to protect against inflation. In recent years, to make people more interested in holding bonds in the face of rising prices, corporations have been issuing "convertible bonds." **Convertible bonds** *can be exchanged for common stocks at some specified price.*

If the stock price goes up very much and you own convertible bonds, you can turn your bonds in and get the high priced stocks in exchange!

The convertible bond lets you sort of "have your cake and eat it too." But you'll be paying for the privilege—either in lower interest stated on the bond, or in the higher price you have to pay to buy it.

Preferred Stocks are sort of halfway between common stocks and bonds. Although preferred stocks do not have a "maturity date" as do bonds, preferred stocks usually pay a fixed dividend each year. But if the company doesn't make any profits it can omit the preferred stock dividends.

There are all kinds of **preferred stocks.** Some let you vote at the stockholders meeting. Some don't. Some give you "bonus dividends" if corporate earnings get above a certain level. Some don't. Some are convertible into common stocks. Some aren't. Some require that during profitable times the corporation must make up any "missed dividends." Some don't.

If a corporation doesn't have enough profit to pay much in dividends, the preferred stockholders get first preference on the available money (after the interest on the bonds is paid, of course).

The common stockholders are last in line. They are the "residual claimants." In lean years they get nothing. But in years of prosperity they get everything that's left over.

Dividends? or capital gains? If you own common stock and if the corporation makes profits, then you may receive some dividends. But maybe not. The board of directors may decide not to pay out any dividends.

Usually **dividends** are paid at a fixed rate, quarterly. If profits increase and stay up for a year or so then the board of directors usually votes an increase in the dividend. When profits go down they usually decrease the dividend.

Some stockholders would rather that the corporation not pay dividends, but put the earnings into expanding the business instead. That would increase the value of the corporation. As the corporation expands and becomes more profitable, what happens to the value of its common stock? It goes up, of course. So if the corporation is profitable but pays no dividends, chances are the value of the stock will be going up.

For some people there's a tax advantage in receiving no dividends, but letting the stock price go up. You must pay income tax on your dividends, of course. But suppose you sell your stock for more than you paid for it. That's a **capital gain!**

Capital gains are usually taxed at less than the regular income tax rate. See the advantage of capital gains instead of dividends? If you happen to be in the upper income brackets where the tax rates are high, whether you get your share of the profits as dividends or as capital gains can make quite a difference!

The Securities and Exchange Commission (SEC) (1934) was set up to regulate the issue of **securities** (stocks and bonds) by corporations, and to keep an eye on the stock exchanges to keep people from rigging prices. Before 1934 a buyer of securities was told the ancient warning—**caveat emptor**—"let the buyer beware."

Since 1934 the SEC requires the business to go through a specific procedure when offering securities for sale. It must issue a **prospectus** giving detailed information about the corporation's financial situation.

It's good that we have the SEC keeping an eye on the securities markets. But that doesn't mean you can't still lose your shirt in the stock market! So beware. And now here's a little bit about what has been called: "the language of business"—that is, accounting.

Business Accounting

There are two basic accounting statements which every business uses. One is the *balance sheet*; the other is the *income statement*. The **balance sheet** shows what the business owns and what it owes. What's left over belongs to the stockholders.

The **income statement** shows how much the business has been earning and how much it has been spending. What's left over is profits. Here's a little more about each of these business accounting statements.

The Balance Sheet. This accounting statement shows the financial situation of the business at a particular time—for example, December 31, 1980. There are two sides to the balance sheet. The left side is the **assets** side. The right side is the **liabilities and ownership** side.

On the left side under assets you'll see listed: cash, money in the bank, accounts receivable, and the dollar value of inventories, buildings, equipment, land, and everything else the business owns. It's all added up to find out the "total assets" of the business.

The right side of the balance sheet shows such things as accounts payable (what the business owes for raw materials, electricity, etc.) bonds outstanding, and other debts owed by the business. All these are added up to get "total liabilities."

The total liabilities (we hope!) will be less than the assets. What's left over is called **net worth.** That's how much more the corporation *owns* than it *owes*. Really, that's what it's worth.

A quick look at the balance sheet tells you quite a lot about a corporation and its financial condition. But it's really quite a simple thing. The income statement is also very helpful—and just as simple.

The Income Statement. This accounting statement is also called the **profit and loss statement** or P & L. It differs from the balance sheet in a very definite way.

The balance sheet is a picture of "the business at rest." You can't look at a balance sheet and tell if the corporation is making money or losing money right now; or if it's producing a little or a lot, or if it's paying a little or a lot in wages. *From the balance sheet you can't tell anything about what the business is doing right now.* All you can tell is *what it owns and what it owes and what's left over* (what it's worth) right now.

The **income statement** shows a picture of "the business in motion." It doesn't show anything about how much the business has in assets or liabilities or net worth. All the income statement shows you is flows of money coming in and money going out.

The income statement (P & L) isn't arranged on two different sides, like the balance sheet. It just starts off with the total amount of money coming in from goods sold. From this is subtracted the cost of producing the goods (cost of materials, labor, electric power, etc.) That gives the **gross profit.**

From the gross profit, deductions are made to cover administration costs, selling costs, interest, and taxes. After all of that is taken off, if there's anything left over it's **profit.** The income statement goes on to show how much of the profit is paid out in dividends to the stockholders, and how much is retained by the corporation as **undistributed profits,** or **surplus** to be used for the expansion of the business.

What's the relationship betweem the income statement and the balance sheet? Sort of like the relationship between a lake and a stream which

flows in at one end and out at the other. The balance sheet is like the lake. It's the situation at any moment—the situation at rest. The income statement is like the stream. It shows the amounts pouring in and the amounts pouring out.

If the amounts pouring in are greater than the amounts pouring out, the lake will get bigger. If the income statement shows a profit, the assets of the corporation will get bigger—and so will the net worth. But if the P & L shows losses? The opposite happens. The asset value goes down. So does net worth.

If losses are made many years in a row, ultimately the net worth will all be gone. Total assets will not be great enough to cover total liabilities. The corporation will be **bankrupt.** Usually before this happens the corporation finds a way to overcome its losses—or else decides to go out of business.

Tables 34-1 and 34-2 show what a balance sheet and an income statement look like. But if you want to see some real balance sheets and income statements, go to your library and ask to see some annual reports of corporations.

The annual report always tells lots of things about what the corporation is doing. Also, it always presents a balance sheet showing all the assets and liabilities and the net worth. And it always shows an income statement of the money coming in and the money going out and the profits (or losses) left over. If you've never seen an annual report you should take a few minutes and go look at one.

Principles, Concepts and Terms Explained in the Appendix

plant, firm, industry
proprietorship
partnership
corporation
common stocks
corporation bonds
convertible bonds
preferred stocks
dividends

capital gains
Securities and Exchange
   Commission (SEC)
balance sheet
income statement
profit and loss (P & L) statement
assets
liabilities

net worth
book value (of stock)
market value (of stock)
gross profit
undistributed profits
surplus
caveat emptor
prospectus

Table 34-1   Example of a Balance Sheet of a Corporation

Assets		Liabilities	
Current Assets:		*Current Liabilities:*	
Cash on hand..............	$ 5,000	Accounts payable.........	$ 30,000
Money in banks...........	25,000	Notes payable..............	40,000
Accounts receivable......	30,000		
Inventories.................	60,000	*Long Term Liabilities:*	
		Mortgage on buildings.................	40,000
		Bonds payable.........	60,000
Fixed Assets:			
Machines and equipment...............	100,000	*Net Worth*	
Buildings and land..........	150,000	Capital:	
		Preferred stock.............	50,000
		Common stock.................	
TOTAL	$370,000	TOTAL	$370,000

This corporation has a net worth of $200,000. Assets ($370,000) minus liabilities ($170,000) equals net worth ($200,000). The preferred stock is valued at $50,000. That leaves $150,000 for the common stockholders. The common stock gets whatever value is left over.

If there are 15,000 shares of common stock, then the "book value" of each share is $10. But the "market value" may be higher or lower.

Table 34-2   Example of an Income (Profit and Loss) Statement

Net Sales (money received for goods sold)......................................		$200,000
Manufacturing costs		
Materials...	$30,000	
Labor...	90,000	
Depreciation..	15,000	
Other operating costs...	5,000	
Total	140,000	
Gross Profit (or "Gross Margin")...		$ 60,000
Selling and Administration Costs...		10,000
Interest and taxes on property, etc..		5,000
Net earnings (profit) before income taxes......................................		$ 45,000
Corporation income taxes..		20,000
Net earnings (profit) after taxes...		$ 25,000
Dividends paid to preferred stockholders.................................		2,000
Dividends paid to common stockholders.................................		13,000
Retained earnings (addition to net worth)......................................		$ 10,000

This corporation is making a profit of $45,000. After income taxes ($20,000) that leaves $25,000 for the stockholders.

The preferred stockholders get $2,000. This corporation pays out $13,000 in common stock dividends and keeps $10,000 of retained earnings.

The $10,000 retained earnings adds to net worth and will show up as *more assets* in the next balance sheet.

35

Public Finance I: Government Spending in Fact and in Theory

Chapter Objectives

- This chapter describes the **historical development** and **present patterns** of **government spending** in this country, and explains the **basic theory of government expenditures.**

- When you finish studying this chapter you will be able to give the highlights of **government spending patterns early in this century** and to contrast those with government spending patterns **in the 1980s.** And you will be able to give some of the **reasons** for the **significant shifts among expenditure categories** which have occurred in recent years.

- You will be able to describe and explain the issues of **fiscal federalism;** the ways in which **federal-state-local expenditure relationships** have been **changing, reasons** for some of these changes, and some of the **effects.**

- You will be able to explain how **changing philosophy** about the role of government in the economy has influenced the **size and structure** of government spending. And you will be able to give the highlights of some of the **recent issues and controversies** regarding government spending.

- Finally, you will be able to explain the **theory of government expenditures:** why is it necessary in a **market economy** for governments to spend money to **allocate the society's resources?** Specifically you will be able to explain: **public goods, market inefficiency and high transactions costs, benefit externalities,** and **income redistribution.**

During the present century the role of government in the economy has increased greatly—from a very minor role to a very major one.

In the early part of this century, all government expenditures—federal, state, and local—amounted to only *about one twelfth* of the national income. Now, in the early 1980s, total government expenditures amount to *about one third* of the national income.

GROWTH IN THE ROLE OF GOVERNMENT

Throughout the last century the role of government in the American economy was small. The government wasn't entirely neutral, of course. It played an important role in establishing and regulating banks and money, it levied tariffs to stimulate industry, it gave great tracts of land to the railroads to stimulate their development, it established land grant colleges for training in agriculture and mechanical skills, and it got involved in several other ways.

But up to the 1900s neither the federal, state, nor local governments were doing very much in the economy. They didn't do very much regulation or control of economic activities, nor were they gathering much money in taxes or doing much government spending.

Government Regulations: Transportation, Banking, Antitrust

In the late 1800s the government's role began to grow. The ICC began regulating the railroads in 1887. The Sherman Antitrust Act was passed in 1890. Remember?

But even before that, in the 1860s the National Banking System was set up to increase the government's control over money and banking. The National Banking System continued until the Federal Reserve System was set up in 1913 and all the national banks were required to join. Also the government got into more regulating when the Pure Food and Drug Act was passed in the early 1900s.

But as you know, it was in the depression years of the 1930s that government's role in the economy really changed. There were more regulations of banking, of money, of securities. The government regulated wages and hours and business practices, and prohibited child labor. Antitrust enforcement was stepped up greatly. Many kinds of goverment regulations were tightened.

More Taxing and Spending

The government has come a long way from its 19th century "hands off" policy. But the biggest change in the role of government wasn't in banking or money or regulations or antitrust.

It was in **public finance**—that is, in taxing money away from the people and businesses and spending it to redirect production into different channels—away from "private" objectives, toward objectives chosen by the government. Government taxing and spending shifts the resources of the economy. The economy produces more "public goods and services" and fewer "private goods and services."

During the last century, local government was the only level of government doing much to provide services for the people. Local governments provided education, police and fire protection, some streets and roads, and some health and welfare services.

The state governments weren't doing much at all. Really, they didn't have much of a role to play. The federal government was doing more than the states. But most federal government activites were concerned with national things—not with providing services for the people.

Increased Government Spending: 1900 into the 1980s

At the beginning of this century, all governments taken together (federal, state and local) were spending only about $50 a year per person. By the early 1980s the per capita expenditure of all governments passed $4,000.

As a percentage of GNP, total government spending increased from about 7 percent at the beginning of the century to more than 30 percent of GNP in the early 1980s. About one third of the total GNP? That's right. That's a far cry from the situation that existed when your grandparents were born!

Figure 35-1 shows a picture of the great increase in government spending during this century. Take a minute now to study that figure.

The Early Decades of the 1900s. In the early decades of the 1900s the governments began taking on more responsibilities—building roads and streets and providing more and better education and welfare services. Also, as the cities grew, expenditures increased for police and fire protection, sanitation, and for other urban services.

World War I pushed federal expenditures up. After the war, expenditures went back down. But not all the way. The national defense program and federal aid to the states for highways kept federal spending up during the 1920s. But by 1929 government spending had only increased from about 7 percent to about 19 percent of GNP.

Rapid Increases Since the 1920s. During the 1920s total government spending per capita was a little more than $100. By the end of the 1930s it was almost $300. By the 1950s it was more than $500. In the early 1960s it was $700, but before 1970 it passed $1,000.

Before 1975, total government spending per capita had passed $2,000, by the late 1970s it was up to about $3,000, and in the early 1980s it passed $4,000. (A lot of the increase represents inflation, of course.)

CHANGING PATTERNS OF GOVERNMENT SPENDING: EARLY 1900s—EARLY 1980s

The gross national product in the United States has increased by about 150 times since the beginning of this century. A 15,000 percent increase, would you believe? That's right. The GNP increased from about $20 billion to *more than $3,000 billion* between 1900 and the early 1980s. A lot of this gigantic increase reflects price increases. But there's a lot of it that doesn't.

As the GNP has been increasing, which gov-

Fig. 35-1   Total Government Spending in the United States: Federal, State, Local (Early 1900s and Early 1980s Compared)

Government spending in the American economy has increased greatly. Chart A doesn't allow for increasing prices or population or growth of GNP or anything. It just shows the dollars spent, then and now.

Chart B shows that even as a percentage of GNP, the growth rate has been very large.

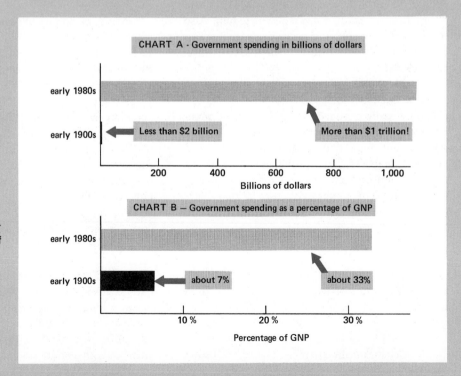

ernment functions have increased as much as GNP? Would you believe *all of them?* That's right.

Since the beginning of this century, *every category of government spending has increased more rapidly than GNP.* Several have expanded *much* more rapidly.

Now you can see why total government spending as a percentage of GNP has increased so much—from less than 10 percent in the early 1900s to more than 30 percent by the 1980s. Of course. If all parts are increasing faster than GNP then the total would have to be! Right? Let's take a look at each of the parts. First, the "defense" budget.

Military and Defense Expenditures

In the early 1900s, defense-related expenditures accounted for about 20 percent of all government expenditures. It's not that the military establishment was all that large. It's just the total expenditures were small.

The 1920s to 1940s. In the mid-1920s, defense related expenditures were quite a lot bigger. But as a percentage of total government spending they were only about half as big—only about 10 percent of the total. Why? Because expenditures for other purposes (mostly education and highways) were increasing so fast.

By 1940 national defense expenditures were increasing rapidly as World War II began spreading across Europe. But defense-related expenditures were still only about 10 percent of the total government spending in ths country. Why? Again, because spending for other things was going up so fast—especially with the New Deal welfare and economic development programs which were started in the 1930s.

World War II and Afterwards. After the United States got into World War II, military spending exploded. Federal spending increased about ten-fold during the war. In 1944-45 the federal government was buying about half of the GNP!

After the war, military spending declined. But by 1950 defense-related spending still made up one third of total government spending in this country. Then expenditures for other things began to increase faster. Defense spending increased too, but not as fast.

Modern Times: Non-Defense Spending Increases Faster than Defense Spending. As non-defense spending at the federal, state, and local levels increased (for education, highways and streets, health and hospitals, welfare, social security, agriculture, police and fire protection, natural resources, etc.) military spending as a percentage of total government spending, began to decline.

By the 1970s, as expenditures to support the Vietnam War wound down and other expenditure functions at all levels of government increased, the military component of total spending dropped to less than 30 percent. By the mid-1970s, military spending as a percentage of total government spending was down to less than 20 percent. In the late 1970s it was down to about 15 percent.

But in 1982 the Reagan administration was calling for budget changes which would sharply reverse the declining trend of defense spending. What did President Reagan's budget projections for the early to mid-1980s call for? Significant increases for defense, and reductions in spending for other functions. By the time you are reading this, defense spending as a percentage of total government spending may again be approaching 20 percent.

Defense Spending as a Percentage of GNP. In the beginning of the century, defense spending made up less than 2 percent of GNP. In the late 1920s it was even less—only about 1 percent of GNP. By 1940 it had only increased to about 2 percent.

Of course it rose dramatically during World War II. But in 1950, defense spending only made up about 8 percent of the GNP. By 1960 it had increased to about 10 percent. During some years of the 1960s the Vietnam War pushed military spending to a little more than 10 percent of

GNP, but in 1970 it was down to less than 10 percent and by the mid-1970s, down to less than 8 percent. In the early 1980s military spending made up less than 6 percent of GNP. But as you just read, the Reagan administration was promising to do something about that.

Social Welfare Spending

As government spending has increased, which functions have increased more than the others? Social welfare is the front-runner, by any measure. In the early part of this century, expenditures by governments on social welfare amounted to only about *one half of one percent* of GNP. By the late 1920s, social welfare expenditures were still less than 1 percent of GNP. By 1950 it was still less than 3 percent.

By 1960 social welfare expenditures had gone up to about 5 percent of GNP. By 1970 it was up to 8 percent. *By the mid-1970s social welfare spending had passed 10 percent of the GNP, to become and remain the biggest single item of government expenditure in the United States.* It now accounts for more than one third of total government expenditures in the country.

Most of the social welfare expenditures come under the social security program initiated in the 1930s. In addition to the social security, unemployment, and welfare programs, social welfare expenditures include expenditures for public housing, health and hospitals, and community development.

At the beginning of this century, social welfare was considered to be a matter of individual or family responsibility—perhaps supplemented by the charity programs of church groups and other organizations. Some local governments provided "old folks homes" for the aged poor and sometimes supplied meager assistance to prevent people from starving.

How different the picture is today! With social welfare spending making up the biggest sin-

gle item of government spending and amounting to more than 10 percent of the GNP, it's clear just how far the United States has moved toward becoming a "welfare state."

Spending for Education

Expenditures for education increased from a little more than one percent of gross national product in the early 1900s, to about 6 percent by the mid-1970s. Throughout most of this century education expenditures were increasing faster than GNP.

By the mid-1920s more than 2 percent of GNP was going into education; by 1940 almost 3 percent, by 1960 almost 4 percent. By the mid-1970s it was up to about 6 percent where it has remained on into the 1980s.

Why have expenditures for education increased so much? Several reasons. One is the increased commitment of government in providing education for everyone—including subsidized college education. Another is the rapid increase in the number of school-age children, which was the trend until recently. Also, increasing emphasis on manpower development and training has pushed spending up.

Cost-push inflation has pushed up education spending, too. Increases in teachers' salaries have not been reflected in increased productivity per teacher; the salary increases have simply pushed up the "cost per student" of education. Unless effective ways can be found to increase teacher productivity, the cost per student will continue to go up.

Spending for Economic Development

In addition to national defense, social welfare, and education, there is only one expenditure item which has more than doubled its percentage of GNP since 1900: economic development. This includes expenditures for natural resource development; programs to assist business, labor, and agriculture; various kinds of research and technological development programs and other programs designed to aid the growth of the economy—either agriculture, industry, or commerce. It also includes the space program.

At the beginning of this century expenditures for economic development accounted for about 1 percent of GNP. By the mid-1920s it exceeded 2 percent. During the 1930s it was expanded under the New Deal programs and by 1940 government economic development programs accounted for more than 5 percent of GNP.

After the depression and war years, economic development expenditures continued to increase in absolute terms, but dropped as a percentage of GNP. In the early 1980s government expenditures for economic development amounted to something more than 3 percent of the GNP.

Beware of Spending Categories

Here's a word of warning—something you should think about. Is all of the spending under the heading "economic development" really spending for economic development? Or is part of it disguised spending for some other purpose?

A lot of economic development spending under the New Deal went to farmers to buy up agricultural surpluses. Was the purpose really "economic development?" Or was the purpose to improve the welfare of the farmers?

What about the space program? Is that entirely concerned with the development of the American economy? Or perhaps also with maintaining military power and national prestige?

Certainly the space program has helped and will continue to help in the development of the American economy. The communications satellites, for one thing, are a great boon to worldwide communications and navigation. But shouldn't some of the space program spending be charged to national defense? Probably so.

Couldn't a lot of our spending for education be charged to economic development? Sure.

So now, a general word of warning: What you see when you look at government spending depends partly on how you choose to look at it. (Or maybe, how *someone else* chooses for you to look at it!)

Anyone could go through the government budgets and group the spending in different ways—under different headings. As a result you could see different things—perhaps come to different conclusions.

So be careful about drawing hard and fast conclusions from any given "breakdown" of government spending—like the breakdown you're reading about in this chapter. Most items of spending can be categorized in two or three different ways—depending on what you're trying to find out—or what you're trying to prove. So beware! Okay? Now a few words about the minor functions of government spending.

Spending for Other Purposes

In transportation, government spending at the turn of the century amounted to about one percent of GNP. By the 1920s it had increased to about 2 percent as government took on more responsibility for highways, roads, and streets. Since the 1920s, government expenditures on transportation—mostly highways, but also airports and rivers and harbors—have just held their own, at about 2 percent of GNP.

General government expenses also have increased from about one percent of GNP to about two percent. Interest expense has increased a lot—from about .5 percent to more than 3 percent.

Foreign relations and foreign aid spending were so small that they don't even show up as percentages of GNP in the early decades of this century. But in 1950, spending for foreign relations and foreign aid amounted to a little more than one percent of GNP. Since then the percentage has declined. Since the mid-1970s expenditures for foreign relations and foreign aid (excluding military aid) have amounted to less than one half of one percent of GNP.

Figure 35-2 shows a picture of what you've been reading about. Stop and take a look at that now.

FISCAL FEDERALISM: FEDERAL-STATE-LOCAL RELATIONSHIPS

Throughout this discussion of the changing functions of government spending, I haven't said anything about *which level of government* (federal, state, or local) was doing the spending.

In a "federal" system of government, each of the "governmental levels" has a role to play.

What is the role of each of these in the United States? And how has this role changed during this century? That's what this section is all about.

At First, Local Governments Were Most Important

In the early 1900s, any services which government needed to provide for the people were provided by the local governments—that is, by the cities, villages, counties, townships, etc. That's the way it had been since the beginning. Education, roads and streets, law and order were all local government functions. There were a few

Fig. 35-2   Government Spending by Purpose Expressed As a Percentage of GNP: Early 1900s and Early 1980s

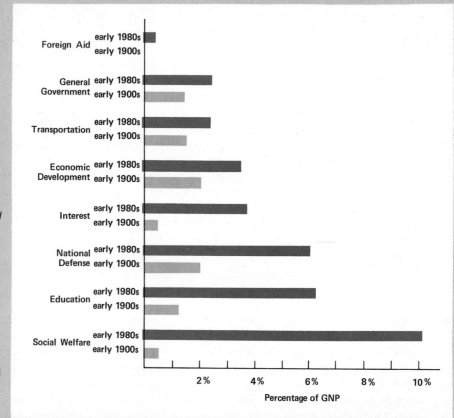

This chart includes *all* levels of government—not just federal spending, but state and local spending, too.

Notice the great expansion of social welfare expenditures, and that national defense expenditures have moved into third place after being in first place for many years.

state police, of course. And Dodge City and a few other places were lucky enough to have a U.S. Marshall. But these were the exceptions.

The federal government was concerned with national defense, money and banking, some regulations of big business, keeping an eye on interstate and foreign commerce, and a few other "big things." There wasn't much immediate contact with the people.

What about the states? They really didn't have much to do. They were hardly providing any services at all. The local governments were the only ones doing that.

Governmental functions "for the people" were performed at the local level and "for the nation as a whole" were performed at the federal level. The local governments were "creatures of the states" so the states had something to say about what the local governments could or couldn't do. The states exercised some legal and police powers, but from the point of view of undertaking programs, generally speaking, they just didn't. How different that is from the picture today!

The Centralization of Government Functions

Today it's a completely different scene from the early 1900s. Government functions and financial responsibilities have become more and more "centralized"—that is, shifted upward to higher levels of government: local to both state and federal, and state to federal.

These days, about the only functions the local governments are still entirely responsible for are local police and fire protection and sanitation services. To be sure, local governments are still providing education, streets and roads, health and hospitals, sometimes public transportation and other public welfare and social services. But they aren't doing *most* of it any more. The state government is heavily involved. So is the federal government. What happened to bring about such a great change?

Need for Coordination

Why did the state and federal governments start paying for highways? and education? and social service? and other things? One reason was the need for coordination.

A road which went only to the boundary of the village couldn't do much to provide transportation throughout the county. A road which went to the county line couldn't do much to provide a statewide road network. And roads going to state lines and ending there didn't do much to provide a national highway system, either! In the early 1900s, would you believe there were lots of roads that just went to the boundary line, and stopped?

Early in this century the federal government started financing highways. First, a system of "post roads" was established connecting the major cities to be used to help in the delivery of mails. You can still go from New York to Boston on the "Boston Post Road"—but it will take you quite a while to get there!

From the post-road beginning, the federal government has continually increased its assistance and influence in developing a nationwide highway system. The modern version of the post road system is the 41,000-mile interstate highway system on which the federal government pays 90 percent of the construction costs. This system was set up in the mid-1950s and is now almost completed. Would the interstate highway system have been constructed if the federal government hadn't gotten involved? Of course not.

Our federalism trend? For 50 years, Centralization!

Using Grants as Inducements

Suppose the federal government has a program it would like to carry out, but the states need to participate. How does the federal government get the states to go along? Offer them money? **Grants-in-aid?** Of course!

Isn't that how the federal government induced the states to build the interstate highway system? Offer them 90 percent grants-in-aid for the construction of the highways! Of course.

The federal government doesn't have the *constitutional power* to tell the state or local governments what to do. But it doesn't need it. All it needs to do is offer them enough money and they will go along. The states do the same thing to the local governments, too.

The need to coordinate has been an important reason for the "upward shifting" or "centralization" of government spending, to be sure. But it hasn't been the biggest reason. The biggest reason, as you might guess, was the need for *money* by the local and state governments.

Inadequate State and Local Revenue Sources

Local governments get their money from local people. Obviously. They get most of it from property taxes—usually levied on houses and land and business properties. You can't collect but limited amounts of money with property taxes. During times of depression it may be impossible for a local government to collect enough tax money to pay for the essential functions— education, police and fire protection, roads and streets, sanitation, social welfare.

So why don't the local governments use other kinds of taxes? The same kinds used by the states? And by the federal government? Sometimes they do. But mostly, they can't. You'll see why in the next chapter. But for now, consider this: If your locality levied a 20 percent tax on your income, what would you do? Move to the suburbs? or to the next town? Probably. Right?

Shifting Local Government Functions to the State Level

During the depression of the 1930s, local governments all over the country were in trou-

ble. They didn't have the money to keep their programs going. So what did they do? They appealed to the state governments for help. And the states responded.

What did the states do? In some states the entire highway system was taken over. The county roads became state roads and the counties were relieved of the burden. Even the main streets in cities often were taken over and financed by the states.

Some states took over the entire education system. Others provided grants-in-aid to the local governments for education. States also provided aid or took over some of the social welfare functions.

Different states responded in different ways. But all over the country the general pattern was the same: centralization of expenditures and functions; shifting the financial burden of local functions upward, to the state level.

Shifting Functions to the Federal Level

What about the states? Where did they get all the money to bail out the local governments? Did they cry "Help!" to the federal government? Yes. And the federal government came to the rescue.

At the same time that the local directors of education, roads, and welfare were in the state capitals crying "Help!" the state directors of education, highways, and welfare were in Washington crying "Help!" Federal help was forthcoming for highways. And for welfare. But for education, not so fast. There was a lot of controversy about federal aid to education.

What About Federal Aid to Education?

Many people were afraid of the idea of letting the federal government start financing education. They were afraid that before long the federal government would be tying some strings to the aid—trying to set standards for teachers, trying to influence curriculum, perhaps even influencing textbook choices.

There were many people in the South who didn't like what some "Northern" history books had to say about the Civil War. They didn't want those books in their schools!

Also, some local school boards were dead set against textbooks which suggested that human beings might have "evolved"—that maybe Adam and Eve weren't created in God's image and placed in the Garden of Eden, after all. Or perhaps there were some unqualified teachers and administrators in various places throughout the country who feared that federal standards would push them out of the system. But for whatever reasons, there were a lot of people arguing against federal aid to education.

Another issue was the question of how much federal money each state should get for education. The wealthy states wanted to get back in proportion to the federal taxes paid by the people in the state. The people in the poor states weren't paying as much in federal taxes. Many of them were unemployed and broke!

But the low income states were the ones where the educational programs were most in need of help. Obviously! If the aid was going to the states which already had plenty of money, there wasn't much point in setting up the program.

Anyway, as a result of all these issues (and maybe others) federal aid to education came slowly. It has been introduced in various ways through relatively small, special-purpose programs, rather than as a planned program of nationwide federal aid to education.

Federal Grants and Direct Expenditures in the 1980s

After all of the changes, what's the pattern of fiscal federalism now? The federal government is making billions of dollars in grants both to the states and to the local governments. The states are making grants of billions of dollars to the local governments too.

About $25 out of every $100 spent by the state governments comes from the federal government. For the local governments, about $40 out of every $100 comes in federal and state grants.

But the grants don't tell the whole story. The federal government makes direct expenditures on its own for education and social welfare. *In the field of social welfare, most of the direct expenditures are made by the federal government.*

More than 80 percent of the expenditures under the social security program are made by the federal government. About one third of total expenditures for health and hospitals are made by the federal government. But in education, direct federal expenditures are much smaller—only about 5 percent of the total.

Most of the federal spending for transportation (highways, airports, etc.) is done through grants to the state and local governments. However, about 15 percent of the total is made up of direct federal expenditures. About half of the total expenditures for economic development and natural resources, including agricultural programs, the space program, national forests, etc., are paid for directly by the federal government.

There's no questions that the federal government is now playing an important role in providing the "people-related" programs which in the early 1900s were the domain of the local governments. The federal government is doing it both through grants and through direct expenditures. More than half of all federal spending is now aimed toward these "people-related" programs.

State Grants and Expenditures

What about the states, in the early 1980s? *The biggest single expenditure item of the state governments is transfers of funds to local governments!* More than one third of total state expenditures go as grants-in-aid.

The biggest *direct* expenditure by state governments is for education. About one fourth of total spending for education is spent by the state governments. Several states have taken over the entire education program.

About one third of all expenditures for hospitals and health are spent by the states. About half of total expenditures for welfare are spent by the states. More than half of direct expenditures for highways are spent by the states. But as you would guess, a lot of money for these program comes in grants from the federal government.

Local Government Functions

It's obvious that the local governments have been successful in getting the state governments and federal government to carry a lot of the cost of providing services to the people. The local governments are still spending a lot of money, of course: for transportation, education, natural resources, agriculture, welfare, housing, urban renewal, health and hospitals, police and fire protection and other things. But *much of this direct spending by local governments is indirect spending by the state and federal governments*—mostly by grants-in-aid.

What's the biggest single expenditure function of the local governments these days? Education. About 80 percent of the expenditures for education in this country are made by local governments. But a lot of the money comes from the states. And some from the federal government. But for all of the other people-related functions (except police and fire protection), local expenditures are small as compared with state and federal expenditures.

"Local Government" Means "Big Cities." Local government includes everything from the big cities like New York, Chicago, Houston, and San Francisco; to the small rural villages and counties and townships scattered all over the country.

Consider this: each of the big cities (economically, and from a taxing-spending point of view) *is much bigger than several of the states!* New York City has more people (by far), produces more product value (by far), and collects and spends more money (by far) than most of the states!

In terms of population and economic activity, New York City is about as big as the entire nation of Australia! Yet when we are talking about "local governments" in the United States, we lump together cities like New York and Los Angeles with places like Rodanthe, North Carolina and Menominee, Michigan and Triadelphia, West Virginia.

Here's the point: Remember that when you're looking at "local government" figures, most of what you are seeing is what's going on in the big cities. The figures from the little places are dwarfed into insignificance.

Suppose someone asks you: "Which levels of government are doing the taxing and spending to provide the government services in the United States?" The answer is: "The federal government, mostly. Next comes the state governments and the big cities. And that's about all." That's right. The small local governments aren't doing enough to show up very much in the total picture.

Which Governments Finance the People-Related Programs?

Most of the cost of the people-related programs is now paid by the state and federal governments. Taking all of the economic and social service programs together—that is, the programs that serve the people—where does the money come from? About half of it is collected by the federal government. The other half is collected by the state and local governments—about one fourth by each.

Federal Grants-in-Aid? or Block Grants?

Over the years, many state and local government leaders have been asking the federal government for block grants. A **block grant** is a "no-strings-attached" gift of money from the federal government to the state or local government. In recent years some block grants have been made, but not many. Almost all intergovernmental grants are grants-in-aid. What's the difference?

A "grant-in-aid" requires (1) that the money must be used for a specified purpose, and (2) that the state or local government must pay some of the cost. Sometimes the state or local share is small—like in the interstate highway program where the federal government pays 90 percent of the construction cost. But sometimes the state or local government pays more than half of the cost.

With block grants, no "matching funds" need to be provided by the receiving governments. But even more important. The receiving governments can use the money any way they want to.

Early in 1976 when President Ford presented his budget message he recommended more use of block grants. The response of some people in the states and localities was: "Great"! But the response of some other people was: "No! Let's not do it!"

Since the beginning, the federal and state grants-in-aid programs have been designed to accomplish two purposes: One is to assist in the financing of state and local programs. The other is to induce the lower levels of government to go along with programs such as interstate highways, unemployment compensation, welfare, and others. Certainly most of the states and cities would not be as involved in welfare programs as they now are, without the federal inducement of grants-in-aid.

So why are some people afraid of replacing grants-in-aid with block grants? It's obvious. They are afraid the state and local governments will abandon some of the federal-induced programs. They're afraid the block-grant money will be spent for things which are of greater interest to the local politicians—things which may not do much to serve the needs of the poor or the unemployed or the minorities in the local areas.

Reagan's "New Federalism" Initiative

In his State of the Union address in early 1982, President Reagan suggested changes which go a lot further than replacing grants-in-aid with block grants. The President proposed that the states take over *nearly four dozen programs* which are now run completely or partly by Washington.

In exchange, the federal government would provide temporary funding which would ultimately run out in the late 1980s. From then on, if the states wanted to continue the programs they could do so with their own funds. The President explained that during the 1990s the states would be able to "preserve, lower or raise taxes on their own, and fund and manage these programs as they see fit."

Controversial? You bet! A daring initiative, to be sure. But at a time when many states are struggling to make ends meet and pay for their present programs, it isn't likely that there will be a quick rush to adopt this **new fiscal federalism.**

So what will happen? It's too early to tell. There will be a lot of controversy about this, that's for sure. Meanwhile, there probably will be some increase in the use of block grants. But we are also likely to see continued use of grants-in-aid.

If you would like to know what's happening currently on this, why not go to the library and find out? You might start by looking up the figures in the latest edition of the *Statistical Abstract of the United States.* And *The New York Times Index* or *The Wall Street Journal Index* would be sure to turn up some interesting articles about what has been going on.

WHY HAS GOVERNMENT SPENDING INCREASED SO MUCH?

Government spending has increased a lot. No question about that. But why? Some things are obvious. Population has expanded. Gross national product has expanded. But *why should government spending increase by more than the rate of population increase? And by more than the rate of increase in GNP? That's what we need to talk about.*

The Great Depression: A New Philosophy

In the early 1900s the laissez-faire philosophy was very strong in this country. People should stand on their own two feet. The government should leave people alone—to prosper, or to starve.

But during the depression of the 1930s, more and more people came to recognize the insecurity of the individual in a modern, interdependent economic system. So they wanted the government to provide economic security. They wanted programs for more equal opportunity, more and better education and training, better health and hospital services, and unemployment payments, old age and survivors insurance and such.

Without the changing ideas about the "proper role" of government, government functions in the American economy could never have expanded so much. But it wasn't just the new ideas that brought on the increased government activities. Changing technology had a lot to do with it, too.

Technological Change: More Capital, More Controls

It wouldn't be easy to list all of the ways that new technology has changed the modern world. Our lives are all different because of it, that's for sure. Modern technology makes us ef-

ficient and lets us earn high incomes without working too hard. It supports the great economic and military power of the modern world. Also it takes away our individuality. It makes us all interdependent. Our economic destinies get all tied together.

Aside from making us all interdependent, new technology has required more government spending. Automobiles and trucks require better highways; modern airlines require better airports; new communications methods require government regulation; new technology makes it possible for an enemy nation to destroy us and new technology makes it very expensive for us to protect ourselves against that possibility.

New technology requires more and better education—and means a tough life for people who don't get much education or training. New technology brings people together in the big cities and increases the social problems. New technology provides new avenues of crime—and makes it more expensive to protect society against crime.

To what extent is technological change responsible for the great increases in government spending since the early 1900s? No one can say for sure. But it's very important. Perhaps more important than anything else.

Private Wealth and Public Poverty

The government didn't just grow up octopus-like and reach out and start doing things. The people asked for it. In the depression they asked for it because they were desperate. But more recently they have been asking for more government spending even in times of prosperity. Why? Because they want more and better government services.

People have been concerned about the gap between their own private standards of living and the standards of public services. People had nice cars, but the highways weren't nearly so comfortable. People had comfortable homes but when the children went to public school they found themselves in poverty-like surroundings. Often the teacher was undertrained (and underpaid) too.

People began to demand higher quality government services. They called on their local, state, and federal legislators to do something about it. And the legislators responded. They taxed (and borrowed) more money, and then spent it to provide better services. One thing we all have discovered: High-standard government services are expensive.

A Summary Comment

Why have government expenditures increased so much? New technology, the high degree of individual interdependence, the psychological impact of the great depression, the increasing wealth of the big middle class, and the high cost of modern military technology—all these have had a lot to do with it.

More and more, people have been demanding things through *government*, rather than through *markets*. And more and more the American economic and political systems have responded to their wishes. So does that mean that the American economic system has changed? Yes. It sure does.

SOME PUBLIC FINANCE ISSUES OF THE 1980s

During the 1970s and early 1980s there were some tough times. You already know that. Did those "tough times" have an impact on government activities and public finance in the United States? Yes. Definitely.

Problems of the States and Cities

Many cities have had great difficulty meeting their financial obligations. Bond buyers have shunned municipal bonds. So interest costs for issuing local bonds have been very high. At one time, Detroit had trouble getting money to meet its obligations and maintain essential services. Even Richmond, Virginia, which has a good record of sound financing, had trouble finding buyers for its bonds.

The states were having difficulties, too. The government of Massachusetts had to make drastic expenditure cut-backs, and it had difficulty obtaining credit to carry on its programs. The state of New York was forced to make big cut-backs in its programs, too.

There have been several bond referendums across the country. The voters have been asked to approve new bond issues so the state and city governments could make new capital expenditures—for highways, buildings, water and sewer systems, other needed facilities. But all across the country voters have been turning down proposed bond issues.

Only large increases in federal grants have prevented either sharp expenditure cut-backs or big tax increases by several state and local governments.

In the case of New York City, a special Act of Congress provided $2.3 billion in loans to prevent financial disaster. The city couldn't pay its debts—and no one would lend more to a broke municipality! Even with the federal help, New York City had to make drastic cuts in spending and drastic tax increases.

The increasing taxes and debt-finance problems of the states and cities during the 1970s generated a move toward fiscal conservatism all over the country. In California, voters passed "Proposition 13" which forced property taxes to be cut. Similar tax cut initiatives were introduced in several other states.

Politicians can't ignore such strong public sentiment. But on the other hand, people keep demanding more and better services. And that could force more borrowing.

State and local borrowing was increasing every year in the 1970s, to the record level of $45 billion in 1977. In 1978 it was down a little, to about $42 billion. But in mid-1979 the total debt of the states and cities amounted to about $300 billion.

Federal Financial Problems

Things haven't looked so healthy at the federal level either—although the federal finance problem is entirely different from the state and local finance problem, as you know. During the 1970s, every year the federal government spent more than it collected in taxes. The deficits ranged from a low of about $5 billion up to about $66 billion. Fiscal year 1976 ended with the highest deficit in history—more than $65 billion. For fiscal year 1977 it was down to about $45 billion, but for fiscal year 1978 it was back up to almost $50 billion.*

President Carter vowed to move toward balancing the budget. Public anti-inflation and anti-deficit sentiment was becoming very strong. Many states passed resolutions calling for a convention to amend the Constitution to require the federal government to operate on a balanced budget.

The deficit for fiscal year 1979 (ending September 30, 1979) had been estimated at about $60 billion. The Carter administration cut back its spending and managed to hold the deficit to less than $30 billion. In January 1979, President Carter called for a "lean and austere" budget for fiscal year 1980, with total spending of $531.6 billion and a projected deficit of $29 billion.

---

*In 1974 the Congressional Budget Reform Act established new federal budget procedures and changed the federal fiscal year from July 1 through June 30, to October 1 through September 30. So "fiscal year 1977" began not on July 1 of 1976, but on October 1 of 1976. Because of this change during the calendar year 1976 there are three months which don't fall in any fiscal year. Fiscal 1976 ended on June 30, 1976. Fiscal 1977 began October 1, 1976. So what about July, August and September of 1976? That's called the "transition quarter" (TQ). If you're looking at federal taxing or spending statistics for 1976 you may see figures for "TQ." That means "July, August, and September of 1976."

In tune with the public sentiment of the times, President Carter's 1980 budget called for spending cuts—not tax increases—to reduce the deficit. What spending cuts? Mostly cuts in spending for social welfare programs. As you might expect the "lean and austere" budget was immediately attacked from several sides.

Senator Kennedy said the budget "asks the poor, the black, the sick, the young, the cities and the unemployed to bear a disproportionate share" of the spending cuts. But as it turned out, not all of the requested cuts were passed by Congress. The deficit for 1980 turned out to be, not $29 billion, but $60 billion.

Reagan's Supply-Side Program

After his inauguration, President Reagan followed through on his campaign promises to try to reduce the role of government in the economy. Tax cuts were pushed through Congress to try to stimulate productivity. Significant spending cuts were called for—except that defense spending was to be increased.

When all of the figures were added up, the projected deficits were big. The economic recession of 1981-82 was reducing tax revenues. It looked like there would be a deficit approaching $60 billion in fiscal 1981, and approaching $100 billion in fiscal '82 and again in '83.

By the spring of 1982 is was clear that many congressional members of the Reagan team were worried about such huge deficits. Planned deficits of $100 billion? That could mean realized deficits of more than $200 billion! But President Reagan stuck by his guns—*no tax increases*, and *no cuts in planned expenditures for defense*.

In 1981 the federal debt had already passed $1 trillion. Interest payments on the government debt were approaching $100 billion. Congressional support for the Reagan program was getting shaky.

What happened after that? I don't know. But in mid-1982 as this book was getting ready to go to press, it appeared that some spending cuts and some tax rate adjustments might be coming.

Suggestion: Go to your library and get the latest issue of the *Economic Report of the President*. Read the president's brief statement in the beginning of the book, then look at the *government finance tables* in the back of the book. Then you'll know for sure what happened!

THE THEORY OF GOVERNMENT EXPENDITURES

The theory of government expenditures is concerned mostly with this fundamental question: Why should governments spend money to direct economic resources? Why does the political process come in and make the choices? What's wrong with just letting the market process take care of things?

Why Do Governments Spend?

Ever since the early part of this book you have known about the neat and efficient way the market process works. People demand things. Demand influences prices, and through the price mechanism, the economy responds. Automatically the wishes of the people are fulfilled. With such a neat system, why should government interfere?

Here's one reason: *Sometimes the market process doesn't work.* Sometimes the price mechanism isn't capable of carrying out the wishes of the society. The special nature of some goods (and some markets) is such that neither the production motivating function nor the rationing function of price can work. With such goods and such markets, the government *must* get involved. Otherwise there's no way that the desired choices can be made.

There are other times when the market process could work all right—but *the people don't like the results the market brings.* Take, for example, education. Is it "in the public interest" for every-

one in the society to have some education? If so, then the government must provide for education. If it's left to private markets, many people will go uneducated.

Whenever private markets wouldn't produce enough of some service (as with education) then the people decide to turn away from the private market. They let government provide the service.

In general, governments must get involved when

1. private markets don't work well, or
2. the results of the private markets aren't considered acceptable.

In a society which has both a democratic government and a market-directed economy, if many people want the government to provide some good or service, then that's just what will happen.

There are four kinds of government-expenditure situations or "cases" we need to look at: (1) the case of public goods, (2) the case of high "transactions costs," (3) the case of externalities, and (4) the case of income redistribution. In case 1 the market process doesn't work at all. In cases 2, 3, and 4, either the market process doesn't work very well, or the society is not satisfied with the results the market process brings.

Public Goods: When Markets Don't Work

There are some goods which by their very nature must be provided by government—that is, if they are going to be provided at all.

Public Goods Are Available to Everyone. Think of community police protection. Or the system of justice. The courts. National defense. Even such things as highway signs and street lights. Once these things are available, *they are available to everyone. With* **public goods** *people enjoy the goods whether they help to pay for them or not!*

Public Goods Are Never Used Up. And here's another thing to think about: *No matter how many people use and enjoy "public goods," the goods are not used up!* Now you know the two essential characterisitcs of "public goods."

It's obvious that if public goods are going to be provided, they must be provided by government. What private citizen would pay for something that's going to be available for everybody? A few might. But how would you like to have to depend on it?

The Rationing Function Reduces Social Welfare. Also, consider this: If a price is charged for the use of a public good, the rationing function of price will start working. People will conserve (use less of) the good. But that would only reduce social welfare! People having to stay home nights to avoid the "out-after-dark-street-light-fee"? Ridiculous.

So it's obvious that the government must provide public goods. As the economy grows and gets more complex, more public goods are required. So the role of government must grow.

Market Inefficiency: High "Transactions Cost"

Sometimes private markets wouldn't work efficiently. Suppose the "marketing activity"—the task of selling the good or service and collecting the money—is very difficult. Very expensive. That is, suppose a lot of society's valuable resources must be used up just in the task of selling the good or service and collecting the money.

For example, suppose we decided to let all the highways, streets, roads and sidewalks be produced by private businesses. The private businesses could sell these services by charging tolls. But you can see what a ridiculous entanglement that would be!

Toll gates and checkpoints all over the place; many thousands of people working as toll col-

lectors, bookkeepers, accountants, turnstile repairers, etc. etc.—and people always looking for little paths to walk on to bypass the sidewalk toll gates!

What a mess! The people really wouldn't be getting full use of the facilities because of the tolls—because of the rationing function of price. Remember? And the cost of collecting the tolls probably would be greater than the cost of building and maintaining the roads, streets, and sidewalks! So what happens? The government does it. (Only on high-volume highways do tolls become feasible. And that's where they're used, of course.)

Benefit Externalities: Desirable Spillovers, or "Third Party" Effects

With externalities, "the market" doesn't reflect the true social costs and benefits. So unless the government gets involved *there will be too few of some goods and too many of others.*

Education is a good example of a service with external social benefits. Your education is important to you. Of course. But it's also important to the society! What kind of a world would you be living in *if you were the only one with any education?* Not so good. Right?

The education of scientists and engineers and other professionals is helpful to the individuals themselves. Sure. But it is also absolutely essential for the operation of a modern economic system. It has long been recognized that education serves the public interest. So education has long been supported by governments.

Many of our present government programs are justified because of **beneficial externalities**—that is, because the total benefit to the society is greater than the sum of the benefits to the individuals. The development of natural resources, land reclamation, conservation programs, research programs, urban transportation systems, dams and lakes, river and harbor improvements, and health and hospital programs all are examples.

Income Redistribution: Sharing the Wealth

Some government expenditures are made to try to increase the incomes of low income people. Sometimes it's done by direct payments. For example, the social security program makes direct payments to retired people and survivors of wage earners. But these aren't the only kinds of "income redistribution" expenditures.

Some government programs are aimed at improving the real incomes of the poor. Often the programs are available for everybody, but it's the low income people who gain the most. Free school lunches and school buses, free parks and recreation areas, subsidized low-cost housing, urban transportation systems, manpower training and job development and placement, assistance to small farmers, small businesses, minority groups—all of these programs are aimed at increasing real incomes of low income people.

Most of these programs generate "benefit externalities." Not only do they benefit the people receiving them. They also have spillover effects which benefit society as a whole.

Economists have developed quite a lot of theory to explain when and why governments should spend money to direct resources in an economic system. Here you've just touched the highlights of this theory. But now, one more point.

Governments Respond to Political Reality

Governments are *political* creatures. What they do must fit the political climate. In a democratic and open society, the government must respond to the attitudes of most of the people. So where does that leave us regarding the theory of government expenditures? Wide open.

How are government expenditure programs actually decided? Usually on the basis of pragmatism. The obvious needs will be taken care of. Beyond that the matter will rest largely on the economic-political philosophy of the people who are making the choices. Ultimately, those things which are politically expedient will be done. Those which are not, will not.

Economic Theory and Public Choice

In the 1980s, any way you measure it the role of government in the economy is great. Expenditures amount to about one-third of GNP. Recent studies have estimated that nearly fifty percent of the people are dependent at least in part for their economic welfare on some kind of government activity or program. So if you want to understand how the American economy functions you need to know something about how governments actually work—how they make the "resource allocation" decisions.

In recent years economists have turned their attention to the analysis of this decision-making process. How do (and/or should) governments actually work out their resource-allocation decisions?

"Public choice" or "collective choice" economics attempts to apply the concepts of microeconomics and marginal analysis in the public-choice-making process. You saw an application of this "marginal social cost equals marginal social benefit" analysis when you were reading about the questions: "How much pollution?" and "How much cleaning up?" "Where is the socially optimum position?" Remember?

Public choice economics also gets into the political arena. It raises questions of the rationality of the voters; of the effects of "log rolling"; of the influence of political parties. It even asks

such questions as: "Is it possible for democratic government to make optimizing decisions?"

Public choice economics is one of the frontiers on which some economists are working. Considerable progress is being made. Perhaps during the 1980s we will see major breakthroughs—greatly improved understanding both of the *process* and of the *efficiency* of collective choice decisions. Then we will know a lot more about resource allocation in our heterogeneous democratic society.

In view of the real-world realities, if some-

one asks you: "Why have government expenditures in the United States increased so greatly during the past few decades?" You can answer: "Because that's what the political process decided."

Public attitudes toward government involvement in the economy have changed greatly. If the attitudes had not changed, the great increases in government spending—for example, the rapid increase in social welfare spending—would not have occurred.

SUMMARY AND SYNTHESIS

During the present century, expenditures by all levels of government have increased from one twelfth of the GNP to one third of GNP. All spending categories have increased over this period—both in absolute terms, and as a percentage of GNP.

In the early 1900s all three levels of government (federal, state, and local combined) were spending only about $50 a year per capita. In the early 1980s, this figure was up to $4,000. A lot of this increase was caused by inflation, of course. But a lot of it was not.

As spending was increasing, the spending patterns were changing. The spending function which has increased the most (by far) has been social welfare spending.

Social welfare spending today is the only spending category that makes up more than 10 percent of GNP. It reached this level in the mid-1970s. In 1960 it had been about 5 percent of GNP. In 1950 it was less than 3 percent. In the 1920s it was less than 1 percent.

The growth of social welfare expenditures has created financial burdens for all levels of government. In 1982 President Reagan recommended that most of the social welfare programs be transferred to the states. But President Reagan's new fiscal federalism recommendations are not likely to be quickly enacted by Congress.

Defense spending as a percentage of GNP has been declining in recent years. It decreased from a little more than 10 percent during the Vietnam War to about 8 percent by the mid-1970s. In the early 1980s, it was down to less than 6 percent of GNP. But the Reagan administration was promising to reverse this trend.

Other major spending categories in the early 1980s are: education, about 6 percent of GNP; economic development, between 3 and 4 percent of GNP; interest expense (remember the trillion dollar federal debt?) between 3 and 4 percent of GNP; transportation and general government, each about 2 percent of GNP; and foreign aid, which makes up less than one half of one percent of GNP.

The history of fiscal federalism in this country shows a picture of continual centralization. In the early 1900s the local governments provided most of the services. Slowly the state and federal governments became involved because of the need for statewide or nationwide coordination.

In the depression years of the 1930s, local governments couldn't finance the desperately needed services in their areas. So they called on the states for help. The states in turn called on Washington. Many functions were moved upward from local to states and from states to the federal government during this time. This centralization of functions continued, up to the 1980s.

Today, for every $100 being spent by the local governments, about $40 comes from state and federal grants. Out of every $100 being spent by the state governments, about $25 comes from federal grants. The federal government also makes direct expenditures on many health, welfare, and social services programs.

Should the federal government use grants-in-aid? Or block grants? Some people argue that we need nationwide standards of health, welfare, and other services and that the federal government should use grants-in-aid to ensure this. Others argue that each state has the right to make up its own mind—that the federal government should provide block grants and let the state and local governments provide whatever programs they wish.

Some reasons for the great increases in government expenditure are: (1) changing ideas about the "proper role" of government; (2) effects of new technology on our interdependence, requiring more regulation, and increasing the costs of national defense, crime prevention, etc.; (3) the desire for high-quality government services to parallel our high living standards; and (of course) (4) inflation.

The public finance picture in the United States was was not all rosy in the early 1980s. The states and cities were having difficulties funding their desired programs because of high interest costs and other problems. Some cities (including New York City) had a narrow brush with bankruptcy during the 1970s. This resulted in a curtailment of programs.

Public attitudes across the country have been increasingly anti-government. One example was the passage of "Proposition 13" in California, limiting the government's powers to increase property taxes. Another was the big Republican victory in the 1980 elections.

At the federal level, deficits have been a persistent problem. Deficits are projected in the neighborhood of $100 billion for 1982 and again for 1983. But it isn't sure that the Congress will go along with this aspect of the Reagan program.

The theory of government expenditures tries to answer the question: "Why do governments spend?" Four important answers are: (1) public goods, (2) high transactions costs, (3) externalities, and (4) income redistribution.

Public goods are goods which must be provided by government if they are to be provided at all, because (1) they are available to everyone whether they pay or not, (2) they are never used up, no matter how much they are used, and (3) since the marginal cost of using these goods is zero, any price placed on them would ration the use without reducing the cost and would reduce the social welfare.

Goods with high transactions costs can't be provided by the market because it might cost more to collect the money than it would to supply the goods! Very wasteful.

With benefit externalities, if the social welfare is to be maximized, the government needs to stimulate the production so that there will be more than private markets would supply. Such things as public education, natural resource development, urban transportation systems, and many others fall into this category.

Finally, government spending is used to share the wealth. Governments provide many things which the lower income people will use more of than upper income people will use. Some examples are: free school lunches, free parks and recreation areas, subsidized low-income housing, and urban transportation.

What determines how much governments actually do spend? And for what? Pragmatism usually plays an important role. Suppose the people in the United States had not been (more or less) in favor of having the government do all these things. Then it wouldn't have happened.

Some economists are now using economic theory to analyze the way governments actually do (and/or should) work out their resource allocation decisions. This area of analysis is called "public choice theory." The results of the public choice theorists seem to indicate that the market does a better job of approaching the social optimum than does the government.

REVIEW EXERCISES

MAJOR CONCEPTS, PRINCIPLES, TERMS (Explain each carefully.)

grants-in-aid

the "new national philosophy"

effects of technological change

private wealth and public poverty

public goods

high "transactions cost"

benefit externalities

income redistribution

public choice economics

OTHER CONCEPTS AND TERMS (Explain each briefly.)

National Banking System

fiscal federalism

centralization of expenditure

federal "post roads"

block grants

matching funds

QUESTIONS (Write out answers or jot down key points.)

1. Describe some of the major changes in government spending patterns between the 1900s and the early 1980s.

2. In recent years "defense" (military) expenditures have been a smaller and smaller part of total government spending in the United States. First describe the *extent* of the change then talk about the reasons for the change.

3. The changes in social welfare spending have been greatest of all. Can you describe the extent of the changes? Then explain some of the reasons? Try.

4. Why has there been relatively so little spending for education by the federal government?

5. Talk about the problem of being misled by the grouping of different kinds of expenditures into "spending categories." (Hint: What category do you suppose the spending by the CIA is hidden in?)

6. The spending functions of the *different levels of government* have changed greatly since the early 1900s. First give highlights of the changes, then give some of the reasons for the changes.

7. Explain some of the uses and advantages and disadvantages of (a) grants-in-aid, as compared with (b) block grants. In which situations do you think "a" should be used? How about "b"? Discuss.

8. The group of governments called "local governments" are really diverse! Explain how diverse. Then discuss the problem this creates for students of public finance.

9. Discuss some of the financial problems of the cities and the states in the mid-to-late 1970s. Then compare the federal financial problems and talk about the *similarities* and the *differences*.

10. Explain why governments spend—that is, explain the highlights of the theory of government expenditures.

36

Public Finance II: Taxes, in Theory and Practice

Chapter Objectives

- In the previous chapter you learned about one side of public finance: **government spending.** In this chapter you will learn about the other side: **taxes.**

- When you finish studying this chapter you will be able to describe the **major changes in taxes collected** between the early part of this century, and today. You will be able to explain the **changing roles** of the **different levels of government,** and the "fiscal federalism" issue from the **taxation point of view.**

- You will be able to **describe and analyze the effects** of various kinds of **taxes on income** including the **individual income tax,** the **payroll tax, and the corporation income tax.** And you will be able to **evaluate** each of these sources of revenue.

- You will be able to **describe and analyze the effects** of various taxes on the **manufacture, purchase, or sale of goods and services,** including primarily **sales and excise taxes,** but also including the **value added tax (VAT).**

- You will be able to **describe and analyze the effects** of various kinds of **taxes on property,** including **real estate and personal property taxes and death and gift taxes.**

- Finally, you will be able to discuss the **theory of taxation: What makes a good tax system?** And you will be able to explain the **complications introduced** by the questions of **shifting and incidence.**

As total government spending in the United States was increasing from about $1 billion at the beginning of the century to about $1 trillion in the early 1980s, what do you suppose was happening to taxes. Increasing too? Of course.

As Spending Increases, Taxes Increase—but Not as Much

As government spending increases, taxes increase, of course. But governments often spend more than they collect in taxes. How do they do that? They make up the difference by borrowing!

Each year when revenues are less than expenditures, the government must borrow, of course. The debt increases. The deficits were especially large in the 1970s and early 1980s as you found out in the previous chapter. Most of the deficits were at the federal level—not at the state and local government levels. Why? One reason was because those weren't easy times for the state and local governments to borrow! Remember?

When the federal government spends more than it takes in, it can create money to make up the difference. That is, it can print up new bonds and sell them and the Federal Reserve banks can buy the bonds and supply the Treasury with new demand deposits to spend.

But when the state and local governments borrow, they can't create money. They must sell their bonds in the bond markets the same way a business sells bonds to raise money. The state and local governments do not have the unlimited borrowing power of the federal government.

A state or local government gets into serious financial difficulty if its tax revenues drop—especially if it has a lot of outstanding debts to be paid off.

FISCAL FEDERALISM: CHANGING PATTERNS OF FEDERAL, STATE, AND LOCAL TAXES

In the early 1980s people were paying taxes at the rate of almost $1 trillion a year. The state and local governments were collecting almost $400 billion a year and the federal government was collecting more than $600 billion.

By the time you are reading this, total tax collections in the country are bound to be higher—maybe even $1.3 trillion, or more! It depends a lot on the rate of inflation and on how fast the GNP increases. If you want to know what happened you can always go to your library and find out in less than 10 minutes.

An Overview of Present Taxing Patterns

You already know a lot about taxes. You know that the *federal government* collects most of the taxes. You know that it collects most of its

money in **income taxes.** And you know that one effect of all these income taxes is to leave people with a lot less money to spend!

You probably also know that the federal government levies **income taxes on corporations,** and that it levies **excise taxes** on alcoholic beverages, cigarettes, gasoline, and several other things. And you know that these taxes make it more expensive to buy the taxed goods.

Most people know that the *states* levy **sales taxes,** because most people have to pay state sales taxes! Most states levy **income taxes,** too. And **excises** on alcoholic beverages and cigarettes and gasoline, and other things. I expect you probably already knew all that, too.

What about the *local governments?* They levy taxes on **property**—mostly real estate: land, houses, and business buildings and equipment and other properties. If you live in a small town or in a rural area, the property tax is probably the major source of local revenue. There are some **business licenses and fees** and a few other things, but mostly, it's the property tax that supports the small local governments.

But suppose you live in a *big city.* What about that? Chances are you are paying to the city some of the same kinds of taxes as you pay to the state: *sales taxes and excises and income taxes.*

See? You didn't have to take economics to find out what kind of taxes the governments are collecting in the United States. You already knew! (How nice it would be if the governments would just let us forget, for a while. Right?)

But the pattern of taxing that exists in the United States now hasn't existed for very long. It's interesting to look back to the early 1900s and see what it looked like then, and to watch how it evolved.

The Changing Size of Federal, State and Local Tax Collections

In the early 1900s the local governments were spending the most. So they were collecting the most taxes. The states weren't spending much, so they weren't collecting much in taxes.

The local governments were collecting about 50 percent of all taxes collected. The federal government was collecting about 40 percent. That left the states with only about 10 percent. And that wasn't very much, considering that *the total only added up to about $1 billion.*

The Federal Level. Throughout the first half of this century, federal taxes generally ranged between 30 and 40 percent of total taxes collected (except during wartime, of course). But after World War II, federal tax collections never dropped back into the 30 to 40 percent range again. Since the 1950s federal tax collections have ranged between 60 and 70 percent of total taxes collected in the country.

The State Level. In the depression years of the 1930s, state tax collections increased from 10 percent to about 30 percent of total taxes collected in the country. Since then state taxes have increased, of course. But the increases have been overshadowed by the great increases in federal tax collections. Since the 1950s the states have been collecting only about 20 percent of the total.

The Local Level. The role of the local governments has really been reversed. Up to the 1930s they were collecting about half of the taxes. Then during the depression, local taxes dropped to about 30 percent of the total—about equal to the states.

Since World War II the picture has been even more different. Local taxes have never again made up more than about 15 percent of the total. In the early 1980s it was less than 15 percent. As I'm sure you could guess, most of the local taxes are collected by the big cities.

Figure 36-1 shows a picture of the changed taxing roles of the three levels of government.

Just about now you may be beginning to wonder about something. From the previous chapter you know that *total expenditures of the state governments are of about the same size as total expenditures of the local governments.* Each is spending about 20 percent of total government spending. Yet their tax collections are quite different. The local governments collect less than 15 percent of the total; the states collect about 20 percent.

Are the local governments borrowing enough money to make up the difference? And if not, where does the money come from? You already know the answer, right? Intergovernmental grants? Of course.

Intergovernmental Grants. *About 40 percent of local spending ($2 out of every $5) is financed by state and federal taxes.* Why?

Politics has a lot to do with it, of course. Local politicians like to be able to provide new things in the local area without having to tax the local people to pay for the things. But aside from that, there's a general feeling that many services are best provided by local government, even though the taxes can best be collected by the state and federal governments. (After you have finished reading about the different kinds of taxes you will understand this statement a lot better.)

New Taxing Patterns: Changing Sources of Tax Revenue

What kinds of taxes are levied in the United States? How much tax revenue comes from each kind of tax? Has there been much change in the kinds of taxes used in this country? Figure 36-2 shows you the answers to these questions.

Figure 36-2 shows that the biggest source of revenue in the 1980s didn't even show up in the picture in the early 1900s. Which tax? The individual income tax. At the other extreme, it shows that the biggest source of revenue in the early 1900s (the property tax) now makes up only a small part of the total.

Why have there been such big shifts in revenue sources? Much of it results from *the great increase in the total amount of revenue to be collected.* The revenue sources of the early 1900s just wouldn't produce that much revenue! Another part of the answer is in *the shift in the role of each*

Fig. 36-1   Taxes Collected by Each Level of Government as a Percentage of Total Taxes Collected in the Country (Early 1900s and Early 1980s)

Look at local government—from first position in the early 1900s to the last position in the 1980s. If it wasn't for the big cities, the "local government bar" for the 1980s would almost shrink out of sight!

Don't forget: the totals in the 1980s are about 1,000 times as big as the totals in the early 1900s!

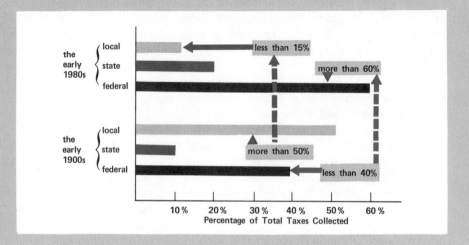

level of government.

The property tax is a good revenue source for the local governments. The income tax is a good revenue source for the federal government. As the role of the local governments has declined and the federal role has increased, income taxes have become more important and property taxes have become less important. Of course.

There are three major kinds of taxes: (1) taxes on income, (2) taxes on the manufacture or sale of goods and services, and (3) taxes on property. When you finish reading the next few sections you will understand them. But first, take time to study Figure 36-2 carefully so that you will know about the present pattern of taxes and about the great changes in the American tax system since the early 1900s.

TAXES ON INCOME

When the U.S. Constitution was amended in 1913 to let the federal government levy taxes on income, that sure touched off a lot of change in the American tax system! Today, about one half of all the tax money collected in this country

comes from taxes on incomes.

The federal government gets about three fourths of its revenues from taxes on income. About one fourth of all state and local tax revenues come from taxes on income.

There are three kinds of taxes which are levied directly on income: *individual income taxes,* *corporation income taxes,* and *payroll taxes.*

The Individual Income Tax

When most people think of the income tax they think of "the individual income tax." The individual income tax is the biggest single source of revenue in the United States.

Almost one third of all taxes collected in this country are "individual income taxes." The federal government gets almost half of its revenue from this tax. The state and local governments get almost 20 percent. This tax will be discussed in detail, later in this section.

The Payroll Tax

The second biggest source of revenue in the United States is the payroll tax. Most of the pay-

Fig. 36-2   Revenue Collected from Each Kind of Tax as a Percentage of Total Revenue Collected in the Country (Early 1900s and Early 1980s)

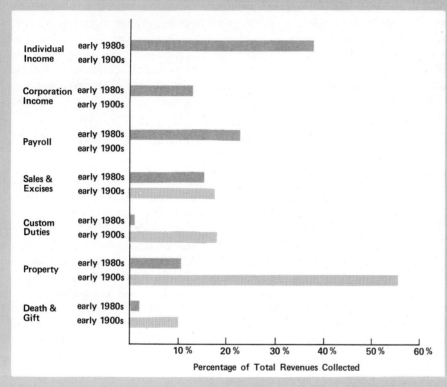

Most of the revenues in the early 1980s came from taxes that didn't even exist in the early 1900s. There were only four major kinds of taxes in the early 1900s: taxes on property, sales and excises, customs duties, and death and gift taxes. The property tax overshadowed all the others.

But today there are five major kinds of taxes. Property taxes, and sales and excises are still important. In addition there are three new sources: taxes on individual incomes, corporation incomes, and payrolls.

roll taxes are collected to finance the social security program. Part of the payroll tax is really a direct tax on income; another part is like an indirect business tax.

Only Part of Payroll Taxes Are Taxes on Income. The last time you received a paycheck, chances are some of the money was withheld for income taxes and some was also withheld for "social security" taxes. The social security tax deduction is the employee's part of the payroll tax. It is a direct tax on the employee's income.

The social security (payroll) tax is levied at a fixed rate. It begins with the first dollar of earnings and is deducted from each paycheck until your total earnings for the year have reached the "maximum taxable amount." After that, any additional earnings are exempt from this tax.

In the beginning, both the rate of the tax (percentage collected) and the "maximum taxable amount" were low. But over the years, expenditures under the social security program have increased greatly. So both the rate and the "maximum taxable amount" have been increased greatly. More on this later.

What about the employer's part of the payroll tax? It's equal to the employee's part. So of the total payroll tax revenue going to Washington to support the social security program half of it comes out of employees' paychecks and the other half is paid by the employer.

The Employer's Part of the Payroll Tax. The employer's part of the payroll tax is not a tax on people's incomes. It is a tax on the business, based on the size of the payroll. Really, it's sort of "extra wage cost" which the employer must pay. Each time an additional worker is hired the tax goes up. *It's like an excise tax on the purchase of labor.*

So how do we handle this payroll tax? Half of it is really a direct tax on the incomes of individuals; the other half is like an excise tax on the purchase of labor. Usually the figure is just lumped together and called "the payroll tax."

But in understanding the tax system, it makes sense to look at it both ways: as the "payroll tax" in total, and then to break it apart—to call half of it "income tax" and the other half "an excise on the hire of labor, paid by businesses."

Other Payroll Taxes.   There are other kinds of payroll taxes too—taxes which are not tied to the social security program. For example, the unemployment compensation (unemployment insurance) programs of the states are financed by payroll taxes levied on the employer.

Also, some cities levy payroll taxes which have nothing to do with the social security program.

City Payroll Taxes. The city payroll tax is usually a "flat-rate individual income tax." With this tax the city can collect revenue from the wage-earners who work in the city (many of whom probably live in the suburbs). The city simply levies a tax (perhaps one percent or two percent or more) on all payrolls. The employers then deduct the tax from all employee paychecks and pay the money to the city government.

This is one way the cities have found of taxing "suburbanites." The people who live outside the city and work in the city can't be taxed by the city on their property. But if they work in the city they sure can be taxed on their incomes!

Federal Payroll Taxes. More than 30 percent of total federal tax revenues come in from the payroll tax. Recently this has been the most rapidly growing source of revenue in the American tax system.

The Corporation Income Tax

The third kind of income tax is the corporation income tax. This is really a tax on the profits of corporations. About 15 percent of the total tax revenue of the federal government comes from the corporation income tax, and about 5 percent of taxes collected by the state and local governments come from corporation income taxes.

Most of the "state and local" corporation income taxes are collected by the states. But a few of the large cities collect corporation income taxes, too. You'll be reading more about corporation income taxes, soon.

How Important are Income Taxes?

How important are income taxes in the total picture of the American tax system? *Income taxes, taken all together, make up about one half of all the taxes collected in the United States.* About 30 percent of total taxes collected come from the individual income tax, about 10 percent from the income tax part of the payroll tax and about 10 percent from the corporation income tax.

The other half of the tax revenues come from sales and excise taxes, including the non-income part of the payroll tax (about 25 percent), from taxes on property (about 15 percent) and from other miscellaneous revenues such as business licenses, automobile licenses, customs duties, etc. (about 10 percent).

Why Levy Taxes on Income?

Why do governments like to collect so much tax on *income?* Here's one good reason: When you put a tax on income you can be sure there's money there to pay the tax. If you collect the tax out of the worker's paycheck, you get your money for sure!

When a tax is levied on property, what if the property owner is unemployed? and broke? You get no money. Maybe you will have to take the property and sell it to get your money. Maybe kick the family out on the street. Nobody wants to do that.

But ease of collection isn't the only reason in favor of the income tax. Even more important is *flexibility*—especially with the individual income tax.

The Individual Income Tax: Flexible Instrument of Taxation

Individual income taxes can be designed to fit the circumstances of the individual taxpayer. A person with a small income and a large family can be treated differently than a person with a large income and a small family. The tax can be designed so that if misfortune strikes—like high medical bills or a bad fire or flood—the tax will be lower.

The tax can be carefully tailored to meet the society's idea of "distributive justice." If income inequality is thought to be too great, then people with higher incomes can be taxed more heavily. Or if the idea of stimulating maximum investment is the objective, the income tax can be designed to leave the big incomes of people and businesses untouched. Then maybe the wealthy people and businesses will invest more and create new jobs and make the economy prosperous.

Yes, the income tax is a very flexible instrument for transferring money from the people to the government. The tough problem, of course, is to get agreement on what the objectives are and what tax design to use. Politicians are always arguing about this.

Individual Income Taxes in the United States

What does the individual income tax look like in the United States? The federal government and most of the states collect individual income taxes. The federal government gets something less than half of its total tax revenue from this source, and the states get about one fifth.

The federal individual income tax has a highly **progressive** rate structure—the rate gets higher as the income gets higher. An individual is permitted a certain amount of tax-free income

(personal exemptions and deductions) and everything over that is "taxable income." As your income goes up, your "marginal tax rate" (tax rate on your marginal, or additional, income) goes up.

Federal individual income tax rates on earned income go up to 50 percent. Once your income is high enough to get you into the "50 percent bracket," half of any additional income you receive will be taxed away. State individual income taxes do not have rates nearly as high as the federal rates, although in some states the tax rate exceeds 15 percent.

Income taxes can be designed to do just about anything!

Yeah. If people agree on what they want to do.

The few large cities which levy taxes on income must keep the rates low (usually 2 or 3 percent) to keep from discouraging people from living there. The states must be careful about that, too. There are still several states which do not levy income taxes. Other things being equal, people with high incomes would rather live in zero-income-tax states. Right?

There's a lot of disagreement. But even so, in general, people seem to agree that with the great revenue requirements of modern governments, the individual income tax is a necessary tool of taxation. And all things considered, it's usually considered to be one of the most desirable (least undesirable?) ways of gathering revenue.

Payroll Taxes: the Wage Earner's Share

The wage earner's share of the payroll tax is really an income tax. But the tax is not progressive. In fact it's **regressive**. The rate stays the same (proportional) until a certain amount of tax has been collected. Then the rate drops to zero. After you have paid the maximum amount of payroll taxes, any income you earn above that is payroll-tax free.

In the 1930s when the social security system was set up, the maximum payroll tax paid by each wage and salary earner was $30 a year. It was increased several times during the 1950s and 60s, but in the early 1970s the maximum was still less than $500 a year. Then the big jumps came.

By 1979 the maximum was up to more than $1,400 per worker. It was estimated that the soaring costs of the social security program would push the maximum up to $3,000 by the mid-1980s, and higher and higher in future years.

Payroll Taxes Are Regressive. The payroll tax is designed to be regressive. People with low wages must pay the full rate of the tax on all of their income. But people with high salaries and wages are only taxed on part of their income. And a wealthy person who just earns income from property, pays nothing! Does that seem fair? How is it justified?

The regressiveness of the employee's share of the payroll tax is justified by this argument: *The person who is paying the payroll tax is not really paying taxes at all, but is "buying insurance."*

The Poor Receive the Benefits. Here's the argument: Under social security, each person is "enrolled in an insurance program" Each person gets considerable benefits from being a member of the program. Therefore each should pay for these benefits. Wealthy people who are not wage earners are not enrolled in the program. They will not get any benefits. Therefore they shouldn't have to pay.

The program was worked out so that the more a person earns the more taxes that person would pay and the more benefits that person would be eligible for. That was the idea. So people didn't complain about the "regressive tax." The benefits of the "insurance" received were clearly great enough to justify the cost— especially for the poor people. When the benefits

received are compared against the tax payments into the program, the total effect is to improve the position of low-income people. No doubt about that!

But some people aren't satisfied with that argument. You might ask: Why is it necessary to tax the money away from low-income earners to finance the program? Why not just finance the program out of a progressive tax system? And keep on distributing benefits the same way as now?

If we did that it would make the social security program almost free to the low-income receivers. It would further reduce income inequality. It would put more burden on the progressive income tax payers. Some people think that would be a good idea.

Recently there has been some talk about bringing in a new kind of tax to assist (or perhaps to replace) the payroll tax. What kind of tax? The "value added" tax (VAT). You'll be reading about the VAT in a few minutes.

The Corporation Income Tax

The corporation income tax is really a profits tax on the corporation. After the corporation receives its revenues and deducts all its costs, it comes out with "profit before corporation income taxes."

The maximum federal tax rate is almost 50 percent. So the federal government is taking about half of the profits of the big corporations. Many of the states also levy corporate income taxes, but at much lower rates.

Why should corporations have to pay income taxes? All of the profits of corporations are really owned by the individuals who own the corporations. Why not just tax the income as it goes to the individuals? Why tax it when it goes to the corporation and then tax it again as it goes to the individuals? It seems like the government is taxing the same income twice. That doesn't seem fair, does it?

A lot of people agree that the "double taxation" resulting from the corporation income tax is not particularly desirable. But corporations don't pay out all of their earnings in dividends. So if there was no corporation income tax, the "retained earnings" of the corporation would not be subject to any income tax at all!

But perhaps this is more important: The corporation income tax is an easy, convenient, politically acceptable way to collect a lot of money. To most people, taxing the profits of a business seems to be an acceptable thing to do.

During 1982 the Reagan administration was working out its future tax program plans. One question being discussed was what to do about the "double taxation" of corporate dividends. Perhaps something will be done. But probably not. Regardless of theoretical issues or questions of equity, it's likely that the government will continue to collect corporation income taxes.

TAXES ON THE MANUFACTURE, PURCHASE, OR SALE OF GOODS AND SERVICES

There are many different kinds of taxes levied on goods and services. Mostly, these taxes can be called either (1) excise taxes, or (2) sales taxes. Even the employer-part of the payroll tax is a kind of excise on the purchase of labor services. Remember? The more labor the business buys, the more payroll taxes it must pay.

The Changing Role of Sales and Excise Taxes

Sales and excise taxes have been important revenue sources for *many centuries*. In the early 1900s, sales and excise taxes made up about 20 percent of total tax revenues in the United States. In the 1930s many of the states levied sales taxes to get the money needed for their own programs and to help out the faltering local governments. Also the federal government levied new excise taxes during the 1930s.

By 1940, almost 30 percent of all taxes collected in this country were sales and excises. But since that time the percentage has declined. Why? Not because of decreases in sales and excise taxes. Of course not. It has been because of the great increases in taxes on incomes and payrolls.

In the late 1970s only about 15 percent of total tax collections in the country were from sales and excises. But if you add in the employer-share of the payroll tax (an excise on the purchase of labor) and add customs duties (excise taxes on imported goods) *the total of taxes in this group adds up to about 25 percent of total taxes collected.*

Sales and Excise Taxes Defined

What are sales taxes? and excise taxes? When someone says "the sales tax" that's really a short name for "the general retail sales tax." *The sales tax is a tax on "things in general."* It applies to everything consumers buy—that is, everything except those goods which are specifically exempted. Most states levy general retail sales taxes and most of them exempt certain goods—usually food and medicines.

An excise tax is a tax on some specific thing. It can be levied at the retail level, in which case it's a consumer's excise. Ot it can be levied at the manufacturing level and be a manufacturer's excise.

Compare a consumer's excise with the general retail sales tax. That's a good way to understand the distinction between the two. Think of it this way: The sales tax applies to *everything* except those items specifically mentioned as exceptions. The consumer's excise tax applies to *nothing* except those items specifically mentioned as taxable. See the difference?

If you wanted to, you could use either consumer's excises or a general retail sales tax and design exactly the same tax system! With excises you're naming a long list of taxable items. With the sales tax you're taxing everything and then naming a long list of exemptions.

Which should you use? the general retail sales tax? or the excise tax? it depends on how many things you wanted to be taxed. If you want almost everything to be taxed, use the general retail sales tax and then make some exemptions if you want to. If you want only a few things to be taxed, use excise taxes and mention the specific things to which the tax will apply.

Manufacturers' Excise Taxes

What about the non-consumer excises?—that is, the excise taxes levied on the producer? the manufacturers' excise? These excises become indirect business taxes—that is, hidden taxes.

When you buy gasoline or cigarettes or alcoholic beverages you know that a large part of the price you're paying goes for excise taxes. But the taxes are hidden in the price of the product.

The prices of almost all manufactured products have some excise taxes hidden in them. But usually not as much as in the prices of gasoline and cigarettes and whiskey and beer! But even when you buy a new car, several hundred dollars of the price goes to pay for manufacturers' excises.

Federal Excise Taxes

In the early 1980s the federal government was collecting about $40 billion in excise taxes. But that's less than 7 percent of total federal revenues. Back in the early part of this century, about 50 percent of all federal revenues came from excises. As recently as 1940, about 30 percent of federal revenues came from excises. But then what happened?

Since 1940 there has been a rapid expansion in income tax revenues, of course. So excise tax revenues have been making up a much smaller percentage of total federal revenues. But if the employer-part of the payroll tax is added in the percentage would go up from less than 7 percent to more than 20 percent! Then if you add the "customs duty" excises, the figure reaches 25

percent! That's a lot of hidden taxes! And *all of us are paying for these taxes in the prices of the things we buy.*

State and Local Sales and Excise Taxes

In the early 1900s the states got most of their money from property taxes just as the local governments did. But *by 1940 more than 50 percent of states revenues were coming from sales and excise taxes.* And since that time the figure has never gone below 50 percent. The only thing that has kept it from rising far above 50 percent is this: In the last two decades the states have been turning more and more to the income tax.

What about the local governments? It isn't easy for them to use sales or excise taxes. Why? You already know. Right? If one locality levies sales or excise taxes, people will drive to the next locality to buy things! Of course! Still, some of the big cities levy cigarette excise taxes and gasoline excise taxes and some others.

In recent years some of the states have been helping out the local governments by collecting sales taxes for them. It works like this: Suppose the state has a 5 percent retail sales tax. And suppose one of the cities or counties in the state would like to levy a 1 percent sales tax. The county or city asks the state to increase the tax rate *in that county or city* from 5 percent to 6 percent. So the state does that. Then it gives the extra money back to the county or city where it was collected.

Evaluation of Sales and Excise Taxes

I suppose the best thing you can say about sales taxes and excises is that *they are good at producing revenue.* No matter what's going on, no matter how bad times might be, there's always some buying and selling going on. If a government levies taxes on these "buying and selling" transactions, it will collect some money. The states discovered this in the depression years of the 1930s. The federal government did too.

Excess Burdens. If sales and excise taxes are such good sources of revenue, why don't we build our entire tax system on sales and excise taxes? One reason is that excises push up the prices of the taxed things and that distorts the economic choices in the society.

With excise taxes, people bear **excess burdens.** Not only do they bear the burden of the taxes they pay. They also bear *the burden of being pushed away from their preferred consumption patterns.*

Regressiveness. Here's another issue: Sales and excise taxes are regressive. They take a larger percentage of poor people's incomes than other people's incomes. Why?

Because poor people spend just about all of their incomes on consumer goods. Most people save (and "invest") some money. So most people don't have to pay retail sales and consumer excise taxes on *all* of their incomes. But the poor people generally do.

But anyway, you can be sure that sales and excise taxes will be with us for a long time. Here's why: They produce a lot of revenue. They aren't too hard to collect. And they are politically acceptable. Most people don't complain too much about them.

Discourages Consumption. In the early 1980s with the Reagan administration's emphasis on "supply-side economics" another advantage was being claimed for sales and excise taxes. These taxes discourage consumption and encourage savings. If the major objective is to increase the productivity of the economy, then it makes sense to consider taxes which discourage consumption and encourage savings. So it may be that regressive taxes are about to take on greater respectability because they discourage consumption.

Customs Duties

One special kind of excise tax is the customs duty. Customs excises have been declining in

importance for many years. In the early 1900s about half of the federal revenue came from this source. Today customs duties produce less than 2 percent of total federal revenues.

A customs duty is a discriminatory excise tax, levied on a foreign product. Usually the purpose is to make the foreign product more expensive so that the American producers can sell their products for higher prices. So customs duties usually are determined, not by the need for revenue, but by the desire to push up the price of foreign products in domestic markets.

The people who buy the taxed imported goods pay the higher price, and the government gets the extra money in taxes. But the people who buy the domestic goods pay the higher price, too! And who gets the extra money then? The American manufacturer? Right.

As the world has been moving toward freer trade, the distorting effects of customs duties have been decreased. You'll be reading more about this in Part Nine, coming up soon.

What About the "Value Added" Tax (VAT)?

In recent years the "value added" tax (VAT) has become a major source of revenue in most of the advanced industrial nations of the world. Almost all of the West European countries collect value added taxes. The tax rate ranges from 8 percent in Britain to about 20 percent in several countries. The government of France collects about one fourth of its total revenues from the VAT. But the United States doesn't levy the VAT at all.*

---

*Since 1976 the state of Michigan has been levying a low-rate (2.35%) valued added tax. Michigan officials say that the results have been highly satisfactory. Some other states are now considering the VAT.

What is the VAT? What advantages does it offer that might explain its wide-spread use? And what are its disadvantages, if any? Is the VAT likely to be levied by the U.S. government? You'll be finding the answers to these questions in this section.

What is the VAT? The VAT is a percentage levy which must be paid by each business in the production-distribution chain. From the mining company that mines the iron ore all the way to the retail company that sells the E string for a bass guitar, each business along the way must pay a tax on the value it adds.

The handful of iron ore isn't worth much. But as it moves through the stages of production, value is added each step along the way. And each time value is added, the business which adds the value must pay the tax on the value added.

Sounds complex? confusing? difficult to administer? It isn't, really. Here's an example that illustrates the kind of VAT system the West European countries are using.

An Example of How the VAT Works. Suppose the VAT rate is 10%. Say a miller buys $10 worth of grain from a farmer and pays the farmer for the grain plus the VAT of $1. The farmer (assuming no "value-added-taxed" inputs were used in producing the grain) pays the $1 to the government. The farmer is just acting as a tax collector for the government.

Then the miller uses the grain to make 100 lbs. of whole grain flour and sells the flour to the local baker for $20, plus the VAT of $2. The miller pays the government $1 ($2, minus the $1 already paid to the farmer). Notice that the miller's "value added" was $10 (output value of $20 minus input cost of $10 = value added of $10) and the amount of the tax the miller paid the government was 10% of "value added," which is one dollar.

The baker uses the 100 lbs. of flour to make 100 loaves of whole grain bread. The baker sells the oven-hot bread to local customers for $1.10

per loaf—$1 for the loaf of bread plus 10¢ for the VAT. For the 100 loaves of bread the baker receives $110 ($100 for the bread and $10 VAT).

Now the baker must pay the government $8. Why $8? Because the value added by the baker was $80. Or you can look at it the other way. The baker has already paid $2 in VAT to the miller. The government has already received that $2—the miller paid the government $1 and the farmer paid $1. So all that's left to be paid is $8—that's exactly 10% of the $80 value which was added by the baker.

Notice that the VAT is stated *separately from the price* at each stage of production. But for the final consumer it usually isn't stated separately. It's just included in the price.

The way the VAT system has been designed in the European countries, the tax is really quite simple to figure and easy to administer and collect. Each business firm (manufacturer, processor, wholesaler, retailer, etc.) adds the full VAT rate (say 10%) to everything they sell (their output product). Then they subtract the total amount of VAT taxes they had to pay when they bought their inputs. And what's left over? The tax on their "value added." And that's what they owe the government.

Arguments for the VAT. What's good about the VAT? It's easy to collect, and even at a low rate it produces a lot of revenue.

Since it's levied on just about everything, the VAT doesn't distort consumer spending patterns. And it doesn't discourage savings or investment, or interfere with incentives or distort business decisions the way income and payroll taxes can.

Also, it's "semi-painless." It's hidden in the prices of consumer goods so there aren't any deductions from people's paychecks. And since the actual tax rate (and no more) is applied to the actual value of all final goods, there is no "pyramiding." That is, there are no "mark-ups on the tax" as occurs with manufacturers excise taxes.

The VAT might help to encourage exports

too. Products for export could be made tax exempt, and the tax could be added to imported goods. That's what the European countries are doing.

With all these things going for it, why don't we have a Federal VAT in this country? Aren't there some arguments against it? Yes, there are.

Arguments against the VAT. The way the VAT works out, it's really nothing more than a sophisticated way of collecting a general retail sales tax. So it's a regressive tax. Many people would reject if for that reason alone.

Another consideration is that the states now get much of their tax revenues from sales taxes. Should the Federal government now come in and impose this "thinly disguised" sales tax, on top of what the states are already collecting? And maybe force the states to limit their use of sales taxes in the future? Some people don't think so.

What about the effect on inflation? You can be sure that one initial impact of the tax will be to push prices up. With higher prices, some workers will get automatic wage increases. And everyone will be pushing for higher wages too. The already serious inflationary spiral of wages and prices could be made worse. But on the other hand, the tax soon would drain off consumer purchasing power and lessen inflationary demand. And if the tax helped to reduce the federal deficit, that would help to slow inflation too.

Will the U.S. Government levy a VAT? There is a lot of concern about the impact of our present federal tax system on the efficiency and growth of the economy. And a lot of people are worried about the great increases in payroll taxes needed to finance the social security program.

Could the VAT help to solve these problems? When members of Congress look at the VAT in Europe some of them conclude "maybe so." But there's some strong opposition. There's no way to guess which way it will go. (Who knows? By the time you're reading this you may already be paying the VAT!)

TAXES ON PROPERTY

When people talk about "the property tax," they are talking about taxes on land, houses, factories, machinery, equipment, railroads, automobiles, TV sets—even bank accounts. Property taxes are levied on real estate, on all business property, and on many kinds of personal property.

There's another kind of tax which can logically be considered a part of the property tax picture: estate (or inheritance) taxes, and the gift taxes which go along with the estate and inheritance taxes. These taxes are levied on property at the time the property owner dies. We'll take a look at these "death taxes" in a few minutes.

The Changing Role of Property Taxes

In the early 1900s more than half of the taxes collected in this country were property taxes. But over the years the property tax has declined greatly in relative importance. Today it accounts for less than 15 percent of the total taxes collected.

Why the shift from property taxes? One reason is that property taxes would not be able to produce the amounts of revenue required in the 1980s. If the billions of dollars of taxes had to be collected from the property owner, nobody could afford to own any private property! Another reason is that property taxes are levied mostly by local governments, and mostly the local governments aren't the ones doing the big spending, these days.

In the 1920s, property taxes were bringing in more than 95 percent of local government revenues. In the early 1980s the percentage was smaller because the big cities turned to sales, excise, and income taxes to meet their growing revenue needs. But even so, property taxes still accounted for more than 70 percent of all local government revenues.

Early in this century the state governments

were getting most of their money from property taxes, too. But by the 1980s most of the states had reduced or eliminated their property taxes and left this source to the local governments. The states have turned to sales and excise and income taxes. Less than 2 percent of total state revenues now come from property taxes.

Why Do Local Governments Rely on Property Taxes?

The property tax is easy for a local government to administer. All they need to do is place an "assessed value" on the property, then multiply that by whatever tax rate they've decided on. Then they know exactly how much taxes each person owes. If the owner doesn't pay, the local government can always take the property and sell it to get its money.

The property tax sometimes is a tough and inhuman way to get revenue. But it does get the revenue! There's no way a person can escape from the property tax. But that doesn't mean it's necessarily a good or equitable tax.

Some Problems with the Property Tax

One problem with the property tax is that equitable "assessed values" are not easy to assign. In times of inflation, values change rapidly. It's hard to keep up with true values. But even if you keep up with true values, that can create serious hardships, too.

It's Unfair to Old People. Consider the retired couple living in their own home. When real estate values go up, their property taxes go up. Either they must put most of their retirement income into paying their property taxes (and live in poverty) or they must rent or sell their home and move into a trailer or some other smaller, lower-valued and lower-taxed place. Does that seem to be a decent thing to do to old people?

It isn't pleasant to see old people forced to move from the homes they have worked for all their lives. Sometimes that's what the property tax does to people. But that's one of the problems with a tax that isn't related to the taxpayer's current income.

It Discourages Property Improvement. Suppose you buy a run-down house on which the property tax is low. Then you have it completely renovated. You have the grounds landscaped. You do great things to improve the appearance of the property, and the neighborhood too.

So what happens? The tax assessor comes by. Up go your taxes! While your neighbor (who believes in letting things go to pot) comes out with lower taxes. See the problem?

It Discourages New Business Locations. When businesses are considering where to build new plants they are discouraged by high property taxes. Local governments frequently give "tax holidays" (an exemption from property taxes for a few years) to businesses to try to induce them to locate in their area.

Why do local governments want businesses to locate in their areas? Because they know that throughout the country many small towns have good schools, good roads, and a low tax burden for their citizens just because there's a big manufacturer or utility plant or some other business located there! One big plant in a small town can pay enough property taxes to carry much of the tax burden.

People and Businesses Move to Avoid the Tax. Do you suppose some of the moves by people and businesses from the cities to the suburbs has been helped along by the property tax? Of course it has.

The central cities usually tax property heavily to try to get the money they need. So people who have nice houses in the city are induced to sell out and get nice houses in the suburbs where property taxes are lower.

You can see some of the problems with the property tax. But local governments will continue to use it. Not because it is theoretically the most justifiable tax, and not because it doesn't have undesirable effects. Certainly, it does. But the important point remains: For the local governments, it works.

The property tax is an effective source of local government revenues. But the big cities are turning to additional sources: income, sales, and excise taxes. Are big cities leaving the property tax? No. They're just adding on other taxes to go with it.

Death and Gift Taxes

Here's another kind of tax on property: the tax levied on the property when the owner dies. "Death taxes" are levied by the federal and state governments. Also, in 1975, as one of its drastic measures to solve its financial crisis, New York City became the first local government in the United States to levy death taxes.

In the early part of this century, as much as one third of total state revenue came from this source. But death and gift taxes have never made up a major part of federal tax revenues.

In the early 1980s death and gift taxes made up a very small percentage of total revenues both for the federal government and for the states. Less than 2 percent of total taxes collected in the United States come from death and gift taxes.

Gift Taxes Must Be Tied to Death Taxes. A death tax could never work unless it was tied together with a gift tax. Suppose you had millions of dollars in assets and the doctors told you you were going to die in a few weeks. And suppose the government doesn't tax gifts but does tax inheritances. What would you do? Give it all away? Of course! So without a gift tax tied to it, death taxes would be meaningless. Everyone, with their last gasp of breath, would give away everything! The way the laws are set up in the United States, it is possible for a person to make tax-exempt gifts year after year and reduce the amount of death taxes.

Arguments About Death and Gift Taxes. There's a lot of disagreement about the subject of death taxes. At one extreme, people suggest that all of a person's wealth should be left to the heirs.

At the other extreme, people suggest that there's no reason why the heirs should receive anything. People should receive incomes and property from their own work and efforts. They shouldn't be given massive fortunes so they can control lots of society's resources without ever having done anything to deserve it—anything, that is, except to be born into a wealthy family!

It isn't likely that there is an easy way to resolve this argument. What the federal and state governments do in the United States is to sort of split the difference. Surely a confiscatory (take it all!) death tax would cause a lot of wealthy people to die penniless. (Just for spite, if for no other reason.)

In terms of the total tax picture, death and gift taxes are not very important. But from the point of view of "social equity" it may be that they are quite significant. These taxes "whittle away" at the huge fortunes and somewhat reduce the wealth received by fortunate heirs. But these taxes still leave children of wealthy parents with a good bit of wealth.

Other Sources of Tax Revenues

There are several other kinds of taxes which in the general picture aren't very important, but which are *very important for some states or localities*.

Most states and localities levy **license taxes** of various kinds—on businesses, automobile drivers, automobiles, dogs, etc. Most localities and some states levy **real estate transfer taxes** which must be paid whenever someone buys a house or a piece of land.

Some states and localities are fortunate enough to have valuable mineral deposits which can be taxed as they are mined, or valuable forests which can be taxed as they are cut. Such taxes are called **"severance taxes."** Some states and localities (especially those in which oil is produced) get a lot of their revenue from severance taxes. There are several other kinds of minor taxes. But for most of the places in the country, most of the tax revenues come from taxes on income, excises, sales, and property.

The State and Local Taxing Pattern Is Very Diverse

Be very careful not to think that any particular state or any particular local government will fit the "average pattern." Each state and each local government is a unique, special case.

Some states still levy property taxes. Some don't. Some rely heavily on income taxes. Others don't levy income taxes at all. Some rely heavily on the general sales tax. Others don't even have a general sales tax.

The differences among localities is even greater—especially as you compare small rural-area governments with the governments of big cities. Big cities levy property taxes to be sure. But in addition they levy taxes on incomes and profits and excises and sales. In some local areas, property taxes are only levied on homes and businesses. In others, property taxes are levied on personal property: automobiles, TV sets, jewelry, stocks and bonds—even money in the bank.

If you want to know about the tax picture for your own state or local government, it's easy to find out. The *Statistical Abstract* would be a good place to start. But if you want to find out all the details, you'll need to contact your state capital or city hall or county seat. If you have time, why don't you take off an afternoon and do that? Your nearest elected representative would be glad to help!

WHAT MAKES A GOOD TAX SYSTEM?

Let's start at the beginning. Governments must somehow transfer some of the society's re-

sources from private to government ownership.

Governments must be able to hire people. Police, judges, jailers, and lawmakers will be needed. Bricks and cement and lumber and furniture will be needed. And some electricity for lights. How is the government going to get these things?

The government could go out and find a building it wanted and say to the owner: "We have decided to confiscate your building." Certainly governments have done such things. So why not just do that all the time? and not worry about levying and collecting taxes?

It wouldn't be fair. A few people would suffer great loss. The lucky ones wouldn't give up anything. Certainly no democratic society would put up with that!

So now do you see why governments levy taxes? Taxes are levied so that when the government takes things away from the private owners, everyone will bear a "fair share" of the burden.

The purpose of a tax system is to distribute the burden of government among the people, in an acceptable way. A good tax system is one which accomplishes that objective.

Fairness and Equitability

How do you decide if a tax is fair? equitable? People would disagree about this, of course. Someone might say: "Let everyone pay the same amount!" Others might say: "Let the rich pay a lot and the poor pay a little!" Still others might say: "Let the poor pay a lot and let the rich keep their money to invest and bring economic growth to the nation!" Others might say other things.

Generally there are two things we look at in trying to decide the fairness of a tax. Two principles are usually considered: the benefit principle and the ability to pay principle.

The Benefit Principle. Some government spending brings direct benefits to specific people. The idea of the benefit principle is that the more benefits a person receives from some program, the more taxes that person should pay to support that program.

Excise taxes on gasoline are justified under the benefit principle. Gasoline tax revenues are used to build and maintain highways. The more gasoline you use, the more taxes you will pay to support the highways. Get the idea?

What about the regressive payroll tax? It's justified on the benefit principle? Sure. Low-income people receive the most benefits, so low-income people have to pay more. That's the idea.

Many kinds of taxes could be justified on the benefit principle—even the property tax, for example. If you own a lot of valuable property, then the local government services (local streets, police and fire protection, etc.) are more important to you than to someone who doesn't own anything. So it could be said that people with more valuable property benefit more and therefore should pay more.

The Ability to Pay Principle. A person with a large income has the ability to pay more taxes than a person with a small income. Obviously. If you take very much from the low income-earner, you don't leave the person enough to live on. But if you take a large share of a big income, you still leave more than enough to live on. That's the idea of "ability to pay."

Generally speaking, the benefit principle and the ability to pay principle are both good ways of evaluating a tax system—of deciding if it is fair and equitable. Most (but not necessarily all) of the taxes in the United States can be justified on the basis of one or the other of these principles.

But **fairness and equitability** aren't all there is. There are two other important questions which need to be asked when you're evaluating a tax system.

One question is: "How much does the tax system distort the workings of the market process?" The other question is: "How much waste (social cost) is involved in collecting the taxes?" These are the questions of **economic neutrality** and **administrative efficiency**.

Economic Neutrality

Some taxes change the prices of things. Some taxes change people's incomes. When either happens, that causes the decisions of people and businesses to change. So the tax is not "neutral." The tax has "side effects" on the economy.

Some taxes are levied for the purpose of having side effects. High tariffs are levied to slow down the flow of foreign goods into domestic markets. Some people probably favor taxes on cigarettes and beer because the high prices may discourage the use of these things.

Whenever a tax is levied on a product and that pushes up the price, the "rationing function of price" comes into play. The tax is not neutral. A non-neutral tax has a distorting effect in the economic system.

Here's an important question: How non-neutral is the income tax? How much do income taxes affect people's incentives to work? to move into higher paying occupations? Are incentives dampened by the income tax? That could be a serious drag on the productivity and growth of the economy! There's a lot of talk about these questions. But no one really knows the answers.

A good tax system is equitable, neutral, efficient.

Administrative Efficiency

A *good* tax needs to be easy (inexpensive) to collect. It needs to be fairly simple and straightforward. Suppose a great battery of accountants and lawyers must be hired just to administer the tax laws. Legal hassles and enforcement problems just burn up valuable resources. What a waste! And the people (the taxpayers) have to pay for all that waste, too!

To be administratively efficient, a tax mustn't require individuals and business to use up a lot of their own time and money just to comply with the tax laws either. The resources used up in transferring goods from private to public hands are a social waste. Some such waste is necessary. But a good tax system is one which holds down this waste—the administrative cost—to a minimum.

SHIFTING AND INCIDENCE: WHO BEARS THE BURDEN?

One reason it's hard to judge a tax system is that we don't know for sure who is bearing the real burden of each tax. As economists would say: we don't know how much **shifting** goes on, so we don't really know who bears the **incidence** of each tax.

Does the person who pays out the cash *really* bear the burden? Or is there some way of getting the cash back by shifting the cost (the incidence) to someone else?

When Can a Tax Be Shifted?

Suppose a tax is levied and you are the one who pays out the cash. Can you get the money back? And shift the incidence of the tax to someone else? That all depends on *whether or not the tax will result in a change of the supply or demand or price of anything you are buying or selling.*

Here's an example. Suppose your state has just levied a new "gross receipts tax" of 3 percent on all grocery stores. For every dollar the grocery store takes in it must pay 3 cents to the government. Can the grocers shift the tax? Probably so.

They might try to shift the tax **backward**—to reduce the wages of the grocery clerks and delivery drivers or get discounts from their suppliers or pay less rent to the people who own the buildings. But it's more likely that they would shift the tax **forward** by raising the prices of their groceries by about 3 percent.

What determines how much a tax can be shifted forward, or backward? Many things. It depends a lot on the **elasticity** of demand and supply for both the inputs (things being bought) and outputs (things being sold). It depends a lot on the market structure, too—that is, on how much **competition** there is. And it depends on whether or not everyone in the industry must pay the tax, or only the people in one locality. In the real world, tax shifting can get complicated. Just watch.

Tax Shifting—a Chain Reaction

Suppose that after the 3 percent gross receipts tax is levied on the grocery stores, the prices of groceries in your area go up about 3 percent. The grocers have shifted the tax forward so that the customers are the ones who really bear the incidence. But is that the end of it? No. That's just the beginning.

Suppose your college buys its groceries from the local grocery stores. Groceries cost more. So the local college increases its dining hall fees.

So the students who work part-time at the local service station get together and convince their employers to give them more wages so they can afford the higher dining hall prices.

Then the service stations raise their prices of their gasoline to cover the high cost of student labor. Then the local trucking companies raise their hauling prices because of the rise in the price of gasoline. Then the local canning factory stops paying Christmas bonuses and raises the price of their canned goods because of the higher cost of shipping by truck.

How far can this chain reaction go? It's already beginning to get a little ridiculous. Right? But now I think you get the idea. It's this: Once the tax is let loose in the economic system, it goes around bumping into different markets and having its "ripple effect" throughout the economic system.

Which Taxes Can Be Shifted?

It's impossible to get any very precise measures of tax shifting and incidence in the real world. Economists can set up model conditions, make certain assumptions, and then show how a certain tax would be shifted and how the final burden would be distributed among the people. But in the real world, it isn't all that easy. Still, economists do know some things about the "shiftability" of different kinds of taxes.

Indirect Business Taxes (Manufacturers Excises). Some taxes are meant to be shifted. The indirect business taxes—excises like the cigarette and gasoline taxes—are meant to be included in the prices of the products. We know that most of these taxes are shifted forward to the consumer.

Sometimes indirect business taxes are even *more than* entirely shifted forward. That is, a 10 percent tax at the manufacturers level may become a 12 percent tax at the retail level. Maybe even higher. Why? Because wholesalers and retailers usually use a "price markup" system for setting their prices.

If the price of the manufacturer's product already has some taxes in it, when the wholesaler and retailer apply their markups, they are adding their *markup on the tax* as well as *on the basic price of the product*. This is called pyramiding. It is sometimes mentioned as one of the undesirable things about indirect business taxes. The consumer pays more taxes than the government gets!

Corporation Income Taxes. These taxes are levied on the profits of the corporation and are not meant to be shifted. In the "model economic system" where every business is doing everything possible to maximize profits, taxes on profits could not be shifted. Why not? Because if the corporation is doing everything it can to make as much profit as possible already, after the tax is levied, what can it do to get more profit, to offset the tax? Nothing.

In the real world it isn't so simple. There are many motives which underlie business decisions *other than* the profit maximizing motive. Suppose the corporate managers feel that large profits would be embarrassing. Large profits may lead to criticism from labor, consumer groups, and government regulatory agencies—might even result in demands for higher wages and government threats of antitrust action!

Suppose the corporation feels that it could raise prices and increase profits. But it doesn't do it right now because it doesn't think it would be a good thing to do, all things considered. Then suppose the government levies a corporate income tax. The corporation might decide to raise its prices and increase its profits to get part of its tax money back. Under these circumstances the tax would be shifted.

Individual Income Taxes. Individual income taxes aren't supposed to be shifted, either. Suppose a person is already doing everything possible to get the highest income possible. Then if the government comes in and taxes part of that income, that's all there is to it.

If you have already *maximized* your income, what more can you do? Nothing. But suppose you haven't really maximized your income. That's a different story.

Suppose the *labor union* goes to the bargaining table and bargains for increases in "take-home" pay. What then? It means that if income taxes are raised, the workers are going to try to shift those taxes to the employers.

It's likely that to some extent labor unions have shifted individual income taxes to businesses. And it's likely that the businesses have shifted them forward in higher prices, to consumers. And it's likely that this process has helped along the speed of *inflation* in the American economy and throughout the modern world.

What about *professional people?* Do they push up their fees and charges because of their high income taxes? When the doctors or lawyers can only afford a new Cadillac every fourth year instead of every third year maybe they decide on a general increase in professional fees.

Are the people who are getting divorces

really paying some of the income taxes for the lawyers? And the people having operations paying some income taxes for the doctors? Are the corporations paying some of the income taxes for the certified public accountants and the business and economic consultants they hire?

We don't have very good answers to any of these questions. It isn't likely that we will ever know precisely. But it's important that you be aware of the chain-reaction effects of different kinds of taxes. And especially, be aware that the person or the business who writes the check or pays the cash isn't necessarily the one who is worse off because of the tax.

How Good is Our Tax System?

Does our tax system distribute the burden of government among the people in an acceptable way? If we knew more about the incidence of different kinds of taxes we could do a much bet-

ter job of answering that question. We would know who winds up with less real income. But we don't know that—not precisely, anyway.

So how can we justify our tax system? Like this: We must somehow transfer resources from private people to the government. Confiscation is totally unacceptable. What's the alternative? A tax system. Even a bad system is better than confiscation.

We know the tax system is far from perfect. It's always being changed by the federal government and the states and the local governments.

The legislators are feeling and responding to the attitudes and wishes of the people. And the people themselves are changing their minds about *what is equitable enough and neutral enough and administratively feasible enough to be acceptable.* An acceptable tax system in any society is one which most of the people are willing to accept. It's determined as much by politics as it is by economics. And *public choice* doesn't always guarantee *optimum social results.* Remember?

SUMMARY AND SYNTHESIS

As government spending has increased over the decades, taxes have increased almost as much. There have been **major shifts in the sources of revenue** (kinds of taxes) used at the different levels of government, and in the amounts of revenue collected from each kind of tax.

In the early 1900s, **local governments** were collecting **more than half** of the taxes, mostly **property taxes.** Today local governments still get **most of their revenues from property taxes,** but they only collect about 15 percent of the total tax revenues.

In the early 1900s the **federal government** was collecting **about 40 percent** of total taxes in the country, mostly from **customs duties and excise taxes.** In the 1980s, the federal government is collecting **more than 60 percent** of total revenues,

with most of it coming from **individual and corporate income taxes and payroll taxes.**

The **state governments** were collecting only **about 10 percent** of total taxes back in the early 1900s, mostly from **property taxes.** In the 1980s the states are collecting **about 20 percent** of total revenues, mostly from **sales and excise and individual and corporation income taxes.**

The taxes which are the **major sources of revenue** in the 1980s did not even exist in the early 1900s: **individual and corporate income, and payroll taxes.** But sales and excises, property taxes, and death and gift taxes have been used far back into history, and these are still important sources of revenue in the 1980s.

The **individual income tax** is the most important single source of revenue and is considered by many to be the **most desirable** (least un-desirable) **form of tax. It is tied to income, and it can be designed to meet the economic circum-stances of the individual taxpayer.**

Income taxes are levied both by the federal government and the state governments and also by some of the **larger cities. The tax is highly progressive** at the federal level, **less progressive** at the state level, and frequently **not progressive** at all when levied by the cities.

The **payroll tax is the tax** which came about under the **social security system** initiated in the 1930s. It is partly a **regressive individual income tax,** and partly **an excise tax** on the "purchase" of labor. In the early 1980s the payroll tax was the second largest source of government revenue.

The **corporation income tax** is a tax on the **profits of corporations.** It amounts to "double taxation" on the income of stockholders. But it is a politically feasible tax and it is likely that it will be continued.

Sales and excise taxes are really the same kinds of things, except that a **sales tax covers everything except exempted items** and an **excise tax covers nothing except specifically mentioned items. Sales taxes** are usually levied on **retail sales. Excises** are often levied at the **wholesale or manufacturing stage** and passed forward as higher prices.

The **relative importance of sales and excise taxes has declined** over the years. But if you add in the **employer-part of the payroll tax** and also add in the **customs duty excises,** the total figure comes to **about 25 percent** of total tax revenues in the country! All of us are paying these taxes in the **higher prices of the things we buy.**

Sales and excise taxes **produce revenue during good times and bad.** But they are **regressive.** And excise taxes can create **excess burdens** and can result in **pyramiding.** But with the **new emphasis on supply-side economics,** some policymakers are suggesting that these taxes are just what we need to discourage consumption and encourage savings.

The **"value added" tax (VAT)** is levied on the "value added" at each stage in the production pro-cess and **passed on** (ultimately) to the **final con-**sumer. These taxes are **widely used in Europe.** Some members of Congress are suggesting that the VAT should be levied in this country, but as of mid-1982 that hasn't happened yet.

Property taxes are levied by local govern-ments because of administrative feasibility. But property taxes discourage improvements and deter business locations and investments. They aren't related to current income, and they aren't always **equitably administered.**

Death and gift taxes need to be tied togeth-er, otherwise a dying person would give away everything! These taxes are used at the **federal level,** and also by **most states.** There is much controversy as to whether or not they should be used—and if so, **how high the rates should be.**

There are many **other sources of tax reve-nues** which individual states or localities levy. **Severance taxes** are major sources of revenue in those states which are fortunate enough to have vast natural resources which can be **taxed as they are removed.**

A good tax system is one which is **equitable, economically neutral, and administratively effi-cient.** Equitability can be justified on the **benefit principle** or on the **ability to pay principle.** Eco-nomic neutrality means that the existence of the tax **doesn't distort the resource flows** (allocation choices) in the society. Administrative efficiency means that you don't **"burn up"** a lot of the so-ciety's resources in the process of collecting the taxes.

It is **difficult to evaluate a tax system** on its equitability, because of the **shifting and incidence** problem. If we don't know who actually bears the burden of the tax, then how can we say if the tax is equitable?

Whenever a tax will result in a **change in the supply or demand or price** of anything, then some **shifting** will occur. The shifting may be ei-ther **backward or forward.** It depends a lot on the **elasticity of demand and supply** for both inputs and outputs, and on the **amount of competition** in these markets. We don't know the **exact re-sults,** but we do know that there is **a lot of shift-ing going on.**

REVIEW EXERCISES

MAJOR CONCEPTS, PRINCIPLES, TERMS (Explain each carefully.)

individual income taxes
payroll taxes
corporation income taxes
sales taxes
excise taxes

"value added" taxes (VAT)
customs duties
property taxes
death and gift taxes
shifting and incidence

OTHER CONCEPTS AND TERMS (Explain each briefly.)

excess burdens
regressive tax
progressive tax
severance tax
license taxes
equitable tax

benefit principle
ability to pay principle
economic neutrality
administrative efficiency
indirect business taxes
pyramiding

QUESTIONS (Write out answers or jot down key points.)

1. As government spending increases, taxes also increase, but spending seems to stay ahead of taxes. How is that possible?
2. Explain this statement: "State and local debts are like private debts."
3. Describe the general taxing pattern in the U.S. economy.
4. Describe the *changing tax sources* of each level of government in the United States, 1900s to the early 1980s.
5. Describe the role of intergovernmental grants in the United States, and discuss this approach to "fiscal federalism." Do you think it's a good approach? Explain why.
6. Give the highlights in the changes in tax revenue sources in the United States since the early 1900s, and give some reasons why these changes occurred.
7. Explain: "The payroll tax is partly an income tax and partly the excise tax."
8. Evaluate the individual income tax as a "good" kind of tax to use.
9. It is said that payroll taxes are regressive. Is it true? Explain.
10. Does the corporation income tax involve double taxation? Explain. What do you think ought to be done about this, if anything? Discuss.
11. Describe and evalute the changing role of sales and excise taxes in the American economic system.
12. Describe and evaluate the VAT. Do you think it should be levied by the U.S. government? Why? or why not?
13. Evaluate the property tax. What are some of the problems?
14. Give an example of tax shifting, where the incidence moves from one person to another and finally gets diffused.
15. Can corporation or individual income taxes be shifted? Discuss.
16. Describe in detail the characteristics of a *good tax system*.

37

The American Economy of the 1980s: an Overview and Synthesis

Chapter Objectives

- All of the previous chapters in Part Eight have discussed **specific parts or sectors of the American economy: agriculture, labor, business, government.** This final chapter in Part Eight provides an **integration and synthesis** of these various parts, and includes **the important role of households** in the economy.

- From this chapter you will gain a more **integrated view** of the economy, and of the **changing productivity, growth,** and **new directions** of the economy.

- When you finish studying this chapter you will be able to explain the **important role of households** and the **difficulty of measuring** this role.

- You will understand the **relative importance of** (and something about the **economic power of) big agriculture, big labor,** and **big business.**

- You will be able to describe **the role of the government** in the economy and to explain several ways in which it has **a major influence** in the American economy.

- Finally, you will be able to describe and discuss some **current issues and special problems** of the American economy in the 1980s: **inflation and unemployment; productivity and growth; foreign competition; environmental problems;** the question of **adequate social control;** and some others.

The American Economy: Growth, and Change

The American economy has been growing and changing rapidly. Many of the conditions which have existed in the past no longer exist: unbridled laissez-faire, great quantities of available land and natural resources, opportunities for great tax-free profits and incomes—all these conditions were characteristics of the American economic system in the past. But not any more.

Today in the American economy there is government involvement in every aspect of economic life. More government spending, more regulations, more controls, more taxes, more assistance to the needy.

It is difficult to get a "conceptual overview picture" of the American economic system. It is made up of so many parts—so many different things. Ultimately, who makes the choices? How are the decisions made? the basic questions answered?

The final sections in this chapter will be talking about the question of how the American economic system is controlled. But first, a quick look at each of the sectors of the American economy—an overview look to see how each is working.

The following sections pull together the highlights from the previous chapters of Part Eight to give you an integrated overview of the American economic system. First, a look at households. Then at agriculture, labor, business and government.

THE ROLE OF HOUSEHOLDS

Households are very important in the economic system. They are the basic consuming unit. They spend the money to buy most of the output of the economy. So they have a lot of influence on the choices about what will be produced, and how much of each.

Most households receive money from the work they do. Many receive income from their property (investments, savings accounts, etc.) and some receive income from government "transfer payments" under the social security program and other assistance programs. Then when the members of the household spend their money, they influence the directions of the economic system.

Households Produce Things for Themselves

Most of the things in the American economy are produced by farms or businesses and then sold to be consumed by someone else. But with the households, it doesn't work that way. Each household is both a producing and a consuming unit.

Households produce meals, wash dishes, wash clothes, perform the functions of purchas-

ing (of groceries, supplies, etc.) transportation, storage, and do-it-yourself carpentry, painting, plumbing, auto repair, electrical repair, minor medical services, and many other productive activities. And what about the production of recreation services? Households do a lot of that: producing music by tapes, producing TV entertainment, providing relaxing, comfortable surroundings in which to enjoy the pleasures of friendship and love.

What is the value of all these goods and services produced and consumed in the households? We don't know, really. There's no way to measure these values, so these outputs don't show up in the GNP. But anyone who lives in a household knows that the productive activities of households are important in the American economic system.

Household Income Redistribution

Another important function of the household is to redistribute income from those who earn it to other family members who need it. Usually the mother with some help from the children will produce such things as meals, housecleaning, washing dishes and clothes and other services. All the members of the household get a share of these services. Usually the father and often the mother will work for money and the money will be spent for things to be shared with everyone in the family.

Throughout history the family has been an important social security unit. That's less true today. The close ties between families have broken down to some extent. In the past, people stuck closer together, worked the land together, and depended on and were responsible to each other. But not so much anymore. Still, even today the household is a very important income redistribution, social security unit—especially for taking care of the young children, but not so much as before for taking care of the older people.

It would be difficult (perhaps impossible) to measure the importance of households in the functioning of the American economy. But they're very important. They buy up the goods and services produced by the economic system, they supply labor and other inputs into the productive process, they produce many services and some goods which they themselves consume, and they operate as important social security and income redistribution units. The **household sector** is a key sector in the American economic system.

THE ROLE OF AGRICULTURE

Less than 5 percent of the people in the United States are now living on farms. That's less than 10 million people. There has been a constant outpouring of people from agriculture over the past 100 years.

Yet farm output has been increasing rapidly all the time. The **productivity** of American agriculture has increased greatly. The big farms have been mostly responsible.

The "Farm Problem"

But still there is a farm problem in the United States. The small, low-output farmers are the problem. Really, it is a problem of **rural poverty**—of farmers who have too little land and capital to work with. Most of them would be better off in some other occupation.

It's likely that if the farm problem is to be solved—that is, if the small, inefficient farmers are to escape rural poverty—a direct antipoverty program will be required: cash payments, educational assistance, training, assistance in consolidating plots of land, and in some cases, assistance in relocation.

American agriculture is highly productive. On the average, each farmer feeds more than 60 people. Output per hour of labor has increased seven-fold since 1929—that is, it has increased by 700 percent!

How did agricultural productivity increase

so much? There has been a technological revolution in American agriculture. Obviously. The machines have been developed and introduced rapidly, together with highly productive seeds and effective agricultural chemicals.

Productivity per person has gone up so much that surplus workers have poured from the rural areas into the urban areas. Some of them have done well in the urban areas. But many have only compounded the problems of rapid urbanization and have joined the ranks of the unemployed.

American Agriculture: Small by Some Measures, but Very Important

Agriculture plays a very important role in the American economy. It provides relatively low-cost food and fibers for the economy. It not only feeds the people in America. It also helps to feed the other people of the world.

But in terms of employment, incomes, and percentage of the total outputs of the economic system, the position of agriculture is small. It has dropped from a major role involving most of the work force during the last century, to a minor one. Today, as an employer of labor in the American economy, agriculture is far down the list.

THE ROLE OF "BIG LABOR"

Powerful labor unions are a predominant feature of the American economic system. This is another fairly recent change in the system. It has only been since the labor legislation of the 1930s that unions have played a powerful role in the American economic system.

But since the 1930s the wages and conditions of working people have been influenced a lot by the **labor unions.** Unions have challenged the giant corporations and have gotten concessions from them. Big labor has served as an effective counterbalance to the power of big businesses in the labor market.

There is no question that unions exercise **monopoly powers** which are strong in times of prosperity and not so strong in times of recession. They use these powers to try to increase their wages and to get other benefits for their members.

Unions influence the government, too. Unions sometimes influence the decisions of legislators. The members of Congress and state legislators don't always do everything organized labor suggests, of course. But no legislators want to go out of their way to get organized labor against them!

THE ROLE OF BIG BUSINESS

The productive heart of the American economy consists mostly of big businesses. Who owns America? The big corporations own a lot of it!

There are more than ten million business firms in the United States. If all of their assets were distributed equally, no one would own very much. But the fact is that *the five largest corporations own more than 10 percent of all of the manufacturing assets in the country.*

Concentration of Corporate Assets

There are over a million corporations in the country. But the 500 largest own more than two thirds of all of the corporate assets. The American economy is mostly a big business economy. **Big business** owns most of the productive assets, hires most of the labor, uses up most of the productive energy and power and produces most of the gross national product.

How is **social control** exercised over these massive enterprises? What keeps them responding to the wishes of society? No one knows exactly how (or how well) it happens. We know the businesses can't ignore the wishes of their customers. But how do they run, on a day-to-day basis?

Who Controls the Corporations?

The corporations are operated on a day-to-day basis by **management people**, located at key spots throughout the corporation. Each manager runs a department or area and keeps things "on stream," producing the proper outputs.

At the top are the vice-presidents—general managers, and above them, the president. The board of directors is in overall control. Usually the general management allows the people in the positions beneath them considerable autonomy, and usually the board of directors allows the president and general managers considerable autonomy.

The control of a big corporation operates sort of like a representative democracy. Once people are chosen for positions of authority, they have quite a lot of freedom to do as they wish. As long as they maintain the confidence of those who have the ultimate power, they are left free to do things their own way.

In the case of a government, it's the party and the voters who will bring their representatives back in line—or else get rid of them. In the case of the big corporation it's the board of directors (and perhaps the few major stockholders) who will have the ultimate say.

The big businesses are not immune from the demands of the buyers of their products. Nor are they immune from the rising costs of their inputs—including the demands of organized labor.

Somehow they must balance off the conflicting forces—of input supplies and prices and output demands and prices—and (they hope!) survive and prosper and grow.

What About the Small Businesses?

There are millions of small businesses in the American economy. They provide opportunities for investment and employment for the millions of people who own and run them. But in terms of the total output of the economy? They don't look very important.

The millions of small retail businesses play

an important role in the daily lives of the households. The little shops provide retail goods and services in out of the way places and at odd hours. Also, there's often a close personal relationship between the owner-managers of these little businesses and their customers.

Most of the little businesses probably couldn't be justified on economic grounds. But so many people have the American dream of being their own boss—of running their own business. Most of them soon discover that being your own boss may create more problems and worries than it solves.

The millions of **small businesses** will continue to be around and will continue to perform an important function in the economy. But the productive heart of the American economy is and will continue to be big business. But the powers of big business are balanced somewhat by big labor and big government.

THE ROLE OF BIG GOVERNMENT IN THE AMERICAN ECONOMY

One important role of government in the American economic system is that of balancing the power of big business and big labor. **Government** tries to look out for the small ones—small businesses and farmers and consumers.

Government also redistributes income to the poor, operates social security, unemployment and other "economic security" programs. It tries to see that each household at least gets enough goods to get by on.

Taxes Always Influence Business Decisions

The federal, state and local governments collect taxes and spend money. As they collect taxes that pulls money away from the businesses and individuals and reduces their "economic choice-making power." At the same time it influences their choices. No business can make an

important decision anymore without first considering the question: "How will this decision affect our *tax* position?"

It isn't just the **tax laws** which influence businesses. There are many **government regulations** and **restrictions** regarding labor practices, environmental protection, antitrust and others which have important effects on business decisions. How much are business decisions changed by federal, state and local tax and other laws? It would be impossible to say.

But you can be sure that the effect is considerable. And certainly some of the effects are not the effects the lawmakers wanted to have in the first place.

We don't really know very much about the indirect effects of the tax laws. But we do know a good bit about the direct effects. The public finance activities of government move a lot of money around—take a lot of money from people and businesses and then spend it in the economy.

Direct Government Influences in the Economy

When governments spend money they operate like a **big household**. Governments spend money to demand the things they want. You already know that about one fourth of all the final goods and services produced in the American economy are being bought by government. That's really a big household!

Governments Usually Buy the Things They Want. Governments go into the markets of the economy and **demand things**. That influences the flow of resources. Products are produced for government which would not have been produced for private buyers. How much demand would there be for fighter planes or police uniforms or army blankets if the government didn't demand them? Not much.

Usually in the American system when a government wants something it doesn't produce it itself. It goes into the market and demands what it wants, just as the households do. Governments enter contracts with private business for the construction of highways, school buildings, dams, army and navy bases, airports, aircraft carriers, police cars, swivel chairs and just about everything else.

Sometimes Governments Produce the Things They Want. But governments in the American economy do produce some things— some goods, but mostly services. Governments produce educational, health, hospital, social welfare, police, fire, judicial, and various other services. Sometimes governments produce such things as paper money and coins, books, highways, ships, city water, and other things.

During World War II the U.S. government went into business in a big way. It built synthetic rubber plants, munitions plants, shipyards, and other plants. At the end of the war the federal government owned more than 10 percent of the nation's productive capacity! But after the war it sold off most of these to private businesses.

Even today the federal government owns and operates several things: national parks and forests and some agricultural enterprises, and it still does some production for national defense. One important economic role of the federal government these days is in the development and control of nuclear power.

Some Other Direct Government Influences. In the American economy, government is much more important in its other roles—of controlling and regulating and directing and influencing things—than in its role as a producer of things.

By contracting with private business and by direct assistance programs, government has a considerable influence on the development of such things as: transportation and communications, natural resource development, housing, small business development, manpower development and training, rejuvenation of the urban areas, financing research for economic growth, aiding depressed areas such as Appalachia, and others.

Government stabilizes farm prices, influences farm production, assists minority groups in entering the mainstream of the economy, levies tariffs on some products, establishes minimum wages and maximum hours and other working conditions, supports research programs to improve technology, and is involved in many other things. Truly, government is an ever-present part of the American economic system.

And what about the macroeconomic influences of government? You know all about monetary and fiscal policy and economic stabilization—about fighting inflation and depression. You know about direct wage and price controls.

The *Employment Act of 1946* and the *Humphrey-Hawkins Act of 1978* both establish a policy of maintaining employment opportunities for everyone. The Council of Economic Advisers (in the Executive Office of the President) keeps an eye on the macro-conditions of the economy and advises on what action should be taken.

Government Is Now a Very Important Part of the Economic System. The American economic system has come a long way from laissez-faire! There's no way to really measure the influence of government in the system. But everyone agrees that it's very important.

It's more important in total than you can see by looking at the size of government spending or by looking at the number of government regulations and restrictions and activities. It's there psychologically, as well as physically.

Government is influencing business decisions and household decisions, day-to-day, all the time. The increased role of government in the American economy in recent decades has brought us a new kind of economic system—one we didn't have before. In some ways, this "new kind of economic system" is one which we don't understand as well as the one we had before.

Who Controls the Role of Government in the Economy?

Remember about the question of social control of the big businesses? About the day-by-day freedom of the management people, but the ultimate control resting in the board of directors and the major stockholders? That really isn't too different from what happens in the governments in the American economy.

Governments respond to the wishes of the people—not perfectly, but they do. They must. They must levy the kinds of taxes people will put up with. They must spend for purposes people are willing to support.

In democratic societies, the policies governments adopt: toward business, labor, welfare, public services, national defense, involvement in anti-Communist wars, etc.—all must reflect the public sentiment (more or less).

But on a day-to-day basis, governments have a great deal of freedom in deciding what to do and how to do it. The federal government does. So do the state and local governments. It takes awhile for the people to exercise their ultimate control and get rid of legislators and policymakers they disagree with. But ultimately, they can.

In the American economic system, is the control of the people over the government adequate? Is it good enough? That's not an easy question to answer. Certainly it could be better. But in the real world of conflicting ideas and differing interests, we aren't going to achieve a "perfect" system.

It's hard to set out practical programs for improving social control over the government's activities in the economy. But this is an important issue. It's one of the issues that will be discussed in the next section—the last section in this chapter. It's one of the major current issues in the American economy.

EVOLVING CURRENT ISSUES IN THE AMERICAN ECONOMY

The American economy has gone through so much change in the last few decades that now it's a different kind of **economic system**. In-creased **government** involvement is one of the big things. But the nature and role of **big business** and **big labor** have changed a lot, too.

Business leadership and labor leadership have become more stable—less boat-rocking. There's more long-range looking at things, and planning. Things are done in a more scheduled way—not so much in fits and spurts anymore. Most people would say it's a better economic system now. But some would disagree. As the changes have occurred, some problems have arisen. We need to take a quick look at some of the problems.

Some Special Problems of the 1980s

What are the major problems of the American economic system in the 1980s? You've run across several in this book already—and surely you are aware of several yourself. A few of the top-priority ones will be highlighted here.

Inflation and Unemployment. The American economy has been more stable since World War II than it was before. But recently there has been the problem of inflation and unemployment at the same time. Why?

The American economy has a lot going for it... but it sure has a lot of problems, too.

Perhaps there's too much **monopoly power** of business and labor, pushing up prices. Or perhaps too much **government interference** in the economy. Or maybe too little government control of the monopoly power of business and labor. Or maybe it's something else.

Economists disagree about this. But everyone agrees that it's a major problem—one for which no solution has yet been worked out. We're going at it with a combination of **theory** and **pragmatism** and **practical politics**. Maybe by the time you're reading this book it will be all worked out. But probably not.

The Slow Growth Rate. The rate of economic growth of the American economy has been slowing down. In recent years it has been slower than the growth rate in several other nations. Why?

Are taxes taking too much of investors' incomes? and of corporate profits? Has the move toward greater income equality removed the incentives needed for rapid growth? for venturesome people to do venturesome things? Or maybe as an economy gets more mature its rate of growth tends to slow down anyway.

Should the government do something to try to step up the growth rate? If so, what? Economists disagree about what to do about this problem, too. This is a problem Reagan's "supply-side economics" was aimed to attack.

The High Cost of Fuel. What about the effect of the high price of oil? Energy is an important part of the cost of production in the American economy.

When the price of energy goes up, prices of production must go up. Then unless productivity per worker goes up and wages go up, what happens? Standards of living of the average American household will go down.

If more of the output of the American economy must go overseas to pay for oil, then either there must be an expansion of output per worker to make up the difference, or there is going to be less for the American people to share. Could it be that the American standard of living must now turn around? and go down?

For so many years everyone has been thinking of getting a bigger house, a second car (or a better second car) or a boat (or a bigger boat) or a color TV set (or a bigger or a second color TV set) etc., etc. It would be pretty tough for most people to have to start thinking about getting a smaller boat or giving up the boat, or getting a smaller TV set or giving up the TV set!

Is it coming to that? Maybe not. But maybe so. The high oil costs have to be made up somehow. The environmental costs aren't going to help, either.

The Environmental Problem. It will cost a lot of money and resources to protect the environment. Cost of production is going to have to go up. You already know about this. Will people have to reduce their standards of living?

We really have been living off the free things of the earth. We have been "living off the land" and not paying the cost of replacing what we have been using up. Now comes the time when we can't do this anymore. So the full cost is going to have to be paid.

Will people now have less? or can productive technology increase rapidly enough to keep standards of living rising? Maybe so. But maybe not. Only time will tell.

New Foreign Competition. During the 1970s and early 1980s, competition from foreign products was intensifying. Worker productivity was increasing more rapidly in Japan, West Germany and several other countries than in the United States.

Our costs of production (and output prices) were going up faster than theirs. So American producers were losing sales (both in this country and abroad) to foreign producers. By the early 1980s several American producers—notably in the automobile and steel industries, but in several other industries as well—were suffering huge losses.

The effects of this new foreign competition were felt throughout the economy, in every sector of the economy. The impact on public policies toward business and labor has been great. During the 1980s many of our economic conditions and policies will be significantly influenced by this new position of the United States in the world economy.

Some Other Problems. There are several other kinds of problems the American economic system has not been able to take care of. You know about them already. The American economy has not been able to meet the needs of the big cities. Economic power is unequally distributed, between big labor and small labor, between big business and small business. Everyone knows that all the things that happen in the American economy don't always add up to what might be called social justice.

Economic opportunities generally are greater for males than for females, greater for whites than for blacks and other minorities. There are regional differences—north to south, east to west, urban to rural. All of these inequalities result in very unequal benefits. Some people derive a lot more benefits from "being an American" than others do!

There are big differences between the rich and the poor. The number of poor people has declined a lot in the last few decades, but there are still a lot of poor people. They probably don't get much consolation from the fact that there aren't as many of them as there used to be.

The Military-Industrial Complex. You already know about this problem. It's a kind of vicious circle. Businesses that depend on government contracts want to get more government contracts. You can't blame them for that. The military forces who are supposed to defend the United States are trying to get the best kinds of armaments and weapons they can get. You can't blame them for that, either. And Congress is caught in the middle.

The industrial representatives and the military representatives urge the adoption of new weapons systems for the good of the nation. The result could be a constantly growing expenditure for military goods. Could it get to the point where it becomes impossible to make a rational choice about how much of society's resources should be directed toward military spending?

The Question of Social Control

How does the American society control its economic system? We know that the market demand has a lot to do with it, of course. But what about control of the big units: big labor, big business, big government?

How do the union members control their unions? The stockholders control their big corporations? The voters control the government? Or do the big unions, big corporations, and big government just go their own way without much control?

Do Things Just Run Themselves? Uncontrolled? Most of the time big unions, big businesses, and big government seem to run along under their own steam. It's only when the people with the ultimate power get dissatisfied with something that they begin to exercise their power.

That seems to be the way it works with the union members controlling their unions, with the stockholders and boards of directors controlling the big corporations, and with the voters in the country controlling the governments—local, state, and federal.

The Ultimate Power to Take Control: Is That Enough? Is this lack of day-by-day control of the big units in the economic system a serious defect in the system? Maybe. But maybe not. When you think about it, isn't it efficient? As long as the results come out all right?

We can all go our own way doing our own thing, leaving all the day-by-day decisions to someone else. But we're always feeling the effects of these little decisions. As long as we are satisfied with the way things are going, we can just let it ride.

But suppose we don't like what we see going on? Then we can get involved. We can play a more active role. Perhaps the price of "maximum social control" in an economic system or a political system is eternal vigilance. But perhaps **eternal vigilance** itself is too great a price to pay for the extra social control gained! (Thinking marginally? Right!)

Perhaps it isn't necessary to have everyone being eternally vigilant. Perhaps it's more efficient to let a few people be vigilant while everyone else does something else. We can all do our daily work, producing the daily bread for ourselves and others.

Isn't that the **socially efficient** way to do things? Isn't that the social efficiency of representative democracy? And wouldn't it seem to be an efficient technique for controlling the big units in the economic system?

Galbraith's Idea of Countervailing Power. Perhaps the "representative democracy approach" is adequate for the union members to control their unions and for the stockholders and boards of directors to control the big corporations, and for the voters to control the government.

But that kind of control certainly isn't going to get the big unions and big businesses to work "for the good of the nation," in response to the best interests of all of the people in the country. Of course not!

That's what **competition** is supposed to do. But with all this bigness there isn't anything like pure competition. So how is "social control for the good of the nation" achieved?

John Kenneth Galbraith has suggested the idea of **countervailing power** as a mechanism for keeping the big units in line. The idea is that the big corporations in *various industries* compete against each other, and the big labor organizations counterbalance the power of the big businesses.

Of course the **government** plays an important balancing role between **business** and **labor,** too. It influences big business and big labor to bend more to the public interest.

How important is countervailing power in keeping big business and big labor in line? And is government doing an adequate job of influencing them? Are these controls adequate for directing the energies of the big units toward the public interest?

People disagree on these issues. I can't tell you the answers because I don't know. But I hope all this helps to give you a realistic picture of the American system and some of the unresolved issues about how it works.

The Very Complex American Economy

The American economy is a **very complex** thing. It's made up of gigantic parts and very tiny parts all intermingled together. There are lots of conflicting forces at work.

I don't suppose anyone will ever be able to develop a complete mental picture of a complex thing like the American economic system. But as you think about the **various components** and the way they fit together, you will come closer to that. The closer you come, the better you'll understand it.

SUMMARY AND SYNTHESIS

The **American economy** of the 1980s is **very complex.** You are a part of it. Everyone is. Everything is.

The **household** is a basic unit in the economy. But we don't spend a great amount of time in **the economic analysis of households.** We can see the household **inflows and outflows.** But we don't know all that much about **what's going on in there.**

We know that households are little production-consumption-want-satisfying units—each a tiny "economic system" But it's **easier** to look at the big units in the economy: big labor, big business, big government. And big agriculture, too. They are easier to see, describe, analyze.

American agriculture is highly productive. But not many Americans are involved in agricultural production. Most workers are involved in trade and service activities. Agriculture plays an important role because much of its output becomes inputs into the processing and manufacturing industries. Also, agriculture has become one of the most productive areas of the American economy. Many of our farm products have no problem competing with foreign products.

The role of big labor is changing rapidly in the 1980s. The changing position of the U.S. economy in the world economy is having a lot to do with that. Workers are accepting trade-offs—giving back past-won gains in exchange for job security—helping businesses compete more effectively against foreign producers—to survive.

Big business is the dominant characteristic of the American economy. Out of the ten million businesses in the United States, only a few hundred own the overwhelming majority of the productive assets and are responsible for by far the greatest proportion of the gross national product in the nation.

In the past decades business productivity in the United States has increased rapidly. But in recent years that productivity increase has slowed down almost to a standstill. This is contributing to the problem of the poor competitive position of American producers in domestic and world markets. In the early 1980s the Reagan administration was using "supply-side economics" in an effort to try to stimulate productivity in this country.

Antitrust policy and government regulation of business have become stronger and tougher over the years—up until the early 1980s. But now productivity growth has become the major objective. This has resulted in some relaxation in the desire to prevent business mergers or to impose costly regulations on business. Now, in the 1980s, many existing regulations are being phased out and all new regulations must be justified by "cost-benefit" analysis. All this is a part of the Reagan administration's "supply-side economics" program.

Big government has been playing an increasingly important role in the economy in recent decades. This important role results from spending and taxing programs as well as regulation activities, income distribution and social welfare programs, and in other ways. Now, in the 1980s, no business can make an intelligent choice—regarding inputs, outputs, location, personnel, or whatever—without first considering the impact of government regulations, and taxes.

In 1982 it was estimated that about one half of the people in the United States depend at least partly for their economic welfare on government activities and programs. The Reagan administration pledged to reduce the role of government in the economy.

There were several special problems facing the American economy in the early 1980s. You have been (and will be) reading about these off and on throughout this book. One serious problem is inflation and unemployment. To fight inflation, interest rates have been very high. This has discouraged investment and helped to turn the economy into recession. Unemployment in early 1982 was higher than at any time since the Great Depression of the 1930s. But inflation seemed to be slowing down.

The slow growth rate and the inability of many American products to compete in the international markets have been harmful to business, labor, government—to all of us. Problems of environmental externalities, questions of the effectiveness of social control over the economic system—all were important issues in the early 1980s. I bet that as you read this, they still are.

Perhaps the most important economic development during the late 1970s and early '80s was the changed competitive position of the American economic system in the world economy. New competition from foreign products was having its impact on every aspect of the economy. Public policies were beginning to be significantly changed to respond to this new world of the 1980s. Businesses were doing a lot of rethinking about their approaches to things. So were the labor organizations. So were the governments—federal, state, and local. So were all of us as we were planning for the future.

In the early 1980s, business, government, labor, households— everyone was just beginning to recognize the dimensions of this new world of the 1980s. We are all just beginning to make some of the changes which in this new world will be required for our survival and prosperity.

The chapters coming up focus directly on the world economy. There you'll be finding out more about all this.

REVIEW EXERCISES

MAJOR CONCEPTS, PRINCIPLES, TERMS (Explain each carefully.)

the inflation and unemployment problem
the environmental problem
the problem of the slow growth rate
the problem of high oil prices
the new foreign competition
countervailing power
the military-industrial complex

OTHER CONCEPTS AND TERMS (Explain each briefly.)

Employment Act of 1946
Humphrey-Hawkins Act (1978)
Council of Economic Advisers

QUESTIONS (Write out answers or jot down key points.)

1. Describe the important function performed by households in the American economic system.
2. Describe some of the basic differences between the American economic system of the early 1900s and the American economic system of today. Do you think these changes in the system were *inevitable?* Do you think they were *good?* Discuss.
3. To try to get a better integrated picture of the American economy, try to give the highlights of the role of each of the following in the economy:
    –households
    –agriculture
    –big labor
    –big business
    –small businesses
    –big government
4. Discuss the problem of the "new foreign competition." How did it come about? What kinds of impacts is it having on each of the various sectors of the economy? and on public policies toward each of these sectors? What do you think the ultimate outcome of all this is likely to be? (Tough questions. Right?)

PART NINE

We're Going To Take A Trip Overseas!

38

International Trade I: The Economics of International Trade, and Trade Restrictions

Chapter Objectives

- This chapter builds on the principles of **comparative advantage, specialization, and trade** which you learned about in Chapter 18. In this chapter those principles are applied to the **economic interrelationships among nations in the real world** of the 1980s.

- When you finish studying this chapter you will be able to **describe the trade patterns** among the various nations of the world, and to indicate how these patterns have **changed over time.**

- You will know about the **techniques used,** and the **economic effects of trade restrictions**—and about the **advantages** which the real world can enjoy from **free trade.**

- You will be able to mention and discuss (refute!) several **arguments** which have been used through the years **to justify restrictions on trade,** and you will be able to use graphs to illustrate and to analyze the effects of tariffs and quotas.

- Finally, you will be able to describe the **changing trade policies** among the nations of the world including the **progress** which has been made under the **General Agreement on Tariffs and Trade (GATT).** And you will know about some of the **issues regarding protectionism and trade restrictions** which are surfacing in the early 1980s.

In Chapter 18 you learned about **comparative advantage** and the gains from trade. The eastside and westside chiefs (King Tuituranga and Queen Isaleilani) traded fish and breadfruit and both came out a lot better. Remember? If you have time it might be a good idea for you to go back and review Chapter 18. A lot of the basic ideas are explained there.

The Basic Economic Principles Apply Everywhere

As you look from one country to another you can see great differences. But as you see dif-ferences, keep this in mind: Economics is economics wherever you find it.

The same economic concepts and principles which apply to people and businesses in the United States apply everywhere. Not only that. The same principles which apply to buyers and sellers in the same town apply to buyers and sellers on different sides of the world.

National boundaries create problems, to be sure. For one thing, most nations have some kinds of restrictions on trade. Also, different countries use different kinds of money. Sometimes that creates problems.

But from the point of view of the opportunity to gain from trade, international trade is just like any other trade. The trading partners benefit in exactly the same way, no matter whether they live in different countries or not.

International Economics: Micro? or Macro?

Do you think international economics is microeconomics? or macroeconomics? Think about it. Microeconomics is concerned with the basic questions: Which products will be produced? by which methods and techniques? and how will the products be shared among the people?

Macroeconomics is concerned with how fast the economy will run—with changes in total demand, total spending, total output and income. So what do you think? Where does international economics fit? Is it both? Of course. It would have to be both.

International Economics Is Partly Microeconomics. International trade influences output choices and input choices in every country in the world. It influences choices of technology—or production techniques. It influences prices for consumer products and prices for inputs.

Truly, product outputs (and their prices) and resource inputs (and their prices) in every nation in the world are influenced a lot by *international economic conditions.* So international economics is microeconomics. There's no question about that. But it's macroeconomics, too.

International Economics Is Partly Macroeconomics. When you are adding up total spending in an economic system, you add consumer spending plus investment spending plus government spending—plus what? Plus spending by foreigners for our goods! Sure.

So what happens if foreigners start spending more for our goods? Total spending goes up? Yes. That pushes the economy to speed up. And it works the other way, too.

Suppose people in this country decided to spend less for domestic goods and more for foreign goods. Total spending in our economy goes down. The economy slows down. What about the foreign economy we are buying more goods from? Total spending there increases. The foreign economy speeds up. Of course.

The World Economy: An Overview of Part Nine

International economics is concerned with the economic relationships among nations. It includes all of the principles and ideas and concepts of economics, applied worldwide.

This chapter is about the economic relationships among nations—about world trade, and about the economic effects of restrictions on trade. The next two chapters talk about the principles and problems of international finance—about the problems which arise because one country's money must be exchanged for another's. Later in Part Nine you'll be reading about the less developed countries (LDCs), and finally about the different economic systems in different countries.

When you finish Part Nine you will have a good picture of how the world economy looks and how it works. Also you'll know about some of the tough problems that will have to be dealt with in the years to come.

INTERNATIONAL TRADE PATTERNS, U.S. AND WORLD

How important is international trade in the world today? In the early 1980s American businesses were getting more than $350 billion a year from sales to foreigners. A lot of businesses and a lot of farmers and a lot of workers depend on sales to foreigners. Obviously, world trade is important to the U.S. economy. But the United States isn't nearly as involved in world trade as are the other nations.

How Important Is International Trade?

The importance of international trade to the United States has been increasing a lot in recent years. Our exports and imports combined only added up to about 8 percent of GNP in 1971. But by 1975 the figure was up to more than 13 percent and by the early 1980s it was more than 20 percent.

But that percentage figure doesn't tell the whole story. How many American products—goods and services—are in *direct competition* with foreign products—both at home and abroad? Many of them, right? More than one third? Probably. And the number has been increasing rapidly.

Most modern nations are more dependent on international trade than is the United States. But none of us could very easily get along without it. And during the 1980s all of us are locked into the arena of fierce international competition.

Imports Serve American Industry, and Consumers Too. American industries would have a tough time getting along without their basic raw material imports: aluminum, chrome, cobalt, nickel, platinum, tin, asbestos and others.

What has happened since 1973 when the OPEC cartel (the Organization of Petroleum Exporting Countries) began pushing up the price of oil? Shortages of gasoline and heating oil? and price increases? and shifts to smaller cars? Of course.

Without international trade, many consumer goods would become more expensive. Consumers would have fewer choices. We would have to get along without (or pay much higher prices for) coffee, chocolate, bananas, coconuts, and a lot of other things. And you wouldn't see imported V.W.'s or Toyotas or Sonys or lots of other things.

Exports Are Vital to Many American Producers and Workers. What about markets for U.S. exports? Important too? You bet they are! Foreign markets absorb from one fifth to one third of our total output of cotton, grains, tobacco, sulphur, coal, textile machinery, metal working machinery, and mining and construction machinery. Also the computer industry and many other industries sell a lot in foreign markets.

You know that the United States imports a lot of cars. You can see them everywhere. But it goes the other way, too. Would you believe that in recent years about 1 out of every 7 autos produced in the United States has been sold overseas? Truly, trade is a two-way street.

U.S. Trade Patterns in the 1980s. There are some charts coming up that will give you a pretty good picture of the position of the United States in world trade. Figures 38-1, 2, 3, and 4 show you this picture. Take a few minutes and study those charts now.

Sources of International Statistics

If you want a more specific or more up-to-date look at what the United States is importing and exporting, and from where and to where, the U.S. Department of Commerce publishes those statistics. Detailed trade statistics are published from time to time in the *Survey of Current*

Fig. 38-1   U.S. Merchandise Exports, Early 1980s: Kinds of Products, Expressed as a Percentage of Total Merchandise Exports

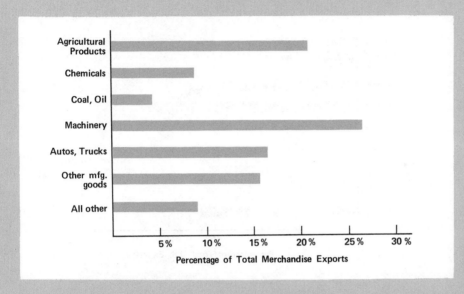

Percentage of Total Merchandise Exports

The U.S. economy has comparative advantage in several kinds of machinery, agricultural products, some kinds of automobiles, chemicals, and other manufactured goods.

Fig. 38-2   U.S. Merchandise Imports, Early 1980s: Kinds of Products Expressed as a Percentage of Total Merchandise Imports

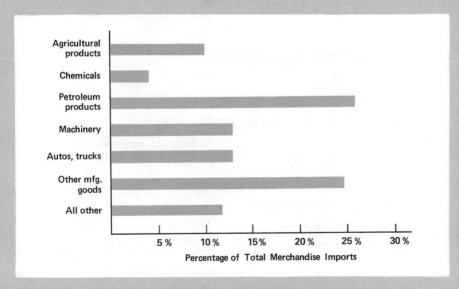

Percentage of Total Merchandise Imports

Automobiles and other manufactured goods make up almost 40 percent of the total. In recent years the cost of petroleum imports has gone up from less than 10 percent to about 25 percent of the total.

Fig. 38-3   Exports of Goods and Services, Early 1980s, By Country of Destination: Expressed as a Percentage of Total Exports of Goods and Services

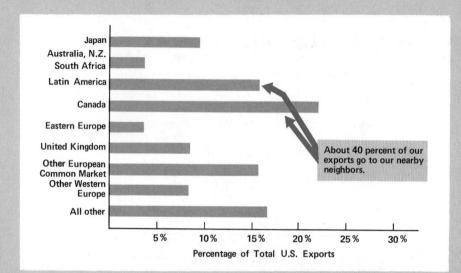

This chart shows the great importance of Canada, the EC, and Latin America as markets for U.S. exports. Japan also buys a lot of American goods and services—but the Japanese sell us a lot more than they buy!

Fig. 38-4   Imports of Goods and Services, Early 1980s, By Country of Origin: Expressed as a Percentage of Total Imports of Goods and Services

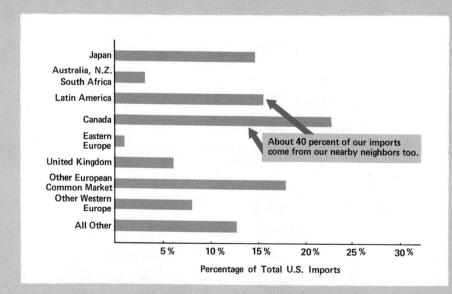

Almost one fourth of our imports come from Canada. This chart also shows the importance of Japan, the EC, and Latin America as sources of our imports.

Business. Or you can always fall back on your trusty friend, *The Statistical Abstract of the United States.*

If you want to look up statistics on lots of countries (not just the United States) a good place to start would be the United Nations *Statistical Yearbook,* and (for more up-to-date statistics) the U.N. *Bulletin of Statistics* (monthly). These U.N. sources carry statistics on world exports by origin and destination, on national income and product for many countries, and a great variety of other statistics.

Other good sources are: *International Financial Statistics,* and the *Balance of Payments Yearbook,* both published by the International Monetary Fund (IMF). The U.S. Department of State—especially the Agency for International Development (AID)—also publishes statistics on other countries, and on world economic conditions.

More Indications of the Importance of International Trade

The bar charts in Figures 38-1, 2, 3, and 4 show you a picture of America's world trade position.

Dependence on Raw Material Imports. About 15 percent of U.S. consumption depends on raw material imports. That's a lot. It would be really tough to try to get along without that 15 percent. But, in the countries of Western Europe, about 75 percent of the final goods output depends on imported raw materials. For Japan the figure is about 90 percent!

For a long time—in fact until after World War II—the American population was small enough and the American "industrial plant" was small enough so that we were almost entirely self-sufficient in raw material inputs—not quite, but almost. But with the population and industrial growth of the last few decades the American economy has become increasingly dependent on imports.

The Need for International Cooperation. When you look at Japan and the other industrialized nations you realize that the problem can't be solved by trying to gain "national self-sufficiency." The problem must be solved through international cooperation. And (as I'm sure you're well aware) that isn't going to be easy to work out.

Now you know something about trade patterns, and about the importance of trade to the United States and some other nations. So it's time to take a look at the economics of trade, and at the subject of trade restrictions.

THE TECHNIQUES AND ECONOMIC EFFECTS OF TRADE RESTRICTIONS

When the government of a country decides to limit the amount of some product coming into the country, how does it do that? Usually by imposing either tariffs or quotas (or both). Most nations are imposing tariffs and quotas on some things all the time. So what happens when they do that? That's what you'll find out in this section.

Tariffs and Quotas

A **tariff** is a tax on an imported good. It's also called a **customs duty.** Sometimes the tax is levied at so much per unit of product; sometimes it's levied as a percentage of the value of the product. The "per unit" tariff is called a **specific tariff;** the "value" tariff is called an **ad valorem tariff.**

Tariff rates can be set high or low. The higher the rate, the more restrictive the tariff. Obviously. If the tariff rate is set high enough it will stop imports of that item!

Who ultimately pays the tariff? The buyers of the imported goods, usually. Prices of the imported goods are increased so the domestic consumers must pay more for it. But another thing: with such high prices for imported goods, domestic producers can also sell their products for higher prices!

Can you see how domestic producers might like to see tariffs imposed on competing foreign goods? Sure. Tariffs can reduce the competition from foreign goods and give domestic producers higher prices and more profits. Already can you begin to see why some people might be in favor of tariffs and quotas? How to make a quick million! More on tariffs, soon. But first, a word about quotas.

Import quotas are limits on the amount of something that can be imported. For example, the United States government might decide that

only one million foreign cars could be imported. The government would issue import licenses to various firms, allowing each firm to import a certain number of cars.

The effect of the quota, of course, would be to create a shortage in the imported car market. So the prices of foreign cars would go up. The importers (at least the ones who get the import licenses) can make big profits.

What about prices and sales of American cars? Domestic producers can sell more cars because there aren't as many foreign cars. And with the higher prices of foreign cars, domestic producers can raise their prices too! Figures 38-5, 6, 7, and 8 show you all this (and more!) on supply and demand graphs. Take a few minutes and study those graphs now.

Fig. 38-5   The Basis for Trade, and International Equilibrium: The "Export Good" Case

Hypothetical example: the United States exports wheat

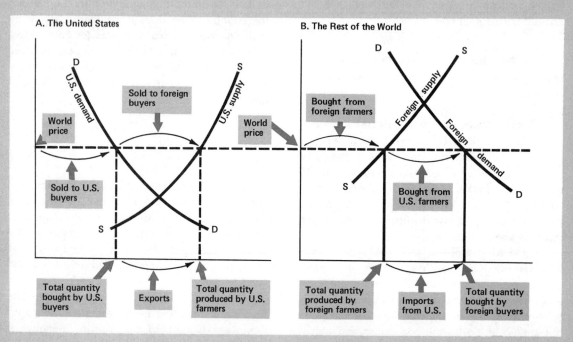

U.S. farmers produce more wheat than Americans are buying, while foreign farmers produce less than foreigners are buying. So at the "going world price" U.S. producers will produce more than enough wheat to supply domestic needs and will ship some overseas.

THE GENERAL ADVANTAGES OF FREE TRADE

What's so good about free trade? It lets people live better. It brings higher standards of living. It increases the "production possibility" for each trading nation. What's the ultimate result? The production possiblity of the whole world is greatly increased.

How does trade increase the production possiblity of the world? By letting the people and businesses in each country specialize. By letting each one do the things which will produce the most output value from the inputs available.

Comparative Advantage, Again

Free trade lets people follow the law of comparative advantage: specialize in the things in which you have comparative advantage and then trade to get the other things you want. So what happens? Everyone produces more output value. The total result is great increases in world output and income, and in living standards of the people.

Here's an example. Suppose you are good at producing posters but not so good at making macrame belts. Suppose you could paint four posters or make one macrame belt in your spare time in one week. Then the opportunity cost to

Fig. 38-6 The Basis for Trade, and International Equilibrium: The "Import Good" Case

Hypothetical example: the United States imports beef

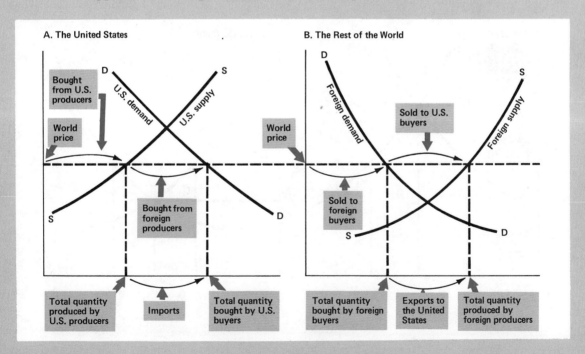

If there wasn't any trade, the price in the United States would be a lot higher. The price in the rest of the world would be a lot lower.

Goods always flow from "plentiful low-price places" to "more scarce, high-price places." So trade always *holds the price up* in the exporting country and *holds the price down* in the importing country.

you of producing one macrame belt is four posters. The opportunity cost to you of producing four posters is one macrame belt.

Suppose people really like your posters and are willing to pay $5 each for them. They also like your belts. They will pay $5 for them, too. In fact the going price on your campus is $5 for a good poster and $5 for a good macrame belt.

It's obvious what you're going to produce. Posters. Right! Suppose you decide you need a macrame belt for yourself. Will you make it for yourself? Or make a poster, sell the poster, and buy the belt? That would be better for you. Of course.

There are some students on your campus

who are very poor at making posters, but who are good at making macrame belts. It would be foolish for them to ever try to make posters. They should make belts and sell them. Then they should buy posters from you.

You can see that there would be a lot more belts and a lot more posters produced on your campus if everyone followed the law of comparative advantage. If you stopped making posters one week in order to make belts, you would reduce the output of posters a lot more than you would increase the output of belts! If the people who couldn't make posters very well stopped making belts to try to make posters, they would reduce the output of belts a lot more than they

Fig. 38-7   How a Tariff Slows or Stops Trade

Here a 50 percent tariff stops all beef imports

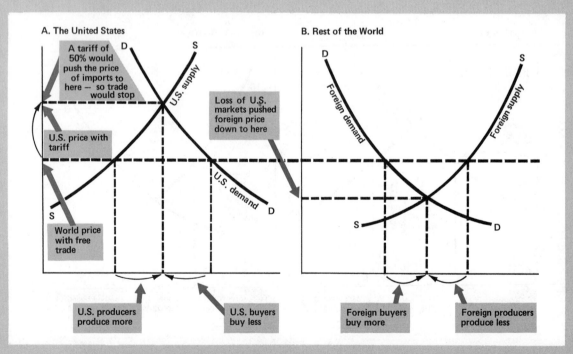

Look! After the tariff the Americans are paying about as much (in total) for beef as they were before. The only difference is: They're getting a lot less beef! The American beef producers are the ones who are getting the extra money.

Look how the foreign producers are hurting! They are selling a lot less and selling it at a lot lower price, too!

would increase the output of posters!

Suppose your college administrators decided there was too much poster-and-belt trading going on. Suppose they decided to prohibit all buying and selling and trading of belts and posters. What would happen? Well, probably you would all ignore the administrators and just keep on doing what you had been doing all along.

But suppose the college adminisration *really could* enforce this anti-trading rule. What would happen? Total output would go down. Costs of belts and posters, to everyone, would go up. That's what always happens when artificial barriers are erected between buyers and sellers.

Trade restrictions force people and businesses *not* to follow the law of comparative advantage. They force people and businesses to shift out of the production of products in which they can produce the greatest output value and into the production of products in which they can only produce smaller output values.

Some Real-World Examples

Does it work out the same way in the real world? with real products? like it does with belts and posters in this example? You bet it does. Exactly. Here are some examples.

Fig. 38-8   The Effect of a Quota: Much Like the Effect of a Tariff

Here, a quota is used to cut back imports by 50 percent

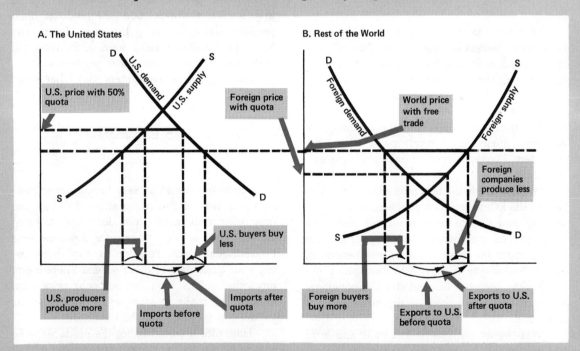

The U.S. quota pushes up the U.S. price, induces U.S. companies to produce more and discourages U.S. buyers from buying. In foreign countries the price is pushed down and production is reduced.

Tariffs result in an *obvious price increase* for the consumers. With quotas the "price effect" isn't so obvious. But prices go up, either way.

The American Economy. Look at the American economy. Fifty states. Some quite similar, many very different from each other. All of the people and businesses in all of the states are completely free to trade with the people and businesses in all of the other states. People, resources, capital—all can flow freely from one place to another, anywhere in the country.

The rapid growth and great productivity of the American economy would have been absolutely impossible if trade among the states had been restricted. The United States is a monumental example of the real-world advantages of free trade.

The European "Economic Community" (EC).* You already know about the "European common market" (the EC). It was set up in 1957 among six European countries: France, Germany, Italy, Belgium, the Netherlands, and Luxembourg.

The idea was to get together and try to reduce trade barriers among the member nations. It was an attempt to achieve "economic integration" among the six countries.

Was the European Common Market (EC) successful? Yes. Quite successful. All of the member nations have enjoyed the advantage of economic integration. Their growth rates have increased. Per capita income has gone up significantly.

Perhaps this is the best indication of the success of the EC: In recent years Denmark, Britain, Ireland, and Greece have requested and have been granted membership. Some people were talking about the possible future membership of Spain. And maybe Turkey. And Portugal.

Today, both the EC and the U.S. economy are outstanding examples of the advantages of free trade.

Who would want to restrict trade and force businesses and workers and farmers to do less

---

*The European "common market" has been called the "European Economic Community" (EEC). In recent years it's also called the "European Community" (EC), so you'll see it referred to both ways.

productive things? to ignore the law of comparative advantage? Who would want to restrict trade and force lower incomes and standards of living on the people in the nation? and in the world? Nobody, right? No. Wrong.

Consider this: Sometimes "maximum living standards for all of the people" is not the uppermost objective in some people's minds. There can be other objectives, of course. Several arguments have been put forth to try to justify trade restrictions. The next section explains some of these arguments.

SOME ARGUMENTS AGAINST FREE TRADE

Free trade generates a lot of competition. Competition is what keeps producers in line. If there's a lot of competition, the producer must produce efficiently, keep the price down, and keep the product quality high. Otherwise the customers will buy from other producers. Competition is good for consumers. But what about for producers?

It's Profitable to Eliminate Competition

Producers would be very happy not to have to put up with all this competition. If you are the only seller in the market you don't have to be so careful about keeping your price down or your product quality up. You don't worry about losing your customers to other sellers. There aren't any other sellers! You can set your price high enough to make profits—even though your production methods may be inefficient.

How nice it would be for the producer to be able to eliminate the controls of competition! But not so nice for the consumers. Competition protects consumers. Without competition, who looks out for the consumers? Nobody. Not very much, anyway.

You can see who might argue for trade restrictions. The domestic producers? Of course! And their workers? Sure.

Politicians working for industrial growth might argue for tariffs and quotas, too—especially the politicians from the areas where the "protected" products are produced. And mayors and governors and senators and representatives all may argue for trade restrictions to stimulate domestic employment and production in their own areas.

Protecting a Threatened Industry

Suppose a foreign country worked out a way of producing a new kind of automobile and producing it very cheaply. Let's call it a "Turtle." Suppose American buyers were all trying to buy these foreign cars.

Take a wild example: suppose nobody in the United States wants to buy a new American car. Everyone wants to buy a Turtle. They like the Turtle twice as much and it only costs half as much as an American car. Can you see what a great economic shock this would be to the city of Detroit? and to the state of Michigan? and to several other places in the United States where cars are produced?

The impact would be felt in industries throughout the country: steel, coal, transport, fabrics, glass, paint, chemicals and many others. What a massive clamor there would be for import restrictions and high tariffs on Turtles! In such an extreme case as this there's no question that some kind of import restriction would be imposed.

So you want to buy a Turtle? You can't. The people who want to buy Turtles may be very unhappy. Some can't get them at all. The ones who can must pay a very high price because of the tariff or quota—the great shortage—very limited supply and very great demand.

But no matter. The trade restrictions will come anyway. But likely, the American producers soon will learn to produce Tortoises and produce them cheaply enough. to compete with Turtles. Then the anti-Turtle tariffs and quotas

can be abolished. But will they be? Maybe so. Maybe not.

The Deck is Stacked Against Free Trade

In a way the deck is stacked against free trade. The people who would like trade to be restricted on a certain product (the producers and workers in the industry, the local politicians, the suppliers, transporters and others) have a strong interest in "protecting the home market" for that product.

Many people have a lot to gain by trade restrictions and they will push hard to get tariffs and quotas against competing goods. But who is pushing hard on the other side—for free trade to improve the real incomes of the consumers? Usually nobody.

Consumers usually don't fight very effectively against trade restrictions. From a tariff on any particular product, the consumers have much less to lose than the producers of the domestic product have to gain!

Not only that. Most people seem to be sort of brainwashed on this issue anyway. Several good-sounding arguments have been used to convince the people that trade restrictions are good for the nation—good for everybody. Some of the arguments have some (limited) validity. Some don't.

The "Infant Industry" Argument

One of the oldest arguments for trade restrictions is this: If we want an industry to get started in this country, we must restrict imports long enough for that industry to get set up and running efficiently. In 1791 Alexander Hamilton (the first U.S. Secretary of the Treasury) in his *Report on Industries and Commerce* used the infant industry argument. Is it a valid argument? Sometimes, yes. But more often than not it has been abused.

The "Infant" Never Wants to Grow Up.
Suppose an industry grows up under the shelter
of a high tariff. When are the domestic producers ready to see the tariff removed? and foreign competition come in? and the price of the
product go down? Never? Right!

The more the industry grows and the
stronger it gets, the better position it is in to
argue for continuing the tariff. But then it must
shift to some other argument—something other
than the "infant industry" argument. So that's
what it does.

Most economists would recommend that if
the government wants to help an industry get
started, subsidies work better than trade restrictions. Subsidies are payments by the government
to the firms in the industry to help them get
started or to help them to keep going or to induce them to expand. When subsidies are used
it's easy to see how much the industry is costing
the taxpayers. But when tariffs and quotas are
used, the cost to the consumer is hidden.

Tariffs Are Excise Taxes. Tariffs are excise taxes. They are mostly shifted forward and
paid by the buyers of the imported products. But
note this: the sellers of the *domestic* product also
receive the higher price. But the extra money
(the tax) doesn't go to the government at all! In
effect, *the government makes it possible for the domestic producers to collect a tax from the buyers of the
product, and to keep the money they collect!*

Another thing. Why should the buyers of
some few particular products carry the entire
burden of subsidizing the industrial growth of
the nation? Doesn't the entire nation stand to
gain? And if so, wouldn't it make more sense for
everybody to help to subsidize the infant industries? Sure.

And here's something else to consider. Subsidies don't distort the price patterns in the
markets of the economy. Trade restrictions do.
But even with all the advantages of the "subsidies" approach, a tariff or quota usually is easier
to impose and easier to "explain to the people."
Do senators or representatives want to tell all the

people back home that they are voting for subsidies to wealthy businesses? You can see the
problem.

The "National Defense" Argument

Suppose some producers in foreign countries have developed some new and very efficient ways to produce aircraft. What if they
could undersell the U.S producers? Should the
U.S. government sit by and watch Boeing and
McDonald-Douglas and Lockheed and all the
others go broke?

Or suppose something like that happened in
the steel industry. Should the steel industry be
allowed to dwindle away and disappear? How
about petroleum? petrochemicals? the merchant
marine? electronics?

Certainly the United States would not want
to be dependent on other nations for the products required for national defense. Luckily most
of our essential products can "hold their own"
against foreign competition. The aircraft, petrochemical, electronics, machinery and several
other industries can do much better than that!

But suppose foreign producers *could* undersell American producers in one of the essential
defense industries. Should the industry be allowed to wither away? Of course not.

Should tariffs or quotas be imposed to protect the threatened defense producers? If that
was the only way to solve the problem, then yes.
Trade restrictions should be imposed. But isn't
there a better way?

Wouldn't it be much better to pay subsidies
to the domestic producers? and let all the taxpayers see what national defense is costing them?
And let *all* the taxpayers carry a share of the
burden? (not just the buyers of a few specific
products?) Of course subsidies would be better.

The national defense argument can be a
very convincing way to justify trade restrictions.
What member of Congress wants to vote against
national security? Anyone who wants to argue
for a tariff or quota will try to think of some way

to use the national defense argument! (and other arguments too of course!)

The "Diversified Economy" Argument

Some smaller nations depend heavily on only one product. This is especially true in the LDCs. Suppose a nation produces only sugar. If there's a steep drop in the world price of sugar, what can they do? Nothing. They suffer.

The countries which depended on natural fibers in the past were seriously hurt by the development of nylon and all the other new synthetic fibers. In the 1970s the countries depending on copra and coconut oil were hurt by the steep drop in world copra prices. But the countries producing sugar reaped big gains from the high world prices of sugar. (Luckily, some of the copra-producing countries also produce sugar!) Cocoa is another product with a history of sharp ups and downs in price. Countries depending on cocoa have had some very good years and some very bad ones.

It's easy to understand why a small nation would like to diversify its economy. No nation wants to put all its eggs in one basket—especially when now and then the basket is sure to tip over! But it isn't always easy to diversify an economy. A small country is not likely to have (or be able to develop) comparative advantage in very many things.

If a small nation tries to force the development of industries which cannot be made to fit the local situation, the economy will suffer. A few protected producers will gain but everyone else will lose. And it's a sure thing that the losers will lose more than the gainers will gain.

What happens when trade is restricted and capital and resources are diverted into uneconomic uses? Standards of living will go down.

What about subsidies? If the government wants to support **diversification**, wouldn't it be better to use subsidies? and let everyone see how much the diversification is costing? and let everyone share in the burden? and not distort prices of goods in the domestic markets? Sure. Subsidies would be better.

Totally Ridiculous (But Cleverly Appealing) Arguments

Why is it that the most ridiculous arguments for trade restrictions are the ones you hear the most? And the ones the most people seem to believe? I don't know why.

I guess it's because for some things in economics, most people need more than common sense to get it figured out right. This section talks about the two most popular of these "ridiculous arguments."

Protect American Workers from Low-wage Foreigners. Suppose you hear an American worker arguing in favor of a tariff or a quota. What argument are you most likely to hear? This one: Tariffs and quotas are necessary, otherwise foreign producers using low-wage workers will flood the American markets with cheap products and put the American workers out of work. That's one of the most often used arguments for tariffs and quotas. And it makes no sense at all.

The "average wage rate" in a country doesn't determine the cost of production of any product! If it did, American producers could never export anything! American producers would be knocked completely out of business by the less developed countries (LDCs)! That's where wages are *really* low. But do the LDCs

How come Some people argue **against** free trade?

'Cause sellers with **less Competition** can make **more profits!**

threaten to take over the world's markets? Of course not.

Which U.S. products compete most successfully in foreign markets? Products made by low-wage American industries? Like textiles? Of course not. The low-wage industries in this country are the *low-productivity industries*. Those are precisely the industries which cannot compete well in foreign markets.

In the high-wage industries—aircraft, computers, petrochemicals, specialized machinery, etc.—American products have no trouble against foreign competition. It's the low-wage *foreign* producers who find it hard to compete against the high-productivity American producers!

A Swiss Watch Industry Example. Here's an example: In January of 1976 in Neuchatel, Switzerland (would you believe?) about 180 employees occupied a Bulova watch company plant to protest its closing. The Swiss watch industry is the largest in the world. But it was hard hit by the 1974-75 recession, and by the high price of the Swiss franc.

But there was another problem for the Swiss. The watchmaking industry in the United States which was knocked out some years ago by high labor cost (that is, by low labor productivity) is now coming back. It's giving the Swiss watch industry cause for concern. Why? Because of electronic digital watches!

These new watches are mass-produced in the United States. Labor productivity on these watches is very high. So does the high wage of American workers give the American digital watch a disadvantage in world markets? Obviously not.

See? It isn't the wage rate that matters. It's the wage as compared with the productivity! Of course.

Per-Unit Labor Cost Comparisons. Back in the 1960s, labor cost per unit of output in the United States was, on the average, much higher than elsewhere in the world.

Labor cost per unit in West Germany (on the average) was only a little more than half as high

as it was in the United States. In Japan the cost was only about 60 percent of the U.S. level. In France it was about 74 percent. In Canada it was about 85 percent and in Italy about 88 percent.

Only in Britain was the average per-unit labor cost higher than in the United States. Still, the high-productivity industries in the United States made out just fine. But the low-productivity ones pleaded for protection against foreign competition.

By the mid-1970s, the picture was very different. Per-unit labor costs in West Germany and Canada (on the average) were just about equal to the United States. In Japan it was about 91 percent of the U.S. average and in France it was about 83 percent. In Italy the per-unit labor cost had pushed up to about 25 percent *higher* than in the United States—which made it equal to Britain.

As you might guess, these statistics aren't meant to be highly precise. They talk about averages—and you know there are always lots of variations around the average! But at least the figures give you some indication of what's been going on. Here's another example—one I think you can see even better.

An Automobile Industry Example. During the mid-1970s the average U.S. autoworker received an annual wage of about $13,000. The average autoworker in West Germany received about $9,000, and in Britain, about $5,600.

So which country has the advantage? You don't know until you know about "value-added" per worker.

In the United States, value added per autoworker came to just about $20,000. In West Germany it came to $11,000 and in Britain it came to slightly less than $5,000. See the picture?

American autoworkers on the average were adding $7,000 more in product value than they were paid in wages. The German workers added about $2,000 more than their wages. And the British? They were paid more than the value of what they produced! (You might wonder how long that could keep going on.)

By now I'm sure you can see how ridiculous

it is to talk about "protecting American workers from the competition of low-wage foreign workers!" It just doesn't make any sense.

Remember this: *It isn't the wage rate that matters. It's the ratio between wages and output.* The efficiency of the workers—the output per hour—must be considered along with the wage rate. If the American worker's output is five times as great, then the worker can be paid five times as much and the product can still compete. But suppose the American worker is only paid four times as much. Then the foreign producer can't compete! Get the point?

Sometimes a Country's Money Is Overvalued.

Suppose there really was a time when foreign products of all kinds were coming in and underselling American products of all kinds. A serious situation? Of course! What should be done? Should we use tariffs and quotas to stop the imports? No. That isn't the answer at all.

What's the problem? The American dollar is **overvalued**. Or to say it differently: foreign monies are **undervalued**. Why aren't foreigners buying American goods? Because *American dollars cost too much!* Foreigners have to give you too much of their money to get the American dollars they need to buy American goods.

What about the Americans? They're buying lots of foreign goods because they can get so much foreign money for an American dollar! You get a lot more for your dollars if you buy a lot of cheap (undervalued) foreign money and then buy foreign goods.

Revalue the Dollar Downward.

So what should be done? Dollars should be sold more cheaply to foreigners. Then more foreigners would buy American dollars and then buy American goods. American buyers then would have to pay more for foreign money, so it would cost them more to buy foreign goods.

After the overvalued dollar is revalued downward, Americans will buy less foreign goods and more American goods. Foreigners will buy more American goods and less of their own

goods. If the revaluation is just right (not too much, not too little) soon trade will come into balance.

Tariffs and quotas wouldn't solve the problem. They might succeed in slowing or stopping trade altogether. But what good is that? to deny both countries the gains from trade? and hold down the standards of living in all the nations involved? That's no solution. A downward revaluation of the dollar would permit trade to flow normally again in response to world demand, supply, and cost conditions.

You don't yet understand much about **money revaluations**. The next two chapters explain the process of financing international trade. After you study those chapters you'll understand all about money revaluations. But now it's time for another ridiculous argument for the tariff.

Keep the Money at Home.

Abraham Lincoln has been accused of saying the following (whether he did or not, I don't know): "If we buy steel rails from another country, we have the rails and they have the money. But if we buy the rails from a domestic producer we have the rails and the money, too!"

What do you think of this argument? If you think about it for a minute you'll realize that this is an argument to end all trade—international and otherwise!

If you make your own shoes you will have your money and your shoes too! If you build your own car you will have your money and your car, too! If everybody follows this philosophy, there won't be any trade! And nobody will have any money, either. Of course not. There won't be any need for money.

What's the purpose of money? To facilitate trade. What does "medium of exchange" mean? Trade facilitator? Of course. Money lets people follow the law of comparative advantage.

Money is useful only because it can be used for buying things—that is, for making trade easier. What is really traded is not money for goods, but goods for goods. If we want foreigners to buy our goods, then we must buy their goods. As we buy their goods, we give them the money they need to buy ours. If we cut off the flow of dollars going out, we also cut off the flow of foreign demand, coming back.

This argument about "keeping the money at home" is a dangerous one because it sounds so appealing. Everyone knows that it's nice to have money. So when someone is arguing for trade restrictions to "keep the country's money at home" it sounds so patriotic—like such a good thing to do for the country. And it seems that with the tariffs and quotas we are all going to have more money. But we aren't, of course.

A few producers will have a lot more money. But the rest of us will have less. That's always the way it is with trade restrictions. Right? Right!

Should Nations Impose Tariffs and Quotas? or Not?

Most economists agree that trade restrictions usually are undesirable. Trade restrictions benefit a few and hurt everyone else. But there's another problem. When one nation begins restricting trade, other nations are likely to do the same.

You Block Our Goods and We'll Block Yours! If the United States puts tariffs and quotas on West German and Japanese steel and cars, then Japan and West Germany are likely to put trade restrictions on American machinery and computers.

So what happens? The American steel and automobile producers make more profits and hire more workers. But the machinery and computer producers lose money and lay off workers. In addition, American consumers have fewer choices. And they pay higher prices for automobiles and for other steel products.

See how trade restrictions tend to hurt the more productive industries? the industries with comparative advantage? and cause expansion of the less efficient industries? the industries which should be trying to increase their productivity-per-worker so that they can hold their own against foreign competition?

And see how the standards of living of the people are reduced? People can't buy as much with their money anymore. It's easy to see why economists generally favor free trade.

But what about the "infant industry" argument? and the "national security" argument? and the "diversified economy" argument? Sometimes these arguments may be valid. But it would be better to accomplish the objectives of industrial growth, national security, and economic diversification by using government subsidies—not tariffs and quotas.

A Rational Approach: Government Investments and Subsidies. A government can design a plan for industrial expansion and national security and economic diversity. It can then set up a system of subsidies and government investments to try to achieve the desired results.

That's the rational way to go about it. But sometimes the **political impediments** are too great. Sometimes trade restrictions are the only realistic alternative.

The question of trade restrictions is very much a political question. It involves power politics and propaganda by businesses, labor, agriculture, political parties and others. Sometimes the only politically feasible way to achieve some national objective is by imposing restrictions on trade. The political realities may make it impossible to use any other approach.

We can hope that as time goes by, the general public will become more aware of the truth about restricting trade—about how much harm it does to almost everyone. Trade is a two-way street. When trade is restricted, both countries lose.

One industry usually gains from a trade restriction. But the total loss is greater than the gain. If we could just get this point across to everyone, I think it would help a lot.

WORLD TRADE POLICIES, PAST AND PRESENT

The advantages of free trade are great. So have the wise politicians in the nations of the world always argued for free trade? You know the answer. No. Quite the opposite. For the past several hundred years, international trade has been entangled with restrictions.

What about the United States? Committed to a philosophy of laissez-faire and minimum government influence, it should be for free trade, right? Perhaps it should. But it hasn't been. Not until recent decades.

The Early Years

Throughout most of its history the United States has kept high tariffs on most manufactured goods. Special interests pushed hard for trade restrictions to give them more monopoly power and higher prices for their products.

The people were the ones who had to pay the higher prices, of course. But the people didn't know what was going on. They were brainwashed by all the arguments you've been reading about in this chapter.

Throughout most of the 1800s and up to the 1930s, U.S. tariffs were generally high. The industrialists fought hard for the tariff. The Republican party, which was in power most of the time from the Civil War until the 1930s, was committed to high tariffs to support industrial growth. Throughout this entire period tariffs on most manufactured imports averaged around 40 to 60 percent of the value of the imported goods. What a sure way to keep prices high and guarantee profits for domestic producers!

The 1930s

As the depression got worse and unemployment became a serious problem world-wide, na-

tions began trying to stop imports. They followed "beggar-thy-neighbor" policies—that is, they froze the foreign sellers out of their domestic markets.

Each nation tried to hold its home markets for domestic producers. That is, each nation tried to cure its own unemployment problem by forcing unemployment on its foreign suppliers. The United States was no exception.

In 1930 Congress passed the **Smoot-Hawley Tariff Act**. That Act pushed America's tariff rates to the highest levels in more than a century. What did it accomplish? It froze a lot of foreign sellers out of American markets, of course. And it put a lot of foreign businesses out of business, too!

And what were the foreign countries doing? The same thing. They were freezing American sellers out of their markets. And putting a lot of American businesses out of business? Sure.

Did all these trade restrictions help to overcome the depression? Of course not. The restrictions only made conditions a lot worse for everybody. How much were all these trade restrictions responsible for the seriousness and length of the great depression? Nobody knows, of course. But everybody knows the trade restrictions hurt a lot.

By 1934, after four miserable years of worsening depression, recovery was trying to get started. By then it was easy to see that beggar-thy-neighbor policies were hurting everybody, impeding the economic recovery. So in 1934 Congress passed the **Reciprocal Trade Agreements Act**. This act gave the president the power to negotiate mutual reductions in trade restrictions: "You cut your tariff and I'll cut mine!"

The General Agreement on Tariffs and Trade (GATT, 1947)

Some tariff cuts were made under the Reciprocal Trade Agreements Act of 1934. But it wasn't until 1947 when 23 nations (including the United States) got together and signed the GATT that the United States became a "relatively free trade" nation.

Under the GATT, U.S. tariffs were cut back to less than half the previous levels—from an average of more than 30 percent of the value of taxed imports down to an average of less than 15 percent of the value of taxed imports.

But beware: These are *average* figures. Tariffs and other restrictions on some things have remained high. Still, since 1947 the United States has been one of the leaders in the "world free trade movement."

The principles adopted by the GATT in 1947 were: equal treatment for all members, elimination of import quotas, and tariff reduction by *multilateral negotiations*—that is, let's *all* get together and cut out tariffs and other trade restrictions at the same time.

The first "round" of **multilateral negotiations** was in 1947. Since then there have been several more "multilateral negotiating sessions." The sixth of these was initiated by President Kennedy in 1962. It was called the "Kennedy Round."

The "Kennedy Round" and the Trade Expansion Act of 1962

In the early 1960s there was increased interest in the United States in moving toward freer world trade. Why? Partly because of the importance of foreign markets for American products

and the desire of American producers to sell freely in foreign markets. But more than that, because in 1957 the European Economic Community (the EC or "Common Market") was set up.

The Desire to Sell to Buyers in EC Countries. Suppose Ford Motor Co. is trying to sell Pintos to a French automobile dealer. The price the French dealer must pay will be pushed up by a tariff. But suppose the French dealer buys Volkswagens from West Germany? Both France and West Germany are in the EC. So there's no tariff on Volkswagens! See the problem?

American producers would like to be able to sell freely to buyers in the Common Market countries, of course. As more nations join the Common Market, free access becomes all the more important! Fortunately, the United States is not the only nation with these objectives.

Japan and Canada and Australia and the Latin American countries and Taiwan and the African countries and the countries of Southeast Asia and the Mideast and even the Communist countries—all would like to be able to sell to customers in the Common Market. So the interest in free trade strengthens!

Congress Moves for Freer Trade. So in 1962 Congress passed the Trade Expansion Act giving the president broad powers to negotiate tariff reductions. On many products tariffs could be cut by 50 percent. On those goods where tariffs were less than 5 percent of the value, the tariff could be dropped entirely.

The 1962 act made allowances to aid any workers or businesses hurt by tariff reductions. This act provided the basis for the United States to play a leading role in the Kennedy Round of multilateral negotiations.

Negotiations under the Kennedy Round continued off and on and were not concluded until 1967. Some of the scheduled tariff reductions were not to go into effect until 1972. It was slow. But that's what you would expect of multilateral negotiations. A good bit of progress was made. On the average, tariffs were cut by about 35 percent.

The "Tokyo Round" and the U.S. Trade Act of 1974

In September of 1973 more than 100 nations (including the United States) met in Tokyo and agreed to start a new round of trade negotiations. Then in 1975, 87 nations began meeting in Geneva to try to work things out.

Not only were negotiations set up to try to reduce tariffs. They were also aimed at reducing quotas, the licensing requirements, the red tape, the fictitious "standards of quality" and the other *novel ways countries use to try to restrict imports without actually passing a law restricting imports.*

In 1974 and early 1975 the world economy suffered the most depressed conditions since the depression of the 1930s. Both the United States and the other nations used domestic programs to try to slow inflation and to deal with the unemployment problem. But did the nations return to the "beggar-thy-neighbor" policies of the 1930s? Fortunately, no.

There were some new import restrictions by a few countries. But there was no general breakdown in the movement toward freer trade.

The **1974 U.S. Trade Act** permitted our GATT negotiators to agree to tariff reductions of up to 60 percent. That's the highest ever.

In March of 1976 the U.S. negotiators presented the U.S. proposal which had been in preparation since the Tokyo meeting in 1973. The U.S. proposal called for cutting tariffs (all those above 7 percent) by a flat rate of 60 percent—the maximum allowed under the Trade Act of 1974.

Japan and the Common Market opposed the U.S. proposal on the basis that agricultural products should not be included with the industrial products. (Both the EC and Japan want to protect their farmers against American farm product imports.)

So how long did the negotiations continue? Would you believe 5½ years? The tariff cuts were not easy to work out. Each nation wants to get the best deal it can (a) for its own producers to be able to enter foreign markets, but without (b) giving up too much of its domestic markets to foreign producers. A lot of time was spent trying to get countries to agree to eliminate **non-tariff barriers** to trade—fictitious quality standards and red tape, etc., imposed to keep out foreign goods.

Finally, in April of 1979 the "trade pact for the 1980s" was completed—several thousand pages long—and signed by the delegates. Were the negotiations successful? Only time will tell about that for sure, because now it's up to the individual nations to do what the pact says (or not). But the pact itself is a big step toward free trade.*

Sir Roy Denman, EC Commissioner for External Affairs called it "one of the great achievements since World War II." U.S. Ambassador Alonzo McDonald said it is the *"most comprehensive and significant results produced by any trade negotiations up to this time."*

The **"Tokyo Round"** pact of 1979 calls for tariff reductions averaging about 33%. It applies to goods which make up about 20% of the value of all world trade. So it covers more than $200 billion worth of the goods which flow in international commerce. The tariff cuts are scheduled to be made over an 8-year period beginning January, 1980.

The Tokyo Round pact also includes "codes of conduct" designed to reduce or eliminate non-tariff barriers to trade. But the success of the "codes of conduct" will depend on how well the nations actually abide by the codes.

---

*In case you want to know more about the Tokyo Round trade pact of 1979, the details together with analysis of some of the effects on the American economy may be found in *The Wall Street Journal*, April 12 and 13, 1979; and also in *Business Week*, May 7, 1979, pp. 34-35.

Developing Trade with the Communist Countries

Since World War II, while trade has been expanding between the United States and the rest of the world, trade with the Communist countries (the USSR, East European countries, China, North Korea, Cuba) has been almost nonexistent. But in the last few years that's changing. Why?

Our establishing political contact with the People's Republic of China helped. Russian interest in U.S. industrial goods has helped, too. But Russia's poor grain harvests have helped even more!

American producers have been watching businesses in other countries benefitting from trade with the Communist countries. Some American producers have been asking: "Why not us, too?"

There is no question that the USSR has a great supply of natural resources which need to be developed. They could be developed with American machinery and management. Russia has timber, oil and gas, nonferrous metals and other resources which they could trade with us in exchange for our high-technology machinery and equipment.

But what about the problem of national defense? In 1975 the Pentagon set up a task force to study this question. The task force concluded that the United States should prohibit the transfer of "design and engineering know-how that could be strategically valuable to Communist nations." But except for that, *product exports should not be restricted.*

You know about the grain-trade agreement with Russia in 1975. Also that year, deals were made with the USSR for the sale of billions of dollars' worth of American agricultural equipment and for plant construction in the USSR. The deals included plants to be built by U.S. manufacturers for making aluminum, paper, and trucks.

In 1979, U.S. "diplomatic recognition" of the People's Republic of China opened an important new avenue of trade. In May of 1979 China was granted most favored nation status. That means Chinese goods now can be imported into the United States with no more restrictions than are imposed on imports from our "most favored" trading partner.

So now, any time the United States reduces the tariff on some product from any other nation (say, Canada), the reduction will automatically apply to imports of that product from China. So the Chinese can now sell goods in U.S. markets on an equal footing with all other foreign producers. Maybe the price of jade earrings (and some other things) will soon be going down!

It is clear that trade restrictions between the United States and the Communist countries are being eased and that our trade with these countries is expanding. There have also been sharp increases in trade between the Communist nations and the EC.

There's no question that this trade is of economic value to the Communist countries—just as it is of economic value to the non-Communist ones. Trade is always a two-way street. But not everyone in the United States is happy with the way things are going. Some people would like more trade with the USSR to be permitted. Others would like less.

There has been a lot of confusing opinion on this issue. A spokesman for Texas Instruments was arguing that we must try to keep our "critical" industrial technology from the USSR, while a spokesman for Control Data Corp. was arguing that the present exporting licensing system is archaic, inconsistent, and too restrictive.

Under the present system, Control Data stands to lose about $500 million in computer sales over the next five years. They argue that controls should be eased—should apply to "new or exotic technology that we are using in defense and not in the commercial world."

From Import Restrictions to Export Restrictions

Here's another interesting change that happened in the 1970s. Usually, nations want to help their domestic producers to sell *more* in foreign markets (and to protect home markets from foreign sellers). But in the 1970s, for several products the emphasis turned around the other way! Shortages of food and raw materials caused some governments to *restrict exports*. And to try to *encourage imports!*

Inflation was a serious problem. If we are exporting our wheat, what happens to the price of bread? It goes up, of course. So what do we do? Restrict exports of wheat! That's what we did for a while. And soybeans too. And scrap steel.

The United States was not the only one to restrict exports. Canada, Brazil, and Australia put export controls on foods. And you already know what the OPEC cartel did with oil!

Some countries levied price controls to fight inflation. Suppose you're in business selling something and the domestic price is controlled—but the foreign price isn't. What do you do? Sell your product to a foreign buyer for a higher price! Of course.

How do nations with price controls protect themselves from this? They restrict exports. Quotas, maybe. Or maybe an export tax which pushes up the price the foreign buyer must pay. It's difficult to have price controls and completely free trade at the same time. You can see why.

Moves Away from Free Trade?

During the 1970s and early 1980s there were pleas for trade restrictions by some industries and labor unions in the United States. The trend toward lower tariffs has hurt some U.S. industries which were previously "protected" from foreign competition.

Also, it has been argued (and with some truth) that both the EC and Japan discriminate against U.S. imports—so why shouldn't we do the same? Now add into the picture high unemployment. Those are the ingredients needed to

trigger a round of "beggar-thy-neighbor" policies. Right?

Several American manufacturers of specialty steels joined with the United Steelworkers union in asking for import restrictions on specialty steel. The companies and the union charged that the foreign sellers were taking advantage of government subsidies in their own countries to undersell American producers in American markets.

The Trade Act of 1974 had set up a panel (called the International Trade Commission) to consider problems like this. The panel considered the question and decided to recommend a quota which would limit American imports of stainless and alloy-tool steel.

This is just one example of the way in which people who are hurt by imports try to keep domestic markets for themselves. (Or perhaps of how foreign sellers try to use special advantages to get into another country's markets!) There will always be some producers arguing (sometimes justifiably) that foreign sellers are using unfair methods to try to steal their customers.

What About the Problem of "Dumping"?

One method of unfair competition in world trade is called **dumping.** What it means is selling your product cheaper, to foreigners. It's "international price discrimination." It's selling to foreigners at less than "full cost of production."

Suppose your regular price is $10 and that price covers your average total cost and brings you an adequate profit. But suppose your marginal cost is only $7. (For a producer with monopoly power, MC is always less than the price. Remember?) So if you can produce another unit for $7 and sell it in a foreign market for $8, that adds a dollar to your profits. And that's "dumping."

Or suppose your government wants to help you to expand—maybe to increase employment or maybe to maintain a diversified economy or maybe for national defense reasons, or for whatever reason. So the government pays you subsidies. That lets you sell the product below cost. And when you do that in foreign markets, that's "dumping."

Or suppose you made a mistake and produced too much and you can't sell all of it. Do you cut the price and take a big loss? Or do you sell as much as you can without cutting the price and then sell the surplus to foreign buyers for half-price? Or for whatever you can get? If you do that, that's "dumping."

What does dumping do to the producers in the importing country? It destroys them! Nobody can compete with foreign products which are being sold below cost. So dumping is absolutely prohibited by all industrial nations. (Some LDCs, which have no domestic producers of the dumped products, often *encourage* dumping. It lets them get imported goods cheaper. But usually the net result is high profits for the importing company—not lower prices for the consumers.) How effective are the anti-dumping laws in the industrial nations? They help a lot. But they don't stop all of the dumping.

Some kinds of dumping are very hard to detect. Enterprising businesses work out all kinds of ways to "dump and hide it." It isn't always easy to find out what the "full cost of production" really is. And an American building contractor can always pay the "full invoice price" for Japanese steel and receive a 20% "cash rebate" under the table. He's maybe several thousand dollars richer and no one the wiser. And he won't pay income taxes on that money, either. See the problem?

In 1979 the Connors Steel Company of Birmingham, Alabama was charging that a Belgian steel firm (with help from the Belgian government) was selling specialized steel beams in this country at prices ranging from 21% to 48% below its European prices. Conners Steel was losing so many customers that it was considering closing its Huntington, West Virginia plant.

American producers brought other dumping charges against foreign producers during the 1970s. The U.S. Treasury Department is responsible for assessing and collecting the fines for dumping. Treasury agents have discovered many cases of "double invoicing" and secret rebates to U.S. importers by Japanese sellers.

In the late 1970s and early 1980s several grand jury investigations on dumping charges were in progress. The investigations could result in criminal penalties and in hundreds of millions of dollars in civil penalties as well. There's one case involving Japanese TV sets that has been under investigation since 1971.

Yes, dumping is a serious problem. And it will continue to be. Why? Because it's so profitable—both for the seller and for the buyer. When a seller wants to lower a price, that makes the buyer happy, too. So it's hard to stop it from happening.

The Three Major Parts of International Economics

At this point you know a lot about the economics of international trade, a lot about the effects of trade restrictions, and a good bit of what's been happening in trade policy. The question of **trade policy** (tariffs, non-tariff barriers, etc.) is one of the important parts of the study of international economics. But there are two more.

There's the question of the **balance of payments** for each nation. How much is it importing and exporting? And how much of its money is flowing into the international money markets?

And there's the question of **exchange rates**. How much Mexican money or Canadian money or Dutch money or Australian money can I buy with one dollar? That depends on the exchange rate, of course.

You already know a lot about trade policies. In the next two chapters you'll be finding out about the other two major issues in international economics: the *balance of payments*, and *exchange rates*.

SUMMARY AND SYNTHESIS

The same basic economic principles which apply within a nation, also apply between nations. Of course! From the point of view of economics, there's no difference! But when the trade is international, it crosses political boundaries and sometimes that complicates things.

International trade is both microeconomics and macroeconomics because it is concerned with both supply, demand, and the price mechanism, and with factors which increase or decrease the size of the spending flow.

International trade has become increasingly important to the American economy, both in the imports of consumer goods and industrial inputs, and in the value of our exports. In the early 1980s our exports and imports combined added up to about 15% of the GNP. For most other countries this figure is higher.

Statistics on international trade can be found in the same sources you use to look up statistics on the American economy. But for more detailed information and statistics you should go to the United Nations' *Statistical Yearbook* and the International Monetary Fund's *International Financial Statistics*.

Most of U.S. exports are manufactured goods—mostly machinery, and automobiles and trucks. Chemical exports are important, and coal has become more important as world oil prices have increased. Also, agricultural products are one of our major exports.

Our biggest import item is petroleum products. But we import a lot of manufactured goods too, including machinery, autos and trucks. We also import chemicals, and some agricultural products—but not nearly as much as we export.

Our biggest trading partner is Canada. The Latin American countries are next. Together, our trade within this hemisphere makes up about 40% of our total trade. Japan and Western Europe make up most of our remaining trade. But our trade with Australia, New Zealand, South Africa,

and Eastern European countries is large enough to be significant.

International cooperation to permit (and not to restrict) trade flows is of great importance in the 1980s. Still, all countries impose some trade restrictions.

Countries levy tariffs and impose import quotas, both of which restrict trade and increase product prices and reduce productivity and living standards.

"Non-tariff" and "non-quota" trade restrictions have become very important in the world of the 1980s. Japan has been especially good at establishing unusual product specifications to exclude foreign products from their market.

Free trade permits producers to follow the law of comparative advantage. The rapid growth of the American economy and the success of the European Common Market are examples of the economic benefits of permitting the free flow of trade over large areas.

In the early development of the United States the infant industry argument was used—we must protect our producers from the competition of more efficient, well-developed foreign producers. But the infant never wants to grow up!

The national defense argument says that we must protect domestic producers in case we need them in time of military emergency. The diversified economy argument says that we want to produce many different kinds of products to protect against world price fluctuations of any one product. This says we don't want to follow the law of comparative advantage.

If the nation establishes policies to support infant industries, or national defense industries, or to diversify the economy, the equitable way to do it is through government subsidies. Then the costs of these policies are clear (not hidden) and the burden is equitably shared—not placed just on the consumers of the restricted products.

The argument that we must "protect American workers from low-wage foreigners" is appealing, but ridiculous. It is only valid if we want to support industries in which we have comparative disadvantage—where worker productivity is low. This approach perpetuates international inefficiency and lowers the standards of living of the people.

The argument "we must keep our money at home" is also seductively appealing. But it's really an argument to end all trade!

The United States has been a high-tariff nation throughout its history, up until the mid-1930s. Throughout the last century and in the early part of this one, tariffs were kept high. This supported high prices for consumers and high profits for businesses. These high profits contributed to industrial growth.

In the early 1930s there was a general breakdown of international trade as nations throughout the world raised their tariffs, trying to support domestic employment. All foreign markets were closed to everybody! This worsened the depression. In 1934 the U.S. Congress passed the Reciprocal Trade Agreements Act which permitted the president to negotiate with other nations for mutual reductions in trade restrictions.

In 1947 the General Agreement on Tariffs and Trade (GATT) was formed. It carries on continuing negotiations to reduce or eliminate trade restrictions. The "Tokyo Round" of multilateral negotiations was started in 1973 and ended in April, 1979 with The Trade Pact for the 1980s. Significant reductions in trade restrictions have been achieved by GATT, and the Tokyo Round negotiations were the most successful of all.

In recent years there has been some relaxation of restrictions on trade with the Soviet Union. But this is a controversial issue.

In the early 1980s, there have been strong pressures from the American steel, automobile, and some other industries to limit foreign imports. And some instances of dumping (foreign producers selling in the United States at less than full cost) have been showing up. So there's still a lot of controversy on the international trade issue.

REVIEW EXERCISES

MAJOR CONCEPTS, PRINCIPLES, TERMS (Explain each carefully.)

comparative advantage
European Common Market (EC) (1957)
the "infant industry" argument
the "national defense" argument
the "diversified economy" argument
the "protect American workers" argument
the "keep the money at home" argument
multilateral negotiations
dumping

OTHER CONCEPTS AND TERMS (Explain each briefly.)

OPEC
LDCs
tariffs
specific tariff
ad valorem tariff
quotas
Smoot-Hawley Tariff Act (1930)

beggar-thy-neighbor policies
Reciprocal Trade Agreements Act (1934)
GATT (1947)
Kennedy Round
Tokyo Round

CURVES AND GRAPHS (Draw, label, and explain each.)

The Basis for Trade and International Equilibrium; The "Export Good" Case
The Basis for Trade and International Equilibrium; The "Import Good" Case
How a Tariff Slows or Stops Trade
The Effect of a Quota: Much like the Effect of a Tariff

QUESTIONS (Write out answers or jot down key points.)

1. Is international economics macroeconomics? or microeconomics? Explain, and give some examples to illustrate your answer.
2. Talk about the importance of international trade to the United States. Give some specific indications of how important it is and compare that with the importance of trade to some other nations.
3. Mention several sources of statistics on international economics, and explain each briefly.
4. Talk about the kinds of products that the U.S. economy is exporting and importing. Why do you think we are exporting and importing those kinds of products? Discuss.
5. Talk about the major "trading partners" of the United States. Who do we buy most of our imports from? Who do we sell most of our exports to? Can you explain this pattern of U.S. trade? Why do you think that's the way it is? Discuss.
6. Explain how the production possibility of the whole world is greatly increased by trade, and illustrate with graphs. (If you need help look back in Chapter 18 and review the production possibility graphs there.)
7. Discuss the issue of free trade. What's good about it? What are some of the problems? Under what circumstances do you think trade should be restricted (if any)? If trade is going to be restricted, what kinds of restrictions do you think should be used? Tariffs? Quotas? Or something else? Discuss in detail.
8. Give some of the highlights in the history of U.S. world trade policy.
9. Give some of the highlights in the new U.S. trade relationships with the communist countries.
10. Describe the international trade conditions in the world in the 1970s, and the multilateral negotiations which were trying to reduce trade restrictions.
11. In most cases when tariffs or quotas might be used, government subsidies could also be used to achieve the same objectives. What are some of the advantages and disadvantages of using the "government subsidies" approach? Discuss.

39 International Trade II: International Finance and the Balance of Payments

Chapter Objectives

- In the previous chapter you learned a lot about **the economics of international trade.** In this chapter you will find out about **international finance** and about the **international balance of payments.**

- When you finish studying this chapter you will be able **to explain how international finance works**—how people in one country **buy or sell money** from another country. And you will know the **meaning and importance** of **devaluation.**

- You will be able to set up a sample **international balance of payments,** to explain and give examples of **debit and credit items in international finance,** and to explain the difference between **capital** and **current** items.

- You will be able to explain **deficits and surpluses:** how they **occur,** what **problems they can create,** and **how they can be "balanced."**

- Finally, you will be able to give the highlights of **recent international balance of payments conditions** for the United States and to give some **reasons why** these conditions have occurred.

When you buy something, you expect to pay for it. Right? But suppose you're buying it from somebody in Canada? or Great Britain? or Argentina? Would you still expect to pay for it? Of course.

How Do You Pay Foreigners for Their Goods?

But how would you pay for it? The people in foreign countries don't want American dollars when they sell their goods. They want Canadian dollars or British pounds or Mexican pesos or whatever kind of money they use.

How would you like to get paid in Japanese yen? or French francs? or some other foreign money? Can't you just see yourself going around town trying to buy a tankful of gas with yen? or francs? or pesos?

If you are a New Yorker and go to California you won't have any problem spending your money. New York dollars and California dollars are the same. But if you are a New Yorker and go to Paris, you *will* have a problem spending your money.

People in Paris don't sell things for American dollars. They sell things for French francs.

So if you are going to buy things in Paris you are going to need some French francs. Where do you get them? Buy them. Where? From the bank, of course.

One Kind of Money Must Be Traded for Another

The money of each country is good only for buying things in that country. So when an American buyer wants to buy something from an Australian seller, American dollars must be exchanged for Australian dollars. Usually it's easy for a person to exchange money.

Would you believe that every day millions of American dollars are used to buy other kinds of money? Pounds and francs and marks and yen and pesos and all? That's right.

People and businesses (and governments) in the United States are buying things from people and businesses in other countries. So they must be buying the other countries' money to pay for all these things.

Why is this so important? What's the big deal about changing the money of one country for the money of another? Just this: It's the need to exchange one kind of money for another that brings up all of the problems of "international finance and the balance of payments."

HOW INTERNATIONAL FINANCE WORKS

How can you buy the money of another country? It's easy. Just go to the bank and do it. Here's how it works.

American banks have deposits of francs in French banks and deposits of pounds in British banks and lire in Italian banks and pesos in Mexican banks and deutsche marks in German banks and yen in Japanese banks—in fact, deposits of local money in other banks all over the world!

Small banks don't have deposits in all these foreign banks. But small banks have "correspondent relationships" with large banks. They can get foreign money from their correspondents. So no matter where you live, chances are you can go to your bank and get a check drawn in any kind of foreign money you want. It's as simple as that!

A Bank "Sells Dollars for Dollars"

Suppose your father needs a guaranteed check for $400 to send to your sister's college, for tuition. He goes to the bank and buys a guaranteed check from the bank. It's usually called a "bank money order."

Your father writes a check on his own checking account and gives it to the bank and he receives the bank's check in exchange. Then he mails the bank's check (money order) to the college. The guaranteed check (money order) is made out by the bank, to be paid to the college. Your father could go to the post office and get a postal money order and it would work exactly the same way.

After it's all over, what has happened? The bank has sold some of its dollars in exchange for some of your father's dollars. That's all. Your father has used American dollars to buy some of the bank's American dollars.

Why would anyone ever want to trade dollars for dollars? Only because the bank's check is guaranteed and is therefore acceptable at all other banks. But your father's check isn't so widely acceptable.

What does all this have to do with changing American dollars for foreign money? Just this: It works exactly the same way!

A Bank "Sells Francs for Dollars"

Suppose your sister happens to be going to college in France. Your father would ask the bank for a check drawn in francs instead of dollars. Your father could then mail the check to the French college to pay your sister's tuition. See how it works exactly the same way?

How can an American bank sell your father a check drawn in French francs? The American bank owns some francs. It has its francs on deposit in a French bank and can write checks on that deposit anytime it wants to.

Foreigners own U.S. dollar accounts in U.S. banks just as Americans own foreign money accounts in foreign banks. It's all very simple. That is, it's all very simple unless things get out of balance. And sometimes that happens.

What If the American Bank Runs out of Francs?

When my bank runs out of francs it can't sell me any more... unless it gets some from somewhere...

BANK

When your father buys francs, that uses up some of the American bank's deposits of francs. Suppose Americans keep buying more and more francs. What happens when the American banks run out of francs? The American bankers might say to the French bankers: "We'll put more dollars in your accounts with us, if you'll put more francs in our accounts with you." Suppose the French bankers agree. That takes care of the problem.

But suppose American consumers keep buying more and more French goods. That means they keep buying more and more French francs to pay for the goods. For a while the French banks may agree to keep putting more and more francs in the American banks' accounts—getting more and more dollar deposits in return. But what if this just keeps going on and on? What happens then?

Sooner or later the time will come when the French bank won't want any more dollars. So they'll stop trading francs for dollars. Then there's a problem. Who will trade good local money for unwanted surpluses of U.S. dollar deposits? Nobody.

Usually Trade Is in Balance—but Not Always

You would think that the French people would be buying dollars from the French banks. Why? Because French people like to buy American goods, of course.

At the same time the Americans are buying French champagne and perfumes and all, the French are buying American computers and chemicals and all. We're using up francs and giving them dollars all the time. They're using up dollars and giving us francs all the time.

The same thing is going on with Japan and Germany and Canada and Argentina and Greece and Libya and Britain and Brazil and everywhere else. It's sort of amazing how it all balances out. Usually it does, though.

But suppose Americans are buying a lot of things from France while the French aren't buying much from America. American banks would run out of francs—and the French banks would get so many dollars they wouldn't want any more.

That's when the problems arise. You'll be reading about the problems later in this chapter, and in the next.

THE IDEA OF A "BALANCE OF PAYMENTS"

From what you have been reading so far, you can see that there must be some kind of "balance" in international payments. When Americans buy foreign goods or services, that uses up American supplies of foreign money. When foreigners buy American goods or services, that uses up the foreigners' supplies of American money.

People in each country are always buying things from foreigners. The foreign money held by the banks in each country is always being added to, and always being used up. If the amounts being added are equal to the amounts being used up, it balances. There's no problem.

You Can't Buy Any More Than You Can Pay for (or Owe for)

Suppose the United States has a lot more exports than imports. What then? Soon the foreigners will run out of U.S. dollars. Then they will have to stop buying U.S. exports—that is, unless they can get more U.S. dollars from somewhere. It works the other way, too.

If Americans are trying to import a lot more than we're exporting, soon we run out of the foreign money we need to buy the foreign products. So unless we can borrow, or buy on credit, we can't import any more.

You can't buy any more than you can pay for (or owe for). If you can't get foreign money, you can't pay for foreign goods! Do you begin to see the importance of a nation's international balance of payments?

Every nation has an "international balance of payments." Wouldn't it be interesting for a nation to know about its international balance of payments? about *all of the sources of new foreign money?* and about *the ways the foreign money balances are being used up?* It sure would! It's one of the critical things that every nation keeps an eye on all the time!

What Is the International Balance of Payments?

Each nation keeps an accounting record of its international transactions. This accounting record is called the "balance of payments." The U.S. balance of payments adds up all of the millions of international transactions between U.S. individuals, businesses, and governments and foreign individuals, businesses, and governments.

The balance of payments shows merchandise imports and exports, payments and receipts for services, money being borrowed or lent or invested—*it shows all the ways that foreigners are getting and using up our money and all the ways that we are getting and using up theirs.* Each nation's international balance of payments shows that nation's trading and financial position with the rest of the world.

THE INTERNATIONAL BALANCE OF PAYMENTS

It has been said: "If you really understand the balance of payments, you really understand international finance. If you don't, you don't." In this section and the following ones you will learn to really understand the balance of payments.

The Balance of Payments Is an Accounting Statement

Just as each business has an accounting statement to show how much it's buying and selling, so does a nation. Just as everyone with a bank account has an accounting statement showing money going in and money going out, so does a nation. But with a nation's accounting statement—that is, with the international balance of payments—there's a big difference.

Businesses and individuals are solely responsible for making all of the transactions recorded on their own accounting statements. But not so for the nation. *The international balance of payments reflects the transactions made by all of the people, businesses, and governments in the country. It reflects all of the trade and money flows: between everyone in the country, and foreigners throughout the rest of the world.*

Millions of individual transactions are summarized in the nation's balance of payments. When you think of all the transactions involved it sounds complex. You'll be surprised how simple and easy to understand it is.

What Does the International Balance of Payments Show?

A nation's balance of payments for any year shows where the nation's **foreign exchange** (bank deposits of foreign money) came from, and where it went. That is, it shows *how the nation acquired its foreign exchange* during that year, and *how it used it up.*

The balance of payments shows how much foreign exchange was earned by selling goods and services to foreigners, and how much came in as loans and investments by foreigners. And it shows how much of the foreign money was used by buying goods and services from foreigners, making gifts to foreigners, and making loans and investments in foreign countries.

The balance of payments also shows whether or not the nation received enough foreign exchange to equal its foreign expenditures. Suppose the nation didn't get enough to meet its needs. The balance of payments shows how the nation got the money to make up the difference. Or maybe the nation received more foreign exchange than it used up. The balance of payments shows what happened to the surplus foreign money received.

Cause for Confusion: Each Transaction Involves Two Kinds of Money

From what's already been said you can see that the balance of payments is really quite a simple statement. But sometimes it appears to be confusing. Why? Mostly because each transaction involves two kinds of money—the money of the importing country and the money of the exporting country.

And another thing: Each transaction can be looked at from either point of view—from the point of view of the importing country, or of the exporting country. The best way I know of to keep from getting confused is to choose one currency and one country and always stick with that. Here's an example showing how we're going to do it.

Suppose your father is in the bank buying a check in francs to pay tuition to your sister's college in France. He writes a check in dollars and receives the bank's check, in francs. This transaction can be thought of in terms of francs: it uses up America's available deposits of francs. Or it can be thought of in terms of dollars: it makes more dollar deposits available to the French banks.

You can look at it either way. But you can't look at it *both ways,* or else you are double-counting. So how do we handle the problem? The next little section talks about that.

Debits and Credits

The international balance of payments shows how a nation gets foreign exchange, and how it uses up foreign exchange. We separate these two kinds of transactions by calling them **credit items** and **debit items.**

A credit item is any transaction which gives a nation more foreign money. A debit item is any transaction which uses up a nation's foreign money. That's one way to look at it.

Here's another way to look at it. You could say that *a debit is any transaction which provides more of your money to foreigners. A credit item is any item which brings back your money from foreigners*— that is, in which foreigners are using up their deposits of your money.

If we try to look at it both ways, it's going to be confusing. So we won't. But which way should we look at it? Which is the best way?

For small or underdeveloped nations like Indonesia or Singapore or Nigeria or Lesotho or Fiji or Nauru it would make a lot of sense to do it the first way: to think of credits as *how they earn their foreign exchange* and to think of debits as *how they spend it up.*

But for a large industrialized nation like the United States which is providing foreign exchange to nations all over the world, it seems to make more sense to look at it the other way—to think of debits as being *transactions which make American dollar deposits available to foreigners* and to think of credits as *transactions in which foreigners are using up their dollar deposits.*

To keep from getting confused by "country hopping" all over the globe, let's just look at everything from the point of view of the United States. Okay? And since we're going to be concentrating on the U.S. balance of payments, let's just decide to do it this way: A **debit** *is any transaction which makes U.S. dollars available to foreigners.* A **credit** *is any transaction which causes foreigners to use up those dollars.*

Some Examples of Debit and Credit Items

What is the U.S. balance of payments? It's an accounting statement of debit and credit items. It's a summary of all the debit and credit transactions between the people, businesses and governments in the United States and the rest of the world, for one year.

What kinds of things are included? You could already guess several of them. And you could guess which items are debits and which ones are credits.

Suppose Americans buy foreign cars or cameras or fly to Europe on British Airways or to the Orient on Japan Airlines. All those transactions give foreigners more U.S. dollars. All debit items? Right.

What about foreigners buying American coal? and machinery? and shipping it via U.S. ships? In all those transactions, foreigners are using up their U.S. dollars. Credit items? Of course.

Suppose the U.S. government gives money to one of the less developed countries (LDCs) so they can build roads to the interior and open up new agricultural land. Does that make dollars available to foreigners? Of course. Another debit item.

What if some of the Saudi Arabians decide

to invest their big oil earnings in General Motors stock. Does that use up their supply of dollars? Sure. It's a credit item.

Debits and Credits Are Not All Alike

You can see from these few examples that not all debit and credit items are alike. Here's another example.

Suppose a group of travelers from Egypt decided to charter a Pan American plane for an around-the-world tour. When they paid Pan Am they would use up some of their dollars. Then they would get a long plane ride and that would be the end of it.

How different that is from the Saudi Arabians investing in General Motors stock! Both are credit items on the U.S. balance of payments. But the plane trip uses up the dollars and that's the end of it.

The GM stock purchase uses up the dollars, *but that's not the end of it.* The Saudi Arabians can always sell the stock and get dollars back if they want to. Meanwhile they can earn dividends on the stock and get more dollars. Also, as stockholders they are part-owners of the corporation and have a voice in the management. It makes a lot of difference how the dollars are used up! Right?

Anything that pushes our dollars into foreign hands is a debit!

When foreigners push the dollars back, that's a Credit!

Current Items and Capital Items

The above example illustrates the two kinds of transactions on the international balance of payments:

    (a) **current items**, which involve no future claims, and

    (b) **capital items**, which do involve future claims.

Americans make dollars available to foreigners on "current items" by:

    (a) buying goods from foreigners,

    (b) buying services from foreigners, and

    (c) giving dollars to foreigners.

On capital items Americans make dollars available to foreigners by:

    (a) investing in foreign countries,

    (b) lending to foreigners, and

    (c) depositing dollars in foreign banks.

The foreigners can use up their dollars in exactly the same ways. *They can use up their dollars on current items and get no future claims against dollars.* They can buy American goods, or American services, or make money gifts to people or organizations in the United States.

But if they wish, *they can use their dollars for capital transactions and get future claims to more dollars.* They can lend to Americans, invest in American stocks, bonds, real estate, etc., or deposit their dollars in American banks or savings institutions.*

Both the current credit items and the capital credit items use up the foreigners' holdings of dollar deposits. But as the years go by it makes a lot of difference which way they have been using up their dollars! Why? Because *each capital credit transaction gives them future claims to more dollars.*

The investments in the United States by foreigners (credit items) lead to the eventual outflow of more dollars to foreigners (debit items). Just as individuals with lots of invest-

ments can pay for what they want with their investment income, also nations with enough foreign investments can pay for the foreign goods they want with the income from their foreign investments.

Debits and Credits, and Deficits and Surpluses

As the foreigners buy American goods they use up their dollar deposits. Credit items. As we buy more goods from them, they get more dollar deposits. Debit items. Of course.

If the "debit merchandise items" (imports) add up to more than the "credit merchandise items" (exports), then we say there's a **deficit** on merchandise transactions. A deficit occurs whenever there are more debits than credits. But if the credit items (exports) add up to more than the debit items (imports) then there's a **surplus** on merchandise transactions.

What about the other kinds of transactions? What about buying services from and selling services to foreigners? Can there be a "deficit" or "surplus" balance on services transactions? Of course. Each of the items—each kind of transaction in the balance of payments—can be "balanced off." The debit items can be subtracted from the credit items to see if there's a deficit or a surplus.

If the debits amount to more than the credits, then the balance (the "net" figure) will show a deficit. If the credits are greater, the balance will show a surplus.

For example, suppose Americans have been making more long-term investments in foreign countries (debits—giving them dollars) than foreigners have been making in the United States (credits—using up dollars). When the "long-term investments" item is balanced, it will show a net deficit—that is, more dollars are being given to foreigners than they are using up.

In a minute you're going to be looking at the U.S. balance of payments. When you do, how are you going to be able to tell if an item is a debit item or a credit item? And how can you tell

---

*American dollars, while they are being held by foreign banks (or foreign branches of U.S. banks) and are available to be loaned, are called Eurodollars. In the early 1980s there were hundreds of billions of dollars flowing through this "Eurodollar money market." Much of the money comes from OPEC oil profits.

if the balance for any group of transactions shows a deficit? or a surplus? Here's how:

> Debit items (and deficit balances) always carry a **minus sign**.
>
> Credit items (and surplus balances) always carry a **plus sign**, or **no sign** at all.

When you look at a balance of payments table you can easily distinguish the debits and the deficits from the credits and the surpluses. Just look at the sign!

The "Overall Balance" and the Role of "Official Transactions"

Each group of items (each major heading on the balance of payments) represents transactions going both ways—both debit and credit transactions. For each one, the **net balance** is figured out—that is, the debits are subtracted from the credits.

Some of the net figures will show a deficit and some will show a surplus, of course. So the next thing you do is just balance off all of these deficit and surplus items to find out if the nation has an **overall deficit** or an **overall surplus** in its balance of payments.

But mustn't the overall balance of payments always balance? Yes. It must. Whenever someone uses dollars to buy American goods, there must be a source of those dollars. They must come from somewhere!

So how can there be an overall deficit? or an overall surplus? The overall deficit or surplus is figured *before* the **official transactions** are considered.

Throughout the year, "official transactions" (also called "official reserve transactions") are being undertaken. These "official transactions" are made by the Federal Reserve and by the central banks in other countries to keep the money flows in balance.

Whenever foreigners are trying to buy more dollars than the commercial banks and other private holders of dollars want to sell, what happens? The Fed sells dollars. The central banks in other countries also own dollars and they may sell some, too. That's how foreigners get the dollars they need to continue buying American goods. Otherwise trade would be cut off.

Or suppose Americans are trying to buy more foreign money (to buy foreign goods and services). And suppose the private holders of foreign money don't want to sell that much. What happens? The Fed buys dollars and pays out some of its holdings of foreign money. The foreign central banks buy dollars and pay out local money, too. So then Americans can buy the foreign money they want. Trade can continue.

What would happen if the Fed and all of the other central banks decided to stop all of these "official transactions"? Suppose foreigners wanted to buy more American goods, but they couldn't get the dollars? And suppose the Fed wouldn't sell any to the foreigners? The foreigners just couldn't buy the American goods!

"But," you say, "if the foreigners wanted the dollars bad enough, they'd find *some way* to get them!" Well, maybe so. Some of them could borrow dollars. Some could buy on credit.

Some foreign buyers would be willing to offer more of their own money in exchange just to get the dollars they wanted. So the international value of the dollar would go up. And, as you'll be finding out soon, such things really do happen. But before we get into that you need to know more about the U.S. balance of payments accounts.

At this point, just remember that "official transactions" are always being undertaken to help keep the supply of dollars (and of every other kind of money) more or less in balance with the foreign demand.

If all of the "non-official" transactions were always in balance (non-official debit items always equal to non-official credit items) then there would be no need for the "official transactions." But during any day or week or month, whenever the non-official items are not in balance—whenever the "balance" shows a net deficit or a net surplus—then official transactions occur.

Does the Balance of Payments Balance? Or Not?

You can always see how far (and which way) the *non-official transactions* are out of balance, by looking to see what *official transactions* were needed to maintain the balance.

Suppose the Fed has been *buying up foreign money and paying out dollars.* Then you know that non-official transactions on the U.S. balance of payments have been running a **surplus.** (Credit items exceed debit items.) Foreigners have been using up more dollars than they have been getting back. The Fed has been supplying them with the extra dollars.

But if the Fed has been *using up its holdings of foreign money to buy up surplus dollars* then you know that non-official transactions on the U.S. balance of payments have been running a **deficit.** (Debit items exceed credit items.) American buyers have been paying out more dollars than foreigners have been using up. The Fed has been buying up the surplus dollars.

So does the balance of payments always balance? or not? You already know the answer. If you include the official transactions, then yes. It always balances. But if you exclude the official transactions, then no. It's almost always out of balance—almost always showing a surplus or a deficit.

Whenever someone says that the **balance of payments** has been running a **deficit** (or a surplus) what they're talking about is the *non-official transactions.* They're talking about the deficit or surplus which had to be offset (balanced) by the official transactions of the central banks.

THE U.S. BALANCE OF PAYMENTS ACCOUNTS

What does the balance of payments show? Exactly what you've been reading about. It shows a summary of all of the current items and the capital items, the debits and credits, the defi-

cits and surpluses.

Table 39-1 shows the U.S. balance of payments accounts for 1981. If you would like to see more recent balance of payments figures, you can find them in your library. They're in the *Survey of Current Business,* in the appendix tables of the *Federal Reserve Bulletin,* in the appendix tables of the *Economic Report of the President,* in the *Statistical Abstract of the United States,* and in several other sources. But these tables will be much easier to understand and interpret after you have studied Table 39-1 and the explanations.

Merchandise Exports and Imports

The first group of transactions on the balance of payments is the current items. The most important of all of the current items is merchandise exports and imports. In 1981, merchandise exports and imports were between $200 and $300 billion for the United States. No other item on the balance of payments is anywhere near as big as the merchandise item.

If you were to look at the U.S. balance of payments for past years you would see that merchandise exports and imports have always been by far the biggest item on the balance of payments. That's true for other countries, too. But after all, that's what you would expect. *Trading things* is mostly what international trade is all about!

Over the years, U.S. exports and imports have been increasing rapidly. In 1950, U.S. merchandise exports and imports amounted to about $10 billion. In 1960, the figure was about $20 billion. By 1970 it was up to more than $40 billion. Then in four years (by 1974) it more than doubled, to about $100 billion. And by 1981? Exports were $236 billion and imports were up to $264 billion!

A good bit of the recent increase has been due to inflation, of course. The high price of oil has had a lot of impact. Still it is clear that there has been an upsurge in world trade.

**Table 39-1   The U.S. Balance of Payments Accounts, 1981
(billions of dollars)**

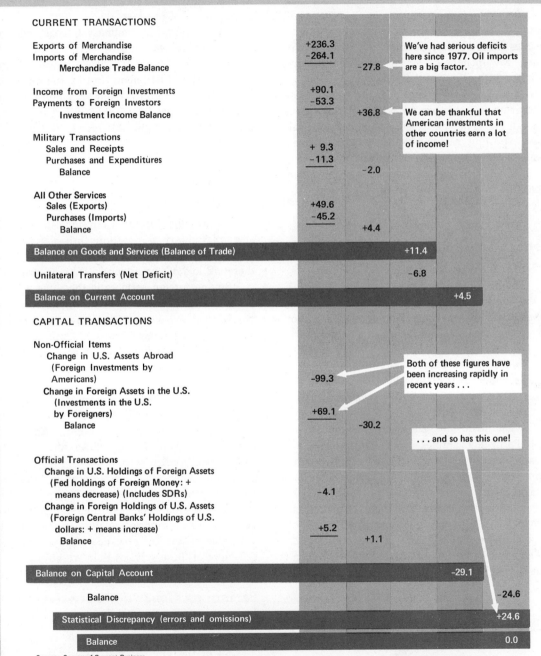

CURRENT TRANSACTIONS		
Exports of Merchandise	+236.3	
Imports of Merchandise	–264.1	
Merchandise Trade Balance		–27.8
Income from Foreign Investments	+90.1	
Payments to Foreign Investors	–53.3	
Investment Income Balance		+36.8
Military Transactions		
Sales and Receipts	+ 9.3	
Purchases and Expenditures	–11.3	
Balance		–2.0
All Other Services		
Sales (Exports)	+49.6	
Purchases (Imports)	–45.2	
Balance		+4.4

Balance on Goods and Services (Balance of Trade)	+11.4

Unilateral Transfers (Net Deficit)	–6.8

Balance on Current Account	+4.5

CAPITAL TRANSACTIONS		
Non-Official Items		
Change in U.S. Assets Abroad		
(Foreign Investments by		
Americans)	–99.3	
Change in Foreign Assets in the U.S.		
(Investments in the U.S.		
by Foreigners)	+69.1	
Balance		–30.2
Official Transactions		
Change in U.S. Holdings of Foreign Assets		
(Fed holdings of Foreign Money: +		
means decrease) (Includes SDRs)	–4.1	
Change in Foreign Holdings of U.S. Assets		
(Foreign Central Banks' Holdings of U.S.		
dollars: + means increase)	+5.2	
Balance		+1.1

Balance on Capital Account	–29.1

Balance	–24.6

Statistical Discrepancy (errors and omissions)	+24.6

Balance	0.0

Annotations in the figure:

"We've had serious deficits here since 1977. Oil imports are a big factor."

"We can be thankful that American investments in other countries earn a lot of income!"

"Both of these figures have been increasing rapidly in recent years . . ."

". . . and so has this one!"

Source: Survey of Current Business
For the sake of clarity and easy comparison the items in this table are grouped differently than as published by the Department of Commerce. The figures in this table are the preliminary figures for 1981 and are subject to revision. Some figures do not add up because of errors, omissions, and statistical discrepancies.

The merchandise imports and exports shown in Table 39-1 reflect *all* of the physical things being shipped out of and shipped into the country. They include imports and exports of all kinds and consumer goods and capital goods: textiles, automobiles, machinery, industrial supplies, raw materials—*every physical thing* being shipped into or out of the country.

It makes no difference how the merchandise import or export is being paid for: perhaps by a foreign aid grant; perhaps by an American business exporting machinery to set up a plant overseas; perhaps by foreign borrowing. It makes no difference. Whatever is shipped out is a merchandise export; whatever is shipped in is a merchandise import.

Foreign Investment Income

The investment income shown in Table 39-1 is the interest and profits earned by the overseas investments of Americans. The net surplus from investment income has increased rapidly in recent years.

In 1970 it was only about $4 billion. In 1974 it was almost $10 billion, by 1978, almost $20 billion, and by 1981 the surplus was almost $40 billion.

What made investment income increase so fast? Partly high interest rates. But also U.S. investments abroad have increased rapidly in recent years—just as foreign investments in the United States also have increased rapidly.

Total income going to foreigners from their American investments only amounted to about $6 billion in 1972. By 1978, it was almost $22 billion. But in 1981 it was more than $53 billion. But that still left us with a *net surplus* of almost $40 billion!

Military Transactions

Until recently, the military transactions item usually showed a large deficit balance ever since the 1950s. But in recent years that has changed—partly because of reductions in U.S. military involvement in foreign countries. But mostly because the foreign governments now are paying more of the costs.

In the 1950s the "military transactions" net deficit balance was ranging between $2 and $3 billion a year; in the late 1960s it was ranging between $3 and $4 billion. But by the mid-1970s it had declined to only about $2 billion per year. And you can see from Table 39-1 that in 1981, military transactions showed a deficit of $2 billion.

Other Services

Technically, income from investments and also all military transactions are classified as "services." But as you can see from the table, there are lots of "other services" transactions.

Buying foreign services is the same as buying foreign goods—except that no goods need to be shipped anywhere. These services include such things as foreign ships hauling American goods, airlines carrying foreign passengers, and the Paris laundry washing the clothes of the American tourists.

Travel and transportation is the biggest "other services" item. It's always a deficit item on the U.S. balance of payments. Americans travel a lot, fly on foreign airlines, and ship a lot of goods on foreign ships.

Some other kinds of services include fees and royalties and other kinds of payments to consultants, engineers, performers, brokers, lawyers, etc. These services usually balance out with a surplus on the U.S. balance of payments. We sell more of these services than we buy.

Balance on Goods and Services: the Balance of Trade

All of the international transactions you've been reading about so far are called "trade items." All of them are included in what is called the balance of trade.

The biggest item in the balance of trade, of course, is **merchandise transactions**: exports and imports. All the other transactions included in the balance of trade are classified as **service items**.

The balance of trade includes all of a country's *buying and selling of goods and services*—and nothing else. Be sure not to confuse "the balance of trade" with the **balance of payments.** *The balance of trade is only a part of the balance of payments.* It's the biggest and perhaps the most important part. But it leaves out a lot of the "money-flow transactions." These money transactions are undertaken to finance a lot of the goods-and-services-flow transactions which show up in the balance of trade.

The U.S. Trade Balance. In 1981 the U.S. trade balance showed a surplus of more than $11 billion. You can see that in Table 39-1.

The table also shows you that the **merchandise trade balance** was in deficit to the tune of almost $30 billion! Our huge merchandise deficits began in 1977 and have continued most of the time ever since.

In January of 1982 the deficit was more than $5 billion. If that continued all year, the deficit would be $60 billion! Our surplus of foreign investment income wouldn't be large enough to offset that! (More on this problem, later.)

Unilateral Transfers

Every year billions of U.S. dollars are given to foreigners. The U.S. government gives money (grants) to other governments; Americans send money (remittances) to foreign relatives and friends and churches and other worthy causes. This has been going on year after year for several decades. These gifts and grants are called **unilateral** (one-way) **transfers.**

The U.S. "net deficit of unilateral transfers" has never dropped below $2 billion a year since World War II. In the early to mid-1970s the figure was running between $3 and $4 billion a year. By 1978 it was up to $5 billion, and by 1981 to almost $7 billion.

The Balance on Current Account

Table 39-1 shows that the U.S. **balance on current account** in 1981 amounted to a surplus of $4.5 billion. The **merchandise deficit** of $27.8 billion was offset mostly by the surplus of **foreign investment** income ($36.8 billion).

How was this $4.5 billion current account surplus "balanced"? By capital transactions? Right. That's what the next section talks about.

"FUTURE CLAIMS" ITEMS: THE CAPITAL TRANSACTIONS

Suppose somebody buys London Bridge and has it dismantled and brings it to the United States to be used as a tourist attraction. That's a "merchandise import." But suppose a person buys London Bridge and leaves it where it is and puts up a tollgate to collect money and make a profit. That's a foreign investment.

What Is (Non-Official) Foreign Investment?

When businesses build factories overseas, or buy machinery and equipment to be used overseas, or pay for any kind of goods which are to be left in the foreign countries to earn income, that's foreign investment.

What about buying foreign bonds? Suppose interest rates on bonds in Germany or Great Britain or France or Japan or some other country happen to be higher than in this country. Wouldn't it be good business for you to exchange some of your dollars for foreign money

If you want to understand all this, you'd better keep looking back at the table!

and buy some of those high-interest foreign bonds? Sure it would. People do that, too.

Not only do private individuals and businesses invest in foreign securities. The U.S. government lends money to foreign governments by buying their bonds. Over the years, the United States has made a lot of dollars available to foreign governments this way.

Suppose foreign banks were offering high interest on savings accounts. Wouldn't it make sense for you to take your dollars out of your American savings account, trade the dollars for foreign money, and then deposit the foreign money in a foreign savings account? and receive more interest? Sure it would. Do people do things like that? Of course they do.

When interest rates in one country get out of balance with interest in other countries, investors shift their liquid assets (money and savings accounts and short-term securities) from one place to another. Investors try to get the highest return on their money.

(You can see how all this could complicate things when a nation is trying to carry out a policy of tight money to control inflation. Money flows in from overseas? Right!)

Short-Term and Long-Term (Non-Official) Capital Transactions

All of the examples you are reading about here are examples of foreign investments—some short-term, some long-term. Investments in buildings and machinery and equipment and long-term securities are called long-term capital transactions. Investments in savings accounts or short-term securities or short-term business loans or buying or selling on credit are short-term capital transactions.

Short-term capital movements are easy to make in a hurry. Sometimes there will be a lot of short-term money flowing into the United States. Maybe it's because of higher interest rates here. Or maybe foreigners think the dollar may appreciate (get more valuable as compared with other kinds of money).

Sometimes it goes the opposite way. People may see better opportunities abroad. So they will start shifting their short-term funds out of U.S. banks and short-term securities, and into banks and short-term securities in other countries.

In Table 39-1, the long-term and short-term capital transactions are lumped together. You can see that non-official net foreign investment by Americans amounted to $99.3 billion. This is a debit item. It makes dollars available to foreigners.

Non-official net foreign investment in the United States amounted to $69.1 billion. That's how they used up a lot of their dollars. Credit item on the U.S. balance of payments? Of course. But not a big enough credit to offset our foreign investment debit. So there was a deficit of $30.2 billion on the non-official capital account for 1981.

Official Transactions: Central Bank Changes in Foreign Exchange Reserves

The official transactions are changes in central bank holdings of foreign money. If all of the unofficial transactions balance out, then there won't be much need for official transactions. But sometimes it doesn't work out that way.

The total amount of dollars being given to foreigners must equal the total amount of dollars being received by foreigners. Obviously. And all of the dollars received by foreigners must either be spent up or given away or lent or deposited or invested—or just held.

But who wants to hold dollars? There's no profit in that. If a business gets some dollars which aren't needed right away, the dollars would be invested in something—maybe U.S. government bonds or Exxon stocks or savings accounts—to get some income. All these investment transactions would use up the surplus dollars and would cause the balance of payments to balance.

But suppose foreign businesses get dollars and they don't want dollars at all. They want their own money so they can pay their workers and buy more raw materials and stay in business! What does the business do with its dollars?

Trades them for local money at the bank. Of course.

But suppose the bank already has all the dollar deposits it wants to hold? The banker might say: "We don't want any more dollars." What then?

You already know what would happen. Right? The central bank could buy up the surplus dollars from the local banks and pay them with local money.

The central banks don't *have* to do that. Maybe sometimes they wouldn't. But in 1981 they sure did! The Fed increased its holdings of foreign money by more than $4 billion, and foreign central banks bought up more than $5 billion in American dollars.

Statistical Discrepancy: Errors and Omissions

Suppose the government statisticians add up and balance out all of the current transactions, and all of the capital transactions including the official transactions—and then find out that *it doesn't balance!*

Maybe there are more debits. Or maybe more credits. What does that prove? It proves that some of the transactions which actually occurred were not recorded.

What do the statisticians do when the payments are out of balance? They put in a debit or credit item big enough to bring the payments into balance. They call this balancing figure **statistical discrepancy.**

Up until recently it was usually small. But since 1978 it's been large and getting larger. In 1981 (Table 39-1) it was up to almost $25 billion!

Sometimes these **errors and omissions** occur innocently. Sometimes transactions just aren't officially recorded. But sometimes errors and omissions are done on purpose.

If a country has tight restrictions on trade or on foreign exchange transactions, some people will try very hard to get around those restrictions. Prohibited or taxed items will be smuggled in. Some people will sneak out of the country

carrying a suitcase full of currency to evade government restrictions.

Americans travelling abroad sometimes deposit dollars in foreign banks. When there is a lot of short-term capital (money) floating around among nations, the errors and omissions figure is likely to be large.

Smuggling can be important, too. It's a pretty sure thing that the marijuana coming in from Mexico isn't showing up on the official merchandise import list! The Mexican sellers wind up with more U.S. dollars than our "recorded imports from Mexico" shows. That's statistical discrepancy.

WHAT ABOUT A CHRONIC PAYMENTS DEFICIT?

Almost every year since the 1940s the U.S. balance of payments has shown a deficit, year after year. How is it possible for Americans to keep pushing more dollars into the hands of foreigners than the foreigners want to spend, give away, lend, or invest in the United States? Isn't there some limit to this? Yes. Of course there is.

Most of the time for the past 25 years and up to the 1970s the U.S. deficit was usually small: no more than $2 or $3 billion a year. In a few years the country even ran surpluses. But in 1970 the deficit leaped to about $10 billion—then in 1971 to the (at that time, unbelievable) figure of $29.8 billion! (You'll hear all about the 1971 crisis in the next chapter.)

The deficits were smaller after 1971, and in 1975 the U.S. balance of payments ran a small surplus. But by 1977 the deficit went into the $30 to $40 billion range. It stayed there during 1978.

In 1979, '80, and '81 it was "saved by the **statistical discrepancy**—billions of U.S. dollars flowing into this country from who-knows-where, to pay for who-knows-what. Except for that, the deficit in 1981 (Table 39-1) would have been about $25 billion! Why such huge deficits? The high price (and high U.S. consumption) of oil was the biggest single factor. More on this in the next chapter, too.

How has the United States financed all these deficits? Were the foreign central banks willing to hold billions of additional dollars, year after year, just letting them pile up? To some extent, yes. But not entirely. Some of the deficit was financed by giving up reserve assets: mostly gold.

After World War II the United States held more than $25 billion in gold. Over the years more than half of that gold has been shipped to foreign central banks to cover some of the U.S. payments deficits.

When a Nation Runs Out of Reserve Assets, What Then?

A nation with a **chronic payments deficit** must do something to overcome the chronic deficit. Otherwise all of its **reserve assets** (gold, SDRs, and foreign money) will run out. Also, its money will become unacceptable at the foreign central banks.

Possible Ways to Cut the Deficit. But what can a nation do? What are the alternatives? If you run your finger down the list of items on the balance of payments (Table 39-1), you can see the kinds of things which would bring the payments into balance.

We could try to export more and import less. We could spend less on overseas military transactions and try to keep Americans from using foreign travel and transportation services. We could try to sell more American services to foreigners.

We could try to cut down on unilateral transfers: Stop giving so much money away. We could also try to discourage Americans from making foreign investments abroad. If we could accomplish all these things, certainly we would take care of the deficit. But how do we do that?

We might try to set up restrictions: on imports, on foreign travel, on foreign investments, etc. But you already know that the "trade restrictions" approach is not a good way to try to solve international economic problems. Isn't there some other way? Yes.

Reduce the International Value of the Dollar? Maybe we should **devalue the dollar**— that is, revalue the dollar downward so that foreigners can buy dollars cheaper. That's what was done in 1971 when the U.S. balance of payments was running the biggest deficit in history. Maybe that's the right approach!

In the next chapter you will find out about devaluation. And you'll also find out about international exchange and about the serious problems of recent years. It talks about exchange rates and floating currencies and gold and SDRs and things like that.

But before you go on, try to spend a good bit of time reviewing (and yes, memorizing) the important kinds of transactions in the balance of payments accounts. You're going to be seeing references to these things in newspapers and magazines all your life. Unless you learn all of it well you won't remember enough to understand it next time. So try to take the time.

SUMMARY AND SYNTHESIS

With international trade, one kind of money must be traded for another. Usually that's no problem. But if **trade is not in balance**, a nation which is **importing** a lot more than it is **exporting**, soon will **run out of foreign money.**

When the **international demand** for a country's money is low, the value of that money in international exchange **will go down.** But if everybody is trying to buy one kind of money (say American dollars), then the value of that kind of money (American dollars) will go up.

The international balance of payments is an accounting statement which shows for one nation all of the ways it has acquired foreign exchange (the money of other nations) and all of the ways that it has used up its foreign exchange.

The balance of payments is made up of debit transactions and credit transactions. A debit transaction on the U.S. balance of payments is any transaction which makes U.S. dollars available to foreigners. A credit is any transaction in which foreigners are using up those dollars.

When we buy things from foreigners or pay them anything for any reason, that's a debit. But when we sell things to foreigners, or receive payments from foreigners for any reason, that's a credit.

Current items are items which are finished in the present and create no future claims on anybody. Capital items are transactions which involve future claims.

A deficit in any category on the balance of payments means that the debit items add up to more than the credit items. A surplus is created whenever the opposite occurs.

If there's a deficit or surplus in the overall balance, then the difference must be made up by official transactions. The central banks provide more (or less) money to bring things into balance.

For example, if the U.S. balance of payments is running a surplus, foreigners are using up their dollars. But the Fed could supply additional dollars to the foreign banking systems. Then the foreign banks can provide dollars so that the foreign buyers can continue to buy American goods. Without these official transactions when foreign banks run out of dollars, foreign buyers would be forced to stop buying American goods.

The largest item on the balance of payments is merchandise exports and imports. In 1981, merchandise exports amounted to $236 billion, and merchandise imports amounted to $264 billion. So there was a deficit of about $28 billion.

Our foreign investment income in 1981 amounted to $90 billion and our payments to foreigners were only $53 billion. So there was a surplus of $37 billion. These figures, both inflows and outflows, have been increasing a lot in recent years. The U.S. surplus has been growing fast, too.

The balance of trade means the balance on goods and services—that is, all current transactions, excluding unilateral transfers. It includes merchandise transactions, income and payments on foreign investments, military transactions, and payments for all other services.

In 1981 the United States received in payment for all other services, $50 billion, and we paid to foreigners $45 billion.

The overall balance on goods and services (the balance of trade) for 1981 showed a surplus of $11 billion.

Capital transactions generate future claims— repayments, and/or payments of interest. If General Motors decides to build a foreign plant, that's a long-term capital transaction. But if you decide to deposit your money in a Swiss bank account, or sell something to someone in England on credit, that's a short-term capital transaction.

In 1981, Americans invested $99 billion in foreign countries, while foreigners invested $69 billion in this country. These investment figures have increased greatly in recent years.

The official transactions are used to offset the surpluses or deficits which are generated by the day-to-day transactions between the businesses and people in the two nations. In 1981, official transactions were large enough to be significant, but were almost in balance.

When a nation continues to run deficits, it can run out of reserve assets. If it can't get any more foreign money, it can't import any more foreign goods! What will happen then? Devaluation? Maybe. That's what you'll be reading about in the next chapter.

REVIEW EXERCISES

MAJOR CONCEPTS, PRINCIPLES, TERMS (Explain each carefully.)

the balance of payments

current item

the balance of trade

capital item

credit item

deficit

debit item

surplus

official transactions

OTHER CONCEPTS AND TERMS (Explain each briefly.)

unilateral transfers

merchandise trade

statistical discrepancy

balance

foreign exchange reserve

"other services"

QUESTIONS (Write out answers or jot down key points.)

1. Explain how a person could buy "foreign exchange"—that is, a "check" drawn in the money of some foreign country. Describe the process.

2. How might the supply of and demand for some kind of money in the world money markets get out of balance? What might happen to cause a surplus? a shortage? Explain.

3. Explain why each nation must have a balance in its money payments with other nations. What would happen if there wasn't a "balance"? Does the statement: "You can't buy any more than you can pay for, or owe for" help to explain it?

4. Explain this statement: "International finance often seems much more confusing than it really is, simply because each transaction involves two kinds of money instead of only one." What's a good way to keep from getting confused?

5. Over past years, the United States has usually run a surplus trade balance, but a deficit "balance of payments." Explain what this statement means. Then give some reasons why it happened that way.

6. Describe the role of central banks in international finance.

7. List some examples of international transactions which would show up as debit items and some which would show up as credit items on the balance of payments. Explain why each is a debit item or credit item.

8. "When you think of all the unrelated kinds of debit items and credit items on the balance of payments it seems like it would be a miracle if it ever came out in balance!" Discuss.

9. Can you list all the items on the international balance of payments, and explain what each one means? Before you leave this chapter it would be a good idea for you to practice until you can do that.

40

International Trade III: The Collapse and Reorganization of the World's Exchange System

Chapter Objectives

- In the two previous chapters you have learned a lot about **the economics of international trade and finance.** This chapter will tell you **what has been happening, what some of the problems are, and what's being done.**

- When you finish studying this chapter you will be able to **explain international exchange rates,** and the meaning of **devaluation.**

- You will be able to explain what has been happening to the **international value of the U.S. dollar** and **to international exchange rates in general, and why.**

- You will be able to **describe the Bretton Woods system** and to explain **why it was set up, how it worked, and why it collapsed.**

- You will be able to explain the **important role** which **gold has played** in the past, and how in recent years the **International Monetary Fund** and **SDRs** have been **"playing the role of gold"** in international finance.

- Finally, you will be able to explain the **dollar crisis** of the late 1970s, the **strong dollar** of the early 1980s, and the **future outlook for "managed floating" exchange rates.**

The world really turned upside down in the 1970s. A real *Poseidon Adventure!* Well, not quite that bad. But in some ways, almost.

ECONOMIC CHANGES IN THE 1970s

Early in the 1970s the international exchange system collapsed. The position of the United States in world trade changed greatly. You found out something about that in the last chapter. Also the position of the U.S. dollar in the world's financial markets really changed. You'll

be reading about that in this chapter.

Between 1973 and 1974 oil prices just about quadrupled—a four-fold increase! Then throughout the 1970s world oil prices went up even more. That forced up the prices of just about everything—fuels, lubricants, chemicals, fertilizers, etc. So worldwide costs of production in industry and agriculture shot upward.

There were world shortages of food. So food prices went higher than ever. So did prices of just about everything else. We had a worldwide inflation like nothing the world had ever known before. And in the mid-1970s, a depression, too. The worst since the 1930s.

As the prices of things went crazy, the traditional relationships between nations—among trading partners—were all pushed out of shape. The prices of some raw materials skyrocketed. The prices of some things went up and just stayed high. But some fell.

The price of sugar shot up from about $200 a ton to more than $1300 a ton. Then it dropped back. The price of copra (for making coconut oil) jumped from less than $200 a ton to about $600 a ton. Then a year later the price was down to $100 a ton.

No, it wasn't really a *Poseidon Adventure*. Not quite. But it was a kind of topsy-turvy "fruit basket-turn-over" world like no one had ever seen before!

Governments Tried to Work Things Out

Through all of this economic turbulence the governments of all countries were doing whatever they could think of (both at home and in world markets) to try to work things out. Everybody was doing something to try to meet the emergency situations brought about by the "new times" of the 1970s.

There were wage-price freezes and monetary and fiscal controls and money devaluations and special trading deals and some trade restrictions and subsidies—all kinds of things going on. You already know about most of the things that were done on the U.S. domestic scene. This chapter will be talking about what happened on the international scene.

Here you'll find out about the collapse of the international exchange system, and about what has been going on since the system collapsed.

HOW THE DOLLAR CRISIS EVOLVED

In August of 1971, President Nixon announced a wage-price freeze. He also made announcements that shattered the world trade and finance arrangements which had existed for the past quarter-century. What had happened to force such drastic action?

The problem was a serious turn for the worse in the U.S. balance of payments deficit. We were pushing more dollars into the hands of foreigners so fast that they didn't want to hold them. Let's go back over the 30 years since World War II and watch exactly what happened.

The Years After World War II: "The Dollar Gap"

In the years just after World War II, the United States was running an international payments surplus. Other countries were trying to spend more American dollars than they were getting. To try to "close the gap" and help foreigners to get the dollars they needed to buy American goods, billions of dollars in grants and loans were made by the U.S. government and by American businesses to foreign governments and banks and businesses.

The U.S. dollars were in very short supply. Why did everybody want dollars? So they could buy U.S. goods, of course.

Most of the industrial products and other things people wanted were available *only from the United States*. The **dollar gap** was severe for many years. If a foreign bank or business had some extra money, they were happy to hold it in the form of "dollar deposits."

Dollars were "as good as gold." They really were! The foreign banks could actually turn in their dollars and get gold if they wanted to—one ounce of gold for $35. But nobody wanted to hold gold.

Why get gold? The dollar was as good as gold. And you could put the dollars in savings accounts or bonds and notes and other securities, and draw interest!

Yes, in the years following World War II, the dollar was really in its heyday. But something happened to turn the tide the other way.

From Surplus to Deficit: "The Dollar Glut"

You know what it's like to run a deficit. It means we're pushing more dollars into the bank accounts of foreigners than they want to use up to buy our goods. Their dollar balances in their U.S. bank accounts keep getting bigger and bigger. Then what happens?

After the foreign banks have many billions of dollars, if the deficit continues, sooner or later the foreign central banks will refuse to accept any more dollars. That would be disastrous. We can't ever let it come to that. (And we won't.) But here's what happened. (It *almost* came to that!)

Following World War II the U.S. government expanded its foreign spending programs. As the programs increased, foreigners kept getting more and more dollars.

But also as time passed, the European and Japanese economies were rebuilt.

Americans began buying VWs and Datsuns and other foreign goods and pushing more dollars into the bank accounts of foreigners. Foreign buyers began buying more of their own goods too—and not using up all these dollars to buy American goods anymore. See the problem?

Then as American wages and prices started leapfrogging each other in the late 1960s and early 1970s, American goods got more overpriced. Both American buyers and foreign buyers switched more and more from U.S. goods to foreign goods. The U.S. **payments deficit** got worse. More "surplus dollars" poured into the bank accounts of foreigners.

What caused the problem? These things: *the U.S. foreign-aid program, the overseas military spending of the Vietnam War and elsewhere, the wage-price spiral at home, and the recovery and rapid growth of the economies of other nations—especially West Germany and Japan.*

By the late 1960s it was clear that the dollar was in trouble. As good as gold? Not anymore. Foreign banks were holding billions of U.S. dollars and they wanted to get rid of them—to trade them for marks or yen, because their customers wanted to buy more things from Germany and Japan and less from the United States. The central banks of foreign countries just kept on absorbing more and more dollars.

Who wanted to trade marks or yen for U.S. dollars? Nobody. But wait! The foreign central banks had a way out. The dollar was as good as gold. Remember? They could use their dollars to buy gold from the United States for $35 an ounce, then sell the gold to Germany or Japan for marks or yen. Of course.

So the dollar really was as good as gold after all! Yes. Except for this: the United States didn't have nearly enough gold to "pay off" all those foreign-owned dollars.

Gold Drains Out: "Convertibility" Is Suspended

In the late 1960s some of the foreign central banks (especially the Bank of France) began using their U.S. dollars to buy gold. That is, they were "converting" their dollars into gold. The U.S. gold supply at Fort Knox began to dwindle.

After World War II, the United States had more than half of the world's monetary gold stock—about **25 billion dollars'** worth. But by the early 1970s more than half of the gold was gone—shipped to foreigners in exchange for dollars. So did our sales of gold use up the foreigners' supplies of dollars? It did not!

In the early 1970s *foreigners still held about 50 billion U.S. dollars!* Suppose all of them demanded gold. The dollar was as good as gold? Not anymore.

On August 15, 1971 when President Nixon announced the wage-price freeze he also announced the immediate "suspension of convertibility" of dollars—no more exchanging dollars for gold—not by central banks, not by anybody. So if foreigners with dollar deposits wanted to get rid of their dollars they could spend them for American goods or for stocks and bonds or for anything else for sale in the United States. But they couldn't trade their dollars for gold anymore. And that's the way it has been ever since.

Another thing the president announced was that the dollar was going to be **revalued downward**—that is, dollars were going to be sold more cheaply in exchange for foreign money. How much more cheaply? That hadn't been decided yet.

The Dollar Exchange Rate Was Allowed to Float

All that had been decided was this: to "cut loose" the **exchange rates** between dollars and all other kinds of money—to let the "price of dollars" (in terms of marks or francs or yen or any other kind of money) float downward.

How far down would the price of dollars float—in terms of marks? and francs? and yen? Nobody knew. But everybody knew that the price of dollars (the exchange rate) would have to go low enough to induce foreigners to spend up (or to hold) the surplus dollars. That is, the price of dollars had to fall to where dollars wouldn't be **overvalued**—to where dollars would be "a good deal," again.

What happened after exchange rates for the dollar were cut loose and allowed to float? We'll get into that in a few minutes. First you need to know more about the issue of exchange rates. And about devaluation.

EXCHANGE RATES AND DEVALUATION

Here's an important thing that influences trade: How much is each nation's money worth in exchange for the money of other nations? How much American money must I give to get one British pound? One German mark? One Canadian dollar? One Mexican peso?

The Importance of Exchange Rates

If I can buy British pounds cheap enough, then I will buy pounds and buy things from Brit-

ain. But if the "price of pounds" is too high, I won't buy any pounds. So I won't buy any British goods. I might decide to buy German marks and then buy things from Germany, instead. Or maybe I would just buy domestic products.

See the importance of having the right exchange rates? If dollars were **undervalued**—that is, being sold to foreigners too cheaply—then too many foreigners will be buying dollars and then buying American goods. Pretty soon the foreigners' supplies of dollars will run out! There will be a **dollar gap**.

It works the other way too, of course. If dollars are **overvalued**—that is, priced too high when sold to foreigners—then foreigners won't trade their money for dollars. And they won't buy American goods.

Also, *if dollars are overvalued in the international money market, that means foreign money is undervalued (as compared with dollars).* So what do Americans do? They trade their overvalued dollars for the undervalued foreign money. Then they buy foreign goods. Of course! A **dollar glut**? Right.

Devaluation Can Cure a Chronic Deficit

Suppose the United States has a **chronic deficit** in its balance of payments. Other nations keep getting more and more U.S. dollars. What then? One answer would be: Change the **exchange rates** between U.S. dollars and other kinds of money.

When U.S. dollars are sold cheaper to foreigners, that makes all American goods cheaper to foreigners. And it makes all foreign goods more expensive to Americans.

The government of each country has a vital interest in its exchange rates. So do the businesses which are selling in foreign markets—and so do the ones who want to protect domestic markets against too much foreign competition.

Yes, exchange rates are of critical importance in the whole international economic scene. A lot of international negotiation and cooperation have been required to keep the system working. But in August of 1971 President Nixon shattered the system. Before we go into that, here's an example of devaluation.

An Example of "Devaluation of the Dollar"

Suppose your father wanted to pay your sister's tuition to a college in France. So he went to the bank and bought a check drawn in francs. He bought **foreign exchange.** He paid 400 U.S. dollars for the "check" (**bill of exchange**).

How many francs did he get? That all depends on the **rate of exchange** between dollars and francs. Of course.

Suppose the rate of exchange is one dollar for five francs (20 cents a franc). Then for 400 U.S. dollars he could buy 2,000 French francs (5 francs = 1 dollar, so 400 dollars equals 2,000 francs). And now, what about the devaluation?

Exactly What Does Devaluation Mean?

Devaluation of the dollar means changing the rate of exchange so that *you get less foreign money for each dollar.* That's what devaluation means, and that's all it means.

In our example, suppose the dollar is devalued to where one dollar can buy only four (instead of five) francs. Then one franc would be worth 25¢ (instead of only 20¢).

After the devaluation your father's $400 will buy only 1600 francs (4 francs = 1 dollar, so 400 dollars equals 1600 francs). But the tuition at your sister's college in Beaujolais is not 1600 francs. It's 2000 francs. After the devaluation, your father is going to have to pay $500 to buy the check for 2,000 francs to pay your sister's tuition!

Devaluation always makes the cost of foreign things go up. A bottle of French champagne that costs 30 francs would cost $6 before the devaluation and $7.50 afterwards. A Peugeot that costs 30,000 francs would cost $6,000 before the devaluation and $7,500 afterwards.

After the devaluation, maybe Americans won't buy so much French champagne or so many Peugeots. Maybe your father will decide that your sister can come back home and go to school at Buies Creek, or Mars Hill or Rexburg just like he did! And maybe she'll fly home on Pan Am or TWA—certainly not on Air France! Those tickets cost more now.

Devaluation Makes Foreign Goods More Expensive

See what devaluation of the dollar does? It causes foreign things to be more expensive. *Devaluation can offset the effects of the American inflation.*

Suppose American prices are high. Devaluation can make the foreign goods high priced, too. Devaluation of the U.S. dollar can convince American buyers to "buy American." But as you already know, that's only half the story. What about the French buyers?

The French person's franc, before the devaluation, would buy only 20¢ worth of American goods. But now? It buys 25¢ worth! A $2,000 Xerox copy machine that once cost 10,000 francs now costs only 8,000 francs! The college in Beaujolais may decide that now Xerox is a better buy than the French photo-copy machine. Suddenly you may begin to see more Pintos and Gremlins and Omnis and Dusters and Cougars and Cutlasses and 'Cudas and Fairmonts showing up on the Champs-Elysees—and fewer Peugeots and Citroens and Renaults on the New York Thruway.

Wait. There's more. When the dollar is devalued, it isn't just devalued against the franc. It's devalued against the money of *all other countries*—Japan and Germany and Britain and Chile and Taiwan and all the others. All foreign goods become more expensive to us; our goods become cheaper to all foreigners.

Now that you understand about the exchange rates and what devaluation is, you can understand what was happening with exchange rates in the 1970s. So let's go back to the beginning—back to the period just after World War II, and trace the events right up through the 1970s.

THE RISE AND FALL OF THE BRETTON WOODS SYSTEM

Following the depression of the 1930s and then the runaway European and Japanese inflations of World War II, international finance and currency exchange rates were in a total mess. During 1944, representatives of the major trading nations met at **Bretton Woods,** New Hampshire to try to work out a new system of exchange rates and to work out other international arrangements for the post-war world.

The International Monetary Fund and the World Bank

The **International Monetary Fund (IMF)** was set up as a sort of "International Federal Reserve bank." It was set up to help countries to exchange their money with each other, and also to decide when a country's money needed to be devalued (to offset domestic inflation, for example).

The IMF started out with 40 member nations. Now there are more than 100. One of the important functions of the IMF is to get the member nations together to work out balance of payments problems.

The agreement at Bretton Woods also set up the **World Bank** (International Bank for Reconstruction and Development—IBRD) to make long-term loans of foreign exchange as needed for reconstruction of war damage, and for development projects in the LDCs.

Over the 40-odd years since its beginning, the World Bank has made billions of dollars of development loans. You'll be reading more about it in the next chapter, which talks about economic development in the LDCs.

Each Nation's Monetary Unit was "Defined in Gold"

At Bretton Woods it was agreed that each nation's money would be valued (for international exchange purposes) in terms of a specified amount of gold. It was agreed that the **gold price** in U.S. dollars would stay at $35 an ounce, just as it had been since 1934. That means "one U.S. dollar" is worth "1/35th of an ounce of gold."

A "gold price" was set for the money of every other country. Once that was done, the exchange rates between all the different countries' money were automatically established. Here are some examples.

Suppose the "gold price" in terms of British pounds was set at 9 pounds for one ounce of gold. That means the British pound is worth 1/9th of an ounce of gold. The pound buys a little more than four times as much gold as the dollar buys. So the pound is worth a little more than four dollars.

Suppose the "gold price" in French francs is set at 175 francs for an ounce. Then the franc is worth 1/175th of an ounce of gold. It takes 5 francs to buy as much gold as one dollar will buy. So one dollar equals 5 francs.

Also you can see that one British pound would be worth a little more than 20 francs. See what a neat system? Once you know the "gold price" in each country's money then you can figure out the "official exchange rates" between any two kinds of money.

A system of exchange rates something like this had already existed for centuries. In the beginning the payments actually were made in gold. It was only later that a system of credits—of "bank account balances"—evolved.

"Devaluation" Means "Less Gold"

Once a system of official exchange rates is set up, if a nation **devalues** its money, what it does is to announce *an increase in the "official gold* *price."* That's how the dollar was "officially devalued"—once in 1971 when the "gold price" was increased from $35 to $38 an ounce, and again in 1973 when the gold price was raised to $42.22 an ounce.

Before, the dollar was worth 1/35th of an ounce of gold. After the 1973 devaluation it was only worth 1/42.22 of an ounce of gold. After the second devaluation it would take $42.22 to buy imported goods which only cost $35 before. But wait. What happened following the Bretton Woods agreement in 1945?

The world managed to live under the Bretton Woods agreement (with some exchange rate adjustments from time to time) from the mid-1940s until the early 1970s. Then the agreement was shattered by President Nixon's August 15 "bombshell." What happened to bring the Bretton Woods system to an end?

The Dollar Becomes the Reserve Currency—"Super Money"

During the early years following World War II the dollar became the world's reserve currency—that is, it became "the medium of exchange for buying other kinds of money." Any nation, bank, or individual was always willing to hold U.S. dollar deposits. Why?

Because dollar deposits were always acceptable in exchange for any other kind of money. Everybody wanted dollars. See how the dollar became a sort of super money? *A money for buying other kinds of money?* Sure.

Suppose you wanted to trade pounds for marks. If you could trade the pounds for dollars, then you could always use the dollars to buy marks! Everybody wanted dollars.

People wanted more dollars than were available. Everybody liked to hold their "extra cash" in dollars. Truly, the dollar was the queen of the international money markets. But pretty soon things started to change—as things always do.

The Beginning of the U.S. Payments Deficit

As the European and Japanese economies recovered, as Americans began buying textiles and radios and tape players and cars and things from abroad, as U.S. overseas military and foreign aid commitments expanded, as American businesses began making more investments abroad—what was happening to the world's supply of U.S. dollars? You know the answer to that. Right?

As more and more dollars accumulated in the accounts of the foreign banks, what could they do with all those dollars? They could hold them. Or invest them. But suppose they didn't want to invest their money in the United States—where interest rates happened to be low. What could they do? They could use the dollars to buy U.S. gold!

The first serious dollar crisis developed in 1968. Foreigners were using their dollar deposits to buy gold. Our gold stocks were dwindling fast.

The officials of the major trading nations hurriedly got together and agreed that the United States would not sell any more gold except through official channels—to the central banks of other countries. That helped for a while. But it didn't solve the problem.

The Payments Deficit Gets Worse

American consumers, businesses, and the government kept right on pushing more dollars into the bank accounts of the foreigners. The chronic balance of payments deficit continued.

In the late 1950s the deficit was around $3 billion a year. It fluctuated around that level until the late 1960s. Then in 1969 the deficit jumped to more than $7 billion. And by early 1971 it was running much higher than ever before.

The U.S. **gold stock** had dwindled from about $25 billion in 1948 to less than $11 billion in 1971. Foreigners were still holding some 50 billion U.S. dollars. Then the dam broke.

The balance of payments figures for the first half of 1971 showed a rapidly increasing U.S. payments deficit. International confidence in the dollar was badly shaken. Everybody who had dollars wanted to get rid of them. It became pretty obvious that the dollar was going to have to be devalued. And who wants to hold dollars when they're going to be devalued? Nobody.

After devaluation, dollars won't buy as much of any other kind of money as before. So everyone was trying to get rid of their dollars before the devaluation came. Everyone was trying to sell dollars and nobody wanted to buy dollars. It was obvious that something had to be done—*immediately!*

President Nixon Shatters the System

President Nixon took decisive action on August 15, 1971—just in the nick of time. He **suspended convertibility** of the dollar (stopped selling gold to central banks or anyone) and announced that the "official exchange rate" between dollars and other currencies was being abandoned.

"Let the dollar float. Let dollars exchange for whatever the foreign bankers will give in exchange for them."

Which way did the dollar "float"? Downward, of course. The supply of dollars was great in the international money markets. Americans were buying a lot of foreign money (to buy foreign goods, make foreign investments, etc.) But not only that. What about the foreigners—banks, businesses, private investors and speculators—

who held billions of U.S. dollars? What were they doing? Trying to get rid of their dollars, of course.

Nobody wants to hold an asset—stocks or bonds or real estate or U.S. dollars or anything else—when they know its value is going to go down! So the supply of dollars was great and the demand was small. So its price (in terms of foreign money) went down. Figure 40-1 shows you what this looks like on supply and demand graphs. Take a minute to study those graphs before you go on to the next section.

TOWARD A NEW SYSTEM OF INTERNATIONAL EXCHANGE

In 1971, *de facto* devaluation (the floating downward of the exchange value of the U.S. dollar) reduced the international exchange value of the dollar by about 10 percent. Then in December, 1971, four months after President Nixon shattered the Bretton Woods system, a new "Bretton Woods-type" meeting was held at the Smithsonian Institution in Washington. There, representatives of the "big ten" trading nations—the major members of the International Monetary Fund (IMF)—began to try to put some of the pieces back together.

The Short-lived Smithsonian Agreement (1971)

At the Smithsonian meeting the agreement was made to officially devalue the dollar (to revalue it downward) by raising the dollar price of gold from $35 to $38 an ounce. Also the Japanese yen and the German mark *were revalued upward,* and some other changes were worked out.

The new **Smithsonian** agreement seemed to work all right for a little more than a year. The U.S. economy was under **wage-price controls** and the "inflationary erosion" of the value of the dollar seemed to be under control. But then what happened?

In January, 1973, President Nixon relaxed the controls over wages and prices. Then confidence in the dollar collapsed. Foreigners began getting rid of their dollars—trading them for other kinds of money—as fast as they could.

In February, 1973, there was another official devaluation. The "gold price" was raised to $42.22 an ounce. But even at the cheaper price nobody wanted to buy or hold dollars.

So it was decided to let the exchange value of the dollar "float" again—to find its own "equilibrium price" in the world's money markets just as it had done between August and December of 1971.

A 25 Percent Devaluation in Less than Two Years

By June of 1973 the total decrease in the exchange value of the "floating dollars"—that is, the actual amount of devaluation since the spring of 1971—amounted to about 25 percent. For example, in the spring of 1971 the dollar would buy 3.6 West German marks; in June of 1973 it would buy only 2.7.

The number of Swiss francs the dollar would buy dropped from 4.3 to 3.1. That might discourage a lot of Americans from going skiing at St. Moritz! And from buying Swiss watches too.

Fig. 40-1 How Floating Exchange Rates Reflect Changes in Demand and Supply

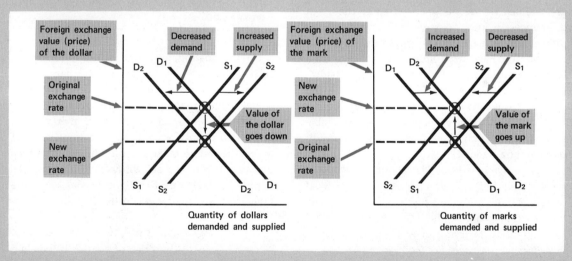

DOLLARS
Supply of and demand for dollars in the international exchange markets.

FOREIGN MONEY (e.g., MARKS)
Supply of and demand for foreign money, by people who are holding dollars.

People begin trying to get rid of their dollars—to exchange them for other kinds of money. So the supply of dollars increases. But people are not willing to trade their foreign money for dollars, so the demand for dollars decreases. So in the international money markets the exchange value of the dollar (the price of one dollar in terms of foreign money) goes down.

People try to use their dollars to buy marks. So the demand for marks increases. But people who have marks are less willing to sell their marks for dollars, so the available supply of marks in the international money markets decreases. So the exchange value of the mark (in terms of dollars) goes up.

The IMF Tries to Put the System Back Together

In July of 1972 the IMF set up a **committee of 20** to begin working on a new long-term international exchange system.

But by mid-1973 most nations had given up on trying to hold fixed exchange rates for their money. So the IMF committee wasn't sure what direction to take. There was a lot of disagreement on the question of **fixed** or **variable** exchange rates.

When the IMF held meetings in September of 1973, some countries were hoping for a new fixed-rate system like the Bretton Woods system. Others were in favor of fixed rates, but with the price of each country's money permitted to move up or down within a limited range. Still others were in favor of letting exchange rates continue to float.

Then what happened? The **oil crisis!** The great shock of the oil price increase, the great differences in inflation rates and economic conditions between nations—all these things probably couldn't have been absorbed within a fixed exchange rate system. If the United States hadn't shattered the system in 1971, chances are the system would have crumbled anyway before 1974. Fixed exchange rates just aren't compatible with such rapid changes in the economic conditions among nations.

By January of 1974, just about all exchange rates were floating. It seemed obvious that fixed exchange rates were not in the cards—certainly not any time soon. So the IMF committee turned their attention to trying to work out *a system of guidelines for "managed floating" exchange rates.*

Managed Floating: Exchange Rate System of the 1980s

So what kind of an international exchange system do we have now? It's a system of "managed floating" exchange rates.

If any country's money gets in short supply, then the exchange rate (price) goes up.

Foreigners must pay more to get it. If any country's money gets in oversupply, its exchange rate (price) goes down. Foreigners can buy it cheaper.

Suppose prices go up a lot in one country. Foreigners aren't going to want to buy those high-priced goods! So nobody wants that country's money. Its price goes down.

But as the price of that country's money goes down, that country's goods get cheaper to foreigners. And that's what brings things back into equilibrium. The **exchange rate** must adjust enough to offset the effect of the **inflation.** With floating rates that's what will tend to happen automatically.

See how floating exchange rates can bring trade between nations into equilibrium? Even though prices in one country may be going up while prices in another country are not? Sure.

How Are the Floating Exchange Rates "Managed"?

With floating exchange rates, the price of each kind of money in the money markets can move freely up or down. The price responds to changes in supply or demand. It works the same way as prices of stocks in the stock markets.

So do people buy and sell different kinds of money hoping to make a profit? In the same way that people buy and sell different kinds of stocks hoping to make a profit? Right! It goes on all the time. So there's a danger in the system.

The Destabilizing Effect of Rumors. What happens to the price of a stock if there's a rumor that the company is going broke? Or if there's a rumor that the company was digging for copper and struck gold? Stock prices are always "floating" in response to supply and demand. So when the rumors hit, prices shoot up or down!

With floating exchange rates, couldn't rumors (about inflation rates and such) push the value of the dollar way up? or way down? And then what would happen to the importers and exporters who are doing business between the United States and West Germany? and Japan? and Switzerland? and Australia? and everywhere?

How can trading partners carry out their business when the exchange value of the dollar is jumping up and down? They can't, of course. That's why the floating rates need to be **managed.** But who does it? and how?

Central Banks Can "Stabilize" Exchange Rates. You already know what the central banks do in international finance. So who do you suppose is going to "manage" the floating exchange rates? The central banks!

Suppose there's a rumor that the inflation rate in the United States is speeding up—that is, the domestic purchasing power of the dollar is going down. What do foreigners start doing with their dollars? They start trading them for marks and francs and yen and guilders and pesos and things. So the value of the dollar (in terms of all these other kinds of money) starts going down.

How can the declining exchange value of the dollar be stopped? Like this: Let the central banks set a "bottom price" (exchange rate) for the dollar and agree to buy all the dollars anyone wants to sell, at that price. Maybe the Deutsche Bundesbank will offer to pay 2.5 marks for one dollar and will buy all the dollars anyone wants to sell, at that price. Then can the value of the dollar go below 2.5 deutsche marks? Of course not.

And the central bank in Switzerland can set the "bottom price" of the dollar in terms of Swiss francs and buy all that are offered at that price. So the price of the dollar (in Swiss francs) can't go any lower than that. The same thing can be done by the central bank of every other country.

It works the other way too, of course. Sup-

pose everyone suddenly gets the idea that the American economy has solved all its inflation problems. And suppose there's a rumor that costs of production are going up much faster in other countries than in the United States. What happens?

Everybody wants to own U.S. dollars. Why? Because everybody thinks dollars will be getting more valuable! People and businesses and banks begin to buy dollars in exchange for marks and francs and drachmas and all. So the value of the dollar (in terms of all these other kinds of money) goes up. The value of the other kinds of money (in terms of dollars) goes down.

What can the central banks do to prevent the exchange value of the dollar from shooting sky high? Sell dollars? Of course.

The Federal Reserve System can accept all kinds of foreign money in exchange for dollars. By supplying a flood of dollars, the Fed (and the foreign central banks who hold dollars) can prevent the foreign exchange value of the dollar from going too high. (That is, prevent the foreign exchange value of the other kinds of money from going too low.)

When Should the Central Banks Intervene? It's usually not too difficult to "manage" the floating exchange rates if all the central banks agree and cooperate with each other. But one serious question is this: When should the value of the dollar (as against the mark or the franc, or whatever) be allowed to float on up? or down? And when should the upward or downward movement be limited by "managing"?

In general terms, the answer is easy: Does the exchange rate need to go up or down to bring that country's trade into equilibrium? maybe because of inflationary changes, for example? If so, then the exchange rate shouldn't be "managed." It should be allowed to move on up

or down as far as necessary to bring that nation's trade into equilibrium.

But suppose the exchange rates for a country's money are being pushed up or down by rumors? by speculators? Then the "money managers" (central banks) should intervene. Then exchange rates should not be permitted to move up or down very much.

But how can you tell if it's an **equilibrating adjustment**? or just a **short-term speculative fluctuation**? Sometimes it isn't easy to know what's happening until after it has already happened!

Some mistakes will be made, sure. But the system will work. Not perfectly, of course. But it will work. *It must work!* It's the kind of international exchange system that exists in the world these days! It looks like it's the kind of system that will be with us for awhile.

Formalizing the System of "Managed Floating Exchange Rates"

In the first couple of years, many people were surprised at how smoothly the floating exchange rate system worked. It wasn't "carefully established." It wasn't "planned." It was the absence of a plan! The planned systems all collapsed. So the **free market forces** took over.

At first the idea was "let's get away from floating exchange rates as soon as we can." But by 1976 many people who had opposed the idea in the first place had changed their minds. They were willing to talk about adopting a floating system on a permanent basis.

The **IMF committee of 20** had a lot of meetings and talks in 1975. In early 1976 they worked out the **Articles of Agreement** which laid the foundation for a future world exchange system—a system of managed floating exchange rates.

The rules of "managed floating" were worked out. Under the Articles of Agreement it's all right (and desirable) for countries to "manage" their exchange rates to smooth out short-term fluctuations. But no nation is supposed to interfere with rate changes which "should" occur—that is, rate changes which reflect **basic changes** in the relative economic circumstances among nations.

Managing the EC Monies: "The Snake" and the "EMS"

The countries of the Common Market have been letting their different kinds of money float, too. But they have had an agreement for "almost fixed" exchange rates among member countries. Suppose the mark and franc and lira and other EC monies are going up (or down) in exchange for U.S. dollars or yen or pesos. That's okay.

But suppose the West German mark is going up in exchange for the Belgian franc. That's what isn't supposed to happen. The EC countries have called their exchange rate stabilization system **the snake.**

The idea of "the snake" is that the average of exchange rates of Common Market nations (as compared with the rest of the world) can wiggle up or down on a chart. The average would be a "wiggling line." But all of the EC countries' monies won't be right on the line. Each country's money is allowed to move up or down around the average. But it's supposed to stay within a range, or a "band" above or below the line. This "snake" system is a sort of "fixed exchange rate system with some flexibility."

In March, 1979 the EC countries set up a new system, sometimes called the "supersnake." Officially it's called the **EMS (European Monetary System).** This new system is supposed to do a better job of doing what the snake was supposed to do. The snake hasn't always worked so well.

With the new EMS there's an **intervention fund** to be used to buy up any kind of European money whenever its supply gets too great and its exchange value begins to fall. Will the new EMS work? That all depends. If changes in the economies of the Common Market countries aren't too great (from one country to another) it can work. But if any big shocks hit the system, it will collapse. That's always the way it is with fixed exchange rates.

When the rates are first set, they reflect the existing circumstances. But as the circumstances change the rates need to change. Otherwise there will be problems of perpetual surpluses for nations with undervalued monies and perpetual deficits for nations with overvalued monies. In the case of the new EMS, some "devaluation adjustments" were made in the early 1980s, but in 1982 the system is still working. As to the future, we'll just have to wait and see what happens.

OTHER CHANGES IN THE INTERNATIONAL EXCHANGE SYSTEM

When the International Monetary Fund (IMF) committee reached its agreement in early 1976, it did more than recognize and set up the rules for "managed floating" exchange rates. It also agreed to reduce the role of gold in international exchange.

What about gold? Maybe we should look at gold for a minute. What role has it been playing? And why? And what's going to happen as the monetary role of gold is diminished?

The Role of Gold in International Trade

How long has gold been important in world trade? For about as far back in history as you can

go. Why? Because it has been valued highly and used as money in many nations.

Suppose all nations use gold as money. And suppose someone in one country wants to buy something from someone in another country. Then there's no problem of changing one kind of money for another!

If you have a little lump of gold, you can use it to buy things in England or France or wherever else you might happen to want to buy something. How nice and simple that is!

The "Specie-flow Price-equilibrating Mechanism." Back in the early 1900s all of the industrial nations were on the **international gold standard.** All of the nations were using gold as domestic currency. And anybody who wanted to could use gold to buy things from foreigners.

Economists developed a model to explain how it all worked out so neatly. The model describes the **specie-flow price-equilibrating mechanism.**

Gold Flows Force Domestic Prices to Adjust. Suppose the Germans are buying a lot of things from the French. What happens to Germany's money (gold)? It flows to France!

When Germany's money flows to France, what happens to prices in Germany? They go down. And in France? They go up.

Increasing the money supply pushes prices up. Inflation. Reducing the money supply pushes prices down.

So prices in Germany go down and prices in France go up. What happens then? French people start buying more of the low-priced German goods—and fewer of their own goods. German people buy less of the high-priced French goods and more of their own goods. See how neatly trade is automatically brought into balance?

How did it happen? The flow of specie (the money metal) caused prices in each country to change. The changed prices brought trade into balance again. A very neat system! Right?

Like most things in the real world, of course, it didn't always work out quite as smoothly as the model suggests. What country wants to see its gold flow out? And its money supply shrink? And prices go down? That brings depression! No country would put up with that, these days. The world hasn't been on an "international gold standard" since the early 1900s.

The Need for a New Reserve Money—"Super Money"

What is gold supposed to do in helping to finance international trade? Simply this: When somebody gets too many francs and wants marks instead, the francs can be traded for gold, then the gold can be traded for marks.

Gold is supposed to be used as **reserve money,** to play the role of **super money**—the medium of exchange for exchanging one country's money for another's. Back before World War I, when the world was on the international gold standard, gold performed this "super money" role very well. But since that time it never has.

From World War II up until the mid-1960s, the **U.S. dollar** was used as "reserve money"—as the world's "super money." But you know what happened to that arrangement. It sort of petered out in the late 1960s and came to an abrupt end in August of 1971.

So what's going to happen next? What can the countries of the world use as "reserve money"? as "super money"? Certainly gold isn't going to do it. There isn't nearly enough of it around. And it doesn't work so well these days anyway.

So what can the world's countries hold that will always be dependable? always acceptable in exchange for any other kind of money? Would you believe SDRs? Maybe so!

What About "Paper Gold"? the SDRs?

Why not let the International Monetary Fund (IMF) do something like the Federal Re-

serve does? Let the IMF create some "super money" (called **SDRs**) which everyone will agree to accept. Then let each country "buy" some "super money" from the IMF.

When the IMF sells the SDRs to all of the countries, the IMF will get lots of all kinds of money in exchange. So the IMF will have bank accounts in all countries, in all kinds of money. That's just in case anybody needs to buy some.

And what do all the countries get? Bank accounts in the IMF? Sure. Bank accounts in SDRs—in "IMF super money."

Then suppose the French banks run low on marks. The French central bank can write an "IMF super money" (SDR) check and buy some marks! Neat? Right!

What do we call this "IMF super money?" **Special drawing rights** (SDRs) would you believe? (Not a very inspired name, I must say! Seems that they could at least have named them zingos or lucky bucks or whallakers or something better than SDRs! But I guess it's too late for that now.)

What do the SDRs do? They give the holder the right to go to the IMF and "draw out" any kind of money. And since the SDRs are always acceptable at the IMF, they're always acceptable by central banks everywhere. They're as good as gold!—and not nearly as much trouble.

The IMF "super money" (SDR) system was suggested as early as 1945, at Bretton Woods, by none other than "the father of modern macroeconomics": John Maynard Keynes. This new idea wasn't actually tried, though, until after the first "crisis of the U.S. dollar" in 1968.

What happened? Did it work? Yes! And it's still working—in fact it's working better than most people expected.

How Do SDRs Work?

When the SDR was introduced in 1968 it was done with a lot of worries and misgivings.

After all, how often do people create a new kind of international "super money"? Never before? Right!

But by the end of the 1970s the SDR was no longer an experiment. Bank deposits of many billions of SDRs were being held by the central banks of all of the major trading nations. The SDR was completely acceptable in exchange for U.S. dollars or Japanese yen or Swiss francs or for any other kind of money.

What is "the SDR"? It's a **monetary unit** just as the U.S. dollar or the Swiss franc is a monetary unit. Central banks can have **bank deposits** of SDRs at the IMF just as you can have bank deposits of dollars at your bank.

Central banks can **write SDR checks** to buy any kind of money they want. When they do that they use up their SDRs. But when they sell their own money they get SDRs back, of course.

How Much Is One SDR Worth? In the beginning the value of the SDR in buying each kind of money was set equal to the exchange value of the U.S. dollar. That made sense at that time because the U.S. dollar was the world's reserve currency (the "super money") which the SDR was being created to replace.

But in 1974 the value of the SDR was changed to a weighted average of the monies of the world's 16 major trading nations. But that turned out to be too complicated. So in January of 1981 the IMF simplified the SDR.

Now the value of the SDR is based on: the U.S. dollar (42%), the German mark (19%), and the British pound, French franc and Japanese yen (13% each). So far it seems that this simplification has made the SDR more popular.

The SDR Has Become the World's New "Super Money." When you go to your library and look the U.S. balance of payments in the latest *Federal Reserve Bulletin* (or whatever), look at the "official reserve assets." You will see "gold" and "foreign currencies" and "SDRs."

Already SDRs have taken over the role of gold in balancing international transactions. SDRs really have become the world's new "super money."

Nowadays, with floating exchange rates, the value of the SDR has become more stable than any other kind of money. Why? Because it's based on the *average exchange value of several different kinds of money!*

New Uses for the SDR. Has the new SDR valuation system worked? Excellently! So SDRs are now being used as the "money unit" in some international transactions.

Suez Canal tolls are quoted in SDRs. International air transport rates seem likely to be set in SDRs, soon. By 1976 some New York banks were offering loans and time (savings) deposits stated in SDRs!

The petroleum exporting (OPEC) countries now quote their oil prices in dollars. But they have been talking about shifting to SDRs. In 1981, seven major London banks began to sell certificates of deposit denominated in SDRs.

Nobody ever pays anybody in SDRs, of course—just like during the last 40 years nobody ever paid anybody in gold. SDRs are used only by central banks for buying and selling different kinds of money. That's all.

The shipping companies don't pay Egypt their Suez Canal fees in SDRs. But the amount of the charge is first figured in SDRs. Then the exchange rate between the SDR and your country's money determines how much of your money you must pay.

Here's an example. Suppose one SDR equals one dollar. If the toll charge is 1,000 SDRs, then the dollar charge will be $1,000. But suppose one SDR equals $2. Then a 1,000 SDR toll charge would equal a toll charge in dollars of $2,000. Get the idea?

Chase Manhattan won't let you withdraw your time deposit in SDRs! (Nobody knows what a handful of SDRs would look like anyway!) But the bank can figure the value of your deposit in SDRs. Then the exchange rate between dollars and SDRs will determine how many dollars you'll get.

SDRs are a new invention. A new kind of international "super money" was badly needed.

So one has been devised. Surely it isn't perfect. But in the early 1980s it seems to be working surprisingly well.

THE DOLLAR CRISIS OF THE LATE 1970s

You already know about the international dollar crisis of 1971. But that wasn't the only one.

After 1971 the international exchange value of the dollar kept floating downward. By 1976 the U.S. dollar would only buy 2.6 West German marks (down from 3.6 in 1971) and only 2.6 Swiss francs (down from 4.3 in 1971). During the mid '70s the dollar was fairly stable. But then in 1977 the U.S. Merchandise Trade deficit jumped to $31 billion—by far the largest in history—and the dollar started going down again.

In the 12-month period ending in October, 1978 the dollar lost 36% of its value against the Swiss franc, 21% against the West German mark, and 31% against the Japanese yen. The week of October 30 opened with near-panic selling of dollars in the money markets in Europe and Japan. It was obvious that something had to be done immediately to rescue the dollar.

President Carter's Rescue Plan

President Carter called his top monetary advisors to the White House for a secret meeting and worked out a plan. On November 1 he announced the plan—the most dramatic package of actions (and the biggest gamble) the United States had ever taken in international finance. The package included:

- Billions of dollars' worth of foreign money to be borrowed by the United States from the foreign central banks to be used to buy dollars in the foreign exchange markets— to increase the demand for dollars, and hold up the price of dollars.

- Sharply higher interest rates in this country (a) to make holding dollars more profitable for foreigners and (b) to let foreigners see that the U.S. was serious about stopping the inflationary decline in the value of the dollar. The Fed immediately raised the discount rate by a full percentage point—a step it had never before taken.

- The sale of $2 billion dollars' worth of SDRs to Germany, Switzerland, and Japan to get more of their money to be used to buy up dollars.

- The sale of 1.5 million ounces of gold per month by the U.S. Treasury to hold down the world price of gold and to pull in more dollars out of the foreign money markets.

- Withdrawal of $3 billion worth of marks, francs, and yen from the U.S. reserve account at the IMF—more money to be used to buy up dollars from foreigners.

- Sale of up to $10 billion worth of high-interest U.S. Treasury securities (denominated in *foreign* money) in the foreign money markets to get more foreign money to be used to buy up dollars.

Did the Plan Work?

So what happened? The immediate response was overwhelmingly positive. The dollar rose sharply in the money markets all over the world. The price of gold dropped $15 an ounce in London and the New York Stock Exchange recorded its biggest single-day advance in history.

It worked in the short run, sure. But a lot of people were worried about the longer run. What if the U.S. trade deficit stays up around $30 or $40 billion dollars a year? And Americans keep investing billions overseas? It won't take long for another dollar glut to develop. And next time the U.S. government will still be deep in debt for all of that foreign money they borrowed in 1978. What then?

That would have been really bad. But luckily, it didn't turn out that way. The dollar continued to increase in value in the foreign exchange markets. By mid-November it was up to its highest level in four months. And it continued its upward trend.

By mid-April, 1979, the dollar had risen (since November, 1978) more than 10% against the mark, 18% against the Swiss franc, and (would you believe?) 22% against the Japanese yen. And all this was happening at the same time that the Fed and the foreign central banks were *selling dollars* to get back the foreign money they had used to buy the dollars back in November!

By April, 1979 the United States had already been able to buy up enough foreign money to pay off a lot of those November loans. And foreign bankers were charging that the U.S. dollar was being allowed to increase in value too much, and too fast!

How did it all happen, so fast? Many things were involved. For one thing, foreigners found out that the United States was serious and determined about (a) protecting the international value of the dollar, and (b) fighting domestic inflation.

Interest rates in the United States were high enough to make dollars a good kind of money to have. And inflation rates increased in several other countries, making the American inflation rate look not so bad. And the U.S. balance of payments figures showed that the trade deficit was going down.

The U.S. Dollar: Glamour Currency of the 1980s?

In October of 1979 the Fed put the brakes on monetary growth. Interest rates in this country rose to their highest levels in modern times. The dollar strengthened.

Throughout 1980 and '81 and on into 1982 money was tight. Interest rates were very high. In early 1982 the U.S. inflation rate seemed to be slowing down. The international value of the dollar continued to increase.

Yes, in the early 1980s everything was looking rosy for the American dollar. And what happened after that? I don't know. This book must go to press, no matter what. So why don't you go to your library and see what happened? It might be interesting to find out.

THE FUTURE OUTLOOK

The world has gone through a period of great change since 1970. The 1970s brought to an end the period during which the United States would play the role of "benevolent protector" for the economies of the other nations of the world. The United States has had to become a tough competitor in international markets. For many years the U.S. economy had been so strong that we had been able to get away with "breaking all the rules of prudent international finance." But not now.

Also the United States can no longer ignore the international consequences in its domestic economic policies.

How do our domestic policies influence our world position? Suppose the economy has unemployment. What should the government do to stimulate more employment. Easy money policy? And cut taxes and increase government spending? Sure.

But when the government cuts taxes and increases spending and runs a deficit, and when the Feds buys bonds and pumps money into the economy, what happens then? Interest rates usually go down. Prices usually go up.

Suppose you were a foreigner holding U.S. dollars. When interest rates on dollars started going down and prices of American goods started going up, what would you do? Get rid of your dollars? Yes! See the problem?

Or suppose the United States is really going all out to fight inflation like in 1981 and '82. That's just fine! When we fight inflation we push up interest rates. People holding dollars can earn more on their dollar holdings.

And we try to cut government spending and increase taxes. People holding dollars feel very confident about the future value of the dollar when they see such things going on.

It shouldn't be necessary for a country like the United States to let its domestic economic policies be completely dictated by international considerations. But the international considerations are important enough that no longer can they be ignored.

Exchange Rates? There's No Perfect Solution

It's too bad that foreign trade has to be complicated by the need to exchange one kind of money for another. But that's the way it is. As long as semi-autonomous economic systems exist, the "money exchange complication" will be with us. All we can do is hope to have an international exchange system that will minimize the complications.

Setting fixed exchange rates for all the different kinds of money in the world is, in a way, like having a "wage-price freeze." If things are more or less "in equilibrium" at the time the freeze comes, then there's no problem. At least, not then. But what happens after that? The basic economic conditions keep changing.

One country will have more inflation than the others; one country will introduce more

high-technology capital than the others; one country will find some new natural resources. All kinds of changes will occur.

As the basic conditions change, the fixed exchange rates will get more and more out of line with reality. Pretty soon one nation's money gets in short supply in the world's money markets (like U.S. dollars after World War II) while another country's money gets in surplus supply (like U.S. dollars in the 1970s).

So what happens? Exchange rates must be adjusted. If the adjustments are too slow in coming, what happens? What happened on August 15, 1971? The collapse of the system! Of course.

A Stable but Flexible System Is Required

What we need is this: a system of exchange rates stable enough to provide for the smooth flow of international trade, yet flexible enough to change as the basic economic conditions among the nations change. That's a tough order to fill. It isn't likely to ever be solved completely, permanently, once and for all.

The solution to this problem, like to most problems of the modern world, is going to have to be a living, changing, evolving solution. There will be some good times, when things go more right than wrong. And there will be some bad times, when things go more wrong than right. The 1970s were mostly bad times.

But in the early 1980s progress was being made. Maybe it'll be possible to keep things flexible enough so that the world's exchange system won't have to collapse again. Let's hope so.

SUMMARY AND SYNTHESIS

The 1970s and early 1980s were times of great changes and upheaval in the international money markets. The impact of quadrupled oil prices and rapidly shifting demands and sup-

plies for various kinds of products caused prices to gyrate upward. It was during the early 1970s that the Bretton Woods exchange rate system collapsed. And it was during this period that the international position of the dollar was drastically changed.

During the post-war period, everyone wanted to hold American dollars. But by the late 1960s and early '70s the world was flooded with dollars, and some people began trading their dollars for gold. The U.S. gold supply was dwindling, so President Nixon "suspended covertibility" and let the value of the dollar in the international markets "float."

Devaluation means charging a lower price for your money when you sell it to foreigners. After the dollar is devalued, foreigners can buy dollars more cheaply. So they can buy American goods more cheaply.

The Bretton Woods system established fixed exchange rates between the monies of different nations. The International Monetary Fund (IMF) was set up to operate as a "world central bank" to assist nations in exchanging their different kinds of money.

The dollar became the world's reserve currency in the period following World War II. But as the United States ran worsening payments deficits, the world was flooded with dollars and the holders of dollars wanted to get rid of them. So the international value of the dollar went down.

After the collapse of the Bretton Woods system in 1971, there were attempts to establish fixed exchange rates again. But with no success. So now we have a system of managed floating exchange rates. The value of the dollar (and other kinds of money which are "floating") are determined by the demand and supply for that money in the international exchange markets.

If more people are trying to buy goods from the United States, they will demand more dollars. So the value of the dollar will go up. Or suppose interest rates happen to be high in the United States. People will want to buy dollars so they can invest in the United States and earn more interest. That would make the value of the dollar go up too.

The floating exchange rates are managed by the central banks. Suppose there is a sudden increase in the demand for dollars. The Fed can sell dollars to stabilize the value of the dollar. Or if foreigners suddenly begin selling lots of dollars, the Fed might use its foreign money reserves to buy up dollars to keep the value from falling very much.

The European Community (EC, or Common Market) has a system of fixed but flexible managed exchange rates among the member nations. Exchange rates are permitted to change, but only within a "band", called the "snake."

Historically, gold has played an important role in international exchange. The "specie-flow price-equilibrating mechanism" has helped to keep international trade in balance for hundreds of years. But since the early 1900s the world has not had a true international gold standard.

The world needs a medium of exchange for exchanging different kinds of money. If gold can't do that, what will? For many years after World War II, the American dollar served in this role. But now we use IMF-created special drawing rights called SDRs.

SDRs are super money deposits at the IMF. The Fed can "write checks" against its SDR deposits and use these checks to buy francs or marks or yen or whatever. This system was set up about ten years ago, and seems to be working well.

In the late 1970s there was another dollar crisis. But President Carter's bold rescue package worked!

With the change of the Fed's policy in October of 1979, interest rates in this country moved up high, and the dollar became a much more desirable asset to hold. So people who had been selling dollars before, began buying dollars.

The international value of the dollar moved up in 1981 and early 1982. What happens to it in the future will depend a lot on (1) the size of U.S. payments deficits, (2) the level of interest rates and (3) the rate of inflation in this country as compared with what is going on in other countries.

Ultimately, the strength of the American economy and the rate of increase in American productivity will have a lot to do with it. And only time will tell about that.

REVIEW EXERCISES

MAJOR CONCEPTS, PRINCIPLES, TERMS (Explain each carefully.)

devaluation

the Bretton Woods system

International Monetary Fund (IMF)

Smithsonian Agreement

floating exchange rates

"managed floating" exchange rates

"the snake" and the "EMS"

the "specie-flow price-equilibrating
mechanism"

SDRs

OTHER CONCEPTS AND TERMS (Explain each briefly.)

the "dollar gap"

the "dollar glut"

exchange rates

de facto devaluation

World Bank (IBRD)

"suspend convertibility"

"official exchange rate"

"buying foreign exchange"

QUESTIONS (Try to write out answers, or jot down highlights.)

1. Explain how the dollar crisis evolved and resulted in the destruction of the Bretton Woods system in August, 1971.
2. What's so important about exchange rates? Discuss.
3. Explain how the rates of exchange between all kinds of money can be established simply by determining the "gold price" in each kind of money.
4. What is "super money"? Explain how the dollar became "super money" and then how it fell from this position and is being replaced by SDRs.
5. Explain how "floating exchange rates" work.
6. Trace the events following the collapse of the Bretton Woods system in August of 1971, up to the late 1970s.
7. Explain this statement: "With changes happening so rapidly in the world of the 1970s, it is doubtful that the Bretton Woods system could have survived much longer anyway."
8. Explain this statement: "With floating exchange rates it isn't as likely that any country would keep running a payments deficit, year after year."
9. Explain how central banks can "manage" the floating exchange rates to prevent them from being too unstable.
10. Describe the changing role of gold in international trade, from the early 1900s to the present.
11. Can you describe the "specie-flow price-equilibrating mechanism"? Try.
12. Describe the history of the SDRs, what they are, how they work, and the present situation.
13. What about the international consequences of domestic economic policies? Do you think the international consequences place a serious restraint on the nation's domestic macroeconomic policies?—that is, on our monetary and fiscal policies? Discuss.
14. It isn't likely that the international payments problem will ever be solved completely, permanently, once and for all. Can you explain why?

41

Economic Development I: Problems of Underdevelopment and the Principles of Economic Growth

Chapter Objectives

- What are the **economic problems** which are facing the **less developed countries (LDCs)** in the 1980s? And **what** (realistically) **can be done** about that? That's what you will be reading about in this chapter and the next.

- When you finish studying this chapter you will be able to **explain what the LDCs are, where they are located,** and something about the **great diversity** among them.

- You will be able to describe the **specific kinds of conditions** which exist in the LDCs. You will understand **the economics of these special circumstances.** And you will be able to explain **what will be required** to **improve conditions** in most LDCs—and **how difficult it will be** for most of them to meet these requirements.

- You will be able to **explain the basic principles of economic growth,** the important role of **savings and investment,** and **different ways** that the "savings and investment" **might be generated.**

- Finally, you will be able to **describe the growth process** as it has actually occurred **in the United States** and in some **other countries.** And you will be able to **relate this past experience** to the **growth problem of the LDCs** in the 1980s.

In the mid-1970s the population of the world passed 4 billion. More than 2½ billion of those people are in less developed countries (LDCs).

By the end of this century the world's population will be more than 6 billion. Maybe almost 7 billion. By then, about 4 out of every 5 people will be living in the LDCs.

What's going to be done to improve the economic circumstances of all these billions of people? Probably in most places in the world, not very much.

Places which can contain their population

growth have a chance. Some will make significant progress. But probably most will not.

SOME EFFECTS OF THE TURBULENT 1970s

You already know about what was going on in the turbulent decade of the 1970s. Worldwide inflation, with crazy price changes. Serious recession, unemployment. Exchange rates all upset—

economic relationships among nations a brand new ball game. And lots of other disruptive changes. Have the LDCs been affected? Of course.

Inflation pushed up the prices of manufactured goods and other things that the LDCs buy. And remember what happened to grain prices? And oil prices? Sure. The LDCs have been hard-hit.

Mounting Payments Deficits of the LDCs

The LDCs usually have a **payments deficit** on current account (that is, not counting capital items, like loans). The deficit is usually covered by loans. In 1973 the combined deficit of all of the LDCs amounted to about $3 billion. But in 1974 it was almost $10 billion! And in 1975 it was $37 billion. And the deficits have been running high ever since.

A lot of the problem was caused by their "unfavorable terms of trade." The high price of oil is a major factor, of course. But it isn't the only factor.

Dependence on One Product

The prices of sugar and copra and some other things have fluctuated widely during the 1970s. What would jumping prices like that do to an economy which produced mostly sugar? Or mostly copra? Or some other product with the prices jumping around?

It would hurt. And that's the way it was in many of the LDCs in the 1970s.

Take the island of Mauritius in the Indian Ocean. About 90 percent of their export earnings come from sugar. For Cuba it's more than three fourths and for Fiji more than half.

And what about Colombia and Ethiopia and Uganda and Rwanda? All of them get more than half of their foreign exchange earnings from coffee. The Caribbean island of Martinique gets more than half of its export earnings from bananas. So does Panama.

Many of the LDCs depend heavily on cocoa, rice, cotton, copra, rubber, tin, copper, iron ore, and jute. What has been happening to the prices of all these things in the 1970s? They have been going up and down. Usually unpredictably.

Worsening "Terms of Trade" for the LDCs

The **terms of trade** of the LDCs have been getting worse. They've been paying a lot more for imports and not getting much more (sometimes less) for their exports.

The LDCs are importing about one seventh of the world's total imports. And they're having problems borrowing enough money to keep their imports flowing in.

The high prices of manufactured goods, foodstuffs, and especially petroleum have been making it very tough for them. The new borrowings (added to their already heavy external debt) has made it difficult for some of them to keep their economic development programs going.

Things haven't been so good for the LDCs. Right? Right! Now that you have that message, let's go back to the beginning and take it step by step.

THE LDCs: A GENERAL OVERVIEW

What are the LDCs? How do you look at a country and tell if it's one? or not? How many of them are there? Where are they? What are they like?

The LDCs Are "Low Income" Countries

Any definition of "less developed countries" is bound to be arbitrary. Some countries which probably should be included, won't be. And some which probably shouldn't be, will be. That would be true of any definition we might choose.

We might define LDCs as countries where the **average income per capita** is less than $700 per year. But please, be careful not to put too much reliance on this "annual income per capita" figure. It really isn't a very good indication of anything. The kind of life you can lead on $700 a year in one place is totally different from the kind of life you can lead on $700 somewhere else!

In Some Places Not Much Cash Income Is Needed. Take the Pacific Island countries, for example. In some of the countries the population is not yet too big. There is plenty of fertile land for growing food. The rivers and lagoons and the ocean provide easy catches of fish and shellfish. Local building materials are easily available and adequate for the climate. So for what do they need an annual income of $700 per capita?

A per capita income of $700 means that a family of 6 would receive $4,200 per year. That's about $80 a week. Most of the traditional rural families on the better-endowed Pacific islands would have difficulty figuring out what to do with all that cash money!

In the mid-1970s most of the rural-traditional families in the Pacific islands were earning less than $10 a week in cash income. But that didn't seem to be enough. There seemed to be a general feeling that $20 a week should be quite adequate. And $30 a week? Unnecessary wealth! (Of course, if they were earning $20 or $30 a week they might soon find that they needed $40! That's the way it seems to be with people.)

In Some Places, Cash Income Is All There Is! Is the traditional Pacific island family in the same situation as a family living in one of the rapidly growing urban areas? Of course not. How well could an urban family of six get by on

$80 a week? Probably not very well.

And remember this: the $700 annual per capita income—the $80 a week for the family of six—is high for the LDCs! In many LDCs the average per capita income is less than half that high. There are more than 25 countries, containing more than a billion people, where average income is less than $200 a year.

If you would like to see some recent figures of per capita income for different countries, the United Nations *Statistical Yearbook* and *Monthly Bulletin of Statistics* would be good places to look. Also the World Bank's *World Development Report* (annual) is an excellent source. But be careful. Many of the statistics are not very accurate. Even if they were accurate, don't forget this: the average figures don't tell you anything about who gets how much of that income.

Grouping Nations by Stage of Development

There are more "less developed countries" in the world than any other kind. The LDCs are just about everywhere—except in two places: North America and Europe.

The "Highly Developed" Countries. The United States and Canada and Western Europe are the places where "high development" is concentrated.

A few nations in other places are not LDCs, of course: Japan, Australia, New Zealand, Iceland, Israel, Puerto Rico, the U.S.S.R. and the oil-rich country of Kuwait all are considered **highly developed countries**—which in the 1970s was usually defined as "a country where annual per capita income is more than $3,500."

About one fifth of the world's population is located in these "highly developed" countries. Then there are several countries which are grouped in the **intermediate development** range—that is, between the "highly developed" countries and the LDCs.

The "Intermediate Development" Countries.
Several of the countries of Eastern Europe fall into this category: Austria, Hungary, Romania, Yugoslavia and others. Spain and Portugal and Greece are also in this group.

Several of the Latin American countries are in this group, too: Argentina, Chile, Uruguay, Costa Rica, Panama, Cuba, and others.

The group includes two countries on the continent of Africa: Libya and South Africa. There are two in Southeast Asia: Hong Kong and Singapore. In the Mideast the oil-rich nation of Saudi Arabia is in this group.

Where Are the LDCs?
Almost all of the African and Asian nations, and several in Latin America, are LDCs.

There are only two African nations which are not LDCs: Libya and South Africa. There are only four Asian nations which are not LDCs: Japan, Hong Kong, Singapore, and the Asian part of the U.S.S.R. More than half of the Latin American nations are LDCs. Those which aren't are in the intermediate range. None have yet gotten into the "highly developed" group.

Where are the LDCs? Like I said: just about everywhere except North America and Europe. Figure 41-1 is a map showing how much of the earth is covered by LDCs.

The Hungry People in the LDCs Want Development.
Most of the world's output is produced by and goes as income to the people in the highly developed countries. It would have to be so. Why? Because that's what highly developed means! High per capita output, and income, of course.

And that explains why so many people in the LDCs are interested in seeing more development. They want to increase their outputs and incomes. For those living near starvation in the cities and in some of the rural areas, you can understand that they want it. They want it *very very much*. You can see why.

A Word of Warning About "Averages"

Whether or not a country shows up in the statistics as "less developed" or "highly developed" depends partly on where the boundary line of the country happens to be.

For example, take "highly developed" Kuwait. Suppose its boundary was erased and it became a part of Iraq. Then suddenly the people in Kuwait would be living in an LDC! But would they be any worse off? Of course not. See the problem?

Or maybe Kuwait's high oil income would be large enough to lift "average income" in Iraq above the LDC level. Then suddenly everyone in Iraq would be living in an "intermediate development" country. But would they be any better off? Of course not.

Could you go throughout the underdeveloped world and find highly developed places? where people are doing highly productive things? where per capita incomes would be high enough to put them up at least into the intermediate development category? Sure.

What about the opposite case? Could you go around in Europe and draw circles around places which, if they were independent countries, would be LDCs? Sure. And you could do it in the United States too. And in Canada and Australia and Japan.

Suppose the boundary lines of Singapore and Hong Kong were erased and these cities became part of the countries which border them. Would the people who live in Singapore and Hong Kong suddenly be living in LDCs? Sure.

The point is this: the world map showing the locations of high development, intermediate development, and LDCs could be made to look a lot different if we made it *a map of small geographic areas* instead of averaging everything within each national border!

The differences between one place and another *within* each LDC are great. The same is true for each highly developed country, too. The poverty which exists in some of the remote areas of Appalachia is no less poverty because it's located in the highly developed U.S.A. than it would be if it were located in Bolivia or Tanzania or Afghanistan or Bangladesh.

But when it's all averaged out, the existence of the poverty is hidden. So don't forget about this "averaging" problem—and now let's talk about some specific things about the LDCs.

SPECIFIC CONDITIONS AND PROBLEMS OF THE LDCs

Most of the countries in the world are LDCs. Does that mean they're all alike? Of course not. The differences among the LDCs are great—sometimes perhaps even greater than the differences between some LDCs and some of the intermediate and highly developed nations.

The Great Differences Between LDCs

Many of the LDCs are small countries. But India and China (both LDCs) are among the largest nations of the world. Some LDCs are sparsely populated. But dense population and rapidly increasing population is the more usual picture.

Some LDCs—India and China and others— have seen the rise and fall of great civilizations in the past. Others—most of the African nations and several in Latin America and Asia and the Pacific—are only now emerging from the traditional societies of the ancient past.

In some the incomes are so low and the opportunities for "living off the land" so meager that malnutrition is everywhere. Actual starvation is a realistic threat to many people. In others, like most of the Pacific island countries, not very many people have to go to bed hungry at night. They may not have many "modern world conveniences." But they are under no threat of starvation.

How different the LDCs are from each other! Often in this chapter you will see references to "the LDCs in general." Be careful to remember about differences. Any generalization you make

about the LDCs is likely to have several exceptions. The only thing that all of them have in common is this: **average income** is very low.

The Inadequate Resource Base

One of the toughest development problems for most of the LDCs is that they don't have much to work with. They lack what's needed for "high productivity": natural resources, infrastructure (roads, harbors, water and sewer systems, electricity, etc.), productive capital (factories, industrial and agricultural machinery and equipment, etc.), and skilled labor.

Most of the LDCs need more fertile land to feed their large and growing populations. Many of them lack adequate sources of minerals or power to support industrialization. The **human resource base** (labor force) could be upgraded, of course. Illiterate people could be taught to be literate, then educated and trained in certain skills—if there was anybody to do all this. But in most cases in the LDCs, there isn't.

What would be the point anyway?—unless some use can be found for the skills they would learn? Without the other ingredients for development there wouldn't be much opportunity for most of the people to be productive anyway.

When you look at the physical and human "resource base" in most of the LDCs you can see that the economic development problem isn't going to be easy to solve.

Unequal Wealth and Income in the LDCs

If the average per capita income is less than $700 per year, can anyone be rich? Sure. In the United States where average income is more than $8,000, can anyone be poor? You already know the answer to that!

Just as there are some very poor people in the United States, there are some very wealthy people in the LDCs. That's one of the serious problems.

Fig. 41-1   Map of the World Showing Location of Less Developed Countries, Countries of Intermediate Development, and Highly Developed Countries

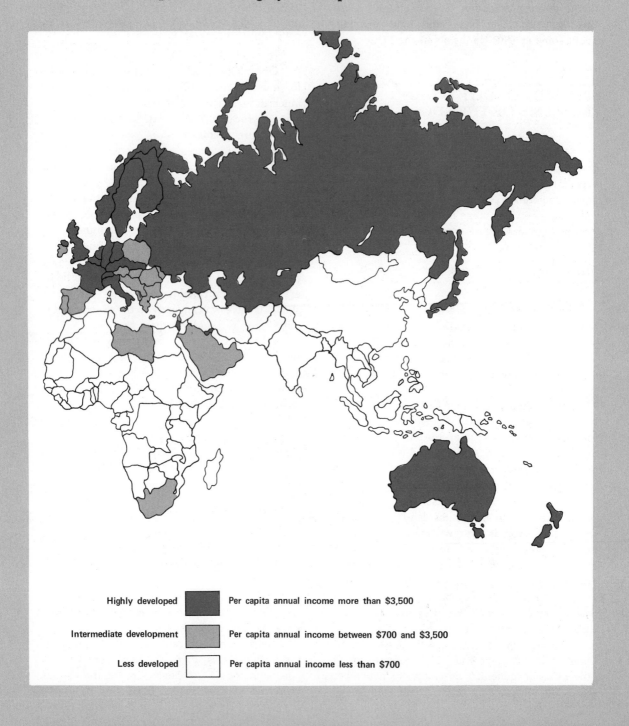

Highly developed		Per capita annual income more than $3,500
Intermediate development		Per capita annual income between $700 and $3,500
Less developed		Per capita annual income less than $700

The United States has about 6 percent of the world's people, but those people receive more than 25 percent of world income. But the almost two thirds of the world population in the LDCs get to share among themselves less than 15 percent of world income.

The extent of **income inequality** in most of the LDCs is much greater than in countries like the United States. In most of the LDCs the wealthy group is very small. But often this small group owns much of the land and other wealth of the country. The few wealthy people live in luxury while the great majority are very poor. How different that is from the highly developed countries!

The LDCs Have No "Middle Income" Group. In countries like the United States there is a large "middle income" group. Most of the people are in that group. But in the LDCs? That group is almost completely missing.

You can see that the small number of wealthy and powerful people in the LDCs might not have much to gain from economic development. Right? And much to lose? Sure.

One of the **impediments to development** in some LDCs is the fact that the "wealthy and powerful few" have no desire to see the kinds of changes which would threaten their positions of wealth and power. Often these are the people who control the government. See the problem?

Not Everybody in the LDCs Wants Change. Maybe the Americans and Europeans and others would like to be helpful—to try to help development to get going—to help to break the **traditional bonds** which keep the masses in poverty—to help increase their **productivity** so they can get more food and clothing and shelter. But maybe some people in some of the LDCs won't welcome these "helpful outsiders" at all!

Maybe now you can see one of the reasons why so many millions of people in the LDCs have been willing to join revolutionary movements (communist and others) to try to overthrow the existing system.

Inequality of income and wealth sure exists

in the United States. So does poverty. So does "political influence" by wealthy and powerful people and organizations. But these problems aren't anything like as serious in the United States and the other advanced countries as they are in some of the LDCs.

What Do the Local People Want?

It's so easy to think of the LDCs in an idealistic "storybook" way—as a lot of simple, primitive people needing help—wanting the good things of the world—people who will welcome and appreciate help in overcoming their poverty.

Even if it was that way, the job wouldn't be easy. But that isn't the way it is. So the job is very difficult. Maybe impossible? Yes. Maybe impossible.

In the discussions in Washington you'll hear people say: "Let's be careful not to force on them our own ideas and ways of doing things. Let's find out what the local people want and then help them to do things their way."

When you think about *the great inequalities of wealth and income and political power* which exist in most of the LDCs you can appreciate the **nonsense** of the question: "What do the local people want?"

The question is: "Which local people?" The wealthy and powerful traditional leaders? The few young people who have just returned from overseas universities and are impatient—often very vocal—sometimes bitter at the great wealth of the highly developed world—and insisting that all of the good things must somehow begin to happen simultaneously? Or do you try to find out what the great majority of the people want?

But remember this: the great majority of the people are not in the habit of thinking much about questions like this. Their great interest is in getting some food so they can have something to eat today. You can't much blame them for that.

See the problem? The U.S.S.R. might have a foreign aid mission doing some things in one of the LDCs and the U.S. Agency for International Development (U.S. AID) might be doing something in the same country, but aimed in the opposite direction. And both might (rightly) claim to be doing "what the local people want"!

Rapid Urbanization in the LDCs

What's the greatest migration of human beings the world has ever known? Remember from the chapter on urbanization? Sure. It's the **migration** that's going on right now between the rural areas and the urban areas throughout the world! And in the LDCs? That's where this problem is most serious.

After World War II the LDCs had about 16 cities with populations of more than 1 million. (A million people makes a pretty big city. Right?) How about in the 1970s? Would you believe four times as many? That's right. More than 60.

But think of this: in another 25 years there will be more than 200! And the cities which were already big will just keep adding millions more all the time! What will all those people be doing? And what will they eat? The prospect is frightening.

There will be millions of **squatters** living in shantytowns, makeshift lean-to temporary shelters—but living there on a permanent basis—and having more babies and making the problem even more impossible for the generation to come.

This problem of **rapid urbanization** is fast becoming a worldwide crisis. In June of 1976 the United Nations held a worldwide conference ("Habitat 76") in Vancouver, B.C., Canada, to try to work out ways to approach this problem.

The conference included representatives from most of the countries of the world, including most of the LDCs. Clearly, this "population-and-urbanization" problem is one of the most serious matters facing the modern world. And it's

in the LDCs where the problem is most acute.

Even so, most of the official delegates to the Habitat conference were not willing to admit the existence of any serious problems in their own countries. So, needless to say, not much was accomplished at Vancouver.

Heavy Dependence on Low-Productivity Agriculture

If you look at the employment statistics for almost any LDC, you'll see that more than half of the labor force—often more than three fourths—is employed in agriculture. That usually means that they are "living off the land"—that is, in **subsistence agriculture**. Often it means that the people aren't employed at all!

Rural families have grown explosively. Often there are more people living on the farm than are needed to work the land. Many of them are really "unemployed." But in the statistics they show up as "employed in agriculture." But they really aren't "producing off the land."

As families get larger and larger this problem gets more and more serious. So what happens? More and more of them move to the cities. The urban problem is compounded.

The Problem of Government Instability

There are many different **kinds of governments** existing in the LDCs. Some of them are autocratic, some are democratic, some are aristocratic. Most are some mixture of two or three of these ingredients.

A few of the LDCs have strong governments committed to strong directions and moving forcefully towards their objectives. But that's the exception—not the rule.

In many of the LDCs in Africa, Latin America, and Asia there has been one revolution after another. Sometimes lots of people have been killed. More often only a few have been killed—just the ones who need to be eliminated to let the next group take over.

In many countries the government hangs on precariously, carefully avoiding conflict, speaking softly, walking on tiptoe, letting each group or power block do their own thing—trying hard to appease all the different groups. That way the "party in power" can hold the political reigns for a little longer.

In a country where there are strong conflicts between the different factions of the population, democracy seems to lead to weak and **indecisive government**. A government which cannot take a strong position and move decisively on things is not in a good position to carry out bold programs for economic development or population control or anything else.

- How can such a government make sound developmental decisions? to **concentrate investments** in a few areas where they can have real development impact, instead of spreading the limited resources in little dribs and drabs throughout the countryside to appease the political pressures?

- How can such a government **resist** the unionized dockworkers or truck drivers or miners who decide to go on strike and double their wages, forcing inflation, and throwing the entire development process out of balance?

- How can such a government take steps to change the **land tenure system** so as to improve agricultural productivity and increase the gross domestic product and release workers from agriculture to join the labor force to help to produce the **infrastructure** and **productive capital** needed for development? It can't. Of course it can't.

Suppose you are a foreign investor, looking for an opportunity to invest somewhere in the world. Would you like to invest in a country with a "pussyfooting government"—one hanging on from day to day by walking softly and not making any tough decisions? Is that where you would want to invest? I doubt it.

Problems of "Militant Nationalism"

Some people in many of the LDCs are making noises that are "militantly nationalistic"— that is, **radical statements** against outsiders, against foreign investment, against foreign managers of foreign-owned plants, and against their foreign-aid donors—especially against the United States, which is by far the biggest foreign-aid donor of them all.

Often (but not always) the statements of militant nationalism are made by some of the young people who have returned from their college days overseas. Sometimes you hear statements such as these:

"We will own the industries in our country. We will have all of the jobs which are available here—including all of the management jobs. If foreigners want to put their money here, they should make gifts. We don't want any profits draining from our country. And we don't think anyone in this country should have to repay any debts to any foreigners."

Those LDCs where such attitudes become official government policies are not likely to develop very fast—if at all. Those who demand the whole cake are not likely to get any cake!

Increasing standards of living will require increasing productivity. No question about that. And increasing productivity is going to require new technology, capital investment, education and training, and experienced management. Foreigners could provide all of that. But no foreign investor is going to put money into anything unless the investor can reasonably expect to own and manage what is built with the money—and then receive an appropriate share of the income generated by the investment.

Given the tenor of the times, it's likely that **nationalistic policies** which block the introduction of foreign capital, management, and skilled labor are going to slow down the development process in many of the LDCs.

Some people in the LDCs have a lot to lose from development and change. They must be quite happy about this slowdown. Could it be that sometimes they are the ones responsible for the militant nationalism?—behind the scenes? I don't know. It probably wouldn't help to find out either. It wouldn't solve the problem.

Traditional Attitudes Impede Development

In many of the LDCs there have been traditional subsistence societies, with mutual sharing as the way of life. This arrangement has served well to meet the economic needs of the people, century after century.

The traditional societies survived through the attitudes of mutual work and sharing. The ideas of "private property" as we think of it in the United States really didn't exist. People did things for their family, their kind, their society.

Nothing completely "belonged" to anyone. So how does that stimulate development? It doesn't. Since nothing belongs to you, why work to get ahead? So who works hard? and saves? and invests? Nobody. So how does the society grow? It doesn't.

Suppose you could afford the time and money to take a trip and spend a few days in several of the LDCs throughout the world. If you did, almost everywhere you would see businesses run by people from outside—people who came (or whose ancestors came) from China, India, and Europe.

You'll see this pattern in much of Africa, Asia, the Pacific islands, even Latin America. It reflects a basic cultural difference between the people who are just now emerging from traditional "sharing" societies and those who had broken loose from those patterns many generations ago.

The Land Tenure Problem

The land ownership pattern is one of the most serious impediments to development in many LDCs. This is a very real problem—one which a lot of the "ordinary people" in the LDCs are upset about. In some countries this problem has contributed to the success of communist revolutions.

What's the problem? In some societies, a small group of wealthy people own the land. All the farmers work as tenants.

In the traditional societies it's somewhat different. Land is owned "communally." All the people in the family group share some "ownership rights" in the land. But nobody owns it outright. So it can't be bought or sold. It can't be used as security for a loan, either.

Sometimes the family group (or its leader) will decide to sell or lease the land. The payments can be split up among the members of the group—or maybe kept by the leader.

Suppose land is leased to a tenant farmer. Who will do long-term improvements?—maybe levelling and drainage? Usually the land owners don't want to. The tenants don't want to, either. So nobody does much. Agriculture stagnates. The society suffers.

And what about the idea of investors building plants on leased land? They would rather not. So development is slowed.

But land reform is not easy to achieve. Many people have deep feelings about land ownership.

Sometimes communist revolutionaries come in and offer to solve the problem. How? Easy. Just take the land—and eliminate the owners, in the process! There's no question that "land reform" has occurred in the countries which have had communist revolutions!

But it doesn't have to be done that way. For example, in Taiwan, land reform was carried out peacefully. The government took the land. But in exchange it gave the owners government bonds.

But by whatever means, sooner or later some changes in the land ownership patterns are going to be required in most of the LDCs. Until then, their development is going to be impeded.

Why Must the LDCs Develop?

Why should the LDCs be so interested in development? Why should they be in such a hurry to depart from their traditional ways of life anyway? Should they let the objective of "keeping up with the world" force them into this "development hangup" that seems to plague all the other nations?

If you stop to think about it, that's a ridiculous question. The intrusion of the modern world on the LDCs has long since happened. The breakdown of the traditional way of life has already happened.

There's a population explosion with millions of people pouring into the urban areas every year. There's just no way to cope with the problem—to meet even the most basic needs of the exploding populations—without development. There's just no choice about that!

If the people in the LDCs are going to make it at all, most of them must have some way to be **productive**. They must have jobs. They must be able to produce something—be able to *earn incomes*. It's either economic development or starvation for a lot of people.

So there's no question that economic development somehow must occur. But how? With all the impediments? One thing is sure: it isn't going to be easy.

Later in these two chapters you'll read about some of the things the LDCs are going to have to do—about which directions development can take, about development planning, about the future prospects for the LDCs. But first we need to talk about some of the economic principles which are important in the development process. Specifically, we need to talk about economic growth.

THE BASIC PRINCIPLES OF ECONOMIC GROWTH

The concept of economic growth can be applied to an individual, a business, a region, a society, a nation, or even to the entire world. Usually it is used to refer to a country—a nation. The simplest meaning of **economic growth** is "increasing capacity to produce," or "increasing productive ability."

The term "economic growth" is often used to mean *"per capita increase in productive ability"*—that is, the ability to produce more output, per person. This is the kind of growth which can provide an increasing standard of living for the people.

But here's a problem. As economic growth begins, population usually begins to expand too. When that happens, the output *per person* may wind up no bigger than it was before. So the average person is no better off than before!

We'll talk more about this problem later. First you will need to understand *the process of economic growth*. The next few pages provide a step-by-step description of the process—of how each economic unit—individual, business, or nation—achieves economic growth.

Economic Growth Requires Saving and Investing

Remember when you were growing corn and tomatoes in your backyard plot? Suppose you had kept on doing that for the past several years. You have worked very hard, but your output has been small.

This year you want to use your labor and land more efficiently. You decide you need more and better capital. You want to get a garden tractor and buy better fertilizer and better seed. How can you do that?

You must save. Or you might borrow from someone else who has saved. But *in order for new capital to become available, someone must save*—that is, *someone must produce output that is not con-*

sumed. Can you see that this must be true?

If everyone consumes everything that's produced, what's left over? Nothing. **Capital,** remember, is anything that we produce and keep to use in future production. If there are no *savings of output* anywhere in the country, that means we are eating up all of our output. Output is like cake. We can't have it and eat it too!

There can't be any new capital to help us produce more *next year* unless we produce more than we consume *this year!* This is another one of those little "obviously true but often forgotten" concepts in economics. If we want some left over to use tomorrow, then we can't eat it all today. And this simple truth is the key to economic growth.

You can increase the productive capacity of your backyard farm by spending less of your income for consumer goods (saving money) and then buying capital goods instead. Anyone can do that—any farmer, any business, any individual. When someone saves money and then spends the savings to get more capital, then that person gets *increased capacity to produce.* That's economic growth.

The more you **save and invest,** the more economic growth you can have. The more your economic growth, the more output you can produce.

What about a society? If all the factors of production are used to satisfy consumer objectives, then productive capacity cannot expand. Growth can't occur. But if many of the input factors are used to make capital goods instead of consumer goods, **productive capacity** will increase. Economic growth will occur.

If the society is "saving and investing" this way, then as the years go by the society's output will get larger and larger. So if the population doesn't expand too much, **standards of living** can go higher and higher.

Economic Growth Means Increasing Capacity to Produce

If we are going to increase the capacity to produce—that is, increase the total amounts of things we are able to produce in a day or month or a year—we must have either *more,* or *better* **factors of production** (labor, land, capital) or else we must learn to make better use of what we have. Obviously! What else is there for use to work with, but the factors of production? Nothing.

If you want to experience "economic growth" you can improve the productivity of your labor (by education, training, observation, trial and error, experience, etc.) or you can save your income and buy (invest in) more and better land or more and better capital.

If a nation wants to experience economic growth it must do the same thing an individual (or business) must do. It must get more and better factors of production (or it must get things better organized so it can make better use of what it has).

A nation usually can't get more land. Land area and the other "free gifts of nature" are just about all given out already! Too bad. But that's the way it is. So if a nation wants economic growth it must concentrate on the other two factors—**labor and capital.**

Essentially, economic growth for any nation hinges on the organization and development of a better labor force (better utilization, education, attitudes, skills, etc.) and somehow getting more and better capital (building more power plants, factories, and producing or importing more machines, equipment, etc.)

Every nation is constantly working to improve its labor skills and to get more and better capital. With improved labor and more and better capital, productive capacity increases. Total output can increase. The **real incomes** of the people can go up.

With economic growth, people can have more and better things—food, transportation, medical care, libraries, refrigerators, telephones, air conditioners, fish hatcheries, colleges, hamburger drive-ins, antipollution devices or whatever the society chooses to produce with its increased productive capacity. But the people can't enjoy any of these extra things if the population expands fast enough to eat up, use up, and wear out all of the increased output!

Economic growth can be a great thing for a society. It can keep a lot of people from starving! In the advanced nations it gives most of us the chance to do our own thing—to relax and enjoy life. In many of the LDCs the very lives of many people depend on it.

But when we choose the path toward economic growth, just as with every other choice, there is a cost.

The Cost of Economic Growth Is Present Consumption

What is the opportunity cost of economic growth? When you save—when you produce things you don't consume—when you use your factors of production to make capital instead of consumer goods—what happens? You give up the opportunity to consume more, today. You are giving up your chance to eat cake today—or even to *have* cake today—when you are using your resources to build a better oven (capital) for baking cakes in the future!

If you're a worker training to improve your skills or a student building an education for the future, you aren't producing anything. At least, not now. Later you will be more productive. But today you produce nothing. Who produces the food to feed you? Someone else must. Some other people must have less so that each trainee and student can eat!

You can see that the opportunity cost of rapid economic growth could be very high. Those factors of production we are using to produce tractors can't also be used to produce canned peas. But nobody eats tractors.

When a poor society produces more tractors (less peas), someone goes hungry. Of course *someday*, with the tractors, the poor society can produce many more cans of peas. Economic growth? Sure.

But until then? The people must force themselves (or be forced) to get by with less food. That's the opportunity cost of economic growth. Is it worth it?

Should some people be forced to go hungry now (maybe even starve?) to bring a better future for the children and grandchildren of tomorrow? What a difficult choice for a society to have to make! But that's the choice many of the LDCs are having to make.

Economic Growth Usually Requires Forced Savings

The problems of economic growth are difficult and serious. Most of the difficulties stem from the "opportunity cost" aspect of growth—the fact that some of the current output must go into improving labor and technology and into building capital for the future. It isn't easy to do this, when all of the output is needed now, for current consumption.

The important thing to understand is that growth requires saving—that is, producing but not consuming. Saving is never easy. Poor people (and poor nations) find it almost impossible to save. Usually a society can't get started on the path of economic growth unless the people are somehow forced to save.

The modern nations have experienced very rapid economic growth over the past century. Large savings were required to bring this about. Most of these savings were forced on most of the people. How? By unequal income distribution!

Most of the people never got the chance to use up much of the output. If they had had a choice they would have used up more. Of course! And most of the economic growth would not have occurred.

In every society, most of the people are prevented from using up as many things as they would like to use up. Either the social process or the political process or the market process limits their consumption. The limited consumption (forced saving) releases the factors of production from making consumer goods, so more capital can be produced. The society must produce fewer consumer goods if it's going to produce more capital goods. So, to grow very much the society must prevent "the masses" from receiving much income.

In an advanced, wealthy society, it's no problem. Everyone can save some. But if everybody is poor, people won't save.

In any one of the LDCs, if all of the output was **equally distributed** among the people, nobody's share would be very large. All of the people would use up all of their shares of the output and still want more. The level of savings would be zero. No growth would occur.

ECONOMIC GROWTH IN DIFFERENT SOCIETIES

In an economy where the **market process** is answering the production and distribution questions, who does most of the saving? And then who uses those savings to demand more capital, factories and machines, research, new technology, and the other things necessary for economic growth? The rich people? and the big corporations? Of course!

In Capitalism, Wealthy People Generate Growth

From the early 1800s to the time of the Great Depression of the 1930s, the great surge of economic growth in the United States was financed mostly by the **high incomes** of the wealthy people and big businesses. These "capitalists" and big businesses developed some very productive capital which brought them large incomes. They spent their large incomes to demand (and thereby to cause the society to produce) more and better capital.

As they acquired more capital their incomes went up even more. So they built even more capital. As this process continued, the economic conditions of the masses improved a little, but not much. Mostly, they stayed poor. But the economy grew by leaps and bounds.

During the late 1800s and early 1900s some very wealthy capitalists had personal incomes (tax free!) of several million dollars a year. You

can't spend several million dollars a year, year after year, on consumer goods. You just can't!— no matter how many mansions and yachts you might buy!

The only thing you can do with that much money is to use it to build more capital. And that brings you even more income. You get even richer. It keeps on snowballing, getting bigger and bigger. There seems to be no way to shut it off!

Suppose your personal income gets up to five million dollars a year. The only way you can keep from getting more and more wealthy is to spend up or give away or somehow get rid of more than $15,000 a day! How would you like to try to do that for a few days?

Economic Growth in the Traditional Society

The "economic process" of growth is essentially the same, no matter what country or society or economic system you happen to be looking at. Saving is essential. Resources and energies must be used *to produce more and better* capital and *to improve the* labor force. That's pretty obvious when you think about it. Right?

Different societies accomplish these results in different ways. In the United States and in most of the other highly developed countries, the *market process* brought about the rapid economic growth. You've just been reading about how that happened.

The high incomes of the "capitalists" (and the low incomes of most of the people) "forced" the society to save. This permitted the growth to occur.

It was painful for the poor people. They suffered. But now we are all sharing the benefits of their sacrifices. It all resulted from **forced savings**—the low incomes of the workers and the high incomes and capital-building of the rich.

How different that is from what happens in the traditional societies! In societies controlled by tradition there usually isn't much growth. If any economic growth occurs it is accomplished in the traditional ways of doing things.

For example, it might be "understood" that all able bodied men must work for three days each month developing roads and digging channels. This **capital-building** would cut down on the time the people could spend catching fish and gathering breadfruit and making tuba and other consumer goods—or just resting.

The amount of consumer goods (or leisure time) would be reduced and the society's investment in capital would be increased. The society is **transforming** consumer goods into capital goods. The society is **saving and investing.**

Suppose the traditions required that the workers go from one family farm to another, clearing brush, planting palm trees, expanding the taro patches and building copra-drying sheds. All these efforts would be "capital-building." The more this sort of thing is done, the more productive the society (economy) will be in the future.

In tradition-oriented societies this is the traditional way capital-building and growth take place. But usually there isn't much growth. The amount of effort usually is only sufficient to maintain the existing capital and to help to keep up with the needs of the expanding local population.

But mostly what's happening these days is the breakdown of these traditional arrangements and the movement of millions of people to the cities. There the task of economic growth is going to have to be approached differently. You'll be reading about that soon.

Growth in the Communist Countries

In societies in which government control over the production and distribution choices is dominant—that is, in the **command-oriented,** communist societies—the government decides how much capital will be produced. The decision becomes a part of the **economic plan** of the country.

If much capital and few consumer goods are included in the plan, then the level of consump-tion in the society will be low and the growth rate will be high. If the amount of consumer goods is small, some people may have to go hungry.

Rapid economic growth has been a major objective of the communist countries. In the **Soviet Union,** thousands of people actually died during the 1920s because of the lack of consumer goods. Both in the Soviet Union and in the **People's Republic of China** there has been a very determined effort by the government to hold down consumption and to build capital.

The growth of the Soviet Union over the past 50 years has been very rapid, especially considering the poor conditions which existed when the Communists took over in 1917.

As Wages Rise, the Growth Rate May Slow Down

The most rapid growth rate of any modern nation in recent years occurred in **Japan** in the 1960s and early 1970s. Japan's relatively low wages held down consumption and profits were high. But by the mid-1970s Japan's wage and material costs began to increase. Since then their growth rate has slowed down.

The market process can be a powerful force for economic growth. But in the beginning it works only if **wages** are low enough and **profits** high enough to generate savings and investment—to direct the factors of production into making more and better capital.

But here's the catch. These days, people don't like to live in poverty while a few wealthy capitalists live like kings. That's the way it was in the last century. But these days—in the world of the 1980s—people in many countries won't put up with that.

Everyone always seems to want a larger share of the output. That has always been true. But these days, *many people have the necessary economic and political* **power** *to be able to get more.*

No longer are people content to "suffer in silence." In the United States and other nations, workers have gained much more power. So have the farmers and fishermen and other economic groups. Also, the voice of the poor has become quite loud and powerful.

These days, the society takes a more **humane attitude** toward people. The government takes money from the rich and gives to the poor. As all this happens, more of society's resources go into consumer goods—TV sets, cars, living room furniture, air conditioners, movies, canned peas, pork chops, TV dinners, outboard motors, disposable diapers, airline travel, electric can openers, and all the other things the "average people" will choose if they have the money.

So now the economy produces more **consumer goods** instead of capital. The growth is not so fast anymore.

The Highly Developed Economy Keeps On Growing

The U.S. economy of the early 1980s has high mass consumption and low profit levels. Even so, growth through the market process continues. How can this be?

It's just that so much growth has already occurred—the economy is now so highly productive—that almost everyone can live well and still there are enough factors of production left over so that new capital can be produced. So growth can continue.

Remember the **snowballing effect** of having a five million dollar annual income? If you ever get that much you can't help getting richer and richer. It's sort of that way for the economy as a whole. In the United States the total productive capacity is great enough to provide high standards of living for the people—and *there are still enough factors of production left over to make even more capital.*

In the United States, even the "ordinary people" have incomes high enough to do some saving if they want to. They can invest in capital if they want to. Or they can just put their savings in the bank and let others do the investing.

In the United States, millions of people save some of their incomes and put the money in

savings accounts to be invested. In addition every year there are billions of dollars of undistributed corporate profits which are invested in capital.

A Summary of the Principles of Economic Growth

The most basic principle of economic growth is really very simple: *If we are going to be more productive tomorrow than we are today, then somehow we must do something today that will result in our increased productivity, tomorrow. Obviously.*

But if we use our efforts today to help us *tomorrow,* we lose the chance to use our efforts today to get what we want today. We give up today's pleasure for the sake of a better tomorrow.

Anything you do today to provide a better way to produce things tomorrow, will mean that you have less to consume (or less leisure time) today.

Economic growth requires choosing *not* to produce consumer goods, but to produce capital goods instead; *not* to spend your time earning money so you can live better today, but to go to school or learn new skills instead; *not* to spend your income for the new car you would like to have, but to spend it for a better set of tools instead.

What's the **opportunity cost** of economic growth? Current consumption? Sure.

Distribution Choices Influence the Growth Rate Indirectly. It's easy to see how the rate of growth is influenced by how the **distribution question** is answered in the society. If everyone gets an equal share, most of the output will be consumed.

But if a few people get a great amount (or if the government takes a great amount) and the majority of the people get very little, then growth can be rapid. The distribution choice influences the growth rate indirectly. Unequal distribution causes "forced savings" and generates a basis for growth.

Production Choices Influence the Growth Rate Directly. The production choice determines the growth rate directly. If the production question is answered by deciding to produce many consumer goods and a few capital goods, the growth rate will be low. But if the decision is made to produce *fewer* consumer goods and *more* capital goods, the growth rate will be higher.

The more economic growth a society experiences, the easier it is for that society to grow even faster. As growth occurs, the society gains *more* and *better* factors of production. This lets the people live better while the economy grows even more.

Those of us in the advanced nations where we work so little and have so much, are truly indebted to our ancestors—not just to our rich ancestors who built the capital and ensured the growth, but also to our poor ancestors who (through no choice of their own) worked long hours and lived in poverty and made possible all this "industrialization" and capital accumulation—all this economic growth.

THE GROWTH PROBLEM IN THE LDCs

If the LDCs are going to generate growth out of their own resources, some people are going to have to go hungry. But many of the people are already hungry. So there isn't much "slack" to get the growth process started.

What about the few wealthy people in the LDCs? Can't they use their money to get growth started? Some, perhaps. But often the wealthy people trade their money for dollars (or pounds or marks or yen or some other foreign money) and then make investments in other countries. Why should they invest in some shaky enterprise in their shaky country?

Any way you look at it, it's easy to see that the LDCs aren't in a favorable position for growth. There are no "easy avenues out." But surely there must be *some* chances. Aren't there?

Yes, there are. And there are several alternatives among which choices must be made. If enough effort is made—in line with the "right" choices—most of the LDCs can look forward to some growth. The next chapter will be talking about that.

SUMMARY AND SYNTHESIS

The turbulent events of the 1970s and early 1980s had a significant impact on conditions in the less developed countries (LDCs). For many countries, prices of their "one product output" fluctuated violently. Many of the LDCs had mounting payments deficits because of worsening terms of trade—especially increased costs of oil and petroleum-related imports.

The LDCs are very different from each other, but there is one thing they have in common: low per capita income.

Almost all of the people live in poverty, there is no "middle income" group, and a very few people are very wealthy. The very wealthy people frequently are happy with the way things are, and are not interested in change.

The LDCs depend heavily on low-productivity agriculture, and there is mass migration from the rural areas to the urban areas. Most have a problem of **government instability**, and the attitudes of the people often hinder economic development. Many of the **traditional attitudes** impede development. Problems with **militant nationalism** discourage foreign investment. **The land tenure problem** hinders development. But if the LDCs are ever going to provide anything other than abject poverty to their people they must develop.

Economic growth means increasing capacity to produce. If output per capita increases, then average standards of living can increase. The cost of economic growth is current consumption. Usually, economic growth requires **forced savings.**

The forced savings required for economic growth **can come about in several ways.** In the past, capitalistic societies have experienced growth through the **high incomes of wealthy people generating savings and investments.**

In an economy in which **equality and sharing** is the way of life, there is **very little saving.** So there is **very little to invest,** and very little opportunity for growth.

The communist countries have used governmental planning involving forced savings, to generate growth. In the capitalistic countries, it was low wages and high incomes and profits of the wealthy that generated growth.

Once an economy is **highly developed,** with a lot of people receiving **incomes so high that they can save,** growth can continue without requiring a lot of the people to live at semi-starvation levels.

The distribution choices in the society influence the growth rate indirectly. The greater the inequality, the greater the pool of savings is likely to be, and therefore the **more investment and the more growth** is likely to occur.

The production choices influence the growth rate directly. Decisions must be made whether to produce **consumer goods or capital goods.** If more and better capital are produced, then **growth will occur.** But if only consumer goods are produced, the society will be **no better off** tomorrow, than today.

The growth problem in the LDCs is especially difficult because the present flow of income is so small it's difficult to generate any savings which could be turned into investment. In the next chapter you'll be reading more about this problem, and about the prospects for doing something about it.

REVIEW EXERCISES

MAJOR CONCEPTS, PRINCIPLES, TERMS (Explain each carefully.)

the "terms of trade" for the LDCs
problem of "militant nationalism"
problem of land tenure
the role of savings and investment
the process of economic growth
income inequality in the LDCs

OTHER CONCEPTS AND TERMS (Explain each briefly.)

economic growth
forced savings
capital accumulation
the LDCs

QUESTIONS (Write out answers or jot down key points.)

1. Many LDCs have been hurt by things which have happened in recent years. Explain.
2. Where are LDCs located?
3. If you lived in one of the LDCs would you be in favor of economic development? Would it depend a lot on whether or not you happened to be one of the wealthy few? Discuss.
4. If you took one LDC and sliced it up into several smaller countries, some of the smaller countries might not be LDCs! Explain.
5. Describe some of the great differences among the LDCs.
6. How does the process of economic growth differ from one society to another?
7. Trying to get economic growth is sort of like trying to borrow money from a bank. Usually the more severely you need it the harder it is to get. Explain.
8. One way of thinking about economic growth is to think of it as "increased production potential per capita." If that's what economic growth is then one way to get it would be to get the population to decline. Right? Discuss.

42

Economic Development II: Issues and Alternatives, Plans and Programs, and Future Prospects for the LDCs

Chapter Objectives

- The last chapter gave you a look at some of the **conditions** in the LDCs, and you learned something about the **principles of economic growth**. This chapter gets into the question of: "**What can be done** about the problems of **growth in the LDCs? How?** And what are the **prospects for success?**"

- When you finish studying this chapter you will know about the **difficulties involved** as the LDCs try to meet their **human capital** and their **physical capital requirements**.

- You will know about the **importance** of the "**capital-output ratio**" question, and about the questions of **balanced growth** and the **dual economy problem**.

- You will be able to **describe** the **development planning process** in the LDCs and explain what a **good development plan** should do.

- You will be able to **describe** and to **evaluate** the present **foreign aid programs** for the LDCs.

- Finally, you will be able to give a **summary overview of the economics of the LDCs**, of their **recent changes**, and of their **future possibilities** for growth.

For the LDCs the choices are not easy. There are always several objectives begging for attention but only enough resources to move toward a very few of the objectives. So the opportunity costs are very obvious and very high.

No matter which choices are made, there will be a lot of people unhappy. Sometimes the LDCs try to move in every direction at once. Then there's no satisfactory progress in any direction.

MEETING THE HUMAN CAPITAL REQUIREMENT

There's no shortage of people in the LDCs! But there is a shortage of **human capital**—that is, the kinds of skilled and productive labor needed for economic development. So how can the "human capital" be developed out of the "teeming masses" of people?

First they need adequate **nourishment**.

(Sometimes even that is out of the question.) Then they need **basic education**—at least to be able to read and understand simple instructions. Then they need to develop **attitudes** of **working** regular hours. And they need to acquire some **basic skills**. If everyone could just go that far, that would be a long step forward. But that isn't enough, of course.

Many people in the labor force need to have advanced skills. A lot of people with supervisory and managerial abilities are required before an economy can develop very much. Such skills develop only slowly.

What About Importing Skilled Labor?

The quickest and easiest way for the LDC to get the kind of skilled and managerial labor required for development is to import it from the developed countries. To some extent that's what's going on, of course. Foreign private investment usually requires **foreign management** and **foreign skilled labor** to go along with it.

But when the unemployed and hungry local people see the foreign workers and managers earning big incomes they say: "We could do those jobs ourselves and be getting all that money!" Often there's strong political pressure to revoke the foreigners' work permits and send them all home.

The word **localization** is one you hear everywhere in the LDCs these days. It means replacing the **expatriate** (foreign) workers and managers with local people and sending the expatriates home.

It's easy to understand why local workers would be in favor of localization, and why politicians would find this a very appealing subject on which to make speeches. But it's also easy to see how the economic development of a country can be slowed and everyone harmed (except the very

few who may get jobs) by **restrictive labor policies**. The country can't develop without the kind of labor force and management capabilities required for development. But that's a choice which the government of each LDC must work out for itself.

What About Education and Training?

As time goes on, education programs can be expanded and special training programs can be set up to develop the needed skills. That's what's happening in almost all of the LDCs—to a much greater extent in some than in others. But there are some problems with this approach, too.

Good education and training programs require the kinds of resources which are in very short supply in the LDCs. Even with adequate resources it would take a long time to develop a skilled labor force. And beyond that, everybody seems to want to get educated in the **liberal arts tradition** and then apply for a scholarship to go to an overseas university! Mostly that's what the mothers and fathers seem to want for their children, too.

But how many make it to the overseas universities? Only very few. And the others? They stay home. But they aren't very well educated for the kinds of lives they're going to lead.

Their "fall-back position" is to try to get a government job and work up through the ranks in the **civil service**. And that's what a lot of them do.

In the LDCs generally, industrial skills are not desired by most of the people. A person who does **"dirty work"** doesn't have as much status as a person who does "clean work"—like clerical or supervisory work.

The LDC which wants to develop most rapidly needs to try to pull in the kinds of labor needed to support development, while simultaneously doing as much as they can to develop "local human capital." But it's really difficult to work out because of the emotional issues involved.

There's a strong appeal to such pleas as: "Let's keep the limited available jobs for ourselves!"—and "Every student should be given an equal chance to prepare and sit for the university entrance exam!" So labor force development comes only slowly.

MEETING THE PHYSICAL CAPITAL REQUIREMENTS

Just as with the human capital requirement, the LDCs can try to meet the physical capital requirement either from its own resources—that is, by producing more than is consumed and selling the surplus and buying capital—or it can try to get the capital from overseas investments or loans or grants.

The Question of Where to Get the Money

If the only capital the LDCs could get would be capital generated from their own productive surpluses there sure wouldn't be much development! Most of the LDCs are hard-pressed to meet the consumption needs of their populations. There's very little "savings" left over for "investment."

The governments of the LDCs are generally happy to accept gifts and grants. Usually they are also quite happy to accept loans for development projects. But some of them aren't quite sure how they feel about private investments by foreigners.

Suppose a major corporation decided to build a new plant employing several hundred workers in Valdosta, Georgia or Waseca, Minnesota or Tonkawa, Oklahoma or Azusa, California. What would the local people think about all this "investment from afar"? New jobs! More income! A new company to pay local taxes! Better schools and better roads and a lot of better things! Great!

But suppose the same company was talking about building the same plant in Uganda or Sri Lanka or Botswana or Surinam? Then there might be all kinds of questions about how much local ownership was going to be allowed and how it was going to be arranged, about whether or not the company would be allowed to "take its profits home," about the kinds of machinery which might be used, the speed with which "localization" would proceed, and lots of other questions.

Most LDCs won't experience nearly enough growth unless they can attract foreign investments. But in some of the LDCs, expressions of nationalism are strong. Sometimes unrealistic restrictions are set on foreign investments.

So what happens? The foreigners don't invest! So the growth of the economy is slowed. The economic circumstances of the people are worsened. But this is the kind of choice that some of the LDCs (that is, the people in power in some of the LDCs) have been making.

The Question of Which Kinds of Capital

What kinds of capital should the LDCs try to attract: The most highly productive capital? Or the kinds of capital which will employ the most labor?

From the point of view of economics it's always best to try to get "the most output with the least input." Right? Of course. So it would seem best to get the most efficient kinds of capital. Then if unemployment is a problem, *work out some other ways to use the unemployed labor*. Of course! But sometimes that isn't so easy to do.

Our economic theory is based on the idea of scarcity. Suppose labor really isn't scarce. Then it really shouldn't be conserved! Under some circumstances, that's conceivable.

Suppose the income distribution consideration is more important than the objective of conserving labor. Could it be possible that capital which requires more labor could be more socially desirable than capital which uses less labor? Yes. It's conceivable.

Of course, low productivity per worker will result. So wage rates must be low. The long run improvement in productivity in the economy (and in wages and living standards, etc.) will be slowed by the introduction of low productivity capital. But focusing on the here and now, there may be circumstances under which the goals of the society would be better achieved by slowing the introduction of the most efficient technology.

The Capital-Output Ratio

One way of getting at the question of "which kinds of capital" is to say "let's try to bring in the kinds of capital which add the most extra output value, per dollar spent on the capital."

Sound familiar? Of course! It's the same concept you've been running into in so many different ways through this book. Spend each dollar so it will do the most good! Sure.

Of course this **capital-output ratio** approach assumes that the objective is "maximum additional output." If it is, then this approach makes sense. But if there's some other objective—**maximizing employment**, or maximizing the **demonstration and training effect** of an investment, or some other, then this "capital-output ratio" guideline won't help much.

The Question of "Balanced Growth"

Should the LDC try to develop several different kinds of economic activity at the same time? Should it emphasize improvements in agriculture? and industrial development? with several different kinds of industries?

And where should all these developments be located? In the biggest city, where things tend to locate? Or at various places throughout the nation? So more of the people can participate without moving to the biggest city?

Many LDCs have emphasized industry over agriculture, and have tried to **diversify:** both into different kinds of industries and into different locations throughout the nation. Some LDCs have tried to develop uneconomic industries

when they could have done better by working to improve agriculture.

Improving the productivity of every farm just a little bit can make a lot of difference. But it isn't very spectacular. You can see why most politicians would rather be associated with the opening of a new steel mill—or of starting the nation's own airline!

The "Dual Economy" Problem

Economic development in the LDCs almost always results in a **dual economy**—a traditional economy and a modern economy existing side by side. Most of the people are living almost as their ancestors lived, while some have moved to the cities and "joined the modern world." The ones who live in the urban areas work for wages and buy the things they need. They live in the "money economy."

The ones in the "money economy" are envied by many of the others. Many of the young people want to break loose from the traditional life—to move to the city and get a job and have all those flashy things.

The idea of **balanced development** as an objective is aimed at overcoming this "dual economy" situation. But as development proceeds there's no way it can really be "balanced." When development is getting going, there are bound to be a lot of people still in the traditional economy, and some of them joining the "modern world."

When you think about it, doesn't a "dual economy" exist to some extent even in a highly developed country like the United States? Yes. If you take a trip through Appalachia or an Indian reservation you can see that it does.

DEVELOPMENT PLANNING IN THE LDCs

All of the LDCs do some "economic development planning." All the countries have their "five-year plans." Frequently the plans depend heavily (sometimes unrealistically) on foreign aid. First let's talk about the development plan itself. Then about foreign aid.

The Development Planning Process

Development planning consists of: (1) deciding what objectives or goals are to be aimed for, and (2) planning how to use the available resources to get to those objectives.

Deciding on the Objectives. Somewhere high in the circles of government, decisions must be made; about pushing for agricultural improvement, or for industrial development; about developing docks and harbors and warehouses at the major port, or pushing roads into the interior; about developing educational and training programs, or health and medical programs; about the "target rate of growth" in output per capita—and about many other questions.

Selecting the objectives is very difficult. Often it consists of deciding: "Let's do everything." Sometimes the **political situation** makes it impossible to strike out any of the "desired objectives" from the plan. But (as you very well know) to **choose everything** as the objective is really *not to choose anything!* Often that's what happens.

Finding Out What There Is to Work With. A good development plan requires a careful analysis of all **existing resources.**

It should include realistic assessments of: the available natural resources, the labor force and its abilities, the amounts of money which can be gathered by government to be used for development, the amounts of foreign capital available (from foreign aid, private investments, etc.), possibilities for importing skilled foreign workers and management and professional people to help to carry out the development programs—re-

alistic assessments of everything which is needed in the development process.

Often it's difficult to get a realistic picture of the "human and natural resource base," and of the capital which can be brought in from outside, or developed at home. But a good development plan needs good estimates of what's available to work with.

What Does a Good Development Plan Do?

Often the economic development plans of the LDCs are quite **unrealistic.** They fail to make the tough choices between alternatives. They fail to face squarely the very meagre human and natural resource situation. Often they plan for much more from foreign aid than will be forthcoming.

If a five-year plan isn't realistic, it's sort of a **five-year dream.** It can talk about the great things that are going to be accomplished over the next five years, but it doesn't make the tough choices. So it really doesn't do much.

Development Planning Requires Hard Choices. A good plan wrestles with the alternatives. It makes the hard choices among objectives. It faces the issue of **serious scarcity** of resources and it explains how progress is going to be made by carefully conserving those things which are available to work with. It describes how the **foreign exchange** is going to be acquired, and how it will be used to introduce and develop the **physical capital** required to meet the (limited number of) chosen objectives.

A good development plan will **deal squarely** with questions of agriculture versus industry, rural versus urban development, the question of income inequality, of population increase, the design and location of education and training programs, the development of infrastructure,

> Many government plans are only wishful dreams.

and the question of where the foreign exchange will come from to finance the investments.

As far as **private investment** is concerned, the plan will spell out government policy on this, including any deterrents or inducements to private foreign investments.

The plan will deal with the issue of expatriate management and labor, and localization. It will make the tough choices between doing something in one place or another; between emphasizing one kind of development or another; between having the benefits of development in a few places, or in several places.

Development Planning Faces "the Economic Problem." The good plan recognizes the strict limitation of the "production possibility curve." Development planning is a kind of **budgeting process.** It looks to see what money and resources are available. Then it works within the constraints to plan for maximum progress toward the chosen objectives. *It tries to work out a practical solution to the country's economic problem.*

One thing a good plan can do is this: It can help to get **foreign aid!** If the LDC has a carefully designed and realistic plan, it can show exactly how much aid is needed to achieve its hard-chosen objectives. So it's in a much better position to ask for foreign aid—and it's much more likely to get the aid it asks for.

Foreign aid is an important source of capital and technical assistance for most of the LDCs. The next section talks about that.

FOREIGN AID TO THE LDCs

Many of the advanced nations give direct **bilateral** aid to LDCs. For example, the United States through the **Agency for International Development** (AID—U.S. Department of State) might provide the money for clearing and draining new agricultural land or building a bridge or a hospital or whatever, in Nigeria or Bolivia or Thailand or wherever.

Most Developed Nations Give Aid to LDCs

This kind of aid is called **official development assistance.** Most of the advanced nations give some of this kind of direct aid. Even the United Kingdom with all of the economic problems now facing that country, continues a flow of official development assistance to many LDCs—usually former British colonies.

By far the largest donor of official development assistance is the United States. Our grants make up about one third of the total. But in terms of "percentage of domestic GNP" the United States is giving less in official development assistance than several other countries.

Grants by the United States amount to less than one fourth of one percent of U.S. GNP. Belgium, Canada, Denmark and Australia all give about one half of one percent of their GNP for official development assistance. France, the Netherlands, and Norway have been giving about .6 percent of their GNP. With Sweden it's up to .7 percent of domestic GNP.

The LDCs, speaking through the **United Nations Conference on Trade and Development (UNCTAD),** say that the developed countries should give at least one percent of their GNP in direct aid to the LDCs. But as yet no nation has done that.

Multilateral Aid

In additional to the direct aid, there are several international organizations which provide aid to the LDCs. The United States is by far the largest contributor to most of these organizations.

There's the **United Nations Development Program (UNDP)** which provides "expert assistance" to the LDCs. For financial assistance there's the **World Bank** and its two affiliates: the **International Finance Corporation (IFC)** and the **International Development Association (IDA).**

The **International Monetary Fund (IMF)** also

has been helping the LDCs to get needed foreign exchange—especially since the oil crisis and other problems of the early 1970s. And there are some other multilateral aid sources.

The World Bank. The World Bank (International Bank for Reconstruction and Development—IBRD) was set up at the Bretton Woods meetings at the same time the international exchange system was set up, just after World War II.

At first the World Bank made loans mostly for post-war reconstruction. But today their loans are aimed toward economic development in the LDCs. World Bank loan commitments in 1978 amounted to almost $9 billion.

The World Bank is made up of more than 130 member nations. Each member has put in some money and holds some stock in the Bank. The United States has paid in about one third of the bank's total capital of about $27 billion.

The Bank can make loans from its own capital, of course. But that isn't all. It can also sell bonds and lend the money it raises, and it can guarantee private loans. So altogether the World Bank can make available many billions of dollars of capital to the LDCs. In addition, the Bank sends experts to help the LDCs with their development planning.

The World Bank has been criticized by some LDCs (and others) as being "too tough" as a lender. The Bank has tried to make only "sound" (self-liquidating) loans. Many loan requests have been turned down. Partly to meet this criticism, the two new organizations were set up.

The IFC and the IDA. The International Finance Corporation (IFC) *provides capital and managerial assistance to private businesses* in the LDCs. In the mid-1970s the United States was pushing for an increase in IFC financing from about $100 million to about $400 million.

The other new World Bank affiliate, the International Development Association (IDA), makes loans on much easier terms (and in much shakier circumstances) than regular World Bank loans. These so-called soft loans may not all be repaid—but that's the idea. If the chance for success in stimulating development seems fairly good, then the IDA is prepared to take that chance.

The IMF Trust Fund. In 1976 the International Monetary Fund arranged to sell one sixth of their gold and use the money to set up a trust fund to help the poorest LDCs to meet their balance of payments emergencies.

Before that there had been a special fund to meet the emergencies which resulted from the high oil prices. The United States has proposed that the new trust fund be partly financed by contributions from the major oil exporting countries—since the high price of oil is to blame for a lot of the problem.

A Summary Statement on Foreign Aid

There's a lot of foreign aid flowing to the LDCs—many billions of dollars every year. But that's not enough to bring very much development very fast, anywhere. The job is just too big.

In many countries, aid can make (and has made) the difference between moving forward and standing still. A small amount of carefully placed aid may be just what is needed to put together the pieces and get things started.

Not all aid has been well placed or well managed, of course. Not all of it has been appreciated, either! But on balance, aid has done some good in just about any country you care to look at. In some countries it has done a lot.

But aid is not going to solve the development problems of the LDCs. In most cases, capital must be generated from domestic sources and also imported by foreign investments. Most of the LDCs either must attract large foreign investments or else must remain "less developed."

THE ECONOMICS OF THE LDCs: A SUMMARY

The problem of the less developed countries is one of mobilizing resources for economic growth. The LDCs need, somehow, to generate investments—to build capital.

The **market system** is great at generating investments. Right? Isn't that how the United States and all of the other advanced "market directed" economies grow so fast? Sure it is.

What About the Market Process for the LDCs?

When labor is plentiful and wages are low and capital is very scarce and highly productive, businesses can be **very profitable.** Such profitable businesses earn lots of money. Then they can invest the money and the economy can grow by leaps and bounds! Sure.

It did happen just that way in the United States and in the other advanced countries. That's what was going on all during the last century and the early part of this one. But it isn't going to happen that way in the less developed countries. Not now. Not during the last quarter of the 1900s. Why? Because conditions in the LDCs are so completely different from the "western world" of the 19th century.

The LDCs Aren't Ready for the Market Process. Certain conditions are necessary before the market process can "break loose" an underdeveloped society and start it on the path of growth. In the LDCs, those conditions don't exist. The people's desires and attitudes are not ready; the labor force isn't ready; the capital with which to begin isn't ready; the governmental stability necessary to make investments "safe" usually isn't ready, either.

More than all those other things combined, consider this: Do you think, these days, that people will accept lives of deprivation and hunger while a few capitalists get richer and richer? That's what happened in the United States and other countries during the 1800s and early 1900s. But today? No, I'm afraid not. Those times have passed.

The market process alone won't do the economic development job for the LDCs. It can't.

The Political Process Must Play a Big Role. Unless the government gets involved and breaks the vicious circle, not much development is likely to occur. So an **increasing role of the state**—economic choice-making by the political process—seems to be required. It looks like that's the name of the game for the LDCs.

The internal conditions of the LDCs aren't ready to let development "grind its way forward" through the market process. Nor are the people patient enough to let it happen that way. The economically advanced nations are always there, offering examples of how life might be—of how life is for the "favored few" of the world.

The people of the "western world" struggled and suffered hardships for centuries as their development was going on. They put up with it. That was "just the way life was." They accepted it that way.

People living in a stone age society never complained because they didn't have steel tools to work with. Of course not! But let a person use a steel tool *just once* and suddenly it's a brand new ball game.

A Taste of "Modern Things" Destroys Traditional Societies

Suppose you were born and raised in a very primitive society. You had always used a stone axe to cut down trees. Then one day a stranger came and let you use a steel axe. How that sharp blade slices through the wood! Unbelievable! After that, would you ever again be satisfied with your stone axe? I doubt it.

Suppose, in your society, if you get a small cut or scratch and it gets infected, you die. Infection causes "blood poisoning" and kills people. Everyone in your society knows that. It has always been that way. Suppose one day you get a scratch and it gets infected. Everyone knows you are going to die. But then a stranger visits your village and rubs ointment on your infected scratch and gives you a shot. The next thing you know the infection is all gone away, just like magic. Wow!

So what happens after that? Will you ever again be contented to die (or to watch someone you love, die) from an infected scratch? I doubt it.

Awareness of better things makes people want better things; modern medicine keeps people alive and lets the population expand. So what happens? There are more people, all wanting more. *Many many more people, all wanting much much more.* Where does the "more" come from? That's the problem.

The **modern nations** have brought to the LDCs just enough things to break the traditional life styles of the past: some better tools and other things, and **modern medicine** to trigger the population explosion. Truly, it's the **progress** in the advanced nations which has brought the **problem** to the LDCs.

The Need for Development Is Becoming More Urgent

As population booms, the family plots of land can't feed all the people. People leave and go to the cities. That's where you can see some of the most miserable economic deprivation you could imagine—in the **urban areas** of the underdeveloped countries.

There aren't many jobs available. It's no wonder the people are clamoring for economic development—for *any kind* of economic development. For income opportunities. For some way to get the basic necessities of life.

Economic development and **population control** are essential. But both of these objectives are extremely difficult to achieve. Resources (manpower and other resources) must be organized and directed toward controlling the population, developing a productive labor force, building capital. But how? There has to be *some slack* to begin with—some capable people and resources to *initiate* the process.

There's **surplus labor** in the cities and on the farms. Those people could be mobilized and trained. But who's going to get the mobilization and training started? And how? **Agriculture** could be made more efficient by land reform and by introducing new technology and capital. That could produce more output. The extra output could be sold in the international markets to get foreign exchange to buy capital.

But who is going to initiate the first step? And don't forget: the people have a strong respect for the traditional ways of doing things. Many **fear change.** Add to that all the taboos, and illiteracy. The economic development and population control programs are going to be difficult to plan and carry out. Who is there to do it?

The Essential Role of Government

The governments of the underdeveloped countries are going to have to play a major role in getting the growth process started and keeping it going. How else can **land reform** be done to convert tiny family plots into efficient farms and break up and utilize the massive landholdings of a few wealthy people and "feudal chiefs"? No other way. The government must do it.

How else can the **surplus labor** be shifted out of agriculture and out of the city slums, and organized, trained, fed, clothed, housed, and put to work building roads, docks and harbors, water systems, power systems, training schools, other development-supporting projects?

How else can **traditions and taboos** be prevented from sabotaging both the population control and economic development efforts? How else can domestic **consumption** be held down and **savings** increased, and then the savings used to support the population control and economic development programs? How else can **foreign aid** be brought in from the advanced nations? and then channelled into the optimum uses?

The government must be involved every step of the way, of course. Even with the very best government effort it's going to be a well nigh impossible task.

What about foreign investment? Unless the government gets some **infrastructure development** started—roads and bridges, docks and harbors, water systems, and other things needed to support development—and unless the **local government** is strong and stable and friendly to foreign investors, not much foreign investment is likely to occur, either.

Population control and economic development will never be easy to achieve in the LDCs. Without a strong and stable government exerting its best efforts to plan and administer the needed programs, nothing much is likely to happen.

Unless you've been in intimate touch with some of these countries you may find it impossible to picture the conditions there. It's hard to visualize what the development process will be like—the kind of *total change* which these societies must undergo as they strike out on the path of "modernization and development."

The Total Social Upheaval of Economic Development

Economic development means the destruction of many treasured beliefs, customs, traditions -- and that's not easy to take!

Development means a **massive upheaval** of the society. It means the destruction of customs and beliefs which have held the society together for a thousand years. Questions of what's right and what's wrong, what's good and what's bad, what's acceptable and what's unacceptable—suddenly they all are going to have different answers. I dare you to try to picture that!

People's relationships to each other must change. Relationships among the members of the immediate family and the extended family, all changed. **Traditional ideas** about rights and duties and responsibilities and obligations, all turned topsy-turvy—all shattered. The sources of honor and prestige and respect, suddenly all different. The whole pattern of what people are supposed to do and what

they aren't supposed to do must be cast in a different mold.

Just in your short lifetime you have seen enough social change in our own society— enough differences of opinion between yourself and your parents and teachers and other "old people" about what is "acceptable behavior"— that I'm sure you have *some idea* how tough it is to work out these changing beliefs about what's good and bad, right and wrong.

Can you guess how tough it must be to get an entire society to go through a complete change of mind on these things? And do it almost overnight? Impossible you say? Right!

Outstanding Governments Are Needed

Can you picture the kind of strong, effective leadership—the kind of power and charisma which will be required to motivate and direct and control the people as the bonds of tradition are shattered? With the people not knowing anymore what is right and what is wrong? Not knowing what they're supposed to do?

The **government leadership** somehow must hold it all together, must keep things moving in the right direction. A tough assignment? Unbelievable!

The world really doesn't have very many of the kinds of governments or of the kinds of leaders who could pull it off. And as you might expect, such outstanding governments and leaders as do exist in the world aren't usually found in the less developed countries.

Often the governments of the LDCs are as tradition-bound as the rest of the society. Often the governments use their powers to **perpetuate the problems.**

Suppose the big landowners are the ones who run the government. Talk about land reform? Forget it! Talk about economic development which will push aside the traditional **hierarchy of chiefdom** and make the "ordinary people" as good as the "royalty"? Forget it!

Do you see the problem? Can you see, now, why a lot of good, honest, intelligent people will join a **communist revolutionary movement** (or any other revolutionary movement) which promises to get rid of the old system?

In many of the underdeveloped countries the only way any improvement in the economic condition of the "common man" is likely, is for the government to change. Often it requires a revolution. That may not be a happy thought. But in some places that's the way it is.

Is Communist Revolution Inevitable in the LDCs?

Does all this mean that communist revolutionaries are going to be the ones to bring economic development to the LDCs? Must the established governments be overthrown in order to break loose the "feudal bonds" of the traditional societies and let development get started?

Is a **revolutionary dictator** required to make it work? Of course not. That isn't the *only* way. But that is *one* way it can be (and is being) done.

Communist revolutionaries have taken over and have shattered pre-existing societies, have swept aside the progress-impeding land ownership patterns, have initiated effective programs for population control, and have done many of the other things necessary for development.

The cost of the "revolution" approach—in terms of human life and individual freedom—has been staggering. Often the development programs have been inefficient and unsuccessful— badly planned and badly administered.

But the fact remains that the "communist revolutionary approach" is one way that it can be done. For millions of people it *is* being done that way.

Isn't there some other way? Some less cruel, more humane way to achieve development? Without such tremendous cost in human lives and suffering? Of course there is—if there's enough **enlightened leadership,** if there's enough concerned and vocal citizenry, if there's enough planning and investment aid and support from the advanced nations, and if there's not too much corruption in the local bureaucra-

cy. But these are big "ifs."

The problem of "how to get it straightened out without a revolution" wouldn't be so tough, except that the kind of leadership needed is so hard to find—in the LDCs or anywhere else in the world.

The Same Problems Must Be Faced, No Matter Who's in Charge

Suppose the communist revolutionaries do take over. Then they face the tough problem. How do they get the talent needed to design **effective plans,** aimed toward wisely chosen goals?

Then, with almost nothing to work with, how do they carry out the almost impossible task of **resource administration** for the entire nation? How do they get everything to start moving and keep moving in the right directions, toward the chosen objectives? Where do those resources and all that talent come from?

It's much easier to sweep aside the old order, "eliminating" anyone who stands in the way, than it is to choose goals, design plans, and effectively administer the labor, land, and capital of a society. Fidel Castro certainly found that out in Cuba. Lenin found it out in Russia in the years following the Bolshevik Revolution.

Brezhnev has found it out more recently. The leaders in the People's Republic of China have found it out, too. You'll be reading more about that in the next chapter.

Here's an important point I don't want you to miss: in the process of economic development in the underdeveloped countries, the things which must be done, the steps that have to be taken are going to be about the same no matter who's in charge—no matter which "banner" is flying from the state house—"capitalism" or "socialism" or "communism" or whatever.

But "who's in charge," and the "banner" that's flying can make a world of difference in **what procedures** *are followed*—in *how the changes are carried out.* In the USSR, for example, land reform was carried out by "eliminating" the landowners; in Taiwan, the land was taken but the owners were given government bonds in exchange.

It's much easier to take land by **firing squad** than by **due process of law,** of course. Quicker, too. But there may be some question about how good a society built on the "firing squad approach" is likely to be—that is, for anybody except the members of the "squad"! Maybe the slower, "due process" way is better after all.

The Market Mechanism Can Help in the Development Process

In the LDCs the **political process** is going to play a major role. No question about it. We can hope the leaders of the nations will know enough about basic **economic principles** (or have advisors who do) so they will be able to make effective use of the **market mechanism** to help them in achieving their objectives.

As you know, whenever it can be used, the **market mechanism**—motivating production and conserving things by using price incentives—is likely to be the most efficient way.

But the "market mechanism" approach is good for another important reason. It leaves people more free, more able to make their own personal choices—to decide where to live and work, which things to do or make, which things to use up and which to conserve and what to trade for what. Yet, even with all this freedom, the society's resources can be directed much more efficiently, much more "optimally" toward the chosen objectives. How's that for a good deal? More **efficiency,** and more **freedom,** too!

Sure.

Will the LDCs succeed in using the market mechanism to increase the efficiency and freedom of their economic systems? Probably some will and some won't. Probably the ones which do will fare better than the others.

Now it's time for a quick final look at some of the immediate problems and prospects of the LDCs.

WHAT ABOUT THE FUTURE OF THE LDCs?

The LDCs have a lot of problems. There are now almost a billion people living in *absolute poverty* in the LDCs. There's a lot to be pessimistic about. But can they make progress? Maybe. There are some signs for cautious optimism.

Recent Growth in the LDCs

In spite of the problems, during the 1960s and 1970s the LDCs had average GNP growth of about 5 percent per year. That's about as high as the average GNP growth rate for the advanced countries! And it's a lot more growth than a lot of people expected in the LDCs. But even so, it isn't as good as you might think.

If GNP is very low, a 5 percent increase isn't much of an increase. Also consider this: the population grew at about 2.5 percent per year in the LDCs. So the **per capita** GNP growth rate was only about 2.5 percent.

In the advanced nations, population grew at only about one percent so their per capita GNP increased by about 4 percent.

Unequal Growth Rates. Here's another problem: Several LDCs (more than 20) grew fairly rapidly while many others grew little—some not at all. In several countries (more than 20) GNP per capita went down.

If all of the LDCs had grown as rapidly as Brazil or Thailand or Lesotho or Gabon or Korea, then there would be a lot more cause for optimism. But they didn't. And even the growth rates of the fastest ones are not going to be adequate unless the flood of population can be stopped.

What about Population Control? Several countries are succeeding in slowing down their population explosion. Japan, Korea, Taiwan, India, Pakistan, China, and some others are having some success.

But don't get excited about the minor successes. The **world population explosion** is not under control—nowhere near it. In about 80 of the LDCs (including total population of about one billion people) the population has been growing at between 2.5% and 3.5% per year. That means the population doubles in less than 30 years!

Even with all the efforts to control it, the world's population continues to explode. It's increasing by more than 100 people per minute— by more than 8,000 per hour—by more than 200,000 people *every day—by a lot more than a million people every week.* It boggles the mind to think about it.

Most of these new people are in the LDCs. What a swift tide for an economic development program to try to swim against!

It isn't just a problem for the LDCs, either. Why not? If for no other reason, here's one: all those people aren't going to just sit down and starve quietly. And even if they would, it wouldn't be a very pleasant thing to watch.

Domestic Investment Rates. Some of the LDCs have been pushing hard for domestic investment. A few have been able to stimulate **domestic investment** of more than 10 percent of GNP. That's very good for a poor country!

In the highly developed countries the average investment doesn't run much higher than about 15 percent of GNP. A few of the LDCs have managed to reach that high. But again, the same problem: When GNP is very low, 10 percent (or even 15 percent) doesn't amount to very much investment.

New Technology. New technology is being introduced in many LDCs. With foreign technical assistance and sometimes foreign entrepreneurs and foreign investment, productivity increases are occurring in some places.

There's more **vocational education**—more training in the new technology. Teachers from the highly developed nations—**Peace Corps volunteers** and others—are helping.

Agricultural Breakthroughs. Agriculture has seen some important breakthroughs, too. The **green revolution** was oversold at first. Now some people are saying it wasn't all that great. But it was (and is) significant.

There really have been some startling increases in the outputs of some crops. The new seed varieties and agricultural chemicals have worked wonders under favorable circumstances. The results in some places in Mexico, the Philippines, Sri Lanka, Pakistan and elsewhere have been good. But the "green revolution" hasn't solved the problem of hunger in the world. Nowhere near it.

The Problems of World Price Changes and Protectionism

The high price of **petroleum** has hurt the LDCs. It will continue to. So will world **inflation.** And so will the shifts in the world demand, away from some of the products of some of the LDCs.

The use of synthetic rubber and fibers has dealt a serious blow to the economies of Malaysia and Indonesia and several other LDCs. In the future there will be more **synthetic replacements** for natural raw materials. And more LDCs will be hurt.

The move to **low cholesterol oils** in cooking and in margarine has hurt the coconut oil-producing areas. The recent development of fructose sugar now may be a threat to those who get their foreign exchange by exporting sugar. And so it goes. You can see why the LDCs would like to get their economies more diversified!

Attempts to Improve the "Terms of Trade." In the 1970s, through the United Nations Conference on Trade and Development (UNCTAD), the LDCs were suggesting a pricing scheme for LDC exports. The prices of what they sell would be based on an index of the prices of the things they must buy. Parity prices for the exports of the LDCs? Yes. That's the idea. But it doesn't seem very likely to be adopted.

Some of the LDCs are looking at what was accomplished by the Organization of Petroleum Exporting Countries (OPEC) cartel. Some of them are tightening up their own "trade associations" and wondering if they can't create a tight cartel and push their prices up, too.

Maybe some of them can. But world markets for most products aren't likely to be rigged as easily as was the market for petroleum. There are too many independent suppliers—and too many good substitutes for most things. Still, in

the years to come we are likely to see more market rigging and monopoly pricing for industrial raw materials—more than we have seen so far.

On the other side, several of the world's industrial nations during the 1970s began increasing their trade barriers (protecting their domestic producers) against some imports from the LDCs—especially textile products and shoes. If this trend continues it will slow the growth of many LDCs.

Needed: World Boom in the 1980s. The LDCs were hurt by the turbulent economic events of the 1970s. Perhaps the best thing for the economies of the LDCs would be a worldwide boom—with increasing world demand for the products of the LDCs.

In boom times the highly developed countries are likely to be more willing to import products from the LDCs and more generous with their "foreign aid" money for the LDCs, too. So while we're waiting (and hoping) for more permanent solutions to the problems of the LDCs, let's all hope for worldwide prosperity in the mid-1980s.

SUMMARY AND SYNTHESIS

Economic development in the LDCs will not be easy to achieve. Effective population controls will be needed. The human capital—the skilled labor and management people—must be developed and/or acquired. But this will not be easy. The appropriate kinds of physical capital must be acquired. But that will not be easy either.

In the labor area, bringing in foreigners to meet the need usually faces serious political problems. And providing (and then getting the local people to take) the kind of skills development and training needed, is difficult. In most places it's a very long-term, often politically un-

acceptable process.

Getting the needed capital is often just as difficult. Many of the LDCs would like to "have their cake and eat it too" when it comes to investments in their country by foreigners. They want the investments, but they want to control the investments. They don't want the owners of the investments to be able to earn any profits and take them home. So what happens? Nobody invests.

The question of which kinds of capital is important. Should they try to maximize the capital-output ratio? Or try to achieve balanced growth?—even if this doesn't maximize the productivity of the investments? In most of the LDCs there are serious disagreements on all of these issues. So there are no clear-cut policies. So nothing much happens.

Almost all of the LDCs use development planning to try to work toward a better economic future. Development planning consists of (1) deciding what objectives or goals are to be aimed for, and (2) planning how to use the available resources to get to those objectives. But neither of these tasks is easy. Everyone wants to achieve all the objectives at once. It's very difficult for development planners in the LDCs to be realistic about the limited resources available to work with. Sometimes the five-year plan is really a five-year dream.

A development plan which does not face the economic problem squarely—which does not make hard choices to not do and to not have certain things—will turn out to be empty promises.

Most of the LDCs receive significant amounts of foreign aid to help them in their development. Most of the developed nations give aid to the LDCs. In addition, several international organizations receive grants from individual nations and then provide aid to the LDCs. There's the United Nations Development Program (UNDP) which provides expert assistance to the LDCs. For financial assistance there's the World Bank and its two affiliates: the International Finance Corporation (IFC) and the International Development Association (IDA). Also, the International Monetary Fund (IMF) has been helping in the financing of some of the LDCs.

In the early 1980s the total amount of foreign aid flowing to the LDCs from all of the non-communist countries was more than $25 billion. But when you consider the number of LDCs and the number of people involved this obviously isn't enough to bring very much development very fast, anywhere. Aid is not going to solve the development problems of the LDCs. Most of the LDCs either must attract large foreign investments or else must remain "LDCs."

Given the economic and political circumstances in most of the LDCs, it appears that the political process must play a big role in getting development going. The people in the LDCs have tasted modern things and they want those things—for the present generation. As fast as population is expanding, productivity must increase just to keep them in the same place!

Government planning and powers of enforcement will be required to break through some of the traditional impediments to development. Economic development causes total social upheaval in a traditional society. Outstanding government leadership is required. But in most of the LDCs that's seriously lacking.

You can see why communist revolution may appeal to a lot of the people. But if revolutionaries take over, then they face the same tough problem. History shows us that communist revolutionaries don't work any development miracles, either!

No matter who's in charge, as the political process plays its role of choosing among objectives, the price mechanism can most efficiently direct resources toward the chosen objectives. With the market mechanism there's more efficiency, and more freedom.

The outlook for the LDCs is not all rosy. In many LDCs significant progress is being made. But some aren't even holding their own against the tide of population growth.

Several are slowing their population explosion. Some have been able to stimulate domestic investment of more than 10 percent of GNP. Some are making progress in introducing technology and in vocational education. And some have increased their agricultural productivity. And some (like Mexico) have struck oil!

It's clear now that a number of the LDCs are going to break free of their vicious circles of poverty and move into paths of sustained growth. But several seem doomed to stay within the vicious circle for the foreseeable future.

REVIEW EXERCISES

MAJOR CONCEPTS, PRINCIPLES, TERMS (Explain each carefully.)

the "human capital" problem
the "physical capital" problem
the "balance of growth" question
the role of development planning
the role of foreign aid
the role of "the market"

OTHER CONCEPTS AND TERMS (Explain each briefly.)

localization   U.S. AID
capital-output ratio   UNDP
dual economy   IFC
"official development assistance"   IDA
multilateral aid   the "green revolution"
the World Bank (IBRD)

QUESTIONS (Write out answers or jot down key points.)

1. Why is it so difficult to develop the needed labor force in the LDCs? Surely there are plenty of *people* there! Discuss.
2. Sometimes policymakers in the LDCs try to "have their cake and eat it too" as far as foreign investments are concerned. Discuss.
3. What about the U.S. contributions for economic development of the LDCs? How much have we been giving? Do you think that's enough? Discuss.
4. Describe the most important of the multilateral aid programs of the early 1980s.
5. Discuss the role of foreign investment in the future of the LDCs.
6. It seems inevitable that in the LDCs, "the state" is going to have to play an increasing role. Can you explain why this is true, and what kinds of things the state is going to have to do?
7. What do you think about the future of the LDCs? How have they been doing recently? What's going to happen next? Discuss.
8. If an LDC has a strong and stable government and good economic planners, much of the development task can be approached through the use of the market mechanism—through the use of the rationing and the production-motivating functions of price. Can you describe some of the specific ways the price mechanism might be used? Try.

43 Economic Systems of the 1980s: Evolving Blends of Economic Planning and the Market Process

Chapter Objectives

- This chapter **describes, analyzes, and evaluates** some of the important kinds of **economic systems** existing **in the world today.** It emphasizes the **different roles** played by the **market process, the social process,** and the **political process** in different countries.

- When you finish studying this chapter you will be able to **describe and evaluate** the important kinds of **economic systems** in the **major nations of the world.**

- You will know about **economic planning** and be able to explain (a) **how the plans are made,** and (b) **how the plans can be carried out** using either **direct allocation** or the **market mechanism.** And you will be able to **evaluate** each of these methods of **plan implementation.**

- You will be able to give some **overview highlights** of the **planned economies of the USSR and the People's Republic of China,** and of the ways these and other **communist economic systems are falling short** of their expectations and are **changing.**

- You will be able to discuss **the changing role of the market process** in the modern world of the 1980s, and the question of **the survival of capitalism.**

Throughout this book you've been reading about economic systems. All of Part Eight was talking about the American economic system and its various parts. Almost all you've been studying in microeconomics and in macroeconomics is concerned with how a **market-directed economic system** works.

You know that the concepts and principles of economics can be applied to an individual, to a business, or the whole society. When concepts and principles are applied to the whole society we're talking about the economic system—what it is, how it's put together, how it works.

Back in Part One you read about the three different processes at work in all economic systems: the **social process** (tradition), the **political process** (government "command"), and the **market process** (the price mechanism). In this chapter you'll be reading about how these processes work in real-world economic systems.

What Is an Economic System?

The **economic system** is what gets the society's economic choices made and carried out. It organizes and directs all of the natural resources and all of the factories and machines and equipment—and all of the people who operate and manage the factories and machines and equip-

ment and everything. Everyone involved in the production of anything is a part of the economic system.

How are the **three basic economic questions** answered? And then how are these decisions carried out? When you know the answers to these questions you understand the basic nature of the economic system.

The economic system is the organized set of procedures the society uses for working out the answers to the basic production and distribution questions. It's the systematic way the society solves its **economic problem!** Of course.

AN INTRODUCTION TO REAL-WORLD ECONOMIC SYSTEMS

Every economic system is made up of some combination of the **social,** the **political,** and the **market processes.** It's a lot easier to talk about "the three processes" than it is to talk about real-world economic systems! Each process has a precise meaning. But when we get into real-world economic systems nothing is very precise anymore.

Each Economic System Is Unique

In each real-world economic system, all three processes—social, political, and market—are at work all the time. And each economic system is changing all the time, too. But we still keep calling each of these evolving real-world systems by the same names.

We still talk about "American capitalism,"

for example. How can that be? It's just that the "system names" aren't very precise. So don't get hung up on the names. How we "label" an economic system really doesn't tell you much about it.

Many times you've heard about "capitalism" and "socialism" and "communism." What do these words mean? That's what this section talks about.

The Economic System Called "Capitalism"

What is **capitalism?** It's an economic system in which the means of production—the factories, tools, equipment, coal mines, oil wells, railroads, etc.—are owned by private individuals, not by the government. **Private ownership** is the distinguishing characteristic of capitalism.

In a capitalistic economic system the owners and workers are free to use their resources, energies, tools, etc. in response to the market process. The workers and owners who respond best—by making the things wanted most—will enjoy the biggest incomes. Of course.

Capitalism has many names. It's called the *free enterprise system* or the *private enterprise system* or the *competitive free enterprise system* or the **laissez-faire** *system.* Laissez-faire is a French term meaning that the government lets the people do whatever they want to do.

If we put together all of the names describing it, capitalism is a system of **laissez-faire-competitive-free-private enterprise.** That's really a pretty good description of what capitalism is. But no "pure system" of capitalism has ever existed in the real world. Some of the effects of such a system would be intolerable!

In **pure capitalism** you're on your own. Entirely. If you break your leg and can't work, unless you've saved enough to get by on, you starve. In "pure capitalism" the government doesn't bail out the ones who can't make it on their own.

With "pure capitalism" we wouldn't have any national, state, or local parks or recreation areas and no public schools or libraries or health and welfare programs. No "public" anything!

Unmodified capitalism would be too harsh to be socially acceptable. Real-world capitalism is always some mixture of socialism and capitalism. The American economic system today is certainly a mixture of capitalism and socialism. So I refer to the American economic system as a system of **mixed socio-capitalism.**

What does it mean to say that the American economic system is "mixed with socialism"? What is socialism?

The Economic System Called "Socialism"

The word **socialism** can mean many things. But it always includes the idea that many economic choices are made and carried out through the political process. If the political process is democratic, then you have **democratic socialism.** If the political process is autocratic or dictatorial, then you have **autocratic socialism.**

Suppose the people could work out a way of mutually sharing all of the work and all of the output of their economic system Then they would have an economic system of **utopian socialism** (which is the same thing as **utopian communism**). The words "socialism" and "communism" come from the same idea. **Socialism** says "society-ism" and **communism** says "community-ism." But that isn't what these words have come to mean in the world today!

In a real-world system, "socialism" means that the government owns and controls some of the industries and it also provides "welfare programs" for the people. The government may own and operate such industries as electric power, coal, oil and gas, transportation, communications, perhaps steel and chemicals, and perhaps others.

One "socialist" country will have more industries under government ownership than another. Also the welfare programs will be different from one socialist country to another.

Is the U.S. Economy Capitalist? In the United States the federal government dredges rivers, builds dams and bridges, produces and sells electric power and chemicals, manages many kinds of natural resources and operates recreation areas. Since 1971 it even operates a nationwide railroad passenger service (Amtrak). And it regulates and controls transportation, communications, electric power, natural gas and several other industries. Is that socialism?

The state governments in the United States are in the insurance business, the liquor business, and various others; local governments are in transportation, water and sewer service, electric power, and other enterprises. Is that socialism?

In the U.S. economy the influence of government touches everybody. No business can afford to make any important decision without first considering the effect of the decision on the taxes it will have to pay. There are licenses, zoning regulations, building codes, pollution regulations, minimum wage laws, and many other government influences.

"Free enterprise" in the United States is really not so free after all. Yet we still refer to the U.S. economy as a "free enterprise" economy—as an economic system of "capitalism."

Capitalism and Socialism May Be Indistinguishable. If the U.S. economic system (with so much governmental influence and control) can be called capitalism, then what is socialism? The truth is that in most real-world cases it isn't very different from the American economic system.

Take the British system for example. A few more of the major industries and resources are owned by the government—coal, transportation, communications, etc. But the British and U.S. economies are really very much alike. Yet we call the U.S. system "capitalism" and the British system "socialism." Why?

Here's one reason: In the United States most people have been taught that socialism is "bad" and capitalism is "good." The Democratic party and the Republican party and the people in general are always doing things to bring about "socialist reforms" in our economic system. But you seldom hear anyone calling the changes "socialist reforms"—not in the United States.

The "Socialist Reforms" of "Mixed Socio-capitalism."

We are constantly making **socialist reforms**. Unemployment and social security benefits, Medicaid and Medicare, public welfare and public assistance, college fellowships with family support, government subsidies for industry, minimum wage laws, Amtrak, TVA, and many other **government interventions** are always chipping away at "raw capitalism."

If you should happen to make a trip to Western Europe and find the "good old American spirit of capitalism" everywhere you go, don't be too surprised. The difference between the **capitalistic socialism** of the Western European countries and the **socialistic capitalism** of the United States really is not always easy to see! The systems are really much more alike than different.

In both places *the demand of the people works through the market process to influence most of the production and distribution choices of the society.* In both places *the political process (government) plays a very important role in making and carrying out the economic choices.*

The truth of the matter is this: The U.S. economy and all these other economies are really systems of **mixed socio-capitalism**. It would eliminate a lot of confusion if we would start calling them by that name!

Economic System? or Political System?

Be careful. Don't confuse the political (governmental) system with the economic system. The two are always related, of course. But they're essentially different things.

Democracy and dictatorship are forms of government. Capitalism and socialism are forms of economic systems. Either capitalism or socialism could exist in a country with either democracy or dictatorship. Sometimes people tie democracy with "laissez-faire-competitive free private enterprise capitalism," and associate socialism and dictatorship. How absurd!

We call the British system "socialism" and the American system "capitalism." But is the British government any less democratic than the American government? No. In some ways the British government is more directly responsive to the people than is the government of the United States!

And what about the United States? There's much more government control over the economic choices now than there was 100 years ago! But has the government become less democratic? I don't think so. All the evidence points the other way. These days, even people without property, blacks, women, and eighteen-year-olds can vote!

What about Communism? Is that different? Let's talk about that.

The Economic System Called "Communism"

Communism is a difficult term to understand. It refers to both a **political system** and an **economic system**. And there are so many different meanings of "communism"!

Communism (with a capital "C") is the name of a **political party**. The Communist party is the group that runs things in the communist countries. What's a Communist country? One where the Communist party is in control, and running things, of course!

The Communist Philosophy and Predictions. Another meaning of the word "communism" is the "**philosophy and predictions** of the communist philosophers": Marx, Engels, Lenin, Mao Tse-tung, others.

For some people the philosophy of communism is a sort of religion. There's a strong belief that the communist doctrine is true and that the predictions are really going to happen. So one definition of a "communist" would be "one who believes in communism"—one who believes the doctrine of communism.

The communist philosophy generally holds that the market process isn't going to work. Pretty soon a few monopolists will gain control and enrich themselves while everyone else suffers.

Then the miserable masses will revolt. They'll kill off all the monopolists and take control. So capitalism will be destroyed. After that the government will be in the hands of the Communist party leaders who will be in control of everything in the nation.

Ultimately there will evolve an economy of abundance. There will be no economic problem of scarcities of material goods—not for anyone. A beautiful world will evolve in which people will no longer be selfish. The wants of everyone will all be satisfied.

People will continue to produce for society because of their love for the society. The government will just "wither away." In such a society of mutual love and trust and respect for each other and where there are no unfilled desires, who needs government? The idea of the coming of the utopian ideal community is where the word "communism" comes from.

What About Utopian Communism?

What about the idea of living in a communal society with a group of other people? The clan in some traditional societies and the family in modern societies operates as a sort of economic commune.

The idea of the commune is that each person works for the group. Each plays his or her role in helping out and they all share things together.

Utopian communism (like "utopian socialism") has never existed except on a small scale among groups of a few people. As a "real-world economic system," it doesn't exist.

The Communist Economic System. The economic system of communism is really an extreme form of socialism. Not just a few major industries but all the factories and mines and stores and restaurants and everything else are government-owned and operated.

The natural forces of the market are not permitted to have much influence on the economic choices. The government owns and directs virtually all of the resources. All the production and distribution decisions are made by the government.

Since the Communist party is in control of the government, the party controls the economic choices. Since the party is controlled by a few people, these few people are really the ones who make the choices for society.

The planned outputs and inputs of the farms and factories are all determined by the government. In the communist system, all of the society's inputs—workers and resources and everything—move according to the government's economic plan.

Industries operate as the government directs. Whether or not the economy will try to produce more heavy machinery and less consumer goods is not determined by private investors. There aren't any private investors! The government decides.

The number of economic decisions which individuals control is very small. People are free to spend their (small) incomes among the few kinds of consumer goods which the "economic plan" calls for.

In general, people's incomes are determined by the work they do and how productive they are. But it is the important people in the party (in the government) who get the most.

ECONOMIC PLANNING

The Communist countries aren't the only ones using economic planning. Government planning in the "mostly market-directed" econo-mies of socio-capitalism is playing an increasing role. It's a trend that got going in Europe in the 1920s, after World War I.

In the United States the trend toward the increasing role of government in the economy didn't really start until the 1930s. The New Deal days? Right. And it has been going on that way most of the time ever since.

And consider this: It's only during this cen-tury—since the time of World War I, in fact—that the several so-called "communist" economic systems have been set up.

"Government economic planning" or "cen-tral economic planning" or just "economic plan-ning" is very important in the world today. Eco-nomic planning is the alternative to the market process for getting the society's economic choices made and carried out.

"Economic planning" is the mechanism of the political process. It's going on everywhere. In the last chapter you read about economic planning in the LDCs. In this section you'll be reading about economic planning in general.

Designing the Plan

The Soviet Union and other communist countries and several non-communist countries (including many LDCs) operate on a five-year plan. The idea is that a set of objectives is laid out in detail, to be achieved during the coming five years. Then all the resources are aimed to-ward fulfilling the plan.

The five-year plan attempts to figure out just exactly how much of each of the various prod-ucts will be produced, and then exactly how each of these will be used—for consumption, or for further production; and if for further produc-tion, for the further production of which things.

Planning Is a Big "Production Possibili-ty" Exercise. You can see that this is like a big "production possibility" or "transformation curve" exercise. Only instead of having only two choices, the choices are almost infinite; and in-stead of knowing for sure exactly how much we

can produce with the available resources, we can only estimate.

How are all these things decided? Through the political process, of course! The government experts (economists) work with the political lead-ers and the production supervisors to get the plans worked out.

All Economic Systems Use Some Plan-ning. Without economic planning, do you sup-pose there would be any state-supported schools or colleges in your state? or a highway system? or any police or fire protection in your town?

Or do you suppose there would be a United States flag on the moon? or an intracoastal wa-terway running from Maine to Mexico? or a Saint Lawrence Seaway? or national parks and recre-ation areas? None of these would exist without economic planning.

The amount of "economic planning" going on in a society indicates the extent to which the political process is making the economic choices. If the government makes most of the choices then there is a lot of economic planning. But when the choices are left up to the market pro-cess, economic planning isn't necessary. Re-sources and products and workers respond to the price mechanism and automatically flow to where they are demanded.

Economic Planning Reduces Individual Choices

Economic planning can make a lot of differ-ence in the lives of the people. It matters wheth-er there is a little or a lot of planning. And it matters how the plans are made.

How much democracy is used in designing the plan? Who gets to have an influence on the objectives? Who decides which resources will be used in which way? If there's a lot of planning, everyone's life is patterned by the plan. So in a society which has a highly planned economy, these questions become very important.

If there is very little economic planning then the market process will be in control of most of the choices. People will respond to the market. The ones who are able to get a lot of money will have a lot of influence. Each person who can get more money can have more influence and can have more things.

In an economy controlled by economic planning, individuals have **less freedom of choice**. If the government of the United States decides to use more resources for Medicare (and to tax you to pay for it) then the society is not going to be able to produce that sporty little car you had wanted to buy—but which because of the high taxes you aren't going to be able to pay for now anyway!

In the Soviet Union, suppose you wanted some new gloves and a warmer coat but the government decided to put more of its resources into the production of a new steel mill. Then the new gloves and warmer coat are not going to be available to you no matter how much you would like to have them.

Economic planning **reduces consumer choice**. But this is not to say that economic planning is always undesirable. Of course not! No intelligent person would suggest that "maximum individual freedom of choice in all things" is the paramount objective!

But the farther we go with economic planning the more we cut down on the individual's freedom of choice. That's a fact we should recognize.

Implementing the Plan

It makes a lot of difference how the plan is carried out, too. Essentially there are two kinds of approaches: (1) the resources can be allocated directly—that is, **ordered** or "directed" to go where and do what the plan requires; or (2) the resources can be **enticed** to do as the plan requires by offering rewards (money).

The first approach can be called "allocation by direct order" or simply **direct allocation**. The second might be called "allocation by incentive." It means using the **price mechanism** to direct the people and resources into the planned activities.

Using the Market Mechanism. In an economic system which relies mostly on the market process, it's just natural for the government's economic plans to be carried out through the "market mechanism."

If the government wants a canal dug, a highway built, or someone to teach in the local school, what does it do? It doesn't *order people* to do these things. Instead, the government **offers to pay** to get the job done.

In the case of the highway, the government can pay a contractor. Then the contractor will hire the labor and buy all the needed things, then build the highway. Or the government might hire the people, buy the rocks and gravel and steel and cement and graders and all the other things and build the highway itself.

In each of these cases you can see that the market mechanism is being used to carry out the plan. People are automatically responding to the **price and profit incentives** offered by the government.

Most of the economic planning decisions in the United States and in the other modern noncommunist countries are carried out by the market mechanism. This means that if you look at the total amounts of money being spent by the national, state, and various local governments, you will get some idea of the total amount of resource use which is being directed by the political process—by governmental "economic plans."

You know that in the United States total government spending amounts to about one third of GNP. That indicates a lot of economic planning? Right.

Direct Allocation. Many of the "political process choices" even in a country like the United States are carried out by direct allocation. Many of the "direct allocations" consist of **private resource-use limitations**.

For example, the uses of almost all of the land in the urban areas of the United States (and in many rural areas too) are restricted by some kind of "zoning" or "land-use restrictions." This means the local government tells you what you can do (and what you cannot do) with "your" (the society's) land.

Governments limit the kinds of activities you can undertake in various places, and governments limit the kinds of resources you can use for what purposes. **Government regulations** are influencing the economic decisions—the resource-use choices—all of the people all of the time.

As population expands and as technology develops, government plays a larger role. That's the way it has been happening.

Economic Planning in the "Non-Market" Economies

In the Soviet Union and the People's Republic of China and the other so-called **communist** countries, economic planning gets into every aspect of life. The plan includes almost all of the **output** and **input** choices. It shows how industry and agriculture will be organized: what kinds of machinery and other inputs will be used, and all the other production details.

But each person's **income** is not predetermined by the plan. In the Soviet Union and in the other communist countries the **productivity principle of distribution** is used just as it is in the United States and in the other "mostly market-directed" economies.

One important difference between the non-market economies and our kind of economy is that they use **resource administration** a lot more than we do to carry out the plans. What is resource administration? The next section talks about that.

RESOURCE ADMINISTRATION? OR THE MARKET MECHANISM?

You already have had a lot of experience with "resource administration." Your college administrators decide how each classroom will be used at each hour of the day, who will live in which dorm, how much land space will be used

for athletic fields and how much for parking lots, and who will get to play in which fields and who will get to park in which lots.

They decide how much floor space will be used for the library, how much for study areas, for student lounges and for faculty lounges, which professors will teach which courses with how many students in which rooms at which times, which students will get to use which of the college's resources, to take which courses. . . . On and on the list could go. This is what it's like with resource administration.

At your college, all of the resource-use choices may be made through very **democratic processes.** The students and faculty may be the ones who have the ultimate say on all of these issues. If so, then everything may be going just fine.

But, likely as not, many of these decisions will be made undemocratically—will be imposed by someone "from above"—who knows what's best for your own good and for the good of your college and is going to give it to you whether you like it or not.

Sometimes your own college administration may be the "dictator." Or it may be your state legislature. Or maybe both. But whoever does it, whenever **autocratic** resource-use planning and administration happens, unless it's done with great wisdom—with great awareness of and sensitivity to the people and issues involved—then problems will arise. Things won't go smoothly. **Morale** will be low.

The **power** to order people around is an essential part of any system of "resource administration." If the administrators are wise and just and if they use **effective leadership** techniques and all that, it can work out just fine. But unfortunately there just don't seem to be enough wise, just, sensitive administrators to go around. So it isn't unusual for problems to arise.

How "Market Mechanism-Type" Incentives Could Be Used

Do you begin to get the idea of what "resource administration" is? When your mom or dad hands you a bucket of paint and tells you to paint the bathroom or hands you a broom and tells you to sweep the steps—and if you feel that you *must* do it (or else face unpleasant consequences)—that's **resource administration**.

How might "market mechanism-type" incentives be used instead? Your mom or dad might offer to pay to get the bathroom painted. They could keep raising the "price" until you (or someone) will gladly grab the brush and start slopping paint all over. Or they could pay to get the steps swept. Obviously.

But what about your college? You know that your college is sort of an "administered economic system." How could it use **market mechanism-type incentives**, instead of "direct allocation"? instead of resource administration? For many things, it couldn't. For some things, it does.

Raises and promotions go to the professors who do a good job (and/or to the ones who please the administrators). Sometimes parking fees are low for the distant lots and high for the close-in ones. But these examples don't really get into the basic resource-use choices for college. Let's take one that does.

A Price System for the "Planned Economy" at Your College. Most colleges need more facilities—more and better buildings, classrooms, listening booths, study areas, and other facilities. But did you ever stop to think of the amount of wasted excess capacity that exists on the college campus at three a.m.? Wow!

Why don't our resource administrators start scheduling classes all night long? Because the faculty and students would revolt, that's why! And because administrators don't like to work nights, either.

Suppose someone began to think about the millions of dollars of savings which might result from running the college all night. Is there any way that people might be *induced* to go to college on the "midnight shift"? Some of the savings might be offered as "bonuses" to the professors and as "scholarships" to the students.

Do you suppose that could work? You bet it could! All it would require is that administrators set the right **price incentives**—the right "bonus" and "scholarship" payments.

Price Adjustments to "Fine-Tune" the Resource Flows. If too many professors and students volunteered for the night shift, the bonuses and scholarships could be reduced. If not enough volunteered, the payments could be raised. Maybe it really ought to be tried. It might work!

The administrators could assign "penalty charges" to professors and students who chose the most desirable class times (like 10 a.m., M.W.F.) and offer "bonus payments" to those who chose the less desirable times.

Eight a.m. and four p.m. classes might carry a two percent bonus; 9:00 a.m., noon, and 3:00 p.m. classes, no bonus and no penalty charge. Then evening and night classes would all carry bonuses of various sizes. For some hours—like midnight on Saturday night, or 8 a.m. Sunday—perhaps the bonus payments would need to be so high that those hours would have to be left idle.

Do you think a system like this could be made to work on your campus? How about all over the country? It's interesting to think about. The savings might run into several millions! But the purpose here is not to recommend it. It's just to show how "market-type" incentives might be used.

Once we get going on this "market mechanism-type" incentive program we might just as well keep going. We could build in bonus payments and penalty charges for professors on the basis of their productivity—how many students they deal with, how much they publish, or whatever measure of productivity is decided on. Each student could make "large-class or small-class" choices and "high-paid prof or low-paid prof" choices and could get rebates or pay extra according to the choices made.

See how it might work? There would be some problems, of course. This approach might not meet our ideas of **equity and justice.** But it sure would take care of the problem of being ordered around by your college administrators! Many professors and students and administrators would perform quite differently under such a system.

Now you know how the price mechanism might be used to carry out economic plans. *Prices are adjusted to get people to go to the chosen places and do the chosen things. This makes it unnecessary to order people around, so policing (watching to see that everyone follows orders) becomes unnecessary.*

The price mechanism can be a very efficient way of getting the resources to do what the plan calls for. Everything just moves automatically!

Do Communist Countries Use the Price Mechanism?

Now that you see what an efficient "resource director" the price mechanism can be, you may wonder why the communist countries use resource administration (direct allocation) instead. One reason is philosophical. They associate wage and profit incentives with their **philosophical adversary: capitalism.**

Anything that looks like capitalism is bad. Anyone who suggests using profit incentives to get resources to move around, soon may be scheduled to go on a long trip—one way.

A second reason is that the Communist party planners haven't been fully aware of the advantages. Understanding the price mechanism and how it works isn't exactly the Communist party leader's cup of tea!

But the truth is that the communist countries *are* using market mechanism-type incentives (the price mechanism) more and more. They are beginning to appreciate the **great efficiency** of the market mechanism as a tool for carrying out economic plans.

They're finding out that an efficient way to get a hole dug is to offer money to anyone who will dig it—and let the digger try to make a "profit" on the job. A good way to get a factory or a hotel or a restaurant or anything else operated *efficiently* is to let the manager work to try to make a **profit.**

Communist Countries Are Using More Incentives. The Soviet Union and its satellite countries are discovering that enterprises which cannot be operated efficiently by government resource-administrators can sometimes be operated very efficiently by a private individual seeking profit.

What's the difference? The profit seeker has a very strong **incentive** to economize and optimize! The November 15, 1971 issue of *U.S. News and World Report* carries the article: "Why Reds Are Turning to Capitalism."

This article describes several instances in which serious inefficiencies had existed in hotels and other service establishments. Then individual managers were allowed to take over the establishments, run them as their own businesses and try to make profits. In most cases the improvements in services and reductions in costs were dramatic!

Throughout the 1970s and on into the '80s there were more and more instances where communist countries were allowing price and profit incentives to work. The People's Republic of China has been moving purposely in that direction. It has established several free enterprise zones. In the early 1980s China was offering incentives to foreigners to set up manufacturing operations in those zones.

On January 1, 1982, a Communist "Soviet satellite" country (Hungary) enacted **economic reform** laws allowing people to form small private enterprise, profit-seeking businesses. The deputy finance minister's comments are reported on page 1 of the March 26, 1982 *Wall Street Jour-*

nal. He said:

"We are saying to our ambitious people, 'unfold your capacities.' It's quite a natural ambition for all human beings to want more than they had yesterday. We must give them the chance."

The Influence of Pragmatism. Are the "Reds turning to capitalism"? No, not really. But there seems to be a movement away from the philosophy that "anything that looks like capitalism must be despised and shunned."

The communist countries are simply indicating their ability to use an approach which has been a hallmark of American life—in economics, in politics, in everything. What approach? **Pragmatism.**

The pragmatic approach aims for results. Try something. If it works, that's good. Do it some more. If it doesn't work, stop doing it. Try something else. Pragmatism recognizes only **effectiveness.**

Pragmatism has been causing Communist countries to use the market mechanism. Why? Because it's **efficient.** It works too well to be ignored.

What about the United States, with its strong laissez-faire philosophy? We have been introducing economic planning techniques which the communist (and other) countries have been developing. Why? Are we swinging over to communism? Of course not! Then why are we using more and more economic planning? Because sometimes that's what seems to work best, that's why!

Are Economic Systems Becoming More Alike?

What's the ultimate result of all these "economic system changes" going to be? Will all the nations eventually wind up with the same kind of economic system? A system with some blend of the market process and government planning? I don't know. Nobody knows. But it doesn't seem likely that anything like that is going to happen very quickly. The philosophical and political impediments are too great to be swept aside easily.

We'll talk more about this question later. First let's take a closer look at what's been going on in some of the "non-market" economies—the economic systems of the Communist countries.

PLANNED ECONOMIES: THE USSR AND CHINA

There are two really big countries which have so-called "Communist" economic systems. Which countries? The People's Republic of China and the Soviet Union, of course.

The economic systems of both of these countries have something in common: **central economic planning** and **resource administration.** Let's talk about how these two systems have been doing. First, the USSR.

The Economy of the USSR

After the Bolshevik (Communist) revolution in 1917 the Soviet system sort of fell apart. The Communist leaders imposed rigid controls, but they didn't know how to get the system put together again.

Lenin's "New Economic Policy." In 1921 Lenin announced his **New Economic Policy**—a "temporary step backward toward capitalism"—and urged people to produce for themselves and to trade and try to make profits. The purpose was to overcome the complete **economic collapse** following the Communist take-over. Remember in the movie *Dr. Zhivago,* or *Reds,* how tough things were?

Beginning in 1928 with the first **five-year plan,** rigid economic **controls** were imposed again. That was more than half a century ago. Today the Soviet economy is still rigidly controlled. No doubt about that! But it's considerably different.

Present-day Planning in the USSR. Consumers now get to have more things. People are ordered around less. Wage and price incentives are used more. The economic plan now responds more to the people's demands for consumer goods—but apparently not very much more.

The plan is worked out by the political leaders in consultation with economists and the production managers.

The question of which goods are to be produced is answered in the plan. Then the managers of the factories and mines and railroads and everything else are given their production quotas.

The major effort has *not* been in the production of consumer goods. The emphasis has been and still is on building capital in basic industries: electric power, transport, mines, chemicals and fertilizers, etc., and on building military power. Recently there has been a lot of effort to overcome the great inefficiency of Soviet agriculture.

How Efficient Is the Soviet System?

In the USSR, factories are run by managers just as they are in the United States. There, the managers have their planned quotas to meet. When the managers are efficient and when all of the raw materials and other inputs arrive on time, things may go just fine. But it doesn't always happen that way.

There are many stories about the things managers do to try to avoid the penalties of falling behind their quotas: hoarding materials, giving false records, holding down output so future quotas won't be too high.

Then there's the story (fictitious, of course) of the Soviet nail factory which met its quota in tons of nails by producing one gigantic nail! And the story (true, they say) of the transportation operation which met its quota of "ton-miles hauled" by hauling carloads of water!

We know that Soviet agriculture has been very unproductive. About one fourth of the Soviet labor force is employed in farming—as compared with about one thirtieth in the United States. And still they haven't been able to produce enough to feed the people.

What about industry? Can we believe the statements of Nobel prize winner Solzhenitzyn? the writer who left Russia and has been proceeding to "tell the world the truth" about what goes on there? Solzhenitzyn says the productivity in manufacturing is incredibly low—as bad as in agriculture. Other reports seem to agree with this.

Recently, Planned Outputs Have Not Been Achieved. During the 1970s, both industrial production and national income fell quite a bit below the amounts planned. In some products, output quotas were met or exceeded. This happened with coal and with eggs. But in electric power, oil, gas, steel, cement, and most agricultural products (grain, meat, milk) outputs fell below the amounts planned.

One of the "bitter jokes" going around Moscow was: "What is 50 meters long and eats cabbage?" Answer: "The line outside the butcher shop."

Clearly, the performance of an economy like the USSR depends on the efficiency with which the economy is planned and then the efficiency with which the plans are administered. Some people are saying that the Brezhnev administration has been shelving problems rather than solving them. In the early 1980s the long lines of people waiting for their food rations, the rapid growth in black markets (free markets), the high inflation rate, and their increasing grain imports would seem to indicate that all was not well.

The Soviet Growth Rate Has Slowed. Back in 1961, Soviet Premier Nikita Khrushchev said that by 1980 the Soviet Union would have the highest per capita GNP in the world. If the growth trends of that time had continued he might have been right. But they didn't.

In the 1960s the Soviet economic growth rate averaged about 5½ percent per year. In the early 1970s it was about 4¾ percent. In the last half of the 1970s it was less than 3 percent.

In the early 1980s, U.S. GNP was about $3 trillion. For the USSR it was about half that size: about $1.5 trillion. With a population of about

270 million—40 million greater than in the United States—the **output per person** is less than half that of the United States.

In 1981 and '82 it was becoming increasingly clear that regardless of its great wealth of natural resources, the USSR was not fulfilling its promises. The economic productivity and growth and increasing standards of living just weren't happening.

The October 19, 1981 *Business Week* article THE STALLED SOVIET ECONOMY: BOGGED DOWN BY PLANNING highlights some of the problems. Also the cover story of the March 1, 1982 *U.S. News and World Report* is COMMUNISM: THE GREAT ECONOMIC FAILURE. This article begins:

> For the 1.5 billion inhabitants of the Communist world, the Marxist promise of a workers' paradise has turned into a nightmare of permanent scarcity, economic stagnation, and discontent.

This article compares the recent performance of the U.S. economy with that of the USSR and of China. It emphasizes China's recent moves toward more free enterprise and the Soviets' reluctance to move very fast in that direction.

What of the future? Can the "science of planning and administration" be improved in the USSR to overcome the inefficiencies? More and more people are beginning to doubt it.

The USSR shows us some of the problems of trying to operate a massive thing like a modern economic system without the help of the automatic market process and the price mechanism.

The Economy of the People's Republic of China

The People's Republic of China has a controlled economy, planned from the top, just as does the USSR. In that respect the two economic systems are alike. But there are lots of really great differences between the two countries. In the 1980s those differences are becoming greater.

China Is One of the LDCs. The USSR is classed as one of the world's highly developed countries. China is ranked as one of the LDCs. Also there are strong ideological differences between the two.

But from the point of view of the **economic system,** the two countries have been quite similar. In both, the **political process**—economic planning and resource administration—has been the name of the game. But beginning in the late 1970s and continuing into the 1980s, China has been making significant moves toward more **free enterprise.** This has been happening to such an extent that their economic system is now undergoing fairly rapid change. Already, in many areas, wage, price, and profit incentives are being openly encouraged. In the early 1980s this was not yet happening in the USSR.

China certainly has one thing that every LDC needs: a strong and gutsy government! The government seems to have been quite successful in transforming the traditional way of life of the people. The people seem to be under control and mobilized and working—being productive. That's very good for a big LDC like China!

China Has Outdistanced Most of the LDCs. In the early 1980s there seems to be general agreement that China is moving forward. Great gains have been made in medicine, public health, and education—and the minimum needs of the population seem to have been supplied. In China you don't see millions of people starving.

There has been a good bit of capital investment and modernization of industry. Some of the other LDCs have done as well and a few may have done better. But it seems clear that China has outdistanced most of them.

Between 1960 and 1976 China had a growth

rate in GNP per capita of about 5 percent. That's fairly high for any country. The fact that their population of over 800 million people has been growing at only 1.7 percent per year (low, for an LDC) has helped a lot. But per capita GNP in the early 1980s was still less than $600.

What About the Future? The 1976 plan was dedicated to some impressive goals: 70 percent mechanization of farming by 1980, and the building of as many as 120 new, modern plants. The new plan reaffirmed strict control by Party committees and detailed supervised planning of almost everything in the economy.

By 1979 it had become clear that some of the planned objectives were not realistic. Top political leaders were charging that the chief economic planners had barged ahead too fast with huge sophisticated projects—that the economy was not ready for these projects and could not support them efficiently.

In early 1979 they began to make some changes. Planned steel production was reduced by 25 percent, pending more development of transportation, electric power, and raw materials. And other production plans were changed. But much more significant: there were beginning moves toward **freer markets** and the use of the **price mechanism** as an important directing force in the economy.

Much is still up in the air about what's happening in the Chinese economy. In the early 1980s it seems to be moving toward **socio-capitalism.** How far it will go in that direction will depend a lot on (a) the successes of these initial moves, and (b) the power of the philosophies and politics of communism to inhibit change.

ECONOMIC PLANNING AND THE MARKET PROCESS IN THE WORLD TODAY

If we want to find out about the basic nature of an economic system, what do we look at? At the processes at work in the system? Of course!

We try to find out the extent to which the **market process** influences the resource choices as compared with the extent to which **economic planning** is in charge of things. Then, for the "economic planning" kinds of choices we ask questions about how the plans are **made** and what techniques are used for **carrying out** the plans.

If we can get answers to these questions then we can see what the economic system is— what it's doing, how it functions. Suppose we look at the world today using this approach. What do we see?

The Economies of Mixed Socio-Capitalism

First, we see in every **non-communist** nation a *basic reliance on the market process, but with many of the resource-use decisions made by the political process—that is, by government plan.*

In most of the economies of mixed **socio-capitalism** the *"political process" decisions are made through some kind of (more or less) democratic process. Then the decisions are carried out by the market mechanism—by using wage, price and profit incentives to get the job done.*

There are several differences among these various economies of socio-capitalism, of course. But the economies of these countries are much more alike than different. The market process plays a major role in all of them. And all of them do a lot of "political process" choosing—that is, "economic planning."

You will see this general pattern in the economies of such different countries as Britain, France, Japan, Sweden, Italy, West Germany, Mexico, Australia, Thailand, Canada, Brazil, Argentina, Ethiopia, the United States (or almost any other non-communist country).

The Non-Market Economies of the Communist Countries

What about the economies of the Soviet Union, the People's Republic of China, Cuba, the East European countries and the other communist countries? Are they really different from the economies of mixed socio-capitalism? Yes they are! They are different on all three counts:

1. They *do not rely on the* **market process** to make the major economic choices;
2. The economic plans are **not very responsive** *to the wishes of the people;* and
3. The plans usually *are carried out by resource administration—not by the market mechanism.*

In the non-market economies, almost all of the economic choices are made by government and are carried out by resource administration. Yes, those systems really are different. But they are changing.

Economic Systems Are Always Changing

All economic systems are changing all the time. The communist countries are finding more ways to use the market mechanism. The economies of mixed socio-capitalism are using more choice-making by the political process.

All nations face the same **basic economic problems**—problems of choosing what to do with the scarce resources of the nation, of saving some output and turning it into capital, of designing programs for education and training, of taking care of the incapable ones, of keeping the economy running smoothly, keeping prices stable, etc.

All nations approach these problems somewhat differently. Some do a better job than others. But all nations keep changing their approaches (their "economic systems") as time goes by.

Economic systems are *living systems*—always changing. It's nice to know about such things as the directions and speed and processes of change. Which way are we headed? how fast? and how is it all happening?

Do Economic Systems Change as the Stage of Development Changes?

Could it be that the stage of economic development in a society will influence the kind of economic system the society will have? Perhaps so.

A Primitive Society May Require "Resource Administration." In a primitive society, custom and tradition seem to do the best job of making the economic choices—of ensuring the survival of the society. But if the economy is ever going to grow, the system must change.

The LDCs need a lot of planning and direction by the **political process**. What would you call such a system? Mixed socio-capitalism? Maybe so. There's no name that fits very well, really.

Economic planning certainly can help an economy on its way up the development path. But as development proceeds, conditions change.

A Complex Economy Is Not Easy to Administer. As a planned economy gets more developed and specialized, the complexity of the planning process may get overwhelming. The task of planning and directing and controlling all the people and resources and things—and doing it efficiently—becomes just about impossible.

In a highly complex "mature modern economy" some indirect way is needed to get all the thousands—no, millions—of little daily choices made and carried out. What "indirect way"? The **price mechanism**? Of course!

Does this explain why the USSR and other communist countries are changing their economic systems? Placing more reliance on the production-motivating and rationing functions of price? Of course it does.

So is it now time for people to start talking about the Soviet economy as "mixed capitalo-communism"? No, I don't think it's time to go that far!

But I don't suppose it makes much difference what you call the so-called "communist" economic systems. Why not? Because we don't have any names that tell us much about what an economic system really is like anyway!

The "Changing Mix" in the Systems of "Mixed Socio-Capitalism"

The United States and Canada and the other countries of mixed socio-capitalism experienced their "economic growth breakthroughs" in another era. Another time. Another world, really!

From Laissez-Faire to Economic Planning. The "capitalist" economies grew up basking in the philosophies and policies of nineteenth century liberalism: laissez-faire, strong property rights, individualism, the Protestant ethic—the inalienable rights (and duties) of all individuals. **Economic growth** was rapid.

But now we see these systems changing rapidly. The **role of the state** has been increasing. Does the stage of development have something to do with it? So it seems.

The "capitalist" economies have become highly industrialized. Population has expanded and become concentrated in the urban areas. These economies have become highly **complex,** highly **interdependent.**

Most of the basic economic needs of most of the people have been taken care of. But now we have a new set of problems and needs—problems and needs which the market process can't take care of very well.

The Market Process Can't Solve All of Today's Problems. The expanding demands of modern society for better "public goods and services"—education, police and fire protection, public health and sanitation, recreation areas, highways, urban transit systems, etc., etc., etc.—require more **political process** choices.

The political process is going to have to be used to tackle the "externalities" problem and the poverty problem and the whole complex of urban problems. Almost any "problem of mod-

ern society" you can think of seems to require some involvement by the political process—some increase in "the role of the state."

The system called "capitalism" has become something else. That's why I've been calling it **mixed socio-capitalism.** The word "capitalism" doesn't describe it very well anymore.

WHAT ABOUT THE SURVIVAL OF CAPITALISM?

Sometimes people talk about the question of "the survival of capitalism." What nonsense. **Capitalism** was the economic system of the mid-nineteenth century, observed and attacked (and incidentally, named) by Karl Marx. That kind of economic system doesn't exist anywhere in the world. It hasn't for more than forty years!

Suppose we stretch the word "capitalism" to mean "any system in which the **market process** plays an important role." What then? As time goes on will the market process continue to be one of the important ways societies make their economic choices? Yes.

The Market Process Will Continue to Be Important

For the foreseeable future the market process will continue to play an important role. No question about it. So if that's the way you want to define capitalism, then okay. Capitalism will survive.

As long as people have individual desires and as long as incentives and rewards are effective ways of motivating people, the market process will keep on influencing social choices. But forevermore? Until the end of time? Who can say? Who cares, anyway?

Consumer demand will never completely direct the resources of any society. But consumer demand won't ever be completely ignored, either.

The market mechanism will continue to be

used as an "implementation tool" to carry out political process choices, too. As more planners come to understand the efficiency of the **market mechanism** you can expect to see it being used more and more as a "plan-implementation device."

Will Private Property Survive?

The market process can't work without some rights of **private property.** Will private property survive? Of course.

You know that private property rights will never be complete and unlimited in any society—but they won't ever be totally revoked, either. Just about everybody in every society gets to own something!

In the United States and the other economies of mixed socio-capitalism we may see more limitations on our private property rights. As the society's productive efforts shift direction—from the old problems of yesterday to the new problems of tomorrow—much of the shift will be a shift from **private objectives** to **social objectives.**

As the shift continues, individuals may lose more rights to do whatever they please with what they own. But this can't go but just so far, or we'll throw out the baby with the bath water! We'll destroy the effectiveness of the market process, and all will suffer.

In the communist countries, private property rights are likely to be expanding. Why? Because as these countries learn more ways to use the market mechanism they're going to have to let people receive more personal rewards—more "private property" as incentives to do outstanding things.

Will Individual Freedom Survive?

What about the freedom of the individual? Are we all going to be free to go our own way? and to claim the rewards of our successes or suffer the hardships of our failures?

When millions of people are crowded to-gether in a little space called "an urban area," then we must work some things out together through the political process. All of us have to go along with some restrictions. But again, we must be careful not to do more harm than good.

In the "free economies," personal freedom already has been reduced. In the "controlled economies," for the sake of increased productivity and efficiency, individual freedom probably will be increased.

Our "Worldly Religions": Capitalism, Socialism, Communism

By now you can see the nonsense of talking about the "survival" of some kind of economic system. When we use labels like "capitalism" or "socialism" or "communism" we spread a blanket over the economic system and hide all the things that are going on!

But these labels—**capitalism, socialism, communism**—words coined by nineteenth century "social protest philosopher-prophets"—have become our "banners" in our "struggle of **worldly religions.**"

It would be better to just forget about the words "capitalism" and "socialism" and "communism." The labels don't describe any of the world's economic systems anyway. If you want to see what the system really is you need to know how the choices are made and carried out. How much social process? political process? and market process? and how does each process work?

If you know these things then you know what kind of economic system the society has. If you don't, then you don't. And whatever it is today, you can be sure that tomorrow it will be different.

Economic Philosophies? or Economic Systems?

The words "capitalism," "socialism," and "communism," refer to **economic philosophies** much more than they refer to economic systems.

The Philosophy of Capitalism. The philosophy of capitalism is the philosophy of the market process—the philosophy of Adam Smith's laissez-faire—of "consumer sovereignty and the invisible hand." It's the philosophy of individual freedom, of private property, of rewards for productivity. The idea is that if people and businesses are left free to make their own choices, everything will come out better for everybody.

This "individual freedom" philosophy of capitalism is strong in the United States. It is also strong in the other non-communist countries, even though most of those countries call themselves "socialist." But there's no real-world economic system anywhere which even comes close to reproducing in the real world the "rugged individualism" philosophy of pure capitalism.

This unmodified "law of the jungle, survival of the fittest" **philosophy of capitalism** was accepted and followed by most business and political leaders of the western world in the last century. This philosophy and the harsh 19th century system was what Marx attacked. He predicted its downfall.

The "downfall" of the system didn't come the way Marx predicted, but it came just the same. Not by revolution but by evolution—by (more or less) orderly change.

No real-world economic system will ever again be built on the "rugged individualist" philosophy of unmodified capitalism. Certainly not. But all real-world systems embody some of the philosophy of capitalism. Even the communist countries use one of the most basic concepts of capitalist philosophy—incentives and rewards—more income for more productivity.

The Philosophy of Socialism. What is the philosophy of socialism? It's a philosophy of working together and sharing, of giving up individual freedoms for the benefit of society. The society (government) should own most of the means of production and the people should work, not for their own betterment, but for the betterment of everybody.

The **philosophy of socialism** seems more "philosophically appealing" to most people than the "self-centered, dog-eat-dog" ideology of capitalism. Everybody knows it's good to be benevolent and to share with others. But when it gets down to the real world, the "benevolent sharing" of socialist philosophy doesn't seem to work out so well.

No modern economic system has ever been able to run on "benevolent sharing." Most people seem to be more productive and do more to help the society toward its objectives if there's a system of incentives and rewards.

What a far cry the philosophy of socialism is from the real-world economic systems called "socialism"! Even farther than the real-world capitalist systems are from the philosophy of capitalism. Real-world systems of **democratic socialism** really are a lot more capitalist than socialist!

So what's a **socialist economic system**? It's a system in which the leaders (and maybe most of the people) proclaim their belief in some version of the socialist philosophy? Right! And a **capitalist economic system** is a system in which the leaders (and maybe most of the people) proclaim their belief in some version of the capitalist philosophy? Sure.

The Philosophy of Communism. What about communism? Is that more "philosophy"—more "worldly religion" than economic system, too? Of course. Communism is a system in which the leaders (and perhaps most of the people) proclaim their belief in the **philosophies of communism**—the beliefs and predictions of Marx and Lenin and Mao Tse-Tung and others.

"Pronouncements of philosophy" don't tell you much about what an economic system looks like! If you want to know what kind of system really exists you have to look and see.

THE MARKET PROCESS: CREATOR OF THE MODERN WORLD

Did you ever stop to think of the great impact which the market process has had on the world? Truly, it was the market process that created the modern world!

The market process provided the power that thrust the world through the industrial revolution. It stimulated savings and investment and great increases in output.

The harshness of it all!—denying things to unproductive people—while the powerful rationing and production-motivating functions of price exercised control—that's what brought the economic breakthroughs which generated the modern world. But now, everywhere you look in the market-directed economies, the "role of the market" is being reduced. Why?

You know why. The results of the market process are often unacceptable these days. Also, society seeks "new-type objectives" which cannot be approached through the market process—cannot be decided on the basis of how people spend their money. So the market process is being bypassed. The political process is getting involved. You already know all about that.

In a brief few hundred years the market process succeeded in ripping out the social control mechanisms that kept society stable and alive for thousands of years. How quickly it broke down the past! And how quickly it generated the modern world!

Is that all over now? Must the market process now be pushed offstage after such a short and brilliant performance? Not entirely. But to some extent, yes.

The Decision-Making and Implementation Questions

In the past the market process performed two functions: (1) it made the decisions, and (2) it carried out the decisions. But now that's being changed. More and more the market process is being used to *carry out decisions which it didn't make*. Decisions made how? By the political process, of course!

For the past few centuries the market process really has been in control. Truly, it has been

the "master mechanism" of social choice. But now? Often the market process is being broken to harness—forced into the role of servant to carry out the deliberate choices of the political process.

In the "capitalist" societies the political process has been taking over more of the **decision-making functions**, leaving the market process with only the **implementation function**. In the non-market economies the political process continues to exercise tight control over the decisions. But more ways are being found to use the powerful forces of the market mechanism to implement the decisions.

What About the Future of the Market Process?

So what's the future for the market process? The market process will never be stripped of all of its decision-making functions. To be sure, products will still be produced in response to what the people are buying!

And as an implementation device? It seems that the market process will be playing an even more important implementation role in the future. Why? Because it's so efficient!

We're all enjoying the benefits of the market process ... of the powerful price mechanism!

People and resources move automatically. Price adjustments can be used to adjust the flows of inputs and outputs. It all works so efficiently, yet no one needs to be ordered around. Fantastic!

The world's economic systems will continue to evolve. As they do, the market process will continue to play an important role in most of them. It will continue to play some role in all of them.

The **laws of economics** tell us that those societies which rely heavily on the **market process** are likely to come out better in the long run than those which don't. Recent events in the communist countries seem to verify this conclusion. Ultimately, time will tell. Right?

I Wish Everybody Knew As Much Economics As You Do

I only wish that all of those who will be influencing the economic decisions—the leaders of the countries all over the world—knew as much basic economics as you do. Just the economics you've learned from this one book, if understood and applied by all the people making the decisions, could make a better world for all of us.

"But," you say, "I really don't know all that much economics." Maybe not. Relative to what you could know or to what you might like to know, maybe not. But if you've really been studying and learning the principles in this book, you know a lot more useful economics than you think.

Right now you know a lot more economics than most people in the world. You know a lot more than some government officials who will be making decisions and choosing policies that

will influence the lives of thousands, maybe millions of people.

Some political leaders have very little understanding of basic economic concepts. That's very unfortunate—especially since the political process is very much involved in making the choices for society.

Some of the "economically illiterate" leaders are in the underdeveloped countries. But not all of them are. Not by a long shot! Many of them are right here—in the federal government and in the government of your own state, city, county, township, school district—everywhere.

It's too bad that so many policymakers know so little about basic economics. But that's the way it is. Some bad choices are bound to result. Be sorry that they don't know more economics. But at the same time, be glad that you do.

This is the end of the last chapter. A short epilogue follows—no big deal—I just wanted to share some parting thoughts with you. But before you go on to that, stop and do some serious thinking about economic planning, the market process, and the evolution of the world's economic systems.

SUMMARY AND SYNTHESIS

Real-world economic systems always consist of some combination of the three basic processes—social, political, and market.

The system called capitalism emphasizes private ownership and the market process. But all systems called capitalism these days are really a mixture of the market process and the social process and might well be called systems of mixed socio-capitalism.

The economic system called socialism emphasizes the fact that political process will play an important role. The so-called communist systems are really systems of extreme socialism under an autocratic form of government. Utopian communism is something else. It has never existed as the economic system of any nation in the real world.

Many kinds of modern problems require some political process choices. Society's ideas about income distribution and social welfare—the impact of high technology on defense spending and on our need for some regulations—the growing population and urbanization—all these and some other factors are causing more government involvement in the market-directed economic systems. Just since World War II, increased government involvement has resulted in significant changes in all of the world's market-directed economic systems.

Economic planning is widely used now. It's a big production possibility exercise. Available resources are assessed and uses are chosen based upon the chosen objectives of society. But economic planning reduces the individual's choices—sometimes a little, sometimes a lot. If the plan is implemented by direct allocation (for example, the military draft) that restricts freedom more than if the plan is implemented using the price mechanism.

In the United States we use several kinds of direct allocation, such as the zoning of land. But most of our plans are carried out through the price mechanism.

In the Soviet Union, the People's Republic of China, and the other so-called Communist countries, more use is being made of the price mechanism. Why? Because it is very efficient. Prices can be set and then adjusted to fine-tune the resource flows.

As the United States and other market-oriented economies move toward more political process choices, the Communist countries are using more price and profit incentives. So are the world's economic systems becoming more alike? Perhaps some. But if so, they have a long way to go before they become very similar.

Both the Soviet Union and the People's Republic of China make autocratic economic plans which are carried out mostly by resource administration. Both of these countries have had some significant successes with their economic plans. But both have encountered serious problems and failures. The economic problems of the Soviet economy in the early 1980s are very serious. And China is trying to improve economic conditions there by turning more toward the price and profit incentives of the market process.

If you want to find out the basic nature of an economic system you need to find out the extent to which it relies on the market process, or on economic planning. Then you need to find out, for the planning part, how the plans are made—democratically or autocratically—and then how the plans are carried out—by resource administration or by the price mechanism.

When you apply these criteria to a nation like the United States and compare it to a nation like the Soviet Union or China, you can see that the two economic systems are widely different.

Economic systems are always changing.

Perhaps a different system (a different mix of mixed socio-capitalism) is required at different stages of economic development. That's what has happened in the American economy, and in Western Europe.

Will capitalism survive? Pure capitalism hasn't. But the essential aspects of capitalism—private property, individual freedom of choice, price and profit incentives—have managed to survive fairly well—but in modified form. These characteristics of the market system are powerful and efficient and hard to kill.

Capitalism, socialism, and communism aren't names which describe real-world economic systems. They are the labels of our "worldly religions"—our economic philosophies and beliefs. These names don't go very far in telling you what an economic system looks like or how it works. If you want to know that, you must look and see which processes are at work, and how they work.

The powerful market process and price mechanism created the modern world. It put a lot of burden and hardship on a lot of people. It kept wages low. It created forced savings, stimulated massive investments and rapid growth. But in recent decades in the modern nations the market process is being bypassed or overruled. What's happening?

More of the decisions—the social choices—are being made by the political process. This leaves the market process with only the implementation function. Why is this happening? Because in modern societies there is a broad range of choices which the society is not willing to leave to the market process. But the implementation function? The powerful forces of the price mechanism are the most efficient yet discovered.

What about the future? The laws of economics tell us that a society which relies heavily on the market process is likely to come out a lot better in the long run than one which doesn't. Recent events in the Communist countries seem to verify this conclusion.

REVIEW EXERCISES

MAJOR CONCEPTS, PRINCIPLES, TERMS (Explain each carefully.)

capitalism
socialism
communism
mixed socio-capitalism
economic planning
resource administration
increasing role of the state in market economies
increasing role of the market in communist countries
the economy of the USSR
the economy of the People's Republic of China
two market functions: decision-making, implementation

OTHER CONCEPTS AND TERMS (Explain each briefly.)

economic system
political system
socialist reforms
pragmatism
direct allocation
allocation by incentive

Lenin's "New Economic Policy"
"five-year plan"
"worldly religions"
philosophy of capitalism
philosophy of socialism
philosophy of communism

QUESTIONS (Write out answers or jot down key points.)

1. "Capitalism—the economic system which was named by and attacked by Karl Marx—no longer exists. So Marx must have been right, after all!" Do you agree? or disagree? Discuss.

2. Think of some things which are now being "administered" at your college, but which might be handled by the "price mechanism" instead. Would you like to see any of these things handled by some kind of "price incentive, reward system"? Discuss.

3. Could it be that economic systems change as the stage of development changes? Discuss.

4. Is it always true that economic planning reduces the choices of individuals? Discuss.

5. It seems likely that in the rigidly-controlled economies of "communism," the market mechanism is going to be used, more and more. Can you explain why this seems likely?

6. Describe capitalism, not as an economic system, but as a philosophy. Do the same for socialism and communism. Now, think back to the last time you heard some people arguing over some economic issue. From listening to what each person said, could you tell how much of which economic philosophies each believed in? Think about it.

7. This chapter suggests that we might all be better off if we could just get rid of the "blanket labels"—the names for our "worldly religions"—capitalism, socialism, communism—and refer to economic systems by describing the highlights instead. What do you think about this idea? Discuss.

8. Suppose you were to rank different real-world economic systems on a scale (from 1 to 10) to indicate how much the "political process" and how much the "market process" was responsible for the choices in that economic system. (Let 1 = pure *political* process, and 10 = pure *market* process.) What number do you think you would assign to the present economic system of the United States? Great Britain? Japan? West Germany? East Germany? the USSR? What number would you assign to the economy of each country, 20 years ago? What do you think the number for each country will be, 20 years from now? Think about it.

Epilogue: Some Parting Words About Economics and You

Welcome to the end of the book. If you've read the whole thing you've seen a lot of economics. If you've learned the concepts well, your eyes are now open to a lot of things you couldn't see before.

You've done a lot of work. Yes. And you're well on your way. So relax for a minute, "Enjoy your achievements. . ." Smile and feel good. You have a right to be proud of yourself.

If you've really been studying hard and learning it well, by now I'm sure you have some new awareness of the world—some sharpened ability to conceptualize reality. You have a new "feel" for things that are going on around you.

You'll be carrying several of these concepts with you, using them as "a way of looking at things" for as long as you live. You have a sound framework that will help you as you further develop your own good common sense, day after day, year after year.

The World Is Your "Econ Lab"

The world is full of illustrations and examples of economic concepts. I'm sure you remember when I said, back in the beginning of the book: "there's no real-world issue or problem that is *purely* economic." Remember? Sure. It's very true, too.

But almost every real-world issue or problem you can think of has *some* important economic aspects. Yes, you can be sure that you will be running into real-world illustrations of economic concepts, all the time.

Everywhere you go (now that you have built this new "window through which to observe the world") you will keep on seeing things you never noticed before. Whenever you go into a bank you'll know a lot more about what's going on. You'll know that when the teller is pushing those accounting machine buttons to print a deposit receipt for you, somewhere in the bank a figure is automatically being added to your checking account. And you'll know that the figure is your money!

As you leave the bank you'll see your friendly branch manager sitting there behind the desk and you'll be tempted to go over and ask if they have created any money today. Go ahead! Ask! I dare you.

Whenever you go into your favorite shoe store you'll see those shoe boxes all around and you'll wonder how much the store keeps in inventory. And you might wonder if the inventory is expanding or contracting.

From now on, whenever you hear the news about employment and unemployment, about Americans spending too much money abroad, about the price of wheat or oil or steel going up, about the increasing GNP, about interest rates going up and bond prices going down, and about all such things, you'll have the good feeling of being "in the know."

Whenever you hear a political demagogue promising to do all kinds of great things for the people, you'll wonder where all the scarce resources needed to do all those great things will come from.

Whenever laws are passed influencing wages or prices, or restricting or subsidizing the supply of something, or regulating market conditions in any way, you will have some idea about whether we will soon be seeing surpluses or shortages.

From now on, whenever you choose corn flakes instead of eggs for breakfast, you might think about how you're influencing the resource-use choices in the economy—about how you're supporting the "Kellogg team" and deserting the "egg team." (You might even wonder if everybody else is switching to corn flakes today, and if, pretty soon, we're all going to be up to someplace in eggs!)

From now on, whenever you have a worrisome choice to make, you'll be aware that you're weighing alternatives, considering opportunity costs—thinking marginally. That's good. Some of your choices may come out better if you think about them that way. I hope so.

You know a lot of economics. You really do! Not enough to handle all the problems economists deal with. Of course not. But as you go through life with your mind turned on you'll be learning more and more economics all the time.

Someday you may understand more economics than some people who majored in it! You can get there quicker by being an econ major—but anyone who knows anything at all about economics knows that a person can't major in everything!

It Takes Scarce Resources to Solve Most Problems

Now that you know some economics, does that make you "materialistic"? There's plenty of talk going around these days against materialism. Everybody knows that big money and big houses and big cars and big steaks and long trips on big airplanes don't bring happiness. No argument on that score.

But everyone who thinks about it will realize that if we want to try to seek an objective—*any* objective—it's going to require some scarce resources—energy, thought, effort, capital, other resources. *"Material inputs" are essential in order to move toward almost any objective you can think of.* That's just the way it is.

Energy is required to move things, to do things, to make things, to change things, to achieve things. And energy is scarce. So we aren't going to be able to move and do and make and change and achieve all the things you might wish plus all the things I might wish plus all the things everyone else might wish.

It's likely that *every major problem you can think of could be at least partly solved if enough scarce resources (material inputs) could be turned in its direction.*

And it's almost just as certain that *no progress toward solving any of these problems is going to be made without the use of some scarce resources (material inputs.)*

If it is true that some scarce resources are needed, then we can't possibly solve all the problems we would like to solve—at least, not all right now. Not all at once. That's the way it is with scarcity.

There just aren't enough resources, enough inputs to do all the things all the people want done. So what can we do? What *must* we do? We must *choose*. Of course. We must decide which problems to solve and which to tolerate for a while.

The Stark Reality of Economics

When you learn economics you experience a stark confrontation with reality. You come face to face with scarcity—and *scarcity is the natural condition of reality.* Once you face it, confront it, recognize it—from then on you live with an awareness of opportunity costs, of substitution, of having to choose between things.

You become painfully aware that every time labor or building materials or electric energy or any other factors are shifted to aim at a new objective or to attack a new problem, someone must pay the cost. Someone must *give up* something.

People *don't like* to give up things! None of us wants to choose this or that. It's so much nicer to have this *and* that. But we can't have this *and* that, *of everything!*

Who Will Make the Sacrifices?

Oh, it's so easy to choose to give up things we never had! "I'll give up the luxury of driving a big car if it will bring a better school system. So everyone else ought to be willing to give up their big cars, too! Of course, I don't happen to have a big car. I only have a motor bike. I sure don't plan to give *that* up! That's not a luxury. It's a necessity!"

Everyone wants someone else to make the sacrifices. Sure. But we aren't going to solve any of society's problems by "volunteering away" the things other people have, while clinging to our own. We aren't going to solve the pollution problem by wishing it on the big business or the local governments or the federal government or anyone else. The same is true of education and law enforcement and everything else.

These problems are society's problems. We're *all* sharing in the benefits of high productivity and individual freedom. And *we're all going to share in the costs.* You can be sure of it.

Solutions to society's problems are not going to be coming along any faster than we ourselves are willing to pay the costs—in taxes, in product prices, in the opportunity costs of *other* goods and services we forfeit, and sometimes in giving up some of our freedoms. It's too bad we're going to have to pay the costs. But we are. You know that now. You know that these are the facts of economics—the facts of the real world—the facts of life.

A Word of Farewell

Now that you are turned on to some of the basic economic concepts, your thoughts never again will be able to escape the fact of scarcity. You'll always have some awareness, now, of the discomfort of opportunity cost.

You'll always be aware that realistic plans and programs to improve anything or to solve any problem, require some means—some effort—some resources—some "scarce factors of production." You will never forget that these factors must come from somewhere. But from where? And then to be used to meet *which* urgent need? These are the really tough questions.

Answering these tough questions can be a very difficult and trying task. If you stop and think about it for a minute you will realize that this difficult and trying task is the thing we've been talking about all along. Sure. It's the economic problem! It's the basic problem of economics—the problem of choosing.

It's the problem of scarcity—of not being able to do all the things we'd like to do—the problem of having to decide, to choose which things to do when we can't do everything—the problem of choosing which objectives to pursue and which to forego, which things to have and which to give up. That's what economics is all about. Surely you'll never forget that.

I hope you will go further in economics. This one book couldn't take you but just so far. But no matter where you go, no matter which objectives you seek, no matter which paths you choose, I hope your choices turn out to be *truly* the right ones, for you.

The right choices are the ones which, many years from now, will let you look back and say:

"How lucky I am to have been wise enough then, to make the right choices—for me." I wish you wisdom in all your choices. Today, and always.

Mathematical Appendix: Fun and Games with Curves and Equations for People Who Hate Math

Do you understand algebra? And enjoy working with it? If so, you may not like this mathematical appendix very much. You'll be able to skim through it very rapidly and understand it very quickly. And you'll probably be bored by the fact that it does everything the longest possible way, step-by-step, with nothing left to the imagination.

But suppose you *don't* understand algebra very well. Or worse still. Suppose you've forgotten all the algebra you ever knew. And suppose algebra always has been a miserable experience for you. Then you'll like this appendix. It was written for you.

So fear not. Just take it carefully, step-by-step. *You will understand it.* Believe it or not, *you may even like it!*

WHY A MATH APPENDIX?

You know that math is a high-powered tool of analysis—in economics, and in just about any other area of scientific study. But the theoretical explanations in this textbook don't require that you understand algebra. If it's true that you can understand the basic principles of economics without understanding algebra, then why bother?

Wouldn't you like to see a little bit of how algebra can be used in economic analysis? That's educational for its own sake. But that isn't all. There are two other very good reasons for including this math appendix.

1. You may be planning to take more advanced courses in economics. You may be (right now) taking courses in college math to prepare yourself for more advanced economics courses. If so, then you'll appreciate this brief look at how equations can be used to deal with some of these principles you've been learning. Also, this exercise may help to make your math courses more meaningful and relevant.

2. Maybe your instructor likes to use equations in class. And maybe the explanations go too fast for you to keep up. (Maybe your algebra isn't as good as your instructor thinks it is!) So wouldn't it be nice to have a place to go to brush up on some of the basics? And to see some applications in economics laid out carefully, step-by-step? That's what you'll find in this appendix.

Many students will not want to (and may not need to) learn the simple algebraic applications explained here. But some will *want* to—may *need* to. If you're one of those, then it's for you that I have written this appendix in this easy, step-by-step way. If algebra somehow has escaped you, here's your chance to start to catch it up—to "be as bright as the rest of 'em."

This mathematical appendix does not go very far. But there's enough here to help you to brush up on some of the basic techniques of algebra. And there's enough to let you see how equations can be helpful in economic analysis.

So here it comes, step-by-step. *I dare you to*

try to get confused, or frustrated—or to hate it. How's that for a challenge?

SOME BASIC CONCEPTS ABOUT CURVES AND THE EQUATIONS WHICH DESCRIBE THEM

Much of the mathematics used in economics consists of (1) translating the curves in a graph into equation form, and then (2) working with those equations. That's exactly what this appendix is all about. So first you need to be sure you understand the basics about these curves and equations.

A Curve Is a Series of (X and Y) Points

After you draw a curve of any kind in a graph, if you choose the value of (size of, or number of units of) X, then you can look at the curve and see the value of (size of, or number of units of) Y. Once the curve is there, if you tell me the X value, I can tell you the Y value.

Eureka! In a situation like this you can say that *the value of Y depends on (is a function of) the value of X!* That gives us a functional relationship:

$$Y = f(X).$$

That little equation doesn't tell you much. It tells you that the value of Y depends on the value of X, and that's all it tells you. You can't figure out the value of Y from that.

An Equation Can Tell You the Relationship Between Values of X and Values of Y

Suppose we did have an equation that would let you figure out the value of Y that corresponds to each value of X. That equation would describe for you the curve in the graph! The curve shows, for each value of X, the corresponding value of Y. Suppose you have an *equation* which shows that. Then that *equation* tells you exactly what the *curve* must look like!

THE EQUATION OF A STRAIGHT-LINE CURVE

To see what all this means, here's a familiar example. Remember the 45-degree line in the Keynesian National Spending = National Income Graph? Suppose you wanted an equation that would let you figure out the value of Y at any point along this line. It would depend on the value of X. Right?

Suppose the value of X is 5. What's the value of Y? It's 5, also. Suppose X is 12. What's Y? It's 12 also. The value of Y is always the same as the value of X! So what's the equation? Here it is:

$$Y = X.$$

Simple, right? Now if you'll take a look at Figure A-1 you'll see it on a graph.

The Equation of a Straight-Line Curve Which Begins at Zero

Suppose you are dealing with *any straight-line curve* beginning at zero—one where Y is *not equal* to X. For example, what if Y goes up only half as fast as X? That's easy too. Here's the equation:

$$Y = \tfrac{1}{2} X, \text{ or}$$

$$Y = 0.5X.$$

Using this equation, how do you find the value of Y? Suppose the value of X is 10. Then the value of Y is ½ of 10.

$$Y = 0.5(10)$$
$$Y = 5$$

Fig. A-1 The Equation of a Straight-Line Curve Which Begins at Zero and Rises at a 45-Degree Angle

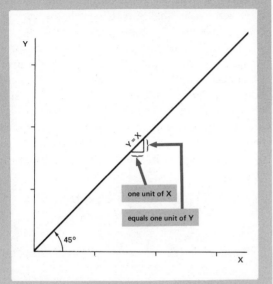

The equation "Y = X" tells you that whatever the value of X may be, that also will be the value of Y. Also, if the value of X increases or decreases, the value of Y will increase or decrease by exactly the same amount. (A look at the curve in the graph shows you that. The equation "Y = X" shows you exactly the same thing.)

Suppose X = 20. Again, use the equation Y = 0.5X.

$$Y = 0.5(20)$$
$$Y = 10$$

The general form of the equation for a straight-line curve which begins at zero is:

$$Y = bX.$$

This says that the value of Y will always be equal to the value of "b" times the value of X. And what's the value of "b"? It's how much Y goes up when X goes up by one unit. This "b" term tells you how steeply the line slopes upward.

If the "b" term happens to be *exactly one*, then Y will go up just as fast as X goes up. You will have a 45° line just as in the Keynesian NS = NI graph. But if "b" is *less than one*, then when the value of X increases by one unit, the value of Y will increase by *less than* one unit. So Y will not go up as fast as X. You can see that when "b" is *less than one* (b < 1) the straight line will not rise as steeply as when "b" = 1. Now if you will take a look at Figure A-2 you'll see how all this looks on a graph.

Fig. A-2 The Equation of a Straight-Line Curve Which Begins at Zero

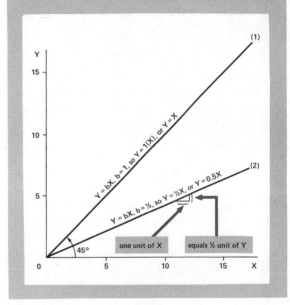

The General Equation of a Straight-Line Curve

Suppose you have a straight-line curve which *does not* begin at zero. What then? Then you must know how high up on the Y axis the straight line begins. That is, you must know the value of Y when X is zero. So you need another term in your equation—a term to show you the "Y intercept" value—where the straight line touches the Y axis—a term to tell you the value of Y when X is zero.

Suppose you have a straight-line curve which begins at 10 on the Y axis and goes up from there. Suppose the curve looks just like curve #2 which started at zero in Figure A-2. The only difference is that this new curve starts with a Y value of 10. So the Y value at each point along the curve is going to be *10 units larger* than it would have been if the curve had started at zero.

Suppose the "Y intercept" is 10 above zero and that for each one unit increase in X, Y increases by half a unit. Can you find the value of Y for each value of X, just as before? Sure. What's the difference? Only this: You must add the Y intercept value—in this case, 10. The equation for this straight-line curve we're talking about is

$$Y = 10 + 0.5X.$$

Using this formula you can find the value of Y which corresponds to any value of X you may choose. For example, suppose $X = 10$. Then

$$Y = 10 + 0.5(10)$$
$$Y = 10 + 5$$
$$Y = 15$$

Now you understand that *the general equation for a straight-line curve* must include two terms. The first term tells you the value of Y when X is zero. It tells you where the curve starts on the Y axis. The second term tells you how much Y goes up each time you add one unit of X. It tells you the slope of the straight-line curve.

The Equation of a Straight Line: Summary Statement

The value of Y, at each value of X, is determined by
(1) the value of Y when $X = 0$ (the "Y intercept" value of Y), and
(2) the rate at which Y increases as X increases (the steepness of the slope of the line).

The generalized equation for the straight-line curve is

$$Y = a + bX.$$

The "a" term tells you the value of Y when X is zero. The "b" term tells you the rate of change in Y as X increases above zero.

With this equation you can define any straight-line curve (any "linear function") in a graph. So what does all this have to do with economics? A lot. You'll be getting into that in just a minute. But first, all of this is illustrated in Figure A-3. Spend enough time with that graph to be sure you understand and will remember all of this. You'll need it in the sections coming up.

Fig A-3   The General Equation of a Straight-Line Curve

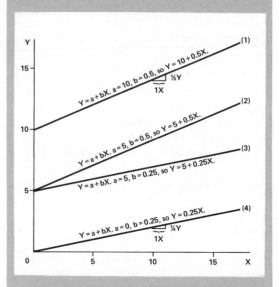

- the larger the "a" term, the higher up the Y axis the curve begins—or, to say it differently, the higher the "Y intercept."
- the larger the "b" term, the steeper the slope of the curve. If the "b" term is *zero* then the line will be *horizontal*.

Some Simplifying Assumptions

Now you understand the equation for a straight-line curve. But what if the curve was a *curved* line? Most real-world functional relationships don't turn out to be linear! Could we describe non-linear curves with equations? Sure we could. But we would need to add additional terms in our equation and that would make the math look more complicated. Fortunately it really isn't necessary to do this to understand the principles. So the rule here is going to be: *Keep it very simple.*

All of the curves (and equations describing them) in this appendix (1) will be straight-line curves, (2) will have positive slope, and (3) will have "b" values between zero and one—that is, the slope of the curve will be somewhere between horizontal, and 45-degree upward slope.

Why are we satisfied to make these simplifying assumptions? Because the basic curve we will be dealing with is the *consumption function* curve. And with the consumption function, these assumptions are realistic enough to illustrate the basic principles.

You can see that if the consumption function is a straight-line curve sloping upward, the marginal propensity to consume (indicated by the upward slope of the curve) is constant. We will assume that to be the case. We will also assume that the price level in this little economy we are talking about is fixed (no inflation or deflation of prices). And now with these simplifying assumptions in place, we're ready to get into the consumption function.

THE STRAIGHT-LINE CONSUMPTION FUNCTION: THE CURVE AND THE EQUATION

The consumption function in the real world is not likely to be a straight line. And certainly it isn't likely to extend all the way to where national income is zero! Still, it isn't too unrealistic to as-

sume that the consumption function is a straight line within the "relevant range" of national income. The important point is this: The principles involved can be illustrated just as well with a straight line as with a curved line. The advantage of using a straight line is that it simplifies the math. It lets us concentrate on the *economics* and not be so concerned with the math.

If your straight-line, upward-sloping curve is a consumption function, then what does the value of Y on that curve tell you? Consumer spending (C)? Of course! And the value of X is national income (NI).[1]

If your curve is a consumption function, what does the "b" term indicate? Think about it. When X increases by one unit, that's a one-unit increase in national income! The "b" term tells how much C goes up. That's the marginal propensity to consume!

You can see that the upward slope of the consumption function curve (indicated by the "b" term in the equation) shows the *marginal propensity to consume*. It indicates *how much more would be spent on consumer goods as national income increases*. When the consumption function is a straight line, the marginal propensity to consume is always the same. It's the slope of the curve. The steeper the curve, the higher the marginal propensity to consume.

Now that you understand all this, you're ready to study Figures A-4 and A-5 where you'll see it explained on graphs. There you'll see how the straight-line equation can be used to figure the size of *consumer spending* for any size of *national income*. Take your time and study the figures thoroughly. Then go on and find out what happens when we bring *investment spending* into the picture.

---

[1]Economists often use the letter "Y" (not NI) as the symbol for national income. Here I have chosen to use the letters NI instead of Y because I think NI will be more familiar to you. Just remember: In other writings in economics you are likely to see the letter Y used to refer to national income.

Fig. A-4 The Straight-Line Consumption Function—the Curve and the Equation

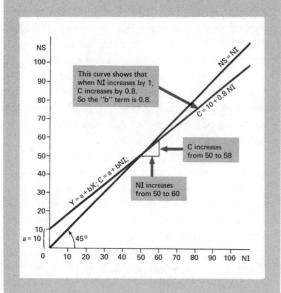

Fig. A-5 Finding the Value of C When You Know the Value of NI

With the equation C=10 + 0.8 NI you can figure out, for any value of NI, the value of C.

Examples:

If NI is 30, then C=10 + 0.8(30), or 10 + 24. C=34.
If NI is 50, then C=10 + 0.8(50), or 10 + 40. C=50.
If NI is 80, then C=10 + 0.8(80), or 10 + 64. C=74.
If NI is 100, then C=10 + 0.8(100), or 10 + 80. C=90.

The graph below illustrates these answers and shows that each one is correct.

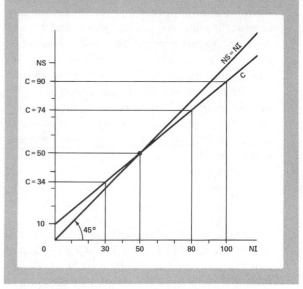

DETERMINING NATIONAL INCOME USING THE C + I EQUATION

The consumption function curve in Figures A-4 and A-5 lets you see for sure how big consumer spending would be at each level of national income. But how big will NI actually be? Suppose consumers are the only ones doing any spending. You can see that macroequilibrium would be at 50. That's the only size of NI where national spending equals NI. But you know that there are likely to be some spending sources other than consumer spending—that is, some injections, right?

How Big Will NI Be? It Depends on (1) Autonomous Injections and (2) Induced Consumer Spending

Assume that the only injections come from *investment spending*. Then (with the consumption

function given) the actual size of NI is going to depend on (1) the size of the investment spending injection and (2) the size of the income multiplier.

You could already figure out the size of the income multiplier, because you know the marginal propensity to consume—it's the "b" coefficient in our consumption function equation. In a minute you'll see how to integrate the multiplier into the equation. But first, the *investment injection* needs to be integrated into our basic "consumption function" equation.

Assume that the only injection is from investment (no government spending injections and no injections from foreigners buying our goods). Then the size of NI is indicated by the following equation:

$$NI = C + I$$

Suppose we assume that the size of the investment injection will be 5, no matter what the size of national income may be. Then the size of NI will be:

$$NI = C + 5$$

How do we solve this? Look at Figure A-4 and you'll see that C = 10 + 0.8 NI. So why not substitute (10 + 0.8 NI) in the above equation, instead of C? No reason not to. So here goes:

$$NI = 10 + 0.8 \text{ NI} + 5.$$

When we solve this equation we'll know the equilibrium size of NI when I = 5. But how do you solve the equation if you've forgotten all your algebra? It's easy. Just watch.

You probably remember that when you work with equations you can do anything you want to on one side of the equation as long as you do exactly the same thing on the other side. That way you don't destroy the equality.

Here we have an equation with NI (which means 1.0 NI) on one side, and 0.8 NI on the other side. If we want to solve this equation for NI, we need to get all of the NI on the same side. So we need to subtract enough NI (equal amounts from both sides) to get rid of all of the NI on one side of the equation. Then we'll see how much NI is left on the other side.

How do we do it? We subtract 0.8 NI from both sides of the equation. That eliminates all of the NI on the right side of the equation and leaves 0.2 NI on the left side of the equation. Here's what it looks like:

$$1.0 \text{ NI} = 10 + 0.8 \text{ NI} + 5$$

$$-0.8 \text{ NI} = -0.8 \text{ NI}$$

$$0.2 \text{ NI} = 10 + 5$$

$$0.2 \text{ NI} = 15$$

Divide both sides by 0.2

$$\frac{0.2 \text{ NI}}{0.2} = \frac{15}{0.2}$$

$$NI = 75$$

The equation is solved! Now it's clear that, given this consumption function, when the investment injection is 5 (that is, I = 5) the equilibrium size of national income is 75. And now if you'll look at Figure A-6 you'll see exactly how this looks on a graph.

Fig. A-6. The Effect of the Investment Injection

When the Investment Injection is 5, the equilibrium size of NI is 75. The C + I curve is the C curve shifted upward by the amount of the investment injection. Here, I = 5.

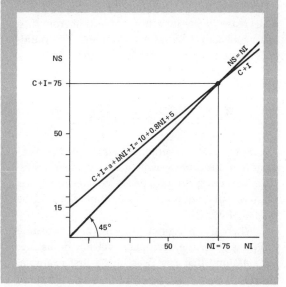

Without any investment injection, the equilibrium national income was 50. With an investment injection of only 5, the equilibrium national income now becomes 75! How is that possible? It's because of the income multiplier. You'll be reading more about all this in a minute. But first, here's another question.

What if the Investment Injection Was Larger? or Smaller?

Suppose the size of the investment injection had been 2? Or 3? Or maybe 7? Or 9? Could you figure out what the equilibrium level of NI would be? Of course you could. You would do it exactly as when the investment injection was 5. Just to be sure, here's a quick run through, assuming that the investment injection is not 5 this time, but 3—that is, I = 3.

$$NI = C + I$$
$$NI = C + 3$$
$$1.0\ NI = 10 + 0.8\ NI + 3$$
$$-0.8\ NI = -0.8\ NI$$
$$0.2\ NI = 10 + 3$$
$$\frac{0.2\ NI}{0.2} = \frac{13}{0.2}$$
$$NI = 65$$

A decrease in the investment injection from 5 to 3 caused NI to decrease from 75 to 65. The multiplier effect working in reverse? Right!

What if the MPC Was Larger? or Smaller?

Now, just for practice, suppose the consumption function wasn't quite so steep. Suppose the marginal propensity to consume was not 0.8, but only 0.75. The multiplier would be smaller. Right?

When the marginal propensity to consume (MPC) is 0.75, the multiplier will not be as big. Let's assume that I = 5 as in the first example, and work it out. Then we'll see what difference it makes when the MPC is 0.75 instead of 0.8.

$$NI = C + I$$
$$NI = C + 5$$
$$1.0\ NI = 10 + 0.75\ NI + 5$$
$$-0.75\ NI = -0.75\ NI$$
$$0.25\ NI = 10 + 5$$

$$\frac{0.25\ NI}{0.25} = \frac{15}{0.25}$$
$$NI = 60$$

See how simple? A decrease in the MPC from 0.8 to 0.75 caused the NI to decrease from 75 to 60. And I'm sure you could show this on a graph too, if you wanted to. But if you'd like to see it first, look at Figure A-7 and that's just what you'll see.

Fig. A-7 The Effect of a Change in the MPC

When the MPC decreases from 0.8 to 0.75 that reduces the upward slope of the C + I curve and reduces the size of the equilibrium NI from 75 as in the previous example to 60 as shown here.

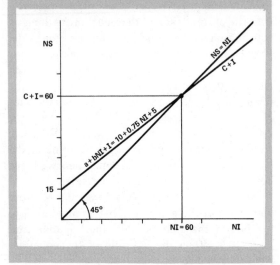

Now you know how to compute the size of national income for (1) different sizes of the investment injection, and (2) different slopes of the straight-line consumption function. Now you can see, understand, and illustrate mathematically both (1) the effect of a change in *the size of the investment injection,* and (2) the effect of a change in *the size of the marginal propensity to consume.*

Now come on. Be honest. Isn't this algebra kind of interesting? And aren't you beginning to see how it can be helpful in figuring out things a lot more quickly than you could without it?

There are even more interesting things coming up. But before you go on, be sure you're learning each step *thoroughly*. Otherwise you're going to start getting confused. And that's no fun. The purpose of this exercise is to have some *fun and games with curves and equations*. Remember? So take your time and try to enjoy it.*

MORE FUN AND GAMES WITH THE "C + I" EQUATION: DERIVING THE INCOME MULTIPLIER

You know that the equation for the consumption function (the C line) is C = a + bNI. And to get the equation for the C + I line you just add the "+I" on each side of the equation.

$$C = a + bNI$$
$$C + I = a + bNI + I.$$

and since C + I = NI we can substitute NI for C + I, and get:

$$NI = a + bNI + I.$$

This equation, like all equations, can be expressed in various ways. Which way should you choose to express it? The way that's *most useful* in helping you to find out what you want to find out.

What are we interested in finding out? The *size of the national income*, and *what happens to it* when the size of the *investment injection* changes! So just watch this:

$$NI = a + bNI + I$$

Now subtract enough NI from both sides of the equation to get rid of all of the NI on one side:

$$-bNI = -bNI$$

And you get:

$$NI - bNI = a + I$$

Now factor out[1] the NI on the left side of the equation and you get:

$$(1-b) NI = a + I$$

Divide both sides by (1−b) and you'll see another way of finding the size of NI[2].

$$NI = \frac{a + I}{(1-b)}$$

What does this equation tell you? It says

---

*Just a reminder: The model we are dealing with is based on some simplifying assumptions, don't forget. We are assuming (1) that the price level in our little economy is fixed, (2) that the only spending sources are C and I, (3) that the investment injection is fixed and does not change as national income changes, and (4) that the consumption function is linear so that the MPC is the same for all levels of NI. We could depart from these simplifying assumptions but that would complicate the math and it really isn't necessary. Our simple model illustrates the principles just fine.

---

[1]In case you've forgotten how to factor a term like "NI − bNI" there are only two little rules you need to be reminded of. (1) a term such as NI which does not have a coefficient, really has the coefficient 1, so "NI" really means "1.0 NI". The other rule is that a term outside the parenthesis means that this term is to be multiplied by each term within the parenthesis.

Logical example: Suppose you have 1 orange + 3 oranges. You have, in fact (1 + 3) oranges. Or suppose you have 1 box of graham crackers at home, and you know your little sister likes to eat graham crackers. If I asked you how many boxes of graham crackers you had at home you might tell me, "Let b equal the amount that my sister has eaten, and I have at home (1 box minus b boxes)." And I might say, "You have (1−b) boxes, right?" Sure. That's factoring.

Now you see why NI − bNI says exactly the same thing as 1.0 NI − bNI, which means exactly the same thing as (1 − b) NI.

[2]This is a neat and helpful little equation, but please be warned that it would only work for values of b ranging between zero and one—that is, for consumption function curves ranging between horizontal and sloping upward at an angle of 45 degrees. But that's the only kind of consumption function anyone is ever likely to encounter!

that "a" (the size of consumer spending when NI = 0) plus I (the amount of the investment injection) divided by (1 − b) gives you the size of the national income. Neat! But what's the real meaning of (1−b)?

The "b" term is the marginal propensity to consume (MPC), remember? So (1−b) is 1−MPC. That's the marginal propensity to save! The larger the "b" term (MPC) the smaller the MPS. So the larger the MPC the smaller this divisor (MPS) will be and the larger NI will be!

Or you can say it the other way. As the "b" term (MPC) gets smaller, the "consumer respending effect" gets smaller and the savings withdrawal gets larger. So the size of the equilibrium NI gets smaller.

Just for fun, let's go through it using the same numbers we were using awhile ago (a = 10, b = 0.8, and I = 5).

$$NI = \frac{a + I}{(1-b)}$$

$$NI = \frac{10 + 5}{(1-0.8)}$$

$$NI = \frac{15}{0.2} = 75.$$

See how the answer comes out the same as when you worked it out the long way, a few minutes ago? Let's do it again with a smaller investment injection (say I = 3):

$$NI = \frac{a + I}{(1 - b)}$$

$$NI = \frac{10 + 3}{(1 - 0.8)}$$

$$NI = \frac{13}{0.2} = 65.$$

And now, for a smaller MPC (say ¾ths, or 0.75)

$$NI = \frac{a + I}{(1 - b)}$$

$$NI = \frac{10 + 5}{(1 - 0.75)}$$

$$NI = \frac{15}{0.25} = 60.$$

What's the logic of this equation? It's really simple once you think about it. The numerator (a + I) tells how big C + I would be when NI = 0. You might call the numerator (a + I) the size of the *autonomous injection* into the income stream. None of this "autonomous injection" is induced by people receiving income.

Once you know the size of the *autonomous injection*, then you need to know how much *additional consumer spending* will be generated by the *multiplier effect*—the effect of the respending of income received.

As NI increases, C increases also. But as C increases, NI increases even more. And that induces even further increases in C. How long does this keep going on? Until the savings withdrawal increases enough to withdraw all of the "autonomous spending." In this case, first the *negative savings* (10, when NI = 0) must be eliminated, and then *positive savings* must expand enough to withdraw all of the investment injection.

The smaller the marginal propensity to consume (MPC), the larger will be the marginal propensity to save (MPS). The larger the MPS, the sooner (1) the *negative savings* will be eliminated and (2) the *positive savings* will be large enough to offset the investment injection. So the smaller the MPC, the larger the MPS, and the smaller will be the size of the equilibrium NI.

You know that you are observing the effect of the "income multiplier." Right? The income multiplier is the "consumer respending effect"— the increase in consumer spending induced by an income increase. The more consumers spend out of an income increase, the larger will be the MPC and the larger will be the income multiplier.

You probably remember the simple formula for the income multiplier. It's $\left(\frac{1}{1\text{-MPC}}\right)$, or $\left(\frac{1}{\text{MPS}}\right)$. How does that relate to the equations we're dealing with now? That's what you'll be finding out in the next section.

The Simple Algebra of the Income Multiplier

If you want to see the income multiplier working, you increase the size of the investment injection and then watch what happens.* Can we *derive* the simple formula for the income multiplier? Sure. First start with the basic equation:

$$C + I = NI$$

So it is obvious that

$$C + I = C + I$$

You know that $C = a + bNI$, so you can substitute $(a + bNI)$ in place of C, and get

$$C + I = a + bNI + I$$

Now if we want to figure out the multiplier we must increase the size of the investment injection. If you change the "I" term to "I + 1" that will increase national income by 1, plus the additional income generated by the multiplier. So the next step is to change I to (I + 1).

$$C + I = a + bNI + I + 1$$

(Note that the C + I term in this case refers to the *new* NI, with the multiple effect of the new investment injection included.) You know that NI = C + I. So you can replace the C + I term with NI, and the equation becomes:

$$NI = a + bNI + I + 1.$$

Now subtract bNI from each side of the equation:

$$-bNI = -bNI$$

And you get

$$NI - bNI = a + I + 1$$

Which when factored (as explained previously) becomes

$$(1 - b)NI = a + I + 1.$$

---

*Or you could increase the size of the "a" term—that is, shift the consumption function upward—increase the size of the "negative savings" injection when NI = 0—and it would work exactly the same. But in this example, we'll just increase the *investment injection* and watch what happens.

Divide both sides of the equation by $(1-b)$ and you get

$$\frac{(1-b)NI}{(1-b)} = \frac{a + I + 1}{(1-b)}$$

Which becomes

$$NI = \frac{a + I + 1}{(1 - b)}.$$

See where this last equation takes you? Right back to the equation you were working with a few minutes ago $\left(NI = \frac{a + I}{(1-b)}\right)$ except that the numerator is changed by "+1." What's the difference between NI, as arrived at by our original formula, and NI as arrived at by this new formula which includes the "+1"?

This new equation which includes the "+1" in the numerator tells us how big the national income will be *with the additional investment injection.* The former equation told us how big the national income would be *without* this new "+1" investment injection. So how much bigger is the new national income with the "+1" injection?

New NI (with +1 Injection) Minus Old NI Equals the Multiplier Effect

Suppose you subtract the old national income (NI without the new injection) from the new national income (NI with the new injection). What do you get? The difference, of course! You'll know how much the national income changed as a result of the additional "+1" investment injection. And if you know that, then you know the size of the income multiplier!

So now, subtract the size of NI *without* the new injection from the size of NI *with* the new injection. The answer will tell you how much NI will change as a result of a change in the size of the investment injection. It will tell you the multiplier effect! So let's do it:

$$\text{Change in NI} = \frac{a + I + 1}{(1 - b)} - \frac{a + I}{(1 - b)}$$

Now simplify the equation by combining the numerator over the denominator

$$\text{Change in NI} = \frac{a + I + 1 - (a + I)}{(1 - b)}$$

When you subtract the $(a + I)$ from the numerator, all there is left up there is 1! So what you get is

$$\text{Change in NI} = \frac{1}{(1 - b)}.$$

What does this equation tell you? Since "b" is the marginal propensity to consume, $(1 - b)$ is the marginal propensity to save. This equation tells you that the income multiplier is "one divided by (that is, the reciprocal of) the marginal propensity to save."

In the example we have been using, "b" has been 0.8, so $(1-b)$ has been 0.2. Divide 0.2 into 1, and you find that the multiplier is 5. Or if you prefer to work with fractions, when MPC is 0.8, that's 8/10 or 4/5, and $1 - 4/5 = 1/5$ (the MPS). When you divide 1 by 1/5 (to divide by a fraction, invert the divisor and multiply, right?) again you see that the multiplier is 5.

Here's another neat little trick. A few minutes ago you were working with this equation:

$$NI = \frac{a + I}{1 - b}$$

Which can also be expressed as

$$NI = (a + I)\left(\frac{1}{1 - b}\right).^*$$

You know that $\left(\frac{1}{1 - b}\right)$ is the income multiplier.

So what does this equation say? Just this: the *autonomous injections* $(a + I)$ times the *multiplier* $\left(\text{that's } \frac{1}{1 - b}\right)$ equals the size of the national income! But you already knew that.

---

*If this second equation doesn't look the same to you as the first, consider this: What's the difference whether you say $\frac{10}{5}$ or $10(\frac{1}{5})$ which is ten times one-fifth. No difference! You come out with 2 either way.

NATIONAL INCOME DETERMINATION WHEN ALL SPENDING SOURCES ARE CONSIDERED: THE C+I+G+F = NI EQUATION

Now that you know how to figure national income when the only spending sources are C and I, you probably could figure out that to include the other spending sources (G and F) you just add them into the equation and figure everything out the same way. And that's exactly what you do. Here goes:

$$NI = C + I + G + F$$

You remember that $C = a + bNI$, so we can substitute this in the equation in place of C and we get

$$NI = a + bNI + I + G + F.$$

Subtract bNI from each side of the equation

$$-bNI = -bNI$$

And you get

$$NI - bNI = a + I + G + F$$

Now factor the NI out of the left-hand side of the equation, as explained previously

$$(1-b)\,NI = a + I + G + F$$

Divide each side of the equation by $(1 - b)$ and this will solve the equation for NI

$$\frac{(1-b)\,NI}{(1-b)} = \frac{a + I + G + F}{(1-b)}$$

$$NI = \frac{a + I + G + F}{(1-b)}$$

This equation can also be expressed as follows:

$$NI = \frac{a}{1-b} + \frac{I}{1-b} + \frac{G}{1-b} + \frac{F}{1-b}$$

Or as follows, to show that what you are doing here is multiplying each one of the autonomous injections by the multiplier, and then adding all these together:

$$NI = \frac{1}{1-b}(a) + \frac{1}{1-b}(I) + \frac{1}{1-b}(G) + \frac{1}{1-b}(F)$$

Suppose you wanted to use this equation to compute the size of the national income. You would need to know the values of a, b, I, G, and F. Once you know these values it's very easy to solve the equation. So let's assume some values for each of these and proceed to work out the answer. Suppose that:

a = $10 billion
b = 0.8
I = $5 billion
G = $2 billion
F = $1 billion

If we put these values into our equation, what we get is:

$$NI = \frac{1}{1 - .8}(\$10) + \frac{1}{1 - .8}(\$5) + \frac{1}{1 - .8}(\$2) + \frac{1}{1 - .8}(\$1)$$

$$NI = \frac{1}{.2}(\$10) + \frac{1}{.2}(\$5) + \frac{1}{.2}(\$2) + \frac{1}{.2}(\$1)$$

$$NI = (5)(\$10) + (5)(\$5) + (5)(\$2) + (5)(\$1)$$

$$NI = \$50 + \$25 + \$10 + \$5$$

$$NI = \$90 \text{ billion}$$

Multiply Each Spending Injection by the Multiplier

You can look at the above computation and see very clearly that the equation says: "Multiply each autonomous spending injection by the multiplier and then add all these together and what you get is the size of the national income."

Of course you could add all of the autonomous injections together and then multiply the whole thing by the multiplier all at once. Or (as in this case) you could multiply each injection by the multiplier and then add them up. It makes no difference. You come out at exactly the same place either way.

From this analysis you can see that it makes no difference where the autonomous injection comes from—from I, or G, or F, or from C when NI is zero (i.e., negative savings), or from any combination of these. The multiplier effect is always the same. Those consumers who are spending 8/10ths (0.8) of their extra income on consumer goods don't care where the extra income came from!

How Do You Find C?

In the equation you just went through, NI turned out to be $90 billion. How big would consumer spending be if NI = $90 billion? When you're dealing with equations that's very easy to figure out. Just watch:

C = a + bNI
C = $10 + 0.8(90)
C = $10 + $72 = $82 billion.

See how easy that is? All we did was to substitute the numbers into the basic equation for the straight-line consumption function curve. It only takes a minute to get the answer, and then if you want to know how much is being pulled out as savings, that's even easier.

S = NI − C
S = 90 − 82
S = $8 billion.

Now compare total injections with total savings. The investment injection is 5, the government injection is 2, and the foreign injection is 1, for total injections of $8 billion. So where is equilibrium NI? Where the savings withdrawal is equal to total injections? Right! That's the way it is when savings is the only withdrawal.

But what if there were some other withdrawals? Taxes, for example? That's what you'll be finding out about in the section coming up. But before you go on, spend a few minutes studying and practicing with Figure A-8. There you'll see a Keynesian NS = NI graph which illustrates the effect of *all of the injections*. And you'll see that the answers you got using equations will come out exactly the same on the graph.

Fig. A-8. Equilibrium NI When All Injections (I, G, and F) Are Considered, and the Only Withdrawal Is Savings

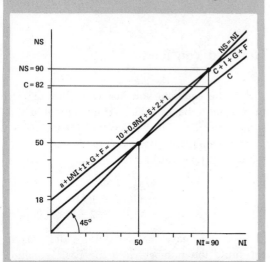

If there were no injections (I + G + F = 0) then equilibrium NI would be 50. But with the injections assumed in this example (5 + 2 + 1 = 8) equilibrium NI increases from 50 to 90—an increase of 40, induced by an injection of 8! The income multiplier must be 5 because 5 times 8 equals 40.

Also $\left(\dfrac{1}{1\text{-MPC}}\right) = \left(\dfrac{1}{1-.8}\right) = \left(\dfrac{1}{.2}\right) = 5,$ and that's the multiplier.

THE EFFECT OF TAX WITHDRAWALS

You know that the government pulls money out of the income stream by collecting taxes. This reduces national income, of course. A tax withdrawal is like a "reverse injection."

You also know that if the income multiplier is 5, one dollar of new injections will result in an additional $5 in NI. Does it work the other way, too? If the government suddenly started pulling out an additional dollar in taxes, would ultimately result in a $5 decrease in national income? Or what? That's what you'll learn to figure out in this section.

All of NI Is Not Disposable Income!

So far, we have been going along on the assumption that disposable income (DI) was the same as NI. But you know that when the government collects taxes, that isn't true. Not all of the NI flows to people and becomes disposable income. So DI is smaller than NI by the amount taken away by taxes. Now to be more realistic we'll say that *disposable income* equals *national income minus taxes*:

$$DI = NI - T$$

It's obvious that the consumption function really reflects DI—not NI. People can't spend for consumer goods the money they must pay as taxes! So the straight-line consumption function equation really isn't:

$$C = a + b \ NI. \text{ It is}$$
$$C = a + b \ DI$$

You know that DI equals NI − T, so let's substitute that in the equation and get

$$C = a + b(NI - T)$$

And multiplying out the b(NI − T) term, we get

$$C = a + bNI - bT.$$

This last equation tells us that the size of the

consumer spending flow will be determined by (1) the size of the consumer spending flow when NI is zero, plus (2) the marginal propensity to consume times the size of the national income, and (3) *minus* the marginal propensity to consume times the tax withdrawal.

The "minus bT" term in this equation shows you that the tax withdrawal is going to pull down the size of consumer spending. You already knew that, of course. But now we're going to play with some algebra and find out *how much* a given tax withdrawal will pull down the size of the national income, and the size of consumer spending. What you will see coming up will look exactly like what you saw a few minutes ago. The only difference is: Now there are taxes.

How Much Will Taxes Reduce NI?

We begin with the same equation as in the earlier example:

$$NI = C + I + G + F$$

Again we substitute for C, but now instead of substituting "a + bNI" we substitute "a + bNI − bT" and get

$$NI = a + bNI - bT + I + G + F$$

Again, subtract bNI from each side of the equation

$$- bNI = - bNI, \text{ and get}$$

$$NI - bNI = a - bT + I + G + F$$

Factor out NI on the left-hand side of the equation

$$(1 - b)NI = a - bT + I + G + F$$

Divide both sides of the equation by (1 − b) just as before. You come out with

$$NI = \frac{a - bT + I + G + F}{(1 - b)}$$

which can be expressed differently as

$$NI = \frac{1}{1-b}(a) - \frac{1}{1-b}(bT) + \frac{1}{1-b}(I) + \frac{1}{1-b}(G) + \frac{1}{1-b}(F)$$

Insert the same figures used before and you get

$$NI = \frac{1}{1-.8}(\$10) - \frac{1}{1-.8}(.8 \times \$2) + \frac{1}{1-.8}(\$5) + \frac{1}{1-.8}(\$2) + \frac{1}{1-.8}(\$1)$$

$$NI = \frac{1}{0.2}(\$10) - \frac{1}{0.2}(\$1.6) + \frac{1}{0.2}(\$5) + \frac{1}{0.2}(\$2) + \frac{1}{0.2}(\$1)$$

$$NI = 5(\$10) - 5(\$1.6) + 5(\$5) + 5(\$2) + 5(\$1)$$

$$NI = \$50 - \$8 + \$25 + \$10 + \$5$$

$$NI = \$82 \text{ billion}$$

So we find that a tax withdrawal of $2 billion reduces NI to $82 billion. With no taxes, NI was $90 billion. Taxes of $2 billion reduced NI to $82 billion? That's $8 billion less!

THE BALANCED-BUDGET MULTIPLIER

Now consider this: The government is spending $2 billion, remember? And that $2 billion injection by the government pushes up national income by $10 billion. A $2 billion injection times a multiplier of 5 equals $10 billion! But when the government collects enough taxes to balance the budget ($2 billion), that only pulls down NI by $8 billion.

What all this says is that the government can balance its budget and still have a stimulating effect on national income! How is that possible? You probably already know, but before you see the answer, first consider this question: With $2 billion now being pulled out in taxes, and with a NI now of $82 billion, how big is consumer spending? How do you find this out? Easy. Use the consumption function equation. But this time you must use the equation which includes the effect of taxes! Here it is:

$$C = a + bNI - bT$$

Now just substitute the numbers we've been using and work it out.

$$C = 10 + (0.8)NI - (0.8)T$$
$$C = 10 + (0.8)\ (\$82) - (0.8)\ (\$2)$$
$$C = 10 + 65.6 - 1.6$$
$$C = 10 + 64$$
$$C = \$74 \text{ billion}$$

Consumer spending is down to $74 billion! It was $82 billion when no taxes were collected. Remember? It's down by $8 billion! So most of that reduction in consumer spending didn't result from the taxes ($2 billion) taken away from the consumers. It resulted in the *lower national income* (down from $90 billion to $82 billion). With lower NI, people have smaller disposable incomes so they spend less.

The initial *direct effect* of the $2 billion in taxes was to reduce consumer spending, not by $2 billion, but by only $1.6 billion. Why?

Look at it this way. When you receive an additional $100, the MPC says that you won't spend it all for consumer goods—only part of it. Suppose the government had taxed away that $100. Would that have reduced consumer spending by $100? No. It would only have reduced it by $100 times the MPC (in this case 0.8 times $100 = $80). Do you get the point?

G Puts More Into the Spending Stream than T Takes Out!

All of government spending (G) is a *direct injection* into the income stream. But *not* all of the tax withdrawal is a withdrawal from the income stream. A part of the tax withdrawal comes from what would have been *saved*. Only that part which comes from what *would have been spent for consumer goods* represents a withdrawal from the income stream.

Now do you understand why there is a "balanced budget multiplier"? I am sure you do. And I'm sure you can see how helpful it is to be able to use algebra to help you to figure out such things.

WHERE COULD YOU GO FROM HERE?

What you've been working with in this appendix is a very simple mathematical model of the economy. This model has been based on many simplifying assumptions, including: (1) a linear consumption function, (2) all autonomous injections (I, G, and F) fixed and (3) the tax withdrawal fixed. So the only variables which could change with changes in income were C and S. Surely this is not entirely realistic.

As you probably would guess, most of these variables change to some extent as national income changes. Actually it would be quite easy to integrate such changes into our model. Just as C changes as NI changes, we could also make the other variables (I, or T, or F, or G) change as income changes. And we could introduce changes in the money supply (M) and changes in the price level (P) into our model. And we could do lots of other things. But let's don't. I think this appendix has gone far enough to serve its purpose without overdoing it.

If you have worked your way through this appendix carefully then I'm certain that you now have some understanding of (and appreciation for) the *usefulness* and *efficiency* of mathematics in economic analysis. And that's the objective which this appendix set out to achieve.

Now you can begin to understand why the economists in Washington who are advising on economic policy are so dependent on mathematical models. They build their models to reflect the most realistic theory and the most accurate statistics they can find. Then, using modern computers they make scientific projections of what would happen if certain tax rates were changed—or if government spending was changed—or if any one or more of dozens of other changes came about. They can project the impact of an increase in the money supply, of an increase in the price of oil, of a reduction in investment spending, of an increase in spending for automobiles or other consumer durables, etc. etc. etc.

There's quite a long way between where you are today and where those high-powered model-building economists are, to be sure. There's a lot of economic theory, mathematics, and econometrics between where you are and where they are. And a lot of serious hard work.

But from this appendix you have a tiny taste of what it's like.

If this sort of thing turns you on, there's no reason why you shouldn't head off in that direction and become a model-building economist. If you want to go that way, remember that you must be *very good*. Nobody needs (or will pay for) a mediocre economist. But if you consider yourself to be bright, hard-working, and highly motivated in this direction, why not go that way? You've got to be doing something ten years from now. Why not mathematical economic analysis? It pays good—and if you like it, it's fun!

Glossary

Concise explanations of
important economic principles,
concepts, and terms.

Note: For a thorough understanding you should consult the index and refer to the appropriate sections in the text.

Ability-to-pay principle. The idea that it is "just" for people who earn more (or own more) to pay more taxes.

Absolute advantage. The ability to produce a good for less cost (less factor inputs) than anyone else.

Acceleration principle. Changes in consumer demand (spending) cause even greater changes in derived demand and therefore in investment spending.

Ad valorem tax. A tax levied on the value of a good.

Aggregate demand. Total spending in the economy, including consumer spending, planned investment, government spending for goods and services, and net exports.

Allocation (of resources and goods). Deciding which resources will be used for which purposes and how the outputs of the economy will be distributed among the people.

Antitrust laws. Laws limiting the growth of and use of monopoly power.

Antitrust policy. Government policy regarding the legal position and the enforcement of restrictions on monopoly power.

Arbitrage. Buying something in one market and selling it in a different market at the same time to make a profit. For example, buying francs in New York and selling them in London when-

ever the price of francs in New York is lower than the price of francs in London.

Arbitration. Letting an impartial third party (the arbitrator) work out the terms of a labor-management contract.

Assets. All those things that are owned, including money, land, buildings, debts others owe you, etc.

Automatic stabilizers. Built-in features of the economic system which tend to stabilize total spending. For example, the progressive income tax which automatically pulls more money out of the income stream as total spending increases, and unemployment payments which automatically push more money into the income stream when the economy slows down.

Average cost (or revenue). The total cost (or revenue), divided by the number of units of output which are produced (or sold).

Average propensity to consume. That fraction (or percentage) of disposable income which is spent for consumer goods.

Average propensity to save. That fraction (or percentage) of disposable income which is not spent for consumer goods, or paid as taxes, or spent for imported goods.

Balanced (government) budget. Government rev-

Note: For a thorough understanding you should consult the index and refer to the appropriate sections in the text.

enues (from taxes and other sources) are great enough to equal government expenditures.

Balance of payments, international. A summary accounting statement showing all transactions (debits and credits) between one nation and all other nations of the world. It shows surplus and deficit balances for each of the various kinds of current and capital transactions. The balance of payments shows how the nation received foreign money, how it used up its foreign money, and whether or not there was a surplus or a deficit which had to be balanced out by using "official reserve transactions."

Balance of trade, international. Total of goods and services exports minus goods and services imports. The largest part of the international balance of payments, but excludes capital items.

Balance of trade deficit. The value of goods and services imported is greater than the value of goods and services exported. The nation is spending more for goods and services than it is receiving from its sales of goods and services.

Balance sheet. A statement showing a firm's financial position: what it owns (assets), what it owes (liabilities), and what's left over (net worth).

Bank holding company. A corporation created for the purpose of holding the stock in one or more commercial banks. Often, bank holding companies also own other financial corporations such as consumer finance companies.

Barter. Exchanging goods for goods without the use of a medium of exchange—that is, without the use of money.

Base year. The year used as the beginning year or "reference" year when constructing a price index or any other index. The index number indicates the percentage change between the base year and the year in question.

Basic Law of Real-World Markets. *See* reflex effect.

Benefit principle. The idea that it is "just" for people who get more benefits from various government expenditures to pay more taxes to

support those expenditures.

Bilateral monopoly. A market structure where there is only one buyer and one seller.

Black market. An "illegal free market" which always tends to develop whenever government restrictions prevent prices from changing to reflect the true demand and supply conditions for that product.

Bonds. Securities sold by governments and businesses to borrow money. People who buy bonds receive the amount of interest stated on the bond certificate and at the "maturity" (pay-off) date stated on the bond, they receive the "principal" (face value stated on the bond).

Boycott. Refusing to do business with a particular firm or to buy some particular product. Labor unions sometimes organize boycotts against the products of nonunion businesses.

Break-even point. The rate of output where the total revenue is just large enough to cover the total cost—that is, where the cost per unit is equal to the price (per unit).

Budget deficit. Expenditures in excess of receipts.

Budget surplus. Receipts in excess of expenditures.

Business cycles. The recurrent speeding up and slowing down of the economy. Macroeconomic fluctuations.

Capital. (1) Factor of production: Things which have been produced and are going to be used as inputs to produce something else. (2) Financial: Assets such as stocks or bonds, or funds available to a business for acquiring capital goods (factors of production). (3) Human: The educated, trained, and experienced human beings in the economy—productive people.

Capital gain. The increase in the value of an asset over time.

Capitalism. One name for an economic system in which private individuals and businesses own the factors of production and make their resource-use decisions based on markets and prices.

Note: For a thorough understanding you should consult the index and refer to the appropriate sections in the text.

Capitalization. Figuring out the capitalized value of an asset. *See also* capitalized value.

Capitalized value. The value of an asset as determined by the amount of (discounted) income which is expected to flow to its owner over the life of asset.

Capital markets. The financial markets in the economy where stocks and bonds are bought and sold, and where businesses obtain funds for long-term investments.

Capital stock. Stock of capital. The total amount of capital (machinery, equipment, infrastructure, etc.) in existence.

Capital transactions (international balance of payments). Long-term foreign investments.

Cartel. A group of sellers who work together to set their prices and outputs and therefore exercise monopoly control in the market for their products.

Cartel, OPEC. The Organization of Petroleum Exporting Countries which brought about the tenfold increase in oil prices between the early 1970s and the early 1980s.

Caveat emptor. A Latin term meaning "Let the buyer beware."

Central bank. The "official bank" of a nation—in the United States, the Federal Reserve System. The central bank regulates other banks, controls the money supply, performs fiscal functions for the government and helps to balance international payments.

Centralization (of government expenditures). The shifting of government expenditure functions upward from the local governments to the state and national governments.

Centralized federalism. *See* federalism.

Ceteris paribus. A Latin term meaning "assuming that everything else remains unchanged." For example, if the price of imported champagne goes down to 50¢ a bottle, *ceteris paribus*, people will buy more imported champagne.

Checkable deposits. Deposits which can be transferred by check, including demand deposits in commercial banks; NOW accounts at savings and loans, mutual savings banks, and some commercial banks; and share drafts at credit unions.

Check clearing. Moving checks from the banks in which they are deposited to the banks against which they are drawn, adding the amounts to the accounts of the people who deposited them and subtracting the amounts from the accounts against which they are written, and transferring funds from the banks against which the checks are written to the banks in which the checks are deposited.

Circular flow (of the economy). A simplified view of a market-directed economic system. It illustrates payments from businesses to households in exchange for input factors, and payments from households to businesses in exchange for output products.

Classical economics (also neoclassical economics). The generally accepted theories of economics of the 1800s and early 1900s. Pre-Keynesian economics. Most of the generally accepted present-day economic theory comes from classical, neoclassical, Keynesian, and neo-Keynesian economics. *See also* neoclassical economics.

Cobweb theorem (or cobweb effect). The tendency for some agricultural markets to be unstable from year to year with low production and high prices in one year, followed by high production and low prices in the following year.

Collective bargaining. Union-management negotiations.

Collusion. Sellers working together to set prices and outputs.

Commercial bank. A privately owned bank that has checking accounts, makes commercial and (usually) consumer loans, and provides other financial services.

Common stock. Ownership shares in a corporation. Shares of common stock are sold by a corporation to get money to buy capital equipment. After the shares have been issued (sold) by the corporation, then the shares can be bought and sold on the stock exchanges. The price of a share of stock is determined by the

Note: For a thorough understanding you should consult the index and refer to the appropriate sections in the text.

demand and supply for that stock on the exchanges, and is influenced by the assets and earnings (and expected future earnings) of the corporation.

Communism. (1) Philosophy: The Marxist ideas and predictions of the ultimate downfall of capitalism and the development of a "classless society" of mutual production and sharing. (2) Economic system: The economic and political system of the Soviet Union, China, and other Communist countries in which there is little private ownership and most of the production and distribution choices are made by the government.

Comparative advantage. The ability to produce a product for an opportunity cost which is lower than anyone else's opportunity cost in producing that product.

Competititon. Opposite of monopoly. Interaction among sellers of a product which tends to hold down prices and maintain product quality because buyers tend to move toward the lower-priced, higher quality products. In any market, the greater the degree of competition the smaller the degree of monopoly power. *See also* pure competition, perfect competition.

Competition, international. *See* international competition.

Competition, monopolistic. *See* monopolistic competition.

Competition, perfect. *See* perfect competition.

Competition, pure. *See* pure competition.

Complementary goods. Goods which are used together, like lumber and nails. If the price of one (lumber) goes down, people will buy more of it so the demand for the other (nails) will increase.

Concave curve. A curve on a graph which bows outward from the zero point, so that it is concave when viewed from the zero point of the graph.

Concentration ratio. A number indicating what percentage of the total output of an industry is produced by the few (usually four) largest firms in the industry. It's a rough way of measuring market structure.

Conglomerate merger. The combining into one firm of two or more previously separate business firms which produce unrelated products. The new combined firm would be called a conglomerate corporation.

Conspicuous consumption. Buying consumer goods for the purpose of "showing off" to impress others. This term was originated by the American economist Thorstein Veblen in the early 1900s.

Constant dollars. Dollar figures which have been deflated (by using a price index) to eliminate the effect of inflation.

Constant returns to scale. There are no economies of scale and no diseconomies of scale. Large plants (firms) can produce just as efficiently as (but no more efficiently than) small ones.

Consumer equilibrium. The consumer's "maximum satisfaction" position, given the consumer's preferences and the existing constraints of the consumer's income, and prices.

Consumer price index (CPI) (cost of living index). The most frequently used measure of changing consumer prices in the United States. Calculated and published by the Bureau of Labor Statistics, U.S. Department of Labor.

Consumer's surplus. The satisfaction (utility) which a consumer receives and doesn't have to pay for. For example, if you are sunburned and would be willing to pay $20 for a tube of lotion and you can buy it for only $4, then you are receiving a consumer's surplus of $16.

Consumption. Expenditures for consumer goods. Also, using up goods and services, or wearing out goods.

Consumption function. The idea that consumer expenditures depend on (are a function of) disposable income.

Consumption function curve. The curve on the Keynesian national income diagram showing the various rates of consumer spending which would occur at the various rates of flow of national income.

Consumption possibility curve (budget line). A straight line on a graph showing the various

Note: For a thorough understanding you should consult the index and refer to the appropriate sections in the text.

combinations of two different goods that could be purchased with a given amount of money. The slope of the line reflects the relative prices of the two goods.

Convertible bonds. Bonds sold by a corporation which permit the owner of the bond to exchange the bond for a specified amount of common stock in the corporation.

Convex curve. A curve on a graph which bows inward toward the zero point, so that it appears convex when viewed from the zero point of the graph.

Corporation. A form of business organization in which the business is a "fictitious person," an entity in its own right. It is owned by stockholders. The stockholders elect the directors, who hire the management. The management runs the corporation, and the corporation usually pays out a part of its profits as dividends to stockholders.

Cost-push inflation. Price increases in the economy caused by increasing input costs (not by increased demand for the output).

Countercyclical policy. Government policy designed to work against "the business cycle." The purpose is to stabilize the rate of output and income and prices in the economy.

Countervailing power. The theory developed by John Kenneth Galbraith, that in a modern economic system like that of the United States, large and powerful economic groups tend to offset and balance each other so that no one can take great unfair advantage of economic power.

Craft union. A trade union. A labor union made up of skilled workers all of whom are in the same trade, or craft.

Crowding-out effect. The idea that too much government borrowing will reduce the funds available to private borrowers, will push up interest rates, and will cause a decrease in private investment spending in the economy.

Currency. Coins and paper money. Also, in international economics the money of another country is often referred to as "foreign currency."

Customs duties. Tariffs. Taxes levied on imported goods.

Cut-throat competition. Using pricing and other policies designed to destroy your competitors.

Decentralized federalism. *See* federalism.

Decreasing returns (to scale). As plants (or firms) get larger, the average (per unit) cost of production goes up—that is, the "output return" for each dollar of input, goes down.

Deficit (government finance). Expenditures by the government are greater than total revenues being collected so that the balance must be made up by borrowing and/or by creating money.

Deficit (international balance of payments). Import items (which cause this country's dollars to flow to foreigners) exceed export items (which cause foreigners to use up their dollars). More dollars are being supplied to foreigners than foreigners are spending in the United States to buy goods, make investments, etc. American dollars held by foreigners (Eurodollars) are increased by the amount of the deficit.

Demand. The functional relationship between the prices which might be charged for a good and the quantities of that good which would be demanded at each of the various prices which might be charged.

Demand curve (or schedule). A curve on a graph (or a table) illustrating the demand function and showing the specific quantity which would be demanded at each price.

Demand deposits. Checking account deposits held by commercial banks. The deposits can be withdrawn "on demand" and can be transferred to others by writing checks.

Demand-pull inflation. Rising prices in the economy caused by increased aggregate demand (total spending) which is not matched by increased aggregate supply (total output).

Demand shift. A change in the demand function so that at each price, the quantity demanded is different than before. On a graph, the demand curve shifts to a different place.

Note: For a thorough understanding you should consult the index and refer to the appropriate sections in the text.

"Demand-side" economics. Economic analysis and/or policy which focuses attention on aggregate demand for output (total spending) and on the factors which influence this. *See also* Keynesian economics.

Deposit multiplier. *See* multiplier effect.

Depreciation. The decline in value of physical capital as it is used up, worn out, or becomes obsolete.

Depression. A serious, prolonged period of high unemployment and low output and income in the economy. Like a recession, only worse.

Derived demand. The demand for inputs. All input demands are "derived from" the fact that there is a final demand for output products.

Devaluation. Reducing the "price" (exchange rate) at which you sell the money of your nation in exchange for the monies of other nations.

Diminishing marginal rate of transformation. Whenever the production possibility curve is concave (as viewed from the zero point of the graph), as more and more production is shifted out of one product and into the other, you get back less and less of the other product. For example, as successive units of product x are "transformed into" product y, the amount of product y received for each unit of product x given up will get successively smaller. *See also* marginal rate of transformation.

Diminishing marginal utility. The idea that the additional satisfaction you get from increasing your consumption of some good or service by one unit, gets smaller as the current rate at which you are consuming it gets greater. Or, the smaller the amount of it you are currently consuming, the greater the amount of additional satisfaction you could get by increasing your consumption rate by one unit. This principle explains why you don't spend *all* of your money on any one thing—like blue jeans, or potato chips.

Diminishing returns, law of (law of variable proportions). If some of the factors of production are fixed (buildings and machinery), output can be increased by adding more variable inputs (labor and materials). But as more and more variable inputs are added and output is expanded more and more, eventually a point will be reached beyond which the extra output received (the returns) from each successive addition of a unit of the variable inputs, will get smaller and smaller. That is, the "returns" from each additional unit of variable input, will diminish.

Discounted value. The *present value* of a sum of money which is to be received at some time in the future. *See also* capitalized value.

Discounting. Finding the *present value* of a sum of money which is not going to be received until sometime in the future.

Discount rate. The interest commercial banks must pay when they borrow money from the Fed. Also, in general, the interest rate.

Discretionary stabilization policy. Government policies to try to stabilize the economy and maintain full employment and which are adjusted by government policymakers at their discretion to reflect changing economic conditions.

Diseconomies of scale (decreasing returns to scale). When a large-scale plant is less efficient than a small-scale plant then there are "diseconomies of scale." The long-run average total cost curve slopes upward.

Disintermediation. Savers take money out of the "financial intermediary" organizations (mostly savings and loan companies) and invest the savings directly in money market funds or other investments without the benefit of the services of a "financial intermediary" to do the investing for them.

Disposable (personal) income. The money households actually have to spend. It's the personal income which is left over after all taxes have been paid and all transfer payments have been received.

Distribution question. The question of how the output of the economic system will be divided up among the people—which people will get how much, and how that will be decided.

Note: For a thorough understanding you should consult the index and refer to the appropriate sections in the text.

Dividends. Payments by corporations to the stockholders.

Division of labor. Breaking down the production process into several small tasks so that each worker can become very specialized in doing one thing. For example, an assembly line.

Dual economy. A less developed country with unbalanced growth where some parts of the economy are modern and efficient and some of the people live by modern standards, while elsewhere in the economy primitive conditions and poverty are widespread.

Dumping (in international trade). Selling goods in foreign markets at prices which are lower than in domestic markets (usually at prices which are below the average total cost of production).

Duopoly. A market structure in which there are only two sellers.

Easy money. Policy of the Fed to keep interest rates low and to supply reserves to the banking system to make it easy for money to be borrowed. The purpose of easy money is to stimulate spending, to reduce unemployment. Opposite of "tight money."

Econometrics. The use of statistical analysis to better understand economic conditions and problems and to make projections of future economic conditions. Widely used in guiding economic policy and planning, both by government and by major corporations.

Economic integration. Eliminating restrictions to the flows of products and factors of production between nations.

Economic man. The "perfectly rational person" who always thinks marginally and maximizes economic welfare and achieves consumer equilibrium. The theory of consumer behavior is built on the assumption that real people function (more often than not) in the same way as would the fictional "economic man."

Economic principle (or law, theory, or model). A precise statement of functional relationships among economic variables. A statement of what causes what, of what would happen if. . . .

Economic rent. That amount of payment to any factor of production which is *above and beyond* the amount which would need to be paid to keep the factor available and doing what it is doing. For example, beach-front property would still be available as beach-front property even if the owners couldn't charge $1,000 a front foot. And John Travolta would still be a movie star even if he wasn't paid so much. Therefore, much of the income of the beach-front property owner and John Travolta is "economic rent."

Economics. The study of how people and families and organizations and societies make and carry out their choices—of what they do and how as they try to maximize their progress toward their objectives—of how they use the things they have (their scarce resources) to achieve their objectives and satisfy their wants. Mostly it's the study of how the market process (the price mechanism) functions and of the principles which underlie those functions, as modified by the traditions of the society and the influences of the political process.

Economics, the science of. Economics as a science consists of the theories, laws, and models of positive economics. It consists of the analysis of causal relationships under assumed model conditions.

Economic system. The organized way in which the production and distribution choices are made and carried out in a nation.

Economies of scale (increasing returns to scale). A larger plant has a lower unit cost of production than a smaller plant, so only larger plants can produce efficiently enough to survive. The long-run total cost curve declines as output increases.

Economizing. Using all of the available resources very carefully so as to maximize progress toward the chosen objectives.

Effective demand. The quantity of a good purchasers are actually buying at the existing price.

Efficiency (maximum). Achieving maximum output value from a given set of inputs, or achieving the desired output with minimum

Note: For a thorough understanding you should consult the index and refer to the appropriate sections in the text.

cost of inputs.

Elastic demand (or supply) (also, *relatively elastic, or price elastic*). When the price changes, the quantity changes by a greater percentage than the price changed, so the elasticity (percentage change in quantity divided by percentage change in price) is numerically greater than one.

Elasticity of demand (or supply). Responsiveness of the quantity demanded (or supplied) to a change in price. Numerically, the elasticity is calculated by dividing the percentage change in price into the percentage change in quantity.

Entrepreneur. The enterprising individual who hires factors of production, organizes and directs the production process, and then sells the output (hopefully) to make a profit.

Equation of exchange. $MV = PQ$. The quantity of money times the velocity at which it turns over, is equal to the total number of units of goods sold times the average price per unit. Sometimes expressed as $MV = PT$, or $MV = OP$, or with other symbols.

Equilibrium. A situation where everything is in balance and there is no tendency to change.

Eurodollars. United States dollar deposits held by (and available to be lent by) foreign banks.

Excess quantity demanded (shortage). Buyers are trying to buy more than the sellers are willing to supply. Whenever the existing market price is below the equilibrium market price, there will be excess quantity demanded and (*ceteris paribus*) the price will rise.

Excess quantity supplied (surplus). Suppliers are trying to sell more than the buyers are willing to buy. Whenever the existing market price is above the equilibrium market price, there will be excess quantity supplied and (*ceteris paribus*) the price will fall.

Excess reserves. Bank reserves held by commercial banks and other depository financial institutions in excess of the amount legally required. Therefore, funds available for making new loans. *See also* required reserves.

Exchange rate. How much foreign money you can get for one unit of your own money, or the price you must pay (in U.S. dollars) to buy a unit of foreign money (say a franc, deutschmark, guilder, etc.).

Exchange value. Economic value. The "going price" for a good.

Excise tax. Tax levied on a specific good—usually levied on the manufacture or sale of the good.

Expenditure possibility curve. *See* consumption possibility curve.

Externality. A "spillover" effect which has either desirable or undesirable effects on the "innocent bystanders" who are a part of neither the production nor the consumption of the product.

Factor of production. Anything used as an input in the production process. In economics, usually grouped as land, labor, capital, and (sometimes) the entrepreneur.

FDIC (Federal Deposit Insurance Corporation). The federal government agency which insures checking accounts and savings accounts at commercial banks.

Featherbedding. Labor practices which try to induce the employer to hire more labor than is needed to do the job.

Federal debt. The total amount of government bonds and other securities which have been sold by the United States government to private individuals and businesses and to the Federal Reserve banks.

Federalism. The relationships among the different levels of government (national, state, and local) in a system of federal government such as that in the United States. *Centralized federalism* means that more of the functions are performed and more of the powers exercised by the highest level of government (our federal government in Washington) and *decentralized* means that more of the power and functions are exercised at the lower levels of government (state, and even more decentralized, local).

Federal Reserve Board. The Board of Governors of the Federal Reserve system which consists of seven members, each appointed by the President to a fourteen-year term. One member's term expires every two years.

Note: For a thorough understanding you should consult the index and refer to the appropriate sections in the text.

Federal Reserve district. One of the twelve geographic subdivisions into which the Federal Reserve system is divided. There is one Federal Reserve bank in each of the twelve districts.

Federal Reserve notes. The paper money which makes up most of the currency in the United States.

Federal Reserve System (The Fed). The central banking system of the United States.

Fiat money. Paper money issued by governments or central banks which is not backed by or convertible into anything, but is money because the government declares it to be legal tender.

Financial intermediary. *See* intermediary, financial.

Fiscal federalism. The financial interrelationships between the federal, state, and local governments. *See also* federalism.

Fiscal policy. Adjusting government expenditures and taxes to try to stabilize the economy and overcome inflation and/or unemployment.

Fixed cost. Cost of production that does not change as output is increased or decreased in the short tun.

Fixed inputs. Those factors of production whose quantity cannot be increased or decreased in the short run. For example, an industrial plant.

Floating exchange rates. Exchange rates (between the monies of different nations) which are allowed to move up or down in response to supply and demand conditions in the foreign exchange markets.

Foreign exchange. The money of any other country. For example, if you exchange dollars for Mexican pesos you are "buying foreign exchange."

Foreign exchange reserves. Foreign money held by the government, or by the central bank. Also SDRs and gold may be held as foreign exchange reserve assets.

Free good. Anything which is available in sufficient quantity that everyone can have all they want without having to pay for it.

Free trade. No tariffs, quotas, or other restrictions are imposed on trade between geographic areas.

Frictional unemployment. The temporary unemployment which occurs when workers are changing jobs.

FSLIC (Federal Savings and Loan Insurance Corporation). The federal agency which insures the savings deposits in savings and loans institutions.

Full-bodied money. Any piece of money which is made from material which is as valuable as the face value of the money. Example: a $50 gold piece which contains $50 worth of gold.

Futures markets. Markets where you can make a contract today to buy something at a specified future date for a price which is agreed on, today. If the price of what you bought goes up between now and the delivery date, you'll make a profit. If it goes down, you'll lose.

Gains from trade. The increased output and income that is generated by the increased efficiency which results from specialization and trade.

GATT (General Agreement on Tariffs and Trade). The international organization set up in 1947 to reduce trade restrictions among nations. Several "rounds" of multilateral negotiations have been undertaken, and significant reductions in trade restrictions have been achieved.

General equilibrium. A situation in which all of the markets in the economy are simultaneously in equilibrium.

GNP. *See* gross national product.

GNP account. *See* national income and product account.

GNP price deflator. The price index number used by the Bureau of Economic Analysis of the U.S. Department of Commerce to "deflate" GNP figures to eliminate the effect of inflation.

Gold certificate. A "dollar bill" which is backed by and convertible into gold. The only gold certificates now in use in the United States are those which are issued by the Treasury and held by the Federal Reserve banks.

Note: For a thorough understanding you should consult the index and refer to the appropriate sections in the text.

Gold standard. An international monetary system in which the monetary unit of each country is defined as a certain amount of gold, and (historically) gold also serves as the medium of exchange within each nation.

Good. Anything people find useful or desirable. Anything people want to have or to use. If the supply of a good is limited, then it is a *scarce good* so it is an *economic good* and it will have a price. If the supply is unlimited, it will be a *free good.* In economics, services are usually included as "goods."

Government securities. Government bonds, Treasury bills, and all other "debt instruments" sold by the government to finance the government debt. *See also* securities.

Grants-in-aid. Grants given by a higher level of government to pay part of the cost of a specific program undertaken by a lower level of government. For example, federal payments to the states to help to pay for the construction of the interstate highway system.

Green revolution, the. Term sometimes used to refer to the "revolutionary" agricultural breakthroughs of the 1960s and 1970s: fast-growing, high-yielding plants and new agricultural chemicals. At one time this was thought to be a possible long-run answer to hunger in the world, but that view seems to have been much too optimistic.

Gresham's Law. "Bad money drives out good money." The idea is that if there are two different types of money in use (for example, gold coins and silver coins) and one is more valuable than the other, people will always spend the less valuable kind and hold the more valuable kind. So the "bad money" drives the "good money" out of circulation.

Gross national product (GNP). Total "gross value" of all goods and services produced in the economy in one year. GNP figures reflect the "annual rate of gross output" of the economy.

Guns vs. butter. A popular expression which refers to the trade-off between production for military purposes and production for civilian purposes. The term arose during World War II, when the idea was that we must produce less butter and release factors of production to produce more guns.

High-powered money. New money that flows into the banking system to provide new reserves and thereby to permit a multiple expansion of the money supply.

Holding company. A corporation which owns a controlling interest in (sometimes all of) the stock in one or more other corporations and thereby owns and controls the other corporations.

Homogeneous. All of the units are identical.

Horizontal merger. Merger between two or more firms which perform the same functions and produce the same things. For example, a merger between two coal mining companies or two automobile producers or two gasoline stations.

Human capital. *See* capital.

Hyperinflation. Very rapid inflation. Runaway inflation.

IMF (International Monetary Fund). The international organization which is concerned with stabilizing exchange rates and working out desirable international financial arrangements between nations.

Imperfect competition. Any market structure in which pure competition does not exist. Some producers have some monopoly power to influence the quantity supplied, and the price.

Implicit cost. The opportunity cost of using something that you own, instead of renting it out or hiring it to someone else and earning money on it.

Import quota. A limit placed on the quantity of a good that can be imported.

Incidence of a tax. The final resting place of the burden of the tax. The person whose real income is reduced by the tax is the one who bears the incidence.

Income accounts. *See* national income and product account.

Note: For a thorough understanding you should consult the index and refer to the appropriate sections in the text.

Income effect. The reduction (or increase) in your real income which occurs when the price of something you buy goes up (or down). If you continue to buy the higher (or lower) priced good, your real income is reduced (or increased).

Income elasticity of demand. Responsiveness of the quantity bought of a good to a change in the incomes of the consumers. If people's incomes go up by one percent and the quantities bought of a certain good increase by more than (less than) one percent, then the demand for this good is said to be "income elastic" ("income inelastic").

Income line. *See* consumption possibility curve.

Income multiplier. Also, investment multiplier. *See* multiplier effect.

Income, real. *See* real income.

Incomes policy. A government policy of direct restraints (such as wage and price controls) on the rate at which money wages and other money incomes can rise. Incomes policies are any form of wage and/or price restraints or controls.

Income statement. *See* profit and loss statement.

Increasing returns (to scale). Larger plants (or firms) can produce more efficiently and at lower cost than smaller ones. As the size of the plant (or firm) increases, the output returns (per unit of input) increase. The long run average total cost curve slopes downward.

Incremental cost (or revenue). A term frequently used in business instead of marginal cost (or revenue).

Indexation. Adjusting various prices and incomes on the basis of changes in the general price level, as indicated by the "price index." Examples: Adjusting social security benefits on the basis of changes in the consumer price index. Adjusting workers' wages based on changes in the cost of living. In some other countries where inflation has become a way of life, indexation is used to adjust the value of a wide range of financial contracts.

Index number. A number showing the percentage change of some variable between a "base year" and the year in question. For example, the consumer price index.

Indifference curve. A curve on a graph showing different combinations between two goods where all combinations along the curve provide equal satisfaction to the consumer whose preferences are represented by the indifference curve. The higher up and more to the right the indifference curve lies in the graph, the higher the level of satisfaction indicated.

Indifference map. A graph containing a series of indifference curves, with each curve representing a different level of satisfaction for the individual whose preferences are illustrated by the indifference graph.

Indirect taxes. Taxes which are levied on products at some stage in the production-distribution process and are included in the final prices of goods. The buyers of the goods pay the taxes but they usually are not aware of how much tax they are paying.

Industrial union. A union open to all workers in an industry regardless of their particular skills or the functions they perform. For example, the United Automobile Workers Union includes machine operators, maintenance personnel, painters, fork-lift operators, and everyone else who wants to join.

Inelastic demand (or supply). Quantities demanded (or supplied) do not respond very much to price changes. A one percent change in price would result in less than one percent change in quantity demanded. Elasticity numerically less than one.

Inferior good. A good which people buy less of as they get more income. Income elasticity is negative, meaning that the demand for the good shifts to the left (decreases) as people's incomes rise. For example, perhaps canned spaghetti, or long-distance bus tickets.

Inflation. Increasing prices of goods and services. An increase in the average price level in the nation.

Infrastructure. The basic physical facilities required to permit an economy to function, such as roads, harbors, water systems, electrical

Note: For a thorough understanding you should consult the index and refer to the appropriate sections in the text.

systems, etc.

Injunction. A court order requiring some person or organization to do or not to do some specific thing, or things. Frequently used in antitrust cases against businesses, and in labor-management cases against unions.

Innovation. Development and introduction of new products, or new production technology.

Input question. The question of which combination of inputs will be used to produce each product. One of the basic questions which must be answered in every economic system.

Interest rate. The percentage return which the lender receives from the borrower. For example, on a bond the interest rate is stated as a percentage of the face value of the bond.

Interest rate, real. *See* real interest rate.

Interest yield. The effective rate of interest which an investor receives. For example, if you can buy for only $500 a perpetual (no maturity) $1,000 bond which pays 5% on its face value, then you will receive an interest yield of 10% on the $500 you invested in the $1,000 bond.

Interlocking directorate. Some of the members of the board of directors of one corporation also are members of the board of directors of a different (perhaps a competing) corporation.

Intermediary, financial. A financial services organization which takes deposits from individuals and invests these in various kinds of income earning assets, so that the savers themselves do not have to make their own investment decisions. Examples: savings and loan associations, credit unions, mutual savings banks, commercial banks.

Intermediate product. Any product which is going to be used as an input in further production. Not a "final product."

Internalization (of externalities). Using such methods as penalty charges or government subsidies to cause a producer's costs and/or revenues to more closely reflect true social costs and benefits.

International balance of payments. *See* balance of payments, international.

International balance of trade. *See* balance of trade, international.

International competition. Competition among producers throughout the world. International competition for American producers has become much more severe in recent decades as the world has moved more toward free trade and as the other major trading nations have become more industrialized and efficient.

Inventories. Stocks of goods held by businesses: raw materials, intermediate products, or final goods waiting to be sold.

Investment (in the economy). Expenditures for new capital goods: buildings, machines, inventories, etc.

Investment bank (or banker). The selling agent for firms which want to issue (sell) new stocks, bonds, or other securities to raise more money.

Investment good. Any capital good. Buildings, machines, inventories, etc.

Investment multiplier. Also, income multiplier. *See* multiplier effect.

Invisible hand. The idea from Adam Smith's *Wealth of Nations* that as people follow their own self interest, they are automatically directed into those activities which will most benefit the society. The idea is that people get their greatest rewards when they best serve the wants of others.

Isocost curve. A straight-line curve on a graph indicating different input combinations of equal cost. The curve is negatively sloped, and the slope represents the price ratio between the two inputs.

Isoquant curve. A negatively sloped curve indicating equal quantities of output which could be produced using different combinations of the two inputs shown on the two axes of the graph. Where the isocost curve is tangent to the isoquant curve, that indicates the least cost combination of these two inputs for producing the quantity of output indicated by the isoquant curve.

Jawboning. Efforts by the government to induce

Note: For a thorough understanding you should consult the index and refer to the appropriate sections in the text.

businesses and labor to go along with government policies even when there is no law which says that they must.

Joint products. Products which when the quantity produced of one is increased, the quantity produced of the other is also automatically increased. For example, sirloin steaks and chuck roast.

Keynesian economics. The theories of macroeconomics initiated by John Maynard Keynes in the 1930's. Emphasis is on the determinants of total spending, especially the relationship between savings and investment and the importance of government withdrawals (taxes), and injections (expenditures). The propensity to consume, the income multiplier, and the effect of the marginal efficiency of capital and interest rates on investment decisions are all parts of Keynesian economics. "Demand-side" economics.

Keynesian-monetarist debate, the. The disagreement about appropriate macroeconomic theory and policy. Keynesians recommend discretionary policy as effective and desirable to smooth out economic fluctuations. Monetarists emphasize the natural tendencies of the market economy to stabilize itself and argue that government attempts to stabilize using Keynesian policies ultimately will be destabilizing.

Keynesian National Income and Spending Graph (the "Keynesian Cross"). A graph showing national spending and income, the consumption function, and the effect of spending injections on the equilibrium level of national income.

Kinked demand curve. Demand curve as seen by the oligopolist seller. The "kink" is at the existing price. The kinked demand curve assumes that if the seller raises the price, other sellers will not. But if the seller lowers the price, all other sellers will do the same. The curve is highly elastic for a price increase and inelastic for a price decrease.

Labor. The factor of production which includes all human effort (both physical and mental)

used in the production of goods or services.

Labor force. The number of people in the population who are either working or seeking work.

Labor participation rate. The percentage of the population which is in the labor force.

Laffer curve. The curve which illustrates the relationship between tax rates and revenues collected. Illustrates the assumption that higher tax rates discourage productivity and encourage people to use tax loopholes so that beyond some point, higher rates will bring lower revenues.

Lags. This term refers to the required "response time" following some economic policy change. Example: Controlling the size of the money supply will control the rate of inflation, but because of lags, the desired result does not occur immediately.

Laissez faire. A French term meaning no government interference in the economic activities of people or businesses. It means to leave people free to do or to make whatever they wish.

Land. The factor of production which includes land itself, plus all of the "free gifts of nature" which come with the land.

Law of demand. The economic principle that says that people will buy more of a good as its price is lowered and less of it as its price is raised.

Law of diminishing marginal utility. *See* diminishing marginal utility.

Law of diminishing returns. *See* diminishing returns, law of.

LDCs. Less developed countries. Countries in which the average income per capita is low (sometimes defined as less than $700 per capita).

Leakages. Withdrawals from the income-spending flow. Also, withdrawals of reserves from the banking system which reduce the potential size of the money supply.

Legal tender. Any kind of money which the government says must be accepted as money for the payment of debts.

Liability. Anything which is owed to others.

Limited liability. The idea that when you own shares of stock in a corporation you are only

Note: For a thorough understanding you should consult the index and refer to the appropriate sections in the text.

liable for the debts of that corporation up to the amount which you paid for the stock. If the corporation owes more debts than it can pay, the stockholders cannot be required to pay those debts which the corporation cannot pay.

Liquidity. Ease with which an asset can be exchanged for other assets (without loss of value). Money is the most liquid asset.

Liquidity preference. The desire to hold money instead of spending it for (or investing it in) less liquid assets.

Localization. A term used in the LDCs which means replacing expatriate (foreign) workers and management people with native citizens.

Long run. A period long enough for all factors of production to become variable so that all of the adjustments required to achieve a "long-run equilibrium" can be made.

Long-run equilibrium. The "model condition" in a market (or an industry) in which all adjustments to demand and cost conditions have been made, all excess profits (or losses) have been eliminated, and there are no existing conditions in the market (or industry) which will induce any further change to occur.

Lorenz curve. A curve showing the percentage of total income which is being received by each of the various income groups in the society.

M₁. The money supply of the nation, defined as the total amount (dollar value) of currency in circulation plus all money in *checkable deposits* in commercial banks, savings and loans, credit unions, and savings banks, plus all travelers checks outstanding.

M₂. The money supply of the nation, defined as M₁ plus money market funds, savings deposits, and a few other highly liquid (near-money) assets.

M₃. The money supply of the nation, defined as M₂, plus large-denomination time deposits such as certificates of deposit (CDs) plus a few other liquid (near-money) assets.

Macroeconomic policy. Government policies designed to try to achieve relatively full employment, stable prices, and an appropriate rate of economic growth. Monetary and fiscal policies. *See also* discretionary stabilization policy, Keynesian-monetarist debate.

Macroeconomics. The study of the rates of flow in the economy (income, employment, output, consumer spending, investment spending, etc.) and of the factors which influence these rates of flow.

Macroequilibrium. Condition in which the size of the spending flow has no tendency to either expand or contract because planned savings (and all other withdrawals) are exactly equal to planned investment (and all other injections). This is not a *stable* equilibrium, because anything which breaks the equality between injections and withdrawals tends to produce a chain reaction which causes the spending flow to change even further in the same direction.

Malthusian problem. The problem of population tending to expand more rapidly than the output of food can expand. A problem first emphasized by Thomas R. Malthus in 1798.

Marginal. A small (one-unit) change in something. A "marginal" unit is an "additional" unit of something.

Marginal cost. Cost of increasing the rate of production by *one output unit* (per day, week, etc.) Cost of the additional variable factors required to expand the production rate by one output unit. At any rate of output (output x) the marginal cost can be found by subtracting total cost at the one-unit smaller output rate (output x − 1) from total cost at the present rate of output (output x).

Marginal efficiency of capital. The expected return from an investment in an additional unit of capital.

Marginal loss. *See* marginal profit.

Marginal physical product (MPP). The additional output (measured in output units) which is produced when one more unit of the variable input is used.

Marginal profit. The additional profit (increase in total profit) which results from increasing the rate of output by one unit. When the marginal revenue received from the sale of an

Note: For a thorough understanding you should consult the index and refer to the appropriate sections in the text.

additional unit is *greater than* the marginal cost of producing the additional unit, then there will be a marginal profit. If MC = MR, marginal profit is zero and total profit is maximized because no more marginal profits are available. If the producer expands output beyond the rate at which MC = MR, then the MR received when the output unit is sold will be less than the MC of producing that additional unit. There will be a marginal loss and total profit will be reduced.

Marginal propensity to consume (MPC). The fraction of an increase in income which is (or would be) spent for consumer goods. For example, if income increased by 10 and consumer spending increased by 7, the marginal propensity to consume would be 7/10ths. The marginal propensity to save would be 3/10ths.

Marginal propensity to save (MPS). The fraction of an increase in income which would *not* be spent for consumer goods. *See also* marginal propensity to consume.

Marginal rate of substitution. The "satisfaction trade-off ratio" between two goods. The ratio shows how much more of one good is required to exactly offset the decrease in satisfaction from the loss of one unit of the other good. It answers the question: "how much x must I get to offset the loss of one unit of y (or vice versa)?" The slope of the indifference curve at each point indicates the marginal rate of substitution between the two goods at that given combination of the two goods.

Marginal rate of transformation. The ratio indicating how much of one product (good x) must be given up in order to release enough inputs to produce one additional unit of some other product (good y). The marginal rate of transformation gives the opportunity cost of a unit of each good in terms of the other good. It is shown by the slope of the production possibility (transformation) curve. *See also* diminishing marginal rate of transformation.

Marginal revenue. The increase in total revenue (per day, week, etc.) that comes from increasing the output rate by one unit and selling that "extra" unit of output. In pure competition, MR always equals the price at which the extra unit is sold. For a seller with monopoly power, MR is always *less than* the price at which the unit is sold, because some revenue is lost when the price is lowered (as it must be) to induce the buyers to buy the additional unit of output.

Marginal revenue product. *See* marginal value product.

Marginal tax rate. The fraction (or percentage) of a small increase in income which must be paid in taxes. The marginal tax rate is the tax rate which applies to the marginal (additional) income.

Marginal utility. The additional satisfaction received from increasing the rate of consumption of some specific good by one unit (per day, week, etc.).

Marginal value product (MVP). Also, marginal revenue product (MRP). The additional revenue received when one additional unit of the variable factor is employed and the marginal physical product of that unit of the variable factor is sold.

Market. The place (actual, or conceptual) where buying and selling take place. It's the place where demand and supply interact and exert their influence on the price, and where the buyers and sellers respond to the existing and changing prices.

Market economy. An economic system in which the market process (demand, supply, and prices) plays an important role in influencing the production and distribution choices.

Market equilibrium price. The price at which the quantity supplied is exactly equal to the quantity demanded. There is no surplus and no shortage in the market. The market equilibrium price may be a short-run price (either above or below the "normal price") or it may be the long-run "normal price."

Market mechanism. The price mechanism. The way in which demand, supply, and prices direct the market economy. *See also* market process, price mechanism.

Market power. Monopoly power. The ability of one seller to influence the market price

Note: For a thorough understanding you should consult the index and refer to the appropriate sections in the text.

through exercising some control over either demand or supply or both.

Market process. The guiding force in the *laissez faire* economy. It operates through demand and supply and prices and directs the production and distribution choices for the society. *See also* market mechanism.

Market structure. The physical characteristics of the market, including such things as: the number and relative sizes of the buyers and sellers, the ease of entry into or exit from the market, and the extent of product differentiation. Examples: Pure competition, oligopoly, monopoly, monopsony, etc.

Maximum efficiency. *See* efficiency (maximum).

MC = MR. Marginal cost equals marginal revenue. This is the most profitable rate of output for the business firm. At this output rate, marginal profit is zero because all opportunities to make marginal profit have already been taken advantage of. At any rate of output at which MC is less than MR (so that marginal profit is available) the firm cannot be maximizing profit because profit can be further increased by expanding output more. When the output rate is expanded to where MC = MR and marginal profit is zero, then all opportunities to increase output and add to profit have been taken. So that's the maximum profit available.

Member bank. A commercial bank which has membership in the Federal Reserve System.

Merger. Creating one firm by joining together two or more previously separate firms.

Merit good. A good or service produced by the government and supplied free to everyone "for the good of the society." For example, public education.

Metro-government. A form of municipal government in which all of the local governments in the metropolitan area give up some of their powers to an areawide metropolitan government body. The metro-government makes plans and exercises control over programs and projects which relate to the entire metropolitan area. There are not many metro-governments in the world. None in the United States.

Microeconomics. The study of how the production and distribution choices are made in an economic system, with primary emphasis on the way in which demand and supply and the price mechanism direct the economic activities of the market economy. The emphasis of microeconomics is on understanding the market process and how it works. *See also* neoclassical economics.

Mixed socio-capitalism (mixed economy). An economic system in which the market process plays a major role but in which the political process also plays an important role. Examples: the U.S. economy, the economies of Western Europe, and most of the economies of the world excluding the so-called Communist nations.

Monetarist economics. The "school of economic ideas and theories" usually associated with Professor Milton Friedman. It places primary emphasis on the size of the money supply in determining macroeconomic conditions and prices in the economy. *See also* Keynesian-monetarist debate.

Monetary policy. Actions designed to stabilize prices and/or employment by adjusting or controlling the availability and/or cost of credit (money).

Money. Anything which is generally acceptable as a medium of exchange.

Money market. The market for short-term borrowing and lending. Therefore, the market for short-term debt instruments such as Treasury bills.

Money supply (money stock). The number of "spendable dollars" in existence at a given moment. May be defined as M_1, M_2, etc.

Monopolistic competition. A market structure in which there are several firms selling differentiated (brand-name) products.

Monopoly. A market structure in which there is only one seller.

Monopoly power. The power to influence the price of a product by exercising some control over the supply of the product. *Same as* market power.

Monopsony. A market structure in which there

Note: For a thorough understanding you should consult the index and refer to the appropriate sections in the text.

is only one buyer.

Moral suasion. A "non-official" tool of monetary policy involving appeals to (and sometimes pressure on) the commercial banks to follow suggested lending policies to influence the availability and cost of credit.

Multilateral foreign aid. Any program of foreign aid in which several nations participate. Example: a United Nations program to aid the less developed countries.

Multiplier effect. The ultimate change is greater than (some multiple of) the initial change. (1) The income (or investment) multiplier: An initial change in spending will result, ultimately, in a larger change in national income because of the consumer respending effect. The larger the marginal propensity to consume (MPC), the smaller the marginal propensity to save (MPS), and the larger the multiplier. $\left(\text{Formula: } \dfrac{1}{1 - \text{MPC}}, \text{ or } \dfrac{1}{\text{MPS}}\right).$

(2) The deposit multiplier: The amount of increase in the money supply which can result from an initial increase in bank reserves. The lower the reserve requirement the higher the multiplier. $\left(\text{Formula: } \dfrac{1}{\text{reserve requirement}}\right).$

National bank. A bank which is chartered by the federal government. National banks are required to be members of the Federal Reserve System.

National Banking System. The system of nationally chartered banks which existed in the U.S. from the time of the Civil War until the Federal Reserve System was established in 1913, at which time all national banks were required to join the Federal Reserve System.

National income. Total income earned in the nation. The sum of wages plus rent plus interest plus profits. Equal to total real value of the nation's output of goods and services. In the national income and product account, GNP minus depreciation and indirect taxes.

National income and product account. The "GNP accounts" which show the income and product flows of the nation and indicate the rate at which the economy is running.

Natural monopoly. An industry in which the most efficient firm is one which is large enough to supply the entire market. The average cost per unit of output goes down as the plant gets larger, so that the least-cost plant is one which supplies the entire market.

Negative income tax. A government program for paying out money to people whose incomes are below a certain level, and collecting taxes from people whose incomes are above that level. Often discussed but never used in the United States.

Neoclassical economics. The accepted basic theories of microeconomics which made up most of the field of economics prior to the development and inclusion of Keynesian economics in the years since the 1920s. The economics of supply and demand and the operation of the price mechanism, of substitution, trade-offs, opportunity costs, and of the way in which *the three basic questions* are answered. *See also* classical economics.

Net national product. GNP minus depreciation. It's the net dollar value of the annual output of the economic system, but it's inflated by the inclusion of indirect business taxes in the prices of the goods.

Net worth. The "ownership value" of a business. If you subtract total liabilities from the value of total assets, the residual is net worth.

Neutrality (of taxes). A neutral tax is one which doesn't cause the economic choices of businesses or individuals to shift—that is, it doesn't cause them to change to different goods, inputs, production methods, locations, etc.

New Deal. The government programs of the 1930s aimed at overcoming the depression. The administration of Franklin D. Roosevelt which introduced a broad range of new government programs and activities in the economy.

Non-price competition. Actions taken by sellers to try to increase their sales without lowering the price. For example, advertising, special

Note: For a thorough understanding you should consult the index and refer to the appropriate sections in the text.

promotions, product differentiation, etc.

Non-tariff barrier (to international trade). Methods used to slow imports, such as establishing unnecessary product specifications and quality standards, unnecessary inspections, requiring many papers to be filled out (red tape) etc. Import quotas are also non-tariff barriers.

Normal price. A price just high enough to cover all of the costs of production including a normal profit for the producer.

Normal profit. A profit high enough to provide the business an adequate return so that it will not leave the industry, but not high enough to serve as an extra enticement to pull other firms into the industry. An industry in which the firms are making normal profits will neither be expanding nor shrinking. Such an industry is said to be in "long-run equilibrium."

Normative economics. That part of economics which is concerned with trying to evaluate the desirability (or undesirability) of economic circumstances, conditions, or programs. *See also* positive economics.

NOW account. A savings account against which a kind of check (called "negotiable order of withdrawal") can be written. NOW accounts only recently have been made legal nationwide.

Oligopoly. A market structure in which there are only a few sellers, so that the actions of any one seller will have an influence on market supply, and price.

Oligopsony. A market in which there are only a few buyers, so that each buyer can influence market demand, and price.

OPEC cartel. *See* cartel, OPEC.

Open economy. An economy which carries on trade with other economies. Opposite of "closed economy."

Open market operations. Buying and selling securities by the central bank in the open securities markets for the purpose of influencing the money supply and/or interest rates.

Opportunity cost. The cost of what you choose, measured in terms of what you must forfeit in order to get what you choose. Also, the amount an input could earn in its best alternative use, and therefore, the income it is forfeiting by not being employed in its best alternative use.

Paradox of thrift. The idea that if everyone tries to be thrifty and save more, the economy will slow down and soon people will lose their jobs (their sources of income) and wind up saving less than before.

Parity prices (for agricultural products). The idea that the prices farmers get for the farm products they sell should go up as much as the prices of the things that farmers buy.

Perfect competition. A market structure in which there are so many buyers and sellers that no one seller or buyer can influence the price, and there are no restrictions on either entry or exit of buyers or sellers. Sometimes defined as a "frictionless system" where there is complete knowledge and instantaneous adjustment to changing market conditions. *See also* pure competition.

Personal income. That part of national income which actually flows to individuals. In the national income and product account, national income *minus* undistributed corporate profits, corporate taxes, and social security taxes, and *plus* social security payments and other transfer payments to individuals.

Phillips Curve. A curve illustrating the trade-off between inflation and unemployment—the more unemployment, the less inflation, and vice versa. Developed by Professor A. W. Phillips.

Planned investment. Spending by businesses to buy fixed capital and inventories. This is the *active demand* for capital goods. Compare unplanned investment, which is keeping money invested in things which the business had planned to sell but has been unable to sell because of slack demand.

Planned savings. Amounts which income receivers are planning to save (not spend for consumer goods) out of their incomes. Not always

Note: For a thorough understanding you should consult the index and refer to the appropriate sections in the text.

equal to realized savings because of the paradox of thrift, and sometimes because of shortages and/or inflationary pressures in the consumer goods markets.

Positive economics. That part of economics which is concerned with cause-and-effect relationships among economic variables. Economic models, theories, and laws are all a part of positive economics. Positive economics is concerned with "what is" and "what will happen if . . . " It is not concerned with questions about "what *should* be." *See also* normative economics.

Present value. *See* capitalized value.

Price discrimination. Selling the same good or service to different buyers for different prices. For example, trying to maximize profits by "charging what the traffic will bear."

Price elasticity of demand. Responsiveness of quantity bought to small changes in the price. *See also* elasticity of demand.

Price index. A percentage number showing the extent of change in a price or in an average group of prices as compared with a "base year." *See also* index number.

Price leadership. The practice in oligopoly markets of one firm announcing price increases (or decreases) and the other firms all follow.

Price mechanism. The rationing and production motivating functions of price, directing the production and distribution activities in the market economy. *See also* market process.

Price supports. Government guarantees to prevent prices from falling, usually for agricultural products, and usually involving the buying of surpluses by the government.

Product differentiation. Making your product a little different from those of your competitors as a means of non-price competition.

Production possibility curve (transformation curve). A curve showing the maximum output combinations of two goods which can be produced with the limited inputs available. The curve shows the opportunity cost of each good in terms of the other.

Productivity. Usually means output *per worker*, or *per worker-hour*, but also can be used to refer to the output-per-unit of the other inputs: capital, and land. Worker productivity determines how high the average standard of living can be.

Productivity, marginal. *See* marginal physical product, marginal value product.

Profit. Total revenue minus total cost. In economic theory, total cost includes a cost to cover the "normal profit" required for the business. Anything above normal profit is called "profit." Also, excess profit.

Profit and loss (P & L) statement (income statement). The accounting statement for a business which shows the sources of revenue (receipts from sales), the various costs which have been incurred, all taxes and other payments which have been made, and what's left over (profit).

Progressive tax. A tax that takes a *larger percentage* of a larger income and a *smaller percentage* of a smaller income.

Propensity to consume. *See* consumption function.

Proportional tax. A tax that takes the same *percentage* of all incomes, large and small.

Protectionism. The policy of "protecting" domestic producer-sellers from the competition of foreign sellers. Protectionism includes the use of protective tariffs, quotas, and other non-tariff barriers designed to stop foreigners from selling in domestic markets.

Protestant ethic. The idea that people are duty-bound to work hard. "The idle mind is the devil's workshop." "Hard work is good for the soul."

"Public choice" economics. The relatively new study of the way economic decisions are made through the political process. Also sometimes called "collective choice" economics. The objective is to better understand both the *process* and the *efficiency* of collective choice decisions regarding resource allocation.

Public goods. Goods which, once provided, are available to everyone, and which no matter how many people enjoy their use, are not

Note: For a thorough understanding you should consult the index and refer to the appropriate sections in the text.

used up. Example: street lights, or mosquito control. If public goods are to be provided, they must be provided by government because it would be (at best) very inefficient or (at worst) impossible to place a "user price" on these goods and have the goods provided by "the market."

Public works programs. Construction projects undertaken by the government for the purpose of employing unemployed people and trying to overcome depression.

Pure competition. A market structure in which there are so many buyers and sellers that no one acting alone can influence the price.

Pure economic rent. *See* economic rent.

Quota. An assigned quantity. In international trade, a quota tells exactly how many units of a product can be imported.

Rate of exchange. The price of the money of one country in terms of the money of another country. It's the price ratio between the two kinds of money. *See also* exchange rate.

Rational expectations theory. The relatively new theory that says the government cannot successfully undertake stabilization policy because the public will not respond in the way the government policymakers intended. The basic idea is that people can foresee that the ultimate results of the government's macroeconomic policies would be harmful to them, and they are too smart to go along and get hurt.

Rationing function of price. The use-limiting, conserving function which price performs. The higher the price, the less the good will be used and the more it will be conserved (rationed).

Reaganomics. The economic policies of the Reagan administration during the early 1980s. Aimed primarily toward controlling inflation and improving the productivity of the economy.

Real income. The goods and services which people receive as a result of their productive efforts. Also, *money income, deflated* by the appropriate price index.

Real interest rate. The rate of interest (actual percentage) minus the rate of inflation. If the stated rate of interest is 12% and the inflation rate is 8%, then the real rate of interest is 4%.

Recession. A slowdown in the rate in which the economy is running. Reduced outputs. Increased unemployment. *See also*, depression.

Reflex effect. Also, the Basic Law of Real-World Markets. The tendency for markets in the real world to automatically return to balanced conditions following any attempt to artificially "rig" the price either too high or too low. The reflex effect is an illustration of the power of the price mechanism (the functions of price) in real-world markets.

Regressive tax. A tax that takes a larger *percentage* of a lower income and a smaller *percentage* of a higher income.

Rent. The return to the owners of the factor of production "land." *See also* economic rent.

Required reserves. Reserves which commercial banks, mutual savings banks, savings and loan associations, credit unions, and other depository financial institutions are required to hold. The amount of required reserves is stated as a percentage of the amount of deposits. The requirement is different for *checkable deposits* than for other deposits and is larger for large banks and financial institutions than for small ones. Most financial institutions are required to hold their reserves in the Federal Reserve bank in their district. *See also* excess reserves.

Response lags. *See* lags.

Revenue sharing. Collection of taxes by a higher level of government (state, or federal) and sharing the revenue with the lower level(s) of government (state, local).

Right-to-work law. A state law saying that no one can be required to join a union as a condition of getting or holding a job.

Savings. Money received as income but not spent for consumer goods. If income is received and spent for investment goods, this is defined as savings, and then investment.

Say's Law. Supply creates its own demand. The

Note: For a thorough understanding you should consult the index and refer to the appropriate sections in the text.

idea is that as people produce and supply more to the market, they automatically demand more from the market. Therefore, total supply and total demand in the economy tend to be equal.

Scarce. Not freely available in sufficient quantities to satisfy everyone's wants for free.

SDRs. Special Drawing Rights. A new kind of international monetary unit created by the major trading nations of the world through the International Monetary Fund (IMF).

Securities. All kinds of financial "paper assets" including government bonds (long-term) and treasury bills (short-term), corporation bonds (long-term) and commercial paper (short-term), all kinds of corporate stocks, and all other kinds of paper financial assets. Short-term securities are usually considered to be those which mature (pay off) in less than one year. *See also* government securities.

Selective credit controls. Controls which try to make money tighter and more difficult to obtain for some kinds of loans than for others. For example, selective controls might be used to try to tighten money which is borrowed for the purchase of new automobiles, or to buy stocks on the stock market, while keeping money more easily available for home mortgages.

Share draft accounts. Deposits at credit unions which can be transferred by checks. The checks are called "share drafts."

Shortage. Buyers are trying to buy more than the sellers are willing to sell at the existing price. *See also* excess quantity demanded.

Short run. A time period which is not long enough for the fixed factors of production to become variable. A time period too short for "long-run" equilibrium to be achieved.

Socialism. (1) Philosophy: The idea that the government (the political process in the society) should play a significant role in making the production and distribution choices for the society (2) Economic system: A system in which the government owns much of the means of production and the political process plays a major role in deciding the production and distribution questions for the society.

Socio-capitalism. *See* mixed socio-capitalism.

Speculation. Buying and selling things in the hope of making profits from price changes.

Stocks. Ownership shares in a corporation. Stockholders vote for the members of the board of directors and in this way have ultimate control of the corporation. *See also* common stock.

Subsidy. A payment by the government to help to support some desired economic activity or to induce businesses to do things which the government wants done.

Substitutes. Two goods, each of which can be used to replace the other. If the price of one of the goods goes up, people will buy less of that one and more of the other.

Substitution effect. Buyers switching to substitute goods whenever the price of a good goes up, and switching from substitute goods to this good whenever the price of this good goes down. When the price of a good goes up, people buy less because of (a) the income effect—they can't buy as much as before, and (b) the substitution effect—they shift their spending to substitute goods which have not gone up in price.

Supply. The functional relationship between prices and quantities supplied. The supply is shown by a schedule or curve indicating the quantity that would be supplied at each price.

Supply-side economics. Theory and policy dealing with factors which influence the size and the rate of growth of productivity and output in the economy. Supply-side economic policies are designed to stimulate more supply of outputs.

Supply-side tax cut. A tax cut aimed toward increasing productivity and output in the economy, and hopefully (ultimately) generating more tax revenues.

Surplus. Quantity supplied in excess of the quantity demanded at the existing price. *See also* excess quantity supplied.

Tariff. A tax levied on imported goods.

Tax-based Incomes Policy (TIP). A government

Note: For a thorough understanding you should consult the index and refer to the appropriate sections in the text.

policy of wage-price controls enforced by tax penalties on those who break the guidelines and tax incentives for those who do not.

Tax incidence. *See* incidence of a tax.

Tax shifting. Transferring some (or all) of the burden of a tax to someone else.

Thrift institutions. Also, "thrifts." Financial services organizations which function primarily as financial intermediaries: savings and loan associations, mutual savings banks, credit unions.

Transfer payment. A "one way" payment where nothing is received in return. Private gifts of money are transfer payments. But most transfer payments are made by the government to private individuals under the social security, welfare, unemployment, and other such programs.

Transformation curve. *See* production possibility curve.

Treasury bill. A short-term debt obligation of the U.S. government. It's like a government bond, only it matures in less than a year (usually 3 or 6 months), and the buyer earns interest by buying the bill at a discount (for less than its face value) and then receiving the face value at maturity.

Tying contract. A contract in which a supplier requires a buyer to buy more than one product, or nothing. For example, an independent service station which sells a certain brand of gas might also be required to carry that same brand of motor oil and car polish.

Underground economy, the. Also called "the informal sector." Includes all economic activities and transactions which do not show up in the national income and product statistics, on which no taxes are paid, and of which there are no official records. Includes illegal activities such as the drug trade, and many legal activities such as cutting your neighbor's grass for money or selling vegetables from your garden (but not reporting the income).

Unemployment rate. The percentage of the labor force which is listed as unemployed.

Unitary elasticity. Elasticity numerically equal to 1. That is, the percentage change in price is exactly equal to the percentage change in the quantity.

Unplanned investment. The value of goods which have been produced for sale but which, because of slack demand, have not been sold. Whenever there is unplanned investment, businesses begin cutting back their production and the economy slows down.

Usury laws. Laws which limit the amount of interest which lending institutions can charge borrowers. Most states have usury laws setting maximum interest rates for various kinds of loans.

Utility. Satisfaction received from the consumption of goods or services. It's the "psychic return" which adds to the welfare (satisfaction) of the consumer.

Utils. Fictitious measurement units used to measure utility hypothetically for the purposes of illustration and analysis.

Value added. The value of the output, less the cost of all of the "semi-finished inputs" which were bought from others. Some value is added at each stage in the production process.

Variable cost. The cost of production which increases and decreases as output is expanded or contracted, in the short-run. The variable cost is the cost of the variable factors.

Variable factors of production. All those inputs which can be adjusted quickly (that is, in the short run) to increase or decrease the output of an existing plant.

Velocity of money. The frequency with which the average dollar is spent. If the average dollar changes hands six times in one year, then the average velocity would be six.

Vertical merger. *See* merger.

Wealth. The total value of everything that is owned (free and clear) at a given moment.

Workable competition. A market structure in which monopoly power exists, but in which there is sufficient competition among the monopolistic units to protect the consumers from serious monopolistic abuses.

Yield. *See* interest yield.

Index